THE K&W GUIDE TO
COLLEGES

FOR STUDENTS WITH LEARNING DISABILITIES OR ATTENTION DEFICIT HYPERACTIVITY DISORDER

9TH EDITION

One of the wonderful things about this *K&W Guide* is that it helps students and their parents plan the best ways to find and use help. With this guide you can map out new, essential connections: with colleges and universities who understand your needs; with appropriate support services on campus; with departments and faculty members who will understand, challenge, and respect you.

Edward M. Hallowell, MD and David Keevil, PsyD

The Hallowell Center

My first exposure to *The K&W Guide to Colleges for Students with Learning Disabilities or Attention Deficit Hyperactivity Disorder* was on a booklist in a college admissions and career planning class. . . . When I first sat down in the quiet evening hours at home, when everyone else was asleep and I do my best thinking, I had the heart thumping and mesmerizing experience one gets when you read something that you feel was written just for you by someone who really understands. The 47 page introduction before the college profiles fits the books dedication: "This book is a labor of love written to help individuals throughout the world who have been identified as having learning disabilities or attention deficit hyperactivity disorder. Just as important, it is for those students who have never been officially identified as learning disabled. And of course, it is an educational tool for all the families, professionals, and friends who know someone who has a learning disability."

Parent of children with learning disabilities and attention deficit disorder

San Francisco, California

You have an excellent resource right at your fingertips! *The K&W Guide to Colleges for Students with Learning Disabilities or Attention Deficit Hyperactivity Disorder* is an excellent starting point for exploring the wide spectrum of assistance provided by DSS offices in every state. Keep in mind that the goal of college is not just getting in, but getting out successfully. Finding an appropriate DSS office to student match can be the key to that success. *The K&W Guide to Colleges for Students with Learning Disabilities or Attention Deficit Hyperactivity Disorder* can help direct you in that roadmap to success.

Dr. Kendra Johnson, Director of the Office for Accessibility at the University of Toledo and president of Transition Game Educational Consultants, Toledo, Ohio

"Many colleges have programs and services for students with learning disabilities. A very informative guidebook you might want to consult is the *The K&W Guide to Colleges for Students with Learning Disabilities or Attention Deficit Hyperactivity Disorder.*

Jeffrey Zaslow

Reporter

K&W is a "godsend"

Dodge Johnson

College Planning

Malvern, PA

PrincetonReview.com

THE K&W GUIDE TO
COLLEGES

FOR STUDENTS WITH LEARNING DISABILITIES OR ATTENTION DEFICIT HYPERACTIVITY DISORDER

9TH EDITION

MARYBETH KRAVETS, MA

AND IMY F. WAX, MS

RANDOM HOUSE, INC.

NEW YORK

The Princeton Review, Inc.
2315 Broadway
New York, NY 10024
E-mail: bookeditor@review.com

ISBN: 978-0-375-76633-6

Printed in the United States of America.

9 8 7 6 5 4 3 2 1

9th Edition

DEDICATION

This book is a labor of love written to help individuals throughout the world who have been identified as having learning disabilities or attention deficit hyperactivity disorder. Just as important, it is for those students who have never been officially identified as learning disabled. In addition, it is an educational tool for all of the families, professionals, and friends who know someone who has a learning disability.

ACKNOWLEDGMENTS

To the families of Marybeth Kravets and Imy F. Wax for their patience and support in this endeavor: Alan, Wendy, Steve, Allison, Connor, Isabel, Mark, Sara, David, Robert, Bennett, Cathy, Dan, Andrea, Benjamin, Howard, Lisa, Bill, Niaya, Ellis, Gary, Debrah, and Greg.

To Deerfield High School and High School District 113 for their ongoing support of learning disability programs and services and their belief in promoting the development of independence for all students and guiding them toward making good decisions about life after high school.

To all of the colleges who provide services and programs to promote the educational endeavors and dreams of students with learning disabilities or attention deficit hyperactivity disorder.

To all of the contributors in the "Thoughts From" section of the *K&W Guide* for sharing their thoughts and experiences with learning disabilities and attention deficit hyperactivity disorder.

To Stephanie Gordon, learning disability specialist, Deerfield High School, Deerfield, Illinois, for her professional assistance.

To Karen Rodgers Photography for the authors' pictures.

CONTENTS

FOREWORD

Edward M. Hallowell, MD and David Keevil, PsyD, The Hallowell Center[1]:

Going to college is a rite of passage. The time for college finally arrives, and with considerable fanfare our children *go*: They go away from home, friends, and family, and go toward a "grown up" life of freedom and independence.

As this time arrives, parents and children often have powerful and competing urges on both sides: To hold on tight and never let go, or to sever all connections and begin anew. Of course many parents tend toward the former urge, while their adolescents yearn for the latter.

When you're a parent, so many instincts protest against letting go. The world is often a cruel and dangerous place, and you are all too aware of your child's newness—their youth and fragility. When you're young, it's blissful to dream of a new life that is entirely yours. So much in our world supports that dream: songs, sitcoms, the exalted fables of popular culture.

If your child has ADHD or LD, you may feel even more acutely the urge to hold tight. Your child may be impulsive; he or she may seem emotionally unprepared for the challenges ahead, and may have only a vague understanding of the sometimes tedious and always disciplined work required at college. You may be particularly aware of all the effort "behind the scenes" that went into getting your child even this far— the homework assistance, the meetings with teachers, the evaluations and treatments—the countless hours of "extra help" along the way.

Your child with ADHD or LD may yearn particularly for the independence of college life. He or she may be awfully tired of feeling dependent on all the help you and others have offered. College may feel like a chance to "throw off the yoke" and finally succeed on one's own, free of dependence.

This tension—between the urge to hold on and the urge to let go—is very real for all of us who are parents, and it is very real for our children. I suppose the good *and* bad news is that this tension is life-long: We never really outgrow these competing urges. They just take on different shapes and sizes as we all continue to grow and mature.

What I want to tell you here—something I'm sure you already understand—is that the way to resolve this conflict is not to choose one side or the other—not to hold on even tighter, or pull away so hard that you are impossible to hold—but to mix them together, to balance them. In order to do this, you need to *stay connected*.

What do I mean by "stay connected"? I mean three things. First, *hold on to what you have*. Second, *stay flexible*. Third, *grow new connections*. Let me tell you a little more about each of these ideas.

HOLD ON TO WHAT YOU HAVE

Maybe it looks as if I'm saying that you shouldn't let go. Actually, some letting go will be essential, for both parent and child. Parents will probably unpack the car, move things into their child's room, get a last hug, and drive away. Students will spend their first night in a college dorm, go to their first campus party, register for classes, and set their own study schedule. But in the midst of all this necessary letting go, remember to hold on to what's important from the past as well.

What *is* important from the past? Every new college student will have his or her own list, but I hope most lists will include these headlines:

- Your parents love you, and will continue to love you no matter what.
- You have a home to return to, where you are welcome.
- You have friends who care about you.
- You have specific strengths and abilities you carry with you.
- You have learned many essential skills for coping with your ADHD or LD, and college is a tremendous opportunity to learn and use many more.

Here's an idea for parents: As your child with ADHD or LD prepares for college, devote some time to making a detailed, truthful, loving, and relentlessly supportive list of what your child will "carry" to college, and offer it to your child as a gift. Here's an idea for new college students with ADHD or LD: Make your own list of what you will carry with you, as a personal, intimate reminder of what is strong and sustaining in your life.

Each list is a testament to the connections that will endure and sustain.

STAY FLEXIBLE

In nature, the best connections—the strongest and most sustaining—are flexible. Think of how a tree sways in the wind, allowing it to stay connected both to the ground and to the air, through its branches and leaves. Connections that are rigid tend to snap and crack apart under strain. Flexibility allows us to grow and flourish.

What does this mean for parents, and for their child with ADHD or LD? It means not to attach too rigidly to any one thing—to any one expectation, to any one vision of the future, to any one marker of "success." Think "trial and error"; think "a different drummer"; think "two steps forward, one and a half steps back."

One of the exciting and dismaying things about people with ADHD is that we do not always follow the pack. We may act impulsively, or "forget" to act at all. We may make associative connections between seven different ideas, but drop the one that's on next Monday's test. These and many other behaviors can lead to difficulty and risk, and they can lead to creativity and discovery.

Parents: If your child goes off to college and marches through in 4 years with a high grade point average, then good for your child! But this may well not happen. If you tie your happiness to such expectations—if your expectations are too rigid—then you may well be disappointed, unhappy, angry, or dismissive. As a result, the connection between you and your child, and between your child and his or her positive self-understanding, may snap and crack apart, and that's not a good thing for anyone. Keep the connections flexible, pliant, and resilient. Cut each other slack, practice forgiveness, and keep your sense of humor.

Expect surprises. Life is always a dress rehearsal, and people flub their lines and miss their cues all the time. People with ADHD or LD may play a love scene when we expected tragedy, or start tap-dancing during the soliloquy. There's nothing to be gained by throwing them off the stage. Rather, find out how your script might be rewritten, and how they can accustom themselves to the action around them. Stay flexible!

GROW NEW CONNECTIONS

Many adolescents with ADHD or LD who head off to college have already received a great deal of help over the years. They may be sick of help! But if they avoid help at college they will be missing one of the most important lessons college has to teach: *How to find and use help*. Think of preparing for college as preparing to find and use help: from teachers, tutors, other students, administrators, friends, and family.

Finding and using help is not the same thing as offering excuses or getting others to do your work. It *is* the same thing as *growing new connections*. College is a community of learners. The vast majority of human beings learn best *in* community—we learn from others and with others. A student who has something to prove by "going it alone" is mistaking a lack of connections for maturity.

One of the wonderful things about this *K & W Guide* is that it helps students and their parents plan the best ways to find and use help. With this guide you can map out new, essential connections: with colleges and universities who understand your needs; with appropriate support services on campus; with departments and faculty members who will understand, challenge, and respect you. Use this guide to start planning now and to further develop your ability to find and use help. Ask yourself: What kind of help might I need? How will I recognize when I need it? How will I go about finding it? How will I ask, and who will I ask? The answers you discover will change and grow as you change and grow. Remember, stay connected, and stay flexible!

IN CLOSING

You have an exciting trip ahead of you, climbing to the top of your own particular mountain. If you have ADHD or LD the path may be particularly challenging and the air particularly thin at times. But you will get there. The people who love and respect you will not stand on the summit with you—that is yours alone. But I hope and trust they will help you along the paths you choose (and the paths that choose you), by remaining connected with you, assisting you in ways you find helpful, and sharing with you the wonder and excitement of your discoveries. Bon voyage!

1   The Hallowell Center, Sudbury, Massachusetts, is dedicated to promoting cognitive and emotional well-being in children and adults. DrHallowell.com.

INTRODUCTION

The K&W Guide was conceived independently by the authors over twenty years ago, but it took until 1987 for the paths of the authors to cross.

Imy Wax is a licensed psychotherapist and educational consultant. She is also the mother of two children—one with a learning disability and the other with a learning disability and Attention Deficit Hyperactivity Disorder (ADHD). The truth is that this book is really a dedication to Imy's daughter, who at the age of two was identified as having multiple learning disabilities, a large delay in her language skills, and a dismal prognosis for her future. Several professionals indicated that a traditional public elementary and high school experience would not be possible, and college was never even mentioned.

Imy was always optimistic, however, and she absolutely refused to accept such a diagnosis. She set goals, became a visionary, and exerted significant influence to allow her daughter to compensate for her limitations. She became an advocate for her daughter. She researched, read every book and every article she could find, and gave herself hope to believe in her child and in herself. Imy made it her goal to understand the learning disability and the strategies that would best contribute to her daughter's well-being.

Imy's daughter ultimately attended both public school and a special private school for students with learning disabilities. When her daughter was in the eighth grade in a private school, Imy volunteered in the College Resource Center at Deerfield High School so that she could get a better grasp on what might be in store for her daughter if she were to enroll in the local public high school. This was in 1987, and the paths of the two authors crossed for the first time.

Marybeth Kravets is the College Counselor at Deerfield High School where Imy volunteered. Deerfield is a public high school that has comprehensive programs and services for students with learning disabilities (LD) and Attention Deficit Hyperactivity Disorder (ADHD). Deerfield High School is also a school from which 98 percent of students matriculate to college, including those students identified as having LD or ADHD. Imy discovered that her daughter could be accommodated in the high school, and that the professionals there had hopes of mainstreaming her into regular college preparatory courses with appropriate accommodations and modifications.

Hidden under Imy's "coat of hope," however, lived the growing anxiety that she experienced every time she listened to a college representative visiting with students at the high school. It seemed to her that all colleges were after the same student, one with at least a 3.0 GPA, an ACT score of 24 or an SAT score of 1000 (out of 1600), a ranking in the top 50 percent of their class, and a four-year curriculum consisting of every subject at Deerfield High School. Imy's daughter had begun the ninth grade with only special education courses, which were individualized to meet her special needs. By junior year, she had mainstreamed into college preparatory courses in English, science, fine arts, and social studies, but was still enrolled in special education classes in math. She was not even close to learning about algebra (the typical freshman curriculum), and she had never taken a foreign language.

One day, Imy asked to meet with Marybeth to talk about her concern that there was not enough information about colleges that were prepared to accommodate students with learning disabilities. As the two began to explore the available resources for information, they realized most guidebooks only offered computer-generated information that said almost the same thing about every college regarding special services and special admissions. Thus began their search for more pertinent information to help Imy in her quest for a possible match for her daughter, and to help Marybeth provide better college counseling for the students at her high school.

The first edition of the book included extensive information about 150 colleges. The ninth edition of *The K&W Guide* has expanded to include more college profiles with detailed information about what these schools do and do not provide. It also gives specific information about documentation guidelines for students with learning disabilities and ADHD, and important information highlighting how services and accommodations are individually tailored for each student at the college level. Through the information provided in this book and the tips and strategies provided to help students identify their priorities and explore their options, students can determine if the services or programs offered at a particular school match their individual needs. In this edition, you'll find:

- Special programs and services for students with multiple learning disabilities and/or ADHD, or for those needing limited accommodations

- Information professionals need to know in order to help, advise, and counsel students and parents in their college search process

- Detailed information about general and special admission procedures, the application process, services, programs, accommodations, remedial or developmental courses, and opportunities for basic skills classes

- Policies and procedures regarding course waivers or substitutions

- General profiles of colleges and universities

- Overview of Student Rights and Responsibilities: U.S. Department of Education

- Information about independent living options for non-traditional learners

The main focus of *The K&W Guide* is to provide comprehensive information about the services or programs available at colleges and universities for students with learning disabilities or ADHD. Many colleges and universities will include students with LD or ADHD in their structured programs or special services. In most high schools, students identified as having only ADHD are categorized under "other health-related disabilities" and protected by Section 504 of the Rehabilitation Act of 1973. These students can request and receive special accommodations in high school and college, as long as they present current and appropriate documentation from a certified professional. It is important for students identified as LD/ADHD to understand that services and accommodations received in high school are not always duplicated in college. Students must self-disclose, request accommodations/services, provide current documentation, and then a determination of appropriate services/accommodations is made on an individual basis.

Colleges that provide descriptions of the level of support and accommodations available on their campuses, whether they are basic services complying with the mandates of Section 504 or enhanced services that go beyond the mandates, provide this population of students with the best opportunity for good decision-making. The end result is that students will choose colleges where the services match their needs.

It is extremely important that readers understand that the fact that a college offers a service or accommodation does not necessarily mean that every student with LD/ADHD can access it. Each student requesting accommodations must submit current and appropriate documentation, and the disability support personnel will determine what accommodations are "reasonable." Too often, students assume that because they received specific services or accommodations in high school, they will receive the same level of services once they enroll in college. This is not the case for all students, and colleges have the right to reexamine the documentation and identify the services they feel are reasonable and appropriate.

Students and their parents are encouraged to visit the college websites and use the internet to research colleges and the support services available, talk to the admissions staff and the directors of the special support services, and visit the campuses. This is a good time to provide a copy of the student's documentation and get an idea of what services and/or accommodations may be offered to the students. Before planning a trip, however, begin with a thorough reading of this guide. Students need to have well-ordered priorities to determine the criteria they will use for selecting an appropriate college.

Students with unique learning needs should approach the college search with the goal of identifying colleges that will fill all of their needs—educationally, culturally, and socially. There is more than one "right" college for any student, learning disabled or not. Although no single source can provide all of the information needed to help students make educated decisions about appropriate college choices, the availability of other resource books with extensive information is very limited. The ultimate goal of *The K&W Guide* is to give descriptive and honest information so that all students have equal access to this knowledge. This guide is the first place to look for colleges providing:

- **Structured Programs:** Schools that have specific programs for students with LD/ADHD that go beyond the mandated services. These services might include special admissions procedures, specialized and trained professionals, compensatory strategies, one-on-one tutoring, Additional fees, compulsory participation, and monitoring.

- **Coordinated Services:** Schools that have some involvement with admissions decisions, voluntary participation, more than just mandated services, small or no fees, and less structure.

- **Basic Services:** Schools that comply with Section 504 mandates that rarely have specialized LD staff, do not have monitoring, and are totally dependent on student advocacy.

The authors gratefully acknowledge the time and effort of all the service providers at the colleges and universities who responded to our request for current information about their services and programs. It is these colleges and others like them that are willing to work closely with learning disabled students, believe in empowering students to articulate their needs, and help students to become independent and successful learners as they pursue a college education.

It is essential that college services and accommodations for individuals with learning disabilities and ADHD be visible, honored, funded, maintained, and expanded to meet the needs of identified students. Because learning disabilities are being identified earlier, diagnosed students are being provided with individualized educational plans to meet their needs, becoming self-advocates, learning compensatory skills, and making the transition in greater numbers from high school to college.

This must be a joint effort. Colleges and universities need to support the efforts and the ongoing learning process of these individuals. Those who believe in the merit of helping these individuals should reach out to those who do not understand. Those who do not understand should open their minds to the fact that learning disabilities are neurological and are life-long; they do not go away. The authors of this guide applaud these students. No child chooses to be born with a learning disability or ADHD. However, if they hold fast to their dreams and aspirations, look beyond the imperfections and hidden handicaps, they can make things happen for themselves.

Marybeth Kravets and Imy Wax

Thoughts From: A Parent

A paradigm shift occurred when I read the chapter heading in the book, *Colleges That Change Lives*, written by Loren Pope, which was titled "The Learning Disabled of Today Will Be the Gifted of Tomorrow." I am the parent of several children each with different learning disabilities, or as I now prefer to say "learning differences." One child has Asperger Syndrome. Although she has exceptionally high intelligence, she has great difficulty dealing with everyday social situations (i.e. school!), has intense interests which border on obsessive/compulsive, has trouble processing and expressing emotions appropriately, finds direct eye contact painful and has a unique learning style. This all can lead to isolation, inappropriate educational placement, misdiagnosis and high risk for anxiety, depression, and even suicide. (*The Oasis Guide to Asperger Syndrome*; Patricia R. Bashe and Barbara L. Kirby.) With her sheer determination and her parent's support, she graduated from a highly selective college and is working in marketing with plans to attend business school.

Another child has ADHD and severe dyslexia. This child spent two years with a vision therapist working on three dimensional vision so the written word would sit flat on a page instead of popping up. This child is highly visual, spatial, artistic, and has bounding and often out of control energy levels. This child was fortunate to attend a small private high school that supported him educationally, but because of a very low reading and comprehension level college was not attempted.

Another child currently in college has ADHD with inattention and mild dyslexia and is an advocate for educational rights. With all the difficult family issues we had to deal with this child was often overlooked in high school. Sadly enough, although I have diagnoses for my children now, I was always a step behind in finding out appropriate and adequate information, gaining access to support professionals and securing correct and thorough diagnoses. Recently, I have delved deeply into all these issues and I am accessing wonderful and extremely helpful information. I know that it is never too late to help my own children and our family, and I want to help other families so they can avoid the pitfalls and challenges that were part of the fabric of our lives.

This is my history. Amazingly enough, for I am a compulsive information and book gatherer, my first exposure to *The K&W Guide to Colleges for Students with Learning Disabilities* was on a booklist in a College Admissions and Career Planning class. Why had I not noticed it in the bookstore or on the pages of Amazon after years of collecting this type of book? When I first sat down in the quiet evening hours at home, when everyone else was asleep and I do my best thinking, I had the heart-thumping and mesmerizing experience one gets when you read something that you feel was written just for you by someone who really understands.

One of the most important things to realize is that the services that were provided to children in the K–12 public educational system under IDEA which places direct responsibility on the schools to identify students with disabilities and provide them services, changes dramatically under Section 504 of the Rehabilitation Act of 1073 and the American with Disabilities Act (ADA) which governs postsecondary school education and places the burden on students to self-identify and request reasonable accommodations. Almost all colleges require recent documentation from trained and certified professionals. Now, more than every before, the student must become his/her own advocate (with parental support if available) and politely demand the services that are their right and will make the difference in a successful college experience.

Before my children entered college I had little familiarity with the wide range of programs that were available to students with documented LD's. (I have since learned that they could have qualified for SAT/ACT accommodations, such as extended testing time.) I was unclear if there should be any mention of special needs on admissions documents (we thought that it might negatively affect the chance of admissions) and did not talk with LD staff at any of the colleges. We believed that with enough hard work our children could make it through their freshman year without any additional support.

We soon discovered that to survive without additional support would result in unnecessary stress and lower grades. With my assistance, we discovered the disabilities resource center that provided extended time on tests in a quiet room, use of a spellchecker, private communication with professors regarding the learning differences and needs, and a variety of other services, many of which were not taken advantage of as yet. Unbeknownst to us at the time (2004), one of the colleges selected by my child had one of the finest structured programs for students with learning differences in the United States. Students must submit a general application to the university admission office and another application to the program. This particular child, who never before wanted to discuss or reveal her learning differences, is now applying to the program to get help with the educational goal of graduating and perhaps continuing on for a medical degree.

When I consumed the information in *The K&W Guide*, I was specifically interested in colleges and universities that offered "structured programs" because my daughter had higher educational needs, and if my son with ADHD and severe dyslexia ever wanted to attend college he would need to be at a school with a very highly structured program. Just a few days ago, I thought a college education was out of the questions for students like him, but slowly the paradigm shift was occurring and I began to think it was possible. I decided to look at programs that were offered at small colleges that I had never heard of before. For example, in *The K&W Guide* I read about tiny University of the Ozarks, a school with an undergraduate enrollment of fewer than 800 students in Clarksville, Arkansas. Students who are admitted to Ozarks' Jones Learning Center are automatically admitted to the university and *no* ACT or SAT scores are required. The school believes that all students are entitled to an education that allows them to compete with other students and the Jones Center provides a total learning environment with individualized personalized instruction and a 4:1 student/staff ratio. The goal is to allow each student to realize their true academic potential, find their own learning style by utilizing strengths and circumventing deficits, and become independent learners and self-advocates.

The thrill of discovering colleges like University of the Ozarks and exploring their websites was palpable. That night I sat down once again to read, but this time it was Loren Pope's exceptional book, *Colleges that Change Lives*. When I came to the chapter entitled, "The Learning Disabled of Today will be the Gifted of

Tomorrow," my heart did stop. I had just been reading about the myriad of colleges and universities who recognized the gifts and the talents of the LD's and Asperger's of the world, and I thought: These students are the new breeding ground of talent and creativity in our country. Aside from the fact that history has proven that some of our greatest minds (Leonardo da Vinci, Albert Einstein) had great trouble with words but were visual, conceptual, and spatial thinkers, Pope contends that these are the same gifts that our modern world needs to foster now. We are entering a new era which has been called the "post-literate" era and the adage "a picture is worth a thousand words" will take on new meaning (Pope, 2000). As the computer's artificial intelligence multiplies and takes on all forms of computations and routine knowledge, the human gift will be the ability to bring imagination, creativity, intuition, serendipity, and connectivity to the task at hand, and this is where dyslexics are outstanding (Pope, 2000).

Rather than hide a LD on the application process, the student should be honest and remember that many of these colleges want to help you and know that many of the world's geniuses come from this group, including Lewis Carroll, Winston Churchill, William Butler Yeats, and Thomas Edison. My paradigm shift was complete when I realized that one day Adelphi University in Garden City, New York; tiny Mitchell College in New London, Connecticut; Westminster College in Fulton, Missouri; and Finlandia University in the rugged Upper Peninsula of Michigan could be the breeding ground for some of our most creative and talented students.

When the revelation hit me, I shared my enthusiasm with my out-of-the-box, brilliant child with Asperger's, who responded, "If this disorder is so wonderful, why don't they call it 'spatial ability' rather than 'dyslexia,'" and I wondered why myself. Just as the new political correctness prefers "learning different" to "learning disable," why label these original and creative thinkers "dys" (abnormal) and "lexia" (lexicon or vocabulary). Why not rename them "pro-spatial" and see what changes occur in their self-confidence and society's perception of their unique and sought after gifts. I will now embark on a "pro-spatial" campaign and see where my efforts lead me. This is my unexpected and wonderful discovery.

THOUGHTS FROM: MICHAEL BARRON, ASSISTANT PROVOST FOR ENROLLMENT SERVICES AND DIRECTOR OF ADMISSIONS, UNIVERSITY OF IOWA

Nearly four decades ago when I first became an admission officer, my mentors and colleagues suggested that I would encounter applicants who had not performed very well in high school. I was told to expect that some of those students would "claim" to have a reading problem and others would actually use the term dyslexia. It seems that many of my admission colleagues were somewhat dubious about the true extent of such a disability. I sadly shake my head now when I look back on those times when many of us simply discounted such students as just being lazy, dumb, or underprepared.

We are blessed today with greater knowledge about such matters, and more important, with compassionate understanding of those individuals who cope with one or more of the growing list of what we now call learning disabilities. Often these students exhibit strong to superior intellectual capacity, but lack the ability to mark the appropriate bubble or write an answer on paper in the prescribed time period. They are a resource that should not be overlooked or swept aside by our application of some of the more odious and inappropriate labels used in the past.

Educational institutions must take risks along with these students in order to help them develop their potential. We have learned that there are many disorders that impact an individual's ability to learn, but do not impair their intellectual capacity. I am pleased to say that now there are many more of my colleagues who understand these needs and, working carefully with disabilities specialists and faculty, are developing ways to provide these students with the opportunity for higher education.

At University of Iowa, staff in the Office of Admissions have taken the time to study and understand these conditions and carefully provide a holistic review of all factors in a student's background when considering their application for admission. When appropriate, we consult with professionals such as those who work in our Student Disability Services office to ensure that we have a clear understanding of the current thinking and research regarding the ability of students with learning disabilities to accommodate their disability and pursue their education. When students with learning disabilities apply for admission and self-identify, we look closely for those who have used the resources available to them to their fullest potential.

A diverse student body with a variety of talents, interests, and backgrounds is necessary in a university. Iowa welcomes applications from students with documented learning disabilities and/or attention deficit disorders. We are looking for students with the ability to do college work as reflected in the strength of the courses they have taken, as well as the compensatory strategies that they have employed during their high school years.

Some students fulfill all of our regular admission requirements despite documented learning disabilities. This does not mean that they no longer need compensatory strategies or a special office to assist them in advising faculty of their special needs. They do. We have also had excellent success at Iowa with students with learning disabilities who do not meet our regular admission requirements; data suggest that with proper attention, as many as eight out of ten such students succeed at the university. Faculty members are recruited to be partners in this process.

We recognize that the decision for students to self-identify as learning disabled is a personal choice. A student's decision not to self-identify is respected. However, it has been our experience that students with learning disabilities who acknowledge the existence of a disability and seek assistance early are more likely to achieve academic success than those who wait for problems to develop. It was not too long ago that such students would probably have never graduated from high school. Even if they did, they could not look forward to a future with very many options for employment.

Thankfully, we are making breakthroughs for many of these students, and are now providing them with access to and opportunities for higher education. While there are intervention and support programs like Iowa's that are beginning to achieve success, we have by no means provided a paradigm that is consistently accepted and used throughout the country. That will only come through public discussion of the successes and failures of those of us who have met the challenge and taken the risk. This book is certainly one of the resources I hope will be widely used in that effort.

While we are working to educate our colleagues, to modify our systems to accommodate these students, and to provide them with the opportunity to obtain the education that they desire, we must also begin to work as partners with industry. It will not be enough to provide an environment where an individual can complete a university degree and yet fail miserably in the world of work because of its lack of understanding and inappropriate job placement procedures. Our experience at Iowa is that these students desperately want to succeed, and they want to stand on the merits of their own achievements. To deny them the opportunity to be an asset at the highest level of their ability is to squander a valuable human resource, creating an unnecessary and unwanted liability for society. I urge students with learning disabilities and their families to use available law to firmly request the services they need and to be patient with those of us in the education establishment as we seek to understand. I also encourage educators at all levels to be sensitive to and aware of these individuals as a resource not to be wasted, and to work diligently to provide educational opportunity to all.

THOUGHTS FROM: ANN DINAN, PHD, ACADEMIC PERFORMANCE COACH AND ASPERGERS COACH

What does it take to be successful in college?

The number one factor with regard to success in college, is making a good choice. That sounds obvious, but so many students choose a college based on a school's sports program (that they are not personally involved with) or where their boy/girlfriend is going to college and they do not use criteria that will adequately support their success. For students with learning disabilities, this decision is even more complicated. You can never underestimate the importance of "fit." Many students who matriculate at my university say that as soon as they stepped foot on campus "it felt like home." I know what they mean, because I felt the same way as an administrator/professor. The students/professors/administrators here actually embody the mission of the university and that is extended to their actions. Inclusion is the prevailing attitude and it is part of the "feel" of the place. It is the little things that create this impression, such as students offering to help you if they see you are juggling a lot of books, or others' automatically holding doors open for everyone. People genuinely care about each other and go the extra mile, and it permeates the atmosphere here. Granted, this is not an environment for everyone. However, it is an environment that is extremely accepting of others. I don't think this characteristic can be underestimated when determining a college for a student with learning disabilities.

When searching for the "right" college/university, I recommend looking at class size (22–25 students or less per class is ideal for most learners), and the degree to which the student will be taught by professors and not teaching assistants. Truthfully, some professors regard teaching as a nuisance that gets in the way of their research. What do the students have to say about their professors and classes? What types of support offices exist on campus? Does the institution have a retention office, program, or plan? Does it have a TRIO program that accepts a small number of students who have disabilities regardless of whether they are first-generation students or not? What types of services/accommodations are offered through the disability office? What is the prevailing attitude toward students with disabilities? What is the relationship between the disabilities office and other support offices and the professors? If you are working with BVR or one of its arms, do they "support" the institution? Does BVR provide financial support to this institution? Are there extra charges for additional tutoring or coaching services? Can the health and counseling office manage the situation if required? How accessible is the campus AND the surrounding environment? Are there any special needs accommodations in the residence halls? What does the orientation program cover—socialization and ensuing social issues can, and do, impact academic performance down the road. Is there a priority registration program for students who either need to have their classes physically close together or who require special permission to get into certain classes? Who is the point person at the university, if one exists, and how closely will the student interact with this person?

Once the student is enrolled, it is never too early to forge a relationship with the head of the disability services office. It is best to do this early in the summer (June) and follow up at the beginning of August. Understand that receiving accommodations at the college level is different than at the high school level. I have encountered many a parent who came into my office with guns drawn based on their experiences in high school. That only serves to put the folks who will help you the most on the defensive. The mission of the disabilities office is for the student to succeed. Everyone is on the same team and retention is everyone's goal. Also, if you suspect a content tutor is going to be needed for one or more subjects, then ask the representative from the disability office about the program during the summer. If a formal program does not exist, ask about the process for finding and hiring a tutor. You will want to line this person up in advance of the first week of school if possible. The same would be true of a time management tutor or coach. Almost every student needs assistance in this area at least the first semester. Think about the type and level of support needed and ask the questions about compatible services. If you are a parent reading this book, consider joining the parents' group on campus. Talking about situations not only gives you inside information but it normalizes many things that go on especially during the freshman year! Finally, if the student is eligible for accommodations, register with the disability office and use the accommodations. And it is not too early to start thinking about graduate school. If the student is going to want accommodations for graduate-level standardized tests, they should make sure they request *and* use accommodations during their tenure because this is a question that the testing bodies ask and apparently take into account when determining accommodations for the tests.

Sometimes all the planning and best thinking will not result in a successful academic experience. I have witnessed this time and time again. So much so, that I created the first full-fledged academic coaching program at the university level. Coaching, as we define it, is a partnership that is designed to help people reach their goals by employing a strength-based model. There are very specific and tangible coaching skills that are employed within this paradigm. All of our coaches are trained and certified by an International Coaching Federation-approved program, and the program has been wildly successful. Students who regularly attended weekly coaching sessions, achieved 100 percent of their goals. Even more remarkable was the fact that these results were achieved within 3 months. Most importantly, the students not only achieved their goals, but they learned skills they can apply to other situations and throughout their lives. Students with disabilities benefited from coaching in the areas of socialization and time management, just to name two categories. Many students with certain disabilities such as Asperger's apply obsessive-compulsive/perfectionistic tendencies to studying and/or test-taking that bog them down. Assigning the students a time management tutor and bringing the tutor on board with the goals helped the students learn necessary management skills. Additionally, students with Asperger's often blurt out answers and have difficulty keeping track of the big picture in class. By working in conjunction with faculty and teachers, greater success was observed. Additionally, the process of adapting to a college roommate is usually a concern of most parents of students with Asperger's or physical disabilities. By working with these students as well as the resident hall assistants on socialization and discussing expectations, potential problems were mitigated. A wrap-around service approach seems to really buoy the student and their chances for success!

The student who inspired our initial coaching program earned a .25 GPA the previous semester before he began coaching. We started working together in January and his first goal was to achieve a 2.0 GPA. Within a few weeks of coaching it was clear he would attain this goal. Much to my amazement, he upped the ante and said his new goal was a 2.5. A few weeks later his GPA AND his new goal was a 3.0 (a solid B average). At mid-term he confidently told me that was going to achieve a 3.5 GPA (Dean's List) by the end of the semester. He narrowly missed this goal but achieved the 3.0 by the end of April! This student not only graduated on time, but is now enrolled in graduate school!

Coaching has been a resounding success for students at all grade levels with varying levels of abilities. Let's hope that by the 10th edition of this book coaching is no longer a novel concept but a recognized accommodation and tool for retention and success of all students!

Ann Dinan, PhD
Director, Learning Assistance Center
Xavier University
Academic Performance Coach
513-503-4246
dinan@xavier.edu

THOUGHTS FROM: LYDIA S. BLOCK, PhD, EDUCATIONAL CONSULTANT, BLOCK EDUCATIONAL CONSULTING, COLUMBUS, OHIO

For many students the idea of attending a large university is very intriguing. These schools offer large sports programs, many majors, different types of living situations, and a multitude of cultural and social activities. Successfully negotiating the large university setting also requires a considerable amount of initiative on the student's part. How do students and their parents know when a large school is a good match? How does a student know that he or she will be able to get what is necessary in terms of academic support and accommodations from a large university? These are important things to find out before applying. *The K&W Guide* is the best resource available to provide families with information gleaned first-hand both from school visitations and directly from the schools' Disability Service Provider.

With few exceptions most large universities have disability service programs to serve students with all disabilities. Some campuses have limited staff to work with students, and students will find that it is up to them to seek the help that they need. By the nature of their size, there is far less personal attention at a large university then at a small school and students must learn to advocate for themselves. Students at large schools must be very independent. The classes are generally large the first year or two, some are taught by graduate students, and it is less likely that a faculty member will be able to get to know a student well. Students must know what they need in terms of academic support and accommodations and be prepared to ask for it. Generally, students are responsible for filing paperwork with the appropriate office to receive accommodation, and for meeting with faculty members to explain their disability.

In addition to knowing what they need in terms of accommodations, students at large universities must also be able to identify when they do not understand material or an assignment. This is true at any school, but a large university offers fewer opportunities for class discussion and often less access to faculty members than a small school. So it is up to the students to seek help when they need it.

Students with attention deficit hyperactivity disorder sometimes find it difficult to structure their academic and social lives at a large university. Students must rely on motivation and their ability to independently make decisions and follow them through. This is a challenge for all college freshmen, but it is particularly difficult for some students with LD and ADHD.

For students who have been successfully involved in activities in high school, and shown the ability to structure their lives and advocate for themselves, a large institution can be full of wonderful opportunities. For certain majors, large schools offer the best programs, noted faculty, and research and internship opportunities. It is important for students to consider what being a student at a large campus environment will be like. When the student visits a large university, it is essential that she sit in on large lecture classes and meet with the disability service provider. These are important steps in realistically evaluating what life would be like in a setting where everything will not always be clearly defined.

The Ten Most Commonly Asked Questions by Parents of College Bound Students with Disabilities

1. Will the disability support services (DSS) provided in college be the same as those provided in high school?

It is important to know that colleges and universities provide accommodations under the requirements of the Americans with Disabilities Act and Section 504 of the 1973 Rehabilitation Act. Neither act requires postsecondary institutions to provide accommodations that fundamentally alter the essential requirements of a course, alter the core curriculum of an academic program, or provide assistance that is considered to be "personal" in nature. Therefore, it is feasible that some accommodations provided in high school may not be provided in postsecondary education. For a detailed explanation of the ADA and Section 504 as it pertains to college and university requirements, visit POSTITT.org//frame/legal/compare.htm.

2. When should we make contact with the disability support (DSS) office?

Because the services provided by a DSS office can vary from minimal to extensive, it is important to determine whether the DSS office can meet individual student need *before* the student enrolls in the institution. Students and parents are strongly encouraged to visit the DSS office as early as their junior year in high school. Each college visit should include a scheduled meeting with the campus DSS office for a detailed investigation of its service offerings.

3. Is my child's written Individualized Education Program (IEP) sufficient to establish college eligibility for disability support services?

An Individualized Education Program (IEP) is a function of the Individuals with Disabilities Education Act (IDEA), a K–12 special education statute. The IDEA does not apply to postsecondary institutions. Thus the IEP while, helpful in establishing a history of using accommodations, does not apply in the postsecondary setting. Colleges will typically require more detailed information of the disability to determine eligibility–information that usually far exceeds what exists within the IEP. A recent psychosocial assessment by a licensed professional will likely be required to establish eligibility for college disability support services. For an example of the most common documentation requirements for students with learning disabilities and attention deficit disorder seeking college accommodations, visit ETS.org.

4. Should my son or daughter disclose their disability on the admission application?

College admissions applications are generally prohibited from asking students if they have a disability; however, whether to disclose the existence of a disability is a personal decision that should be considered carefully. For example, if a student has overcome significant odds and achieved academically, disclosing the disability in a personal statement highlights their record of accomplishment and could be a benefit. If electing to disclose, the goal is to highlight your academic strengths, not your weaknesses. Whether you choose to disclose or not, postsecondary institutions are not required to waive or lower its admission criteria because a student has a disability.

5. **Are there existing scholarships specifically for students with disabilities?**

Colleges and universities typically offer scholarships for students meeting a wide variety of criteria and characteristics, including disability status. Check with both the college's office of financial aid and scholarship, as well as the DSS office to inquire what is available. Many national organizations serving individuals with disabilities offer scholarships and thus, parents and students should also inquire directly with these organizations. For a comprehensive listing of organizations, review the free listing of Web Resources for Assisting College Students with Disabilities at DAS.kucrl.org/iam/resources.html

6. **Will my son or daughter's disability qualify him/ her for a single residence hall room?**

As with all accommodation requests at the postsecondary level, qualification for a single residence hall room will be evaluated on an individualized basis. Students should make their request known to the DSS office before they enroll. The exact nature of the student's disability and the resulting impact on both the student and the potential roommate(s) will be one of the determining factors.

7. **Will the DSS staff have expertise in my child's disability?**

The professional training and background of the DSS office professional staff can vary immensely from campus to campus. Some may have specific certification in learning disabilities and cognitive disorders, while others may have a generalist background in such fields as counseling, education, or social work, among a few. When investigating the service offered by the DSS office, do not hesitate to inquire about the expertise, training, and credentials of the professional staff.

8. **Are private tutors available?**

The U.S. Department of Education Office of Civil Rights has been consistent in its findings that tutoring is a "personal service" and therefore, postsecondary institutions are under no obligation to provide it. On most college campuses however, some form of tutoring will be available. Students with disabilities will have access to existing tutoring services on the same basis as other students. Some campuses with comprehensive DSS services may indeed provide specialized, private professional tutoring for students with disabilities, although there may be a fee associated with this specialized service.

9. **Will the college keep me informed of my child's academic progress?**

Colleges and universities view enrolled students as adults and will generally place limits on divulging personal information of its students. Further, the Family Educational Rights and Privacy Act (FERPA) limits some of the information the college and DSS office can share with parents without written permission from the student. Therefore, parents should assume that neither the DSS office nor the college will release information relating to a student's academic progress. For a detailed explanation of FERPA, visit Ed.gov/offices/OM/fpco/ferpa.

10. **Is there a centralized resource that can provide me with detailed information on the DSS offices throughout the country as we begin the college selection process?**

Yes! You have an excellent resource right at your fingertips! *The K & W Guide to Colleges for Students with Learning Disabilities or Attention Deficit Hyperactivity Disorder* is an excellent starting point for exploring the wide spectrum of assistance provided by DSS offices in every state. Keep in mind that the goal of college is not just getting in, but getting out *successfully.* Finding an appropriate DSS office to student match can be the key to that success. *The K & W Guide to Colleges for Students with Learning Disabilities or Attention Deficit Hyperactivity Disorder* can help direct you in that roadmap to success.

Reprinted with permission from Dr. Kendra Johnson, President of Transition Game Educational Consultants, an educational consulting firm specializing in assisting students with disabilities with the transition to college, and the co-author of the book, *100 Things Every College Student with a Disability Ought to Know*.

INFORMATION FROM AN ATTORNEY ON DISABILITY LAW

Obtaining Accommodations for College Students with Disabilities By Matt Cohen, Esq.

Matt Cohen has represented children and adults with disabilities in regard to public and higher education for approximately 25 years. He regularly writes on disability law topics and lectures regularly on these subjects throughout the United States.

Although some children with disabilities may have impairments that are so severe that college is not a realistic option for them, many others have the potential to be highly successful in college and beyond, particularly if provided the appropriate accommodations that they need to function within the college environment. However, the procedures for obtaining accommodations are very different in relation to getting into and participating in higher education than they are in elementary and high school. In the public school system, the responsibility lies with the school district to identify children suspected of having disabilities, to evaluate them (with parental consent), and to develop and implement individualized educational programs (IEPs) or Section 504 plans designed to meet their unique needs. Unfortunately, the Individuals with Disabilities Education Act (IDEA)—the law governing special education—does not apply to higher education.

Further, while Section 504 applies to many colleges and universities, the rules for how it applies are different than within public elementary and high schools. Eligibility under the IDEA or Section 504 in public school does NOT automatically ensure that a student will be eligible for accommodations in college or, if eligible, will automatically qualify for the same services or accommodations. In order to maximize the likelihood that the student will receive appropriate accommodations in college, the parents, the student, and the school district must begin planning well before the child applies for college. Some of these steps will be briefly highlighted below.

The Right to Accommodations

Two different federal laws govern the right to accommodations in relation to higher education. The first is the Americans with Disabilities Act of 1990 (the ADA), which has two different sections that are relevant to higher education. Title II of the ADA regulates local and state governmental entities, which includes public colleges and universities. Title III of the ADA regulates what are called places of public accommodation. All private colleges and universities are places of public accommodation. However, those schools that are religiously-affiliated are exempt from the coverage of the ADA.

In addition to regulating the provision of "reasonable accommodations" within colleges and universities, the ADA also provides the right to reasonable accommodations from agencies that administer the tests that are used for college and graduate admissions and for licensing upon graduation. Thus, the ACT, SAT, MCAT, LSAT, etc. are all operated by organizations that are required to comply with the requirements of the ADA.

The second law which governs the right to reasonable accommodations in higher education is Section 504 of the Rehabilitation Act of 1973. Section 504 provides very similar protections as the ADA, but with one significant difference. In order for Section 504 to be applicable, the organization must be a recipient of federal financial assistance. While most colleges and universities do receive federal financial assistance and are therefore governed by Section 504, not all do. Thus, the non-discrimination laws apply to all colleges and universities except those that are religiously-affiliated and do not receive federal financial assistance.

What Needs to Happen during High School?

First, all students in special education should have a transition plan in place starting at the age of 16. This plan should include the student's input about long-term goals; assessment of the student's continuing needs; and the development and implementation of a plan to facilitate the student's accomplishment of realistic postsecondary goals. This plan, when done right, can often provide important support for students to prepare them for college, before they even get there. The transition plan can ADHDress not only academic and vocational goals, but life skills, organizational or executive functioning needs, social deficits, and a variety of other issues that may impact students' ability to function successfully in college even if they meet the college's admissions criteria.

Secondly, students need to identify what schools may be appropriate for them to consider, in light of their disability. Consulting *The K&W Guide* and meeting with college counselors can be invaluable in helping to determine whether particular colleges or even types of colleges are realistic for the students, with or without the provision of accommodations. If the student is going to take the SAT and/or ACT, the school and the family must take the necessary steps to secure accommodations on those tests. For those students who do not test well on such tests, it is worth investigating colleges that place less emphasis on those tests or don't require them at all (See www/fairtest.org for a list), a trend which has gained momentum recently.

Finally, before a student in special education graduates, the school district is required to complete a document called a Summary of Performance. This document is supposed to identify the nature of the student's disability, the accommodations currently being provided in school, the progress to date, and services and/or supports that need to be continued. The Summary of Performance, required by law beginning in 2005, can be of enormous value both in documenting the nature of the student's disability and in providing support for the provision of particular accommodations. It is so new that not all schools are fully familiar with it, so parents should be sure that this is provided to them before the student graduates.

Who is Entitled to Accommodations Under the Disability Rights Laws?

Under both the ADA and Section 504, a person is entitled to reasonable accommodations if that person meets a number of criteria. First, the person must have a physical or mental impairment which substantially limits a major life activity. There are a variety of different major life activities, but one of the most important, for purposes of accommodations in college, is the major life activity of learning. Secondly, the person must meet the general qualifications for participation in the program or activity for which special access is being requested, either with or without accommodations. Finally, the person must establish that there is a need for specific accommodations and that these accommodations are "reasonable."

These criteria are very different from those used under the IDEA for children in special education. Unlike the public schools, where the responsibility lies with the school to identify, evaluate, and plan a program for children suspected of having a disability, the ADA and Section 504 place the responsibility for establishing the presence of a disability with the student seeking the accommodation. In other words, if the student wants reasonable accommodations, the student must come forward, identify that there is a disability, document the disability and the need for accommodation, and specifically request the provision of such accommodations. The burden is on the student, not the college. In fact, under these laws, the college may not ask questions about disabilities in the application/admissions process and the student need not disclose the existence of a disability.

Students seeking information about how a particular college will respond to the student's disability and whether it will have appropriate services to meet the student's needs can and should contact the school's office of disability services. The disability services staff will be able to share information about the types of services that are provided, the types of students that are effectively served by the college or university, and help the students to determine when and what information to share (pre- or post-application) in securing accommodations.

Although this is less often an issue, it should also be pointed out that under both laws, students are protected from discrimination if they have a history of disability or are perceived to have a disability. Thus, a school could not discriminate against an individual who is HIV Positive but has no symptoms, simply because of their HIV-Positive status. This would be discrimination based on the student being regarded as having a disability, even though they were not at that time actually disabled.

The Need for Documentation

Because the burden rests with the student to document that there actually is a disability, it is important that the student keep careful records of the existence of the impairment. This requires several different kinds of documentation. Colleges and universities are interested in the student's history in relation to the disability. Clinical reports which first provide the diagnosis and which track the progression of the diagnosis are useful in establishing that the disability has been present on a long-standing basis. Secondly, colleges are interested in current evaluations, typically within the past three years if not more current. Often, evaluations can be obtained from the school districts during this period, which may provide the necessary information. However, under some circumstances, the student may need to obtain outside clinical evaluations. This may be necessary for several reasons. First, if the student does not have a current school district evaluation, the outside evaluation may be the only option for obtaining current diagnostic material. Secondly, and particularly for students who are high functioning or even gifted, or who have more subtle disabilities, more sophisticated private testing may provide data that offers support for the presence of a disability that does not surface in the public school's testing.

In addition to clinical material, the colleges and universities are very interested in whether the student has been receiving special education and/or Section 504 services. Colleges tend to be more receptive to the provision of accommodations when the student has a history of having received special education or Section 504 accommodations for a long period of time. Colleges tend to be more skeptical of the student's entitlement to accommodations if the student went through most or all of school without assistance and only became eligible for services late in high school. Unfortunately, there is a sense that some students deliberately seek eligibility around the junior year of high school for the primary purpose of obtaining accommodations on the SAT and ACT and for purposes of accommodations in college. While this may sometimes happen, there are also many students whose disability does not become a major problem or become obvious until the rigors of high school expose the problems that the students had previously been able to cope with successfully. Nonetheless, providing documentation of a prior history of accommodations is very useful in establishing both general eligibility for accommodations and justifying the need for the particular accommodations being requested. The graduate exam administrators (for the MCAT, LSAT, etc.) also look closely at whether there is a history of accommodation in high school and college, so these processes have a domino effect as the student progresses through school.

While students with late-diagnosed disabilities are not excluded from being considered for accommodations, there is no question that those students are viewed with greater scrutiny and may need even more documentation to establish that they have a real impairment and require accommodations. Notably, recent research has suggested that the criteria for diagnosing AD/HD may be modified to allow for diagnosis based on symptoms that manifest themselves in adolescence, rather than in childhood, because of growing information that suggests that not all students with AD/HD meet criteria in elementary school. This may make it easier for some late-diagnosed students to make the case for eligibility.

Obtaining Accommodations After Admission

As indicated, the school may not ask questions that directly or indirectly seek to identify whether a student has a disability during the application process. However, some students may choose to share information about their disability during the application process or even use the disability as material in application essays for sharing ways that they have coped with adversity or otherwise. Whether to share and what to share in the application process is a difficult decision, which should typically be made in consultation with parents, college counselors, and even the disabilities services staff at the college the student is interested in attending.

Once the student has been admitted, however, and wants accommodations, the student must contact the office of disability services, present documentation of a disability, and formally request accommodations. A wide variety of accommodations are available, from preferential seating to extra time for assignments or tests; from use of a note-taker to use of a tape recorder or word processor for completion of assignments. The nature of potential accommodations is at one level limitless, in that there is no specified list. Instead, accommodations are developed to respond to the needs of the particular individual. On the other hand, just because a student seeks a particular accommodation, or even received that accommodation previously in public school, does not mean that the college or university is obligated to provide it.

Unlike special education, the college or university is not obligated to provide individual tutoring or 1-1 aides. If they elect to do so, as some do, they may charge extra fees for those services. The colleges must make their own judgment as to whether a request for a particular accommodation is "unduly burdensome" rather than reasonable. That determination will be based on a variety of factors, including but not limited to the quality of the student's documentation supporting the need for the accommodation, whether the student has a history of receiving the accommodation, the size of the college and its ability to provide the accommodation, and whether the college feels the accommodation simply goes beyond what is reasonable for the student.

In addition, the college has the right to refuse requested accommodations if the college believes and can establish that the proposed accommodation will "fundamentally alter" the basic mission, organization, or mode of operation of the school. This comes up most often in circumstances when the student is requesting a total waiver of a particular requirement for graduation, such as exemption from math or foreign language requirements. Under some circumstances, alternatives to these requirements can be agreed upon which will work for the student and satisfy the school, but this is not always the case.

What to do if the accommodation is not being provided?

Unlike public school, where the school district is charged with the responsibility for insuring compliance with the IEP or 504 plan, there is less direct responsibility for enforcement placed on the college or university. At the outset, schools handle the process of alerting faculty of the accommodation plan in a variety of ways. In some cases the office of disability services takes initial responsibility for notifying the faculty, while in other colleges the burden is put on the student to bring the accommodations' plan to the attention of the faculty member. Once the plan has been presented, the staff person is supposed to carry the plan out, but implementation often varies with the personality, understanding, and sensitivity of the individual staff member. Where there is a problem with compliance, the student is advised to follow a series of steps:

1) Try to work it out directly with the faculty member

2) Seek the help of the office of disability services staff

3) Seek to work things out with higher-ups in the particular department or dean's office

4) Determine what the school's internal grievance procedure is. Typically, schools have two sets of grievance procedures, a general grievance procedure relating to any problem involving a student, and a specific grievance procedure for handling disability related complaints. In consultation with the office of disability services staff, parents, and perhaps private counsel, the student may opt to file exclusively via the disability grievance route, the general grievance route, or both. In either event, the student should be aware that there are typically specific timelines and documentation requirements set forth in the grievance procedures.

5) If these efforts are unsuccessful, or if the problem is sufficiently severe to warrant more serious action, the student may file complaints with the U.S. Department of Education, Office for Civil Rights or the U.S. Department of Justice, for violation of Section 504 or the ADA respectively.

Obviously, these are last resort measures and students are best off resolving matters informally and amicably within the school structure whenever possible.

When seeking to obtain reasonable accommodations, documentation is critical. The standards for qualifying for accommodations are generally getting tougher, rather than easier, so parents and students should be thorough in gathering as much information about the student's difficulties–both historically and currently–as possible. School records, clinical data, anecdotal information, and evidence of the actual impact of the impairment are all critical in order for the student to receive recognition as a person with a disability and obtain the desired accommodations. Once the accommodations have been secured, the student must develop and judiciously implement self-advocacy skills to insure that the accommodations are provided as intended and as needed. When in doubt, students should seek assistance from their office of disability services, or if necessary, from outside agencies such as the Office for Civil Rights (www.ed.gov./about/offices/list/ocr and www.hhs.gov.ocr), or from knowledgeable lawyers. Students and parents can obtain more information about disability rights in higher education and the process of securing accommodations at two excellent websites: Heath.gwu.edu and Ahead.org.

Matt Cohen, Esq.
Monahan & Cohen
225 West Washington Street, Suite 2300
Chicago, IL 60606
312-419-0252
www.monahan-cohen.com
mdcspedlaw@earthlink.net

GUIDELINES FOR DOCUMENTATION OF LEARNING DISABILITIES OR ATTENTION DEFICIT HYPERACTIVITY DISORDER

Students with disabilities may arrive as freshmen knowing what strategies have worked best for them in a previous learning environment, or they may become injured or diagnosed after they arrive at college and face some unanticipated adjustments to learning and living in a campus environment. In either case, they are asked by institutions of higher learning to provide clinical documentation to assist the school in determining what, if any, accommodations are appropriate now: The mere history of services at an earlier age and in a previous setting may not reflect the intellectual functioning, demands, and routines of the new environment.

Rather than expect clinicians to guess how little or how much information is needed, documentation guidelines have been developed over time which are designed to capture the current functional strengths and limitations of each student seeking accommodations. It gives the disability service provider the opportunity to start a conversation with students based on solid information, and promotes communication with professionals to clarify the information, leading to the best opportunity to serve students well.

Our documentation guidelines are designed to parallel those of testing agencies and professional licensure examinations to minimize the need for frequent, expensive re-testing. Whatever postsecondary setting the student may enter, this information can lead to the development of excellent self-advocacy skills designed to help schools and employers provide the most productive environment possible.

Louise H. Russell, Director
Student Disability Resources
Harvard University

One of the more confusing things about applying to college as a student with a learning disability or Attention Deficit Hyperactivity Disorder is answering the questions: "What documentation should I send?" and "How will the college use that documentation?" It is important to keep in mind that documentation of your disability cannot be considered during the admission process unless you are requesting special consideration of your application. In cases of special consideration, your disability documentation may help the review committee understand the nature of your learning disability and how it impacted your high school studies. It may also help to explain why you did not complete some high school classes commonly required for admission to your favorite college or university.

Though documentation may be important during the admission process, for most students current, comprehensive documentation becomes critical for receiving appropriate accommodations guaranteed under either the ADA or Section 504. Guidelines for documenting learning disabilities or ADHD in postsecondary-age individuals are provided by the individual colleges or universities. These guidelines are used to verify the existence of a student's disability and may determine what accommodations are appropriate to support each student's enrollment.

IDEA no longer requires that a disability be re-evaluated every three years. It is true that learning disabilities do not go away with age, but the nature of the disability may change and functional limitations may result in difficulties not experienced until college. For this reason, many colleges and universities are requiring that documentation of disability be "current," in many cases within the last three years.

Comprehensive documentation, including measures of aptitude, achievement, and information processing are essential for any college or university to implement the best possible academic accommodation plan. Accommodations are to be provided based on the individual student's functional limitations and each evaluation should point to a link between the test scores and the recommendations the evaluator is making regarding the student's needs. Students sometimes believe that because an evaluator made recommendations in his or her documentation report that those recommendations will be followed. This may not be true. The postsecondary service provider must be able to identify how the functional limitations of the disability necessitate a particular accommodation.

Documentation of learning disabilities or ADHD should include results of a clinical interview with a medical, family, school, and psychosocial history. This information not only helps to ADHD to the credibility of a diagnosis of the disability, it also frequently helps the service provider to understand the full scope of a student's needs.

Providing comprehensive, current documentation of your disability in the form of a report compiled by a well-trained professional will help to assure you the most appropriate support services in college. Make sure you do everything you can to set the stage for your success!

Diane C. Quinn, Ed. Past Director,
The S.A.L.T. Center
The University of Arizona

GUIDELINES FOR REQUESTING ACCOMMODATIONS DUE TO A LEARNING DISABILITY

INTRODUCTION

Students requesting accommodations are required to submit documentation to determine eligibility in accordance with Section 504 of the Rehabilitation Act of 1973 and the Americans with Disabilities Act (ADA). A diagnosis of a learning disability does not necessarily qualify a student for academic accommodations under the law. To establish that a student is covered under Section 504 and the ADA, the documentation must indicate that the disability *substantially* limits some major life activity, including learning. Individual colleges or universities will determine eligibility and appropriate services, case by case, based on the quality, current testing, and completeness of the documentation submitted.

REQUIREMENTS OF THE COMPONENTS OF DOCUMENTATION

A Qualified Professional Must Conduct the Evaluation: The assessment must be administered by a trained and qualified (i.e., certified and/or licensed) professional.

Documentation Must be Current: Reasonable accommodations are based on the current impact of the disability on academic performance. A diagnostic evaluation should be age appropriate and relevant to the student's learning environment, and show the student's current level of functioning.

Documentation Must Include a Specific Diagnosis: The report must include a clear and direct statement that a learning disability does or does not exist and must rule out alternative explanations of learning problems. Terms such as "learning difficulty," "appears," "suggests," or "probable" do not support a conclusive diagnosis.

Documentation Must be Comprehensive: It must include a summary containing relevant historical information, instructional interventions, related services, and age of initial diagnosis. The documentation must also include objective data regarding aptitude, achievement, and information processing. Test scores (standard scores, percentiles, and grade equivalents) must be included in the documentation.

Recommendations for Accommodations: A diagnostic report may include specific recommendations for accommodations. Prior history of an accommodation, without a demonstration of a current need, does not in and of itself warrant the provision of a like accommodation. Each accommodation recommended should include a rationale and the evaluation should support the recommendations with specific test results or clinical observations.

EXAMPLES OF TYPICAL MEASURES USED IN ADULT ASSESSMENT OF LEARNING DISABILITIES

(This is intended to serve only as a guide for clinicians.)

Aptitude

   a. Wechsler Adult Intelligence Scale-3rd Edition (WAIS-III)

   b. Wechsler Adult Intelligence Scale-Revised (WAIS-R)

   c. Stanford Binet Intelligence Scale-4th and 5th Edition (SB IV, V)

   d. Woodcock-Johnson Psychoeducational Battery—3rd Edition: Tests of Cognitive Ability

   e. Woodcock-Johnson Psychoeducational Battery—Revised: Tests of Cognitive Ability

   f. Kaufman Adolescent and Adult Intelligence Test

Achievement

    a. Wechsler Individual Achievement Tests II (WIAT II)

    b. Wechsler Individual Achievement Test (WIAT)

    c. Woodcock-Johnson Psychoeducational Battery—3rd Edition: Tests of Achievement (WJ-III)

    d. Woodcock-Johnson Psychoeducational Battery—Revised: Tests of Achievement (WJ-R)

    e. Stanford Test of Academic Skills (TASK)

    f. Scholastic Abilities Test for Adults (SATA)

Assessments such as the **Wide Range Achievement Test (WRAT-III)** are not considered a comprehensive measure of achievement and must be accompanied by a comprehensive measure such as one of those listed above. All instruments selected to measure these areas must be age appropriate.

Information Processing

    a. Subtests of the WAIS-R or WAIS-III

    b. Subtests of the Woodcock-Johnson Psycho educational Battery: Tests of Cognitive Ability c. Wechsler Memory Scales-Revised or 3rd Edition

GENERAL GUIDELINES FOR REQUESTING ACCOMMODATIONS FOR ATTENTION DEFICIT HYPERACTIVITY DISORDER

Introduction

Students requesting accommodations or services because of AD/HD are required to submit documentation to determine eligibility in accordance with Section 504 of the Rehabilitation Act of 1973 and the Americans with Disabilities Act (ADA). A diagnosis of AD/HD does not necessarily qualify a student for academic accommodations under the law. To establish that a student is covered under Section 504 and the ADA, the documentation must indicate that the disability substantially limits some major life activity, including learning. For students previously diagnosed who have not continuously received medical and educational support, a comprehensive evaluation may be necessary to determine whether academic accommodations are appropriate.

REQUIREMENTS OF THE COMPONENTS OF DOCUMENTATION

A Qualified Professional Must Conduct the Evaluation: The assessment must be administered by a trained and qualified (i.e., certified and/or licensed) professional, who has had direct experience with adolescents and adults with AD/HD.

Documentation Must Be Current: Reasonable accommodations are based on the current impact of the disability on academic performance. In most cases, this means that a diagnostic evaluation should be age appropriate and relevant to the students learning environment, and show the students current level of functioning.

Documentation Must Include a Specific Diagnosis: The report must include a specific diagnosis of AD/HD based on the DSM-IV diagnostic criteria. It is recommended that the diagnostic criteria used to support the diagnosis be included. The diagnosis must avoid the use of terms such as "suggests," "is indicative of," or "attentional problems."

Documentation Must Include Evidence of Current Impairment

Statement of Presenting Problem

A history of the individual's presenting attentional symptoms including evidence of ongoing hyperactive-impulsive or inattentive behaviors that significantly impair functioning in an academic setting.

Diagnostic Interview

Information from a structured interview may include:

- Family history

- Educational history

- Developmental history

- Medical history

- Social history

- Review of prior psycho-educational reports

- Description of current functional limitations pertaining to an educational setting

- Relevant history of therapeutic treatment

Documentation Must Include Relevant Testing Information

Psychoeducational assessments help determine the current impact of the disorder on the individual's ability to function in an academic setting. The report must include objective data, which might include, but not be limited to psychological assessments, educational assessments, rating scales, memory function tests, attention or tracking tests, or continuous performance tests. The report should include a score report page(s) presenting the tests, sub tests, standard scores, and percentiles.

Current Plan for Treatment and Effects of Medication

Plans should summarize current treatment including the use of medications. The report should indicate whether or not the individual was evaluated while on medication, and whether the use of medications mitigates the impact of the disorder on the individual's ability to function in an academic setting.

Recommendations for Accommodations

A diagnostic report may include specific recommendations for accommodation(s). It is important to note that a prior history of an accommodation, without demonstrating a current need, may not warrant the provision of similar accommodation. Each accommodation recommended should include a rationale. The evaluation should also support the recommendations with specific test results or clinical observations. Each college will make the final determination of what accommodations is appropriate based on documentation provided.

GETTING READY

The purpose of *The K&W Guide* is to help students with learning disabilities or attention deficit disorder acquire the basic knowledge necessary to begin the college exploration process and get ready to make appropriate college selections.

TO GET READY STUDENTS NEED TO:

- Understand their strengths and weaknesses.
- Be able to articulate the nature of their learning disabilities.
- Understand the compensatory skills developed to accommodate the learning differences.
- Describe the services they received in high school.
- Identify short-term and long-term goals.
- Select appropriate college choices to match individual needs.

GUIDELINES FOR THE SEARCH AND SELECTION PROCESS

Self Assessment

- What is the student's disability?
- When was the disability diagnosed?
- What is the student's level of performance in high school?
- Is the student enrolled in college-prep courses, modified courses, or individualized, special-education courses?
- What are the student's individual strengths and weaknesses?
- Is it easier for the student to learn from a lecture, from reading the material, or from having the material read to her?
- Does the student perform better on written assignments or oral presentations?
- Which subjects are easier, and which are more difficult?
- What are the student's favorite and least favorite courses and why?
- What are the student's short-term and long-term goals?
- Are these goals realistic?
- Is the student striving to improve in academic areas?
- What accommodations are being provided?
- Is the student actively utilizing resource assistance and learning compensatory strategies?
- What does the student plan to study in college?
- What skills and competencies are required for the career goals being pursued?
- When were the last diagnostic tests given?
- What level of services/accommodations are needed in college? Structured programs, comprehensive services, or basic services?

ARTICULATION

- Does the student understand the disability?

- Can the student describe the disability?

- Does the student comprehend how the disability impacts learning?

- Can the student explain the nature of the disability?

- Can the student explain the accommodations being utilized as well as any curriculum modifications received?

- Can the student explain necessary accommodations to teachers?

ACADEMIC ASSESSMENT

Does the student have difficulty with written language?

- Using appropriate words

- Organizing thoughts

- Writing lengthy compositions

- Using correct punctuation and sentence structure

- Expressing thoughts clearly

Does the student have trouble with verbal expression?

- Retrieving appropriate words

- Understanding what others are saying

- Using words in the correct context

- Carrying on conversations

Does the student have a problem with hand-eye coordination?

- Finding certain information on a page

- Performing tasks that require fine motor coordination

Does the student get frustrated reading?

- Decoding unfamiliar words

- Understanding reading assignments

- Completing reading assignments within a time frame

Does the student often misspell words?

- Mix up the sequence of letters

- Become confused when spelling irregular words

Does the student experience difficulty performing mathematics?

- Multiplication table and fractions

- Sequencing of steps of various mathematical questions

Does the student have difficulty concentrating?

- Fidgets or squirms

- Distracted by noises

- Difficulty following instructions
- Difficulty finishing assignments

What are the student's study habits?

- Attentive in class for an extended period of time
- Easily distracted
- Needs extra time to respond to questions
- Note-taking skills
- Memory
- Time management
- Time orientation
- Organization

How is the student's handwriting ability?

- Assignments are difficult to read
- Appropriate capitalization used
- Stays within the lines when writing
- Leaves enough space between words

EXPLORATION AND TIMELINES

Sophomore year

- Explore options.
- Consider taking the PLAN (if available)- request appropriate testing accommodations.
- Meet with counselor and case manager.
- Review testing and documentation.
- Review course registration for junior year. Students considering four year colleges/universities should be enrolled in as many main mainstreamed, college preparatory courses as possible.
- Write to colleges or use college web sites to explore for information.
- Contact the service providers on the college campus.
- Work on developing good self-advocacy skills.
- Understand learning style and strengths and challenges.
- Understand the disability.

Junior year

- Consider taking the PSAT—request appropriate testing accommodations
- Review achievement level.
- Review course registration for senior year. Students considering four year colleges/universities should be enrolled in as many main mainstreamed, college preparatory courses as possible.
- Write to colleges or use college web sites to explore for information.
- Review the level of services in high school.

- Identify the level of services needed in college.

- Be able to articulate the disability.

- Be comfortable asking for support and accommodations.

- Participate in the IEP process and be actively involved in the IEP meeting.

- Visit colleges.

- Register for the ACT/SAT, standardized or non-standardized.

- Request necessary updated psychoeducational testing (Including the WAIS-R).

Senior year

- Submit general applications.

- Submit special applications (if required).

- Schedule interviews (if appropriate).

- Write essays (if required).

- Disclose disability to college.

- Release current psychoeducational testing.*

- Release documentation of other health-related disabilities.*

- Be sure that the documentation includes a description of the disability and recommended accommodations.

- Be sure to get copies of the entire special education file including testing assessments and IEP summaries to have in your personal files after graduation.

Students under the age of eighteen must have their parents' signature to release information to each of the colleges.

CAMPUS VISITS

- The student should call to make an arrangement for a visit.

- Visit while classes are in session.

- Meet with admissions and special support service providers.

- Take a guided tour.

- Attend a class.

- Eat a meal on campus.

- Drive around the boundaries of the campus.

- Take pictures, take notes, and talk to students on campus.

- Take parents or family members along (but not in the interview).

- Pick up college catalogue, view book, video, and support service brochures.

- Write thank-you notes.

INTERVIEWS

To prepare for interviews, students should know:

- Strengths and weaknesses.
- The accommodations needed.
- How to describe learning disability.

If an interview is required prior to an admission decision:

- View the interview as an opportunity.
- Prepare a list of questions.
- Know that interviews, if required, are either required of all applicants or required for a special program or special admission practice.

Questions the Director of Support Services may ask:

- When was the learning disability first diagnosed?
- What type of assistance has the student been receiving in high school?
- What kind of accommodations will the student need in college?
- Can the student describe the learning difficulties?
- Can the student articulate strengths and weaknesses?
- How has the disability affected the student's learning?
- What high school courses were easy (or more difficult)?
- Is the student comfortable with the learning disability?
- Can the student self-advocate?
- What does the student plan to choose as a major?
- Is the student motivated?

Questions students and/or parents may ask:

- What are the admission requirements?
- Is there any flexibility in admission policy? Course substitutions? GPA?
- What is the application procedure?
- Is a special application required?
- What auxiliary testing is required?
- Are there extra charges or fees for the special programs or services?
- Are there remedial or developmental courses?
- What is the procedure for requesting waivers or substitutions?
- Who is the contact person for learning disabilities?
- What are the academic qualifications of the individual who provides services to students with learning disabilities?

- What services and accommodations are available: Testing accommodations? Note takers? Books on tape? Skills classes? Support groups? Priority registration? Professional tutors? Peer tutors? Advising? Computer-aided technology? Scribes? Proctors? Oral tests? Use of computers and spell-checker in class? Use of calculators in class? Distraction-free environment for tests? Learning disability specialists? Advocacy with professors? Faculty in-services?

- How long has the program been in existence?

- How many students are receiving services?

- How long can students access services?

- What is the success rate of students receiving services?

For a successful interview:

- Develop a list of questions.

- Know the accommodations needed.

- Provide new information.

- Practice interviewing.

- Be able to describe strengths and weaknesses.

- Talk about extracurricular activities.

- Take notes.

- Get the business card of the interviewer.

- Try to relax.

- Have fun!

LETTERS OF RECOMMENDATION

- Obtain descriptive letters from counselors, teachers, and case managers.

- Have recommenders address learning style, degree of motivation, level of achievement, abilities, attitudes, self-discipline, determination, creativity, mastery of subject matter, academic risks, and growth.

- Have a teacher describe the challenge in a difficult course.

- Advise recommenders when letters are due.

We have just highlighted some of the areas of importance. Now it is time to begin to use the information in this guide that describes the various programs and services that can be found at hundreds of colleges and universities in the United States.

College Interview Preparation Form For Students With Learning Disabilities/ADHD

NAME: _____ DATE: _____

ADDRESS: _____ PHONE: _____

_____

Description of Disability:

_____

_____

When Diagnosed:

_____

_____

Special Help Received:

Tutoring _____

LD Resource _____

Remedial Reading _____

Study Skills _____

Other _____

Which were helpful and why?

_____

_____

_____

_____

Current High School:

_____

Describe this school:

_____

_____

_____

GPA _____

SAT _____

ACT _____

Comment on your abilities in the following areas and describe them:

_____

_____

Memory:

_____

Attention:

_____

Time Management:

_____

Time Orientation:

_____

Describe strategies you have used to compensate for your learning disability:

_____

Why were these strategies successful/unsuccessful for you?

_____

_____

_____

When was your last diagnostic testing?

_____

_____

What is taking these kinds of tests like for you?

_____

_____

_____

Describe your skills in the following areas. If your learning disability interferes in any of these areas, describe strategies you have used to compensate:

_____

Reading

_____

Writing

_____

Spelling

_____

Math

_____

Test-taking

_____

Note-taking

_____

What is your favorite subject? Least favorite?

_____

_____

_____

How would your favorite teacher describe you?

_____

_____

_____

How would your least favorite teacher describe you?

_____

_____

_____

What do you see as your own personal strengths?

_____

_____

What are your weaknesses?

_____

_____

What kinds of activities are you involved in?

_____

_____

_____

What do you hope to get out of college?

_____

_____

What do you want in an LD college program?

_____

_____

Which of the following services will be appropriate for you?

Extended Time Tests   _____

Distraction Reduced
Environment for Tests   _____

Taped Texts   _____

LD Specialist   _____

Skills Courses in Time
Management/Test Taking/
Organization/Note taking   _____

Tutors   _____

Note takers   _____

Counseling   _____

Reduced Course Load   _____

Study Skills   _____

Support Group   _____

What are your career interests?

_____

_____

_____

STUDENTS WITH DISABILITIES PREPARING FOR POSTSECONDARY EDUCATION: KNOW YOUR RIGHTS AND RESPONSIBILITIES

U.S. Department of Education
Margaret Spellings
Secretary
June 2006

More and more high school students with disabilities are planning to continue their education in postsecondary schools, including vocational and career schools, two- and four- year colleges, and universities. As a student with a disability, you need to be well informed about your rights and responsibilities as well as the responsibilities postsecondary schools have toward you. Being well informed will help ensure you have a full opportunity to enjoy the benefits of the postsecondary education experience without confusion or delay.

The information in this pamphlet, provided by the Office for Civil Rights (OCR) in the U. S. Department of Education, explains the rights and responsibilities of students with disabilities who are preparing to attend postsecondary schools. This pamphlet also explains the obligations of a postsecondary school to provide academic adjustments, including auxiliary aids and services, to ensure the school does not discriminate on the basis of disability.

OCR enforces Section 504 of the Rehabilitation Act of 1973 (Section 504) and Title II of the Americans with Disabilities Act of 1990 (Title II), which prohibit discrimination on the basis of disability. Practically every school district and postsecondary school in the United States is subject to one or both of these laws, which have similar requirements.

Although both school districts and postsecondary schools must comply with these same laws, the responsibilities of postsecondary schools are significantly different from those of school districts.

Moreover, you will have responsibilities as a postsecondary student that you do not have as a high school student. OCR strongly encourages you to know your responsibilities and those of postsecondary schools under Section 504 and Title II. Doing so will improve your opportunity to succeed as you enter postsecondary education.

The following questions and answers provide more specific information to help you succeed.

As a student with a disability leaving high school and entering postsecondary education, will I see differences in my rights and how they are addressed?

Yes. Section 504 and Title II protect elementary, secondary and postsecondary students from discrimination. Nevertheless, several of the requirements that apply through high school are different from the requirements that apply beyond high school. For instance, Section 504 requires a school district to provide a free appropriate public education (FAPE) to each child with a disability in the district's jurisdiction. Whatever the disability, a school district must identify an individual's education needs and provide any regular or special education and related aids and services necessary to meet those needs as well as it is meeting the needs of students without disabilities.

Unlike your high school, your postsecondary school is not required to provide FAPE. Rather, your postsecondary school is required to provide appropriate academic adjustments as necessary to ensure that it does not discriminate on the basis of disability. In addition, if your postsecondary school provides housing to nondisabled students, it must provide comparable, convenient and accessible housing to students with disabilities at the same cost.

Other important differences you need to know, even before you arrive at your postsecondary school, are addressed in the remaining questions.

May a postsecondary school deny my admission because I have a disability?

No. If you meet the essential requirements for admission, a postsecondary school may not deny your admission simply because you have a disability.

Do I have to inform a postsecondary school that I have a disability?

No. However, if you want the school to provide an academic adjustment, you must identify yourself as having a disability. Likewise, you should let the school know about your disability if you want to ensure that you are assigned to accessible facilities. In any event, your disclosure of a disability is always voluntary.

What academic adjustments must a postsecondary school provide?

The appropriate academic adjustment must be determined based on your disability and individual needs. Academic adjustments may include auxiliary aids and modifications to academic requirements as are necessary to ensure equal educational opportunity. Examples of such adjustments are arranging for priority registration; reducing a course load; substituting one course for another; providing note takers, recording devices, sign language interpreters, extended time for testing and, if telephones are provided in dorm rooms, a TTY in your dorm room; and equipping school computers with screen-reading, voice recognition, or other adaptive software or hardware.

In providing an academic adjustment, your postsecondary school is not required to lower or effect substantial modifications to essential requirements. For example, although your school may be required to provide extended testing time, it is not required to change the substantive content of the test. In addition, your postsecondary school does not have to make modifications that would fundamentally alter the nature of a service, program, or activity or would result in undue financial or administrative burdens. Finally, your postsecondary school does not have to provide personal attendants, individually prescribed devices, readers for personal use or study, or other devices or services of a personal nature, such as tutoring and typing.

If I want an academic adjustment, what must I do?

You must inform the school that you have a disability and need an academic adjustment. Unlike your school district, your postsecondary school is not required to identify you as having a disability or assess your needs.

Your postsecondary school may require you to follow reasonable procedures to request an academic adjustment. You are responsible for knowing and following these procedures. Postsecondary schools usually include, in their publications providing general information, information on the procedures and contacts for requesting an academic adjustment. Such publications include recruitment materials, catalogs and student handbooks, and are often available on school web sites. Many schools also have staff whose purpose is to assist students with disabilities. If you are unable to locate the procedures, ask a school official, such as an admissions officer or counselor.

When should I request an academic adjustment?

Although you may request an academic adjustment from your postsecondary school at any time, you should request it as early as possible. Some academic adjustments may take more time to provide than others. You should follow your school's procedures to ensure that your school has enough time to review your request and provide an appropriate academic adjustment.

Do I have to prove that I have a disability to obtain an academic adjustment?

Generally, yes. Your school will probably require you to provide documentation that shows you have a current disability and need an academic adjustment.

What documentation should I provide?

Schools may set reasonable standards for documentation. Some schools require more documentation than others. They may require you to provide documentation prepared by an appropriate professional, such as a medical doctor, psychologist or other qualified diagnostician. The required documentation may include one or more of the following: a diagnosis of your current disability; the date of the diagnosis; how the diagnosis was reached; the credentials of the professional; how your disability affects a major life activity; and how the disability affects your academic performance. The documentation should provide enough information for you and your school to decide what is an appropriate academic adjustment.

Although an Individualized Education Program (IEP) or Section 504 plan, if you have one, may help identify services that have been effective for you, it generally is not sufficient documentation. This is because postsecondary education presents different demands than high school education, and what you need to meet these new demands may be different. Also in some cases, the nature of a disability may change.

If the documentation that you have does not meet the postsecondary school's requirements, a school official must tell you in a timely manner what additional documentation you need to provide. You may need a new evaluation in order to provide the required documentation.

Who has to pay for a new evaluation?

Neither your high school nor your postsecondary school is required to conduct or pay for a new evaluation to document your disability and need for an academic adjustment. This may mean that you have to pay or find funding to pay an appropriate professional for an evaluation. If you are eligible for services through your state vocational rehabilitation agency, you may qualify for an evaluation at no cost to you. You may locate your state vocational rehabilitation agency through the following Department of Education website: Ed.gov/about/offices/list/osers/rsa/index.html.

Once the school has received the necessary documentation from me, what should I expect?

The school will review your request in light of the essential requirements for the relevant program to help determine an appropriate academic adjustment. It is important to remember that the school is not required to lower or waive essential requirements. If you have requested a specific academic adjustment, the school may offer that academic adjustment or an alternative one if the alternative would also be effective. The school may also conduct its own evaluation of your disability and needs at its own expense.

You should expect your school to work with you in an interactive process to identify an appropriate academic adjustment. Unlike the experience you may have had in high school, however, do not expect your postsecondary school to invite your parents to participate in the process or to develop an IEP for you.

What if the academic adjustment we identified is not working?

Let the school know as soon as you become aware that the results are not what you expected. It may be too late to correct the problem if you wait until the course or activity is completed. You and your school should work together to resolve the problem.

May a postsecondary school charge me for providing an academic adjustment?

No. Furthermore, it may not charge students with disabilities more for participating in its programs or activities than it charges students who do not have disabilities.

What can I do if I believe the school is discriminating against me?

Practically every postsecondary school must have a person—frequently called the Section 504 Coordinator, ADA Coordinator, or Disability Services Coordinator—who coordinates the school's compliance with Section 504 or Title II or both laws. You may contact this person for information about how to address your concerns.

The school must also have grievance procedures. These procedures are not the same as the due process procedures with which you may be familiar from high school. However, the postsecondary school's grievance procedures must include steps to ensure that you may raise your concerns fully and fairly and must provide for the prompt and equitable resolution of complaints.

School publications, such as student handbooks and catalogs, usually describe the steps you must take to start the grievance process. Often, schools have both formal and informal processes. If you decide to use a grievance process, you should be prepared to present all the reasons that support your request.

If you are dissatisfied with the outcome from using the school's grievance procedures or you wish to pursue an alternative to using the grievance procedures, you may file a complaint against the school with OCR or in a court. You may learn more about the OCR complaint process from the brochure *How to File a Discrimination Complaint with the Office for Civil Rights*, which you may obtain by contacting us at the addresses and phone numbers below, or at Ed.gov/ocr/docs/howto.html.

If you would like more information about the responsibilities of postsecondary schools to students with disabilities, read the OCR brochure *Auxiliary Aids and Services for Postsecondary Students with Disabilities: Higher Education's Obligations Under Section 504 and Title II of the ADA*. You may obtain a copy by contacting us at the address and phone numbers below, or at Ed.gov/ocr/docs/auxaids.html.

Students with disabilities who know their rights and responsibilities are much better equipped to succeed in postsecondary school. We encourage you to work with the staff at your school because they, too, want you to succeed. Seek the support of family, friends, and fellow students, including those with disabilities. Know your talents and capitalize on them, and believe in yourself as you embrace new challenges in your education.

To receive more information about the civil rights of students with disabilities in education institutions, you may contact us at:

Customer Service Team
Office for Civil Rights
U.S. Department of Education
Washington, DC 20202-1100
Phone: 800-421-3481
TDD: 877-521-2172
E-mail: ocr@ed.gov
Website: www.ed.gov/ocr

Source: U.S. Department of Education, Office for Civil Rights. Students with Disabilities Preparing for Postsecondary Education: Know Your Rights and Responsibilities. Washington, DC, 2006.

How to Use This Guide

The K&W Guide to Colleges for Students with Learning Disabilities or Attention Deficit Disorder includes information on colleges and universities that offer services to students with learning disabilities. No two colleges are identical in the programs or services they provide, but there are some similarities. For the purpose of this guide, the services and programs at the various colleges have been grouped into three categories.

Structured Programs (SP)

Colleges with Structured Programs offer the most comprehensive services for students with learning disabilities. The director and/or staff are certified in learning disabilities or related areas. The director is actively involved in the admission decision and, often, the criteria for admission may be more flexible than general admission requirements. Services are highly structured and students are involved in developing plans to meet their particular learning styles and needs. Often students in Structured Programs sign a contract agreeing to actively participate in the program. There is usually an additional fee for the enhanced services. Students who have participated in a Structured Program or Structured Services in high school such as Learning Disabilities Resource Program, individualized or modified coursework, tutorial assistance, academic monitoring, note-takers, test accommodations, or skill classes might benefit from exploring colleges with Structured Programs.

COORDINATED SERVICES (CS)

Coordinated Services differ from Structured Programs in that the services are not as comprehensive. These services are provided by at least one certified learning disability specialist. The staff is knowledgeable and trained to provide assistance to students to develop strategies for their individual needs. The director of the program or services may be involved in the admission decision, or be in a position to offer recommendations to the admissions office on the potential success of the applicant, or to assist the students with an appeal if denied admission to the college. Receiving these services generally requires specific documentation of the learning disability—students are encouraged to self-identify prior to entry. Students voluntarily request accommodations or services in the Coordinated Services category, and there may be specific skills courses or remedial classes available or required for students with learning disabilities who are admitted probationally or conditionally. High school students who may have enrolled in some modified or remedial courses, utilized test accommodations, required tutorial assistance, but who typically requested services only as needed, might benefit from exploring colleges with Coordinated Services.

SERVICES (S)

Services is the least comprehensive of the three categories. Colleges offering Services generally are complying with the federal mandate requiring reasonable accommodations to all students with appropriate and current documentation. These colleges routinely require documentation of the disability in order for the students with LD/ADHD to receive accommodations. Staff and faculty actively support the students by providing basic services to meet the needs of the students. Services are requested on a voluntarily basis, and there may be some limitations as to what is reasonable and the degree of services available. Sometimes, just the small size of the student body allows for the necessary personal attention to help students with learning disabilities succeed in college. High school students who require minimum accommodations, but who would find comfort in knowing that services are available, knowing who the contact person is, and knowing that this person is sensitive to students with learning disabilities, might benefit from exploring colleges providing Services.

CATEGORIES USED TO DESCRIBE THE PROGRAMS AND SERVICES AT COLLEGES AND UNIVERSITIES

The categories on the following pages describe the topics of information presented in this guide. Each college in the book is profiles on two pages, beginning with pertinent information describing the learning disability program or services. This is followed by special admission procedures, then specific information about services offered, and concludes with general college information. Please note the statement preceding the section on services and accommodations which states "Services and Accommodations are determined individually for each student based on current and appropriate documentation." Some categories are answered with: N/A (not applicable) because not all colleges were able to fit into every category included in this guide; NR (not reported) because some colleges were unable to provide the information we requested; and Y/N (Yes/No) because the answer is dependent on individual situations.

The authors have made a conscientious effort to provide the most current information possible. However, names, costs, dates, policies, and other information are always subject to change, and colleges of particular interest or importance to the reader should be contacted directly for verification of the data.

SCHOOL PROFILES

JACKSONVILLE STATE UNIVERSITY

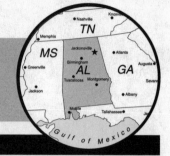

700 Pelham Road North, Jacksonville, AL 36265
Phone: 256-782-5268 • Fax: 256-782-5953
E-mail: info@jsu.edu • Web: www.jsu.edu
Support: CS • Institution: 4-year public

LEARNING DISABILITY PROGRAM AND SERVICES

Under Disability Support Services (DSS), the Academic Center for Excellence offers support for students with learning disabilities and ADHD. It is an inclusive service community that promotes academic excellence and empowers students for success. Once students have been admitted, DSS assists the qualified student with a documented disability in receiving academic support services. Accommodations are based solely on the supporting documentation. Required documents for a student with learning disabilities are current intelligence tests, current achievement tests, certified professional validation of the LD, or high school records that document prior identification and/or services. Students with IQs below 85 do not qualify for services. Each student with appropriate documentation of a learning disability will develop an individualized postsecondary program (IPP). The IPP is prepared from the documentation received, input from the student (and parents, if appropriate), and the staff in support services. Copies of the IPP are given to the student who is responsible for identifying himself or herself and giving a copy to each instructor.

LD/ADHD ADMISSIONS INFORMATION

College entrance tests required: Yes
Interview required: No
Essay recommended: No
Documentation required for LD: Psychoeducational evaluation with a diagnosis from a qualified professional
Documentation required for ADHD: Diagnosis from a qualified professional. (Actual documentation can vary, depending on the type or amount of accommodations requested.)
Submitted to: Support Program/Services
Special Ed. HS course work accepted: Yes

Specific course requirements: NR
Separate application required: No
# of LD applications submitted each year: 100
# of LD applications accepted yearly: 100
Total # of students receiving LD services: 100
Acceptance into program means acceptance into college: Students must be admitted and enrolled in the university first and then request services.

ADMISSIONS

All applicants must meet the general entrance requirements. The middle 50 percent of the applicants have an ACT of 18–22. All students must have at least 3 years of English, and no more than 4 of the 15 required courses in high school may be in vocational courses. Interviews are recommended but not required. Students with an ACT below 16 may enter through successful completion of a summer bridge program. The program, Experiencing Success in Education and Life, offers skill-building classes. Students with an ACT between 16 and 19 are conditionally admitted.

ADDITIONAL INFORMATION

DSS is funded to provide programming only for sensory impaired (blind/low vision and deaf/hard of hearing). However, they do, of course, provide services for all disabilities. Disability Support Services will provide services to any student with LD/ADHD with appropriate documentation, and accommodations are based solely on the supporting documentation. DSS requires formal documentation (current—within the past 3 years), and the academic accommodations needed are determined from this documentation. Services available may include note-takers, readers, scribes, priority registration, assistive technology, testing modifications, distraction-free environment for tests, and an Individualized Postsecondary Program. Academic Success Skills offers skills classes in time management, test strategies, organizational skills, as well as other areas. These courses are offered for college credit. All students have access to tutoring, supplemental instruction, structured study sessions, and online tutorials. Students Involved with Disabilities is a support group for students with disabilities whose purpose is to spread disability awareness on campus and throughout the community.

LEARNING DISABILITY PROGRAM/SERVICES

Learning Disability Program/Services: Academic Center for Excellence
Director: Dan Miller
  E-mail: dss@jsu.edu
  Telephone: 256-782-8380
  Fax: 256-782-8383

LEARNING DISABILITY SERVICES

Requests for the following/services accommodations will be evaluated individually based on appropriate and current documentation.

Allowed in exams
  Calculator: Yes
  Dictionary: Yes
  Computer: Yes
  Spellchecker: Yes
Extended test time: Yes
Scribes: Yes
Proctors: Yes
Oral exams: Yes
Note-takers: Yes

Distraction-reduced environment: Yes
Tape recording in class: Yes
Books on tape from RFBD: Yes
Taping of books not from RFBD: Yes
Accommodations for students with
  ADHD: Yes
Reading machine: Yes
Other assistive technology: Yes
Priority registration: Yes

Added costs for services: No
LD specialists: Yes
Professional tutors: No
Peer tutors: 40
Max. hours/wk. for services:
  Unlimited
How professors are notified of
  LD/ADHD: By both student and
  director

GENERAL ADMISSIONS INFORMATION

Director of Admissions: Martha Mitchell
Telephone: 256-782-5268

ENTRANCE REQUIREMENTS

Academic units required: 3 English, 4 academic electives. High school diploma is required, and GED is accepted. TOEFL required of all international applicants: minimum paper TOEFL 500, minimum computer TOEFL 173.

Application deadline: Rolling
Notification: Rolling
Average GPA: 2.99
ACT Composite middle 50% range:
  17–23

SAT Math middle 50% range:
  400–530
SAT Critical Reading middle 50%
  range: 420–530
SAT Writing middle 50% range: NR

Graduated top 10% of class: 3%
Graduated top 25% of class: 13%
Graduated top 50% of class: 34%

COLLEGE GRADUATION REQUIREMENTS

Course waivers allowed: Yes
In what course: Individual case-by-case decisions
Course substitutions allowed: Yes
In what course: Individual case-by-case decisions

ADDITIONAL INFORMATION

Environment: Located in a small town about 75 miles from Birmingham.

Student Body
  Undergrad enrollment: 7,096
  Women: 58%
  Men: 42%
  Percent out-of-state: 12%

Cost Information
  In-state tuition: $4,040
Out-of-state tuition: $8,080
  Room & board: $3,312
Housing Information
  University housing: Yes
  Percent living on campus: 15%

Greek System
  Fraternity: Yes
  Sorority: Yes
Athletics: Division I

THE U. OF ALABAMA IN HUNTSVILLE

301 Sparkman Drive, Huntsville, AL 35899
Phone: 256-824-6070 • Fax: 256-824-6073
E-mail: admitme@uah.edu • Web: www.uah.edu
Support: S • Institution type: 4-year public

LEARNING DISABILITY PROGRAM AND SERVICES

The Office of Student Development Services offers a variety of services and accommodations to assist students with disabilities in eliminating barriers they encounter in pursuing higher education. The office's main objective is to provide access to academic, social, cultural, recreational, and housing opportunities at the university. A student is considered registered with Disability Support Services (DSS) when they have completed all application paperwork, their intake/registration paperwork has been approved, and they have had an interview with a 504 Coordinator. The services offered through this office encourage students to achieve and maintain autonomy.

LD/ADHD ADMISSIONS INFORMATION

College entrance tests required: Yes
Interview required: No
Essay recommended: No
Documentation required for LD: Psychoeducational evaluation
Documentation required for ADHD: Yes
Submitted to: Support Program/Services
Specific course requirements: NR

Special Ed. HS course work accepted: Yes
Separate application required: Yes
# of LD applications submitted each year: NR
# of LD applications accepted yearly: NR
Total # of students receiving LD services: 167
Acceptance into program means acceptance into college: Students must be admitted and enrolled in the university first and then request services.

ADMISSIONS

Admission is based on grades and test scores. Additionally, applicants should have 4 years of English, 3 years of social studies, 3 years of math, 2 years of science, and a total of 20 Carnegie units.

ACT	SAT	GPA
17 or below	700 or below	3.25
18	740	3.00
19	790	2.75
20–21	860	2.50
22	920	2.25
23	970	2.00
24 or above	1010 or above	1.15

There is no special LD admission process. If a student becomes subject to academic suspension, the suspension is for a minimum of one term, and the student must petition the Admissions Committee for approval to reenroll.

ADDITIONAL INFORMATION

Students should forward their documentation to Services for Students with Disabilities. Student Development Services provides the mandated services, including testing accommodations, distraction-free environments for tests, readers, proctors, scribes, note-takers, peer tutoring on an unlimited basis, specialized adaptive computers, and study skills classes that can be taken for credit. Math labs, chemistry labs, writing centers, and tutorial services are available for all students on campus. Additionally, all students have access to skills classes in time management, test-taking strategies, and study skills. Services and accommodations are available for undergraduate and graduate students.

LEARNING DISABILITY PROGRAM/SERVICES

Learning Disability Program/Services: Student Development Services
Director: Jared Dinehart, PhD
  E-mail: dineharj@uah.edu
  Telephone: 256-824-6203
  Fax: 256-824-6672

LEARNING DISABILITY SERVICES

Requests for the following/services accommodations will be evaluated individually based on appropriate and current documentation.

Allowed in exams
  Calculator: Yes
  Dictionary: Yes
  Computer: Yes
  Spellchecker: Yes
Extended test time: Yes
Scribes: Yes
Proctors: Yes
Oral exams: Yes
Note-takers: Yes

Distraction-reduced environment: Yes
Tape recording in class: Yes
Books on tape from RFBD: Yes
Taping of books not from RFBD: Yes
Accommodations for students with ADHD: Yes
Reading machine: Yes
Other assistive technology: Yes
Priority registration: Yes

Added costs for services: No
LD specialists: No
Professional tutors: 3
Peer tutors: 10
Max. hours/wk. for services: Unlimited
How professors are notified of LD/ADHD: By both student and director

GENERAL ADMISSIONS INFORMATION

Director of Admissions: John Maxon
Telephone: 256-824-6070

ENTRANCE REQUIREMENTS

Academic units required: 4 English, 3 math, 3 science, 4 social studies, 6 academic electives. High school diploma is required, and GED is accepted. ACT with or without writing component accepted. TOEFL required of all international applicants: minimum paper TOEFL 500, minimum computer TOEFL 173.

Application deadline: 8/15
Notification: Students are notified when application is complete.
Average GPA: 3.31
ACT Composite middle 50% range: 21–27

SAT Math middle 50% range: 500–640
SAT Critical Reading middle 50% range: 480–630
SAT Writing middle 50% range: NR

Graduated top 10% of class: 26%
Graduated top 25% of class: 52%
Graduated top 50% of class: 78%

COLLEGE GRADUATION REQUIREMENTS

Course waivers allowed: Yes
In what course: Individual case-by-case decisions
Course substitutions allowed: Yes
In what course: Individual case-by-case decisions

ADDITIONAL INFORMATION

Environment: The university is located on 337 acres 100 miles north of Birmingham and 100 miles south of Nashville.

Student Body
  Undergrad enrollment: 5,529
  Women: 49%
  Men: 51%
  Percent out-of-state: 14%

Cost Information
  In-state tuition: $4,848
Out-of-state tuition: $10,224
  Room & board: $5,110
Housing Information
  University housing: Yes
  Percent living on campus: 17%

Greek System
  Fraternity: Yes
  Sorority: Yes
Athletics: Division II

THE U. OF ALABAMA AT TUSCALOOSA

PO Box 870132, Tuscaloosa, AL 35487-0132
Phone: 205-348-5666 • Fax: 205-348-9046
E-mail: admissions@ua.edu • Web: www.ua.edu
Support: S • Institution type: 4-year public

LEARNING DISABILITY PROGRAM AND SERVICES

The Office of Disability Services (ODS) serves as the central contact point for students with disabilities. The goal of ODS is to provide an environment that ensures an individual is viewed on the basis of ability, not disability. ODS works individually with students to determine appropriate and reasonable academic accommodations and to ensure that students' academic performances are evaluated apart from the limiting effects of disability. Any student enrolled with a documented LD is eligible for services and accommodations. Students must provide documentation, including a written report of an LD evaluation, a summary of areas of testing, actual test scores, overall summary and diagnosis, and recommendations and suggested strategies for student, professors, and academic advisors. The Office of Disability Services may request further testing.

LD/ADHD ADMISSIONS INFORMATION

College entrance tests required: Yes
Interview required: No
Essay recommended: No
Documentation required for LD: Appropriate professional reports measuring the student's aptitude and achievement; a report on the history of the student's disability and past accommodations. Demonstrate a substantial limitation to a major life activity as a result of the condition; rationale for accommodations using test results to support the need.
Documentation required for ADHD: Appropriate professional narrative report that must include the results of tests measuring the student's aptitude and achievement; a report on the history of the student's disability and past accommodations; demonstrate a substantial limitation to a major life activity as a result of the condition; rationale for recommended accommodations using test results to support the need.

Submitted to: Support Program/Services
Specific course requirements: NR
Special Ed. HS course work accepted: No
Separate application required: Yes
# of LD applications submitted each year: NR
# of LD applications accepted yearly: NR
Total # of students receiving LD services: 150–160
Acceptance into program means acceptance into college: Students must be admitted and enrolled in the university first and then request services.

ADMISSIONS

All students must meet regular entrance requirements. An interview with the Office of Disabilities is recommended. Students with an acceptable GPA but low test scores, or vice versa, may be considered for Summer Trial Admissions. Students who fall within this category are encouraged to submit teacher/counselor recommendations that could substantiate the student's potential for success. Students admitted through Summer Trial Admissions will be required to attend the summer session and enroll in an appropriate math class and either psychology or child development. Additionally, students will take a study skills lab, which will provide strategies and during which the student's notes taken during the classes will be monitored. The strategies are practical rather than theoretical. Students need a 2.0 GPA in the summer courses to be admitted for the fall.

ADDITIONAL INFORMATION

Accommodations are tailored to individual needs according to diagnostic testing. Accommodations include early registration; testing modifications; academic aids such as taping lectures and the use of calculators, dictionaries, spellcheckers, note-takers, and taped materials; and reading assistance. The Center for Teaching and Learning (CTL) Independent Study Lab is available for all students. Students can use videotapes, computer software, and other self-paced materials for review of math, chemistry, physics, biology, statistics, and other selected classes; study and reading skills; and graduate entrance exam preparation. Individual tutoring is offered for select classes. Math review and help sessions offered through small group review sessions. The CTL offers reading comprehension workshops, as well as workshops in study skills and time management. The Writing Center is staffed by instructors from the University of Alabama's English Department who provide individual assistance in developing the composition skills necessary to complete university course work.

LEARNING DISABILITY PROGRAM/SERVICES

Learning Disability Program/Services: Office of Disability Services
Director: Judy Thorpe
  E-mail: jthorpe@aalan.ua.edu
  Telephone: 205-348-4285
  Fax: 205-348-0804

LEARNING DISABILITY SERVICES

Requests for the following/services accommodations will be evaluated individually based on appropriate and current documentation.

Allowed in exams
  Calculator: Yes
  Dictionary: Yes
  Computer: Yes
  Spellchecker: Yes
Extended test time: Yes
Scribes: Yes
Proctors: Yes
Oral exams: Yes
Note-takers: Yes

Distraction-reduced environment: Yes
Tape recording in class: Yes
Books on tape from RFBD: Yes
Taping of books not from RFBD: Yes
Accommodations for students with
  ADHD: Yes
Reading machine: Yes
Other assistive technology: Yes
Priority registration: Yes

Added costs for services: No
LD specialists: No
Professional tutors: No
Peer tutors: 22
Max. hours/wk. for services: NR
How professors are notified of
  LD/ADHD: By student

GENERAL ADMISSIONS INFORMATION

Director of Admissions: Mary K. Spiegel
Telephone: 205-348-8197

ENTRANCE REQUIREMENTS

Academic units required: 4 English, 3 math, 3 science (2 science labs), 1 foreign language, 3 social studies, 1 history, 5 academic electives. **Academic units recommended:** 4 English, 3 math, 3 science (2 science labs), 1 foreign language, 3 social studies, 1 history, 5 academic electives. High school diploma is required, and GED is accepted. ACT with or without Writing component accepted. TOEFL required of all international applicants: minimum paper TOEFL 500, minimum computer TOEFL 173.

Application deadline: NR
Notification: Rolling
Average GPA: 3.40
ACT Composite middle 50% range:
  21–27

SAT Math middle 50% range:
  500–630
SAT Critical Reading middle 50%
  range: 500–630
SAT Writing middle 50% range: NR

Graduated top 10% of class: 39%
Graduated top 25% of class: 54%
Graduated top 50% of class: 79%

COLLEGE GRADUATION REQUIREMENTS

Course waivers allowed: No
Course substitutions allowed: Yes
In what course: Substitutions are sometimes granted, but no courses are waived. Typically, substitutions are most often granted for math courses. Courses cannot be substituted if doing so would substantially alter the nature of the program or if the course is required as part of the student's major or for any type of certification or licensure.

ADDITIONAL INFORMATION

Environment: The university is located 55 miles from the city of Birmingham.

Student Body
  Undergrad enrollment: 19,237
  Women: 53%
  Men: 47%
  Percent out-of-state: 24%

Housing Information
  In-state tuition: $4,864
  Out-of-state tuition: $13,516
  Room & board: $5,025
  University housing: Yes
  Percent living on campus: 29%

Greek System
  Fraternity: Yes
  Sorority: Yes
Athletics: Division I

The University of Alabama at Tuscaloosa

UNIVERSITY OF ALASKA—ANCHORAGE

3211 Providence Drive, Anchorage, AK 99508-8046
Phone: 907-786-1480 • Fax: 907-786-4888
E-mail: enroll@uaa.alaska.edu • Web: www.uaa.alaska.edu
Support: S • Institution type: 4-year public

AK

Anchorage
★

Gulf of Alaska

LEARNING DISABILITY PROGRAM AND SERVICES

The University of Alaska—Anchorage provides equal opportunities for students who have disabilities. Academic support services are available to students with learning disabilities. Staff trained to work with students with disabilities coordinate these services. To allow time for service coordination, students are encouraged to contact the Disability Support Services (DSS) office several weeks before the beginning of each semester. Ongoing communication with the staff throughout the semester is encouraged.

LD/ADHD ADMISSIONS INFORMATION

College entrance tests required: Yes
Interview required: No
Essay recommended: No
Documentation required for LD: Yes
Documentation required for ADHD: Yes
Submitted to: NR
Learning Disability Program/Services: NR
Special Ed. HS course work accepted: Yes

Specific course requirements: NR
Separate application required: No
# of LD applications submitted each year: NR
# of LD applications accepted yearly: NR
Total # of students receiving LD services: 90 plus
Acceptance into program means acceptance into college: The University of Alaska—Anchorage has open enrollment; students are accepted to the university and then may request services.

ADMISSIONS

All students must meet the same admission requirements. The university has an open enrollment policy. However, admission to specific programs of study may have specific course work or testing criteria that all students will have to meet. While formal admission is encouraged, the university has an open enrollment policy that allows students to register for courses in which they have the adequate background. Open enrollment does not guarantee subsequent formal admission to certificate or degree programs. Individuals with learning disabilities are admitted via the standard admissions procedures that apply to all students submitting applications for formal admission. Students with documentation of a learning disability are eligible to receive support services once they are enrolled in the university. LD students who self-disclose during the admission process are referred to DSS for information about services and accommodations.

ADDITIONAL INFORMATION

Slingerland language arts classes are available for all students in the areas of vocabulary building and study skills. There is no separate tutoring for students with learning disabilities. Tutorial help is available for all students in the reading and writing labs and the Learning Resource Center. With appropriate documentation, students with LD or ADHD may have access to accommodations such as testing modifications, distraction-free testing environments, scribes, proctors, note-takers, calculators, dictionaries, and computers in exams, and access to assistive technology. Services and accommodations are available for undergraduate and graduate students.

LEARNING DISABILITY PROGRAM/SERVICES

Learning Disability Program/Services: Disability Support Services
Director: Kaela Parks
E-mail: aydss@uaa.alaska.edu
Telephone: 907-786-4530
Fax: 907-786-4531

LEARNING DISABILITY SERVICES

Requests for the following/services accommodations will be evaluated individually based on appropriate and current documentation.

Allowed in exams
  Calculator: Yes
  Dictionary: Yes
  Computer: Yes
  Spellchecker: Yes
Extended test time: Yes
Scribes: Yes
Proctors: Yes
Oral exams: Yes
Note-takers: Yes

Distraction-reduced environment: Yes
Tape recording in class: Yes
Books on tape from RFBD: Yes
Taping of books not from RFBD: Yes
Accommodations for students with ADHD: Yes
Reading machine: Yes
Other assistive technology: Yes
Priority registration: Yes

Added costs for services: No
LD specialists: No
Professional tutors: No
Peer tutors: Yes
Max. hours/wk. for services: Unlimited
How professors are notified of LD/ADHD: By student

GENERAL ADMISSIONS INFORMATION

Director of Admissions: Al Kastar
Telephone: 907-786-1480

ENTRANCE REQUIREMENTS

Academic units recommended: 4 English, 2 math, 3 science, 1 foreign language, 3 social studies, 1 history. High school diploma is required, and GED is accepted. TOEFL required of all international applicants: minimum paper TOEFL 450.

Application deadline: 7/1
Notification: Rolling
Average GPA: 3.08
ACT Composite middle 50% range: 18–24

SAT Math middle 50% range: 450–570
SAT Critical Reading middle 50% range: 440–580
SAT Writing middle 50% range: NR

Graduated top 10% of class: 9%
Graduated top 25% of class: 28%
Graduated top 50% of class: 59%

COLLEGE GRADUATION REQUIREMENTS

Course waivers allowed: Yes
In what course: Individual case-by-case decisions
Course substitutions allowed: Yes
In what course: Individual case-by-case decisions

ADDITIONAL INFORMATION

Environment: The University of Alaska is an urban campus on 350 acres 7 miles from downtown Anchorage.

Student Body
  Undergrad enrollment: 10,064
  Women: 62%
  Men: 38%
  Percent out-of-state: 6%

Cost Information
  In-state tuition: $3,600
Out-of-state tuition: $11,970
  Room & board: $6,930
Housing Information
  University housing: Yes
  Percent living on campus: 5%

Greek System
  Fraternity: Yes
  Sorority: Yes
Athletics: Division II

UNIVERSITY OF ALASKA—FAIRBANKS

PO Box 757480, Fairbanks, AK 99775-7480
Phone: 907-474-7500 • Fax: 907-474-5379
E-mail: admissions@uaf.edu • Web: www.uaf.edu
Support: S • Institution type: 4-year public

LEARNING DISABILITY PROGRAM AND SERVICES

The University of Alaska is committed to providing equal opportunity to students with disabilities. Disability Services at The University of Alaska—Fairbanks provides assistance to students with permanent or temporary disabilities. The purpose of Services for Students with Disabilities (SSD) is to enable students who have disabilities to be successful in college. Campus services include the Academic Advising Center, which is responsible for advising incoming freshmen and students with undeclared majors. It provides explanations of programs and their requirements and assists students with choosing majors, selecting electives, and choosing classes consistent with their academic and career goals. Student Support Services provides academic and personal support, including developmental classes and tutoring for students who are economically disadvantaged, do not have a parent who graduated from college, or have a documented disability. Disabled Students of UAF is an organizations that provides peer support groups for UAF students experiencing disabilities. The Student Development and Learning Center provides tutoring, individual instruction in basic skills and counseling, career-planning services, and assessment testing. Disability Services welcomes inquiries and seeks to make the college experience a success for students with disabilities.

LD/ADHD ADMISSIONS INFORMATION

College entrance tests required: Yes
Interview required: No
Essay recommended: No
Documentation required for LD: Yes
Documentation required for ADHD: Yes
Submitted to: Disability Services
Special Ed. HS course work accepted: Yes

Specific course requirements: NR
Separate application required: No
# of LD applications submitted each year: NR
# of LD applications accepted yearly: NR
Total # of students receiving LD services: 30–40
Acceptance into program means acceptance into college: Students must be admitted and enrolled in the university first and then request services.

ADMISSIONS

The university has a liberal admissions policy. To qualify for admission, freshman students must meet one of the following requirements: The associate's degree program requires a high school diploma or GED, and students must maintain a C average with 14 credits to enter a bachelor's degree program; the bachelor's degree program requires a high school diploma with a 2.0 GPA, and admission to specific programs requires different combinations of GPA and high school courses. Students must also complete, with a minimum GPA of 2.5, a core curriculum including 4 years of English, 3 years of math, 3 years of social sciences, and 3 years of natural or physical sciences. Foreign language courses are recommended. Students can be provisionally accepted if they make up course deficiencies with a C or better in each of the developmental or university courses and complete nine credits of general degree requirements with a C or better. Being accepted to the university does not depend on minimum test scores; however, these test scores are used to determine placement in English, math, and other freshman-level courses.

ADDITIONAL INFORMATION

Services include individual counseling to determine necessary accommodations; arrangements for special services such as readers, scribes, and note-takers; advocacy with faculty and staff; assistance to faculty and staff in determining appropriate accommodations; help in determining specific needs for students with learning disabilities; and referral to campus and community agencies for additional services. Basic study-skills classes are offered for all students and may be taken for credit. Services and accommodations are provided for undergraduate and graduate students.

LEARNING DISABILITY PROGRAM/SERVICES

Learning Disability Program/Services: Disability Services
Director: Mary Matthews
  E-mail: fydso@uaf.edu
  Telephone: 907-474-7043
  Fax: 907-474-5777
Contact Person: Same as above

LEARNING DISABILITY SERVICES

Requests for the following/services accommodations will be evaluated individually based on appropriate and current documentation.

Allowed in exams
  Calculator: No
  Dictionary: Yes
  Computer: Yes
  Spellchecker: Yes
Extended test time: Yes
Scribes: Yes
Proctors: Yes
Oral exams: Yes

Note-takers: Yes
Distraction-reduced environment: Yes
Tape recording in class: Yes
Books on tape from RFBD: Yes
Taping of books not from RFBD: Yes
Accommodations for students with
  ADHD: Yes
Reading machine: Yes
Other assistive technology: Yes

Priority registration: No
Added costs for services: No
LD specialists: No
Professional tutors: No
Peer tutors: No
Max. hours/wk. for services: N/A
How professors are notified of
  LD/ADHD: By student

GENERAL ADMISSIONS INFORMATION

Director of Admissions: Nancy Dix
Telephone: 907-474-7500

ENTRANCE REQUIREMENTS

Academic units required: 4 English, 3 math, 3 science (1 science lab), 3 social studies, 3 academic electives.
Academic units recommended: 2 foreign language. High school diploma is required, and GED is not accepted. ACT with or without Writing component accepted. TOEFL required of all international applicants: minimum paper TOEFL 550, minimum computer TOEFL 213.

Application deadline: 8/1
Notification: Rolling
Average GPA: 3.19
ACT Composite middle 50% range:
  18–25

SAT Math middle 50% range:
  450–590
SAT Critical Reading middle 50%
  range: 450–600
SAT Writing middle 50% range: NR

Graduated top 10% of class: 15%
Graduated top 25% of class: 35%
Graduated top 50% of class: 64%

COLLEGE GRADUATION REQUIREMENTS

Course waivers allowed: No
In what course: N/A
Course substitutions allowed: Yes
In what course: Depends on documentation

ADDITIONAL INFORMATION

Environment: The university is in a small town close to Fairbanks.

Student Body
  Undergrad enrollment: 4,684
  Women: 57%
  Men: 43%
  Percent out-of-state: 13%

Cost Information
  In-state tuition: $3,870
Out-of-state tuition: $12,810
  Room & board: $6,030
Housing Information
  University housing: Yes
  Percent living on campus: 27%

Greek System
  Fraternity: Yes
  Sorority: Yes
Athletics: Division II

University of Alaska—Fairbanks

ARIZONA STATE UNIVERSITY

PO Box 870112, Tempe, AZ 85287-0112
Phone: 480-965-7788 • Fax: 480-965-3610
E-mail: ugradinq@asu.edu • Web: www.asu.edu
Support: CS • Institution type: 4-year public

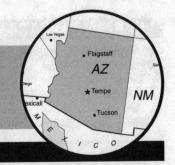

LEARNING DISABILITY PROGRAM AND SERVICES

ASU's Disabled Student Resources (DSR) program strives to facilitate resources, services, and auxiliary aids to allow each qualified student with disabilities to equitably access educational, social, and career opportunities. Students utilizing the services through the DSR program are mainstreamed in all courses. Support is available, but students need to be assertive and have a desire to succeed. The services are geared to the needs of the particular student and are individually based. Each student is encouraged to seek out methods for attaining the highest possible goals. All services and accommodations are provided on request on an individual basis as appropriate for qualified/eligible individuals with learning disabilities. The goal of DSR is to assist the student in becoming academically and socially independent. The DSR staff includes professionals who facilitate a wide range of academic support services and accommodations. The center also provides consultation on disability issues to the surrounding community.

LD/ADHD ADMISSIONS INFORMATION

College entrance tests required: Yes
Interview required: No
Essay recommended: No
Documentation required for LD: Psychoeducational evaluation
Documentation required for ADHD: Same as above
Submitted to: Disability Student Resources
Special Ed. HS course work accepted: Yes

Specific course requirements: NR
Separate application required: No
# of LD applications submitted each year: 163
# of LD applications accepted yearly: 150
Total # of students receiving LD services: 359
Acceptance into program means acceptance into college: Students must be admitted and enrolled in the university first and then request services.

ADMISSIONS

Students with LD submit the regular ASU application. Students should self-disclose their LD and submit documentation. Courses required: 4 years of English, 4 years of math, 3 years of science, 2 years of social science, and 1 year of fine arts. Arizona residents should rank in the top quarter or have a 22 ACT/930 SAT or a 3.0 GPA in core courses. Nonresidents should rank in the top quarter or have a 24 ACT/1010 SAT or a 3.0 GPA in core courses. Nonresidents who have a strong high school background and who rank in the top 50 percent or have a GPA of 2.5–2.9 will be considered individually. To appeal a denial, applicants should write a letter stating reasons for wanting to attend ASU and describing their ability for success, send three recommendations demonstrating their motivation and perseverance, and send a transcript showing gradual upward trend in courses and grades. Appeals are reviewed by admissions and disability support personnel. If applicants are ultimately denied after an appeal or 6 hours of credits or less is desired per semester, a nondegree-seeking application is available. Transcripts are not required. Students can earn up to 15 nondegree hours to be applied toward a degree program. Nondegree candidates may live in residential housing at ASU, attend ASU, and participate in the local community college. After completing 24 credits and maintaining a GPA of 2.0, the student may apply for regular admission at ASU.

ADDITIONAL INFORMATION

Academic support accommodations include consultation, individualized program recommendations, registration information and advisement referrals, academic tutoring, access to the Computer Technology Center, learning strategies instruction, library research assistance, supplemental readers in coordination with RFBD, mastery of Alternative Learning Techniques Lab, in-class note-taking, testing accommodations, and diagnostic testing referrals. DSR provides in-service training for faculty/staff. Services and accommodations are available for undergraduate and graduate students. DSR will accept current diagnosis of ADHD that are based on appropriate diagnostic information given by a licensed/certified professional. The diagnosis must be written on professional letterhead and include a clinical history, instruments used for the diagnosis, narrative, DSM–IV diagnosis, and recommendations for accommodations. All students have access to skills classes in time management, note-taking strategies, test-taking, and career awareness.

LEARNING DISABILITY PROGRAM/SERVICES

Learning Disability Program/Services: Disability Student Resources
Director: Carol Takao
  E-mail: Carol.Takao@asu.edu
  Telephone: 602-965-1234
  Fax: 602-965-0441
Contact Person: Phyllis Jones
  E-mail: Phyllis.Jones@asu.edu
  Telephone: 602-965-1234
  Fax: 602-965-0441

LEARNING DISABILITY SERVICES

Requests for the following/services accommodations will be evaluated individually based on appropriate and current documentation.

Allowed in exams
  Calculator: Yes
  Dictionary: Yes
  Computer: Yes
  Spellchecker: Yes
Extended test time: Yes
Scribes: Yes
Proctors: Yes
Oral exams: Yes
Note-takers: Yes

Distraction-reduced environment: Yes
Tape recording in class: Yes
Books on tape from RFBD: Yes
Taping of books not from RFBD: Yes
Accommodations for students with
  ADHD: Yes
Reading machine: Yes
Other assistive technology: Yes
Priority registration: Yes

Added costs for services: No
LD specialists: Yes
Professional tutors: No
Peer tutors: Yes
Max. hours/wk. for services: 3
How professors are notified of
  LD/ADHD: By student

GENERAL ADMISSIONS INFORMATION

Director of Admissions: Martha Byrd
Telephone: 480-965-7788

ENTRANCE REQUIREMENTS

Academic units required: 4 English, 4 math, 3 science (3 science labs), 2 foreign language, 1 social studies, 1 history, 1 fine arts. High school diploma is required, and GED is accepted. ACT without Writing component accepted. TOEFL required of all international applicants: minimum paper TOEFL 500, minimum computer TOEFL 173.

Application deadline: Rolling
Notification: Rolling
Average GPA: 3.30
ACT Composite middle 50% range:
  20–26

SAT Math middle 50% range:
  490–620
SAT Critical Reading middle 50%
  range: 480–600
SAT Writing middle 50% range: NR

Graduated top 10% of class: 28%
Graduated top 25% of class: 55%
Graduated top 50% of class: 83%

COLLEGE GRADUATION REQUIREMENTS

Course waivers allowed: No
In what course: N/A
Course substitutions allowed: N/A
In what course: N/A

ADDITIONAL INFORMATION

Environment: Arizona State University is a city school about five miles from Phoenix.

Student Body
  Undergrad enrollment: 38,984
  Women: 49%
  Men: 51%
  Percent out-of-state: 25%

Cost Information
  In-state tuition: $4,591
  Out-of-state tuition: $15,750
  Room & board: $6,900
Housing Information
  University housing: Yes
  Percent living on campus: 17%

Greek System
  Fraternity: Yes
  Sorority: Yes
Athletics: Division I

NORTHERN ARIZONA UNIVERSITY

PO Box 4084, Flagstaff, AZ 86011-4084
Phone: 928-523-5511 • Fax: 928-523-0226
E-mail: undergraduate.admissions@nau.edu • Web: www.nau.edu
Support: S • Institution type: 4-year public

LEARNING DISABILITY PROGRAM AND SERVICES

Disability Support Services (DSS) promotes educational opportunities for students with disabilities at Northern Arizona University. DSS assists students in their persistence to graduate by providing resources, services, and auxiliary aids so that they may realize their life goals. The goal of DSS is to assist students in achieving their academic goals while at the same time creating an environment conducive to learning and building students' self-esteem. The belief is that by receiving supportive assistance, the student will become an independent learner and self-advocate.

LD/ADHD ADMISSIONS INFORMATION

College entrance tests required: Yes
Interview required: No
Essay recommended: No
Documentation required for LD: Current psychoeducational
  evaluation
Documentation required for ADHD: Yes
Submitted to: Disability Support Services
Special Ed. HS course work accepted: Yes

Specific course requirements: NR
Separate application required: No
# of LD applications submitted each year: NR
# of LD applications accepted yearly: NR
Total # of students receiving LD services: 117
**Acceptance into program means acceptance into
  college:** Students must be admitted and enrolled in the
  university first and then request services.

ADMISSIONS

There are no special admissions criteria for students with learning disabilities. General admission requirements for unconditional admission include: 4 years of English, 4 years of math; 2 years of social science with 1 year being American history; 2–3 years of science lab with additional requirements; 1 year of fine arts; and 2 years of a foreign language. (Students may be admitted conditionally with course deficiencies, but not in both math and science). In-state residents should have a 2.5 GPA, be in the top 50 percent of their high school class (a 3.0 GPA or being in the upper 25 percent of their graduating class is required for nonresidents), or earn an SAT combined score of 930 (1010 for nonresidents) or an ACT score of 22 (24 for nonresidents). Conditional admissions is possible with a 2.5–2.99 GPA or being in the top 50 percent of their graduating class and strong ACT/SAT scores. Exceptional admission may be offered to 10 percent of the new freshmen applicants or transfer applicants.

ADDITIONAL INFORMATION

Skills classes are available in note-taking, study techniques, reading, memory and learning, overcoming math anxiety, speed reading, time management, test-taking strategies. The university offers the following courses: How to Make Math Easy, How to Get Started Writing, How to Edit Writing, and How to Prepare for Final Exams. All services and accommodations are available for undergraduate and graduate students.

LEARNING DISABILITY PROGRAM/SERVICES

Learning Disability Program/Services: Disability Support Services
Director: Jane Mulrooney
  E-mail: jane.mulrooney@nau.edu
  Telephone: 928-523-8773
  Fax: 928-523-8747
Contact Person: Terry Alban
  E-mail: disability.support@nau.edu
  Telephone: 928-523-8773
  Fax: 928-523-8747

LEARNING DISABILITY SERVICES

Requests for the following/services accommodations will be evaluated individually based on appropriate and current documentation.

Allowed in exams
  Calculator: Yes
  Dictionary: Yes
  Computer: Yes
  Spellchecker: Yes
Extended test time: Yes
Scribes: Yes
Proctors: Yes
Oral exams: Yes
Note-takers: Yes

Distraction-reduced environment: Yes
Tape recording in class: Yes
Books on tape from RFBD: Yes
Taping of books not from RFBD: Yes
Accommodations for students with ADHD: Yes
Reading machine: Yes
Other assistive technology: Yes
Priority registration: Yes

Added costs for services: No
LD specialists: No
Professional tutors: No
Peer tutors: 100
Max. hours/wk. for services: Unlimited
How professors are notified of LD/ADHD: By student

GENERAL ADMISSIONS INFORMATION

Director of Admissions: Chris Lynch
Telephone: 928-523-6053

ENTRANCE REQUIREMENTS

Academic units required: 4 English, 4 math, 3 science (1 science lab), 2 foreign language, 2 social studies, 1 history, 1 fine arts. High school diploma is required, and GED is accepted. TOEFL required of all international applicants: minimum paper TOEFL 525, minimum computer TOEFL 195.

Application deadline: Rolling
Notification: Rolling
Average GPA: 3.40
ACT Composite middle 50% range: 20–25

SAT Math middle 50% range: 450–530
SAT Critical Reading middle 50% range: NR
SAT Writing middle 50% range: 430–510

Graduated top 10% of class: 17%
Graduated top 25% of class: 47%
Graduated top 50% of class: 80%

COLLEGE GRADUATION REQUIREMENTS

Course waivers allowed: No
Course substitutions allowed: Yes
In what course: There is a math substitution (not waiver) program for individuals with a math learning disability. It only applies to the liberal studies math requirement.

ADDITIONAL INFORMATION

Environment: The university is located on 320 acres in an urban area 2 hours from Phoenix.

Student Body
  Undergrad enrollment: 14,325
  Women: 60%
  Men: 40%
  Percent out-of-state: 19%

Cost Information
  In-state tuition: $4,376
Out-of-state tuition: $13,316
  Room & board: $6,260
Housing Information
  University housing: Yes
  Percent living on campus: 38%

Greek System
  Fraternity: Yes
  Sorority: Yes
Athletics: Division I

Northern Arizona University

UNIVERSITY OF ARIZONA

PO Box 210040, Tucson, AZ 85721-0040
Phone: 520-621-3237 • Fax: 520-621-9799
E-mail: appinfo@arizona.edu • Web: www.arizona.edu
Support: SP • Institution type: 4-year public

LEARNING DISABILITY PROGRAM AND SERVICES

The Strategic Alternative Learning Techniques (SALT) challenges students with LD to succeed in their pursuit of higher education. Supporting the ideal of education for life, SALT encourages and provides experiences and opportunities to build students' confidence beyond the classroom. SALT encourages growth and independence, training individuals to improve learning, expression, and decision making. A major philosophy is to provide intensive service for the first year with the goal of increasing independence as the student learns the coping strategies to succeed in college. The following guidelines clarify the process of documenting LD at the University of Arizona: Assessment and testing must be comprehensive and include a diagnostic interview and results of a neuropsychological or psychoeducational evaluation; a specific diagnosis and actual test scores; evaluation by a qualified professional. The report must be current and recommended accommodations should include a rationale that correlates the accommodations to specific test results and clinical observations. Students providing documentation express a desire to qualify for consideration as an individual with a disability. Being identified as LD/ADHD does not afford any individual automatic access to university accommodations or for privileges as an individual with disabilities. The university has established guidelines to meet diverse needs while maintaining the integrity of academic and non-academic programming.

LD/ADHD ADMISSIONS INFORMATION

College entrance tests required: Yes
Interview required: Yes
Essay recommended: Yes
Documentation required for LD: A complete diagnostic battery including measures of aptitude/intellectual functioning, cognitive/information processing, and academic achievement. See http://drc.arizona.edu/drc/ldprotocol.shtml.
Documentation required for ADHD: Same as above.

Specific course requirements: NR
Submitted to: Admissions, SALT, and Disability Resource Center
Special Ed. HS course work accepted: No
Separate application required: Yes, for SALT
# of LD applications submitted each year: 500 plus
# of LD applications accepted yearly: 160–200
Total # of students receiving LD services: 565
Acceptance into program means acceptance into college: Students are admitted to the university and then will be considered for SALT.

ADMISSIONS

Most students with LD meet the general admission requirements: ACT 24 (22 in-state) or SAT 1010 (930 in-state); top 25 percent of class (top 50 percent in-state), or 3.0 GPA (2.5 in-state) and 4 English, 4 math, 3 science, 2 social studies, 2 foreign language, and 1 fine arts. Candidates with disabilities, desiring special consideration, are expected to provide all documentation they feel necessary to represent the specific circumstances. If the candidate has LD/ADHD and is requesting special consideration through admissions, the student should submit all documentation of the disability directly to UA admissions. Students may apply to SALT at any time beginning in August preceding senior year of high school. A student may submit documentation with the SALT application as well, but one copy must accompany the UA application for admission to receive special consideration. Notification of admissions to SALT will start December 1, and continue monthly until enrollment is capped. Once SALT is filled, a waiting list will be established in mid-March.

ADDITIONAL INFORMATION

DRC basic services include advocacy, auxiliary aids for classroom accommodations, and special testing; there is no charge for these services. SALT enhanced services provide a full-service program with academic monitoring, registration assistance, staff contact and trained learning specialists, tutoring, a writing enhancement program, a specially equipped computer learning laboratory, and personalized tutorial services. Each student works with a trained specialist to identify learning preferences, learning strategies, and appropriate compensatory, productive learning techniques. There is a fee for enhanced services. Support services include both academic programs and counseling components. Students receive assistance with academic planning and registration followed by regularly scheduled staff contact to monitor progress. A drop-in center is available for study, tutoring, and student/staff interaction. The SALT program is staffed by persons trained and experienced in working with students with LD.

LEARNING DISABILITY PROGRAM/SERVICES

Learning Disability Program/Services: Disability Resource Center/SALT
Director: Jeff Orgera
 E-mail: saltctr@arizona.edu
 Telephone: 520-621-1242 V/TTY
 Fax: 520-621-9448
Contact Person: Autumn Palmer
 E-mail: autumn@u.arizona.edu
 Telephone: 520-621-5285
 Fax: 520-621-3260

LEARNING DISABILITY SERVICES

Requests for the following/services accommodations will be evaluated individually based on appropriate and current documentation.

Allowed in exams
 Calculator: Yes
 Dictionary: Yes
 Computer: Yes
 Spellchecker: Yes
Extended test time: Yes
Scribes: Yes
Proctors: Yes
Oral exams: Yes
Note-takers: Yes

Distraction-reduced environment: Yes
Tape recording in class: Yes
Books on tape from RFBD: Yes
Taping of books not from RFBD: Yes
Accommodations for students with ADHD: Yes
Reading machine: Yes
Other assistive technology: Yes
Priority registration: No

Added costs for services: Yes for SALT
LD specialists: Yes
Professional tutors: No
Peer tutors: Yes
Max. hours/wk. for services: Unlimited
How professors are notified of LD/ADHD: By student

GENERAL ADMISSIONS INFORMATION

Director of Admissions: Paul Kohn
Telephone: 520-621-3237

ENTRANCE REQUIREMENTS

Academic units required: 4 English, 4 math, 3 science (3 science labs), 2 foreign language, 1 social studies, 1 history, 1 fine art. **Academic units recommended:** 4 English, 4 math, 3 science (3 science labs), 2 foreign language, 2 social studies, 1 history, 1 fine art. High school diploma is required, and GED is accepted. ACT with or without Writing component accepted.

Application deadline: 4/1
Notification: Rolling
Average GPA: 3.36
ACT Composite middle 50% range: 20–26

SAT Math middle 50% range: 500–630
SAT Critical Reading middle 50% range: 490–600
SAT Writing middle 50% range: NR

Graduated top 10% of class: 34%
Graduated top 25% of class: 62%
Graduated top 50% of class: 87%

COLLEGE GRADUATION REQUIREMENTS

Course waivers allowed: No
Course substitutions allowed: Yes
In what course: Course substitutions are typically in math or second language; approval must come from college/major department.

ADDITIONAL INFORMATION

Environment: Situated in downtown Tucson on 325 acres, the university is surrounded by the Santa Catalina Mountain range in the Sonora Desert.

Student Body
 Undergrad enrollment: 28,013
 Women: 53%
 Men: 47%
 Percent out-of-state: 33%

Cost Information
 In-state tuition: $4,594
Out-of-state tuition: $14,800
 Room & board: $7,850
Housing Information
 University housing: Yes
 Percent living on campus: 20%

Greek System
 Fraternity: Yes
 Sorority: Yes
Athletics: Division I

University of Arizona

HARDING UNIVERSITY

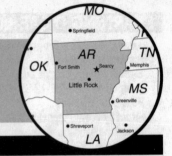

PO Box 12255, Searcy, AR 72149
Phone: 501-279-4407 • Fax: 501-279-4129
E-mail: admissions@harding.edu • Web: www.harding.edu
Support: CS • Institution type: 4-year private

LEARNING DISABILITY PROGRAM AND SERVICES

The philosophy and goals of Student Support Services (SSS) are to foster an institutional climate supportive of the success of high-risk students. SSS strives to deliver a program of services that result in increasing the college retention and graduation rates. Students receive a high level of personal attention to and support for their needs. Students meet with an academic counselor concerning their specific needs. Students meet with an academic counselor to discuss their specific needs and goals to better understand what they are. There are workshops that provide students with hands-on learning, and a ropes course that teaches skills ranging from communication to trust to working as a team. The mission of the Academic Resources Center is to serve as a central location that provides information and services needed by students to achieve academic success such as: a learning environment that is individualized, personal, and supportive; support by means of supplementary materials for additional drill and practice in course skills; provide tutorial and counseling programs that prepare students to function effectively, efficiently and confidently; assess learning and study skills, and provide materials to develop needed skills; and identify individual learning styles that contribute to effective adjustment to the teaching-learning situation.

LD/ADHD ADMISSIONS INFORMATION

College entrance tests required: Yes
Interview required: No
Essay recommended: Yes
Documentation required for LD: Current psychological evaluation (preferred senior year in high school) by licensed professional
Documentation required for ADHD: Evaluation by medical doctor
Submitted to: Both Admissions Office and Support Program/Services

Special Ed. HS course work accepted: No
Specific course requirements: NR
Separate application required: No
# of LD applications submitted each year: 100
# of LD applications accepted yearly: 100
Total # of students receiving LD services: 78
Acceptance into program means acceptance into college: Students must be admitted and enrolled in the university first and then request services.

ADMISSIONS

Admission criteria for students with learning disabilities are the same as for regular applicants. Students who score 18 or below on the ACT (or equivalent SAT) are admitted into the Developmental Studies Program. Transfer students with low GPAs are accepted on probation. Course requirements include 4 English, 3 math, 3 social studies, 2 science, 2 foreign language (recommended). The minimum GPA is a 2.0. The director of SSS makes admission decisions for the program and the Admissions Office determines admissibility into the university. Students may self-disclose in the admission process, and this information could be used as one component in making an admission decision.

ADDITIONAL INFORMATION

Testing accommodations are provided with documented evidence of a disability, and include extended time on exams, readers, taking the test in parts with breaks, using a computer with spellchecker, and providing a distraction-free environment. Classroom accommodations may include a computer with spellchecker, extra time for proofreading and editing of written assignments, note-takers, books on tape, and taping outside reading assignments. Each semester the student signs a permission form designating which professors should receive letters. Skills classes for college credit are offered. The CAPS (coaches and players) mentoring program targets primarily students with ADHD, but students without this disability may be admitted into this program with the recommendation from an instructor or SSS staff member. Both coach and player sign a contract and are expected to meet and contact each other by phone weekly. The coach and player complete a workout sheet that requires the player (student) to complete a study schedule and report on assignment deadlines. If tutors are needed, the coach helps to make the appointments. As players, students will meet regularly with their coaches and may expect their coaches to be a friend and share their experiences; help players formulate their game plans (study plans), get organized, and with that all-important survival skill—time management—and serve as a liaison between the players and university staff or faculty.

LEARNING DISABILITY PROGRAM/SERVICES

Learning Disability Program/Services: Student Support Services (SSS)
Director: Jim Johnston, EdD
  E-mail: jjohnston@harding.edu
  Telephone: 501-279-4416
  Fax: 501-279-4217
Contact Person: Teresa McLeod, MEd
  E-mail: tmcleod@harding.edu
  Telephone: 501-279-4019
  Fax: 501-279-4217

LEARNING DISABILITY SERVICES

Requests for the following/services accommodations will be evaluated individually based on appropriate and current documentation.

Allowed in exams
  Calculator: Yes
  Dictionary: Yes
  Computer: Yes
  Spellchecker: Yes
Extended test time: Yes
Scribes: Yes
Proctors: Yes
Oral exams: Yes
Note-takers: Yes

Distraction-reduced environment: Yes
Tape recording in class: Yes
Books on tape from RFBD: Yes
Taping of books not from RFBD: Yes
Accommodations for students with ADHD: Yes
Reading machine: Yes
Other assistive technology: Yes
Priority registration: Yes

Added costs for services: No
LD specialists: Yes
Professional tutors: 1
Peer tutors: 15
Max. hours/wk. for services: Unlimited
How professors are notified of LD/ADHD: By both student and director

GENERAL ADMISSIONS INFORMATION

Director of Admissions: Glenn Dillard
Telephone: 800-477-4407

ENTRANCE REQUIREMENTS

Academic units required: 4 English, 3 math, 2 science, 3 social studies, 3 academic electives. **Academic units recommended:** 4 English, 4 math, 4 science, 2 foreign language, 4 social studies, 2 academic electives. High school diploma is required, and GED is accepted. ACT with or without Writing component accepted. TOEFL required of all international applicants: minimum paper TOEFL 500, minimum computer TOEFL 175.

Application deadline: 7/1
Notification: Rolling
Average GPA: 3.40
ACT Composite middle 50% range: 20–27

SAT Math middle 50% range: 470–630
SAT Critical Reading middle 50% range: 480–620
SAT Writing middle 50% range: 470–600

Graduated top 10% of class: 27%
Graduated top 25% of class: 49%
Graduated top 50% of class: 75%

COLLEGE GRADUATION REQUIREMENTS

Course waivers allowed: No
Course substitutions allowed: No

ADDITIONAL INFORMATION

Environment: The university is located on 200 acres in a small town 50 miles northeast of Little Rock.

Student Body
  Undergrad enrollment: 3,995
  Women: 53%
  Men: 47%
  Percent out-of-state: 71%

Cost Information
  Tuition: $11,250
  Room & board: $5,442
Housing Information
  University housing: Yes
  Percent living on campus: 73%

Greek System
  Fraternity: Yes
  Sorority: Yes
Athletics: Division II

Harding University

U. OF ARKANSAS—FAYETTEVILLE

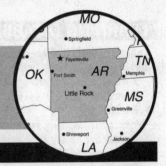

232 Silas Hunt Hall, Fayetteville, AR 72701
Phone: 479-575-5346 • Fax: 479-575-7515
E-mail: uofa@uark.edu • Web: www.uark.edu
Support: S • Institution type: 4-year public

LEARNING DISABILITY PROGRAM AND SERVICES

The goals of Student Support Services (SSS) are to offer holistic personal and professional development opportunities. We have academic tools and instruction for intellectual growth; exclusive hallmark events that offer a matchless SSS experience; collaborative enrichment opportunities with UA faculty, staff, and departments; a friendly environment consisting of a helpful, approachable, and caring staff; new-age, reliable, and technologically advanced services and equipment; a centrally located facility outfitted with suitable furniture and inviting staff offices and a quiet place to study. The Enhanced Learning Center offers tutoring services to all University of Arkansas students free of charge. Supplemental Instruction (SI) is an academic enrichment program that increases student performance and retention. SI offers enrolled students regularly scheduled, out-of-class review sessions in historically difficult courses. Sessions are led by experienced students who excel in the difficult subject matter. SI is free to all UA students.

LD/ADHD ADMISSIONS INFORMATION

College entrance tests required: Yes
Interview required: No
Essay recommended: No
Documentation required for LD: Psychoeducational evaluation
Documentation required for ADHD: Yes
Submitted to: Student Support Services
Specific course requirements of all applicants: Yes

Separate application required: No
# of LD applications submitted each year: NR
# of LD applications accepted yearly: NR
Total # of students receiving LD services: NR
Acceptance into program means acceptance into college: Students must be admitted and enrolled prior to requesting services.

ADMISSIONS

Guaranteed general admission to the University of Arkansas requires a minimum GPA of 3.0 and an ACT score of 20 (or SAT of 930). Students who do not meet qualifications may be admitted on the basis of individual review of their application portfolios. Course requirements include: 4 years of English, 4 years of math, 3 years of social studies, 3 years of science, and 2 electives to be chosen from English, foreign languages, oral communication, mathematics, computer science, natural sciences, and social studies. SSS is a federally funded program, and there are a limited number of participants who can be served. An applicant must meet the following qualification criteria: Have an academic need, ACT score of 27 or below, and a high school or college GPA of 3.0 or below. In addition, applicants must meet one or more of the following: first generation college student; did not graduate with a four-year degree; meet federal income eligibility requirements; and/or have a documented disability with the Center for Students with Disabilities.

ADDITIONAL INFORMATION

The University of Arkansas is committed to ensuring student success through a powerful convergence of programs and services. While at the university, we help students meet their challenges confidently. SSS has a friendly, resourceful, and helpful staff committed to helping students make great grades, better understand textbooks, take excellent notes, manage time, and explore career and graduate school options. SSS is dedicated to helping students succeed.

LEARNING DISABILITY PROGRAM/SERVICES

Learning Disability Program/Services: Student Support Services
Director: Anne L. Jannarone
  Telephone: 479-575-3104
  Fax: 479-575-7445
Contact Person: Administrative Assistant
  Telephone: 479-575-3104
  E-mail: ada@uark.edu

LEARNING DISABILITY SERVICES

Requests for the following/services accommodations will be evaluated individually based on appropriate and current documentation.

Allowed in exams
  Calculator: NR
  Dictionary: NR
  Computer: NR
  Spellchecker: NR
Extended test time: NR
Scribes: NR
Proctors: NR
Oral exams: NR
Notetakers: NR

Distraction-reduced environment: NR
Tape recording in class: NR
Books on tape from RFBD: NR
Taping of books not from RFBD: NR
Accommodations for students with ADHD: NR
Reading machine: NR
Other assistive technology: NR
Priority registration: NR

Added costs for services: No
LD specialists: No
Professional tutors: NR
Peer tutors: N/A
Max. hours/wk. for services: N/A
How professors are notified of LD/ADHD: Student

GENERAL ADMISSIONS INFORMATION

Director of Admissions: Dawn Medley
Telephone: 479-575-53

ENTRANCE REQUIREMENTS

Academic units required: 4 English, 4 math, 3 science (2 science labs), 3 social studies, 2 academic electives. Academic units recomended: 2 foreign language. High school diploma is required, and GED is accepted. ACT with or without Writing component accepted. TOEFL required of all international applicants: minimum paper TOEFL 550, minimum computer TOEFL 213.

Application deadline: 8/15
Notification: Rolling
Average GPA: 3.60
ACT Composite middle 50% range: 22–28

SAT Math middle 50% range: 530–650
SAT Critical Reading middle 50% range: 510–630
SAT Writing middle 50% range: 510–640

Graduated top 10% of class: 32%
Graduated top 25% of class: 61%
Graduated top 50% of class: 88%

COLLEGE GRADUATION REQUIREMENTS

Course waivers allowed: N/A
Course substitutions allowed: N/A

ADDITIONAL INFORMATION

Environment: Urban area about 200 miles northwest of Little Rock.

Student Body
  Undergrad enrollment: 14,350
  Women: 50%
  Men: 50%
  Percent out-of-state: 21%

Cost Information
  In-state tuition: $4,590
Out-of-state tuition: $12,724
  Room & board: $6,522
Housing Information
  University housing: Yes
  Percent living on campus: 29%

Greek System
  Fraternity: Yes
  Sorority: Yes
Athletics: Division I

University of Arkansas—Fayetteville

UNIVERSITY OF THE OZARKS

415 College Avenue, Clarksville, AR 72830
Phone: 479-979-1227 • Fax: 479-979-1355
E-mail: jdecker@ozarks.edu • Web: www.ozarks.edu
Support: SP • Institution type: 4-year private

LEARNING DISABILITY PROGRAM AND SERVICES

The Jones Learning Center (JLC) believes that students with specific learning disabilities are entitled to services that allow them to compete with other students. The Learning Center program emphasizes a total learning environment. Instruction is individualized and personalized. Enhanced services include individualized programming, a technology unit, centralized accessibility, and a supportive atmosphere with a low student/faculty ratio, which provides students even greater opportunity to realize their true academic potential. Ideas, instructional materials, and activities are presented on a variety of different levels commensurate with the educational needs of the individual student. This program is very comprehensive in every area. At the beginning of each semester, the course load and needs of the student are assessed to determine what services will be needed.

LD/ADHD ADMISSIONS INFORMATION

College entrance tests required: Yes
Interview required: Yes
Essay recommended: Yes
Documentation required for LD: Psychoeducational evaluation
Documentation required for ADHD: Psychoeducational and medical evaluation
Submitted to: Jones Learning Center
Special Ed. HS course work accepted: Yes

Specific course requirements of all applicants: No
Separate application required: Yes
# of LD applications submitted each year: 50–60
# of LD applications accepted yearly: 25–30
Total # of students receiving LD services: 30–40
Acceptance into program means acceptance into college: Students admitted to the Learning Center are automatically accepted to the university.

ADMISSIONS

Students complete a special application. Applicants must be 18 or older, complete high school or obtain a GED, demonstrate average or above-average IQ, have a learning disability or attention deficit hyperactivity disorder as a primary disability, provide diagnostic information from previous evaluations, complete the admissions packet, visit campus, and participate in a 2-day psychoeducational evaluation that includes interviews. Applicants with some areas of concern for the Admissions Committee may be admitted on a 1-year trial basis. This conditional admission is only available to students applying to the Jones Learning Center. There are no specific high school courses and no minimum ACT/SAT scores required for admission. Admission decisions are made by the Admissions Committee. Motivation is a key factor in the admission decision. Students are encouraged to begin the application to the Jones Learning Center during the spring semester of their junior year or early in the senior year. The JLC has a rolling admission policy. Once students are admitted into the JLC, they are automatically admitted to the university.

ADDITIONAL INFORMATION

Students are assigned to a program coordinator who is responsible for the individualized planning of the students' program of study, acts as an advocate, and monitors the students' progress. Students receive help understanding learning styles, utilizing strengths, circumventing deficits, building skills, and becoming independent learners and self-advocates. Skills classes are offered in study skills (for credit), writing (for credit), reading, and math. Enhanced services include testing accommodations, one-to-one administration of a test with a reader and staff to take dictation if needed, assistive technology including Dragon Dictate and a Kurzweil Scanner/Reader, peer tutoring, and note-takers. Developmental services include opportunities to improve basic skills in reading, writing, and math. Students with ADHD and/or LD may receive services from the Learning Center.

LEARNING DISABILITY PROGRAM/SERVICES

Learning Disability Program/Services: Jones Learning Center
Director: Julia Frost
  E-mail: jfrost@ozarks.edu
  Telephone: 479-979-1401
  Fax: 479-979-1477
Contact Person: Bonnie Starkey
  E-mail: bstarkey@ozarks.edu
  Telephone: 479-979-1301
  Fax: 479-979-1477

LEARNING DISABILITY SERVICES

Requests for the following/services accommodations will be evaluated individually based on appropriate and current documentation.

Allowed in exams
  Calculator: Yes
  Dictionary: No
  Computer: Yes
  Spellchecker: Yes
Extended test time: Yes
Scribes: Yes
Proctors: Yes
Oral exams: Yes
Note-takers: Yes

Distraction-reduced environment: Yes
Tape recording in class: Yes
Books on tape from RFBD: No
Taping of books not from RFBD: Yes
Accommodations for students with ADHD: Yes
Reading machine: Yes
Other assistive technology: Yes
Priority registration: Yes

Added costs for services: Yes
LD specialists: Yes
Professional tutors: 15
Peer tutors: 100–125
Max. hours/wk. for services: Unlimited
How professors are notified of LD/ADHD: By both student and director

GENERAL ADMISSIONS INFORMATION

Director of Admissions: Jana Hart
Telephone: 800-264-8600

ENTRANCE REQUIREMENTS

Academic units required: 4 English, 4 math, 3 science (2 science labs), 2 foreign language, 1 social studies, 2 history. **Academic units recommended:** 4 English, 4 math, 3 science (2 science labs), 2 foreign language, 1 social studies, 2 history. High school diploma is required, and GED is accepted. TOEFL required of all international applicants: minimum paper TOEFL 500, minimum computer TOEFL 173.

Application deadline: Rolling
Notification: Rolling
Average GPA: 3.40
ACT Composite middle 50% range: 19–25

SAT Math middle 50% range: 440–550
SAT Critical Reading middle 50% range: 490–560
SAT Writing middle 50% range: NR

Graduated top 10% of class: 23%
Graduated top 25% of class: 44%
Graduated top 50% of class: 77%

COLLEGE GRADUATION REQUIREMENTS

Course waivers allowed: No
Course substitutions allowed: Yes
In what course: College algebra and foreign language

ADDITIONAL INFORMATION

Environment: The university is located on 56 acres, 100 miles northwest of Little Rock. Clarksville is a town of 5,000 residents in the Arkansas River Valley.

Student Body
  Undergrad enrollment: 622
  Women: 54%
  Men: 46%
  Percent out-of-state: 30%

Cost Information
  Tuition: $14,170
  Room & board: $5,080
Housing Information
  University housing: Yes
  Percent living on campus: 64%

Greek System
  Fraternity: No
  Sorority: No
Athletics: Division III

University of the Ozarks

CALIFORNIA POLYTECHNIC STATE UNIVERSITY—SAN LUIS OBISPO

Admissions Office, Cal Poly, San Luis Obispo, CA 93407
Phone: 805-756-2311 • Fax: 805-756-5400
E-mail: admissions@calpoly.edu • Web: www.calpoly.edu
Support: CS • Institution type: 4-year public

LEARNING DISABILITY PROGRAM AND SERVICES

The goal of the program is to assist students with learning disabilities use their learning strengths. The Disability Resources Center (DRC) assists students with disabilities in achieving access to higher education, promotes personal and educational success, and increases the awareness and responsiveness of the campus community. DRC is actively involved with students and faculty and provides a newsletter and open house to keep the college population aware of what it is and what it does. Incoming students are encouraged to meet with DRC staff to receive assistance in the planning of class schedules. This allows for the selection of appropriate classes to fit particular needs and personal goals. It is the responsibility of each student seeking accommodations and services to provide a written, comprehensive psychological and/or medical evaluation verifying the diagnosis. The Cal Poly Student Learning Outcomes model promotes students' personal growth and the development of self-advocacy for full inclusion of qualified students with verified disabilities. The promotion of student self-reliance and responsibility are necessary adjuncts to educational development. For learning disabilities, the assessments must be done by a licensed educational psychologist, psychologist, neurologist, or LD specialist. The diagnosis of ADHD must be done by a licensed therapist, educational psychologist, psychologist, neurologist, or physician.

LD/ADHD ADMISSIONS INFORMATION

College entrance tests required: Yes
Interview required: No
Essay recommended: No
Documentation required for LD: Refer to www.drc.calpoly.edu.
Documentation required for ADHD: Refer to
   www.drc.calpoly.edu.
Submitted to: Disability Resource Center
Special Ed. HS course work accepted: Yes

Specific course requirements of all applicants: Yes
Separate application required: No
# of LD applications submitted each year: 100–150
# of LD applications accepted yearly: 50–70
Total # of students receiving LD services: 250–325
Acceptance into program means acceptance into
   college: Students must be admitted and enrolled in the
   university first and then request services.

ADMISSIONS

Students with LD must meet the same admission criteria as all applicants and should submit a general admission application to the Admissions Office. General requirements include 4 years of English, 3 years of math, 1 year of U.S. history or government, 1 year of science lab, 2 years of a foreign language, 1 year of fine arts, and 3 years of academic electives. On a case-by-case basis, foreign language substitutions may be allowed. Some courses taken in the Special Education Department may be accepted. All documentation should be sent directly to the Support Program, and students who self-disclose will receive information. Admission decisions are made by the Admissions Office.

ADDITIONAL INFORMATION

Incoming students are strongly urged to schedule an appointment with DRC to receive assistance in the planning of classes. Academic accommodations are designed to meet a student's disability-related needs without fundamentally altering the nature of the instructional program and are not intended to provide remediation. Supportive services may include academic advising, alternative format materials, assistive listening devices, note-taking, taped textbooks, test accommodations, tutorial services, and writing assistance. DRC may recommend the services of the Academic Skills Center of Student Academic Services and enrollment in English and math classes offering additional support. There are also a peer mentoring program, Partners for Success, and a career mentoring program available to all students. Students requesting accommodations, which include using a computer, dictionary, or spellchecker during an exam, will need the professor's permission. The university can provide some free psychoeducational assessment services, but there is a lengthy waiting period for these limited services. Services and accommodations are available to undergraduate and graduate students.

LEARNING DISABILITY PROGRAM/SERVICES

Learning Disability Program/Services: Disability Resource Center (DRC)
Director: J. Trey Duffy
  E-mail: duffy@calpoly.edu
  Telephone: 805-756-1395
  Fax: 805-756-5451
Contact Person: Dr. Steven Kane
  E-mail: skane@calpoly.edu
  Telephone: 805-756-1395
  Fax: 805-756-5451

LEARNING DISABILITY SERVICES

Requests for the following/services accommodations will be evaluated individually based on appropriate and current documentation.

Allowed in exams
  Calculator: Yes
  Dictionary: Yes
  Computer: Yes
  Spellchecker: Yes
Extended test time: Yes
Scribes: Yes
Proctors: Yes
Oral exams: Yes

Note-takers: Yes
Distraction-reduced environment: Yes
Tape recording in class: Yes
Books on tape from RFBD: Yes
Taping of books not from RFBD: Yes
Accommodations for students with ADHD: Yes
Reading machine: Yes
Other assistive technology: Yes

Priority registration: Yes
Added costs for services: No
LD specialists: Yes
Professional tutors: No
Peer tutors: NR
Max. hours/wk. for services: Depends on service
How professors are notified of LD/ADHD: By student

GENERAL ADMISSIONS INFORMATION

Director of Admissions: James Maraviglia
  Telephone: 805-756-2311

ENTRANCE REQUIREMENTS

Academic units required: 4 English, 3 math, 3 science (1 science lab), 2 foreign language, 2 social studies, 1 history, 1 academic elective, 1 visual/performing arts. High school diploma is required, and GED is accepted. ACT with or without Writing component accepted. TOEFL required of all international applicants: minimum paper TOEFL 550, minimum computer TOEFL 213.

Application deadline: 11/30
Notification: Rolling
Average GPA: 3.70
ACT Composite middle 50% range: 23–28

SAT Math middle 50% range: 560–670
SAT Critical Reading middle 50% range: 520–620
SAT Writing middle 50% range: NR

Graduated top 10% of class: 39%
Graduated top 25% of class: 76%
Graduated top 50% of class: 97%

COLLEGE GRADUATION REQUIREMENTS

Course waivers allowed: No
Course substitutions allowed: Yes
In what course: On a case-by-case basis, individuals may be granted course substitutions (not waivers) in quantitative reasoning (in very limited non-math-related majors) by the Vice President of Academic Affairs and foreign language substitutions with department approval.

ADDITIONAL INFORMATION

Environment: The campus is located 100 miles north of Santa Barbara.

Student Body
  Undergrad enrollment: 17,671
  Women: 43%
  Men: 57%
  Percent out-of-state: 6%

Cost Information
  In-state tuition: $4,350
Out-of-state tuition: $10,170
  Room & board: $8,453
Housing Information
  University housing: Yes
  Percent living on campus: 20%

Greek System
  Fraternity: Yes
  Sorority: Yes
Athletics: Division I

CALIFORNIA STATE POLYTECHNIC UNIVERSITY—POMONA

3801 West Temple Avenue, Pomona, CA 91768
Phone: 909-869-3210 • Fax: 909-869-4529
E-mail: admissions@csupomona.edu • Web: www.csupomona.edu
Support: CS • Institution type: 4-year public

LEARNING DISABILITY PROGRAM AND SERVICES

The mission of the Office of Disabled Student Services (DSS) is to help students with disabilities compete on an equal basis with their nondisabled peers by providing reasonable accommodations. This will allow them access to any academic program or facilitate participation in any university activity that is offered to fellow students. The major purposes of DSS are to determine reasonable accommodations based on disability as assessed by knowledgeable professionals; emphasize self-advocacy, maximize learning experience and continuously assess students' needs, actively recruit and increase retention and graduation rates of students with disabilities, and provide greater educational equity; facilitate the university in meeting requirements of the Americans with Disabilities Act; and prepare students with disabilities for life, leadership, and careers in a changing world.

LD/ADHD ADMISSIONS INFORMATION

College entrance tests required: Yes
Interview required: No
Essay recommended: No
Documentation required for LD: Report with scores for aptitude and achievement testing
Documentation required for ADHD: Diagnostic information and historical data should be summarized in a report.
Submitted to: Disabled Student Services
Special Ed. HS course work accepted: Yes

Specific course requirements of all applicants: Yes
Separate application required: No
# of LD applications submitted each year: NR
# of LD applications accepted yearly: NR
Total # of students receiving LD services: 155
Acceptance into program means acceptance into college: Students must be admitted and enrolled in the university first and then request services.

ADMISSIONS

Students must meet the university's regular entrance requirements, including C or better in the subject requirements of 4 years of English, 3 years of math, 1 year of U.S. history, 2 years of science lab, 2 years of a foreign language, 1 year of visual or performing arts, and 3 years of academic electives and a qualifiable eligibility index based on high school GPA and scores on either ACT or SAT. Special admits are very limited. Applicants with LD are encouraged to complete college-prep courses. However, if students are unable to fulfill a specific course requirement because of a learning disability, alternative college-prep courses may be substituted. Substitutions may be granted in foreign language, science lab, and math. Substitutions may be authorized on an individual basis after review and recommendation by applicant's guidance counselor in consultation with the Director of DSS. Course substitutions could limit access to some majors. Students are encouraged to self-disclose a learning disability if it would help to explain lower grades. Students who self-disclose are reviewed by DSS, which provides a recommendation to admissions.

ADDITIONAL INFORMATION

Support services include counseling, advocacy services, registration, note-takers, readers, tutors, testing accommodations, and specialized equipment. Skills classes are not offered through DSS, but are available in other departments in the areas of reading skills, test preparation, test-taking strategies, and study skills. Services and accommodations are available to undergraduate and graduate students. Cal Poly offers a summer program for any high school student.

California

LEARNING DISABILITY PROGRAM/SERVICES

Learning Disability Program/Services: Disabled Student Services
Director: Dr. Catherine Schmitt Whitaker
  E-mail: clschmitt@csupomona.edu
  Telephone: 909-869-5257
  Fax: 909-869-3271

LEARNING DISABILITY SERVICES

Requests for the following/services accommodations will be evaluated individually based on appropriate and current documentation.

Allowed in exams
  Calculator: Yes
  Dictionary: Yes
  Computer: Yes
  Spellchecker: Yes
Extended test time: Yes
Scribes: Yes
Proctors: Yes
Oral exams: Yes
Note-takers: Yes

Distraction-reduced environment: Yes
Tape recording in class: Yes
Books on tape from RFBD: Yes
Taping of books not from RFBD: Yes
Accommodations for students with ADHD: Yes
Reading machine: Yes
Other assistive technology: Yes
Priority registration: Yes

Added costs for services: No
LD specialists: Yes
Professional tutors: No
Peer tutors: Yes
Max. hours/wk. for services: 2
How professors are notified of LD/ADHD: By student

GENERAL ADMISSIONS INFORMATION

Director of Admissions: Dr. George R. Bradshaw, Director, Admissions and Outreach
  Telephone: 909-869-3427

ENTRANCE REQUIREMENTS
Academic units required: 4 English, 3 math, 2 science (2 science labs), 2 foreign language, 1 social studies, 1 history, 1 academic elective, 1 visual/performing arts. **Academic units recommended:** 4 math. High school diploma is required, and GED is accepted. ACT with or without Writing component accepted. TOEFL required of all international applicants: minimum paper TOEFL 525, minimum computer TOEFL 195.

Application deadline: 11/30
Notification: Rolling
Average GPA: 3.24
ACT Composite middle 50% range: 17–23

SAT Math middle 50% range: 450–590
SAT Critical Reading middle 50% range: 430–540
SAT Writing middle 50% range: NR

Graduated top 10% of class: NR
Graduated top 25% of class: NR
Graduated top 50% of class: NR

COLLEGE GRADUATION REQUIREMENTS

Course waivers allowed: No
Course substitutions allowed: Yes
In what course: On a case-by-case basis, individuals may be granted course substitutions (not waivers) in quantitative reasoning (in very limited non-math-related majors) by the Vice President of Academic Affairs and foreign language substitutions with department approval.

ADDITIONAL INFORMATION

Environment: The university is located on 1,437 acres in a suburban area 30 miles east of Los Angeles.

Student Body
  Undergrad enrollment: 18,040
  Women: 43%
  Men: 57%
  Percent out-of-state: 2%

Cost Information
  In-state tuition: $3,012
Out-of-state tuition: $13,002
  Room & board: $7,212
Housing Information
  University housing: Yes
  Percent living on campus: 12%

Greek System
  Fraternity: Yes
  Sorority: Yes
Athletics: Division II

CALIFORNIA STATE U.—CHICO

400 West First Street, Chico, CA 95929-0722
Phone: 530-898-4428 • Fax: 530-898-6456
E-mail: info@csuchico.edu • Web: www.csuchico.edu
Support: CS • Institution type: 4-year public

LEARNING DISABILITY PROGRAM AND SERVICES

The goal of Disability Student Services (DSS) is to facilitate accommodation requests and provide the support services necessary to ensure equal access to university programs for students with disabilities. This goal is consistent with university policy and federal and state laws. DSS provides a variety of services to university students at no charge. DSS advisers who specialize in various disabilities are available to assist students with individual accommodations. It is the student's responsibility to initiate accommodation requests early to ensure proper coordination of services. Students must provide current and appropriate documentation to support their requests for services/accommodations.

LD/ADHD ADMISSIONS INFORMATION

College entrance tests required: Yes
Interview required: No
Essay recommended: No
Documentation required for LD: Psychoeducational evaluation
Documentation required for ADHD: Yes
Submitted to: Disability Student Services
Special Ed. HS course work accepted: Yes

Specific course requirements of all applicants: Yes
Separate application required: No
# of LD applications submitted each year: NR
# of LD applications accepted yearly: NR
Total # of students receiving LD services: 300
Acceptance into program means acceptance into college: Students must be admitted and enrolled in the university first and then request services.

ADMISSIONS

There are no special admission procedures for students with learning disabilities. Applicants must meet the general admission requirements that are based on GPA, test scores, and subject requirements. Course requirements include 4 years of English, 3 years of math, 1 year of U.S. history, 1 year of science, 2 years of a foreign language, and 1 year of visual/performing arts. Applicants with disabilities are encouraged to complete college-prep courses. If the applicant is judged unable to fulfill a specific course requirement because of a verified disability, alternate college-prep courses may be substituted for specific subject requirements. Substitutions may be authorized on an individual basis after review and recommendation by the high school counselor or academic advisor in consultation with the director of a CSU DSS.

ADDITIONAL INFORMATION

General accommodations may include: priority registration, note-takers, readers, scribes, test accommodations, computer access assistance, LD assessment, and liaison with faculty and administration. Students are also eligible for certain retention services programs, including the Academic Learning Forum and tutoring at the Student Learning Center. Advisors are available to discuss all accommodation requests. There is a Math Lab, Writing Center, Tutoring Center, and Student Learning Center available to all students. The university is committed to making electronic information available to all students. Designated computer stations throughout campus have adaptive hardware and software installed. Software, hardware, and equipment include Open Book Unbound Reading System, Kurzweil Reading System, DeckTalk PC, Couble Talk LT, Vocal/Window Eyes, Jaws for Windows, Ducksberry Software, and ZoomText Plus. Most computers are networked for library and Internet access.

LEARNING DISABILITY PROGRAM/SERVICES

Learning Disability Program/Services: Disability Student Services
Director: Billie Jackson
  E-mail: bfjackson@csuchico.edu
  Telephone: 530-898-5959
  Fax: 530-898-4411
Contact Person: Van Alexander
  E-mail: valexander@csuchico.edu
  Telephone: 530-898-5959
  Fax: 530-898-4411

LEARNING DISABILITY SERVICES

Requests for the following/services accommodations will be evaluated individually based on appropriate and current documentation.

Allowed in exams	**Distraction-reduced environment:** Yes	**Added costs for services:** No
Calculator: Yes	**Tape recording in class:** Yes	**LD specialists:** Yes
Dictionary: Yes	**Books on tape from RFBD:** Yes	**Professional tutors:** 25
Computer: Yes	**Taping of books not from RFBD:** Yes	**Peer tutors:** 25
Spellchecker: Yes	**Accommodations for students with**	**Max. hours/wk. for services:** Varies
Extended test time: Yes	**ADHD:** Yes	**How professors are notified of**
Scribes: Yes	**Reading machine:** Yes	**LD/ADHD:** By student
Proctors: Yes	**Other assistive technology:** Yes	
Oral exams: Yes	**Priority registration:** Yes	
Note-takers: Yes		

GENERAL ADMISSIONS INFORMATION

Director of Admissions: John Swiney
Telephone: 530-898-4428

ENTRANCE REQUIREMENTS

Academic units required: 4 English, 3 math, 2 science (2 science labs), 2 foreign language, 2 social studies, 1 academic elective, 1 visual/performing arts. High school diploma is required, and GED is accepted. ACT with or without Writing component accepted. TOEFL required of all international applicants: minimum paper TOEFL 500.

Application deadline: 11/30	**SAT Math middle 50% range:**	**Graduated top 10% of class:** 35%
Notification: 3/1	460–580	**Graduated top 25% of class:** 76%
Average GPA: 3.15	**SAT Critical Reading middle 50%**	**Graduated top 50% of class:** 100%
ACT Composite middle 50% range:	**range:** 450–560	
18–23	**SAT Writing middle 50% range:** NR	

COLLEGE GRADUATION REQUIREMENTS

Course waivers allowed: No
In what course: N/A
Course substitutions allowed: No
In what course: N/A

ADDITIONAL INFORMATION

Environment: The university is located in a small town 100 miles from Sacramento.

Student Body	**Cost Information**	**Greek System**
Undergrad enrollment: 14,927	**In-state tuition:** $2,520	**Fraternity:** Yes
Women: 53%	**Out-of-state tuition:** $12,690	**Sorority:** Yes
Men: 47%	**Room & board:** $8,314	**Athletics:** Division II
Percent out-of-state: 1%	**Housing Information**	
	University housing: Yes	
	Percent living on campus: 13%	

CALIFORNIA STATE U.—FULLERTON

800 North State College Boulevard, Fullerton, CA 92834-6900
Phone: 714-773-2370 • Fax: 714-278-2356
E-mail: admissions@fullerton.edu • Web: www.fullerton.edu
Support: CS • Institution type: 4-year public

LEARNING DISABILITY PROGRAM AND SERVICES

The Student Support Services Program is a wide network of support services that help ensure academic and personal success in college. The program is designed to increase retention and graduation rates for underrepresented students. Students are encouraged to fulfill their academic and career potential by participating in an exceptional support environment. Each participant is teamed with an academic counselor for one-on-one mentoring and advisement. The emphasis is on providing students with personal attention and access to support services that include academic advisement; tutoring (referrals for individual and group tutoring including review sessions in select courses and development of study group); co-curricular events; peer mentoring for first-time freshmen; workshops and study-skills courses in reading, writing, math and other subjects, as well as time management; counseling; and an introduction to campus resources.

LD/ADHD ADMISSIONS INFORMATION

College entrance tests required: Yes
Interview required: No
Essay recommended: No
Documentation required for LD: Psychoeducational evaluation
Documentation required for ADHD: Yes
Submitted to: Student Support Services
Special Ed. HS course work accepted: No

Specific course requirements of all applicants: Yes
Separate application required: No
# of LD applications submitted each year: NR
# of LD applications accepted yearly: NR
Total # of students receiving LD services: NR
Acceptance into program means acceptance into college: Students must be admitted and enrolled prior to requesting services.

ADMISSIONS

Students are admitted on an eligibility index based on high school GPA for a full complement of college-prep courses and scores on either the ACT or SAT. Lower GPA requires higher scores on the test. Other factors such as impaction and residency status are also considered. The foreign language requirement for admission may be waived in rare cases when supported by the testing data supporting a relevant learning disability. All students must submit either the ACT or SAT Reasoning Test. These tests should be taken no later than December so that the results are available in January. All applicants must have the following years of study: 2 social science, 4 English, 3 math, 2 science (science with a lab, 1 biological and 1 physical), and 2 foreign language. The GPA is calculated based on the college-preparatory pattern only completed in grades 10, 11, and if available, 12. College-preparatory courses can only be counted toward the required units if you have earned at least a C in the course. Grades of D or less cannot be validated by a higher second semester grade in any of the following disciplines: social science/history, English, laboratory science, visual/performing arts, and electives. Students must have earned at least grades of C or higher in all semesters of English, other lab sciences than chemistry, social sciences/history, and visual/performing arts to have the course counted toward the required preparatory units. Applicants within the local area will be required to meet the minimum eligibility requirement of 2900 based on GPA and SAT result or a 694 based on GPA and ACT result. Students outside of the local area should not anticipate receiving an admissions decision until late January or February. If requested to forward a high school transcript, send only a transcript that contains your first semester senior grades (seventh semester grades) posted to the record.

ADDITIONAL INFORMATION

The Intensive Learning Experience (ILE) program is designed not only to monitor the progress of any students in fulfilling remedial compliance requirements, but also to help students make successful progress in fulfilling the requirements for graduation via intensive counseling and academic advising. Staff of the program advise and inform students on class planning, study skills, transfer work, campus resources, time management, and campus organizations. Their goal is to give students the essential skills to not only survive academically and socially, but also be successful at CSUF. If not exempt from the English Placement Test (EPT) and Entry Level Mathematics (ELM), every new freshman must pass the EPT and/or ELM to move into the GE-level mathematics and English courses. If the student does not pass, he/she must take a developmental English and/or math course to fulfill the remedial compliance requirements. Each semester, ILE provides students with an accommodation letter for each class requested. For students to receive the appropriate accommodations in their classes, students must present a current accommodation letter to each of their professors at the beginning of the semester or at such time as the disability is verified.

LEARNING DISABILITY PROGRAM/SERVICES

Learning Disability Program/Services: Student Support Services
Director: Paul K. Miller
  E-mail: pmiller@fullerton.edu
  Telephone: 714-278-3112
  Fax: 714-278-2408
Contact Person: Doug Liverpool or Debra Fletcher
  E-mail: dliverpool@fullerton.edu or dfletcher@fullerton.edu
  Telephone: 714-278-3112
  Fax: 714-278-2408

LEARNING DISABILITY SERVICES

Requests for the following/services accommodations will be evaluated individually based on appropriate and current documentation.

Allowed in exams
  Calculator: Yes
  Dictionary: Yes
  Computer: Yes
  Spellchecker: Yes
Extended test time: Yes
Scribes: Yes
Proctors: Yes
Oral exams: Yes
Note-takers: Yes

Distraction-reduced environment: Yes
Tape recording in class: Yes
Books on tape from RFBD: Yes
Taping of books not from RFBD: Yes
Accommodations for students with ADHD: Yes
Reading machine: Yes
Other assistive technology: Yes
Priority registration: Yes

Added costs for services: No
LD specialists: Yes
Professional tutors: No
Peer tutors: No
Max. hours/wk. for services: Varies
How professors are notified of LD/ADHD: By student

GENERAL ADMISSIONS INFORMATION

Director of Admissions: Nancy Dority
Telephone: 714-773-2370

ENTRANCE REQUIREMENTS

Academic units required: 4 English, 3 math, 2 science (2 science labs), 2 foreign language, 2 history, 1 academic elective, 1 visual/performing arts. High school diploma is required, and GED is accepted. TOEFL required of all international applicants: minimum paper TOEFL 500, minimum computer TOEFL 173.

Application deadline: 4/15
Notification: Rolling
Average GPA: 3.20
ACT Composite middle 50% range: 17–23

SAT Math middle 50% range: 440–560
SAT Critical Reading middle 50% range: 420–530
SAT Writing middle 50% range: NR

Graduated top 10% of class: 15%
Graduated top 25% of class: 45%
Graduated top 50% of class: 81%

COLLEGE GRADUATION REQUIREMENTS

Course waivers allowed: No
Course substitutions allowed: Yes
In what course: Those students with a documented severe math disbility may be allowed a substitution for the math general education requirement.

ADDITIONAL INFORMATION

Environment: The university is located 35 miles from Los Angeles.

Student Body
  Undergrad enrollment: 25,261
  Women: 60%
  Men: 40%
  Percent out-of-state: 1%

Cost Information
  In-state tuition: $3,010
  Out-of-state tuition: $13,180
  Room & board: $3,953
Housing Information
  University housing: Yes
  Percent living on campus: 2%

Greek System
  Fraternity: Yes
  Sorority: Yes
Athletics: Division I

California State University—Fullerton

CALIFORNIA STATE U.—LONG BEACH

1250 Bellflower Boulevard, Long Beach, CA 90840
Phone: 562-985-5471 • Fax: 562-985-4973
E-mail: eslb@csulb.edu • Web: www.csulb.com
Support: CS • Institution type: 4-year public

LEARNING DISABILITY PROGRAM AND SERVICES

The Office of Disabled Student Services (DSS) is a student support program within the Division of Student Services. Its mission is to assist students with disabilities as they secure their university degrees at California State University—Long Beach (CSULB). They provide services to over 1,300 students each semester. Over 3,000 students with disabilities have graduated from CSULB with support from the program. The program staff are committed to helping students with disabilities build a better future. To meet this goal, the Disabled Student Services program provides support services for in-classroom activities, career development resources, use of and training on adaptive computer equipment and access devices, disability related counseling, and academic advisement. If you have any questions, please contact the DSS office at 562-985-5401.

LD/ADHD ADMISSIONS INFORMATION

College entrance tests required: Yes
Interview required: No
Essay recommended: Yes
Documentation required for LD: Acceptable documentation should consist of a psychoeducational report and/or other professional verification. Documentation should be dated within the past 3 years from time of application. Note: Individual Educational Plans (IEPs) are not generally an acceptable form of verification for the California State University (CSU) system.
Documentation required for ADHD: A psychoeducational report and/or other professional verification from an appropriately licensed professional with a DSM–IV diagnosis and/or medical verification

Submitted to: Both Admissions and Disabled Student Services
Special Ed. HS course work accepted: N/A
Specific course requirements of all applicants: Yes
Separate application required: Yes
# of LD applications submitted each year: 50–100
# of LD applications accepted yearly: 20–40
Total # of students receiving LD services: 300–400
Acceptance into program means acceptance into college: Students must be admitted and enrolled prior to requesting services.

ADMISSIONS

Freshmen applicants must have completed each of the courses in the comprehensive pattern of college-preparatory subject requirements with a grade of C or higher prior to high school graduation and must have a qualifiable index based on their high school GPA in approved college-preparatory courses taken in the 10th through 12th grades and test scores. There is a special admission process for California residents who may not meet the regular admission requirements due to a disability but who are otherwise qualified. These students may appeal for special consideration. The Stephen Benson Program (SBP) facilitates this process by providing additional information about the applicant's circumstances to admissions. SBP evaluates documentation of the learning disability, and decisions are made by the Admissions Office. A student wishing to be considered for special admission must apply through regular admission procedures. California residents should submit the following information to SBP: personal statement letter describing interest in attending, two letters of recommendation, transcripts (unofficial accepted), a copy of SAT or ACT or transcripts of 60 transferable units from a community college, verification of specific learning disability, photograph of applicant, and a completed Special Admission Information Form and checklist of these requirements.

ADDITIONAL INFORMATION

The Stephen Benson Program for Students with LD was created to serve the needs of CSULB students who have a diagnosed learning disability. SBP provides a support system to assist students in attaining academic goals. The program provides counseling for clarification of issues related to learning disabilities, makes recommendations for accommodations, and fosters self-advocacy in students. Students with documented disabilities are entitled to one hour of tutoring per class, per week. All of the tutoring is done through the Learning Assistance Center. Special testing accommodation for course-related examinations are arranged through the Support Services Program. These accommodations include readers, writers, monitors, extended time, and alternative testing locations. Additional support services could include note-taking, readers, and registration assistance if appropriate.

LEARNING DISABILITY PROGRAM/SERVICES

Learning Disability Program/Services: Disabled Student Services
Director: David Sanfilippo
  E-mail: dss@csulb.edu
  Telephone: 562-985-5401
  Fax: 562-985-7183
Contact Person: Valerie Iapello
  E-mail: dss@csulb.edu
  Telephone: 562-985-5401
  Fax: 562-985-7183

LEARNING DISABILITY SERVICES

Requests for the following/services accommodations will be evaluated individually based on appropriate and current documentation.

Allowed in exams
  Calculator: Yes
  Dictionary: Yes
  Computer: Yes
  Spellchecker: Yes
Extended test time: Yes
Scribes: Yes
Proctors: Yes
Oral exams: Yes
Note-takers: Yes

Distraction-reduced environment: Yes
Tape recording in class: Yes
Books on tape from RFBD: Yes
Taping of books not from RFBD: Yes
Accommodations for students with ADHD: Yes
Reading machine: Yes
Other assistive technology: Yes
Priority registration: Yes

Added costs for services: No
LD specialists: Yes
Professional tutors: No
Peer tutors: 4–7
Max. hours/wk. for services: NR
How professors are notified of LD/ADHD: By student

GENERAL ADMISSIONS INFORMATION

Director of Admissions: Tom Enders
Telephone: 562-985-5471

ENTRANCE REQUIREMENTS

Academic units recommended: 4 English, 3 math, 2 science (2 science labs), 2 foreign language, 1 social study, 1 history, 1 academic elective, 1 fine arts. High school diploma is required, and GED is accepted. ACT with or without Writing component accepted. TOEFL required of all international applicants: minimum paper TOEFL 525.

Application deadline: 11/30
Notification: Rolling
Average GPA: 3.35
ACT Composite middle 50% range: 17–23

SAT Math middle 50% range: 460–580
SAT Critical Reading middle 50% range: 440–550
SAT Writing middle 50% range: NR

Graduated top 25% of class: NR
Graduated top 25% of class: 82%
Graduated top 50% of class: 100%

COLLEGE GRADUATION REQUIREMENTS

Course substitutions allowed: Yes
In what course: Math and other general education courses as needed, on a case-by-case basis by way of an appeal through Academic Affairs

ADDITIONAL INFORMATION

Environment: The campus is located south of Los Angeles.

Student Body
  Undergrad enrollment: 29,540
  Women: 60%
  Men: 40%
  Percent out-of-state: 1%

Cost Information
  In-state tuition: $3,116
Out-of-state tuition: $11,000
  Room & board: $7,536
Housing Information
  University housing: Yes
  Percent living on campus: 7%

Greek System
  Fraternity: Yes
  Sorority: Yes
Athletics: Division I

California State University—Long Beach

CALIFORNIA STATE U.—NORTHRIDGE

PO Box 1286 Northridge, Northridge, CA 91330-8365
Phone: 818-677-2270 • Fax: 818-677-5088
E-mail: lorraine.newlon@csun.edu • Web: www.csun.edu
Support: CS • Institution type: 4-year public

LEARNING DISABILITY PROGRAM AND SERVICES

The Office of Disabled Student Services recognizes that students with learning disabilities can be quite successful in a university setting if appropriate educational support services are offered to them. In an effort to assist students with learning disabilities in reaching their full potential, the program offers a comprehensive and well-coordinated system of educational support services that allow students to be judged on the basis of their ability rather than disability. The professional staff includes LD specialists trained in the diagnosis of learning disabilities and the provision of educational support services. Additionally, the program employs graduate students (educational support specialists) who work under the direction of the professional staff and assist students with study skills, time management procedures, test-taking techniques, and other individualized programs.

LD/ADHD ADMISSIONS INFORMATION

College entrance tests required: Yes
Interview required: Yes
Essay recommended: No
Documentation required for LD: The documentation must contain a specific diagnosis and a concise description of the functional limitations imposed by the disability; a diagnostic interview, an assessment of aptitude, academic achievement, and information processing as well as a diagnosis with functional limitations are recommended.
Documentation required for ADHD: Neuropsychological assessment signed by your physician, other licensed health care professional, or rehabilitation counselor. A specific diagnosis that indicates a concise description of the functional limitations

Submitted to: Disabled Student Services
Special Ed. HS course work accepted: Yes
Specific course requirements of all applicants: Yes
Separate application required: No
# of LD applications submitted each year: 70–150
# of LD applications accepted yearly: 50
Total # of students receiving LD services: 350–400
Acceptance into program means acceptance into college: Students must be admitted and enrolled in the university first and then request services.

ADMISSIONS

There is no special admission process. However, the Special Admission Committee of Students with Disabilities Resources makes recommendations to the Admissions Office. Students must get a C or better in 4 years of English, 3 years of math, 1 year of U.S. history, 1 year of science, 2 years of a foreign language, 1 year of visual/performing arts, and 3 years of academic electives. Students with LD may request course substitutions. An eligibility index combining GPA and ACT or SAT is used, and grades used are from 10th through 12th grade (bonus points for honor courses). Index is calculated by multiplying GPA by 800 and adding SAT or multiplying GPA by 200 and adding 10 times the ACT. California residents need an index of 2900 using SAT or 694 using ACT. Nonresidents must have a minimum index of 3502 (SAT) or 842 (ACT). No test scores needed if GPA is a 3.0 plus for residents or 3.61 for nonresidents.

ADDITIONAL INFORMATION

Services and accommodations are available to students with appropriate documentation: calculators, dictionary, computer and spellchecker for tests, extended testing time, scribes, proctors, oral exams, note-takers, distraction-free testing environments, tape recorder in class, books on tape, and priority registration. Testing accommodations may be arranged without the integrity of the test being sacrificed. The Computer Access Lab provides computers along with professional assistance. The program and the CSUN Career Center work cooperatively to assist students with LD in planning and attaining career goals. Diagnostic testing is available for students who suspect they may have a learning disability. Counselors are available to assist students with social/emotional needs as well as academic requirements. Assistance in developing appropriate learning strategies is provided on an individual basis. Additionally, a support group for students with LD meets regularly. There are also workshops, a reader service, and note-takers. Services and accommodations are available for undergraduate and graduate students.

LEARNING DISABILITY PROGRAM/SERVICES

Learning Disability Program/Services: Office of Disabled Student Services
Director: Dr. Mary Ann Cummins Prager
  E-mail: mary.ann.cummins.prager@csun.edu
  Telephone: 818-677-2684
  Fax: 818-677-4929
Contact Person: Dr. Jennifer Zvi
  E-mail: jennifer.zvi@csun.edu
  Telephone: 818-677-2684
  Fax: 818-677-4929

LEARNING DISABILITY SERVICES

Requests for the following/services accommodations will be evaluated individually based on appropriate and current documentation.

Allowed in exams
  Calculator: Yes
  Dictionary: Yes
  Computer: Yes
  Spellchecker: Yes
Extended test time: Yes
Scribes: Yes
Proctors: Yes
Oral exams: Yes
Note-takers: Yes

Distraction-reduced environment: Yes
Tape recording in class: Yes
Books on tape from RFBD: Yes
Taping of books not from RFBD: Yes
Accommodations for students with
  ADHD: Yes
Reading machine: Yes
Other assistive technology: Yes
Priority registration: Yes

Added costs for services: No
LD specialists: Yes
Professional tutors: No
Peer tutors: No
Max. hours/wk. for services: 2
How professors are notified of
  LD/ADHD: By student

GENERAL ADMISSIONS INFORMATION

Director of Admissions: Lorraine Newlon
  Telephone: 818-677-2270

ENTRANCE REQUIREMENTS

Academic units required: 4 English, 3 math, 1 science (2 science labs), 2 foreign language, 2 history, 1 academic elective, 1 visual/performing arts. High school diploma is required, and GED is accepted. TOEFL required of all international applicants: minimum paper TOEFL 500.

Application deadline: 11/30
Notification: Rolling
Average GPA: 3.10
ACT Composite middle 50% range: NR

SAT Math middle 50% range: NR
SAT Critical Reading middle 50% range: NR
SAT Writing middle 50% range: NR

Graduated top 25% of class: 10%
Graduated top 25% of class: 33%
Graduated top 50% of class: 33%

COLLEGE GRADUATION REQUIREMENTS

Course waivers allowed: No
In what course: N/A
Course substitutions allowed: Yes
In what course: Individual case-by-case decisions

ADDITIONAL INFORMATION

Environment: The university has a large suburban campus in the San Fernando Valley northwest of Los Angeles.

Student Body
  Undergrad enrollment: 20,955
  Women: 59%
  Men: 41%
  Percent out-of-state: 1%

Cost Information
  In-state tuition: $3,042
  Out-of-state tuition: $15,600
  Room & board: $5,801
Housing Information
  University housing: Yes
  Percent living on campus: 8%

Greek System
  Fraternity: Yes
  Sorority: Yes
Athletics: Division II

CAL. STATE U.—SAN BERNARDINO

5500 University Parkway, San Bernardino, CA 92407-2397
Phone: 909-537-5188 • Fax: 909-537-7034
E-mail: moreinfo@mail.csusb.edu • Web: www.csusb.edu
Support: CS • Institution type: 4-year public

LEARNING DISABILITY PROGRAM AND SERVICES

The Learning Disability Program is dedicated to assuring each student an opportunity to experience equity in education. Each student must complete an assessment, and then the staff helps to develop compensatory methods for handling assignments and classroom projects. Careful attention is paid to helping the student acquire learning skills and formulating and implementing specific strategies for note-taking and management of written materials. Recommendations are designed for each student as a result of a psychometric assessment, personal interview, and academic requirements. The emphasis of the plan is to assist the students with a learning disability in finding techniques to deal with it in college and in the job market.

LD/ADHD ADMISSIONS INFORMATION

College entrance tests required: Yes
Interview required: Yes
Essay recommended: No
Documentation required for LD: Yes
Documentation required for ADHD: Yes
Submitted to: Services for Students with Disabilities
Special Ed. HS course work accepted: No

Specific course requirements of all applicants: Yes
Separate application required: Yes
# of LD applications submitted each year: 75–101
# of LD applications accepted yearly: 45–66
Total # of students receiving LD services: 140–156
Acceptance into program means acceptance into college: Students must be admitted and enrolled in the university first and then request services.

ADMISSIONS

Applicants with learning disabilities must follow the same application procedure as all students. Entrance requirements include a minimum GPA of 2.0; 4 years of English, 3 years of math, 1 year of U.S. history, 1 year of science, 2 years of a foreign language, 1 year of visual/performing arts, and 3 years of electives from any of the previous areas (including agriculture). The middle 50 percent have an ACT of 15–19 and SAT of 800–1020. Special admission may be requested through the Learning Disability Program if the student has a deficiency in course entrance requirements. The Director of the LD Program provides recommendations on the admissibility of those students who do not meet regular admissions requirements. Occasionally, the special admit will consider students who are below the required GPA or test scores. These requirements can be substituted, and the student can make up the deficiency on campus once enrolled.

ADDITIONAL INFORMATION

Services and accommodations for students with appropriate documentation could include the following: the use of calculators, dictionaries, computers, or spellchecker during exams; extended time on tests; distraction-free testing environments; oral exams; note-takers; proctors; scribes; tape recorders in class; books on tape; assisting technology; and priority registration. Specific services include assessment counseling and testing accommodations. Students on academic probation have two quarters to raise their GPA to a 2.0. The LD Program provides continual academic support.

LEARNING DISABILITY PROGRAM/SERVICES

Learning Disability Program/Services: Services to Students with Disabilities
Director: Dr. Beth Jaworski
  E-mail: bjaworsk@csusb.edu
  Telephone: 909-537-3589
  Fax: 909-537-7090
Contact Person: Doron A. Dula
  E-mail: ddula@csusb.edu
  Telephone: 909-537-5240
  Fax: 909-537-7090

LEARNING DISABILITY SERVICES

Requests for the following/services accommodations will be evaluated individually based on appropriate and current documentation.

Allowed in exams
  Calculator: Yes
  Dictionary: Yes
  Computer: Yes
  Spellchecker: Yes
Extended test time: Yes
Scribes: Yes
Proctors: Yes
Oral exams: Yes
Note-takers: Yes

Distraction-reduced environment: Yes
Tape recording in class: Yes
Books on tape from RFBD: Yes
Taping of books not from RFBD: Yes
Accommodations for students with ADHD: Yes
Reading machine: Yes
Other assistive technology: Yes
Priority registration: Yes

Added costs for services: No
LD specialists: Yes
Professional tutors: No
Peer tutors: No
Max. hours/wk. for services: N/A
How professors are notified of LD/ADHD: By student

GENERAL ADMISSIONS INFORMATION

Director of Admissions: Dr. Milton Clark
Telephone: 909-537-5032

ENTRANCE REQUIREMENTS
Academic units required: 4 English, 3 math, 2 science (2 science labs), 2 foreign language, 1 social studies, 1 history, 1 academic elective, 1 visual/performing arts. High school diploma is required, and GED is accepted. ACT without Writing component accepted. TOEFL required of all international applicants: minimum paper TOEFL 500, minimum computer TOEFL 173.

Application deadline: Rolling
Notification: Rolling
Average GPA: 3.19
ACT Composite middle 50% range: 16–21

SAT Math middle 50% range: 400–520
SAT Critical Reading middle 50% range: 400–510
SAT Writing middle 50% range: NR

Graduated top 10% of class: 18%
Graduated top 25% of class: 35%
Graduated top 50% of class: 90%

COLLEGE GRADUATION REQUIREMENTS

Course waivers allowed: Yes
In what course: Evaluated individually based on appropiate and current documentation
Course substitutions allowed: Yes
In what course: General education, math

ADDITIONAL INFORMATION

Environment: The university is located in a suburban area in the foothills of the San Bernadino Mountains.
Student Body
  Undergrad enrollment: 12,926
  Women: 65%
  Men: 35%
  Percent out-of-state: 2%

Cost Information
  In-state tuition: $3,110
  Out-of-state tuition: $8,136
  Room & board: $7,517
Housing Information
  University housing: Yes
  Percent living on campus: 10%

Greek System
  Fraternity: Yes
  Sorority: Yes
Athletics: Division II

California State University—San Bernardino

COLLEGE OF THE SISKIYOUS

800 College Avenue, Weed, CA 96094
Phone: 530-938-5555 • Fax: 530-938-5367
E-mail: registration@siskiyous.edu • Web: www.siskiyous.edu
Support: CS • Institution type: 2-year public

LEARNING DISABILITY PROGRAM AND SERVICES

The Disabled Student Programs and Services Office (DSP&S) is dedicated to meeting the needs of students with disabilities. The goal of DSP&S is to assist students to overcome barriers to allow access to the college's regular programs and activities. Support services are provided for students with a wide variety of disabilities. Any student who has a documented disability and demonstrates a need for a service that is directly related to the educational limitation is eligible for support services.

LD/ADHD ADMISSIONS INFORMATION

College entrance tests required: Yes
Interview required: No
Essay recommended: No
Documentation required for LD: Appropriate testing results within last 3 years
Documentation required for ADHD: Yes
Submitted to: Disabled Student Programs and Services
Special Ed. HS course work accepted: Yes

Specific course requirements of all applicants: No
Separate application required: Yes
# of LD applications submitted each year: 90–100
# of LD applications accepted yearly: 100
Total # of students receiving LD services: 100
Acceptance into program means acceptance into college: Students must be admitted and enrolled in the university first and then request services.

ADMISSIONS

Students with LD/ADHD who self-disclose during the admission process may receive advice from DSP&S during the admission process. Basically, this advice would provide descriptions of appropriate courses the students may take and the services and accommodations they may be eligible to receive. There are not any minimum admission requirements for a specific class rank, GPA, or ACT/SAT score. Applicants must have a high school diploma or equivalent certification.

ADDITIONAL INFORMATION

There is an LD specialist available in the Learning Disability Programs and Services Office. There are support services available for students who have a documented disability and demonstrate a need for a service that is directly related to their educational limitations. They may include academic advising, registration assistance, and the development of an individualized educational plan, LD assessment, tutoring, readers, note-takers, testing accommodations, and adaptive educational equipment. The COS High Tech Center is designed to provide computer access and technology to students with disabilities to educate and prepare them for academic success and today's work force. In addition, all students have access to skills classes in areas such as time management, organization, study strategies, and test-taking strategies.

LEARNING DISABILITY PROGRAM/SERVICES

Learning Disability Program/Services: Disabled Student Programs and Services
Director: Dr. Kathleen Gabriel
  E-mail: gabriel@siskiyous.edu
  Telephone: 530-938-5297
  Fax: 530-938-5375
Contact Person: Same as above

LEARNING DISABILITY SERVICES

Requests for the following/services accommodations will be evaluated individually based on appropriate and current documentation.

Allowed in exams
  Calculator: Yes
  Dictionary: Yes
  Computer: Yes
  Spellchecker: Yes
Extended test time: Yes
Scribes: Yes
Proctors: Yes
Oral exams: Yes
Note-takers: Yes

Distraction-reduced environment: Yes
Tape recording in class: Yes
Books on tape from RFBD: Yes
Taping of books not from RFBD: Yes
Accommodations for students with ADHD: Yes
Reading machine: Yes
Other assistive technology: Yes
Priority registration: No

Added costs for services: No
LD specialists: Yes
Professional tutors: 2
Peer tutors: 70
Max. hours/wk. for services: Unlimited
How professors are notified of LD/ADHD: By student

GENERAL ADMISSIONS INFORMATION

Director of Admissions: Theresa Winkelman
Telephone: 530-938-5555

ENTRANCE REQUIREMENTS

High school diploma or equivalent is required. There are no specific requirements for courses, GPA, class rank, or test scores. TOEFL required of all international applicants: minimum paper TOEFL 470, minimum computer TOEFL 150.

Application deadline: Rolling
Notification: Rolling
Average GPA: NR
ACT Composite middle 50% range: NR

SAT Math middle 50% range: NR
SAT Critical Reading middle 50% range: NR
SAT Writing middle 50% range: NR

Graduated top 10% of class: NR
Graduated top 25% of class: NR
Graduated top 50% of class: NR

COLLEGE GRADUATION REQUIREMENTS

Course waivers allowed: No
Course substitutions allowed: Yes
In what course: Students can petition for a substitute course.

ADDITIONAL INFORMATION

Environment: The college is located at the base of Mt. Shasta.

Student Body
  Undergrad enrollment: 1,153
  Women: 57%
  Men: 43%
  Percent out-of-state: 10%

Cost Information
  In-state tuition: $806
  Out-of-state tuition: $5,906
  Room & board: $6,020
  Housing Information
    University housing: Yes
    Percent living on campus: 9%

Greek System
  Fraternity: No
  Sorority: No
Athletics: Intercollegiate

LOYOLA MARYMOUNT UNIVERSITY

One LMU Drive, Suite 100, Los Angeles, CA 90045
Phone: 310-338-2750 • Fax: 310-338-2797
E-mail: admissions@lmu.edu • Web: www.lmu.edu
Support: S • Institution type: 4-year private

LEARNING DISABILITY PROGRAM AND SERVICES

The Office of Disability Support Services (DSS) provides specialized assistance and resources that enable students with physical, perceptual, emotional, and learning disabilities to achieve maximum independence while they pursue their educational goals. Assisted by staff specialists from all areas of the university, the DSS office works to eliminate physical and attitudinal barriers. To be eligible for services, students must provide documentation of the disability from a licensed professional. At the Learning Resource Center (LRC), students can receive tutoring in over 250 LMU classes, attend workshops, and access assistance in writing, reading, and math with LRC specialists.

LD/ADHD ADMISSIONS INFORMATION

College entrance tests required: Yes
Interview required: No
Essay recommended: No
Documentation required for LD: Current psychoeducational evaluation within the past 3 years
Documentation required for ADHD: Psychoeducational evaluation, transcripts, accommodations in high school, SAT/ACT scores/accommodations, and IEP/504, if attended public high school
Submitted to: Disability Support Services
Special Ed. HS course work accepted: Yes

Specific course requirements: NR
Separate application required: Yes
# of LD applications submitted each year: NR
# of LD applications accepted yearly: NR
Total # of students receiving LD services: 81
Acceptance into program means acceptance into college: Students must be admitted and enrolled in the university first and then request services.

ADMISSIONS

There is no special admissions process for students with learning disabilities or attention deficit hyperactivity disorder. The admission decision will be based on the student's GPA, SAT/ACT scores, strength of curriculum, application essay, letters of recommendation, and extracurricular activities. Enrolled students have an average GPA of 3.3, 25 ACT, and 1130 SAT Reasoning. Students are encouraged to have completed 4 years of English, 3 years of social sciences, 3 years of a foreign language, 3 years of math (4 years for engineering and science), and 1 year of an academic elective.

ADDITIONAL INFORMATION

There is a Learning Resource Center where all students can find specialists and tutors. There is course-specific tutoring, study-skills programs (which include learning time management, overcoming test anxiety, conquering math word problems, mastering the textbook, preparing for exams, and studying efficiently), and other academic support programs with full-time professional staff members prepared to assist with writing, reading, math, ESL, and DSS. Assistive technology includes equipment that enlarges print, Window Bridge 21000, screen-reading program, Kurzweil Reader, and Dragon Dictate. Specific accommodations for LD students with appropriate documentation could include priority registration, note-takers, readers, transcribers, alternate testing conditions, taped books, and advocacy.

LEARNING DISABILITY PROGRAM/SERVICES

Learning Disability Program/Services: Office of Disability Support Services (DSS)
Director: Priscilla F. Levine, LCSW
  E-mail: plevine@lmu.edu
  Telephone: 310-338-4535
  Fax: 310-338-7657

LEARNING DISABILITY SERVICES

Requests for the following/services accommodations will be evaluated individually based on appropriate and current documentation.

Allowed in exams
  Calculator: Yes
  Dictionary: Yes
  Computer: Yes
  Spellchecker: Yes
Extended test time: Yes
Scribes: Yes
Proctors: Yes
Oral exams: Yes
Note-takers: Yes

Distraction-reduced environment: Yes
Tape recording in class: Yes
Books on tape from RFBD: Yes
Taping of books not from RFBD: No
Accommodations for students with ADHD: Yes
Reading machine: Yes
Other assistive technology: Yes
Priority registration: Yes

Added costs for services: No
LD specialists: No
Professional tutors: No
Peer tutors: 80
Max. hours/wk. for services: 1
How professors are notified of LD/ADHD: By student

GENERAL ADMISSIONS INFORMATION

Director of Admissions: Matt Fissinger
Telephone: 310-338-2750

ENTRANCE REQUIREMENTS

Academic units recommended: 4 English, 3 math, 2 science (2 science labs), 3 foreign language, 3 social studies, 1 academic elective. High school diploma is required, and GED is accepted. TOEFL required of all international applicants: minimum paper TOEFL 550, minimum computer TOEFL 213.

Application deadline: Rolling
Notification: Rolling
Average GPA: 3.60
ACT Composite middle 50% range: NR

SAT Math middle 50% range: 540–640
SAT Critical Reading middle 50% range: 530–630
SAT Writing middle 50% range: NR

Graduated top 10% of class: 30%
Graduated top 25% of class: 66%
Graduated top 50% of class: 99%

COLLEGE GRADUATION REQUIREMENTS

Course waivers allowed: No
Course substitutions allowed: No

ADDITIONAL INFORMATION

Environment: The university is located on 125 acres in a suburban setting close to Los Angeles.

Student Body
  Undergrad enrollment: 5,590
  Women: 59%
  Men: 41%
  Percent out-of-state: 23%

Cost Information
  Tuition: $27,710
  Room & board: $8,709
Housing Information
  University housing: Yes
  Percent living on campus: 60%

Greek System
  Fraternity: Yes
  Sorority: Yes
Athletics: Division I

MENLO COLLEGE

1000 El Camino Real, Atherton, CA 94027
Phone: 650-543-3753 • Fax: 650-543-4496
E-mail: admissions@menlo.edu • Web: www.menlo.edu
Support: CS • Institution type: 4-year private

LEARNING DISABILITY PROGRAM AND SERVICES

The Menlo College Academic Success Center (ASC) welcomes all students including those with learning, psychological, and attention challenges. In its new configuration with the Bowman Library, now the Learning Community Commons, services have broadened to include library staff and resources. Students who present proper documentation of a disability may qualify for accommodations. All students are welcome to utilize the services of the Academic Success Center.

LD/ADHD ADMISSIONS INFORMATION

College entrance tests required: Yes
Interview required: No
Essay recommended: Yes
Documentation required for LD: Psychoeducational evaluation that is current and provides measurements of aptitude, academic achievement, and informational processing
Documentation required for ADHD: Documentation should be within the past 3 years and require credentials of the professional, length of time since diagnosis, provisions taken to ameliorate the functional impairment, and description of academic challenges and limitations to date.

Submitted to: Academic Success Center
Special Ed. HS course work accepted: No
Specific course requirements: NR
Separate application required: No
# of LD applications submitted each year: NR
# of LD applications accepted yearly: NR
Total # of students receiving LD services: 200
Acceptance into program means acceptance into college: Students must be admitted and enrolled prior to requesting services.

ADMISSIONS

Students are admitted to Menlo College on their own merits, without regard to disability. If students choose to self-disclose their learning challenges, they are encouraged to meet with the Academic Success Center in advance of their arrival to arrange for early set-up of accommodations. Menlo values the individual strengths and diversity that students bring to Menlo, so we choose not to follow a specific formula when making our admission decisions. Each applicant is reviewed individually, and the acceptance decisions are based on many factors including the strength of your course curriculum, the school you attend(ed), and your grades and test scores. In addition, we consider your extracurricular activities, community involvement, employment, and leadership roles. Menlo College is most interested in the quality of students' activities, rather than the quantity. The Philler Curtis Transition to College Program is a comprehensive approach to help students who wish to improve academic performance and transition more smoothly to the rigors of college academics. There is no separate admission process for the Philler Curtis Program. Simply indicate anywhere on your application or in your essay that you wish to be considered for the program. An interview with students and parents is strongly advised for those considering the Philler Curtis Program.

ADDITIONAL INFORMATION

The Philler Curtis Transition to College Program is not a program for students with disabilities, but many students who want a strong bridge to college choose to enroll in this program. Participants arrive on campus approximately 1 month early to take part in a series of classes, on- and off-campus activities, and seminars designed to let them experience the first semester before it actually begins. The Transition to College period lasts approximately 3 weeks, during which time the students become familiar with college academics and their new environment and have an opportunity to experience how their decisions will impact their ability to succeed in college. Each participant receives a thorough learning assessment. The results of this assessment are used to build the Menlo College Learning Portfolio and to make sure that if the student is dealing with undiscovered learning issues, appropriate action will be taken to help the student learn to deal effectively with those issues. Transition to College Month costs $5,000 and includes tuition, room and board, all scheduled activities, and a complete learning assessment. There is no additional cost for ongoing support, which could include testing accommodations, academic and technical support, advocacy, registration assistance, individual education plans, residence hall and athletic programs on learning skills and time- and task-management strategies, and certifying student's enrollment for books on tape.

LEARNING DISABILITY PROGRAM/SERVICES

Learning Disability Program/Services: Academic Success Center
Director: Janet Miller, MA, CET
  E-mail: jmiller@menlo.edu
  Telephone: 650-543-3854
  Fax: 650-543-4120
Contact Person: Janet Miller or Judy Wasmann
  E-mail: jmiller@menlo.edu or jwasserman@menlo.edu
  Telephone: 650-543-3854
  Fax: 650-543-4120

LEARNING DISABILITY SERVICES

Requests for the following/services accommodations will be evaluated individually based on appropriate and current documentation.

Allowed in exams
  Calculator: Yes
  Dictionary: Yes
  Computer: Yes
  Spellchecker: Yes
Extended test time: Yes
Scribes: Yes
Proctors: Yes
Oral exams: No
Note-takers: Yes

Distraction-reduced environment: Yes
Tape recording in class: Yes
Books on tape from RFBD: No
Taping of books not from RFBD: Yes
Accommodations for students with ADHD: Yes
Reading machine: Yes
Other assistive technology: Yes
Priority registration: No

Added costs for services: No
LD specialists: Yes
Professional tutors: No
Peer tutors: 6–10
Max. hours/wk. for services: N/A
How professors are notified of LD/ADHD: By both student and director

GENERAL ADMISSIONS INFORMATION

Director of Admissions: Greg Smith
Telephone: 650-543-3753

ENTRANCE REQUIREMENTS

Academic units recommended: 4 English, 3 math, 3 science (1 science lab), 2 foreign language, 3 social studies, 3 history. Recommendation from teacher or counselor and a student essay required. High school diploma is required, and GED is accepted. ACT with or without Writing component accepted. TOEFL required of all international applicants: minimum paper TOEFL 500, minimum computer TOEFL 173.

Application deadline: NR
Notification: Rolling
Average GPA: NR
ACT Composite middle 50% range: NR

SAT Math middle 50% range: NR
SAT Critical Reading middle 50% range: NR
SAT Writing middle 50% range: NR

Graduated top 10% of class: NR
Graduated top 25% of class: NR
Graduated top 50% of class: NR

COLLEGE GRADUATION REQUIREMENTS

Course waivers allowed: No
Course substitutions allowed: Yes
In what course: Math, foreign language

ADDITIONAL INFORMATION

Environment: Menlo College is within easy reach of the San Francisco Bay Area.

Student Body
  Undergrad enrollment: 725
  Women: 42%
  Men: 58%
  Percent out-of-state: 22%

Cost Information
  Tuition: $25,920
  Room & board: $9,800
Housing Information
  University housing: Yes
  Percent living on campus: 58%

Greek System
  Fraternity: No
  Sorority: No
Athletics: Division III

OCCIDENTAL COLLEGE

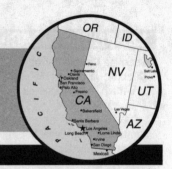

1600 Campus Road, Office of Admission, Los Angeles, CA 90041
Phone: 323-259-2700 • Fax: 323-341-4875
E-mail: admission@oxy.edu • Web: www.oxy.edu
Support: S • Institution type: 4-year private

LEARNING DISABILITY PROGRAM AND SERVICES

The Center for Academic Excellence (CAE) coordinates academic support services for all students, including those with disabilities, who want to enhance their academic success. Students who have a documented disability requiring academic accommodation and who wish to apply for academic accommodation in addition to the general academic support services need to make an appointment with the Coordinator of Academic Support Services as far in advance of the semester of enrollment as possible. The purpose of this meeting is to acquaint the student with the available resources, determine the accommodations required by the student, and complete appropriate forms requesting services. If relevant documentation has not been previously submitted to the CAE, students should bring it to this meeting. The documentation should support assessments completed within the past 3 years. Accommodations for students with documented disabilities are determined by individual student needs.

LD/ADHD ADMISSIONS INFORMATION

College entrance tests required: Yes
Interview required: N/A
Essay recommended: N/A
Documentation required for LD: Psychoeducational evaluation
Documentation required for ADHD: Psychoeducational evaluation
Submitted to: Center for Academic Excellence
Special Ed. HS course work accepted: NR

Specific course requirements: NR
Separate application required: N/A
# of LD applications submitted each year: NR
# of LD applications accepted yearly: NR
Total # of students receiving LD services: NR
Acceptance into program means acceptance into college: Students must be admitted and enrolled prior to requesting services.

ADMISSIONS

There are no special admissions criteria for students with learning disabilities. The college will assess and balance a variety of academic factors to determine the overall scholastic strength of each applicant. An applicant who wishes to have his or her disability considered as a factor in the admission process must identify the disability and provide an explanation of why it is a factor at the time of application. If the applicant wishes the disability to be considered a factor, it may be necessary to provide appropriate documentation of the disability at the time of application for admission.

ADDITIONAL INFORMATION

The most typically successful student at Occidental College is a self-advocate who understands and can explain his or her academic needs, when appropriate, to professors and others providing academic assistance. The student seeks assistance related to the disability, as needed, from the CAE coordinator. If concerns or questions arise, the student contacts the coordinator of the CAE to resolve or clarify. If extended time for exams, note-taking, alternative formats to text, or other academic accommodations are needed, the student carries out his or her responsibilities for receiving these accommodations, including timely scheduling of exam proctoring appointments, communicating with professors, seeking out student note-takers, and notifying the CAE of assigned readings. Alternative courses to the foreign language requirement are offered on a case-by case basis and with presentation of psychoeducational documentation that specifically justifies the need in the area of foreign language. In such cases, the student will make arrangements through the coordinator of Academic Support Services. Occidental College does not provide daily support and consultation for learning disabled students. Students are encouraged to find fellow students as note-takers, and the college will make available two-ply paper for use by volunteer note-takers and will honor volunteer note-takers with bookstore gift certificates. Students enrolled at Occidental College who have not been previously diagnosed and who have reason to suspect they may have a learning disability or ADHD are encouraged to meet with the coordinator of Academic Support Services to determine appropriate action. Occidental College does not administer diagnostic assessments, but will assist students in making arrangements to be tested by a qualified professional. The cost of the evaluation is the responsibility of the student.

LEARNING DISABILITY PROGRAM/SERVICES

Learning Disability Program/Services: Occidental College Center for Academic Excellence
Director: Raul Villa
  E-mail: rhvilla@oxy.edu
  Telephone: 323-259-2545
  Fax: 323-259-1402
Contact Person: Linda Whitney, Coordinator
  E-mail: lwhitney@oxy.edu
  Telephone: 323-259-2849
  Fax: 323-259-1402

LEARNING DISABILITY SERVICES

Requests for the following/services accommodations will be evaluated individually based on appropriate and current documentation.

Allowed in exams
  Calculator: Yes
  Dictionary: Yes
  Computer: Yes
  Spellchecker: Yes
Extended test time: Yes
Scribes: Yes
Proctors: Yes
Oral exams: No
Note-takers: Yes

Distraction-reduced environment: Yes
Tape recording in class: Yes
Books on tape from RFBD: Yes
Taping of books not from RFBD: NR
**Accommodations for students with
  ADHD:** Yes
Reading machine: Yes
Other assistive technology: Yes
Priority registration: N/A

Added costs for services: No
LD specialists: No
Professional tutors: 5
Peer tutors: 25–35
Max. hours/wk. for services: NR
**How professors are notified of
  LD/ADHD:** By student

GENERAL ADMISSIONS INFORMATION

Director of Admissions: Vince Cuseo
Telephone: 323-259-2700

ENTRANCE REQUIREMENTS

Academic units recommended: 4 English, 4 math, 3 science (2 science labs), 3 foreign language, 2 social studies, 2 history, 2 academic electives. High school diploma is required, and GED is accepted. ACT with or without Writing component accepted. TOEFL required of all international applicants: minimum paper TOEFL 600, minimum computer TOEFL 250.

Application deadline: 1/10
Notification: 4/1
Average GPA: NR
ACT Composite middle 50% range:
  NR

SAT Math middle 50% range:
  610–690
**SAT Critical Reading middle 50%
  range:** 600–690
SAT Writing middle 50% range: NR

Graduated top 10% of class: 61%
Graduated top 25% of class: 89%
Graduated top 50% of class: 100%

COLLEGE GRADUATION REQUIREMENTS

Course waivers allowed: No
Course substitutions allowed: Yes
In what course: Foreign language

ADDITIONAL INFORMATION

Environment: Occidental College is located in northeast Los Angeles.

Student Body
  Undergrad enrollment: 1,864
  Women: 56%
  Men: 44%
  Percent out-of-state: 53%

Cost Information
  Tuition: $32,800
  Room & board: $9,552
Housing Information
  University housing: Yes
  Percent living on campus: 70%

Greek System
  Fraternity: Yes
  Sorority: Yes
Athletics: Division III

REEDLEY COLLEGE

995 North Reed Avenue, Reedley, CA 93654
Phone: 559-638-3641 • Fax: 559-638-5040
E-mail: emerzian@scccd.org • Web: www.reedleycollege.com
Support: CS • Institution type: 2-year public

LEARNING DISABILITY PROGRAM AND SERVICES

The Disabled Student Program and Services (DSP&S) focuses on abilities, not disabilities. DSP&S offers services to students with learning disabilities beyond those provided by conventional programs at the college and enables students to pursue their individual educational, vocational, and personal goals successfully. The Learning Disabilities Program assesses the needs and skill levels of each student, tailoring a specific educational course of study designed to bring out the best in an individual at a college level. The instructional program in reading, writing, math, and other academics prepares students to function in the classroom, in their vocation, and throughout life. The LD Program provides special instruction and attention for students with specific educational needs not available in mainstream classes.

LD/ADHD ADMISSIONS INFORMATION

College entrance tests required: No
Interview required: Yes
Essay recommended: No
Documentation required for LD: Psychoeducational evaluation
Documentation required for ADHD: Yes
Submitted to: Disabled Student Program and Services
Special Ed. HS course work accepted: Yes

Specific course requirements of all applicants: No
Separate application required: No
# of LD applications submitted each year: NR
# of LD applications accepted yearly: NR
Total # of students receiving LD services: 200
Acceptance into program means acceptance into college: Students must be admitted and enrolled in the university first and then request services.

ADMISSIONS

Reedley is an open-door admission college. Students present a high school diploma, certificate of high school completion equivalent, or LD/special education test results. There is no minimum GPA or required courses required for admission. ACT/SAT tests are not required for admission. There is a separate application to access services for students with learning disabilities. This application, however, is submitted after admission.

ADDITIONAL INFORMATION

The LD Program offers the following services: LD assessments, learning strategies instruction from an LD specialist, small class sessions, adaptive instruction, matriculation and integration with mainstream classes, individualized student contact, and specialized educational counseling. In addition, students can access the following accommodations if they provide appropriate documentation: the use of calculators, dictionaries, computers, or spellchecker in exams; extended time on tests; scribes; proctors; oral exams; note-takers; tape recorder in class; books on tape; assistive technology; and priority registration. American Sign Language may be substituted for foreign language, and students are responsible for providing information about their disability to their professors.

LEARNING DISABILITY PROGRAM/SERVICES

Learning Disability Program/Services: Disabled Students Program and Services (DSP&S)
Director: Dr. Janice Emerzian
  E-mail: janice.emerzian@scccd.com
  Telephone: 559-638-0332
  Fax: 559-638-0382

LEARNING DISABILITY SERVICES

Requests for the following/services accommodations will be evaluated individually based on appropriate and current documentation.

Allowed in exams
  Calculator: Yes
  Dictionary: Yes
  Computer: Yes
  Spellchecker: Yes
Extended test time: Yes
Scribes: Yes
Proctors: Yes
Oral exams: Yes
Note-takers: Yes

Distraction-reduced environment: Yes
Tape recording in class: Yes
Books on tape from RFBD: Yes
Taping of books not from RFBD: Yes
Accommodations for students with ADHD: Yes
Reading machine: Yes
Other assistive technology: Yes
Priority registration: Yes

Added costs for services: No
LD specialists: Yes
Professional tutors: No
Peer tutors: Yes
Max. hours/wk. for services: Unlimited
How professors are notified of LD/ADHD: By student

GENERAL ADMISSIONS INFORMATION

Director of Admissions: Letty Alvarez
Telephone: 559-638-3641

ENTRANCE REQUIREMENTS
High school diploma is required, and GED is accepted.

Application deadline: Rolling
Notification: Continuous
Average GPA: NR
ACT Composite middle 50% range: NR

SAT Math middle 50% range: NR
SAT Critical Reading middle 50% range: NR
SAT Writing middle 50% range: NR

Graduated top 10% of class: NR
Graduated top 25% of class: NR
Graduated top 50% of class: NR

COLLEGE GRADUATION REQUIREMENTS

ADDITIONAL INFORMATION

Environment: The college is located 30 miles southeast of Fresno.

Student Body
  Undergrad enrollment: 7,434
  Women: 62%
  Men: 38%
  Percent out-of-state: 1%

Cost Information
  In-state tuition: $1,400
  Out-of-state tuition: $4,980
  Room & board: $3,820
Housing Information
  University housing: Yes
  Percent living on campus: 18%

Greek System
  Fraternity: No
  Sorority: No
Athletics: NJCAA

SAN DIEGO STATE UNIVERSITY

5500 Campanile Drive, San Diego, CA 92182-7455
Phone: 619-594-6336 • Fax: 619-594-1250
E-mail: admissions@sdsu.edu• Web: www.sdsu.edu
Support: CS • Institution type: 4-year public

LEARNING DISABILITY PROGRAM AND SERVICES

The Learning Disability Program at San Diego State is under the umbrella of Disabled Student Services (DSS). The LD Program is designed to provide assessment, accommodations, and advocacy. Students must provide documentation prior to receiving services. Students with learning disabilities may be assessed using nationally standardized batteries. The university believes that students with learning disabilities can be successful at San Diego State and will try to provide the appropriate services to foster their success.

LD/ADHD ADMISSIONS INFORMATION

College entrance tests required: Yes
Interview required: No
Essay recommended: No
Documentation required for LD: WAIS–III and WJ–III
Documentation required for ADHD: Diagnosis and evidence to support functional limitations related to ADHD.
Submitted to: Disabled Student Services
Special Ed. HS course work accepted: No

Specific course requirements of all applicants: Yes
Separate application required: Yes
# of LD applications submitted each year: NR
# of LD applications accepted yearly: NR
Total # of students receiving LD services: 275
Acceptance into program means acceptance into college: Students must be admitted and enrolled in the university first and then request services.

ADMISSIONS

Students with learning disabilities who are not admissible by the general admission criteria or who are denied admission may request a review through special admission. Students need to write a letter to the Director of the LD Program explaining why they feel they should be admitted. Three recommendations are required for special admit. No student will be admitted with a GPA below 2.0. Students must provide documentation verifying the disability and meeting the California State definition of a learning disability. The Director of Disabled Student Services reviews documentation and makes a recommendation to the Admissions Office.

ADDITIONAL INFORMATION

Students are encouraged to get volunteer note-takers from among other students enrolled in the class. Students with learning disabilities may request permission to tape a lecture. Students will also need permission from the professor to use a calculator, dictionary, computer, or spellchecker in exams. Tutoring services are provided at no charge. High Tech Center is a learning center available for all students with disabilities. Services and accommodations are available for undergraduates and graduate students.

LEARNING DISABILITY PROGRAM/SERVICES

Learning Disability Program/Services: Learning Disability Program/Disabled Student Services
Director: Mary Shojai
  E-mail: mshojai@mail.sdsu.edu
  Telephone: 619-594-6473
  Fax: 619-594-4315
Contact Person: Margo Behr
  E-mail: mbehr@mail.sdsu.edu
  Telephone: 619-594-6473
  Fax: 619-594-4315

LEARNING DISABILITY SERVICES

Requests for the following/services accommodations will be evaluated individually based on appropriate and current documentation.

Allowed in exams
  Calculator: Yes
  Dictionary: No
  Computer: Yes
  Spellchecker: NR
Extended test time: Yes
Scribes: Yes
Proctors: Yes
Oral exams: No
Note-takers: Yes

Distraction-reduced environment: Yes
Tape recording in class: Yes
Books on tape from RFBD: Yes
Taping of books not from RFBD: Yes
Accommodations for students with ADHD: Yes
Reading machine: Yes
Other assistive technology: Yes
Priority registration: Yes

Added costs for services: No
LD specialists: Yes
Professional tutors: 2
Peer tutors: 1–20
Max. hours/wk. for services: Depends on need
How professors are notified of LD/ADHD: By student

GENERAL ADMISSIONS INFORMATION

Director of Admissions: Beverly Arata
Telephone: 619-594-6336

ENTRANCE REQUIREMENTS

Academic units required: 4 English, 3 math, 2 science (2 science labs), 2 foreign language, 1 social studies, 1 history, 1 academic elective, 1 visual/performing arts. **Academic units recommended:** 4 math. High school diploma is required, and GED is accepted. ACT with or without Writing component accepted. TOEFL required of all international applicants: minimum paper TOEFL 550, minimum computer TOEFL 213.

Application deadline: 11/30
Notification: 3/1
Average GPA: 3.45
ACT Composite middle 50% range: 19–24

SAT Math middle 50% range: 480–590
SAT Critical Reading middle 50% range: 460–570
SAT Writing middle 50% range: NR

Graduated top 10% of class: NR
Graduated top 25% of class: NR
Graduated top 50% of class: NR

COLLEGE GRADUATION REQUIREMENTS

Course waivers allowed: No
Course substitutions allowed: Yes
In what course: Varies; must be directly related to disability

ADDITIONAL INFORMATION

Environment: San Diego State is located on 300 acres 12 miles from the ocean.

Student Body
  Undergrad enrollment: 28,527
  Women: 58%
  Men: 42%
  Percent out-of-state: 5%

Cost Information
  In-state tuition: $3,120
  Out-of-state tuition: $13,290
  Room & board: $10,093
Housing Information
  University housing: Yes
  Percent living on campus: 13%

Greek System
  Fraternity: Yes
  Sorority: Yes
Athletics: Division I

San Diego State University

SAN FRANCISCO STATE UNIVERSITY

1600 Holloway Avenue, San Francisco, CA 94132
Phone: 415-338-6486 • Fax: 415-338-7196
E-mail: ugadmit@sfsu.edu • Web: www.sfsu.com
Support: CS • Institution type: 4-year public

LEARNING DISABILITY PROGRAM AND SERVICES

The Disability Program and Resource Center (DPRC) is available to promote and provide equal access to the classroom and campus-related activities. A full range of support services is provided so that students may define and achieve personal autonomy at SFSU. The staff is sensitive to the diversity of disabilities, including those only recently recognized as disabilities requiring reasonable accommodations. Confidential support services are available. All students registered with DPRC are eligible for disability management advising. This consists of helping students access services from DPRC; manage DPRC services and school in general; problem-solve conflicts/concerns that are disability-related with individuals, programs, and services on campus; and understand "reasonable accommodation" under the law. Generally, the campus community is sensitive, but if an oversight occurs, students do have protection under Section 504 and the ADA. Students are encouraged to contact DPRC for guidance in pursuing a grievance. Resolution of a violation can often be achieved informally without completing the formal grievance procedure.

LD/ADHD ADMISSIONS INFORMATION

College entrance tests required: Yes
Interview required: Yes
Essay recommended: No
Documentation required for LD: Psychoeducational evaluation
Documentation required for ADHD: Psychoeducational evaluation
Submitted to: Disability Program and Resource Center (DPRC)
Special Ed. HS course work accepted: Yes

Specific course requirements of all applicants: Yes
Separate application required: Yes
# of LD applications submitted each year: NR
# of LD applications accepted yearly: NR
Total # of students receiving LD services: 250
Acceptance into program means acceptance into college: Students must be admitted and enrolled in the university first and then request services.

ADMISSIONS

Students with LD apply to the university through the regular application process. If the student is not eligible for regular admission for a disability-related reason, DPRC can provide special admissions assistance. To obtain special admissions assistance, students need to register with the DPRC office, provide verification of the disability, and notify the Admissions Office that the DPRC has the appropriate verification. When these steps have been taken, the Admissions Office will consult with the DPRC before making a decision. The admissions contact person can request substitutions of high school courses in math, foreign language, and science. Students with LD who are judged unable to fulfill specific requirements may take course substitutions. Substitutions are authorized on an individual basis after review and recommendation by the high school or community college counselor. Students taking substitutions must have 15 units of college-prep study. High school case managers may write summaries and provide a clinical judgment. The DPRC wants information about achievement deficits and may require the student to attend an admissions interview.

ADDITIONAL INFORMATION

The DPRC offers a drop-in center with available tutorial services. The DPRC can also arrange for test accommodations and note-takers and will advocate for the student. The staff is very involved and offers comprehensive services through a team approach. There are no developmental courses offered at the university. However, there are skills classes. Students with documented LD may request assistance in locating tutors. Other services may include registration assistance, campus orientation, note-takers, readers, test-taking assistance, tutoring, disability-related counseling, and referral information.

LEARNING DISABILITY PROGRAM/SERVICES

Learning Disability Program/Services: Disability Programs and Resource Center
Director: Gene Chelberg
  E-mail: chelberg@sfsu.edu
  Telephone: 415-338-2472
  Fax: 415-338-1041
Contact Person: Deidre Defreese, Associate Director
  E-mail: defreese@sfsu.edu
  Telephone: 415-338-6356
  Fax: 415-338-1041

LEARNING DISABILITY SERVICES

Requests for the following/services accommodations will be evaluated individually based on appropriate and current documentation.

Allowed in exams
  Calculator: Yes
  Dictionary: Yes
  Computer: Yes
  Spellchecker: Yes
Extended test time: Yes
Scribes: Yes
Proctors: Yes
Oral exams: Yes
Note-takers: Yes

Distraction-reduced environment: Yes
Tape recording in class: Yes
Books on tape from RFBD: Yes
Taping of books not from RFBD: Yes
Accommodations for students with
  ADHD: Yes
Reading machine: Yes
Other assistive technology: Yes
Priority registration: Yes

Added costs for services: No
LD specialists: Yes
Professional tutors: No
Peer tutors: Yes
Max. hours/wk. for services: Limited
How professors are notified of
  LD/ADHD: By student

GENERAL ADMISSIONS INFORMATION

Director of Admissions: Valerie Perry
Telephone: 415-338-2037

ENTRANCE REQUIREMENTS

Academic units required: 4 English, 3 math, 2 science (2 science labs), 2 foreign language, 1 social studies, 1 history, 1 visual/performing arts. **Academic units recommended:** 1 academic elective. High school diploma is required, and GED is accepted. ACT with or without Writing component accepted. TOEFL required of all international applicants: minimum paper TOEFL 550, minimum computer TOEFL 173.

Application deadline: Rolling
Notification: Rolling
Average GPA: 3.12
ACT Composite middle 50% range:
  18–23

SAT Math middle 50% range:
  440–560
SAT Critical Reading middle 50%
  range: 440–560

SAT Writing middle 50% range:
  440–550
Graduated top 10% of class: NR
Graduated top 25% of class: NR
Graduated top 50% of class: NR

COLLEGE GRADUATION REQUIREMENTS

Course waivers allowed: Yes
In what course: Individual case-by-case decisions
Course substitutions allowed: Yes
In what course: Individual case-by-case decisions in subjects where impact of disability is evident.

ADDITIONAL INFORMATION

Environment: The school is located in downtown San Francisco on a 130-acre campus.

Student Body
  Undergrad enrollment: 23,843
  Women: 59%
  Men: 41%
  Percent out-of-state: 1%

Cost Information
  In-state tuition: $3,000
  Out-of-state tuition: $12,690
  Room & board: $10,000
Housing Information
  University housing: Yes
  Percent living on campus: 15%

Greek System
  Fraternity: Yes
  Sorority: Yes
Athletics: Division II

SAN JOSE STATE UNIVERSITY

One Washington Square, San Jose, CA 95112-0001
Phone: 408-283-7500 • Fax: 408-924-2050
E-mail: contact@sjsu.edu • Web: www.sjsu.com
Support: CS • Institution type: 4-year public

LEARNING DISABILITY PROGRAM AND SERVICES

The goal of the Disability Resource Center (DRC) is to provide appropriate academic adjustments and support services to students with disabilities while training them to become self-advocates and develop maximum independence. The DRC provides services to students and consultation to faculty to educate every department so that they best serve students with disabilities. To request services students must self identify and meet with a DRC counselor to create a student file. Documentation of the disability should verify a disability and support the requests for accommodations or academic adjustments.

LD/ADHD ADMISSIONS INFORMATION

College entrance tests required: Yes
Interview required: No
Essay recommended: No
Documentation required for LD: WJ–R III, Parts 1–2; WAIS and WJ–R, Part 2. The DRC will accept the WIAT II test results: standard scores are required for all assessments.
Documentation required for ADHD: Documentation from a licensed professional who is trained/specialized in ADHD and is licensed to use the DSM–IV criteria for ADHD diagnosis.
Submitted to: Disability Resource Center
Special Ed. HS course work accepted: No

Specific course requirements of all applicants: Yes
Separate application required: No
# of LD applications submitted each year: NR
# of LD applications accepted yearly: NR
Total # of students receiving LD services: 652
Acceptance into program means acceptance into college: Students must be admitted and enrolled in the university first and then request services.

ADMISSIONS

Students with LD apply directly to the Admissions Office; there is no special handling of the student's applications through the DRC. All assessments and disability verifications go direct to DRC for establishment of a confidential file. (The assessment should include the WJ–R Parts 1 and 2 or the WAIS–III and WJ–R Part 2 and other skills tests.) Students must have at least a 2.0 GPA, and a sliding scale is used combining GPA and test scores. Only courses from grades 10–12 are used to compute GPA. High school courses required include 4 years of English, 3 years of math, 1 year of science lab, 1 year of U.S. history, 2 years of a foreign language, 1 year of visual/performing arts, and 3 years of academic electives. Foreign language admission requirements can be waived for students with learning disabilities if their high school sends a letter stating that other college-prep courses have been substituted for the foreign language. Those students not meeting general entrance criteria can petition the Exceptional Admissions Committee of the Admissions Office. These students must submit a personal statement and two letters of recommendation, plus disclosure of their learning disability, to be eligible for special consideration. The Admissions Committee has a representative from Disabled Student Services.

ADDITIONAL INFORMATION

No skills courses are offered by the DRC, nor is tutoring offered by the DRC. Referral for skills courses and tutoring is made to regular university services. Recent changes in SJSU policy require that any remediation needed in math and English be cleared during students' first years. Transfer students must have completed oral communication, English 1A equivalent, critical thinking, and math past intermediate algebra. Books on tape are provided through RFB. Students who request the use of a calculator in an exam will need to secure permission from the professor, as well as have appropriate documentation identifying that this is a necessary accommodation to compensate for the disability. Some accommodations include note-taking, priority registration, test accommodations, adaptive technology, disability management, learning disability assessment, readers, academic counseling, and faculty and staff consultation to assist with access and recommend accommodations. Students who are transferring to San Jose State University from another campus in California do not need to provide new documentation of the learning disability.

LEARNING DISABILITY PROGRAM/SERVICES

Learning Disability Program/Services: Disability Resource Center
Director: Martin Schulter
 E-mail: mschulter@drc.sjsu.edu
 Telephone: 408-924-6000
 Fax: 408-924-5999

LEARNING DISABILITY SERVICES

Requests for the following/services accommodations will be evaluated individually based on appropriate and current documentation.

Allowed in exams
 Calculator: Yes
 Dictionary: Yes
 Computer: Yes
 Spellchecker: Yes
Extended test time: Yes
Scribes: Yes
Proctors: Yes
Oral exams: Yes
Note-takers: Yes

Distraction-reduced environment: Yes
Tape recording in class: Yes
Books on tape from RFBD: Yes
Taping of books not from RFBD: Yes
Accommodations for students with ADHD: Yes
Reading machine: Yes
Other assistive technology: Yes
Priority registration: Yes

Added costs for services: No
LD specialists: Yes
Professional tutors: No
Peer tutors: No
Max. hours/wk. for services: Case-by-case basis
How professors are notified of LD/ADHD: By student

GENERAL ADMISSIONS INFORMATION

Director of Admissions: John Loera
Telephone: 408-924-2550

ENTRANCE REQUIREMENTS

Academic units required: 4 English, 3 math, 2 science (2 science labs), 2 foreign language, 1 social studies, 1 history, 1 academic elective, 1 visual/performing arts. **Academic units recommended:** 4 math, 3 science. High school diploma is required, and GED is accepted. ACT with Writing component required. TOEFL required of all international applicants: minimum paper TOEFL 550, minimum computer TOEFL 213.

Application deadline: 3/1
Notification: Rolling
Average GPA: 3.13
ACT Composite middle 50% range: 16–23

SAT Math middle 50% range: 440–570
SAT Critical Reading middle 50% range: NR
SAT Writing middle 50% range: NR

Graduated top 10% of class: NR
Graduated top 25% of class: NR
Graduated top 50% of class: NR

COLLEGE GRADUATION REQUIREMENTS

Course waivers allowed: Yes
In what course: General education quantitative reasoning substitutions made on case-by-case basis
Course substitutions allowed: Yes
In what course: General education quantitative reasoning substitutions made on case-by-case basis; must be disability related

ADDITIONAL INFORMATION

Environment: The university is located on 117 acres in an urban area in the center of San Jose.

Student Body
 Undergrad enrollment: 22,521
 Women: 51%
 Men: 49%
 Percent out-of-state: 1%

Cost Information
 In-state tuition: $3,609
 Out-of-state tuition: $11,187
 Room & board: $8,415
Housing Information
 University housing: Yes
 Percent living on campus: 7%

Greek System
 Fraternity: Yes
 Sorority: Yes
Athletics: Division I

SANTA CLARA UNIVERSITY

500 El Camino Real, Santa Clara, CA 95053
Phone: 408-554-4700 • Fax: 408-554-5255
E-mail: ugadmissions@scu.edu • Web: www.scu.edu
Support: CS • Institution type: 4-year private

LEARNING DISABILITY PROGRAM AND SERVICES

The primary mission of Disabilities Resources (DR) is to enhance academic progress, promote social involvement, and build bridges connecting the various services of the university for all students. This goal is met by providing academic intervention programs, opportunities to increase students' personal understanding of their disability, role models, and community outreach. Disabilities Resources is a resource area within the Drahmann Center that helps to ensure equal access to all academic and programmatic activities for students with disabilities. This goal is met through the provision of Academic Support Services, contact with other university offices, educational programming on disability issues for the university, and, most importantly, assistance in teaching students effective self-advocacy skills under the student development model. Students with disabilities must have documentation of their disability from a qualified professional. Students must submit proper documentation to obtain services through the Office of Disability Resources. The documentation needs to have been completed within the past 3 years to be valid and must include a diagnostic statement; the date of the disability's onset, if appropriate; what procedures and measures (formal or informal) were used to assess the condition; what functional limitations there are and how they will affect academics; if appropriate, all psychometric testing results (standard scores and percentile scores); and, if appropriate, what the examiners' recommendations are for specific academic accommodations and/or auxiliary aids that specifically meet the student's needs. For students seeking academic accommodations for a documented disability of attention deficit hyperactivity disorder, a form, obtained from Disabilities Resources, must be completed by a certified medical professional addressing a treatment plan.

LD/ADHD ADMISSIONS INFORMATION

College entrance tests required: Yes
Interview required: Yes
Essay recommended: Yes
Documentation required for LD: Psychoeducational evaluation
Documentation required for ADHD: Documentation must be completed by a qualified professional.
Submitted to: Disability Resources
Special Ed. HS course work accepted: No

Specific course requirements of all applicants: Yes
Separate application required: No
# of LD applications submitted each year: NR
# of LD applications accepted yearly: NR
Total # of students receiving LD services: 125
Acceptance into program means acceptance into college: Students must be admitted and enrolled in the university first and then request services.

ADMISSIONS
All students submit the same general application. Santa Clara takes pride in the personal nature of its admission process. All applicants are carefully reviewed. Freshman applicants are offered admission based on high school record, ACT/SAT (will mix and match the best Math and Verbal scores from multiple SAT tests), one letter of recommendation, and personal factors. Applicants with disabilities are encouraged to write a personal statement to assist the Admission Committee in evaluating the application. Recommended course requirements include 4 years of English, 3 years of math, 3 years of social studies, 2 years of science labs, and 3 years of a foreign language (4 years recommended).

ADDITIONAL INFORMATION
The Disabilities Resources staff meets individually with students. Some of the academic accommodations provided by DR include note-taking, library assistance, proofreading, and test accommodations. Other support services include priority registration, tutoring or academic counseling, and workshops on legal issues and self-advocacy. The DR is in the process of purchasing computer-aided technology to assist the students. Graduate students with learning disabilities are offered the same services and accommodations as those provided for undergraduate students. Students can be better served if the professional documentation they submit specifically identifies the accommodations needed for the student to be successful in college. This should include the student's strengths and weaknesses and any required modifications. Examples of possible accommodations are priority registration, extended time for exams, scribes, note-takers, and textbooks on tape. All students have access to peer tutoring, a drop-in Math Lab, and a drop-in Writing Center. Some accommodations would need to be approved by the professor.

LEARNING DISABILITY PROGRAM/SERVICES

Learning Disability Program/Services: Disability Resources (DR)
Director: Ann Ravenscroft
  E-mail: eravenscroft@scu.edu
  Telephone: 408-554-4111
  Fax: 408-554-2709
Contact Person: Same as above

LEARNING DISABILITY SERVICES

Requests for the following/services accommodations will be evaluated individually based on appropriate and current documentation.

Allowed in exams
  Calculator: Yes
  Dictionary: Yes
  Computer: Yes
  Spellchecker: Yes
Extended test time: Yes
Scribes: Yes
Proctors: Yes
Oral exams: Yes
Note-takers: Yes

Distraction-reduced environment: Yes
Tape recording in class: Yes
Books on tape from RFBD: Yes
Taping of books not from RFBD: No
Accommodations for students with ADHD: Yes
Reading machine: No
Other assistive technology: Yes
Priority registration: Yes

Added costs for services: No
LD specialists: Yes
Professional tutors: No
Peer tutors: 50
Max. hours/wk. for services: 1
How professors are notified of LD/ADHD: By both student and director

GENERAL ADMISSIONS INFORMATION

Director of Admissions: Sandra Hayes
Telephone: 408-554-525

ENTRANCE REQUIREMENTS

Academic units required: 4 English, 3 math, 2 science, 2 foreign language, 3 social studies, 1 academic elective.
Academic units recommended: 4 English, 4 math, 3 science, 3 foreign language, 3 social studies, 1 academic elective. High school diploma is required, and GED is accepted. ACT with or without Writing component accepted. TOEFL required of all international applicants: minimum paper TOEFL 550, minimum computer TOEFL 213.

Application deadline: 1/15
Notification: Rolling
Average GPA: 3.54
ACT Composite middle 50% range: 24–29

SAT Math middle 50% range: 560–670
SAT Writing middle 50% range: 550–650
SAT Writing middle 50% range: NR

Graduated top 10% of class: 37%
Graduated top 25% of class: 72%
Graduated top 50% of class: 100%

COLLEGE GRADUATION REQUIREMENTS

Course waivers allowed: No
Course substitutions allowed: Yes
In what course: Foreign language

ADDITIONAL INFORMATION

Environment: The university is located 1 hour south of San Francisco in Silicon Valley, 3 miles from San Jose airport.

Student Body
  Undergrad enrollment: 4,592
  Women: 55%
  Men: 45%
  Percent out-of-state: 36%

Cost Information
  Tuition: $30,900
  Room & board: $10,380
Housing Information
  University housing: Yes
  Percent living on campus: 52%

Greek System
  Fraternity: No
  Sorority: No
  Athletics: Division I

SANTA MONICA COLLEGE

1900 Pico Boulevard, Santa Monica, CA 90405
Phone: 310-434-4000 • Fax: 310-434-3645
E-mail: admission@smc.edu • Web: www.smc.edu
Support: CS • Institution type: 2-year public

LEARNING DISABILITY PROGRAM AND SERVICES

The Santa Monica College Learning Disabilities Program is designed to provide support services to students with learning disabilities who are enrolled in regular college classes. The college is dedicated to helping students with learning disabilities achieve their goals by identifying those eligible for special services according to state-mandated guidelines and by assisting them in becoming independent, optimally functioning college students. These goals are met by screening, testing, and certifying learning disabilities according to state guidelines; developing individual plans and recommending appropriate academic accommodations to provide academic equity for LD students; and teaching compensatory learning strategies and fostering self-awareness of learning strengths and weaknesses. Before a student can receive these support services, the student must be evaluated to determine eligibility for the program. This evaluation is achieved in an 8-week assessment workshop (HD1H or 2H). During this time, students discover their learning strengths and weaknesses through a series of tasks. Both academic and thinking skills are assessed. Test results will be compared to guidelines provided by the State of California, in accordance with federal mandates, to determine whether a student qualifies for ongoing support services as a learning disabled student. The LD specialist will interpret test results and will make individual recommendations on how to improve learning and study strategies. Orientations explaining the assessment process are offered regularly throughout the year.

LD/ADHD ADMISSIONS INFORMATION

College entrance tests required: No
Interview required: No
Essay recommended: No
Documentation required for LD: Psychoeducational
   evaluation
Documentation required for ADHD: Medical doctor's letter
Submitted to: Center for Students with Disabilities
Special Ed. HS course work accepted: Yes

Specific course requirements: NR
Separate application required: No
# of LD applications submitted each year: 120
# of LD applications accepted yearly: 100
Total # of students receiving LD services: 300
**Acceptance into program means acceptance into
   college:** Students must be admitted and enrolled in the
   university first and then request services.

ADMISSIONS

Students may enroll at Santa Monica College if they have graduated from high school, are 18 years of age or older, or are 16 years of age or older and submit a Student Score Report for passing the California High School Proficiency examination. Students taking courses leading to degrees or certificates or wish to transfer to a four-year college or university should file an application for admissions and schedule time for assessments. Assessment tests are required to enroll in English or math courses unless the student meets the exemption criteria. Students should arrange for transcripts from the high school and/or previous college work be sent to the college. Students must complete orientation. Orientations can be completed in person or online. After the orientation, the student will be able to proceed with enrollment. Printed applications are processed at a lower priority than the online applications; therefore, submission of the printed application will result in a significantly lower priority date for enrollment.

ADDITIONAL INFORMATION

After the assessment process, an individual plan is developed with recommendations for needed skills training and appropriate accommodations. Following is a list of services that the student may be eligible for as indicated in the personal plan: study-strategies workshops, drop-in tutoring appointments that are available for short-term help, and long-term tutoring. Students should see their contact instructor to discuss their needs. The LD program has help available in math and English. There are many options available for tutoring campus-wide. Additional accommodations or services could include test proctoring, if recommended as an appropriate accommodation on the Student Educational Contract, which will provide a quiet, distraction-free environment; priority registration for fall and spring only; volunteer note-takers for students who have difficulty listening and taking notes at the same time; tape-recording lectures (but it is also possible to request the assistance of a student in the class who is a good note-taker and willing to volunteer); books on tape for students who have severe reading difficulties; access to the High Tech Training Center, which includes assistive technology training, word-processing classes, computer-assisted instruction, introduction to the Internet, and open lab times to get help or work on an assignment; academic advisement; and on- and off-campus referrals.

LEARNING DISABILITY PROGRAM/SERVICES

Learning Disability Program/Services: Learning Disability Program/Center for Students with Disabilities
Director: Mary Jane Weil
  E-mail: weil_Mary-Jane@smc.edu
  Telephone: 310-434-4265
  Fax: 310-434-4272
Contact Person: George Marcopulos
  E-mail: marcopulos_george@smc.edu
  Telephone: 310-434-4684
  Fax: 310-434-4272

LEARNING DISABILITY SERVICES

Requests for the following/services accommodations will be evaluated individually based on appropriate and current documentation.

Allowed in exams		
Calculator: Yes	**Distraction-reduced environment:** Yes	**Added costs for services:** No
Dictionary: Yes	**Tape recording in class:** Yes	**LD specialists:** Yes
Computer: Yes	**Books on tape from RFBD:** Yes	**Professional tutors:** No
Spellchecker: Yes	**Taping of books not from RFBD:** Yes	**Peer tutors:** Yes
Extended test time: Yes	**Accommodations for students with ADHD:** Yes	**Max. hours/wk. for services:** N/A
Scribes: No	**Reading machine:** Yes	**How professors are notified of LD/ADHD:** By student
Proctors: Yes	**Other assistive technology:** Yes	
Oral exams: Yes	**Priority registration:** Yes	
Note-takers: Yes		

GENERAL ADMISSIONS INFORMATION

Director of Admissions: Brenda Simmons
Telephone: 310-434-4000

ENTRANCE REQUIREMENTS

Academic units recommended: 16 total (4 English, 3 math, 3 science, 4 social studies, and 2 foreign language). No ACT/SAT required. High school diploma or GED accepted. TOEFL required of all international applicants: minimum paper TOEFL 450, minimum computer TOEFL 133.

Application deadline: Rolling	**SAT Math middle 50% range:** NR	**Graduated top 10% of class:** NR
Notification: Rolling	**SAT Writing middle 50% range:** NR	**Graduated top 25% of class:** NR
Average GPA: NR	**SAT Writing middle 50% range:** NR	**Graduated top 50% of class:** NR
ACT Composite middle 50% range: NR		

COLLEGE GRADUATION REQUIREMENTS

Course waivers allowed: Yes
In what course: Math proficiency exam
Course substitutions allowed: Yes
In what course: Math proficiency exam

ADDITIONAL INFORMATION

Environment: Santa Monica College is located in West Los Angeles.

Student Body	Cost Information	Greek System
Undergrad enrollment: 18,326	**In-state tuition:** $0	**Fraternity:** No
Women: 55%	**Out-of-state tuition:** $3,576	**Sorority:** No
Men: 45%	**Housing Information**	**Athletics:** NJCAA
Percent out-of-state: NR	**University housing:** Yes, off campus	

SANTA ROSA JUNIOR COLLEGE

1501 Mendocino Avenue, Santa Rosa, CA 95401
Phone: 707-527-4685 • Fax: 707-527-4798
E-mail: admininfo@santarosa.edu • Web: www.santarosa.edu
Support: CS • Institution type: 2-year public

LEARNING DISABILITY PROGRAM AND SERVICES

The Disability Resources Department provides students with disabilities equal access to a community college education through specialized instruction, disability-related support services, and advocacy activities. Santa Rosa Junior College is a state-supported school that accepts all students with learning disabilities who apply and meet the mandatory state eligibility requirements that verify their learning disability. If a student is eligible for the program, an IEP is developed and implemented. Students may participate in a combination of special and mainstream college classes with appropriate support services as needed. The college encourages and fosters autonomy, independence, and responsibility in students with disabilities and challenges them to become self-advocates. The college also creates a campus climate in which diverse learning styles are respected and equal access for students with disabilities can be realized.

LD/ADHD ADMISSIONS INFORMATION

College entrance tests required: No
Interview required: No
Essay recommended: No
Documentation required for LD: WAIS–III, WJ–III
Documentation required for ADHD: Yes
Submitted to: Disability Resources
Special Ed. HS course work accepted: Yes

Specific course requirements of all applicants: No
Separate application required: No
# of LD applications submitted each year: 150–200
# of LD applications accepted yearly: 125–175
Total # of students receiving LD services: 500
Acceptance into program means acceptance into college: Students must be admitted and enrolled in the university first and then request services.

ADMISSIONS

Admission to Santa Rosa is open to students with a high school diploma or a GED. There are no specific requirements for admission. Students with learning disabilities must meet state eligibility requirements verifying a learning disability to qualify for services. Students must demonstrate: average to above-average intellectual ability, adequate measured achievement in at least one academic area or employment setting, a severe processing deficit in one or more areas, a severe discrepancy between aptitude and achievement in one or more academic areas, and adaptive behavior appropriate to a college setting. Students may also qualify on the basis of a communicative disorder and head injuries. All students must demonstrate appropriate behavior and an ability to benefit from the instructional program.

ADDITIONAL INFORMATION

The Learning Skills Program offers small specialized classes in the following areas for nontransferable credit: basic academic skills, guidance/independent living, sensory-motor integration, and speech and language. Support services include assessment for learning disabilities, counseling, tutoring, speech/language skills development, and liaison. Skills classes are offered in spelling, writing, math, study strategies, computers, and art process. All of these courses may be taken for college credit.

LEARNING DISABILITY PROGRAM/SERVICES

Learning Disability Program/Services: Disability Resources Department
Director: Patie Wegman
  E-mail: pwegman@santarosa.edu
  Telephone: 707-527-4278
  Fax: 707-524-1768
Contact Person: Marcy Stinnett
  E-mail: pwegman@santarosa.edu
  Telephone: 707-527-4278
  Fax: 707-524-1768

LEARNING DISABILITY SERVICES

Requests for the following/services accommodations will be evaluated individually based on appropriate and current documentation.

Allowed in exams
  Calculator: Yes
  Dictionary: Yes
  Computer: Yes
  Spellchecker: Yes
Extended test time: Yes
Scribes: Yes
Proctors: Yes
Oral exams: Yes
Note-takers: Yes

Distraction-reduced environment: Yes
Tape recording in class: Yes
Books on tape from RFBD: Yes
Taping of books not from RFBD: Yes
Accommodations for students with
  ADHD: Yes
Reading machine: Yes
Other assistive technology: Yes
Priority registration: Yes

Added costs for services: No
LD specialists: Yes
Professional tutors: 10
Peer tutors: No
Max. hours/wk. for services: N/A
How professors are notified of
  LD/ADHD: By student

GENERAL ADMISSIONS INFORMATION

Director of Admissions: Ricardo Navarrette
Telephone: 707-527-4685

ENTRANCE REQUIREMENTS

The college has an open-door admissions policy. GED or high school diploma required. **Academic units recommended:** 16 total (4 English, 3 math, 3 science, 4 social studies, and 2 foreign language.) TOEFL required of all international applicants: minimum paper TOEFL 475, minimum computer TOEFL 153.

Application deadline: Rolling
Notification: Rolling
Average GPA: NR
ACT Composite middle 50% range:
  NR

SAT Math middle 50% range: NR
SAT Writing middle 50% range: NR
SAT Writing middle 50% range: NR

Graduated top 10% of class: NR
Graduated top 25% of class: NR
Graduated top 50% of class: NR

COLLEGE GRADUATION REQUIREMENTS

Course waivers allowed: Yes
In what course: Student must attempt math course/s before a waiver is granted.
Course substitutions allowed: No

ADDITIONAL INFORMATION

Environment: The college is located on 93 acres with easy access to San Francisco.

Student Body
  Undergrad enrollment: 28,233
  Women: 59%
  Men: 41%
  Percent out-of-state: 2%

Cost Information
  In-state tuition: $26 per unit
  Out-of-state tuition: $4,104
  Room & board: $2,100
Housing Information
  University housing: Yes
  Percent living on campus: 22%

Greek System
  Fraternity: Yes
  Sorority: Yes
Athletics: Intercollegiate

SIERRA COLLEGE

5000 Rocklin Road, Rocklin, CA 95677
Phone: 916-789-0553 • Fax: 916-789-2967
E-mail: gmodder@sierracollege.edu • Web: www.sierracollege.edu
Support: CS • Institution type: 2-year public

LEARNING DISABILITY PROGRAM AND SERVICES

The goals of the program are to assist students with learning disabilities in reaching their academic/vocational goals, help the students strengthen and develop their perceptual skills, and provide the support needed to maximize student success. Sierra College subscribes to the psychometric-evaluation model established by the California Community College System. This six-step process includes intake screening, measured achievement, ability level, processing deficit, aptitude-achievement discrepancy, and eligibility recommendation. Students are evaluated individually through the Learning Disabilities Orientation course. This is a mainstreamed program with no special classes, but it does provide support and accommodations for students with learning disabilities.

LD/ADHD ADMISSIONS INFORMATION

College entrance tests required: No
Interview required: No
Essay recommended: No
Documentation required for LD: WAIS–III, WJ–III
Documentation required for ADHD: Yes
Submitted to: Disabled Student Program and Services
Special Ed. HS course work accepted: Yes

Specific course requirements: NR
Separate application required: No
# of LD applications submitted each year: NR
# of LD applications accepted yearly: NR
Total # of students receiving LD services: 350
Acceptance into program means acceptance into college: Students must be admitted and enrolled in the university first and then request services.

ADMISSIONS

Sierra College has an open admissions policy for those students who meet the regular entrance requirements. ACT/SAT are not required, and there are no cutoffs for GPA, class rank, or test scores. Additionally, no specific courses are required for admission. Any student who holds a high school diploma or GED is admitted. Services are provided to all enrolled students with appropriate documentation.

ADDITIONAL INFORMATION

To receive services and accommodations, students must meet the eligibility requirements set forth by the state of California for students with learning disabilities. Skills courses are available in reading, math, writing, study strategies, English as a second language, and spelling. These skills classes are offered for college credit. In addition, students can get assistance in test-taking techniques, priority registration, and peer tutoring. Other services include assessment and evaluation of learning disabilities, individual education plans, identification of students' learning styles and modalities, perceptual training programs, test-taking facilitation, compensatory learning strategies/techniques, computer-assisted instruction, and classroom accommodations.

LEARNING DISABILITY PROGRAM/SERVICES

Learning Disability Program/Services: Learning Opportunities Center/Disabled Student Programs and Services (DSP&S)
Director: Kaylene Hallberg
  E-mail: khallberg@sierracollege.edu
  Telephone: 916-789-2939
Contact Person: Denise Stone
  E-mail: dstone@sierracollege.edu
  Telephone: 916-789-2697
  Fax: 916-789-2967

LEARNING DISABILITY SERVICES

Requests for the following/services accommodations will be evaluated individually based on appropriate and current documentation.

Allowed in exams
  Calculator: Yes
  Dictionary: Yes
  Computer: Yes
  Spellchecker: Yes
Extended test time: Yes
Scribes: No
Proctors: Yes
Oral exams: Yes
Note-takers: Yes

Distraction-reduced environment: Yes
Tape recording in class: Yes
Books on tape from RFBD: Yes
Taping of books not from RFBD: Yes
Accommodations for students with ADHD: Yes
Reading machine: No
Other assistive technology: Yes
Priority registration: Yes

Added costs for services: No
LD specialists: Yes
Professional tutors: No
Peer tutors: Approximately 100
Max. hours/wk. for services: Unlimited
How professors are notified of LD/ADHD: By student

GENERAL ADMISSIONS INFORMATION

Director of Admissions: Pat Efseaff
Telephone: 916-781-0430

ENTRANCE REQUIREMENTS

The college has an open admissions policy. High school diploma or GED is accepted. ACT/SAT are not required for admission.

Application deadline: Rolling
Notification: Rolling
Average GPA: NR
ACT Composite middle 50% range: NR

SAT Math middle 50% range: NR
SAT Writing middle 50% range: NR
SAT Writing middle 50% range: NR

Graduated top 10% of class: NR
Graduated top 25% of class: NR
Graduated top 50% of class: NR

COLLEGE GRADUATION REQUIREMENTS

Course waivers allowed: Yes
In what course: Waivers are provided on an individual basis.
Course substitutions allowed: Yes
In what course: Substitutions are provided on an individual basis.

ADDITIONAL INFORMATION

Environment: The school is located on a 327-acre campus in a rural setting with easy access to Sacramento.

Student Body
  Undergrad enrollment: 20,173
  Women: 56%
  Men: 44%

Cost Information
  In-state tuition: $20 per unit
  Out-of-state tuition: $160 per unit
  Room & board: $4,800–$7,400
  Housing Information
  University housing: Yes
  Percent living on campus: 1% (150 students)

Greek System
  Fraternity: No
  Sorority: No
  Athletics: Intercollegiate

SONOMA STATE UNIVERSITY

1801 East Cotati Avenue, Rohnert Park, CA 94928
Phone: 707-664-2778 • Fax: 707-664-2060
E-mail: admitme@sonoma.edu • Web: www.sonoma.edu
Support: S • Institution type: 4-year public

LEARNING DISABILITY PROGRAM AND SERVICES

The goal of Disabled Student Services (DSS) is to provide reasonable accommodations and equal access to the educational process while helping students with disabilities become self-advocates. Services at Sonoma State University are provided primarily through two offices on campus. DSS offers support services and advocacy, and Learning Skills Services provides academic support and skill development. One-on-one sessions and workshops are given by specialists in various subject areas. In addition, a campus tutorial program offers individual peer tutoring. Appropriate documentation for LD/ADHD student is required and must be completed by a qualified professional. The documentation should be submitted to DSS.

LD/ADHD ADMISSIONS INFORMATION

College entrance tests required: Yes
Interview required: No
Essay recommended: Yes
Documentation required for LD: WAIS–R, WAIS–III, WS–R, TAPS, TVPS, TOMAL
Documentation required for ADHD: Yes
Submitted to: Disabled Student Services
Special Ed. HS course work accepted: No

Specific course requirements of all applicants: Yes
Separate application required: Yes
# of LD applications submitted each year: 40–50
# of LD applications accepted yearly: 20–25
Total # of students receiving LD services: 200
Acceptance into program means acceptance into college: Students must be admitted and enrolled in the university first and then request services.

ADMISSIONS

Admission is based on a combination of high school GPA, test scores, and college-preparatory classes. Courses include 4 years of English, 3 years of math, 1 year of social studies, 2 years of science, 2 years of a foreign language, 1 year of visual/performing arts, and 3 years of academic electives. SAT/ACT score requirements depend on the GPA. However, a 2.0 GPA is the absolute minimum. Students with learning disabilities submit a general application. If a limited number of required courses are missing, students can be granted a conditional admission, and these courses must be made up in college. Students not meeting either regular or conditional admissions may initiate a request for special admissions by writing a letter to the DSS director providing information about strengths, weaknesses, and why special admission is needed. LD diagnostic evaluation and two letters of recommendations are also required for conditional admission. All special admission applicants are interviewed in person or by phone. Special admission is only available to designated groups of students. Special admissions applicants need to submit a letter to Linda Lipps describing what subject areas are missing or if the GPA or SAT/ACT are low. The staff of DSS makes recommendations, but the final decision is made by the Office of Admissions.

ADDITIONAL INFORMATION

DSS does not offer skills classes or tutoring. Reading, writing, and math are offered through the Learning Skills Services. Tutorial assistance is available in the Tutorial Center. There are no LD specialists in the DSS; however, there are disability management advisors who authorize accommodations. With appropriate documentation, some of the services or accommodations offered include the use of calculators, dictionaries, computers, or spellchecker during exams; extended time on tests; scribes; proctors; oral exams; note-takers; distraction-free testing environments; tape recorder in class; taped text; and priority registration.

LEARNING DISABILITY PROGRAM/SERVICES

Learning Disability Program/Services: Disabled Student Services
Director: Rosa T. (Rose) Lawrence
  E-mail: rose.lawrence@sonoma.edu
  Telephone: 707-664-2677
  Fax: 707-664-3330
Contact Person: Aurelia Melgar
  Telephone: 707-664-2677
  Fax: 707-644-3330

LEARNING DISABILITY SERVICES

Requests for the following/services accommodations will be evaluated individually based on appropriate and current documentation.

Allowed in exams
  Calculator: Yes
  Dictionary: Yes
  Computer: Yes
  Spellchecker: Yes
Extended test time: Yes
Scribes: Yes
Proctors: No
Oral exams: Yes
Note-takers: Yes

Distraction-reduced environment: Yes
Tape recording in class: Yes
Books on tape from RFBD: Yes
Taping of books not from RFBD: Yes
Accommodations for students with
  ADHD: Yes
Reading machine: Yes
Other assistive technology: Yes
Priority registration: Yes

Added costs for services: No
LD specialists: No
Professional tutors: No
Peer tutors: 40–45
Max. hours/wk. for services: 4
How professors are notified of
  LD/ADHD: By student

GENERAL ADMISSIONS INFORMATION

Director of Admissions: Gustavo Flores
Telephone: 707-664-2778

ENTRANCE REQUIREMENTS

Academic units required: 4 English, 3 math, 2 science (1 science lab), 2 foreign language, 1 history, 3 academic electives, 1 visual/performing arts, 1 U.S. government. High school diploma is required, and GED is accepted. TOEFL required of all international applicants: minimum paper TOEFL 500, minimum computer TOEFL 173.

Application deadline: 1/31
Notification: Rolling
Average GPA: 3.23
ACT Composite middle 50% range:
  18–23

SAT Math middle 50% range:
  450–560
SAT Critical Reading middle 50%
  range: 450–550
SAT Writing middle 50% range: NR

Graduated top 10% of class: NR
Graduated top 25% of class: NR
Graduated top 50% of class: NR

COLLEGE GRADUATION REQUIREMENTS

Course waivers allowed: Yes
In what course: Allowed sometimes in math by petition; the university offers an alternative math class to fulfill the general education requirements.
Course substitutions allowed: Yes
In what course: Students may substitute foreign language only.

ADDITIONAL INFORMATION

Environment: The school is located on 220 acres with easy access to San Francisco.

Student Body
  Undergrad enrollment: 7,112
  Women: 63%
  Men: 37%
  Percent out-of-state: 1%

Cost Information
  In-state tuition: $3,616
  Out-of-state tuition: $10,170
  Room & board: $8,465
Housing Information
  University housing: Yes
  Percent living on campus: 35%

Greek System
  Fraternity: Yes
  Sorority: Yes
Athletics: Division II

STANFORD UNIVERSITY

Office of Undergraduate Admission, Montag Hall, Stanford, CA 94305-3020
Phone: 650-723-2091 • Fax: 650-723-6050
E-mail: admission@stanford.edu • Web: www.stanford.edu
Support: CS • Institution type: 4-year private

LEARNING DISABILITY PROGRAM AND SERVICES

Since its creation in 1983, the Disability Resource Center (DRC) has provided direct academic services for students with learning disabilities. It also serves as an advocacy group to assist students who encounter accessibility problems and facilitate special arrangements for housing and campus activities. If a new student mentions having a disability in the admissions process, the Admissions Office, with the student's permission, notifies the DRC of the student's acceptance to the university. A DRC staff member will then contact the student to inquire about his or her accommodations and academic adjustment needs.

LD/ADHD ADMISSIONS INFORMATION

College entrance tests required: Yes
Interview required: No
Essay recommended: No
Documentation required for LD: Psychoeducational evaluation
Documentation required for ADHD: Yes
Submitted to: Disability Resource Center
Special Ed. HS course work accepted: No

Specific course requirements: NR
Specific course requirements of all applicants: Yes
Separate application required: No
# of LD applications submitted each year: NR
# of LD applications accepted yearly: NR
Total # of students receiving LD services: NR
Acceptance into program means acceptance into college: Students must be admitted and enrolled prior to requesting services.

ADMISSIONS

Stanford seeks to enroll students with excellent academic records who show evidence of personal achievement outside the classroom and who have used the resources available to them to their fullest potential. The policy on the admissions of students with learning disabilities makes clear there is no separate academic program. Students should take a strong college-preparatory curriculum, including honors and Advanced Placement courses. Applicants must submit the ACT with Writing or the SAT Reasoning Test, plus three SAT Subject Tests. The university will look at ACT/SAT test scores in context of the learning disability. Typically, applicants to Stanford rank in the top 10 percent from a public high school or the top 20–30 percent in a private high school.

ADDITIONAL INFORMATION

Students seeking services or accommodations for specific learning disabilities or attention deficit hyperactivity disorder must submit psychoeducational evaluations that are recent enough to reflect current levels of functioning. There are no skill courses offered. Tutoring is available on campus through the Center for Teaching and Learning. A peer support group is available. Other accommodations can include note-taking services, typist/scribe services, reader services, letters to professors for course/exam accommodations, and exam room accommodation. Services and accommodations are offered to undergraduate and graduate students.

LEARNING DISABILITY PROGRAM/SERVICES

Learning Disability Program/Services: Disability Resource Center
Director: Joan Bisagno, PhD
 E-mail: joan.bisagno@stanford.edu
 Telephone: 650-723-1066
 Fax: 650-725-5301

LEARNING DISABILITY SERVICES

Requests for the following/services accommodations will be evaluated individually based on appropriate and current documentation.

Allowed in exams
 Calculator: NR
 Dictionary: NR
 Computer: NR
 Spellchecker: NR
Extended test time: Yes
Scribes: Yes
Proctors: Yes
Oral exams: Yes
Note-takers: Yes

Distraction-reduced environment: Yes
Tape recording in class: Yes
Books on tape from RFBD: Yes
Taping of books not from RFBD: Yes
Accommodations for students with
 ADHD: Yes
Reading machine: Yes
Other assistive technology: Yes
Priority registration: Yes

Added costs for services: No
LD specialists: Yes
Professional tutors: No
Peer tutors: Yes
Max. hours/wk. for services: Varies
How professors are notified of
 LD/ADHD: By student

GENERAL ADMISSIONS INFORMATION

Director of Admissions: Rick Shaw
Telephone: 650-723-2091

ENTRANCE REQUIREMENTS

Academic units recommended: 4 English, 4 math, 3 science (3 science labs), 3 foreign language, 2 social studies, 1 history. High school diploma is required, and GED is accepted.

Application deadline: 12/15
Notification: 4/1
Average GPA: 4.30
ACT Composite middle 50% range:
 28–33

SAT Math middle 50% range:
 680–780
SAT Critical Reading middle 50%
 range: 660–760
SAT Writing middle 50% range:
 660–760

Graduated top 10% of class: 89%
Graduated top 25% of class: 98%
Graduated top 50% of class: 100%

COLLEGE GRADUATION REQUIREMENTS

Course waivers allowed: No
In what course: N/A
Course substitutions allowed: No
In what course: N/A

ADDITIONAL INFORMATION

Environment: Stanford University is located about 30 minutes south of San Francisco.

Student Body
 Undergrad enrollment: 6,391
 Women: 48%
 Men: 52%
 Percent out-of-state: 54%

Cost Information
 Tuition: $32,994
 Room & board: $10,367
Housing Information
 University housing: Yes
 Percent living on campus: 90%

Greek System
 Fraternity: Yes
 Sorority: Yes
Athletics: Division I

U. OF CALIFORNIA—BERKELEY

Office of Undergraduate Admissions, 110 Sproul Hall #5800,
Berkeley, CA 94720-5800 • Phone: 510-642-3175 • Fax: 510-642-7333
E-mail: ouars@uclink.berkeley.edu • Web: www.berkeley.edu
Support: CS • Institution type: 4-year public

LEARNING DISABILITY PROGRAM AND SERVICES

The Disabled Student Program (DSP) seeks to ensure that students with disabilities have equal access to educational opportunities and student life at UC—Berkeley. DSP works to sustain a supportive environment that provides appropriate and necessary disability-related accommodations, enables students to demonstrate their knowledge and skills, facilitates students' success in academic pursuits, and promotes independence. DSP's services assist students as they develop their skills and the qualities needed to meet their educational, personal, and professional goals. DSP also works to support the efforts of the campus community to ensure full participation of students with disabilities in every aspect of university life. DSP is a recipient of a TRIO Student Support Services Grant. Funds are used to provide a variety of services for students, helping them to complete graduation requirements and plan successful post-graduation educations or careers. For services, DSP must have verification of the disability on file. Students with LD must submit a psychoeducational evaluation completed by a qualified professional. Students with ADHD must submit a letter from a qualified professional who has an expertise in diagnosing ADHD in adults. Additional testing may be requested if it is deemed necessary for the planning and provision of appropriate accommodations and services.

LD/ADHD ADMISSIONS INFORMATION

College entrance tests required: Yes
Interview required: No
Essay recommended: Yes
Documentation required for LD: Current WAIS and WJ
Documentation required for ADHD: Yes
Submitted to: Disabled Student Program
Special Ed. HS course work accepted: No

Specific course requirements of all applicants: Yes
Separate application required: No
# of LD applications submitted each year: NR
# of LD applications accepted yearly: NR
Total # of students receiving LD services: 242
Acceptance into program means acceptance into college: Students must be admitted and enrolled in the university first and then request services.

ADMISSIONS

An LD specialist and admission specialist are available to meet with students with LD interested in applying to UC Berkeley. These specialists will review the applicant's high school or college transcript and give advice on how to proceed with the application. DSP works closely with the Office of Admissions and Records. There are two tiers for admission: Tier I is an automatic admission; Tier II applicants may need other criteria to be admitted. The impact of a disability could be a factor in an admission for a Tier II applicant. When an applicant indicates on the application that there is a disability, DSP contacts the applicant to request information, documentation of the disability, and a statement from the applicant about the impact of the disability on his or her life and academic achievement. DSP uses this information to answer questions about the applicant from the Admissions Office. UC—Berkeley seeks to identify students with disabilities who have a high potential for success if provided with appropriate accommodation and support services. In general, applicants have taken 4 years of English, 2 years of social science, 3 years of math (4 years recommended), 2 years of science (3 recommended), 2 years of a foreign language (3 years recommended), 1 year of visual/performing arts, and 1 year of an academic elective from previous areas.

ADDITIONAL INFORMATION

DSP staff provide the following services: recommending and ensuring the provision of academic accommodations; consulting with instructors about accommodations; authorizing auxiliary services; teaching academic strategies and study skills; promoting on-campus awareness; providing academic advising, adaptive technology, support groups, and a special section of the course "Facilitating Success" for students with LD and ADHD that centers on understanding learning differences, maximizing strengths, academic planning, research, writing, exam preparation, and using university resources; enabling priority registration; providing specialists to help in developing problem-solving strategies and solutions to difficult problems; conducting a series of informational workshops on topics like understanding disabilities and individual learning styles; improving reading, writing, and research efficiency; memory strategies, self-advocacy; computer applications that facilitate learning; and career or graduate school planning. Specialists may recommend a reduced course load.

LEARNING DISABILITY PROGRAM/SERVICES

Learning Disability Program/Services: Disabled Students' Program
Director: Ed Rogers
  E-mail: erogers@berkeley.edu
  Telephone: 510-642-0518
  Fax: 510-643-9686
Contact Person: Connie Chiba
  E-mail: cchiba@berkeley.edu
  Telephone: 510-642-0518
  Fax: 510-643-9686

LEARNING DISABILITY SERVICES

Requests for the following/services accommodations will be evaluated individually based on appropriate and current documentation.

Allowed in exams
  Calculator: Yes
  Spellchecker: Yes
Extended test time: Yes
Scribes: Yes
Proctors: Yes
Oral exams: Yes
Note-takers: Yes

Distraction-reduced environment: Yes
Tape recording in class: Yes
Books on tape from RFBD: Yes
Taping of books not from RFBD: Yes
Accommodations for students with ADHD: Yes
Reading machine: Yes
Other assistive technology: Yes

Priority registration: Yes
Added costs for services: No
LD specialists: Yes
Professional tutors: No
Peer tutors: Student Learning Center
max. hours/wk. for services: NR
How professors are notified of LD/ADHD: By student

GENERAL ADMISSIONS INFORMATION

Director of Admissions: Camila Hicks
Telephone: 510-642-3175

ENTRANCE REQUIREMENTS

Academic units required: 4 English, 3 math, 2 science (2 science labs), 2 foreign language, 2 social studies, 2 history, 1 academic elective, 1 visual/performing arts. **Academic units recommended:** 4 English, 4 math, 3 science (3 science labs), 3 foreign language, 2 social studies, 2 historys, 1 academic elective, 1 visual/performing arts. High school diploma is required, and GED is accepted. SAT Reasoning or ACT with Writing component required plus 2 SAT Subject Tests. TOEFL required of all international applicants: minimum paper TOEFL 550, minimum computer TOEFL 213.

Application deadline: 11/30
Notification: Decisions available on website by 3/31
Average GPA: 3.93
ACT Composite middle 50% range: NR

SAT Math middle 50% range: 620–740
SAT Critical Reading middle 50% range: 580–710
SAT Writing middle 50% range: 590–710

Graduated top 10% of class: 98%
Graduated top 25% of class: 100%
Graduated top 50% of class: 100%

COLLEGE GRADUATION REQUIREMENTS

Course waivers allowed: Yes
In what course: Math waivers are considered on a case-by-case basis.
Course substitutions allowed: Yes
In what course: Foreign language requirement can be substituted with cultural courses on a case-by-case basis.

ADDITIONAL INFORMATION

Environment: The 1,232-acre campus is in an urban area 10 miles east of San Francisco.

Student Body
  Undergrad enrollment: 23,863
  Women: 54%
  Men: 46%
  Percent out-of-state: 11%

Cost Information
  In-state tuition: $7,780 (fees)
  Out-of-state tuition: $26,484
  Room & board: $11,630
Housing Information
  University housing: Yes
  Percent living on campus: 35%

Greek System
  Fraternity: Yes
  Sorority: Yes
Athletics: Division I

U. OF CALIFORNIA—LOS ANGELES

1147 Murphy Hall, Box 951436, Los Angeles, CA 90095-1436
Phone: 310-825-3101 • Fax: 310-206-1206
E-mail: ugadm@saonet.ucla.edu • Web: www.ucla.edu
Support: CS • Institution type: 4-year public

LEARNING DISABILITY PROGRAM AND SERVICES

UCLA complies with state, federal, and university guidelines that mandate full access for students with disabilities, including learning disabilities. UCLA complies with the requirement to provide reasonable accommodations for documented students to allow them to participate in their academic program to the greatest extent possible. Students with other documented types of learning disabilities, including attention deficit hyperactive disorder and traumatic brain injury, are also served by the LD program. The UCLA LD program is coordinated by a full-time learning disabilities specialist and offers a full range of accommodations and services. Services are individually designed and include counseling, special test arrangements, note-taker services, readers, priority enrollment, adaptive technology, and individual tutoring. An active support group provides opportunities for students to discuss mutual concerns and enhance learning strategies. Workshops and speakers address skill development and topics of interest. In the Peer Mentor Program, continuing students with learning disabilities serve as resources to entering students.

LD/ADHD ADMISSIONS INFORMATION

College entrance tests required: Yes
Interview required: No
Essay recommended: Yes
Documentation required for LD: Psychoeducational documentation
Documentation required for ADHD: An assessment for ADHD must be current and completed by a qualified professional.
Submitted to: Office for Students with Disabilities
Special Ed. HS course work accepted: No

Specific course requirements of all applicants: Yes
Separate application required: No
# of LD applications submitted each year: NR
# of LD applications accepted yearly: NR
Total # of students receiving LD services: 225–300
Acceptance into program means acceptance into college: Students must be admitted and enrolled in the university first and then request services.

ADMISSIONS

There are no special admissions criteria for students with learning disabilities. In an academic review, the university will assess and balance a variety of academic factors to determine the overall scholastic strength of each applicant. UCLA does not use a formula. The comprehensive review includes the remainder of the freshman applicants after the academic review. While commitment to intellectual development and academic progress continues to be of primary importance, the personal statement also forms an integral part of this review. All applicants are required to submit the SAT or ACT and SAT Subject Tests (including the Writing Test, Mathematics Level I or II, and either English Literature, Foreign Language, Science, or Social Studies). To be competitive, students usually score in the high 20s on the ACT or high 1100s on the SAT I and between 500–600 on each of the SAT Subject Tests. Required high school courses are 4 years of English, 2 years of history/social science, 3 years of math, 2 years of a foreign language (3 years recommended), 2 years of science lab (3 years recommended), and 2 years of electives. Additional criteria are based on an eligibility index using test scores and class rank. Selected students are admitted for winter. Admissions readers pay attention to significant obstacles and challenges related in personal statements. The LD specialists provide disability-related information to admissions staff.

ADDITIONAL INFORMATION

The LD Program includes tutors for individual classes, peer mentors, support group meetings, learning skills workshops, advocacy, referrals to campus resources, priority enrollment, orientation program, LD screening, and disability management counseling by four LD specialists including disability awareness, learning, and time management strategies, self-advocacy skills, and interpretation of evaluation reports. Compensations could include alternatives in printed materials: (taped textbooks, computerized voice synthesizer, and RFBD); test-taking procedures (extended time, proctor to assist with reading and writing, distraction-free test area, computer for essay exams, alternative test formats, including essay-type rather than multiple choice-type or taped exams rather than written exams, or use of calculator or spellchecker); note-taking (note-takers or taped lectures); writing essays and papers (word processors with voice synthesizers or composition tutors); reduced course load; extended time to complete a program; and tutors for individual classes.

LEARNING DISABILITY PROGRAM/SERVICES

Learning Disability Program/Services: Office for Students with Disabilities
Director: Kathy Molini
  E-mail: kmolini@saonet.ucla.edu
  Telephone: 310-825-1501
  Fax: 310-825-9656

LEARNING DISABILITY SERVICES

Requests for the following/services accommodations will be evaluated individually based on appropriate and current documentation.

Allowed in exams
  Calculator: Yes
  Dictionary: Yes
  Computer: Yes
  Spellchecker: Yes
Extended test time: Yes
Scribes: Yes
Proctors: Yes
Oral exams: No
Note-takers: Yes

Distraction-reduced environment: Yes
Tape recording in class: Yes
Books on tape from RFBD: Yes
Taping of books not from RFBD: Yes
Accommodations for students with
  ADHD: Yes
Reading machine: Yes
Other assistive technology: Yes
Priority registration: Yes

Added costs for services: No
LD specialists: Yes
Professional tutors: No
Peer tutors: Yes
Max. hours/wk. for services:
  Unlimited
How professors are notified of
  LD/ADHD: By both student and
  director

GENERAL ADMISSIONS INFORMATION

Director of Admissions: Dr. Vu T. Tran
Telephone: 310-825-3101

ENTRANCE REQUIREMENTS

Academic units required: 4 English, 3 math, 2 science (2 science labs), 2 foreign language, 2 history, 1 academic elective, 1 visual/performing arts. **Academic units recommended:** 4 English, 4 math, 3 science (3 science labs), 3 foreign language, 2 historys, 1 academic elective, 1 visual/performing arts. High school diploma is required, and GED is accepted. SAT Reasoning or ACT with Writing component required plus 2 SAT Subject Tests. TOEFL required of all international applicants: minimum paper TOEFL 550, minimum computer TOEFL 220.

Application deadline: 11/30
Notification: Rolling
Average GPA: 4.14
ACT Composite middle 50% range:
  24–30

SAT Math middle 50% range:
  610–720
SAT Critical Reading middle 50%
  range: 570–690
SAT Writing middle 50% range:
  590–700

Graduated top 10% of class: 97%
Graduated top 25% of class: 100%
Graduated top 50% of class: 100%

COLLEGE GRADUATION REQUIREMENTS

Course waivers allowed: No
Course substitutions allowed: Yes
In what course: Foreign language and math as appropriate based on documentation, history, and recommendation

ADDITIONAL INFORMATION

Environment: The university is located on 419 acres in an urban area of Los Angeles.

Student Body
  Undergrad enrollment: 25,432
  Women: 56%
  Men: 44%
  Percent out-of-state: 2%

Cost Information
  In-state tuition: $6,141
  Out-of-state tuition: $24,825
  Room & board: $12,415
Housing Information
  University housing: Yes
  Percent living on campus: 40%

Greek System
  Fraternity: Yes
  Sorority: Yes
Athletics: Division I

University of California—Los Angeles

U. OF CALIFORNIA—SAN DIEGO

9500 Gilman Drive, 0021, La Jolla, CA 92093-0021
Phone: 858-534-4831 • Fax: 858-534-5723
E-mail: admissionsinfo@ucsd.edu • Web: www.ucsd.edu
Support: CS • Institution type: 4-year public

LEARNING DISABILITY PROGRAM AND SERVICES

The primary objective of the Office for Students with Disabilities (OSD) is to integrate mainstream students with learning disabilities into campus programs, services, and activities. Academic accommodations are designed to meet disability-related needs without fundamentally altering the program; are not remedial; and may include part-time enrollment, exception to minimum academic progress requirements, substitution of course work required for graduation, and alternative test formats. This program is not intended to provide remediation. Students seeking accommodations must provide a comprehensive written evaluation that meets the following requirements: Assessment must be comprehensive and include aptitude (WAIS–R with subtest scores and/or WJ–R), achievement (WJ–R), information processing (WAIS–R subtests or WJ–R-cognitive portions) tests completed within 3 years; diagnostic report with written summary of educational, medical, family histories and behavioral observation; test scores, testing procedures followed, interpretation, dates, and evaluator; specified intracognitive and/or cognitive-achievement discrepancies; statement of how the LD substantially interferes with the student's educational progress; and recommendations for academic accommodations. OSD's peer mentoring program is designed to match new students who have disabilities (mentees) with continuing students (mentors) who have the same major, interests, and/or disabilities. Mentors and mentees meet as a group once a week throughout the academic year. The group provides for informal meetings and serve as a place to receive emotional support from several students who understand and have something in common. The group also gives students a place where they can feel comfortable discussing issues. Topics covered in the past include problem-solving techniques, study strategies, test-taking problems, and social issues.

LD/ADHD ADMISSIONS INFORMATION

College entrance tests required: Yes
Interview required: No
Essay recommended: Yes
Documentation required for LD: Psychoeducational evaluation, WAIS, WJ–R
Documentation required for ADHD: Documentation from the student's doctor
Submitted to: Office for Students with Disabilities

Specific course requirements of all applicants: Yes
Separate application required: Yes
# of LD applications submitted each year: 40–50
# of LD applications accepted yearly: 50
Total # of students receiving LD services: 150
Acceptance into program means acceptance into college: Student must be admitted and enrolled in the university first and then reviewed for LD services.

ADMISSIONS
There is no special admissions process for students with learning disabilities. All applicants must meet the same admission criteria. Students need to check the disability information on the application if they wish to receive information about university resources and services available. Course requirements include 2 years of social science (including U.S. history and 0.5 year government), 4 years of English, 3 years of math, 2 years of science labs, 2 years of a foreign language (courses taken in 7th or 8th grade may be used to fulfill part of this requirement), and 2 years of electives. There is an eligibility index based on ACT/SAT and GPA, such as 2.82 GPA and 36 ACT/1590–1600 SAT up to 3.29 GPA and 12 ACT/490–570 SAT. Meeting the eligibility index requirements does not guarantee admission. The minimum GPA for a California resident is 2.8 and for a nonresident a 3.4. Students must submit three SAT Subject Tests. There is a Summer Bridge Program for conditional admits that is available to a specific group of students.

ADDITIONAL INFORMATION
Depending on the nature of the disability and level of functional limitation coordination may include the following: note-takers; readers; peer mentoring; priority registration; typists; problem resolution assistance; peer mentoring; extended time for tests; distraction-free testing environment; calculators, dictionaries, computers, or spellcheckers in exams; scribes; proctors; tape recorders in class; peer tutoring; and priority registration. Course substitutions are dependent on the college and major requirements. Skills classes are offered for all students in study and time management and skill building.

LEARNING DISABILITY PROGRAM/SERVICES

Learning Disability Program/Services: Office for Students with Disabilities (OSD)
Director: Roberta J. Gimblett
  E-mail: rgimblett@ucsd.edu
  Telephone: 858-534-4382
  Fax: 858-534-4650

LEARNING DISABILITY SERVICES

Requests for the following/services accommodations will be evaluated individually based on appropriate and current documentation.

Allowed in exams
  Calculator: Yes
  Dictionary: Yes
  Computer: Yes
  Spellchecker: Yes
Extended test time: Yes
Scribes: Yes
Proctors: Yes
Oral exams: Yes
Note-takers: Yes

Distraction-reduced environment: Yes
Tape recording in class: Yes
Books on tape from RFBD: Yes
Taping of books not from RFBD: Yes
Accommodations for students with ADHD: Yes
Reading machine: Yes
Other assistive technology: Yes
Priority registration: Yes

Added costs for services: No
LD specialists: Yes
Professional tutors: No
Peer tutors: 200–300
Max. hours/wk. for services: Unlimited
How professors are notified of LD/ADHD: By student

GENERAL ADMISSIONS INFORMATION

Director of Admissions: Mae Brown
Telephone: 858-534-4831

ENTRANCE REQUIREMENTS

Academic units required: 4 English, 3 math, 2 science labs, 2 foreign language, 2 history, 2 academic elective, 1 visual/performing arts. **Academic units recommended:** 4 English, 4 math, 3 science labs, 3 foreign language, 2 history, 1 academic elective, 1 visual/performing arts. High school diploma is required, and GED is accepted. SAT Reasoning Test or ACT with Writing component required. TOEFL required of all international applicants: minimum paper TOEFL 550.

Application deadline: 11/30
Notification: Rolling
Average GPA: 3.90
ACT Composite middle 50% range: 23–29

SAT Math middle 50% range: 600–700
SAT Critical Reading middle 50% range: 540–660
SAT Writing middle 50% range: NR

Graduated top 10% of class: 99%
Graduated top 25% of class: 100%
Graduated top 50% of class: 100%

COLLEGE GRADUATION REQUIREMENTS

Course waivers allowed: Yes
In what course: Course waivers are dependent on college and major requirements.
Course substitutions allowed: Yes
In what course: Course substitution is dependent on college and major requirements.

ADDITIONAL INFORMATION

Environment: The university has a suburban campus north of downtown San Diego.

Student Body
  Undergrad enrollment: 20,679
  Women: 52%
  Men: 48%
  Percent out-of-state: 3%

Cost Information
  In-state tuition: $6,685
  Out-of-state tuition: $23,961
  Room & board: $9,657
Housing Information
  University housing: Yes
  Percent living on campus: 33%

Greek System
  Fraternity: Yes
  Sorority: Yes
Athletics: Division II

U. OF CALIFORNIA—SANTA BARBARA

1210 Cheadle Hall, U. of California, Santa Barbara, CA 93106-2014
Phone: 805-893-2881 • Fax: 805-893-2676
E-mail: admissions@sa.ucsb.edu • Web: www.ucsb.edu
Support: CS • Institution type: 4-year public

LEARNING DISABILITY PROGRAM AND SERVICES

The Disabled Student Program (DSP) is a department within the Division of Student Affairs that works to increase the retention and graduation ratio of students with temporary and permanent disabilities, assure equal access to all educational and academic programs, and foster student independence. The university is strongly committed to maintaining an environment that guarantees students with disabilities full access to educational programs and activities. The DSP office serves as a campus liaison regarding issues and regulations related to students with disabilities. DSP provides reasonable accommodations to students with learning disabilities and specific accommodations are determined on an individual basis. Admitted students should send LD documentation to DSP and schedule an appointment with the LD specialist. Accommodations and academically related services are not designed to provide remediation, but to accommodate a perceptual disorder that impairs the student's ability to acquire, process, or communicate information. Each accommodation will be made available to the extent that it does not compromise the academic integrity of the student's program. In all cases, it is the student's responsibility to communicate special needs to the professor and/or DSP.

LD/ADHD ADMISSIONS INFORMATION

College entrance tests required: Yes
Interview required: No
Essay recommended: Yes
Documentation required for LD: WAIS–III; WJ–R;
   Achievement R or III (preferred), NDRT
Documentation required for ADHD: Yes
Submitted to: Disabled Student Program
Special Ed. HS course work accepted: No

Specific course requirements of all applicants: Yes
Separate application required: No
# of LD applications submitted each year: NR
# of LD applications accepted yearly: NR
Total # of students receiving LD services: 300
Acceptance into program means acceptance into college: Students must be admitted and enrolled in the university first and then request services.

ADMISSIONS

There is no special application for students with learning disabilities. All students must meet the same admission criteria. However, students may self-disclose the existence of a learning disability. Students should use their autobiographical statement to address their disability and how they have coped with it in high school. All documentation is submitted to the Office of Admissions, including tests and letters that could be helpful in determining the student's ability to succeed in college. Special circumstances qualifying students for special action admissions is viewed on a case-by-case basis, such as waiving foreign language, math, and science. General admission requirements include 4 years of English, 3 years of math, 1 year of world history, 1 year of U.S. history, 2 years of science labs, 2 years of a foreign language, 2 years of academic electives. The ACT or SAT is required and three SAT Subject Tests in English Composition, Math, and one other additional subject. DSP does not admit students but may consult with the Office of Admissions. Admission decisions are made by admissions officers and consultation from an LD specialist regarding documentation submitted.

ADDITIONAL INFORMATION

Academic accommodations may include substitution of courses required for graduation, nonremedial individualized tutoring, and instruction in reading and writing strategies and in compensatory study skills. Academic support services include priority registration; aids with reading, writing, note-taking, test-taking, and proofreading; and liaison with faculty. Skills classes and tutoring are provided through CLASS, the Campus Learning Assistance Program. These classes are available for all students on campus. DSP Office does not have the space to provide areas for testing accommodations, but individual professors assist by securing space. Students are not required to attend a summer program or special orientation. However, DSP orientation is highly recommended prior to the fall quarter. Services and accommodations are available for undergraduate and graduate students.

LEARNING DISABILITY PROGRAM/SERVICES

Learning Disability Program/Services: Disabled Student Program (DSP)
Director: Gary White
  E-mail: gary.white@ucsb.edu
  Telephone: 805-893-2182
  Fax: 805-893-7127
Contact Person: Claudia Batty
  E-mail: claudia.batty@ucsb.edu
  Telephone: 805-893-8897
  Fax: 805-893-7127

LEARNING DISABILITY SERVICES

Requests for the following/services accommodations will be evaluated individually based on appropriate and current documentation.

Allowed in exams
  Calculator: Yes
  Dictionary: No
  Computer: Yes
  Spellchecker: Yes
Extended test time: Yes
Scribes: Yes
Proctors: Yes
Oral exams: No

Note-takers: Yes
Distraction-reduced environment: Yes
Tape recording in class: Yes
Books on tape from RFBD: Yes
Taping of books not from RFBD: Yes
Accommodations for students with
  ADHD: Yes
Reading machine: Yes
Other assistive technology: Yes

Priority registration: Yes
Added costs for services: No
LD specialists: Yes
Professional tutors: No
Max. hours/wk. for services: 1
How professors are notified of
  LD/ADHD: By student

GENERAL ADMISSIONS INFORMATION

Director of Admissions: Christine Van Gieson
Telephone: 805-893-3641

ENTRANCE REQUIREMENTS

Academic units required: 4 English, 3 math, 2 science (2 science labs), 2 foreign language, 2 social studies, 2 history, 2 academic electives, 1 visual/performing arts. **Academic units recommended:** 4 math, 3 science (3 science labs), 3 foreign language. High school diploma is required, and GED is accepted. SAT Reasoning Test or ACT with Writing component required plus 2 SAT Subject Tests. TOEFL required of all international applicants: minimum paper TOEFL 500, minimum computer TOEFL 173.

Application deadline: 11/30
Notification: 3/15
Average GPA: 3.74
ACT Composite middle 50% range:
  22–28

SAT Math middle 50% range:
  540–660
SAT Critical Reading middle 50% range: 530–650
SAT Writing middle 50% range: NR

Graduated top 10% of class: 96%
Graduated top 25% of class: 98%
Graduated top 50% of class: 100%

COLLEGE GRADUATION REQUIREMENTS

Course waivers allowed: No
Course substitutions allowed: Yes
In what course: Substitutions depend on documentation and an attempt by the student to take the course. Typically, the requests for substitutions are in math and foreign language. Requests for substitutions of course work are reviewed by a committee.

ADDITIONAL INFORMATION

Environment: The university is located on 813 acres in a small city 10 miles west of Santa Barbara.

Student Body
  Undergrad enrollment: 18,210
  Women: 55%
  Men: 45%
  Percent out-of-state: 4%

Cost Information
  In-state tuition: $7,277
  Out-of-state tuition: $25,960
  Room & board: $11,493
Housing Information
  University housing: Yes
  Percent living on campus: 31%

Greek System
  Fraternity: Yes
  Sorority: Yes
Athletics: Division I

University of California—Santa Barbara

UNIVERSITY OF REDLANDS

1200 East Colton Avenue, Redlands, CA 92373
Phone: 909-793-2121 • Fax: 909-793-2029
E-mail: admissions@redlands.edu • Web: www.redlands.edu
Support: S • Institution type: 4-year private

LEARNING DISABILITY PROGRAM AND SERVICES

Students identified as learning disabled are eligible for tutoring and individual assistance from Academic Support Services. While the university does not have a formal program for students with learning disabilities, the goal is to help students succeed in college once they are enrolled. Although the services and accommodations offered are minimal, they do comply with the mandates of Section 504 of the Rehabilitation Act of 1973. Academic Support Services is sensitive to the needs of students with disabilities and strives to provide the services and accommodations that are identified in the professional documentation.

LD/ADHD ADMISSIONS INFORMATION

College entrance tests required: Yes
Interview required: No
Essay recommended: Yes
Documentation required for LD: Psychoeducational evaluation
Documentation required for ADHD: Yes
Submitted to: Disabled Student Service
Special Ed. HS course work accepted: No

Specific course requirements of all applicants: Yes
Separate application required: No
# of LD applications submitted each year: NR
# of LD applications accepted yearly: 50–70
Total # of students receiving LD services: 200
Acceptance into program means acceptance into college: Students must be admitted and enrolled in the university first and then request services.

ADMISSIONS

Students with learning disabilities are required to submit the general application form and meet the same admission standards as all applicants. Redlands strongly recommends a college-preparatory program that includes 4 years of English and 2 or 3 years each of foreign language, science labs, and social studies. Three years of math up to and including Algebra II is required. The middle 50 percent of the class has between 1060 and 1240 SAT Reasoning Test and between 22 and 27 ACT. Faculty admits are for those students whose GPAs or SAT/ACT scores do not meet admissions standards, but who show promise of success in college. The Director of Academic Support Services is involved in the admission decision for students with learning disabilities.

ADDITIONAL INFORMATION

Each service provided by Academic Support Services encourages students to take personal responsibility for their academic success. Study skills courses are available as well as basic skills classes in math, writing, and learning strategies. Students have access to tutoring on a one-on-one basis. The peer tutoring program provides friendly, supportive assistance for most academic subjects. Peer tutors must have faculty recommendations in the subjects they wish to tutor and at least a 3.0 GPA in the area they tutor. The Director of Academic Support Services will work with students to assist them in identifying their needs and securing appropriate accommodations. Additionally, students may make individual appointments for assistance with time management and study skills. However, it is the students' responsibility to seek out help and request assistance.

LEARNING DISABILITY PROGRAM/SERVICES

Learning Disability Program/Services: Academic Support and Disabled Student Services
Director: Jen Ostermiller
  E-mail: jen_ostermiller@redlands.edu
  Telephone: 909-748-8108
  Fax: 909-335-5297

LEARNING DISABILITY SERVICES

Requests for the following/services accommodations will be evaluated individually based on appropriate and current documentation.

Allowed in exams
  Calculator: Yes
  Dictionary: Yes
  Computer: Yes
  Spellchecker: Yes
Extended test time: Yes
Scribes: Yes
Proctors: Yes
Oral exams: Yes
Note-takers: Yes

Distraction-reduced environment: Yes
Tape recording in class: Yes
Books on tape from RFBD: Yes
Taping of books not from RFBD: No
Accommodations for students with ADHD: Yes
Reading machine: No
Other assistive technology: Yes
Priority registration: N/A

Added costs for services: No
LD specialists: No
Professional tutors: No
Peer tutors: 50–80
Max. hours/wk. for services: Unlimited
How professors are notified of LD/ADHD: By both student and director

GENERAL ADMISSIONS INFORMATION

Director of Admissions: Paul Driscoll
Telephone: 909-748-8074

ENTRANCE REQUIREMENTS

Academic units required: 4 English, 3 math, 2 science (1 science lab), 2 foreign language, 2 social studies.
Academic units recommended: 4 English, 4 math, 3 science (1 science lab), 3 foreign language, 2 social studies, 1 history. High school diploma is required, and GED is accepted. ACT without Writing component accepted. TOEFL required of all international applicants: minimum paper TOEFL 550, minimum computer TOEFL 213.

Application deadline: 4/1
Notification: Rolling
Average GPA: 3.58
ACT Composite middle 50% range: 22–26

SAT Math middle 50% range: 540–630
SAT Critical Reading middle 50% range: 540–630
SAT Writing middle 50% range: NR

Graduated top 10% of class: 37%
Graduated top 25% of class: 67%
Graduated top 50% of class: 94%

COLLEGE GRADUATION REQUIREMENTS

Course waivers allowed: No
Course substitutions allowed: Yes
In what course: Math and foreign language

ADDITIONAL INFORMATION

Environment: The university is located on 130 acres in a small town 60 miles east of Los Angeles.

Student Body
  Undergrad enrollment: 2,310
  Women: 57%
  Men: 43%
  Percent out-of-state: 29%

Cost Information
  Tuition: $28,476
  Room & board: $9,360
Housing Information
  University housing: Yes
  Percent living on campus: 67%

Greek System
  Fraternity: Yes
  Sorority: Yes
Athletics: Division III

University of Redlands

UNIVERSITY OF SAN FRANCISCO

2130 Fulton Street, San Francisco, CA 94117
Phone: 415-422-6563 • Fax: 415-422-2217
E-mail: admission@usfca.edu • Web: www.usfca.edu
Support: CS • Institution type: 4-year private

LEARNING DISABILITY PROGRAM AND SERVICES

The University of San Francisco believes that students with learning disabilities are capable of succeeding and becoming contributing members of the university community and society. To this end, USF provides educational support and assistance to those students whose goals are successful completion of college and who take an active participatory role in their own education. Services provided enable students to achieve grades that accurately reflect their ability, promote healthy self-images, remediate deficit areas, and promote USF's LD program by conducting in-services for faculty, admissions, and other staff; providing brochures and advertising services; and working closely with faculty to provide accommodations to students with learning disabilities. USF does not provide diagnostic testing for LD or ADHD. However, students can request a screening or consultation.

LD/ADHD ADMISSIONS INFORMATION

College entrance tests required: Yes
Interview required: No
Essay recommended: No
Documentation required for LD: Current psychoeducational assessment report by a qualified professional verifying the presence of a specific learning disability
Documentation required for ADHD: Comprehensive neuropsychological or psychoeducational assessment report by a qualified professional clearly stating the presence of ADHD.
Submitted to: Both Admissions Office and Student Disability Services

Special Ed. HS course work accepted: Yes
Specific course requirements: NR
Separate application required: No
# of LD applications submitted each year: 100
# of LD applications accepted yearly: 80
Total # of students receiving LD services: 200
Acceptance into program means acceptance into college: Students must be admitted and enrolled in the university first and then request services.

ADMISSIONS

All applicants must meet the entrance requirements (examples: GPA, ACT, SAT, letters of recommendation). Once a student is admitted, disclosure of a disability will allow the student to work with faculty, staff, and Student Disability Services (SDS) to obtain reasonable accommodations. If a student who is a borderline admit self-discloses on the regular application form, the Director of Student Disability Services reviews the documentation and gives an evaluation before an admission decision is made. The final decision is made jointly between the Director of Student Disability Services and the Office of Admissions.

ADDITIONAL INFORMATION

Services include trained tutors, instruction in study skills and coping strategies, academic advising, maintaining regular contact with the LD coordinator, diagnostic testing, individual or small group instruction for educational building, and helping students improve their understanding of their learning disability. Assistive technology includes Kurzweil, Dragon Naturally Speaking, and so on. Extended time for course examinations may be a reasonable accommodation for students with specific types of disabilities. SDS reviews the documentation submitted by the student as part of the intake process and indicates extended time on a letter of accommodation when appropriate. Students with attention deficit hyperactivity disorder request services through SDS. A comprehensive neuropsychological or psychoeducational assessment report by a qualified professional clearly stating the presence of this disorder is required. The University of San Francisco's Learning and Writing Center aims to help all students to connect with one another and with professional staff members to achieve their academic best. Services in the Learning Center include tutors, academic workshops, and opportunities for study group information, and computer and other learning resources. The Writing Center provides professional writing assistance. For a complete and comprehensive listing of documentation guidelines and how to access services, please visit the website: www.usfca.edu/acadserv/academic/services/sds.

LEARNING DISABILITY PROGRAM/SERVICES

Learning Disability Program/Services: Student Disability Services
Director: Tom Merrell
  E-mail: merrellt@usfca.edu
  Telephone: 415-422-6876
  Fax: 415-422-5906
Contact Person: Teresa Ong
  E-mail: ongt@usfca.edu
  Telephone: 415-422-6876
  Fax: 415-422-5906

LEARNING DISABILITY SERVICES

Requests for the following/services accommodations will be evaluated individually based on appropriate and current documentation.

Allowed in exams
  Calculator: Yes
  Dictionary: Yes
  Computer: Yes
  Spellchecker: Yes
Extended test time: Yes
Scribes: Yes
Proctors: Yes
Oral exams: Yes

Note-takers: Yes
Distraction-reduced environment: Yes
Tape recording in class: Yes
Books on tape from RFBD: Yes
Taping of books not from RFBD: Yes
Accommodations for students with ADHD: Yes
Reading machine: Yes
Other assistive technology: Yes

Priority registration: Yes
Added costs for services: No
LD specialists: Yes
Professional tutors: 20
Peer tutors: 100
Max. hours/wk. for services: 3
How professors are notified of LD/ADHD: By student

GENERAL ADMISSIONS INFORMATION

Director of Admissions: Mike Hughes
Telephone: 415-422-6563

ENTRANCE REQUIREMENTS

Academic units recommended: 4 English, 3 math, 2 science (2 science labs), 2 foreign language, 3 social studies, 6 academic electives, 1 chemistry, and 1 biology or physics is required of nursing and science applicants. High school diploma is required, and GED is accepted. ACT with Writing component required. TOEFL required of all international applicants: minimum paper TOEFL 550, minimum computer TOEFL 213.

Application deadline: 2/1 priority
Notification: Within 4 weeks of completed application
Average GPA: 3.47
ACT Composite middle 50% range: 21–26

SAT Math middle 50% range: 500–620
SAT Critical Reading middle 50% range: 510–620
SAT Writing middle 50% range: NR

Graduated top 10% of class: 21%
Graduated top 25% of class: 59%
Graduated top 50% of class: 91%

COLLEGE GRADUATION REQUIREMENTS

Course waivers allowed: Yes
In what course: Foreign language, math
Course substitutions allowed: Yes
In what course: Foreign language, math

ADDITIONAL INFORMATION

Environment: The University of San Francisco is located on 52 acres in the heart of the city.

Student Body
  Undergrad enrollment: 4,796
  Women: 66%
  Men: 34%
  Percent out-of-state: 24%

Cost Information
  Tuition: $28,420
  Room & board: $10,580
Housing Information
  University housing: Yes
  Percent living on campus: 48%

Greek System
  Fraternity: Yes
  Sorority: Yes
Athletics: Division I

University of San Francisco

UNIVERSITY OF SOUTHERN CALIFORNIA

Admissions Office: Student Administrative Services, 700 Childs Way,
Los Angeles, CA 90089-0911 • Phone: 213-740-1111 • Fax: 213-740-6364
E-mail: admitusc@usc.edu • Web: www.usc.edu
Support: CS • Institution type: 4-year private

LEARNING DISABILITY PROGRAM AND SERVICES

Disability Services and Programs is responsible for delivery of services to students with learning disabilities. It offers a comprehensive support program in the areas of educational therapy, content area tutoring, study skills instruction, special exam administration, liaison with textbook-taping services, advocacy, and network referral system. The learning specialists, graduate assistants, and learning assistants are available to students for academic therapy. A computer lab is available for computer-assisted learning and for word processing when working with a staff person. After admission, students with LD are counseled by advisors who dialogue with the learning specialist and who are sensitive to special needs. Educational counseling is done by the learning specialist. Off-campus referrals are made to students desiring comprehensive diagnostic testing. The support structure for students with documented learning disabilities is one that is totally individualized; there is no special program per se. Support is given at the request of the student. The learning disabilities specialist and/or grad assistants at USC are prepared to act as advocates when appropriate for any student experiencing academic problems that are related to the learning disability. USC aims to assure close, personal attention to its students even though it is a large campus.

LD/ADHD ADMISSIONS INFORMATION

College entrance tests required: Yes
Interview required: No
Essay recommended: Yes
Documentation required for LD: WAIS–III, WJ–II (achievement)
Documentation required for ADHD: Yes
Submitted to: Disability and Services and Programs
Special Ed. HS course work accepted: Yes

Specific course requirements of all applicants: Yes
Separate application required: NR
# of LD applications submitted each year: NR
# of LD applications accepted yearly: NR
Total # of students receiving LD services: 350
Acceptance into program means acceptance into college: Students must be admitted and enrolled in the university first and then request services.

ADMISSIONS

There are no special admissions for students with learning disabilities. Course requirements include 4 years of English, 3 years of math, 2 years of natural science, 2 years of social studies, 2 years of a foreign language, and 4 year-long electives. (The foreign language requirement is not waived in the admission process). It is helpful for comparison purposes to have both timed and untimed SAT or ACT test results. Transfer students are admitted on the basis of their college course work as well as the high school record. It is the student's responsibility to provide recent educational evaluations for documentation as part of the admissions application process. Testing must be current within 3 years, or 5 years for transfer or returning students.

ADDITIONAL INFORMATION

The services provided are modifications that are determined to be appropriate for students with LD. During the first 3 weeks of each semester, students are seen on a walk-in basis by the staff in the LD Support Services. Students requesting assistance must have a planning appointment with an LD specialist or grad assistant; provide a copy of the current class schedule; and be sure that eligibility has been determined by documenting specific learning disabilities. Learning assistance most often involves one-on-one attention for academic planning, scheduling, organization, and methods of compensation. Students may have standing appointments with learning assistants and subject tutors. After one "no-show" or three canceled appointments, standing appointments will be canceled. Course accommodations could include taping of lectures, note-taking, extended time for tests, use of word processor, proofreader, limiting scheduling of consecutive exams, and advocacy. Other services include support groups, counseling, and coaching.

LEARNING DISABILITY PROGRAM/SERVICES

Learning Disability Program/Services: Disability Services and Programs
Director: Edward Roth, PhD
  E-mail: eroth@usc.edu
  Telephone: 213-740-0776
  Fax: 213-740-8216
Contact Person: Dr. Patricia Tobey
  E-mail: ptobey@usc.edu
  Telephone: 213-740-0776
  Fax: 213-740-8216

LEARNING DISABILITY SERVICES

Requests for the following/services accommodations will be evaluated individually based on appropriate and current documentation.

Allowed in exams
  Calculator: NR
  Dictionary: NR
  Computer: Yes
  Spellchecker: Yes
Extended test time: Yes
Scribes: Yes
Proctors: Yes
Oral exams: No
Note-takers: Yes

Distraction-reduced environment: Yes
Tape recording in class: Yes
Books on tape from RFBD: Yes
Taping of books not from RFBD: Yes
Accommodations for students with ADHD: Yes
Reading machine: Yes
Other assistive technology: Yes
Priority registration: No

Added costs for services: No
LD specialists: Yes
Professional tutors: Yes
Peer tutors: 15
Max. hours/wk. for services: 2
How professors are notified of LD/ADHD: By both student and director

GENERAL ADMISSIONS INFORMATION

Director of Admissions: L. Katharine Harrington
Telephone: 213-740-6753

ENTRANCE REQUIREMENTS

Academic units required: 4 English, 3 math, 2 science (2 science labs), 2 foreign language, 2 social studies, 4 academic electives. **Academic units recommended:** 4 English, 4 math, 3 science (3 science labs), 3 foreign language, 3 social studies, 4 academic electives. High school diploma is required, and GED is not accepted. ACT with Writing component required.

Application deadline: 1/10
Notification: 4/1
Average GPA: 3.71
ACT Composite middle 50% range: 28–32

SAT Math middle 50% range: 650–740
SAT Critical Reading middle 50% range: 630–720
SAT Writing middle 50% range: 640–720

Graduated top 10% of class: 86%
Graduated top 25% of class: 97%
Graduated top 50% of class: 100%

COLLEGE GRADUATION REQUIREMENTS

Course waivers allowed: No
Course substitutions allowed: Yes
In what course: Students may petition for substitution for foreign language. LD specialtist decides if appeal is valid and writes a letter recommending course substitutions. Course valid for substitutions include literature in translation, linguistics, and classics.

ADDITIONAL INFORMATION

Environment: The university is located on 150 acres in an urban area, 2 miles south of downtown Los Angeles.

Student Body
  Undergrad enrollment: 16,449
  Women: 50%
  Men: 50%
  Percent out-of-state: 34%

Cost Information
  Tuition: $33,314
  Room & board: $10,144
Housing Information
  University housing: Yes
  Percent living on campus: 36%

Greek System
  Fraternity: Yes
  Sorority: Yes
Athletics: Division I

University of Southern California

UNIVERSITY OF THE PACIFIC

3601 Pacific Avenue, Stockton, CA 95211
Phone: 209-946-2211 • Fax: 209-946-2413
E-mail: admissions@pacific.edu • Web: www.pacific.edu
Support: S • Institution type: 4-year private

LEARNING DISABILITY PROGRAM AND SERVICES

There is no special program for students with learning disabilities, but the university does have a Learning Disabilities Support Program. This program offers assistance through tutoring, study skills classes, support groups, and testing accommodations. Documentation for LD must include psychoeducational evaluations from a professional. The documentation for ADHD must be from a medical doctor. Documentation should be sent to the Director of the Educational Resource Center. Students register for services after admission by contacting the Educational Resource Center. Student confidentiality is protected. The ultimate goal is for the student to earn a degree that is unmodified and unflagged. Faculty and staff are dedicated to providing students with learning disabilities all reasonable accommodations so that they may enjoy academic success. The LD Support Program helps keep UOP in compliance with the Americans with Disabilities Act and Section 504 of the Rehabilitation Act. Compliance is accomplished without compromising UOP standards, placing undue financial or administrative burden on the university, fundamentally altering the nature of programs, or extending unreasonable accommodations.

LD/ADHD ADMISSIONS INFORMATION

College entrance tests required: Yes
Interview required: No
Essay recommended: Yes
Documentation required for LD: Psychoeducational evaluation (no more than 3 to 5 years old)
Documentation required for ADHD: Yes (no more than 3 years old)
Submitted to: Office of Services for Students with Disabilities
Special Ed. HS course work accepted: Yes

Specific course requirements: NR
Separate application required: Yes
# of LD applications submitted each year: NR
# of LD applications accepted yearly: NR
Total # of students receiving LD services: 140–160
Acceptance into program means acceptance into college: Students must be admitted and enrolled in the university first and then request services.

ADMISSIONS

UOP welcomes students with learning disabilities. Although there is no special admission procedure, students are given special consideration. There is no minimum ACT/SAT requirement. There are two alternative methods for admissions: (1) probationary admissions for the marginal student—C/D average with no special requirements, but the university advisor is notified of status; no required test score; and no quota regarding the number of students admitted; and (2) special admissions—students who begin college courses in the summer prior to freshman year and receive at least a C average in two courses and one study skills class (can take those courses at any local community college).

ADDITIONAL INFORMATION

All admitted students are eligible for LD services with the appropriate assessment documentation. Academic Support Services offers services to improve learning opportunities for students with LD and are provided within reasonable limits. These services could include diagnostic assessment, accommodations for academic needs, taped texts, readers, tutorials for academic courses, and referrals to appropriate resources. Other related services include career development and guidance, counseling, and LD support groups. The Educational Resource Center is open to all students on campus. Skills courses for credit are available in reading, study skills, writing, and math. Services and accommodations are available for undergraduate and graduate students. The university offers a special summer program for precollege freshmen students with learning disabilities.

LEARNING DISABILITY PROGRAM/SERVICES

Learning Disability Program/Services: Office of Services for Students with Disabilities
Director: Lisa Cooper (Educational Resource Center)
  E-mail: lcooper@pacific.edu
  Telephone: 209-946-2458
  Fax: 209-946-2278
Contact Person: Daniel Nuss, Coordinator
  E-mail: dnuss@pacific.edu
  Telephone: 209-946-2879
  Fax: 209-946-2278

LEARNING DISABILITY SERVICES

Requests for the following/services accommodations will be evaluated individually based on appropriate and current documentation.

Allowed in exams
  Calculator: Yes
  Dictionary: Yes
  Computer: Yes
  Spellchecker: Yes
Extended test time: Yes
Scribes: Yes
Proctors: Yes
Oral exams: Yes
Note-takers: Yes

Distraction-reduced environment: Yes
Tape recording in class: Yes
Books on tape from RFBD: Yes
Taping of books not from RFBD: Yes
Accommodations for students with ADHD: Yes
Reading machine: Yes
Other assistive technology: Yes
Priority registration: Yes

Added costs for services: No
LD specialists: No
Professional tutors: Yes
Peer tutors: 80
Max. hours/wk. for services: 2
How professors are notified of LD/ADHD: By director

GENERAL ADMISSIONS INFORMATION

Director of Admissions: Marc McGee
Telephone: 209-946-2211

ENTRANCE REQUIREMENTS

Academic units recommended: 4 English, 3 math, 2 science lab, 2 foreign language, 3 social studies, 3 academic electives, 1 fine arts/performing arts. High school diploma is required, and GED is accepted. TOEFL required of all international applicants: minimum paper TOEFL 475, minimum computer TOEFL 150.

Application deadline: 1/10
Notification: 3/15
Average GPA: 3.46
ACT Composite middle 50% range: 22–27

SAT Math middle 50% range: 540–670
SAT Critical Reading middle 50% range: 500–620
SAT Writing middle 50% range: 500–610

Graduated top 10% of class: 42%
Graduated top 25% of class: 72%
Graduated top 50% of class: 93%

COLLEGE GRADUATION REQUIREMENTS

Course waivers allowed: Yes
Course substitutions allowed: Yes

ADDITIONAL INFORMATION

Environment: The university is located on 150 acres 90 miles east of San Francisco.

Student Body
  Undergrad enrollment: 3,535
  Women: 56%
  Men: 44%
  Percent out-of-state: 13%

Cost Information
  Tuition: $26,920
  Room & board: $8,700
Housing Information
  University housing: Yes
  Percent living on campus: 57%

Greek System
  Fraternity: Yes
  Sorority: Yes
Athletics: Division I

University of the Pacific

WHITTIER COLLEGE

13406 Philadelphia Street, PO Box 634, Whittier, CA 90608
Phone: 562-907-4238 • Fax: 562-907-4870
E-mail: admission@whittier.edu • Web: www.whittier.edu
Support: S • Institution type: 4-year private

LEARNING DISABILITY PROGRAM AND SERVICES

The Director of Disability Services provides assistance to students with documented disabilities. Accommodation requests are made through the director's office. Students with disabilities must make their needs known to the Director of Learning Support Services (LSS) to receive accommodations. To arrange for services, students must self-disclose the disability and make an individual appointment to discuss their accommodation requests with the director. Learning Support Services offers additional services: peer tutoring, workshops on study skills, and basic English and math skills assistance. These services are provided at no cost.

LD/ADHD ADMISSIONS INFORMATION

College entrance tests required: Yes
Interview required: No
Essay recommended: No
Documentation required for LD: The evaluation must minimally include the administration of a measure of intellectual ability (e.g., WAIS–III) and a measure of academic achievement (e.g., WAIS–II; WJ–III). The diagnosis of a learning disability must be based on established clinical criteria (e.g., DSM–IV).
Documentation required for ADHD: The documentation must be submitted by a clinician who is qualified to diagnose and treat psychological disorders. The evaluative methods used to establish the diagnosis should be indicated. A diagnosis consistent with established clinical criteria (e.g., DSM–IV) must be given. Indication of the person's present symptoms and their degree of impairment (e.g., Global Assessment of Function score) should be provided.
Submitted to: Disability Services

Specific course requirements of all applicants: Yes
Separate application required: No
# of LD applications submitted each year: 25–30
# of LD applications accepted yearly: NR
Total # of students receiving LD services: 22
Acceptance into program means acceptance into college: Student must be admitted and enrolled in the university first and then reviewed for LD services.

ADMISSIONS

There is no special admissions process for students with disabilities. All applicants are expected to meet the same admission criteria. Students must submit the ACT or SAT Reasoning and have a minimum of a 2.0 GPA; the recommended courses include 4 years of English, 3–4 years of math, 2–3 years of a foreign language, 2–3 years of social studies, and 2–3 years of science labs.

ADDITIONAL INFORMATION

The use of calculators, dictionaries, computers, or spellcheckers in exams would be considered on a case-by-case basis, depending on appropriate documentation and student needs. Students with appropriate documentation will have access to note-takers, readers, extended exam times, alternative exam locations, proctors, scribes, oral exams, books on tape, and priority registration. All students have access to a Math Lab, a Writing Center, a Learning Lab, and academic counseling.

LEARNING DISABILITY PROGRAM/SERVICES

Learning Disability Program/Services: Disability Services
Director: Rosalba B. Rios, MS
  E-mail: rrios@whittier.edu
  Telephone: 562-907-4840
  Fax: 562-907-4827

LEARNING DISABILITY SERVICES

Requests for the following/services accommodations will be evaluated individually based on appropriate and current documentation.

Allowed in exams
  Calculator: Yes
  Dictionary: Yes
  Computer: Yes
  Spellchecker: Yes
  Extended test time: Yes
  Scribes: Yes
  Proctors: Yes
  Oral exams: No
  Note-takers: Yes

Distraction-reduced environment: Yes
Tape recording in class: Yes
Books on tape from RFBD: Yes
Taping of books not from RFBD: Yes
Accommodations for students with
  ADHD: Yes
Reading machine: Yes
Other assistive technology: Yes
Priority registration: Yes

Added costs for services: No
LD specialists: No
Professional tutors: No
Peer tutors: 15–30
Max. hours/wk. for services:
  Unlimited
How professors are notified of
  LD/ADHD: By both student and director

GENERAL ADMISSIONS INFORMATION

Director of Admissions: Lisa Meyer, Vice President of Enrollment
Telephone: 562-907-4238

ENTRANCE REQUIREMENTS

Academic units required: 3 English, 3 math, 2 science (2 science lab), 2 foreign language, 2 social studies.
Academic units recommended: 4 English, 3 math, 3 science (3 science labs), 3 foreign language, 4 social studies. High school diploma is required, and GED is accepted. ACT with Writing component required. TOEFL required of all international applicants: minimum paper TOEFL 550, minimum computer TOEFL 230.

Application deadline: 2/1
Notification: Rolling
Average GPA: 3.12
ACT Composite middle 50% range:
  22–24

SAT Math middle 50% range:
  480–590
SAT Critical Reading middle 50%
  range: 480–590
SAT Writing middle 50% range: NR

Graduated top 10% of class: 27%
Graduated top 25% of class: 57%
Graduated top 50% of class: 88%

COLLEGE GRADUATION REQUIREMENTS

Course waivers allowed: Yes
In what course: Foreign language, math
Course substitutions allowed: Yes
In what course: Foreign language as an admissions requirement

ADDITIONAL INFORMATION

Environment: The college is on a suburban campus 20 miles southeast of Los Angeles.

Student Body
  Undergrad enrollment: 1,313
  Women: 54%
  Men: 46%
  Percent out-of-state: 30%

Cost Information
  Tuition: $27,906
  Room & board: $8,334
Housing Information
  University housing: Yes
  Percent living on campus: 59%

Greek System
  Fraternity: Yes
  Sorority: Yes
Athletics: Division III

COLORADO STATE U.—PUEBLO

Admissions, 2200 Bonforte Boulevard, Pueblo, CO 81001
Phone: 719-549-2461 • Fax: 719-549-2419
E-mail: info@colostate-pueblo.edu • Web: www.colostate-pueblo.edu
Support: S • Institution type: 4-year public

LEARNING DISABILITY PROGRAM AND SERVICES

The Disabilities Services Office, an affiliate of the Learning Assistance Center, strives to provide optimal services to students who have disabilities to enhance learning and increase retention. Students with LD or ADHD are encouraged to submit additional documentation, as well as letters of recommendation from counselors, teachers, or special education specialists. Documentation must include a comprehensive psychological evaluation with diagnostic and descriptive information of the disability to the learning environment with recommendations for specific accommodations.

LD/ADHD ADMISSIONS INFORMATION

College entrance tests required: Yes
Interview required: No
Essay recommended: No
Documentation required for LD: The most recent aptitude and achievement tests and narrative explaining the results: completed within the past 3 years and conducted using adult measures.
Documentation required for ADHD: Documentation must come from an appropriate diagnostician; include early impairment and current impairment and should include a diagnostic battery; include a diagnostic report and a summary; and be current (completed within the past 3 years).
Submitted to: Disability Services Office

Specific course requirements: NR
Separate application required: No
# of LD applications submitted each year: NR
# of LD applications accepted yearly: NR
Total # of students receiving LD services: NR
Acceptance into program means acceptance into college: Students must be admitted and enrolled in the university first and then request services.

ADMISSIONS

All first-time freshmen must submit their high school transcripts with GPA and ACT/SAT scores along with the general application. There is no special admission procedure for students with disabilities, but all information submitted will be considered in making an admission decision. Twenty percent of the freshmen applicants are eligible for admission based on criteria in addition to GPA and test scores. Students who do not meet the general admission criteria should submit letters of recommendation with information describing their ability to be successful in the university curriculum. Since there are no course requirements for admission, only recommendations, waivers are not necessary.

ADDITIONAL INFORMATION

Skills classes are offered in note-taking strategies, study skills, and textbook-reading strategies. The request for the use of a dictionary, computer, or spellchecker during exams will depend on the student's documented needs and permission from the professor. Students with specific needs are encouraged to provide documentation that specifically identifies the disability and the accommodations identified to compensate for it. Services and accommodations are available for undergraduate and graduate students.

LEARNING DISABILITY PROGRAM/SERVICES

Learning Disability Program/Services: Disability Resource Office
Director: John Meister
  E-mail: john.meister@colostate-pueblo.edu
  Telephone: 719-549-2663
  Fax: 719-549-2195

LEARNING DISABILITY SERVICES

Requests for the following/services accommodations will be evaluated individually based on appropriate and current documentation.

Allowed in exams
  Calculator: Yes
  Dictionary: Yes
  Computer: Yes
  Spellchecker: Yes
Extended test time: Yes
Scribes: Yes
Proctors: Yes
Oral exams: Yes
Note-takers: Yes

Distraction-reduced environment: Yes
Tape recording in class: Yes
Books on tape from RFBD: Yes
Taping of books not from RFBD: Yes
Accommodations for students with ADHD: Yes
Reading machine: Yes
Other assistive technology: Yes
Priority registration: No

Added costs for services: No
LD specialists: No
Professional tutors: No
Peer tutors: No
Max. hours/wk. for services: As needed
How professors are notified of LD/ADHD: By student

GENERAL ADMISSIONS INFORMATION

Director of Admissions: Joseph Marshall
Telephone: 719-549-2462

ENTRANCE REQUIREMENTS

Academic units recommended: 4 English, 3 math, 3 science (2 science labs), 2 foreign language, 2 social studies, 1 history. High school diploma is required, and GED is accepted. ACT with or without Writing component accepted. TOEFL required of all international applicants: minimum paper TOEFL 500, minimum computer TOEFL 173.

Application deadline: 8/1
Notification: As received
Average GPA: 3.10
ACT Composite middle 50% range: 18–23

SAT Math middle 50% range: 410–530
SAT Critical Reading middle 50% range: 400–510
SAT Writing middle 50% range: NR

Graduated top 10% of class: 0%
Graduated top 25% of class: 7%
Graduated top 50% of class: 32%

COLLEGE GRADUATION REQUIREMENTS

Course substitutions allowed: Yes
In what course: Possibly math with appropriate documentation

ADDITIONAL INFORMATION

Environment: The university is located in an urban area 100 miles south of Denver.

Student Body
  Undergrad enrollment: 4,104
  Women: 59%
  Men: 41%
  Percent out-of-state: 3%

Cost Information
  In-state tuition: $4,115
  Out-of-state tuition: $14,750
  Room & board: $7,450
Housing Information
  University housing: Yes
  Percent living on campus: 15%

Greek System
  Fraternity: Yes
  Sorority: Yes
Athletics: Division II

REGIS UNIVERSITY

3333 Regis Boulevard, A-12, Denver, CO 80221-1099
Phone: 303-458-4900 • Fax: 303-964-5534
E-mail: regisadm@regis.edu/college.asp • Web: www.regis.edu
Support: CS • Institution type: 4-year private

LEARNING DISABILITY PROGRAM AND SERVICES

Regis University does not have a specific structured program for students with LD/ADHD. Regis's philosophy is a commitment to ensure equal opportunities for students with disabilities to succeed by providing equal access. Disability Services provides services to all students with documented disabilities on an individualized basis. The Freshman Commitment Program is not specifically for students with LD/ADHD, though students with disabilities may be in the program. This program is not connected with Disability Services. Recommendations from high school teachers and evidence of extracurricular activities, as well as all other information a student provides, are considered for inclusion in this program. The goals of the Commitment Program are to provide a means for underachieving students to enter college and the support needed to be successful learners and help students develop the analytical processes that lead to high achievement. Students remain in the program for two semesters. To be successful, students must attend and pass all required commitment courses with a C or better; cannot fall below a 2.0 GPA in noncommitment courses; may not participate in varsity sports, forensics, or other activities that could interfere with class attendance; and must limit outside work, events, or other extracurricular activities that could impact their scholastic success.

LD/ADHD ADMISSIONS INFORMATION

College entrance tests required: Yes
Interview required: No
Essay recommended: No
Documentation required for LD: Psychoeducational evaluation
Documentation required for ADHD: Testing by a certifiied professional
Submitted to: Disability Services

Specific course requirements: NR
Separate application required: No
# of LD applications submitted each year: 90
# of LD applications accepted yearly: 20
Total # of students receiving LD services: 1–150
Acceptance into program means acceptance into college: Students are reviewed by Freshman Commitment and a recommendation is provided to the Admissions Committee for a final decision.

ADMISSIONS

There is no special admission procedure for students with learning disabilities. Although an interview is not required, the college would prefer that the student visit the school and have a minimum GPA of 2.56, an SAT of 930, or ACT of 20 and 15 academic units. Students may be considered with 17 ACT or 810 SAT and 2.3 GPA. Students need to show sufficient evidence of motivation and ability to succeed in college, even though they may not have the required GPA or test scores. Recommendations from counselors and evidence of extracurricular activities will be used in the committee's decision-making process. Students admitted on probation are typically students with stronger test scores and lower GPAs. These students are admitted into the college's degree program on one semester probation. They must have a 2.0 GPA to return the second semester. Other students may be admitted into the Freshman Commitment Program. These students usually have lower test scores and C-plus average, and the probationary admission is for two semesters.

ADDITIONAL INFORMATION

Disability Services provides the following services for students with appropriate documentation: self-advocacy training; test-taking and learning strategies assistance; a mentoring program; note-takers; readers; scribes; extended testing time; course substitutions; and priority registration. Students in the Commitment Program remain for one year and, with successful completion, are officially admitted to the college. They must pass all required commitment courses with a C or better, not fall below a 2.0 GPA in non-Commitment course work, and agree not to participate in varsity sports or other activities that may interfere with class attendance while involved in the program. There are learning support courses, study groups, and tutorials as needed. Three study rooms are staffed by tutors during the daytime and in the evening. All students must pass 3 hours of math, but there is a math learning support course or a remedial math class available for students to take prior to taking the regular college algebra class. The program offers learning support classes in reading skills, writing skills, and study skills, which apply toward elective credit. Special advising, tutoring, diagnostic academic testing, and study and testing assistance are other services offered.

LEARNING DISABILITY PROGRAM/SERVICES

Learning Disability Program/Services: Disability Services
Director: Marijo (Joie) Williams
  E-mail: mwillia@regis.edu
  Telephone: 303-458-4941
  Fax: 303-964-3647

LEARNING DISABILITY SERVICES

Requests for the following/services accommodations will be evaluated individually based on appropriate and current documentation.

Allowed in exams
  Calculator: Yes
  Dictionary: Yes
  Computer: Yes
  Spellchecker: Yes
Extended test time: Yes
Scribes: Yes
Proctors: Yes
Oral exams: Yes
Note-takers: Yes

Distraction-reduced environment: Yes
Tape recording in class: Yes
Books on tape from RFBD: Yes
Taping of books not from RFBD: Yes
Accommodations for students with ADHD: Yes
Reading machine: Yes
Other assistive technology: Yes
Priority registration: Yes

Added costs for services: No
LD specialists: Yes
Professional tutors: No
Peer tutors: 22
Max. hours/wk. for services: Unlimited
How professors are notified of LD/ADHD: By student

GENERAL ADMISSIONS INFORMATION

Director of Admissions: Vic Davolt
Telephone: 303-458-4900

ENTRANCE REQUIREMENTS

Academic units recommended: 4 English, 2 math, 2 science, 2 foreign language, 2 social studies, 1 history. High school diploma is required, and GED is accepted. TOEFL required of all international applicants: minimum paper TOEFL 550, minimum computer TOEFL 213.

Application deadline: Rolling
Notification: Rolling
Average GPA: 3.24
ACT Composite middle 50% range: 21–26

SAT Math middle 50% range: 480–600
SAT Critical Reading middle 50% range: 490–590
SAT Writing middle 50% range: NR

Graduated top 10% of class: 21%
Graduated top 25% of class: 47%
Graduated top 50% of class: 79%

COLLEGE GRADUATION REQUIREMENTS

Course waivers allowed: Yes
In what course: All students must take 3 hours of math. Foreign culture courses are substituted for foreign language if the documentation verifies a disability.
Course substitutions allowed: Yes
In what course: All students must take 3 hours of math. Foreign culture courses are substituted for foreign language if the documentation verifies a disability.

ADDITIONAL INFORMATION

Environment: The university is on a 90-acre campus in a suburban area of Denver.

Student Body
  Undergrad enrollment: 5,430
  Women: 62%
  Men: 38%
  Percent out-of-state: 24%

Cost Information
  Tuition: $23,700
  Room & board: $8,190
Housing Information
  University housing: Yes
  Percent living on campus: 8%

Greek System
  Fraternity: No
  Sorority: No
Athletics: Division II

U. OF COLORADO—BOULDER

552 UCB, Boulder, CO 80309-0552
Phone: 303-492-6301 • Fax: 303-492-7115
E-mail: apply@colorado.edu • Web: www.colorado.edu/prospective
Support: CS • Institution type: 4-year public

LEARNING DISABILITY PROGRAM AND SERVICES

The Academic Access and Resource Program (AAR) is a component of Disability Services. The AAR Program provides services to students with nonvisible disabilities such as learning disabilities, attention deficit hyperactivity disorder, head injuries, and psychiatric disabilities. The philosophy is that a student with a disability can be successful in a competitive postsecondary environment given self-acknowledgment of the disability and appropriate support services. Inherent in this philosophy is the importance of the student understanding his or her diagnostic profile so that relevant learning strategies can be learned and applied. The goal is for the student to become an independent learner who takes ownership and responsibility for the learning process. This process begins with the student understanding his or her areas of strengths and weaknesses, then building both awareness of needs and the development of appropriate compensatory strategies and building a network of resources. A profile of individual strengths and weaknesses is developed between the student and diagnostician. This information enables the student to understand how learning occurs and how strategies may be developed. Students need to be aware that there are no waivers or substitutions provided at the university. The goal of the program is to help students be successful within this academic community and provide them with skills and tools to be productive members of society.

LD/ADHD ADMISSIONS INFORMATION

College entrance tests required: Yes
Interview required: No
Essay recommended: No
Documentation required for LD: See documentation
  requirements on the Disability Services website at
  www.colorado.edu/disabilityservices.
Documentation required for ADHD: See documentation
  requirements on the Disability Services website at
  www.colorado.edu/disabilityservices.
Submitted to: Disability Services

Specific course requirements of all applicants: Yes
Separate application required: No
# of LD applications submitted each year: NR
# of LD applications accepted yearly: NR
Total # of students receiving LD services: 300–350
**Acceptance into program means acceptance into
  college:** Student must be admitted and enrolled in the
  university first and then reviewed for LD services.

ADMISSIONS

There is no special admission process for students with LD. All students are considered under the same competitive admissions criteria. All application information should be submitted to admissions by February 15, but documentation should be submitted directly to Disability Services. For the College of Arts and Sciences, minimum academic requirements include 4 years of English, 3 years of math, 3 years of natural science (must include chemistry or physics and 2 years science lab), 3 years of social science (including geography), and 3 years of foreign language. UC—Boulder is a competitive institution and admitted students must meet the same requirements as all other students. Graduation requirements are never waived. Students with documented LD/ADHD who struggle with foreign language learning may qualify for enrollment in the Modified Foreign Language Program. Students who struggle with math need to speak with a disability specialist about options for satisfying this requirement. SAT or the ACT for admission consideration. Your highest scores are used in the admission decision. Students' highest scores are used in the admission decision. Combined highest subsection scores are used if the same test is taken more than once.

ADDITIONAL INFORMATION

Services are provided through Disability Services, of which AAR is a component. The AAR Program provides an opportunity to meet with a disability specialist to work on academic strategies. If tutoring is needed, the disability specialist can refer the student to the appropriate resources, but the student pays for the service. Other services include advocacy and support, an evening Writing Lab, an Assistive Technology Lab, and a career program for students with disabilities. Lectures may be taped with the professor's permission. Priority registration is provided only if it directly responds to the disability. Support services and accommodations are available to undergraduate and graduate students who provide documentation of a disability. Students may seek an assessment to determine the possibility of the existence of a learning disability. The AAR will respond to all students with appropriate documentation who request services.

LEARNING DISABILITY PROGRAM/SERVICES

Learning Disability Program/Services: Disability Services
Director: Cindy Donahue
  E-mail: dsinfo@colorado.edu
  Telephone: 303-492-8671
  Fax: 303-492-5601
Contact Person: Jim Cohn, Coordinator of Academic Resource Team
  E-mail: dsinfo@colorado.edu
  Telephone: 303-492-8671
  Fax: 303-492-5601

LEARNING DISABILITY SERVICES

Requests for the following/services accommodations will be evaluated individually based on appropriate and current documentation.

Allowed in exams
  Calculator: Yes
  Dictionary: No
  Computer: Yes
  Spellchecker: Yes
Extended test time: Yes
Scribes: Yes
Proctors: Yes
Oral exams: No
Note-takers: Yes

Distraction-reduced environment: Yes
Tape recording in class: Yes
Books on tape from RFBD: Yes
Taping of books not from RFBD: Yes
Accommodations for students with ADHD: Yes
Reading machine: No
Other assistive technology: Yes
Priority registration: Yes

Added costs for services: No
LD specialists: Yes
Professional tutors: No
Peer tutors: No
Max. hours/wk. for services: Varies
How professors are notified of LD/ADHD: By student

GENERAL ADMISSIONS INFORMATION

Director of Admissions: Kevin MacLennan
Telephone: 303-492-6301

ENTRANCE REQUIREMENTS

Academic units required: 4 English, 3 math, 3 science (2 science labs), 3 foreign language, 3 social studies, 1 history, 1 geography. High school diploma is required, and GED is accepted. ACT with or without Writing component accepted. TOEFL required of all international applicants: minimum paper TOEFL 500, minimum computer TOEFL 173.

Application deadline: 1/15
Notification: Rolling
Average GPA: 3.53
ACT Composite middle 50% range: 23–28

SAT Math middle 50% range: 540–650
SAT Critical Reading middle 50% range: 520–630
SAT Writing middle 50% range: NR

Graduated top 10% of class: 23%
Graduated top 25% of class: 54%
Graduated top 50% of class: 90%

COLLEGE GRADUATION REQUIREMENTS

Course waivers allowed: No
Course substitutions allowed: Yes
In what course: Decisions on academic requirements are within the domain of the academic deans. Decisions are made on an individualized basis. There are no waivers/substitutions for entrance to College of Arts and Science.

ADDITIONAL INFORMATION

Environment: The school is located at the base of the Rocky Mountains, 45 minutes from Denver.

Student Body
  Undergrad enrollment: 25,495
  Women: 47%
  Men: 53%
  Percent out-of-state: 31%

Cost Information
  In-state tuition: $5,375
  Out-of-state tuition: $23,825
  Room & board: $8,300
Housing Information
  University housing: Yes
  Percent living on campus: 26%

Greek System
  Fraternity: Yes
  Sorority: Yes
Athletics: Division I

University of Colorado—Boulder

UNIVERSITY OF COLORADO—COLORADO SPRINGS

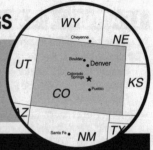

Admissions Office, PO Box 7150, Colorado Springs, CO 80933-7150
Phone: 719-262-3383 • Fax: 719-262-3116
E-mail: admrec@uccs.edu • Web: www.uccs.edu
Support: CS • Institution type: 4-year public

LEARNING DISABILITY PROGRAM AND SERVICES

University of Colorado—Colorado Springs is committed to providing equal educational opportunity for all students who meet the academic admission requirements. The purpose of Disability Services is to provide comprehensive support to meet the individual needs of students with disabilities. Students are expected to utilize the resources of Disability Services to the degree they determine necessary.

LD/ADHD ADMISSIONS INFORMATION

College entrance tests required: Yes
Interview required: No
Essay recommended: No
Documentation required for LD: WAIS–II, WJ–III or alternative testing from a qualified professional
Documentation required for ADHD: Documentation from a qualified professional who has diagnosed the student's ADHD
Submitted to: Disability Services
Special Ed. HS course work accepted: No

Specific course requirements of all applicants: Yes
Separate application required: No
# of LD applications submitted each year: NR
# of LD applications accepted yearly: NR
Total # of students receiving LD services: 40
Acceptance into program means acceptance into college: Student must be admitted and enrolled in the university first and then reviewed for LD services.

ADMISSIONS

An applicant's learning disability is not considered in an admission decision. All applicants are required to meet the Minimum Academic Preparation Standards (MAPS), including 4 years of English, 3 years of math (4 years for engineering and business), 3 years of natural science, 2 years of social science, 2 years of a foreign language, and 1 year of an elective; fine and performing arts are encouraged. Courses taken before 9th grade are accepted as long as the documentation provided shows that the courses were completed. American Sign Language is a qualified substitute for a foreign language.Successfully completing 2 years of a foreign language will satisfy the foreign language requirement regardless of whether the courses were taken before the 9th grade. Students with deficiencies may be admitted to the university provided they meet the other admission standards of test scores, rank in class, and GPA (minimum of 2.8), provided they make up any deficiencies in the MAPS prior to graduation.

ADDITIONAL INFORMATION

Students with learning disabilities receive information in their acceptance letter about contacting Disability Services if they wish to request accommodations or services. Students must request services and submit appropriate documentation. Students must meet with Disability Services to discuss support services and/or accommodations that are appropriate. Strategy development is offered in study skills, reading, test performance, stress reduction, time management, and writing skills. Disability Services offers the use of volunteers who use carbonless paper provided by the support services. Services and accommodations are available for undergraduate and graduate students with learning disabilities. Tutors are available for all university students in labs; tutors are also provided for students with disabilities.

LEARNING DISABILITY PROGRAM/SERVICES

Learning Disability Program/Services: Disability Services
Director: Kaye Simonton
  E-mail: ksimonton@uccs.edu
  Telephone: 719-262-3354
  Fax: 719-262-3195

LEARNING DISABILITY SERVICES

Requests for the following/services accommodations will be evaluated individually based on appropriate and current documentation.

Allowed in exams
  Dictionary: Yes
  Computer: Yes
  Spellchecker: Yes
Extended test time: Yes
Scribes: Yes
Proctors: Yes
Oral exams: Yes
Note-takers: No

Distraction-reduced environment: Yes
Tape recording in class: Yes
Books on tape from RFBD: Yes
Taping of books not from RFBD: Yes
Accommodations for students with
  ADHD: Yes
Reading machine: Yes
Other assistive technology: Yes
Priority registration: No

Added costs for services: No
LD specialists: Yes
Professional tutors: No
Peer tutors: No
Max. hours/wk. for services: N/A
How professors are notified of
  LD/ADHD: By student

GENERAL ADMISSIONS INFORMATION

Director of Admissions: Steve Ellis
Telephone: 719-262-3375

ENTRANCE REQUIREMENTS

Academic units required: 4 English, 3 math, 3 science (2 science labs), 2 foreign language, 2 social studies, 1 academic elective. **Academic units recommended:** 4 English, 4 math, 3 science (2 science labs), 2 foreign language, 2 social studies, 1 academic elective. High school diploma is required, and GED is accepted. ACT with or without Writing component accepted. TOEFL required of all international applicants: minimum paper TOEFL 550, minimum computer TOEFL 213.

Application deadline: 7/1
Notification: Rolling
Average GPA: 3.36
ACT Composite middle 50% range:
  20–25

SAT Math middle 50% range:
  470–610
SAT Critical Reading middle 50%
  range: 470–590
SAT Writing middle 50% range:
  450–560

Graduated top 10% of class: 16%
Graduated top 25% of class: 42%
Graduated top 50% of class: 78%

COLLEGE GRADUATION REQUIREMENTS

Course waivers allowed: No
In what course: N/A
Course substitutions allowed: Yes
In what course: American Sign Language is accepted as a foreign language.

ADDITIONAL INFORMATION

Environment: The university has an urban campus 70 miles south of Denver.

Student Body
  Undergrad enrollment: 6,098
  Women: 60%
  Men: 40%
  Percent out-of-state: 7%

Cost Information
  In-state tuition: $5,490
  Out-of-state tuition: $22,950
  Room & board: $7,662
Housing Information
  University housing: Yes
  Percent living on campus: 10%

Greek System
  Fraternity: No
  Sorority: Yes
Athletics: Division II

UNIVERSITY OF DENVER

Office of Admission, 2197 South University Boulevard, Denver, CO 80208
Phone: 303-871-2036 • Fax: 303-871-3301
E-mail: admission@du.edu • Web: www.du.edu/admission
Support: SP • Institution type: 4-year private

LEARNING DISABILITY PROGRAM AND SERVICES

Learning Effectiveness Program (LEP) is a comprehensive program structured to provide students with individualized support. LEP counselors work one-on-one with students to determine their learning strengths and develop skills that will make them successful university students. Three crucial areas of skill development are encouraged: self-advocacy, articulation of strengths and weaknesses, and independent learning strategies. Cognitive strategy development is a basic part of individual sessions with a learning specialist. Students participate in regular course work and do not take special classes. One major focus of the LEP is reducing anxiety about learning in a college environment. Students learn how to focus on higher-level thought processes to compensate for lower-level processing deficits. They are also taught nontraditional study skills designed to increase reading, writing, and memory. Students are treated as responsible adults and are expected to participate in the program willingly.

LD/ADHD ADMISSIONS INFORMATION

College entrance tests required: Yes
Interview required: No
Essay recommended: Yes
Documentation required for LD: A full psychoeducational evaluation completed within the past 3 years. Ideally, an aptitude test and achievement test, though not strictly tied to a discrepancy model for diagnosis.
Documentation required for ADHD: Psychoeducational evaluation or comprehensive neuropsychological by qualified professional stating the presence of ADHD
Submitted to: Learning Effectiveness Program
Special Ed. HS course work accepted: No

Specific course requirements: NR
Separate application required: Yes
# of LD applications submitted each year: 300
# of LD applications accepted yearly: 95
Total # of students receiving LD services: NR
Acceptance into program means acceptance into college: Student must be admitted first to the university to enroll in the LEP.

ADMISSIONS

Admission to the university and LEP are two distinct processes. All potential candidates with LD/ADHD must submit a general admissions application, essay, recommendations, activity sheet, high school transcript, and ACT/SAT scores. Applicants must be admitted to the university prior to being admitted to the LEP Program. Students applying to LEP must also provide documentation of LD/ADHD; recent diagnostic tests; the completed LEP Intake Form provided on disclosure of an LD; and a letter from a counselor, teacher, or LD specialist. The verification form from an appropriate specialist is critical and should describe the student's learning deficit and the support services necessary for success. Strengths, weaknesses, maturity level, ability to handle frustration, and feelings about limitations should also be included in documentation sent to the LEP. A successful background in college-prep classes is desirable. The minimum GPA is 3.1. A campus visit and interview are recommended after submission of all documentation and testing. Interviews should be scheduled as far in advance as possible.

ADDITIONAL INFORMATION

LEP services are only available to students who are enrolled in the program. The LEP is a fee-for-service program that provides services beyond the mandated services provided under Section 504. There is a $2,550 fee per year for this program. The director and associate director are LD specialists, and the staff is composed of professionals in a variety of academic disciplines. The LEP provides a variety of services designed to support each student's academic experience, including individual academic counselors, professional tutoring, and organizational and study strategies specialists. Our philosophy emphasizes student responsibility, self-awareness, and self-advocacy. Students who feel that they need only basic accommodations and do not wish to participate in the comprehensive program should contact Disability Services Program at 303-871-2455 to make those arrangements. The use of a calculator, dictionary, computer, and/or spellchecker requires the professor's permission. Services and accommodations are available for undergraduate and graduate students. Learning disability assessments are available on campus.

LEARNING DISABILITY PROGRAM/SERVICES

Learning Disability Program/Services: Learning Effectiveness Program/Disability Services Program
Director: Ted F. May Director, LEP/DSP
  E-mail: tmay@du.edu
  Telephone: 303-871-2372
  Fax: 303-871-3939
Contact Person: Jane Parks, Enrollment Coordinator, Learning Effectiveness Program
  E-mail: jparks2@du.edu
  Telephone: 303-871-2372
  Fax: 303-871-3939

LEARNING DISABILITY SERVICES

Requests for the following/services accommodations will be evaluated individually based on appropriate and current documentation.

Allowed in exams	**Distraction-reduced environment:** Yes	**Added costs for services:** Yes
Calculator: Yes	**Tape recording in class:** Yes	**LD specialists:** Yes
Computer: Yes	**Taping of books not from RFBD:** Yes	**Professional tutors:** 30
Spellchecker: No	**Accommodations for students with**	**Peer tutors:** Yes
Extended test time: Yes	**ADHD:** Yes	**Max. hours/wk. for services:**
Scribes: Yes	**Reading machine:** Yes	Unlimited
Proctors: Yes	**Other assistive technology:** Yes	**How professors are notified of**
Oral exams: Yes	**Priority registration:** Yes	**LD/ADHD:** By student
Note-takers: Yes		

GENERAL ADMISSIONS INFORMATION

Director of Admissions: Tom Willoughby, Vice Chancellor for Enrollment
Telephone: 303-871-3383

ENTRANCE REQUIREMENTS

Academic units recommended: 4 English, 4 math, 4 science (2 science labs), 3 foreign language, 2 social studies, 2 history. Interview required. Essay required. High school diploma is required, and GED is accepted. ACT with or without Writing component accepted. TOEFL required of all international applicants: minimum paper TOEFL 525, minimum computer TOEFL 193.

Application deadline: 1/15	**SAT Math middle 50% range:**	**Graduated top 10% of class:** 35%
Notification: 3/15	540–650	**Graduated top 25% of class:** 67%
Average GPA: 3.58	**SAT Critical Reading middle 50%**	**Graduated top 50% of class:** 92%
ACT Composite middle 50% range:	**range:** 530–640	
23–28	**SAT Writing middle 50% range:** NR	

COLLEGE GRADUATION REQUIREMENTS

Course waivers allowed: No
Course substitutions allowed: Yes
In what course: In the area of foreign language, students may qualify to take substitution courses that still expose them to new cultures and identities but do not have the intensive grammar component.

ADDITIONAL INFORMATION

Environment: The university has a 230-acre campus 7 miles southeast of Denver.

Student Body	**Cost Information**	**Greek System**
Undergrad enrollment: 5,092	**Tuition:** $28,400	**Fraternity:** Yes
Women: 55%	**Room & board:** $8,000	**Sorority:** Yes
Men: 45%	**Housing Information**	**Athletics:** Division I
Percent out-of-state: 53%	**University housing:** Yes	
	Percent living on campus: 46%	

University of Denver

UNIVERSITY OF NORTHERN COLORADO

UNC Admissions Office, Campus Box 10, Greeley, CO 80639
Phone: 970-351-2881 • Fax: 970-351-2984
E-mail: admissions.help@unco.edu • Web: www.unco.edu
Support: S • Institution type: 4-year public

LEARNING DISABILITY PROGRAM AND SERVICES

Although the university does not offer a formal LD program, individual assistance is provided whenever possible. The Disability Access Center (DAC) provides access, accommodations, and advocacy for UNC students who have documented disabilities. Academic needs are determined by the documentation and a student interview. Students with disabilities have an equal opportunity to pursue their educational goals. DAC provides test accommodations, adaptive hardware and software, learning strategies, organizational skills, and a reader program. Students requesting accommodations at UNC must provide test instruments from a certified professional that measures general intellect, aptitude, and more specific information processing tests; academic and vocational measures of achievement; and a clinical interview, which is the primary measure of previous educational and psychological functioning. Suggestions of reasonable accommodations that may be appropriate at the postsecondary level are encouraged. These recommendations should be supported by the diagnosis. Students with ADHD must provide a medical or clinical diagnosis from a developmental pediatrician, neurologist, and psychiatrist, licensed clinical or educational psychologist, family physician, or a combination of such professionals.

LD/ADHD ADMISSIONS INFORMATION

College entrance tests required: Yes
Interview required: Yes
Essay recommended: No
Documentation required for LD: Current psychological evaluation, including aptitude and achievement. See the site map for documentation guidelines at www.unco.edu/dss.
Documentation required for ADHD: See the site map for documentation guidelines at www.unco.edu/dss.
Submitted to: Disability Access Center
Special Ed. HS course work accepted: Yes

Specific course requirements of all applicants: Yes
Separate application required: No
# of LD applications submitted each year: 100-120
# of LD applications accepted yearly: NR
Total # of students receiving LD services: 160
Acceptance into program means acceptance into college: Students must be admitted and enrolled in the university first and then request services.

ADMISSIONS
There is no special admission process for students with learning disabilities. All students with disabilities are admitted to UNC under the standard admission requirements of the university. The university uses class rank, GPA, and test scores to determine a selection index. UNC requires 3 years of math, and the classes must be college-prep. Pre-Algebra does not count. UNC recommends 4 years of English, 3 years of history/social sciences, and 3 years of natural science. When UNC evaluates a transcript for admissions, they only look at the math. The UNC has a special window for admitting students who do not meet UNC's freshman admission requirements but want to earn full admission into a degree program. Students wishing to participate in this program need to call the Admissions Office. Each applicant is judged on an individual basis. Students do not need to be LD to apply for this DAC program but must have a documented disability. To assist in determining eligibility for the program, current medical/clinical information is necessary. To receive services, students must request accommodations upon arrival at UNC. Students enrolled in the Challenge Program must take 12 hours of college credit and earn a GPA of 2.0 after one or two semesters to remain at UNC.

ADDITIONAL INFORMATION
Services for individuals with LD/ADHD includes learning strategies, organizational skills, and advocacy skills; reader program; test accommodations; assistance in arranging for note-takers; and assistive technology, including voice synthesizers, screen readers, screen enlargers, scanners, voice-recognition computer systems, large monitors, and word processing with spellchecker. Workshops are offered in student skills, organizational skills, study strategies, and time management. These workshops are electives and are not for credit. There is a support group for students with LD/ADHD, facilitated by DAC staff, which assists students in developing a support network. Services and accommodations are available for undergraduate and graduate students.

LEARNING DISABILITY PROGRAM/SERVICES

Learning Disability Program/Services: Disability Access Center
Director: Nancy Kauffman
  E-mail: nancy.kauffman@unco.edu
  Telephone: 970-351-2289
  Fax: 970-351-4166

LEARNING DISABILITY SERVICES

Requests for the following/services accommodations will be evaluated individually based on appropriate and current documentation.

Allowed in exams
  Calculator: Yes
  Dictionary: Yes
  Computer: Yes
  Spellchecker: Yes
Extended test time: Yes
Scribes: Yes
Proctors: Yes
Oral exams: Yes
Note-takers: Yes

Distraction-reduced environment: Yes
Tape recording in class: Yes
Books on tape from RFBD: Yes
Taping of books not from RFBD: Yes
Accommodations for students with ADHD: Yes
Reading machine: Yes
Other assistive technology: Yes
Priority registration: Yes

Added costs for services: No
LD specialists: No
Professional tutors: No
Peer tutors: 20
Max. hours/wk. for services: Varies
How professors are notified of LD/ADHD: By student

GENERAL ADMISSIONS INFORMATION

Director of Admissions: Gary Gullickson
Telephone: 970-351-2881

ENTRANCE REQUIREMENTS
Academic units required: 3 math. **Academic units recommended:** 4 English, 3 science (1 science lab), 3 social studies. High school diploma is required, and GED is accepted. ACT with or without Writing component accepted. TOEFL required of all international applicants: minimum paper TOEFL 520, minimum computer TOEFL 190.

Application deadline: 8/1
Notification: Rolling
Average GPA: 3.20
ACT Composite middle 50% range: 20–24

SAT Math middle 50% range: 470–580
SAT Critical Reading middle 50% range: 470–580
SAT Writing middle 50% range: NR

Graduated top 10% of class: 12%
Graduated top 25% of class: 31%
Graduated top 50% of class: 67%

COLLEGE GRADUATION REQUIREMENTS

Course waivers allowed: No
Course substitutions allowed: No

ADDITIONAL INFORMATION

Environment: The university is located on 240 acres in a small town 50 miles north of Denver.

Student Body
  Undergrad enrollment: 10,610
  Women: 61%
  Men: 39%
  Percent out-of-state: 9%

Cost Information
  In-state tuition: $3,840
  Out-of-state tuition: $12,380
  Room & board: $6,832
Housing Information
  University housing: Yes
  Percent living on campus: 32%

Greek System
  Fraternity: Yes
  Sorority: Yes
Athletics: Division I

WESTERN STATE COLLEGE OF COLORADO

600 North Adams Street, Gunnison, CO 81231
Phone: 970-943-2119 • Fax: 970-943-2212
E-mail: discover@western.edu • Web: www.western.edu
Support: S• Institution type: 4-year public

LEARNING DISABILITY PROGRAM AND SERVICES

Disability Services, located in Western's Learning Assistance Center, coordinates support services for all qualified students with disabilities. We offer a variety of resources and accommodations to assist students as they pursue their academic and career goals. While providing a supportive environment, we encourage students to develop independence and take responsibility for their academic experiences. Personal consultation and workshops are available to help students improve learning, problem-solving, and self-advocacy skills.

LD/ADHD ADMISSIONS INFORMATION

College entrance tests required: Yes
Interview required: No
Essay recommended: No
Documentation required for LD: Psychoeducational
  evaluation
Documentation required for ADHD: Yes
Submitted to: Disability Services
Special Ed. HS course work accepted: Yes

Specific course requirements of all applicants: Yes
Separate application required: No
# of LD applications submitted each year: NR
# of LD applications accepted yearly: NR
Total # of students receiving LD services: NR
Acceptance into program means acceptance into
  college: Students must be admitted and enrolled prior to
  requesting services.

ADMISSIONS

Admission to Western depends on academic performance and background, standardized test scores, and personal attributes. In addition to general admissions requirements, Western State recommends a personal essay and recommendations from teachers, counselors, or others who know the student's academic ability. The college tries to admit those students who have demonstrated their ability to succeed. Normally, students are admitted if they meet the following criteria: graduate from an accredited high school; have a cumulative GPA of 2.5 or better (on a 4.0 scale of college-prep courses) and/or rank in the upper two-thirds of the student's graduating class; and score 20 or higher on the ACT or 950 on the SAT. Western recommends 4 years of English, 3 years of mathematics to include Algebra II, 2 years of natural science, and 2 years of social science. Modern language and computer science units are also important.

ADDITIONAL INFORMATION

Students who choose to register for Learning Disability Program/Services typically do so soon after acceptance to Western. A Disability Services registration packet will be sent to accepted students who contact our office. We encourage students to meet with our staff during a campus visit or New Student Orientation and attend our Disability Services Welcome and Information Session, which is offered at the beginning of each semester to help students become familiar with policies, procedures, and resources. Some of the services used by students include, but are not limited to, test accommodations, taped textbooks, readers, scribes, note-takers, and assistance with academic advising and course registration. Individual learning skills assistance is availalble through appointments and workshops, our staff works with students to help them develop effective learning skills and study strategies in areas such as reading, memory, test taking, note-taking, organization, and time management. We encourage students who wish to enhance motivation, develop an understanding of individual learning styles, and improve academic performance to use the Learning Assistance Center's resources.

LEARNING DISABILITY PROGRAM/SERVICES

Learning Disability Program/Services: Disability Services
Director: Julie Luekenga
  E-mail: jluekenga@western.edu
  Telephone: 970.943.7056
  Fax: 970.943.3409

LEARNING DISABILITY SERVICES

Requests for the following/services accommodations will be evaluated individually based on appropriate and current documentation.

Allowed in exams
  Calculator: Yes
  Dictionary: No
  Computer: Yes
  Spellchecker: Yes
Extended test time: Yes
Scribes: Yes
Proctors: Yes
Oral exams: Yes
Note-takers: Yes

Distraction-reduced environment: Yes
Tape recording in class: Yes
Books on tape from RFBD: Yes
Taping of books not from RFBD: Yes
Accommodations for students with ADHD: Yes
Reading machine: Yes
Other assistive technology: Yes
Priority registration: Yes

Added costs for services: No
LD specialists: No
Professional tutors: No
Peer tutors: NR
Max. hours/wk. for services: NR
How professors are notified of LD/ADHD: By student

GENERAL ADMISSIONS INFORMATION

Director of Admissions: Assistant Vice President Tim Albers
Telephone: 970-943-2119

ENTRANCE REQUIREMENTS
Academic units required: 4 English, 3 math, 2 science (2 science labs), 2 social studies, 2 history, 3 academic electives. **Academic units recommended:** 4 English, 4 math, 3 science, 2 foreign language, 3 social studies, 3 history. High school diploma is required, and GED is accepted. ACT with or without Writing component accepted. TOEFL required of all international applicants: minimum paper TOEFL 550, minimum computer TOEFL 213.

Application deadline: 8/1
Notification: Rolling
Average GPA: 2.99
ACT Composite middle 50% range:
  18–23

SAT Math middle 50% range:
  460–550
SAT Critical Reading middle 50% range: 440–550
SAT Writing middle 50% range: NR

Graduated top 10% of class: 5%
Graduated top 25% of class: 21%
Graduated top 50% of class: 52%

COLLEGE GRADUATION REQUIREMENTS

Course waivers allowed: No
Course substitutions allowed: Yes
In what course: Math substitutions may be approved for students with documented math learning disabilies, when appropriate.

ADDITIONAL INFORMATION

Environment: Western State College of Colorado is located in the heart of the Rocky Mountains.

Student Body
  Undergrad enrollment: 2,152
  Women: 40%
  Men: 60%
  Percent out-of-state: 25%

Cost Information
  In-state tuition: $3,140
  Out-of-state tuition: $11,750
  Room & board: $7,200
Housing Information
  University housing: Yes
  Percent living on campus: 38%

Greek System
  Fraternity: Yes
  Sorority: Yes
Athletics: Division II

FAIRFIELD UNIVERSITY

1073 North Benson Road, Fairfield, CT 06824-5195
Phone: 203-254-4100 • Fax: 203-254-4199
E-mail: admis@mail.fairfield.edu • Web: www.fairfield.edu
Support: CS • Institution type: 4-year private

LEARNING DISABILITY PROGRAM AND SERVICES

The university provides services for students with disabilities through Student Support Services. There is no learning disability program, only services that are available for all students with disabilities. These services are designed to provide equal access to the learning environment. Students are supported while being encouraged to be self-advocates. Students with learning disabilities must provide documentation from an appropriate testing agent. For students with learning disabilities. Students with ADHD must have documentation from appropriate professionals who can provide behavior rating scales, ruling out other disabilities, and showing the onset of the ADHD between ages 7–12. All documentation should be submitted to Student Support Services.

LD/ADHD ADMISSIONS INFORMATION

College entrance tests required: Yes
Interview required: No
Essay recommended: No
Documentation required for LD: Psychoeducational evaluation
Documentation required for ADHD: Neuropsychological evaluation
Submitted to: Student Support Services
Special Ed. HS course work accepted: Yes

Specific course requirements of all applicants: Yes
Separate application required: No
# of LD applications submitted each year: NR
# of LD applications accepted yearly: NR
Total # of students receiving LD services: 150
Acceptance into program means acceptance into college: Students must be admitted and enrolled in the university first and then request services.

ADMISSIONS

There is no special admissions process for students with learning disabilities. Admission criteria include ranking in top 40 percent of graduating class or better; maintaining a B average; scoring 25 ACT; counselor recommendations; and college-prep courses including 4 years of English, 3–4 years of math, 2–4 years of a foreign language, 1–3 years of science lab, and 2–3 years of history. Courses taken in the Special Education Department may be acceptable. The mid 50 percent SAT Reasoning Test scores are 1120–1270, and ACT scores are 26–29. Once students have been admitted and have enrolled, they may initiate contact for services.

ADDITIONAL INFORMATION

Skills courses are offered in study skills, note-taking strategies, time management skills, and strategies for success. These skills courses are not for credit. Students are offered meetings with a professional who has a background in teaching students with disabilities. Letters are sent to professors on students' request. All students have access to content tutoring and a Writing Center. Services and accommodations are available for undergraduate and graduate students.

LEARNING DISABILITY PROGRAM/SERVICES

Learning Disability Program/Services: Student Support Services
Director: David Ryan-Soderlund
  E-mail: drsoderlund@mail.fairfield.edu
  Telephone: 203-254-4000 ext. 2615
  Fax: 203-254-5542

LEARNING DISABILITY SERVICES

Requests for the following/services accommodations will be evaluated individually based on appropriate and current documentation.

Allowed in exams
  Calculator: Yes
  Dictionary: Yes
  Computer: Yes
  Spellchecker: Yes
Extended test time: Yes
Scribes: Yes
Proctors: Yes
Oral exams: Yes
Note-takers: Yes

Distraction-reduced environment: Yes
Tape recording in class: Yes
Books on tape from RFBD: Yes
Taping of books not from RFBD: Yes
Accommodations for students with ADHD: Yes
Reading machine: Yes
Other assistive technology: Yes
Priority registration: No

Added costs for services: No
LD specialists: Yes
Professional tutors: No
Peer tutors: 90–120
Max. hours/wk. for services: Unlimited
How professors are notified of LD/ADHD: By student

GENERAL ADMISSIONS INFORMATION

Director of Admissions: Karen Pelligrino
Telephone: 203-254-4100

ENTRANCE REQUIREMENTS

Academic units required: 4 English, 3 math, 2 science (2 science labs), 2 foreign language, 2 social studies, 2 history, 1 academic elective. **Academic units recommended:** 4 English, 4 math, 3 science (2 science labs), 4 foreign language, 2 social studies, 2 history, 1 academic elective. High school diploma is required, and GED is not accepted. ACT with or without Writing component accepted. TOEFL required of all international applicants: minimum paper TOEFL 550, minimum computer TOEFL 213.

Application deadline: 1/15
Notification: 4/1
Average GPA: 3.47
ACT Composite middle 50% range: 25–27

SAT Math middle 50% range: 550–640
SAT Critical Reading middle 50% range: 540–630
SAT Writing middle 50% range: 780

Graduated top 10% of class: 12%
Graduated top 25% of class: 26%
Graduated top 50% of class: 98%

COLLEGE GRADUATION REQUIREMENTS

Course substitutions allowed: Yes
In what course: Foreign language, math (must have severe impairment)

ADDITIONAL INFORMATION

Environment: The university is located on 200 acres in a suburban area 60 miles northeast of New York City.

Student Body
  Undergrad enrollment: 3,675
  Women: 57%
  Men: 43%
  Percent out-of-state: 78%

Cost Information
  Tuition: $31,450
  Room & board: $9,980
Housing Information
  University housing: Yes
  Percent living on campus: 67%

Greek System
  Fraternity: No
  Sorority: No
Athletics: Division I

MITCHELL COLLEGE

437 Pequot Avenue, New London, CT 06320
Phone: 860-701-5011 • Fax: 860-444-1209
E-mail: admissions@mitchell.edu • Web: www.mitchell.edu
Support: SP • Institution type: 2-year and 4-year private

LEARNING DISABILITY PROGRAM AND SERVICES

Mitchell College is dedicated to providing a student-centered supportive learning environment that addresses the educational needs of all students, including those with LD, through associate's and baccalaureate degree programs. The Academic Support Center offers The Learning Resource Center whose mission is to provide a spectrum of academic support services to students with disabilities at three levels of support; a Tutoring Center for all students; and a Testing Center to monitor, proctor and administer tests and exams. There are three levels of support for the LRC. Level I, which encompasses the most comprehensive enhanced services, is a fee-based program that includes individual or small-group appointments, guided reading or study sessions, regularly scheduled skills mini-workshops, and collaboration with academic advisors and other CARES staff; allows for review and modification of course selections or credit loads if necessary; and ensures documented modifications and/or accommodations. Level II offers non-fee-based, standard support services, including weekly consultation and review sessions, and accommodations and modifications. Level III provides accommodations and modifications. The staff is comprised of specialists trained to work with students who have difficulties with reading, mathematics, writing, and organization.

LD/ADHD ADMISSIONS INFORMATION

College entrance tests required: No
Interview required: No
Essay recommended: Yes
Documentation required for LD: Cognitive testing and an aptitude and achievement test reflecting reading, writing, and math standard scores
Documentation required for ADHD: The documentation that was appropriate for the student's school/school district is acceptable.
Submitted to: Admissions Office

Specific course requirements: NR
Separate application required: No
# of LD applications submitted each year: 400
# of LD applications accepted yearly: 300
Total # of students receiving LD services: 215
Acceptance into program means acceptance into college: Students are reviewed by both the program and the Admissions Office, but the final decision is with the Admissions Office. Once admitted, students may request services.

ADMISSIONS
Students with LD may apply for admission through the LRC program. Students must submit high school transcript; documentation of LD/ADHD, current assessment information; and aptitude and achievement test scores (reading, writing, and math) reflecting all subtest and summative scores in the form of standard scores and/or percentile ranks, ACT/SAT, and recommendations from LD teacher(s) and counselors. Students must submit a writing sample that is part of the formal application. LRC staff may request a student interview following a review of the completed application. High school courses should be within a mainstream and/or inclusion framework, with a consistent C or better performance reflected in the core academic subjects. Evidence of commitment, motivation, and preparedness for college-level study is desired. The SAT/ACT is required but admission is more dependent on student potential and desire to be successful than what he/she has necessarily done in the past. The director and LRC staff reviews all LRC applicants and make a recommendation to the Admissions Office. Mitchell notifies applicants of a decision as soon as all of the credentials are received and reviewed.

ADDITIONAL INFORMATION
Students accepted into the LRC program are expected to work with their assigned learning specialists at least 4 hours per week in individual and small group sessions. The LRC students must fulfill all degree requirements. Academic Coaching for Empowerment (ACE) helps students with ADHD complete daily tasks and address hidden effects on grades, attendance, and student success. ACE pairs students with individual LRC coaches who help students evaluate and replace ineffective daily planning habits, learn about the effects of ADHD, and how it impacts their daily lives. STEP is a 4-week optional intensive summer program for incoming freshmen to strengthen study skills, improve basic academic skills, identify personal learning style, and earn college credits.

LEARNING DISABILITY PROGRAM/SERVICES

Learning Disability Program/Services: Learning Resource Center
Director: Peter F. Love, PhD
  E-mail: love_p@mitchell.edu
  Telephone: 860-701-5071
  Fax: 860-701-5090

LEARNING DISABILITY SERVICES

Requests for the following/services accommodations will be evaluated individually based on appropriate and current documentation.

Allowed in exams
  Calculator: Yes
  Dictionary: Yes
  Computer: Yes
  Spellchecker: Yes
Extended test time: Yes
Scribes: Yes
Proctors: Yes
Oral exams: Yes
Note-takers: Yes

Distraction-reduced environment: Yes
Tape recording in class: Yes
Books on tape from RFBD: Yes
Taping of books not from RFBD: Yes
Accommodations for students with
  ADHD: Yes
Reading machine: Yes
Other assistive technology: Yes
Priority registration: N/A

Added costs for services: Yes
LD specialists: Yes
Professional tutors: 10–12
Peer tutors: No
Max. hours/wk. for services: 4
How professors are notified of
  LD/ADHD: By student

GENERAL ADMISSIONS INFORMATION

Director of Admissions: Kim Hodges
Telephone: 860-701-5011

ENTRANCE REQUIREMENTS

Academic units recommended: 4 English, 3 math, 3 science, 2 social studies, 2 history, 2 academic electives. High school diploma is required, and GED is accepted. TOEFL required of all international applicants: minimum paper TOEFL 500.

Application deadline: Rolling
Notification: Rolling
Average GPA: 2.80
ACT Composite middle 50% range:
  15–17

SAT Math middle 50% range:
  350–460
SAT Critical Reading middle 50%
  range: 360–460
SAT Writing middle 50% range: NR

Graduated top 10% of class: 3%
Graduated top 25% of class: 15%
Graduated top 50% of class: 35%

COLLEGE GRADUATION REQUIREMENTS

Course waivers allowed: No
Course substitutions allowed: Yes
In what course: Varies based on the student's history with the subject area and the school policies and procedures

ADDITIONAL INFORMATION

Environment: The 65-acre campus sits on a former estate located in a safe and quiet residential area of historic New London.

Student Body
  Undergrad enrollment: 762
  Women: 54%
  Men: 46%
  Percent out-of-state: 36%

Cost Information
  Tuition: $20,382
  Room & board: $9,795
Housing Information
  University housing: Yes
  Percent living on campus: 85%

Greek System
  Fraternity: No
  Sorority: No
Athletics: Division III

SOUTHERN CONNECTICUT STATE U.

SCSU—Admissions House, 131 Farnham Ave., New Haven, CT 06515-1202
Phone: 203-392-5656 • Fax: 203-392-5727
E-mail: adminfo@scsu.ctstateu.edu • Web: www.southernct.edu
Support: CS • Institution type: 4-year public

LEARNING DISABILITY PROGRAM AND SERVICES

The purpose of the Disability Resource Office (DRO) is to ensure educational equity for students with disabilities. The DRO works to provide access to full participation in all aspects of campus life. The DRO assists students in arranging for individualized accommodations and support services. The DRO is a resource for students, faculty, and the university at large. Use of DRO services is voluntary and confidential. The DRO provides academic, career, and personal support for all university students with disabilities, including students with specific learning disabilities and attention deficit hyperactivity disorder. The DRO is a component of Student Supportive Services.

LD/ADHD ADMISSIONS INFORMATION

College entrance tests required: Yes
Interview required: No
Essay recommended: No
Documentation required for LD: Psychoeducational
Documentation required for ADHD: Yes
Submitted to: Disability Resource Office
Special Ed. HS course work accepted: Yes

Specific course requirements of all applicants: Yes
Separate application required: No
# of LD applications submitted each year: NR
# of LD applications accepted yearly: NR
Total # of students receiving LD services: 400
Acceptance into program means acceptance into college: Students must be admitted and enrolled in the university first and then request services.

ADMISSIONS

There is no special admissions process for students with learning disabilities. All applicants must meet the same criteria. Course requirements include 4 years of English, 3 years of math, 2 years of science, 2 years of a foreign language, 2 years of social studies, and 2 years of history. Conditional admission is considered and based on the following: WAIS scores and sub scores, achievement tests, SAT/ACT scores, and transcript. Applicants who wish DRO to be involved in the admission decision should note "disability" on the application that goes to the Admissions Office. They should also submit current psychoeducational testing information to DRO.

ADDITIONAL INFORMATION

The DRO assists students in arranging for individualized accommodations and support services. Services are available to both prospective and current students as follows: prospective students should attend one of the several workshops offered each fall for prospective students and their parents seeking information regarding the program, and should obtain an application to the university. Current students should make an appointment with the office and bring educational documentation, including achievement testing and psychoeducational evaluation, or medical documentation. Services include course selection and registration assistance; course and testing accommodations; support from learning specialists in developing time management and study skills, identifying strengths and weaknesses, and acquiring compensatory strategies; contact with faculty and university departments; and advocacy and self-advocacy information and training. Services and accommodations are available for undergraduate and graduate students.

LEARNING DISABILITY PROGRAM/SERVICES

Learning Disability Program/Services: Disability Resource Office (DRO)
Director: Suzanne Tucker
  E-mail: tuckers1@southernct.edu
  Telephone: 203-392-6828
  Fax: 203-392-6829
Contact Person: Debbie Fairchild
  E-mail: fairchildd1@southernct.edu

LEARNING DISABILITY SERVICES

Requests for the following/services accommodations will be evaluated individually based on appropriate and current documentation.

Allowed in exams
  Calculator: Yes
  Dictionary: Yes
  Computer: Yes
  Spellchecker: Yes
Extended test time: Yes
Scribes: Yes
Proctors: Yes
Oral exams: Yes
Note-takers: Yes

Distraction-reduced environment: Yes
Tape recording in class: Yes
Books on tape from RFBD: Yes
Taping of books not from RFBD: Yes
Accommodations for students with
  ADHD: Yes
Reading machine: Yes
Other assistive technology: Yes
Priority registration: No

Added costs for services: No
LD specialists: Yes
Professional tutors: No
Peer tutors: Yes
Max. hours/wk. for services: .5
How professors are notified of
  LD/ADHD: By student

GENERAL ADMISSIONS INFORMATION

Director of Admissions: Sharon Brenner
Telephone: 203-392-5656

Entrance Requirements

Academic units required: 4 English, 3 math, 2 science (1 science lab), 2 foreign language, 2 social studies, 2 history. **Academic units recommended:** 4 math, 3 foreign language. High school diploma is required, and GED is accepted. ACT with Writing component required. TOEFL required of all international applicants: minimum paper TOEFL 525, minimum computer TOEFL 1.

Application deadline: 7/1
Notification: Rolling
Average GPA: NR
ACT Composite middle 50% range:
  NR

SAT Math middle 50% range:
  420–520
SAT Critical Reading middle 50%
  range: 430–530
SAT Writing middle 50% range: NR

Graduated top 10% of class: 5%
Graduated top 25% of class: 22%
Graduated top 50% of class: 57%

COLLEGE GRADUATION REQUIREMENTS

Course waivers allowed: Yes
In what course: Foreign language
Course substitutions allowed: Yes
In what course: Foreign Language

Additional Information

Environment: The university is located in an urban area 35 miles south of Hartford and 90 miles from New York City.

Student Body
  Undergrad enrollment: 8,309
  Women: 62%
  Men: 38%
  Percent out-of-state: 6%

Cost Information
  In-state tuition: $3,187
  Out-of-state tuition: $10,315
  Room & board: $8,101
Housing Information
  University housing: Yes
  Percent living on campus: 31%

Greek System
  Fraternity: Yes
  Sorority: Yes
Athletics: Division II

UNIVERSITY OF CONNECTICUT

2131 Hillside Road, Unit 3088, Storrs, CT 06268-3088
Phone: 860-486-3137 • Fax: 860-486-1476
E-mail: beahusky@uconn.edu • Web: www.uconn.edu
Support: CS • Institution type: 4-year public

LEARNING DISABILITY PROGRAM AND SERVICES

The major goal of the University Program for College Students with LD (UPLD) is to assist qualified students with LD to become independent and successful learners within the regular university curriculum. The program is designed to complement and support, but not to duplicate, the university's existing campus services and programs. Three types of program services are offered along a continuum leading to independence: direct instruction, in which students meet with learning specialists weekly to learn compensatory skills to strengthen learning strategies; monitoring for students who need periodic contact; and consultation with UPLD staff on a student-initiated basis. Most students find that it is beneficial to access services at the direct instruction level and progress at an individual rate through the UPLD Continuum as they experience increasing confidence and competence. UPLD staff is available to help student's access additional campus resources. Staff of UPLD is not qualified to serve as academic advisors. In cases where the disability does not include a specific LD, such as ADHD, students can receive support services from the Center for Students with Disabilities (CSD). Students diagnosed with LD and ADHD have services coordinated through UPLD and CSD.

LD/ADHD ADMISSIONS INFORMATION

College entrance tests required: Yes
Interview required: No
Essay recommended: No
Documentation required for LD: Psychoeducational
  evaluation
Documentation required for ADHD: Psychoeducational
  evaluation
Submitted to: University Program for College Students with LD

Specific course requirements of all applicants: Yes
Separate application required: No
# of LD applications submitted each year: 40
# of LD applications accepted yearly: 40
Total # of students receiving LD services: 150
**Acceptance into program means acceptance into
  college:** Students must be admitted and enrolled in the
  university first and then request services.

ADMISSIONS

There is no separate application or process for students with LD, and they must meet regular admissions criteria. The typical profile is rank in top third of class; 3.2 GPA in college-prep courses; and SAT 1100-plus or ACT 24. Transfer students need a cumulative GPA of 2.5 and must be in good standing at their current institution. To access services, students must refer themselves to UPLD and submit documentation meeting university guidelines for documentation of a specific LD. Documentation must verify eligibility and support requests for reasonable accommodations, academic adjustments, and/or auxiliary aids. Testing must be comprehensive and current. Minimally, domains to be addressed include aptitude, achievement (current levels of functioning in reading, math, and written language), and information processing. There must be clear and specific evidence and identification of an LD. Actual test scores must be provided, including interpretation of the results. The assessments must be conducted by qualified professionals. A written summary about relevant educational, medical, and family histories that relate to LD must be included. Recommendations for accommodations should be based on objective evidence of a current substantial limitation to learning, and descriptions of any accommodation and/or auxiliary aid used in high school or college should be discussed. IEPs and Section 504 plans are useful but not sufficient.

ADDITIONAL INFORMATION

Trained staff works with students on developing learning strategies and offers individual structured sessions. Learning specialists help students develop self-advocacy, identify and monitor needs, and develop individualized goals. Reasonable accommodations are determined on a case-by-case basis. The CSD coordinates requests for proctors or scribes and provides services to students with ADHD without a diagnosed LD. The university has a formal course substitution policy for students with LD that requires current, valid diagnostic evidence that the nature and severity of the LD precludes completion of courses in foreign language or math despite the provision of accommodations. A waiver of a subject in high school does not guarantee a substitution at the university.

LEARNING DISABILITY PROGRAM/SERVICES

Learning Disability Program/Services: University Program for College Students with LD
Director: David Parker, PhD
  E-mail: david.parker@uconn.edu
  Telephone: 860-486-0178
  Fax: 860-486-5799

LEARNING DISABILITY SERVICES

Requests for the following/services accommodations will be evaluated individually based on appropriate and current documentation.

Allowed in exams
  Calculator: Yes
  Dictionary: Yes
  Computer: Yes
  Spellchecker: Yes
Extended test time: Yes
Scribes: Yes
Proctors: Yes
Oral exams: Yes
Note-takers: Yes

Distraction-reduced environment: Yes
Tape recording in class: Yes
Books on tape from RFBD: Yes
Taping of books not from RFBD: Yes
Accommodations for students with ADHD: Yes
Reading machine: Yes
Other assistive technology: Yes
Priority registration: Yes

Added costs for services: No
LD specialists: Yes
Professional tutors: No
Peer tutors: No
Max. hours/wk. for services: 2
How professors are notified of LD/ADHD: By student

GENERAL ADMISSIONS INFORMATION

Director of Admissions: Lee H. Melvin
Telephone: 860-486-3137

ENTRANCE REQUIREMENTS

Academic units required: 4 English, 3 math, 2 science (2 science labs), 2 foreign language, 2 social studies, 3 academic electives. **Academic units recommended:** 3 foreign language. High school diploma is required, and GED is accepted. ACT with Writing component required. TOEFL required of all international applicants: minimum paper TOEFL 550, minimum computer TOEFL 213.

Application deadline: 2/1
Notification: Rolling
Average GPA: NR
ACT Composite middle 50% range: 23–27

SAT Math middle 50% range: 560–660
SAT Critical Reading middle 50% range: 530–630
SAT Writing middle 50% range: 540–630

Graduated top 10% of class: 38%
Graduated top 25% of class: 81%
Graduated top 50% of class: 98%

COLLEGE GRADUATION REQUIREMENTS

Course waivers allowed: No
Course substitutions allowed: Yes
In what course: Based on documented evidence of significant impairment, some students qualify for course substitutions in foreign language or math courses.

ADDITIONAL INFORMATION

Environment: The University of Connecticut is located 30 miles northeast of Hartford.

Student Body
  Undergrad enrollment: 16,006
  Women: 51%
  Men: 49%
  Percent out-of-state: 23%

Cost Information
  In-state tuition: $6,816
  Out-of-state tuition: $20,760
  Room & board: $8,850
Housing Information
  University housing: Yes
  Percent living on campus: 71%

Greek System
  Fraternity: Yes
  Sorority: Yes
Athletics: Division I

UNIVERSITY OF HARTFORD

200 Bloomfield Avenue, West Hartford, CT 06117
Phone: 860-768-4296 • Fax: 860-768-4961
E-mail: admissions@mail.hartford.edu • Web: www.hartford.edu
Support: CS • Institution type: 2-year and 4-year private

LEARNING DISABILITY PROGRAM AND SERVICES

The Learning Plus (LP) program facilitates equal opportunity for academic achievement and is available to any student diagnosed with LD. Program objectives include helping students' understand their strengths and weaknesses; providing learning strategies; developing students' self-advocacy skills; connecting students with campus resources; developing students' decision-making skills; facilitating appropriate testing modifications for students; providing information to faculty and students regarding LD, classroom accommodations and testing modifications, and legal rights and responsibilities; and protecting the confidentiality of student records. Learning Plus services include direct strategies, in which students are assigned to an LP tutor and meet weekly for instruction in metacognitive skills, such as information processing or organizational strategies; Check-In, where students meet every other week with tutors for monitoring and organizational strategies; and Drop-In, for as-needed assistance. Service determination depends on semester standing, GPA, and course curricula. Freshmen are assigned to Direct Strategies Instruction. Students with documentation are advised to contact the Director of LP during the first week of classes. The director will discuss the disability, appropriate services, and classroom accommodations. Students are encouraged to discuss effective accommodations with professors. To receive services and accommodations from Learning Plus, students should submit comprehensive documentation to the LP director, not admissions, after being accepted to the university.

LD/ADHD ADMISSIONS INFORMATION

College entrance tests required: Yes
Interview required: No
Essay recommended: No
Documentation required for LD: WAIS and achievement
testing
Documentation required for ADHD: WAIS and achievement
testing
Submitted to: Learning Plus

Specific course requirements of all applicants: Yes
Separate application required: No
# of LD applications submitted each year: NR
# of LD applications accepted yearly: NR
Total # of students receiving LD services: 100–300
**Acceptance into program means acceptance into
college:** Students must be admitted and enrolled in the
university first and then request services.

ADMISSIONS

Students with LD do not apply to the Learning Plus Program, but do apply directly to one of the nine colleges within the university. If admitted, students with LD may then elect to receive the support services offered. The Admissions Committee pays particular attention to the student's individual talents and aspirations, especially as they relate to programs available at the university. Some borderline applicants may be admitted as a summer admission. Course requirements include 4 years of English, 3–3.5 years of math, 2 years of science, 2 years of social studies, plus electives. Substitutions are allowed on rare occasions and depend on the student's disability and intended major. Students may also apply to Hillyer College, which is a two-year program with more flexible admission criteria. This is a developmental program, with flexible admission standards, offering many services. Hillyer provides students with the opportunity to be in a college atmosphere and, if successful, transfer into the four-year program. Hillyer is not necessarily for students with LD, though some students with LD are enrolled.

ADDITIONAL INFORMATION

Learning Plus is voluntary, and students are required to seek assistance and maintain contact. All modifications are determined on a case-by-case, course-by-course basis. Students are responsible for disclosing their LD to their professors. Skills classes are offered in study skills and math. Students can also receive one individual appointment weekly, consisting of learning strategies from masters-level professionals. Instruction focuses on time management, organization strategies, reading, writing, mathematics, and course-specific study techniques. Some students with LD choose not to avail themselves of Learning Plus services. That is their privilege. The Director of Learning Plus maintains confidential files of all documentation should students request services at anytime during their college career.

LEARNING DISABILITY PROGRAM/SERVICES

Learning Disability Program/Services: Learning Plus
Director: Lynne Golden
   E-mail: golden@mail.hartford.edu
   Telephone: 860-768-5129

LEARNING DISABILITY SERVICES

Requests for the following/services accommodations will be evaluated individually based on appropriate and current documentation.

Allowed in exams
  Calculator: Yes
  Dictionary: No
  Computer: Yes
  Spellchecker: Yes
Extended test time: Yes
Scribes: No
Proctors: Yes
Oral exams: No
Note-takers: Yes

Distraction-reduced environment: Yes
Tape recording in class: Yes
Books on tape from RFBD: Yes
Taping of books not from RFBD: No
Accommodations for students with
  ADHD: Yes
Reading machine: No
Other assistive technology: No
Priority registration: No

Added costs for services: No
LD specialists: Yes
Professional tutors: NR
Peer tutors: No
Max. hours/wk. for services: NR
How professors are notified of
  LD/ADHD: By student

GENERAL ADMISSIONS INFORMATION

Director of Admissions: Richard Zeiser
Telephone: 860-768-4296

ENTRANCE REQUIREMENTS

Academic units required: 4 English, 3 math, 2 science, 2 social studies, 2 history, 4 academic electives.
Academic units recommended: 3.5 math, 3 science, 2 foreign language, 3 social studies. High school diploma is required, and GED is accepted. TOEFL required of all international applicants: minimum paper TOEFL 550, minimum computer TOEFL 213.

Application deadline: Rolling
Notification: Rolling
Average GPA: NR
ACT Composite middle 50% range:
  21–25

SAT Math middle 50% range:
  490–590
SAT Critical Reading middle 50%
  range: 480–580
SAT Writing middle 50% range:
  540–630

Graduated top 10% of class: NR
Graduated top 25% of class: NR
Graduated top 50% of class: NR

COLLEGE GRADUATION REQUIREMENTS

Course waivers allowed: Yes
In what course: On rare occasions—depends on students' disabilities and majors.
Course substitutions allowed: Yes
In what course: Foreign language, math

ADDITIONAL INFORMATION

Environment: The university is located on 320 acres in a residential section of West Hartford, 90 minutes from Boston.

Student Body
  Undergrad enrollment: 5,318
  Women: 51%
  Men: 49%
  Percent out-of-state: 61%

Cost Information
  Tuition: $24,576
  Room & board: $9,922
Housing Information
  University housing: Yes
  Percent living on campus: 66%

Greek System
  Fraternity: Yes
  Sorority: Yes
Athletics: Division I

UNIVERSITY OF NEW HAVEN

300 Orange Avenue, West Haven, CT 06516
Phone: 203-932-7319 • Fax: 203-931-6093
E-mail: adminfo@newhaven.edu • Web: www.newhaven.edu
Support: S • Institution type: 4-year private

LEARNING DISABILITY PROGRAM AND SERVICES

The primary responsibility of the Disability Services and Resource Office (DSR) is to provide services and support that promote access to the university's educational programs and services for students with disabilities. Students must self-identify and submit documentation of a disability and the need for accommodations. Documentation should be submitted once the student is accepted to the university along with a signed DSR Intake form to request accommodations. Students must also follow the established policies and procedures for making arrangements for accommodations each semester. Staff members act as advocates, liaisons, planners, and troubleshooters. Staff is responsible for assuring access, but at the same time, they avoid creating an artificial atmosphere of dependence on services that cannot reasonably be expected after graduation. The Center for Learning Resources (CLR) offers free tutoring for all students, including students with disabilities. The Office of Academic Services offers academic assistance to all students. Academic skills counselors work one-on-one with students to strengthen their abilities and develop individualized study strategies, which focus on reading, note-taking, time management, learning/memory, and test-taking skills.

LD/ADHD ADMISSIONS INFORMATION

College entrance tests required: Yes
Interview required: No
Essay recommended: No
Documentation required for LD: Intelligence test/achievement test including information processing
Documentation required for ADHD: Comprehensive neuropsychological or psychoeducational assessment report by a qualified professional clearly stating the presence of ADHD
Submitted to: Disability Services and Resources

Special Ed. HS course work accepted: Yes
Specific course requirements: NR
Separate application required: No
# of LD applications submitted each year: NR
# of LD applications accepted yearly: NR
Total # of students receiving LD services: NR
Acceptance into program means acceptance into college: Students must be admitted and enrolled in the university first and then request services.

ADMISSIONS

All applicants must meet the same admission requirements. SAT or ACT required. Students must submit a personal essay, and letter of recommendation. Foreign language is not required for admission. Students with learning disabilities may self-disclose if they feel that it would positively affect the admissions decision. Students admitted as a conditional admit are limited to four classes for the first semester.

ADDITIONAL INFORMATION

DSR provides services that include the coordination of classroom accommodations, such as extended time for exams; use of a tape recorder, calculator, note-takers, and so on; access to readers, scribes, or books on tape; assistance during the course registration process; proctoring of tests when accommodations cannot be arranged for in the classroom; proctoring of English course post-tests and the Writing Proficiency Exam; and training in time management, organization, and test anxiety management. The office includes testing rooms and a mini computer lab with some adaptive software. The center for learning resources has a Math Lab, Writing Lab, and Computer Lab. The CLR presents free workshops on preparing resumes and preparing for the Writing Proficiency Exam. The Office of Academic Services presents free workshops on improving study skills, such as getting organized, textbook and lecture note-taking techniques, and test preparation and strategies.

LEARNING DISABILITY PROGRAM/SERVICES

Learning Disability Program/Services: Disability Services and Resources
Director: Linda Copney-Okeke
  E-mail: lcokeke@newhaven.edu
  Telephone: 203-932-7331
  Fax: 203-931-6082

LEARNING DISABILITY SERVICES

Requests for the following/services accommodations will be evaluated individually based on appropriate and current documentation.

Allowed in exams
  Calculator: Yes
  Dictionary: Yes
  Computer: Yes
  Spellchecker: Yes
Extended test time: Yes
Scribes: Yes
Proctors: Yes
Oral exams: Yes
Note-takers: Yes

Distraction-reduced environment: Yes
Tape recording in class: Yes
Books on tape from RFBD: Yes
Taping of books not from RFBD: Yes
**Accommodations for students with
  ADHD:** Yes
Reading machine: No
Other assistive technology: Yes
Priority registration: No

Added costs for services: No
LD specialists: No
Professional tutors: No
Peer tutors: N/A
Max. hours/wk. for services:
  Unlimited
**How professors are notified of
  LD/ADHD:** By student

GENERAL ADMISSIONS INFORMATION

Director of Admissions: Jane Sangeloty
Telephone: 203-932-7319

ENTRANCE REQUIREMENTS

Academic units required: 4 English, 3 math, 2 science, 2 history, 3 academic electives. **Academic units recommended:** 2 foreign language, 2 social studies. High school diploma is required, and GED is accepted. TOEFL required of all international applicants: minimum paper TOEFL 520, minimum computer TOEFL 190.

Application deadline: NR
Notification: Rolling
Average GPA: 3.00
ACT Composite middle 50% range:
  NR

SAT Math middle 50% range:
  450–570
**SAT Critical Reading middle 50%
  range:** 460–560
SAT Writing middle 50% range: NR

Graduated top 10% of class: 14%
Graduated top 25% of class: 35%
Graduated top 50% of class: 67%

COLLEGE GRADUATION REQUIREMENTS

Course waivers allowed: No
Course substitutions allowed: Yes
In what course: Courses that are not essential to the student's program of study

ADDITIONAL INFORMATION

Environment: The campus is located close to New Haven and 75 miles from New York City.

Student Body
  Undergrad enrollment: 2,627
  Women: 45%
  Men: 55%
  Percent out-of-state: 38%

Cost Information
  Tuition: $22,380
  Room & board: $9,415
Housing Information
  University housing: Yes
  Percent living on campus: 60%

Greek System
  Fraternity: Yes
  Sorority: Yes
Athletics: Division II

University of New Haven

WESTERN CONNECTICUT STATE U.

Undergraduate Admissions Office, 181 White St., Danbury, CT 06810-6855
Phone: 203-837-9000 • Fax: 203-837-8338
E-mail: admissions@wcsu.edu • Web: www.wcsu.edu
Support: CS • Institution type: 4-year public

LEARNING DISABILITY PROGRAM AND SERVICES

Two primary purposes of Students with Disabilities Services are to provide the educational development of disabled students and improve understanding and support in the campus environment. Students with learning disabilities will be assisted in receiving the services necessary to achieve their goals. Western Connecticut recognizes your right to reasonable accommodations and necessary services as a student qualified to be enrolled at this university. The Office of Disability Services directs and coordinates such services for students with disabilities that impact their educational experience. We provide advocacy, early registration, confidential counseling, empowerment counseling, complaint processing, accommodation planning, accommodation referrals, referrals to other university services, exam proctoring, accessibility, and other important services that are of value and consequence to students.

LD/ADHD ADMISSIONS INFORMATION

College entrance tests required: Yes
Interview required: No
Essay recommended: No
Documentation required for LD: Psychoeducational evaluation or other documentation from a qualified professional
Documentation required for ADHD: Psychoeducational evaluation or other documentation from a qualified professional
Submitted to: Disability Services
Special Ed. HS course work accepted: Yes

Specific course requirements of all applicants: Yes
Separate application required: No
# of LD applications submitted each year: NR
# of LD applications accepted yearly: NR
Total # of students receiving LD services: NR
Acceptance into program means acceptance into college: Students must be admitted and enrolled in the university first and then request services.

ADMISSIONS

Students with learning disabilities submit the general application form. No alternative admission policies are offered. Students should have a 2.5 GPA (C-plus or better), with the average SAT of 894 (ACT may be substituted). Courses required include 4 years of English, 3 years of math, 2 years of science, 2 science labs, 2 years of a foreign language (3 years of a foreign language recommended), 1 year of social studies, 1 year of history, and 3 years of electives. Students are encouraged to self-disclose their disability on the application and submit documentation to be used after admission to determine services and accommodations.

ADDITIONAL INFORMATION

Services include priority registration, tutoring, testing accommodations, and advocacy and counseling. The university does not offer any skills classes. The university offers a special summer program for precollege freshmen with learning disabilities. Services and accommodations are available for undergraduate and graduate students.

LEARNING DISABILITY PROGRAM/SERVICES

Learning Disability Program/Services: Disability Services
Director: Jack Sikora
  E-mail: sikoraj@wcsu.edu
  Telephone: 203-837-8946
  Fax: 203-837-8848

LEARNING DISABILITY SERVICES

Requests for the following/services accommodations will be evaluated individually based on appropriate and current documentation.

Allowed in exams
  Calculator: Yes
  Dictionary: No
  Computer: Yes
  Spellchecker: Yes
Extended test time: Yes
Scribes: Yes
Proctors: Yes
Oral exams: Yes
Note-takers: Yes

Distraction-reduced environment: Yes
Tape recording in class: Yes
Books on tape from RFBD: Yes
Taping of books not from RFBD: Yes
Accommodations for students with
  ADHD: Yes
Reading machine: No
Other assistive technology: Yes
Priority registration: Yes

Added costs for services: No
LD specialists: Yes
Professional tutors: 1
Peer tutors: N/A
Max. hours/wk. for services: N/A
How professors are notified of
  LD/ADHD: By both student and director

GENERAL ADMISSIONS INFORMATION

Director of Admissions: William Hawkins, Enrollment Management Officer
Telephone: 203-837-9000

ENTRANCE REQUIREMENTS

Academic units required: 4 English, 3 math, 2 science (2 science labs), 2 foreign language, 1 social studies, 1 history. **Academic units recommended:** 3 foreign language. High school diploma is required, and GED is accepted. TOEFL required of all international applicants: minimum paper TOEFL 550, minimum computer TOEFL 213.

Application deadline: Rolling
Notification: Rolling
Average GPA: NR
ACT Composite middle 50% range:
  NR

SAT Math middle 50% range:
  440–540
SAT Critical Reading middle 50% range: 450–550
SAT Writing middle 50% range: NR

Graduated top 10% of class: 4%
Graduated top 25% of class: 24%
Graduated top 50% of class: 62%

COLLEGE GRADUATION REQUIREMENTS

Course waivers allowed: Yes
In what course: As required depending on the student's disability
Course substitutions allowed: Yes
In what course: As required depending on the student's disability

ADDITIONAL INFORMATION

Environment: The university is located on 315 acres, 60 miles from New York City.

Student Body
  Undergrad enrollment: 4,480
  Women: 54%
  Men: 46%
  Percent out-of-state: 9%

Cost Information
  In-state tuition: $7,100
  Out-of-state tuition: $15,000
  Room & board: $7,193
Housing Information
  University housing: Yes
  Percent living on campus: 34%

Greek System
  Fraternity: Yes
  Sorority: Yes
Athletics: Division III

UNIVERSITY OF DELAWARE

116 Hullihen Hall, Newark, DE 19716-6210
Phone: 302-831-8123 • Fax: 302-831-6905
E-mail: admissions@udel.edu • Web: www.udel.edu
Support: CS • Institution type: 4-year public

LEARNING DISABILITY PROGRAM AND SERVICES

The University of Delaware is committed to providing reasonable and timely academic accommodations for students with disabilities. The Academic Services Center (ASC) focuses primarily on serving students with learning disabilities and ADHD. ASC is not a program but rather a center that provides services and accommodations to help students. ASC works jointly with other offices. The staff has been trained to understand LD and ADHD and is available to assist faculty in providing accommodations for students whose documentation is complete. Independent, highly motivated students will do well at the university.

LD/ADHD ADMISSIONS INFORMATION

College entrance tests required: Yes
Interview required: No
Essay recommended: Yes
Documentation required for LD: Yes
Documentation required for ADHD: Yes
Submitted to: Academic Success Services
Special Ed. HS course work accepted: NR

Specific course requirements of all applicants: Yes
Separate application required: NR
# of LD applications submitted each year: NR
# of LD applications accepted yearly: NR
Total # of students receiving LD services: NR
Acceptance into program means acceptance into college: Student must be admitted and enrolled in the university first and then reviewed for LD services.

ADMISSIONS

Students must be otherwise qualified for university admissions, which means they must meet university and college admissions criteria. In other words, students are admitted on the basis of their abilities. General admission requirements include essays, letters of recommendations, and 4 years of English, 2 years of math (4 recommended), 3 years of science, 2 years of social studies (4 recommended), 2 years of a foreign language (4 recommended), and 2 years of electives. Once admitted, students are encouraged to self-disclose their individual disability by returning a form they receive during orientation or by making an appointment to discuss their needs with an ASC staff member. Documentation sent as part of the admissions application does not constitute the official notification to the university that the student is seeking services. The Admissions Office requests documentation sent directly from a psychologist or medical doctor.

ADDITIONAL INFORMATION

With appropriate documentation, students with LD could be eligible for some of the following services: the use of calculators, computers, and spellcheckers in exams; extended time on tests; proctors; oral exams; note-takers; distraction-free environments for tests; tape recorders in class; books on tape; and priority registration. There are one-credit courses offered through the School of Education that assist students in their study skills, critical thinking, and problem solving. In addition, the ASC offers a college intensive literacy course for students who need additional assistance. Students with ADHD are provided assistance jointly by the ASC and the Center for Counseling and Student Development. All students have access to a Writing Center, a Math Center, and tutoring and study skills workshops in the Academic Services Center.

LEARNING DISABILITY PROGRAM/SERVICES

Learning Disability Program/Services: Academic Success Services
Director: Lysbet J. Murray
  E-Mail: lysbet@udel.edu
  Telephone: 302-831-1639
  Fax: 302-831-4128

LEARNING DISABILITY SERVICES

Requests for the following/services accommodations will be evaluated individually based on appropriate and current documentation.

Allowed in exams
  Calculator: Yes
  Dictionary: No
  Computer: Yes
  Spellchecker: Yes
Extended test time: Yes
Scribes: No
Proctors: Yes
Oral exams: Yes
Note-takers: Yes

Distraction-reduced environment: Yes
Tape recording in class: Yes
Books on tape from RFBD: Yes
Taping of books not from RFBD: Yes
Accommodations for students with ADHD: Yes
Reading machine: Yes
Other assistive technology: Yes
Priority registration: Yes

Added costs for services: No
LD specialists: Yes
Professional tutors: No
Peer tutors: 100
Max. hours/wk. for services: NR
How professors are notified of LD/ADHD: By both student and director

GENERAL ADMISSIONS INFORMATION

Director of Admissions: Lou Hirsh
Telephone: 302-831-1209

ENTRANCE REQUIREMENTS

Academic units required: 4 English, 2 math, 3 science (2 science labs), 2 foreign language, 2 social studies, 2 history, 2 academic electives. **Academic units recommended:** 4 English, 4 math, 4 science (3 science labs), 4 foreign language, 2 social studies, 2 history, 2 academic electives. High school diploma is required, and GED is accepted. ACT with Writing component required. TOEFL required of all international applicants: minimum paper TOEFL 550, minimum computer TOEFL 213.

Application deadline: 1/15
Notification: 3/15
Average GPA: 3.60
ACT Composite middle 50% range: 23–28

SAT Math middle 50% range: 560–660
SAT Critical Reading middle 50% range: 540–640
SAT Writing middle 50% range: 540–650

Graduated top 10% of class: 39%
Graduated top 25% of class: 80%
Graduated top 50% of class: 98%

COLLEGE GRADUATION REQUIREMENTS

Course waivers allowed: No
Course substitutions allowed: Yes
In what course: Math and foreign language course substitution decisions are made on a case-by-case basis. Students are asked to attempt the class and work closely with a tutor before submitting a petition for a substitution.

ADDITIONAL INFORMATION

Environment: The 1,100-acre campus is in a small town 12 miles southwest of Wilmington and midway between Philadelphia and Baltimore.

Student Body
  Undergrad enrollment: 15,211
  Women: 58%
  Men: 42%
  Percent out-of-state: 60%

Cost Information
  In-state tuition: $6,980
  Out-of-state tuition: $17,690
  Room & board: $7,366
Housing Information
  University housing: Yes
  Percent living on campus: 47%

Greek System
  Fraternity: Yes
  Sorority: Yes
Athletics: Division I

University of Delaware

AMERICAN UNIVERSITY

4400 Massachusetts Avenue, Northwest, Washington, DC 20016-8001
Phone: 202-885-6000 • Fax: 202-885-1025
E-mail: admissions@american.edu • Web: www.american.edu
Support: SP • Institution type: 4-year private

LEARNING DISABILITY PROGRAM AND SERVICES

The focus of the Learning Services Program is to assist students with their transition from high school to college during their freshman year. The Learning Services Program is a mainstream program offering additional support in college writing and finite math. The Academic Support Center (ASC) provides services for students with learning disabilities. These services are provided to promote full participation in academic programs and other campus activities. The Disability Support Services and the Academic Support Center have the specific responsibility for reviewing professionally prepared documentation of a disability, determining effective and reasonable modification for a disability, verifying a disability for faculty and other persons, and recommending course and learning accommodations on behalf of the university. Support continues to be available until graduation.

LD/ADHD ADMISSIONS INFORMATION

College entrance tests required: Yes
Interview required: No
Essay recommended: Yes
Documentation required for LD: Recent psychoeducational evaluation, including a test of aptitude such as the WAIS and a test of achievement such as WJ–III.
Documentation required for ADHD: A complete psychoeducational report is preferred. If ADHD has been diagnosed by a medical doctor, a report or letter must meet published guidelines.
Submitted to: Disability Support Services
Special Ed. HS course work accepted: Yes

Specific course requirements of all applicants: Yes
Separate application required: Yes
# of LD applications submitted each year: 65–125
# of LD applications accepted yearly: 40–50
Total # of students receiving LD services: 175–200
Acceptance into program means acceptance into college: Student must be admitted and enrolled in the university first and then reviewed for LD services.

ADMISSIONS

Students with LD must be admitted to the university and then to the Learning Services Program. Students who wish to have program staff consult with the Admissions Office about their LD during the admissions process must submit a supplemental application to the Learning Services Program that requires documentation of the LD. Students using a common application should indicate interest in the program on their application. Special education courses taken in high school may be accepted if they meet the criteria for the Carnegie Units. The academic credentials of successful applicants with LD fall within the range of regular admissions criteria: the mean GPA is 2.9 for LD admits and 3.2 for regularly admitted students; ACT ranges from 24–29 for regular admits and 24–28 for LD admits or SAT 1110–1270 for regular admits and 1131 for LD admits. American Sign Language is an acceptable substitution for foreign language. The admission decision is made by a special Admissions Committee and is based on the high school record, recommendations, and all pertinent diagnostic reports. For selected students, admission to the university will be contingent on enrollment in the program; for others, the Learning Services Program will be optional though strongly recommended. Conditional admission is offered to some students through the Excel Program.

ADDITIONAL INFORMATION

Students have an academic advisor experienced in advising students with LD. All entering freshmen have the same requirements, including college writing (a section is reserved for students in the program) and college reading. Students meet weekly with a learning specialist for individual tutorial sessions that help them further develop college-level reading, writing, and study strategies. Peer tutors assist with course content tutoring. Individual and group counseling is offered through Psychological Services. The staff of the program will consult professors with students' written permission. All modifications are based on diagnostic testing and educational recommendations, and students are held to the same academic standards but may meet these standards through nontraditional means. As sophomores, basic skills tutorial sessions are offered on an as-needed basis.

LEARNING DISABILITY PROGRAM/SERVICES

Learning Disability Program/Services: Academic Support Center
Director: Kathy Schwartz
  E-mail: kschwar@american.edu
  Telephone: 202-885-3360
  Fax: 202-885-1042

LEARNING DISABILITY SERVICES

Requests for the following/services accommodations will be evaluated individually based on appropriate and current documentation.

Allowed in exams
  Calculator: Yes
  Dictionary: Yes
  Computer: Yes
  Spellchecker: Yes
Extended test time: Yes
Scribes: Yes
Proctors: Yes
Oral exams: Yes
Note-takers: Yes

Distraction-reduced environment: Yes
Tape recording in class: Yes
Books on tape from RFBD: Yes
Taping of books not from RFBD: Yes
**Accommodations for students with
  ADHD:** Yes
Reading machine: Yes
Other assistive technology: Yes
Priority registration: Yes

Added costs for services: Yes
LD specialists: Yes
Professional tutors: No
Peer tutors: 20–40
Max. hours/wk. for services:
  Unlimited
**How professors are notified of
  LD/ADHD:** By both student and
  director

GENERAL ADMISSIONS INFORMATION

Director of Admissions: Dr. Sharon M. Alston, Director, Undergraduate Admissions
Telephone: 202-885-6000

ENTRANCE REQUIREMENTS

Academic units required: 4 English, 3 math, 2 science (2 science labs), 2 foreign language, 2 social studies, 3 academic electives. **Academic units recommended:** 4 English, 4 math, 4 science, 3 foreign language, 4 social studies, 4 academic electives. High school diploma is required, and GED is accepted. ACT with Writing component required. TOEFL required of all international applicants: minimum paper TOEFL 590, minimum computer TOEFL 213.

Application deadline: 1/15
Notification: 4/1
Average GPA: 3.2
ACT Composite middle 50% range:
  26–30

SAT Math middle 50% range:
  580–670
**SAT Critical Reading middle 50%
  range:** 600–690
SAT Writing middle 50% range: NR

Graduated top 10% of class: 47%
Graduated top 25% of class: 82%
Graduated top 50% of class: 98%

COLLEGE GRADUATION REQUIREMENTS

Course waivers allowed: No
Course substitutions allowed: No

ADDITIONAL INFORMATION

Environment: The university is located on 77 acres close to the Capitol.

Student Body
  Undergrad enrollment: 5,788
  Women: 62%
  Men: 38%
  Percent out-of-state: 75%

Cost Information
  Tuition: $29,206
  Room & board: $11,570
Housing Information
  University housing: Yes
  Percent living on campus: 75%

Greek System
  Fraternity: Yes
  Sorority: Yes
Athletics: Division I

THE CATHOLIC U. OF AMERICA

620 Michigan Avenue, Northeast, Washington, DC 20064
Phone: 202-319-5305 • Fax: 202-319-6533
E-mail: cua-admissions@cua.edu • Web: www.cua.edu
Support: CS • Institution type: 4-year private

LEARNING DISABILITY PROGRAM AND SERVICES

The university does not have a specially designated program for students with learning disabilities but offers comprehensive support services and accommodations. The university has an Advisory Committee on students with LD composed of faculty members and administrators with expertise in a variety of specialized areas. The committee assists Students with LD that might preclude their full participation in university academic activities. The goals of the services are to facilitate academic success, support personal growth, and encourage self-advocacy. Students with LD are required to meet the same academic standards as other students. Students must submit current diagnostic verification of the LD. To initiate services and accommodations, students make an appointment with an advisor who will consult with students to determine appropriate accommodations and coordinate services.

LD/ADHD ADMISSIONS INFORMATION

College entrance tests required: Yes
Interview required: No
Documentation required for LD: Diagnostic interview, assessment of aptitude, and measure of academic achievement and information processing; comprehensive assessment battery (i.e., WJ–III and WAIS–III); quantitative and qualitative information including all subscale/subtest scores; objective evidence of a substantial limitation to learning.
Documentation required for ADHD: Comprehensive assessment that includes a clinical summary of objective historical information, a complete psychoeducational assessment.
Submitted to: Disability Support Services
Special Ed. HS course work accepted: Yes

Specific course requirements: NR
Separate application required: Yes
# of LD applications submitted each year: NR
# of LD applications accepted yearly: NR
Total # of students receiving LD services: NR
Acceptance into program means acceptance into college: Students must be admitted and enrolled in the university first and then request services.

ADMISSIONS

Students with LD may apply for admission through the regular admission procedures or may request a special admissions review. If an otherwise intellectually qualified applicant feels that there are weaknesses in admissions material due to a preexisting learning disability and voluntarily informs the Office of Admissions, the application will be referred to a special Admissions Committee for review. The review process will be used to provide a fuller assessment of the total student than what regular admissions material might provide. Applicants wishing to be considered under the special admissions policy for students with LD/ADHD should submit the following along with regular admissions requirements: diagnostic reports certifying the LD and the ability to do college work; three teacher evaluations from the students' most recent teachers of math, English, and one other subject; a supervised handwritten writing sample on a topic of the applicant's choice; and an optional interview. These procedures are intended to enhance each applicant's opportunity for admission to the university and will not be used to discriminate against the individual.

ADDITIONAL INFORMATION

Services include advocacy, advising and referral to tutoring or study skills, faculty consultation and support, assistance in arranging note-takers and recorded texts, support and positive feedback, tape-recording, extended time on tests, priority registration, and reasonable extension of deadlines on written papers. The Academic Tutoring and Learning Assistance Services offers individual and group tutoring, information concerning study strategies, writing skills assistance, counseling, and an ADHD/LD support group. Students with LD that impair the ability to learn a foreign language (two semesters required for graduation) may apply for a substitution by providing LD documentation, completing basic language testing, writing a letter formally requesting the substitution, and meeting with an LD advisor. If granted a foreign language substitution, students meet with the Associate Dean of Arts and Sciences to determine alternate courses.

LEARNING DISABILITY PROGRAM/SERVICES

Learning Disability Program/Services: Disability Support Services
Director: Emily Singer
  E-Mail: cua-disabilityservices@cua.edu
  Telephone: 202-319-5211 tty 202-299-2899
  Fax: 202-319-5126

LEARNING DISABILITY SERVICES

Requests for the following/services accommodations will be evaluated individually based on appropriate and current documentation.

Allowed in exams
  Calculator: Yes
  Dictionary: Yes
  Computer: Yes
  Spellchecker: Yes
Extended test time: Yes
Scribes: Yes
Proctors: Yes
Oral exams: Yes
Note-takers: Yes

Distraction-reduced environment: Yes
Tape recording in class: Yes
Books on tape from RFBD: Yes
Taping of books not from RFBD: Yes
Accommodations for students with ADHD: Yes
Reading machine: Yes
Other assistive technology: Yes
Priority registration: Yes

Added costs for services: No
LD specialists: Yes
Professional tutors: No
Peer tutors: 55–100
Max. hours/wk. for services: 3
How professors are notified of LD/ADHD: By student

GENERAL ADMISSIONS INFORMATION

Director of Admissions: Christine Mica
Telephone: 202-319-5305

ENTRANCE REQUIREMENTS

Academic units recommended: 4 English, 3 math, 3 science (1 science lab), 2 foreign language, 4 social studies, 1 fine arts or humanities. High school diploma is required, and GED is accepted. ACT with Writing component required. TOEFL required of all international applicants: minimum paper TOEFL 560, minimum computer TOEFL 220.

Application deadline: 2/15
Notification: 3/15
Average GPA: 3.32
ACT Composite middle 50% range: 22–27

SAT Math middle 50% range: 520–620
SAT Critical Reading middle 50% range: 520–620
SAT Writing middle 50% range: NR

Graduated top 10% of class: 25%
Graduated top 25% of class: 53%
Graduated top 50% of class: 87%

COLLEGE GRADUATION REQUIREMENTS

Course waivers allowed: No
Course substitutions allowed: Yes
In what course: Foreign language

ADDITIONAL INFORMATION

Environment: The university is situated in northeast Washington, DC, within minutes of the Capitol.

Student Body
  Undergrad enrollment: 3,083
  Women: 56%
  Men: 44%
  Percent out-of-state: 94%

Cost Information
  Tuition: $27,700
  Room & board: $10,808
Housing Information
  University housing: Yes
  Percent living on campus: 68%

Greek System
  Fraternity: Yes
  Sorority: Yes
Athletics: Division III

The Catholic University of America

THE GEORGE WASHINGTON UNIVERSITY

2121 I Street Northwest, Suite 201, Washington, DC 20052
Phone: 202-994-6040 • Fax: 202-994-0325
E-mail: gwadm@gwu.edu • Web: www.gwu.edu
Support: CS • Institution type: 4-year private

LEARNING DISABILITY PROGRAM AND SERVICES

Disability Support Services (DSS) was established to provide support to learning disabled students so that they might participate fully in university life, derive the greatest benefit from their educational experiences, and achieve maximum personal success. There is no LD program at GWU with a fee for service. Students with LD/ADHD are served through DSS. Services are designed to eliminate competitive disadvantages in an academic environment while preserving academic integrity. The staff is committed to providing student-centered services that meet the individual needs of each student. The ultimate goal of DSS is to assist students with disabilities as they gain knowledge to recognize strengths, accommodate differences, and become strong self-advocates. Staff are available to discuss issues such as course load, learning strategies, academic accommodations, and petitions for course waivers or substitutions. DSS offers individual assistance in addressing needs not provided through routine services. Students with LD must provide documentation, including a comprehensive diagnostic interview, psychoeducational evaluation, and a treatment plan; test scores and an interpretation of overall intelligence, information processing, executive functioning, spatial ability, memory, motor ability, achievement skills, reading, writing, and math; and a specific diagnosis and description of the student's functional limitations in an educational setting.

LD/ADHD ADMISSIONS INFORMATION

College entrance tests required: Yes
Interview required: No
Essay recommended: N/A
Documentation required for LD: Psychoeducational evaluation
Documentation required for ADHD: Psychoeducational evaluation
Submitted to: Disability Support Services
Special Ed. HS course work accepted: No

Specific course requirements: NR
Separate application required: No
# of LD applications submitted each year: NR
# of LD applications accepted yearly: NR
Total # of students receiving LD services: 283
Acceptance into program means acceptance into college: Student must be admitted and enrolled in the university and then reviewed for services with Disability Support Services.

ADMISSIONS

GWU does not discriminate on the basis of disability in the recruitment and admission of students. There are no separate admissions procedures or criteria for disabled students. The minimal course requirements include 2 years of math (4 recommended), 4 years of English, 2 years of a foreign language (4 recommended), 2–3 years of social sciences (4 recommended), and 2–3 years of science (4 recommended). The score range for the ACT is 25–30 and for the SAT 1160–1320. The SAT Subject Tests are optional. Since there is no automatic referral from admissions or other campus offices, students are encouraged to contact DSS directly prior to or at the time of admission.

ADDITIONAL INFORMATION

Students need to make a specific request for services or accommodations. Based on the documentation, the Director of DSS authorizes the needed academic adjustments. DSS provides services without charge, including advocacy, readers, scribes, test proctors, LD advising, and assistance with registration and note-taking. Students may be referred for additional services, including diagnostic testing, tutors, and specialized noncredit courses that are available on a fee basis. There is a learning disabilities support group that meets twice throughout the academic year. This group focuses on issues important to students with LD/ADHD. In addition to providing an opportunity for peer support, the group discusses topics ranging from study strategies, note-taking, and the planning of papers, to social issues facing the GWU student with LD/ADHD. Also, there is a Disability Resource Association, which is a student organization that has a speakers bureau and offers support groups.

LEARNING DISABILITY PROGRAM/SERVICES

Learning Disability Program/Services: Disability Support Services
Director: Christy Willis
  E-Mail: cwillis@gwu.edu
  Telephone: 202-994-8250
  Fax: 202-994-7610

LEARNING DISABILITY SERVICES

Requests for the following/services accommodations will be evaluated individually based on appropriate and current documentation.

Allowed in exams
  Calculator: Yes
  Dictionary: Yes
  Computer: Yes
  Spellchecker: Yes
Extended test time: Yes
Scribes: Yes
Proctors: Yes
Oral exams: Yes
Note-takers: Yes

Distraction-reduced environment: Yes
Tape recording in class: Yes
Books on tape from RFBD: Yes
Taping of books not from RFBD: Yes
Accommodations for students with ADHD: Yes
Reading machine: Yes
Other assistive technology: Yes
Priority registration: Yes

Added costs for services: No
LD specialists: Yes
Professional tutors: No
Peer tutors: No
Max. hours/wk. for services: Unlimited
How professors are notified of LD/ADHD: By student

GENERAL ADMISSIONS INFORMATION

Director of Admissions: Kathryn Napper
Telephone: 202-994-6040

ENTRANCE REQUIREMENTS

Academic units required: 4 English, 2 math, 2 science (1 science lab), 2 foreign language, 2 social studies.
Academic units recommended: 4 English, 4 math, 4 science, 4 foreign language, 4 social studies. High school diploma is required, and GED is not accepted. ACT with or without Writing component accepted. Essay, teacher and counselor recommendations are required. TOEFL required of all international applicants: minimum paper TOEFL 550, minimum computer TOEFL 300.

Application deadline: 1/15
Notification: 3/15
Average GPA: NR
ACT Composite middle 50% range: 25–30

SAT Math middle 50% range: 590–680
SAT Critical Reading middle 50% range: 590–690
SAT Writing middle 50% range: NR

Graduated top 10% of class: 59%
Graduated top 25% of class: 80%
Graduated top 50% of class: 99%

COLLEGE GRADUATION REQUIREMENTS

Course waivers allowed: No
Course substitutions allowed: Yes
In what course: Determination is made on a case-by-case basis, primarily in the areas of math and foreign language.

ADDITIONAL INFORMATION

Environment: The university has an urban campus three blocks from the White House.

Student Body
  Undergrad enrollment: 10,563
  Women: 56%
  Men: 44%
  Percent out-of-state: 98%

Cost Information
  Tuition: $34,000
  Room & board: $11,000
Housing Information
  University housing: Yes
  Percent living on campus: 67%

Greek System
  Fraternity: Yes
  Sorority: Yes
Athletics: Division I

BARRY UNIVERSITY

11300 North East Second Avenue, Miami Shores, FL 33161-6695
Phone: 305-899-3100 • Fax: 305-899-2971
E-mail: Des-forms@mail.barry.edu • Web: www.barry.edu
Support: SP • Institution type: 4-year private

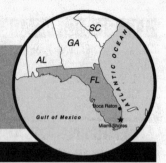

LEARNING DISABILITY PROGRAM AND SERVICES

Barry University offers a special program for students with LD. The Clinical Center for Advanced Learning Program (CCAL) is a comprehensive, intensive, highly structured, and individualized approach to assisting students with LD throughout their college careers. It is designed to move students gradually toward increasing self-direction in academic, personal, and career activities. This program affirms Barry University's commitment to expand college opportunities to students with LD and provide the specialized services that can enhance college success. To apply to the CCAL Program students must complete and return to CCAL the general Barry application for admission and the CCAL Application; write a 1–2 page personal statement on how the student would benefit from the CCAL Program; have a personal interview with the CCAL; sign the Informed Consent Form and present this form to their high school for documentation to be released; forward psychoeducational evaluation report including the WAIS–R; achievement tests, and information processing testing, and provide a copy of the most recent IEP, high school transcript, and a letter of recommendation from a school counselor or LD specialist. It is important for students with LD to understand the need for a commitment to working with the CCAL Program to achieve success at college.

LD/ADHD ADMISSIONS INFORMATION

College entrance tests required: Yes
Interview required: Yes
Essay recommended: Yes
Documentation required for LD: Psychoeducational evaluation
Documentation required for ADHD: Psychoeducational evaluation, childhood history
Submitted to: CCAL
Special Ed. HS course work accepted: Yes

Specific course requirements of all applicants: NR
Separate application required: No
# of LD applications submitted each year: 125
# of LD applications accepted yearly: 25
Total # of students receiving LD services: 45
Acceptance into program means acceptance into college: Student must be admitted and enrolled in the university first and then request services from CCAL.

ADMISSIONS

Students with learning disabilities must meet the regular admission criteria for the university, which includes 2.0 GPA, ACT of 17 or above or SAT of 800 or above, and 4 years of English, 3–4 years of math, 3 years of natural science, and 3–4 years of social science. However, there is a process of individual review by learning disability professionals for those students who have a diagnosed disability and who do not meet the general admission criteria. These students must have an interview and provide appropriate and current LD documentation. An essay is required for admission into the LD Program. Students admitted to the CCAL Program will be expected to meet all requirements established for them and those of the specific university program in which they enroll.

ADDITIONAL INFORMATION

The CCAL Program includes a full range of professionally managed and intensive support services that includes the following: individual diagnostic evaluation allowing for development of a personalized educational plan; intensive scheduled classes to improve math, reading, and written and oral communication skills; individual and small-group subject-area tutoring; instruction in learning and study strategies based on individual needs; academic advising; assistance in developing interpersonal skills; individual and small-group personal, academic, and career counseling; assistance in obtaining study aids; computer access; special test administration services; advocacy with faculty; and an optional summer college transition program. Additionally, all students have access to math labs, writing centers, reading clinics, and educational seminars. All instructional staff hold advanced degrees in their area of specialization. Services are available for both undergraduate and graduate students.

LEARNING DISABILITY PROGRAM/SERVICES

Learning Disability Program/Services: Clinical Center for Advanced Learning Program (CCAL)
Director: Leslie Rouder
  E-Mail: lrouder@mail.barry.edu
  Telephone: 305-899-3488
  Fax: 305-899-3056

LEARNING DISABILITY SERVICES

Requests for the following/services accommodations will be evaluated individually based on appropriate and current documentation.

Allowed in exams
  Calculator: Yes
  Dictionary: Yes
  Computer: Yes
  Spellchecker: Yes
Extended test time: Yes
Scribes: Yes
Proctors: Yes
Oral exams: Yes
Note-takers: Yes

Distraction-reduced environment: Yes
Tape recording in class: Yes
Books on tape from RFBD: Yes
Taping of books not from RFBD: Yes
**Accommodations for students with
  ADHD:** Yes
Reading machine: Yes
Other assistive technology: Yes
Priority registration: No

Added costs for services: Yes
LD specialists: Yes
Professional tutors: 13
Peer tutors: No
Max. hours/wk. for services:
  Unlimited
**How professors are notified of
  LD/ADHD:** By both student and
  director

GENERAL ADMISSIONS INFORMATION

Director of Admissions: Marcia Nance
Telephone: 305-899-3100

ENTRANCE REQUIREMENTS

Academic units recommended: 4 English, 3 math, 3 science, 3 social studies. High school diploma is required, and GED is accepted. ACT with or without Writing component accepted. TOEFL required of all international applicants: minimum paper TOEFL 550, minimum computer TOEFL 213.

Application deadline: Rolling
Notification: Rolling
Average GPA: 3.12
ACT Composite middle 50% range:
  18–22

SAT Math middle 50% range:
  480–530
**SAT Critical Reading middle 50%
  range:** 480–540
SAT Writing middle 50% range: NR

Graduated top 10% of class: NR
Graduated top 25% of class: NR
Graduated top 50% of class: 100%

COLLEGE GRADUATION REQUIREMENTS

Course waivers allowed: No
Course substitutions allowed: No

ADDITIONAL INFORMATION

Environment: The university is located seven miles from Miami.

Student Body
  Undergrad enrollment: 2,800
  Women: 50%
  Men: 50%
  Percent out-of-state: 16%

Cost Information
  Tuition: $24,000
  Room & board: $7,850
Housing Information
  University housing: Yes
  Percent living on campus: 40%

Greek System
  Fraternity: Yes
  Sorority: Yes
Athletics: Division II

BEACON COLLEGE

105 East Main Street, Leesburg, FL 34748
Phone: 352-787-7249 • Fax: 352-787-0721
E-mail: admissions@beaconcollege.edu • Web: www.beaconcollege.edu
Support: SP • Institution type: 4-year private

LEARNING DISABILITY PROGRAM AND SERVICES

The philosophy of Beacon College is to offer LD/ADHD students academic programs supplemented by appropriate accommodations and support services that will help them prepare for meaningful participation in society. The purpose of Beacon College is to create a campus community that facilitates academic and personal success. The mission of Beacon College is to offer academic degree programs to students with learning disabilities. To accomplish this, the college provides Associate of Arts and Bachelor of Arts programs in human services and liberal studies. The human services programs provide a practical experience in the professional fields associated with public and community services. The liberal studies program provides a broad-based liberal arts education for students seeking intellectual growth and personal change. Liberal studies exposes students to a variety of subjects designed to establish a basis for effective life-long learning and attainment of personal goals. Beacon serves students with language-based learning disabilities, math disabilities, ADHD, auditory and visual processing differences, expressive/receptive language deficits, and read/writing disabilities.

LD/ADHD ADMISSIONS INFORMATION

College entrance tests required: No
Interview required: Yes
Essay recommended: Yes
Documentation required for LD: Psychoeducational evaluation; WAIS–III with subtest scores; WJ–III with age or grade equivalency scores in reading, writing, and math
Documentation required for ADHD: Psychoeducational evaluation; WAIS–III with subtest scores; WJ–III with age or grade equivalency scores in reading, writing, and math
Submitted to: Admissions Office
Special Ed. HS course work accepted: Yes

Specific course requirements of all applicants: No
Separate application required: No
# of LD applications submitted each year: 87
# of LD applications accepted yearly: 54
Total # of students receiving LD services: 112
Acceptance into program means acceptance into college: Students are admitted directly into the college and the program simultaneously.

ADMISSIONS

Applicants must submit current (completed within the last 2 years) academic reports and test scores, recent psychoeducational evaluations documenting a learning disability, and records that may help clarify students' learning problems. Students must also submit a high school transcript, personal statements, and three recommendation forms. All applicants must have a high school diploma or the GED. Each applicant must have an interview prior to an admission decision being made. There are no specific high school courses required for admission, and courses taken in a special education curriculum are accepted. The college does not require either the ACT or SAT. The admission decision is made by the Admissions Committee. Beacon may admit students on a provisional basis.

ADDITIONAL INFORMATION

Beacon College is a growing program (fall of 2000) that serves college students with documented learning disabilities who each have the ability, desire, and perseverance to earn either an AA or BA degree. Some students are recent high school graduates, while others are older students who transfer from other colleges or who attend after being in the workforce. Beacon serves a culturally diverse group of men and women from 22 different states. Small class sizes, averaging 10 students per class, help the college meet the needs of the individual students. Beacon's Academic Mentoring Program guides students with a focus on self-awareness, time management/organization skills, and strategies for academic success. The Field Placement Program assists students with goal setting, career exploration, and obtaining work experience. Students gain life skills through living within the Leesburg community in apartments leased by the college. Beacon students graduate with a college academic degree and the life skills to live independently. In addition to the ability to set personal goals, graduates are also prepared to seek gainful employment or explore additional academic or vocational training.

LEARNING DISABILITY PROGRAM/SERVICES

Learning Disability Program/Services: Beacon College
Director: Deborah Brodbeck, President
  E-Mail: admissions@beaconcollege.edu
  Telephone: 352-787-7660
  Fax: 352-787-0721
Contact Person: Carolyn A. Scott, Director of Admissions
  E-Mail: cscott@becon.edu
  Telephone: 352-315-9269
  Fax: 352-787-0721

LEARNING DISABILITY SERVICES

Requests for the following/services accommodations will be evaluated individually based on appropriate and current documentation.

Allowed in exams
  Calculator: Yes
  Dictionary: Yes
  Computer: Yes
  Spellchecker: Yes
Extended test time: Yes
Scribes: Yes
Proctors: Yes
Oral exams: Yes
Note-takers: Yes

Distraction-reduced environment: Yes
Tape recording in class: Yes
Books on tape from RFBD: Yes
Taping of books not from RFBD: Yes
Accommodations for students with ADHD: Yes
Reading machine: Yes
Other assistive technology: Yes
Priority registration: N/A

Added costs for services: No
LD specialists: Yes
Professional tutors: 5–6
Peer tutors: No
Max. hours/wk. for services: Unlimited
How professors are notified of LD/ADHD: By both student and director

GENERAL ADMISSIONS INFORMATION

Director of Admissions: Carolyn A. Scott
Telephone: 352-315-9269

ENTRANCE REQUIREMENTS

Academic units required: 4 English, 1 math, 1 science, 1 social studies, 2 history, 3 academic electives. High school diploma is required, and GED is accepted. ACT with or without Writing component accepted.

Application deadline: 8/20
Notification: Rolling
Average GPA: NR
ACT Composite middle 50% range: NR

SAT Math middle 50% range: NR
SAT Critical Reading middle 50% range: NR
SAT Writing middle 50% range: NR

Graduated top 10% of class: NR
Graduated top 25% of class: NR
Graduated top 50% of class: NR

COLLEGE GRADUATION REQUIREMENTS

Course waivers allowed: Yes
In what course: Math
Course substitutions allowed: Yes
In what course: Math

ADDITIONAL INFORMATION

Environment: The college is located in the city of Leesburg, 1 hour from Orlando.

Student Body
  Undergrad enrollment: 112
  Women: 43%
  Men: 57%
  Percent out-of-state: 80%

Cost Information
  Tuition: $23,900
  Room & board: $7,200
Housing Information
  University housing: Yes
  Percent living on campus: 95%

Greek System
  Fraternity: NR
  Sorority: NR
Athletics: NR

FLORIDA A&M UNIVERSITY

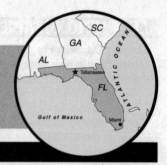

Suite G-9, Foote-Hilyer Administration Center, Tallahassee, FL 32307
Phone: 850-599-3796 • Fax: 850-599-3069
E-mail: admission@famu.edu • Web: www.famu.edu
Support: SP • Institution type: 4-year public

LEARNING DISABILITY PROGRAM AND SERVICES

Florida A&M offers an education for students with LD and meets the challenge consistent with the objective indicated by the LDEC club name: "Excellence Through Caring." The goals of the Learning Development and Evaluation Center (LDEC) are threefold: First, students with specific learning disabilities can successfully pursue college-level studies with a reasonable level of expectation for degree success. Second, preparation for college-level studies for students with specific learning disabilities should begin early. Third, postsecondary students should actively engage in developmental learning. The need for life-long learning is evident in the ever-changing society and, for the learning disabled person, is mandatory for continued success. Tutoring for developmental learning is a major component. The program does not offer blanket accommodations, but services offered are very comprehensive, such as preparation classes for tests, adapted courses, opportunities for test retakes, alternative courses, and academic activities structured according to students' diagnostic evaluations. A reduced course load is considered a viable option to maintaining an acceptable GPA. The LDEC is a multifaceted program that provides psychoeducational evaluation, personalized accommodations, and comprehensive support services.

LD/ADHD ADMISSIONS INFORMATION

College entrance tests required: Yes
Interview required: No
Essay recommended: Yes
Documentation required for LD: Psychoeducational
 evaluation no more than 3 years old
Documentation required for ADHD: Letter from a physician
 on official letterhead
Submitted to: LEDC
Special Ed. HS course work accepted: No

Specific course requirements of all applicants: Yes
Separate application required: Yes
# of LD applications submitted each year: 40–50
# of LD applications accepted yearly: 20–25
Total # of students receiving LD services: 275
**Acceptance into program means acceptance into
 college:** Students are admitted directly into LDEC and attend
 the summer LD program as part of special admissions to the
 university.

ADMISSIONS
Acceptance into the LDEC does not ensure admission to the university. If students with learning disabilities apply and are rejected, they may ask for special admission consideration and send verifying information of a learning disability. The Office of Admissions gives all information to the LDEC director for a recommendation for admission to the university based on acceptance into the LDEC program. Applicants must have a regular high school diploma, take the ACT/SAT, have a recent psychoeducational evaluation, and attend a summer program. Most students who have learning disabilities and who seek admission through the LDEC enter Florida A&M through the special admission process. ACT scores should be 12 or higher. The required GPA is 1.7 or above.

ADDITIONAL INFORMATION
Specific course offerings in reading, study skills, English, and math with additional class meetings and assignments to meet the individual needs of the students are available. Students must register for reading and student life-skills courses each semester until the student and program staff feel that optimal learning development skills have been reached. When appropriate, students may have a peer tutor attend classes and take notes (student and tutor will exchange notes in the LDEC), or the peer tutor may only need to help the student organize notes from a taped lecture. LDEC offers a 2-week summer transition program (required for incoming students with LD) to students entering 11th or 12th grade or recent graduates from high school. This program provides students a chance to focus on certain skills such as memory and technological skills or a particular academic area. Mastery of the College Study Skills Institute provides a firm foundation for students with learning disabilities to enhance success in college and their future employment.

LEARNING DISABILITY PROGRAM/SERVICES

Learning Disability Program/Services: Learning Development and Evaluation Center (LDEC)
Director: Dr. Nathaniel Holmes
  Telephone: 850-599-3180
  Fax: 850-561-2513
Contact Person: Donna C. Shell
  Telephone: 850-599-3180
  Fax: 850-561-2513

LEARNING DISABILITY SERVICES

Requests for the following/services accommodations will be evaluated individually based on appropriate and current documentation.

Allowed in exams
  Calculator: Yes
  Dictionary: Yes
  Computer: Yes
  Spellchecker: Yes
Extended test time: Yes
Scribes: Yes
Proctors: Yes
Oral exams: Yes
Note-takers: Yes

Distraction-reduced environment: Yes
Tape recording in class: Yes
Books on tape from RFBD: Yes
Taping of books not from RFBD: Yes
Accommodations for students with ADHD: Yes
Reading machine: Yes
Other assistive technology: Yes
Priority registration: No

Added costs for services: No
LD specialists: Yes
Professional tutors: NR
Peer tutors: 10
Max. hours/wk. for services: 45
How professors are notified of LD/ADHD: By both student and director

GENERAL ADMISSIONS INFORMATION

Director of Admissions: Danielle Kennedy-Lamar
Telephone: 850-599-3796

ENTRANCE REQUIREMENTS

Academic units required: 4 English, 3 math, 3 science (1 science lab), 2 foreign language, 3 social studies, 3 academic electives. **Academic units recommended:** 4 English, 3 math, 3 science, 2 foreign language, 3 social studies, 3 academic electives with at least 2.5 GPA. High school diploma is required, and GED is accepted. SAT 1010 or ACT 21 with or without Writing component accepted. TOEFL required of all international applicants: minimum paper TOEFL 500, minimum computer TOEFL 173.

Application deadline: 5/9
Notification: Rolling
Average GPA: 3.00
ACT Composite middle 50% range: 19–22

SAT Math middle 50% range: 440–550
SAT Critical Reading middle 50% range: 440–550
SAT Writing middle 50% range: NR

Graduated top 10% of class: NR
Graduated top 25% of class: NR
Graduated top 50% of class: NR

COLLEGE GRADUATION REQUIREMENTS

Course waivers allowed: No
Course substitutions allowed: Yes
In what course: Varies; it depends on the major elective requirements and the disability of the individual. Substitutions used rather than waivers.

ADDITIONAL INFORMATION

Environment: The university is located on 419 acres 169 miles west of Jackson.

Student Body
  Undergrad enrollment: 9,967
  Women: 58%
  Men: 42%
  Percent out-of-state: 27%

Cost Information
  In-state tuition: $3,047
  Out-of-state tuition: $14,243
  Room & board: $5,492
Housing Information
  University housing: Yes
  Percent living on campus: 75%

Greek System
  Fraternity: Yes
  Sorority: Yes
Athletics: Division I

FLORIDA ATLANTIC UNIVERSITY

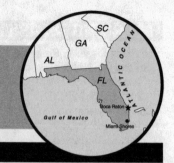

777 Glades Road, PO Box 3091, Boca Raton, FL 33431-0991
Phone: 561-297-3040 • Fax: 561-297-2758
E-mail: UGRecruitment@fau.edu • Web: www.fau.edu
Support: CS • Institution type: 4-year public

LEARNING DISABILITY PROGRAM AND SERVICES

The Office for Students with Disabilities (OSD) offers equal access to a quality education by providing reasonable accommodations to qualified students. Students who have a documented LD may receive strategy tutoring from an LD specialist by appointment. Students are expected to be self-sufficient and strong self-advocates. There is a Counseling Center with professionally trained staff to help students with interpersonal conflicts and concerns, test anxiety, poor concentration, and guidance services.

LD/ADHD ADMISSIONS INFORMATION

College entrance tests required: Yes
Interview required: No
Essay recommended: No
Documentation required for LD: Test of aptitude (WAIS preferred), achievement battery, tests of information processing. Performed on adult scale.
Documentation required for ADHD: Diagnostician's report, including standardized assessment of attention and 2 behavioral rating scales
Submitted to: Office for Students with Disabilities
Special Ed. HS course work accepted: Yes

Specific course requirements of all applicants: Yes
Separate application required: Yes
# of LD applications submitted each year: NR
# of LD applications accepted yearly: NR
Total # of students receiving LD services: NR
Acceptance into program means acceptance into college: Student must be admitted and enrolled in the university first (they can appeal a denial) and then request services.

ADMISSIONS

There is no special application process for students with LD. However, students with LD may be eligible to substitute for certain admission requirements. Students not meeting admission criteria may be admitted by a faculty admission committee if they possess the potential to succeed in university studies or will enhance the university. Supporting documentation explaining circumstances that adversely affected the student's past academic performances will be required. An admissions counselor will assess each applicant in developing supporting materials to be presented to the committee by the Director of Admissions. Students are expected to have a minimum ACT of 20 or SAT of 860. A sliding scale is used with GPA and test scores. Students who self-disclose and are admitted are then reviewed for services. In some cases, these students are reviewed by the OSD, which provides a recommendation to admissions. Typical courses required for admission include 4 years of English, 3 years of math (Algebra I and higher), 3 years of science, 2 years of a foreign language, 3 years of social studies, and 4 electives.

ADDITIONAL INFORMATION

Students must provide documentation including an aptitude (WAIS preferred) and achievement battery. The diagnostician's report must indicate standardized assessment measures on attention, reported history, and corroboration of current symptoms using two rating scales. With appropriate documentation, students may receive the following accommodations or services: the use of calculators, dictionaries, computers, or spellchecker during exams; extended time on tests; distraction-free environment for tests; oral exams; proctors; scribes; tape recorders in class; textbooks on tape; note-takers; and course substitutions. Skills classes are offered in study skill techniques and organizational strategies. There are occasionally instances where a student is unable to master a particular course because of a disability. In those cases, course substitutions may be permitted if the course in question is not essential to the degree program or related to a licensing requirement. If a student feels he or she may be eligible for a course substitution, the student must first contact OSD for information regarding the substitution process.

LEARNING DISABILITY PROGRAM/SERVICES

Learning Disability Program/Services: Office for Students with Disabilities (OSD)
Director: Nicole Rokos, MEd
  E-Mail: nrokos@fau.edu
  Telephone: 561-297-3880
  Fax: 561-297-2184

LEARNING DISABILITY SERVICES

Requests for the following services/accommodations will be evaluated individually based on appropriate and current documentation.

Allowed in exams
  Calculator: Yes
  Dictionary: No
  Computer: Yes
  Spellchecker: Yes
Extended test time: Yes
Scribes: Yes
Proctors: Yes
Oral exams: Yes
Note-takers: Yes

Distraction-reduced environment: Yes
Tape recording in class: Yes
Books on tape from RFBD: Yes
Taping of books not from RFBD: Yes
Accommodations for students with ADHD: Yes
Reading machine: Yes
Other assistive technology: Yes
Priority registration: No

Added costs for services: No
LD specialists: Yes
Professional tutors: NR
Peer tutors: 1–10
Max. hours/wk. for services: Unlimited
How professors are notified of LD/ADHD: By both student and director

GENERAL ADMISSIONS INFORMATION

Director of Admissions: Barbara Pletcher
Telephone: 561-297-3040

ENTRANCE REQUIREMENTS

Academic units required: 4 English, 3 math, 3 science (2 science labs), 2 foreign language, 3 social studies, 4 academic electives. High school diploma is required, and GED is accepted. ACT without Writing component accepted. TOEFL required of all international applicants: minimum paper TOEFL 550, minimum computer TOEFL 300.

Application deadline: 6/1
Notification: NR
Average GPA: 3.40
ACT Composite middle 50% range: 19–24

SAT Math middle 50% range: 480–570
SAT Critical Reading middle 50% range: 480–570
SAT Writing middle 50% range: NR

Graduated top 10% of class: NR
Graduated top 25% of class: NR
Graduated top 50% of class: NR

COLLEGE GRADUATION REQUIREMENTS

Course waivers allowed: Yes
In what course: Substitutions rather than waivers when possible for math and foreign language requirements (depending on major)
Course substitutions allowed: Yes
In what course: Varies; it depends on the major requirements and the disability. Substitutions used rather than waivers when possible.

ADDITIONAL INFORMATION

Environment: The university is located on 1,000 acres one and a half miles from the ocean and in proximity to Miami and Fort Lauderdale.

Student Body
  Undergrad enrollment: 19,951
  Women: 60%
  Men: 40%
  Percent out-of-state: 5%

Cost Information
  In-state tuition: $3,327
  Out-of-state tuition: $16,391
  Room & board: $8,280
Housing Information
  University housing: Yes
  Percent living on campus: 5%

Greek System
  Fraternity: Yes
  Sorority: Yes
Athletics: Division I

FLORIDA STATE UNIVERSITY

PO Box 3062400, Tallahassee, FL 32306-2400
Phone: 850-644-6200 • Fax: 850-644-0197
E-mail: admissions@admin.fsu.edu • Web: www.fsu.edu
Support: CS • Institution type: 4-year public

LEARNING DISABILITY PROGRAM AND SERVICES

The Student Disability Resource Center (SDRC) is the primary advocate for students with disabilities. The center works with faculty and staff to provide accommodations for the unique needs of students both in and out of the classroom. Learning specialists meet individually with students who have LD/ADHD, or other impairments. FSU is noted for its sensitivity to students with disabilities. By providing support services at no cost to students with disabilities, the Student Disability Resource Center offers an opportunity for students with disabilities to achieve their academic and personal goals. Students who self-disclose their disability must complete a request for services form to receive accommodations. LD documentation must be no more than 3 years old and submitted from a licensed psychologist.

LD/ADHD ADMISSIONS INFORMATION

College entrance tests required: Yes
Interview required: No
Essay recommended: Yes
Documentation required for LD: Psychoeducational evaluation
Documentation required for ADHD: Yes
Submitted to: Both Admissions Office and Student Disability Resource Center
Special Ed. HS course work accepted: Yes

Specific course requirements of all applicants: Yes
Separate application required: Yes
# of LD applications submitted each year: NR
# of LD applications accepted yearly: NR
Total # of students receiving LD services: 300
Acceptance into program means acceptance into college: Students must be admitted and enrolled in the university first and then request services.

ADMISSIONS

Students with LD or ADHD who are borderline candidates for admission are encouraged to self-disclose in the admission process. These students can choose to apply for special consideration based on a disability. Special consideration is specifically designed for students who do not meet general admissions requirements. A disability subcommittee reviews the documentation, personal statement, recommendations, transcripts, and ACT/SAT scores to determine eligibility for admissions. Under certain circumstances, students may be offered summer admission. Florida students applying to the university should present at least a B-plus average in all academic subjects 24 ACT or 1100 SAT. The profile for non-Florida applicants is higher. While the writing component of the ACT and/or SAT is required, FSU does not currently use it as part of the total composite/score. Course requirements include 4 English, 3 math, 3 science, 3 social studies, 2 foreign language, and 3 academic elective units. Auditions required for music, dance, or the BFA degree in theater. A departmental application is required of all students wishing to major in motion picture, television, and recording arts. Through the Center for Academic Retention and Enhancement (CARE), Florida State University offers a special admission program dedicated to assisting those who have been disadvantaged due to economic, educational, or cultural circumstances. CARE provides a comprehensive program of orientation and academic support designed to ease the transition from high school to college and build a strong academic foundation. Most of the participants selected will be first-generation college students from financially disadvantaged backgrounds who will enter CARE in the summer.

ADDITIONAL INFORMATION

Students who choose to disclose their disability to receive accommodations must complete a Request for Services from the SDRC. For an LD, documentation less than 3 years old is required from a licensed psychologist. Staff members assist students in exploring their needs and determining the necessary services and accommodations. Academic accommodations include alternative testing/extended time, editing, note-takers, registration assistance, tutors, and study partners. Learning specialists meet individually with students with LD/ADHD. Services include teaching study skills, memory enhancement techniques, organizational skills, test-taking strategies, stress management techniques, ways to structure tutoring for best results, skills for negotiating accommodations with instructors, and supportive counseling. Advocates for Disability Awareness act as a support group for students with disabilities. Through their participation, students and others in the university community involved develop skills in leadership, self-advocacy, and career development.

LEARNING DISABILITY PROGRAM/SERVICES

Learning Disability Program/Services: Student Disability Resource Center
Director: Bea Awoniyi
  E-Mail: bawoniyi@admin.fsu.edu
  Telephone: 850-644-9566
  Fax: 850-644-7164

LEARNING DISABILITY SERVICES

Requests for the following services/accommodations will be evaluated individually based on appropriate and current documentation.

Allowed in exams
  Calculator: Yes
  Dictionary: Yes
  Computer: Yes
  Spellchecker: Yes
Extended test time: Yes
Scribes: Yes
Proctors: Yes
Oral exams: Yes
Note-takers: Yes

Distraction-reduced environment: Yes
Tape recording in class: Yes
Books on tape from RFBD: Yes
Taping of books not from RFBD: Yes
Accommodations for students with ADHD: Yes
Reading machine: Yes
Other assistive technology: Yes
Priority registration: Yes

Added costs for services: No
LD specialists: Yes
Professional tutors: NR
Peer tutors: No
Max. hours/wk. for services: N/A
How professors are notified of LD/ADHD: By student

GENERAL ADMISSIONS INFORMATION

Director of Admissions: Janice Finney
Telephone: 850-644-6200

ENTRANCE REQUIREMENTS

Academic units required: 4 English, 3 math, 3 science (2 science labs), 2 foreign language, 3 social studies, 2 history, 3 academic electives. **Academic units recommended:** 4 English, 4 math, 4 science (2 science labs), 4 foreign language, 3 social studies, 2 history, 3 academic electives. High school diploma is required, and GED is accepted. ACT with Writing component required. TOEFL required of all international applicants: minimum paper TOEFL 550, minimum computer TOEFL 213.

Application deadline: 2/14
Notification: 11/1, 12/13, 2/14, 3/28
Average GPA: 3.62
ACT Composite middle 50% range: 23–27

SAT Math middle 50% range: 540–630
SAT Critical Reading middle 50% range: 530–620
SAT Writing middle 50% range: 510–600

Graduated top 10% of class: 26%
Graduated top 25% of class: 63%
Graduated top 50% of class: 94%

COLLEGE GRADUATION REQUIREMENTS

Course waivers allowed: No
In what course: N/A
Course substitutions allowed: Yes
In what course: Foreign language, math.

ADDITIONAL INFORMATION

Environment: Suburban campus in Tallahassee

Student Body
  Undergrad enrollment: 30,841
  Women: 56%
  Men: 44%
  Percent out-of-state: 12%

Cost Information
  In-state tuition: $2,465
  Out-of-state tuition: $15,596
  Room & board: $6,778
  Housing Information
  University housing: Yes
  Percent living on campus: 15%

Greek System
  Fraternity: Yes
  Sorority: Yes
  Athletics: Division I

LYNN UNIVERSITY

3601 North Military Trail, Boca Raton, FL 33431-5598
Phone: 561-237-7000 • Fax: 561-237-7100
E-mail: admission@lynn.edu • Web: www.lynn.edu
Support: SP • Institution type: 4-year private

LEARNING DISABILITY PROGRAM AND SERVICES

The Comprehensive Support Program has experts in the field of learning pedagogy and nontraditional methodology providing extensive academic support for students with learning differences. This program includes unlimited tutoring, testing accommodations, distraction-free testing, specialized classes, expert instructors who teach in a multimodality assessment format, workshops on anxiety and testing, progress updates, mid-term grades, and more. The Metamorphosis Coaching Program addresses specific executive functioning issues for students with ADHD through weekly coaching, tutors trained in brain-based learning techniques, and weekly experiential activities. This program uses a diagnostic coaching model to address behavioral issues specific to college students with ADHD such as organization skills, procrastination issues, time management, impulsivity, focus and attention, and study skills. The weekly experiential learning component immerses students in bodily-kinesthetic and naturalist activities. The lessons learned through this intrapersonal reflective process provides students with valuable insights about themselves and the way they learn best.

LD/ADHD ADMISSIONS INFORMATION

College entrance tests required: Yes
Interview required: No
Essay recommended: Yes
Documentation required for LD: Psychoeducational evaluations
Documentation required for ADHD: DSM–IV diagnosis or documentation from a physcian
Submitted to: Admissions Office

Special Ed. HS course work accepted: Yes
Separate application required: No
# of LD applications submitted each year: 750
# of LD applications accepted yearly: 300
Total # of students receiving LD services: 350
Acceptance into program means acceptance into college: Student must be admitted and enrolled in the university first and then offered services through ACA.

ADMISSIONS

Students submit the general admission application and admissions criteria depend on the level of services required. Students needing the least restrictive services need college-prep courses. Some students are admitted provisionally and others admitted conditionally into the Frontiers Program with an ACT of 18 or lower or SAT of 850 or lower and 2.0 GPA. Students admitted conditionally take a reduced course load, no science the first semester, and 1.5 hours of scheduled tutoring. The program director/staff make a final recommendation to admission regarding the admission of students to the Advancement Program. Interviews are encouraged. Comprehensive Support Program ($5,350 per semester plus regular tuition) applicants must provide: transcript, SAT/ACT, personal statement, counselor recommendation, and current psychoeducational evaluation. Metamorphosis Coaching Program ($3,475 for freshmen plus regular tuition) applicants must provide: transcript, SAT/ACT, personal statement, counselor recommendation, and current psychoeducational evaluation and/or verification of ADHD diagnosis or other related executive processing issues.

ADDITIONAL INFORMATION

All tests are monitored and advocacy work with faculty is provided by the director. Students needing support after 1 year will continue in the program for specific tutoring, test accommodations, and program guidance. Other features include: skills classes for credit in Language and Learning Development; professional tutors; individual study strategy sessions to enhance study and organizational skills and test anxiety; updates to parents of tutorial and testing center utilization; parent/student advocate discusses issues with parents, students, and professors; EDU 100 Language and Learning course for freshmen in developing strategies for college achievement; midterm faculty progress reports updating students and parents on academic success; alternative test procedures; academic advising and schedule planning; selected core courses taught in a multimodality style and/or with alternative performance assessment to meet students' individual needs; 1-day Comprehensive Support Program Orientation; Comprehensive Support Program advisor monitors students on probation. All Comprehensive Support Program instructors and tutors trained in learning styles and techniques to stay current on new strategies and concepts. All incoming freshman and transfer students are required to take two tutoring sessions per week. Summer classes and case study meetings are available.

LEARNING DISABILITY PROGRAM/SERVICES

Learning Disability Program/Services: Institute for Achievement and Learning
Director: Dr. Marsha A. Glines
  E-Mail: mglines@lynn.edu
  Telephone: 561-237-7881
  Fax: 561-237-7873
Contact Person: Admissions Office
  E-Mail: admission@lynn.edu
  Telephone: 561-237-7900
  Fax: 561-237-7100

LEARNING DISABILITY SERVICES

Requests for the following services/accommodations will be evaluated individually based on appropriate and current documentation.

Allowed in exams
  Calculator: Yes
  Dictionary: Yes
  Computer: Yes
  Spellchecker: Yes
Extended test time: Yes
Scribes: Yes
Proctors: Yes
Oral exams: Yes
Note-takers: No

Distraction-reduced environment: Yes
Tape recording in class: Yes
Books on tape from RFBD: No
Taping of books not from RFBD: No
Accommodations for students with
  ADHD: Yes
Reading machine: Yes
Other assistive technology: Yes
Priority registration: No

Added costs for services: Yes
LD specialists: Yes
Professional tutors: 46
Peer tutors: No
Max. hours/wk. for services:
  Unlimited
How professors are notified of
  LD/ADHD: By student

GENERAL ADMISSIONS INFORMATION

Director of Admissions: Brett Ormandy
Telephone: 561-237-7836

ENTRANCE REQUIREMENTS

Academic units required: 4 English, 4 math, 4 science, 2 social studies, 2 history. High school diploma is required, and GED is accepted. ACT with or without Writing component accepted. TOEFL required of all international applicants: minimum paper TOEFL 500, minimum computer TOEFL 173.

Application deadline: NR
Notification: Rolling—continuous
Average GPA: 2.64
ACT Composite middle 50% range:
  16–20

SAT Math middle 50% range:
  400–510
SAT Critical Reading middle 50%
  range: 410–500
SAT Writing middle 50% range: NR

Graduated top 10% of class: 2%
Graduated top 25% of class: 10%
Graduated top 50% of class: 33%

COLLEGE GRADUATION REQUIREMENTS

Course waivers allowed: No
Course substitutions allowed: No

ADDITIONAL INFORMATION

Environment: The university is located on 123 acres in a suburban area on Florida's Gold Coast.

Student Body
  Undergrad enrollment: 2,300
  Women: 50%
  Men: 50%
  Percent out-of-state: 38%

Cost Information
  Tuition: $27,350
  Room & board: $9,650
Housing Information
  University housing: Yes
  Percent living on campus: 47%

Greek System
  Fraternity: Yes
  Sorority: Yes
Athletics: Division II

UNIVERSITY OF CENTRAL FLORIDA

PO Box 160111, Orlando, FL 32816-0111
Phone: 407-823-3000 • Fax: 407-823-5625
E-mail: admission@mail.ucf.edu • Web: www.ucf.edu
Support: CS • Institution type: 4-year public

LEARNING DISABILITY PROGRAM AND SERVICES

The Office of Student Disability Services provides information and individualized services consistent with the student's documented disability. To be eligible for disability-related services, individuals must have a documented disability as defined by applicable federal and state laws. Individuals seeking services are required to provide recent documentation from an appropriate health care provider or professional. See www.sds.ucf.edu for specific documentation required.

LD/ADHD ADMISSIONS INFORMATION

College entrance tests required: Yes
Interview required: No
Essay recommended: No
Documentation required for LD: Psychoeducational evaluation
Documentation required for ADHD: Yes
Submitted to: Admissions Office
Special Ed. HS course work accepted: No

Specific course requirements of all applicants: Yes
Separate application required: No
# of LD applications submitted each year: NR
# of LD applications accepted yearly: NR
Total # of students receiving LD services: NR
Acceptance into program means acceptance into college: Students must be admitted and enrolled prior to requesting services.

ADMISSIONS

Admission to the University of Central Florida requires graduation from an accredited high school with certain high school academic units, a cumulative high school GPA in those academic units, and SAT or ACT test scores. Course requirements include 4 years of English (at least 3 with substantial writing requirements); 3 years of mathematics (Algebra I and above); 3 years of natural science (at least 2 with labs); 3 years of social science; 2 sequential years of the same foreign language; 3 elective years (preferably from English, mathematics, natural science, social science, or foreign language areas). Students with disabilities who have not taken a foreign language in high school must submit, along with appropriate documentation, a letter from a school official verifying that not taking a foreign language was an accommodation for the disability. If a student needs special admission consideration based on a disability, the student should send the requested appropriate documentation to the Undergraduate Admissions Office. Satisfying minimum requirements does not guarantee admission to UCF since preference will be given to those students whose credentials indicate the greatest promise of academic success.

ADDITIONAL INFORMATION

The University Writing Center (UWC) provides free writing support to all undergraduates and graduates at the University of Central Florida. The Student Academic Resource Center (SARC) provides high-quality academic support programs, including tutoring and supplemental instruction, retention programs, academic advising programs, and various other academic programs and services. The Math Lab provides tutoring for students enrolled in mathematics courses.

LEARNING DISABILITY PROGRAM/SERVICES

Learning Disability Program/Services: Student Disibility Services
Director: Dr. Philip Kalfin
  E-Mail: sds@mail.ucf.edu
  Telephone: 407-823-2371
  Fax: 407-823-2372

LEARNING DISABILITY SERVICES

Requests for the following services/accommodations will be evaluated individually based on appropriate and current documentation.

Allowed in exams
  Calculator: Yes
  Dictionary: Yes
  Computer: Yes
  Spellchecker: Yes
Extended test time: Yes
Scribes: Yes
Proctors: Yes
Oral exams: No
Note-takers: Yes

Distraction-reduced environment: Yes
Tape recording in class: Yes
Books on tape from RFBD: Yes
Taping of books not from RFBD: Yes
Accommodations for students with ADHD: Yes
Reading machine: Yes
Other assistive technology: Yes
Priority registration: Yes

Added costs for services: No
LD specialists: Yes
Professional tutors: No
Peer tutors: N/A
Max. hours/wk. for services: Varies
How professors are notified of LD/ADHD: By student

GENERAL ADMISSIONS INFORMATION

Director of Admissions: Dr. Gordon Chavis
Telephone: 407-823-3000

ENTRANCE REQUIREMENTS

Academic units required: 4 English, 3 math, 3 science (2 science labs), 2 foreign language, 3 social studies, 4 academic electives. High school diploma is required, and GED is accepted. ACT with Writing component required. TOEFL required of all international applicants: minimum paper TOEFL 550, minimum computer TOEFL 213.

Application deadline: 5/1
Notification: Rolling
Average GPA: 3.57
ACT Composite middle 50% range: 22–27

SAT Math middle 50% range: 540–640
SAT Critical Reading middle 50% range: 520–610
SAT Writing middle 50% range: 500–590

Graduated top 10% of class: 35%
Graduated top 25% of class: 77%
Graduated top 50% of class: 93%

COLLEGE GRADUATION REQUIREMENTS

Course waivers allowed: No
Course substitutions allowed: Yes
In what course: With appropriate documentation, math and foreign language may be substituted with selected other courses.

ADDITIONAL INFORMATION

Environment: The main campus of UCF is located 13 miles east of Orlando.

Student Body
  Undergrad enrollment: 39,298
  Women: 55%
  Men: 45%
  Percent out-of-state: 5%

Cost Information
  In-state tuition: $3,492
  Out-of-state tuition: $17,017
  Room & board: $8,000
  Housing Information
  University housing: Yes
  Percent living on campus: 25%

Greek System
  Fraternity: Yes
  Sorority: Yes
Athletics: Division I

UNIVERSITY OF FLORIDA

201 Criser Hall, Box 114000, Gainesville, FL 32611-4000
Phone: 352-392-1365 • Fax: 352-392-3987
E-mail: ourwebrequests@registrar.ufl.edu • Web: www.ufl.edu
Support: CS • Institution type: 4-year public

LEARNING DISABILITY PROGRAM AND SERVICES

The University of Florida offers a full range of support services designed to assist students with learning disabilities. Support services are individually tailored to each student's needs, and those services may be modified to meet the specific demands and requirements of individual courses. Advisement and support services are available to students on an as-needed basis. Assistance can be provided regarding registration, learning strategies, classroom accommodations, and the University of Florida petition process.

LD/ADHD ADMISSIONS INFORMATION

College entrance tests required: Yes
Interview required: No
Essay recommended: No
Documentation required for LD: Psychoeducational evaluation
Documentation required for ADHD: Psychoeducational evaluation
Submitted to: Admissions Office
Special Ed. HS course work accepted: Yes

Specific course requirements of all applicants: Yes
Separate application required: No
# of LD applications submitted each year: NR
# of LD applications accepted yearly: NR
Total # of students receiving LD services: 650
Acceptance into program means acceptance into college: Student must be admitted and enrolled in the university first (they can appeal a denial) and then request services.

ADMISSIONS

The student with learning disabilities applies to the university under the same guidelines as all other students. However, students with learning disabilities may request a separate review. Students should submit a personal statement describing how their learning disabilities may have had an impact on their GPA or standardized test scores, if applicable. The required SAT or ACT varies according to the student's GPA. Students denied admission may petition for a review of their application. This review process petition should be directed to the director of the Office of Student Services (OSS).

ADDITIONAL INFORMATION

Skills workshops are offered in reading, note-taking, memory, and time management. OSS sponsors Preview, an early registration and orientation program. Assistance can be provided regarding learning strategies, classroom accommodations, and petitions. Services are available to focus on strategic learning strategies and success strategies.

LEARNING DISABILITY PROGRAM/SERVICES

Learning Disability Program/Services: Disability Resource Center
Director: Jim Faubel
 E-Mail: jimrf@dso.ufl.edu
 Telephone: 352-392-8565 ext 200
 Fax: 352-392-8570

LEARNING DISABILITY SERVICES

Requests for the following services/accommodations will be evaluated individually based on appropriate and current documentation.

Allowed in exams
 Calculator: Yes
 Dictionary: No
 Computer: Yes
 Spellchecker: Yes
Extended test time: Yes
Scribes: Yes
Proctors: Yes
Oral exams: Yes
Note-takers: Yes

Distraction-reduced environment: Yes
Tape recording in class: Yes
Books on tape from RFBD: Yes
Taping of books not from RFBD: Yes
**Accommodations for students with
 ADHD:** Yes
Reading machine: Yes
Other assistive technology: Yes
Priority registration: Yes

Added costs for services: No
LD specialists: Yes
Professional tutors: No
Peer tutors: No
Max. hours/wk. for services: N/A
**How professors are notified of
 LD/ADHD:** By student

GENERAL ADMISSIONS INFORMATION

Director of Admissions: William Kolb, Associate University Registrar
Telephone: 352-392-1365

ENTRANCE REQUIREMENTS

Academic units required: 4 English, 3 math, 3 science (2 science labs), 2 foreign language, 3 social studies, 3 academic electives. High school diploma is required, and GED is accepted. ACT with Writing component required.

Application deadline: 1/17
Notification: March
Average GPA: 3.80
ACT Composite middle 50% range:
 25–29

SAT Math middle 50% range:
 580–690
**SAT Critical Reading middle 50%
 range:** 560–670
SAT Writing middle 50% range:
 24–29

Graduated top 10% of class: NR
Graduated top 25% of class: NR
Graduated top 50% of class: NR

COLLEGE GRADUATION REQUIREMENTS

Course waivers allowed: Yes
In what course: Foreign language and math
Course substitutions allowed: Yes
In what course: Students may petition for substitutions in foreign language and math courses. These cases are individually decided on a case-by-case basis.

ADDITIONAL INFORMATION

Environment: The university is located on 2,000 acres 115 miles north of Orlando.

Student Body
 Undergrad enrollment: 34,534
 Women: 54%
 Men: 46%
 Percent out-of-state: 5%

Cost Information
 In-state tuition: $3,206
 Out-of-state tuition: $17,791
 Room & board: $6,590
Housing Information
 University housing: Yes
 Percent living on campus: 22%

Greek System
 Fraternity: Yes
 Sorority: Yes
Athletics: Division I

University of Florida

BRENAU UNIVERSITY

500 Washington Street Southeast, Gainesville, GA 30501
Phone: 770-534-6100 • Fax: 770-538-4306
E-mail: wcadmissions@lib.brenau.edu • Web: www.brenau.edu
Support: SP • Institution type: 4-year private

LEARNING DISABILITY PROGRAM AND SERVICES

The Brenau Learning Center is a program for students with a diagnosed learning disability or attention deficit hyperactivity disorder. Students must also have average to above average academic aptitude with an adequate high school preparation for college studies. The program is designed to provide support services for students as they attend regular college courses. It also offers a more structured learning environment, as well as the freedom associated with college living. Full-time students enroll in four or five courses per semester. Learning Center students receive academic advising from the college, as well as the director of the program. Students have the opportunity to register early, which allows them to take required courses at the appropriate time in their college career. Many students become inactive in the program as they experience success and require less assistance. They may reenter the program at any time. Brenau University attempts to offer a more personalized caring approach to college education. Faculty is very supportive of students who request extra help. So, in addition to receiving special services from the Learning Center, staff, and tutors, the student is being educated in an environment conducive to learning.

LD/ADHD ADMISSIONS INFORMATION

College entrance tests required: Yes
Interview required: Yes
Essay recommended: Yes
Documentation required for LD: Psychological report
Documentation required for ADHD: Physician's report for ADHD. If the student also has learning disabilities, a psychological report would be needed.
Submitted to: Admissions Office
Special Ed. HS course work accepted: Yes

Specific course requirements of all applicants: NR
Separate application required: Yes
# of LD applications submitted each year: 10 to 15
# of LD applications accepted yearly: 12
Total # of students receiving LD services: NR
Acceptance into program means acceptance into college: Students can be reviewed by the LD program director but must be admitted and enrolled in the university first and then request services.

ADMISSIONS

Regular admission criteria include a minimum SAT of 900 or ACT of 18 and a GPA of 2.5. Applicants with an LD not meeting regular admission criteria may be admitted through a Learning Center Admission and must participate in the LD program. These students should be college-able, motivated, and have appropriate high school preparation. Students must have the intellectual potential and academic foundation to be successful. Applicants must provide documentation. Not all students with a diagnosed LD are eligible for the program; the learning differences must not be the primary result of emotional problems. Both the Director of the LC and the Director of Admissions make a decision after reviewing SAT/ACT scores; academic performance and preparation; counselors' recommendations and other letters of reference; test results contained in the psychological evaluation; and a campus interview.

ADDITIONAL INFORMATION

Learning Center students can register early and receive regular academic advising from the director of the program. Study skills, including word processing, reading, and math skills classes are offered for credit. At all service levels, students may take tests in an extended-time format during which oral assistance is available. Learning Center students begin tutoring with professional tutors during the first week of the term and contract to regularly attend tutoring sessions throughout the semester. All LC students may receive 1 hour of educational support per week in addition to scheduled tutoring. Students may be tutored in one to four academic classes per semester. Skills classes in word processing, time management, study skills, and research may be taken for credit. LD services and accommodations are available for undergraduate and graduate students. Courses are offered in the summer, and entering freshman are encouraged to attend. Summer school allows students to get ahead with courses and take a reduced course load the first year.

LEARNING DISABILITY PROGRAM/SERVICES

Learning Disability Program/Services: Learning Center (LC)
Director: Vincent Yamilkoski, EdD
  E-Mail: vyamilkoski@lib.brenau.edu
  Telephone: 770-534-6134
  Fax: 770-297-5883
Contact Person: Diana Mulkey
  E-Mail: dmulkey@ub.brenau.edu
  Telephone: 770-534-6133
  Fax: 770-297-5883

LEARNING DISABILITY SERVICES

Requests for the following services/accommodations will be evaluated individually based on appropriate and current documentation.

Allowed in exams
  Calculator: Yes
  Dictionary: Yes
  Computer: Yes
  Spellchecker: Yes
Extended test time: Yes
Scribes: Yes
Proctors: Yes
Oral exams: Yes
Note-takers: Yes

Distraction-reduced environment: Yes
Tape recording in class: Yes
Books on tape from RFBD: Yes
Taping of books not from RFBD: Yes
Accommodations for students with ADHD: Yes
Reading machine: Yes
Other assistive technology: Yes
Priority registration: Yes

Added costs for services: No
LD specialists: Yes
Professional tutors: 15–20
Peer tutors: No
Max. hours/wk. for services: 9
How professors are notified of LD/ADHD: By both student and director

GENERAL ADMISSIONS INFORMATION

Director of Admissions: Scott Briell
Telephone: 770-538-4704

ENTRANCE REQUIREMENTS

High school diploma is required, and GED is accepted. ACT without Writing component accepted. SAT 900 or ACT 18 and 2.5 GPA. TOEFL required of all international applicants: minimum paper TOEFL 550, minimum computer TOEFL 173.

Application deadline: NR
Notification: Rolling
Average GPA: NR
ACT Composite middle 50% range: 19–23

SAT Math middle 50% range: 450–540
SAT Critical Reading middle 50% range: 450–560
SAT Writing middle 50% range: 450–560

Graduated top 10% of class: NR
Graduated top 25% of class: NR
Graduated top 50% of class: NR

COLLEGE GRADUATION REQUIREMENTS

Course waivers allowed: No
Course substitutions allowed: No

ADDITIONAL INFORMATION

Environment: Brenau University is in a small city setting in the foothills of the Blue Ridge Mountains 50 miles northeast of Atlanta.

Student Body
  Undergrad enrollment: 796
  Women: 100%
  Men: 0%
  Percent out-of-state: 9%

Cost Information
  Tuition: $15,450
  Room & board: $8,350
Housing Information
  University housing: Yes
  Percent living on campus: 59%

Greek System
  Fraternity: No
  Sorority: Yes
Athletics: NAIA

EMORY UNIVERSITY

Boisfeuillet Jones Center, Atlanta, GA 30322
Phone: 404-727-6036 • Fax: 404-727-4303
E-mail: admiss@emory.edu • Web: www.emory.edu
Support: CS • Institution type: 4-year private

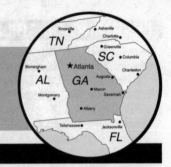

LEARNING DISABILITY PROGRAM AND SERVICES

Emory University ensures that all services/accommodations are accessible to students with disabilities. Accommodations are made on an individualized basis. Students are responsible for seeking available assistance and establishing their needs. The goals of Disability Services (DS) include coordinating services to provide equal access to programs, services, and activities; reducing competitive disadvantage in academic work; providing individual counseling and referral; serving as an advocate for student needs; providing a variety of support services; and serving as a liaison between students and university officers or community agencies. Documentation for LD must include intelligence tests, specific cognitive processing, oral language assessment, social-emotional assessment, significant specific achievement deficits relative to potential, assessment instruments appropriate for adult population, and recommendations regarding accommodations for the student in an academic setting. ADHD documentation must include reported history of symptoms by age 7, self-report of three major behaviors from DSM–IV items, observations from two professionals, mandatory corroboration of behaviors by another adult (parent, relative, etc.), documentation on two rating scales of ADHD behaviors, and recommendations regarding suggested accommodations.

LD/ADHD ADMISSIONS INFORMATION

College entrance tests required: Yes
Interview required: No
Essay recommended: No
Documentation required for LD: Specific documentation
    criteria available upon request
Documentation required for ADHD: Yes
Submitted to: Disability Services
Special Ed. HS course work accepted: No

Specific course requirements of all applicants: Yes
Separate application required: No
# of LD applications submitted each year: NR
# of LD applications accepted yearly: NR
Total # of students receiving LD services: NR
Acceptance into program means acceptance into
    college: Students must be admitted and enrolled in the
    university first and then request services.

ADMISSIONS

Students with learning disabilities are required to submit everything requested by the Office of Admissions for regular admissions. Nonstandardized SAT/ACT may be submitted. Teacher and/or counselor recommendations may be weighted more heavily in the admissions process. A professional diagnosis of the learning disability with recommended accommodations is helpful. Essentially, each student with a disability is evaluated individually and admitted based on potential for success in the Emory environment, taking into consideration the necessary accommodations requested. Documentation is required for services, not admissions. Once admitted, the Admissions Office sends a self-identification form in the acceptance packet to each student who discloses a learning disability.

ADDITIONAL INFORMATION

The needs of students with LD are met through counseling and referral advocacy, and a variety of support services. Deans are notified by a report each semester of students who have self-identified as having LD. Tutoring is offered in most subjects on a one-on-one basis or in small groups. Students also are eligible for priority registration. Skills classes are offered, and the coordinator can monitor and track students to follow their progress. The coordinator meets with students to assess needs and develop an IEP. The coordinator is also an advocate for students and provides information to faculty to help with their understanding of providing accommodations to students with LD. DSS sends memos to professors to support student accommodation requests. The staff of DSS acknowledges they have sufficient verification to support the request and then provides the professor with the identified accommodations necessary. The Emory Students Enabling Association provides a support network for students with disabilities.

LEARNING DISABILITY PROGRAM/SERVICES

Learning Disability Program/Services: Office of Disablility Services
Director: Gloria Weaver
  E-Mail: gloria.weaver@emory.edu
  Telephone: 404-727-6016
  Fax: 404-727-1126
Contact Person: Jessalyn Smiley
  E-Mail: jessalyn.p.smiley@emory.edu
  Telephone: 404-727-6016
  Fax: 404-727-1126

LEARNING DISABILITY SERVICES

Requests for the following services/accommodations will be evaluated individually based on appropriate and current documentation.

Allowed in exams
  Calculator: Yes
  Dictionary: Yes
  Computer: Yes
  Spellchecker: Yes
Extended test time: Yes
Scribes: Yes
Proctors: Yes
Oral exams: Yes
Note-takers: Yes

Distraction-reduced environment: Yes
Tape recording in class: Yes
Books on tape from RFBD: Yes
Taping of books not from RFBD: Yes
Accommodations for students with ADHD: Yes
Reading machine: No
Other assistive technology: Yes
Priority registration: Yes

Added costs for services: No
LD specialists: Yes
Professional tutors: Yes
Peer tutors: Yes
Max. hours/wk. for services: NR
How professors are notified of LD/ADHD: By student

GENERAL ADMISSIONS INFORMATION

Director of Admissions: Dan Walls
Telephone: 800-727-6036

ENTRANCE REQUIREMENTS

Academic units required: 4 English, 3 math, 2 science (2 science labs), 2 foreign language, 2 social studies, 2 history, 2 academic electives. **Academic units recommended:** 4 math, 3 science, 3 foreign language. High school diploma is required, and GED is not accepted. ACT with Writing component required.

Application deadline: 1/15
Notification: 4/1
Average GPA: 3.72
ACT Composite middle 50% range: 27–31

SAT Math middle 50% range: 660–740
SAT Critical Reading middle 50% range: 640–730
SAT Writing middle 50% range: NR

Graduated top 10% of class: 85%
Graduated top 25% of class: 95%
Graduated top 50% of class: 100%

COLLEGE GRADUATION REQUIREMENTS

Course waivers allowed: No
Course substitutions allowed: No

ADDITIONAL INFORMATION

Environment: The 631-acre campus is in a suburban section 5 miles northeast of Atlanta.

Student Body
  Undergrad enrollment: 6,546
  Women: 58%
  Men: 42%
  Percent out-of-state: 71%

Cost Information
  Tuition: $32,100
  Room & board: $9,938
Housing Information
  University housing: Yes
  Percent living on campus: 66%

Greek System
  Fraternity: Yes
  Sorority: Yes
Athletics: Division III

GEORGIA SOUTHERN UNIVERSITY

PO Box 8024, Statesboro, GA 30460
Phone: 912-681-5391 • Fax: 912-486-7240
E-mail: admissions@georgiasouthern.edu • Web: www.georgiasouthern.edu
Support: CS • Institution type: 4-year public

LEARNING DISABILITY PROGRAM AND SERVICES

Georgia Southern University wants all students to have a rewarding and pleasant college experience. The university offers a variety of services specifically tailored to afford students with learning disabilities an equal opportunity for success. These services are in addition to those provided to all students and to the access provided by campus facilities. Opportunities available through the Disabled Student Services Program, include special registration, which allows students to complete the course registration process without going through the standard procedure, and academic/personal assistance for students who are having difficulty with passing a class and need help with time management, note-taking skills, study strategies, and self-confidence. The university has a support group designed to help students with disabilities deal with personal and academic problems related to their disability.

LD/ADHD ADMISSIONS INFORMATION

College entrance tests required: Yes
Interview required: No
Essay recommended: No
Documentation required for LD: Psychoeducational evaluation
Documentation required for ADHD: Yes
Submitted to: Disabled Student Services
Special Ed. HS course work accepted: Yes

Specific course requirements of all applicants: Yes
Separate application required: No
# of LD applications submitted each year: NR
# of LD applications accepted yearly: NR
Total # of students receiving LD services: 236
Acceptance into program means acceptance into college: Students must be admitted and enrolled in the university first and then request services.

ADMISSIONS

There is no special admissions procedure for students with learning disabilities. The university system feels that all applicants must meet the same minimum requirements. Courses required for admission include 4 years of English, 3 years of math, 3 years of science, 2 years of a foreign language, and 3 years of social studies. The minimum SAT Reasoning is 1000 or ACT 21. State minimum requirements for each portion of the SAT/ACT are 430 Critical Reading, 400 Math/17 English, 17 Math. The minimum GPA is 2.0. Students who do not meet the admission criteria may be considered for deferred admission through the Eagle Incentive Program. Students must have a 920–990 SAT, Writing portion required, or 20 ACT (composite). Students' high school academic GPA should be 2.0-plus, and students should complete the college-preparatory curriculum of 4 units of English, 4 units of math, 3 units of science (at least 2 science labs), 3 units of social sciences, and 2 units of foreign language (same language). This is a program offered during the summer for students provisionally accepted (meaning that they have been deferred admission) for fall admission to prove their success by taking 7 credit hours and earning a C or better cumulative average on all courses attempted.

ADDITIONAL INFORMATION

To ensure the provision of services, the Disabled Student Services office requests that any student with learning disabilities who will need accommodations and/or assistance identify himself or herself as a student with a disability as soon as possible by either returning the Voluntary Declaration of Disability form found in the admissions acceptance packet or by contacting the Disabled Student Services Office directly. Services or accommodations could include accommodations for all standardized tests and professional licensure exams, advocacy when needed to ensure provision of accommodations, assistance in arranging academic accommodations in classes, assistance with obtaining acceptable documentation of the disabling condition, and early registration. Following the completion of documentation requirements, students meet with a DSS staff member for a drafting of an accommodation letter. The purpose of the Learning Support Program is to provide any students who have been admitted with inadequate skills in reading, composition, and/or mathematics the opportunity to develop those skills to entry-level competency for regular freshman credit hours. If results of the placement tests reflect a need for assistance in developing academic skills of those who qualify for admission, students will be enrolled in a portion or in all of the Learning Support curriculum.

LEARNING DISABILITY PROGRAM/SERVICES

Learning Disability Program/Services: Disabled Student Services
Director: Wayne Akins
  E-Mail: cwatkins@gsix2.cc.gasou.edu
  Telephone: 912-871-1566
  Fax: 912-871-1419

LEARNING DISABILITY SERVICES

Requests for the following services/accommodations will be evaluated individually based on appropriate and current documentation.

Allowed in exams
  Calculator: Yes
  Dictionary: Yes
  Computer: Yes
  Spellchecker: Yes
Extended test time: Yes
Scribes: Yes
Proctors: Yes
Oral exams: Yes
Note-takers: Yes

Distraction-reduced environment: Yes
Tape recording in class: Yes
Books on tape from RFBD: Yes
Taping of books not from RFBD: Yes
Accommodations for students with
  ADHD: Yes
Reading machine: No
Other assistive technology: No
Priority registration: Yes

Added costs for services: No
LD specialists: Yes
Professional tutors: No
Peer tutors: Yes
Max. hours/wk. for services:
  Unlimited
How professors are notified of
  LD/ADHD: By student

GENERAL ADMISSIONS INFORMATION

Director of Admissions: Susan Davies
Telephone: 912-681-5533

ENTRANCE REQUIREMENTS

Academic units required: 4 English, 4 math, 3 science (2 science labs), 2 foreign language, 3 social studies. High school diploma is required, and GED is not accepted. ACT with or without Writing component accepted. TOEFL required of all international applicants: minimum paper TOEFL 500, minimum computer TOEFL 173.

Application deadline: 5/1
Notification: Continuous
Average GPA: 3.14
ACT Composite middle 50% range:
  21–24

SAT Math middle 50% range:
  510–590
SAT Critical Reading middle 50%
  range: 510–580
SAT Writing middle 50% range: NR

Graduated top 10% of class: 14%
Graduated top 25% of class: 38%
Graduated top 50% of class: 68%

COLLEGE GRADUATION REQUIREMENTS

Course waivers allowed: No
Course substitutions allowed: Yes
In what course: Substitutions have only been granted in foreign language and a deficit area.

ADDITIONAL INFORMATION

Environment: The campus is in a small town close to Savannah.

Student Body
  Undergrad enrollment: 13,752
  Women: 49%
  Men: 51%
  Percent out-of-state: 4%

Cost Information
  In-state tuition: $2,560
  Out-of-state tuition: $10,144
  Room & board: $6,500
Housing Information
  University housing: Yes
  Percent living on campus: 26%

Greek System
  Fraternity: Yes
  Sorority: Yes
Athletics: Division I

GEORGIA STATE UNIVERSITY

PO Box 4009, Atlanta, GA 30302-4009
Phone: 404-651-2365 • Fax: 404-651-4811
E-mail: admissions@gsu.edu • Web: www.gsu.edu
Support: CS • Institution type: 4-year public

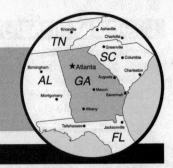

LEARNING DISABILITY PROGRAM AND SERVICES

Georgia State University is committed to helping each student, including those students with disabilities; realize his or her full potential. This commitment is fulfilled through the provision of reasonable accommodations to ensure equitable access to its programs and services for all qualified students with disabilities. In general, the university will provide accommodations for students with disabilities on an individualized and flexible basis. It is the student's responsibility to seek available assistance and make his or her needs known. All students are encouraged to contact the Office of Disability Services and/or Student Support Services in the early stages of their college planning. The pre-admission services include information regarding admission requirements and academic support services. Students should register with both services before classes begin. This will assure that appropriate services are in place prior to the first day of classes. As a rule, the university does not waive academic requirements because of any disability. Therefore, the student should carefully evaluate degree requirements early in his or her studies. The only exception to this policy is if there is a documented learning disability that would hinder the learning of a foreign language, in which case a student may petition for a substitution in the foreign language requirement.

LD/ADHD ADMISSIONS INFORMATION

College entrance tests required: Yes
Interview required: No
Essay recommended: No
Documentation required for LD: Psychological evaluation
  meeting the Georgia Board of Regents guidelines listed at
  www.gsu.edu/rcld.
Documentation required for ADHD: See guidelines for
  Georgia Board of Regents listed at www.gsu.edu/rcld.
Submitted to: Office of Disability Services
Special Ed. HS course work accepted: No

Specific course requirements of all applicants: Yes
Separate application required: No
# of LD applications submitted each year: NR
# of LD applications accepted yearly: NR
Total # of students receiving LD services: 163
**Acceptance into program means acceptance into
  college:** Students must be admitted and enrolled in the
  university first and then request services.

ADMISSIONS

Students with LD must meet the same admission criteria as all other applicants. The university uses a predicted GPA of 2.1 for admission to a degree program or a GPA of 1.8 for admission to Learning Support Systems. This is determined by the ACT/SAT I score and the high school GPA. The higher the GPA, the lower the ACT/SAT can be and vice versa. Course requirements include 4 years of English, 3 years of science, 3 years of math, 3 years of social science, and 2 years of a foreign language. (Substitutions are allowed for foreign language if the student has documentation that supports the substitution). Students may appeal an admission decision if they are denied and could be offered a probationary admission. If a student contacts the Office of Disability Services and provides documentation of an LD, the office will write the Admissions Office and verify the existence of the LD.

ADDITIONAL INFORMATION

To receive LD services, students must submit documentation that evaluates intelligence; academic achievement in reading, math, and written language; auditory/phonological processing; language skills; visual-perceptual-spatial-constructural capabilities; attention; memory; executive function; motor skills; and social-emotional behavior. Student Support Services provides individual and group counseling, tutoring, advocacy, taped texts, advising, readers, learning lab, computer training, and referral for diagnosis of LD. The University Counseling Center provides study skills training; test-taking strategies; note-taking skills; textbook-reading skills; test anxiety and stress management, time management, and organizational techniques; thesis and dissertation writing; and personal counseling. Passport is a special section of the Personal and Academic Development Seminar Class offered through the Learning Support Program and is specifically designed for students with LD. The Office of Disability Services offers advisement, a study lab, readers, and testing accommodations.

LEARNING DISABILITY PROGRAM/SERVICES

Learning Disability Program/Services: Margaret A. Staton Office of Disability Services
Director: Rodney E. Pennamon
  E-Mail: dismail@langate.gsu.edu
  Telephone: 404-463-9044
  Fax: 404-463-9049
Contact Person: Louise Bedrossian
  E-Mail: dismail@langate.gsu.edu
  Telephone: 404-463-9044
  Fax: 404-463-9049

LEARNING DISABILITY SERVICES

Requests for the following services/accommodations will be evaluated individually based on appropriate and current documentation.

Allowed in exams
  Calculator: Yes
  Dictionary: Yes
  Computer: Yes
  Spellchecker: Yes
Extended test time: Yes
Scribes: No
Proctors: Yes
Oral exams: No
Note-takers: Yes

Distraction-reduced environment: Yes
Tape recording in class: Yes
Books on tape from RFBD: Yes
Taping of books not from RFBD: Yes
Accommodations for students with ADHD: Yes
Reading machine: Yes
Other assistive technology: Yes
Priority registration: Yes

Added costs for services: No
LD specialists: Yes
Professional tutors: No
Peer tutors: No
Max. hours/wk. for services: Based on need and availability of space and staff
How professors are notified of LD/ADHD: By student

GENERAL ADMISSIONS INFORMATION

Director of Admissions: Nannette Commander
  Telephone: 404-651-2365

ENTRANCE REQUIREMENTS

Academic units required: 4 English, 4 math, 3 science (2 science labs), 2 foreign language, 2 social studies, 1 history. High school diploma is required, and GED is not accepted. ACT with Writing component required. TOEFL required of all international applicants: minimum paper TOEFL 525, minimum computer TOEFL 213.

Application deadline: 3/1
Notification: Rolling
Average GPA: 3.33
ACT Composite middle 50% range: 20–25

SAT Math middle 50% range: 500–600
SAT Critical Reading middle 50% range: 490–590
SAT Writing middle 50% range: NR

Graduated top 10% of class: NR
Graduated top 25% of class: NR
Graduated top 50% of class: NR

COLLEGE GRADUATION REQUIREMENTS

Course waivers allowed: Yes
Course substitutions allowed: Yes
In what course: Foreign language course substitutions, not waivers, are approved by appeal in a limited number of cases based on psychological evaluation and finding of significant language disability.

ADDITIONAL INFORMATION

Environment: The university's campus is in an urban area in Atlanta.

Student Body
  Undergrad enrollment: 18,478
  Women: 61%
  Men: 39%
  Percent out-of-state: 7%

Cost Information
  In-state tuition: $4,202
  Out-of-state tuition: $16,808
  Room & board: $7,990
Housing Information
  University housing: Yes
  Percent living on campus: 13%

Greek System
  Fraternity: Yes
  Sorority: Yes
Athletics: Division I

REINHARDT COLLEGE

7300 Reinhardt College Circle, Waleska, GA 30183
Phone: 770-720-5526 • Fax: 770-720-5899
E-mail: admissions@reinhardt.edu • Web: www.reinhardt.edu
Support: SP • Institution type: 4-year private

LEARNING DISABILITY PROGRAM AND SERVICES

The Academic Support Office (ASO) provides assistance to students with specific learning abilities or attention deficit hyperactivity disorder. Students are enrolled in regular college courses. The program focuses on compensatory skills and provides special services in academic advising and counseling, individual and group tutoring, assistance in writing assignments, note-taking, testing accommodations, and taped texts. The ASO was established in 1982 to provide assistance to students with learning disabilities who meet regular college entrance requirements, have a diagnosed LD, and may or may not have received any LD services in the past due to ineligibility for high school services or a recent diagnosis.

LD/ADHD ADMISSIONS INFORMATION

College entrance tests required: Yes
Interview required: Yes
Essay recommended: Yes
Documentation required for LD: Yes
Documentation required for ADHD: Yes
Submitted to: Admissions Office
Special Ed. HS course work accepted: No

Specific course requirements of all applicants: Yes
Separate application required: Yes
# of LD applications submitted each year: 70
# of LD applications accepted yearly: 30
Total # of students receiving LD services: 70
Acceptance into program means acceptance into
   college: Students are admitted jointly by the college and
   ASO.

ADMISSIONS
Applicants with learning disabilities should request an ASO admission packet from admissions; complete the regular application; check the ASO admission box; fill out the supplemental form from ASO; provide IEPs from as many years of high school as possible, psychological evaluations documenting the disability, and three references addressing aptitude, motivation, ability to set realistic goals, interpersonal skills, and readiness for college; and submit SAT/ACT scores. Students applying to the ASO program may be asked to interview with the ASO staff. Admission decisions are made by the Admission office with recommendations from the program director. General admission criteria includes a 2.00 GPA or better in academic subjects, and the admission decision is based SAT/ACT scores, high school grades, and a personal interview, if requested by college personnel. Course requirements include 4 years of English, 4 years of math, 3 years of social studies, and 3 years of natural sciences, while foreign language is preferred.

ADDITIONAL INFORMATION
The ASO is staffed by four full-time faculty members. Additional tuition is required for students enrolled in ASO tutorials. A generous financial aid program is available to all qualified students. Academic support services include faculty-led tutorials (for a fee), academic advisement and counseling, and accommodative services for students with documented LD/ADHD such as individualized testing, note-takers, and the coordination of taped texts. All students admitted and enrolled in the ASO Program attend a regular student orientation program plus have an interview and orientation with the staff from the ASO Program.

LEARNING DISABILITY PROGRAM/SERVICES

Learning Disability Program/Services: Academic Support Office (ASO)
Director: Sylvia Robertson
 E-Mail: srr@reinhardt.edu
 Telephone: 770-720-5567
 Fax: 770-720-5602

LEARNING DISABILITY SERVICES

Requests for the following services/accommodations will be evaluated individually based on appropriate and current documentation.

Allowed in exams
 Calculator: Yes
 Dictionary: No
 Computer: Yes
 Spellchecker: Yes
Extended test time: Yes
Scribes: Yes
Proctors: Yes
Oral exams: Yes
Note-takers: Yes

Distraction-reduced environment: Yes
Tape recording in class: Yes
Books on tape from RFBD: Yes
Taping of books not from RFBD: No
**Accommodations for students with
 ADHD:** Yes
Reading machine: Yes
Other assistive technology: Yes
Priority registration: Yes

Added costs for services: Yes
LD specialists: Yes
Professional tutors: 4
Peer tutors: No
Max. hours/wk. for services:
 Unlimited
**How professors are notified of
 LD/ADHD:** By both student and
 director

GENERAL ADMISSIONS INFORMATION

Director of Admissions: Julie Cook
Telephone: 770-720-5524

ENTRANCE REQUIREMENTS

Academic units required: 4 English, 4 math, 3 science, 3 social studies. **Academic units recommended:** 2 foreign language. High school diploma is required, and GED is accepted. ACT with or without Writing component accepted. TOEFL required of all international applicants: minimum paper TOEFL 500, minimum computer TOEFL 150.

Application deadline: No deadline
Notification: Rolling beginning 8/1
Average GPA: 2.88
ACT Composite middle 50% range:
 17–21

SAT Math middle 50% range:
 430–540
**SAT Critical Reading middle 50%
 range:** 450–550
SAT Writing middle 50% range: NR

Graduated top 10% of class: NR
Graduated top 25% of class: NR
Graduated top 50% of class: 75%

COLLEGE GRADUATION REQUIREMENTS

Course waivers allowed: No
Course substitutions allowed: No

ADDITIONAL INFORMATION

Environment: The college is located on a 600-acre campus in a small town 40 miles from Atlanta.

Student Body
 Undergrad enrollment: 1,008
 Women: 58%
 Men: 42%
 Percent out-of-state: 12%

Cost Information
 Tuition: $15,500
 Room & board: $5,270
Housing Information
 University housing: Yes
 Percent living on campus: 61%

Greek System
 Fraternity: No
 Sorority: No
Athletics: NAIA

UNIVERSITY OF GEORGIA

Undergraduate Admissions, Terrell Hall, Athens, GA 30602
Phone: 706-542-8776 • Fax: 706-542-1466
E-mail: undergrad@admissions.uga.edu • Web: www.uga.edu
Support: CS • Institution type: 4-year public

LEARNING DISABILITY PROGRAM AND SERVICES

The purpose of the Learning Disabilities Center (LDC) is to provide support and direct services to students who demonstrate a specific LD so that they may function as independently as possible while at the university. The objectives of the program are to assist students in understanding their disability, coordinate information about other support services, recommend modifications for the Regents Exam (required to graduate) and program of study where appropriate, and consult with faculty. All UGA students whose LD have been confirmed by the LDC are eligible for support services. Students must meet the learning disability criteria acceptable by the Georgia Board of Regents, including documentation completed within the past 3 years; average broad cognitive functioning; specific cognitive processing deficits; social-emotional assessment that doesn't suggest a primary emotional basis for results; oral language assessment; significant specific achievement deficits relative to potential documented in the areas of written language, reading, and math; and utilization of assessment instruments with appropriate age norms. All standardized measures must be represented by standard scores or percentile ranks based on published norms.

LD/ADHD ADMISSIONS INFORMATION

College entrance tests required: Yes
Interview required: No
Essay recommended: No
Documentation required for LD: See www.coe.uga.edu for Board of Regents criteria for LD and ADHD.
Documentation required for ADHD: Yes
Submitted to: Learning Disabilities Center
Special Ed. HS course work accepted: No

Specific course requirements of all applicants: Yes
Separate application required: Yes
# of LD applications submitted each year: NR
# of LD applications accepted yearly: NR
Total # of students receiving LD services: 225–275
Acceptance into program means acceptance into college: Students must be admitted and enrolled in the university first and then request services.

ADMISSIONS

Students with LD are encouraged to self-disclose on the general application form. This disclosure sets the process in motion, and the Admissions Office notifies the LDC. LDC contacts the applicant, offers to discuss services available, and then refers the student's name back to admissions. LDC provides the Admissions Office with a diagnosis to assist with an admission decision. Students must submit documentation of their disability to be considered for special admissions. The Admissions Office may be flexible with GPA and test scores, but students should take college-prep courses in high school. GPA is the most important criterion, and the sub score on the verbal section of the ACT/SAT is weighted more heavily than math. Required SAT and GPA are adjusted in relation to general admission averages. The final decision is made by the Admissions Office.

ADDITIONAL INFORMATION

Specialists help with learning strategies for courses. Students meet with LD specialists to register quarterly and design a schedule that considers their LD along with curriculum requirements. Students are assisted in communicating their disabilities and learning needs with their instructors. Course substitutions for foreign language may be approved with appropriate documentation. Modifications for assignments and tests are designed to meet students' specific needs. Skills classes for college credit are offered to all students at UGA in study techniques, time management, problem-solving, research paper writing, and career selection. Students with ADHD are serviced by Disability Services.

LEARNING DISABILITY PROGRAM/SERVICES

Learning Disability Program/Services: Learning Disabilities Center
Director: Dr. Karen Kalivoda
  E-Mail: voda@uga.edu
  Telephone: 706-542-8719
  Fax: 706-542-7719

LEARNING DISABILITY SERVICES

Requests for the following services/accommodations will be evaluated individually based on appropriate and current documentation.

Allowed in exams
  Calculator: Yes
  Dictionary: Yes
  Computer: Yes
  Spellchecker: Yes
Extended test time: Yes
Scribes: Yes
Proctors: Yes
Oral exams: Yes
Note-takers: Yes

Distraction-reduced environment: Yes
Tape recording in class: Yes
Books on tape from RFBD: Yes
Taping of books not from RFBD: Yes
Accommodations for students with
  ADHD: Yes
Reading machine: Yes
Other assistive technology: Yes
Priority registration: Yes

Added costs for services: No
LD specialists: Yes
Professional tutors: Yes
Peer tutors: No
Max. hours/wk. for services: N/A
How professors are notified of
  LD/ADHD: By student

GENERAL ADMISSIONS INFORMATION

Director of Admissions: Nancy McDuff
Telephone: 706-542-8776

ENTRANCE REQUIREMENTS

Academic units required: 4 English, 4 math, 3 science (2 science labs), 2 foreign language, 3 social studies.
Academic units recommended: 4 English, 4 math, 3 science (2 science labs), 3 foreign language, 1 social studies, 2 history, 1 academic elective. High school diploma is required, and GED is accepted. ACT with Writing component required. TOEFL required of all international applicants: minimum paper TOEFL 550, minimum computer TOEFL 213.

Application deadline: 1/15
Notification: Rolling
Average GPA: 3.76
ACT Composite middle 50% range:
  24–29

SAT Math middle 50% range:
  570–660
SAT Critical Reading middle 50%
  range: 560–660
SAT Writing middle 50% range:
  550–650

Graduated top 10% of class: 48%
Graduated top 25% of class: 84%
Graduated top 50% of class: 98%

COLLEGE GRADUATION REQUIREMENTS

Course waivers allowed: Yes
In what course: Foreign language
Course substitutions allowed: Yes
In what course: Foreign language

ADDITIONAL INFORMATION

Environment: The university is located on a large campus 80 miles from Atlanta.

Student Body
  Undergrad enrollment: 25,055
  Women: 57%
  Men: 43%
  Percent out-of-state: 11%

Cost Information
  In-state tuition: $4,630
  Out-of-state tuition: $16,850
  Room & board: $6,375
Housing Information
  University housing: Yes
  Percent living on campus: 27%

Greek System
  Fraternity: Yes
  Sorority: Yes
Athletics: Division I

UNIVERSITY OF IDAHO

UI Admissions Office, PO Box 444264, Moscow, ID 83844-4264
Phone: 208-885-6326 • Fax: 208-885-9119
E-mail: admappl@uidaho.edu • Web: www.uihome.uidaho.edu/uihome
Support: S • Institution type: 4-year public

LEARNING DISABILITY PROGRAM AND SERVICES

Student Support Services (SSS) is an Educational Assistance Program that offers participating students academic and personal support services necessary to reach their educational goals. Designed to complement existing resources on campus, this federally funded program offers students opportunities to identify and pursue educational and career goals, establish and improve academic performance, and balance the challenges of university and personal life. SSS provides highly individualized assistance, which often makes the difference in a student's persistence with his or her educational plan. Tutoring is available from 1 to 3 hours per week, per class. One hour per week is with a professional counselor, the rest with peer tutors. A math specialist is available. Enrollment is limited to the first 200 students on a first-come, first-served basis. To qualify for services, a student must be a U.S. citizen; accepted for enrollment or currently enrolled; and be either first generation, financially limited, or physically or learning disabled. In addition, a student must show a need for and a potential to benefit from the SSS Program.

LD/ADHD ADMISSIONS INFORMATION

College entrance tests required: Yes
Interview required: No
Essay recommended: No
Documentation required for LD: Psychoeducational
  evaluation
Documentation required for ADHD: Yes
Submitted to: Student Support Services
Special Ed. HS course work accepted: NR

Specific course requirements of all applicants: Yes
Separate application required: NR
# of LD applications submitted each year: NR
# of LD applications accepted yearly: NR
Total # of students receiving LD services: 100
**Acceptance into program means acceptance into
  college:** Student must be admitted and enrolled in the
  university first and then reviewed for LD services.

ADMISSIONS

Students must meet the general admission requirements. The following index is used for general admission: GPA 3.0 and no ACT/SAT required; GPA 2.6–2.99 and ACT 15-plus or SAT 790-plus; GPA 2.5–2.59 and ACT 17-plus or SAT 870-plus; GPA 2.4–2.49 and ACT 19-plus or SAT 930-plus; GPA 2.30–2.39 and ACT 21-plus or SAT 1000-plus; GPA 2.20–2.29 and ACT 23-plus or SAT 1070-plus; and 2.0 GPA in 4 years of English, 3 years of math, 1 year of humanities or foreign language, 2.5 years of social science, 3 years of natural science, plus electives. A freshman applicant who does not qualify for regular admission may be considered for provisional admission. A student seeking provisional admission must submit a written statement and three letters of recommendation. The student statement should include the student's goals, educational and/or professional objectives, an explanation of past academic performance, information and/or documentation regarding any extenuating circumstances, and anything else that may be pertinent to the applicant's request. The file is reviewed by the Admissions Committee. A staff person from SSS is part of the special Admissions Committee for students with disabilities who do not meet regular admissions criteria. Students admitted specially or on probation must successfully complete 14 credits in four core areas over three semesters.

ADDITIONAL INFORMATION

Students with LD who participate in the SSS Program receive assistance with learning strategies, organization and time management, career advisory and employment readiness, advocacy, academic advisory, and instruction in unprepared areas in reading, writing, and math. An academic plan is mutually developed, and students take an active role in their education. Students with LD who exhibit a need for and the potential to benefit from the SSS Program are eligible to participate. Currently, there are 125 students with LD and 15–20 students with ADHD receiving services. There are no LD specialists, but the Director and Senior Program Counselor of SSS have had extensive training. The Office of Student Disability Services serves as a clearinghouse to direct students with disabilities to various services on campus. The SSS Computer Lab has software programs that are useful for students with LD. All students have access to the Tutoring and Academic Assistance Center, Math and Statistics Center, and the Writing Center. The Tutoring and Learning Services (TLS) learning specialist offers in-depth help with learning strategies and basic academic skill development. She can help students develop reading and writing skills, as well as learn new approaches to memorizing, note-taking, and test preparation. TLS also provides small group tutoring in many introductory courses, primarily in sciences, engineering, and foreign languages. Student Support Services provide one-on-one assistance with a professional academic counselor and individualized tutoring in one to two courses per semester.

LEARNING DISABILITY PROGRAM/SERVICES

Learning Disability Program/Services: Student Support Services
Director: Gloria R. Jensen
  E-Mail: dss@uidaho.edu
  Telephone: 208-885-7200
  Fax: 208-885-9404

LEARNING DISABILITY SERVICES

Requests for the following services/accommodations will be evaluated individually based on appropriate and current documentation.

Allowed in exams	Distraction-reduced environment: Yes	Added costs for services: No
Calculator: Yes	Tape recording in class: Yes	LD specialists: No
Dictionary: Yes	Books on tape from RFBD: Yes	Professional tutors: No
Computer: Yes	Taping of books not from RFBD: Yes	Peer tutors: Yes
Spellchecker: Yes	Accommodations for students with	Max. hours/wk. for services: NR
Extended test time: Yes	ADHD: Yes	How professors are notified of
Scribes: Yes	Reading machine: No	LD/ADHD: By student
Proctors: Yes	Other assistive technology: Yes	
Oral exams: Yes	Priority registration: Yes	
Note-takers: Yes		

GENERAL ADMISSIONS INFORMATION

Director of Admissions: Dan Davenport
Telephone: 208-885-7616

ENTRANCE REQUIREMENTS

Academic units required: 4 English, 3 math, 3 science (1 science lab), 1 foreign language, 2 social studies, 1 academic elective. High school diploma is required, and GED is accepted. ACT with or without Writing component accepted. TOEFL required of all international applicants: minimum paper TOEFL 525, minimum computer TOEFL 193.

Application deadline: 8/1	**SAT Math middle 50% range:** 490–620	**Graduated top 10% of class:** 20%
Notification: Rolling	**SAT Critical Reading middle 50% range:** 480–600	**Graduated top 25% of class:** 45%
Average GPA: 3.36		**Graduated top 50% of class:** 77%
ACT Composite middle 50% range: 20–26	**SAT Writing middle 50% range:** 460–560	

COLLEGE GRADUATION REQUIREMENTS

Course waivers allowed: No
Course substitutions allowed: Yes
In what course: Math and foreign language: Students must request substitutions by petition.

ADDITIONAL INFORMATION

Environment: The university is located on a 800-acre campus in a small town 90 miles south of Spokane, Washington.

Student Body	Cost Information	Greek System
Undergrad enrollment: 8,636	In-state tuition: $4,200	Fraternity: Yes
Women: 45%	Out-of-state tuition: $13,800	Sorority: Yes
Men: 55%	Room & board: $5,696	Athletics: Division I
Percent out-of-state: 26%	**Housing Information**	
	University housing: Yes	
	Percent living on campus: 90%	

University of Idaho

DePaul University

One East Jackson Boulevard, Chicago, IL 60604-2287
Phone: 312-362-8300 • Fax: 312-362-5749
E-mail: admitdpu@depaul.edu • Web: www.depaul.edu
Support: CS • Institution type: 4-year private

LEARNING DISABILITY PROGRAM AND SERVICES

Productive Learning Strategies (PLuS) is designed to service students with learning disabilities and/or attention deficit hyperactivity disorder who are motivated to succeed in college. The immediate goals are to provide learning strategies based on students' strengths and weaknesses to assist students in the completion of course work. The ultimate goal is to impart academic and study skills that will enable the students to function independently in the academic environment and competitive job market. PLuS provides intensive help on a one-on-one basis. It is designed to assist with regular college courses, improve learning deficits, and help the student learn compensatory skills. Students can choose to work with learning disability specialists with whom they can meet for up to 2 hours per week.

LD/ADHD ADMISSIONS INFORMATION

College entrance tests required: Yes
Interview required: Yes
Essay recommended: No
Documentation required for LD: WAIS–III, academic achievement and information processing measures (could include Woodcock-Johnson psychoeducational battery and/or WIAT–II)
Documentation required for ADHD: Report with background information, DSM–IV criteria, and symptoms that met diagnosis and recommendations for academic accomodations

Submitted to: Productive Learning Strategies
Special Ed. HS course work accepted: Yes
Specific course requirements of all applicants: Yes
Separate application required: Yes
# of LD applications submitted each year: 50–75
# of LD applications accepted yearly: 50–75
Total # of students receiving LD services: 125–140
Acceptance into program means acceptance into college: Students must be admitted and enrolled in the university first and then request services.

ADMISSIONS

There is no separate admission process for students with learning disabilities. Students with learning disabilities must be accepted to DePaul University before they can be accepted to PLuS. The diagnostic testing that is required, if done within the last 3 to 5 years, will be used in the evaluation. General admission criteria includes a GPA of 2.5, a top 40 percent class rank, and ACT 21 or SAT 1000. Students should have 4 years of English, 3 years of math, 2 years of science, and 2 years of social studies (1 history). Students with appropriate documentation may request substitutions in entrance requirements. Students may elect to self-disclose the disability during the admission process and submit their application to the attention of the PLuS Program. If the student does not have the required testing, PLuS will administer the appropriate assessments. Some students who are considered to have high potential but who have borderline admission criteria may qualify for admissions through the Bridge Program. This is an enhancement program for incoming freshmen. Bridge students may have an ACT of 18–20 or an SAT of 850–880. (This program is not for students with learning disabilities, though some students are learning disabled.) Bridge students must begin in a summer program prior to freshman year. Some students can be admitted on a probationary basis as special students. Adult students (over 24) can be admitted through the Adult Admissions Program.

ADDITIONAL INFORMATION

PLuS is housed in the Reading and Learning Lab, and the program is only available to students with learning disabilities and/or attention deficit hyperactivity disorder. Some accommodations are offered through the Office for Students with Disabilities. Students who do the best at DePaul and the PLuS program are students who are highly motivated and who have received LD resource support in grade school and high school but were enrolled in mainstream classes. Accommodations include extended time of exams, separate and distraction-free space to take exams, and books on tape. Services provided by PLuS include advocacy with professors 2 hours per week with a learning disabilities specialist to receive direct instruction in learning strategies, coping strategies, and mentoring. Students can choose to participate in this fee-for-service component of the program. Services and accommodations are available for undergraduate and graduate students.

LEARNING DISABILITY PROGRAM/SERVICES

Learning Disability Program/Services: Productive Learning Strategies
Director: Coordinator: Karen Meyer
 E-Mail: kmeyer@depaul.edu
 Telephone: 773-325-7290
 Fax: 773-325-7396

LEARNING DISABILITY SERVICES

Requests for the following services/accommodations will be evaluated individually based on appropriate and current documentation.

Allowed in exams
 Calculator: Yes
 Dictionary: Yes
 Computer: Yes
 Spellchecker: Yes
Extended test time: Yes
Scribes: Yes
Proctors: Yes
Oral exams: Yes
Note-takers: No

Distraction-reduced environment: Yes
Tape recording in class: Yes
Books on tape from RFBD: No
Taping of books not from RFBD: Yes
Accommodations for students with
 ADHD: Yes
Reading machine: No
Other assistive technology: Yes
Priority registration: Yes

Added costs for services: No
LD specialists: Yes
Professional tutors: No
Peer tutors: No
Max. hours/wk. for services: 2
How professors are notified of
 LD/ADHD: By student

GENERAL ADMISSIONS INFORMATION

Director of Admissions: Carlene Klass
Telephone: 312-362-8146

ENTRANCE REQUIREMENTS

Academic units required: 4 English, 3 math, 2 science (2 science labs), 2 social studies, 4 academic electives. High school diploma is required, and GED is accepted. ACT with or without Writing component accepted. TOEFL required of all international applicants: minimum paper TOEFL 550, minimum computer TOEFL 213.

Application deadline: Rolling
Notification: Rolling
Average GPA: 3.40
ACT Composite middle 50% range:
 21–26

SAT Math middle 50% range:
 510–620
SAT Critical Reading middle 50%
 range: 510–630
SAT Writing middle 50% range:
 520–610

Graduated top 10% of class: 19%
Graduated top 25% of class: 47%
Graduated top 50% of class: 79%

COLLEGE GRADUATION REQUIREMENTS

Course waivers allowed: Yes
In what course: Foreign language (LD and ADHD), math (LD in math only)
Course substitutions allowed: Yes
In what course: Foreign language (LD and ADHD), math (LD in math only)

ADDITIONAL INFORMATION

Environment: DePaul has a three-acre urban campus located in Chicago's Lincoln Park area three miles north of the downtown area.

Student Body
 Undergrad enrollment: 14,465
 Women: 56%
 Men: 44%
 Percent out-of-state: 16%

Cost Information
 Tuition: $22,365
 Room & board: $9,414
Housing Information
 University housing: Yes
 Percent living on campus: 19%

Greek System
 Fraternity: Yes
 Sorority: Yes
Athletics: Division I

EASTERN ILLINOIS UNIVERSITY

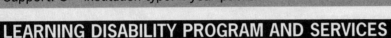

600 Lincoln Avenue, Charleston, IL 61920
Phone: 217-581-2223 • Fax: 217-581-7060
E-mail: admissions@eiu.edu • Web: www.eiu.edu
Support: S • Institution type: 4-year public

LEARNING DISABILITY PROGRAM AND SERVICES

EIU will provide services as deemed effective and reasonable to assist students with LD to obtain access to the proper university programs. Students applying to the university who are requesting support services and/or accommodations from the Office of Disability Services are required to submit documentation to verify eligibility under Section 504. The assessment and diagnosis of specific LD must be conducted by a qualified professional. The written diagnostic evaluation report should include the following information: diagnostic report clearly stating the LD and the rationale for the diagnosis; the tests administered and the specific scores, including grade level scores, standard scores, and percentile scores; descriptive written text beyond that which is provided on a typical IEP and including qualitative information about the student's abilities; recommendations for accommodations that include specific suggestions based on the diagnostic evaluation results and supported by the diagnosis; and identifying information about the evaluator/diagnostician. The diagnostic tests should be current, having been completed within the past 3 years, and should be comprehensive and include a battery of more than one test and/or subtest. The report should also include at least one instrument to measure aptitude or cognitive ability and at least one measurement in reading, written language, and math.

LD/ADHD ADMISSIONS INFORMATION

College entrance tests required: Yes
Interview required: No
Essay recommended: No
Documentation required for LD: Adult normal educational psychoeducational evaluation
Documentation required for ADHD: Completion of our ADHD documentation form by a licensed mental health professional
Submitted to: Office of Disability Services
Special Ed. HS course work accepted: Yes

Specific course requirements of all applicants: Yes
Separate application required: No
# of LD applications submitted each year: NR
# of LD applications accepted yearly: NR
Total # of students receiving LD services: NR
Acceptance into program means acceptance into college: Students must be admitted and enrolled in the university first and then request services.

ADMISSIONS

All applicants must meet the same admission criteria. General admission requires students to rank in the top half of the class and have a minimum ACT of 18 or SAT of 860, or rank in the top three-quarters of the class and have a minimum ACT of 22 or SAT of 1020. Additionally, all students must have 4 years of English, 3 years of math, 3 years of social science, 3 years of science labs, and 2 years of electives. Once admitted, students with LD or ADHD must provide appropriate documentation to access services and accommodations.

ADDITIONAL INFORMATION

Students should meet with the Office of Disability Services to discuss accommodations or make further arrangements as needed. Some services provided include priority registration, alternate format for classroom materials, note-takers, assistance locating tutors and liaison with tutors to develop effective study strategies, proctors, and liaison with instructors. Skills classes can be arranged in time management, note-taking, test-taking, and study strategies.

LEARNING DISABILITY PROGRAM/SERVICES

Learning Disability Program/Services: Office of Disability Services
Director: Kathy Waggoner
  E-Mail: klwaggoner@eiu.edu
  Telephone: 217-581-6583
  Fax: 217-581-7208

LEARNING DISABILITY SERVICES

Requests for the following services/accommodations will be evaluated individually based on appropriate and current documentation.

Allowed in exams
  Calculator: Yes
  Dictionary: Yes
  Computer: Yes
  Spellchecker: Yes
Extended test time: Yes
Scribes: Yes
Proctors: Yes
Oral exams: Yes
Note-takers: Yes

Distraction-reduced environment: Yes
Tape recording in class: Yes
Books on tape from RFBD: Yes
Taping of books not from RFBD: Yes
**Accommodations for students with
  ADHD:** Yes
Reading machine: Yes
Other assistive technology: Yes
Priority registration: Yes

Added costs for services: No
LD specialists: No
Professional tutors: NR
Peer tutors: No
Max. hours/wk. for services: N/A
**How professors are notified of
  LD/ADHD:** By student

GENERAL ADMISSIONS INFORMATION

Director of Admissions: Brenda Major
Telephone: 217-581-2223

ENTRANCE REQUIREMENTS

Academic units required: 4 English, 3 math, 3 science (3 science labs), 3 social studies, 2 academic electives.
Academic units recommended: 2 foreign language. High school diploma is required, and GED is accepted. ACT with or without Writing component accepted. TOEFL required of all international applicants: minimum paper TOEFL 500, minimum computer TOEFL 173.

Application deadline: Rolling
Notification: Rolling; upon receipt of
  application
Average GPA: 3.05
ACT Composite middle 50% range:
  19–24

SAT Math middle 50% range: NR
**SAT Critical Reading middle 50%
  range:** NR
SAT Writing middle 50% range: NR

Graduated top 10% of class: 9%
Graduated top 25% of class: 28%
Graduated top 50% of class: 62%

COLLEGE GRADUATION REQUIREMENTS

Course waivers allowed: No
Course substitutions allowed: No

ADDITIONAL INFORMATION

Environment: The university is in a small town 50 miles south of the University of Illinois.

Student Body
  Undergrad enrollment: 10,477
  Women: 58%
  Men: 42%
  Percent out-of-state: 1%

Cost Information
  In-state tuition: $5,207
  Out-of-state tuition: $15,620
  Room & board: $6,660
Housing Information
  University housing: Yes
  Percent living on campus: 42%

Greek System
  Fraternity: Yes
  Sorority: Yes
  Athletics: Division I

ILLINOIS STATE UNIVERSITY

Admissions Office, Campus Box 2200, Normal, IL 61790-2200
Phone: 309-438-2181 • Fax: 309-438-3932
E-mail: admissions@ilstu.edu • Web: www.ilstu.edu
Support: CS • Institution type: 4-year public

LEARNING DISABILITY PROGRAM AND SERVICES

The mission of the Disability Concerns Office is to ensure the full and equal participation for persons with disabilities in the university community through empowering individuals, promoting equal access, encouraging self-advocacy, reducing attitudinal and communication barriers, and providing appropriate accommodation. The Disability Concerns Program is designed to work with students who have learning disabilities on becoming academically and socially successful while attending Illinois State University. After a review of the appropriate documentation by the coordinator of the learning disability services and a consultation, accommodations can then be determined based on the needs of the individual.

LD/ADHD ADMISSIONS INFORMATION

College entrance tests required: Yes
Interview required: No
Essay recommended: No
Documentation required for LD: A psychoeducational evaluation (adult assessment) including specific areas of the disability; the impact the disability has on the academic performance; and accommodations suggested
Documentation required for ADHD: Psychoeducational evaluation
Submitted to: Support Program/Services
Special Ed. HS course work accepted: Yes

Specific course requirements of all applicants: Yes
Separate application required: No
# of LD applications submitted each year: NR
# of LD applications accepted yearly: NR
Total # of students receiving LD services: 92
Acceptance into program means acceptance into college: Students must be admitted and enrolled in the university first and then request services.

ADMISSIONS

Admissions criteria for students with learning disabilities are the same as for other students at this time. Applicants with questions should contact the Disability Concerns Office. In general, students are admissible if they are in the top three-fourths of their high school class and have an ACT of 23 or better. High school courses required include: 4 years of English, 3 years of math, 2 years of social science, 2 years of science, and 2 years of electives. Students with learning disabilities who are borderline admits or who are denied admission may self-disclose and ask to be reviewed by Disability Concerns. The director will review the documentation and make a recommendation to admissions.

ADDITIONAL INFORMATION

The following are options for accommodations based on appropriate documentation and needs: note-takers, peer tutors, readers, scribes, taped textbooks, computers, testing accommodations, conference with LD specialist, and quiet study rooms. LMS (Learning Through Mini-Sessions) are designed to help students make college academics and college life a little less stressful. Sessions could include stress management, self-advocacy, test anxiety, communication skills, and organizational skills.

LEARNING DISABILITY PROGRAM/SERVICES

Learning Disability Program/Services: Disability Concerns
Director: Ann M. Caldwell
  E-Mail: amcaldwell@ilstu.edu
  Telephone: 309-438-5853
  Fax: 309-438-7713
Contact Person: Sheryl Hogan
  E-Mail: sjhogan@ilstu.edu
  Telephone: 309-438-5853
  Fax: 309-438-7713

LEARNING DISABILITY SERVICES

Requests for the following services/accommodations will be evaluated individually based on appropriate and current documentation.

Allowed in exams		
Calculator: Yes	**Distraction-reduced environment:** Yes	**Added costs for services:** No
Dictionary: No	**Tape recording in class:** Yes	**LD specialists:** Yes
Computer: Yes	**Books on tape from RFBD:** No	**Professional tutors:** No
Spellchecker: Yes	**Taping of books not from RFBD:** No	**Peer tutors:** 30–40
Extended test time: Yes	**Accommodations for students with ADHD:** Yes	**Max. hours/wk. for services:** NR
Scribes: Yes	**Reading machine:** Yes	**How professors are notified of LD/ADHD:** By both student and director
Proctors: Yes	**Other assistive technology:** Yes	
Oral exams: Yes	**Priority registration:** No	
Note-takers: Yes		

GENERAL ADMISSIONS INFORMATION

Director of Admissions: Molly Arnold
Telephone: 309-438-2181

ENTRANCE REQUIREMENTS

Academic units required: 4 English, 3 math, 2 science (2 science labs), 2 foreign language, 2 social studies, 2 academic electives. High school diploma is required, and GED is accepted. ACT with or without Writing component accepted. TOEFL required of all international applicants: minimum paper TOEFL 550, minimum computer TOEFL 213.

Application deadline: 3/1	**SAT Math middle 50% range:** NR	**Graduated top 10% of class:** 11%
Notification: Rolling	**SAT Critical Reading middle 50% range:** NR	**Graduated top 25% of class:** 38%
Average GPA: NR	**SAT Writing middle 50% range:** NR	**Graduated top 50% of class:** 81%
ACT Composite middle 50% range: 22–26		

COLLEGE GRADUATION REQUIREMENTS

Course waivers allowed: No
Course substitutions allowed: Yes
In what course: Determined on an individual basis

ADDITIONAL INFORMATION

Environment: The university is located on 850 acres in a small town 125 miles south of Chicago and 180 miles north of St. Louis.

Student Body	Cost Information	Greek System
Undergrad enrollment: 17,824	**In-state tuition:** $6,150	**Fraternity:** Yes
Women: 57%	**Out-of-state tuition:** $12,840	**Sorority:** Yes
Men: 43%	**Room & board:** $6,148	**Athletics:** Division I
Percent out-of-state: 2%	**Housing Information**	
	University housing: Yes	
	Percent living on campus: 36%	

Illinois State University

LINCOLN COLLEGE

300 Keokuk Street, Lincoln, IL 62656
Phone: 800-569-0556 • Fax: 217-732-7715
E-mail: admission@lincolncollege.com • Web: www.lincolncollege.edu
Support: CS • Institution type: 4-year private

LEARNING DISABILITY PROGRAM AND SERVICES

Lincoln College is committed to enhancing student achievement through supportive service community efforts in combination with parental involvement. The college offers personal attention and a number of supportive services to assist students. The Academic Enrichment Program meets every day to improve fundamental learning skills in writing, reading, mathematics, and oral communication. Study skills and habits are also emphasized. Tutoring is assigned, and each student's course schedule is strictly regulated. The Breakfast Club is for students who are failing two or more classes. These students meet with the college president and the academic dean to discuss ways to change direction and achieve academic success. Class attendance is monitored, and faculty members inform the dean weekly if a student has missed class. Advisors help students to change counterproductive behaviors regarding attendance. CASP (Concerned About Student Progress) warnings are sent the fifth week of each semester to provide an early indicator of below-average performance and allow students time to recover and change behaviors. The Connection Program targets incoming freshmen who may benefit from an established peer group. These groups of 8–10 students meet with professors and foster awareness and build relationships.

LD/ADHD ADMISSIONS INFORMATION

College entrance tests required: Yes
Interview required: No
Essay recommended: No
Documentation required for LD: Students must provide current documentation (i.e., not older than 3 years). This documentation may include a psychological evaluation, an IEP, a Section 504 Plan, or a summary of performance.
Documentation required for ADHD: Same as above
Submitted to: Office of Disability Services
Special Ed. HS course work accepted: Yes

Specific course requirements of all applicants: NR
Separate application required: No
# of LD applications submitted each year: NR
# of LD applications accepted yearly: NR
Total # of students receiving LD services: NR
Acceptance into program means acceptance into college: Students are admitted and enrolled at the college and then reviewed for supportive services.

ADMISSIONS

There is no special admissions process for students with learning disabilities. Students must submit the general application, a high school transcript, and counselor recommendations. Students with sub-17 ACT scores are required to attend the 1-week Academic Development Seminar prior to the fall semester. After completing the Academic Development Seminar, a student's probationary status is removed. Students may be admitted and placed into a split semester, which means the student will take two courses per nine weeks if this is recommended by the Academic Development Seminar.

ADDITIONAL INFORMATION

Lincoln College offers the Academic Development Seminar for students the week before fall semester starts. Students learn writing and speaking skills, effective library skills, and science lab orientation. They develop effective student techniques; lab and field orientation; methods to evaluate social science graphs, charts, and maps; and concepts and values in the humanities. The Academic Writing Seminar is also offered one week in the summer to cover crucial college skills such as writing skill development, note-taking techniques, exam tips, speaking skills, writing to define and classify, college expectations, analytical thinking and writing, and writing to understand and evaluate. Lincoln also has a special program for students with ADHD. The Academy for Collegiate Collaboration for Effective Student Success (ACCESS) is designed for students with ADHD to receive services from private coaches trained to support students. Tuition is $1,000 per semester plus $500 for ACCESS prep course prior to the fall semester.

LEARNING DISABILITY PROGRAM/SERVICES

Learning Disability Program/Services: The Office for Disability Services
Director: Stephanie Gaddy, EdD
  E-Mail: sgaddy@lincolncollege.edu
  Telephone: 800-569-0556
  Fax: 217-732-7715

LEARNING DISABILITY SERVICES

Requests for the following services/accommodations will be evaluated individually based on appropriate and current documentation.

Allowed in exams
  Calculator: Yes
  Dictionary: No
  Computer: Yes
  Spellchecker: Yes
Extended test time: Yes
Scribes: No
Proctors: Yes
Oral exams: Yes
Note-takers: No

Distraction-reduced environment: Yes
Tape recording in class: Yes
Books on tape from RFBD: Yes
Taping of books not from RFBD: No
**Accommodations for students with
  ADHD:** Yes
Reading machine: No
Other assistive technology: No
Priority registration: Yes

Added costs for services: Yes for
  ACCESS Program
LD specialists: Yes
Professional tutors: 15
Peer tutors: 20–30
Max. hours/wk. for services:
  Unlimited
**How professors are notified of
  LD/ADHD:** By student

GENERAL ADMISSIONS INFORMATION

Director of Admissions: Anthony Schilling, Executive Director of Enrollment Management
Telephone: 800-569-0556 ext. 254

ENTRANCE REQUIREMENTS

16 total recommendations, including 4 English, 3 math, 3 science, 3 social studies, and 2 foreign language. ACT of 16 or higher admitted without restriction. Those with an ACT of 15 or lower may be admitted upon review by the Admission Committee. These students must complete and pass the academic development seminar. TOEFL required of all international applicants, minimum paper TOEFL 480, minimum computer TOEFL 157.

Application deadline: Rolling
Notification: Rolling
Average GPA: 2.25
ACT Composite middle 50% range:
  NR

SAT Math middle 50% range: NR
**SAT Critical Reading middle 50%
  range:** NR
SAT Writing middle 50% range: NR

Graduated top 10% of class: 5
Graduated top 25% of class: 10
Graduated top 50% of class: 65

COLLEGE GRADUATION REQUIREMENTS

Course waivers allowed: Yes
In what course: Freshman Orientation
Course substitutions allowed: Yes
In what course: Freshman Orientation

ADDITIONAL INFORMATION

Environment: The college has a suburban campus in Normal, Illinois and a small town campus in Lincoln.

Student Body
  Undergrad enrollment: 700
  Women: 45%
  Men: 55%
  Percent out-of-state: 5%

Cost Information
  Tuition: $14,300
  Room & board: $5,600
Housing Information
  University housing: Yes
  Percent living on campus: 83%

Greek System
  Fraternity: No
  Sorority: No
  Athletics: NJCAA

LOYOLA UNIVERSITY—CHICAGO

820 North Michigan Avenue, Chicago, IL 60611
Phone: 312-915-6500 • Fax: 312-915-7216
E-mail: admission@luc.edu • Web: www.luc.edu
Support: CS • Institution type: 4-year private

LEARNING DISABILITY PROGRAM AND SERVICES

Every student with a disability is unique and her or his requests for services will be considered on a case-by-case basis. Services for Students with Disabilities work closely with several Loyola departments and outside agencies to ensure that their educational needs are met. The goal of Services for Students with Disabilities is to maximize each student's potential in assisting him or her to develop and maintain independence. Our philosophy encourages self-awareness, self-determination, self-advocacy, and independence in an accessible learning environment. Encouragement is given to all students to visit the Learning Assistance Center and Services for Students with Disabilities to explore the services available. The Office of Services for Students with Disabilities is part of the Learning Assistance Center.

LD/ADHD ADMISSIONS INFORMATION

College entrance tests required: Yes
Interview required: No
Essay recommended: No
Documentation required for LD: Psychoeducational
  evaluation
Documentation required for ADHD: Yes
Submitted to: Students with Disabilities
Special Ed. HS course work accepted: Yes

Specific course requirements of all applicants: Yes
Separate application required: No
# of LD applications submitted each year: NR
# of LD applications accepted yearly: NR
Total # of students receiving LD services: NR
**Acceptance into program means acceptance into
  college:** Students must be admitted and enrolled prior to
  requesting services.

ADMISSIONS

There is no special admissions procedure for students with disabilities. All admission applications are handled on a case-by-case basis by the Admissions Office for the Undergraduate Admissions. The following units or courses are suggested for admission to Loyola University—Chicago: 4 years of English (required), 3–4 years of math, 3 years of social science, 2 or more years of a foreign language, and 3–4 years of natural or physical science. Each application is reviewed individually and thoroughly. The writing sample, counselor recommendations, student activities, grades (minimum 3.2 GPA), and standardized test scores are all considered to determine if Loyola will be a good academic match for the strengths and abilities of the applicant. Loyola does not require or use the new written sections on the SAT and ACT for admission or placement.

ADDITIONAL INFORMATION

The Office of Services for Students with Disabilities is part of the Learning Assistance Center, which offers individual and group sessions for improving learning, tutorial services, and in-class workshops. Many students with disabilities work closely with both the coordinator and a learning assistance counselor. Students are encouraged to meet with the coordinator of services for students with disabilities during the first 2 weeks of each semester to determine accommodations and services for the current semester. Documentation should provide a clear description of the recommended accommodations, connect these to the impact of the condition, provide possible alternatives to the recommended accommodations, and include a statement of the level of need (or consequences of not receiving) the accommodations. The Learning Enrichment for Academic Progress (LEAP) Program takes otherwise strong freshman students with low ACT/SAT scores and offers them an extensive, 2-week seminar each August to shape study skills and habits. This program is not specifically for students with LD. The Academic Success Program is offered during the school year and is for all students who could benefit from extensive work on study strategies and college survival skills.

LEARNING DISABILITY PROGRAM/SERVICES

Learning Disability Program/Services: Services for Students with Disabilities
Director: Maggie Rogers
  E-Mail: aroger1@luc.edu
  Telephone: 773-508-2741
  Fax: 773-508-3123

LEARNING DISABILITY SERVICES

Requests for the following services/accommodations will be evaluated individually based on appropriate and current documentation.

Allowed in exams
  Calculator: Yes
  Dictionary: Yes
  Computer: Yes
  Spellchecker: Yes
Extended test time: Yes
Scribes: Yes
Proctors: Yes
Oral exams: Yes
Note-takers: Yes

Distraction-reduced environment: Yes
Tape recording in class: Yes
Books on tape from RFBD: Yes
Taping of books not from RFBD: Yes
Accommodations for students with ADHD: Yes
Reading machine: Yes
Other assistive technology: Yes
Priority registration: Yes

Added costs for services: N/A
LD specialists: Yes
Professional tutors: No
Peer tutors: 20
Max. hours/wk. for services: NR
How professors are notified of LD/ADHD: By both student and director

GENERAL ADMISSIONS INFORMATION

Director of Admissions: April Hansen
Telephone: 773-508-3079

ENTRANCE REQUIREMENTS

Academic units required: 4 English, 3 math, 3 science, 3 social studies, 1 history, 1 academic elective.
Academic units recommended: 4 English, 4 math, 4 science, 2 foreign language, 3 social studies, 2 history, 3 academic electives. High school diploma is required, and GED is accepted. ACT with or without Writing component accepted. TOEFL required of all international applicants: minimum paper TOEFL 550, minimum computer TOEFL 213.

Application deadline: Rolling
Notification: Rolling
Average GPA: 3.53
ACT Composite middle 50% range: 23–28

SAT Math middle 50% range: 520–640
SAT Critical Reading middle 50% range: 530–640
SAT Writing middle 50% range: 520–620

Graduated top 10% of class: 32%
Graduated top 25% of class: 67%
Graduated top 50% of class: 95%

COLLEGE GRADUATION REQUIREMENTS

Course waivers allowed: Yes
In what course: Waiver for math and foreign language if documentation supports the request.
Course substitutions allowed: Yes
In what course: Substitution for math and foreign language if documentation supports the request.

ADDITIONAL INFORMATION

Environment: The campus is located in downtown Chicago, just east of Lake Michigan.

Student Body
  Undergrad enrollment: 9,076
  Women: 65%
  Men: 35%
  Percent out-of-state: 32%

Cost Information
  Tuition: $26,450
  Room & board: $9,930
Housing Information
  University housing: Yes
  Percent living on campus: 36%

Greek System
  Fraternity: Yes
  Sorority: Yes
  Athletics: Division I

Loyola University —Chicago

NATIONAL-LOUIS UNIVERSITY

122 South Michigan Avenue, Chicago, IL 60603
Phone: 312-261-3550
E-mail: nlnuinfo@wheeling1.nl.edu • Web: www.nl.edu
Support: SP • Institution type: 4-year private

LEARNING DISABILITY PROGRAM AND SERVICES

The Center for Academic Development is designed to assist students with learning disabilities to pursue and complete a college education. It is a supportive program for students admitted by the university and enrolled in regular and developmental college courses. While the total services furnished in this program are provided by the university to all students who might experience difficulty with a regular college curriculum, emphasis is placed on individual program planning, tutoring, monitoring, arranged counseling, and special testing for the learning disabled. The center provides peer tutoring, contact with faculty, academic advising, and career and emotional counseling for students who make reasonable progress toward a degree in one of the college programs.

LD/ADHD ADMISSIONS INFORMATION

College entrance tests required: Yes
Interview required: No
Essay recommended: No
Documentation required for LD: At least WAIS–III; WJ–III
Documentation required for ADHD: Yes
Submitted to: Center for Academic Development
Special Ed. HS course work accepted: No

Specific course requirements of all applicants: NR
Separate application required: No
# of LD applications submitted each year: NR
# of LD applications accepted yearly: NR
Total # of students receiving LD services: 25
Acceptance into program means acceptance into college: Students must be admitted and enrolled in the university first and then request services.

ADMISSIONS

Students must meet regular admission requirements of a 2.0 GPA in nonremedial academic courses. Applicants should be high school graduates in the top half of their graduating class. Applicants must submit 119 ACT or 750 SAT. Some students who do not meet these criteria may be admitted on a provisional basis as summer admits or as high-potential students. A student's learning environment may make a change in academic performance; therefore, applications are considered from students who do not meet the general admission criteria to be admitted as high-potential students. Such students may be admitted on a provisional basis and referred for appropriate assistance to the Center for Academic Development or other academic and student support services. Criteria used in determining admissibility could include work experience, demonstrated leadership in community or extracurricular activities, motivation and attitude toward learning, and career objectives. In addition, letters of support reflecting the applicant's academic work or ability may be required. A personal interview may also be required. Some students may be asked to sit for the university's skills assessment prior to admission and the results of these tests will be used as a basis for the admission decision. Interested students should indicate on the supplemental application form the nature of their learning disability and return the form to the Admissions Office. An informal assessment session is held with the applicants by a learning specialist. Students submit reports to admissions with authorization for release of information. Students should submit a statement from a diagnostician that they can function at college level. Social service or psychiatric reports should also be submitted. The learning specialist evaluates reports and admits 10 students each fall, and these students must participate in the Summer Bridge Program and LD counseling group.

ADDITIONAL INFORMATION

The Center for Academic Development is staffed by specialists. Special services include: Summer Bridge Program; developmental reading, writing, and math courses; special advising and orientation; assistance in registration; individualized tutoring and monitoring; organizational and student skill training; academic and career counseling; and an arrangement with faculty for modification of course presentation and examination. The PACE Program, housed on a separate campus, is a noncredit transition program for students with low IQ scores who want to experience residential living and develop life skills. These students have the opportunity to get work experience as teacher aides or in human resources. The decision to accept or reject a student for admission is based on the following criteria: the student should be between the ages of 18 and 30 and have identified learning problems that have interfered with school performance through his or her academic career. Generally, students accepted into the PACE Program have a range of cognitive and processing difficulties, a high probability of difficulty with a regular college curriculum, even with the provision of various support services, and sufficient emotional stability to adjust to all aspects of the program. They also have the ability to participate in most activities.

LEARNING DISABILITY PROGRAM/SERVICES

Learning Disability Program/Services: Center for Academic Development
Director: Erin Haulotte
  E-Mail: Erin.Haulotte@nl.edu
  Telephone: 847-947-5491
  Fax: 847-947-5610

LEARNING DISABILITY SERVICES

Requests for the following services/accommodations will be evaluated individually based on appropriate and current documentation.

Allowed in exams
  Calculator: Yes
  Dictionary: Yes
  Computer: Yes
  Spellchecker: Yes
Extended test time: Yes
Scribes: Yes
Proctors: Yes
Oral exams: No
Note-takers: Yes

Distraction-reduced environment: Yes
Tape recording in class: Yes
Books on tape from RFBD: Yes
Taping of books not from RFBD: No
Accommodations for students with ADHD: Yes
Reading machine: No
Other assistive technology: Yes
Priority registration: Yes

Added costs for services: Yes for PACE
LD specialists: Yes
Professional tutors: 5
Peer tutors: 5
Max. hours/wk. for services: 2
How professors are notified of LD/ADHD: By both student and director

GENERAL ADMISSIONS INFORMATION

Director of Admissions: Pat Patillo
Telephone: 847-465-0575

ENTRANCE REQUIREMENTS

Academic units recommended: 4 English, 3 math, 2 science (1 science lab), 2 foreign language, 3 social studies. High school diploma is required, and GED is accepted.

Application deadline: NR
Notification: NR
Average GPA: NR
ACT Composite middle 50% range: 15–20

SAT Math middle 50% range: NR
SAT Critical Reading middle 50% range: NR
SAT Writing middle 50% range: NR

Graduated top 10% of class: 0%
Graduated top 25% of class: 29%
Graduated top 50% of class: 89%

COLLEGE GRADUATION REQUIREMENTS

Course waivers allowed: No
Course substitutions allowed: Yes

ADDITIONAL INFORMATION

Environment: There are five locations in the Chicago area.

Student Body
  Undergrad enrollment: 3,545
  Women: 72%
  Men: 28%
  Percent out-of-state: 1%

Cost Information
  Tuition: $13,095
  Room & board: $6,336
Housing Information
  University housing: Yes
  Percent living on campus: 5%

Greek System
  Fraternity: No
  Sorority: No
Athletics: Division I

NORTHERN ILLINOIS UNIVERSITY

Office of Admissions, Williston Hall 101, NIU, DeKalb, IL 60115-2857
Phone: 815-753-0446 • Fax: 815-753-1783
E-mail: admissions-info@niu.edu • Web: www.reg.niu.edu
Support: CS • Institution type: 4-year public

LEARNING DISABILITY PROGRAM AND SERVICES

The main goal of the Center for Access-Ability Resources (CAAR) is to create and maintain a supportive atmosphere to assist students with LD in developing self-esteem, self-advocacy skills, and effective strategies for college success. CAAR is staffed by personnel who are supportive and sensitive to students. CAAR provides a comprehensive range of support services that are integrated within the university resources. Assistance must be requested by the student. The LD coordinator assists students in identifying appropriate accommodations, compensatory and remediation strategies, and in the utilization of both on- and off-campus resources. Not all students are eligible for services. It is the responsibility of CAAR to see that qualified students who request services are provided appropriate accommodations. Instructors can also verify student accommodation requests through CAAR. The goal is to enhance student success through an individualized program of support services. To request and initiate services, students must submit to CAAR the necessary and appropriate official documentation verifying the disability.

LD/ADHD ADMISSIONS INFORMATION

College entrance tests required: Yes
Interview required: No
Essay recommended: No
Documentation required for LD: Psychoeducational evaluation—prefer within 3 years and with adult based norms
Documentation required for ADHD: Documentation from diagnostician/physician verifying diagnosis, diagnostic tests/criteria, medications, and functional impact
Submitted to: Center for Access Ability Resources
Special Ed. HS course work accepted: No

Specific course requirements of all applicants: Yes
Separate application required: No
# of LD applications submitted each year: NR
# of LD applications accepted yearly: NR
Total # of students receiving LD services: 150–180
Acceptance into program means acceptance into college: Students admitted may request services. Students denied admission may appeal the decision, and once admitted, they may request services.

ADMISSIONS

Regular admission requires a 50–99 percent class rank and 19 ACT or a 34–49 percent class rank and 23 ACT. Course requirements include 4 years of English, 2–3 years of math, 2–3 years of sciences, 3 years of social studies, and 1–2 years of a foreign language, art, or music. Substitutions may be allowed with appropriate documentation. Students with LD apply through regular admissions but can self-disclose the LD and request that their application be given special consideration if they feel that their entrance tests scores or high school performance was adversely affected by special circumstances related to a documented disability. Special admission consideration for students with disabilities applies only to freshmen applicants who do not meet standard admission criteria and/or have already been denied admission. The special admission process involves completing the standard NIU application and attaching a special consideration letter asking that the application be given special consideration based on a diagnosed disability. It helps to describe the disability. This alerts admissions to forward the application to CAAR. CAAR will need the following: (1) documentation of the disability with a personal statement explaining student's interest in attending NIU, student's academic and career goals, and any other information the student would like to share; (2) three letters of recommendation from persons who have worked with the student in an academic setting; and (3) any additional information about the disability that is pertinent. The admission process begins when all requested information has been received. Students may be contacted for an on-campus interview with a CAAR coordinator. CAAR staff make a recommendation to the Admissions Office, who will notify students of the admission decision.

ADDITIONAL INFORMATION

Academic resources include priority registration, exam accommodations, limited tutoring, individualized study-skill learning-strategy advisement and instruction by LD specialists, reading and study techniques course taught by an LD specialist, foreign language course substitution with documentation, and taped texts. Other requests for course substitutions will be reviewed individually. Advocacy services include orientation, self-advocacy training, and liaison with faculty, information on LD/ADHD-related events, and in-service training for faculty. Advisement resources include academic advising, referrals to university counseling, and support and consultation by staff. Diagnostic evaluation for LD and ADHD are offered through referral to private diagnostician. Not all students are eligible for all services.

LEARNING DISABILITY PROGRAM/SERVICES

Learning Disability Program/Services: Center for Access-Ability Resources
Director: Nancy Kasinski
  E-Mail: nancyk@niu.edu
  Telephone: 815-753-9734
  Fax: 815-753-9570
Contact Person: Garth Rubin
  E-Mail: grubin@niu.edu
  Telephone: 815-753-9750
  Fax: 815-753-9570

LEARNING DISABILITY SERVICES

Requests for the following services/accommodations will be evaluated individually based on appropriate and current documentation.

Allowed in exams
  Calculator: Yes
  Dictionary: Yes
  Computer: Yes
  Spellchecker: Yes
Extended test time: Yes
Scribes: Yes
Proctors: Yes
Oral exams: Yes
Note-takers: Yes

Distraction-reduced environment: Yes
Tape recording in class: Yes
Books on tape from RFBD: Yes
Taping of books not from RFBD: Yes
Accommodations for students with
  ADHD: Yes
Reading machine: Yes
Other assistive technology: Yes
Priority registration: Yes

Added costs for services: No
LD specialists: Yes
Professional tutors: NR
Peer tutors: No
Max. hours/wk. for services:
  Unlimited
How professors are notified of
  LD/ADHD: By student

GENERAL ADMISSIONS INFORMATION

Director of Admissions: Robert Burk
Telephone: 815-753-0446

ENTRANCE REQUIREMENTS
Academic units required: 4 English, 2 math, 2 science (1 science lab), 1 foreign language, 2 social studies, 1 history. **Academic units recommended:** 4 math, 4 science (2 science labs), 2 foreign language, 3 social studies. High school diploma is required, and GED is accepted. TOEFL required of all international applicants: minimum paper TOEFL 525, minimum computer TOEFL 1.

Application deadline: 8/1
Notification: Rolling
Average GPA: NR
ACT Composite middle 50% range: 19–24

SAT Math middle 50% range: NR
SAT Critical Reading middle 50% range: NR
SAT Writing middle 50% range: NR

Graduated top 10% of class: 9%
Graduated top 25% of class: 34%
Graduated top 50% of class: 74%

COLLEGE GRADUATION REQUIREMENTS

Course waivers allowed: No
Course substitutions allowed: Yes
In what course: Primarily for foreign language if disability severely impacts the learning of foreign language. Substitutions are not given for core competency math classes (general education).

ADDITIONAL INFORMATION

Environment: The school is located on 460 acres in a small town 65 miles from Chicago.

Student Body
  Undergrad enrollment: 18,025
  Women: 53%
  Men: 47%
  Percent out-of-state: 4%

Cost Information
  In-state tuition: $7,230
  Out-of-state tuition: $12,290
  Room & board: $5,010
Housing Information
  University housing: Yes
  Percent living on campus: 33%

Greek System
  Fraternity: Yes
  Sorority: Yes
  Athletics: Division I

NORTHWESTERN UNIVERSITY

PO Box 3060, 1801 Hinman Avenue, Evanston, IL 60204-3060
Phone: 847-491-4100 • Fax: 847-467-5771
E-mail: ug-admission@northwestern.edu • Web: www.northwestern.edu
Support: CS • Institution type: 4-year private

LEARNING DISABILITY PROGRAM AND SERVICES

It is the policy at Northwestern University to ensure that no qualified student with a disability is denied the benefit of, excluded from participation in, or subjected to discrimination in any university program or activity. The mission of Services for Students with Disabilities is to ensure that all undergraduate, graduate, and professional school students with disabilities can fully participate in academic programming and all other facets of university life on campus. To fulfill this mission, Services for Students with Disabilities has five primary goals: (1) gather and evaluate documentation information and requests to determine eligibility for accommodations and services; (2) provide, coordinate, and facilitate reasonable accommodations and services; (3) recommend modifications to improve access to university facilities and transportation services; (4) provide information and training on disability-related topics to university faculty and staff; and (5) serve as a resource on disability information for the university community and visitors. Students with disabilities have the responsibility to meet qualifications and maintain essential institutional standards for courses, programs, and activities; self-identify as an individual with a disability when an accommodation is needed and seek information, counsel, and assistance as necessary in a timely fashion; demonstrate and/or provide documentation describing (from an appropriate professional) how the disability limits participation in courses, programs, services, and activities; and follow published procedures for obtaining reasonable accommodations, academic adjustments, and/or auxiliary aids and services.

LD/ADHD ADMISSIONS INFORMATION

College entrance tests required: Yes
Interview required: No
Essay recommended: Yes
Documentation required for LD: A current psychoeducational evaluation with a clear statement of the diagnosis, scores from the tests administered, and explanations of the appropriate academic accommodations
Documentation required for ADHD: A diagnostic report from an appropriate professional that includes documentation of current symptons that meet the diagnostic criteria for ADHD and a description of why the student's condition necessitates an accommodation
Submitted to: Services for Students with Disabilities
Special Ed. HS course work accepted: No

Specific course requirements of all applicants: NR
Separate application required: No
# of LD applications submitted each year: NR
# of LD applications accepted yearly: NR
Total # of students receiving LD services: 100–120
Acceptance into program means acceptance into college: Students must be admitted and enrolled in the university first and then request services.

ADMISSIONS

There is no special admissions procedure for students with learning disabilities. All applicants must meet the general admission criteria. Most students have taken AP and honors courses in high school and been very successful in these competitive college-prep courses. ACT/SAT tests are required, and SAT Subject Tests are recommended.

ADDITIONAL INFORMATION

Services are available for all students with disabilities and include a Writing Center, comprehensive assistive technology, support groups, and individualized counseling. There are LD specialists on staff, and all of the staff has knowledge in all disability categories. Students with learning disabilities must provide current psychoeducational evaluations normed on an adult population. Students with ADHD must provide a letter from an appropriate professional that includes a diagnosis, functional limitations, and recommendations. This documentation should be submitted to Services for Students with Disabilities. Reasonable accommodations are individualized and flexible based on the nature of the disability and the academic environment. Some of the accommodations provided, with appropriate documentation, could include note-taking services; materials in e-text and/or audio format; testing accommodations, such as extended time and alternative test environment; scribe and reader services; screening for learning disabilities; and building study skills.

LEARNING DISABILITY PROGRAM/SERVICES

Learning Disability Program/Services: Services for Students with Disabilities
Director: Margie Roe
  E-Mail: m-roc@northwestern.edu
  Telephone: 847-491-2960
  Fax: 847-467-5531

LEARNING DISABILITY SERVICES

Requests for the following services/accommodations will be evaluated individually based on appropriate and current documentation.

Allowed in exams
  Calculator: Yes
  Dictionary: Yes
  Computer: Yes
  Spellchecker: Yes
Extended test time: Yes
Scribes: Yes
Proctors: Yes
Oral exams: Yes
Note-takers: Yes

Distraction-reduced environment: Yes
Tape recording in class: Yes
Books on tape from RFBD: Yes
Taping of books not from RFBD: Yes
Accommodations for students with ADHD: Yes
Reading machine: Yes
Other assistive technology: Yes
Priority registration: Yes

Added costs for services: No
LD specialists: Yes
Professional tutors: No
Peer tutors: No
Max. hours/wk. for services: Unlimited
How professors are notified of LD/ADHD: By both student and director

GENERAL ADMISSIONS INFORMATION

Director of Admissions: Keith Todd
  Telephone: 847-491-7271

ENTRANCE REQUIREMENTS

Academic units recommended: 4 English, 3 math, 2 science (2 science labs), 2 foreign language, 2 social studies, 1 academic elective. High school diploma or equivalent is not required. ACT with Writing component required. TOEFL required of all international applicants: minimum paper TOEFL 600, minimum computer TOEFL 250.

Application deadline: 1/1
Notification: 4/15
Average GPA: NR
ACT Composite middle 50% range: 29–33

SAT Math middle 50% range: 670–760
SAT Critical Reading middle 50% range: 650–740
SAT Writing middle 50% range: 650–740

Graduated top 10% of class: 83%
Graduated top 25% of class: 97%
Graduated top 50% of class: 100%

COLLEGE GRADUATION REQUIREMENTS

Course waivers allowed: No
Course substitutions allowed: Yes
In what course: On case-by-case basis

ADDITIONAL INFORMATION

Environment: The Evanston campus, which houses the undergraduate schools, is located approximately 15 miles from downtown Chicago.

Student Body
  Undergrad enrollment: 8,060
  Women: 53%
  Men: 47%
  Percent out-of-state: 75%

Cost Information
  Tuition: $33,408
  Room & board: $10,266
Housing Information
  University housing: Yes
  Percent living on campus: 65%

Greek System
  Fraternity: Yes
  Sorority: Yes
  Athletics: Division I

ROOSEVELT UNIVERSITY

430 South Michigan Avenue, Chicago, IL 60605
Phone: 312-341-3515 • Fax: 312-341-3523
E-mail: applyRU@roosevelt.edu • Web: www.roosevelt.edu
Support: CS • Institution type: 4-year private

LEARNING DISABILITY PROGRAM AND SERVICES

The goal of the Learning and Support Services Program (LSSP) is to provide a highly individualized support system that will help students discover their learning style. The staff works with each student individually on reading comprehension, writing skills, note-taking, study skills, time management skills, and test-taking skills. Roosevelt's small classroom size provides an opportunity for students to get to know their professors, and the faculty has been very responsive to the needs of LSSP students. The program is for students who would otherwise experience difficulty with a regular college curriculum. Emphasis is placed on individual program planning, tutoring, arranged counseling, and modified test-taking. The program helps students to define their strengths so that they can overcome their weaknesses and become independent, successful college students.

LD/ADHD ADMISSIONS INFORMATION

College entrance tests required: Yes
Interview required: Yes
Essay recommended: Yes
Documentation required for LD: Psychoeducational evaluation by licensed psychologist
Documentation required for ADHD: Diagnostic workup from psychologist
Submitted to: Learning and Support Services Program
Special Ed. HS course work accepted: No

Specific course requirements of all applicants: Yes
Separate application required: No
# of LD applications submitted each year: NR
# of LD applications accepted yearly: NR
Total # of students receiving LD services: 25–30
Acceptance into program means acceptance into college: Students must be admitted through the regular university admissions process, and once enrolled, may request services.

ADMISSIONS

There is not a separate admissions process through LSSP. However, it is recommended that students write a letter to the LSSP director to request services and state the purpose and reason for seeking help. After reviewing the letter, LSSP staff holds an informal interview assessment with the student. Applicants send reports to the LSSP with authorization for release of information. These reports should include the following: (1) most recent transcript and confidential records; (2) health and academic history; (3) test results and reports, including achievements, individual IQ, or other measurements of academic performance; and (4) the latest IEP. The LSSP staff will evaluate the reports and a meeting will be held to determine eligibility into LSSP. Students may be admitted during the summer with probationary status.

ADDITIONAL INFORMATION

The Learning and Support Services Program is only available to students with learning disabilities. Assistance is available in course selection, required course readings, assignments, and more. A major department advisor is assigned to each student. Depending on individual needs, tutoring assistance may include course-related training, reading, writing, and spelling. Help is offered in specific problem areas such as note-taking, basic skills improvement, time management, and organization. Qualified counseling psychologists help students cope with personal concerns and advise them on career goals. Students are encouraged to use Roosevelt's Learning Resource Center and Writing Laboratory. Services and accommodations are available to undergraduate and graduate students.

LEARNING DISABILITY PROGRAM/SERVICES

Learning Disability Program/Services: Learning and Support Services Program
Director: Nancy Litke
  E-Mail: nlitke@roosevelt.edu
  Telephone: 312-341-3810
  Fax: 312-341-2471

LEARNING DISABILITY SERVICES

Requests for the following services/accommodations will be evaluated individually based on appropriate and current documentation.

Allowed in exams
  Calculator: Yes
  Dictionary: Yes
  Computer: Yes
  Spellchecker: Yes
Extended test time: Yes
Scribes: Yes
Proctors: Yes
Oral exams: Yes
Note-takers: Yes

Distraction-reduced environment: Yes
Tape recording in class: Yes
Books on tape from RFBD: Yes
Taping of books not from RFBD: Yes
Accommodations for students with ADHD: Yes
Reading machine: No
Other assistive technology: Yes
Priority registration: No

Added costs for services: Yes
LD specialists: Yes
Professional tutors: 3
Peer tutors: Yes
Max. hours/wk. for services: NR
How professors are notified of LD/ADHD: By student

GENERAL ADMISSIONS INFORMATION

Director of Admissions: Gwen Kanelos
Telephone: 312-341-3515

ENTRANCE REQUIREMENTS
Academic units required: 4 English, 3 math, 3 science (2 science labs), 2 social studies, 1 history, 2 academic electives. **Academic units recommended:** 4 English, 4 math, 3 science (2 science labs), 2 foreign language, 2 social studies, 2 history, 2 academic electives. High school diploma is required, and GED is accepted. ACT with or without Writing component accepted. TOEFL required of all international applicants: minimum paper TOEFL 525, minimum computer TOEFL 197.

Application deadline: 8/21
Notification: Rolling
Average GPA: 3.00
ACT Composite middle 50% range:
  19–25

SAT Math middle 50% range:
  470–590
SAT Critical Reading middle 50% range: 500–630
SAT Writing middle 50% range: NR

Graduated top 10% of class: 3%
Graduated top 25% of class: 11%
Graduated top 50% of class: 33%

COLLEGE GRADUATION REQUIREMENTS

Course waivers allowed: Yes
In what course: Varies. Each request is considered individually and subject to department approval.
Course substitutions allowed: Yes
In what course: Varies. Each request is considered individually and subject to department approval.

ADDITIONAL INFORMATION

Environment: Roosevelt University is located in an urban area in downtown Chicago and in Schaumburg, Illinois which is 20 miles West of Chicago.

Student Body
  Undergrad enrollment: 6,500
  Women: 67%
  Men: 33%
  Percent out-of-state: 8%

Cost Information
  Tuition: $15,340
  Room & board: $6,000–10,000
Housing Information
  University housing: Yes
  Percent living on campus: 15%

Greek System
  Fraternity: Yes
  Sorority: Yes
Athletics: NR

SHIMER COLLEGE

Shimer College, 3424 South State Street, Chicago, IL 60616
Phone: 312-235-3500 • Fax: 312-235-3501
E-mail: admission@shimer.edu • Web: www.shimer.edu
Support: S • Institution type: 4-year private

LEARNING DISABILITY PROGRAM AND SERVICES

Shimer has no specific program for students with learning disabilities. Some students with relatively mild learning disabilities who have been unsuccessful in other settings have been successful at Shimer because of the unusual approach to education. Shimer offers an integrated curriculum where students read original sources and not textbooks. Students gather to discuss the books in small groups. Shimer has been able to meet the needs of students with learning disabilities who are motivated to seek this kind of education. Students are responsible for seeking the supportive help they want. Class sizes vary from 8 to 12 students, and a great deal of individual attention is available to all students.

LD/ADHD ADMISSIONS INFORMATION

College entrance tests required: No
Interview required: Yes
Essay recommended: Yes
Documentation required for LD: Psychoeducational evaluation
Documentation required for ADHD: No
Submitted to: Admissions
Special Ed. HS course work accepted: Yes

Specific course requirements of all applicants: NR
Separate application required: No
# of LD applications submitted each year: NR
# of LD applications accepted yearly: NR
Total # of students receiving LD services: NR
Acceptance into program means acceptance into college: Students must be admitted and enrolled in the university first and then request services.

ADMISSIONS

The goal of Shimer is to select students who will benefit from and contribute to its intellectual community. Each applicant is considered on an individual basis. Motivation, intellectual curiosity, and commitment to a rigorous and integrative educational program are important qualifications. Shimer will consider the application of any individual who has the potential to perform well. Admissions standards are the same for all students. Admission is based on whether or not the college feels it can provide the services necessary for successful learning. Students are encouraged to have a personal interview, which can be conducted by telephone; write a personal essay; submit ACT/SAT scores; submit letters of recommendation; and have their psychoeducational reports sent to the Admissions Office. There is no minimum GPA or specific high school courses required. ACT/SAT scores are considered in the admission decision, but they are not required. Writing samples and other personal contact will be used by the Admissions Committee to make an evaluation. A visit to campus is encouraged, and an interview is highly recommended and, in some cases, required. The essay portion of the application asks the applicant to provide an analysis of academic experience and offers the opportunity to demonstrate creative talent. These essays are major criteria in determining candidacy for admission. Shimer will accept a limited number of students on a threshold basis. These students often lack specific evidence of academic achievement, but they are able to convince the Admissions Committee of their commitment and potential. These students receive special guidance. Continuation after one semester is dependent on academic achievement.

ADDITIONAL INFORMATION

Skills courses are offered to all students for credit in writing, reading, math, study strategies, and learning strategies. The skills developed in these courses do not depend on earlier study in the core curriculum, so most do not have prerequisites. Classes are never larger than 12 students. All courses are conducted through discussion, and all course reading is from original sources. Extraordinary support is available to all students by faculty, staff, and other students.

LEARNING DISABILITY PROGRAM/SERVICES

Learning Disability Program/Services: Disability Services
Director: Elaine Vincent
E-Mail: e.vincent@shimer.edu
Telephone: 312-235-3500
Fax: 312-235-3051

LEARNING DISABILITY SERVICES

Requests for the following services/accommodations will be evaluated individually based on appropriate and current documentation.

Allowed in exams
  Calculator: Yes
  Dictionary: Yes
  Computer: Yes
  Spellchecker: Yes
Extended test time: Yes
Scribes: No
Proctors: No
Oral exams: Yes
Note-takers: No

Distraction-reduced environment: Yes
Tape recording in class: Yes
Books on tape from RFBD: Yes
Taping of books not from RFBD: Yes
Accommodations for students with ADHD: Yes
Reading machine: No
Other assistive technology: No
Priority registration: No

Added costs for services: No
LD specialists: No
Professional tutors: Yes
Peer tutors: 1–3
Max. hours/wk. for services: Unlimited
How professors are notified of LD/ADHD: By student

GENERAL ADMISSIONS INFORMATION

Director of Admissions: Elaine Vincent
Telephone: 312-235-3500

ENTRANCE REQUIREMENTS

Academic units recommended: 4 English, 4 math, 3 science (1 science lab), 3 foreign language, 1 social studies, 2 history, 3 academic electives. High school diploma or equivalent is not required. ACT without Writing component accepted. TOEFL required of all international applicants: minimum paper TOEFL 625, minimum computer TOEFL 263.

Application deadline: Rolling
Notification: Rolling
Average GPA: 3.10
ACT Composite middle 50% range: NR

SAT Math middle 50% range: NR
SAT Critical Reading middle 50% range: NR
SAT Writing middle 50% range: NR

Graduated top 10% of class: NR
Graduated top 25% of class: NR
Graduated top 50% of class: NR

COLLEGE GRADUATION REQUIREMENTS

Course waivers allowed: No
Course substitutions allowed: No

ADDITIONAL INFORMATION

Environment: Shimer is located in Chicago on the campus of the Illinois Institute of Technology.

Student Body
  Undergrad enrollment: 81
  Women: 49%
  Men: 51%
  Percent out-of-state: 60%

Cost Information
  Tuition: $21,000
  Room & board: $8,000
Housing Information
  University housing: Yes
  Percent living on campus: 40%

Greek System
  Fraternity: No
  Sorority: No
Athletics: Intramural

SOUTHERN ILLINOIS U.—CARBONDALE

MC 4710, Carbondale, IL 62901
Phone: 618-536-4405 • Fax: 618-453-4609
E-mail: joinsiuc@siu.edu • Web: www.siuc.edu
Support: SP • Institution type: 4-year public

LEARNING DISABILITY PROGRAM AND SERVICES

The Achieve Program is an academic support program for students with learning disabilities. The program provides comprehensive academic support services to meet the needs of students with previously diagnosed learning disabilities. Students interested in Achieve apply to the program and provide supporting documentation. All appropriate applicants must complete a 2-day battery of diagnostic tests prior to entering the program. There are fees for application, diagnostic testing, and support services offered by Achieve. Students are accepted on a first-come, first-served basis providing they qualify for the program. Students are enrolled in regular college courses and never restricted from any courses. Students are enrolled as full-time students freshman year but restricted to 12 semester hours.

LD/ADHD ADMISSIONS INFORMATION

College entrance tests required: Yes
Interview required: Yes
Essay recommended: Yes
Documentation required for LD: For DSS, psychoeducational evaluation. For Achieve Program, psychoeducational testing, from the earliest to the most recent, regardless of its age; candidates to perform a comprehensive diagnostic battery of tests
Documentation required for ADHD: Diagnostic statements from professionals with experience diagnosing ADHD
Submitted to: Achieve Program
Special Ed. HS course work accepted: No

Specific course requirements of all applicants: Yes
Separate application required: Yes
# of LD applications submitted each year: 200
# of LD applications accepted yearly: 50
Total # of students receiving LD services: 130
Acceptance into program means acceptance into college: Students are offered admission to the university and admission to Project Achieve.

ADMISSIONS

Application to the university and the program are separate. University application requires a general application form, SAT/ACT scores, and transcript. Students with an ACT of 21 or SAT equivalent and 4 years of English, 3 years of math, 3 years of science, 3 years of social studies, and electives are automatically admissible to the university. Applicants to Achieve Program are required to provide: Achieve application, $50 application fee, recent photo, and documentation of the LD. There is a fee of $1,000 for diagnostic testing (some fee waivers available), which is required before admissions. The Achieve application can be submitted any time during high school (the earlier the better). Students who self-disclose on their applications will have them reviewed by the program, which provides a recommendation to admissions. The required 21 ACT or SAT equivalent can be reviewed for Achieve Program applicants. Students not automatically admitted may be admitted through the Center for Basic Skills. In addition a two-year Associates Program will consider admitting students not meeting minimum standards for regular admission.

ADDITIONAL INFORMATION

Students take tests in five subject areas and are assigned specific classes within those course areas. Peer tutors assist students with understanding course material, studying and preparing for exams, homework assignments, projects, written work, and time management. Note-takers are hired to go into classes and take notes for students who demonstrate difficulty with visual-motor, auditory-memory-to-motor, and auditory comprehension tasks. Students must attend classes even if they are receiving note-taking support. Students may take exams in the Achieve Office, and receive extended time, as well as a reader or writer if needed. Students may have textbooks and other written material taped. Some students will benefit from remediation of reading, spelling, math, and/or organizational deficits. Achieve students may take a developmental writing course before attempting the required English course. Graduate assistants work with students on a one-on-one basis so that the students have individual attention. Students have access to individualized tutoring, taped texts, test accommodations, remedial classes, developmental writing course, test proctoring, and advocacy service.

LEARNING DISABILITY PROGRAM/SERVICES

Learning Disability Program/Services: Achieve Program
Director: Kathleen Plesko
  E-Mail: kplesko@siu.edu
  Telephone: 618-453-7754
  Fax: 618-453-7000

LEARNING DISABILITY SERVICES

Requests for the following services/accommodations will be evaluated individually based on appropriate and current documentation.

Allowed in exams
  Calculator: Yes
  Dictionary: Yes
  Computer: Yes
  Spellchecker: Yes
Extended test time: Yes
Scribes: Yes
Proctors: Yes
Oral exams: Yes
Note-takers: Yes

Distraction-reduced environment: Yes
Tape recording in class: Yes
Books on tape from RFBD: Yes
Taping of books not from RFBD: Yes
Accommodations for students with ADHD: Yes
Reading machine: Yes
Other assistive technology: Yes
Priority registration: Yes

Added costs for services: Yes
LD specialists: Yes
Professional tutors: 20–40
Peer tutors: 50–80
Max. hours/wk. for services: Unlimited
How professors are notified of LD/ADHD: By both student and director

GENERAL ADMISSIONS INFORMATION

Director of Admissions: Jim Carl, Interim Dean of Admissions
  Telephone: 618-536-4405

ENTRANCE REQUIREMENTS

Academic units required: 4 English, 3 math, 3 science (3 science labs), 3 social studies, 2 academic electives. High school diploma is required, and GED is accepted. ACT with or without Writing component accepted. TOEFL required of all international applicants: minimum paper TOEFL 520, minimum computer TOEFL 190.

Application deadline: NR
Notification: Rolling
Average GPA: NR
ACT Composite middle 50% range: 19–24

SAT Math middle 50% range: 460–610
SAT Critical Reading middle 50% range: 460–610
SAT Writing middle 50% range: 340–550

Graduated top 10% of class: 9%
Graduated top 25% of class: 28%
Graduated top 50% of class: 61%

COLLEGE GRADUATION REQUIREMENTS

Course waivers allowed: Yes
In what course: Waivers or substitutions are granted by committee within the student's department. Individual decisions are made for each student request regarding curriculum. Achieve will provide input for the committee's review.
Course substitutions allowed: Yes
In what course: Waivers or substitutions are granted by committee within the student's department. Individual decisions are made for each student request regarding curriculum. Achieve will provide input for the committee's review.

ADDITIONAL INFORMATION

Environment: The campus lies at the edge of the Shawnee National Forest 6 hours south of Chicago.

Student Body
  Undergrad enrollment: 16,217
  Women: 43%
  Men: 57%
  Percent out-of-state: 14%

Cost Information
  In-state tuition: $5,310
  Out-of-state tuition: $13,276
  Room & board: $6,138
Housing Information
  University housing: Yes
  Percent living on campus: 28%

Greek System
  Fraternity: Yes
  Sorority: Yes
Athletics: Division I

SOUTHERN ILLINOIS U.—EDWARDSVILLE

PO Box 1600, Edwardsville, IL 62026-1080
Phone: 618-650-3705 • Fax: 618-650-5013
E-mail: admissions@siue.edu • Web:
Support: CS • Institution type: 4-year public

LEARNING DISABILITY PROGRAM AND SERVICES

SIUE's philosophy is to assist students in becoming as independent as possible, and every effort has been made to eliminate barriers to learning. SIUE offers a full range of resources to support students with disabilities and help them attain their educational goals. Reaching goals starts with pre-admission planning and an assessment of the student's abilities and interests. The coordinator in the Office of Disabled Student Services (ODSS) will develop an understanding of the student's individual needs through counseling and academic advising. Early planning and testing will ensure that special needs are taken into consideration and that students can enjoy the full benefit of an educational experience at SIUE. Students are encouraged to contact the ODSS as soon as they decide to enroll at the university in order to plan an individualized support program. SIUE does not have special classes for students with learning disabilities; however, the university does offer academic development classes for all students who need to develop their math, reading, and writing skills. New Horizons is an organization for students, faculty, and staff who are concerned with issues facing students with disabilities on campus. New Horizons' activities include advocacy, fund-raising, guest speakers, and social activities.

LD/ADHD ADMISSIONS INFORMATION

College entrance tests required: Yes
Interview required: No
Essay recommended: No
Documentation required for LD: Psychoeducational
  evaluation preferred, but IEP's are accepted.
Documentation required for ADHD: Same as above. In
  addition, letters from physicians and therapists are accepted.
Submitted to: Office of Disabled Student Services
Special Ed. HS course work accepted: NR

Specific course requirements of all applicants: Yes
Separate application required: No
# of LD applications submitted each year: NR
# of LD applications accepted yearly: NR
Total # of students receiving LD services: 87
**Acceptance into program means acceptance into
  college:** Student must be admitted and enrolled in the
  university first and then reviewed for LD services.

ADMISSIONS
Students with learning disabilities are required to submit the same general application form as all other students. Students should submit documentation of their learning disability in order to receive services once enrolled. This documentation should be sent to ODSS. Regular admissions criteria recommend: 4 years of English, 3 years of math, 3 years of science, 3 years of social science, 2 years of a foreign language or electives (students with deficiencies need to check with the Office of Admissions); a class rank in the top two-thirds, and an ACT minimum of 17 (the average is 21) or SAT of 640–680. Students denied admission may appeal the decision.

ADDITIONAL INFORMATION
The advisers of ODSS will assist students with learning disabilities with pre-admission planning, including an assessment of abilities and interests. Counseling and academic advisement provides assistance in developing an understanding of individual needs. Skills classes are available in math, writing, and reading. Current resources include testing accommodations, assistance in writing/reading exams, assistance with library research, tutoring, and volunteer note-takers. In addition, the coordinator of ODSS acts as a liaison with faculty and staff regarding learning disabilities and accommodations needed by students. Services and accommodations are available for undergraduate and graduate students.

LEARNING DISABILITY PROGRAM/SERVICES

Learning Disability Program/Services: Office of Disabled Student Services
Director: Jane Floyd-Hendey
  E-Mail: jfloydh@siue.edu
  Telephone: 618-650-3782
  Fax: 618-650-5691

LEARNING DISABILITY SERVICES

Requests for the following services/accommodations will be evaluated individually based on appropriate and current documentation.

Allowed in exams	**Distraction-reduced environment:** Yes	**Added costs for services:** No
Calculator: Yes	**Tape recording in class:** Yes	**LD specialists:** Yes
Dictionary: Yes	**Books on tape from RFBD:** NR	**Professional tutors:** No
Computer: Yes	**Taping of books not from RFBD:** No	**Peer tutors:** No
Spellchecker: Yes	**Accommodations for students with**	**Max. hours/wk. for services:** 47
Extended test time: Yes	**ADHD:** Yes	**How professors are notified of**
Scribes: Yes	**Reading machine:** Yes	**LD/ADHD:** By student
Proctors: Yes	**Other assistive technology:** Yes	
Oral exams: Yes	**Priority registration:** Yes	
Note-takers: Yes		

GENERAL ADMISSIONS INFORMATION

Director of Admissions: Todd Burrell
Telephone: 618-650-3705

ENTRANCE REQUIREMENTS

Academic units required: 4 English, 3 math, 3 science (3 science labs), 3 social studies, 2 academic electives.
Academic units recommended: 2 foreign language. High school diploma is required, and GED is accepted. TOEFL required of all international applicants: minimum paper TOEFL 550, minimum computer TOEFL 213.

Application deadline: 5/31	**SAT Math middle 50% range:** NR	**Graduated top 10% of class:** 18%
Notification: Rolling	**SAT Critical Reading middle 50%**	**Graduated top 25% of class:** 44%
Average GPA: NR	**range:** NR	**Graduated top 50% of class:** 79%
ACT Composite middle 50% range:	**SAT Writing middle 50% range:** NR	
19–25		

COLLEGE GRADUATION REQUIREMENTS

Course waivers allowed: Yes
In what course: Foreign language, math
Course substitutions allowed: Yes
In what course: Math

ADDITIONAL INFORMATION

Environment: The university is located on 2,664 acres 18 miles northeast of St. Louis.

Student Body	**Cost Information**	**Greek System**
Undergrad enrollment: 10,886	**In-state tuition:** $4,758	**Fraternity:** Yes
Women: 55%	**Out-of-state tuition:** $11,895	**Sorority:** Yes
Men: 45%	**Room & board:** $6,500	**Athletics:** Division II
Percent out-of-state: NR	**Housing Information**	
	University housing: Yes	
	Percent living on campus: 27%	

U. OF ILLINOIS AT URBANA-CHAMPAIGN

901 West Illinois Street, Urbana, IL 61801
Phone: 217-333-0302 • Fax: 217-333-0903
E-mail: ugradadmissions@uiuc.edu • Web: www.uiuc.edu
Support: CS • Institution type: 4-year public

LEARNING DISABILITY PROGRAM AND SERVICES

The Division of Rehabilitation Education Services (DRES) assists qualified students with disabilities in the pursuit of their higher education objectives. Professional staff are available at DRES to assist university students in the following areas: planning and implementing academic accommodations, compensatory strategies, academic coaching, obtaining additional aids (e.g., interpreters, readers/writer), obtaining modified test accommodations, counseling, and priority registration/scheduling assistance.

LD/ADHD ADMISSIONS INFORMATION

College entrance tests required: Yes
Interview required: No
Essay recommended: No
Documentation required for LD: Diagnostic interviews (developmental, medical, family histories); cognitive abilities (WAIS–III); cognitive processing (WJ–III); and achievement scores with a diagnosis by a qualified professional
Documentation required for ADHD: Evidence of early impairment, extensive interview, developmental history, consideration of alternate diagnostic hypothesis, and psychological testing when appropriate. Documentation needs to include a diagnosis by a qualified professional.
Submitted to: Division of Rehabilitation Services
Special Ed. HS course work accepted: Yes

Specific course requirements of all applicants: NR
Separate application required: Yes
# of LD applications submitted each year: NR
# of LD applications accepted yearly: NR
Total # of students receiving LD services: 175
Acceptance into program means acceptance into college: Students must be admitted and enrolled in the university first and then request services.

ADMISSIONS

Applicants with LD are expected to meet the same admission criteria as all other applicants. Any tests for undergraduate and graduate admissions taken with accommodations are considered as competitive. Applicants whose qualifications are slightly below a college's admission guidelines are encouraged to use the "Background Statement" section on the application to provide additional information that could be useful in understanding the student's academic history. Students are encouraged to provide diagnostic evidence from a licensed clinical examiner. The university admits students to particular colleges on the basis of class rank, GPA, ACT/SAT scores, extracurricular activities, personal statements, achievements and challenge of curriculum. Prospective students should contact the appropriate college for complete course requirements. Required courses include 4 years of English, 3 years of math, 2 years of a foreign language, 2 years of social science, and 2 science labs. In 2006 the middle 50 percent admitted to the College of Liberal Arts had an ACT of 26–30 or SAT Reasoning Test of 1210–1390 and rank in the 85 percentile–96 percentile. The middle 50 percent admitted to the College of Business had an ACT of 28–31 or SAT Reasoning Test of 1240–1380 and a class rank in the 88–97 percentile.

ADDITIONAL INFORMATION

Accommodations are individually student centered. The student is expected to declare and document all concurrent disabilities for which services are expected. The design and implementation of accommodations depend on the student's perspective of his or her functional limitations relative to the academic requirements of each course. Timely communication to the learning disability specialist of any situations that are projected to need accommodations during the semester is essential. Individual inquiries and early contacts prior to campus residency strengthen the process of accommodation. Students with LD/ADHD can work with a specialist to develop compensatory strategies and get assistance with the coordination of academic accommodations and tutorial recommendations. Reading and study skills workshops and writer's workshops are available for all students. Skills classes are offered in time management, test anxiety, stress management, and study strategies

LEARNING DISABILITY PROGRAM/SERVICES

Learning Disability Program/Services: Division of Disability Resources and Educational Services (DRES)
Director: Brad Hedrick
  E-Mail: bhedrick@uiuc.edu
  Telephone: 217-333-4600
  Fax: 217-333-0248
Contact Person: Kim Collins, PhD
  E-Mail: bhedrick@uiuc.edu
  Telephone: 217-333-4603
  Fax: 217-333-0248

LEARNING DISABILITY SERVICES

Requests for the following services/accommodations will be evaluated individually based on appropriate and current documentation.

Allowed in exams
  Calculator: Yes
  Dictionary: Yes
  Computer: Yes
  Spellchecker: Yes
Extended test time: Yes
Scribes: Yes
Proctors: Yes
Oral exams: Yes
Note-takers: Yes

Distraction-reduced environment: Yes
Tape recording in class: Yes
Books on tape from RFBD: Yes
Taping of books not from RFBD: Yes
Accommodations for students with ADHD: Yes
Reading machine: Yes
Other assistive technology: Yes
Priority registration: Yes

Added costs for services: No
LD specialists: Yes
Professional tutors: 175–225
Peer tutors: 15–35
Max. hours/wk. for services: Unlimited
How professors are notified of LD/ADHD: By student

GENERAL ADMISSIONS INFORMATION

Director of Admissions: Stacey Kostell
Telephone: 217-333-4626

ENTRANCE REQUIREMENTS

Academic units required: 4 English, 3 math, 2 science (2 science labs), 2 foreign language, 2 social studies, 2 academic electives. High school diploma is required, and GED is accepted. ACT without Writing component accepted. TOEFL required of all international applicants: minimum paper TOEFL 550, minimum computer TOEFL 213.

Application deadline: 1/2
Notification: 12/15
Average GPA: NR
ACT Composite middle 50% range: 25–30

SAT Math middle 50% range: 620–740
SAT Critical Reading middle 50% range: 540–670
SAT Writing middle 50% range: NR

Graduated top 10% of class: 55%
Graduated top 25% of class: 96%
Graduated top 50% of class: 99%

COLLEGE GRADUATION REQUIREMENTS

Course waivers allowed: No
Course substitutions allowed: Yes
In what course: Course substitutions for foreign language and math are available via a petition process through the student's college.

ADDITIONAL INFORMATION

Environment: The university has an urban campus 130 miles south of Chicago.

Student Body
  Undergrad enrollment: 30,721
  Women: 47%
  Men: 53%
  Percent out-of-state: 7%

Cost Information
  In-state tuition: $7,042
  Out-of-state tuition: $21,128
  Room & board: $7,716
Housing Information
  University housing: Yes
  Percent living on campus: 50%

Greek System
  Fraternity: Yes
  Sorority: Yes
Athletics: Division I

WESTERN ILLINOIS UNIVERSITY

One University Circle, 115 Sherman Hall, Macomb, IL 61455-1390
Phone: 309-298-3157 • Fax: 309-298-3111
E-mail: wiuadm@wiu.edu • Web: www.wiu.edu
Support: CS • Institution type: 4-year public

LEARNING DISABILITY PROGRAM AND SERVICES

Western Illinois University is committed to justice, equity, and diversity. Academically qualified students who have disabilities are an important part of our student body. Providing equal opportunities for students with disabilities is a campus-wide responsibility and commitment. Disability Support Services is responsible for coordinating support services for students who have disabilities. It is important to note that while services are available, there is no formal program for students with learning disabilities. WIU does not provide any remedial programs or offer any specialized curriculum. Students requesting accommodations must provide documentation verifying the specific learning disability. P.R.I.D.E. (Promoting the Rights of Individuals with Disabilities Everywhere) is an organization composed of students with and without disabilities. Members work together to remove attitudinal barriers within the university community. The group sponsors awareness-raising activities and serves as a resource for faculty, staff, and students.

LD/ADHD ADMISSIONS INFORMATION

College entrance tests required: Yes
Interview required: No
Essay recommended: No
Documentation required for LD: Current documentation (no more than 3 years old), presenting concerns, developmental, educational, and accommodation history, tests of IQ; information processing and academic achievement, interpretive summary of testing; and a definitive diagnostic statement.
Documentation required for ADHD: Current documentation (no more than 3 years old): a comprehensive report; information from self-report and third-party; information regarding medication and any effects the medication has on performance in an academic setting; and a definitive diagnostic statement.

Submitted to: Disability Support Services
Special Ed. HS course work accepted: N/A
Specific course requirements of all applicants: NR
Separate application required: Yes
# of LD applications submitted each year: NR
# of LD applications accepted yearly: NR
Total # of students receiving LD services: 100–120
Acceptance into program means acceptance into college: Students must be admitted and enrolled in the university first and then request services.

ADMISSIONS

Students with learning disabilities must meet the same admission criteria as all applicants, which includes 4 English, 3 social studies, 3 math, 3 science, and 2 electives. Applicants must also have an ACT 22/SAT 1010 and a 2.2 GPA or ACT 18/SAT 850 and rank in the top 40 percent of their class and have a 2.2 GPA. Students not meeting these standards may be considered for alternative admission. The application should be supported by a letter of recommendation from the counselor and a letter of appeal from the student. The Academic Services Program provides an opportunity for admission to a limited number of students yearly who do not meet the regular WIU admissions. Students considered for alternative admissions must have an ACT of 15 and a high school cumulative GPA of 2.2. Students admitted in the Academic Services Program are chosen on the basis of demonstrated academic potential for success. Several criteria are considered including GPA, grade patterns, references, and student letter expressing interest in the program.

ADDITIONAL INFORMATION

There are tutoring support services available to all students through laboratories for writing and math, staffed by the English and Mathematics Departments. Students can receive one-on-one help with study skills including time management, note-taking skills, and exam preparation. There is tutoring available, but no guarantee for tutoring in all subjects. Some tutors charge $4 –$7 per hour, and some tutorials offered through the Office of Academic Services are free. Academic Advisors in the Academic Services Program monitor student progress during each semester for students admitted in the program. These students are provided with tutorial support throughout freshman year, and enroll in appropriate courses and introductory courses in their majors. The goal of the program is to promote the development of skills necessary for students to achieve academic success at WIU.

LEARNING DISABILITY PROGRAM/SERVICES

Learning Disability Program/Services: Disability Support Services (DSS)
Director: Tara Miller
  E-Mail: T-Miller@wiu.edu
  Telephone: 309-298-2512
  Fax: 309-298-2361
Contact Person: Robin Hyman
  E-Mail: R-Hyman@wiu.edu
  Telephone: 309-298-2512
  Fax: 309-298-2361

LEARNING DISABILITY SERVICES

Requests for the following services/accommodations will be evaluated individually based on appropriate and current documentation.

Allowed in exams
  Calculator: Yes
  Dictionary: Yes
  Computer: Yes
  Spellchecker: Yes
Extended test time: Yes
Scribes: Yes
Proctors: Yes
Oral exams: Yes
Note-takers: Yes

Distraction-reduced environment: Yes
Tape recording in class: Yes
Books on tape from RFBD: No
Taping of books not from RFBD: No
Accommodations for students with ADHD: Yes
Reading machine: No
Other assistive technology: Yes
Priority registration: Yes

Added costs for services: No
LD specialists: Yes
Professional tutors: No
Peer tutors: No
Max. hours/wk. for services: N/A
How professors are notified of LD/ADHD: By student

GENERAL ADMISSIONS INFORMATION

Director of Admissions: Eric Campbell
Telephone: 309-298-1968

ENTRANCE REQUIREMENTS

Academic units recommended: 4 English, 3 math, 3 science, 3 social studies, 2 electives. 2 High school diploma is required, and GED is accepted. ACT with or without Writing component accepted. TOEFL required of all international applicants: minimum paper TOEFL 550, minimum computer TOEFL 213.

Application deadline: 5/15
Notification: Within 24–48 hours after receiving application.
Average GPA: NR
ACT Composite middle 50% range: 18–23

SAT Math middle 50% range: NR
SAT Critical Reading middle 50% range: NR
SAT Writing middle 50% range: NR

Graduated top 10% of class: 7%
Graduated top 25% of class: 23%
Graduated top 50% of class: 59%

COLLEGE GRADUATION REQUIREMENTS

Course substitutions allowed: Yes
In what course: Students may submit a request for course subsitutions to the Council on Admission, Graduation, and Academic Standards for review.

ADDITIONAL INFORMATION

Environment: The university is located in a rural area 75 miles from Peoria.

Student Body
  Undergrad enrollment: 11,327
  Women: 48%
  Men: 52%
  Percent out-of-state: 7%

Cost Information
  In-state tuition: $6,900
  Out-of-state tuition: $9,390
  Room & board: $6,145
Housing Information
  University housing: Yes
  Percent living on campus: 45%

Greek System
  Fraternity: Yes
  Sorority: Yes
Athletics: Division I

ANDERSON UNIVERSITY

1100 East Fifth Street, Anderson, IN 46012
Phone: 765-641-4080 • Fax: 765-641-4091
E-mail: info@anderson.edu • Web: www.anderson.edu
Support: CS • Institution type: 4-year private

LEARNING DISABILITY PROGRAM AND SERVICES

It is the philosophy of Anderson University that those students who are qualified and have a sincere motivation to complete a college education should be given every opportunity to work toward that goal. Students with specific learning disabilities may be integrated into any of the many existing services at the Kissinger Learning Center or more individual programming may be designed. Students receive extensive personal contact through the program. The director of the program schedules time with each student to evaluate personal learning style in order to assist in planning for the most appropriate learning environment. One of the most successful programs is individual or small group tutorial assistance. Social and emotional support is also provided. The college strives to provide the maximum amount of services necessary to assist students with learning disabilities in their academic endeavors, while being careful not to create an overdependency.

LD/ADHD ADMISSIONS INFORMATION

College entrance tests required: Yes
Interview required: Yes
Essay recommended: Yes
Documentation required for LD: WISC–R or WAIS–R (completed within the past 3 years); the student's most recent IEP is helpful.
Documentation required for ADHD: TOVA; Written diagnosis/testing
Submitted to: Kissinger Learning Center
Special Ed. HS course work accepted: N/A

Specific course requirements of all applicants: Yes
Separate application required: No
# of LD applications submitted each year: 15–25
# of LD applications accepted yearly: 20
Total # of students receiving LD services: 48
Acceptance into program means acceptance into college: It is a joint decision between admissions and the program.

ADMISSIONS

Students with specific learning disabilities who apply to Anderson do so through the regular admission channels. The university recommends that students have the following courses in their high school background: 4 years of English, 3 years of mathematics, 2 years of a foreign language, 3 years of science, and 3 years of social studies. Also considered in the evaluation of each application is the student's seriousness of purpose; personality and character; expressed willingness to live within the standards of the Anderson University community; and service to school, church, and community. Documentation of a specific learning disability must be included with the application. We encourage students to self-disclose because they may qualify for special consideration and be admitted through the LD program. Failure to disclose could result in nonacceptance based on standardized class scores, GPA, etc. Upon request for consideration for the program, prospective students are expected to make an on-campus visit, at which time a personal interview is arranged with the program director. All applicants are considered on an individual basis.

ADDITIONAL INFORMATION

Freshmen enrolled in the program are typically limited to 12–13 credit hours of course work during the first semester, including a 2-hour study skills class. As students become more independent and demonstrate the ability to deal with increased hours, an additional course load may be considered. There are currently 42 students with LD and 41 students with ADHD receiving accommodations or services. Depending on the specific needs of the student, all or a selected number of services may be provided including: assistance with advising, study skills instruction, time management, career counseling, alternative testing situations, and advocacy/liaison. The Kissinger Learning Center offers a variety of services, including a writing assistance program directed by a faculty member of the English Department. Individuals needing further assistance receive a diagnostic evaluation, which enables staff to work more efficiently with school personnel in creating programs to fit the needs of students with learning disabilities. Students are fully integrated into the university and are expected to meet the same academic standards as all other students.

LEARNING DISABILITY PROGRAM/SERVICES

Learning Disability Program/Services: Kissinger Learning Center
Director: Rinda Vogelgesang
  E-Mail: rsvogelgesang@anderson.edu
  Telephone: 765-641-4226
  Fax: 765-641-3851

LEARNING DISABILITY SERVICES

Requests for the following services/accommodations will be evaluated individually based on appropriate and current documentation.

Allowed in exams
  Calculator: NR
  Dictionary: Yes
  Computer: Yes
  Spellchecker: Yes
Extended test time: Yes
Scribes: Yes
Proctors: Yes
Oral exams: Yes
Note-takers: Yes

Distraction-reduced environment: Yes
Tape recording in class: Yes
Books on tape from RFBD: Yes
Taping of books not from RFBD: No
Accommodations for students with ADHD: Yes
Reading machine: Yes
Other assistive technology: Yes
Priority registration: No

Added costs for services: No
LD specialists: Yes
Professional tutors: 1
Peer tutors: 25
Max. hours/wk. for services: Unlimited
How professors are notified of LD/ADHD: By both student and director

GENERAL ADMISSIONS INFORMATION

Director of Admissions: Jim King
Telephone: 765-641-4084

ENTRANCE REQUIREMENTS

Academic units required: 4 English, 3 math, 3 science (3 science labs), 2 foreign language, 1 social studies, 1 history.
Academic units recommended: 4 English, 4 math, 4 science (4 science labs), 3 foreign language, 3 social studies, 2 history, 5 academic electives. High school diploma is required, and GED is not accepted. ACT with Writing component required. TOEFL required of all international applicants: minimum paper TOEFL 515, minimum computer TOEFL 187.

Application deadline: 7/1
Notification: Rolling
Average GPA: 3.33
ACT Composite middle 50% range: 20–26

SAT Math middle 50% range: 460–580
SAT Critical Reading middle 50% range: 460–580
SAT Writing middle 50% range: NR

Graduated top 10% of class: 22%
Graduated top 25% of class: 46%
Graduated top 50% of class: 78%

COLLEGE GRADUATION REQUIREMENTS

Course waivers allowed: No
Course substitutions allowed: No

ADDITIONAL INFORMATION

Environment: Anderson University is located on 100 acres 40 miles northeast of Indianapolis.

Student Body
  Undergrad enrollment: 2,194
  Women: 58%
  Men: 42%
  Percent out-of-state: 34%

Cost Information
  Tuition: $19,990
  Room & board: $6,460
Housing Information
  University housing: Yes
  Percent living on campus: 63%

Greek System
  Fraternity: No
  Sorority: No
Athletics: Division III

INDIANA UNIVERSITY

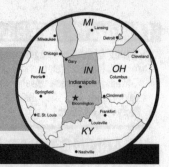

300 North Jordan Avenue, Bloomington, IN 47405-1106
Phone: 812-855-0661 • Fax: 812-855-5102
E-mail: iuadmit@indiana.edu • Web: www.iub.edu
Support: CS • Institution type: 4-year public

LEARNING DISABILITY PROGRAM AND SERVICES

The goal of the Office of Disabled Student Services is to provide services that enable students with disabilities to participate in, and benefit from all university programs and activities. There is no specific program for students with LD. However there is a Learning Disabilities Coordinator who provides supportive services necessary to help students pursue their academic objectives. The Briscoe Academic Support Center offers free assistance to all IU students, night and day. During the day, the center is used for study groups, meetings, and advising, and in the evenings it provides free tutoring, advising, and academic support to assist with course assignments and studying. No appointments are necessary. Students with LD must provide current and appropriate psychoeducational evaluations that address: aptitude; achievement; information processing; clear and specific evidence and identification of an LD; test scores/data must be included; evaluations must be done by a qualified professional; and current IEPs are helpful. Students with ADHD must provide documentation that includes: a clear statement of ADHD with a current diagnosis, including a description of supporting symptoms; current testing, preferably within 3 years; a summary of assessment procedures and evaluations used; a summary supporting diagnosis; medical history; suggestions of reasonable accommodations; and current IEP is helpful.

LD/ADHD ADMISSIONS INFORMATION

College entrance tests required: Yes
Interview required: No
Essay recommended: No
Documentation required for LD: A comprehensive psychoeducational evaluation completed after age 16 with adult normed tests that that meets school's documentation guidelines (online at www.indiana.edu/~iubdss/)
Documentation required for ADHD: A current, comprehensive evaluation that meets school's documentation guidelines for attention deficit hyperactivity disorder (online at www.indiana.edu/~iubdss/)
Submitted to: Office of Disabled Student Services
Special Ed. HS course work accepted: No

Specific course requirements of all applicants: Yes
Separate application required: Yes
# of LD applications submitted each year: NR
# of LD applications accepted yearly: NR
Total # of students receiving LD services: NR
Acceptance into program means acceptance into college: Students must be admitted and enrolled in the university first and then request services.

ADMISSIONS

There is no special admission process for students with learning disabilities. Each applicant is reviewed individually. IU is concerned with the strength of the college-prep program, including senior year, grade trends, and the student's class rank. Students falling below the minimum standards may receive serious consideration for admission if their grades have been steadily improving in a challenging college-prep program. Conversely, declining grades and/or a program of less demanding courses are often reasons to deny admission. The minimum admission standards include: 4 years of English, 3 years of math, 1 year of science, 2 years of social science, plus additional courses in math, science, social science and/or foreign language to be competitive for admission. Indiana residents must complete Core 40 which includes a minimum of 28 semesters of college-prep courses. Nonresidents must complete a minimum of 32 semester college-prep classes. All students should be enrolled in at least 3–4 college-prep courses each semester. Students usually rank in the top one-third out-of-state and top half in-state. Students must take either the ACT with Writing or the SAT Reasoning.

ADDITIONAL INFORMATION

The LD specialist assists students with LD on an individual basis. Accommodations can be made to provide: test modifications, referrals to tutors, peer note-takers, books on tape, adaptive technology, and priority registration for students needing books on tape. Students must provide appropriate documentation. Students need to request a letter from DSS to give to their professors. Two years of a foreign language are required for a degree from the College of Arts and Sciences. Students with a disability that impacts their ability to learn a foreign language must attempt taking one and the dean will monitor the student's sincere effort to succeed. If the student is unsuccessful, there will be a discussion of alternatives. There are special math courses and one is a remedial course for credit. Currently, there are approximately 400 students with LD/ADHD receiving services.

LEARNING DISABILITY PROGRAM/SERVICES

Learning Disability Program/Services: Disability Services for Students (DSS)
Director: Martha P. Jacques
  E-Mail: iubdss@indiana.edu
  Telephone: 812-855-7578
  Fax: 812-855-7650
Contact Person: Jody K. Ferguson
  E-Mail: iubdss@indiana.edu
  Telephone: 812-855-3508
  Fax: 812-855-7650

LEARNING DISABILITY SERVICES

Requests for the following services/accommodations will be evaluated individually based on appropriate and current documentation.

Allowed in exams
  Calculator: Yes
  Dictionary: Yes
  Computer: Yes
  Spellchecker: Yes
Extended test time: Yes
Scribes: Yes
Proctors: Yes
Oral exams: Yes
Note-takers: Yes

Distraction-reduced environment: Yes
Tape recording in class: Yes
Books on tape from RFBD: Yes
Taping of books not from RFBD: Yes
Accommodations for students with
  ADHD: Yes
Reading machine: Yes
Other assistive technology: Yes
Priority registration: Yes

Added costs for services: No
LD specialists: Yes
Professional tutors: No
Peer tutors: Yes
Max. hours/wk. for services: Varies
How professors are notified of
  LD/ADHD: By student

GENERAL ADMISSIONS INFORMATION

Director of Admissions: Mary Ellen Anderson
Telephone: 812-855-0661

ENTRANCE REQUIREMENTS

Academic units required: 4 English, 3 math, 1 science (1 science lab), 2 social studies, 4 academic electives.
Academic units recommended: 4 math, 3 science, 3 foreign language, 3 social studies. High school diploma is required, and GED is accepted. ACT with Writing component required.

Application deadline: NR
Notification: NR
Average GPA: 3.50
ACT Composite middle 50% range:
  22–27

SAT Math middle 50% range:
  510–630
SAT Critical Reading middle 50%
  range: 490–610
SAT Writing middle 50% range: NR

Graduated top 10% of class: 27%
Graduated top 25% of class: 61%
Graduated top 50% of class: 95%

COLLEGE GRADUATION REQUIREMENTS

Course waivers allowed: No
Course substitutions allowed: Yes
In what course: There are processes to request accommodations and substitutions in regard to math and foreign language for eligible students with LD. Students are required to attempt the course.

ADDITIONAL INFORMATION

Environment: The university is located in a small town 45 minutes from Indianapolis.

Student Body
  Undergrad enrollment: 29,258
  Women: 52%
  Men: 48%
  Percent out-of-state: 30%

Cost Information
  In-state tuition: $7,110
  Out-of-state tuition: $19,500
  Room & board: $6,352
Housing Information
  University housing: Yes
  Percent living on campus: 36%

Greek System
  Fraternity: Yes
  Sorority: Yes
Athletics: Division I

INDIANA WESLEYAN UNIVERSITY

4201 South Washington Street, Marion, IN 46953-4974
Phone: 765-677-2138 • Fax: 765-677-2333
E-mail: admissions@indwes.edu • Web: www.indwes.edu
Support: S • Institution type: 4-year private

LEARNING DISABILITY PROGRAM AND SERVICES

The services offered at IWU are designed to assist students who have documented Learning Disabilities through advocacy and provision of appropriate accommodations. Student Support Services (SSS) provides tutoring, counseling, note-takers, and test accommodations. The Learning Center is available to all students who seek assistance with raising the quality of their academic work. Developmental educational courses are offered in reading improvement, fundamentals of communication, and skills for academic success.

LD/ADHD ADMISSIONS INFORMATION

College entrance tests required: Yes
Interview required: No
Essay recommended: No
Documentation required for LD: Standardized intelligence or psychometric testing or other documentation related to disability. Documentation should demonstrate a diagnosis of an impairment that significantly impacts a major life area.
Documentation required for ADHD: Same as the LD requirement
Submitted to: Student Support Services
Special Ed. HS course work accepted: Yes

Specific course requirements of all applicants: NR
Separate application required: No
# of LD applications submitted each year: NR
# of LD applications accepted yearly: NR
Total # of students receiving LD services: 40
Acceptance into program means acceptance into college: Students are admitted to the university and to the program simultaneously.

ADMISSIONS

The Office of Admissions seeks students with at least a 2.6 GPA and an ACT of 18 or SAT Reasoning Test of 880. Students not meeting these requirements may be accepted on a conditional status and be required to enroll in a student success program designed to enhance their academic skills. Students with learning disabilities may self-disclose their LD or ADHD through a personal statement attached to the application for admission. There is a separate application for requesting services/accommodations for disabilities that is submitted after a student has been accepted and enrolled.

ADDITIONAL INFORMATION

All admitted students are given the Compass English Proficiency Test. If they score below 10.7, they are required to take developmental reading, writing, and study skills classes. An SAT verbal score below 350 or ACT English below 14 will also be indicators that the student should take developmental reading and fundamentals of communication classes. With appropriate documentation students with LD/ADHD may be eligible for some of the following services or accommodations: the use of a calculator, dictionary, computer, or spellchecker in exams; extended time on tests; scribes; proctors; oral exams; note-takers; distraction-free environment; tape recorder in class; books on tape; assistive technology; priority registration; and workshops for all students in time management, test-taking skills, reading, and stress management. The Center for Student Support Services offers academic and personal counseling services for students at the university. Course-specific small group tutoring is available in which groups of up to five students are placed with student tutors for weekly tutoring sessions that run the length of the semester. Additionally there are monthly academic 'check-ups' for students under probationary, conditional, or provisional status. Other services available through the center include study skills assessment and help, test anxiety strategies, personal counseling, short-term assessment and counseling for students with mental health issues, crisis intervention, referral facilitation for medication management/long-term therapy, and tips for recognizing and addressing typical student mental health concerns.

LEARNING DISABILITY PROGRAM/SERVICES

Learning Disability Program/Services: Student Support Services
Director: Nathan L. Herring M.A.
  E-Mail: nathan.herring@indwes.edu
  Telephone: 765-677-2257
  Fax: 765-677-2140

LEARNING DISABILITY SERVICES

Requests for the following services/accommodations will be evaluated individually based on appropriate and current documentation.

Allowed in exams	**Distraction-reduced environment:** Yes	**Added costs for services:** No
Calculator: Yes	**Tape recording in class:** Yes	**LD specialists:** No
Dictionary: Yes	**Books on tape from RFBD:** Yes	**Professional tutors:** No
Computer: Yes	**Taping of books not from RFBD:** Yes	**Peer tutors:** 40–50
Spellchecker: Yes	**Accommodations for students with**	**Max. hours/wk. for services:** NR
Extended test time: Yes	**ADHD:** Yes	**How professors are notified of**
Scribes: Yes	**Reading machine:** Yes	**LD/ADHD:** By student
Proctors: Yes	**Other assistive technology:** Yes	
Oral exams: Yes	**Priority registration:** Yes	
Note-takers: Yes		

GENERAL ADMISSIONS INFORMATION

Director of Admissions: Danny Solms
Telephone: 765-677-2138

ENTRANCE REQUIREMENTS

Academic units recommended: 4 English, 3 math, 3 science, 2 foreign language, 3 social studies, 5 academic electives, 1 health/physical education. High school diploma is required, and GED is accepted. ACT without Writing component accepted. TOEFL required of all international applicants: minimum paper TOEFL 550, minimum computer TOEFL 213.

Application deadline: 8/1	**SAT Math middle 50% range:**	**Graduated top 10% of class:** 24%
Notification: Rolling	490–610	**Graduated top 25% of class:** 59%
Average GPA: 3.46	**SAT Critical Reading middle 50%**	**Graduated top 50% of class:** 86%
ACT Composite middle 50% range:	**range:** 490–590	
21–26	**SAT Writing middle 50% range:** NR	

COLLEGE GRADUATION REQUIREMENTS

Course waivers allowed: Yes
In what course: Dependent on course of study and specific disability. Assessed on an individual basis.
Course substitutions allowed: Yes
In what course: Dependent on course of study and specific disability. Assessed on an individual basis.

ADDITIONAL INFORMATION

Environment: The university is located on a 50-acre campus in a rural city 65 miles from Indianapolis and 50 miles south of Fort Wayne.

Student Body	**Cost Information**	**Greek System**
Undergrad enrollment: 2,785	**Tuition:** $18,284	**Fraternity:** No
Women: 62%	**Room & board:** $6,368	**Sorority:** No
Men: 38%	**Housing Information**	**Athletics:** NAIA
Percent out-of-state: 46%	**University housing:** Yes	
	Percent living on campus: 80%	

MANCHESTER COLLEGE

604 East College Avenue, North Manchester, IN 46962
Phone: 260-982-5055 • Fax: 260-982-5239
E-mail: admitinfo@manchester.edu • Web: www.manchester.edu
Support: CS • Institution type: 4-year private

LEARNING DISABILITY PROGRAM AND SERVICES

Manchester College does not have a specific program for students with learning disabilities. The college is, however, very sensitive to all students. The key word at Manchester College is "success," which means graduating in 4 years. The college wants all students to be able to complete their degree in 4 years. The college does provide support services to students identified as disabled to allow them to be successful. The goal is to assist students in their individual needs.

LD/ADHD ADMISSIONS INFORMATION

College entrance tests required: Yes
Interview required: Yes
Essay recommended: No
Documentation required for LD: Psychoeducational evaluation
Documentation required for ADHD: Yes
Submitted to: Learning Support Services
Special Ed. HS course work accepted: Yes

Specific course requirements of all applicants: Yes
Separate application required: No
# of LD applications submitted each year: NR
# of LD applications accepted yearly: NR
Total # of students receiving LD services: 20–30
Acceptance into program means acceptance into college: Students must be admitted and enrolled in the university first and then request services.

ADMISSIONS

Students with learning disabilities submit the regular application form, and are required to meet the same admission criteria as all other applicants. Course requirements include 4 years of English, 2 years of math (3 years recommended), 2 years of science (3 years recommended), 2 years of science labs (3 years of science labs recommended), 2 years of a foreign language required, 2 years of social studies, 1 year of history (2 years recommended), and 1 year of an elective (2 years recommended). Average ACT is 22 or SAT Reasoning 990. Students are admitted to the college and use the support services as they choose. If special consideration for admission is requested, it is done individually, based on potential for graduation from the college. Manchester considers a wide range of information in making individual admission decisions. Students are encouraged to provide information beyond what is required on the application form if they believe it will strengthen their application or help the college to understand the students' performance or potential. Students who self-disclose the existence of a learning disability and are denied can ask to appeal the decision and have their application reviewed in a "different" way. The key question that will be asked is if the student can graduate in 4 years or, at the most, 5 years.

ADDITIONAL INFORMATION

College Study Skills, for one credit, is offered. A support group meets biweekly. No developmental or remedial courses are offered. A Learning Center provides tutoring for all students at the college. A course is offered presenting college level study skills with opportunities for students to apply these skills in their current course texts. Specific topics include time management, note-taking, vocabulary, text study techniques, test-taking, and memory strategies. Other topics include: college expectations, learning styles and assessments, self-management, and educational and career planning. Students in the ADAPT program are each assigned to one of these two academic advisors. Meeting often with their advisees, advisors discuss the transition from high school to college and other issues related to college success at Manchester.

LEARNING DISABILITY PROGRAM/SERVICES

Learning Disability Program/Services: Learning Support Services
Director: Denise L.S. Howe, EdS
  E-Mail: dshowe@manchester.edu
  Telephone: 260-982-5076
  Fax: 260-982-5043

LEARNING DISABILITY SERVICES

Requests for the following services/accommodations will be evaluated individually based on appropriate and current documentation.

Allowed in exams
  Calculator: No
  Dictionary: No
  Computer: Yes
  Spellchecker: Yes
Extended test time: Yes
Scribes: Yes
Proctors: Yes
Oral exams: Yes
Note-takers: Yes

Distraction-reduced environment: Yes
Tape recording in class: Yes
Books on tape from RFBD: No
Taping of books not from RFBD: No
Accommodations for students with ADHD: Yes
Reading machine: No
Other assistive technology: No
Priority registration: No

Added costs for services: No
LD specialists: Yes
Professional tutors: No
Peer tutors: Yes
Max. hours/wk. for services: Unlimited
How professors are notified of LD/ADHD: By both student and director

GENERAL ADMISSIONS INFORMATION

Director of Admissions: Jolane Rohr
Telephone: 260-982-5055

ENTRANCE REQUIREMENTS

Academic units required: 4 English, 2 math, 2 science (2 science labs), 2 foreign language, 2 social studies, 1 history, 1 academic elective. **Academic units recommended:** 4 English, 3 math, 3 science (3 science labs), 2 foreign language, 2 social studies, 2 history, 2 academic electives. High school diploma is required, and GED is accepted. ACT with or without Writing component accepted. TOEFL required of all international applicants: minimum paper TOEFL 550, minimum computer TOEFL 213.

Application deadline: NR
Notification: Rolling
Average GPA: NR
ACT Composite middle 50% range: 18–24

SAT Math middle 50% range: 470–580
SAT Critical Reading middle 50% range: 460–580
SAT Writing middle 50% range: NR

Graduated top 10% of class: NR
Graduated top 25% of class: NR
Graduated top 50% of class: NR

COLLEGE GRADUATION REQUIREMENTS

Course waivers allowed: No
Course substitutions allowed: No

ADDITIONAL INFORMATION

Environment: The college is located in North Manchester, 35 miles west of Fort Wayne.

Student Body
  Undergrad enrollment: 1,058
  Women: 53%
  Men: 47%
  Percent out-of-state: 10%

Cost Information
  Tuition: $19,800
  Room & board: $7,260
Housing Information
  University housing: Yes
  Percent living on campus: 74%

Greek System
  Fraternity: No
  Sorority: No
Athletics: Division III

UNIVERSITY OF INDIANAPOLIS

1400 East Hanna Avenue, Indianapolis, IN 46227-3697
Phone: 317-788-3216 • Fax: 317-788-3300
E-mail: admissions@uindy.edu • Web: www.uindy.edu
Support: SP • Institution type: 4-year private

LEARNING DISABILITY PROGRAM AND SERVICES

The University of Indianapolis offers a full support system for students with learning disabilities called BUILD (Baccalaureate for University of Indianapolis Learning Disabled). The goal of this program is to help students with learning disabilities reach their academic potential. Helen Keller expressed this goal best, "Although the world is full of suffering, it is also full of the overcoming of it." All students with LD at the University have reasonable modifications available to them at no extra charge. The BUILD program offers accommodations significantly more in depth than just minimal requirements. Services are extensive, and the staff is very supportive and knowledgeable about learning disabilities.

LD/ADHD ADMISSIONS INFORMATION

College entrance tests required: Yes
Interview required: Yes
Essay recommended: No
Documentation required for LD: Current IQ tests and reading and math achievement tests that have been completed within the past 3 years
Documentation required for ADHD: Appropriate testing results and recommendations by a qualified professional
Submitted to: BUILD
Special Ed. HS course work accepted: No

Specific course requirements of all applicants: Yes
Separate application required: Yes
# of LD applications submitted each year: 50
# of LD applications accepted yearly: 25
Total # of students receiving LD services: 35
Acceptance into program means acceptance into college: Students must be admitted by the university and then admitted to BUILD. If not accepted by admissions, a committee confers.

ADMISSIONS

Admission to BUILD program occurs after a student has been accepted as a regular student, and students with LD must meet the university admissions requirements. Recommended courses for general admission include: 4 years of English, 3 years of math, 3 years of science, 2 years of science lab, 2 years of a foreign language, and 3 years of social studies. However, flexibility is allowed to consider individual strengths. Students are encouraged to self-disclose their learning disability. It is important for the university to know the circumstances of a student's learning, but self-disclosing also allows the student to learn how the university views disabilities. To seek admission to the university and to BUILD, students must submit the following: regular application for admission; BUILD application; high school transcript; current documentation regarding IQ scores, reading and math proficiency levels, primary learning style, and major learning difficulty; recommendations from a mainstream teacher or guidance counselor of students with LD discussing the applicant's main areas of strength and weakness; and an optional letter from an employer. After the directors of BUILD review the information, interviews will be arranged for those applicants being considered for final selection. Acceptance into the BUILD Program is determined by the program director.

ADDITIONAL INFORMATION

The director assigns tutors to each student in BUILD. All students must have at least 2 hours per week of individualized tutoring. Books on CD, test modifications, and group study are also provided. Course substitution is a possibility. BUILD offers three special courses to meet university requirements for English and math proficiency, all other classes are regular classes. Students are limited to 12 hours each semester until they can demonstrate academic success indicating they can handle the demands of a heavier course load. Other services include: a specialized study skills course; specialized note-taking paper; test-taking arrangements; private study area; advice with course selection and career planning; possible course substitution; diagnostic testing referrals; and other aids such as books on tape, compressed-time tape recorders, and computers.

LEARNING DISABILITY PROGRAM/SERVICES

Learning Disability Program/Services: Baccalaureate for University of Indianapolis Learning Disabled (BUILD)
Director: Candace Joles
  E-Mail: cjoles@uindy.edu
  Telephone: 317-788-3536
  Fax: 317-788-3585
Contact Person: Kim Cantaou
  E-Mail: kcantaou@uindy.edu
  Telephone: 317-788-3536
  Fax: 317-788-3585

LEARNING DISABILITY SERVICES

Requests for the following services/accommodations will be evaluated individually based on appropriate and current documentation.

Allowed in exams
  Calculator: Yes
  Dictionary: Yes
  Computer: Yes
  Spellchecker: Yes
Extended test time: Yes
Scribes: Yes
Proctors: Yes
Oral exams: Yes
Note-takers: No

Distraction-reduced environment: Yes
Tape recording in class: Yes
Books on tape from RFBD: Yes
Taping of books not from RFBD: No
Accommodations for students with ADHD: Yes
Reading machine: Yes
Other assistive technology: Yes
Priority registration: Yes

Added costs for services: Yes
LD specialists: Yes
Professional tutors: 17
Peer tutors: No
Max. hours/wk. for services: Unlimited
How professors are notified of LD/ADHD: By both student and director

GENERAL ADMISSIONS INFORMATION

Director of Admissions: Ron Wilks
Telephone: 317-788-3517

ENTRANCE REQUIREMENTS

Academic units required: 4 English, 3 math, 2 science (1 science lab), 1 social studies, 1 history, 3 academic electives. **Academic units recommended:** 4 English, 4 math, 3 science (2 science labs), 2 foreign language, 1 social studies, 1 history, 3 academic electives. High school diploma is required, and GED is accepted. ACT with or without Writing component accepted. TOEFL required of all international applicants: minimum paper TOEFL 500, minimum computer TOEFL 173.

Application deadline: NR
Notification: Rolling
Average GPA: 3.12
ACT Composite middle 50% range: 19–24

SAT Math middle 50% range: 460–570
SAT Critical Reading middle 50% range: 450–550
SAT Writing middle 50% range: NR

Graduated top 10% of class: 23%
Graduated top 25% of class: 50%
Graduated top 50% of class: 80%

COLLEGE GRADUATION REQUIREMENTS

Course waivers allowed: No
Course substitutions allowed: Yes
In what course: Modern language requirements

ADDITIONAL INFORMATION

Environment: The 60-acre campus in a suburban neighborhood is located 10 miles south of downtown Indianapolis.

Student Body
  Undergrad enrollment: 3,800
  Women: 68%
  Men: 32%
  Percent out-of-state: 25%

Cost Information
  Tuition: $18,700
  Room & board: $7,380
Housing Information
  University housing: Yes
  Percent living on campus: 36%

Greek System
  Fraternity: No
  Sorority: No
Athletics: Division II

UNIVERSITY OF NOTRE DAME

220 Main Building, Notre Dame, IN 46556
Phone: 574-631-7505 • Fax: 574-631-8865
E-mail: admissions@nd.edu • Web: www.nd.edu
Support: S • Institution type: 4-year private

LEARNING DISABILITY PROGRAM AND SERVICES

It is the mission of the Office for Students with Disabilities (OSD) to ensure that Notre Dame students with disabilities have access to the programs and facilities of the university. OSD is committed to forming partnerships with students to share the responsibility of meeting individual needs. At the University of Notre Dame, students with disabilities may use a variety of services intended to reduce the effects that a disability may have on their educational experience. Services do not lower course standards or alter essential degree requirements but instead give students an equal opportunity to demonstrate their academic abilities. Students can initiate a request for services by registering with the Office for Students with Disabilities and providing information that documents the disability. Individual assistance is provided in selecting the services that will provide access to the academic programs and facilities of the university.

LD/ADHD ADMISSIONS INFORMATION

College entrance tests required: Yes
Interview required: No
Essay recommended: No
Documentation required for LD: The university follows the guidelines developed by the Associate for Higher Education and Disability.
Documentation required for ADHD: Same as above
Submitted to: Office for Students with Disabilities
Special Ed. HS course work accepted: N/A

Specific course requirements of all applicants: Yes
Separate application required: No
# of LD applications submitted each year: NR
# of LD applications accepted yearly: NR
Total # of students receiving LD services: 0–75
Acceptance into program means acceptance into college: Students must be admitted and enrolled in the university first and then request services.

ADMISSIONS

The university does not have a special admission process for students with learning disabilities. All students submit the same application and are expected to meet the same admission criteria. Admission to the university is highly competitive. The university seeks to enroll an exceptionally distinguished student body from among its broadly diverse and richly talented applicant pool. The Admissions Office prides itself on reviewing each application individually and with care. Students are expected to have 4 years of English, 4 years of math, 4 years of science, 2 years of a foreign language, 2 years of social studies, and 3 years of additional courses from these mentioned areas.

ADDITIONAL INFORMATION

Services for students with learning disabilities or attention deficit hyperactivity disorder include taped textbooks, note-takers, assistance with developing time management skills and learning strategies, and screening and referral for diagnostic testing. All students with disabilities are given assistance in developing a positive working relationship with faculty, facilitation of classroom accommodations, liaison with Vocational Rehabilitation and other state and local agencies, informal academic, personal and vocational counseling, and referral to other university resources. If it is difficult for a student to learn a foreign language because of a disability, the student may request to take another course, such as sign language, in order to fulfill the foreign language requirement. The impact of the disability on learning a foreign language must be well documented and the substitution cannot significantly alter the student's academic program. Currently 20 students with LD and 29 students with ADHD are receiving services and accommodations. Undergraduates and graduates with appropriate documentation are eligible to request services and accommodations.

LEARNING DISABILITY PROGRAM/SERVICES

Learning Disability Program/Services: Office for Students with Disabilities
Director: Scott Howland
  E-Mail: showland@nd.edu
  Telephone: 574-631-7157
  Fax: 574-631-2133

LEARNING DISABILITY SERVICES

Requests for the following services/accommodations will be evaluated individually based on appropriate and current documentation.

Allowed in exams
  Calculator: Yes
  Dictionary: Yes
  Computer: Yes
  Spellchecker: Yes
Extended test time: Yes
Scribes: Yes
Proctors: Yes
Oral exams: Yes
Note-takers: Yes

Distraction-reduced environment: Yes
Tape recording in class: Yes
Books on tape from RFBD: Yes
Taping of books not from RFBD: Yes
**Accommodations for students with
  ADHD:** Yes
Reading machine: Yes
Other assistive technology: Yes
Priority registration: Yes

Added costs for services: No
LD specialists: No
Professional tutors: NR
Peer tutors: No
Max. hours/wk. for services:
  Unlimited
**How professors are notified of
  LD/ADHD:** By student

GENERAL ADMISSIONS INFORMATION

Director of Admissions: Dan Saracino
Telephone: 574-631-7505

ENTRANCE REQUIREMENTS
Academic units required: 4 English, 4 math, 4 science, 2 foreign language, 2 social studies, 3 academic electives.
Academic units recommended: 4 English, 4 math, 4 science, 4 foreign language, 4 social studies. High school diploma is required, and GED is not accepted. ACT with or without Writing component accepted. TOEFL required of all international applicants: minimum paper TOEFL 600, minimum computer TOEFL 250.

Application deadline: 12/31
Notification: 4/10
Average GPA: NR
ACT Composite middle 50% range:
  31–33

SAT Math middle 50% range:
  630–740
**SAT Critical Reading middle 50%
  range:** 600–720
SAT Writing middle 50% range:
  580–710

Graduated top 10% of class: 85%
Graduated top 25% of class: 97%
Graduated top 50% of class: 100%

COLLEGE GRADUATION REQUIREMENTS

Course waivers allowed: No
Course substitutions allowed: Yes
In what course: Students with supportive documentation can receive a substitution course for the foreign language requirement.

ADDITIONAL INFORMATION

Environment: The university is located in a suburban area about 1.5 hours from Chicago.

Student Body
  Undergrad enrollment: 8,346
  Women: 47%
  Men: 53%
  Percent out-of-state: 92%

Cost Information
  Tuition: $32,900
  Room & board: $8,730
Housing Information
  University housing: Yes
  Percent living on campus: 76%

Greek System
  Fraternity: No
  Sorority: No
Athletics: Division I

University of Notre Dame

UNIVERSITY OF SAINT FRANCIS (IN)

2701 Spring Street, Fort Wayne, IN 46808
Phone: 260-434-3279 • Fax: 260-434-7590
E-mail: admis@sf.edu • Web: www.sf.edu
Support: CS • Institution type: 4-year private

LEARNING DISABILITY PROGRAM AND SERVICES

The Student Learning Center assists and acts as an advocte for students with disabilities. Students are encouraged to be self-advocates, as well as, develop skills to become independent learners. The Learning Center strives to provide students with disabilities with special services and acadmic support needed to achieve success in the college environment. Students with disabilities are encouraged to meet with the Learning Center Director, prior to the start of the school year, to discuss the types of accommodations necessary to provide the best opportunity for academic success.

LD/ADHD ADMISSIONS INFORMATION

College entrance tests required: NR
Interview required: No
Essay recommended: No
Documentation required for LD: The most recent psychological evaluation and the student's last individual education plan (within 3 years).
Documentation required for ADHD: Yes
Submitted to: Both Admissions Office and Student Learning Center

Special Ed. HS course work accepted: No
Specific course requirements of all applicants: NR
Separate application required: No
# of LD applications submitted each year: NR
# of LD applications accepted yearly: NR
Total # of students receiving LD services: NR
Acceptance into program means acceptance into college: Students must be admitted and enrolled in the university first and then request services.

ADMISSIONS

There is no special admission process for students with learning disabilities. Entrance is based on an overall evaluation of the student's high school transcript, recommendations, and tests. The minimum ACT is 19 or SAT is 800. Automatic admission is given to students with a 920 SAT. College-prep course requirements include 4 years of English, 3 years of math, 2 years of science labs, 2 years of social studies, and 2 years of a foreign language. The minimum GPA is 2.2. Some students may be asked to come to campus for an interview and/or to write a personal statement or essay. Students may be admitted "on warning," on a 13-hour limit or a part-time basis.

ADDITIONAL INFORMATION

Incoming freshmen may be asked to take placement exams in reading, writing, and math to determine appropriate beginning level courses. Curriculum consideration is given to applicants whose test scores show that a limited number of credit hours would be helpful. Skills classes are offered in reading, writing, and math. The writing consultant helps students with all phases of the research paper or essay writing process including forming and refining ideas, planning a rough draft, revising, editing, and proofreading. Specialized services provided by the Student Learning Center are: accommodations on admission placement exams, alternative exam site, extended exam time, reading of exams or reading directions, carbonless paper for note-taking, assistance in ordering taped texts, altered exam procedures, large print, LD specialist for individuial assistance, peer tutors, academic progress monitoring with two reports per semester, letter to professors regarding accommodations, assistance with study and organizational skills, and assistance in facilitating a positive relationship with faculty and staff. Help is also available in the areas of time management, efficient study reading, memory techniques, concentration and motivation, test-taking strategies, and note-taking techniques.

LEARNING DISABILITY PROGRAM/SERVICES

Learning Disability Program/Services: Student Learning Center
Director: Michelle Kruyer
  E-Mail: mkruyer@sf.edu
  Telephone: 219-434-7677
  Fax: 219-434-3183

LEARNING DISABILITY SERVICES

Requests for the following services/accommodations will be evaluated individually based on appropriate and current documentation.

Allowed in exams
  Calculator: Yes
  Dictionary: Yes
  Computer: Yes
  Spellchecker: Yes
Extended test time: Yes
Scribes: Yes
Proctors: Yes
Oral exams: Yes
Note-takers: Yes

Distraction-reduced environment: Yes
Tape recording in class: Yes
Books on tape from RFBD: Yes
Taping of books not from RFBD: No
Accommodations for students with ADHD: Yes
Reading machine: Yes
Other assistive technology: Yes
Priority registration: No

Added costs for services: No
LD specialists: Yes
Professional tutors: Yes
Peer tutors: Yes
Max. hours/wk. for services: Unlimited
How professors are notified of LD/ADHD: By both student and director

GENERAL ADMISSIONS INFORMATION

Director of Admissions: Matthew P. Nettleton
Telephone: 260-434-3279

ENTRANCE REQUIREMENTS

Academic units recommended: 4 English, 3 math, 2 science (2 science labs), 2 foreign language, 2 social studies. High school diploma is required, and GED is accepted. TOEFL required of all international applicants: minimum paper TOEFL 500.

Application deadline: NR
Notification: Rolling
Average GPA: 2.90
ACT Composite middle 50% range: 17–22

SAT Math middle 50% range: 420–540
SAT Critical Reading middle 50% range: 430–530
SAT Writing middle 50% range: NR

Graduated top 10% of class: 12%
Graduated top 25% of class: 32%
Graduated top 50% of class: 73%

COLLEGE GRADUATION REQUIREMENTS

Course waivers allowed: Yes
Course substitutions allowed: Yes

ADDITIONAL INFORMATION

Environment: The 70-acre campus is located west of Fort Wayne.

Student Body
  Undergrad enrollment: 1,413
  Women: 66%
  Men: 34%
  Percent out-of-state: 8%

Cost Information
  Tuition: $15,500
  Room & board: $5,500
Housing Information
  University housing: Yes
  Percent living on campus: 16%

Greek System
  Fraternity: No
  Sorority: No
  Athletics: NAIA

University of Saint Francis (IN)

UNIVERSITY OF SOUTHERN INDIANA

8600 University Boulevard, Evansville, IN 47712
Phone: 812-464-1765 • Fax: 812-465-7154
E-mail: enroll@usi.edu • Web: www.usi.edu
Support: S • Institution type: 4-year public

LEARNING DISABILITY PROGRAM AND SERVICES

Staff provides resources to assist students with disabilities so they can participate in educational programming. This mission is accomplished by offering student support and advocacy, being available for student and faculty consultation, coordinating accommodation services, and serving as a centralizing service for disability information for the university. While most of the services offered through the Counseling Center are available to all currently-enrolled USI students and do not require any special registration, disability resources are provided only to students with professionally documented disabilities and do require registration. There are no additional costs to a qualified student for the provision of reasonable and appropriate accommodations for a disability.

LD/ADHD ADMISSIONS INFORMATION

College entrance tests required: Yes
Interview required: N/A
Essay recommended: No
Documentation required for LD: University's learning disability verification form filled out by the appropriate professional, including a complete diagnostic report or diagnostic narrative. Testing older than 3 years is not accepted.
Documentation required for ADHD: University's attention deficit hyperactivity disorder verification form filled out by the appropriate professional, including a complete diagnostic report or diagnostic narrative. Testing older than 3 years is not accepted.
Submitted to: Counseling Center
Special Ed. HS course work accepted: Yes

Specific course requirements of all applicants: NR
Separate application required: No
# of LD applications submitted each year: 20–30
# of LD applications accepted yearly: 20–30
Total # of students receiving LD services: 82
Acceptance into program means acceptance into college: Students must be admitted and enrolled in the university first and then request services.

ADMISSIONS

Admissions criteria are the same for all students; however, the Admissions Office will always work with students on an individual basis if needed. In general, students with a 3.6 GPA or higher are admitted with honors. Students with a 2.0–3.5 GPA are admitted in good standing, and students with a GPA below a 2.0 are accepted conditionally. The conditional admissions procedure is for new freshmen who earned below a 2.0 in English, math, science, and social studies. The following are required for those admitted conditionally: freshman seminar, 2.0 GPA, registration through the University Division rather than a specific major, and enrollment in no more than 12 credit hours. ACT/SAT scores are used for placement purposes. The college accepts courses taken the Special Education Department of the high school.

ADDITIONAL INFORMATION

In order to use resources, documentation of an LD must be provided by the student. Skills classes are offered in basic grammar, algebra review, reading, and study skills. Credit is given for the hours, but the grades are Pass/No Pass. There are no note-takers, but special supplies are provided to allow the students to get other students to carbon their notes in class. Other services include; readers/taping services; test accommodations; tutor referral; advocacy and counseling; and career planning. Services and accommodations are available for undergraduate and graduate students.

LEARNING DISABILITY PROGRAM/SERVICES

Learning Disability Program/Services: Support Services Contact Information Counseling Center
Director: James Browning
  E-mail: lmsmith@usi.edu
  Telephone: 812-464-1867
  Fax: 812-461-5288

LEARNING DISABILITY SERVICES

Requests for the following services/accommodations will be evaluated individually based on appropriate and current documentation.

Allowed in exams
  Calculator: Yes
  Dictionary: Yes
  Computer: Yes
  Spellchecker: Yes
Extended test time: Yes
Scribes: Yes
Proctors: Yes
Oral exams: Yes
Note-takers: Yes

Distraction-reduced environment: Yes
Tape recording in class: Yes
Books on tape from RFBD: Yes
Taping of books not from RFBD: Yes
Accommodations for students with ADHD: Yes
Reading machine: Yes
Other assistive technology: Yes
Priority registration: Yes

Added costs for services: No
LD specialists: No
Professional tutors: NR
Peer tutors: 56
Max. hours/wk. for services: Unlimited
How professors are notified of LD/ADHD: By student

GENERAL ADMISSIONS INFORMATION

Director of Admissions: Eric H. Otto
Telephone: 812-464-1765

ENTRANCE REQUIREMENTS

Academic units recommended: 4 English, 4 math, 3 science, 2 foreign language, 2 social studies, 2 history, 2 academic electives. High school diploma is required, and GED is accepted. ACT with Writing component required. TOEFL required of all international applicants: minimum paper TOEFL 525, minimum computer TOEFL 197.

Application deadline: 8/15
Notification: Rolling
Average GPA: 2.97
ACT Composite middle 50% range: 17–23

SAT Math middle 50% range: 420–540
SAT Critical Reading middle 50% range: 420–530
SAT Writing middle 50% range: NR

Graduated top 10% of class: 9%
Graduated top 25% of class: 27%
Graduated top 50% of class: 61%

COLLEGE GRADUATION REQUIREMENTS

Course waivers allowed: No
Course substitutions allowed: Yes
In what course: Math, physical education

ADDITIONAL INFORMATION

Environment: The university is located on 300 acres in a suburban area 150 miles south of Indianapolis.

Student Body
  Undergrad enrollment: 9,045
  Women: 60%
  Men: 40%
  Percent out-of-state: 9%

Cost Information
  In-state tuition: $4,460
  Out-of-state tuition: $10,631
  Room & board: $6,492
Housing Information
  University housing: Yes
  Percent living on campus: 27%

Greek System
  Fraternity: Yes
  Sorority: Yes
Athletics: Division II

University of Southern Indiana

VINCENNES UNIVERSITY

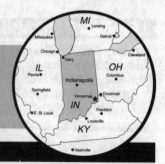

1002 North First Street, Vincennes, IN 47591
Phone: 800-742-9198 • Fax: 812-888-8888
E-mail: vuadmit@vinu.edu • Web: www.vinu.edu
Support: SP • Institution type: 2-year public

LEARNING DISABILITY PROGRAM AND SERVICES

Students Transition into Education Program (STEP) is a LD support program for students in the mainstream. Students' strengths rather than deficits are the emphasis; compensatory techniques rather than remediation are the thrust. STEP is designed to give students the opportunity to develop their own unique abilities, achieve their highest academic potential, and develop a sense of self-worth and the skills needed to function and learn independently in college. STEP students take four semesters in Coping in College I–IV: The course teaches requisite social, study, and self-awareness skills and serves as a support group. The curriculum is practical and emphasizes active thinking, independent learning, student accountability, and the acquisition of specific strategies proven to improve academic performance. Coping in College I addresses self-advocacy, compensatory techniques, coping, adaptation, stress, and socialization; II emphasizes socialization and metacognitive skills; III further develops social skills and solidifies study skills; IV emphasizes career planning, job-search, and social skills, and includes the STEP retreat. Cope Student Support Services is a program designed to help students with all aspects of the college experience. This is a Trio Program requiring that the student meet one of three requirements: first generation college student, low income, or disabled.

LD/ADHD ADMISSIONS INFORMATION

College entrance tests required: No
Interview required: No
Essay recommended: No
Documentation required for LD: Psychoeducational
evaluation
Documentation required for ADHD: Yes
Submitted to: STEP
Special Ed. HS course work accepted: Yes

Specific course requirements of all applicants: NR
Separate application required: Yes
# of LD applications submitted each year: 400
# of LD applications accepted yearly: 60
Total # of students receiving LD services: 100–120
Acceptance into program means acceptance into
  college: Students must apply separately to the university
  and STEP or Cope. Students will be accepted to the
  university first and then to the STEP or Cope.

ADMISSIONS

Students with learning disabilities must submit the general application form to Vincennes University. Vincennes offers open-door admissions to any student with a high school diploma or the GED. SAT or ACT scores are required for all Health Occupations majors. SAT and ACT scores are not required for other majors, however they are used for placement in course levels appropriate to a student's academic preparation. If students have not taken the SAT or ACT, they will be required to take a placement test before they can register for classes. Students with learning disabilities must apply separately to STEP: Send the STEP application; psychological evaluation; and letters of recommendation from LD specialists, counselors, or teachers. The transcript is of less importance and the recommendations are more important. Once accepted, students reserve a spot with a deposit of $110 to STEP. Deposits are refundable if students do not matriculate to Vincennes. Admission to the program is based on completion of the application process, determination of student eligibility, available funding, and space remaining. Space in the program is limited. Early application is important, and the deadline date is February 1. Students applying to Cope should apply separately to the university prior to applying to STEP.

ADDITIONAL INFORMATION

STEP benefits include an LD specialist for individualized tutoring/remediation, professional/peer tutoring, specialized remedial and/or support classes, weekly academic monitoring, coordinated referral to Counseling/Career Center, special classes, note-taking paper, reduced class load, auditing class before taking test modifications, papers rather than tests, and alternative ways to demonstrate competency. STEP does not exempt students from classes, class requirements, or provide taped books and note-takers. Cope provides individual counselor to assist with needs; tutoring; progress reports; academic advising; appropriate accommodations; academic support groups; and workshops on study skills, test anxiety, self-esteem, and interview skills. The Study Skills Center is open to all students and offers free tutoring; classes in spelling, success strategies, and learning strategies; individualized materials to help improve performance in problem areas; assessment center; and a study skills lab.

LEARNING DISABILITY PROGRAM/SERVICES

Learning Disability Program/Services: Students Transition into Education Program (STEP)
Director: Jane Kavanaugh
  E-Mail: jkavanaugh@vinu.edu
  Telephone: 812-888-4485
  Fax: 812-888-5531
Contact Person: Jane Kavanaugh, Jane Hunckler, and Susan Laue
  E-Mail: jkavanaugh@vinu.edu
  Telephone: 812-888-4214 or 812-888-4212
  Fax: 812-888-5531

LEARNING DISABILITY SERVICES

Requests for the following services/accommodations will be evaluated individually based on appropriate and current documentation.

Allowed in exams
  Calculator: Yes
  Dictionary: Yes
  Computer: Yes
  Spellchecker: Yes
Extended test time: Yes
Scribes: Yes
Proctors: Yes
Oral exams: Yes
Note-takers: Yes

Distraction-reduced environment: Yes
Tape recording in class: Yes
Books on tape from RFBD: Yes
Taping of books not from RFBD: Yes
Accommodations for students with ADHD: Yes
Reading machine: Yes
Other assistive technology: Yes
Priority registration: Yes

Added costs for services: Yes
LD specialists: Yes
Professional tutors: 10–20
Peer tutors: 25–45
Max. hours/wk. for services: N/A
How professors are notified of LD/ADHD: By both student and director

GENERAL ADMISSIONS INFORMATION

Director of Admissions: Phyllis Carling
Telephone: 800-742-9198

ENTRANCE REQUIREMENTS

Application deadline: Rolling
Notification: Rolling
Average GPA: NR
ACT Composite middle 50% range: NR

SAT Math middle 50% range: NR
SAT Critical Reading middle 50% range: NR
SAT Writing middle 50% range: NR

Graduated top 10% of class: NR
Graduated top 25% of class: NR
Graduated top 50% of class: NR

COLLEGE GRADUATION REQUIREMENTS

Course waivers allowed: NR
Course substitutions allowed: NR

ADDITIONAL INFORMATION

Environment: The school is located on 95 acres 45 minutes south of Terre Haute.

Student Body
  Undergrad enrollment: 4,700
  Women: 40%
  Men: 60%
  Percent out-of-state: 5%

Cost Information
  In-state tuition: $3,100
  Out-of-state tuition: $8,600
  Room & board: $6,400
Housing Information
  University housing: Yes
  Percent living on campus: 44%

Greek System
  Fraternity: Yes
  Sorority: Yes
Athletics: NJCAA

DRAKE UNIVERSITY

2507 University Avenue, Des Moines, IA 50311-4505
Phone: 515-271-3181 • Fax: 515-271-2831
E-mail: admission@drake.edu • Web: www.choose.drake.edu
Support: S • Institution type: 4-year private

LEARNING DISABILITY PROGRAM AND SERVICES

The Disability Resource Centers' purpose is to facilitate and enhance the opportunity for students with any type of disability to successfully complete their postsecondary education. The DRC is committed to enriching the academic experience of Drake students with disabilities through individualized assessment of accommodations and resource needs. To initiate a request for services, students should contact the DRC. An appointment will be made with a staff member to begin the registration process. Students are encouraged to meet with a DRC counselor each semester to identify accommodations that are needed. It is the students' responsibility to self-identify that they have a learning disability; to provide professional documentation of their disability; and to request the accommodations that they need. The DRC office maintains a collection of information on disabilities, and there are many sources on the instruction and evaluation of students with disabilities. DRC encourages faculty, staff, and students to contact the office if they are interested in this type of information.

LD/ADHD ADMISSIONS INFORMATION

College entrance tests required: Yes
Interview required: No
Essay recommended: No
Documentation required for LD: Psychoeducational
  evaluation
Documentation required for ADHD: Yes
Submitted to: Disability Resource Center
Special Ed. HS course work accepted: Yes

Specific course requirements of all applicants: NR
Separate application required: No
# of LD applications submitted each year: NR
# of LD applications accepted yearly: NR
Total # of students receiving LD services: NR
Acceptance into program means acceptance into
  college: Student must be admitted and enrolled in the
  university first and then reviewed for LD services.

ADMISSIONS

There is no special admission process for students with learning disabilities. All applicants are expected to meet the same admission criteria, including 16 academic college-prep courses with a minimum of 4 years of English, 2 years of math, 2 years of science, 2 years of social studies, 1 year of history, and 2 years of a foreign language; 21 ACT or 970 SAT; and a minimum of a 2.0 GPA. Students must be admitted and enrolled in the university prior to seeking accommodations or services for a learning disability.

ADDITIONAL INFORMATION

The DRC can offer students appointments at the pre-admission and pre-enrollment stages; review of Drake's policies and procedures regarding students with disabilities; identification and coordination of classroom accommodations; assessment of service needs; note-takers, scribes, and readers; referral to appropriate campus resources; advocacy and liaison with the university community; and training on the use of assistive technology. Services provided by the DRC do not lower any course standards or change any requirements of a particular degree. The services are intended to allow equal access and provide an opportunity for students with disabilities to demonstrate their abilities.

LEARNING DISABILITY PROGRAM/SERVICES

Learning Disability Program/Services: Disability Resource Center
Director: Michelle Laughlin
E-Mail: michelle.laughlin@drake.edu
Telephone: 515-271-1835
Fax: 515-271-1855

LEARNING DISABILITY SERVICES

Requests for the following services/accommodations will be evaluated individually based on appropriate and current documentation.

Allowed in exams	**Distraction-reduced environment:** Yes	**Added costs for services:** No
Calculator: Yes	**Tape recording in class:** Yes	**LD specialists:** No
Dictionary: Yes	**Books on tape from RFBD:** Yes	**Professional tutors:** No
Computer: Yes	**Taping of books not from RFBD:** Yes	**Peer tutors:** 30–40
Spellchecker: Yes	**Accommodations for students with**	**Max. hours/wk. for services:**
Extended test time: Yes	**ADHD:** Yes	Unlimited
Scribes: Yes	**Reading machine:** Yes	**How professors are notified of**
Proctors: Yes	**Other assistive technology:** Yes	**LD/ADHD:** By student
Oral exams: Yes	**Priority registration:** No	
Note-takers: Yes		

GENERAL ADMISSIONS INFORMATION

Director of Admissions: Laura Linn
Telephone: 515-271-3182

ENTRANCE REQUIREMENTS

Academic units recommended: 4 English, 3 math, 2 science, 2 foreign language, 4 social studies. High school diploma is required, and GED is accepted. ACT with or without Writing component accepted. TOEFL required of all international applicants: minimum paper TOEFL 545, minimum computer TOEFL 252.

Application deadline: 3/1	**SAT Math middle 50% range:**	**Graduated top 10% of class:** 40%
Notification: Rolling	540–660	**Graduated top 25% of class:** 68%
Average GPA: 3.62	**SAT Critical Reading middle 50%**	**Graduated top 50% of class:** 92%
ACT Composite middle 50% range:	**range:** 520–650	
23–28	**SAT Writing middle 50% range:** NR	

COLLEGE GRADUATION REQUIREMENTS

Course waivers allowed: No
Course substitutions allowed: Yes
In what course: Documentation must be provided and is considered on a case-by-case basis.

ADDITIONAL INFORMATION

Environment: The campus is located in the suburbs of Des Moines.

Student Body	**Cost Information**	**Greek System**
Undergrad enrollment: 3,191	**Tuition:** $22,270	**Fraternity:** Yes
Women: 56%	**Room & board:** $6,500	**Sorority:** Yes
Men: 44%	**Housing Information**	**Athletics:** Division I
Percent out-of-state: 61%	**University housing:** Yes	
	Percent living on campus: 67%	

GRAND VIEW COLLEGE

1200 Grandview Avenue, Des Moines, IA 50316-1599
Phone: 515-263-2810 • Fax: 515-263-2974
E-mail: admissions@gvc.edu • Web: www.gvc.edu
Support: CS • Institution type: 4-year private

LEARNING DISABILITY PROGRAM AND SERVICES

The Academic Success Program is available for all students on campus. The objective of the program is to provide a variety of learning environments and teaching techniques. Academic Success provides academic support programs, services and courses designed to optimize student performance. Students who participate in the Center for Academic and Career Success Program make a smoother transition to Grand View, develop social and academic networks essential to their success, and benefit from informal student-faculty-staff interactions. Grand View is committed to enriching the academic experience of every qualified student with LD and endorses reasonable accommodations for participation in all programs and activities. Students are encouraged to make an appointment in the Academic Success Center to review college policies and procedures, request accommodations, develop an accommodation plan, or discuss personal advocacy issues.

LD/ADHD ADMISSIONS INFORMATION

College entrance tests required: Yes
Interview required: No
Essay recommended: No
Documentation required for LD: Verification of learning disabilities by licensed psychologist required
Documentation required for ADHD: Verification of learning disabilities by licensed psychologist required
Submitted to: Academic Success Program
Special Ed. HS course work accepted: Yes

Specific course requirements of all applicants: No
Separate application required: No
# of LD applications submitted each year: NR
# of LD applications accepted yearly: NR
Total # of students receiving LD services: 15
Acceptance into program means acceptance into college: Students must be admitted and enrolled prior to requesting services.

ADMISSIONS

There is no special admissions process for students with LD and ADHD. There is a probationary admit for students with an 18 ACT and a 2.0 high school GPA and below. This is offered to students who show that they are committed and have the potential for success at college.

ADDITIONAL INFORMATION

Academic Success Center provides resources which complement classroom instruction enabling students to optimize their academic experience. Students can receive help with reading rate and reading comprehension, study skills, organizational skills, developing a personal management plan, test-taking strategies, writing skills, personalized instruction in math, and peer tutoring. The Career Center provides services, resources, and educational opportunities by assisting students in developing, evaluating, initiating, and implementing personal career and life plans. Faculty members serve as academic advisors. Core courses can have substitutions options. Other services or accommodations offered for students with appropriate documentation include the use of calculators, computers, or spellcheckers; extended testing time; scribes; proctors; oral exams; note-takers; a distraction-free environment for taking tests; tape-recording of lectures; and services for students with ADHD. There is one professional staff member who is certified in LD.

LEARNING DISABILITY PROGRAM/SERVICES

Learning Disability Program/Services: Academic Success
Director: Carolyn Wassenaar
  E-Mail: cwassenaar@gve.edu
  Telephone: 515-263-2971
  Fax: 515-263-2840

LEARNING DISABILITY SERVICES

Requests for the following services/accommodations will be evaluated individually based on appropriate and current documentation.

Allowed in exams
  Calculator: Yes
  Dictionary: Yes
  Computer: Yes
  Spellchecker: Yes
Extended test time: Yes
Scribes: Yes
Proctors: Yes
Oral exams: Yes
Note-takers: Yes

Distraction-reduced environment: Yes
Tape recording in class: Yes
Books on tape from RFBD: Yes
Taping of books not from RFBD: Yes
Accommodations for students with ADHD: Yes
Reading machine: No
Other assistive technology: No
Priority registration: Yes

Added costs for services: No
LD specialists: Yes
Professional tutors: 1
Peer tutors: NR
Max. hours/wk. for services: Unlimited
How professors are notified of LD/ADHD: By both student and director

GENERAL ADMISSIONS INFORMATION

Director of Admissions: Diane Schafer Johnson
Telephone: 515-263-2810

ENTRANCE REQUIREMENTS

Academic units recommended: 4 English, 3 math, 3 science, 2 foreign language, 3 social studies. High school diploma is required, and GED is accepted. ACT without Writing component accepted. TOEFL required of all international applicants: minimum paper TOEFL 550, minimum computer TOEFL 210.

Application deadline: 8/15
Notification: Rolling
Average GPA: 3.15
ACT Composite middle 50% range: 18–22

SAT Math middle 50% range: 440–590
SAT Critical Reading middle 50% range: 400–590
SAT Writing middle 50% range: 460–470

Graduated top 10% of class: 14%
Graduated top 25% of class: 36%
Graduated top 50% of class: 68%

COLLEGE GRADUATION REQUIREMENTS

Course waivers allowed: No
Course substitutions allowed: Yes
In what course: We have included acceptable substitions/options within our core.

ADDITIONAL INFORMATION

Environment: Located in Des Moines

Student Body
  Undergrad enrollment: 1,644
  Women: 68%
  Men: 32%
  Percent out-of-state: 6%

Cost Information
  Tuition: $16,000
  Room & board: $5,422
Housing Information
  University housing: Yes
  Percent living on campus: 35%

Greek System
  Fraternity: No
  Sorority: No
Athletics: NAIA

GRINNELL COLLEGE

1103 Park Street, Grinnell, IA 50112-1690
Phone: 641-269-3600 • Fax: 641-269-4800
E-mail: askgrin@grinnell.edu • Web: www.grinnell.edu
Support: S • Institution type: 4-year private

LEARNING DISABILITY PROGRAM AND SERVICES

Grinnell College is dedicated to educating young people whose achievements show a high level of intellectual capacity, initiative, and maturity. Every year, this highly qualified group of students includes people with learning disabilities. Grinnell is committed to providing academic adjustments and reasonable accommodations for students with disabilities who are otherwise qualified for admission. Many of Grinnell's characteristics make it a positive educational environment for all students: an open curriculum, small classes, easy access to professors, and openness to diversity. The Director of Academic Advising coordinates services for students with LD, arranges for academic accommodations, acts as a liaison to the faculty, and offers personal, individual assistance. Once students are admitted and they accept the offer of admission, Grinnell likes to plan with them for any reasonable accommodation they will need in order to enjoy a successful experience. Students have the responsibility to make their needs known. The most important factors for college success are seeking help early and learning to be self-advocates. Students are encouraged to notify the Director of Academic Advising about their needs before they arrive for the first semester. For planning purposes, sooner is always better.

LD/ADHD ADMISSIONS INFORMATION

College entrance tests required: Yes
Interview required: No
Essay recommended: No
Documentation required for LD: Current written evaluation from qualified professional indicating results from psychoeducational testing that indicates a specific diagnosis of a learning disability
Documentation required for ADHD: Current written evaluation from qualified professional indicating results from appropriate testing with a specific diagnosis of ADHD
Submitted to: Academic Advising
Special Ed. HS course work accepted: N/A

Specific course requirements of all applicants: NR
Separate application required: No
# of LD applications submitted each year: NR
# of LD applications accepted yearly: NR
Total # of students receiving LD services: 25
Acceptance into program means acceptance into college: Students must be admitted and enrolled in the university first and then request services.

ADMISSIONS

Grinnell welcomes applications from students with learning disabilities. While the same admissions standards apply to all students, the college does accept nonstandardized test scores. Students are advised to document their needs in the application for admission and how learning disabilities may have affected their secondary school performance. Interviews are encouraged. Grinnell is looking for a strong scholastic record from high school, recommendations, satisfactory results on the ACT/SAT, and specific units of high school course work, including 4 years of English, 3 years of math, 3 years of social studies, 3 years of science, and 3 years of a foreign language. Applicants with appropriate documentation may substitute for some entrance requirements such as foreign language. The middle 50 percent range for the ACT is 28–31 and 1238–1433 for the SAT. Over 85 percent of the admitted students are from the top 20 percent of the class. The minimum GPA is a 2.5. Students are encouraged to have an interview either on or off campus.

ADDITIONAL INFORMATION

Students need to meet with professors and the director of Academic Advising to plan for their individual needs. The Office of Academic Advising coordinates services for students and arranges for academic accommodations. The ADA Task Force ensures compliance with the Americans with Disabilities Act. The Reading Lab helps students improve reading speed, vocabulary, and reading comprehension. The Director of Academic Advising assists students with LD in identifying effective academic strategies. The Science and Math Learning Center provides instruction in math and science courses for students who want to strengthen their background in these areas. Student tutoring will help students make arrangements for tutoring at no charge. Additional resources include referral for LD testing, reduced course loads, untimed exams, personal counseling, and volunteers who are willing to read to students with learning disabilities. Skills classes for credit are offered in reading, writing, and math.

LEARNING DISABILITY PROGRAM/SERVICES

Learning Disability Program/Services: Academic Advising Office
Director: Joyce M. Stern, Dean for Student Academic Support and Advising
  E-Mail: sternjm@grinnell.edu
  Telephone: 641-269-3702
  Fax: 641-269-3710

LEARNING DISABILITY SERVICES

Requests for the following services/accommodations will be evaluated individually based on appropriate and current documentation.

Allowed in exams
  Calculator: Yes
  Dictionary: Yes
  Computer: Yes
  Spellchecker: Yes
Extended test time: Yes
Scribes: Yes
Proctors: Yes
Oral exams: Yes
Note-takers: Yes

Distraction-reduced environment: Yes
Tape recording in class: Yes
Books on tape from RFBD: Yes
Taping of books not from RFBD: Yes
Accommodations for students with ADHD: Yes
Reading machine: Yes
Other assistive technology: Yes
Priority registration: No

Added costs for services: No
LD specialists: No
Professional tutors: 7
Peer tutors: 50
Max. hours/wk. for services: Unlimited
How professors are notified of LD/ADHD: By both student and director

GENERAL ADMISSIONS INFORMATION

Director of Admissions: James Sumner
Telephone: 641-269-3600

ENTRANCE REQUIREMENTS

Academic units recommended: 4 English, 4 math, 4 science (3 science labs), 4 foreign language, 4 social studies. High school diploma is required, and GED is accepted. ACT with or without Writing component accepted. TOEFL required of all international applicants: minimum paper TOEFL 550, minimum computer TOEFL 220.

Application deadline: 1/20
Notification: 4/1
Average GPA: NR
ACT Composite middle 50% range: 29–32

SAT Math middle 50% range: 620–720
SAT Critical Reading middle 50% range: 630–740
SAT Writing middle 50% range: NR

Graduated top 10% of class: 64%
Graduated top 25% of class: 90%
Graduated top 50% of class: 100%

COLLEGE GRADUATION REQUIREMENTS

Course waivers allowed: No
Course substitutions allowed: No

ADDITIONAL INFORMATION

Environment: The college is located on 95 acres in a small town 55 miles east of Des Moines.

Student Body
  Undergrad enrollment: 1,555
  Women: 54%
  Men: 46%
  Percent out-of-state: 87%

Cost Information
  Tuition: $28,566
  Room & board: $7,700
Housing Information
  University housing: Yes
  Percent living on campus: 88%

Greek System
  Fraternity: No
  Sorority: No
Athletics: Division III

INDIAN HILLS COMMUNITY COLLEGE

623 Indian Hills Drive, Building 12, Ottumwa, IA 52501
Phone: 800-726-2585 • Fax: 641-683-5184
E-mail: bhenderso@ihcc.cc.ia.us • Web: www.ihcc.cc.ia.us
Support: S • Institution type: 2-year public

LEARNING DISABILITY PROGRAM AND SERVICES

The Success Center provides academic and physical accommodations and services for students with disabilities based on documented needs. Students with a documented learning disability or attention deficit hyperactivity disorder must provide current documentation which has been completed by a qualified professional such as a school counselor, physician, psychologist, or other health care professional. Statements must include: a description of the disability, a statement of how the disability prohibits one or more major life activities and is a barrier to the student's full participation in the program, and a description of the specific accommodations which might be provided. All requests for accommodations should be made as far in advance as possible. Students enrolling in credit programs are encouraged to make their requests for accommodations at the time they are applying for admission and preferably no later than 6 weeks prior to the beginning of each academic term. All student requests are dealt with in a confidential manner.

LD/ADHD ADMISSIONS INFORMATION

College entrance tests required: N/A
Interview required: No
Essay recommended: No
Documentation required for LD: WAIS–III, WJ–III
Documentation required for ADHD: Yes
Submitted to: Success Center
Special Ed. HS course work accepted: Yes

Specific course requirements of all applicants: NR
Separate application required: Yes
# of LD applications submitted each year: 20–45
# of LD applications accepted yearly: 45
Total # of students receiving LD services: 45
Acceptance into program means acceptance into college: Students must be admitted and enrolled in the university first and then request services.

ADMISSIONS

Indian Hills Community College is an "open-door" institution. All students must present a high school diploma or GED or must earn one while enrolled in order to receive a college degree. ACT/SAT tests are not required, and there are no specific high school courses required for admission. Although an interview is not required, it is highly recommended. Students enroll with widely varying levels of achievement and differing goals, and some discover that they can move ahead more quickly. Applicants are required to submit a portfolio, which is reviewed by a selection committee. Many eventually enter one or more of the Indian Hills credit courses. A decision to move into college credit courses is made by staff members, parents, and the student involved.

ADDITIONAL INFORMATION

IHCC believes that all students have value and their goal is to empower students to achieve their full potential in an academic setting. At the Success Center students can find assistance in skill upgrading, academic support, and career counseling. All students have access to skills classes in study skills and specialized vocabulary skills. Other services include computer labs, developmental classes, peer tutoring, and professional tutoring. There are currently approximately 35 students with learning disabilities and 10 with attention deficit hyperactivity disorder receiving accommodations or services.

LEARNING DISABILITY PROGRAM/SERVICES

Learning Disability Program/Services: Success Center
Director: Mary Stewart
  E-Mail: mstewart@indianhills.edu
  Telephone: 641-683-5218
  Fax: 641-683-5184
Contact Person: Marva Philipsen
  E-Mail: mphilipsen@indianhills.edu
  Telephone: 641-683-5238
  Fax: 641-683-5184

LEARNING DISABILITY SERVICES

Requests for the following services/accommodations will be evaluated individually based on appropriate and current documentation.

Allowed in exams
  Calculator: Yes
  Dictionary: Yes
  Computer: Yes
  Spellchecker: Yes
Extended test time: Yes
Scribes: Yes
Proctors: Yes
Oral exams: Yes
Note-takers: Yes

Distraction-reduced environment: Yes
Tape recording in class: Yes
Books on tape from RFBD: Yes
Taping of books not from RFBD: Yes
Accommodations for students with ADHD: Yes
Reading machine: Yes
Other assistive technology: Yes
Priority registration: No

Added costs for services: No
LD specialists: Yes
Professional tutors: 9
Peer tutors: 20–30
Max. hours/wk. for services: Unlimited
How professors are notified of LD/ADHD: By both student and director

GENERAL ADMISSIONS INFORMATION

Director of Admissions: Sally Harris
Telephone: 800-726-2585

ENTRANCE REQUIREMENTS

Academic Units Recommended: 4 English, 3 math, 3 science, 4 social studies, 2 foreign language. Some majors require specific math courses. Open admissions. High school diploma or GED equivalent accepted.

Application deadline: Rolling
Notification: Rolling
Average GPA: NR
ACT Composite middle 50% range: NR

SAT Math middle 50% range: NR
SAT Critical Reading middle 50% range: NR
SAT Writing middle 50% range: NR

Graduated top 10% of class: NR
Graduated top 25% of class: NR
Graduated top 50% of class: NR

COLLEGE GRADUATION REQUIREMENTS

Course waivers allowed: No
Course substitutions allowed: No

ADDITIONAL INFORMATION

Environment: The college is located on 400 acres about 2 hours east of Iowa City or west of Des Moines.

Student Body
  Undergrad enrollment: 3,700
  Women: 50%
  Men: 50%
  Percent out-of-state: 9%

Cost Information
  In-state tuition: $105 per credit
  Out-of-state tuition: $158 per credit
  Room & board: $4,400
Housing Information
  University housing: Yes
  Percent living on campus: 15%

Greek System
  Fraternity: No
  Sorority: No
Athletics: NJCAA

Iowa State University

100 Alumni Hall, Ames, IA 50011-2011
Phone: 515-294-5836 • Fax: 515-294-2592
E-mail: admissions@iastate.edu • Web: www.iastate.edu
Support: CS • Institution type: 4-year public

LEARNING DISABILITY PROGRAM AND SERVICES

ISU is committed to providing equal opportunities and facilitating the personal growth and development of all students. The LD specialist assists students with issues relating to LD, provides a review of most current LD evaluation and documentation to determine the accommodations needed, offers assistance in articulating needs to faculty and staff, and may serve as a liaison in student/staff negotiations. Documentation should include demographic data about the student and examiner's qualifications; behavioral observation of the way students present themselves, verbal and nonverbal communication, interpersonal skills and behavior during testing; a narrative describing developmental and educational history; a description of the effect of the LD on academic learning; a report of the results of an assessment of intellectual functioning (including WAIS–R or WISC—R); a report of the results of academic testing including Woodcock-Johnson; testing for foreign language substitute; and specific recommendations concerning academic compensatory strategies and whether the student qualifies for specific academic accommodations.

LD/ADHD ADMISSIONS INFORMATION

College entrance tests required: Yes
Interview required: No
Essay recommended: No
Documentation required for LD: Psychoeducational evaluation
Documentation required for ADHD: Psychoeducational evaluation
Submitted to: Student Disability Resources
Special Ed. HS course work accepted: Yes

Specific course requirements of all applicants: Yes
Separate application required: N/A
# of LD applications submitted each year: NR
# of LD applications accepted yearly: NR
Total # of students receiving LD services: NR
Acceptance into program means acceptance into college: Students must be admitted and enrolled in the university first and then request services.

ADMISSIONS

If a student is LD and does not meet minimum requirements, the student can request a review. However, this is not a program for students with extreme deficits. Iowa State is looking for students who can succeed, have good verbal skills, and have an upward trend in grades. Students not meeting high school course requirements, but who are otherwise qualified, may be admitted after an individual review. The pattern on the ACT, not just the score, will be considered. General admission requirements include 4 English, 3 math, 3 science, 2 social studies (3 liberal arts and sciences plus 2 foreign language), ACT 19 (SAT is accepted); 3 high school foreign language satisfies the requirement to graduate from Iowa State; requirements for students from out-of-state may be more difficult; there is an admission index indicating student rank and ACT scores. There is a Summer Trial Program for students not regularly admissible through test scores or class rank: Students must take six credits and get C or better. These students are often in the top 75 percent of their class but may not have a 25 ACT. For students entering in the fall of 2009, a Regent Admission Index (RAI) score will be calculated for each applicant based on the following equation: RAI = (2 x ACT composite score) + (1 x high school rank) + (20 x high school GPA) + (5 x number of high school courses completed in the core subject areas). Applicants with a 245 RAI and who meet the minimum high school course requirements will automatically be offered admission. Applicants who achieve less than a 245 RAI score and who meet the minimum high school course requirements may also be offered admission, but their applications will be reviewed on an individual basis.

ADDITIONAL INFORMATION

The Academic Learning Lab is a "learning-how-to-learn" center designed to help all students. Counselors work one-on-one to evaluate and identify problem study habits and devise strategies to improve them. The Learning Lab and Tutoring and Student Support Services are in one area called the Academic Success Center (ASC). ASC coordinates services including counseling, teaching reading, and study skills, and provides a list of tutors. The Writing Center is available to all students. The LD specialist provides information about readers, note-takers, and scribes. Peer Supplemental Instruction (SI) is an academic assistance program attached to very difficult courses. SI leaders attend classes and conduct biweekly sessions to help students learn and study the course material. Student Support Services is a federally funded program for students with LD and others qualified to receive academic support in the form of free tutoring and skill-building workshops.

LEARNING DISABILITY PROGRAM/SERVICES

Learning Disability Program/Services: Student Disability Resources
Director: Steve Moats
  E-Mail: smoats@iastate.edu
  Telephone: 515-294-7220
  Fax: 515-294-2397
Contact Person: John Hirschman
  E-Mail: smoats@iastate.edu
  Telephone: 515-294-7220
  Fax: 515-294-2397

LEARNING DISABILITY SERVICES

Requests for the following services/accommodations will be evaluated individually based on appropriate and current documentation.

Allowed in exams
  Calculator: Yes
  Dictionary: Yes
  Computer: Yes
  Spellchecker: Yes
Extended test time: Yes
Scribes: Yes
Proctors: Yes
Oral exams: No
Note-takers: Yes

Distraction-reduced environment: Yes
Tape recording in class: Yes
Books on tape from RFBD: Yes
Taping of books not from RFBD: Yes
Accommodations for students with
  ADHD: Yes
Reading machine: Yes
Other assistive technology: Yes
Priority registration: No

Added costs for services: No
LD specialists: Yes
Professional tutors: No
Peer tutors: Varies
Max. hours/wk. for services: 0.5
How professors are notified of
  LD/ADHD: By student

GENERAL ADMISSIONS INFORMATION

Director of Admissions: Mark Harding
Telephone: 515-294-0815

ENTRANCE REQUIREMENTS

Academic units required: 4 English, 3 math, 3 science (2 science labs), 2 foreign language, 2 social studies.
Academic units recommended: 4 English, 4 math, 4 science (3 science labs), 3 foreign language, 4 social studies. High school diploma is required, and GED is accepted. ACT with or without Writing component accepted. TOEFL required of all international applicants: minimum paper TOEFL 500, minimum computer TOEFL 173.

Application deadline: 7/1
Notification: Rolling
Average GPA: 3.50
ACT Composite middle 50% range:
  22–27

SAT Math middle 50% range:
  540–690
SAT Critical Reading middle 50%
  range: 510–640
SAT Writing middle 50% range: NR

Graduated top 10% of class: 27%
Graduated top 25% of class: 60%
Graduated top 50% of class: 93%

COLLEGE GRADUATION REQUIREMENTS

Course waivers allowed: NR
Course substitutions allowed: NR

ADDITIONAL INFORMATION

Environment: Iowa State University is located on a 1,000-acre campus about 30 miles north of Des Moines.

Student Body
  Undergrad enrollment: 20,035
  Women: 43%
  Men: 57%
  Percent out-of-state: 21%

Cost Information
  In-state tuition: $5,352
  Out-of-state tuition: $16,110
  Room & board: $6,445
Housing Information
  University housing: Yes
  Percent living on campus: 37%

Greek System
  Fraternity: Yes
  Sorority: Yes
Athletics: Division I

LORAS COLLEGE

1450 Alta Vista, Dubuque, IA 52004-0178
Phone: 800-245-6727 • Fax: 563-588-7119
E-mail: admissions@loras.edu • Web: www.loras.edu
Support: SP • Institution type: 4-year private

LEARNING DISABILITY PROGRAM AND SERVICES

Loras College provides a supportive, comprehensive program for the motivated individual with a learning disability. Students can be successful in Loras' competitive environment if they have had adequate preparation, are willing to work with program staff, and take responsibility for their own learning. The LD Program staff has two full-time specialists to serve as guides and advocates, encouraging and supporting students to become independent learners. Students with LD who are enrolled in college-preparatory courses in high school are the most appropriate candidates for the Loras program. Often high school students who previously were in LD programs, but are not currently receiving services, are appropriate candidates for the program if they have taken college-prep classes.

LD/ADHD ADMISSIONS INFORMATION

College entrance tests required: Yes
Interview required: Yes
Essay recommended: Yes
Documentation required for LD: Diagnostic evaluation, including IQ and achievement testing, completed within the past 3 years
Documentation required for ADHD: Diagnostic evaluation, including IQ and achievement testing, completed within the past 3 years
Submitted to: Admissions Office
Special Ed. HS course work accepted: Yes

Specific course requirements of all applicants: NR
Separate application required: Yes
# of LD applications submitted each year: 60–70
# of LD applications accepted yearly: 20–30
Total # of students receiving LD services: 50–60
Acceptance into program means acceptance into college: Students are admitted into the LD Program and the College simultaneously. The decision is made by the LD Program director.

ADMISSIONS

Students may contact program staff in their junior year and request an early assessment of their chances for admission; the admission process will be explained and students will receive an application. Students should arrange for an evaluation documenting the learning disability if the evaluation is more than 2 years old, to include the WAIS–R, as well as achievement/diagnostic tests of reading, written expression, and math and send the evaluation when completed. Transcript with 4 years of English, 3 years of math, 3 years of social studies, 2–3 years of science; ACT/SAT; and 3 letters of recommendation should be submitted by November 1 if students are applying for the Enhanced Program. Criteria for admission include strong average intelligence, class rank close to or above 50 percent, 2.0 GPA (minimum), 16 ACT or 750 SAT (minimum). Students must be able to present their needs, strengths, and interests in a required interview with the LD Program director, scheduled for those who are invited to visit after all materials have been received. An admission decision is made by the Director of the LD Program.

ADDITIONAL INFORMATION

The Loras LD Program provides two levels of service: Enhanced and Mandated. The Enhanced Program for the first year students includes a two-credit class, Learning Strategies, both semesters of the first year; an individual meeting with program staff each week, and tutors, as needed. Upperclass, continuing students and transfer students receive the same support with the exception of the class. The students in the Enhanced Program are also eligible to receive Mandated Services, which include note-takers, taped textbooks, and a place to take extended time tests in a quiet room. Students in the Enhanced Program are charged a fee for services; those receiving only Mandated Services are not. Students who want Mandated Services are not required to self-disclose their need for services until after they are accepted to Loras. However, those who want the more comprehensive Enhanced Program should make their intention known on the application and submit all materials before the deadline of November 1 of their senior year.

LEARNING DISABILITY PROGRAM/SERVICES

Learning Disability Program/Services: Learning Disabilities Program
Director: Dianne Gibson
  E-Mail: dianne.gibson@loras.edu
  Telephone: 563-588-7134
  Fax: 563-588-7071
Contact Person: Rochelle Fury
  E-Mail: rochelle.fury@loras.edu
  Telephone: 563-588-7134
  Fax: 563-588-7071

LEARNING DISABILITY SERVICES

Requests for the following services/accommodations will be evaluated individually based on appropriate and current documentation.

Allowed in exams
  Calculator: Yes
  Dictionary: Yes
  Computer: Yes
  Spellchecker: Yes
Extended test time: Yes
Scribes: Yes
Proctors: Yes
Oral exams: Yes
Note-takers: Yes

Distraction-reduced environment: Yes
Tape recording in class: Yes
Books on tape from RFBD: Yes
Taping of books not from RFBD: Yes
Accommodations for students with ADHD: Yes
Reading machine: Yes
Other assistive technology: Yes
Priority registration: Yes

Added costs for services: Yes
LD specialists: Yes
Professional tutors: No
Peer tutors: 5–15
Max. hours/wk. for services: Unlimited
How professors are notified of LD/ADHD: By student

GENERAL ADMISSIONS INFORMATION

Director of Admissions: Sharon Lyons
Telephone: 563-588-7829

ENTRANCE REQUIREMENTS

Academic units recommended: 4 English, 3 math, 3 science, 3 social studies, 3 history. High school diploma is required, and GED is accepted. TOEFL required of all international applicants: minimum paper TOEFL 550, minimum computer TOEFL 213.

Application deadline: Rolling
Notification: Rolling
Average GPA: 3.22
ACT Composite middle 50% range: 20–25

SAT Math middle 50% range: 503–625
SAT Critical Reading middle 50% range: 453–575
SAT Writing middle 50% range: NR

Graduated top 10% of class: 13%
Graduated top 25% of class: 34%
Graduated top 50% of class: 65%

COLLEGE GRADUATION REQUIREMENTS

Course waivers allowed: Yes
In what course: Waivers are possible for math after attempting math course work; no foreign language waivers are necessary because there is no foreign language requirement.
Course substitutions allowed: No

ADDITIONAL INFORMATION

Environment: The college is located on 66 hilltop acres in northeast Iowa overlooking the Mississippi River.

Student Body
  Undergrad enrollment: 1,565
  Women: 50%
  Men: 50%
  Percent out-of-state: 45%

Cost Information
  Tuition: $19,990
  Room & board: $6,095
Housing Information
  University housing: Yes
  Percent living on campus: 60%

Greek System
  Fraternity: Yes
  Sorority: Yes
Athletics: Division III

Loras College

MORNINGSIDE COLLEGE

1501 Morningside Avenue, Sioux City, IA 51106-1751
Phone: 712-274-5511 • Fax: 712-274-5101
E-mail: mscadm@morningside.edu • Web: www.morningside.edu
Support: CS • Institution type: 4-year private

LEARNING DISABILITY PROGRAM AND SERVICES

Students with learning disabilities can and do succeed in college. However, students with different learning styles may need assistance in order to be truly successful students. Morningside College's Learning Disabilities Program, Focus, provides courses, tutoring, and academic adjustments tailored to for each student's needs. Morningside College will require supportive data to verify that a disability exists. These may include, but are not necessarily limited to, the following: high school records; specific plans recommended by qualified professionals and/or consultants; and satisfactory medical determination as required.

LD/ADHD ADMISSIONS INFORMATION

College entrance tests required: Yes
Interview required: Yes
Essay recommended: Yes
Documentation required for LD: Please call for details.
Documentation required for ADHD: Please call for details.
Submitted to: Academic Support Center
Special Ed. HS course work accepted: N/A

Specific course requirements of all applicants: NR
Separate application required: Yes
# of LD applications submitted each year: 30
# of LD applications accepted yearly: 10–15
Total # of students receiving LD services: 15–20
Acceptance into program means acceptance into college: Students must be admitted and enrolled prior to requesting services.

ADMISSIONS

Morningside's selective admissions program is based on the following criteria: class rank, college preparatory course work, GPA, ACT or SAT, essay participation recommended but not required, character, and personal abilities. Students with ACT of 20 or SAT of 1410, and either ranked in the top half of their class or have achieved a high school GPA of 2.5 meet the academic standards for admissions. First-year students who have been out of high school more than 5 years are not required to submit ACT or SAT test scores but are required to take math and/or English placement assessments. Students who have not completed high school may be admitted on the basis of a GED score.

ADDITIONAL INFORMATION

Examples of potential reasonable accommodations for students might include the following: note-taking, copies of instructor's notes, tape-recording of class, reasonable equipment modification, preferential seating, books on tape, test-taking accommodations, word processor adaptations, and reader service. The Academic Support Center is open to all students. Academic Support Center staff helps students improve or strengthen their academics by providing free assistance in writing techniques. Writing specialists are available to help students with the basics as well as help proficient writers who want assistance for particular writing assignments or projects. The specialists do not proofread, but they can help students see the strengths and weaknesses of their paper. Staff and student tutors are available in the Academic Support Center for students who want help in areas such as accounting, biology, chemistry, economics, history, math, science, religion, and sociology.

LEARNING DISABILITY PROGRAM/SERVICES

Learning Disability Program/Services: Academic Support Center
Director: Robbie Rohlena
E-Mail: rohlena@morningside.edu
Telephone: 800-831-0806, ext. 5104
Fax: 712-274-5101

LEARNING DISABILITY SERVICES

Requests for the following services/accommodations will be evaluated individually based on appropriate and current documentation.

Allowed in exams
Calculator: Yes
Dictionary: Yes
Computer: Yes
Spellchecker: Yes
Extended test time: Yes
Scribes: Yes
Proctors: Yes
Oral exams: Yes
Note-takers: Yes

Distraction-reduced environment: Yes
Tape recording in class: Yes
Books on tape from RFBD: Yes
Taping of books not from RFBD: Yes
Accommodations for students with ADHD: Yes
Reading machine: Yes
Other assistive technology: No
Priority registration: No

Added costs for services: Yes
LD specialists: Yes
Professional tutors: 5–10
Peer tutors: 5–15
Max. hours/wk. for services: Unlimited
How professors are notified of LD/ADHD: By director

GENERAL ADMISSIONS INFORMATION

Director of Admissions: Joel Weyand
Telephone: 712-274-5511

ENTRANCE REQUIREMENTS

Academic units recommended: 3 English, 2 math, 2 science, 3 social studies. High school diploma is required, and GED is accepted. ACT with or without Writing component accepted. TOEFL required of all international applicants: minimum paper TOEFL 450, minimum computer TOEFL 133.

Application deadline: NR
Notification: Rolling
Average GPA: 3.37
ACT Composite middle 50% range: 20–25

SAT Math middle 50% range: NR
SAT Critical Reading middle 50% range: NR
SAT Writing middle 50% range: NR

Graduated top 10% of class: 14%
Graduated top 25% of class: 43%
Graduated top 50% of class: 78%

COLLEGE GRADUATION REQUIREMENTS

Course waivers allowed: No
Course substitutions allowed: No

ADDITIONAL INFORMATION

Environment: Morningside College is located in Sioux City, Iowa, 90 miles north of Omaha, Nebraska and 75 miles south of Sioux Falls, South Dakota.

Student Body
Undergrad enrollment: 1,191
Women: 54%
Men: 46%
Percent out-of-state: 31%

Cost Information
Tuition: $18,932
Room & board: $6,227
Housing Information
University housing: Yes
Percent living on campus: 64%

Greek System
Fraternity: Yes
Sorority: Yes
Athletics: NAIA

SAINT AMBROSE UNIVERSITY

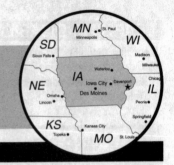

518 West Locust Street, Davenport, IA 52803-2898
Phone: 563-333-6300 • Fax: 563-333-6297
E-mail: admit@sau.edu/ • Web: www.sau.edu
Support: CS • Institution type: 4-year private

LEARNING DISABILITY PROGRAM AND SERVICES

St. Ambrose University's Services for Students with Disabilities is two-dimensional. The first dimension is the education of the faculty to specific needs of students. The second dimension is the development of services that allow programmatic access to students with disabilities. The key to both dimensions is the Coordinator of Services for Students with Disabilities who prepares seminars for faculty and staff to advise students. Students with learning disabilities are provided with an individual program of services. Services do not lower academic standards, but rather help "level the playing field" for individuals with LD. The coordinator works with students to develop skills and select accommodations to compensate for their learning disabilities and become their own advocates. Students with disabilities at St. Ambrose University may use a variety of services or reasonable accommodations intended to reduce the effects that a disability may have on their performance in a traditional academic setting.

LD/ADHD ADMISSIONS INFORMATION

College entrance tests required: Yes
Interview required: No
Essay recommended: No
Documentation required for LD: Ability test, achievement test, information processing test
Documentation required for ADHD: DSM–IV diagnosis by a licensed clinical professional
Submitted to: Services for Students with Disabilities
Special Ed. HS course work accepted: Yes

Specific course requirements of all applicants: NR
Separate application required: No
# of LD applications submitted each year: NR
# of LD applications accepted yearly: NR
Total # of students receiving LD services: 155–165
Acceptance into program means acceptance into college: Students must be admitted and enrolled in the university first and then request services.

ADMISSIONS

Students meeting minimum admission requirements are not required to send additional information for admission purposes, but it is helpful in providing effective services. The general admission criteria include minimum ACT 20 or minimum 950 SAT; 2.5 GPA; and no specific courses are required. However, students are encouraged to take 4 years of English, 3 years of math, 3 years of science, 3 years of social studies, and 3 years of foreign language. Students not meeting minimum requirements for admission may request special consideration by (1) submitting a regular application accompanied by a letter including a description of the LD, how the student has compensated for academic deficits, what resources were utilized in high school, and whether the student has independently requested accommodations; (2) submitting written assessment of learning problems (including all test scores) done by a certified professional, clearly stating that the student is LD and/or ADHD; (3) submitting recommendations from teachers who have firsthand knowledge of the student's academic abilities; and (4) scheduling a meeting with the Coordinator of Services. Students who have completed junior year may also attend the Summer Transition Program to assess their ability for regular admission. Students who do not meet the criteria are encouraged to contact the coordinator for additional consideration

ADDITIONAL INFORMATION

Students may have access to the following services: academic advising; advocacy; alternate exam arrangements including extended time, separate testing room, readers, scribes, or use of a computer; books on tape; assistive technology; equipment loans; LD specialist to provide one-on-one learning skills instruction; liaison with outside agencies; screening and referral for diagnosis of learning disabilities; and other accommodations. A 4-week Summer Transition Program is available for college-bound students with learning disabilities who have completed junior year in high school. Students do not have to be admitted to St. Ambrose to participate, and completion of the program does not guarantee admission to the college. Students take Intro to Psychology, tutoring, and study skills sessions, where they receive instruction on study skills, note-taking, textbook reading, memorization strategies, and test preparation; LD seminar, an informal discussion group on topics such as rights and responsibilities of LD, selecting accommodations, understanding LD, and self-advocacy; Socializing in College, which relates to making new friends, dealing with stress, and communication skills. Tutors attend the psych class and assist students in applying learning skills to their course work.

LEARNING DISABILITY PROGRAM/SERVICES

Learning Disability Program/Services: Services for Students with Disabilities
Director: Ryan C. Saddler
  E-Mail: SaddlerRyanC@sau.edu
  Telephone: 563-333-6275
  Fax: 563-333-6248

LEARNING DISABILITY SERVICES

Requests for the following services/accommodations will be evaluated individually based on appropriate and current documentation.

Allowed in exams
  Calculator: Yes
  Dictionary: Yes
  Computer: Yes
  Spellchecker: Yes
Extended test time: Yes
Scribes: Yes
Proctors: Yes
Oral exams: Yes
Note-takers: Yes

Distraction-reduced environment: Yes
Tape recording in class: Yes
Books on tape from RFBD: Yes
Taping of books not from RFBD: Yes
Accommodations for students with ADHD: Yes
Reading machine: Yes
Other assistive technology: Yes
Priority registration: Yes

Added costs for services: No
LD specialists: Yes
Professional tutors: NR
Peer tutors: No
Max. hours/wk. for services: Unlimited
How professors are notified of LD/ADHD: By both student and director

GENERAL ADMISSIONS INFORMATION

Director of Admissions: Meg Halligan
Telephone: 563-333-6311

ENTRANCE REQUIREMENTS

Academic units recommended: 4 English, 3 math, 2 science (2 science labs), 3 foreign language, 3 social studies, 1 history, 4 academic electives. High school diploma is required, and GED is accepted. ACT with Writing component required. TOEFL required of all international applicants: minimum paper TOEFL 500, minimum computer TOEFL 213.

Application deadline: NR
Notification: Rolling
Average GPA: 3.18
ACT Composite middle 50% range: 19–24
SAT Math middle 50% range: NR

SAT Critical Reading middle 50% range: NR
SAT Writing middle 50% range: NR

Graduated top 10% of class: 16%
Graduated top 25% of class: 35%
Graduated top 50% of class: 61%

COLLEGE GRADUATION REQUIREMENTS

Course waivers allowed: Yes
In what course: Foreign language, PE substitutions
Course substitutions allowed: Yes
In what course: Foreign language, PE substitutions

ADDITIONAL INFORMATION

Environment: The campus is located in an urban area 180 miles west of Chicago.

Student Body
  Undergrad enrollment: 2,728
  Women: 61%
  Men: 39%
  Percent out-of-state: 46%

Cost Information
  Tuition: $20,580
  Room & board: $7,525
Housing Information
  University housing: Yes
  Percent living on campus: 48%

Greek System
  Fraternity: No
  Sorority: No
Athletics: NAIA

University of Dubuque

2000 University Avenue, Dubuque, IA 52001-5050
Phone: 319-589-3200 • Fax: 319-589-3690
E-mail: admssns@dbq.edu • Web: www.disq.edu
Support: CS • Institution type: 4-year private

LEARNING DISABILITY PROGRAM AND SERVICES

The University of Dubuque meets the requirements of the American Disability Act and provides reasonable accommodations for qualified students. The goal of the Academic Support Center is to assist all students to achieve success in college. Those wishing to receive accommodations need to meet with the Director of the Academic Support Center. A written formal request must be submitted. Documentation regarding the disability must be provided.

LD/ADHD ADMISSIONS INFORMATION

College entrance tests required: Yes
Interview required: No
Essay recommended: Yes
Documentation required for LD: Psychoeducational evaluation
Documentation required for ADHD: Yes
Submitted to: Academic Support Center
Special Ed. HS course work accepted: Yes

Specific course requirements of all applicants: Yes
Separate application required: Yes
# of LD applications submitted each year: NR
# of LD applications accepted yearly: NR
Total # of students receiving LD services: NR
Acceptance into program means acceptance into college: Students must be admitted and enrolled prior to requesting services.

ADMISSIONS

An applicant for admission to the University of Dubuque should be a graduate of a high school or have an equivalent (GED). Applicants should have a minimum of 15 high school units of which 10 should be from academic fields (English, social studies, natural science, mathematics, foreign language). Preference is given to students in the upper one-half of their graduating class and who have an ACT score of 18 or higher. A limited number of students may be granted provisional admittance based on counselor recommendations and evidence of potential for college success. These students are admitted to the University of Dubuque Opportunity Program. The Opportunity Program provides consistent tutoring and grade monitoring in a welcoming environment.

ADDITIONAL INFORMATION

The Academic Support Center provides help for all University of Dubuque students and seminary students needing one-on-one assistance with course work, writing, study skills, and other academic matters. Students can improve their grades and study habits with the assistance of tutors, who help with a variety of subjects. The Academic Support Center's professional tutors and peer tutors have expertise in almost all academic areas taught. Specific accommodations for students with learning disabilities include the following: textbooks on tape and numerous resource materials, duplicate note pads for students who need class notes taken for them, test monitoring for students who are overly anxious about time constraints of regular classroom testing, tests read aloud to students when necessary, monitoring of progress by the Director of the Academic Support Center, and advocacy for students with academic disabilities. The Academic Support Center is dedicated to helping students get the most out of college. It offers free supplemental and supportive assistance for students in all majors and at all grade-point levels.

LEARNING DISABILITY PROGRAM/SERVICES

Learning Disability Program/Services: Academic Support Center
Director: Susanna Robey
  E-Mail: srobey@dbq.edu
  Telephone: 563-589-3218
  Fax: 563-589-3722

LEARNING DISABILITY SERVICES

Requests for the following services/accommodations will be evaluated individually based on appropriate and current documentation.

Allowed in exams
  Calculator: Yes
  Dictionary: Yes
  Computer: Yes
  Spellchecker: Yes
Extended test time: Yes
Scribes: Yes
Proctors: Yes
Oral exams: Yes
Note-takers: Yes

Distraction-reduced environment: Yes
Tape recording in class: Yes
Books on tape from RFBD: Yes
Taping of books not from RFBD: No
Accommodations for students with ADHD: Yes
Reading machine: No
Other assistive technology: Yes
Priority registration: N/A

Added costs for services: No
LD specialists: Yes
Professional tutors: 5
Peer tutors: 15
Max. hours/wk. for services: Unlimited
How professors are notified of LD/ADHD: By student

GENERAL ADMISSIONS INFORMATION

Director of Admissions: Jesse James
Telephone: 563-589-3214

ENTRANCE REQUIREMENTS

Academic units required: 4 English, 3 math, 3 science, 3 social studies, 3 academic electives. High school diploma is required, and GED is accepted. ACT with or without Writing component accepted. TOEFL required of all international applicants: minimum paper TOEFL 500, minimum computer TOEFL 275.

Application deadline: NR
Notification: Rolling
Average GPA: 3.00
ACT Composite middle 50% range: 18–23

SAT Math middle 50% range: 410–560
SAT Critical Reading middle 50% range: 400–540
SAT Writing middle 50% range: NR

Graduated top 10% of class: 10%
Graduated top 25% of class: 25%
Graduated top 50% of class: 65%

COLLEGE GRADUATION REQUIREMENTS

Course waivers allowed: No
Course substitutions allowed: No

ADDITIONAL INFORMATION

Environment: The University of Dubuque is located in Dubuque, Iowa on the Mississippi River.

Student Body
  Undergrad enrollment: 1,234
  Women: 42%
  Men: 58%
  Percent out-of-state: 57%

Cost Information
  Tuition: $17,960
  Room & board: $6,200
Housing Information
  University housing: Yes
  Percent living on campus: 85%

Greek System
  Fraternity: Yes
  Sorority: Yes
Athletics: Division III

UNIVERSITY OF IOWA

107 Calvin Hall, Iowa City, IA 52242
Phone: 319-335-3847 • Fax: 319-333-1535
E-mail: admissions@uiowa.edu • Web: www.uiowa.edu
Support: CS • Institution type: 4-year public

LEARNING DISABILITY PROGRAM AND SERVICES

The mission of LD/ADHD Services in the University of Iowa's Student Disability Services (SDS) is to facilitate individualized academic accommodations for eligible students. Each student has an assigned staff adviser who assists the student in identifying appropriate course accommodations, communicating classroom needs to faculty, accessing other related services and resources. Students with LD/ADHD who believe they will need disability services in order to have an equal educational opportunity are encouraged to self-disclose their disability to SDS as soon as possible. Students who self-disclose when applying for admission will be contacted by SDS with information about LD/ADHD services at Iowa. They are encouraged to schedule an on-campus interview with the LD/ADHD coordinator to learn more about disability services for students with LD/ADHD and about the university.

LD/ADHD ADMISSIONS INFORMATION

College entrance tests required: Yes
Interview required: No
Essay recommended: No
Documentation required for LD: Psychoeducational evaluation, www.uiowa.edu/~sds
Documentation required for ADHD: Psychoeducational evaluation, www.uiowa.edu/~sds
Submitted to: Admissions Office
Special Ed. HS course work accepted: Yes

Specific course requirements of all applicants: NR
Separate application required: No
# of LD applications submitted each year: NR
# of LD applications accepted yearly: NR
Total # of students receiving LD services: 120–200
Acceptance into program means acceptance into college: Students must be admitted and enrolled in the university first and then request services.

ADMISSIONS

General admissions require 4 years of English, 3 years of math, 3 years of social studies, 3 years of science, and 2 years of a foreign language. In-state residents must rank in top 50 percent of class or present an admission index score of 90. Nonresidents must rank in the top 30 percent or present an admission index of 100 (students with scores between 90–100 will be considered). The College of Engineering requires an ACT of 25 with a math score of 25 (minimum). There is a "special considerations" procedure for students not meeting general admission requirements who do not believe their academic record accurately reflects their ability to do college work. Students must submit a general application, transcript, and test scores; a letter disclosing the disability and requesting "special consideration," describing how the disability affected academic performance and what accommodations and compensation strategies are used to strengthen performance in deficit areas; a description of resources used and a statement explaining why the student may not have completed high school requirements, if applicable; letters from two people, not related, who can attest to the applicant's ability to be successful; and a diagnostic report verifying the disability and providing information about both the process and findings of the diagnostic assessment. The report should contain specific recommendations concerning the eligible academic accommodations, including whether the student qualifies for foreign language or math substitutions, and be signed by a licensed professional with the license number.

ADDITIONAL INFORMATION

Students requesting services and resources from Student Disability Services must self-disclose and provide satisfactory evidence of their disability-related eligibility for services. It is the responsibility of each student to determine whether or not to utilize services for which he or she is eligible. Services available through SDS for which students may be eligible on a case-by-case basis include the following: pre-admission information, new student orientation, assistance in communicating with faculty and administrators, note-taking assistance, alternative examination services, obtaining audiotapes of required reading materials, referrals to other university resources for counseling, tutoring, study skills development, and time management training. SDS notes that due to the high demand for tutoring at the university, tutors are not always available for all courses.

LEARNING DISABILITY PROGRAM/SERVICES

Learning Disability Program/Services: Student Disability Services (SDS)
Director: Dau-shen Ju, PhD
  E-Mail: daushen-ju@uiowa.edu
  Telephone: 319-335-1462
  Fax: 319-335-3973

LEARNING DISABILITY SERVICES

Requests for the following services/accommodations will be evaluated individually based on appropriate and current documentation.

Allowed in exams
  Calculator: Yes
  Dictionary: Yes
  Computer: Yes
  Spellchecker: Yes
Extended test time: Yes
Scribes: Yes
Proctors: Yes
Oral exams: No
Note-takers: Yes

Distraction-reduced environment: Yes
Tape recording in class: Yes
Books on tape from RFBD: No
Taping of books not from RFBD: Yes
Accommodations for students with
  ADHD: Yes
Reading machine: Yes
Other assistive technology: Yes
Priority registration: Yes

Added costs for services: No
LD specialists: Yes
Professional tutors: NR
Peer tutors: 50–60
Max. hours/wk. for services: 1
How professors are notified of
  LD/ADHD: By student

GENERAL ADMISSIONS INFORMATION

Director of Admissions: Michael Barron
Telephone: 319-335-3847

ENTRANCE REQUIREMENTS

Academic units required: 4 English, 3 math, 3 science, 2 foreign language, 3 social studies. **Academic units recommended:** 4 foreign language. High school diploma is required, and GED is accepted. ACT without Writing component accepted. TOEFL required of all international applicants: minimum paper TOEFL 600, minimum computer TOEFL 250.

Application deadline: 4/1
Notification: Rolling
Average GPA: 3.56
ACT Composite middle 50% range:
  23–27

SAT Math middle 50% range:
  540–670
SAT Critical Reading middle 50%
  range: 520–650
SAT Writing middle 50% range: NR

Graduated top 10% of class: 23%
Graduated top 25% of class: 54%
Graduated top 50% of class: 93%

COLLEGE GRADUATION REQUIREMENTS

Course waivers allowed: No
Course substitutions allowed: Yes
In what course: High school math deficiency, general education foreign language requirement, or both

ADDITIONAL INFORMATION

Environment: The university is on a 1,900-acre campus in a small city 180 miles east of Des Moines.

Student Body
  Undergrad enrollment: 19,915
  Women: 53%
  Men: 47%
  Percent out-of-state: 37%

Cost Information
  In-state tuition: $5,373
  Out-of-state tuition: $18,548
  Room & board: $6,912
Housing Information
  University housing: Yes
  Percent living on campus: 30%

Greek System
  Fraternity: Yes
  Sorority: Yes
Athletics: Division I

UNIVERSITY OF NORTHERN IOWA

1227 West Twenty-seventh Street, Cedar Falls, IA 50614-0018
Phone: 319-273-2281 • Fax: 319-273-2885
E-mail: admissions@uni.edu • Web: www.uni.edu
Support: S • Institution type: 4-year public

LEARNING DISABILITY PROGRAM AND SERVICES

The Office of Disability Services is dedicated to serving the special needs of students at the University of Northern Iowa. The Office of Disability Services works with students to ensure that all persons with disabilities have access to university activities, programs, and services. Specialized services are provided to enhance the overall academic, career, and personal development of each person with a physical, psychological, or learning disability. Services are available to currently enrolled students, who must apply for services, and provide appropriate documentation to substantiate the claimed disability. RUN (Restrict Us Not) is a recognized student organization, sponsored by the Office of Disability Services.

LD/ADHD ADMISSIONS INFORMATION

College entrance tests required: Yes
Interview required: N/A
Essay recommended: No
Documentation required for LD: NR
Documentation required for ADHD: NR
Submitted to: Office of Disabilities Services
Special Ed. HS course work accepted: Yes

Specific course requirements of all applicants: Yes
Separate application required: No
# of LD applications submitted each year: NR
# of LD applications accepted yearly: NR
Total # of students receiving LD services: 75
Acceptance into program means acceptance into
    college: Students must be admitted and enrolled in the
    university first and then request services.

ADMISSIONS

There is no special admission process for students with learning disabilities. Students with disabilities are considered for admission on the same basis as all other applicants, and must meet the same academic standards. Students must have 4 years of English, 3 years of math, 3 years of science, 3 years of social studies, and 2 years of academic electives (can be foreign language). The university will accept college-preparatory courses taken through the special education department of the high school. Students must rank in the top half of their class and submit either the ACT or the SAT.

ADDITIONAL INFORMATION

Services available include individualized pre-enrollment interview and orientation to disability services, preferred registration, a list of students interested in serving as academic aides, alternative testing arrangements, and auxiliary aides. The Center for Academic Achievement services all students at UNI who wish to receive additional academic support outside of the classroom. The center provides students with a variety of supportive services that will enhance academic achievement and success. Students may access help in writing assistance in any of their classes. Students may schedule a single appointment to work on a specific assignment or a regular appointment to work on a variety of assignments. Assistance with math skills is also available in the math lab. Services include one-on-one and small group instruction, individual instruction and practice through a variety of self-instructional modes, and review lessons to support the development and practice of concepts/skills taught in math courses. Drop-in hours are available.

LEARNING DISABILITY PROGRAM/SERVICES

Learning Disability Program/Services: Office of Disability Services
Director: David Towle, PhD
    E-Mail: david.towle@uni.edu
    Telephone: 319-273-2676
    Fax: 319-273-6884
Contact Person: Jane Slykhuis, Coordinator
    E-Mail: jane.slykhuis@uni.edu
    Telephone: 319-273-2676
    Fax: 319-273-6884

LEARNING DISABILITY SERVICES

Requests for the following services/accommodations will be evaluated individually based on appropriate and current documentation.

Allowed in exams
    Calculator: Yes
    Dictionary: No
    Computer: Yes
    Spellchecker: Yes
Extended test time: Yes
Scribes: Yes
Proctors: No
Oral exams: Yes
Note-takers: Yes

Distraction-reduced environment: Yes
Tape recording in class: Yes
Books on tape from RFBD: Yes
Taping of books not from RFBD: Yes
Accommodations for students with ADHD: Yes
Reading machine: Yes
Other assistive technology: No
Priority registration: Yes

Added costs for services: No
LD specialists: No
Professional tutors: No
Peer tutors: Yes
Max. hours/wk. for services: 1
How professors are notified of LD/ADHD: By both student and director

GENERAL ADMISSIONS INFORMATION

Director of Admissions: Roland Carrillo
Telephone: 319-273-2701

ENTRANCE REQUIREMENTS

Academic units required: 4 English, 3 math, 3 science, 3 social studies, 2 academic electives. **Academic units recommended:** 1 science lab, 2 foreign language. High school diploma is required, and GED is accepted. ACT with or without Writing component accepted. TOEFL required of all international applicants: minimum paper TOEFL 550, minimum computer TOEFL 213.

Application deadline: 8/15
Notification: Rolling
Average GPA: NR
ACT Composite middle 50% range: 21–26

SAT Math middle 50% range: 461–660
SAT Critical Reading middle 50% range: 490–621
SAT Writing middle 50% range: NR

Graduated top 10% of class: 18%
Graduated top 25% of class: 47%
Graduated top 50% of class: 89%

COLLEGE GRADUATION REQUIREMENTS

Course waivers allowed: Yes
In what course: The university is in the process of establishing guidelines for waiver/substitutions in math and foreign language
Course substitutions allowed: Yes
In what course: Case-by-case basis for math and foreign language

ADDITIONAL INFORMATION

Environment: The campus is in a small town about 1.5 hours from Des Moines.

Student Body
    Undergrad enrollment: 10,453
    Women: 57%
    Men: 43%
    Percent out-of-state: 5%

Cost Information
    In-state tuition: $5,086
    Out-of-state tuition: $13,002
    Room & board: $5,740
Housing Information
    University housing: Yes
    Percent living on campus: 38%

Greek System
    Fraternity: Yes
    Sorority: Yes
Athletics: Division I

WALDORF COLLEGE

106 South Sixth Street, Forest City, IA 50436
Phone: 641-585-8112 • Fax: 641-585-8125
E-mail: admissions@waldorf.edu • Web: www.waldorf.edu
Support: SP • Institution type: 4-year private

LEARNING DISABILITY PROGRAM AND SERVICES

The Learning Disabilities Program (LDP) fully integrates students with learning disabilities into mainstream courses. The program features a special orientation session, academic advising, tutoring, specialized services, and developmental courses. The LDP takes a holistic approach to address the social, emotional, and academic needs of the person with a learning disability. The LDP is learning strategies based. Students are accepted as individuals with the potential to succeed in college. The students have the opportunity to participate fully in college life and to experience academic success. Students benefit from a 12:1 student/instructor ratio; each student is provided a laptop computer to use while in attendance. To be eligible for the Waldorf LDP, students must meet the following criteria: have psychological and achievement test results, preferably no more than 2 years old; have been involved with intervention on some level during high school; and exhibit a positive attitude and potential for good college success when appropriate learning strategies and coping skills are used.

LD/ADHD ADMISSIONS INFORMATION

College entrance tests required: Yes
Interview required: Yes
Essay recommended: NR
Documentation required for LD: Psychoeducational
  evaluation
Documentation required for ADHD: Yes
Submitted to: Learning Disability Program
Special Ed. HS course work accepted: Yes

Specific course requirements of all applicants: NR
Separate application required: NR
# of LD applications submitted each year: NR
# of LD applications accepted yearly: NR
Total # of students receiving LD services: 30
**Acceptance into program means acceptance into
  college:** Students are either admitted directly into the
  college and then must request LDP or are reviewed by LDP
  committee and a joint decision is made.

ADMISSIONS

There is no special admissions process for students with learning disabilities. LDP students go through the regular admission procedures. General admission requirements include 4 years of English, 2 years of math and science; ACT 18 minimum; and a 2.0 GPA. There is a probationary admission for students not meeting the regular criteria. Students will be asked to participate in a special interview, either by phone or in person, in order to be considered for LDP. The number of spaces in LDP is limited. The stronger candidates are reviewed and admitted by the Office of Admissions; the students with weaker records, who have a documented learning disability, are reviewed by the LDP director and the Office of Admissions and they make a joint decision on admission.

ADDITIONAL INFORMATION

Services in the LDP include the following: specialized academic advising regarding schedules and academic classes; priority time and scheduling with the learning specialist; counseling services available upon referral or request; special orientation for LDP students at the beginning of the academic year, prior to the arrival of the other students; tutor time above and beyond the regular services available to all students; academic coaches who work one-on-one with students; specialized materials and/or technology for LD students; priority assignment for developmental and study skills classes; as-needed academic and psychological testing with a learning-style emphasis; instructor notification of learning disability; and academic progress monitoring that will be shared with the student, and parents if permission is given. There are skills classes for credit in study skills, math/pre-algebra, reading, and writing. There is a 1-day LD orientation prior to the beginning of the regular freshman orientation in the fall.

LEARNING DISABILITY PROGRAM/SERVICES

Learning Disability Program/Services: Learning Disability Program
Director: Michelle Sprout Murray
  E-Mail: murraym@waldorf.edu
  Telephone: 641-584-8207
  Fax: 641-584-8194

LEARNING DISABILITY SERVICES

Requests for the following services/accommodations will be evaluated individually based on appropriate and current documentation.

Allowed in exams
  Calculator: Yes
  Dictionary: Yes
  Computer: Yes
  Spellchecker: Yes
Extended test time: Yes
Scribes: No
Proctors: Yes
Oral exams: Yes
Note-takers: Yes

Distraction-reduced environment: Yes
Tape recording in class: Yes
Books on tape from RFBD: Yes
Taping of books not from RFBD: No
Accommodations for students with
  ADHD: Yes
Reading machine: No
Other assistive technology: No
Priority registration: Yes

Added costs for services: Yes
LD specialists: Yes
Professional tutors: 5
Peer tutors: 25
Max. hours/wk. for services:
  Unlimited
How professors are notified of
  LD/ADHD: By director

GENERAL ADMISSIONS INFORMATION

Director of Admissions: Scott Pitcher
Telephone: 641-585-8112

ENTRANCE REQUIREMENTS

Academic units recommended: 4 English, 3 math, 3 science, 2 foreign language, 4 history. High school diploma is required, and GED is accepted. TOEFL required of all international applicants: minimum paper TOEFL 500, minimum computer TOEFL 173.

Application deadline: NR
Notification: Rolling
Average GPA: NR
ACT Composite middle 50% range: NR

SAT Math middle 50% range: NR
SAT Critical Reading middle 50% range: NR
SAT Writing middle 50% range: NR

Graduated top 10% of class: NR
Graduated top 25% of class: NR
Graduated top 50% of class: NR

COLLEGE GRADUATION REQUIREMENTS

Course waivers allowed: No
Course substitutions allowed: Yes
In what course: NR

ADDITIONAL INFORMATION

Environment: The campus is in a small town 2.5 hours from Des Moines.

Student Body
  Undergrad enrollment: 573
  Women: 53%
  Men: 47%
  Percent out-of-state: 25%

Cost Information
  Tuition: $15,700
  Room & board: $5,670
Housing Information
  University housing: Yes
  Percent living on campus: 71%

Greek System
  Fraternity: No
  Sorority: No
Athletics: NAIA

KANSAS STATE UNIVERSITY

119 Anderson Hall, Manhattan, KS 66506
Phone: 785-532-6250 • Fax: 785-532-6393
E-mail: kstate@ksu.edu • Web: www.consider.k-state.edu
Support: CS • Institution type: 4-year public

LEARNING DISABILITY PROGRAM AND SERVICES

Kansas State provides a broad range of support services to students with learning disabilities through Disabled Student Services (DSS), as well as through numerous other university departments. Under DSS the Services for Learning Disabled Students serves as a liaison between students and instructors. The goals of the program are to recommend and provide accommodations and assistance tailored to the students' needs. Faculty and staff are sensitive to the special needs of the students and will work with them in their pursuit of educational goals. DSS works with students to plan accommodations that best aid the students to overcome areas of difficulty. DSS does not modify or reduce the content of courses. Rather, DSS helps to set up ways for students to demonstrate academic knowledge without interference from the disability. To qualify for services students must provide DSS with documentation of a learning disability that includes: a complete record of all testing administered; a signed statement from a professional documenting LD; and information about strengths and weaknesses to help plan accommodations best suited to the student's needs. Many of the services provided take time to arrange. Consequently, students are encouraged to apply for services early in the process of planning for college.

LD/ADHD ADMISSIONS INFORMATION

College entrance tests required: Yes
Interview required: No
Essay recommended: No
Documentation required for LD: WAIS–III; Woodcock-Johnson; within 3 years
Documentation required for ADHD: Yes
Submitted to: Disabled Student Services
Special Ed. HS course work accepted: Yes

Specific course requirements of all applicants: NR
Separate application required: No
# of LD applications submitted each year: 268
# of LD applications accepted yearly: NR
Total # of students receiving LD services: 380–421
Acceptance into program means acceptance into college: Students must be admitted and enrolled in the university first and then request services.

ADMISSIONS

There is no special admissions process for students with learning disabilities. Applicants must either have a 21 on the ACT or 980 SAT Reasoning, rank in the top third of their senior class, or have a 2.0 GPA (2.5 GPA for out-of-state students) in the Kansas precollege curriculum. If applicants don't meet these criteria, they may be admitted as an exception. Exceptions option: If students have encountered unusual situations that keep them from meeting the requirements they should contact the Office of Admissions. As many as 10 percent of new freshmen may be offered admission based on other measures of their ability to succeed at K-State. High schools may recommend approval of course substitutions to the Regents. Special consideration may be given when requested. The Director of Support Services may be asked to consult with admissions on individual applicants.

ADDITIONAL INFORMATION

To access support services students must provide DSS with verification of LD. A signed statement documenting LD qualifies students for services. Specific information about strengths and weaknesses help DSS plan accommodations best suited to students' needs. Students should contact Services for LD Students for services. Many services take time to arrange so early applications are encouraged. Students with LD are eligible for services such as test-taking accommodations, readers, assistance in obtaining taped texts, note-takers, taped lectures, and priority registration. Tutoring is offered in some freshman/sophomore classes. All students may attend an orientation meeting prior to registration freshman year. Special courses are offered in Enhanced University Experience to learn note-taking, textbook-reading, and test-taking skills; math review for students experiencing difficulty with arithmetic computations; intermediate algebra; and college algebra. Services are available for undergrads and graduate students.

LEARNING DISABILITY PROGRAM/SERVICES

Learning Disability Program/Services: Disability Support Services (DSS)
Director: Andrea Blair, MEd
 E-mail: andreab@ksu.edu
 Telephone: 785-532-6441
 Fax: 785-532-6457

LEARNING DISABILITY SERVICES

Requests for the following services/accommodations will be evaluated individually based on appropriate and current documentation.

Allowed in exams
 Calculator: Yes
 Dictionary: Yes
 Computer: Yes
 Spellchecker: Yes
 Extended test time: Yes
 Scribes: Yes
 Proctors: Yes
 Oral exams: Yes
 Note-takers: Yes

Distraction-reduced environment: Yes
Tape recording in class: Yes
Books on tape from RFBD: Yes
Taping of books not from RFBD: Yes
**Accommodations for students with
 ADHD:** Yes
Reading machine: Yes
Other assistive technology: Yes
Priority registration: Yes

Added costs for services: No
LD specialists: Yes
Professional tutors: No
Peer tutors: No
Max. hours/wk. for services: 3
**How professors are notified of
 LD/ADHD:** By both student and
 director

GENERAL ADMISSIONS INFORMATION

Director of Admissions: Larry Moeder
Telephone: 785-532-6250

ENTRANCE REQUIREMENTS

Academic units recommended: 4 English, 3 math, 3 science, 2 social studies, 1 history, 1 computer technology.
High school diploma is required, and GED is accepted. ACT with or without Writing component accepted.

Application deadline: NR
Notification: Rolling
Average GPA: NR
ACT Composite middle 50% range:
 21–27

SAT Math middle 50% range: NR
**SAT Critical Reading middle 50%
 range:** NR
SAT Writing middle 50% range: NR

Graduated top 10% of class: 23%
Graduated top 25% of class: 49%
Graduated top 50% of class: 78%

COLLEGE GRADUATION REQUIREMENTS

Course waivers allowed: Yes
In what course: Substitutions only. No waivers. Math and foreign language are most frequently requested.
Course substitutions allowed: Yes
In what course: Substitutions only. No waivers. Math and foreign language are most frequently requested.

ADDITIONAL INFORMATION

Environment: The university is located on 664 acres in a suburban area 125 miles west of Kansas City.

Student Body
 Undergrad enrollment: 18,591
 Women: 49%
 Men: 51%
 Percent out-of-state: 14%

Cost Information
 In-state tuition: $4,830
 Out-of-state tuition: $13,890
 Room & board: $5,912
Housing Information
 University housing: Yes
 Percent living on campus: 27%

Greek System
 Fraternity: Yes
 Sorority: Yes
Athletics: Division I

PITTSBURG STATE UNIVERSITY

1701 South Broadway, Pittsburg, KS 66762
Phone: 620-235-4251 • Fax: 620-235-6003
E-mail: psuadmit@pittstate.edu • Web: www.pittstate.edu
Support: CS • Institution type: 4-year public

LEARNING DISABILITY PROGRAM AND SERVICES

The Learning Center at Pittsburgh State University is committed to providing appropriate educational and related services to students with LD. PSU works hard to help meet the transition needs of new students with identified LD. The specific type of assistance is determined on an individual basis. Previous records and an interview determine the type and degree of assistance appropriate for the student. The main purpose of the LD Assistance Team is to assist students in understanding and preparing assignments and completing tests. They provide a minimum amount of tutoring but look to respective departments to provide these services. The key to their services is assistance. They do not provide content, information, or answers that do not reflect knowledge obtained by the student. Bright, highly motivated students with LD who are confident that they can succeed with hard work and supervision are welcomed to explore the educational possibilities at PSU.

LD/ADHD ADMISSIONS INFORMATION

College entrance tests required: No
Interview required: No
Essay recommended: No
Documentation required for LD: A recent IEP or a current diagnosis
Documentation required for ADHD: A recent 504 Plan or a current diagnosis
Submitted to: Learning Center
Special Ed. HS course work accepted: Yes

Specific course requirements of all applicants: NR
Separate application required: Yes
# of LD applications submitted each year: NR
# of LD applications accepted yearly: NR
Total # of students receiving LD services: 15–20
Acceptance into program means acceptance into college: Students must be admitted and enrolled in the university first and then request services.

ADMISSIONS

Students must meet the regular admissions criteria to the university. Applicants must meet one of the following: score an ACT composite of 21 or higher, rank in the top one-third of graduating class, or complete the precollege curriculum with a 2.0 or higher GPA (GPA) on a 4.0 scale (2.5 GPA for out-of-state students). The precollege curriculum includes: 4 years of English, 3 years of science (at least 1 must be chemistry), 3 years of math, 3 years of social sciences, and 1 semester of computer technology. Foreign language is recommended but not required. There are provisions for a small number of exceptions to the qualified admission standards above. Upon acceptance they should visit the campus in the spring, request to visit with a member of the Learning Disabilities Assistance Team, attend a summer orientation program on campus, and forward a copy of the most recent Individualized Education Program or documentation from the high school or doctor stating the nature of the LD. Once on campus, students should contact the team for an appointment to plan their study schedule at the learning center.

ADDITIONAL INFORMATION

Specific assistance is determined on an individual basis based on documentation and an interview. Services provided by the Learning Disabilities Assistance Team include: academic advising and planning; study skills strategies; testing modifications that include extended time for tests, reading multiple-choice and true-false tests verbatim, reading and defining words on a test (if the definition of that word does not give the student an unfair advantage in answering questions), and reading and explaining what is being asked on short answer and essay tests; reading and helping the student understand the notes they took in class or the notes they took from their tape-recorded lectures; writing or typing a tape recorded assignment prepared by the student; and reading and explaining the assignment to the student. They will also monitor the student's class attendance, study schedule, and free time schedule.

LEARNING DISABILITY PROGRAM/SERVICES

Learning Disability Program/Services: Learning Center
Director: Dr. Jamie Wood
  E-mail: jwood@pittstate.edu
  Telephone: 620-235-4193
  Fax: 620-235-6102

LEARNING DISABILITY SERVICES

Requests for the following services/accommodations will be evaluated individually based on appropriate and current documentation.

Allowed in exams
  Calculator: Yes
  Dictionary: Yes
  Computer: Yes
  Spellchecker: Yes
Extended test time: Yes
Scribes: No
Proctors: Yes
Oral exams: Yes
Note-takers: No

Distraction-reduced environment: Yes
Tape recording in class: Yes
Books on tape from RFBD: No
Taping of books not from RFBD: No
**Accommodations for students with
  ADHD:** Yes
Reading machine: Yes
Other assistive technology: No
Priority registration: No

Added costs for services: No
LD specialists: Yes
Professional tutors: 5
Peer tutors: 2
Max. hours/wk. for services: 40
**How professors are notified of
  LD/ADHD:** By director

GENERAL ADMISSIONS INFORMATION

Director of Admissions: Melinda Roelfs
Telephone: 620-235-4251

ENTRANCE REQUIREMENTS

Academic units recommended: 4 English, 3 math, 3 science, 3 social studies, 1 computer technology. High school diploma is required, and GED is accepted. ACT with or without Writing component accepted. TOEFL required of all international applicants: minimum paper TOEFL 520, minimum computer TOEFL 190.

Application deadline: Rolling
Notification: Rolling
Average GPA: 3.30
ACT Composite middle 50% range:
  19–24

SAT Math middle 50% range: NR
**SAT Critical Reading middle 50%
  range:** NR
SAT Writing middle 50% range: NR

Graduated top 10% of class: 13%
Graduated top 25% of class: 36%
Graduated top 50% of class: 67%

COLLEGE GRADUATION REQUIREMENTS

Course waivers allowed: No
In what course: N/A
Course substitutions allowed: No
In what course: N/A

ADDITIONAL INFORMATION

Environment: 120 miles from Kansas City and Tulsa

Student Body
  Undergrad enrollment: 5,517
  Women: 49%
  Men: 51%
  Percent out-of-state: 23%

Cost Information
  In-state tuition: $3,036
  Out-of-state tuition: $10,366
  Room & board: $4,844
Housing Information
  University housing: Yes
  Percent living on campus: 18%

Greek System
  Fraternity: Yes
  Sorority: Yes
Athletics: Division II

University of Kansas

Office of Admiss. and Scholarships, 1502 Iowa Street, Lawrence, KS 66045
Phone: 785-864-3911 • Fax: 785-864-5017
E-mail: adm@ku.edu • Web: www.ku.edu
Support: CS • Institution type: 4-year public

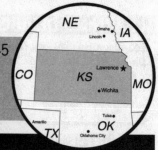

LEARNING DISABILITY PROGRAM AND SERVICES

The university accommodates the student with LD by understanding the student's ability and individualizing the services as much as possible. KU's philosophy is one of mainstreaming students with disabilities, including LD. Thus, there are no special classes, resource rooms, tutoring services, or other services specifically for the student with an LD. Course requirements and academic standards are not reduced. Rather, once the LD is adequately documented, the student receives classroom accommodations to meet specific individual needs. The Services for Students with Disabilities (SSD) also serves as a referral agent to other resources at the university and in the Lawrence community. Integration and mainstreaming, decentralized services with appropriate accommodations centrally coordinated, and student involvement and responsibility are critical aspects of the university's philosophy. Documentation is necessary and should include a recent diagnostic report of LD, and LD programs and progress will need to be identified. Students are encouraged to begin planning early so that programs are in place at the beginning of the semester to facilitate studies. The goal of SSD is to facilitate independence in preparation for needs after graduation.

LD/ADHD ADMISSIONS INFORMATION

College entrance tests required: Yes
Interview required: No
Essay recommended: No
Documentation required for LD: WAIS–III; WJ–III
Documentation required for ADHD: Yes
Submitted to: Services for Students with Disabilities
Special Ed. HS course work accepted: Yes

Specific course requirements of all applicants: NR
Separate application required: No
# of LD applications submitted each year: NR
# of LD applications accepted yearly: NR
Total # of students receiving LD services: 256
Acceptance into program means acceptance into college: Student must be admitted and enrolled in the university first (they can appeal a denial) and then request services.

ADMISSIONS

All applicants are admitted using the same criteria. Students unable to meet admission criteria because of LD should submit a personal statement providing additional information, such as no foreign language taken in high school because of the LD. Applicants should contact SSD for information and an early assessment of needs. It is important to include recent documentation or diagnosis, samples of students' work, and parent and student statements regarding educational history. Regular admission requires (1) 2.5 GPA in Board of Regents courses including 4 years of English, 3 years of college-prep math, 3 years of natural science, 3 years of social science, 2 years of a foreign language, (2) an ACT of 24 and a 2.0 GPA, or (3) a 3.0 GPA and no cutoff on the ACT. The university is very concerned that a student with LD be competitive in this academic environment. If admission criteria are not met because of LD, the applicant should submit documentation and counselor recommendation, and the director of SSD will review and make a recommendation to the Admissions Office to waive requirements.

ADDITIONAL INFORMATION

Skill workshops are available in study skills, time management, listening, note-taking, calculus, speed and reading comprehension, learning a foreign language, and preparing for exams. SSD also serves as an advocate or liaison for students. Tutoring services for students who meet qualifications are available through Supportive Educational Services at no cost. Private tutors can also be hired by the student for specific subjects. In neither instance are the tutors specifically trained regarding learning disabilities. SSD does not offer a reduced standard for academic performance, special classes, supplemental instruction, a learning center, special tutorial program, or exemption to graduation requirements. Services and accommodations are available for undergraduate and graduate students.

LEARNING DISABILITY PROGRAM/SERVICES

Learning Disability Program/Services: Services for Students with Disabilities
Director: Mary Ann Rasnak
  E-mail: mrasnak@ku.edu
  Telephone: 785-864-2620
  Fax: 785-864-2817

LEARNING DISABILITY SERVICES

Requests for the following services/accommodations will be evaluated individually based on appropriate and current documentation.

Allowed in exams
  Calculator: Yes
  Dictionary: Yes
  Computer: Yes
  Spellchecker: Yes
Extended test time: Yes
Scribes: Yes
Proctors: Yes
Oral exams: Yes
Note-takers: Yes

Distraction-reduced environment: Yes
Tape recording in class: Yes
Books on tape from RFBD: Yes
Taping of books not from RFBD: Yes
Accommodations for students with ADHD: Yes
Reading machine: Yes
Other assistive technology: Yes
Priority registration: No

Added costs for services: No
LD specialists: Yes
Professional tutors: NR
Peer tutors: 75
Max. hours/wk. for services: Unlimited
How professors are notified of LD/ADHD: By both student and director

GENERAL ADMISSIONS INFORMATION

Director of Admissions: Lisa Pinamonti Kress
Telephone: 785-864-3911

ENTRANCE REQUIREMENTS
Academic units required: 4 English, 3 math, 3 science, 3 social studies, 2 foreign language, 1 computer technology (1 unit) **Academic units recommended:** 4 English, 4 math, 3 science, 2 foreign language, 3 social studies, 1 computer technology (1 unit). High school diploma is required, and GED is accepted. ACT with Writing component required.

Application deadline: 4/1
Notification: Rolling
Average GPA: 3.40
ACT Composite middle 50% range: 22–28

SAT Math middle 50% range: NR
SAT Critical Reading middle 50% range: NR
SAT Writing middle 50% range: NR

Graduated top 10% of class: 28%
Graduated top 25% of class: 55%
Graduated top 50% of class: 88%

COLLEGE GRADUATION REQUIREMENTS

Course waivers allowed: No
Course substitutions allowed: Yes
In what course: Foreign language, math

ADDITIONAL INFORMATION

Environment: The 1,000-acre campus is located in a small city 40 miles west of Kansas City.

Student Body
  Undergrad enrollment: 20,979
  Women: 50%
  Men: 50%
  Percent out-of-state: 23%

Cost Information
  In-state tuition: $5,513
  Out-of-state tuition: $14,483
  Room & board: $5,747
Housing Information
  University housing: Yes
  Percent living on campus: 22%

Greek System
  Fraternity: Yes
  Sorority: Yes
Athletics: Division I

BLUEGRASS COMMUNITY AND TECHNICAL COLLEGE

208 Oswald Building, Cooper Drive, Lexington, KY 40506
Phone: 859-257-4872 • Fax: 859-257-2634
E-mail: eabel10@uky.edu • Web: www.bluegrass.kctcs.edu
Support: S • Institution type: 2-year public

LEARNING DISABILITY PROGRAM AND SERVICES

Bluegrass Community and Technical College (BCTC) has made a firm commitment to providing high-quality postsecondary education to persons with disabilities. The Office of Services for Students with Disabilities seeks to ensure equal access and full participation for persons with disabilities in postsecondary education, and empower students to obtain the life skills necessary for a fulfilling, productive lifestyle after leaving BCTC. Students can request services by visiting Disability Support Services (DSS). Full participation in the DSS program is encouraged from the initial admission contact throughout the student's academic career. Positive peer contacts as well as guidance from the DSS coordinator and other faculty and staff also play a major role in encouraging participation in the DSS program.

LD/ADHD ADMISSIONS INFORMATION

College entrance tests required: No
Interview required: No
Essay recommended: No
Documentation required for LD: A comprehensive assessment battery and the resulting diagnostic report, which includes a diagnostic interview, assessment of aptitude, academic achievement, information processing, and diagnosis.
Documentation required for ADHD: A comprehensive assessment battery and the resulting diagnostic report, which includes a diagnostic interview, assessment of aptitude, academic achievement, information processing, and diagnosis.

Submitted to: Services for Students with Disabilities
Special Ed. HS course work accepted: Yes
Specific course requirements of all applicants: NR
Separate application required: No
# of LD applications submitted each year: NR
# of LD applications accepted yearly: NR
Total # of students receiving LD services: NR
Acceptance into program means acceptance into college: Students must be admitted and enrolled at LCC and then may request services.

ADMISSIONS

BCTC offers open-door admission to all applicants who meet the following requirements: proof of a high school diploma or the GED; ACT for placement not admission; 4 years of English, Algebra I and II, biology, chemistry or physics, U.S. history, and geometry. Any areas of deficiency can be made up at BCTC before enrolling in college courses; there is no required GPA or class rank. Students may live in the residence halls at the University of Kentucky and attend classes at BCTC, which is located on the same campus as the university. There is an articulation agreement between BCTC and the University of Kentucky. Students wishing to apply to Project Success must submit a separate application, call for an appointment, and bring supporting materials.

ADDITIONAL INFORMATION

DSS provides a full range of services, including academic advising, career counseling, supportive counseling, specialized computer software, recorded textbooks, note-takers, readers, writers/scribes, tutors, and testing accommodation. The DSS coordinator serves as student liaison with college faculty, staff, and administrators; vocational rehabilitational counselors; and various other social service agencies. A case-management approach is used to ensure continuity of services between agencies. LD assessments are available on campus for $175–$200. Study Strategies is offered for college credit. The Athena Club is a student organization created to assume an advocacy role on behalf of students with disabilities at BCTC through education, recruiting, support groups, and social opportunities.

LEARNING DISABILITY PROGRAM/SERVICES

Learning Disability Program/Services: Disability Support Services
Director: Veronica Miller
E-mail: veronica.miller@kctcs.edu
Telephone: 859-246-6530
Fax: 859-246-4678

LEARNING DISABILITY SERVICES

Requests for the following services/accommodations will be evaluated individually, based on appropriate and current documentation.

Allowed in exams
Calculator: Yes
Dictionary: Yes
Computer: Yes
Spellchecker: Yes
Extended test time: Yes
Scribes: Yes
Proctors: Yes
Oral exams: Yes
Note-takers: Yes

Distraction-reduced environment: Yes
Tape recording in class: Yes
Books on tape from RFBD: Yes
Taping of books not from RFBD: Yes
Accommodations for students with ADHD: Yes
Reading machine: Yes
Other assistive technology: Yes
Priority registration: No
Added costs for services: No

LD specialists: No
Professional tutors: NR
Peer tutors: Yes
Max. hours/wk. for services: 2
How professors are notified of LD/ADHD: By director

GENERAL ADMISSIONS INFORMATION

Director of Admissions: Shelblie Hugle
Telephone: 859-257-4872

ENTRANCE REQUIREMENTS

Academic units recommended: 4 English, 3 math, 3 science, 3 U.S. history. Course deficiencies can be made up at BCTC. Open admissions. High school diploma or GED accepted. ACT is used for placement but not for admissions. GPA and class rank are not required.

Application deadline: NR
Notification: NR
Average GPA: NR
ACT Composite middle 50% range: NR

SAT Math middle 50% range: NR
SAT Critical Reading middle 50% range: NR
SAT Writing middle 50% range: NR

Graduated top 10% of class: NR
Graduated top 25% of class: NR
Graduated top 50% of class: NR

COLLEGE GRADUATION REQUIREMENTS

Course waivers allowed: No
Course substitutions allowed: Yes
In what course: Students may request subsitutions for courses with the approriate documentation

ADDITIONAL INFORMATION

Environment: The college is located on the campus of the University of Kentucky.

Student Body
Women: 58%
Men: 42%
Percent out-of-state: 5%

Cost Information
In-state tuition: $3,000
Out-of-state tuition: $7,700
Room & board: $5,840
Housing Information
University housing: Yes
Percent living on campus: 1%

Greek System
Fraternity: Yes
Sorority: No
Athletics: Intramural

EASTERN KENTUCKY UNIVERSITY

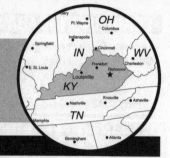

SSB CPO 54, 521 Lancaster Avenue, Richmond, KY 40475
Phone: 859-622-2106 • Fax: 859-622-8024
E-mail: admissions@eku.edu. • Web: www.eku.edu
Support: CS • Institution type: 4-year public

LEARNING DISABILITY PROGRAM AND SERVICES

The mission of Project SUCCESS is to respond effectively and efficiently to the individual educational needs of eligible university students with learning disabilities through a cost-effective, flexible program of peer tutors, workshops, group support, and program referral. Upon admittance Project SUCCESS develops an individualized program of services that serve to enhance the academic success of each student. The services a student utilizes will be determined in a conference between the student and the program director. All services are offered free of charge to the student. EKU also offers a summer transition program for students with learning disabilities. The program is designed to smooth the transition between high school and college. To apply for participation in Project SUCCESS, students are encouraged to visit both the campus and the Office of Services for Students with Disabilities. The student will be asked to fill out an application and provide appropriate, current documentation of the disability. The application for services through Project SUCCESS is in no way connected to admission to EKU.

LD/ADHD ADMISSIONS INFORMATION

College entrance tests required: Yes
Interview required: Yes
Essay recommended: No
Documentation required for LD: Adult scales for both aptitude and achievement; usually the WAIS and the Woodcock-Johnson Test of Achievement
Documentation required for ADHD: Specific details of diagnosis describing functional limitations; please refer to our "Disability Documentation Guidelines"
Submitted to: Project SUCCESS

Special Ed. HS course work accepted: Yes
Specific course requirements of all applicants: Yes
Separate application required: Yes
# of LD applications submitted each year: 60
# of LD applications accepted yearly: 50
Total # of students receiving LD services: 225
Acceptance into program means acceptance into college: Students must be in the process of admittance to apply to Project SUCCESS.

ADMISSIONS

There are no special admissions criteria for students with learning disabilities. Students must be admitted and enrolled in the university in order to be eligible for entrance into Project SUCCESS. Full admission includes a 2.0 GPA and high school diploma, GED, or distance-learning degree; ACT 18 (with no score below 18 in English, Math, and Reading); and students must meet the Kentucky precollege curriculum or its equivalent ACT scores of 21 in English, 20 in Math, 22 in Reading, and 21 in Science Reasoning. Students not meeting probationary admission (2.0 GPA, GED, or distance-learning diploma, etc; ACT 15–17) may apply to attend EKU through a retention support program by applying for special admission. Collaborating retention support programs include Project SUCCESS.

ADDITIONAL INFORMATION

Project SUCCESS services provided include one-on-one tutoring, note-taking services, books on tape, test accommodations, advocacy, weekly seminars. Skills classes are offered in study skills, reading skills, weekly workshops in transition, time management, learning and study strategies, test-taking skills, developmental math, developmental reading, and developmental writing. Planning to Win is a summer transitions program specifically designed for high school juniors and graduating seniors with learning disabilities, attention deficit hyperactivity disorder, and other cognitive disorders. The program is geared towards high school students who are planning to attend college in the fall, as well as those who are only exploring postsecondary educational options at any college. Students will attend 2 days of educational and inspiring workshops and fellowship with current college students, and spend the night in an EKU residence hall. All services and accommodations are available for undergraduate and graduate students.

LEARNING DISABILITY PROGRAM/SERVICES

Learning Disability Program/Services: Project SUCCESS
Director: Teresa Belluscio
  E-mail: Teresa.belluscio@eku.edu
  Telephone: 859-622-2933
  Fax: 859-622-6794

LEARNING DISABILITY SERVICES

Requests for the following services/accommodations will be evaluated individually based on appropriate and current documentation.

Allowed in exams	**Distraction-reduced environment:** Yes	**Added costs for services:** No
Calculator: Yes	**Tape recording in class:** Yes	**LD specialists:** Yes
Dictionary: Yes	**Books on tape from RFBD:** Yes	**Professional tutors:** No
Computer: Yes	**Taping of books not from RFBD:** Yes	**Peer tutors:** 25
Spellchecker: Yes	**Accommodations for students with**	**Max. hours/wk. for services:**
Extended test time: Yes	**ADHD:** Yes	Unlimited
Scribes: Yes	**Reading machine:** Yes	**How professors are notified of**
Proctors: Yes	**Other assistive technology:** Yes	**LD/ADHD:** By student
Oral exams: Yes	**Priority registration:** Yes	
Note-takers: Yes		

GENERAL ADMISSIONS INFORMATION

Director of Admissions: Stephen Byrn
Telephone: 859-622-2106

ENTRANCE REQUIREMENTS

Academic units required: 4 English, 3 math, 3 science (1 science lab), 2 foreign language, 3 social studies, 7 academic electives, 3 health, 1.5 physical education, and 1 art. High school diploma is required, and GED is accepted. ACT with or without Writing component accepted. TOEFL required of all international applicants: minimum paper TOEFL 500, minimum computer TOEFL 173.

Application deadline: 8/1	**SAT Math middle 50% range:**	**Graduated top 10% of class:** NR
Notification: Rolling	440–550	**Graduated top 25% of class:** NR
Average GPA: 3.12	**SAT Critical Reading middle 50%**	**Graduated top 50% of class:** NR
ACT Composite middle 50% range:	**range:** NR	
18–23	**SAT Writing middle 50% range:** NR	

COLLEGE GRADUATION REQUIREMENTS

Course waivers allowed: Yes
In what course: Waivers and substitutions are determined on a case-by-case basis.
Course substitutions allowed: Yes
In what course: Waivers and substitutions are determined on a case-by-case basis.

ADDITIONAL INFORMATION

Environment: The university is located on 350 acres in a small town 20 miles south of Lexington.

Student Body	**Cost Information**	**Greek System**
Undergrad enrollment: 12,813	**In-state tuition:** $5,192	**Fraternity:** Yes
Women: 60%	**Out-of-state tuition:** $14,538	**Sorority:** Yes
Men: 40%	**Room & board:** $4,906	**Athletics:** Division I
Percent out-of-state: 12%	**Housing Information**	
	University housing: Yes	
	Percent living on campus: 26%	

THOMAS MORE COLLEGE

333 Thomas More Parkway, Crestview Hill, KY 41017-3495
Phone: 859-344-3332 • Fax: 859-344-3444
E-mail: admissions@thomasmore.edu • Web: www.thomasmore.edu
Support: S • Institution type: 4-year private

LEARNING DISABILITY PROGRAM AND SERVICES

Thomas More College's Student Support Services program is committed to the individual academic, personal, cultural/social, and financial needs of the student. It is committed to promoting sensitivity and cultural awareness of the population served and to promoting varied on/off campus services and events that enhance the student's educational opportunities. A variety of support services are offered, including developmental courses, peer tutoring, and individual counseling. Students with deficits in speech/language, study skills, written expression, ongoing additional skills, perceptual skills, reading, speaking, math, fine motor, and ADHD with or without LD are admissible. Students may need 5 years to graduate. The college offers small classes, excellent faculty, and solid preparation for the future.

LD/ADHD ADMISSIONS INFORMATION

College entrance tests required: Yes
Interview required: No
Essay recommended: No
Documentation required for LD: Psychoeducational
    evaluation
Documentation required for ADHD: Yes
Submitted to: Student Support Services
Special Ed. HS course work accepted: Yes

Specific course requirements of all applicants: Yes
Separate application required: No
# of LD applications submitted each year: NR
# of LD applications accepted yearly: NR
Total # of students receiving LD services: 10
Acceptance into program means acceptance into
    college: Students must be admitted and enrolled in the
    university first and then request services.

ADMISSIONS

There is no separate application required for an applicant with learning disabilities. All students must submit the general application for admission. A Student Support Services staff person is part of the Admissions Committee. Students with learning disabilities may be conditionally admitted so that they can receive extra support. General admission criteria include a recommendation for 4 years of English, 2 years of math, 2 years of science, 2 years of social studies, and 2 years of a foreign language. Foreign language, and possibly math requirements, may be substituted for: ACT 19–23 or 950 SAT; rank in top half of class; and a B-minus average. The college can waive ACT/SAT scores after considering the student's LD status. A WAIS–R is not required, but diagnostic testing is encouraged before enrolling, as it is required to be on file before students can access services.

ADDITIONAL INFORMATION

Students with learning disabilities could be limited to 12–13 hours the first semester. Student progress will be monitored. Some students may be required to take developmental courses based on the college's assessment of reading, writing, and math skills. Skills classes are paired with World History, and there is college credit for skill classes in study skills, reading, and math. Some students are admitted on a conditional status and are given additional support through Student Support Services.

LEARNING DISABILITY PROGRAM/SERVICES

Learning Disability Program/Services: Student Support Services
Director: Barbara S. Davis
E-mail: barb.davis@thomasmore.edu
Telephone: 606-344-3521
Fax: 606-433-3638

LEARNING DISABILITY SERVICES

Requests for the following services/accommodations will be evaluated individually based on appropriate and current documentation.

Allowed in exams
  Calculator: No
  Dictionary: NR
  Computer: No
  Spellchecker: No
Extended test time: Yes
Scribes: Yes
Proctors: Yes
Oral exams: Yes
Note-takers: Yes

Distraction-reduced environment: Yes
Tape recording in class: Yes
Books on tape from RFBD: NR
Taping of books not from RFBD: Yes
Accommodations for students with
  ADHD: Yes
Reading machine: No
Other assistive technology: No
Priority registration: No

Added costs for services: No
LD specialists: No
Professional tutors: 2
Peer tutors: 15
Max. hours/wk. for services:
  Unlimited
How professors are notified of
  LD/ADHD: By student

GENERAL ADMISSIONS INFORMATION

Director of Admissions: Angela Griffin-Jones, Vice President for Enrollment Management and Marketing
Telephone: 859-344-3332

ENTRANCE REQUIREMENTS

Academic units required: 4 English, 3 math, 3 science (1 science lab), 2 foreign language, 3 social studies.
Academic units recommended: 2 arts appreciation and computer literacy. High school diploma is required, and GED is accepted. TOEFL required of all international applicants: minimum paper TOEFL 515, minimum computer TOEFL 187.

Application deadline: Rolling
Notification: Rolling
Average GPA: 2.88
ACT Composite middle 50% range:
  19–24

SAT Math middle 50% range:
  460–600
SAT Critical Reading middle 50%
  range: 460–580
SAT Writing middle 50% range: NR

Graduated top 10% of class: 7%
Graduated top 25% of class: 31%
Graduated top 50% of class: 85%

COLLEGE GRADUATION REQUIREMENTS

Course waivers allowed: Yes
In what course: Foreign language and math
Course substitutions allowed: No

ADDITIONAL INFORMATION

Environment: The college is located on a 160-acre campus 8 miles from Cincinnati.

Student Body
  Undergrad enrollment: 1,371
  Women: 51%
  Men: 49%
  Percent out-of-state: 38%

Cost Information
  Tuition: $19,500
  Room & board: $6,150
Housing Information
  University housing: Yes
  Percent living on campus: 20%

Greek System
  Fraternity: No
  Sorority: No
  Athletics: Division III

UNIVERSITY OF KENTUCKY

100 Funkhouser Building, Lexington, KY 40506
Phone: 859-257-2000 • Fax: 859-257-3823
E-mail: admission@uky.edu • Web: www.uky.edu
Support: CS • Institution type: 4-year public

LEARNING DISABILITY PROGRAM AND SERVICES

The goal of the Disability Resource Center is to provide equal access to students who are eligible. We advocate for reasonable accommodations, removal of barriers, and acceptance of different learning methods. In partnership with students, faculty, and staff, our purpose is to achieve an accessible educational environment where students with disabilities have an equal opportunity to fully participate in all aspects of the university community. Students with learning disabilities may find the transition to college challenging. Typical concerns may include one or more of the following: slow reading/processing rate; poor memory skills; problems organizing and sequencing ideas; frequent spelling errors; difficulty taking notes; low math reasoning; problems with basic math operations; poor study skills; difficulty organizing, planning, and completing tasks. With reasonable classroom accommodations and individualized learning strategies, students can generally learn to compensate for these problems and manage their academic expectations competently. It is recommended that students with learning disabilities who are preparing to enter University of Kentucky register with the Disability Resource Center (DRC) soon after acceptance. The DRC can play a vital role in providing students with information, strategies, other campus resources, and support to improve their efforts in making these transitions and completing their educational degree programs. Students must provide a current psychological assessment or medical assessment using adult measures and complete results as documentation of their diagnosis to the DRC, and schedule an appointment to discuss their accommodation needs. IEPs or 504 Plans or Transition Plans are useful but cannot be used to document a disability.

LD/ADHD ADMISSIONS INFORMATION

College entrance tests required: Yes
Interview required: No
Essay recommended: No
Documentation required for LD: A current comprehensive psychoeducational report
Documentation required for ADHD: A current psychological report or medical statement indicating diagnosis
Submitted to: Disability Resources Center
Special Ed. HS course work accepted: No

Specific course requirements of all applicants: Yes
Separate application required: No
# of LD applications submitted each year: 200–250
# of LD applications accepted yearly: 200–250
Total # of students receiving LD services: 550–600
Acceptance into program means acceptance into college: Students must be admitted and enrolled prior to requesting services.

ADMISSIONS

The University of Kentucky subscribes to a selective admission policy. The academic criteria are established by a faculty committee of the University Senate. The admission decision is based on factors, including cumulative high school grade point average, completion of the precollege curriculum, ACT or SAT Reasoning score results, and special talents and abilities. High school minimum GPA is 2.0 to 2.49 with an average of 3.55. High school courses required: 4 English, 3 math, 3 science, 2 foreign language, 3 social studies, 5 academic electives, 1 health/physical education, and 1 visual/performing arts.

ADDITIONAL INFORMATION

The Academic Enhancement Program, referred to as The Study, helps students reach their academic goals. The Study includes academic study groups, tutoring, and learning skills workshops. Programs are purposefully designed to foster interactions that promote learning strategies and attitudes toward academic life that are characteristic of successful college students. The Writing Center offers free individual or group consultations for students, faculty, and staff. The Writing Center provides help for many kinds of writing: class assignments, creative writing, dissertations, scholarly monographs, grant applications, reports, articles, scholarship applications, and more. The Math Resource Center (Mathskeller) is specifically designed for students studying mathematics courses at the University of Kentucky, and tutors are free and available.

LEARNING DISABILITY PROGRAM/SERVICES

Learning Disability Program/Services: Disability Resource Center
Director: Jake Karnes
E-mail: jkarnes@uky.edu
Telephone: 859-257-2754
Fax: 859-257-1980

Contact Person: Leisa Pickering, PhD
E-mail: jkarnes@uky.edu
Telephone: 859-257-2754
Fax: 859-257-1980

LEARNING DISABILITY SERVICES

Requests for the following services/accommodations will be evaluated individually based on appropriate and current documentation.

Allowed in exams
 Calculator: No
 Dictionary: No
 Computer: Yes
 Spellchecker: No
Extended test time: Yes
Scribes: Yes
Proctors: Yes
Oral exams: Yes
Note-takers: No

Distraction-reduced environment: Yes
Tape recording in class: Yes
Books on tape from RFBD: Yes
Taping of books not from RFBD: Yes
Accommodations for students with ADHD: Yes
Reading machine: Yes
Other assistive technology: Yes
Priority registration: Yes

Added costs for services: No
LD specialists: Yes
Professional tutors: NR
Peer tutors: N/A
Max. hours/wk. for services: Unlimited
How professors are notified of LD/ADHD: By student

GENERAL ADMISSIONS INFORMATION

Director of Admissions: Donald Witt
Telephone: 859-257-2000

ENTRANCE REQUIREMENTS

Academic units required: 4 English, 3 math, 3 science, 2 foreign language, 3 social studies, 5 academic electives, 2 fine or performing arts, 1 health and physical education. **Academic units recommended:** 4 English, 4 math, 4 science, 2 foreign language, 3 social studies, 3 academic electives, 2 fine or performing arts, 1 Health and physical education. High school diploma is required, and GED is accepted. ACT with or without Writing component accepted. TOEFL required of all international applicants: minimum paper TOEFL 527, minimum computer TOEFL 197.

Application deadline: 2/15
Notification: Rolling
Average GPA: 3.55
ACT Composite middle 50% range: 22–27

SAT Math middle 50% range: 520–640
SAT Critical Reading middle 50% range: 510–630
SAT Writing middle 50% range: NR

Graduated top 10% of class: 28%
Graduated top 25% of class: 57%
Graduated top 50% of class: 86%

COLLEGE GRADUATION REQUIREMENTS

Course waivers allowed: No
Course substitutions allowed: Yes
In what course: Possibly in math, statistics, logic, and foreign language, depending on the individual circumstances.

ADDITIONAL INFORMATION

Environment: The university is located on 687 acres in the city of Lexington.

Student Body
 Undergrad enrollment: 18,416
 Women: 52%
 Men: 48%
 Percent out-of-state: 17%

Cost Information
 In-state tuition: $5,782
 Out-of-state tuition: $13,242
 Room & board: $7,262
Housing Information
 University housing: Yes
 Percent living on campus: 29%

Greek System
 Fraternity: Yes
 Sorority: Yes
Athletics: Division I

WESTERN KENTUCKY UNIVERSITY

Potter Hall 117, 1906 College Heights Boulevard,
Bowling Green, KY 42101-1020 • Phone: 270-745-2551
Fax: 270-745-6133 • E-mail: admission@wku.edu • Web: www.wku.edu
Support: CS • Institution type: 4-year public

LEARNING DISABILITY PROGRAM AND SERVICES

The goal of the Office of Affirmative Action is to foster the full and self-directed participation of persons with disabilities attending the university. The service is established to facilitate the participation of students at Western Kentucky University by providing information on services, acting as liaison with faculty and staff for reasonable accommodation, and providing learning disability services. Office for Disability Services (ODS) coordinates support services so that students can be self-sufficient and can develop to their maximum academic potential. To be eligible for these services, documentation from a licensed professional must be provided. This documentation must be no more than 3 years old, state the nature of the disability, and clearly describe the kinds of accommodations recommended. Once accepted students should provide the documentation; discuss the disability and ways to accommodate special needs; arrange to take placement tests and register for classes early; contact instructors to learn what each instructor will require in terms of grading criteria, amount of weekly reading, and number and types of homework assignments and tests; order books on tape; and request alternative testing conditions, note-takers, and readers. Students needing specialized help beyond that offered by the university may need to seek financial assistance.

LD/ADHD ADMISSIONS INFORMATION

College entrance tests required: Yes
Interview required: Yes
Essay recommended: No
Documentation required for LD: Psychoeducational evaluation or Completed Student Disability Verification Form (providing by SDS)
Documentation required for ADHD: Psychoeducational evaluation or Completed Student Verification Form by a licensed professional. Documentation must be no more than two pages.
Submitted to: Office for Disability Services
Special Ed. HS course work accepted: Yes

Specific course requirements of all applicants: Yes
Separate application required: No
# of LD applications submitted each year: 100
# of LD applications accepted yearly: 100
Total # of students receiving LD services: 380
Acceptance into program means acceptance into college: Students must be admitted and enrolled in the university first and then request services.

ADMISSIONS

There is no special admissions process for students with learning disabilities. All applicants must meet the same admission criteria. High school courses required include: 4 years of English, 3 years of math, 2 years of social science, and 2 years of science lab (biology, physics, and chemistry). In-state residents must have a minimum 2.3 GPA or 18 ACT; out-of-state students must have a minimum 2.3 GPA and 18 ACT or 990 SAT. Factors considered for admission are ACT/SAT, high school performance, any postsecondary record, recommendations, personal qualifications and conduct, interview, and complete and accurate information listed on the application for admission. Students can be admitted by exception through the Director of Admissions. Western Kentucky University's community college will admit students who do not meet high school course requirements.

ADDITIONAL INFORMATION

The program for students with LD offers students: adapted test administrations; taped textbooks; short-term loan of special equipment; reading referral services; faculty liaison; peer tutoring; academic, personal, and career counseling; and assistance with the Reading and Learning labs. Academic advisors assist students in course selection. The university combines intensive academic advisement with special seminars to provide support during the freshman year. The University Counseling Services Center provides assistance in personal, social, emotional, and intellectual development. Skills classes are offered in math, reading, vocabulary, study skills, and English through the community college. College credit is given for these classes. Services and accommodations are available for undergraduate and graduate students.

LEARNING DISABILITY PROGRAM/SERVICES

Learning Disability Program/Services: Office for Student Disability Services
Director: Matt Davis, Coordinator
   E-mail: matt.davis@wku.edu
   Telephone: 502-745-5004
   Fax: 502-745-3623

LEARNING DISABILITY SERVICES

Requests for the following services/accommodations will be evaluated individually based on appropriate and current documentation.

Allowed in exams
  Calculator: Yes
  Dictionary: Yes
  Computer: Yes
  Spellchecker: Yes
Extended test time: Yes
Scribes: Yes
Proctors: Yes
Oral exams: Yes
Note-takers: Yes

Distraction-reduced environment: Yes
Tape recording in class: Yes
Books on tape from RFBD: Yes
Taping of books not from RFBD: Yes
Accommodations for students with
  ADHD: Yes
Reading machine: No
Other assistive technology: Yes
Priority registration: Yes

Added costs for services: No
LD specialists: Yes
Professional tutors: 25
Peer tutors: 20
Max. hours/wk. for services:
  Unlimited
How professors are notified of
  LD/ADHD: By both student and
  director

GENERAL ADMISSIONS INFORMATION

Director of Admissions: Dr. Dean R. Kahler
Telephone: 270-745-2551

ENTRANCE REQUIREMENTS

Academic units required: 4 English, 3 math, 3 science (1 science lab), 2 foreign language, 3 social studies, 1.5 credits each: health and physical education, history, performing arts. High school diploma is required, and GED is accepted. ACT with or without Writing component accepted. TOEFL required of all international applicants: minimum paper TOEFL 525, minimum computer TOEFL 197.

Application deadline: 8/1
Notification: Immediately
Average GPA: 3.15
ACT Composite middle 50% range:
  18–24

SAT Math middle 50% range:
  450–560
SAT Critical Reading middle 50%
  range: 440–550
SAT Writing middle 50% range: NR

Graduated top 10% of class: 17%
Graduated top 25% of class: 39%
Graduated top 50% of class: 69%

COLLEGE GRADUATION REQUIREMENTS

Course waivers allowed: Yes
In what course: Courses that can be substituted are handled on a case-by-case basis.
Course substitutions allowed: Yes
In what course: NR

ADDITIONAL INFORMATION

Environment: The university is located on 200 acres in a suburban area 65 miles north of Nashville.

Student Body
  Undergrad enrollment: 15,415
  Women: 58%
  Men: 42%
  Percent out-of-state: 17%

Cost Information
  In-state tuition: $5,952
  Out-of-state tuition: $14,440
  Room & board: $5,348
Housing Information
  University housing: Yes
  Percent living on campus: 31%

Greek System
  Fraternity: Yes
  Sorority: Yes
Athletics: Division I

LOUISIANA COLLEGE

1140 College Drive, PO Box 560, Pineville, LA 71359-0560
Phone: 318-487-7259 • Fax: 318-487-7550
E-mail: admissions@lacollege.edu • Web: www.lacollege.edu
Support: SP • Institution type: 4-year private

LEARNING DISABILITY PROGRAM AND SERVICES

The goal of the Program to Assist Student Success (PASS) is to facilitate the academic success of students with disabilities and to serve as an advocate for the students. This highly individualized, limited enrollment program provides support services and personal attention to students who need special academic counseling, tutoring, or classroom assistance. Three levels of services are provided. Level I students are required to attend weekly individual counseling and tutoring sessions; the emphasis at this level is to provide individualized help to ensure the student's successful transition to college and to compensate for any identifiable disability. Level II students have, at a minimum, completed 24 hours of college credit at Louisiana College with at least a 2.5 GPA. Regularly scheduled individual counseling sessions continue to be provided; all other services continue to be available to the student as needed. Level III students have learned to compensate for their disability and are independently achieving college success; these students will have their progress monitored by the staff, and tutoring will continue to be available. Any student not maintaining a 2.5 GPA must remain in or return to Level I.

LD/ADHD ADMISSIONS INFORMATION

College entrance tests required: Yes
Interview required: Yes
Essay recommended: Yes
Documentation required for LD: Current professional evaluation
Documentation required for ADHD: Current medical evaluation
Submitted to: Program to Assist Student Services
Special Ed. HS course work accepted: Yes

Specific course requirements of all applicants: NR
Separate application required: Yes
# of LD applications submitted each year: 15–20
# of LD applications accepted yearly: 8–13
Total # of students receiving LD services: 44
Acceptance into program means acceptance into college: Student must be admitted and enrolled in the university first and then request admission to PASS.

ADMISSIONS
All qualified applicants to PASS must submit the regular application, meet the general criteria for admission to Louisiana College, and have a diagnosed learning or physical disability. Successful applicants must have the intellectual potential (average to superior), the appropriate academic foundation (class standing and/or ACT/SAT scores), and the personal desire and motivation to succeed. The PASS director and staff make the final decision about admission to the program after reviewing the following: 20 or above on ACT or 930 or above on SAT; 4 years of English, 3 years of science, 3 years of social studies, and 3 years of math; 2.0 GPA; counselor's recommendation and other letters of reference; psychological or medical reports; and an essay outlining why the student feels he or she can succeed in college. At least one personal interview with student and parent(s) is required. Students are encouraged to apply early and there is an application evaluation fee of $25. Students may appeal to the Appeals Board if they are denied admission.

ADDITIONAL INFORMATION
Tutoring sessions are conducted in most subjects taken by Level I students. Additional tutorial help is available at the higher levels as needed. The PASS staff will carefully work with individual professors and the student's academic advisor to coordinate and accommodate the student's learning needs. Students admitted to PASS will remain in the program as long as they are at Louisiana College. Noncompliance with any component of the program may result in a student's dismissal from the program. Skills classes are offered in study techniques, test-taking strategies, and time management through orientation, and private tutoring from a PASS staff member. Incoming freshmen are encouraged to attend one summer session (5 weeks) to become familiar with the campus and college life.

LEARNING DISABILITY PROGRAM/SERVICES

Learning Disability Program/Services: Program to Assist Student Success (PASS)
Director: Betty P. Matthews
  E-mail: pass@lacollege.edu
  Telephone: 318-487-7629
  Fax: 318-487-7285

LEARNING DISABILITY SERVICES

Requests for the following services/accommodations will be evaluated individually based on appropriate and current documentation.

Allowed in exams	**Distraction-reduced environment:** Yes	**Added costs for services:** Yes
Calculator: Yes	**Tape recording in class:** Yes	**LD specialists:** Yes
Dictionary: Yes	**Books on tape from RFBD:** Yes	**Professional tutors:** 3
Computer: Yes	**Taping of books not from RFBD:** Yes	**Peer tutors:** 50–60
Spellchecker: Yes	**Accommodations for students with**	**Max. hours/wk. for services:** 10
Extended test time: Yes	**ADHD:** Yes	**How professors are notified of**
Scribes: Yes	**Reading machine:** No	**LD/ADHD:** By both student and
Proctors: Yes	**Other assistive technology:** No	director
Oral exams: Yes	**Priority registration:** No	
Note-takers: Yes		

GENERAL ADMISSIONS INFORMATION

Director of Admissions: Scarlett Pourciau
Telephone: 318-487-7259

ENTRANCE REQUIREMENTS

Academic units required: 4 English, 3 math, 3 science (2 science labs), 2 social studies, 1 history, 4 academic electives. **Academic units recommended:** 2 foreign language. High school diploma is required, and GED is accepted. TOEFL required of all international applicants: minimum paper TOEFL 550, minimum computer TOEFL 213.

Application deadline: 8/15	**SAT Math middle 50% range:**	**Graduated top 10% of class:** 23%
Notification: Rolling	440–600	**Graduated top 25% of class:** 47%
Average GPA: 3.40	**SAT Critical Reading middle 50%**	**Graduated top 50% of class:** 78%
ACT Composite middle 50% range:	range: 440–570	
21–26	**SAT Writing middle 50% range:** NR	

COLLEGE GRADUATION REQUIREMENTS

Course waivers allowed: No
Course substitutions allowed: Yes
In what course: Appeals for substitutions must be made to special committee. However, the director of PASS rarely makes a recommendation.

ADDITIONAL INFORMATION

Environment: The college is located on 81 acres in a small town, 1 mile northeast of Alexandria.

Student Body	**Cost Information**	**Greek System**
Undergrad enrollment: 1,014	**Tuition:** $9,750	**Fraternity:** Yes
Women: 56%	**Room & board:** $3,740	**Sorority:** Yes
Men: 44%	**Housing Information**	**Athletics:** Division III
Percent out-of-state: 8%	**University housing:** Yes	
	Percent living on campus: 56%	

LOUISIANA STATE UNIVERSITY

110 Thomas Boyd Hall, Baton Rouge, LA 70803
Phone: 225-578-1175 • Fax: 225-578-4433
E-mail: admissions@lsu.edu • Web: www.lsu.edu
Support: CS • Institution type: 4-year public

LEARNING DISABILITY PROGRAM AND SERVICES

The purpose of the Office of Disability Services (ODS) is to assist any student who finds his or her disability to be a barrier to achieving educational and/or personal goals. The office provides support services to students with learning disabilities. These services are provided to encourage students with LD/ADHD to achieve success in college. The consequences of a disability may include specialized requirements; therefore, the particular needs of each student are considered on an individual basis. ODS dedicates its efforts to meeting both the needs of students with disabilities and the interests of faculty, staff, and the university as a whole. It is the practice of ODS that issues concerning accommodations of students with disabilities in academic and other programs and activities be resolved between the student requesting the accommodation and the university employee representing the department within which the academic program or service is located. After intervention, if the student does not find the provision of an accommodation satisfactory, the student may file a formal grievance.

LD/ADHD ADMISSIONS INFORMATION

College entrance tests required: Yes
Interview required: No
Essay recommended: No
Documentation required for LD: WAIS–III; WJ–III
Documentation required for ADHD: Yes
Submitted to: Office of Disability Services
Special Ed. HS course work accepted: No

Specific course requirements of all applicants: NR
Separate application required: Yes
# of LD applications submitted each year: NR
# of LD applications accepted yearly: NR
Total # of students receiving LD services: 475
Acceptance into program means acceptance into college: Students must be admitted and enrolled in the university first and then request services.

ADMISSIONS

There is no special admissions process for students with learning disabilities. All applicants must meet the general admission requirements, including: 4 years of English, 3 years of math (including Algebra I and II and an advanced math), 3 sciences in biology, chemistry, and physics, 3 social studies in American and world history or world geography or History of Western Civilization and 1 additional social studies, 2 years of a foreign language, 0.5 years of computers, and 1.5 academic electives, plus 1 additional math/science elective. ACT 20 or above or SAT 910 or above, (exact scores are dependent on an individual student record); 2.3 GPA. LSU will consider the total high school record: rigor of courses completed, grades, test scores, educational objectives, school leadership, and breadth of experiences in and out of the classroom. Minimum expectations for consideration for admission are 3.0 academic on 18 units of college-preparatory high school courses as outlined in the LSU Core, a 1030 SAT (Critical Reading and Math), and a 22 Composite ACT. If an applicant does not meet the general admission criteria but is borderline, the student can be admitted through the Access Program.

ADDITIONAL INFORMATION

Specialized support services are based on individual disability-based needs. Services available include disability management counseling; adaptive equipment loan; note-takers; referral for tutoring; assistance with enrollment and registration; liaison assistance and referral to on-campus and off-campus resources; supplemental orientation to the campus; and advocacy on behalf of students with campus faculty, staff, and students. Learning Assistance Center is open to all students on campus. Computer labs, science tutoring, math lab, learning-skills assistance, supplemental instruction, and skills classes in time management, test-taking strategies, note-taking skills, reading skills, and study skills are available. The decision to provide accommodations and services is made by the SSD after reviewing documentation. Currently there are 175 students with LD and 300 students with ADHD receiving services and accommodations.

LEARNING DISABILITY PROGRAM/SERVICES

Learning Disability Program/Services: Office of Disability Services (ODS)
Director: Benjamin Cornwell
  E-mail: bjcornw@lsu.edu
  Telephone: 225-578-4401
  Fax: 225-578-4560
Contact Person: Wendy Devall
  E-mail: bjcornw@lsu.edu
  Telephone: 225-578-4310
  Fax: 225-578-4560

LEARNING DISABILITY SERVICES

Requests for the following services/accommodations will be evaluated individually based on appropriate and current documentation.

Allowed in exams
  Calculator: Yes
  Dictionary: Yes
  Computer: Yes
  Spellchecker: Yes
Extended test time: Yes
Scribes: Yes
Proctors: Yes
Oral exams: Yes
Note-takers: Yes

Distraction-reduced environment: Yes
Tape recording in class: Yes
Books on tape from RFBD: Yes
Taping of books not from RFBD: Yes
Accommodations for students with ADHD: Yes
Reading machine: Yes
Other assistive technology: Yes
Priority registration: Yes

Added costs for services: No
LD specialists: Yes
Professional tutors: No
Peer tutors: No
Max. hours/wk. for services: Unlimited
How professors are notified of LD/ADHD: By student

GENERAL ADMISSIONS INFORMATION

Director of Admissions: Cleve Brooks
Telephone: 225-578-1175

ENTRANCE REQUIREMENTS

Academic units required: 4 English, 3 math, 3 science, 2 foreign language, 3 social studies, 3 academic electives.
Academic units recommended: 4 math. High school diploma is required, and GED is accepted. ACT with Writing component required. TOEFL required of all international applicants: minimum paper TOEFL 550, minimum computer TOEFL 213.

Application deadline: 4/15
Notification: Rolling
Average GPA: 3.47
ACT Composite middle 50% range: 22–27

SAT Math middle 50% range: 540–660
SAT Critical Reading middle 50% range: 520–630
SAT Writing middle 50% range: NR

Graduated top 10% of class: 25%
Graduated top 25% of class: 53%
Graduated top 50% of class: 83%

COLLEGE GRADUATION REQUIREMENTS

Course waivers allowed: No
Course substitutions allowed: No

ADDITIONAL INFORMATION

Environment: The campus is in an urban area in Baton Rouge.

Student Body
  Undergrad enrollment: 25,301
  Women: 52%
  Men: 48%
  Percent out-of-state: 13%

Cost Information
  In-state tuition: $4,419
  Out-of-state tuition: $12,720
  Room & board: $6,498
Housing Information
  University housing: Yes
  Percent living on campus: 23%

Greek System
  Fraternity: Yes
  Sorority: Yes
Athletics: Division I

NICHOLLS STATE UNIVERSITY

PO Box 2004, Thibodaux, LA 70310
Phone: 985-448-4507 • Fax: 985-448-4929
E-mail: nicholls@nicholls.edu • Web: www.nicholls.edu
Support: S • Institution type: 4-year public

LEARNING DISABILITY PROGRAM AND SERVICES

The Center for the Study of Dyslexia offers assistance to serious, capable students with learning disabilities at Nicholls State University who seek to earn an undergraduate degree. They believe that everyone has the right and the obligation to pursue the fulfillment of their learning potential. The center's programs are data driven, goal oriented, and committed to change. The center is committed to continually questioning and evaluating its own practices. It has its own research program and has close ties with leading scholars and researchers in dyslexia. The center is impressed with multisensory, linguistic, and direct instructional approaches, but to maintain its own integrity, it projects an orientation that is objective, open-minded, and directed toward the future. The goals of the center are focused on the need to increase the understanding of dyslexia and to upgrade and improve the accessibility and quality of the services that individuals with dyslexia depend upon to help them to become self-sufficient, well-adjusted, and contributing members of society.

LD/ADHD ADMISSIONS INFORMATION

College entrance tests required: Yes
Interview required: Yes
Essay recommended: NR
Documentation required for LD: Psychoeducational
  evaluation
Documentation required for ADHD: Psychoeducational
  evaluation
Submitted to: Office for Students with Disabilities
Special Ed. HS course work accepted: Yes

Specific course requirements of all applicants: Yes
Separate application required: Yes
# of LD applications submitted each year: 0–60
# of LD applications accepted yearly: 0–50
Total # of students receiving LD services: 0–100
**Acceptance into program means acceptance into
  college:** Student must be admitted and enrolled in the
  university first and then request to be reviewed for services.

ADMISSIONS

There is no special admissions process for students with learning disabilities. The college has an open admissions policy for all graduates of high school or a GED. The college recommends that students have 4 years of English, 3 years of math, 3 years of science, 3 years of social studies, and 2 years of a foreign language. ACT/SAT are not required for admission. The average high school GPA is 2.7, and the average ACT is 20. There are a limited number of openings in the center, and students should apply early to assure space. The program seeks highly motivated students who have been diagnosed as having a learning disability. Admission decisions are made after careful review of all submitted documentation. The final decision is based on selecting the option best suited to providing a successful experience at NSU for the student.

ADDITIONAL INFORMATION

The Dyslexia Center provides a support system; equipment; remediation; academic planning; resources; and assistance. With the student's permission, letters requesting appropriate classroom and testing accommodations are written to professors. Typical accommodations may include but are not limited to extended time; use of an electronic dictionary; oral reader; or use of a computer. Students meet weekly with an identified program coordinator and are enrolled in regular college classes. Other campus services for students with disabilities include the Office for Students with Disabilities; the Testing Center for special testing accommodations such as extended time or a quiet room; the Tutorial Learning Center for tutoring assistance; the university Counseling Center, which provides counseling directed at self-encouragement, self-esteem, assertiveness, stress management, and test anxiety; and the computer lab for assistance with written assignments. Assessment is available for a fee for students applying to the university.

LEARNING DISABILITY PROGRAM/SERVICES

Learning Disability Program/Services: Office of Disability Services
Director: Stacey Guidry
   E-mail: stacey.guidry@nicholls.edu
   Telephone: 985-448-4429
   Fax: 985-449-7009
Contact Person: Gerald Sanders
   E-mail: stacey.guidry@nicholls.edu
   Telephone: 985-448-4430
   Fax: 985-449-7009

South River High School
201 Central Avenue East
Edgewater, MD 21037

LEARNING DISABILITY SERVICES

Requests for the following services/accommodations will be evaluated individually based on appropriate and current documentation.

Allowed in exams
  Calculator: Yes
  Dictionary: Yes
  Computer: Yes
  Spellchecker: Yes
Extended test time: Yes
Scribes: Yes
Proctors: Yes
Oral exams: Yes
Note-takers: No

Distraction-reduced environment: Yes
Tape recording in class: Yes
Books on tape from RFBD: Yes
Taping of books not from RFBD: No
Accommodations for students with ADHD: Yes
Reading machine: No
Other assistive technology: Yes
Priority registration: No

Added costs for services: No
LD specialists: No
Professional tutors: 3
Peer tutors: No
Max. hours/wk. for services: NR
How professors are notified of LD/ADHD: By student

GENERAL ADMISSIONS INFORMATION

Director of Admissions: Becky Durocher
  Telephone: 985-448-4510

ENTRANCE REQUIREMENTS

Academic units required: 4 English, 3 math, 3 science, 2 foreign language, 3 social studies, 2 history, 1 academic elective. High school diploma is required, and GED is accepted. ACT with or without Writing component accepted. TOEFL required of all international applicants: minimum paper TOEFL 500, minimum computer TOEFL 173.

Application deadline: Rolling
Notification: Rolling
Average GPA: 3.11

SAT Math middle 50% range: NR
SAT Critical Reading middle 50% range: NR
SAT Writing middle 50% range: NR
ACT Composite middle 50% range: 18–23

Graduated top 10% of class: 37%
Graduated top 25% of class: 46%
Graduated top 50% of class: 61%

COLLEGE GRADUATION REQUIREMENTS

Course waivers allowed: No
Course substitutions allowed: No

ADDITIONAL INFORMATION

Environment: The university is in a small town 1 hour from New Orleans.

Student Body
  Undergrad enrollment: 6,086
  Women: 62%
  Men: 38%
  Percent out-of-state: 4%

Cost Information
  In-state tuition: $3,000
  Out-of-state tuition: $8,500
  Room & board: $4,038
Housing Information
  University housing: Yes
  Percent living on campus: 18%

Greek System
  Fraternity: Yes
  Sorority: Yes
Athletics: Division I

UNIVERSITY OF NEW ORLEANS

AD 103, Lakefront, New Orleans, LA 70148
Phone: 504-280-6595 • Fax: 504-280-5522
E-mail: admissions@uno.edu • Web: www.uno.edu
Support: S • Institution type: 4-year public

LEARNING DISABILITY PROGRAM AND SERVICES

The University of New Orleans is committed to providing all students with equal opportunities for academic and extracurricular success. The Disabled Student Services (DSS) office coordinates all services and programs. In addition to serving its primary function as a liaison between the student and the university, the office provides a limited number of direct services to students with all kinds of permanent and temporary disabilities. Services begin when a student registered with the university contacts the DSS office, provides documentation of the disability, and requests assistance. DSS encourages student independence, program accessibility, and a psychologically supportive environment, so students may achieve their educational objectives. DSS also seeks to educate the campus community about disability issues.

LD/ADHD ADMISSIONS INFORMATION

College entrance tests required: Yes
Interview required: No
Essay recommended: No
Documentation required for LD: Psychoeducational evaluation completed within the past 3 years
Documentation required for ADHD: Specific diagnosis of ADHD based on the DSM–IV diagnostic criteria
Submitted to: Disabled Student Services
Special Ed. HS course work accepted: Yes

Specific course requirements of all applicants: NR
Separate application required: Yes
# of LD applications submitted each year: NR
# of LD applications accepted yearly: NR
Total # of students receiving LD services: NR
Acceptance into program means acceptance into college: Students must be admitted and enrolled in the university first and then request services.

ADMISSIONS

UNO does not have any special admissions process for students with LD. Students with LD should submit the general application form and are expected to meet the same admission standards as all other applicants. Students who graduate from state-approved high schools must complete the Louisiana Board of Regents core curriculum and require no more than one developmental/remedial course and one of the following: (1) ACT composite score of 23 or greater (SAT Reasoning Test 1060) or (2) GPA of 2.5 or greater with an ACT (SAT equivalent) of 18 or greater on the English and/or Math sub scores or (3) Rank in top 25 percent of class. Out-of-state and homeschooled students who do not meet the core curriculum must satisfy all items in 1–3 or have a composite ACT score of 26 or greater (SAT Reasoning 1170) and require no more than 1 developmental/remedial course. Courses required include: 4 English, 3 math, 3 science, 2 science labs, 2 foreign language, 3 social studies, 1 history, and 2 electives. Any student denied admission may apply to the College Life Program, designed as an alternative admission for "high-risk" students (not only students with learning disabilities). This program is for students who need assistance in one or more academic areas. The students remain with this program until they are able to remediate their deficits and then transfer into the appropriate college.

ADDITIONAL INFORMATION

DSS provides regular support services to all UNO students. Only those students who self identify and/or present appropriate written documentation of a disability shall be eligible for academic accommodations. To access accommodations through ODS students must submit appropriate documentation of disability and of the disability-related need for any specific accommodations being requested to the ODS staff. Accommodations are decided on a case-by-case basis and may include tape-recorded lectures, volunteer note-taker, alternate format text books, extended time on examinations, examinations in a distraction-reduced environment, reader, scribe, and use of a word processor with spellchecker for exams. Accommodations for students with ADHD are also decided on a case-by-case basis and could include: extended time for examinations; writing directly on the test without a scantron; examinations in a distraction-reduced environment; tape-recorded lectures; and volunteer note-taker. Drop-in tutoring for math and writing is available in the Learning Resource Center and testing centers in the library for test-taking, adaptive technology, and/or test administration. Developmental courses are offered in math and English, and skills classes are available for assistance in study techniques. PREP START is a special summer outreach program for recent high school graduates to gain admission to the university.

LEARNING DISABILITY PROGRAM/SERVICES

Learning Disability Program/Services: Disabled Student Services
Director: Janice G. Lyn, PhD
  E-mail: jlyn@uno.edu
  Telephone: 504-280-6222
  Fax: 504-280-3975

Contact Person: Amy King
  E-mail: jlyn@uno.edu
  Telephone: 504-280-7284
  Fax: 504-280-3998

LEARNING DISABILITY SERVICES

Requests for the following services/accommodations will be evaluated individually based on appropriate and current documentation.

Allowed in exams
  Calculator: Yes
  Dictionary: Yes
  Computer: Yes
  Spellchecker: Yes
Extended test time: Yes
Scribes: Yes
Proctors: Yes
Oral exams: Yes
Note-takers: Yes

Distraction-reduced environment: Yes
Tape recording in class: Yes
Books on tape from RFBD: Yes
Taping of books not from RFBD: Yes
Accommodations for students with ADHD: Yes
Reading machine: Yes
Other assistive technology: Yes
Priority registration: No

Added costs for services: No
LD specialists: No
Professional tutors: No
Peer tutors: No
Max. hours/wk. for services: Referred to Learning Resource Center
How professors are notified of LD/ADHD: By both student and director

GENERAL ADMISSIONS INFORMATION

Director of Admissions: Robert J Hensley
Telephone: 504-280-6595

ENTRANCE REQUIREMENTS

Academic units required: 4 English, 3 math, 3 science, 2 foreign language, 3 social studies, 2 history, 1 academic elective, 1 computer literacy or science (0.5 units required). High school diploma is required, and GED is accepted. ACT with or without Writing component accepted. TOEFL required of all international applicants: minimum paper TOEFL 525, minimum computer TOEFL 195.

Application deadline: 8/20
Notification: Rolling
Average GPA: 3.11
ACT Composite middle 50% range: 20–24

SAT Math middle 50% range: 480–620
SAT Critical Reading middle 50% range: 450–610
SAT Writing middle 50% range: NR

Graduated top 10% of class: 14%
Graduated top 25% of class: 33%
Graduated top 50% of class: 66%

COLLEGE GRADUATION REQUIREMENTS

Course waivers allowed: No
Course substitutions allowed: Yes
In what course: Foreign language and math substitutions may be requested through individual colleges with appropriate documentation

ADDITIONAL INFORMATION

Environment: The university is located on 345 acres in downtown New Orleans.

Student Body
  Undergrad enrollment: 9,156
  Women: 54%
  Men: 46%
  Percent out-of-state: 4%

Cost Information
  In-state tuition: $3,292
  Out-of-state tuition: $10,336
  Room: $4,734
  Housing Information
  University housing: Yes
  Percent living on campus: 2%

Greek System
  Fraternity: Yes
  Sorority: Yes
Athletics: Division I

SOUTHERN MAINE COMM. COLLEGE

Two Fort Road, South Portland, ME 04106
Phone: 207-741-5800 • Fax: 207-741-5760
E-mail: menrollmentservices@smccme.edu • Web: www.smccme.edu
Support: S • Institution type: 2-year public

LEARNING DISABILITY PROGRAM AND SERVICES

The Disability Services program is designed to offer academic support to students through various individualized services. Students can get professional faculty tutoring in their most difficult courses; learn about their specific learning style; improve concentration and memory; study more efficiently for tests; learn how to better manage their time; learn the basic skills that are the foundation of their specific technology; and use a computer toward processing, Internet research, and other computer applications. The NoveNET Learning Lab at SMTC uses a specially designed set of lessons and offers an alternative to adult education or other classes to complete high school level math, science, and English. The Learning Lab is a good place to become reacquainted with oneself as a learner: Students can start using it anytime during the school year and work at their own pace; they can study only the lessons that they need; they can work at home on their own personal computer; there is an instructor available during regular lab hours; the instruction meets SMTC's prerequisite admissions requirements; it has day and evening hours; and it allows students to earn credit for work in math courses in the lab by credit-by-examination.

LD/ADHD ADMISSIONS INFORMATION

College entrance tests required: Yes
Interview required: No
Essay recommended: No
Documentation required for LD: Psychoeducational evaluation
Documentation required for ADHD: Students should contact the Disability Services office to obtain a copy of the ADHD documentation guidelines.
Submitted to: Disability Services
Special Ed. HS course work accepted: Yes

Specific course requirements of all applicants: No
Separate application required: No
# of LD applications submitted each year: NR
# of LD applications accepted yearly: NR
Total # of students receiving LD services: 75
Acceptance into program means acceptance into college: Students must be admitted and enrolled in the university first and then request services.

ADMISSIONS

All students must meet the same admission criteria. There is no special admissions process for students with learning disabilities. All students have access to disability services, including those with a diagnosed learning disability. Applicants must submit a high school transcript, essay, and recommendation. Interviews are required. Students must have 2 years of algebra, and 1 of year biology, physics, or chemistry for most programs. SAT is required for applicants to the associate's degree programs who have been out of high school 2 years or less. The ACT is not required. Students are expected to have a C average with at least a C in prerequisite courses. Assessment tests sometimes are required as well.

ADDITIONAL INFORMATION

Students with diagnosed LD, as well as any student with academic needs, are provided with tutoring by faculty and students; access to NoveNET; access to resources in study skills in the form of personal advising/counseling, skill inventories, and study guides; and for LD, access to academic accommodations such as untimed exams, testing in a quiet area, and note-takers or readers. Other services are learning assessments; faculty consulting; curriculum development; preparation of materials to assist students in all courses; study skills counseling; academic advising; counseling and support for students with learning disabilities; and access to multimedia self-teaching materials including computer-assisted instruction, videotapes, audio cassettes, microcomputers, and tape recorders. The college administers the ASSET test to any student who has not provided scores from the ACT or SAT.

LEARNING DISABILITY PROGRAM/SERVICES

Learning Disability Program/Services: Disability Services
Director: Mark Krogman
  E-mail: mkrogman@smccme.edu
  Telephone: 207-741-5629
  Fax: 207-741-5653
Contact Person: Joyce Leslie, Learning Assistance Center
  E-mail: mkrogman@smccme.edu
  Telephone: 207-741-5534
  Fax: 207-741-5752

LEARNING DISABILITY SERVICES

Requests for the following services/accommodations will be evaluated individually based on appropriate and current documentation.

Allowed in exams
  Calculator: Yes
  Dictionary: Yes
  Computer: Yes
  Spellchecker: Yes
Extended test time: Yes
Scribes: Yes
Proctors: Yes
Oral exams: Yes
Note-takers: Yes

Distraction-reduced environment: Yes
Tape recording in class: Yes
Books on tape from RFBD: Yes
Taping of books not from RFBD: Yes
Accommodations for students with ADHD: Yes
Reading machine: Yes
Other assistive technology: Yes
Priority registration: Yes

Added costs for services: No
LD specialists: No
Professional tutors: 3
Peer tutors: 3
Max. hours/wk. for services: 3
How professors are notified of LD/ADHD: By both student and director

GENERAL ADMISSIONS INFORMATION

Director of Admissions: Odilia Silveira-Harmon
Telephone: 207-741-5800

ENTRANCE REQUIREMENTS

Academic units recommended: 4 English, 3 math, 1 lab science. High school diploma is required, and GED is accepted.

Application deadline: Rolling
Notification: Rolling
Average GPA: 2.2 minimum

SAT Math middle 50% range: NR
SAT Critical Reading middle 50% range: NR
SAT Writing middle 50% range: NR
ACT Composite middle 50% range: NR

Graduated top 10% of class: NR
Graduated top 25% of class: NR
Graduated top 50% of class: NR

COLLEGE GRADUATION REQUIREMENTS

Course waivers allowed: Yes
In what course: Limited
Course substitutions allowed: Yes
In what course: Limited

ADDITIONAL INFORMATION

Environment: The college, part of the Maine Technical College System, is located on a 50-acre campus.

Student Body
  Undergrad enrollment: 4,689
  Women: 49%
  Men: 51%
  Percent out-of-state: 3%

Cost Information
  In-state tuition: $2,660
  Out-of-state tuition: $5,600
  Room & board: $6,400
Housing Information
  University housing: Yes

  Percent living on campus: 4%
Greek System
  Fraternity: No
  Sorority: No
Athletics: NAIA

UNITY COLLEGE

PO Box 532, Unity, ME 04988-0532
Phone: 207-948-3131 • Fax: 207-948-6277
E-mail: admissions@unity.edu • Web: www.unity.edu
Support: CS • Institution type: 4-year private

LEARNING DISABILITY PROGRAM AND SERVICES

Unity College offers services for students with learning disabilities and encourages them to begin their studies in the summer prior to freshman year in the Summer Institute. The institute provides an opportunity for students to become familiar with the college and is an effective way to prepare for college course work. The Learning Resource Center (LRC) provides a program for bright, highly motivated students. Once admitted, students with learning disabilities follow a carefully coordinated program that combines regular course work, supportive services, and intensive individual work on academic course support. The LD specialist meets regularly with students, monitoring progress and ensuring personal contact. The LRC's staff is composed of faculty members, a learning disabilities specialist, and peer tutors. The staff is available to help students develop effective learning strategies, with special emphasis placed on individual student needs. Most importantly, the LRC gives necessary attention to each student's academic and personal growth. With the support of the LRC, students can gain confidence, knowledge, and skills to complete a high-quality college education.

LD/ADHD ADMISSIONS INFORMATION

College entrance tests required: Yes
Interview required: Yes
Essay recommended: NR
Documentation required for LD: WAIS–III
Documentation required for ADHD: Yes
Submitted to: Learning Resource Center
Special Ed. HS course work accepted: Yes

Specific course requirements of all applicants: Yes
Separate application required: No
# of LD applications submitted each year: NR
# of LD applications accepted yearly: NR
Total # of students receiving LD services: 60–75
Acceptance into program means acceptance into college: Student must be admitted and enrolled in the university prior to requesting services from the Learning Resource Center.

ADMISSIONS

To apply for admission students with learning disabilities should submit the general college application and the results of recent diagnostic testing, including a WAIS–R. Students should submit other diagnostic materials that indicate their level of functioning. SAT and ACT scores are not required but should be submitted if available. Students also must send two letters of recommendation and their official high school transcript. The Office of Admissions may require an on-campus interview, on-campus testing, or submission of additional supporting materials. Students with learning disabilities may request an interview with the director of Student Support Services. Other students may be admitted with the stipulation that they attend the Summer Institute and be successful prior to being admitted as a student for the fall semester. Other factors used in the admission decision include special talents, leadership, activities, and personality. Students not regularly admissible are reviewed by the LD specialist, who provides a recommendation to admissions, and a joint decision is made.

ADDITIONAL INFORMATION

Unity College offers services to assist eligible students who need additional academic support or accommodations. Students should fill out a request for academic support services as soon as notification of acceptance is received. During an initial consultation with the learning specialist, a student's eligibility for services is determined. In order to assess a student's eligibility for accommodations students must submit documentation no more than 3 years old. A student's high school Individualized Education Program (IEP), although very helpful information in the documentation process, is not sufficient for determining eligibility for services in college. The Summer Institute ($1,495), required of some incoming freshmen, is a 4-week precollege program offering basic academic skills in writing, math, study strategies, computers, Unity College orientation, as well as the natural environment of Maine. The institute includes credit and noncredit courses and individual tutorial assistance. Students meet with academic advisors and pre-register for fall courses. A learning disability specialist is on staff and services during the school year include specialized academic advising, support groups, taped texts, tutoring on a one-on-one basis or in small groups, and skills remediation in reading, math, spelling, written language, and learning techniques. Special courses, mostly for credit, are offered in composition, math, reading, college survival skills, and study skills. This program is curriculum based, designed to foster independence and allow students to achieve maximum academic goals and maximum potential.

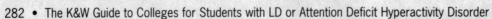

LEARNING DISABILITY PROGRAM/SERVICES

Learning Disability Program/Services: Learning Resource Center (LRC)
Director: James Horan
  E-mail: jreed@unity.edu
  Telephone: 207-948-3131, ext. 241
Contact Person: Ann Dailey
  E-mail: jreed@unity.edu
  Telephone: 207-948-3131, ext. 236

LEARNING DISABILITY SERVICES

Requests for the following services/accommodations will be evaluated individually based on appropriate and current documentation.

Allowed in exams
  Calculator: Yes
  Dictionary: Yes
  Computer: Yes
  Spellchecker: Yes
Extended test time: Yes
Scribes: Yes
Proctors: Yes
Oral exams: Yes
Note-takers: Yes

Distraction-reduced environment: Yes
Tape recording in class: Yes
Books on tape from RFBD: Yes
Taping of books not from RFBD: Yes
Accommodations for students with ADHD: Yes
Reading machine: No
Other assistive technology: No
Priority registration: Yes

Added costs for services: No
LD specialists: Yes
Professional tutors: Yes
Peer tutors: Yes
Max. hours/wk. for services: Unlimited
How professors are notified of LD/ADHD: By both student and director

GENERAL ADMISSIONS INFORMATION

Director of Admissions: John Craig
Telephone: 207-948-3131

ENTRANCE REQUIREMENTS

Academic units required: 4 English, 2 science. **Academic units recommended:** 4 math, 2 foreign language, 4 social studies. High school diploma is required, and GED is accepted. TOEFL required of all international applicants: minimum paper TOEFL 500, minimum computer TOEFL 1.

Application deadline: Rolling
Notification: Rolling
Average GPA: 2.70
ACT Composite middle 50% range: NR

SAT Math middle 50% range: 500–510
SAT Critical Reading middle 50% range: 480–500
SAT Writing middle 50% range: NR

Graduated top 10% of class: 3%
Graduated top 25% of class: 13%
Graduated top 50% of class: 48%

COLLEGE GRADUATION REQUIREMENTS

Course waivers allowed: Yes
In what course: Waivers are handled on an individual basis.
Course substitutions allowed: Yes
In what course: Substitutions are handled on an individual basis.

ADDITIONAL INFORMATION

Environment: The college is located on 185-acres in a rural community about 20 miles from Waterville.

Student Body
  Undergrad enrollment: 512
  Women: 31%
  Men: 69%
  Percent out-of-state: 67%

Cost Information
  Tuition: $17,690
  Room & board: $6,630
Housing Information
  University housing: Yes
  Percent living on campus: 90%

Greek System
  Fraternity: Yes
  Sorority: Yes
Athletics: NAIA

UNIVERSITY OF MAINE AT MACHIAS

Office of Admissions, Nine O'Brien Avenue, Machias, ME 04654
Phone: 207-255-1318 • Fax: 207-255-1363
E-mail: ummadmissions@maine.edu • Web: www.umm.maine.edu
Support: S • Institution type: 4-year public

LEARNING DISABILITY PROGRAM AND SERVICES

The University of Maine at Machias offers a personal approach to education. Students with documented disabilities may request modifications, accommodations, or auxiliary aids that will enable them to participate in and benefit from all postsecondary educational programs and activities. Students must provide current documentation completed within the past 3 years. This documentation should be submitted to the Student Resources Coordinator who works one-on-one with any student who needs academic support. This support takes the form of working with methods specific to the LD. All accommodation requests must be processed through the Student Resources Coordinator.

LD/ADHD ADMISSIONS INFORMATION

College entrance tests required: Yes
Interview required: No
Essay recommended: No
Documentation required for LD: WJ–III (full battery) or WISC–IV completed within past 3 years
Documentation required for ADHD: Doctor's letter explaining degree of the problem
Submitted to: Both Admissions and Student Resources
Special Ed. HS course work accepted: Yes

Specific course requirements of all applicants: Yes
Separate application required: No
# of LD applications submitted each year: NR
# of LD applications accepted yearly: NR
Total # of students receiving LD services: NR
Acceptance into program means acceptance into college: Students must be admitted and enrolled in the university first and then request services.

ADMISSIONS

There is no special admissions process for students with LD and ADHD. An interview is strongly suggested. Applicants in general have a 1000 on the SAT, rank in the top 50 percent of their senior class, and have a 3.0 GPA. Students seeking admission to an associate's degree program should have a C average and rank in the top two-thirds of their senior class.

ADDITIONAL INFORMATION

One-on-one services are available on request. One-on-one assistance is offered in the following areas: learning style and learning strategies, time management skills, organizing and writing papers, basic study skills, anxiety management, major and career focus, assistance using the library, information and/or referrals, advocacy, and peer tutoring. For a student to obtain a waiver or substitution of a course, a Disabilities Committee meets to evaluate the student's documentation and make a recommendation to the Vice President of Academic Affairs.

LEARNING DISABILITY PROGRAM/SERVICES

Learning Disability Program/Services: Student Resources
Director: Jean Schild
  E-mail: jschild@acad.umm.maine.edu
  Telephone: 207-255-1228
  Fax: 208-255-4864

LEARNING DISABILITY SERVICES

Requests for the following services/accommodations will be evaluated individually based on appropriate and current documentation.

Allowed in exams
  Calculator: Yes
  Dictionary: Yes
  Computer: Yes
  Spellchecker: Yes
Extended test time: Yes
Scribes: Yes
Proctors: Yes
Oral exams: Yes
Note-takers: Yes

Distraction-reduced environment: Yes
Tape recording in class: Yes
Books on tape from RFBD: No
Taping of books not from RFBD: Yes
Accommodations for students with ADHD: Yes
Reading machine: No
Other assistive technology: Yes
Priority registration: Yes

Added costs for services: No
LD specialists: No
Professional tutors: No
Peer tutors: 14
Max. hours/wk. for services: Unlimited
How professors are notified of LD/ADHD: By director

GENERAL ADMISSIONS INFORMATION

Director of Admissions: Stewart Bennett
Telephone: 207-255-1318

ENTRANCE REQUIREMENTS
Academic units required: 4 English, 3 math, 2 science (2 science labs), 2 social studies. **Academic units recommended:** 2 foreign language, 3 academic electives. High school diploma is required, and GED is accepted. ACT with or without Writing component accepted. TOEFL required of all international applicants: minimum paper TOEFL 500, minimum computer TOEFL 173.

Application deadline: 8/15
Notification: Rolling
Average GPA: 2.80
ACT Composite middle 50% range: 19–21

SAT Math middle 50% range: 400–540
SAT Critical Reading middle 50% range: 410–540
SAT Writing middle 50% range: NR

Graduated top 10% of class: 15%
Graduated top 25% of class: 31%
Graduated top 50% of class: 69%

COLLEGE GRADUATION REQUIREMENTS

Course waivers allowed: Yes
In what course: The student's petition for a waiver goes through a Disabilities Committee who make recommendation to the Vice President of Academic Affairs for final determination.
Course substitutions allowed: Yes
In what course: The student's petition for a substitution goes through a Disabilities Committee who make recommendation to the Vice President of Academic Affairs for final determination.

ADDITIONAL INFORMATION

Environment: The rural campus is located 85 miles east of Bangor.

Student Body
  Undergrad enrollment: 625
  Women: 67%
  Men: 33%
  Percent out-of-state: 24%

Cost Information
  In-state tuition: $4,650
  Out-of-state tuition: $12,510
  Room & board: $5,962
Housing Information
  University housing: Yes
  Percent living on campus: 43%

Greek System
  Fraternity: Yes
  Sorority: Yes
Athletics: NAIA

UNIVERSITY OF NEW ENGLAND

11 Hills Beach Road, Biddeford, ME 04005-9599
Phone: 207-602-2297 • Fax: 207-602-5900
E-mail: admissions@une.edu • Web: www.une.edu
Support: S • Institution type: 4-year private

LEARNING DISABILITY PROGRAM AND SERVICES

The University of New England's Disability Services exists to ensure that the university fulfills the part of its mission that seeks to promote respect for individual differences and ensure that no one person who meets the academic and technical standards requisite for admission to and the continued enrollment at the university is denied benefits or subjected to discrimination at UNE solely by reason of the disability. Toward this end, and in conjunction with federal and state laws, the university both accepts and provides reasonable accommodations for qualified students. Students with learning disabilities or attention deficit hyperactivity disorder must provide current documentation that identifies the specific disability. All documentation should be submitted to Disability Services.

LD/ADHD ADMISSIONS INFORMATION

College entrance tests required: Yes
Interview required: No
Essay recommended: N/A
Documentation required for LD:
  Psychoeducational/neuropsychological evaluation
Documentation required for ADHD:
  Psychoeducational/neuropsychological evaluation
Submitted to: Disability Services
Special Ed. HS course work accepted: Yes

Specific course requirements of all applicants: Yes
Separate application required: No
# of LD applications submitted each year: NR
# of LD applications accepted yearly: NR
Total # of students receiving LD services: NR
Acceptance into program means acceptance into college: Students must be admitted and enrolled in the university first and then request services.

ADMISSIONS

All applicants must meet the same admission criteria. There is no separate process for students with LD/ADHD. General admission criteria include 4 years of English, 2–4 years of math, 2–4 years of social studies, 2–4 years of science, and 2–4 years of a foreign language. It is recommended that students submit an essay and have an interview. Interviews are especially helpful for borderline applicants. After being admitted, students may submit documentation to Disability Services in order to request accommodations and services.

ADDITIONAL INFORMATION

Documentation requirements have been established by the Disability Services. Students with learning disabilities should submit psychoeducational assessment reports based on adult-normed tests of ability and achievement. Students with ADHD must also submit appropriate documentation from a qualified professional. Services could include priority registration, note-takers, scribes, proctors, and books on tape through the Recordings for the Blind and Dyslexic. Accommodations could include the use of a calculator, dictionary, computer, or spellchecker during exams; reduced-distraction site for exams; extended time on tests; oral exams; and assistive technology. All students have access to tutoring.

LEARNING DISABILITY PROGRAM/SERVICES

Learning Disability Program/Services: Disability Services
Director: Susan Church, Coordinator
  E-mail: schurch@une.edu
  Telephone: 207-283-0170
  Fax: 207-294-5971

LEARNING DISABILITY SERVICES

Requests for the following services/accommodations will be evaluated individually based on appropriate and current documentation.

Allowed in exams
  Calculator: Yes
  Dictionary: Yes
  Computer: Yes
  Spellchecker: Yes
Extended test time: Yes
Scribes: Yes
Proctors: Yes
Oral exams: Yes
Note-takers: No

Distraction-reduced environment: Yes
Tape recording in class: Yes
Books on tape from RFBD: Yes
Taping of books not from RFBD: Yes
Accommodations for students with
  ADHD: Yes
Reading machine: Yes
Other assistive technology: Yes
Priority registration: Yes

Added costs for services: No
LD specialists: No
Professional tutors: 5
Peer tutors: 15
Max. hours/wk. for services:
  Unlimited
How professors are notified of
  LD/ADHD: By student

GENERAL ADMISSIONS INFORMATION

Director of Admissions: Alan Liebrecht
Telephone: 207-602-2297

ENTRANCE REQUIREMENTS

Academic units required: 4 English, 3 math, 3 science (2 science labs), 2 social studies, 3 foreign language, 2 history. **Academic units recommended:** 4 math, 4 science (3 science labs), 2 foreign language, 4 social studies, 4 history, 4 academic electives. High school diploma is required, and GED is accepted. ACT with or without Writing component accepted. TOEFL required of all international applicants: minimum paper TOEFL 550, minimum computer TOEFL 213.

Application deadline: Rolling
Notification: Rolling
Average GPA: 3.20
ACT Composite middle 50% range:
  NR

SAT Math middle 50% range:
  470–580
SAT Critical Reading middle 50%
  range: 540–570
SAT Writing middle 50% range: NR

Graduated top 10% of class: 17%
Graduated top 25% of class: 49%
Graduated top 50% of class: 86%

COLLEGE GRADUATION REQUIREMENTS

Course waivers allowed: No
Course substitutions allowed: Yes
In what course: Substitutions are permitted on a case-by-case basis only after a reasonable attempt has been made to succeed in any given course.

ADDITIONAL INFORMATION

Environment: The 121-acre campus is in a rural area 16 miles east of Portland.

Student Body
  Undergrad enrollment: 1,698
  Women: 77%
  Men: 23%
  Percent out-of-state: 59%

Cost Information
  Tuition: $22,940
  Room & board: $9,255
Housing Information
  University housing: Yes
  Percent living on campus: 66%

Greek System
  Fraternity: No
  Sorority: No
Athletics: Division III

FROSTBURG STATE UNIVERSITY

FSU, 101 Braddock Road, Frostburg, MD 21532
Phone: 301-687-4201 • Fax: 301-687-7074
E-mail: fsuadmissions@frostburg.edu • Web: www.frostburg.edu
Support: S • Institution type: 4-year public

LEARNING DISABILITY PROGRAM AND SERVICES

Frostburg State provides comprehensive support services for students with learning disabilities to assist them in achieving their potential. To be eligible for the Frostburg State University support services, admitted students must provide records of evaluation that are no more than 3 years old. Services include advising and counseling by a qualified counselor familiar with each student's needs, assistance in course selection, guaranteed schedules, liaison with faculty, representation at Academic Standards Committee meetings, tutoring, and study skills workshops. The goal of the program is to provide appropriate support services to enhance learning and to strive for student self-advocacy and understanding of and independence in their learning styles.

LD/ADHD ADMISSIONS INFORMATION

College entrance tests required: Yes
Interview required: No
Essay recommended: No
Documentation required for LD: Psychoeducational evaluation
Documentation required for ADHD: Yes
Submitted to: Disability Support Services
Special Ed. HS course work accepted: Yes

Specific course requirements of all applicants: NR
Separate application required: No
# of LD applications submitted each year: NR
# of LD applications accepted yearly: NR
Total # of students receiving LD services: 240
Acceptance into program means acceptance into college: Students must be admitted and enrolled in the university first and then request services. There is an appeal procedure for students who are denied admission.

ADMISSIONS

There is no special admission procedure for students with learning disabilities. All students must complete the mainstream program in high school and meet all of the requirements for the university and the state. There is a Student Support Services/Disabled Student Services information form that must be completed by students to enroll in these programs. Admission to FSU is determined by the Admissions Office, which assesses an applicant's likelihood of success in a regular college program with support service assistance. Course requirements include 4 English, 3 math, 3 science, 2 science lab, 2 foreign language, and 3 social studies. If you have not taken the required courses, you may be admitted to the university with the understanding that courses in the deficient area(s) must be completed during the first year if you want to continue your studies. The average SAT Reasoning is 980 or ACT 21.

ADDITIONAL INFORMATION

Basic skills courses are available in time management, study techniques, organizational skills, and test-taking strategies. Other services include note-takers, dictation services, and readers. There is an orientation course to the university taught by an LD specialist. Students with LD or ADHD must provide current and appropriate documentation to receive support services. Students who believe they may have a learning disability, but who have not been tested, may request testing and assessment for no fee. Other services are available at FSU. Tutoring is available to all FSU students through the Learning Center and the Writing Center. Additional tutoring is available to those students selected to participate in the Student Support Services program. Academic advising on course selection and academic rules and regulations is available to all students through DSS and the Learning Center. The monitoring program, coordinated by the Diversity Center, is designed to increase the graduation rate of FSU students. On at least two occasions during each semester, monitoring forms are issued to faculty for those students participating in the monitoring program. These monitoring forms ask faculty to report on a student's performance and progress. The forms are then returned to the student's monitor and are shared with the student. Students with disabilities can have a DSS staff member as their monitor.

LEARNING DISABILITY PROGRAM/SERVICES

Learning Disability Program/Services: Disability Support Services
Director: Leroy Pullen
  E-mail: lpullen@frostburg.edu
  Telephone: 301-687-4483
  Fax: 301-687-4671

LEARNING DISABILITY SERVICES

Requests for the following services/accommodations will be evaluated individually based on appropriate and current documentation.

Allowed in exams
  Calculator: Yes
  Dictionary: Yes
  Computer: Yes
  Spellchecker: Yes
Extended test time: Yes
Scribes: Yes
Proctors: Yes
Oral exams: Yes
Note-takers: Yes

Distraction-reduced environment: Yes
Tape recording in class: Yes
Books on tape from RFBD: Yes
Taping of books not from RFBD: Yes
**Accommodations for students with
  ADHD:** Yes
Reading machine: No
Other assistive technology: No
Priority registration: NR

Added costs for services: No
LD specialists: No
Professional tutors: 7
Peer tutors: Yes
Max. hours/wk. for services: Varies
**How professors are notified of
  LD/ADHD:** By student

GENERAL ADMISSIONS INFORMATION

Director of Admissions: Trisha Gregory
Telephone: 301-687-4201

ENTRANCE REQUIREMENTS
Academic units required: 4 English, 3 math, 3 science (2 science labs), 2 foreign language, 3 social studies. High school diploma is required, and GED is accepted. ACT with or without Writing component accepted. TOEFL required of all international applicants: minimum paper TOEFL 550, minimum computer TOEFL 213.

Application deadline: Rolling
Notification: Rolling
Average GPA: 3.06
ACT Composite middle 50% range:
  18–21

SAT Math middle 50% range:
  450–550
**SAT Critical Reading middle 50%
  range:** 450–550
SAT Writing middle 50% range: NR

Graduated top 10% of class: 10%
Graduated top 25% of class: 32%
Graduated top 50% of class: 73%

COLLEGE GRADUATION REQUIREMENTS

Course waivers allowed: No
Course substitutions allowed: Yes
In what course: Students may appeal for any course to be substituted. Appeals are determined on a case-by-case basis.

ADDITIONAL INFORMATION

Environment: The university in located on 260 acres in the Appalachian Highlands in a small town 150 miles northwest of Baltimore.

Student Body
  Undergrad enrollment: 4,246
  Women: 49%
  Men: 51%
  Percent out-of-state: 11%

Cost Information
  In-state tuition: $6,230
  Out-of-state tuition: $14,400
  Room & board: $6,442
Housing Information
  University housing: Yes
  Percent living on campus: 35%

Greek System
  Fraternity: Yes
  Sorority: Yes
  Athletics: Division III

McDANIEL COLLEGE

Two College Hill, Westminster, MD 21157
Phone: 410-857-2230 • Fax: 410-857-2757
E-mail: admissions@mcdaniel.edu • Web: www.mcdaniel.edu
Support: CS • Institution type: 4-year private

LEARNING DISABILITY PROGRAM AND SERVICES

The goal of the college is to assist students with learning disabilities. More time is given to freshmen and transfer students to help with the transition into WMC. The Academic Skills Program is an optional service that is primarily for students with learning disabilities and ADHD, but there may be other students with disabilities who have a documented need for this service. The Academic Skills Center (ASC) provides three levels of services: Within Level I (no fee), students receive appropriate accommodations, tutoring, and access to monthly support groups, and for 2 hours a semester, students meet with an ASC coordinator. During Level II ($1,000 fee), the ASC provides Level I services and prescheduling of courses, consulting with an ASC coordinator, access to a study lab, 5 hours per week of study skills tutoring, and assignment to an ASC mentor. At Level III ($1,500 fee), the ASC provides services from Level I and Level II and diagnostic testing, planning, developmental implementation, and evaluation of a yearly individualized academic program. Student Academic Support Services works with each student on a case-by-case basis to determine and implement appropriate accommodations based on documentation.

LD/ADHD ADMISSIONS INFORMATION

College entrance tests required: Yes
Interview required: No
Essay recommended: Yes
Documentation required for LD: WAIS–III, psychoeducational testing that has been completed within the past 3 years
Documentation required for ADHD: Yes
Submitted to: Academic Skills Center
Special Ed. HS course work accepted: No

Specific course requirements of all applicants: Yes
Separate application required: Yes
# of LD applications submitted each year: 100
# of LD applications accepted yearly: 55
Total # of students receiving LD services: 150
Acceptance into program means acceptance into college: Students must be admitted and enrolled in the university first and then request services.

ADMISSIONS

The admission process is the same for all applicants. General admission criteria include a minimum 2.75 GPA in core academic courses including 4 years of English, 3 years of math, 3 years of science, 3 years of social studies, and 3 years of a foreign language (substitutions are allowed in foreign language if appropriate). Students with a 3.5 GPA do not have to submit an ACT or SAT Reasoning Test. The average ACT is 21, and the average SAT is 1000. Any LD or ADHD documentation should be sent to ASC to be used after a student is admitted and enrolled.

ADDITIONAL INFORMATION

Enrolled new students must attend one guidance day during the summer prior to freshman year to select classes. Students with learning disabilities should attend an orientation meeting before college begins and schedule individual appointments with the ASC coordinator. All students must pass one math course. There is a basic math class and two math review courses for students needing more math foundation prior to taking the required course. One skills class is offered, and students have access to unlimited tutoring.

LEARNING DISABILITY PROGRAM/SERVICES

Learning Disability Program/Services: Academic Skills Center
Director: Kevin Selby, Acting Director
  E-mail: kselby@mcdaniel.edu
  Telephone: 410-857-2504
  Fax: 410-386-4617

LEARNING DISABILITY SERVICES

Requests for the following services/accommodations will be evaluated individually based on appropriate and current documentation.

Allowed in exams
  Calculator: Yes
  Dictionary: Yes
  Computer: Yes
  Spellchecker: Yes
Extended test time: Yes
Scribes: Yes
Proctors: Yes
Oral exams: Yes
Note-takers: Yes

Distraction-reduced environment: Yes
Tape recording in class: Yes
Books on tape from RFBD: Yes
Taping of books not from RFBD: Yes
Accommodations for students with
  ADHD: Yes
Reading machine: Yes
Other assistive technology: Yes
Priority registration: Yes

Added costs for services: Yes
LD specialists: Yes
Professional tutors: Yes
Peer tutors: 10
Max. hours/wk. for services:
  Unlimited
How professors are notified of
  LD/ADHD: By student

GENERAL ADMISSIONS INFORMATION

Director of Admissions: M. Martha O'Connell
Telephone: 410-857-2273

ENTRANCE REQUIREMENTS
Academic units required: 4 English, 3 math, 3 science (3 science labs), 3 foreign language, 3 social studies, 2 history. **Academic units recommended:** 4 English, 4 math, 4 science (3 science labs), 4 foreign language, 3 social studies, 3 history. High school diploma is required, and GED is accepted. ACT with or without Writing component accepted. TOEFL required of all international applicants: minimum paper TOEFL 550, minimum computer TOEFL 213.

Application deadline: 2/1
Notification: 4/1
Average GPA: 3.49
ACT Composite middle 50% range:
  20–25

SAT Math middle 50% range:
  500–610
SAT Critical Reading middle 50%
  range: 490–600
SAT Writing middle 50% range: NR

Graduated top 10% of class: 29%
Graduated top 25% of class: 56%
Graduated top 50% of class: 91%

COLLEGE GRADUATION REQUIREMENTS

Course waivers allowed: Yes
In what course: Foreign language
Course substitutions allowed: Yes
In what course: Foreign language

ADDITIONAL INFORMATION

Environment: The college is located on 160 acres in a small town 30 miles northwest of Baltimore.

Student Body
  Undergrad enrollment: 1,723
  Women: 56%
  Men: 44%
  Percent out-of-state: 29%

Cost Information
  Tuition: $26,000
  Room & board: $5,600
Housing Information
  University housing: Yes
  Percent living on campus: 78%

Greek System
  Fraternity: Yes
  Sorority: Yes
  Athletics: Division III

TOWSON UNIVERSITY

8000 York Road, Towson, MD 21252-0001
Phone: 410-704-2113 • Fax: 410-704-3030
E-mail: admissions@towson.edu • Web: www.new.towson.edu
Support: CS • Institution type: 4-year public

LEARNING DISABILITY PROGRAM AND SERVICES

Towson University does not have a separate program for students with learning disabilities and/or attention deficit hyperactivity disorder. The university policy is to ask students what their needs are rather than to present them with a plan to which they must adapt. There is involvement in class selection. Professors are notified of students' disabilities, which eliminates the need for students to explain or prove their disability. Towson University also offers all students tutorial services, a reading center, and a writing lab. All students requesting services and/or accommodations must have an interview with the director of Support Services to establish what is necessary. Towson University's program for students with learning disabilities is individualistic, as the severity and compensating skills of the students are unique.

LD/ADHD ADMISSIONS INFORMATION

College entrance tests required: Yes
Interview required: No
Essay recommended: No
Documentation required for LD: Current psychoeducational evaluation
Documentation required for ADHD: Current psychiatrist or psychologist report
Submitted to: Disability Support Services
Special Ed. HS course work accepted: Yes

Specific course requirements of all applicants: Yes
Separate application required: No
# of LD applications submitted each year: NR
# of LD applications accepted yearly: NR
Total # of students receiving LD services: 400
Acceptance into program means acceptance into college: Students must be admitted and enrolled in the university first and then request services.

ADMISSIONS

There is no question on the application that inquires about a learning disability. Students with learning disabilities who want special consideration and/or services should provide documentation and information about their learning disability. Exceptions to published entrance requirements are made by a committee for students with documented learning disabilities. Credentials are reviewed by a committee that has some flexibility in interpreting scores. Students submitting documentation should send copies to the Admissions Office and Disability Support Services. Interviews are recommended. The mid 50 percent SAT range for applicants is 1020–1180. Priority admission is granted to applicants with a GPA of 3.0 and 4 years of English, 3 years of social science, 3 years of science lab, 3 years of math, 2 years of a foreign language (waived with appropriate documentation), and an 1100 SAT. Courses taken in special education may be considered. Applicants with lower GPAs and test scores will be considered after their seventh-semester grades on a space-available basis, with priority given to those with the highest GPA.

ADDITIONAL INFORMATION

Towson University provides students with learning disabilities with necessary accommodations based on recent psychoeducational evaluations. The Learning Center provides reading and study skills development services. The Writing Lab provides assistance for students who need improvement in writing skills. A quiet study area is available. Additionally, Disability Support Services provides note-takers; a resource room to be used for a quiet place to take a test; extended testing times and other testing arrangements; student advocacy; interpretation of documentation; authorization of accommodations; assistance with the implementation of reasonable accommodations; scribes and readers; short-term instructional support in time management, study, and test-taking strategies; reading and writing assistance; assistive technology; and referrals for other services. Students must be registered with Reading for the Blind to get taped textbooks. Those textbooks not available through RFB may be requested from Disability Support Services.

LEARNING DISABILITY PROGRAM/SERVICES

Learning Disability Program/Services: Disability Support Services
Director: Susan Willemin
  E-mail: swillemin@towson.edu
  Telephone: 410-704-2638
  Fax: 410-704-4247
Contact Person: Donna Eichelberger
  E-mail: swillemin@towson.edu
  Telephone: 410-704-2638
  Fax: 410-704-4247

LEARNING DISABILITY SERVICES

Requests for the following services/accommodations will be evaluated individually based on appropriate and current documentation.

Allowed in exams
  Calculator: Yes
  Dictionary: No
  Computer: Yes
  Spellchecker: Yes
Extended test time: Yes
Scribes: Yes
Proctors: Yes
Oral exams: Yes
Note-takers: Yes

Distraction-reduced environment: Yes
Tape recording in class: Yes
Books on tape from RFBD: Yes
Taping of books not from RFBD: Yes
Accommodations for students with ADHD: Yes
Reading machine: Yes
Other assistive technology: Yes
Priority registration: Yes

Added costs for services: No
LD specialists: Yes
Professional tutors: No
Peer tutors: Yes
Max. hours/wk. for services: Varies
How professors are notified of LD/ADHD: By student

GENERAL ADMISSIONS INFORMATION

Director of Admissions: Louise Shulack
Telephone: 410-704-368

ENTRANCE REQUIREMENTS

Academic units required: 4 English, 3 math, 3 science (3 science labs), 2 foreign language, 3 social studies, 6 academic electives. **Academic units recommended:** 4 English, 4 math, 3 science (3 science labs), 4 foreign language, 4 social studies. High school diploma is required, and GED is accepted. ACT with Writing component required. TOEFL required of all international applicants: minimum paper TOEFL 500, minimum computer TOEFL 173.

Application deadline: 2/15
Notification: Rolling
Average GPA: 3.45
ACT Composite middle 50% range: 20–24

SAT Math middle 50% range: 490–590
SAT Critical Reading middle 50% range: 480–580
SAT Writing middle 50% range: 480–580

Graduated top 10% of class: 23%
Graduated top 25% of class: 54%
Graduated top 50% of class: 89%

COLLEGE GRADUATION REQUIREMENTS

Course waivers allowed: No
Course substitutions allowed: Yes
In what course: Course substitutions are based on individual need and current documentation.

ADDITIONAL INFORMATION

Environment: The school is located on 306 landscaped and wooded acres minutes from downtown Baltimore.

Student Body
  Undergrad enrollment: 14,760
  Women: 61%
  Men: 39%
  Percent out-of-state: 17%

Cost Information
  In-state tuition: $7,090
  Out-of-state tuition: $16,300
  Room & board: $7,506
Housing Information
  University housing: Yes
  Percent living on campus: 23%

Greek System
  Fraternity: Yes
  Sorority: Yes
  Athletics: Division I

U. OF MARYLAND—COLLEGE PARK

Mitchell Building, College Park, MD 20742-5235
Phone: 301-314-9395 • Fax: 301-314-9693
E-mail: um-admit@uga.umd.edu • Web: www.umd.edu
Support: CS • Institution type: 4-year public

LEARNING DISABILITY PROGRAM AND SERVICES

The goal of the Disability Support Services is to coordinate accommodations and services for students with learning disabilities and physical disabilities. Services are offered through the Learning Assistance Service as well through accommodations as provided by the Disability Support Services. Students are expected to facilitate contact with instructors and negotiate any special accommodations. Students may request assistance from the service office with handling interactions with instructors. Commonly used services include testing assistance, note-takers, readers, and priority registration. Besides the standard accommodations, students receive support through special study skills course workshops, mentoring, and support groups.

LD/ADHD ADMISSIONS INFORMATION

College entrance tests required: Yes
Interview required: No
Essay recommended: No
Documentation required for LD: Psychoeducational evaluation (including aptitude and achievement testing)
Documentation required for ADHD: Psychoeducational evaluation (including aptitude and achievement testing)
Submitted to: Both Admissions and Disability Support Services
Special Ed. HS course work accepted: Yes

Specific course requirements of all applicants: Yes
Separate application required: No
# of LD applications submitted each year: NR
# of LD applications accepted yearly: NR
Total # of students receiving LD services: 450
Acceptance into program means acceptance into college: Students must be admitted and enrolled in the university first and then request services.

ADMISSIONS

There is no special or alternative admissions process for students with learning disabilities. Applicants with learning disabilities must meet general admissions criteria. The admission decision is based on courses taken in high school, which include 4 years of English, 3 years of social studies, 2 years of science lab, 3 years of math, and 2 years of a foreign language; GPA; SAT/ACT; class rank; personal statement; recommendations; and the psychoeducational evaluation. All freshmen applicants must submit a personal statement for admissions. The student may submit supporting documentation, which will be considered during the decision-making process. The learning disabilities coordinator may review the documentation and make a recommendation to the admissions office. The final decision rests with the Office of Admissions.

ADDITIONAL INFORMATION

There is a math lab and writing center available for all students. There is no centralized tutoring service. However, limited free tutoring is available through departments. For most tutoring needs, students need to hire their own tutors. There are approximately 450 students with either LD or ADHD currently receiving services or accommodations on campus. Note-takers are volunteers and could be students enrolled in the course. There is a mentoring program and support programs for students with disabilities. Priority registration is available. Services and accommodations are available to undergraduate and graduate students. There is a summer program for high school students. While it is not specifically for those with learning disabilities, these students could benefit from the program. The university is currently working on developing a special summer program for students with learning disabilities.

LEARNING DISABILITY PROGRAM/SERVICES

Learning Disability Program/Services: Disability Support Service (DSS)
Director: Jo Ann Hutchinson, PhD, CRC, LCPC
   E-mail: jahutch@umd.edu
   Telephone: 301-314-7682
   Fax: 301-405-0813

LEARNING DISABILITY SERVICES

Requests for the following services/accommodations will be evaluated individually based on appropriate and current documentation.

Allowed in exams
   Calculator: Yes
   Dictionary: No
   Computer: Yes
   Spellchecker: Yes
Extended test time: Yes
Scribes: Yes
Proctors: Yes
Oral exams: Yes
Note-takers: Yes

Distraction-reduced environment: Yes
Tape recording in class: Yes
Books on tape from RFBD: Yes
Taping of books not from RFBD: Yes
Accommodations for students with
   ADHD: Yes
Reading machine: Yes
Other assistive technology: Yes
Priority registration: Yes

Added costs for services: No
LD specialists: Yes
Professional tutors: No
Peer tutors: Yes
Max. hours/wk. for services:
   Unlimited
How professors are notified of
   LD/ADHD: By student

GENERAL ADMISSIONS INFORMATION

Director of Admissions: Barbara Gill
Telephone: 301-314-8350

ENTRANCE REQUIREMENTS
Academic units required: 4 English, 3 math, 3 science (2 science labs), 2 foreign language, 3 social studies.
Academic units recommended: 4 math. High school diploma is required, and GED is accepted. ACT with Writing component required. TOEFL required of all international applicants: minimum paper TOEFL 575, minimum computer TOEFL 232.

Application deadline: 1/20
Notification: 4/1
Average GPA: 3.89
ACT Composite middle 50% range:
   NR

SAT Math middle 50% range:
   600–710
SAT Critical Reading middle 50%
   range: 570–680
SAT Writing middle 50% range: NR

Graduated top 10% of class: 50%
Graduated top 25% of class: 83%
Graduated top 50% of class: 99%

COLLEGE GRADUATION REQUIREMENTS

Course waivers allowed: No
Course substitutions allowed: Yes
In what course: Foreign language, math

ADDITIONAL INFORMATION

Environment: The university is in a small town setting within proximity to Washington, DC and Baltimore.

Student Body
   Undergrad enrollment: 24,590
   Women: 49%
   Men: 51%
   Percent out-of-state: 22%

Cost Information
   In-state tuition: $7,800
   Out-of-state tuition: $20,145
   Room & board: $8,562
Housing Information
   University housing: Yes
   Percent living on campus: 42%

Greek System
   Fraternity: Yes
   Sorority: Yes
   Athletics: Division I

U. OF MARYLAND—EASTERN SHORE

Office of Admissions, Backbone Road, Princess Anne, MD 21853
Phone: 410-651-6410 • Fax: 410-651-7922
E-mail: ccmills@mail.umes.edu • Web: www.umes.edu
Support: CS • Institution type: 4-year public

LEARNING DISABILITY PROGRAM AND SERVICES

Disabled Student Services assures the commitment of the university to provide access and equal opportunity to students with disabilities admitted to the university. The Office of Services for Students with Disabilities (OSSD) assures the commitment of the University of Maryland—Eastern Shore to provide access and equal opportunities to the students with disabilities that are admitted to the university. Although there is no special curriculum for students with disabilities, OSSD is designed to assist students in maximizing their academic potential. OSSD maintains a comprehensive support network for students with disabilities. The office provides consultation with university staff, faculty, administrators, and student body to increase awareness of the needs of students with disabilities and eliminate accessibility barriers. The OSSD's focus is on supporting the positive development of students with disabilities.

LD/ADHD ADMISSIONS INFORMATION

College entrance tests required: Yes
Interview required: No
Essay recommended: Yes
Documentation required for LD: Psychoeducational evaluation
Documentation required for ADHD: Yes
Submitted to: Disabled Student Services
Special Ed. HS course work accepted: Yes

Specific course requirements of all applicants: Yes
Separate application required: No
# of LD applications submitted each year: 30–40
# of LD applications accepted yearly: NR
Total # of students receiving LD services: 25–35
Acceptance into program means acceptance into college: Students must be admitted and enrolled in the university first and then request services.

ADMISSIONS

There is no special admissions process for students with disabilities. All applicants must meet the same criteria. General admission requirements include 4 years of English, 3 years of math, 2 years of a foreign language, and 3 years of social studies; minimum SAT of 750 and minimum GPA of 2.5 are recommended. In-state students who have a high school diploma and minimum C average may be admitted on the basis on the predictive index weighing SAT scores and GPA. The PACE Summer Program is a 6-week residential program designed to provide basic skills enhancement and college orientation for any applicant whose high school GPAs and/or SAT scores do not meet the criteria for admission to the university. For those who do not meet regular admission standards, participation and success in the program is required as a preliminary step to admission to the university. The program offers students an opportunity to enhance their proficiency in the following fundamental skills areas: math, science, reading/study skills, writing, and college orientation. In addition, students learn to use the library to conduct research, go on cultural and scientific field trips, receive tutoring, attend seminars with key university personnel, and receive group counseling and basic skills testing. Upon successful completion of the summer program, students may be admitted to the university. Evaluation of student performance in the program will include the successful completion of math, writing, and science components, as well as the student's positive social development and adjustment to university life.

ADDITIONAL INFORMATION

Tutoring is available in every subject for all students. Developmental skills classes are extensions of the university's academic program. At some point in their educational careers, students may find themselves in need of planned instructional assistance in reading, study skills, math, and writing skills. These tutorials are taught and directed by professional staff specialists. The emphasis will be on assisting students to master college-level basic skills as required in their academic programs. As a result of their performance on their placement tests, many students are required to successfully complete the fundamental classes of reading/study skills, math, or writing. Additional accommodations for students with LD could include tape recorders; test proctoring; recorded materials; recorded text; note-takers; and an LD support group. The PACE Summer Program is a 6-week residential program designed to provide access and opportunity for those applicants who want to improve their chances of being admitted to the University of Maryland—Eastern Shore. Applicants who have SAT scores and/or high school GPAs that do not meet the regular admissions criteria are given an opportunity to attend the PACE Program as a pre-admission opportunity to attend UMES.

LEARNING DISABILITY PROGRAM/SERVICES

Learning Disability Program/Services: Disabled Student Services
Director: Dorling K. Joseph
  E-mail: djoseph@mail.umes.edu
  Telephone: 410-651-6461
  Fax: 410-651-6322

LEARNING DISABILITY SERVICES

Requests for the following services/accommodations will be evaluated individually based on appropriate and current documentation.

Allowed in exams
  Calculator: Yes
  Dictionary: Yes
  Computer: Yes
  Spellchecker: Yes
Extended test time: Yes
Scribes: Yes
Proctors: Yes
Oral exams: Yes
Note-takers: Yes

Distraction-reduced environment: Yes
Tape recording in class: Yes
Books on tape from RFBD: NR
Taping of books not from RFBD: Yes
Accommodations for students with
  ADHD: Yes
Reading machine: No
Other assistive technology: No
Priority registration: No

Added costs for services: No
LD specialists: Yes
Professional tutors: No
Peer tutors: No
Max. hours/wk. for services:
  Unlimited
How professors are notified of
  LD/ADHD: By student

GENERAL ADMISSIONS INFORMATION

Director of Admissions: Cheryl Collier-Mills
Telephone: 410-651-6410

ENTRANCE REQUIREMENTS

Academic units required: 4 English, 3 math, 2 science (2 science labs), 2 foreign language, 3 social studies, 6 academic electives. High school diploma is required with 2.5 GPA, and GED is accepted. TOEFL required of all international applicants: minimum paper TOEFL 500, minimum computer TOEFL 1.

Application deadline: 7/15
Notification: Rolling
Average GPA: 2.68
ACT Composite middle 50% range:
  NR

SAT Math middle 50% range: NR
SAT Critical Reading middle 50%
  range: NR
SAT Writing middle 50% range: NR

Graduated top 10% of class: NR
Graduated top 25% of class: NR
Graduated top 50% of class: NR

COLLEGE GRADUATION REQUIREMENTS

Course waivers allowed: Yes
In what course: All pending core course requirements
Course substitutions allowed: Yes
In what course: Foreign language, math

ADDITIONAL INFORMATION

Environment: The university is located on a 600-acre campus in a rural area 15 miles south of Salisbury.

Student Body
  Undergrad enrollment: 2,704
  Women: 57%
  Men: 43%
  Percent out-of-state: 29%

Cost Information
  In-state tuition: $5,080
  Out-of-state tuition: $10,000
  Room & board: $6,130
Housing Information
  University housing: Yes
  Percent living on campus: 56%

Greek System
  Fraternity: Yes
  Sorority: Yes
Athletics: Division I

AMERICAN INTERNATIONAL COLLEGE

1000 State Street, Springfield, MA 01109-3184
Phone: 413-205-3201 • Fax: 413-205-3051
E-mail: inquiry@www.aic.edu • Web: www.aic.edu
Support: SP • Institution type: 4-year private

LEARNING DISABILITY PROGRAM AND SERVICES

American International College believes that individuals who have LD can compensate for their difficulties and achieve success in the college environment. AIC feels that the Supportive Learning Services Program (SLSP) has all of the components necessary to allow for a successful college career for a student with LD. The college models compensatory techniques and teaching strategies to enable students to be effective in college and plan for their future. Students receiving supportive learning services may elect to participate in the comprehensive services offered by the Curtis Blake Center. Metacognitive strategies are taught to help students use their intellect more efficiently. Students are mainstreamed and may receive a minimum of 2 hours of tutoring/studying strategies weekly. Students create an IEP with their tutor freshman year and may take as few as four courses each semester. Students generally stay in the program for 4 years. In addition to comprehensive services, AIC also offers a limited services component that allows students with LD to reserve 5–10 hours of professional tutoring to be used over the semester. Additional hours can also be arranged for a fee.

LD/ADHD ADMISSIONS INFORMATION

College entrance tests required: Yes
Interview required: No
Essay recommended: No
Documentation required for LD: WAIS–III and accompanying diagnosis, relevant diagnostic results of achievement testing
Documentation required for ADHD: Diagnosis of ADHD and psychoeducational assessment
Submitted to: Supportive Learning Services Program
Special Ed. HS course work accepted: No

Specific course requirements of all applicants: No
Separate application required: No
# of LD applications submitted each year: 300
# of LD applications accepted yearly: 35
Total # of students receiving LD services: 95
Acceptance into program means acceptance into college: Simultaneous admission decisions are made by the program and admissions.

ADMISSIONS

In addition to submitting an application to admissions, students interested in applying for the support program must also contact the coordinator of SLSP. Applicants must schedule an on-campus interview with admissions and SLSP. Applicants must submit the results of the WAIS–R and accompanying report, relevant diagnostic material, and information about supportive assistance in the past. The college requires a high school transcript and ACT/SAT scores. There should be a strong indication of achievement and motivation in the fields of knowledge studied. The majority of applicants have a GPA of 2.0–3.0. Courses required include 16 academic units from English, math, science, and social studies. Foreign language is not required. The admission decision is made simultaneously between admissions and SLSP.

ADDITIONAL INFORMATION

At the heart of the services provided is a minimum of 2 hours of regularly scheduled direct, one-on-one assistance provided by a learning specialist. The specialist develops a tailored support program based on a student's needs. Priority is given to practical assistance to help students negotiate demands of the curriculum. Provisions can be made for more basic remediation of the student's learning difficulties. Specialists assist in course selection, organizing work and study schedules, and as a resource. Students have access to skills seminars in many areas. Classes in reading, spelling, math, study strategies, time management, written language, and handwriting are offered. The Supportive Learning Services Center is only open to students who are participating in the program. Services and accommodations are available to undergraduate and graduate students.

LEARNING DISABILITY PROGRAM/SERVICES

Learning Disability Program/Services: Supportive Learning Services Program
Director: Professor Mary M. Saltus
  E-mail: sls@aic.edu
  Telephone: 413-205-3426
  Fax: 413-205-3908
Contact Person: Anne Midura
  E-mail: sls@aic.edu
  Telephone: 413-205-3426
  Fax: 413-205-3908

LEARNING DISABILITY SERVICES

Requests for the following services/accommodations will be evaluated individually based on appropriate and current documentation.

Allowed in exams
  Calculator: Yes
  Dictionary: No
  Computer: Yes
  Spellchecker: Yes
Extended test time: Yes
Scribes: Yes
Proctors: Yes
Oral exams: Yes
Note-takers: No

Distraction-reduced environment: Yes
Tape recording in class: Yes
Books on tape from RFBD: Yes
Taping of books not from RFBD: Yes
Accommodations for students with ADHD: Yes
Reading machine: Yes
Other assistive technology: Yes
Priority registration: Yes

Added costs for services: Yes
LD specialists: Yes
Professional tutors: 9
Peer tutors: No
Max. hours/wk. for services: 5
How professors are notified of LD/ADHD: By both student and director

GENERAL ADMISSIONS INFORMATION

Director of Admissions: Peter Miller
Telephone: 413-205-3201

ENTRANCE REQUIREMENTS
Academic units required: 4 English, 2 math, 2 science (1 science lab), 1 social studies, 1 history, 5 academic electives. **Academic units recommended:** 4 English, 3 math, 2 science (1 science lab), 2 foreign language, 1 social studies, 1 history, 3 academic electives. High school diploma is required, and GED is accepted. ACT with or without Writing component accepted. TOEFL required of all international applicants: minimum paper TOEFL 500, minimum computer TOEFL 173.

Application deadline: Rolling
Notification: Rolling
Average GPA: 2.90
ACT Composite middle 50% range: NR

SAT Math middle 50% range: 430–580
SAT Critical Reading middle 50% range: 430–520
SAT Writing middle 50% range: NR

Graduated top 10% of class: 15%
Graduated top 25% of class: 25%
Graduated top 50% of class: 70%

COLLEGE GRADUATION REQUIREMENTS

Course waivers allowed: No
Course substitutions allowed: No

ADDITIONAL INFORMATION

Environment: The school is located on 58 acres in Springfield, 75 miles west of Boston and 30 miles north of Hartford.

Student Body
  Undergrad enrollment: 1,227
  Women: 53%
  Men: 47%
  Percent out-of-state: 40%

Cost Information
  Tuition: $19,800
  Room & board: $8,900
Housing Information
  University housing: Yes
  Percent living on campus: 55%

Greek System
  Fraternity: Yes
  Sorority: Yes
Athletics: Division II

BOSTON COLLEGE

140 Commonwealth Ave., Devlin Hall 208, Chestnut Hill, MA 02467-3809
Phone: 617-552-3100 • Fax: 617-552-0798
E-mail: ugadmis@bc.edu• Web: www.bc.edu
Support: CS • Institution type: 4-year private

LEARNING DISABILITY PROGRAM AND SERVICES

There is no specific program at Boston College for students with LD. The Academic Development Center (ADC) offers instructional support to faculty and graduate students, special services to students with LD, and tutoring and skills workshops to all Boston College students. The ADC provides academic support to more that 250 BC students with LD. The ADC aims to help students with LD to become independent learners who understand their abilities and disabilities and can act effectively as self-advocates. The ADC also offers free tutoring to all students at BC. All tutors receive training and must be recommended or approved by the chair of the department for which the student will tutor. Students who are seeking support services are required to submit documentation to verify eligibility. Testing must be current, comprehensive, and performed by a certified LD specialist or licensed psychologist, and there must be clear and specific evidence of an LD. Educational recommendations regarding the impact of the disability and accommodations recommended at the postsecondary level must be included. Documentation for ADHD must include an in depth evaluation from the psychiatrist/psychologist/physician who made the diagnosis as well as specific educational recommendations.

LD/ADHD ADMISSIONS INFORMATION

College entrance tests required: Yes
Interview required: No
Essay recommended: Yes
Documentation required for LD: Psychoeducational evaluation
Documentation required for ADHD: Yes
Submitted to: Academic Development Center
Special Ed. HS course work accepted: No

Specific course requirements of all applicants: NR
Separate application required: No
# of LD applications submitted each year: NR
# of LD applications accepted yearly: NR
Total # of students receiving LD services: NR
Acceptance into program means acceptance into college: Students must be admitted and enrolled in the university first and then request services.

ADMISSIONS

Students with LD who self-disclose during the admission process may receive a second review by the Committee on Learning Disabilities. Some students may be given the option of a summer admit into a transition program for the summer prior to freshman year. General admission requirements for BC are very competitive. The mid 50 percent for the SAT is 1230–1370. SAT Subject Tests are required in Writing, Math, and one additional subject. It is recommended that students have 4 years of English, 4 years of a foreign language, 4 years of math, 3 years of science, and 3 years of social studies. All students must submit an essay, and interviews are recommended. Students with LD who may be deficient in foreign language or math skills should provide documentation and request a substitution for these courses. Documentation of the LD should be sent to the Office of Admissions. Students are encouraged to self-disclose during the admission process.

ADDITIONAL INFORMATION

Services offered by the ADC include a summer transition program for entering freshmen students with LD, screening sessions for students who may have LD, individual consultations with a learning specialist, letters to faculty confirming and explaining the LD, reduced course load during the academic year combined with summer school, access to textbooks on tape, testing in a distraction-free room, workshops on study skills and time management, and small group seminars on learning strategies.

LEARNING DISABILITY PROGRAM/SERVICES

Learning Disability Program/Services: Academic Development Center
Director: Dr. Kathleen Duggan
  E-mail: kathleen.duggan@bc.edu
  Telephone: 617-552-8055
  Fax: 617-552-6075

LEARNING DISABILITY SERVICES

Requests for the following services/accommodations will be evaluated individually based on appropriate and current documentation.

Allowed in exams
  Calculator: NR
  Dictionary: NR
  Computer: Yes
  Spellchecker: Yes
Extended test time: Yes
Scribes: Yes
Proctors: Yes
Oral exams: No
Note-takers: Yes

Distraction-reduced environment: Yes
Tape recording in class: Yes
Books on tape from RFBD: Yes
Taping of books not from RFBD: No
Accommodations for students with
  ADHD: Yes
Reading machine: Yes
Other assistive technology: Yes
Priority registration: Yes

Added costs for services: No
LD specialists: Yes
Professional tutors: No
Peer tutors: Yes
Max. hours/wk. for services: N/A
How professors are notified of
  LD/ADHD: By both student and
  director

GENERAL ADMISSIONS INFORMATION

Director of Admissions: John L. Mahoney Jr.
Telephone: 617-552-3100

ENTRANCE REQUIREMENTS

Academic units recommended: 4 English, 4 math, 3 science (3 science labs), 4 foreign language, 3 social studies. High school diploma is required, and GED is accepted. ACT with Writing component required. TOEFL required of all international applicants: minimum paper TOEFL 600, minimum computer TOEFL 250.

Application deadline: 1/1
Notification: 4/15
Average GPA: NR
ACT Composite middle 50% range:
  NR

SAT Math middle 50% range:
  640–720
SAT Critical Reading middle 50%
  range: 610–700
SAT Writing middle 50% range:
  610–700

Graduated top 10% of class: 80%
Graduated top 25% of class: 95%
Graduated top 50% of class: 99%

COLLEGE GRADUATION REQUIREMENTS

Course waivers allowed: No
Course substitutions allowed: Yes
In what course: Foreign language

ADDITIONAL INFORMATION

Environment: The campus is located six miles from downtown Boston.

Student Body
  Undergrad enrollment: 9,020
  Women: 52%
  Men: 48%
  Percent out-of-state: 71%

Cost Information
  Tuition: $33,000
  Room & board: $11,438
Housing Information
  University housing: Yes
  Percent living on campus: 82%

Greek System
  Fraternity: No
  Sorority: No
Athletics: Division I

BOSTON UNIVERSITY

121 Bay State Road, Boston, MA 02215
Phone: 617-353-2300 • Fax: 617-353-9695
E-mail: admissions@bu.edu • Web: www.bu.edu
Support: CS • Institution type: 4-year private

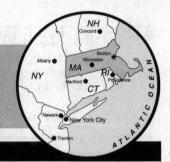

LEARNING DISABILITY PROGRAM AND SERVICES

Boston University recognizes that many students with a learning disability, attention deficit hyperactivity disorder, or a mental disability can succeed in a university if they are provided with support services and appropriate accommodations. The Office of Disability Services, including its division of Learning Disability Support Services (LDSS), is committed to assisting individuals with disabilities in achieving fulfillment and success in all aspects of university life. As part of the Office of the Vice President and Dean of Students, the primary objective of LDSS is to foster academic excellence, personal responsibility, and leadership growth in students with disabilities through vigorous programming and the provision of reasonable accommodation services. LDSS seeks to further this commitment through the promotion of independence and self-advocacy in students with LD, ADHD, or other cognitive disabilities. The university does not waive program requirements or permit substitutions for required courses. Several degree programs have foreign language or mathematics requirements. The university considers these degree requirements essential to its programs.

LD/ADHD ADMISSIONS INFORMATION

College entrance tests required: Yes
Interview required: No
Essay recommended: No
Documentation required for LD: Psychoeducational evaluation with adult normed instruments that has been completed within the past 3 years
Documentation required for ADHD: Clinical and psychoeducational evaluation that has been completed within the past 3 years
Submitted to: Learning Disability Support Services

Special Ed. HS course work accepted: No
Specific course requirements of all applicants: Yes
Separate application required: No
# of LD applications submitted each year: NR
# of LD applications accepted yearly: NR
Total # of students receiving LD services: 550
Acceptance into program means acceptance into college: Students must be admitted and enrolled in the university first and then request to be considered for services.

ADMISSIONS

All admissions decisions are made on an individual basis by the Office of Undergraduate Admissions. Because requirements may vary substantially depending on the college or program within the university, students are encouraged to contact BU for information regarding admissions requirements. BU expects that students with disabilities, including those with LD, will meet the same competitive admissions criteria as their peers without disabilities. Thus, there are no special admissions procedures for applicants with LD. The Office of Disability Services does not participate in any way in the application process or in admissions decisions. Admissions is based on the strength of a student's secondary school record. For most programs at BU, the minimum requirements for consideration include 4 years of English, 3 years of mathematics (through precalculus), 3 years of history and/or social science, 3 years of science (with laboratory components), and 2 years of a foreign language. Teacher and counselor recommendations and other personal qualifications as demonstrated by extracurricular activities are evaluated and weighed before admission decisions are made. The essay is considered a significant part of the application process. Activities in and out of school are important, and it is helpful if there is a match between the student's experiences or academic interests and the opportunities available at Boston University.

ADDITIONAL INFORMATION

LDSS offers support services to students with LD/ADHD, including access to academic accommodations for which the student is eligible, counseling and support in self-advocacy, assistive technology, and LDSS skills workshops for academic and study strategies, note-taking, time management, and self-advocacy. Students are active in the accommodation process and should notify faculty about the implementation of approved accommodations. Students needing more extensive support may enroll in LDSS Comprehensive Services, a fee-based program offering one-on-one strategy tutoring with a professional learning specialist. Tutoring covers writing development, critical reading, note-taking, study skills, testing strategies, time management, and organization. Tutoring is tailored to the student's learning profile of strengths and weaknesses, academic program, access to other resources, and personal goals. The enhanced services strategy plan is designed in collaboration with the student, the learning specialist, and LDSS professional staff. To be considered for LDSS, admitted students must submit the results of a comprehensive evaluation completed within the past 3 years, including (but not limited to) level intelligence and achievement testing.

LEARNING DISABILITY PROGRAM/SERVICES

Learning Disability Program/Services: Learning Disability Support Services
Director: Allan Macurdy
  E-mail: amacurdy@bu.edu
  Telephone: 617-353-3658
  Fax: 617-353-9646
Contact Person: Dr. Lorraine Wolf, Clinical Director
  E-mail: lwolf@bu.edu
  Telephone: 617-353-3658
  Fax: 617-353-9446

LEARNING DISABILITY SERVICES

Requests for the following services/accommodations will be evaluated individually based on appropriate and current documentation.

Allowed in exams
  Calculator: No
  Dictionary: No
  Computer: Yes
  Spellchecker: Yes
Extended test time: Yes
Scribes: Yes
Proctors: Yes
Oral exams: Yes
Note-takers: Yes

Distraction-reduced environment: Yes
Tape recording in class: Yes
Books on tape from RFBD: Yes
Taping of books not from RFBD: Yes
Accommodations for students with ADHD: Yes
Reading machine: No
Other assistive technology: Yes
Priority registration: No

Added costs for services: Yes
LD specialists: Yes
Professional tutors: 6–10
Peer tutors: No
Max. hours/wk. for services: 4
How professors are notified of LD/ADHD: By student

GENERAL ADMISSIONS INFORMATION

Director of Admissions: Kelly A. Walter
Telephone: 617-353-2300

ENTRANCE REQUIREMENTS

Academic units required: 4 English, 3 math, 3 science (3 science labs), 2 foreign language, 3 social studies.
Academic units recommended: 4 English, 4 math, 4 science (4 science labs), 4 foreign language, 4 social studies. High school diploma is required, and GED is accepted. ACT with Writing component required. TOEFL required of all international applicants: minimum paper TOEFL 550, minimum computer TOEFL 215.

Application deadline: 1/1
Notification: 3/31
Average GPA: 3.46
ACT Composite middle 50% range: 25–29

SAT Math middle 50% range: 600–690
SAT Critical Reading middle 50% range: 580–680
SAT Writing middle 50% range: 590–690

Graduated top 10% of class: 53%
Graduated top 25% of class: 87%
Graduated top 50% of class: 99%

COLLEGE GRADUATION REQUIREMENTS

Course waivers allowed: No
Course substitutions allowed: No

ADDITIONAL INFORMATION

Environment: The university is located on a 131-acre campus in an urban area.

Student Body
  Undergrad enrollment: 16,479
  Women: 60%
  Men: 40%
  Percent out-of-state: 77%

Cost Information
  Tuition: $33,330
  Room & board: $10,480
Housing Information
  University housing: Yes
  Percent living on campus: 66%

Greek System
  Fraternity: Yes
  Sorority: Yes
Athletics: Division I

Boston University

CLARK UNIVERSITY

950 Main Street, Worcester, MA 01610-1477
Phone: 508-793-7431 • Fax: 508-793-8821
E-mail: admissions@clarku.edu • Web: www.clarku.edu
Support: CS • Institution type: 4-year private

LEARNING DISABILITY PROGRAM AND SERVICES

The learning disabilities services at Clark University, based within the Academic Advising Center (AAC), was developed to advocate and support the needs of the student with learning disabilities in a college environment. Strategies are developed to help the student with learning disabilities cope with the increased demands of the college curriculum. Resources are available to students who experience difficulties and who may require some support or wish to learn more about their own learning styles. Support services in the AAC are coordinated with services offered by the university's Writing Center, Math Clinic, and Dean of Students. The most successful students are the ones who accept their disability, develop good self-advocacy skills, and are capable of good time management. The ultimate goal of special services is to help students improve their self-awareness and self-advocacy skills and assist them in being successful and independent in college.

LD/ADHD ADMISSIONS INFORMATION

College entrance tests required: Yes
Interview required: No
Essay recommended: No
Documentation required for LD: An evaluation completed within the past three years by a qualified diagnostician. This may include a clinical or educational psychoeducational evaluation.
Documentation required for ADHD: Documentation diagnosing the disability by a relevantly trained physician and/or other relevantly trained professionals
Submitted to: Academic Advising Center
Special Ed. HS course work accepted: N/A

Specific course requirements of all applicants: Yes
Separate application required: No
# of LD applications submitted each year: NR
# of LD applications accepted yearly: NR
Total # of students receiving LD services: 550
Acceptance into program means acceptance into college: Students must be admitted and enrolled in the university first and then request services.

ADMISSIONS

Special Services and the Office of Undergraduate Admissions work together in considering students for admission. Admission is based on ability rather than disability. Applicants must meet standard admissions requirements. An interview with Clark's Special Services Office is highly recommended. If a student requires any classroom accommodations or support services, a diagnostic assessment completed within the past 2 years must be submitted, documenting the learning disability. This documentation is needed to evaluate the applicant's needs and determine what services the university can provide. The university looks at a student's upward trend in high school, as well as the challenge of the curriculum and the number of mainstream courses the student has taken. Some special education courses in freshman year may be allowed if they have been followed by a college-prep curriculum during the rest of high school. The Director of Special Services makes a recommendation to the Admissions Office about the applicant, but the final decision rests with the Office of Admissions. The university values diversity in their applicants, but most students have taken 4 years of English, 3 years of mathematics, 3 years of science, 2 years of both a social science and a foreign language, and other credit electives, including the arts, recognized in the curriculum. The university feels that successful candidates for admission should have a strong senior-year course load (at least four, preferably five, solid academic courses).

ADDITIONAL INFORMATION

An early orientation program 2 days prior to general orientation is designed to meet the needs of entering students with LD. This program is highly recommended as it provides intensive exposure to academic services on campus. Students take a reading comprehension and writing exam, and results are used to match students to the most appropriate academic program. Graduate students work with students on time management and organizational skills. Although note-takers are available, Special Services supplements this accommodation with the taping of lectures and highly recommends that students use a cassette recorder with a count. It is also recommended that freshmen students take only three courses in their first semester. All students must complete one math course in basic algebra prior to graduating. The overall GPA of freshmen receiving services from Special Services is a 2.7. Clark offers space to an outside LD specialist who will provide tutoring and services for a fee. Services and accommodations are available to undergrads and graduates.

LEARNING DISABILITY PROGRAM/SERVICES

Learning Disability Program/Services: Academic Advising Center
Director: Jane Daigneault
 E-mail: jdaigneault@clarku.edu
 Telephone: 508-793-7468
 Fax: 508-421-3700

LEARNING DISABILITY SERVICES

Requests for the following services/accommodations will be evaluated individually based on appropriate and current documentation.

Allowed in exams
 Calculator: Yes
 Dictionary: Yes
 Computer: Yes
 Spellchecker: Yes
Extended test time: Yes
Scribes: No
Proctors: Yes
Oral exams: No
Note-takers: Yes

Distraction-reduced environment: Yes
Tape recording in class: Yes
Books on tape from RFBD: Yes
Taping of books not from RFBD: No
**Accommodations for students with
 ADHD:** Yes
Reading machine: No
Other assistive technology: Yes
Priority registration: No

Added costs for services: No
LD specialists: Yes
Professional tutors: No
Peer tutors: No
Max. hours/wk. for services: N/A
**How professors are notified of
 LD/ADHD:** By both student and
 director

GENERAL ADMISSIONS INFORMATION

Director of Admissions: Harold Wingood
Telephone: 508-793-7431

ENTRANCE REQUIREMENTS

Academic units recommended: 4 English, 3 math, 3 science (2 science labs), 2 foreign language, 2 social studies, 2 history. High school diploma is required, and GED is accepted. ACT with or without Writing component accepted. TOEFL required of all international applicants: minimum paper TOEFL 550, minimum computer TOEFL 213.

Application deadline: 1/15
Notification: 4/1
Average GPA: 3.45
ACT Composite middle 50% range:
 23–29

SAT Math middle 50% range:
 540–640
**SAT Critical Reading middle 50%
 range:** 550–670
SAT Writing middle 50% range: NR

Graduated top 10% of class: 31%
Graduated top 25% of class: 71%
Graduated top 50% of class: 96%

COLLEGE GRADUATION REQUIREMENTS

Course waivers allowed: No
Course substitutions allowed: NR

ADDITIONAL INFORMATION

Environment: The university is located on 45 acres in a small city 38 miles west of Boston.

Student Body
 Undergrad enrollment: 2,175
 Women: 60%
 Men: 40%
 Percent out-of-state: 62%

Cost Information
 Tuition: $31,200
 Room & board: $5,900
Housing Information
 University housing: Yes
 Percent living on campus: 74%

Greek System
 Fraternity: No
 Sorority: No
Athletics: Division III

CURRY COLLEGE

1071 Blue Hill Avenue, Milton, MA 02186
Phone: 617-333-2210 • Fax: 617-333-2114
E-mail: curryadm@curry.edu • Web: www.curry.edu
Support: SP • Institution type: 4-year private

LEARNING DISABILITY PROGRAM AND SERVICES

The Program for Advancement of Learning (PAL) at Curry College is a comprehensive individualized program for students with specific learning disabilities. Students in PAL participate fully in Curry College course work and extracurricular activities. The goal of PAL is to facilitate students' understanding of their individual learning styles and help them achieve independence as learners. Students' empowerment is developed via intensive study of their own strengths, needs, and learning styles. PAL is a place where students are honored for the strengths and talents they bring to the learning process and are given the chance to demonstrate their abilities. PAL students are leaders on campus. The PAL summer program is a 3-week course that is strongly recommended for new students to ease the transition to college and provide excellent preparation.

LD/ADHD ADMISSIONS INFORMATION

College entrance tests required: No
Interview required: No
Essay recommended: Yes
Documentation required for LD: Diagnostic evaluation with narrative report. Testing must have been administered within 3 years of the submission of the student's application and include comprehensive cognitive testing (WAIS–III or WJ–III) results and achievement testing in reading (word recognition and reading comprehension), written language (must include written expression), and math (computation and reasoning). The WRAT or other abbreviated achievement measures are not accepted.
Documentation required for ADHD: Yes

Submitted to: Program for the Advancement of Learning (PAL)
Special Ed. HS course work accepted: Yes
Specific course requirements of all applicants: NR
Separate application required: Yes
# of LD applications submitted each year: 900
# of LD applications accepted yearly: 400
Total # of students receiving LD services: 275
Acceptance into program means acceptance into college: Students must be admitted and enrolled in the university first and then request services.

ADMISSIONS

Applicants must submit the regular application, the application fee, their official transcript, SAT or ACT (recommended) scores, and counselor or teacher recommendations. Courses required for general admission include 4 English, 3 math, 2 science, 2 science lab, 1 social studies, 1 history, and 5 electives. For admission into the Program for Advancement in Learning, the following needs to be submitted diagnostic evaluations and other material that describe a specific learning disability; testing that includes the WAIS–III or WAIS–R accompanied by a narrative report, administered within 2 years of application; achievement testing indicating current levels in areas such as reading, written language, and math. An IEP or its equivalent is requested, if available. Interviews on campus are strongly recommended, and may be required of some applicants. Space is limited for the program. Students applying to PAL are not required to submit SAT or ACT. Admission decisions are made jointly by PAL and the Office of Admissions.

ADDITIONAL INFORMATION

PAL students must commit to the program for at least 1 year and have the option to continue with full or partial support beyond the first year. A 3-week 3-credit summer PAL orientation session is strongly recommended. Students meet regularly with their own PAL instructor who is a learning specialist. The focus is on using the student's strengths to improve skills in areas such as listening, speaking, reading, writing, organization and time management, note-taking, and test-taking. Students also receive help with readings, papers, and assignments for classes as the basis for learning about their unique learning style. The specialist reviews diagnostic testing to help the student understand the profile of strengths and needs. Students earn three credits toward graduation for the first year. Skills classes, for credit, are offered through the Essential Skills Center in developmental reading, writing, and math. Another special offering is diagnostic testing, which available through the Educational Diagnostic Center at PAL.

LEARNING DISABILITY PROGRAM/SERVICES

Learning Disability Program/Services: Program for Advancement of Learning (PAL)
Director: Dr. Lisa Ijiri
  E-mail: pal@curry.edu
  Telephone: 617-333-2250
  Fax: 617-333-2018
Contact Person: Tish Pieper, Admissions Counselor
  E-mail: pal@curry.edu
  Telephone: 617-333-2250
  Fax: 617-333-2018

LEARNING DISABILITY SERVICES

Requests for the following services/accommodations will be evaluated individually based on appropriate and current documentation.

Allowed in exams	Distraction-reduced environment: Yes	Added costs for services: Yes
Calculator: Yes	Tape recording in class: Yes	LD specialists: Yes
Dictionary: Yes	Books on tape from RFBD: Yes	Professional tutors: Yes
Computer: Yes	Taping of books not from RFBD: Yes	Peer tutors: No
Spellchecker: Yes	Accommodations for students with	Max. hours/wk. for services: 2.5
Extended test time: Yes	ADHD: Yes	How professors are notified of
Scribes: No	Reading machine: Yes	LD/ADHD: By student
Proctors: Yes	Other assistive technology: Yes	
Oral exams: NR	Priority registration: No	
Note-takers: NR		

GENERAL ADMISSIONS INFORMATION

Director of Admissions: Jane Patricia Fidler
Telephone: 617-333-2210

ENTRANCE REQUIREMENTS

Academic units required: 4 English, 3 math, 2 science (2 science labs), 1 social studies, 1 history, 5 academic electives. High school diploma is required, and GED is accepted. ACT with or without Writing component accepted. TOEFL required of all international applicants: minimum paper TOEFL 500, minimum computer TOEFL 173.

Application deadline: 4/1	**SAT Math middle 50% range:** NR	**Graduated top 10% of class:** 5%
Notification: Rolling	**SAT Critical Reading middle 50%**	**Graduated top 25% of class:** 22%
Average GPA: 2.30	**range:** NR	**Graduated top 50% of class:** 65%
ACT Composite middle 50% range: NR	**SAT Writing middle 50% range:** NR	

COLLEGE GRADUATION REQUIREMENTS

Course waivers allowed: No
Course substitutions allowed: Yes
In what course: Varies

ADDITIONAL INFORMATION

Environment: Curry's 120-acre campus is minutes from metropolitan Boston.

Student Body	Cost Information	Greek System
Undergrad enrollment: 1,709	Tuition: $18,900	Fraternity: No
Women: 53%	Room & board: $7,200	Sorority: No
Men: 47%	Housing Information	Athletics: Division III
Percent out-of-state: 40%	University housing: Yes	
	Percent living on campus: 60%	

DEAN COLLEGE

Office of Admissions, 99 Main Street, Franklin, MA 02038-1994
Phone: 508-541-1508 • Fax: 508-541-8726
E-mail: admission@dean.edu • Web: www.dean.edu
Support: SP • Institution type: 2-year private

LEARNING DISABILITY PROGRAM AND SERVICES

Dean College faculty and staff are committed to maintaining a caring and nurturing environment. While much of this support comes in the form of informal, face-to-face interactions, students will find that a number of programs have been developed specifically to provide students with structured guidance in both academics and student life. The Learning Center offers student academic support and assistance through the Berenson Writing Center, the Math Tutoring Program, Disability Support Services, and course-specific tutoring. Personalized Learning Services offers a comprehensive system of support for students with documented learning disabilities. Learning specialists work with students to develop customized programs that address both short-term goals and the skills needed to create a foundation for success in future academic and professional settings. The goal of PLS is to assist students in becoming confident, successful, independent learners. This program is designed to help all students achieve their academic goals. The FACTS (Financial, Academic, and Career, Transfer, and Student life) Advising Center provides comprehensive assistance and information to students. Students are assigned a personal advising team to guide them as they move through the academic year.

LD/ADHD ADMISSIONS INFORMATION

College entrance tests required: Yes
Interview required: Yes
Essay recommended: Yes
Documentation required for LD: WAIS–III, WJ–III
Documentation required for ADHD: Comprehensive documentation
Submitted to: Disability Support Services
Special Ed. HS course work accepted: Yes

Specific course requirements of all applicants: NR
Separate application required: Yes
# of LD applications submitted each year: 125
# of LD applications accepted yearly: 50
Total # of students receiving LD services: 100
Acceptance into program means acceptance into college: Student must be admitted and enrolled in the university first and then reviewed for LD services.

ADMISSIONS

There is no special admission process for students with learning disabilities. All students submit the same general application. Every application is carefully reviewed by admissions, and students are selected based on their academic performance in high school, recommendations, and personal accomplishments. Students who self-disclose and submit documentation may have their materials reviewed by the LD specialist, who will make a recommendation to admissions. There is no simple formula applied to an application. Dean strives to make the best match between what it offers as an institution and each student's skills, interests, and abilities. Interviews are highly recommended. Students should have college-prep, including 4 years of English and 3 years of math. Interviews are not required, but students must submit a counselor's recommendation. SAT/ACT are required, but viewed as less important than school record. Students who do not meet the general admission requirements may be considered for conditional admission through successful completion of the Summer Bridge Program.

ADDITIONAL INFORMATION

Accommodations may include, but are not limited to, taped texts; access to computers, scribes, and note-takers; alternative testing modes; and extended time for testing. The Learning Center provides free academic assistance and support services for all students through tutoring, workshops, and study groups. Professional and peer tutors are available throughout the day to assist students in developing writing, math, and study skills and provide course-specific tutoring. PLS offers tutorial support to students with documented LD, unique learning styles, or other diagnosed learning needs. Students meet one-on-one or in small groups with LD specialist weekly. Learning and study strategies taught by the specialist include test-taking, test preparation, note-taking, time management, academic organization, reading comprehension, research and writing skills, and self-awareness and advocacy. The fee is $700–$3,500 per semester.

LEARNING DISABILITY PROGRAM/SERVICES

Learning Disability Program/Services: Disability Support Services
Director: Erin Lowery-Corkran, PhD
 E-mail: elowery-corkran@dean.edu
 Telephone: 508-541-1764
 Fax: 508-541-1829
Contact Person: Liane Albert
 E-mail: elowery-corkran@dean.edu
 Telephone: 508-541-1768
 Fax: 508-541-1829

LEARNING DISABILITY SERVICES

Requests for the following services/accommodations will be evaluated individually based on appropriate and current documentation.

Allowed in exams	**Distraction-reduced environment:** Yes	**Added costs for services:** Yes
Calculator: Yes	**Tape recording in class:** Yes	**LD specialists:** Yes
Dictionary: Yes	**Books on tape from RFBD:** No	**Professional tutors:** 25
Computer: Yes	**Taping of books not from RFBD:** No	**Peer tutors:** 12–18
Spellchecker: Yes	**Accommodations for students with**	**Max. hours/wk. for services:** 5
Extended test time: Yes	**ADHD:** Yes	**How professors are notified of**
Scribes: Yes	**Reading machine:** Yes	**LD/ADHD:** By both student and
Proctors: Yes	**Other assistive technology:** Yes	director
Oral exams: Yes	**Priority registration:** No	
Note-takers: Yes		

GENERAL ADMISSIONS INFORMATION

Director of Admissions: Paul Vaccaro
Telephone: 508-541-1508

ENTRANCE REQUIREMENTS

Academic units required: 4 English, 3 math, 1 science (1 science lab), 1 social studies, 1 history. **Academic units recommended:** 4 English, 2 math, 2 science (1 science lab), 1 foreign language, 2 social studies, 2 history, 1 academic elective. High school diploma is required, and GED is accepted. ACT with or without Writing accepted.

Application deadline: Rolling	**SAT Math middle 50% range:**	**Graduated top 10% of class:** NR
Notification: Rolling	380–490	**Graduated top 25% of class:** NR
Average GPA: 2.0	**SAT Critical Reading middle 50%**	**Graduated top 50% of class:** NR
ACT Composite middle 50% range:	**range:** 390–490	
15–20	**SAT Writing middle 50% range:** NR	

COLLEGE GRADUATION REQUIREMENTS

Course waivers allowed: No
Course substitutions allowed: No

ADDITIONAL INFORMATION

Environment: The campus is in a small town near Boston.

Student Body	**Cost Information**	**Greek System**
Undergrad enrollment: 1,106	**Tuition:** $24,000	**Fraternity:** No
Women: 48%	**Room & board:** $10,350	**Sorority:** No
Men: 52%	**Housing Information**	**Athletics:** NJCAA
Percent out-of-state: 53%	**University housing:** Yes	
	Percent living on campus: 88%	

EMERSON COLLEGE

120 Boylston Street, Boston, MA 02116-4624
Phone: 617-824-8600 • Fax: 617-824-8609
E-mail: admission@emerson.edu • Web: www.emerson.edu
Support: CS • Institution type: 4-year private

LEARNING DISABILITY PROGRAM AND SERVICES

Emerson College is committed to providing equal access to its academic, residential, and social activities to all qualified students. The college makes every effort to accommodate individuals with disabilities according to ADA and Section 504 of the Rehabilitation Act. Emerson offers services through the Disabilities Services Office (DSO) to students with documented physical, visual, hearing, learning, or psychiatric disabilities. The Disabilities Service Coordinator is the primary contact person for all students with disabilities. Emerson does not require students with disabilities to register with the DSO; however, students with accommodation needs will need to register to take advantage of the services. Students must register in a timely manner to have accommodations or services in place when needed. Students must also provide appropriate documentation of their disabilities. This documentation must be prepared by qualified professionals and will serve as a basis for determining appropriate accommodations.

LD/ADHD ADMISSIONS INFORMATION

College entrance tests required: Yes
Interview required: No
Essay recommended: No
Documentation required for LD: Students typically supply documentation recommended by ETS (Educational Testing Service) (for example, the WAIS–III).
Documentation required for ADHD: Yes
Submitted to: Disabilities Service Office
Special Ed. HS course work accepted: N/A

Specific course requirements of all applicants: Yes
Separate application required: No
# of LD applications submitted each year: NR
# of LD applications accepted yearly: NR
Total # of students receiving LD services: NR
Acceptance into program means acceptance into college: Student must be admitted and enrolled in the college to request services.

ADMISSIONS

Admission is competitive. In choosing candidates for the entering class, Emerson looks for students who present academic promise in their secondary school record, recommendations, and writing competency, as well as personal qualities as seen in extracurricular activities, community involvement, and demonstrated leadership. There is no separate application for students with learning disabilities. A complete application includes the Emerson application form and application fee, application essay, an official secondary school transcript, two letters of recommendation (one from a guidance counselor/college advisor and the other from a teacher of an academic subject), and official SAT or ACT test results. The academic preparation of successful candidates should include 4 years of English and 3 years each of math, science, social science, and a single foreign language.

ADDITIONAL INFORMATION

Emerson offers services through its Disability Services Office to students with documented disabilities. Services are determined on an individual basis and are dependent on the appropriate documentation. The college's Learning Assistance Center offers reading tutorials, writing assistance, and seminars on such topics as strengthening study skills, improving time management, and conducting library searches. Course-specific tutorials can also be arranged.

LEARNING DISABILITY PROGRAM/SERVICES

Learning Disability Program/Services: Disability Services Office
Director: Dr. Anthony Bashir
  E-mail: dso@emerson.edu
  Telephone: 617-824-8415
  Fax: 617-824-8941

LEARNING DISABILITY SERVICES

Requests for the following services/accommodations will be evaluated individually based on appropriate and current documentation.

Allowed in exams
  Calculator: Yes
  Dictionary: Yes
  Computer: Yes
  Spellchecker: Yes
Extended test time: Yes
Scribes: Yes
Proctors: Yes
Oral exams: Yes
Note-takers: Yes

Distraction-reduced environment: Yes
Tape recording in class: Yes
Books on tape from RFBD: No
Taping of books not from RFBD: No
Accommodations for students with
  ADHD: Yes
Reading machine: Yes
Other assistive technology: Yes
Priority registration: N/A

Added costs for services: No
LD specialists: Yes
Professional tutors: No
Peer tutors: 14
Max. hours/wk. for services: 4
How professors are notified of
  LD/ADHD: By both student and
  director

GENERAL ADMISSIONS INFORMATION

Director of Admissions: Sara S. Ramirez
Telephone: 617-824-8600

ENTRANCE REQUIREMENTS

Academic units required: 4 English, 3 math, 3 science, 3 foreign language, 3 social studies. **Academic units recommended:** 4 English, 3 math, 3 science, 3 foreign language, 3 social studies, 4 academic electives. High school diploma is required, and GED is accepted. ACT with Writing component required. TOEFL required of all international applicants: minimum paper TOEFL 550, minimum computer TOEFL 213.

Application deadline: 1/5
Notification: 4/1
Average GPA: 3.59
ACT Composite middle 50% range:
  24–29

SAT Math middle 50% range:
  550–640
SAT Critical Reading middle 50%
  range: 580–670
SAT Writing middle 50% range:
  580–660

Graduated top 10% of class: 36%
Graduated top 25% of class: 78%
Graduated top 50% of class: 98%

COLLEGE GRADUATION REQUIREMENTS

Course waivers allowed: Yes
In what course: Documentation-specific
Course substitutions allowed: Yes
In what course: Documentation-specific

ADDITIONAL INFORMATION

Environment: Emerson's campus is located on Boston Common in the heart of the city's theater district.

Student Body
  Undergrad enrollment: 3,216
  Women: 55%
  Men: 45%
  Percent out-of-state: 63%

Cost Information
  Tuition: $25,248
  Room & board: $10,870
Housing Information
  University housing: Yes
  Percent living on campus: 42%

Greek System
  Fraternity: Yes
  Sorority: Yes
Athletics: Division III

FITCHBURG STATE COLLEGE

160 Pearl Street, Fitchburg, MA 01420-2697
Phone: 978-665-3144 • Fax: 978-665-4540
E-mail: admissions@fsc.edu • Web: www.fsc.edu
Support: S • Institution type: 4-year public

LEARNING DISABILITY PROGRAM AND SERVICES

The Disability Services Office provides individually tailored support services and programs for students with disabilities. Disability Services empowers eligible students to succeed by striving to assure equal access and opportunity of curricular and extracurricular activities. Student autonomy is encouraged through the provision of reasonable accommodations, services, and training in the use of assistive technology, self-advocacy, and leadership. Disability Services is responsible for verifying student eligibility for accommodations and for coordinating accommodations across campus. Students must request services themselves and must provide appropriate documentation to support the need for such services. Once students have obtained copies of their disability documentation from their high school (or medical provider who is most familiar with their needs and their disabilities), they should complete and sign the Statement of Learning Needs and Release of Information forms. Documentation must clearly state the diagnosis, describe the symptoms that impact the student's ability to function in the educational environment, and provide specific recommendations for accommodations.

LD/ADHD ADMISSIONS INFORMATION

College entrance tests required: Yes
Interview required: No
Essay recommended: No
Documentation required for LD: Psychoeducational or neuropsychological evaluation, including cognitive and achievement testing
Documentation required for ADHD: Letter from an appropriate diagnostician along with any relevant neuropsychological testing
Submitted to: Disability Services Office

Special Ed. HS course work accepted: Yes
Specific course requirements of all applicants: Yes
Separate application required: No
# of LD applications submitted each year: NR
# of LD applications accepted yearly: NR
Total # of students receiving LD services: 80
Acceptance into program means acceptance into college: Students must be admitted and enrolled in the college prior to requesting services.

ADMISSIONS

The Admissions Office forwards folders for students with documented disabilities who have waived the ACT/SAT or foreign language entrance requirement or have requested evaluation by the Admissions Advocacy Committee for Students with Disabilities. Students may opt to have an interview with the Office of Disability Services. Review by the Admissions Advocacy Committee can be requested by the candidate. General admission requirements include 4 English, 3 math, 3 science, 2 social science, 2 foreign language, and 2 electives. GPA is based on all college-prep courses and weighs honors and Advanced Placement courses. The college looks for a minimum weighted GPA of 3.0. However, the Admissions Committee will consider applicants with GPAs between 2.0 and 2.99 if they submit SAT/ACT scores meeting the sliding scale requirements. Applicants who do not meet the sliding scale requirements will be considered on an individual basis for a limited number of admission exceptions. Meeting the minimum GPA and SAT/ACT requirements does not guarantee admission to the college. Applicants who meet the 3.0 GPA requirements do not have to use the sliding scale for admission, but still must submit competitive SAT/ACT scores if they are applying within 3 years of high school graduation.

ADDITIONAL INFORMATION

Disability Services provides individually tailored support services, programs, and academic accommodations for students with documented disabilities. Services available include: an adaptive computer lab, tape recorders, testing accommodations, note-takers, readers, interpreters, support groups, coaching, and consultation with the faculty. The adaptive computer lab houses a voice-activated computer system, Braille printer, Kurzweil 3000 reading program, scanner with print recognition, screen enlargement programs, a closed circuit television, and speech synthesizers. Students with disabilities needing testing accommodations for placement exams or other standardized tests must submit requests for accommodations. Extended-time, out-of-classroom testing, oral exams, and other alternative testing are options offered to students with disabilities. Course waivers may be available to students with disabilities who need the accommodation of a reduced course load. Waivers are granted by the Dean of Curriculum and Instruction.

LEARNING DISABILITY PROGRAM/SERVICES

Learning Disability Program/Services: Disability Services
Director: Dawn K. Stevenson, MEd, OTR/L
  E-mail: dstevenson@fsc.edu
  Telephone: 978-665-3427
  Fax: 978-665-3021

LEARNING DISABILITY SERVICES

Requests for the following services/accommodations will be evaluated individually based on appropriate and current documentation.

Allowed in exams	**Distraction-reduced environment:** Yes	**Added costs for services:** No
Calculator: No	**Tape recording in class:** Yes	**LD specialists:** No
Dictionary: Yes	**Books on tape from RFBD:** Yes	**Professional tutors:** 2–5
Computer: Yes	**Taping of books not from RFBD:** No	**Peer tutors:** 15–30
Spellchecker: Yes	**Accommodations for students with**	**Max. hours/wk. for services:**
Extended test time: Yes	**ADHD:** Yes	Unlimited
Scribes: Yes	**Reading machine:** Yes	**How professors are notified of**
Proctors: Yes	**Other assistive technology:** Yes	**LD/ADHD:** By student
Oral exams: Yes	**Priority registration:** Yes	
Note-takers: No		

GENERAL ADMISSIONS INFORMATION

Director of Admissions: Lynn Petrillo
Telephone: 978-665-3144

ENTRANCE REQUIREMENTS

Academic units required: 4 English, 3 math, 3 science (2 science labs), 2 foreign language, 1 social studies, 1 history, 2 academic electives. **Academic units recommended:** 4 math. High school diploma is required, and GED is accepted. TOEFL required of all international applicants: minimum paper TOEFL 550, minimum computer TOEFL 213.

Application deadline: Rolling	**SAT Math middle 50% range:**	**Graduated top 10% of class:** NR
Notification: Rolling	460–550	**Graduated top 25% of class:** NR
Average GPA: 2.95	**SAT Critical Reading middle 50%**	**Graduated top 50% of class:** NR
ACT Composite middle 50% range:	**range:** 460–560	
NR	**SAT Writing middle 50% range:** NR	

COLLEGE GRADUATION REQUIREMENTS

Course waivers allowed: Yes
In what course: Varies
Course substitutions allowed: No

ADDITIONAL INFORMATION

Environment: 45-acre campus is located 50 miles from Boston.

Student Body	**Cost Information**	**Greek System**
Undergrad enrollment: 3,157	In-state tuition: $5,000	Fraternity: Yes
Women: 57%	Out-of-state tuition: $10,260	Sorority: Yes
Men: 43%	Room & board: $6,270	Athletics: Division III
Percent out-of-state: 5%	**Housing Information**	
	University housing: Yes	
	Percent living on campus: 41%	

MOUNT IDA COLLEGE

777 Dedham Street, Newton, MA 02459
Phone: 617-928-4553 • Fax: 617-928-4507
E-mail: admissions@mountida.edu • Web: www.mountida.edu
Support: SP • Institution type: 4-year private

LEARNING DISABILITY PROGRAM AND SERVICES

The Learning Opportunities Program (LOP) provides additional academic support for students with LD. The program focuses on developing and strengthening individual learning styles that create successful, independent learners. Students are mainstreamed in a regular degree curriculum. Mount Ida goes the extra mile for all its students, and the LOP is a natural extension of this philosophy. Students discover a supportive environment where a positive, successful experience is the goal. An important component of the LOP is the mentoring relationship with individual learning specialists. Mount Ida also has the Horizon Program to serve the needs of students not accepted into the LOP but who still demonstrate some academic promise and the ability to contribute to the college community. Horizon is a nondegree, transitional program; students take a reduced number of academic classes bolstered by non-academic support classes and tutorials; students who have achieved a minimum 2.0 GPA are eligible to transfer into LOP after their first year. The goal of Horizon is to improve the quality of the college experience by providing a support network so students can better understand themselves, exchanging feelings and personal learning histories, and discovering a commonality that they are not alone in dealing with LD.

LD/ADHD ADMISSIONS INFORMATION

College entrance tests required: Yes
Interview required: No
Essay recommended: Yes
Documentation required for LD: WAIS–III
Documentation required for ADHD: Yes
Submitted to: Admissions
Special Ed. HS course work accepted: Yes

Specific course requirements of all applicants: NR
Separate application required: Yes
# of LD applications submitted each year: 100
# of LD applications accepted yearly: 70–90
Total # of students receiving LD services: 60–90
Acceptance into program means acceptance into college: Students are admitted first to the college and then to the LOP.

ADMISSIONS

There is no special admissions process for students with learning disabilities. Open admissions is available. ACT/SAT are not required for admission. An interview is strongly recommended. Students with disabilities should submit the WAIS–R, a test indicating appropriate reading grade level, and evaluative documentation of the learning disability. Some students may be admitted into a pilot program called Horizon, which is a special admit program. It is a transition program prior to entering the LOP that reduces academic challenges and increases support.

ADDITIONAL INFORMATION

In the Learning Skills Laboratory, students have the opportunity to work with Mount Ida faculty and students to improve study skills. Tutoring provided by professional tutors who are learning specialists is available two times per week. Each tutoring session is private and strategy based. These meetings focus on developing self-advocacy skills and independent learning skills. Other services include reduced course load; enrollment in basic English, if needed; extended testing times; note-taking; diagnostic testing; course substitutions; and counseling. Study skills courses in math and English are available. Additional support and content tutoring are offered in the Academic Success Center. The college also runs a Freshman Experience course that focuses on building the skills necessary to facilitate student success specifically for students who may be under prepared for college. Students work to identify and strengthen their individual learning styles.

LEARNING DISABILITY PROGRAM/SERVICES

Learning Disability Program/Services: Learning Opportunities Program (LOP)
Director: Jill Mehler
  E-mail: jmehler@mountida.edu
  Telephone: 617-928-4648
  Fax: 617-928-4648

LEARNING DISABILITY SERVICES

Requests for the following services/accommodations will be evaluated individually based on appropriate and current documentation.

Allowed in exams	**Distraction-reduced environment:** Yes	**Added costs for services:** Yes
Calculator: Yes	**Tape recording in class:** Yes	**LD specialists:** Yes
Dictionary: Yes	**Books on tape from RFBD:** Yes	**Professional tutors:** 7–10
Computer: No	**Taping of books not from RFBD:** Yes	**Peer tutors:** No
Spellchecker: Yes	**Accommodations for students with**	**Max. hours/wk. for services:** 2
Extended test time: Yes	**ADHD:** Yes	**How professors are notified of**
Scribes: No	**Reading machine:** Yes	**LD/ADHD:** By student
Proctors: No	**Other assistive technology:** Yes	
Oral exams: Yes	**Priority registration:** No	
Note-takers: No		

GENERAL ADMISSIONS INFORMATION

Director of Admissions: Elizabeth Storinge
Telephone: 617-928-4553

ENTRANCE REQUIREMENTS

Academic units required: 4 English. **Academic units recommended:** 3 math, 3 science, 2 foreign language, 2 social studies, 2 history. High school diploma is required, and GED is accepted. ACT without Writing component accepted. TOEFL required of all international applicants: minimum paper TOEFL 525, minimum computer TOEFL 197.

Application deadline: Rolling	**SAT Math middle 50% range:** NR	**Graduated top 10% of class:** NR
Notification: Rolling	**SAT Critical Reading middle 50%**	**Graduated top 25% of class:** NR
Average GPA: 2.0–2.9	**range:** NR	**Graduated top 50% of class:** NR
ACT Composite middle 50% range:	**SAT Writing middle 50% range:** NR	
NR		

COLLEGE GRADUATION REQUIREMENTS

Course waivers allowed: Yes
In what course: No foreign language requirement
Course substitutions allowed: Yes
In what course: Depends on the major and the learning style issues; not a usual accommodation

ADDITIONAL INFORMATION

Environment: Mount Ida's 85-acre campus is in a suburban neighborhood eight miles west of Boston.

Student Body	**Cost Information**	**Greek System**
Undergrad enrollment: 439	**Tuition:** $19,800	**Fraternity:** No
Women: 66%	**Room & board:** $10,225	**Sorority:** No
Men: 34%	**Housing Information**	**Athletics:** Division III
Percent out-of-state: 38%	**University housing:** Yes	
	Percent living on campus: 72%	

NORTHEASTERN UNIVERSITY

360 Huntington Avenue, 150 Richards Hall, Boston, MA 02115
Phone: 617-373-2200 • Fax: 617-373-8780
E-mail: admissions@neu.edu • Web: www.northeastern.edu
Support: SP • Institution type: 4-year private

LEARNING DISABILITY PROGRAM AND SERVICES

The Disability Resource Center (DRC) offers ongoing support and counseling services, academic advising, student advocacy, and help with course and exam modifications for students with LD. Students who apply to the university must have the LD documented through a recent evaluation and must have the willingness to use the resources and services of the program. Students work on a one-to-one basis and in small groups with a learning disabilities specialist. There is no charge for basic support services. Persons with LD who need intensive support may be interested in the independent, highly structured LD program. Students meet with a psychologist and LD specialist who act as primary advisors to explore students' learning strengths and weaknesses and develop specific goals for each quarter. On the basis of individual need, each student receives 3 to 5 hours of one-on-one tutoring weekly. This privately sponsored program, only for students with LD, has an additional cost of $1,400 per quarter.

LD/ADHD ADMISSIONS INFORMATION

College entrance tests required: Yes
Interview required: Yes
Essay recommended: No
Documentation required for LD: Extensive psychoeducational evaluations performed within the past 3 years (see the university's website for more information)
Documentation required for ADHD: Extensive psychoeducational evaluations performed within the past three years (See the university's website for more information)
Submitted to: Disability Resource Center
Special Ed. HS course work accepted: Decided by the director of the program

Specific course requirements of all applicants: Yes
Separate application required: Yes
# of LD applications submitted each year: 25–50
# of LD applications accepted yearly: 10–20
Total # of students receiving LD services: 350
Acceptance into program means acceptance into college: Student must be admitted and enrolled in the university first and then request LD services from DRC or admission to the LD program.

ADMISSIONS

There are two separate application processes involved in admission to Northeastern. Admission requirements to the university are the same for all students, and any student may be eligible for help in the Disability Resource Center. General applicants have a 3.0 GPA and an average SAT of 1150 or ACT of 25. Depending on the program, courses, and diagnosis of the student's learning disability, courses may be substituted for admission. Students apply to the DRC program after admission to the university. There is a separate application and interview needed for the Learning Disability Program, which is the independent program. Students must partake in a full battery of tests that may last for 6–10 hours for this program and must also submit previous diagnostic tests. These students must have an interview. Notification of acceptance is sent from the Office of Admissions.

ADDITIONAL INFORMATION

DRC services include note-taking, readers and scribes, liaison and advocacy services, counseling and referral services, support groups, and basic skills courses taught by LD specialists in time management, learning strategies, study strategies, social skills, and perceptual skills. There are currently 35 students enrolled in the program, and there are always students waiting to be admitted. Documentation must address attention, perception, motor abilities, language, memory, processing speed, organization, emotional factors, and general intellectual and academic functioning. Services and accommodations are available for undergraduate and graduate students.

LEARNING DISABILITY PROGRAM/SERVICES

Learning Disability Program/Services: Disability Resource Program (DRC)
Director: Dean G. Ruth Kukiela Bork
 E-mail: r.bork@neu.edu
 Telephone: 617-373-2675 (v), 617-373-2730 (tty)
 Fax: 617-373-7800
Contact Person: Debbie Auerbach
 E-mail: r.bork@neu.edu
 Telephone: 617-373-4428 (v), 617-373-2730 (tty)
 Fax: 617-373-7800

LEARNING DISABILITY SERVICES

Requests for the following services/accommodations will be evaluated individually based on appropriate and current documentation.

Allowed in exams
 Calculator: Yes
 Dictionary: Yes
 Computer: Yes
 Spellchecker: Yes
Extended test time: Yes
Scribes: Yes
Proctors: Yes
Oral exams: Yes
Note-takers: Yes

Distraction-reduced environment: Yes
Tape recording in class: Yes
Books on tape from RFBD: Yes
Taping of books not from RFBD: Yes
Accommodations for students with ADHD: Yes
Reading machine: Yes
Other assistive technology: Yes
Priority registration: N/A

Added costs for services: Yes
LD specialists: Yes
Professional tutors: 1–8
Peer tutors: Yes
Max. hours/wk. for services: Unlimited
How professors are notified of LD/ADHD: By student

GENERAL ADMISSIONS INFORMATION

Director of Admissions: Ronne Patrick Turner
Telephone: 617-373-2200

ENTRANCE REQUIREMENTS
Academic units required: 4 English, 3 math, 3 science (2 science labs), 2 foreign language, 2 social studies, 2 history. **Academic units recommended:** 4 math, 4 science (4 science labs), 4 foreign language. High school diploma is required, and GED is accepted. ACT with Writing component required. TOEFL required of all international applicants: minimum paper TOEFL 550, minimum computer TOEFL 213.

Application deadline: 1/15
Notification: decisions released between 3/15 and 4/1
Average GPA: NR
ACT Composite middle 50% range: 24–28

SAT Math middle 50% range: 590–680
SAT Critical Reading middle 50% range: 560–650
SAT Writing middle 50% range: NR

Graduated top 10% of class: 38%
Graduated top 25% of class: 76%
Graduated top 50% of class: 95%

COLLEGE GRADUATION REQUIREMENTS

Course waivers allowed: No
Course substitutions allowed: Yes
In what course: Foreign language course substitutions as well as a math class specifically for students with dyscalculia are available with approval from the learning disabilities specialist.

ADDITIONAL INFORMATION

Environment: The school is located on 55 acres in the city of Boston.

Student Body
 Undergrad enrollment: 15,195
 Women: 50%
 Men: 50%
 Percent out-of-state: 65%

Cost Information
 Tuition: $29,910
 Room & board: $10,970
Housing Information
 University housing: Yes
 Percent living on campus: 49%

Greek System
 Fraternity: Yes
 Sorority: Yes
Athletics: Division I

PINE MANOR COLLEGE

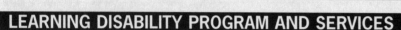

400 Heath Street, Chestnut Hill, MA 02467-2332
Phone: 617-731-7104 • Fax: 617-731-7102
E-mail: admission@pmc.edu • Web: www.pmc.edu
Support: CS • Institution type: 2-year and 4-year private

LEARNING DISABILITY PROGRAM AND SERVICES

The Learning Resource Center (LRC) is an expression of the college's strong commitment to the individual learning experience. The LRC supports and challenges students to realize their maximum academic potential in the way that best suits their individual learning styles. There are five professional tutors—writing tutors, math tutors, learning specialists, and the director—who provide tutoring that is individually tailored to the learning style and needs of the student. The tutoring is not content-oriented, but rather strategy-based and process-oriented. The LRC hopes that students with learning disabilities enter college with some compensatory techniques and study skills. The learning specialists furnish guidance and academic skills assistance to students whose learning disabilities create a gap between their true capacity and daily performance. The LRC serves the whole college population free of charge, whether or not a student has a documented learning disability.

LD/ADHD ADMISSIONS INFORMATION

College entrance tests required: Yes
Interview required: No
Essay recommended: Yes
Documentation required for LD: WAIS–R or WISC–R with all sub scores reported, achievement testing, and/or WJ–III
Documentation required for ADHD: Yes
Submitted to: Learning Resource Center
Special Ed. HS course work accepted: Yes

Specific course requirements of all applicants: NR
Separate application required: No
# of LD applications submitted each year: NR
# of LD applications accepted yearly: NR
Total # of students receiving LD services: 35–50
Acceptance into program means acceptance into college: Students must be admitted and enrolled at the college prior to requesting services from the LRC.

ADMISSIONS

All applicants submit the same general application. Although not required, an interview is highly recommended. The average ACT is 19, and the average SAT is 870. Courses required are 4 years of English, 3 years of math, 2 years of science, and 4 years of social studies. Courses taken in special education are accepted. Admissions decisions are made by the Office of Admissions. However, the director of the LRC assists in interpreting testing and documentation and makes a recommendation to the Office of Admissions. Students are encouraged to self-disclose during the admission process. There is a special optional response form that is used by the LRC after the student is accepted.

ADDITIONAL INFORMATION

LRC staff work with students on a regular, once- or twice-a-week, basis or on a drop-in basis. Students also work closely with their academic advisors. LRC tutors offer diagnosis and remediation for students in academic difficulty, enrichment for successful students, and assistance to faculty and staff. The LRC can also obtain recorded textbooks and arrange for tutors and diagnostic testing. In addition, allowing for the following accommodations has proved useful to students with disabilities: reduced course loads each semester; additional time to complete exams, quizzes, or written assignments; and separate, distraction-free room for examinations. Basic skills classes are offered in reading, math, learning strategies, written language, study strategies, and time management.

LEARNING DISABILITY PROGRAM/SERVICES

Learning Disability Program/Services: Learning Resource Center (LRC)
Director: Mary Walsh
  E-mail: walshmar@pmc.edu
  Telephone: 617-731-7181
  Fax: 617-731-7631

LEARNING DISABILITY SERVICES

Requests for the following services/accommodations will be evaluated individually based on appropriate and current documentation.

Allowed in exams
  Calculator: Yes
  Dictionary: Yes
  Computer: Yes
  Spellchecker: Yes
Extended test time: Yes
Scribes: Yes
Proctors: Yes
Oral exams: Yes
Note-takers: Yes

Distraction-reduced environment: Yes
Tape recording in class: Yes
Books on tape from RFBD: Yes
Taping of books not from RFBD: No
Accommodations for students with ADHD: Yes
Reading machine: No
Other assistive technology: Yes
Priority registration: No

Added costs for services: No
LD specialists: Yes
Professional tutors: 5
Peer tutors: No
Max. hours/wk. for services: 3
How professors are notified of LD/ADHD: By both student and director

GENERAL ADMISSIONS INFORMATION

Director of Admissions: Bill Nichols
Telephone: 617-731-7167

ENTRANCE REQUIREMENTS

Academic units recommended: 4 English, 3 math, 2 science, 2 foreign language, 4 social studies. High school diploma is required, and GED is accepted. ACT with or without Writing component accepted. TOEFL required of all international applicants: minimum paper TOEFL 475, minimum computer TOEFL 150.

Application deadline: Rolling
Notification: Rolling
Average GPA: 2.40
ACT Composite middle 50% range: 15–19

SAT Math middle 50% range: 340–450
SAT Critical Reading middle 50% range: 360–480
SAT Writing middle 50% range: NR

Graduated top 10% of class: 0%
Graduated top 25% of class: 23%
Graduated top 50% of class: 49%

COLLEGE GRADUATION REQUIREMENTS

Course waivers allowed: Yes
In what course: Mathematics
Course substitutions allowed: Yes
In what course: Mathematics

ADDITIONAL INFORMATION

Environment: Pine Manor is located on a 79-acre campus in Chestnut Hill, five miles west of Boston.

Student Body
  Undergrad enrollment: 477
  Women: 100%
  Percent out-of-state: 24%

Cost Information
  Tuition: $15,538
  Room & board: $9,500
  Housing Information
    University housing: Yes
    Percent living on campus: 74%

Greek System
  Fraternity: No
  Sorority: No
Athletics: Division III

SMITH COLLEGE

Seven College Lane, Northampton, MA 01063
Phone: 413-585-2500 • Fax: 413-585-2527
E-mail: admission@smith.edu • Web: www.smith.edu
Support: S • Institution type: 4-year private

LEARNING DISABILITY PROGRAM AND SERVICES

Smith College does not have a formal LD program. However, the college is both philosophically committed and legally required to enable students with documented disabilities to participate in college programs by providing reasonable accommodations for them. The Office of Disabilities Services (ODS) facilitates the provision of services and offers services aimed to eliminate barriers through modification of the program when necessary. A student may voluntarily register with ODS by completing a disability identification form and providing documentation of the disability, after which proper accommodations will be determined. Students with disabilities who need academic services are asked to make their needs known and file timely request forms for accommodations in course work each semester with ODS. The college cannot make retroactive accommodations. Students are encouraged to tell professors about the accommodations needed. The college is responsible for providing that, within certain limits, students are not denied the opportunity to participate in college programs on the basis of a disability. The college will provide support services to students with appropriate evaluations and documentation. Students should contact the ODS for consultation and advice.

LD/ADHD ADMISSIONS INFORMATION

College entrance tests required: Yes
Interview required: Yes
Essay recommended: Yes
Documentation required for LD: WAIS–III; WRAT; Woodcock Johnson Acheivement Battery, and possibly the Nelson-Denny Test. A comprehensive psychoeducational evaluation is required.
Documentation required for ADHD: Physician letter with diagnosis, symptoms and severity, treatment, and recommendations
Submitted to: Office of Disability Services
Special Ed. HS course work accepted: No

Specific course requirements of all applicants: NR
Separate application required: Yes
# of LD applications submitted each year: NR
# of LD applications accepted yearly: NR
Total # of students receiving LD services: 80
Acceptance into program means acceptance into college: Students must be admitted to and enrolled in the university first and then request services.

ADMISSIONS

There is no special admissions procedure for students with learning disabilities. Tests that evaluate cognitive ability, achievement, and information processing should be included with the regular application. It is also helpful to have a letter from a diagnostician documenting services that will be needed in college. SAT and three SAT Subject Tests are required, or the ACT without SAT Subject Tests. Leniency may be granted in regard to a high school's waiving of foreign language requirements due to a learning disability. High school courses recommended are 4 years of English composition and literature, 3 years of a foreign language (or 2 years in each of 2 languages), 3 years of math, 2 years of science, and 2 years of history.

ADDITIONAL INFORMATION

Because college and departmental requirements are implemented for sound academic reasons, Smith College does not provide waivers for required courses for students with LD. The support services assist students to meet their requirements through modifications to programs when necessary. Courses are available in quantitative skills, study skills, and time management skills. The Special Needs Action Group for Support is a cross-disability, student-led group that meets regularly to provide support and peer mentoring and plan activities. Support services include readers, note-takers, scribes, assistive listening devices, typists, computing software and hardware, books on tape, writing counseling (more and/or longer appointments), peer tutoring, and time management/study skills training. If peer tutors are not available, other tutorial services may be sought. The college will not provide services that create an undue burden for the college.

LEARNING DISABILITY PROGRAM/SERVICES

Learning Disability Program/Services: Office of Disability Services (ODS)
Director: Laura Rauscher Coordinator
  E-mail: lrausche@smith.edu
  Telephone: 413-585-2071
  Fax: 413-585-2206

LEARNING DISABILITY SERVICES

Requests for the following services/accommodations will be evaluated individually based on appropriate and current documentation.

Allowed in exams
  Calculator: Yes
  Dictionary: No
  Computer: Yes
  Spellchecker: Yes
Extended test time: Yes
Scribes: Yes
Proctors: No
Oral exams: Yes
Note-takers: Yes

Distraction-reduced environment: Yes
Tape recording in class: Yes
Books on tape from RFBD: Yes
Taping of books not from RFBD: Yes
Accommodations for students with
  ADHD: Yes
Reading machine: Yes
Other assistive technology: Yes
Priority registration: Yes

Added costs for services: No
LD specialists: No
Professional tutors: 2
Peer tutors: Yes
Max. hours/wk. for services:
  Unlimited
How professors are notified of
  LD/ADHD: By both student and
  director

GENERAL ADMISSIONS INFORMATION

Director of Admissions: Debra Shaver
Telephone: 413-585-2500

ENTRANCE REQUIREMENTS

Academic units recommended: 4 English, 3 math, 3 science (3 science labs), 3 foreign language, 2 history.
High school diploma or equivalent is not required. ACT with or without Writing component accepted. TOEFL required of all international applicants: minimum paper TOEFL 600, minimum computer TOEFL 250.

Application deadline: 1/15
Notification: 4/1
Average GPA: 4.00
ACT Composite middle 50% range:
  25–29

SAT Math middle 50% range:
  560–670
SAT Critical Reading middle 50%
  range: 580–700
SAT Writing middle 50% range:
  640–730

Graduated top 10% of class: 61%
Graduated top 25% of class: 91%
Graduated top 50% of class: 100%

COLLEGE GRADUATION REQUIREMENTS

Course waivers allowed: No
Course substitutions allowed: Yes
In what course: Foreign language

ADDITIONAL INFORMATION

Environment: The 204-acre campus is located in a small city 85 miles west of Boston and 15 minutes from Amherst.

Student Body
  Undergrad enrollment: 2,598
  Women: 100%
  Percent out-of-state: 78%

Cost Information
  Tuition: $32,320
  Room & board: $10,880
Housing Information
  University housing: Yes
  Percent living on campus: 88%

Greek System
  Fraternity: No
  Sorority: No
  Athletics: Division III

SPRINGFIELD COLLEGE

263 Alden Street, Springfield, MA 01109
Phone: 413-748-3136 • Fax: 413-748-3694
E-mail: admissions@spfldcol.edu • Web: www.springfieldcollege.edu
Support: CS • Institution type: 4-year private

LEARNING DISABILITY PROGRAM AND SERVICES

Springfield College is committed to providing an equal educational opportunity and full participation in college activities for persons with disabilities. The Office of Student Support Services provides services that ensure that students with disabilities are given an equal educational opportunity and the opportunity for full participation in all college programs and activities. In addition to supporting students with disabilities, Student Support Services works with students who are having academic difficulty. Students can receive services by meeting with the director of Student Support Services to verify eligibility for services, identify student needs, and determine appropriate services and accommodations. To receive services, students must provide documentation of their learning disabilities; the documentation must be current and comprehensive and contain specific evidence and identification of a learning disability. Documentation should not be older than 3 years.

LD/ADHD ADMISSIONS INFORMATION

College entrance tests required: Yes
Interview required: No
Essay recommended: Yes
Documentation required for LD: Psychoeducational evaluation
Documentation required for ADHD: Psychological and medical report by a licensed professional
Submitted to: Office of Student Support Services
Special Ed. HS course work accepted: No

Specific course requirements of all applicants: NR
Separate application required: No
# of LD applications submitted each year: NR
# of LD applications accepted yearly: NR
Total # of students receiving LD services: 150–160
Acceptance into program means acceptance into college: Students must be admitted to and enrolled in the university first and then request services.

ADMISSIONS

There is no special admissions process for students with learning disabilities. All applicants must submit the same general application and meet the same admission criteria. There is no minimum GPA required, though the average GPA is a 3.0. Courses required include 4 years of English, 3 years of math, 2 years of history, and 2–3 years of science. Personal statements and interviews are required. Admissions decisions are made by the Office of Admissions.

ADDITIONAL INFORMATION

Services provided through the Office of Student Support Services include taped textbooks, taped lectures, readers, alternative testing, note-takers, tutors, computers with spell-check, reduced course loads, study skills and time management training, course accommodations, and assistance with course selection. Services and accommodations that may be appropriate for students with attention deficit hyperactivity disorder include testing accommodations, tape recording of lectures, assistance organizational skills, assistance with study skills, and access to adaptive technology. Services and accommodations that may be appropriate for students with learning disabilities include taped textbooks, readers, note-takers, tape recording of lectures, testing accommodations, reduced course load, assistance with study skills, assistance with organizational skills, and adaptive technology. Students experiencing academic difficulties may benefit from working one-on-one with an academic coach. Academic coaches help students put together a plan for success by focusing on each student's academic strengths and weaknesses. Academic coaches are available to help students address problems that impede academic progress, such as procrastination, time mismanagement, and related issues. Academic coaches develop plans to strengthen specific academic skills after an initial assessment. Tutoring is available for any Springfield College student who needs it. Faculty-approved tutors provide individual or small group sessions to students who are concerned about their academic performance.

LEARNING DISABILITY PROGRAM/SERVICES

Learning Disability Program/Services: Student Support Services
Director: Deb Dickens
  E-mail: ddickens@spfldcol.edu
  Telephone: 413-748-3768
  Fax: 413-748-3937

LEARNING DISABILITY SERVICES

Requests for the following services/accommodations will be evaluated individually based on appropriate and current documentation.

Allowed in exams
  Calculator: Yes
  Dictionary: Yes
  Computer: Yes
  Spellchecker: Yes
Extended test time: Yes
Scribes: Yes
Proctors: Yes
Oral exams: Yes
Note-takers: Yes

Distraction-reduced environment: Yes
Tape recording in class: Yes
Books on tape from RFBD: Yes
Taping of books not from RFBD: Yes
Accommodations for students with ADHD: Yes
Reading machine: Yes
Other assistive technology: Yes
Priority registration: No

Added costs for services: No
LD specialists: Yes
Professional tutors: No
Peer tutors: No
Max. hours/wk. for services: Unlimited
How professors are notified of LD/ADHD: By both student and director

GENERAL ADMISSIONS INFORMATION

Director of Admissions: Mary DeAngelo
Telephone: 413-748-3136

ENTRANCE REQUIREMENTS

Academic units recommended: 4 English, 3 math, 3 science, 2 foreign language, 2 social studies, 4 academic electives. High school diploma is required, and GED is accepted. TOEFL required of all international applicants: minimum paper TOEFL 525.

Application deadline: 4/11
Notification: Rolling
Average GPA: NR
ACT Composite middle 50% range: NR

SAT Math middle 50% range: 450–550
SAT Critical Reading middle 50% range: 440–550
SAT Writing middle 50% range: NR

Graduated top 10% of class: 14%
Graduated top 25% of class: 35%
Graduated top 50% of class: 76%

COLLEGE GRADUATION REQUIREMENTS

Course waivers allowed: Yes
In what course: Foreign language
Course substitutions allowed: Yes
In what course: Foreign language

ADDITIONAL INFORMATION

Environment: The campus is in a suburban area about 30 minutes north of Hartford.

Student Body
  Undergrad enrollment: 12,046
  Women: 51%
  Men: 49%
  Percent out-of-state: 66%

Cost Information
  Tuition: $22,000
  Room & board: $8,350
Housing Information
  University housing: Yes
  Percent living on campus: 85%

Greek System
  Fraternity: Yes
  Sorority: Yes
Athletics: Division III

U. OF MASSACHUSETTS—AMHERST

University Admissions Center, 37 Mather Drive, Amherst, MA 01003-9291
Phone: 413-545-0222 • Fax: 413-545-4312
E-mail: mail@admissions.umass.edu • Web: www.umass.edu
Support: CS • Institution type: 4-year public

LEARNING DISABILITY PROGRAM AND SERVICES

Learning Disabilities Support Services (LDSS) is a support service for all students with LD. Students are eligible for services if they can document their LD with the appropriate diagnostic evidence. To be eligible, all students must provide one or more of the following types of documentation: an IEP indicating LD from elementary or secondary school, a report from a state-certified assessment center indicating LD, and/or psychoeducational test results to be interpreted in the LDSS. Not all students with learning problems have learning disabilities. Only students with disabilities may be served by LDSS. Students whose predominate disability is a form of ADHD are served by the Program for Students with Medical Disabilities and not LDSS. Each student enrolled in LDSS is assigned a case manager who is a graduate student in education, counseling, or a related field. Case managers have prior relevant professional experience and are supervised by professional staff. Students work with the same case manager on three objectives for the entire academic year: understanding and obtaining accommodations needed, identifying and utilizing resources, and identifying and implementing learning strategies to compensate for the disability. The goal of LDSS is for students to become independent self-advocates by the time they graduate.

LD/ADHD ADMISSIONS INFORMATION

College entrance tests required: Yes
Interview required: N/A
Essay recommended: Yes
Documentation required for LD: Formal psychoeducational evaluation
Documentation required for ADHD: Formal psychoeducational evaluation
Submitted to: Both Admissions and LD Support Services
Special Ed. HS course work accepted: No

Specific course requirements of all applicants: Yes
Separate application required: Yes
# of LD applications submitted each year: NR
# of LD applications accepted yearly: NR
Total # of students receiving LD services: 407
Acceptance into program means acceptance into college: Students must be admitted to and enrolled in the university first and then request services.

ADMISSIONS

There are no special admissions criteria for students with learning disabilities. General admission requirements recommend that students be in the top 35 percent of their class with a 3.0 GPA, SAT of 1140, or ACT of 24. Course requirements include 4 years of English, 3 years of math, 3 years of social studies, 2 years of science, and 2 years of a foreign language (this can be waived if it is part of the disability). Massachusetts students with learning disabilities do not need to submit ACT/SAT results. All admissions and support documents go through the Admissions Office. All applicants who check the learning disabilities box are reviewed individually by learning disabilities specialists. If any information is missing, the applicant will be notified. There is no quota on the number of students with LD who can be admitted to the university. Students who are otherwise qualified and have taken college-preparatory courses in high school should submit a recent IEP and documentation.

ADDITIONAL INFORMATION

Students and case managers prepare learning style sheets for professors. These forms are requests for various accommodations, such as untimed exams, extended time on assignments, alternate forms of tests, and note-taking. At midsemester, each professor who received an accommodation sheet receives a request from LDSS asking for the student's grades, attendance, and performance. There is individual tutoring weekly for most introductory level courses and math skills, study skills, language arts, written expression, time management, learning strategies, and organizational skills. Tutors are graduate students trained to work with LD. Students with LD can request to substitute a foreign language with cultural courses. Disability Student Network is an organization designed to support the needs of students with disabilities. Faculty Friends is a group of instructors nominated by Disability Student Network as outstanding in teaching and meeting the needs of students with disabilities.

LEARNING DISABILITY PROGRAM/SERVICES

Learning Disability Program/Services: LD Support Services
Director: Madeline L. Peters
  E-mail: mlpeters@stuaf.umass.edu
  Telephone: 413-545-0892
  Fax: 413-577-0122

LEARNING DISABILITY SERVICES

Requests for the following services/accommodations will be evaluated individually based on appropriate and current documentation.

Allowed in exams
  Calculator: Yes
  Dictionary: Yes
  Computer: Yes
  Spellchecker: Yes
Extended test time: Yes
Scribes: Yes
Proctors: Yes
Oral exams: Yes
Note-takers: Yes

Distraction-reduced environment: Yes
Tape recording in class: Yes
Books on tape from RFBD: Yes
Taping of books not from RFBD: Yes
Accommodations for students with ADHD: Yes
Reading machine: Yes
Other assistive technology: Yes
Priority registration: No

Added costs for services: No
LD specialists: Yes
Professional tutors: Yes
Peer tutors: Yes
Max. hours/wk. for services: 1
How professors are notified of LD/ADHD: By both student and director

GENERAL ADMISSIONS INFORMATION

Director of Admissions: Kevin Kelly
Telephone: 413-545-0222

ENTRANCE REQUIREMENTS

Academic units required: 4 English, 3 math, 2 science (2 science labs), 2 foreign language, 2 social studies, 2 academic electives. High school diploma is required, and GED is accepted. ACT without Writing component accepted. TOEFL required of all international applicants: minimum paper TOEFL 550, minimum computer TOEFL 213.

Application deadline: 1/15
Notification: Rolling
Average GPA: 3.46
ACT Composite middle 50% range: NR

SAT Math middle 50% range: 530–640
SAT Critical Reading middle 50% range: 510–620
SAT Writing middle 50% range: NR

Graduated top 10% of class: 23%
Graduated top 25% of class: 58%
Graduated top 50% of class: 94%

COLLEGE GRADUATION REQUIREMENTS

Course waivers allowed: No
Course substitutions allowed: Yes
In what course: The Colleges of Arts and Sciences require foreign language. This requirement is never waived; however, if documented disabilities prevent a student from learning a foreign language, a student can ask for a foreign language modification.

ADDITIONAL INFORMATION

Environment: The university is located on 1,405 acres in a small town 90 miles west of Boston.

Student Body
  Undergrad enrollment: 19,299
  Women: 49%
  Men: 51%
  Percent out-of-state: 18%

Cost Information
  In-state tuition: 9,456
  Out-of-state tuition: $17,070
  Room & board: $6,517
Housing Information
  University housing: Yes
  Percent living on campus: 62%

Greek System
  Fraternity: Yes
  Sorority: Yes
Athletics: Division I

WHEATON COLLEGE (MA)

Office of Admissions, Norton, MA 02766
Phone: 508-286-8251 • Fax: 508-286-8271
E-mail: admission@wheatoncollege.edu • Web: www.wheatoncollege.edu
Support: S • Institution type: 4-year private

LEARNING DISABILITY PROGRAM AND SERVICES

Wheaton College encourages life-long learning by assisting students to become self-advocates and independent learners. The college does not have a special program for students with LD. The Assistant Dean for College Skills serves as the 504/ADA coordinator. Students with LD can access services through the dean. The Academic Advising Center houses the Dean of Academic Advising who holds drop-in office hours and assists students with petitions to the Committee on Admissions and Academic Standing, Orientation, and Probation; general advising; and incomplete grade resolution. The advising staff can assist with pressing advising questions. Students also have access to tutors, peer advisors, and preceptors who offer assistance with study strategies. All students have access to these services.

LD/ADHD ADMISSIONS INFORMATION

College entrance tests required: No
Interview required: No
Essay recommended: No
Documentation required for LD: WAIS–III, WJR, Wexler Memory Scales; aptitude and achievement testing; diagnostic interview; clinical summary, accompanied with rationale for diagnosis and accomodations
Documentation required for ADHD: The tests mentioned above and tests for attention and distractability
Submitted to: Academic Support Services
Special Ed. HS course work accepted: Yes

Specific course requirements of all applicants: NR
Separate application required: No
# of LD applications submitted each year: NR
# of LD applications accepted yearly: NR
Total # of students receiving LD services: 120
Acceptance into program means acceptance into college: Students must be admitted to and enrolled in the university first and then request services.

ADMISSIONS

All applicants must meet the same admission standards. Students with LD may choose to meet with the Assistant Dean for College Skills. Wheaton College does not require the ACT/SAT for admission. It is strongly suggested that students take 4 years of English, 3–4 years of math, 3–4 years of a foreign language, 2 years of social studies, and 3–4 years of science. Students are encouraged to take AP and honors courses and courses in visual/performing arts. Wheaton will accept courses taken in the special education department. Students with LD are encouraged to self-disclose and provide current documentation. All LD testing information should be sent to both admissions and support services.

ADDITIONAL INFORMATION

Services for students with LD can include classroom accommodations, college skills workshops, course tutoring program, general advising, and study strategy tutoring as well as strategy workshops. Reasonable accommodations are available for students with appropriate documentation. There is a summer program available for students who wish to participate. Proctors are not offered because Wheaton has an honor code for exams.

LEARNING DISABILITY PROGRAM/SERVICES

Learning Disability Program/Services: Academic Support Services
Director: Martha Bledsoe, Assistant Dean for Studies and Disability Services
  E-mail: mbledsoe@wheatonma.edu
  Telephone: 508-286-8215
  Fax: 508-286-5621

LEARNING DISABILITY SERVICES

Requests for the following services/accommodations will be evaluated individually based on appropriate and current documentation.

Allowed in exams
  Calculator: Yes
  Dictionary: Yes
  Computer: Yes
  Spellchecker: Yes
Extended test time: Yes
Scribes: Yes
Proctors: No
Oral exams: Yes
Note-takers: Yes

Distraction-reduced environment: Yes
Tape recording in class: Yes
Books on tape from RFBD: Yes
Taping of books not from RFBD: Yes
Accommodations for students with ADHD: Yes
Reading machine: Yes
Other assistive technology: Yes
Priority registration: No

Added costs for services: No
LD specialists: No
Professional tutors: 7
Peer tutors: N/A
Max. hours/wk. for services: Unlimited
How professors are notified of LD/ADHD: By student

GENERAL ADMISSIONS INFORMATION

Director of Admissions: Gail Berson
Telephone: 508-286-8251

ENTRANCE REQUIREMENTS

Academic units recommended: 4 English, 4 math, 3 science (2 science labs), 4 foreign language, 2 social studies, 2 history. High school diploma is required, and GED is accepted. TOEFL required of all international applicants: minimum paper TOEFL 550, minimum computer TOEFL 213.

Application deadline: 1/15
Notification: 4/1
Average GPA: 3.50
ACT Composite middle 50% range: 25–28

SAT Math middle 50% range: 580–670
SAT Critical Reading middle 50% range: 600–680
SAT Writing middle 50% range: NR

Graduated top 10% of class: 53%
Graduated top 25% of class: 83%
Graduated top 50% of class: 99%

COLLEGE GRADUATION REQUIREMENTS

Course waivers allowed: No
Course substitutions allowed: Yes
In what course: Foreign language

ADDITIONAL INFORMATION

Environment: The college is located 35 miles from Boston and 15 miles from Providence, Rhode Island.

Student Body
  Undergrad enrollment: 1,550
  Women: 62%
  Men: 38%
  Percent out-of-state: 67%

Cost Information
  Tuition: $34,365
  Room & board: $8,150
Housing Information
  University housing: Yes
  Percent living on campus: 96%

Greek System
  Fraternity: No
  Sorority: No
Athletics: Division III

WHEELOCK COLLEGE

200 The Riverway, Boston, MA 02215
Phone: 617-879-2206 • Fax: 617-879-2449
E-mail: undergrad@wheelock.edu • Web: www.wheelock.edu
Support: CS • Institution type: 4-year private

LEARNING DISABILITY PROGRAM AND SERVICES

The Disability Services Program in the Office of Academic Advising and Assistance (OAAA) at Wheelock College ensures that students with disabilities can actively participate in all facets of college life. They also provide and coordinate support services and programs that will enable students to maximize their educational potential. Students are encouraged to be independent individuals who know their strengths and develop compensatory skills for academic success. When working with students, the two major goals are to help with becoming independent and assisting in developing self-advocacy skills. Students with LD are encouraged to self-disclose to OAAA. Students are required to provide documentation from a qualified professional. Disability Services will assist in identifying appropriate accommodations based on the documentation provided.

LD/ADHD ADMISSIONS INFORMATION

College entrance tests required: Yes
Interview required: N/A
Essay recommended: NR
Documentation required for LD: Cognitive, achievement, and aptitude testing
Documentation required for ADHD: Medical diagnosis and treatment plan provided by an MD or psychologist
Submitted to: Disability Services Program
Special Ed. HS course work accepted: Yes

Specific course requirements of all applicants: Yes
Separate application required: N/A
# of LD applications submitted each year: NR
# of LD applications accepted yearly: NR
Total # of students receiving LD services: 67
Acceptance into program means acceptance into college: Students must be admitted to and enrolled in the university first and then request services.

ADMISSIONS

There is no special admissions process for students with LD and ADHD. All applicants are expected to meet the general admission criteria. All students should have 4 years of English, 1 year of U.S. history and additional social studies, 3 years of college-prep math, and at least 1 year of science lab. Substitutions are not allowed for entrance requirements. Wheelock will accept courses in high school that were taken in the Special Education Department. Students should feel free to self-disclose their disabilities in the application process. Students must submit a copy of a graded paper written within the past year. It should be a minimum of 250 words and can be on any subject. Some examples are an English composition, a history thesis, a psychology report, or a literary critique.

ADDITIONAL INFORMATION

With appropriate documentation, students may be eligible for the following services or accommodations: priority registration, letters informing the instructors of the disability and what reasonable accommodations the student will need, individual sessions with a learning specialist to help with time management, academic, and organizational skills support. The Writing Center is available for all students interested in assistance with writing skills, and peer tutors work one-on-one with the students. Students may request referrals for peer tutors, and study groups are available. In addition, workshops on the following topics are offered throughout the academic year: academic survival skills, reading skills, and evaluation of students' learning styles. Other academic support services include academic advising, note-takers, textbooks on tape, testing modifications, readers, scribes, and referrals for diagnostic testing.

LEARNING DISABILITY PROGRAM/SERVICES

Learning Disability Program/Services: Disability Support Services
Director: Paul Hastings
　E-mail: phastings@wheelock.edu
　Telephone: 617-879-2304
　Fax: 617-879-2163

LEARNING DISABILITY SERVICES

Requests for the following services/accommodations will be evaluated individually based on appropriate and current documentation.

Allowed in exams
　Calculator: Yes
　Dictionary: Yes
　Computer: Yes
　Spellchecker: Yes
Extended test time: Yes
Scribes: Yes
Proctors: Yes
Oral exams: Yes
Note-takers: Yes

Distraction-reduced environment: Yes
Tape recording in class: Yes
Books on tape from RFBD: Yes
Taping of books not from RFBD: Yes
Accommodations for students with ADHD: Yes
Reading machine: Yes
Other assistive technology: Yes
Priority registration: Yes

Added costs for services: No
LD specialists: Yes
Professional tutors: No
Peer tutors: 25
Max. hours/wk. for services: Unlimited
How professors are notified of LD/ADHD: By student

GENERAL ADMISSIONS INFORMATION

Director of Admissions: Lynne Harding
Telephone: 617-879-2206

ENTRANCE REQUIREMENTS
Academic units required: 4 English, 3 math, 2 science (1 science lab), 2 social studies. High school diploma is required, and GED is accepted. ACT with or without Writing component accepted. TOEFL required of all international applicants: minimum paper TOEFL 500, minimum computer TOEFL 173.

Application deadline: 3/1
Notification: Rolling
Average GPA: 2.90
ACT Composite middle 50% range: 16–19

SAT Math middle 50% range: 410–550
SAT Critical Reading middle 50% range: 430–550
SAT Writing middle 50% range: 440–560

Graduated top 10% of class: 8%
Graduated top 25% of class: 35%
Graduated top 50% of class: 70%

COLLEGE GRADUATION REQUIREMENTS

Course waivers allowed: No
Course substitutions allowed: No

ADDITIONAL INFORMATION

Environment: Wheelock College is located in the Fenway area of Boston, two miles from downtown.

Student Body
　Undergrad enrollment: 717
　Women: 96%
　Men: 4%
　Percent out-of-state: 48%

Cost Information
　Tuition: $24,235
　Room & board: $9,910
Housing Information
　University housing: Yes
　Percent living on campus: 70%

Greek System
　Fraternity: No
　Sorority: No
Athletics: Division III

ADRIAN COLLEGE

110 South Madison Street, Adrian, MI 49221
Phone: 517-265-5161 • Fax: 517-264-3331
E-mail: admissions@adrian.edu • Web: www.adrian.edu
Support: CS • Institution type: 4-year private

LEARNING DISABILITY PROGRAM AND SERVICES

Adrian College has extensive academic support services for all students with disabilities. The more the students are mainstreamed in high school, the greater their chances of success at Adrian in their mainstream program. There is no special or separate curriculum for students with learning disabilities. Project EXCEL is the umbrella program for all services at Adrian. EXCEL supports 160 students yearly with scholarships and services aimed at persistence, retention, and graduation. Students qualify who are first-generation college students, come from low-income households, and/or are students with disabilities. Services offered to EXCEL participants include unlimited, free tutoring; skills development courses; educational opportunities; career assessments; and scholarship software. Any member of the Academic Services staff can be of assistance with online and paper-pencil assessments and programs exploring careers and scholarships. The members of the Academic Services staff are retention specialists trained in many facets of student success who can help with academic needs.

LD/ADHD ADMISSIONS INFORMATION

College entrance tests required: Yes
Interview required: No
Essay recommended: No
Documentation required for LD: Current psychoeducational evaluation
Documentation required for ADHD: Current evaluation
Submitted to: ACCESS
Special Ed. HS course work accepted: Yes

Specific course requirements of all applicants: NR
Separate application required: Yes
# of LD applications submitted each year: 10
# of LD applications accepted yearly: NR
Total # of students receiving LD services: 37
Acceptance into program means acceptance into college: Students must be admitted to and enrolled in the university first and then request services.

ADMISSIONS

Students with learning disabilities must meet regular admission criteria. Students should demonstrate the ability to do college-level work through an acceptable GPA in college-preparatory classes such as 4 years of English and 2 years of math, social studies, science, and a foreign language; ACT (17-plus) or SAT scores; and a psychological report. Furthermore, by their senior year in high school, students should, for the most part, be mainstreamed. Courses taken in special education will be considered for admission. The applications of students who self-disclose are reviewed by Academic Services staff, not to determine admissions, but to start a documentation file. There is a special admissions program designed for students who demonstrate academic potential. This Special Admissions Support Program (SASP) requires students to sign a contract and maintain a certain GPA by the first semester each of the first two semesters.

ADDITIONAL INFORMATION

Course adaptations help to make courses more understandable. Skills classes are available in reading, math, study skills, and research paper writing, and students are granted credit toward their GPA. Support services and accommodations are available, if appropriate, in the following areas: extended time on tests; distraction-free testing environments; scribes; note-takers; proctors; use of calculators, dictionaries, spellcheckers, and computers during exams; taped textbooks; and reading machines. Tutorial assistance is available for all students, and there are three full-time and one part-time LD specialists on staff. The Enrichment Program supports specially admitted first-year students. The Academic Services staff works collaboratively with college faculty to support the learning environment of Enrichment Program students throughout the first year. The program provides study tools to students as they adjust to the new and challenging environment in which they find themselves. The goals of the program are to enhance student experiences in the classroom, encourage active involvement in learning, and lead to first-year success. Some of the opportunities included in the program include skills-building classes, tutoring, frequent academic counseling with Academic Services, and possible participation in EXCEL

LEARNING DISABILITY PROGRAM/SERVICES

Learning Disability Program/Services: ACCESS, Academic Services
Director: Jane McCloskey
  E-mail: jmccloskey@adrian.edu
  Telephone: 517-265-5161, ext. 4093
  Fax: 517-264-3331
Contact Person: Carol Tapp
  E-mail: jmccloskey@adrian.edu
  Telephone: 517-265-5161, ext. 4094
  Fax: 517-264-3331

LEARNING DISABILITY SERVICES

Requests for the following services/accommodations will be evaluated individually based on appropriate and current documentation.

Allowed in exams
  Calculator: Yes
  Dictionary: No
  Computer: Yes
  Spellchecker: Yes
Extended test time: Yes
Scribes: Yes
Proctors: Yes
Oral exams: Yes
Note-takers: Yes

Distraction-reduced environment: Yes
Tape recording in class: Yes
Books on tape from RFBD: Yes
Taping of books not from RFBD: Yes
**Accommodations for students with
  ADHD:** Yes
Reading machine: Yes
Other assistive technology: No
Priority registration: No

Added costs for services: No
LD specialists: Yes
Professional tutors: No
Peer tutors: 30–40
Max. hours/wk. for services:
  Unlimited
**How professors are notified of
  LD/ADHD:** By both student and
  director

GENERAL ADMISSIONS INFORMATION

Director of Admissions: Ms. Janel A. Sutkus
Telephone: 517-265-5161

ENTRANCE REQUIREMENTS

Academic units recommended: 4 English, 2 math, 2 science (1 science lab), 2 foreign language, 2 social studies, 1 history, 3 academic electives. High school diploma is required, and GED is accepted. ACT with or without Writing component accepted. TOEFL required of all international applicants: minimum paper TOEFL 500, minimum computer TOEFL 173.

Application deadline: 8/15
Notification: Rolling
Average GPA: 3.10
ACT Composite middle 50% range:
  18–23

SAT Math middle 50% range: NR
**SAT Critical Reading middle 50%
  range:** NR
SAT Writing middle 50% range: NR

Graduated top 10% of class: 13%
Graduated top 25% of class: 32%
Graduated top 50% of class: 61%

COLLEGE GRADUATION REQUIREMENTS

Course waivers allowed: No
Course substitutions allowed: No

ADDITIONAL INFORMATION

Environment: The school is located on 100 acres in a residential section of Michigan 35 miles northeast of Ann Arbor.

Student Body
  Undergrad enrollment: 1,010
  Women: 54%
  Men: 46%
  Percent out-of-state: 20%

Cost Information
  Tuition: $17,000
  Room & board: $6,000
Housing Information
  University housing: Yes
  Percent living on campus: 77%

Greek System
  Fraternity: Yes
  Sorority: Yes
Athletics: Division III

Adrian College

CALVIN COLLEGE

3201 Burton Street Southeast, Grand Rapids, MI 49546
Phone: 616-526-6106 • Fax: 616-526-6777
E-mail: admissions@calvin.edu • Web: www.calvin.edu
Support: CS • Institution type: 4-year private

LEARNING DISABILITY PROGRAM AND SERVICES

The mission of Student Academic Services is to ensure that otherwise qualified students are able to benefit from a distinctly Christian education based on liberal arts. The Coaching Program is for students with learning disabilities and/or ADHD and other students who specifically need help with time management and study skills. The coaches give suggestions and feedback as well as encouragement on how to manage academics with other areas of life. First-year students are encouraged to apply for the Coaching Program at the beginning of the fall semester. Once admitted, the student with a learning disability or ADHD may take advantage of all academic services. The student must understand, however, that academic standards at Calvin are rigorous. By taking advantage of appropriate services and by means of individual effort, it is assumed that academic progress will be made. The student and the disability coordinator maintain open communication with the appropriate faculty members to ensure academic integrity as well as reasonable expectations.

LD/ADHD ADMISSIONS INFORMATION

College entrance tests required: Yes
Interview required: No
Essay recommended: No
Documentation required for LD: Psychoeducational evaluation
Documentation required for ADHD: Clear statement of DSM–IV diagnosis, with a description of assessment procedures including behavior rating scales, vigilance, and sustained attention deficit hyperactivity disorder.
Submitted to: Student Academic Services

Special Ed. HS course work accepted: No
Specific course requirements of all applicants: Yes
Separate application required: No
# of LD applications submitted each year: NR
# of LD applications accepted yearly: NR
Total # of students receiving LD services: 106
Acceptance into program means acceptance into college: Students must be admitted to and enrolled in the university first and then request services.

ADMISSIONS

There are no special admissions criteria for students with LD. Applicants are expected to have an ACT of 20 (19 English and 20 Math) or SAT of 810 (390 Verbal and 420 Math). The mid 50 percent for ACT is 23–25, and for SAT, it is 1090–1320. Courses required include: 3 English, 1 algebra, 1 geometry, and a minimum of 2 in any two of the following fields: social science, language, or natural science; one of the foreign language, math, social science, and natural science fields must include at least 3 years of study. The mid 50 percent GPA is 3.3–3.9. The Access Program provides an alternate entry track for first-time students who show promise of being successful at Calvin, but who cannot meet all of the admissions standards. The students are provided with placement testing in math and/or English, special advising, and enrollment in a college thinking and learning course during their first semester at Calvin. Depending on the outcome of the placement testing, additional developmental courses may be required as a condition of admission. The Access Program helps students develop new approaches, methods, and skills for learning by means of placement testing, academic advising, Academic Services Courses (ASC), and consultation with students' professors.

ADDITIONAL INFORMATION

The Office of Student Academic Services is a learning center is open to all students. SAS provides tutoring in most core and upper-level courses by trained upperclass students. Tutors meet with students each week to assist them in learning course content and in developing good approaches to learning. Classes are available in English, math, and study skills. These classes may be taken for college credit. The Coaching Program is an interactive relationship with another student who learns about the student's disability and learning style and then provides direction and strategies for the student. The program provides support in the areas of education and self-advocacy, time management and avoiding procrastination, note-taking, providing environments for studying, taking tests, and general organizational skills. Services and accommodations are offered to undergraduate and graduate students. Students who self-disclose and are admitted to the college are then reviewed for services.

LEARNING DISABILITY PROGRAM/SERVICES

Learning Disability Program/Services: Student Academic Services
Director: James Mackenzie, PhD
  E-mail: jmackenz@calvin.edu
  Telephone: 616-957-6113
  Fax: 616-957-8551
Contact Person: June DeBoer
  E-mail: jmackenz@calvin.edu
  Telephone: 616-957-6937
  Fax: 616-957-7066

LEARNING DISABILITY SERVICES

Requests for the following services/accommodations will be evaluated individually based on appropriate and current documentation.

Allowed in exams
  Calculator: Yes
  Dictionary: No
  Computer: Yes
  Spellchecker: Yes
Extended test time: Yes
Scribes: Yes
Proctors: Yes
Oral exams: No
Note-takers: Yes

Distraction-reduced environment: Yes
Tape recording in class: Yes
Books on tape from RFBD: Yes
Taping of books not from RFBD: Yes
Accommodations for students with ADHD: Yes
Reading machine: No
Other assistive technology: Yes
Priority registration: Yes

Added costs for services: No
LD specialists: Yes
Professional tutors: 2
Peer tutors: 65–70
Max. hours/wk. for services: Unlimited
How professors are notified of LD/ADHD: By student

GENERAL ADMISSIONS INFORMATION

Director of Admissions: Dale Kuiper
Telephone: 616-526-6110

ENTRANCE REQUIREMENTS
Academic units required: 3 English, 3 math, 2 science, 2 social studies, 3 academic electives. **Academic units recommended:** 4 English, 3 math, 2 science (1 science lab), 2 foreign language, 3 social studies, 3 academic electives. High school diploma is required, and GED is accepted. ACT with or without Writing component accepted. TOEFL required of all international applicants: minimum paper TOEFL 550, minimum computer TOEFL 213.

Application deadline: 8/15
Notification: Rolling
Average GPA: 3.57
ACT Composite middle 50% range: 23–28

SAT Math middle 50% range: 550–670
SAT Critical Reading middle 50% range: 540–663
SAT Writing middle 50% range: NR

Graduated top 10% of class: 26%
Graduated top 25% of class: 54%
Graduated top 50% of class: 80%

COLLEGE GRADUATION REQUIREMENTS

Course waivers allowed: No
Course substitutions allowed: Yes
In what course: Foreign language with documentation

ADDITIONAL INFORMATION

Environment: The college is located on a 370-acre campus in a suburban area seven miles southeast of Grand Rapids.

Student Body
  Undergrad enrollment: 4,040
  Women: 54%
  Men: 46%
  Percent out-of-state: 41%

Cost Information
  Tuition: $20,245
  Room & board: $7,040
Housing Information
  University housing: Yes
  Percent living on campus: 58%

Greek System
  Fraternity: No
  Sorority: No
Athletics: Division III

FERRIS STATE UNIVERSITY

1201 South State St., Center for Student Services, Big Rapids, MI 49307
Phone: 231-591-2100 • Fax: 231-591-3944
E-mail: admissions@ferris.edu • Web: www.ferris.edu
Support: CS • Institution type: 4-year public

LEARNING DISABILITY PROGRAM AND SERVICES

Ferris State University is committed to a policy of equal opportunity for qualified students. The mission of Disabilities Services is to serve and advocate for students with disabilities, empowering them for self-reliance and independence. Ferris State does not have a program for students with learning disabilities, but does provide a variety of support services and accommodations for students with documented learning disabilities that interfere with the learning process. Ferris State does not, however, attempt to rehabilitate learning disabilities. To obtain support services, students need to meet with a special needs counselor in the Academic Support Center. Students will complete a request for services application and a release form allowing the university to obtain a copy of the documentation of the disability. Documentation for LD/ADHD must be current and be submitted by a qualified professional. Professional development is offered to faculty and staff.

LD/ADHD ADMISSIONS INFORMATION

College entrance tests required: Yes
Interview required: No
Essay recommended: No
Documentation required for LD: Psychoeducational report: WAIS–III and KTEA, WRAT, WIAT, or Woodcock-Johnson Battery
Documentation required for ADHD: ADHD behavior checklist report must contain a diagnosis, scores and/or results of behavior ratings, and the evaluator's credentials.
Submitted to: Disabilities Services
Special Ed. HS course work accepted: Yes

Specific course requirements of all applicants: NR
Separate application required: Yes
# of LD applications submitted each year: 60–75
# of LD applications accepted yearly: 60–75
Total # of students receiving LD services: NR
Acceptance into program means acceptance into college: Students must be admitted to and enrolled in the university first and then request services.

ADMISSIONS

Students with learning disabilities must submit the general application form and should meet the same entrance criteria as all students. Qualified persons with disabilities may not be denied or subjected to discrimination in admission. There is no limit on the number of students admitted with disabilities. ACT scores are used for placement only and may not have an adverse effect on applicants with disabilities. No pre-admission inquiry regarding a possible disability can be made. Therefore, students with LD/ADHD are encouraged to self-disclose and provide information as to the extent of the disability. Sometimes a pre-admission interview is required if the GPA is questionable. In general, students should have a 2.0 GPA, but some programs require a higher GPA and specific courses. Diverse curricula offerings and a flexible admissions policy allow for the admission of most high school graduates and transfer students. Some programs are selective in nature and require the completion of specific courses and/or a minimum GPA. The special needs counselor is involved in the admissions decision when there is a question about academic preparedness.

ADDITIONAL INFORMATION

Disability Services provides services and accommodations to students with LD or ADHD with appropriate documentation. These could include the Arkenstone Reading System; calculators for exams; Dragon Dictate voice interactive software; assistance with membership in Recording for the Blind and Dyslexic; extended testing times for essay tests and/or exams; texts on tape, additional classroom material on tape, and use of four-track tape players; spellchecker for essay tests or exams; note-takers; standing tutoring appointments; word processing for essay tests; use of tape players in class; copies of overheads or PowerPoint presentations; quiet areas; educational counseling; and Kurtzweil/JAWS. Student Development Services offers tutoring for most courses. Flex tutoring is designed for in-depth clarification and review of subject material, and workshop tutoring is designed for short-term, walk-in assistance. The Collegiate Skills Program is designed to help academically underprepared students succeed in college by offering assistance in reading, writing, and study skills. Students also have an opportunity to develop skills in goal setting, decision making, and time management. The Academic Skills Center offers special instruction to assist students in improving their academic performance. Additionally, the following are offered: admission assistance, early registration, counseling/career awareness, academic assistance, campus advocacy, case conferences with referring agencies, and referrals to appropriate university and community agencies.

LEARNING DISABILITY PROGRAM/SERVICES

Learning Disability Program/Services: Disabilities Services
Director: Eunice Merwin
  E-mail: EuniceMerwin@ferris.edu
  Telephone: 231-591-3772
  Fax: 231-591-5398
Contact Person: Eunice Merwin/Kerstin Rios
  E-mail: EuniceMerwin@ferris.edu
  Telephone: 231-595-3772/231-591-5039

LEARNING DISABILITY SERVICES

Requests for the following services/accommodations will be evaluated individually based on appropriate and current documentation.

Allowed in exams
  Calculator: Yes
  Dictionary: Yes
  Computer: Yes
  Spellchecker: Yes
Extended test time: Yes
Scribes: Yes
Proctors: Yes
Oral exams: Yes
Note-takers: Yes

Distraction-reduced environment: Yes
Tape recording in class: Yes
Books on tape from RFBD: Yes
Taping of books not from RFBD: Yes
Accommodations for students with ADHD: Yes
Reading machine: Yes
Other assistive technology: Yes
Priority registration: No

Added costs for services: No
LD specialists: Yes
Professional tutors: 5
Peer tutors: 100
Max. hours/wk. for services: NR
How professors are notified of LD/ADHD: By director

GENERAL ADMISSIONS INFORMATION

Director of Admissions: Craig Westman
Telephone: 800-433-7747

ENTRANCE REQUIREMENTS

Academic units recommended: 4 English, 4 math, 3 science (1 science lab), 2 foreign language, 2 social studies, 2 history, 3 academic electives. High school diploma is required, and GED is accepted. ACT with or without Writing component accepted. TOEFL required of all international applicants: minimum paper TOEFL 500, minimum computer TOEFL 173.

Application deadline: 8/4
Notification: Rolling
Average GPA: 3.18
ACT Composite middle 50% range: 18–23

SAT Math middle 50% range: NR
SAT Critical Reading middle 50% range: NR
SAT Writing middle 50% range: NR

Graduated top 10% of class: NR
Graduated top 25% of class: NR
Graduated top 50% of class: NR

COLLEGE GRADUATION REQUIREMENTS

Course waivers allowed: No
Course substitutions allowed: No

ADDITIONAL INFORMATION

Environment: The university is located on 600 acres 50 miles north of Grand Rapids.

Student Body
  Undergrad enrollment: 11,030
  Women: 47%
  Men: 53%
  Percent out-of-state: 5%

Cost Information
  In-state tuition: $7,200
  Out-of-state tuition: $14,640
  Room & board: $7,220
Housing Information
  University housing: Yes
  Percent living on campus: 38%

Greek System
  Fraternity: Yes
  Sorority: Yes
Athletics: Division II

FINLANDIA UNIVERSITY

601 Quincy Street, Hancock, MI 49930
Phone: 877-202-5491
E-mail: admissions@finlandia.edu • Web: www.finlandia.edu
Support: SP • Institution type: 4-year private

LEARNING DISABILITY PROGRAM AND SERVICES

Through Suomi's Learning Disabilities Program, students will receive individual counseling, tutoring, academic advising, career counseling, and lots of support and encouragement. The LD program is designed for students who need personalized attention and additional education before entering a liberal arts or career program. Careful academic planning is performed by the LD director to ensure that students carry a reasonable credit load that is sequential and well balanced and that focuses on reading, written assignments, and other course requirements. The faculty is supportive, and written and verbal communication between the LD director and faculty is frequent. Student performance is monitored, and there are weekly scheduled meetings. The director is the advisor and support person overseeing and coordinating each individual's program. Self-advocacy and compensatory skills are goals rather than remediation. There is a 7-day orientation prior to freshman year. Advisors work with students during the orientation to plan the best course of study, provide advice and assurance that the student will get what is needed in the program, provide encouragement, and may even be able to match the student with professors whose style of teaching best complements the student's style of learning.

LD/ADHD ADMISSIONS INFORMATION

College entrance tests required: No
Interview required: No
Essay recommended: No
Documentation required for LD: Test results from a medical doctor and/or a prior educational facility
Documentation required for ADHD: Test results from a medical doctor and/or a prior educational facility
Submitted to: Learning Disabilities Program
Special Ed. HS course work accepted: No

Specific course requirements of all applicants: NR
Separate application required: No
# of LD applications submitted each year: NR
# of LD applications accepted yearly: NR
Total # of students receiving LD services: 15–20
Acceptance into program means acceptance into college: Students are reviewed jointly by the LD program and the Office of Admissions to reach an admission decision.

ADMISSIONS

General admission requirements must be met by all applicants. ACT/SAT are not required for admission. Students with learning disabilities should submit an evaluation that has been completed within the past 3 years, documenting the learning disability; an IEP; and a handwritten essay by the student describing the learning disability. Sometimes a telephone interview or visitation is requested to help determine a student's eligibility for the program. An applicant must have the academic ability and background for work on a college level. Each applicant is evaluated individually by the director of the LD program and the admissions staff. Depending on the high school information provided, some students will be given the dual designation of LD/pro-college if the director of the program feels the student may be at risk.

ADDITIONAL INFORMATION

The program director provides professors with a disability data sheet to request accommodations and also meets individually with faculty regarding student needs. Special services offered include alternative testing, individual counseling, career counseling, auxiliary aids and services, academic advising, computer-based instruction, group and individualized courses, support from the Teaching/Learning Center, and support from Student Support Services. The director of the program is certified to teach students with learning disabilities and will help them set up a plan for growth and strength in areas that are challenging. Students will meet with their advisor once a week for as much or as little time as is needed. Students may take skills classes, for noncollege credit, in reading and study strategies. A 1-week summer orientation program is required for incoming freshmen.

LEARNING DISABILITY PROGRAM/SERVICES

Learning Disability Program/Services: Disability Student Services
Director: Kirsti Arko
    E-mail: kirsti.arko@finlandia.edu
    Telephone: 906-487-7276
    Fax: 906-487-7535

LEARNING DISABILITY SERVICES

Requests for the following services/accommodations will be evaluated individually based on appropriate and current documentation.

Allowed in exams
  Calculator: Yes
  Dictionary: Yes
  Computer: Yes
  Spellchecker: Yes
Extended test time: Yes
Scribes: Yes
Proctors: Yes
Oral exams: Yes
Note-takers: Yes

Distraction-reduced environment: Yes
Tape recording in class: Yes
Books on tape from RFBD: Yes
Taping of books not from RFBD: Yes
Accommodations for students with
  ADHD: Yes
Reading machine: Yes
Other assistive technology: No
Priority registration: No

Added costs for services: No
LD specialists: Yes
Professional tutors: 7
Peer tutors: 5
Max. hours/wk. for services:
  Unlimited
How professors are notified of
  LD/ADHD: By both student and
  director

GENERAL ADMISSIONS INFORMATION

Director of Admissions: Ben Larson
Telephone: 877-202-5491

ENTRANCE REQUIREMENTS

High school diploma or GED accepted. Applicants must have the academic ability and background to work on a college level. ACT/SAT not required. TOEFL required of all international applicants, minimum paper TOEFL 400, minimum computer TOEFL 97.

Application deadline: Rolling
Notification: Rolling
Average GPA: 2.8
ACT Composite middle 50% range:
  NR

SAT Math middle 50% range: NR
SAT Critical Reading middle 50%
  range: NR
SAT Writing middle 50% range: NR

Graduated top 10% of class: 15%
Graduated top 25% of class: 33%
Graduated top 50% of class: 70%

COLLEGE GRADUATION REQUIREMENTS

Course waivers allowed: No
Course substitutions allowed: Yes
In what course: Math

ADDITIONAL INFORMATION

Environment: The school is located in a beautiful and rugged area of the Upper Peninsula of Michigan.

Student Body
  Undergrad enrollment: 515
  Women: 69%
  Men: 31%
  Percent out-of-state: 24%

Cost Information
  Tuition: $17,414
  Room & board: $5,800
Housing Information
  University housing: Yes
  Percent living on campus: 45%

Greek System
  Fraternity: No
  Sorority: No
Athletics: Intramural and varsity sports

GRAND VALLEY STATE UNIVERSITY

One Campus Drive, Allendale, MI 49401
Phone: 616-331-2025 • Fax: 616-331-2000
E-mail: go2gvsu@gvsu.edu • Web: www.gvsu.edu
Support: S • Institution type: 4-year public

LEARNING DISABILITY PROGRAM AND SERVICES

The Office of Academic Support at Grand Valley State University provides academic support services and accommodations that enhance the learning environment for students with disabilities and helps educate the university community on disability issues. In addition to the regular services the university offers student skill assessment, academic and career advising, specialized tutoring, textbooks on tape, note-taking assistance, alternative test-taking assistance, peer mentoring, and counseling. OAS provides students with memoranda documenting their disability. The documentation will contain information on the nature of the disability and what academic accommodations the student may need.

LD/ADHD ADMISSIONS INFORMATION

College entrance tests required: Yes
Interview required: No
Essay recommended: No
Documentation required for LD: Psychoeducational evaluation
Documentation required for ADHD: Yes
Submitted to: Office of Academic Support
Special Ed. HS course work accepted: Yes

Specific course requirements of all applicants: Yes
Separate application required: Yes
# of LD applications submitted each year: 20–55
# of LD applications accepted yearly: 11
Total # of students receiving LD services: 263
Acceptance into program means acceptance into college: Students must be admitted to and enrolled in the university first and then request services.

ADMISSIONS

Students are given the opportunity to provide documentation of their LD or ADHD. Information is reviewed by the Office of Academic Support and Admissions. Students interested in special accommodations need to submit both the regular admissions application and a separate application for the program. An evaluation report should include the summary of a comprehensive diagnostic interview. Standardized tests are required for admission. General admission requirements include 4 years of English, 3 years of math, 3 years of social science, and 2 years of science. The average ACT score is 23 or 1050–1080 SAT Reasoning and a 2.8 GPA.

ADDITIONAL INFORMATION

Once admitted into the program students may request that an instructor progress report be sent to each of their professors. The purpose of this report is to inform students of their current academic standing in a class. Academic Support staff provide the following services: working with students to help them improve their academic weaknesses and increase their areas of strength; academic and career advising; specialized tutoring in addition to the general tutoring available for all students; seminars on reading textbooks, note-taking, time management, and test-taking strategies; tape recording of texts not available through RFBD; alternative test-taking; peer mentoring; and counseling. There is also the Organization for the Achievement of Disabled Students, which is a student organization whose goal is to advance the educational and career goals of students with disabilities.

LEARNING DISABILITY PROGRAM/SERVICES

Learning Disability Program/Services: Academic Support (OAS)
Director: Kathleen Vanderveen
   E-mail: vandervk@gvsu.edu
   Telephone: 616-331-2490
   Fax: 616-331-3440
Contact Person: Sandy Sall or Pat DeJoug
   E-mail: vandervk@gvsu.edu
   Telephone: 616-331-2490
   Fax: 616-331-3440

LEARNING DISABILITY SERVICES

Requests for the following services/accommodations will be evaluated individually based on appropriate and current documentation.

Allowed in exams
   Calculator: Yes
   Dictionary: Yes
   Computer: Yes
   Spellchecker: Yes
Extended test time: Yes
Scribes: Yes
Proctors: Yes
Oral exams: Yes
Note-takers: Yes

Distraction-reduced environment: Yes
Tape recording in class: Yes
Books on tape from RFBD: Yes
Taping of books not from RFBD: No
Accommodations for students with ADHD: Yes
Reading machine: No
Other assistive technology: Yes
Priority registration: Yes

Added costs for services: No
LD specialists: No
Professional tutors: No
Peer tutors: 140
Max. hours/wk. for services: 4
How professors are notified of LD/ADHD: By student

GENERAL ADMISSIONS INFORMATION

Director of Admissions: Jodi Chycinski
Telephone: 616-331-2025

ENTRANCE REQUIREMENTS

Academic units required: 4 English, 3 math, 2 science (1 science lab), 2 foreign language, 3 social studies.
Academic units recommended: 4 English, 4 math, 4 science (2 science labs), 2 foreign language, 3 social studies, 1 computer science, 1 fine arts. High school diploma is required, and GED is accepted. ACT without Writing component accepted. TOEFL required of all international applicants: minimum paper TOEFL 550, minimum computer TOEFL 213.

Application deadline: 5/1
Notification: Rolling
Average GPA: 3.53
ACT Composite middle 50% range: 22–26

SAT Math middle 50% range: NR
SAT Critical Reading middle 50% range: NR
SAT Writing middle 50% range: NR

Graduated top 10% of class: 21%
Graduated top 25% of class: 55%
Graduated top 50% of class: 90%

COLLEGE GRADUATION REQUIREMENTS

Course waivers allowed: No
Course substitutions allowed: No

ADDITIONAL INFORMATION

Environment: The campus is located 12 miles from Grand Rapids, Michigan.

Student Body
   Undergrad enrollment: 19,388
   Women: 61%
   Men: 39%
   Percent out-of-state: 4%

Cost Information
   In-state tuition: $6,220
   Out-of-state tuition: $13,000
   Room & board: $6,600
Housing Information
   University housing: Yes
   Percent living on campus: 27%

Greek System
   Fraternity: Yes
   Sorority: Yes
Athletics: Division II

MICHIGAN STATE UNIVERSITY

250 Administration Building, East Lansing, MI 48824-1046
Phone: 517-355-8332 • Fax: 517-353-1647
E-mail: admis@msu.edu • Web: www.msu.edu
Support: CS • Institution type: 4-year public

LEARNING DISABILITY PROGRAM AND SERVICES

MSU is serious in its commitment to helping students no matter what the disability. Their mission is to be an advocate for the inclusion of students with disabilities into the total university experience. The Resource Center for Persons with Disabilities' (RCPD) purpose is to respond to the needs of students by providing resources that equalize their chances for success, support their full participation in all university programs, and act as a resource for the university community and the community at large. The RCPD will facilitate reasonable accommodations for persons with disabilities, coordinate the identification of students with disabilities, and provide referrals. Students must provide recent documentation and history in the form of a school report, a psychologist's assessment or certification by another recognized authority, and contain a clearly stated diagnosis. The RCPD will help facilitate reasonable accommodations for students.

LD/ADHD ADMISSIONS INFORMATION

College entrance tests required: Yes
Interview required: No
Essay recommended: No
Documentation required for LD: Psychoeducational evaluation
Documentation required for ADHD: Yes—a verification form for documentation of ADHD
Submitted to: RCPD
Special Ed. HS course work accepted: No

Specific course requirements of all applicants: Yes
Separate application required: No
# of LD applications submitted each year: NR
# of LD applications accepted yearly: NR
Total # of students receiving LD services: 360
Acceptance into program means acceptance into college: Students must be admitted to and enrolled in the university first and then request services.

ADMISSIONS

Admission for students with learning disabilities to the university is based on the same criteria used for all other students. Courses required include 4 years of English, including instruction and practice in writing; 3 years of mathematics, including a calculus preparatory class; 3 years of social science with at least 1 year of history and 1 year in such areas as sociology, anthropology, economics, geography, government, political science, and psychology; 2 years of college-preparatory science from the disciplines of biology, chemistry, physics, and earth science; and 2 years of a foreign language. The College Achievement Admissions Program (CAAP) is an alternative admissions procedure for students who have academic potential but who would be unable to realize that potential without special support services due to their economic, cultural, or educational background. Students with learning disabilities should not send any documentation to the Office of Admissions. All documentation should be sent to the RCPD.

ADDITIONAL INFORMATION

Specialists are available by appointment to provide information to students. Accommodations include priority registration, study skills training and tutoring, assistive technology and training, taped texts, voice output computers, taping of lectures, extended time on tests, readers or scribes, quiet rooms for tests, advocacy assistance from specialists and letters to professors, support groups through the RCPD, and consultation with service providers. Various other resources on campus such as the Learning Resource Center, Office of Supportive Services, MSU Counseling Center, and Undergraduate University Division of Academic Advising. The Learning Resource Center works with students with learning disabilities on an individual basis to help the student learn to utilize appropriate learning strategies and mediate his or her learning environment.

LEARNING DISABILITY PROGRAM/SERVICES

Learning Disability Program/Services: Resource Center for Persons with Disabilities
Director: Michael Hudson
  E-mail: mjh@msu.edu
  Telephone: 517-353-9642
  Fax: 517-438-3191
Contact Person: Elaine High
  E-mail: mjh@msu.edu
  Telephone: 517-432-4266
  Fax: 517-432-3191

LEARNING DISABILITY SERVICES

Requests for the following services/accommodations will be evaluated individually based on appropriate and current documentation.

Allowed in exams
  Calculator: Yes
  Dictionary: No
  Computer: Yes
  Spellchecker: Yes
Extended test time: Yes
Scribes: Yes
Proctors: Yes
Oral exams: Yes
Note-takers: Yes

Distraction-reduced environment: Yes
Tape recording in class: Yes
Books on tape from RFBD: Yes
Taping of books not from RFBD: Yes
Accommodations for students with ADHD: Yes
Reading machine: Yes
Other assistive technology: Yes
Priority registration: Yes

Added costs for services: No
LD specialists: Yes
Professional tutors: 3
Peer tutors: 10
Max. hours/wk. for services: Unlimited
How professors are notified of LD/ADHD: By student

GENERAL ADMISSIONS INFORMATION

Director of Admissions: James Cotter, Acting Director
Telephone: 517-355-8332

ENTRANCE REQUIREMENTS

Academic units required: 4 English, 3 math, 2 science, 2 foreign language, 2 social studies, 1 history. High school diploma is required, and GED is accepted. ACT with Writing component required. TOEFL required of all international applicants: minimum paper TOEFL 550, minimum computer TOEFL 213.

Application deadline: 8/1
Notification: Rolling—12–14 weeks after submission of application
Average GPA: 3.61
ACT Composite middle 50% range: 22–27

SAT Math middle 50% range: 530–600
SAT Critical Reading middle 50% range: 500–630
SAT Writing middle 50% range: 490–610

Graduated top 10% of class: 29%
Graduated top 25% of class: 69%
Graduated top 50% of class: 95%

COLLEGE GRADUATION REQUIREMENTS

Course waivers allowed: No
Course substitutions allowed: No

ADDITIONAL INFORMATION

Environment: Michigan State is located 1 hour from Ann Arbor and 1.5 hours from Detroit.

Student Body
  Undergrad enrollment: 35,521
  Women: 54%
  Men: 46%
  Percent out-of-state: 8%

Cost Information
  In-state tuition: $8,000
  Out-of-state tuition: $20,310
  Room & board: $6,044
Housing Information
  University housing: Yes

  Percent living on campus: 41%
Greek System
  Fraternity: Yes
  Sorority: Yes
Athletics: Division I

Michigan State University

NORTHERN MICHIGAN UNIVERSITY

1401 Presque Isle Avenue, Marquette, MI 49855
Phone: 906-227-2650 • Fax: 906-227-1747
E-mail: admiss@nmu.edu • Web: www.nmu.edu
Support: S • Institution type: 4-year public

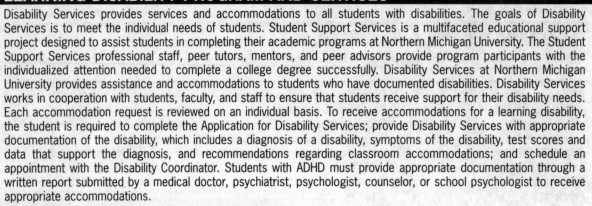

LEARNING DISABILITY PROGRAM AND SERVICES

Disability Services provides services and accommodations to all students with disabilities. The goals of Disability Services is to meet the individual needs of students. Student Support Services is a multifaceted educational support project designed to assist students in completing their academic programs at Northern Michigan University. The Student Support Services professional staff, peer tutors, mentors, and peer advisors provide program participants with the individualized attention needed to complete a college degree successfully. Disability Services at Northern Michigan University provides assistance and accommodations to students who have documented disabilities. Disability Services works in cooperation with students, faculty, and staff to ensure that students receive support for their disability needs. Each accommodation request is reviewed on an individual basis. To receive accommodations for a learning disability, the student is required to complete the Application for Disability Services; provide Disability Services with appropriate documentation of the disability, which includes a diagnosis of a disability, symptoms of the disability, test scores and data that support the diagnosis, and recommendations regarding classroom accommodations; and schedule an appointment with the Disability Coordinator. Students with ADHD must provide appropriate documentation through a written report submitted by a medical doctor, psychiatrist, psychologist, counselor, or school psychologist to receive appropriate accommodations.

LD/ADHD ADMISSIONS INFORMATION

College entrance tests required: Yes
Interview required: No
Essay recommended: No
Documentation required for LD: WAIS–III or Stanford Binet–4, achievement testing
Documentation required for ADHD: Stanford Binet–1
Submitted to: Disability Services
Special Ed. HS course work accepted: Yes

Specific course requirements of all applicants: NR
Separate application required: Yes
# of LD applications submitted each year: NR
# of LD applications accepted yearly: 150
Total # of students receiving LD services: 150
Acceptance into program means acceptance into college: Students must be admitted to and enrolled in the university first and then request services.

ADMISSIONS
There are no special admissions for students with learning disabilities. All students submit the same general application and are expected to have an ACT of 19 or higher and a high school GPA of at least 2.25. There are no specific high school courses required for admissions, though the university recommends 4 years of English, 4 years of math, 3 years of history/social studies, 3 years of science, 3 years of a foreign language, 2 years of fine or performing arts, and 1 year of computer instruction. Applicants who do not meet all of the criteria will be fully considered by the Admission Review Committee. Applicants may be asked to take a pre-admission test or supply further information. A review of the applicant's academic background and potential for success may result in admission into the applicant's program of choice or admission on probation or into the College Transitions Program. Students will be asked to agree to certain conditions as part of their enrollment. Applicants denied admission may appeal to the Admissions Review Committee. Appeal letters should be submitted to the Director of Admissions.

ADDITIONAL INFORMATION
The director of disability services works on a one-on-one basis with students as needed, and will also meet with students who do not have specific documentation if they request assistance. Skill classes are offered in reading, writing, math, study skills, sociocultural development, and interpersonal growth. No course waivers are granted for graduation requirements from NMU because the university views waivers as an institutional failure to educate its students with disabilities. Substitutions, however, are granted when appropriate. Services and accommodations are available for undergraduate and graduate students. Student Support Services provides each student with an individual program of educational support services, including academic advising; basic skill building in reading, math, and writing; counseling; career advisement; developmental skill building; mentoring; support groups and study groups; tutoring from paraprofessionals; specialized tutors; group tutoring or supplemental instruction; and workshops on personal development and study skills improvement.

LEARNING DISABILITY PROGRAM/SERVICES

Learning Disability Program/Services: Disability Services
Director: Lynn Walden, Coordinator
 E-mail: lwalden@nmu.edu
 Telephone: 906-227-1737
 Fax: 906-227-1714

LEARNING DISABILITY SERVICES

Requests for the following services/accommodations will be evaluated individually based on appropriate and current documentation.

Allowed in exams
 Calculator: Yes
 Dictionary: Yes
 Computer: Yes
 Spellchecker: Yes
Extended test time: Yes
Scribes: Yes
Proctors: Yes
Oral exams: No
Note-takers: Yes

Distraction-reduced environment: Yes
Tape recording in class: Yes
Books on tape from RFBD: No
Taping of books not from RFBD: Yes
**Accommodations for students with
 ADHD:** Yes
Reading machine: No
Other assistive technology: Yes
Priority registration: Yes

Added costs for services: No
LD specialists: No
Professional tutors: No
Peer tutors: Yes
Max. hours/wk. for services: 2–4
**How professors are notified of
 LD/ADHD:** By director

GENERAL ADMISSIONS INFORMATION

Director of Admissions: Ms. Gerri Daniels
Telephone: 800-682-9797

ENTRANCE REQUIREMENTS

Academic units recommended: 4 English, 4 math, 3 science, 3 foreign language, 3 social studies. High school diploma is required, and GED is accepted. ACT with or without Writing component accepted. TOEFL required of all international applicants: minimum paper TOEFL 500, minimum computer TOEFL 173.

Application deadline: Rolling
Notification: Rolling
Average GPA: 3.04
ACT Composite middle 50% range:
 19–25

SAT Math middle 50% range: NR
**SAT Critical Reading middle 50%
 range:** NR
SAT Writing middle 50% range: NR

Graduated top 10% of class: NR
Graduated top 25% of class: NR
Graduated top 50% of class: NR

COLLEGE GRADUATION REQUIREMENTS

Course waivers allowed: No
Course substitutions allowed: Yes
In what course: Substitutions permitted to fulfill graduation requirements with appropriate documentation.

ADDITIONAL INFORMATION

Environment: The campus is located in an urban area about 300 miles north of Milwaukee, Wisconsin.

Student Body
 Undergrad enrollment: 8,498
 Women: 53%
 Men: 47%
 Percent out-of-state: 20%

Cost Information
 In-state tuition: $5,860
 Out-of-state tuition: $9,600
 Room & board: $6,874
Housing Information
 University housing: Yes
 Percent living on campus: 35%

Greek System
 Fraternity: Yes
 Sorority: Yes
Athletics: Division II

UNIVERSITY OF MICHIGAN

1220 Student Activities Building, Ann Arbor, MI 48109-1316
Phone: 734-764-7433 • Fax: 734-936-0740
E-mail: ugadmiss@umich.edu • Web: www.umich.edu
Support: CS • Institution type: 4-year public

LEARNING DISABILITY PROGRAM AND SERVICES

The philosophy of Services for Students with Disabilities (SSD) is based on the legal actions described in Section 504 of the Rehabilitation Act of 1973. SSD services are dependent on self-advocacy of the students and are nonintrusive, giving the students the responsibility to seek out assistance. SSD offers selected student services that are not provided by other University of Michigan offices or outside organizations. SSD assists students in negotiating disability-related barriers to the pursuit of their education; strives to improve access to university programs, activities, and facilities; and promotes increased awareness of disability issues on campus. SSD encourages inquiries for information and will confidentially discuss concerns relating to a potential or recognized disability and, if requested, provide appropriate referrals for further assistance.

LD/ADHD ADMISSIONS INFORMATION

College entrance tests required: Yes
Interview required: No
Essay recommended: No
Documentation required for LD: Psychoeducational evaluation
Documentation required for ADHD: Clinical report that goes beyond verifying the diagnosis and gives objective evidence for a functional impairment that requires academic accommodations
Submitted to: Services for Students with Disabilities
Special Ed. HS course work accepted: No

Specific course requirements of all applicants: Yes
Separate application required: No
# of LD applications submitted each year: NR
# of LD applications accepted yearly: NR
Total # of students receiving LD services: 300–350
Acceptance into program means acceptance into college: Students must be admitted to and enrolled in the university first and then request services.

ADMISSIONS

Students with learning disabilities are expected to meet the same admission requirements as their peers. Courses required include 4 years of English, 2 years of a foreign language (4 years recommended), 3 years of math (4 years recommended including algebra, trigonometry, and geometry), 2 years of biological and physical sciences (3 years recommended), 3 years of history and the social sciences (2 years of history recommended, including 1 year of U.S. history). One year of hands-on computer study is strongly recommended, as is 1 year in the fine or performing arts, or equivalent preparation. Score range for the ACT is 25–29, and for the SAT, it is 1170–1340. There is no set minimum GPA as it is contingent on several other factors. For students with learning disabilities, the Admissions Office will accept untimed test scores and letters of recommendation from LD specialists. When applying for admission to the University of Michigan, students with learning disabilities are encouraged to self-identify on the application form or by writing a cover letter.

ADDITIONAL INFORMATION

All accommodations are based on documented needs by the student. Services for students with learning disabilities include volunteer readers, volunteer tutors, referral for psychoeducational assessments, selected course book loans for taping, Franklin Spellers, free cassette tapes, APH 4-track recorders, advocacy and referrals, advocacy letters to professors, limited scholarships, newsletters, volunteer note-takers, carbonized notepaper, free photocopying of class notes, free course notes service for some classes, assisted earlier registration, adaptive technology, and library reading rooms. SSD also provides appropriate services for students with other health-related disabilities, such as ADHD. There is a special summer program at the university for high school students with learning disabilities. Services and accommodations are available for undergraduates and graduates.

LEARNING DISABILITY PROGRAM/SERVICES

Learning Disability Program/Services: Services for Students with Disabilities (SSD)
Director: Stuart Segal, PhD, Coordinator and Virginia Grubaugh
  E-mail: ssegal@umich.edu
  Telephone: 734-763-3000
  Fax: 734-936-3947

LEARNING DISABILITY SERVICES

Requests for the following services/accommodations will be evaluated individually based on appropriate and current documentation.

Allowed in exams	**Distraction-reduced environment:** Yes	**Added costs for services:** No
Calculator: Yes	**Tape recording in class:** Yes	**LD specialists:** Yes
Dictionary: Yes	**Books on tape from RFBD:** No	**Professional tutors:** No
Computer: Yes	**Taping of books not from RFBD:** No	**Peer tutors:** No
Spellchecker: Yes	**Accommodations for students with**	**Max. hours/wk. for services:** NR
Extended test time: Yes	**ADHD:** Yes	**How professors are notified of**
Scribes: Yes	**Reading machine:** Yes	**LD/ADHD:** By student
Proctors: No	**Other assistive technology:** Yes	
Oral exams: No	**Priority registration:** Yes	
Note-takers: Yes		

GENERAL ADMISSIONS INFORMATION

Director of Admissions: Theodore L. Spencer
Telephone: 734-764-7433

ENTRANCE REQUIREMENTS

Academic units required: 4 English, 3 math, 2 science, 2 foreign language, 3 social studies. **Academic units recommended:** 4 English, 4 math, 2 science (1 science lab), 4 foreign language, 3 social studies, 2 history, 2 academic electives. High school diploma is required, and GED is accepted. ACT with Writing component required. TOEFL required of all international applicants: minimum paper TOEFL 570, minimum computer TOEFL 230.

Application deadline: 2/1	**SAT Math middle 50% range:**	**Graduated top 10% of class:** 90%
Notification: Rolling	630–730	**Graduated top 25% of class:** 99%
Average GPA: 3.72	**SAT Critical Reading middle 50%**	**Graduated top 50% of class:** 100%
ACT Composite middle 50% range:	**range:** 580–690	
27–31	**SAT Writing middle 50% range:** NR	

COLLEGE GRADUATION REQUIREMENTS

Course waivers allowed: Yes
In what course: Foreign language
Course substitutions allowed: Yes
In what course: Foreign language

ADDITIONAL INFORMATION

Environment: The campus is located in a suburban area about 30 minutes west of Detroit.

Student Body	**Cost Information**	**Greek System**
Undergrad enrollment: 25,422	**In-state tuition:** $9,609	**Fraternity:** Yes
Women: 50%	**Out-of-state tuition:** $28,381	**Sorority:** Yes
Men: 50%	**Room & board:** $7,838	**Athletics:** Division I
Percent out-of-state: 32%	**Housing Information**	
	University housing: Yes	
	Percent living on campus: 35%	

AUGSBURG COLLEGE

2211 Riverside Avenue South, Minneapolis, MN 55454
Phone: 612-330-1001 • Fax: 612-330-1590
E-mail: admissions@augsburg.edu • Web: www.augsburg.edu
Support: SP • Institution type: 4-year private

LEARNING DISABILITY PROGRAM AND SERVICES

The Center for Learning and Adaptive Student Services (CLASS) program affirms that Augsburg College's commitment to provide a high-quality liberal arts education for students is by assisting students in developing self-confidence, independence, and self-advocacy skills in an academic setting. Augsburg has a commitment to recruit, retain, and graduate students with learning disabilities who demonstrate the willingness and ability to participate in college-level learning. Typically, the program provides a very intensive level of support to students during the early phases of their college career, while at the same time, teaching them self-advocacy and independence skills. As students master these skills, they gradually assume an increasing degree of responsibility. It is expected that over time, CLASS students will develop the ability to advocate for themselves, gain working knowledge of the accommodations they need, and acquire the skills to access those accommodations independently.

LD/ADHD ADMISSIONS INFORMATION

College entrance tests required: Yes
Interview required: Yes
Essay recommended: No
Documentation required for LD: Cognitive testing (e.g., WAIS–III), achievement testing (e.g., Woodcock-Johnson), measures of information processing and memory; documentation must have been completed within the past 3 years
Documentation required for ADHD: Same as above with additional measures of attention and concentration
Submitted to: CLASS
Special Ed. HS course work accepted: N/A

Specific course requirements of all applicants: Yes
Separate application required: Yes
# of LD applications submitted each year: 140–160
# of LD applications accepted yearly: 70–90
Total # of students receiving LD services: 50–80
Acceptance into program means acceptance into college: Students must be admitted to and enrolled in the university first and then request services.

ADMISSIONS

Applicants with learning disabilities must first complete the Augsburg application form. Students with a 2.5 GPA who rank in top half of their class or scored at least a 20 ACT are automatically admissible. Courses required include 4 years of English, 3 years of math, 3 years of science, 2 years of a foreign language, and 3 years of social studies (4 recommended). Students complete a brief application form and submit LD documentation directly to CLASS. The written diagnostic report must contain a definite statement that an LD is present. Specific recommendations about accommodations and academic strengths and weaknesses are valuable. A formal interview will be scheduled to allow the student to provide information and receive more details about accommodations at Augsburg. Students admitted on probation or as high-risk students must take a study skills class and earn a 2.0 GPA for the first year.

ADDITIONAL INFORMATION

Students admitted into CLASS are given individual assistance from application through graduation by learning specialists. Academic support includes assistance with registration and advising, guidance with course work, assistance with writing, instruction in learning strategies and compensatory techniques, help with improving basic skills, and advocacy. Accommodations include testing arrangements, access to computers and training, taped texts, allowing the use of Kurzweil software, assistance in securing note-takers, assistance in obtaining tutors, and foreign language alternatives. There are also many community resources available. Currently, there are 190 students with learning disabilities receiving services and accommodations. Undergraduates and graduates can access support services.

LEARNING DISABILITY PROGRAM/SERVICES

Learning Disability Program/Services: Center for Learning and Adaptive Student Services (CLASS)
Director: Karena Jones, Disability Specialist
  E-mail: class@augsburg.edu
  Telephone: 612-330-1053
  Fax: 612-230-edu

LEARNING DISABILITY SERVICES

Requests for the following services/accommodations will be evaluated individually based on appropriate and current documentation.

Allowed in exams
  Calculator: Yes
  Dictionary: Yes
  Computer: Yes
  Spellchecker: Yes
Extended test time: Yes
Scribes: Yes
Proctors: Yes
Oral exams: Yes
Note-takers: Yes

Distraction-reduced environment: Yes
Tape recording in class: Yes
Books on tape from RFBD: Yes
Taping of books not from RFBD: No
Accommodations for students with ADHD: Yes
Reading machine: No
Other assistive technology: Yes
Priority registration: No

Added costs for services: No
LD specialists: Yes
Professional tutors: No
Peer tutors: 40–80
Max. hours/wk. for services: As needed
How professors are notified of LD/ADHD: By student

GENERAL ADMISSIONS INFORMATION

Director of Admissions: Carrie Carroll
Telephone: 612-330-1001

ENTRANCE REQUIREMENTS

Academic units required: 4 English, 3 math, 3 science, 2 foreign language, 3 social studies. **Academic units recommended:** 4 social studies, 2 history. High school diploma is required, and GED is accepted. ACT with or without Writing component accepted. TOEFL required of all international applicants: minimum paper TOEFL 550, minimum computer TOEFL 213.

Application deadline: 8/15
Notification: Rolling
Average GPA: 3.22
ACT Composite middle 50% range: 20–25

SAT Math middle 50% range: 500–635
SAT Critical Reading middle 50% range: 510–640
SAT Writing middle 50% range: 475–598

Graduated top 10% of class: 16%
Graduated top 25% of class: 34%
Graduated top 50% of class: 66%

COLLEGE GRADUATION REQUIREMENTS

Course waivers allowed: No
Course substitutions allowed: Yes
In what course: Foreign language

ADDITIONAL INFORMATION

Environment: The college is located on 25 acres near downtown Minneapolis.

Student Body
  Undergrad enrollment: 2,783
  Women: 56%
  Men: 44%
  Percent out-of-state: 14%

Cost Information
  Tuition: $22,900
  Room & board: $6,604
Housing Information
  University housing: Yes
  Percent living on campus: 52%

Greek System
  Fraternity: No
  Sorority: No
Athletics: Division III

THE COLLEGE OF ST. CATHERINE

2004 Randolph Avenue, St. Paul, MN 55105
Phone: 651-690-8850 • Fax: 651-690-8824
E-mail: admissions@stkate.edu • Web: www.stkate.edu
Support: CS • Institution type: 4-year private

LEARNING DISABILITY PROGRAM AND SERVICES

The O'Neill Learning Center houses the special learning programs for students with learning disabilities. Accommodations are made on an individual basis. The center's staff works with students and departments to provide reasonable and appropriate accommodations for access to and fair treatment in college programs and activities. The Learning Center and the Counseling Center offer staff in-services to help them accommodate students with learning disabilities. A reduced course load is strongly suggested for the student's first semester. Services include information sessions, faculty consultations, and early registration. While the college does not have all of the resources that students with learning disabilities may need, it is committed to responding flexibly to individual needs.

LD/ADHD ADMISSIONS INFORMATION

College entrance tests required: Yes
Interview required: No
Essay recommended: No
Documentation required for LD: Psychoeducational evaluation completed within the past 3 years
Documentation required for ADHD: A diagnosis from an accredited professional along with a psychoeducational assessment to measure the impact of the condition
Submitted to: O'Neill Learning Center
Special Ed. HS course work accepted: Yes

Specific course requirements of all applicants: NR
Separate application required: No
# of LD applications submitted each year: NR
# of LD applications accepted yearly: NR
Total # of students receiving LD services: 40–45
Acceptance into program means acceptance into college: Students must be admitted to and enrolled in the university first and then request services.

ADMISSIONS

There is no special admission procedure for students with learning disabilities, though the college tends to give special consideration if students self-disclose this information. Disclosure can help explain test scores, difficulties with certain course work, and so on. The Director of Services for Students with Disabilities serves on the Admissions Committee. The College of St. Catherine does not discriminate on the basis of disability in admission. A student may enter as a LEAP student which provides special advising, limited course load, and a course in strategies for success.

ADDITIONAL INFORMATION

To access services, the student and counselor discuss the anticipated demands of the courses for which the student is registered and develop accommodation letters. The letters identify the learning strategies and accommodations that will be used. For example, tape-recorded books, testing accommodations, and note-takers are some of the more frequently offered accommodations. The specific nature of the disability is not addressed. The accommodation plan will include the student's preference for notifying the instructor of the need for accommodations. Drop-in help is available on a one-on-one basis from student assistants in writing, study skills, and time management. Students with learning disabilities also have access to support groups and practice in self-advocacy.

LEARNING DISABILITY PROGRAM/SERVICES

Learning Disability Program/Services: O'Neill Learning Center
Director: Barbara Mandel
    E-mail: bjmandel@stkate.edu
    Telephone: 651-590-6563
    Fax: 651-690-6718

LEARNING DISABILITY SERVICES

Requests for the following services/accommodations will be evaluated individually based on appropriate and current documentation.

Allowed in exams
  Calculator: Yes
  Dictionary: Yes
  Computer: Yes
  Spellchecker: Yes
Extended test time: Yes
Scribes: Yes
Proctors: Yes
Oral exams: Yes
Note-takers: Yes

Distraction-reduced environment: Yes
Tape recording in class: Yes
Books on tape from RFBD: Yes
Taping of books not from RFBD: Yes
Accommodations for students with ADHD: Yes
Reading machine: Yes
Other assistive technology: Yes
Priority registration: Yes

Added costs for services: No
LD specialists: Yes
Professional tutors: No
Peer tutors: 25–35
Max. hours/wk. for services: Unlimited
How professors are notified of LD/ADHD: By both student and director

GENERAL ADMISSIONS INFORMATION

Director of Admissions: Cal Mosley
Telephone: 651-690-8850

ENTRANCE REQUIREMENTS

Academic units recommended: 4 English, 3 math, 2 science, 4 foreign language, 2 social studies. High school diploma is required, and GED is accepted. ACT with or without Writing component accepted. TOEFL required of all international applicants: minimum paper TOEFL 500, minimum computer TOEFL 173.

Application deadline: NR
Notification: Rolling
Average GPA: 3.63
ACT Composite middle 50% range: 22–27

SAT Math middle 50% range: 495–650
SAT Critical Reading middle 50% range: 518–660
SAT Writing middle 50% range: NR

Graduated top 10% of class: 34%
Graduated top 25% of class: 75%
Graduated top 50% of class: 95%

COLLEGE GRADUATION REQUIREMENTS

Course waivers allowed: No
Course substitutions allowed: Yes
In what course: Math, foreign language

ADDITIONAL INFORMATION

Environment: The college is located on 110 acres in an urban area in central St. Paul, Minnesota.

Student Body
  Undergrad enrollment: 3,511
  Women: 97%
  Men: 3%
  Percent out-of-state: 10%

Cost Information
  Tuition: $22,620
  Room & board: $6,432
Housing Information
  University housing: Yes
  Percent living on campus: 37%

Greek System
  Fraternity: No
  Sorority: Yes
Athletics: Division III

The College of St. Catherine

MINNESOTA STATE U.—MOORHEAD

Owens Hall, MSU—Moorhead, Moorhead, MN 56563
Phone: 218-477-2161 • Fax: 218-477-4374
E-mail: dragon@mnstate.edu • Web: www.mnstate.edu
Support: S • Institution type: 4-year public

LEARNING DISABILITY PROGRAM AND SERVICES

The university is committed to ensuring that all students have equal access to programs and services. The office of Services to Students with Disabilities (SSD) addresses the needs of students who have disabilities. The purpose of SSD is to provide services and accommodations to students with disabilities, work closely with faculty and staff in an advisory capacity, assist in the development of reasonable accommodations for students, and provide equal access for otherwise qualified individuals with disabilities. Any Moorhead State student with a documented learning disability is eligible for services. SSD will assist in the development of reasonable accommodations for students with disabilities. To be eligible to receive services, students must provide appropriate documentation. This documentation should identify the nature and extent of the disability and provide information on the functional limitations as related to the academic environment. The documentation should provide recommended reasonable accommodations. Requests that would alter the academic standards are not granted. Students are responsible for monitoring their progress with faculty, requesting assistance, and meeting university standards.

LD/ADHD ADMISSIONS INFORMATION

College entrance tests required: Yes
Interview required: No
Essay recommended: No
Documentation required for LD: Completion of a disability verification form, psycheducational evaluation
Documentation required for ADHD: Yes
Submitted to: Services for Students with Disabilities
Special Ed. HS course work accepted: Yes

Specific course requirements of all applicants: Yes
Separate application required: NR
# of LD applications submitted each year: NR
# of LD applications accepted yearly: NR
Total # of students receiving LD services: 25–50
Acceptance into program means acceptance into college: Students must be admitted to and enrolled in the university first and then request services.

ADMISSIONS

There are no special admissions for students with learning disabilities. All students must meet the same criteria, including ranking in the top half of their class or the following scores on standardized college admission tests: ACT 21-plus, PSAT 90-plus, or SAT 900-plus. They must also have 4 years of English, 3 years of math (2 algebra and 1 geometry), 3 years of science (1 biological science, 1 physical science, and at least 1 course that includes significant laboratory experience), 3 years of social studies (including American History and at least 1 course that includes significant emphasis on geography), 3 electives chosen from at least two of the following: world language, world culture, and visual/performing arts. The New Center offers an alternative way to begin university studies to students who reside within the MSU service region. If a student does not meet the above admission requirements, his or her application will be reviewed on the basis of strength of college-preparation course work, GPA, probability of success, academic progression, as well as class rank and test scores. Supplemental information may be requested before an admission decision can be made. The New Center offers small, interdisciplinary courses that meet MSUM's liberal studies requirement for graduation. Enrollment is limited. Students who do not meet New Center admission criteria will be admitted to the Gateway Program—a partnership offered by MSUM and Minnesota State Community and Technical College with courses taught on the MSUM campus.

ADDITIONAL INFORMATION

Examples of general accommodations or services include the following: extended testing times, distraction-free testing environments, taped texts, note-taking, assistive technology, scribes, readers, extra time for assignment completion, tape-recording lectures, faculty liaisons, strategy development, priority registration, and individual support. Skills courses are offered in study skills and test anxiety, and students may earn credits for these courses. Services and accommodations are available for undergraduate and graduate students.

LEARNING DISABILITY PROGRAM/SERVICES

Learning Disability Program/Services: Disability Services
Director: Greg Toutges, Coordinator
  E-mail: toutges@mnstate.edu
  Telephone: 218-477-5859
  Fax: 218-477-2430

LEARNING DISABILITY SERVICES

Requests for the following services/accommodations will be evaluated individually based on appropriate and current documentation.

Allowed in exams
  Calculator: Yes
  Dictionary: Yes
  Computer: Yes
  Spellchecker: Yes
Extended test time: Yes
Scribes: Yes
Proctors: Yes
Oral exams: Yes
Note-takers: Yes

Distraction-reduced environment: Yes
Tape recording in class: Yes
Books on tape from RFBD: Yes
Taping of books not from RFBD: Yes
Accommodations for students with ADHD: Yes
Reading machine: Yes
Other assistive technology: Yes
Priority registration: Yes

Added costs for services: No
LD specialists: No
Professional tutors: No
Peer tutors: Yes
Max. hours/wk. for services: 1
How professors are notified of LD/ADHD: By both student and director

GENERAL ADMISSIONS INFORMATION

Director of Admissions: Gina Monson
Telephone: 218-477-2161

ENTRANCE REQUIREMENTS

Academic units required: 4 English, 3 math, 3 science (1 science lab), 3 social studies, 3 academic electives. High school diploma is required, and GED is accepted. ACT with or without Writing component accepted. TOEFL required of all international applicants: minimum paper TOEFL 500, minimum computer TOEFL 173.

Application deadline: 8/1
Notification: Rolling
Average GPA: NR
ACT Composite middle 50% range: 19–24
SAT Math middle 50% range: 465–535
SAT Critical Reading middle 50% range: 480–580
SAT Writing middle 50% range: NR
Graduated top 10% of class: 10%
Graduated top 25% of class: 28%
Graduated top 50% of class: 63%

COLLEGE GRADUATION REQUIREMENTS

Course waivers allowed: Yes
In what course: Depends on the disability and requirements of the student's major
Course substitutions allowed: Yes
In what course: Depends on the disability and requirements of the student's major

ADDITIONAL INFORMATION

Environment: The university has a suburban campus 240 miles northwest of Minneapolis.

Student Body
  Undergrad enrollment: 6,854
  Women: 59%
  Men: 41%
  Percent out-of-state: 43%

Cost Information
  In-state tuition: $4,464
  Out-of-state tuition: $6,500
  Room & board: $4,974
Housing Information
  University housing: Yes
  Percent living on campus: 21%

Greek System
  Fraternity: Yes
  Sorority: Yes
Athletics: Division II

ST. OLAF COLLEGE

1520 St. Olaf Avenue, Northfield, MN 55057
Phone: 507-786-3025 • Fax: 507-786-3832
E-mail: admissions@stolaf.edu • Web: www.stolaf.edu
Support: S • Institution type: 4-year private

LEARNING DISABILITY PROGRAM AND SERVICES

The goal of the services at St. Olaf is to provide equal access to a St. Olaf education for all students with disabilities. Because it is a small institution, they are able to work individually with students to reach this goal. Its purpose is to create and maintain an environment in which students may achieve their fullest potential, limited to the least extent possible by individual disabilities. All faculty, staff, and students of the college are expected to adhere to this philosophy of equal access to educational opportunity and assume broad responsibility for its implementation. Students must provide a clear statement of diagnosed disability, summary of symptoms, list all assessments and relevant scores, description of functional limitations, statement of why the disability qualifies the applicant for accommodations, and a list of recommended educational accommodations. The diagnosis must be made by a qualified professional who is not related to the student and who is practicing in an area in which the disability has been diagnosed. In addition, the documentation provided must be within the past 5 years and be on official letterhead.

LD/ADHD ADMISSIONS INFORMATION

College entrance tests required: Yes
Interview required: NR
Essay recommended: NR
Documentation required for LD: Psychoeducational evaluation
Documentation required for ADHD: Medical only documentation is not acceptable. Provide the same documentation as for LD.
Submitted to: Student Disabilities Services

Special Ed. HS course work accepted: NR
Specific course requirements of all applicants: Yes
Separate application required: No
# of LD applications submitted each year: 3,500
# of LD applications accepted yearly: 750
Total # of students receiving LD services: NR
Acceptance into program means acceptance into college: Students must be admitted to and enrolled in the university first and then request services.

ADMISSIONS

All applicants must meet the same competitive admission criteria. There is no separate application process for students with learning disabilities or attention deficit hyperactivity disorder. Students are encouraged to self-disclose the disability in a personal statement. The mid 50 percent score range for the ACT is 25–30, and for the SAT it is 1170–1380. It's recommended that students have a strong academic curriculum that includes 4 years of English, 3–4 years of math, 3–4 years of social studies, 3–4 years of science, and 2–4 years of a foreign language. High school diploma is required, and GED is accepted. The TOEFL is required of all international applicants with a minimum score of 550. Once admitted, students with documented disabilities should have their current documentation sent to the Academic Support Center.

ADDITIONAL INFORMATION

All students have access to tutoring, math clinics, writing centers, study skills assistance, and weekly meetings a counselor, if necessary. Other accommodations and services are available with appropriate documentation, including extended testing times; distraction-free testing environments; the use of a calculator, spellchecker, or computer during exams; scribes; readers; note-takers; and taped texts.

LEARNING DISABILITY PROGRAM/SERVICES

Learning Disability Program/Services: Student Disability Services
Director: Ruth Bolstad
 E-mail: bolstadr@stolaf.edu
 Telephone: 507-786-3288
 Fax: 507-786-3923

LEARNING DISABILITY SERVICES

Requests for the following services/accommodations will be evaluated individually based on appropriate and current documentation.

Allowed in exams
 Calculator: Yes
 Dictionary: No
 Computer: Yes
 Spellchecker: Yes
Extended test time: Yes
Scribes: Yes
Proctors: Yes
Oral exams: Yes
Note-takers: Yes

Distraction-reduced environment: Yes
Tape recording in class: Yes
Books on tape from RFBD: Yes
Taping of books not from RFBD: Yes
**Accommodations for students with
 ADHD:** Yes
Reading machine: Yes
Other assistive technology: Yes
Priority registration: Yes

Added costs for services: No
LD specialists: No
Professional tutors: No
Peer tutors: 200–250
Max. hours/wk. for services: 3
**How professors are notified of
 LD/ADHD:** By student

GENERAL ADMISSIONS INFORMATION

Director of Admissions: Jill Lynch, Interim Director
Telephone: 507-646-3304

ENTRANCE REQUIREMENTS

Academic units required: 4 English, 2 math, 2 science (1 science lab), 2 foreign language, 1 social studies, 1 history, 2 academic electives. **Academic units recommended:** 4 English, 4 math, 4 science (2 science labs), 4 foreign language, 2 social studies, 2 history, 4 academic electives. High school diploma is required, and GED is accepted. ACT with or without Writing component accepted. TOEFL required of all international applicants: minimum paper TOEFL 550, minimum computer TOEFL 213.

Application deadline: NR
Notification: Rolling
Average GPA: 3.67
ACT Composite middle 50% range:
 25–30

SAT Math middle 50% range:
 590–700
**SAT Critical Reading middle 50%
 range:** 580–700
SAT Writing middle 50% range: NR

Graduated top 10% of class: 51%
Graduated top 25% of class: 83%
Graduated top 50% of class: 99%

COLLEGE GRADUATION REQUIREMENTS

Course waivers allowed: No
Course substitutions allowed: Yes
In what course: Alternatives are rarely considered. A subcommittee must recommend substitutions, and a faculty committee makes the decision. Most often a student is required to try a language with support from the department, tutors, labs, and study groups first.

ADDITIONAL INFORMATION

Environment: The college is located on 350 acres in a small town near Minneapolis.

Student Body
 Undergrad enrollment: 2,993
 Women: 56%
 Men: 44%
 Percent out-of-state: 42%

Cost Information
 Tuition: $28,200
 Room & board: $7,400
Housing Information
 University housing: Yes
 Percent living on campus: 96%

Greek System
 Fraternity: No
 Sorority: No
 Athletics: Division III

St. Olaf College

UNIVERSITY OF ST. THOMAS (MN)

2115 Summit Avenue, Mail #32F, St. Paul, MN 55105-1096
Phone: 651-962-6150 • Fax: 651-962-6160
E-mail: admissions@stthomas.edu • Web: www.stthomas.edu
Support: S • Institution type: 4-year private

LEARNING DISABILITY PROGRAM AND SERVICES

The mission of the Enhancement Program and Specialized Services is to ensure that all students with disabilities achieve their educational, career, and personal goals. Comprehensive support services and accommodations are offered that will allow the student equal access to all the university programs and facilities. Students qualify for services through the Enhancement Program once they have self-disclosed their disability and presentated appropriate documentation of an LD/ADHD. Qualified students, along with the Enhancement Program staff, work to realize their potential for academic success. The staff acknowledges that individuals with documented disabilities have unique learning needs. Reasonable accommodations are arranged on an individual basis based on the student's disability and the requirements of a particular course. For students to be eligible for these services, documentation from a licensed professional is required. The documentation should state the nature of the disability and the types of accommodations recommended by the licensed professional. The Enhancement Program represents an institutional commitment to individual guidance for students to develop the skills necessary to become independent life-long learners.

LD/ADHD ADMISSIONS INFORMATION

College entrance tests required: Yes
Interview required: No
Essay recommended: No
Documentation required for LD: A psychoeducational assessment completed within the past 3 years and results from the Woodcock-Johnson Test of Achievement and Weschler Adult Intelligence Scale
Documentation required for ADHD: An assessment completed within the past 3 years and a letter outlining DSM–IV diagnosis, symptoms, and methods used to diagnose
Submitted to: Enhancement Program and Specialized Services

Special Ed. HS course work accepted: Yes
Specific course requirements of all applicants: Yes
Separate application required: No
# of LD applications submitted each year: 35
# of LD applications accepted yearly: NR
Total # of students receiving LD services: 250
Acceptance into program means acceptance into college: Students must be admitted to and enrolled in the university and then request services.

ADMISSIONS

There are general requirements for admission; some exceptions are made on a case-by-case basis. The general requirements include an ACT score of 20–21, a GPA of 3.0, or a rank within the top 35–40 percent of a student's class; recommendations; and an essay. If it is known that a student has a disability, the Office of Admissions may ask the Director of the Enrichment Program to assess the documentation. The Office of Admissions has the final decision, but the Director of the Enhancement Program may be asked to provide information and recommendations. Students can be admitted on a probationary status. They will be required to develop an academic contract with a counselor and meet with that person regularly throughout the semester. Students cannot get an F in any of their classes. They must maintain this for two semesters, and if they do, they are then admitted unconditionally.

ADDITIONAL INFORMATION

Comprehensive services are available through a collaborative effort of the Enhancement Program counselors, the Accommodations Coordinator, and student employees. Academic and personal counseling pertaining to the student's specific disability is offered. Reasonable accommodations such as note-takers, readers, and scribes; books on tape; alternate testing arrangements; and course/program modifications are offered, if appropriate. The student's skills are assessed through a pre-screening interview to see if further testing is necessary, and the staff will collaborate with outside agencies for complete diagnostic services. The Enhancement Program offers a testing, tutoring, and technology center that houses adaptive technology. Additionally, they offer one-on-one tutoring that emphasizes strategies to improve course content and retention.

LEARNING DISABILITY PROGRAM/SERVICES

Learning Disability Program/Services: Enhancement Program—Disability Services
Director: Kimberly Schumann
E-mail: kjschumann@stthomas.edu
Telephone: 651-962-6315
Fax: 651-962-5965

LEARNING DISABILITY SERVICES

Requests for the following services/accommodations will be evaluated individually based on appropriate and current documentation.

Allowed in exams
 Calculator: Yes
 Dictionary: Yes
 Computer: Yes
 Spellchecker: Yes
Extended test time: Yes
Scribes: Yes
Proctors: Yes
Oral exams: Yes
Note-takers: Yes

Distraction-reduced environment: Yes
Tape recording in class: Yes
Books on tape from RFBD: Yes
Taping of books not from RFBD: Yes
Accommodations for students with ADHD: Yes
Reading machine: Yes
Other assistive technology: Yes
Priority registration: Yes

Added costs for services: No
LD specialists: No
Professional tutors: No
Peer tutors: Yes
Max. hours/wk. for services: Unlimited
How professors are notified of LD/ADHD: By both student and director

GENERAL ADMISSIONS INFORMATION

Director of Admissions: Marla Friederichs
Telephone: 651-962-6151

ENTRANCE REQUIREMENTS

Academic units required: 3 math. **Academic units recommended:** 4 English, 4 math, 2 science, 4 foreign language, 2 social science/history. High school diploma is required, and GED is accepted. ACT with or without Writing component accepted. TOEFL required of all international applicants: minimum paper TOEFL 550, minimum computer TOEFL 213.

Application deadline: NR
Notification: Rolling
Average GPA: 3.53
ACT Composite middle 50% range: 22–27

SAT Math middle 50% range: 530–640
SAT Critical Reading middle 50% range: 510–640
SAT Writing middle 50% range: NR

Graduated top 10% of class: 19%
Graduated top 25% of class: 29%
Graduated top 50% of class: 40%

COLLEGE GRADUATION REQUIREMENTS

Course waivers allowed: No
Course substitutions allowed: Yes
In what course: Students may petition to have their math or foreign language requirement substituted.

ADDITIONAL INFORMATION

Environment: The University of St. Thomas is located five miles from downtown St. Paul.

Student Body
 Undergrad enrollment: 5,682
 Women: 50%
 Men: 50%
 Percent out-of-state: 16%

Cost Information
 Tuition: $24,808
 Room & board: $7,000
Housing Information
 University housing: Yes
 Percent living on campus: 43%

Greek System
 Fraternity: No
 Sorority: No
 Athletics: Division III

WINONA STATE UNIVERSITY

Office of Admissions, Winona State University, Winona, MN 55987
Phone: 507-457-5100 • Fax: 507-457-5620
E-mail: admissions@winona.edu • Web: www.winona.edu
Support: S • Institution type: 4-year public

LEARNING DISABILITY PROGRAM AND SERVICES

The Disability Resource Center serves Winona State University students and faculty by providing a complex of advising and academic support services and programs that enhance student success, student identification with and commitment to the university, and student persistence to graduation. If a student has been diagnosed with a disability, the student should bring the documentation to the DRC. The coordinator will assist the student in determining which services would be most beneficial and how to obtain them.

LD/ADHD ADMISSIONS INFORMATION

College entrance tests required: Yes
Interview required: No
Essay recommended: No
Documentation required for LD: Psychoeducational evaluation
Documentation required for ADHD: Yes
Submitted to: Disability Resource Center
Special Ed. HS course work accepted: N/A

Specific course requirements of all applicants: Yes
Separate application required: Yes
# of LD applications submitted each year: NR
# of LD applications accepted yearly: NR
Total # of students receiving LD services: 50–100
Acceptance into program means acceptance into college: Students must be admitted and enrolled prior to requesting services.

ADMISSIONS

There is no special admissions process for students with learning disabilities. Winona State University admissions requirements include an ACT score of 21-plus or a ranking in the top 50 percent of the applicant's graduating class with an ACT score of 18. The student's academic transcript will be reviewed to see that he or she has completed the Minnesota State University preparation requirements. Admissions decisions are processed in 15–20 days following the receipt of the student's complete application.

ADDITIONAL INFORMATION

The Winona State University Disability Resource Center has many services to help students with disabilities. Some of these services include advising (academic, career, and personal), readers, auditory textbooks, testing accommodations, study skills seminars, and academic tutoring days. The Writing Center offers all WSU students free, individualized instruction in all aspects of writing. The mission of the Writing Center is to help students in all disciplines use writing as an effective tool for learning, communication, self-expression, and critical thinking. To this end, staff in the Writing Center work closely with students, faculty, and administrators to help students become capable, successful writers. Supplemental Instruction (SI) is an academic assistance program that utilizes peer-assisted study sessions. SI sessions are regularly scheduled, informal review sessions in which students compare notes, discuss readings, develop organizational tools, and predict test items. Students learn how to integrate course content and study skills while working together under the guidance of a student who has already excelled in the course. Tutoring is offered by several different departments and programs, including the Academic Assistance Center, Chemistry Department, and the Math Department. Tutoring is offered both on a drop-in basis and by arranged one-on-one appointments.

LEARNING DISABILITY PROGRAM/SERVICES

Learning Disability Program/Services: Disability Resource Center
Director: Nancy Dumke
   E-mail: DRC@winona.edu
   Telephone: 507-457-2391
   Fax: 507-457-2957

LEARNING DISABILITY SERVICES

Requests for the following services/accommodations will be evaluated individually based on appropriate and current documentation.

Allowed in exams
   Calculator: Yes
   Dictionary: Yes
   Computer: Yes
   Spellchecker: Yes
Extended test time: Yes
Scribes: Yes
Proctors: Yes
Oral exams: Yes
Note-takers: Yes

Distraction-reduced environment: Yes
Tape recording in class: Yes
Books on tape from RFBD: Yes
Taping of books not from RFBD: Yes
Accommodations for students with ADHD: Yes
Reading machine: Yes
Other assistive technology: Yes
Priority registration: Yes

Added costs for services: No
LD specialists: No
Professional tutors: 1–4
Peer tutors: 5–13
How professors are notified of LD/ADHD: By both student and director

GENERAL ADMISSIONS INFORMATION

Director of Admissions: Carl Stange
Telephone: 507-457-5100

ENTRANCE REQUIREMENTS

Academic units required: 4 English, 3 math, 3 science (3 science labs), 2 foreign language, 2 social studies, 1 history, 1 academic elective. High school diploma is required, and GED is accepted. ACT with or without Writing component accepted. TOEFL required of all international applicants: minimum paper TOEFL 550, minimum computer TOEFL 270.

Application deadline: Rolling
Notification: Rolling
Average GPA: 3.30
ACT Composite middle 50% range: 21–24

SAT Math middle 50% range: NR
SAT Critical Reading middle 50% range: NR
SAT Writing middle 50% range: NR

Graduated top 10% of class: 13%
Graduated top 25% of class: 28%
Graduated top 50% of class: 42%

COLLEGE GRADUATION REQUIREMENTS

Course waivers allowed: No
Course substitutions allowed: Yes
In what course: Course substitutions are more likely, depending on the documentation. Decisions are made on a case-by-case situation.

ADDITIONAL INFORMATION

Environment: The campus is located 90 miles south of Minneapolis.

Student Body
   Undergrad enrollment: 7,608
   Women: 62%
   Men: 38%
   Percent out-of-state: 36%

Cost Information
   In-state tuition: $5,800
   Out-of-state tuition: $10,290
   Room & board: $6,300
Housing Information
   University housing: Yes
   Percent living on campus: 33%

Greek System
   Fraternity: Yes
   Sorority: Yes
Athletics: Division II

U. OF SOUTHERN MISSISSIPPI

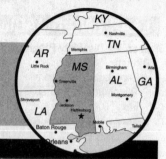

118 College Drive, #5166, Hattiesburg, MS 39406
Phone: 601-266-5000 • Fax: 601-266-5148
E-mail: admissions@usm.edu • Web: www.usm.edu
Support: S • Institution type: 4-year public

LEARNING DISABILITY PROGRAM AND SERVICES

The philosophy of USM is to provide services to students with learning disabilities and give them the maximum opportunity to complete a college education. The Office for Disability Accommodations (ODA) is USM's designated office to verify eligibility for accommodations under the American with Disabilities Act and develop and coordinate plans for the provision of such accommodations. After receiving documentation of a student's disability, ODA works with the student to develop a plan for the provision of reasonable accommodations that are specific to his or her disabilities.

LD/ADHD ADMISSIONS INFORMATION

College entrance tests required: Yes
Interview required: No
Essay recommended: No
Documentation required for LD: Psychoeducational evaluation
Documentation required for ADHD: Yes
Submitted to: Office of Disability Accommodations
Special Ed. HS course work accepted: NR

Specific course requirements of all applicants: Yes
Separate application required: No
# of LD applications submitted each year: NR
# of LD applications accepted yearly: NR
Total # of students receiving LD services: NR
Acceptance into program means acceptance into college: Students must be admitted and enrolled prior to requesting services.

ADMISSIONS

There is no special application for students with learning disabilities. Freshmen have specific curriculum, GPA, and test score requirements. The mean ACT is 18, and the mean SAT is 850. The minimum GPA is 2.0. Course requirements include 4 years of English, 3 years of math, 3 years of social studies, 3 years of science, and 2 electives. The admission decision for students with learning disabilities is made by the director of OSSD. An interview is not required, but it is preferred. The university offers a pre-admission summer program.

ADDITIONAL INFORMATION

To receive reasonable accommodations for a disability, students must file an application with OSS and provide current documentation of a disability. After an application is filed, students schedule an appointment with the OSS coordinator, complete an intake form, and establish a plan for reasonable accommodations and services. The OSS helps students locate tutors, note-takers, and other ancillary aids for their classwork. The office works with vocational rehabilitation to pay for these services. The office staff works with students on a one-on-one basis to determine how they learn best. There are remedial programs in math, writing, and reading.

LEARNING DISABILITY PROGRAM/SERVICES

Learning Disability Program/Services: Office for Disability Accommodations
Director: Suzy B. Hebert, Coordinator
  E-mail: suzanne.hebert@usm.edu
  Telephone: 601-266-5024
  Fax: 601-266-6035

LEARNING DISABILITY SERVICES

Requests for the following services/accommodations will be evaluated individually based on appropriate and current documentation.

Allowed in exams
  Calculator: NR
  Dictionary: NR
  Computer: NR
  Spellchecker: NR
Extended test time: Yes
Scribes: Yes
Proctors: Yes
Oral exams: Yes
Note-takers: Yes

Distraction-reduced environment: Yes
Tape recording in class: Yes
Books on tape from RFBD: Yes
Taping of books not from RFBD: Yes
Accommodations for students with ADHD: Yes
Reading machine: Yes
Other assistive technology: Yes
Priority registration: Yes

Added costs for services: No
LD specialists: No
Professional tutors: No
Peer tutors: No
Max. hours/wk. for services: Varies
How professors are notified of LD/ADHD: By student

GENERAL ADMISSIONS INFORMATION

Director of Admissions: NR
Telephone: 601-266-5000

ENTRANCE REQUIREMENTS
Academic units required: 4 English, 3 math, 3 science (3 science labs), 1 social studies, 2 history, 2 academic electives, 1 semester course in computer applications. **Academic units recommended:** 4 English, 3 math, 3 science (3 science labs), 2 foreign language, 1 social studies, 2 history, 2 academic electives, 1 semester course in computer applications. High school diploma is required, and GED is accepted. ACT with or without Writing component accepted. TOEFL required of all international applicants: minimum paper TOEFL 525.

Application deadline: Rolling
Notification: Rolling
Average GPA: 3.07
ACT Composite middle 50% range:
  18–24

SAT Math middle 50% range:
  438–593
SAT Critical Reading middle 50% range: 448–583
SAT Writing middle 50% range: NR

Graduated top 10% of class: NR
Graduated top 25% of class: NR
Graduated top 50% of class: NR

COLLEGE GRADUATION REQUIREMENTS

Course waivers allowed: No
Course substitutions allowed: Yes

ADDITIONAL INFORMATION

Environment: The university is located on 840 acres in a small city 90 miles southeast of Jackson.

Student Body
  Undergrad enrollment: 12,122
  Women: 61%
  Men: 39%
  Percent out-of-state: 11%

Cost Information
  In-state tuition: $4,594
  Out-of-state tuition: $10,622
  Room & board: $5,070
Housing Information
  University housing: Yes
  Percent living on campus: 21%

Greek System
  Fraternity: Yes
  Sorority: Yes
Athletics: Division I

EVANGEL COLLEGE

111 North Glenstone, Springfield, MO 65802
Phone: 417-865-2811 • Fax: 417-520-0545
E-mail: admissions@evangel.edu • Web: www.evangel.edu
Support: CS • Institution type: 4-year private

LEARNING DISABILITY PROGRAM AND SERVICES

The Academic Support Center supports the needs of all students at Evangel College. The center focuses on assisting students with improving academic skills so that they remain successful in college. The center offers study skills assistance, tutorial services, and individual college planning. Group and individual support counseling is also available. Classes covering study skills are offered for credit.

LD/ADHD ADMISSIONS INFORMATION

College entrance tests required: Yes
Interview required: No
Essay recommended: No
Documentation required for LD: Psychoeducational diagnostic evaluation
Documentation required for ADHD: Yes
Submitted to: Academic Support Center
Special Ed. HS course work accepted: Yes

Specific course requirements of all applicants: NR
Separate application required: No
# of LD applications submitted each year: NR
# of LD applications accepted yearly: NR
Total # of students receiving LD services: 35
Acceptance into program means acceptance into college: Students must be admitted to and enrolled in the university first and then request services.

ADMISSIONS

There is no special application for students with learning disabilities. All students must meet the same admission criteria. Evangel College looks at the completed application. ACT test scores are required. Students should have at least a 2.0 GPA, a pastor's recommendation, and a high school recommendation. Course requirements include 3 years of English, 2 years of math, 2 years of social science, and 1 year of science. Students with documented LD can request a substitute for specific courses if their disability impacts their ability to learn that particular subject. Special admission to the SOAR Program is offered to students with ACT scores between 14–17. These students will be enrolled in study skills as well as other proficiency classes.

ADDITIONAL INFORMATION

Some study skills classes are required for students who are admitted conditionally. The Academic Support Center offers tutoring, at no cost, in a variety of courses. The center offers resources in such topics as personal growth, goal setting, self-concept enrichment, stress management, memory and concentration, test-taking, underlining, note-taking, outlining, reading a textbook, research, writing term papers, time scheduling, reading efficiency, and vocabulary. Additional resources include the design and implementation of individualized programs with an instructor, personal professional counseling at no charge, career counseling with the Director of Career Development Services, reading labs for increased reading speed, and tutoring in other classes at no charge. SOAR is designed to assist selected provisionally admitted students during the first two semesters of college. SOAR courses focus on specific modules such as assessment and skills review in reading, math, and writing; study skills application; and career planning.

LEARNING DISABILITY PROGRAM/SERVICES

Learning Disability Program/Services: Academic Development Center
Director: Dr. Laynah Rogers
  E-mail: rogers@evangel.edu
  Telephone: 417-865-2811
  Fax: 417-865-9599

LEARNING DISABILITY SERVICES

Requests for the following services/accommodations will be evaluated individually based on appropriate and current documentation.

Allowed in exams
  Calculator: Yes
  Dictionary: Yes
  Computer: Yes
  Spellchecker: Yes
Extended test time: Yes
Scribes: Yes
Proctors: Yes
Oral exams: Yes
Note-takers: Yes

Distraction-reduced environment: Yes
Tape recording in class: Yes
Books on tape from RFBD: Yes
Taping of books not from RFBD: Yes
Accommodations for students with ADHD: Yes
Reading machine: Yes
Other assistive technology: Yes
Priority registration: No

Added costs for services: No
LD specialists: Yes
Professional tutors: 1
Peer tutors: 5
Max. hours/wk. for services: Unlimited
How professors are notified of LD/ADHD: By both student and director

GENERAL ADMISSIONS INFORMATION

Director of Admissions: Charity Waltner
Telephone: 417-865-2811

ENTRANCE REQUIREMENTS

Academic units recommended: 3 English, 2 math, 1 science (1 science lab), 2 foreign language, 2 social studies, 3 academic electives. High school diploma is required, and GED is accepted. TOEFL required of all international applicants: minimum paper TOEFL 490.

Application deadline: 8/15
Notification: Rolling
Average GPA: NR
ACT Composite middle 50% range: NR

SAT Math middle 50% range: NR
SAT Critical Reading middle 50% range: NR
SAT Writing middle 50% range: NR

Graduated top 10% of class: NR
Graduated top 25% of class: NR
Graduated top 50% of class: NR

COLLEGE GRADUATION REQUIREMENTS

Course waivers allowed: No
Course substitutions allowed: Yes
In what course: Math

ADDITIONAL INFORMATION

Environment: The college is located on 80 acres in an urban area 225 miles west of St. Louis.

Student Body
  Undergrad enrollment: 1,616
  Women: 56%
  Men: 44%
  Percent out-of-state: 60%

Cost Information
  Tuition: $13,530
  Room & board: $5,120
Housing Information
  University housing: Yes
  Percent living on campus: 82%

Greek System
  Fraternity: Yes
  Sorority: Yes
Athletics: Division II

KANSAS CITY ART INSTITUTE

4415 Warwick Boulevard, Kansas City, MO 64111-1762
Phone: 816-474-5225 • Fax: 816-802-3309
E-mail: admiss@kcai.edu • Web:www.kcai.edu
Support: CS • Institution type: 4-year private

LEARNING DISABILITY PROGRAM AND SERVICES

The Academic Resource Center (ARC) is committed to the educational development of students at the Kansas City Art Institute. A recognition of the individual cognitive and creative styles of students of art and design is reflected in the comprehensive support service offered. The goal is to foster independent thinking and problem solving, resourcefulness, and personal responsibility. All KCAI students are invited to take advantage of the services provided by the ARC. Services are aimed at enhancing a student's experience throughout his or her academic career. The staff takes a holistic approach and is committed to the educational, personal, and evolving professional development of all students. Students with formal documentation of a disability are encouraged to contact the ARC for assistance in arranging accommodations or developing self-advocacy strategies.

LD/ADHD ADMISSIONS INFORMATION

College entrance tests required: Yes
Interview required: No
Essay recommended: No
Documentation required for LD: IEP, Section 504, or psychological report
Documentation required for ADHD: IEP, Section 504, or psychological report
Submitted to: Both the Admissions Office and the Academic Resource Center
Special Ed. HS course work accepted: Yes

Specific course requirements of all applicants: NR
Separate application required: No
# of LD applications submitted each year: NR
# of LD applications accepted yearly: NR
Total # of students receiving LD services: NR
Acceptance into program means acceptance into college: Students must be admitted to and enrolled in the university first and then request services.

ADMISSIONS
Students with learning disabilities must demonstrate art ability through a portfolio review and meet a combination of academic criteria, like all other applicants, but with a more specialized evaluation. Admitted students should have a minimum ACT of 20 or SAT of 950 and a 2.5 GPA. Students must have had at least 4 years of high school English. If the criteria are not met, applicants are considered in depth via an Admissions Committee. An interview is recommended.

ADDITIONAL INFORMATION
Students are given assistance in the ARC on an individual basis. Students will consult with their academic advisors each semester about progress in their academic degree program. Advisors help assess progress toward a degree and provide guidance in course selection. Peer advisors are also available. The learning specialist helps students gain a more complete understanding of their individual learning styles, skills, strengths, and weaknesses to cope with the great demands of college courses. Assistance is available through study groups and one-on-one tutoring sessions to improve reading, writing, study, testing, and time management skills.

LEARNING DISABILITY PROGRAM/SERVICES

Learning Disability Program/Services: Academic Resource Center (ARC)
Director: Andrea Khan
  E-mail: akhan@kcai.edu
  Telephone: 816-802-3466
  Fax: 816-802-3480
Contact Person: Katherine Keller
  E-mail: akhan@kcai.edu
  Telephone: 816-802-3485
  Fax: 816-802-3480

LEARNING DISABILITY SERVICES

Requests for the following services/accommodations will be evaluated individually based on appropriate and current documentation.

Allowed in exams
  Calculator: Yes
  Dictionary: Yes
  Computer: Yes
  Spellchecker: Yes
Extended test time: Yes
Scribes: Yes
Proctors: Yes
Oral exams: Yes
Note-takers: Yes

Distraction-reduced environment: Yes
Tape recording in class: Yes
Books on tape from RFBD: Yes
Taping of books not from RFBD: Yes
Accommodations for students with ADHD: Yes
Reading machine: No
Other assistive technology: Yes
Priority registration: Yes

Added costs for services: No
LD specialists: Yes
Professional tutors: 1
Peer tutors: 4
Max. hours/wk. for services: Unlimited
How professors are notified of LD/ADHD: By both student and director

GENERAL ADMISSIONS INFORMATION

Director of Admissions: Larry Stone
Telephone: 816-802-3304

ENTRANCE REQUIREMENTS
Academic units recommended: 4 English, 3 math, 3 science, 3 social studies, 3 academic electives, 4 fine arts. High school diploma is required, and GED is accepted. TOEFL required of all international applicants: minimum paper TOEFL 550, minimum computer TOEFL 213.

Application deadline: NR
Notification: Rolling
Average GPA: 3.30
ACT Composite middle 50% range: 20–24

SAT Math middle 50% range: 450–580
SAT Critical Reading middle 50% range: 480–630
SAT Writing middle 50% range: NR

Graduated top 10% of class: 11%
Graduated top 25% of class: 33%
Graduated top 50% of class: 65%

COLLEGE GRADUATION REQUIREMENTS

Course waivers allowed: No
Course substitutions allowed: No

ADDITIONAL INFORMATION

Environment: The campus is located in an urban area in Kansas City.

Student Body
  Undergrad enrollment: 665
  Women: 57%
  Men: 43%
  Percent out-of-state: 69%

Cost Information
  Tuition: $24,000
  Room & board: $7,500
Housing Information
  University housing: Yes
  Percent living on campus: 20%

Greek System
  Fraternity: Yes
  Sorority: Yes
  Athletics: None

Kansas City Art Institute

MISSOURI STATE UNIVERSITY

901 South National, Springfield, MO 65897
Phone: 417-836-5517 • Fax: 417-836-6334
E-mail: info@missouristate.edu • Web: www.missouristate.edu
Support: SP • Institution type: 4-year public

LEARNING DISABILITY PROGRAM AND SERVICES

The Learning Diagnostic Clinic (LDC) is an academic support facility to assist students with learning disabilities. The staff includes psychologists and learning specialists. The LDC provides two levels of academic support to qualified individuals: One level of services includes those services that comprise basic accommodations guaranteed to the qualified students with disabilities under the law; these services are offered at no cost. The second level is called Project Success, an academic support program for college students with learning disabilities who desire more comprehensive services. This program provides academic and emotional support that will help to ease the student's transition to higher learning and the opportunity to function independently. Students applying to Project Success are required to have a psychoeducational evaluation by the LDC staff to ensure that the program is suitable for their needs and able provide appropriate accommodations. The fee for testing is $500. If background and documentation do not support a diagnosis of LD, alternatives and suggestions are discussed with the student. If the student wishes to appeal a decision not to provide services, he or she is referred to the ADA/504 compliance officer.

LD/ADHD ADMISSIONS INFORMATION

College entrance tests required: Yes
Interview required: No
Essay recommended: NR
Documentation required for LD: Psychoeducational
  evaluation
Documentation required for ADHD: Letter from student's
  current physician
Submitted to: Learning Diagnostic Clinic
Special Ed. HS course work accepted: No

Specific course requirements of all applicants: NR
Separate application required: No
# of LD applications submitted each year: NR
# of LD applications accepted yearly: NR
Total # of students receiving LD services: 200
**Acceptance into program means acceptance into
  college:** Students must be admitted and enrolled at the
  university first and then may request an application to LDC or
  Project Success.

ADMISSIONS

Students with LD must meet the same requirements for admission as all other applicants. There is a special application to be completed as well as a required evaluation fee for students requesting special services. Eligibility for admissions is based on a sliding scale determined by ACT scores and class rank. Course requirements include 4 English, 3 mathematics (Algebra I or higher, including Algebra II), 3 social studies (must include American History and at least one semester of Government), 2 science (not including general science, and one unit must be a laboratory course), and 1 visual and performing arts, plus 3 additional core courses selected from any combination of two or more of the above subject areas and/or foreign language. Computer science may also be used (prerequisite of Algebra I or higher). Steps in the application procedure to Project Success: (1) gain acceptance to the university, (2) self-identify and request an application at LDC, (3) submit application and information, and (4) personal interview and testing or referred to other services. The student is accepted or offered alternative suggestions. The university admits a limited number of students who do not meet the above requirements but who demonstrate an academic potential not reflected in their standard performance measures. Students who wish to be considered for admission as an exception to the policy should contact the Admissions Office for information on the appeal process. Students are encouraged to request this information before submitting their application.

ADDITIONAL INFORMATION

Students must self-identify to request accommodations. Appropriate accommodations are determined by the director and the student. The student is assigned to a graduate assistant who maintains contact, monitors progress, and assesses the effectiveness of accommodations. Project Success staff provides intensive remediation, focusing on written language and mathematics strategies. Caseworkers provide assistance with advocacy skills. Tutors trained by the LDC are available to students enrolled in the Project Success program; the fee for this level of accommodations is $1,000 per semester. Basic services from the LDC may include assistance in obtaining recorded textbooks, testing accommodations, counseling, advisement, and note-taking assistance; there is no fee for these basic services.

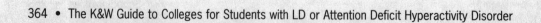

LEARNING DISABILITY PROGRAM/SERVICES

Learning Disability Program/Services: Learning Diagnostic Clinic (LDC)
Director: Steve Capps, PhD
  E-mail: stevencapps@missouristate.edu
  Telephone: 417-836-4787
  Fax: 417-836-5475
Contact Person: Douglas Gere, MS, LPC
  E-mail: stevencapps@missouristate.edu
  Telephone: 417-836-4787

LEARNING DISABILITY SERVICES

Requests for the following services/accommodations will be evaluated individually based on appropriate and current documentation.

Allowed in exams
  Calculator: Yes
  Dictionary: Yes
  Computer: Yes
  Spellchecker: Yes
Extended test time: Yes
Scribes: Yes
Proctors: Yes
Oral exams: Yes
Note-takers: Yes

Distraction-reduced environment: Yes
Tape recording in class: Yes
Books on tape from RFBD: Yes
Taping of books not from RFBD: Yes
Accommodations for students with
  ADHD: Yes
Reading machine: Yes
Other assistive technology: Yes
Priority registration: Yes

Added costs for services: No
LD specialists: Yes
Professional tutors: No
Peer tutors: Yes
Max. hours/wk. for services: N/A
How professors are notified of
  LD/ADHD: By both student and director

GENERAL ADMISSIONS INFORMATION

Director of Admissions: Don Simpson
Telephone: 417-836-5521

ENTRANCE REQUIREMENTS

Academic units required: 4 English, 3 math, 2 science (1 science lab), 3 social studies, 3 academic electives. High school diploma is required, and GED is accepted. ACT with or without Writing component accepted. TOEFL required of all international applicants: minimum paper TOEFL 500, minimum computer TOEFL 173.

Application deadline: 7/20
Notification: NR
Average GPA: 3.57
ACT Composite middle 50% range: 21–26

SAT Math middle 50% range: NR
SAT Critical Reading middle 50% range: NR
SAT Writing middle 50% range: NR

Graduated top 10% of class: 22%
Graduated top 25% of class: 49%
Graduated top 50% of class: 81%

COLLEGE GRADUATION REQUIREMENTS

Course waivers allowed: No
Course substitutions allowed: Yes
In what course: Varies

ADDITIONAL INFORMATION

Environment: The 200-acre rural campus is located 170 miles from Kansas City and 120 miles from St. Louis.

Student Body
  Undergrad enrollment: 14,463
  Women: 56%
  Men: 44%
  Percent out-of-state: 7%

Cost Information
  In-state tuition: $5,400
  Out-of-state tuition: $10,300
  Room & board: $5,294
Housing Information
  University housing: Yes
  Percent living on campus: 24%

Greek System
  Fraternity: Yes
  Sorority: Yes
Athletics: Division I

UNIVERSITY OF MISSOURI—COLUMBIA

230 Jesse Hall, Columbia, MO 65211
Phone: 573-882-7786 • Fax: 573-882-7887
E-mail: MU4U@missouri.edu • Web: www.missouri.edu
Support: CS • Institution type: 4-year public

LEARNING DISABILITY PROGRAM AND SERVICES

The mission of Disability Support Services is to encourage the educational development of students with a disability and improve the understanding and support of the campus environment by providing assistance to students with a documented disability and encouraging independence, serving as a liaison and advocate, and working with students to ensure equal access to all programs and services. The Office for Disability Services (ODS) provides accommodations and support services within the resources of the university. The goal of the program is to promote independence and self-advocacy. In addition, ODS assists other college departments in providing access to services and programs in the most integrated setting possible.

LD/ADHD ADMISSIONS INFORMATION

College entrance tests required: Yes
Interview required: No
Essay recommended: No
Documentation required for LD: Students with LD must provide the most recent documentation indicating ability and achievement and IQ testing performed by a qualified professional.
Documentation required for ADHD: Students with ADHD must have written documentation from a qualified professional stating client history, tests given, diagnosis, and accommodations recommended.
Submitted to: Disability Support Services
Special Ed. HS course work accepted: Yes

Specific course requirements of all applicants: Yes
Separate application required: No
# of LD applications submitted each year: NR
# of LD applications accepted yearly: NR
Total # of students receiving LD services: 610
Acceptance into program means acceptance into college: Students must be admitted to and enrolled in the university first and then request services.

ADMISSIONS
There are no special admissions for students with learning disabilities. General admission is based on high school curriculum, ACT scores, and class rank. Applicants must have 4 years of English, 4 years of math, 3 years of social studies, 3 years of science, 2 years of a foreign language, and 1 unit of fine arts. Math, science, and foreign language requirements may be satisfied by completion of courses in middle school, junior high, or senior high. Any student with an ACT of 24 with the required courses is automatically admissible. Students with 23 ACT or 1050–1090 SAT need to rank within the top 52 percent of their graduating class. Students with 22 ACT or 1010–1040 SAT need to rank within the top 46 percent of their class. Students with 21 ACT or 970–1000 SAT need to rank within the top 31 percent of their class. Students with 19 ACT or 890–920 SAT need to rank within the top 22 percent of their class. Students with 18 ACT or 840–880 SAT need to rank within the top 14 percent of their class. Students with 17 ACT or 800–830 SAT need to rank within the top 6 percent of their class; ACT below 17 or SAT below 800 does not meet regular admission standards. Graduates of Missouri high schools who do not meet the standards for regular admission may be admitted on a conditional basis through a summer session program.

ADDITIONAL INFORMATION
Auxiliary aids and classroom accommodations include note-takers, lab assistants, readers, and specialized equipment. Testing accommodations include time extensions, quiet rooms, readers, scribes, or adaptive equipment. The learning disabilities specialist offers support and counseling in the areas of time management, study skills, learning styles, and other academic and social issues. Group support is also available. Disabilities Services offers a mentoring program to provide first-year students the opportunity to meet with upperclassmen with disabilities. The Learning Center works cooperatively with ODS to provide individual tutoring free of charge. Other services include writing assistance, math assistance, test reviews, help with reading comprehension, and study skills training.

LEARNING DISABILITY PROGRAM/SERVICES

Learning Disability Program/Services: Office of Disability Services (ODS)
Director: Sarah Colby Weaver, PhD
  E-mail: weavers@missouri.edu
  Telephone: 573-882-4696
  Fax: 573-884-9272

LEARNING DISABILITY SERVICES

Requests for the following services/accommodations will be evaluated individually based on appropriate and current documentation.

Allowed in exams
  Calculator: Yes
  Dictionary: Yes
  Computer: Yes
  Spellchecker: Yes
Extended test time: Yes
Scribes: Yes
Proctors: Yes
Oral exams: Yes
Note-takers: Yes

Distraction-reduced environment: Yes
Tape recording in class: Yes
Books on tape from RFBD: Yes
Taping of books not from RFBD: Yes
**Accommodations for students with
  ADHD:** Yes
Reading machine: Yes
Other assistive technology: Yes
Priority registration: Yes

Added costs for services: No
LD specialists: Yes
Professional tutors: 7
Peer tutors: 120
Max. hours/wk. for services:
  Unlimited
**How professors are notified of
  LD/ADHD:** By student

GENERAL ADMISSIONS INFORMATION

Director of Admissions: Barbara Rupp
Telephone: 573-882-7786

ENTRANCE REQUIREMENTS

Academic units required: 4 English, 4 math, 3 science (1 science lab), 2 foreign language, 3 social studies, 1 fine arts. High school diploma is required, and GED is accepted. ACT with or without Writing component accepted. TOEFL required of all international applicants: minimum paper TOEFL 500, minimum computer TOEFL 173.

Application deadline: Rolling
Notification: Rolling
Average GPA: NR
ACT Composite middle 50% range:
  23–28

SAT Math middle 50% range:
  540–650
**SAT Critical Reading middle 50%
  range:** 530–650
SAT Writing middle 50% range: NR

Graduated top 10% of class: 27%
Graduated top 25% of class: 57%
Graduated top 50% of class: 87%

COLLEGE GRADUATION REQUIREMENTS

Course waivers allowed: No
Course substitutions allowed: No

ADDITIONAL INFORMATION

Environment: The university is located on 1,350 acres in a small town.

Student Body
  Undergrad enrollment: 21,258
  Women: 51%
  Men: 49%
  Percent out-of-state: 13%

Cost Information
  In-state tuition: $7,308
  Out-of-state tuition: $16,890
  Room & board: $7,000
Housing Information
  University housing: Yes
  Percent living on campus: 37%

Greek System
  Fraternity: Yes
  Sorority: Yes
Athletics: Division I

University of Missouri—Columbia

WASHINGTON U. IN ST. LOUIS

Campus Box 1089, One Brookings Drive, St. Louis, MO 63130-4899
Phone: 314-935-6000 • Fax: 314-935-4290
E-mail: admissions@wustl.edu • Web: www.wustl.edu
Support: CS • Institution type: 4-year private

LEARNING DISABILITY PROGRAM AND SERVICES

The Disability Resource Center recognizes that there are many types of disabilities that can hinder a student in showing his or her true academic ability. It is the goal of the DRC to treat students with disabilities as individuals with specific needs and provide services responsive to those needs. The DRC provides a wide range of services and accommodations to help remove barriers posed by the students' disabilities. Students are encouraged to be their own advocates and have the major responsibility for securing services and accommodations. Reasonable accommodations will be made to assist students in meeting their individual needs. It is the goal of the DRC to incorporate students with disabilities into the mainstream of the university community. Any student who has a permanent or temporary psychological or physical disability is eligible for services. Students must self-identify and provide current documentation. The director of the DRC will work with the student to identify appropriate accommodations and services based on documentation and previous experiences. Most accommodations result from communication and agreements between the students and the classroom instructors.

LD/ADHD ADMISSIONS INFORMATION

College entrance tests required: Yes
Interview required: No
Essay recommended: No
Documentation required for LD: Adult-based psychoeducational evaluation
Documentation required for ADHD: Adult-based psychoeducational evaluation
Submitted to: Disability Resource Center
Special Ed. HS course work accepted: NR

Specific course requirements of all applicants: NR
Separate application required: Yes
# of LD applications submitted each year: NR
# of LD applications accepted yearly: NR
Total # of students receiving LD services: 114
Acceptance into program means acceptance into college: Students must be admitted to and enrolled in the university first and then request services.

ADMISSIONS
Washington University gives full consideration to all applicants for admission. There is no special admissions process for students with learning disabilities. Students may choose to voluntarily identify themselves as learning disabled in the admissions process. If they chose to self-identify, details of the history and treatment of their disability, of how they have met different academic requirements in light of the disability, and the relationship between the disability and the students' academic record help the university to understand more fully the applicants' profiles. This information can be helpful in the application process to explain, for example, lower grades in certain subjects. Washington University is a competitive school and looks for students with rigorous academic preparation, including 4 years of English, 3–4 years of math, 3–4 years of science, and 3–4 years of social studies. Two years of a foreign language are preferred but not required.

ADDITIONAL INFORMATION
The Learning Center services focus on reading, writing, vocabulary, time management, and study techniques. Skills classes are offered in time management, rapid reading, and self-advocacy, but they are not for credit. Common services and accommodations include, but are not limited to, readers or scribes, note-takers, campus orientation, assistance in obtaining accommodations for professional exams, referral for disability evaluation, audio taping class lectures, extra time to complete exams, alternative exam formats, and distraction-free exam sites. Services and accommodations are available for undergraduate and graduate students.

LEARNING DISABILITY PROGRAM/SERVICES

Learning Disability Program/Services: Disability Resources
Director: Christine Duden Street
　E-mail: Christine_street@wustl.edu
　Telephone: 314-935-4153
　Fax: 314-935-7559
Contact Person: Zachary McBee
　E-mail: zachary_mcbee@wustl.edu.
　Telephone: 314-935-4062
　Fax: 314-935-8272

LEARNING DISABILITY SERVICES

Requests for the following services/accommodations will be evaluated individually based on appropriate and current documentation.

Allowed in exams
　Calculator: Yes
　Dictionary: Yes
　Computer: Yes
　Spellchecker: Yes
Extended test time: Yes
Scribes: Yes
Proctors: Yes
Oral exams: Yes
Note-takers: Yes

Distraction-reduced environment: Yes
Tape recording in class: Yes
Books on tape from RFBD: Yes
Taping of books not from RFBD: Yes
Accommodations for students with ADHD: Yes
Reading machine: Yes
Other assistive technology: Yes
Priority registration: No

Added costs for services: No
LD specialists: Yes
Professional tutors: No
Peer tutors: No
Max. hours/wk. for services: Unlimited
How professors are notified of LD/ADHD: By both student and director

GENERAL ADMISSIONS INFORMATION

Director of Admissions: Nanette Tarbouni
Telephone: 314-935-6000

ENTRANCE REQUIREMENTS

Academic units recommended: 4 English, 4 math, 4 science (4 science labs), 2 foreign language, 4 social studies, 4 history. High school diploma is required, and GED is accepted. ACT with or without Writing component accepted. TOEFL required of all international applicants: minimum paper TOEFL 550, minimum computer TOEFL 213.

Application deadline: 1/15
Notification: 4/1
Average GPA: NR
ACT Composite middle 50% range: 30–33

SAT Math middle 50% range: 700–780
SAT Critical Reading middle 50% range: 670–750
SAT Writing middle 50% range: NR

Graduated top 10% of class: 95%
Graduated top 25% of class: 100%
Graduated top 50% of class: 100%

COLLEGE GRADUATION REQUIREMENTS

Course waivers allowed: No
Course substitutions allowed: Yes
In what course: Foreign language and math are not required for most majors.

ADDITIONAL INFORMATION

Environment: The Washington University campus is located on 169 acres seven miles west of St. Louis.

Student Body
　Undergrad enrollment: 6,601
　Women: 50%
　Men: 50%
　Percent out-of-state: 89%

Cost Information
　Tuition: $34,500
　Room & board: $11,252
Housing Information
　University housing: Yes
　Percent living on campus: 72%

Greek System
　Fraternity: Yes
　Sorority: Yes
Athletics: Division III

WESTMINSTER COLLEGE

501 Westminster Avenue, Fulton, MO 65251-1299
Phone: 573-592-5251 • Fax: 573-592-5255
E-mail: admissions@westminster-mo.edu • Web: www.westminster-mo.edu
Support: SP • 7Institution type: 4-yearprivate

LEARNING DISABILITY PROGRAM AND SERVICES

The goal of the Learning Disabilities Program is to give students with learning disabilities the special attention they need to succeed in basically the same academic program as that pursued by other admitted students. Westminster offers the students a supportive environment, small classes, and professors who are readily accessible. The LD staff offers intensive instruction in reading, writing, and study skills. Much of the instruction is conducted on a one-on-one basis and is directed to the student's specific problem. Close supervision of the curriculum is essential in the student's freshman year, and the student's progress is monitored for any difficulties that may arise. The staff is LD certified, and faculty members have the specific role of providing LD support.

LD/ADHD ADMISSIONS INFORMATION

College entrance tests required: Yes
Interview required: Yes
Essay recommended: Yes
Documentation required for LD: WAIS-R, WISC–III and written evaluation completed within the past 2 years; Woodcock-Johnson Test for Achievement
Documentation required for ADHD: Connors Parent/Teacher Rating Scale and/or various behavioral assessments
Submitted to: Admissions
Special Ed. HS course work accepted: No

Specific course requirements of all applicants: Yes
Separate application required: Yes
# of LD applications submitted each year: 40–60
# of LD applications accepted yearly: 14–17
Total # of students receiving LD services: 15–20
Acceptance into program means acceptance into college: Students are admitted jointly to the LD program and the college.

ADMISSIONS

There is a special application and admissions procedure for students with learning disabilities. Students submit a completed Westminster College application form and a separate application form for the LD program; results of an eye and hearing exam, WAIS-R, WJ-III, and achievement tests; SAT scores of 900-plus or ACT scores of 19-plus; two copies of their high school transcript; recent reports from school counselors, learning specialists, psychologists, or physicians who have diagnosed the disability; four recommendations from counselors or teachers familiar with their performance; and an evaluation from an educational specialist. An on-campus interview is required. Following the interview and a review of the file, the director and assistant director of the program confer and reach an admission decision usually within 1 week after the visit. Students are either admitted directly into the college and then reviewed for LD services or admitted into the LD program, which results in an admission to the college.

ADDITIONAL INFORMATION

Students are mainstreamed and need a solid college-prep background in high school. There is a fee of $1,800 for the first year of the program and $900 each year thereafter. Students have access to unlimited tutoring. Learning resources include audio tapes of textbooks; self-instructional materials; special classes in study, reading, and listening skills; test-taking, time management, and English composition strategies; and word processors to assist in writing instruction. There is also the Student Development Center, which is a learning center that is open to all students.

LEARNING DISABILITY PROGRAM/SERVICES

Learning Disability Program/Services: Learning Disabilities Program
Director: Hank Ottinger
  E-mail: ottingh@jwestminster-mo.edu
  Telephone: 573-592-5304
  Fax: 573-592-5191

LEARNING DISABILITY SERVICES

Requests for the following services/accommodations will be evaluated individually based on appropriate and current documentation.

Allowed in exams
  Calculator: Yes
  Dictionary: No
  Computer: Yes
  Spellchecker: Yes
Extended test time: Yes
Scribes: Yes
Proctors: Yes
Oral exams: Yes
Note-takers: Yes

Distraction-reduced environment: Yes
Tape recording in class: Yes
Books on tape from RFBD: Yes
Taping of books not from RFBD: Yes
**Accommodations for students with
  ADHD:** Yes
Reading machine: Yes
Other assistive technology: Yes
Priority registration: No

Added costs for services: Yes
LD specialists: Yes
Professional tutors: 2.5
Peer tutors: 20
Max. hours/wk. for services:
  Unlimited
**How professors are notified of
  LD/ADHD:** By director

GENERAL ADMISSIONS INFORMATION

Director of Admissions: Patrick T. Kirby
Telephone: 800-475-3361

ENTRANCE REQUIREMENTS

Academic units required: 4 English, 3 math, 2 science (2 science labs). **Academic units recommended:** 2 foreign language, 2 social studies, 2 academic electives. High school diploma is required, and GED is accepted. ACT with or without Writing component accepted. TOEFL required of all international applicants: minimum paper TOEFL 550, minimum computer TOEFL 213.

Application deadline: Rolling
Notification: Rolling
Average GPA: 3.46
ACT Composite middle 50% range:
  22–27

SAT Math middle 50% range:
  490–640
**SAT Critical Reading middle 50%
  range:** 460–640
SAT Writing middle 50% range:
  470–640

Graduated top 10% of class: 17%
Graduated top 25% of class: 49%
Graduated top 50% of class: 82%

COLLEGE GRADUATION REQUIREMENTS

Course waivers allowed: No
Course substitutions allowed: Yes
In what course: Students can petition the academic dean for substitute courses in any area.

ADDITIONAL INFORMATION

Environment: The 250-acre college campus is located in a small town 20 miles east of Columbia, Missouri.

Student Body
  Undergrad enrollment: 936
  Women: 43%
  Men: 57%
  Percent out-of-state: 26%

Cost Information
  Tuition: $15,500
  Room & board: $6,420
Housing Information
  University housing: Yes
  Percent living on campus: 85%

Greek System
  Fraternity: Yes
  Sorority: Yes
Athletics: Division III

Montana State U.—Billings

1500 University Drive, Billings, MT 59101
Phone: 406-657-2158 • Fax: 406-657-2051
E-mail: cjohannes@msubillings.edu • Web: www.msubillings.edu
Support: S • Institution type: 4-year public

LEARNING DISABILITY PROGRAM AND SERVICES

The mission of Disability Support Services is to encourage the educational development of students with disabilities and improve the understanding and support of the campus environment by providing assistance to students with disabilities, encouraging independence, and providing a supportive emotional atmosphere; serving as a liaison and advocate; and working with students to ensure equal access to all programs and services. MSU—Billings has a policy of providing reasonable accommodations to qualified students with a documented disability. Students requiring accommodations such as exam accessibility or reader services are encouraged to contact Disability Support Services at least 4 weeks before services are required. The guidelines utilized for providing services to students with LD are that (1) the student must meet the definition of LD set forth by the National Joint Committee on LD; (2) the student must have an LD diagnosed by a professional qualified to diagnose and a statement of the disability, and a summary of the student's academic strengths and weaknesses must be included; (3) quantitative data acceptable for documentation must include standardized and informal measures including case histories, interviews, and previous records that confirm the learning problem; (4) DSS reserves the right to determine whether a student qualifies for services.

LD/ADHD ADMISSIONS INFORMATION

College entrance tests required: Yes
Interview required: No
Essay recommended: No
Documentation required for LD: Psychoeducational evaluation
Documentation required for ADHD: Yes
Submitted to: Disability Support Services
Special Ed. HS course work accepted: Yes

Specific course requirements of all applicants: Yes
Separate application required: No
# of LD applications submitted each year: NR
# of LD applications accepted yearly: NR
Total # of students receiving LD services: NR
Acceptance into program means acceptance into college: Students must be admitted to and enrolled in the university first and then request services.

ADMISSIONS

There is no special admission process for students with learning disabilities. All students must meet the same admission criteria. Freshmen applicants must meet one of the following conditions: ACT of 22 or SAT of 920, a 2.5 GPA; or rank in the top half of the class. Students must have 4 years of English, 3 years of math (students are encouraged to take math in their senior year), 3 years of social studies, 2 years of science lab (1 year must be earth science, biology, chemistry, or physics), and 2 years chosen from foreign language, computer science, visual/performing arts, and/or vocational education that meet the Office of Public Instruction guidelines. Students not meeting the college-preparatory requirements have four options: They can (1) apply for an exemption by writing a letter and addressing their special needs, talents, or other reasons; (2) enroll part-time in a summer session; (3) enroll as a part-time student with seven or fewer credits the first semester; or (4) attend a community college or other college and attempt at least 12 credits or make up any deficiency.

ADDITIONAL INFORMATION

Students must request services, provide documentation specifying a learning disability or ADHD, make an appointment for an intake with DSS, meet with professors at the beginning of each semester, and work closely with DSS. DSS must keep documentation and intake on file, make a determination of accommodations, issue identification cards to qualified students, and serve as a resource and a support system. Services include course and testing accommodations, alternative testing, priority scheduling, technical assistance, liaison and referral services, taped textbooks, and career, academic, and counseling referrals. The use of a computer, calculator, dictionary, or spellchecker is at the discretion of the individual professor and based on the documented needs of the student. Services and accommodations are available for undergraduate and graduate students.

LEARNING DISABILITY PROGRAM/SERVICES

Learning Disability Program/Services: Disability Support Services (DSS)
Director: Trudy Carey
  E-mail: tcarey@msubillings.edu
  Telephone: 406-657-2283
  Fax: 406-657-2187

LEARNING DISABILITY SERVICES

Requests for the following services/accommodations will be evaluated individually based on appropriate and current documentation.

Allowed in exams
  Calculator: Yes
  Dictionary: No
  Computer: Yes
  Spellchecker: Yes
Extended test time: Yes
Scribes: Yes
Proctors: Yes
Oral exams: No
Note-takers: Yes

Distraction-reduced environment: Yes
Tape recording in class: Yes
Books on tape from RFBD: Yes
Taping of books not from RFBD: Yes
Accommodations for students with ADHD: Yes
Reading machine: Yes
Other assistive technology: Yes
Priority registration: Yes

Added costs for services: No
LD specialists: No
Professional tutors: 1
Peer tutors: 10–20
Max. hours/wk. for services: Unlimited
How professors are notified of LD/ADHD: By student

GENERAL ADMISSIONS INFORMATION

Director of Admissions: Stacy Klippenstein
Telephone: 406-657-2307

ENTRANCE REQUIREMENTS

Academic units required: 4 English, 3 math, 2 science (2 science labs), 3 social studies, 2 foreign language, visual/performing arts, or computer science. High school diploma is required, and GED is accepted. ACT without Writing component accepted. TOEFL required of all international applicants: minimum paper TOEFL 500, minimum computer TOEFL 173.

Application deadline: 7/1
Notification: Rolling
Average GPA: 3.10
ACT Composite middle 50% range: 19–24

SAT Math middle 50% range: 470–590
SAT Critical Reading middle 50% range: 440–580
SAT Writing middle 50% range: NR

Graduated top 10% of class: 8%
Graduated top 25% of class: 25%
Graduated top 50% of class: 63%

COLLEGE GRADUATION REQUIREMENTS

Course waivers allowed: Yes
In what course: In foreign language and math under strict guidelines
Course substitutions allowed: Yes
In what course: In foreign language and math under strict guidelines

ADDITIONAL INFORMATION

Environment: The campus is in an urban area in Billings, Montana.

Student Body
  Undergrad enrollment: 4,207
  Women: 63%
  Men: 37%
  Percent out-of-state: 8%

Cost Information
  In-state tuition: $4,850
  Out-of-state tuition: $13,900
  Room & board: $4,310
Housing Information
  University housing: Yes
  Percent living on campus: 11%

Greek System
  Fraternity: No
  Sorority: No
Athletics: Division II

MONTANA TECH OF THE U. OF MT

1300 West Park Street, Butte, MT 59701
Phone: 406-496-4178 • Fax: 406-496-4710
E-mail: admissions@mtech.edu • Web: www.mtech.edu
Support: CS • Institution type: 4-year public

LEARNING DISABILITY PROGRAM AND SERVICES

All persons with disabilities have the right to participate fully and equally in the programs and services of Montana Tech. Tech is committed to making the appropriate accommodations. The primary contact and resource person for students with disabilities is the Dean of Students. The dean serves as a general resource for all students who may need assistance. Availability of services from Disability Services is subject to a student's eligibility for these and any other services. Students must provide appropriate and current documentation prior to requesting and receiving services or accommodations. All faculty and staff at the college are responsible for assuring access by providing reasonable accommodations. The Montana Tech Learning Center offers a variety of services to help students achieve their full academic potential. Tutors are available to help all students with course work in an assortment of subject areas. The Learning Center addresses the importance of developing basic college success skills.

LD/ADHD ADMISSIONS INFORMATION

College entrance tests required: Yes
Interview required: No
Essay recommended: No
Documentation required for LD: Accommodation recommendations from a certified professional
Documentation required for ADHD: Yes
Submitted to: Disability Services
Special Ed. HS course work accepted: No

Specific course requirements of all applicants: Yes
Separate application required: No
# of LD applications submitted each year: NR
# of LD applications accepted yearly: NR
Total # of students receiving LD services: NR
Acceptance into program means acceptance into college: Students must be admitted to and enrolled in the university first and then request services.

ADMISSIONS

There is no special admission process for students with LD or ADHD. Applicants must have a 22 ACT or 920 SAT Reasoning, or be in the upper 50 percent of their high school class, or have a 2.5 GPA. The GED is accepted. Students must have 14 academic high school credits, including 4 years of English, 2 years of science, 3 years of math, 3 years of social studies, and 2 years from other academic areas, including foreign language, computer science, visual/performing arts, and vocational education. Interviews are not required, and special education courses in high school are not accepted. Students who do not meet any of the general admission criteria may ask to be evaluated considering other factors. Students with LD/ADHD are encouraged to self-disclose in the admissions process.

ADDITIONAL INFORMATION

The following types of services are offered to students with disabilities: responses to requests for accommodation, assistance in working with faculty members, text accommodation in concert with instructors, access to assistive technology, note-taking, disability evaluation and testing, and career services. Documentation to receive services should be sent directly to Disability Services. The Learning Center houses computer stations for students. In addition, Montana Tech offers compensatory classes for students with LD in both math and English. Services and accommodations are available for undergraduate and graduate students.

LEARNING DISABILITY PROGRAM/SERVICES

Learning Disability Program/Services: Disability Services
Director: Eletha Suttey or Paul Beatty
  E-mail: esuttey@mtech.edu or pbeatty@mtech.edu
  Telephone: 406-496-3730
  Fax: 406-496-3710

LEARNING DISABILITY SERVICES

Requests for the following services/accommodations will be evaluated individually based on appropriate and current documentation.

Allowed in exams
  Calculator: No
  Dictionary: No
  Computer: Yes
  Spellchecker: No
Extended test time: Yes
Scribes: Yes
Proctors: Yes
Oral exams: Yes
Note-takers: Yes

Distraction-reduced environment: Yes
Tape recording in class: Yes
Books on tape from RFBD: Yes
Taping of books not from RFBD: Yes
Accommodations for students with ADHD: No
Reading machine: Yes
Other assistive technology: Yes
Priority registration: No

Added costs for services: No
LD specialists: Yes
Professional tutors: 2
Peer tutors: 0–12
Max. hours/wk. for services: Unlimited
How professors are notified of LD/ADHD: By both student and director

GENERAL ADMISSIONS INFORMATION

Director of Admissions: Tony Campeau
Telephone: 406-469-4632

ENTRANCE REQUIREMENTS

Academic units required: 4 English, 3 math, 2 science (2 science labs), 3 social studies, 2 years combined of a foreign language, visual/performing arts, computer science, or vocational education units. **Academic units recommended:** 4 English, 4 math, 4 science (2 science labs), 2 foreign language. High school diploma is required, and GED is accepted. ACT with Writing component required. TOEFL required of all international applicants: minimum paper TOEFL 525, minimum computer TOEFL 195.

Application deadline: Rolling
Notification: Rolling
Average GPA: 3.20
ACT Composite middle 50% range: 19–24

SAT Math middle 50% range: 490–610
SAT Critical Reading middle 50% range: 450–570
SAT Writing middle 50% range: NR

Graduated top 10% of class: 14%
Graduated top 25% of class: 35%
Graduated top 50% of class: 68%

COLLEGE GRADUATION REQUIREMENTS

Course waivers allowed: No
Course substitutions allowed: No

ADDITIONAL INFORMATION

Environment: The campus is located 65 miles from Helena.

Student Body
  Undergrad enrollment: 1,913
  Women: 44%
  Men: 56%
  Percent out-of-state: 12%

Cost Information
  In-state tuition: $5,606
  Out-of-state tuition: $14,766
  Room & board: $5,594
Housing Information
  University housing: Yes
  Percent living on campus: 16%

Greek System
  Fraternity: No
  Sorority: No
Athletics: NAIA

ROCKY MOUNTAIN COLLEGE

1511 Poly Drive, Billings, MT 59102-1796
Phone: 406-657-1026 • Fax: 406-657-1189
E-mail: admissions@rocky.edu • Web: www.rocky.edu
Support: CS • Institution type: 4-year private

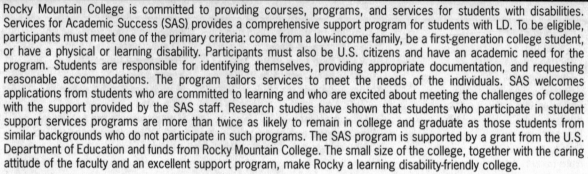

LEARNING DISABILITY PROGRAM AND SERVICES

Rocky Mountain College is committed to providing courses, programs, and services for students with disabilities. Services for Academic Success (SAS) provides a comprehensive support program for students with LD. To be eligible, participants must meet one of the primary criteria: come from a low-income family, be a first-generation college student, or have a physical or learning disability. Participants must also be U.S. citizens and have an academic need for the program. Students are responsible for identifying themselves, providing appropriate documentation, and requesting reasonable accommodations. The program tailors services to meet the needs of the individuals. SAS welcomes applications from students who are committed to learning and who are excited about meeting the challenges of college with the support provided by the SAS staff. Research studies have shown that students who participate in student support services programs are more than twice as likely to remain in college and graduate as those students from similar backgrounds who do not participate in such programs. The SAS program is supported by a grant from the U.S. Department of Education and funds from Rocky Mountain College. The small size of the college, together with the caring attitude of the faculty and an excellent support program, make Rocky a learning disability-friendly college.

LD/ADHD ADMISSIONS INFORMATION

College entrance tests required: Yes
Interview required: No
Essay recommended: No
Documentation required for LD: Psychoeducational
evaluation
Documentation required for ADHD: Yes
Submitted to: Services for Academic Success
Special Ed. HS course work accepted: No

Specific course requirements of all applicants: Yes
Separate application required: Yes
# of LD applications submitted each year: 10–20
# of LD applications accepted yearly: 10–20
Total # of students receiving LD services: 30–40
Acceptance into program means acceptance into
college: Students must be admitted to and enrolled in the
university first and then request services.

ADMISSIONS

There is no special admissions application for students with learning disabilities. All applicants must meet the same criteria, which include an ACT of 21 or SAT of 1000, a GPA of 2.5, and courses in English, math, science, and social studies. There is the opportunity to be considered for a conditional admission if scores or grades are below the cutoffs. However, to identify and provide necessary support services as soon as possible, students with disabilities are encouraged to complete a Services for Academic Success application form at the same time they apply for admission to Rocky Mountain College. Recommended courses for admissions include 4 years of English, 3 years of math, 3 years of social science, 2 years of science lab, and 2 years of a foreign language.

ADDITIONAL INFORMATION

SAS provides a variety of services tailored to meet a student's individual needs. Services are free to participants and include developmental course work in reading, writing, and mathematics, study skills classes, tutoring in all subjects, academic, career, and personal counseling, graduate school counseling, accommodations for students with learning disabilities, alternative testing arrangements, taping of lectures or textbooks, cultural and academic enrichment opportunities, and advocacy. SAS staff meets with each student to talk about the supportive services the student needs and then develop a semester plan. Skills classes for college credit are offered in math, English, and studying techniques.

LEARNING DISABILITY PROGRAM/SERVICES

Learning Disability Program/Services: Services for Academic Success (SAS)
Director: Dr. Jane Van Dyk
  E-mail: vandykj@rocky.edu
  Telephone: 406-657-1128
  Fax: 406-259-9751

LEARNING DISABILITY SERVICES

Requests for the following services/accommodations will be evaluated individually based on appropriate and current documentation.

Allowed in exams
  Calculator: Yes
  Dictionary: Yes
  Computer: Yes
  Spellchecker: Yes
Extended test time: Yes
Scribes: Yes
Proctors: Yes
Oral exams: Yes
Note-takers: Yes

Distraction-reduced environment: Yes
Tape recording in class: Yes
Books on tape from RFBD: Yes
Taping of books not from RFBD: Yes
Accommodations for students with
  ADHD: Yes
Reading machine: No
Other assistive technology: Yes
Priority registration: Yes

Added costs for services: No
LD specialists: Yes
Professional tutors: 2
Peer tutors: 30
Max. hours/wk. for services:
  Unlimited
How professors are notified of
  LD/ADHD: By both student and
  director

GENERAL ADMISSIONS INFORMATION

Director of Admissions: Laurie Rodriguez
Telephone: 406-657-1026

ENTRANCE REQUIREMENTS

Academic units required: 4 English, 2 math, 2 science (1 science lab), 1 foreign language, 2 social studies, 2 history. **Academic units recommended:** 4 English, 3 math, 2 science (2 science lab), 2 foreign language, 2 social studies, 2 history. High school diploma is required, and GED is accepted. ACT with Writing component required. TOEFL required of all international applicants: minimum paper TOEFL 525, minimum computer TOEFL 197.

Application deadline: Rolling
Notification: Rolling
Average GPA: 3.34
ACT Composite middle 50% range:
  19–24

SAT Math middle 50% range:
  450–570
SAT Critical Reading middle 50%
  range: 460–590
SAT Writing middle 50% range: NR

Graduated top 10% of class: 21%
Graduated top 25% of class: 43%
Graduated top 50% of class: 78%

COLLEGE GRADUATION REQUIREMENTS

Course waivers allowed: No
Course substitutions allowed: No

ADDITIONAL INFORMATION

Environment: The campus is located in a small town over 500 miles north of Denver, Colorado.

Student Body
  Undergrad enrollment: 817
  Women: 55%
  Men: 45%
  Percent out-of-state: 38%

Cost Information
  Tuition: $16,389
  Room & board: $5,608
Housing Information
  University housing: Yes
  Percent living on campus: 53%

Greek System
  Fraternity: No
  Sorority: No
Athletics: NAIA

UNIVERSITY OF MONTANA

Lommasson Center 103, Missoula, MT 59812
Phone: 406-243-6266 • Fax: 406-243-5711
E-mail: admiss@umontana.edu • Web: www.umt.edu
Support: S • Institution type: 4-year public

LEARNING DISABILITY PROGRAM AND SERVICES

Disability Services for Students (DSS) ensures equal access to the university by students with disabilities. DSS is a stand-alone student affairs office at the university. It is staffed by more than 10 full-time professionals. Students with learning disabilities have the same set of rights and responsibilities of and the same set of services and accommodations offered to other students with disabilities. Written documentation from a qualified diagnostician containing the diagnosis and functional limitation of the LD must be provided to DSS. It should be noted that DSS does not operate the same way many special education programs in secondary schools do. At the university, students have a right to access education, not a right to education. This means that DSS treats students as adults who succeed or fail on their own merits. Students should determine their needs, initiate requests for accommodations, and follow up with the delivery of those rights. DSS refrains from seeking out individuals for interventionist actions. Once a student makes his or her disability and needs known to DSS, DSS will provide the accommodations that will grant the student the right of equal access. Transitioning from high school to college is enhanced when students grasp and apply the principles of self-advocacy.

LD/ADHD ADMISSIONS INFORMATION

College entrance tests required: Yes
Interview required: No
Essay recommended: No
Documentation required for LD: A current and comprehensive diagnostic report completed within the past 3 to 5 years.
Documentation required for ADHD: A current and comprehensive diagnostic report completed within 3 to 5 years.
Submitted to: Disability Services for Students

Special Ed. HS course work accepted: N/A
Specific course requirements of all applicants: Yes
Separate application required: Yes
# of LD applications submitted each year: NR
# of LD applications accepted yearly: NR
Total # of students receiving LD services: 152
Acceptance into program means acceptance into college: Students must be admitted to and enrolled in the university first and then request services.

ADMISSIONS

Admissions criteria are the same for all applicants. However, consideration will be given to students who do not meet the general admissions criteria. General admission criteria include 22 on the ACT or 1030 on the SAT; ranking in the upper half of the class; and a 2.5 GPA. DSS will act as an advocate for students with learning disabilities during the admission process. Applicants not meeting admission criteria may request and receive a review of their eligibility by an Admissions Committee. Students should send documentation verifying the disability directly to the DSS office. Documentation should include a complete and current, having been completed within the past 3 to 5 years, psychological evaluation written by a qualified professional stating the diagnosis. In the report, there should also be the list of apptitude and achievement tests the student has taken, relevant history, functional limitations, and recommended accommodations.

ADDITIONAL INFORMATION

Students with LD can expect reasonable accommodations to suit their individual needs. Accommodations may include a direct service or academic adjustment, but they will not reduce the academic standards of the institution. Academic assistants at the university provide auxiliary services such as reading textbooks and other instructional materials, scribing assignments or tests, assisting in library research, and proofreading materials. Other services may include academic adjustments, admissions assistance, assistive technology, auxiliary aids, consultation with faculty, counseling, course waiver assistance, letter of verification, note-taking, orientation, priority registration, scribes, study skills course, test accommodations services, and tutoring services. Academic adjustments may include extended testing times, substitute course requirements, or lecture notes from instructors.

LEARNING DISABILITY PROGRAM/SERVICES

Learning Disability Program/Services: Disability Services for Students (DSS)
Director: James Marks
  E-mail: jim.marks@umontana.edu
  Telephone: 406-243-2243
  Fax: 406-243-5330

LEARNING DISABILITY SERVICES

Requests for the following services/accommodations will be evaluated individually based on appropriate and current documentation.

Allowed in exams
  Calculator: Yes
  Dictionary: Yes
  Computer: Yes
  Spellchecker: Yes
Extended test time: Yes
Scribes: Yes
Proctors: Yes
Oral exams: Yes
Note-takers: Yes

Distraction-reduced environment: Yes
Tape recording in class: Yes
Books on tape from RFBD: Yes
Taping of books not from RFBD: Yes
Accommodations for students with ADHD: Yes
Reading machine: Yes
Other assistive technology: Yes
Priority registration: Yes

Added costs for services: Yes
LD specialists: No
Professional tutors: No
Peer tutors: Yes
Max. hours/wk. for services: N/A
How professors are notified of LD/ADHD: By student

GENERAL ADMISSIONS INFORMATION

Director of Admissions: Jed Liston
Telephone: 406-243-6266

ENTRANCE REQUIREMENTS

Academic units required: 4 English, 3 math, 2 science (2 science labs), 3 social studies, 2 history, 2 academic electives, and choice of 2 units in foreign language, computer science, visual/performing arts, or vocational education. **Academic units recommended:** 2 foreign language. High school diploma is required, and GED is accepted. ACT with or without Writing component accepted. TOEFL required of all international applicants: minimum paper TOEFL 500, minimum computer TOEFL 173.

Application deadline: Rolling
Notification: Rolling
Average GPA: 3.26
ACT Composite middle 50% range:
  20–25

SAT Math middle 50% range:
  480–600
SAT Critical Reading middle 50% range: 480–600
SAT Writing middle 50% range:
  470–590

Graduated top 10% of class: 16%
Graduated top 25% of class: 40%
Graduated top 50% of class: 70%

COLLEGE GRADUATION REQUIREMENTS

Course waivers allowed: No
Course substitutions allowed: Yes
In what course: Determined case-by-case

ADDITIONAL INFORMATION

Environment: The university's urban campus is 200 miles from Spokane.

Student Body
  Undergrad enrollment: 11,572
  Women: 54%
  Men: 46%
  Percent out-of-state: 27%

Cost Information
  In-state tuition: $4,900
  Out-of-state tuition: $13,900
  Room & board: $5,860
Housing Information
  University housing: Yes
  Percent living on campus: 24%

Greek System
  Fraternity: Yes
  Sorority: Yes
Athletics: Division I

University of Montana

UNIVERSITY OF MONTANA—WESTERN

710 South Atlantic, Dillon, MT 59725
Phone: 406-683-7331 • Fax: 406-683-7493
E-mail: admissions@umwestern.edu • Web: www.umwestern.edu
Support: S • Institution type: 4-year public

LEARNING DISABILITY PROGRAM AND SERVICES

Western Montana College strives to accommodate all students with special needs. These needs may be physical, social, and/or academic. Almost all services are free to the student. The Associate Dean of Students is in charge of making special accommodations available to students with learning disabilities. If an applicant has a documented learning disability and requests special accommodations for a class, he or she must contact the Associate Dean of Students so that arrangements can be made. The professor of the class, the Associate Dean, and the student will meet to set up an IEP for that class, and documentation will be kept on file in the Student Life Office.

LD/ADHD ADMISSIONS INFORMATION

College entrance tests required: Yes
Interview required: No
Essay recommended: No
Documentation required for LD: Psychoeducational evaluation
Documentation required for ADHD: Psychoeducational evaluation
Submitted to: Disability Services
Special Ed. HS course work accepted: Yes

Specific course requirements of all applicants: NR
Separate application required: No
# of LD applications submitted each year: NR
# of LD applications accepted yearly: NR
Total # of students receiving LD services: 21
Acceptance into program means acceptance into college: Students must be admitted to and enrolled in the university first and then request services.

ADMISSIONS

The college has no special requirements other than those outlined by the state Board of Regents: a valid high school diploma or GED. Criteria for general admission includes 4 years of English, 3 years of math, 3 years of science, 3 years of social studies, and 2 years from foreign language, computer science, visual/performing arts, or vocational education; a 2.5 GPA (minimum 2.0 for students with learning disabilities); a 20 ACT or 960 SAT; and ranking within the top 50 percent of the applicant's class. Students with documented learning disabilities may request waivers or substitutions in courses affected by the disability. Because Western Montana is a small university, each individual can set up an admissions plan. There is a 15 percent window of exemption for some students who do not meet admission requirements. These students can be admitted provisionally if they provide satisfactory evidence that they are prepared to pursue successfully the special courses required.

ADDITIONAL INFORMATION

Students who present appropriate documentation may be eligible for some of the following services or accommodations: the use of calculators, dictionaries, computers, or spellcheckers during tests; extended time on tests; distraction-free environments for tests; proctors; scribes; oral exams; note-takers; tape recorders in class; books on tape; and priority registration. The Learning Center offers skill-building classes in reading, writing, and math. These classes do not count toward a student's GPA, but they do for athletic eligibility. Students whose ACT or entrance tests show that they would profit from such instruction will be placed in courses that will best meet their needs and ensure a successful college career. Free tutoring is available in most areas on a drop-in basis and/or at prescribed times. Services and accommodations are available for undergraduate and graduate students.

LEARNING DISABILITY PROGRAM/SERVICES

Learning Disability Program/Services: Disability Services
Director: Nicole Hazelbaker
  E-mail: n_hazelbaker@umwestern.edu
  Telephone: 406-683-7565
  Fax: 406-683-7570

LEARNING DISABILITY SERVICES

Requests for the following services/accommodations will be evaluated individually based on appropriate and current documentation.

Allowed in exams
  Calculator: Yes
  Dictionary: Yes
  Computer: Yes
  Spellchecker: Yes
Extended test time: Yes
Scribes: Yes
Proctors: Yes
Oral exams: Yes
Note-takers: Yes

Distraction-reduced environment: Yes
Tape recording in class: Yes
Books on tape from RFBD: Yes
Taping of books not from RFBD: Yes
Accommodations for students with ADHD: Yes
Reading machine: No
Other assistive technology: No
Priority registration: Yes

Added costs for services: No
LD specialists: No
Professional tutors: 3
Peer tutors: 6
Max. hours/wk. for services: Unlimited
How professors are notified of LD/ADHD: By both student and director

GENERAL ADMISSIONS INFORMATION

Director of Admissions: Eric Murray
Telephone: 406-683-7665

ENTRANCE REQUIREMENTS

Academic units required: 4 English, 3 math, 3 science (2 science labs), 3 social studies, 4 academic electives. High school diploma is required, and GED is accepted. ACT with Writing component required. TOEFL required of all international applicants: minimum paper TOEFL 500, minimum computer TOEFL 173.

Application deadline: 7/1
Notification: Rolling
Average GPA: 2.99
ACT Composite middle 50% range: 16–22

SAT Math middle 50% range: 430–520
SAT Critical Reading middle 50% range: 410–510
SAT Writing middle 50% range: NR

Graduated top 10% of class: 5%
Graduated top 25% of class: 18%
Graduated top 50% of class: 49%

COLLEGE GRADUATION REQUIREMENTS

Course waivers allowed: Yes
In what course: General education courses
Course substitutions allowed: Yes
In what course: General education courses

ADDITIONAL INFORMATION

Environment: The college is located on 20 acres in a small town about 60 miles south of Butte, Montana.

Student Body
  Undergrad enrollment: 1,159
  Women: 59%
  Men: 41%
  Percent out-of-state: 15%

Cost Information
  Out-of-state tuition: $12,300
  In-state tuition: $3,538
  Room & board: $4,920
Housing Information
  University housing: Yes
  Percent living on campus: 30%

Greek System
  Fraternity: No
  Sorority: No
  Athletics: NAIA

UNION COLLEGE (NE)

3800 South Forty-eighth Street, Lincoln, NE 68506-4300
Phone: 402-486-2504 • Fax: 402-486-2566
E-mail: ucenroll@ucollege.edu • Web: www.ucollege.edu
Support: CS • Institution type: 4-year private

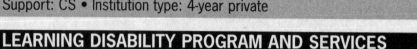

LEARNING DISABILITY PROGRAM AND SERVICES

The Teaching Learning Center (TLC) is a specialized program serving the Union College student with learning disabilities/dyslexia and has now expanded to serve all students with disabilities. The TLC offers assistance to the serious, capable student with learning disabilities who seeks to earn an undergraduate degree in a Christian environment. To qualify for accommodations, a student must have an IQ commensurate with college achievement; have a diagnosis based on current data, which will be reviewed by the TLC staff; complete admission procedures to Union College; take the ACT or SAT; apply to the TLC and provide needed information; and arrange for a 2-day visit to campus to complete diagnostic/prescriptive testing to determine needed accommodations and remediation. Students with LD in the program enroll in regular college classes, though a light load is initially recommended.

LD/ADHD ADMISSIONS INFORMATION

College entrance tests required: Yes
Interview required: No
Essay recommended: No
Documentation required for LD: Psychoeducational evaluation, preferably WAIS–III and/or WJ–III
Documentation required for ADHD: Yes
Submitted to: Teaching Learning Center
Special Ed. HS course work accepted: Yes

Specific course requirements of all applicants: Yes
Separate application required: Yes
# of LD applications submitted each year: 60–70
# of LD applications accepted yearly: NR
Total # of students receiving LD services: 80–90
Acceptance into program means acceptance into college: Students are admitted to the Teaching Learning Center program and the college jointly.

ADMISSIONS

There is no special admission process for students with learning disabilities. All applicants are expected to meet the same admission criteria, including having a 2.5 GPA, scoring 16-plus on the ACT, and the course requirements of 3 years of English, 2 years of natural science, 2 years of history, 2 years of algebra, and 3 years selected from English, math, natural science, social studies, religion, modern foreign language, or vocational courses. Students with course deficiencies can be admitted and make up the deficiencies in college. The staff from the Teaching Learning Center may review documentation from some applicants and provide a recommendation to the Office of Admissions regarding an admission decision. The final decision for admission into the program is made by the TLC. Special admission status is for students with no immediate plans to graduate. Temporary admission status is valid on a semester-by-semester basis, allowing students to secure official transcripts from high school or other colleges. This status is limited to three semesters. Conditional admission status is for students who lack certain entrance requirements, such as math, English, history, or science, which must be satisfied within the first year of attendance. A 3-semester-hour course taken in college to remove an entrance deficiency is equivalent to 1 full year of a high school course.

ADDITIONAL INFORMATION

Reasonable accommodation is an individualized matter determined in consultation between the student, parents, project staff, and appropriate faculty members. Accommodations may include texts on tape, oral testing, individual testing, extended time/alternate assignments, note-takers, remediation, academic tutoring (additional fee), counseling, instruction in word processing, and assistance with term papers. Skills classes for college credit are offered in reading, spelling, math, and writing. The Technology Resource Center for learning disabilities provides information on available technology such as: four-track tape player (fits in your hand), personal voice organizer, Language Master 600 (voice powered, hand-held dictionary, thesaurus, and word games), Calcu-Talk (scientific and financial talking calculator, plus laser printer, character recognition scanner, and two personal computers with screen filters. Software includes Arkenstone (reads written page), Dragon Dictate (control computer by voice), Grammatik (analyzes and corrects grammar), Kurzweil (combines with scanner to convert written test to spoken word), Inspiration (allows the visual person to organize thoughts in outline and cluster form), and Telepathic II (word-prediction engine).

LEARNING DISABILITY PROGRAM/SERVICES

Learning Disability Program/Services: Teaching Learning Center (TLC)
Director: Debbie Forshee-Sweeney
  E-mail: tlc@ucollege.edu
  Telephone: 402.486.2506
  Fax: 402.486.2691
Contact Person: Terri Ingram
  E-mail: tlc@ucollege.edu
  Telephone: 402-486-2506
  Fax: 402-486-2895

LEARNING DISABILITY SERVICES

Requests for the following services/accommodations will be evaluated individually based on appropriate and current documentation.

Allowed in exams
  Calculator: Yes
  Dictionary: Yes
  Computer: Yes
  Spellchecker: Yes
Extended test time: Yes
Scribes: Yes
Proctors: Yes
Oral exams: Yes
Note-takers: Yes

Distraction-reduced environment: Yes
Tape recording in class: Yes
Books on tape from RFBD: Yes
Taping of books not from RFBD: Yes
Accommodations for students with ADHD: Yes
Reading machine: Yes
Other assistive technology: Yes
Priority registration: No

Added costs for services: Yes
LD specialists: Yes
Professional tutors: 3
Peer tutors: 15–25
Max. hours/wk. for services: 5
How professors are notified of LD/ADHD: By both student and director

GENERAL ADMISSIONS INFORMATION

Director of Admissions: Huda McClelland
Telephone: 402-486-2051

ENTRANCE REQUIREMENTS
Academic units required: 3 English, 2 math, 2 science (1 science lab), 1 social studies, 2 history, 3 academic electives. **Academic units recommended:** 4 English, 3 math, 3 science, 1 foreign language. High school diploma is required, and GED is accepted. ACT with or without Writing component accepted. TOEFL required of all international applicants: minimum paper TOEFL 550, minimum computer TOEFL 213.

Application deadline: 8/1
Notification: Rolling
Average GPA: NR
ACT Composite middle 50% range: 19–25

SAT Math middle 50% range: NR
SAT Critical Reading middle 50% range: NR
SAT Writing middle 50% range: NR

Graduated top 10% of class: 17%
Graduated top 25% of class: 14%
Graduated top 50% of class: 57%

COLLEGE GRADUATION REQUIREMENTS

Course waivers allowed: No
Course substitutions allowed: No

ADDITIONAL INFORMATION

Environment: The college has a suburban campus near Lincoln.

Student Body
  Undergrad enrollment: 845
  Women: 56%
  Men: 44%
  Percent out-of-state: 79%

Cost Information
  Tuition: $13,990
  Room & board: $4,720
Housing Information
  University housing: Yes
  Percent living on campus: 58%

Greek System
  Fraternity: No
  Sorority: No
Athletics: Division III

UNIVERSITY OF NEBRASKA—LINCOLN

1410 Q Street, Lincoln, NE 68588-0256
Phone: 402-472-2023 • Fax: 402-472-0670
E-mail: admissions@unl.edu • Web: www.unl.edu
Support: S • Institution type: 4-year public

LEARNING DISABILITY PROGRAM AND SERVICES

Services for Students with Disabilities (SSD) provide special assistance to students with disabilities through individualized help and counseling. Because adjustment to college life and its academic demands are a new experience for disabled students and there are special challenges confronting them, SSD is committed to providing students with the support that will help them to reach their academic goals. SSD coordinates and delivers the services required to accommodate a disability. All accommodation requests are initiated at the SSD office with appropriate documentation. Once the accommodations are approved, the individual student is responsible for requesting services each semester from the SSD office.

LD/ADHD ADMISSIONS INFORMATION

College entrance tests required: Yes
Interview required: No
Essay recommended: No
Documentation required for LD: Psychoeducational evaluation
Documentation required for ADHD: Psychoeductional evaluation is preferred; a doctor's statement is required.
Submitted to: Services for Students with Disabilities
Special Ed. HS course work accepted: N/A

Specific course requirements of all applicants: NR
Separate application required: No
# of LD applications submitted each year: NR
# of LD applications accepted yearly: NR
Total # of students receiving LD services: NR
Acceptance into program means acceptance into college: Students must be admitted and enrolled prior to requesting services.

ADMISSIONS

There is no special admission process for students with disabilities. All applicants are expected to meet the same admission criteria, including an ACT of 20 or higher or an SAT of 950 or higher; or rank in the top half of their graduating class along with meeting the course requirements of 4 units of math, 4 units of English, 3 units of social sciences, 3 units of natural sciences, and 2 units of a foreign language. There is an appeal process for deferred students.

ADDITIONAL INFORMATION

Accommodations are provided in an individualized manner for all students. Reasonable accommodations include extended time on exams, a separate testing area, a reader, a scribe, an interpreter, taped exams, Braille or large print exams, spelling assistance, the use of computer or other adaptive equipment for exams, a classroom note-taker, a tape recorder in the classroom, C Print captioning for classes, and alternative formats, which include Braille, e-text, and taped textbooks. Other services provided include intercampus transportation coordination, priority registration, and assistance with advocacy.

LEARNING DISABILITY PROGRAM/SERVICES

Learning Disability Program/Services: Services for Students with Disabilities
Director: Veva Cheney
E-mail: vcheney@unc.edu
Telephone: 402-472-3787
Fax: 402-472-0080

LEARNING DISABILITY SERVICES

Requests for the following services/accommodations will be evaluated individually based on appropriate and current documentation.

Allowed in exams
Calculator: Yes
Dictionary: No
Computer: Yes
Spellchecker: Yes
Extended test time: Yes
Scribes: Yes
Proctors: Yes
Oral exams: Yes
Note-takers: Yes

Distraction-reduced environment: Yes
Tape recording in class: Yes
Books on tape from RFBD: Yes
Taping of books not from RFBD: Yes
Accommodations for students with ADHD: Yes
Reading machine: Yes
Other assistive technology: Yes
Priority registration: Yes

Added costs for services: No
LD specialists: No
Professional tutors: No
Peer tutors: No
Max. hours/wk. for services: N/A
How professors are notified of LD/ADHD: By both student and director

GENERAL ADMISSIONS INFORMATION

Director of Admissions: Alan Cerveny
Telephone: 402-472-2023

ENTRANCE REQUIREMENTS

Academic units required: 4 English, 4 math, 3 science (1 science lab), 2 foreign language, 3 social studies.
Academic units recommended: 1 history. High school diploma is required, and GED is accepted. ACT with or without Writing component accepted. TOEFL required of all international applicants: minimum paper TOEFL 525, minimum computer TOEFL 193.

Application deadline: 5/1
Notification: Rolling
Average GPA: NR
ACT Composite middle 50% range: 22–28

SAT Math middle 50% range: 530–670
SAT Critical Reading middle 50% range: 510–650
SAT Writing middle 50% range: NR

Graduated top 10% of class: 25%
Graduated top 25% of class: 53%
Graduated top 50% of class: 83%

COLLEGE GRADUATION REQUIREMENTS

Course waivers allowed: No
Course substitutions allowed: Yes
In what course: Foreign language

ADDITIONAL INFORMATION

Environment: UNL is located in Lincoln, Nebraska, which is the capital and the second-largest city in the state.

Student Body
Undergrad enrollment: 17,371
Women: 46%
Men: 54%
Percent out-of-state: 14%

Cost Information
In-state tuition: $5,540
Out-of-state tuition: $14,450
Room & board: $6,523
Housing Information
University housing: Yes
Percent living on campus: 45%

Greek System
Fraternity: Yes
Sorority: Yes
Athletics: Division I

WAYNE STATE COLLEGE

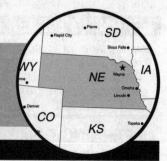

1111 Main Street, Wayne, NE 68787
Phone: 402-375-7234 • Fax: 402-375-7204
E-mail: admit1@wsc.edu • Web: www.wsc.edu
Support: S • Institution type: 4-year public

LEARNING DISABILITY PROGRAM AND SERVICES

Students with LD and ADHD are provided an individualized, cooperatively planned program of accommodations and services that are integrated within existing college services and programs. Accommodations and services are matched to the individual student's needs and are provided free of charge. Students Taking Responsibility in Development and Education (STRIDE) is a program of student support services that includes individual attention, academic and personal support, and disability services. STRIDE services help new students adjust more quickly and fully to college life. Students with disabilities are one of the populations eligible for STRIDE. STRIDE expects students to place a high priority on academic performance, invest the time and effort needed for college-level learning, and take advantage of the services and programs available. Students with LD or ADHD must complete a special application for STRIDE and submit written information that verifies the disability diagnosis.

LD/ADHD ADMISSIONS INFORMATION

College entrance tests required: Yes
Interview required: No
Essay recommended: No
Documentation required for LD: Psychoeducational
  evaluation
Documentation required for ADHD: Yes
Submitted to: STRIDE
Special Ed. HS course work accepted: Yes

Specific course requirements of all applicants: NR
Separate application required: No
# of LD applications submitted each year: NR
# of LD applications accepted yearly: NR
Total # of students receiving LD services: NR
**Acceptance into program means acceptance into
  college:** Students must be admitted to and enrolled in the
  university first and then request services.

ADMISSIONS
Admission to Wayne State College is open to all high school graduates or students with a GED or equivalent. The college recommends that students take 4 years of English, 3 years of math, 3 years of social studies, and 2 years of science. Foreign language is not an entrance or graduation requirement. High school special education courses are accepted.

ADDITIONAL INFORMATION
Through the STRIDE Program, students have access to the following personal support services: a summer STRIDE precollege experience; a STRIDE peer mentor program; and academic, personal, and career counseling. Academic support services include academic advising and course selection guidance; a Succeeding in College course; one-on-one peer tutoring; professional tutoring; and individual study skills assistance in time management and organization, note-taking, study techniques, and test-taking strategies. STRIDE provides a cooperatively planned program of disability-related services and accommodations, which include assistance in arranging accommodations, tape-recorded textbooks and materials, and alternative exam arrangements.

LEARNING DISABILITY PROGRAM/SERVICES

Learning Disability Program/Services: STRIDE: Students Taking Responsibility in Development and
Education
Director: Jamie Mackling
E-mail: jamackl1@wsc.edu
Telephone: 402-375-7321
Fax: 402-375-7058

LEARNING DISABILITY SERVICES

Requests for the following services/accommodations will be evaluated individually based on appropriate and current documentation.

Allowed in exams
  Calculator: Yes
  Dictionary: Yes
  Computer: Yes
  Spellchecker: Yes
Extended test time: Yes
Scribes: Yes
Proctors: Yes
Oral exams: Yes
Note-takers: Yes

Distraction-reduced environment: Yes
Tape recording in class: Yes
Books on tape from RFBD: Yes
Taping of books not from RFBD: Yes
Accommodations for students with
  ADHD: Yes
Reading machine: Yes
Other assistive technology: No
Priority registration: Yes

Added costs for services: No
LD specialists: No
Professional tutors: No
Peer tutors: 35
Max. hours/wk. for services:
  Unlimited
How professors are notified of
  LD/ADHD: By student

GENERAL ADMISSIONS INFORMATION

Director of Admissions: Lois Ash
Telephone: 402-375-7234

ENTRANCE REQUIREMENTS
Academic units recommended: 4 English, 3 math, 2 science, 3 social studies. High school diploma is required, and GED is accepted. TOEFL required of all international applicants: minimum paper TOEFL 550, minimum computer TOEFL 213.

Application deadline: 8/1
Notification: Rolling
Average GPA: 3.22
ACT Composite middle 50% range:
  18–24

SAT Math middle 50% range: NR
SAT Critical Reading middle 50%
  range: NR
SAT Writing middle 50% range: NR

Graduated top 10% of class: 11%
Graduated top 25% of class: 29%
Graduated top 50% of class: 58%

COLLEGE GRADUATION REQUIREMENTS

Course waivers allowed: No
Course substitutions allowed: No

ADDITIONAL INFORMATION

Environment: The college is located in a rural area 45 miles southwest of Sioux City, Iowa.

Student Body
  Undergrad enrollment: 2,748
  Women: 56%
  Men: 44%
  Percent out-of-state: 14%

Cost Information
  In-state tuition: $3,800
  Out-of-state tuition: $6,700
  Room & board: $4,470
Housing Information
  University housing: Yes
  Percent living on campus: 45%

Greek System
  Fraternity: Yes
  Sorority: Yes
  Athletics: Division II

University of Nevada—Las Vegas

4505 Maryland Parkway, Box 451021, Las Vegas, NV 89154-1021
Phone: 702-774-8658 • Fax: 702-774-8008
E-mail: Undergraduate.Recruitment@ccmail.nevada.edu
Web: www.unlv.edu • Support: S • Institution type: 4-year public

LEARNING DISABILITY PROGRAM AND SERVICES

The Disability Resource Center (DRC) provides academic accommodations for students with documented disabilities who are otherwise qualified for university programs. Compliance with Section 504 requires that reasonable academic accommodations be made for students with disabilities. These accommodations may include note-taking, testing accommodations, books on tape, readers, tutoring, priority registration, transition training, assistance with course registration and class monitoring, counseling, and information of the laws pertaining to disabilities. The center also serves as a resource area for all disability issues affecting students, faculty, and staff. To establish services, students will need to provide the DRC with appropriate documentation of their disability. For each semester a student wishes to receive assistance, a review of current documentation and assessment of the course needs will be made to determine the appropriate academic accommodations. On some occasions, decisions are based on input from the students, faculty, and the designated DRC staff.

LD/ADHD ADMISSIONS INFORMATION

College entrance tests required: No
Interview required: No
Essay recommended: No
Documentation required for LD: Psychoeducational evaluation (no more than 3 years old)
Documentation required for ADHD: Yes
Submitted to: Disability Resource Center
Special Ed. HS course work accepted: No

Specific course requirements of all applicants: Yes
Separate application required: No
# of LD applications submitted each year: NR
# of LD applications accepted yearly: NR
Total # of students receiving LD services: 450
Acceptance into program means acceptance into college: Any student attending classes at UNLV who has a documented disability may apply for accommodations through the Learning Enhancement Services.

ADMISSIONS

All applicants are expected to meet the same admission criteria, which include a 2.5 GPA and 13.5 college-prep courses or a 3.0 GPA and no specific high school courses. ACT/SAT results are not required for admission, but are used for placement. Students are encouraged to self-disclose their learning disability and request information about services. DRC will assess the student's documentation and write a recommendation to the Office of Admissions based on the director's opinion of the student's chance for success. Students denied admission may request assistance for an appeal through the director of the Disability Resource Center. This requires a special application with an explanation of the circumstances of previous academic performance. Students (not the parents) should call DRC to inquire about initiating an appeal of the denial. Some of these students may be offered admission by alternative criteria. If admitted on probation, the students must maintain a 2.0 GPA for the first semester. Others can enter on special status as a part-time student, take 15 credits, and then transfer into the university.

ADDITIONAL INFORMATION

The Disabilities Resource Center offers help to all students on campus who have a diagnosed disability. Following the evaluation, students meet with the DRC director and staff to develop a plan for services. Students are encouraged to only enroll in 12 credit hours the first semester, including courses in abilities or skill development. Psychological services are available through the Counseling Office. Workshops are offered in time management, organization, test-taking strategies, and note-taking skills. The DRC offers workshops to teach classroom success techniques and self-advocacy skills. Assistance is provided year-round to active students. Students remain active by signing a new contract for service before each semester. The DRC hires enrolled students to be note-takers, readers, scribes, and proctors. Services are available to undergraduate and graduate students.

LEARNING DISABILITY PROGRAM/SERVICES

Learning Disability Program/Services: Disability Resource Center (DRC)
Director: Clark Hochstetler
E-mail: DRC@unlv.edu
Telephone: 702-895-0866
Fax: 702-895-0651

LEARNING DISABILITY SERVICES

Requests for the following services/accommodations will be evaluated individually based on appropriate and current documentation.

Allowed in exams
 Calculator: Yes
 Dictionary: Yes
 Computer: Yes
 Spellchecker: Yes
Extended test time: Yes
Scribes: Yes
Proctors: Yes
Oral exams: Yes
Note-takers: Yes

Distraction-reduced environment: Yes
Tape recording in class: Yes
Books on tape from RFBD: NR
Taping of books not from RFBD: Yes
Accommodations for students with ADHD: Yes
Reading machine: Yes
Other assistive technology: Yes
Priority registration: Yes

Added costs for services: No
LD specialists: No
Professional tutors: No
Peer tutors: Yes
Max. hours/wk. for services: 2
How professors are notified of LD/ADHD: By both student and director

GENERAL ADMISSIONS INFORMATION

Director of Admissions: Pamela Hicks, Director of Undergraduate Recruitment
Telephone: 702-774-8658

ENTRANCE REQUIREMENTS

Academic units required: 4 English, 3 math, 3 science (2 science labs), 3 social studies. **Academic units recommended:** 4 English, 3 math, 3 science (2 science labs), 3 social studies. High school diploma is required, and GED is accepted. ACT with or without Writing component accepted. TOEFL required of all international applicants: minimum paper TOEFL 500.

Application deadline: 4/1
Notification: Rolling
Average GPA: 3.34
ACT Composite middle 50% range: 18–24

SAT Math middle 50% range: 450–580
SAT Critical Reading middle 50% range: 440–560
SAT Writing middle 50% range: NR

Graduated top 10% of class: 18%
Graduated top 25% of class: 47%
Graduated top 50% of class: 82%

COLLEGE GRADUATION REQUIREMENTS

Course waivers allowed: No
Course substitutions allowed: Yes
In what course: Foreign language is only required for English majors; substitutions are available. Math is required for graduation. All requests go to Academic Standards Committee after initial approval from the college advisor, chair of the department, and dean.

ADDITIONAL INFORMATION

Environment: The university is located on 355 acres in an urban area minutes from downtown Las Vegas.

Student Body
 Undergrad enrollment: 20,607
 Women: 56%
 Men: 44%
 Percent out-of-state: 22%

Cost Information
 In-state tuition: $3,060
 Out-of-state tuition: $12,527
 Room & board: $9,000
Housing Information
 University housing: Yes
 Percent living on campus: 7%

Greek System
 Fraternity: Yes
 Sorority: Yes
Athletics: Division I

University of Nevada—Las Vegas

UNIVERSITY OF NEVADA—RENO

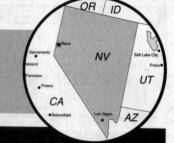

Mail Stop 120, Reno, NV 89557
Phone: 775-784-4700 • Fax: 775-784-4283
E-mail: asknevada@unr.edu • Web: www.unr.edu
Support: CS • Institution type: 4-year public

LEARNING DISABILITY PROGRAM AND SERVICES

The Disability Resource Center was created to meet the unique educational needs of students with disabilities. The purpose of the DRC is to ensure that students with disabilities have equal access to participate in, contribute to, and benefit from all university programs. Their goal is to act as a catalyst for elimination of barriers and increase awareness of students with disabilities attending the university. The DRC staff is available to provide students with sensitive and individualized assistance at the student's request. Students who wish to request academic accommodations must provide the DRC with documentation of a verified disability. Appropriate services are determined and provided based on the student's specific disability and the academic requirements of the appropriate department. Students need to request their desired accommodations at least 4 weeks prior to their actual need for accommodations. Students requesting accommodations must sign a Release of Information form, giving DRC permission to discuss the student's educational situation with other professionals with a legitimate need to know. Students requesting accommodations will also be required to sign a student contract defining the student's responsibilities in receiving services.

LD/ADHD ADMISSIONS INFORMATION

College entrance tests required: No
Interview required: No
Essay recommended: No
Documentation required for LD: Prefer for cognitive testing the WAIS–III and WJ–III; prefer achievement testing the WJ–III, KTEA, and/or Nelson Denny
Documentation required for ADHD: Prefer that documentation for ADHD include a psychoeducational evaluation but this is not mandatory. Documentation must include DSM–IV diagnosis by an appropriate certified professional.
Submitted to: Disability Resource Center
Special Ed. HS course work accepted: No

Specific course requirements of all applicants: Yes
Separate application required: Yes
# of LD applications submitted each year: NR
# of LD applications accepted yearly: NR
Total # of students receiving LD services: NR
Acceptance into program means acceptance into college: Students must be admitted to and enrolled in the university first and then request services.

ADMISSIONS

There is no special admission process for students with LD or attention deficit hyperactivity disorder. However, students with LD/ADHD are encouraged to self-disclose if they do not meet general admission requirements and to provide documentation. Admissions will consult with the DRC director during the admission process. General admission criteria include a 2.5 GPA; an ACT score of 20 in English and Math or SAT Verbal or Math of 500; 4 years of English, 3 years of math, 3 years of social studies, 3 years of natural science, and 0.5 years of computer literacy. Students may appeal to use a substitute course for one of the required courses for admission. Students who do not meet the general admission criteria may appeal. Some students may be admitted on appeal and brought in under a special admit.

ADDITIONAL INFORMATION

DRC provides accommodations and services tailored to the individual needs of each student. When appropriate, reasonable accommodations can include the following: reader services and books on tape; note-taking services; alternative testing accommodations, proctors, and scribes; adaptive computer equipment access; accommodations counseling; registration assistance; faculty liaisons; learning strategies instruction; course substitutions; Math 019/119 (a two-semester course equivalent to Math 120); referrals to campus and community services; and other appropriate services as necessary. There is also a Writing Center, tutorial program, Math Lab, Counseling Center, and Women's Resource Center.

LEARNING DISABILITY PROGRAM/SERVICES

Learning Disability Program/Services: Disability Resource Center
Director: Mary Zabel
  E-mail: mzabel@unr.edu
  Telephone: 775-784-6000
  Fax: 775-784-6955
Contact Person: Mary Anne Christensen
  E-mail: maryac@unr.edu
  Telephone: 775-784-6000
  Fax: 775-784-6955

LEARNING DISABILITY SERVICES

Requests for the following services/accommodations will be evaluated individually based on appropriate and current documentation.

Allowed in exams
  Calculator: Yes
  Dictionary: Yes
  Computer: Yes
  Spellchecker: Yes
Extended test time: Yes
Scribes: Yes
Proctors: Yes
Oral exams: Yes
Note-takers: Yes

Distraction-reduced environment: Yes
Tape recording in class: Yes
Books on tape from RFBD: Yes
Taping of books not from RFBD: Yes
Accommodations for students with ADHD: Yes
Reading machine: Yes
Other assistive technology: Yes
Priority registration: No

Added costs for services: No
LD specialists: Yes
Professional tutors: No
Peer tutors: 50
Max. hours/wk. for services: NR
How professors are notified of LD/ADHD: By student

GENERAL ADMISSIONS INFORMATION

Director of Admissions: Melissa Choroszy
Telephone: 775-784-4700

ENTRANCE REQUIREMENTS

Academic units required: 4 English, 3 math, 3 science (2 science labs), 3 social studies. High school diploma is required, and GED is not accepted.

Application deadline: Rolling
Notification: Rolling
Average GPA: 3.36
ACT Composite middle 50% range: 20–25

SAT Math middle 50% range: 480–600
SAT Critical Reading middle 50% range: 470–590
SAT Writing middle 50% range: NR

Graduated top 10% of class: NR
Graduated top 25% of class: NR
Graduated top 50% of class: NR

COLLEGE GRADUATION REQUIREMENTS

Course waivers allowed: No
Course substitutions allowed: Yes
In what course: Foreign language (depending on declared major)

ADDITIONAL INFORMATION

Environment: In an urban area 200 miles east of San Francisco

Student Body
  Undergrad enrollment: 11,605
  Women: 55%
  Men: 45%
  Percent out-of-state: 18%

Cost Information
  In-state tuition: $3,200
  Out-of-state tuition: $12,700
  Room & board: $8,800
Housing Information
  University housing: Yes
  Percent living on campus: 14%

Greek System
  Fraternity: Yes
  Sorority: Yes
Athletics: Division I

University of Nevada—Reno

COLBY-SAWYER COLLEGE

541 Main Street, New London, NH 03257-7835
Phone: 603-526-3700 • Fax: 603-526-3452
E-mail: admissions@colbysawyer.edu • Web: www.colby-sawyer.edu
Support: CS • Institution type: 4-year private

LEARNING DISABILITY PROGRAM AND SERVICES

The goal of the Academic Development Center is to offer students with LD the same opportunities that the college extends to other students. This includes providing individualized, free of charge academic support services designed to enable Colby-Sawyer College students to realize their full academic potential. By way of implementation, the Academic Development Center staff are trained to meet the academic needs of the entire student body by providing supplemental assistance to those who need help in specific courses and/or development of basic study skills, seek academic achievement beyond their already strong level, and/or have learning styles with diagnosed differences.

LD/ADHD ADMISSIONS INFORMATION

College entrance tests required: Yes
Interview required: No
Essay recommended: Yes
Documentation required for LD: Psychoeducational evaluation—aptitude and achievement results
Documentation required for ADHD: Diagnostic interview and substantiation and statement of diagnosis
Submitted to: Academic Development Center
Special Ed. HS course work accepted: Yes

Specific course requirements of all applicants: Yes
Separate application required: No
# of LD applications submitted each year: NR
# of LD applications accepted yearly: NR
Total # of students receiving LD services: 75
Acceptance into program means acceptance into college: Students must be admitted to and enrolled in the university first and then request services.

ADMISSIONS

There is no special admissions process for students with learning disabilities. Students must submit one recommendation from their counselor and one from a teacher. An essay is also required. It is recommended that students have at least 15 units of college-preparatory courses. Students with documented learning disabilities may substitute courses for math or foreign language if those are the areas of deficit. Students' GPA is evaluated in terms of factors that may have affected GPA, as well as a subjective assessment of students' chances of succeeding in college.

ADDITIONAL INFORMATION

Essential to the success of the Academic Development Center is the informal, individualized, nonjudgmental nature of the learning that occurs during tutoring sessions. Tutors must qualify for their jobs by maintaining a GPA of 3.3 with no less than an A-minus in every course they designate as part of their area of expertise. Other services provided include classroom modifications (students meet with a learning specialist to develop a profile, which includes the student's learning style, learning strengths and weaknesses, and recommendations to professors for accommodations), special learning specialists assist students in improving study skills and/or developing writing skills, and academic advising (each student has a faculty advisor interested in student progress who confers with students at regular intervals to set and achieve goals and select courses). There are currently 50 students with LD and 25 students with ADHD receiving services.

LEARNING DISABILITY PROGRAM/SERVICES

Learning Disability Program/Services: Academic Development Center
Director: Ann Chalker, MA
  E-mail: achalker@colby-sawyer.edu
  Telephone: 603-526-3711
  Fax: 603-526-3115

LEARNING DISABILITY SERVICES

Requests for the following services/accommodations will be evaluated individually based on appropriate and current documentation.

Allowed in exams
  Calculator: Yes
  Dictionary: Yes
  Computer: Yes
  Spellchecker: Yes
Extended test time: Yes
Scribes: Yes
Proctors: Yes
Oral exams: Yes
Note-takers: Yes

Distraction-reduced environment: Yes
Tape recording in class: Yes
Books on tape from RFBD: Yes
Taping of books not from RFBD: No
Accommodations for students with ADHD: Yes
Reading machine: Yes
Other assistive technology: Yes
Priority registration: No

Added costs for services: No
LD specialists: Yes
Professional tutors: 2–3
Peer tutors: 12–15
Max. hours/wk. for services: 5
How professors are notified of LD/ADHD: By student

GENERAL ADMISSIONS INFORMATION

Director of Admissions: Joseph Chillo
Telephone: 603-526-3700

ENTRANCE REQUIREMENTS
Academic units required: 4 English, 3 math, 2 science (2 science labs), 2 foreign language, 3 social studies. High school diploma is required, and GED is accepted. TOEFL required of all international applicants: minimum paper TOEFL 500, minimum computer TOEFL 173.

Application deadline: 4/1
Notification: Rolling
Average GPA: 2.84
ACT Composite middle 50% range: 18–21

SAT Math middle 50% range: 450–540
SAT Critical Reading middle 50% range: 430–550
SAT Writing middle 50% range: NR

Graduated top 10% of class: NR
Graduated top 25% of class: NR
Graduated top 50% of class: NR

COLLEGE GRADUATION REQUIREMENTS

Course waivers allowed: No
Course substitutions allowed: Yes
In what course: Substitutions are usually unnecessary, but can be made under special circumstances.

ADDITIONAL INFORMATION

Environment: The college has an 80-acre campus in a small town.

Student Body
  Undergrad enrollment: 954
  Women: 65%
  Men: 35%
  Percent out-of-state: 71%

Cost Information
  Tuition: $24,700
  Room & board: $9,490
Housing Information
  University housing: Yes
  Percent living on campus: 87%

Greek System
  Fraternity: No
  Sorority: No
Athletics: Division III

NEW ENGLAND COLLEGE

26 Bridge Street, Henniker, NH 03242
Phone: 603-428-2223 • Fax: 603-428-3155
E-mail: admission@nec.edu • Web: www.nec.edu
Support: CS • Institution type: 4-year private

LEARNING DISABILITY PROGRAM AND SERVICES

The Academic Advising and Support Center provides services for all students in a welcoming and supportive environment. Students come to the center with a variety of academic needs. Some want help writing term papers. Some feel they read too slowly. Others are confused and anxious about their ability to perform as college students. Some students may have learning disabilities. The center provides individual or small group tutoring, academic counseling, and referral services. Tutoring is available in most subject areas. The center focuses primarily on helping students make a successful transition to New England College while supporting all students in their effort to become independent and successful learners. The support services meet the needs of students who do not require a formal, structured program, but who can find success when offered support and advocacy by a trained and experienced staff in conjunction with small classes and personal attention by faculty. Typically, these students have done well in mainstream programs in high school when given assistance. Students with learning disabilities are encouraged to visit NEC and the Pathways Center to determine whether the support services will adequately meet their academic needs.

LD/ADHD ADMISSIONS INFORMATION

College entrance tests required: No
Interview required: No
Essay recommended: No
Documentation required for LD: WAIS (to include the subtest scores), Woodcock-Johnson Reading and Writing
Documentation required for ADHD: Same as above. A physician's diagnosis does not meet the requirement.
Submitted to: Academic Advising and Support Center
Special Ed. HS course work accepted: NR

Specific course requirements of all applicants: Yes
Separate application required: No
# of LD applications submitted each year: NR
# of LD applications accepted yearly: NR
Total # of students receiving LD services: NR
Acceptance into program means acceptance into college: Students must be admitted to and enrolled in the university first and then request services.

ADMISSIONS

Students with learning disabilities submit the general New England College application. Students should have a 2.0 GPA. SAT/ACT results are optional. Course requirements include 4 years of English, 2 years of math, 2 years of science, and 2 years of social studies. Documentation of the learning disability should be submitted along with counselor and teacher recommendations. An interview is recommended. Successful applicants have typically done well in mainstream programs in high school when given tutorial and study skills assistance.

ADDITIONAL INFORMATION

Students may elect to use the Pathways Center services with regular appointments or only occasionally in response to particular or difficult assignments. The center provides tutoring in content areas; computer facilities; study skills instruction; time management strategies; writing support in planning, editing, and proofreading; referrals to other college services; and one-on-one writing support for first-year students taking WR 101–102. Students are encouraged to use the word processors to generate writing assignments and to use the tutors to help plan and revise papers. The writing faculty works closely with the center to provide coordinated and supportive learning for all students. The Skills Center has its own building, and the director is an LD specialist. Professional tutors work with students individually and in small groups. These services are provided in a secure and accepting atmosphere. Currently, 20 percent of the student body has a diagnosed LD, and 10 percent have a diagnosed ADHD.

LEARNING DISABILITY PROGRAM/SERVICES

Learning Disability Program/Services: Academic Advising and Support Center.
Director: Anna Carlson
  E-mail: acarslon@nec.edu
  Telephone: 603-428-2218
  Fax: 603-428-2433

LEARNING DISABILITY SERVICES

Requests for the following services/accommodations will be evaluated individually based on appropriate and current documentation.

Allowed in exams
  Calculator: Yes
  Dictionary: No
  Computer: Yes
  Spellchecker: Yes
Extended test time: Yes
Scribes: Yes
Proctors: Yes
Oral exams: Yes
Note-takers: No

Distraction-reduced environment: Yes
Tape recording in class: Yes
Books on tape from RFBD: Yes
Taping of books not from RFBD: No
Accommodations for students with ADHD: Yes
Reading machine: No
Other assistive technology: No
Priority registration: No

Added costs for services: No
LD specialists: Yes
Professional tutors: 7–10
Peer tutors: 5–7
Max. hours/wk. for services: 4
How professors are notified of LD/ADHD: By student

GENERAL ADMISSIONS INFORMATION

Director of Admissions: Paul Miller
Telephone: 603-428-2223

ENTRANCE REQUIREMENTS

Academic units required: 4 English, 2 math, 2 science (1 science lab), 2 social studies. **Academic units recommended:** 4 English, 3 math, 3 science (2 science labs), 2 foreign language, 3 social studies. High school diploma is required, and GED is accepted. TOEFL required of all international applicants: minimum paper TOEFL 550, minimum computer TOEFL 213.

Application deadline: Rolling
Notification: Rolling
Average GPA: 2.70
ACT Composite middle 50% range: 14–21

SAT Math middle 50% range: 400–520
SAT Critical Reading middle 50% range: NR
SAT Writing middle 50% range: 400–510

Graduated top 10% of class: 6%
Graduated top 25% of class: 15%
Graduated top 50% of class: 37%

COLLEGE GRADUATION REQUIREMENTS

Course waivers allowed: No
Course substitutions allowed: No

ADDITIONAL INFORMATION

Environment: The college is located in the town of Henniker on 212 acres 17 miles west of Concord.

Student Body
  Undergrad enrollment: 1,039
  Women: 49%
  Men: 51%
  Percent out-of-state: 68%

Cost Information
  Tuition: $23,936
  Room & board: $8,456
Housing Information
  University housing: Yes
  Percent living on campus: 67%

Greek System
  Fraternity: Yes
  Sorority: Yes
Athletics: Division III

RIVIER COLLEGE

420 South Main Street, Nashua, NH 03060
Phone: 603-897-8219 • Fax: 603-891-1799
E-mail: rivadmit@rivier.edu • Web: www.rivier.edu
Support: S • Institution type: 4-year private

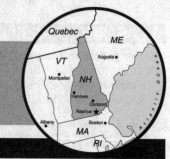

LEARNING DISABILITY PROGRAM AND SERVICES

Rivier College recognizes that learning styles differ from person to person. The college is committed to providing supports that allow all otherwise qualified individuals with disabilities an equal educational opportunity. Special Needs Services provides the opportunity for all individuals who meet academic requirements to be provided auxiliary services, facilitating their earning of a college education. To be eligible for support services, students are required to provide appropriate documentation of their disabilities to the coordinator of Special Needs Services. This documentation shall be provided from a professional in the field of psychoeducational testing or a physician and shall be current (completed within the past 3 to 5 years). This information will be confidential and is kept in the coordinator's office for the purpose of planning appropriate support services. To access services, students must contact the coordinator of Special Needs Services before the start of each semester to schedule an appointment and provide documentation; together the coordinator and the student will discuss and arrange for support services specifically related to the disability.

LD/ADHD ADMISSIONS INFORMATION

College entrance tests required: Yes
Interview required: No
Essay recommended: Yes
Documentation required for LD: Psychoeducational evaluation
Documentation required for ADHD: Yes
Submitted to: Special Needs Services
Special Ed. HS course work accepted: NR

Specific course requirements of all applicants: NR
Separate application required: No
# of LD applications submitted each year: NR
# of LD applications accepted yearly: NR
Total # of students receiving LD services: NR
Acceptance into program means acceptance into college: Students must be admitted to and enrolled in the university first and then request services.

ADMISSIONS

There is no special admissions process for students with LD. All applicants must meet the same criteria. Students should have a combined SAT of 820, a GPA in the top 80 percent of their graduating class, and take college-prep courses in high school. Courses required include 4 years of English, 2 years of a foreign language (though this may be substituted), 1 year of science, 3 years of math, 2 years of social science, and 4 years of academic electives. Applicants not meeting the general admission requirements may inquire about alternative admissions. The college offers a probational admit option that requires students to maintain a minimum 2.0 GPA their first semester.

ADDITIONAL INFORMATION

Services available include academic, career, and personal counseling; preferential registration; classroom accommodations including tape recording of lectures, extended times for test completion, testing free from distractions, and note-takers; student advocacy; a writing center for individualized instruction in writing; and individualized accommodations as developed by the coordinator of Special Needs Services with the student. Skills classes are offered in English and math, and students may take these classes for college credit. Services and accommodations are available for undergraduate and graduate students.

LEARNING DISABILITY PROGRAM/SERVICES

Learning Disability Program/Services: Special Needs Services
Director: Dina DiGregorio Karlon
  E-mail: dkarlon@rivier.edu
  Telephone: 603-897-8497
  Fax: 603-897-8887

LEARNING DISABILITY SERVICES

Requests for the following services/accommodations will be evaluated individually based on appropriate and current documentation.

Allowed in exams
  Calculator: Yes
  Dictionary: No
  Computer: Yes
  Spellchecker: Yes
Extended test time: Yes
Scribes: Yes
Proctors: Yes
Oral exams: Yes
Note-takers: Yes

Distraction-reduced environment: Yes
Tape recording in class: Yes
Books on tape from RFBD: Yes
Taping of books not from RFBD: No
Accommodations for students with
  ADHD: Yes
Reading machine: Yes
Other assistive technology: Yes
Priority registration: Yes

Added costs for services: No
LD specialists: No
Professional tutors: No
Peer tutors: No
Max. hours/wk. for services: N/A
How professors are notified of
  LD/ADHD: By both student and
director

GENERAL ADMISSIONS INFORMATION

Director of Admissions: David A. Boisvert
Telephone: 603-897-8219

ENTRANCE REQUIREMENTS

Academic units recommended: 4 English, 3 math, 1 science (1 science lab), 2 foreign language, 2 social studies, 1 history, 4 academic electives. High school diploma is required, and GED is accepted. ACT without Writing component accepted. TOEFL required of all international applicants: minimum paper TOEFL 500, minimum computer TOEFL 173.

Application deadline: 8/30
Notification: Rolling
Average GPA: 2.87
ACT Composite middle 50% range:
  NR

SAT Math middle 50% range:
  420–530
SAT Critical Reading middle 50%
  range: 420–530
SAT Writing middle 50% range:
  430–520

Graduated top 10% of class: 0%
Graduated top 25% of class: 0%
Graduated top 50% of class: 80%

COLLEGE GRADUATION REQUIREMENTS

Course waivers allowed: No
Course substitutions allowed: Yes
In what course: Each course subtitution is looked at individually.

ADDITIONAL INFORMATION

Environment: The college is located on 60 acres in a suburban area 40 miles north of Boston.

Student Body
  Undergrad enrollment: 1,387
  Women: 78%
  Men: 22%
  Percent out-of-state: NR

Cost Information
  Tuition: $20,970
  Room & board: $7,942
Housing Information
  University housing: Yes
  Percent living on campus: 62%

Greek System
  Fraternity: No
  Sorority: No
Athletics: Division III

UNIVERSITY OF NEW HAMPSHIRE

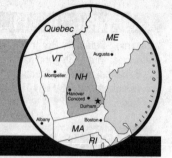

Four Garrison Avenue, Durham, NH 03824
Phone: 603-862-1360 • Fax: 603-862-0077
E-mail: admissions@unh.edu • Web: www.unh.edu
Support: CS • Institution type: 4-year public

LEARNING DISABILITY PROGRAM AND SERVICES

UNH encourages students to self-disclose within the admissions procedure. There is no LD program. Rather services/accommodations are based on student self-disclosure and obtaining the proper guidelines for documentation of LD/ADHD. Support for Students with Disabilities is where students with documented disabilities can receive those accommodations and academic services that enable them to have equal access to the classroom. Additionally, students can learn and further develop their self-advocacy skills and increase their knowledge about communicating regarding their disability. Students need to be aware that being tested for a learning disability, having old documentation (more than 3 years old), or being previously coded in secondary education in and of itself does not necessarily mean that the student will be currently qualified with a disability under federal laws in college. UNH does not offer a program for subject area tutorial, nor are LD specialists on staff. Services and accommodations at UNH can be defined as those generic activities offered to ensure educational opportunity for any student with a documented disability. All students with LD/ADHD must provide current and appropriate documentation to qualify for services.

LD/ADHD ADMISSIONS INFORMATION

College entrance tests required: Yes
Interview required: No
Essay recommended: No
Documentation required for LD: Current WAIS–III or other cognitive measure (full battery) and WJ–III, WIAT, or other achievement measure (full battery)
Documentation required for ADHD: Full medical and educational history and DSM–IV diagnosis within the past 3 years.
Submitted to: Support for Students with Disabilities

Special Ed. HS course work accepted: NR
Specific course requirements of all applicants: Yes
Separate application required: No
# of LD applications submitted each year: NR
# of LD applications accepted yearly: NR
Total # of students receiving LD services: NR
Acceptance into program means acceptance into college: Students must be admitted to and enrolled in the university first and then request services.

ADMISSIONS

Admissions criteria are the same for all applicants. Typically, students who are admitted to the university are in the top 30 percent of their class, have a B average in college-preparatory courses, and have taken 4 years of college-prep math, 3–4 years of a science lab, and 3–4 years of a foreign language; SAT average range is 1050–1225, but there are no cutoffs (or equivalent ACT). There are no alternative options for admissions. ACCESS has no involvement in any admissions decision. However, there is a member of the admissions staff with a background in special education.

ADDITIONAL INFORMATION

Academic accommodations provided, based on documentation, include the following: individually scheduled meetings with ACCESS coordinator for guidance, advising, and referrals; mediation and advocacy; note-takers; scribes; proctors; readers; taped texts; extended exam times; distraction-free rooms for exams; alternative methods for exam administration; pre-registration priority scheduling; reduced course load; and faculty support letters. UNH does not provide a university-wide service or program for subject area tutoring; it is the student's responsibility to secure subject area tutoring. However, the Center for Academic Resources provides all students with drop-in tutoring in selected courses, referrals to free academic assistance opportunities and to private pay tutors, individualized study skills assistance, and peer support for academic and personal concerns. There is a federally funded grant that allows some students to receive free peer tutoring and reading/writing assistance with a specialist.

LEARNING DISABILITY PROGRAM/SERVICES

Learning Disability Program/Services: Support for Students with Disabilities
Director: Maxine Little
  E-mail: maxine.little@unh.edu
  Telephone: 603-862-2607
Fax: 603-862-4043

LEARNING DISABILITY SERVICES

Requests for the following services/accommodations will be evaluated individually based on appropriate and current documentation.

Allowed in exams	**Distraction-reduced environment:** Yes	**Added costs for services:** No
Calculator: Yes	**Tape recording in class:** Yes	**LD specialists:** Yes
Dictionary: Yes	**Books on tape from RFBD:** Yes	**Professional tutors:** No
Computer: Yes	**Taping of books not from RFBD:** Yes	**Peer tutors:** No
Spellchecker: Yes	**Accommodations for students with**	**Max. hours/wk. for services:** Varies
Extended test time: Yes	**ADHD:** Yes	**How professors are notified of**
Scribes: Yes	**Reading machine:** Yes	**LD/ADHD:** By student
Proctors: Yes	**Other assistive technology:** Yes	
Oral exams: Yes	**Priority registration:** Yes	
Note-takers: Yes		

GENERAL ADMISSIONS INFORMATION

Director of Admissions: Robert McGann
Telephone: 603-862-1360

ENTRANCE REQUIREMENTS

Academic units required: 4 English, 3 math, 3 science (3 science labs), 2 foreign language, 3 social studies.
Academic units recommended: 4 English, 4 math, 3 science (3 science labs), 3 foreign language, 3 social studies, 1 academic elective. High school diploma is required, and GED is accepted. ACT with Writing component required. TOEFL required of all international applicants: minimum paper TOEFL 550, minimum computer TOEFL 213.

Application deadline: 2/1	**SAT Math middle 50% range:**	**Graduated top 10% of class:** 20%
Notification: 4/15	510–620	**Graduated top 25% of class:** 61%
Average GPA: 3.0	**SAT Critical Reading middle 50%**	**Graduated top 50% of class:** 97%
ACT Composite middle 50% range:	**range:** 500–600	
NR	**SAT Writing middle 50% range:** NR	

COLLEGE GRADUATION REQUIREMENTS

Course waivers allowed: No
Course substitutions allowed: Yes
In what course: In foreign language on a case-by-case basis by a petition process

ADDITIONAL INFORMATION

Environment: The university is located in a rural area about 1 hour north of Boston.

Student Body	**Cost Information**	**Greek System**
Undergrad enrollment: 11,523	**In-state tuition:** $9,700	**Fraternity:** Yes
Women: 57%	**Out-of-state tuition:** $21,500	**Sorority:** Yes
Men: 43%	**Room & board:** $7,584	**Athletics:** Division I
Percent out-of-state: 43%	**Housing Information**	
	University housing: Yes	
	Percent living on campus: 57%	

CALDWELL COLLEGE

Nine Ryerson Avenue, Caldwell, NJ 07006-6195
Phone: 973-618-3500 • Fax: 973-618-3600
E-mail: admissions@caldwell.edu • Web: www.caldwell.edu
Support: CS • Institution type: 4-year private

LEARNING DISABILITY PROGRAM AND SERVICES

Caldwell College offers students with disabilities a support program through the Learning Center and the Office of Disability Services. Students with documentation of an LD are fully integrated into college degree programs of study, and, in addition, are offered support services. The Office of Disability Services functions as a service coordinator for students with disabilities, advocating with faculty for reasonable accommodations in accordance with the Americans with Disabilities Act.

LD/ADHD ADMISSIONS INFORMATION

College entrance tests required: Yes
Interview required: No
Essay recommended: No
Documentation required for LD: WAIS and Woodcock-Johnson psychoeducational battery. Revised WJPB–J.
Documentation required for ADHD: Letter from a physician
Submitted to: Learning Center
Special Ed. HS course work accepted: Yes

Specific course requirements of all applicants: Yes
Separate application required: No
# of LD applications submitted each year: NR
# of LD applications accepted yearly: NR
Total # of students receiving LD services: NR
Acceptance into program means acceptance into college: Students must be admitted to and enrolled in the university first and then request services.

ADMISSIONS

There is no special admissions process for students with LD and ADHD. There is a pre-freshman summer program for students considered at risk for success in the fall. The decision to advise a student for this program may be based on low SAT/ACT scores or a borderline (1.9) GPA. This conditional admission program is available to all applicants regardless of a disability. The mid 50 percent SAT score for general admissions is 900. Additionally, students generally have a minimum GPA of 2.0 and have 16 high school academic units including 4 English, 2 years of a foreign language, 2 years of math, 2 years of science, and 1 year of history. With appropriate documentation, applicants with LD may request to substitute some of the required courses with other high school courses.

ADDITIONAL INFORMATION

There is one LD specialist on staff, and no fee is charged for tutoring or other services. Individual tutoring sessions with a professional learning specialist are offered to help students improve organizational skills and promote self-advocacy. Meetings are also scheduled to facilitate advocacy in the form of accommodation letters to faculty and coordinating peer tutoring. There is a Writing Center, a Learning Center, supplemental instruction, and peer tutoring available for all students. The library is equipped with various programs to assist students with disabilities. Caldwell College acknowledges that some students need to strengthen their academic skills before entering into the rigors of college-level work. Therefore, a full complement of courses are available to skill deficient students in the areas of mathematics, composition, and reading. The grades in these courses are calculated into the GPA. Caldwell College administers a placement test to all incoming freshman. The test assesses skills in reading, writing, and mathematics. Test performance is one factor in assigning students to developmental courses. Exit criteria for these courses are a grade of C or higher and attainment of a proficiency level on the placement test. English and reading requirements must be completed by the end of the second semester. Math requirements must be met by the end of the fourth semester.

LEARNING DISABILITY PROGRAM/SERVICES

Learning Disability Program/Services: Office of Disability Services/Learning Center
Director: Abbe Benowitz, Coordinator
  E-mail: abenowitz@caldwell.edu
  Telephone: 973-618-3645
  Fax: 973-618-3488
Contact Person: Abbe Benowitz
  E-mail: abenowitz@caldwell.edu
  Telephone: 973-618-3645
  Fax: 973-618-3488

LEARNING DISABILITY SERVICES

Requests for the following services/accommodations will be evaluated individually based on appropriate and current documentation.

Allowed in exams
  Calculator: Yes
  Dictionary: Yes
  Computer: Yes
  Spellchecker: Yes
Extended test time: Yes
Scribes: Yes
Proctors: Yes
Oral exams: Yes
Note-takers: Yes

Distraction-reduced environment: Yes
Tape recording in class: Yes
Books on tape from RFBD: Yes
Taping of books not from RFBD: Yes
Accommodations for students with ADHD: Yes
Reading machine: Yes
Other assistive technology: Yes
Priority registration: No

Added costs for services: No
LD specialists: Yes
Professional tutors: 5
Peer tutors: 30–40
Max. hours/wk. for services: Unlimited
How professors are notified of LD/ADHD: By both student and director

GENERAL ADMISSIONS INFORMATION

Director of Admissions: Dr. Richard Ott
Telephone: 973-618-3500

ENTRANCE REQUIREMENTS

Academic units required: 4 English, 2 math, 2 science (1 science lab), 2 foreign language, 1 history, 5 academic electives. High school diploma is required, and GED is accepted. TOEFL required of all international applicants: minimum paper TOEFL 500.

Application deadline: 4/1
Notification: Continuous
Average GPA: 3.03
ACT Composite middle 50% range: NR

SAT Math middle 50% range: 430–530
SAT Critical Reading middle 50% range: 440–520
SAT Writing middle 50% range: NR

Graduated top 10% of class: 7%
Graduated top 25% of class: 14%
Graduated top 50% of class: 47%

COLLEGE GRADUATION REQUIREMENTS

Course waivers allowed: No
Course substitutions allowed: Yes
In what course: Students may receive substitutions in foreign language if documentation supports the need for it.

ADDITIONAL INFORMATION

Environment: The campus is located 10 miles from Newark, New Jersey and 20 miles from New York City.

Student Body
  Undergrad enrollment: 1,563
  Women: 67%
  Men: 33%
  Percent out-of-state: 14%

Cost Information
  Tuition: $20,000
  Room & board: $7,600
Housing Information
  University housing: Yes
  Percent living on campus: 26%

Greek System
  Fraternity: No
  Sorority: No
  Athletics: Division II

FAIRLEIGH DICKINSON UNIVERSITY— FLORHAM CAMPUS

285 Madison Avenue, Madison, NJ 07940
Phone: 800-338-8803 • Fax: 973-443-8088
E-mail: globaleducation@fdu.edu • Web: www.fdu.edu
Support: SP • Institution type: 4-year private

LEARNING DISABILITY PROGRAM AND SERVICES

The Regional Center for College Students with LD offers a structured plan of intensive advisement, academic support, and counseling services that is tailored to the unique needs of students with LD. The goal is to provide a framework within which college students with LD will develop the confidence to succeed in their studies and the independence to do their best. Planning, learning strategies, professional tutors, counseling, and accommodations are the cornerstones of the Regional Center. Staffed by professionals with services at both the Teaneck and the Madison campus, the LD program and special services are free of charge. Assistance to students is intensive, and the program is fully integrated into the course work. Students are in touch with faculty on a regular basis. The program encourages involvement in the community, particularly service-type activities relevant to the students with LD. Performance data are routinely reviewed to identify students in need of more intensive help. Upon admission, students are invited to attend a summer orientation session. During this time, students meet with center staff to develop an IEP to develop a class schedule with the right balance.

LD/ADHD ADMISSIONS INFORMATION

College entrance tests required: Yes
Interview required: No
Essay recommended: No
Documentation required for LD: Psychoeducational evaluation, WAIS–III, WJ-III, WIAT
Documentation required for ADHD: This is not applicable to the Regional Center Program.
Submitted to: Regional Center for College Students with LD
Special Ed. HS course work accepted: Yes

Specific course requirements of all applicants: Yes
Separate application required: Yes
# of LD applications submitted each year: 250
# of LD applications accepted yearly: 60–75
Total # of students receiving LD services: 165
Acceptance into program means acceptance into college: Decisions are made jointly by Admissions and LD program.

ADMISSIONS

Admissions decisions are made jointly by the Admissions Office and the LD program director. Criteria include documentation of LD made by licensed professionals dated within 24 months of the application, IQ in the average to above-average range, evidence of adequate performance in mainstream college-prep high school courses, and evidence of motivation as reflected in recommendations. Students enrolled in all special education high school classes are usually not admissible. Lower level mainstream classes are acceptable from high schools offering different levels in the same subjects. ACT or SAT results are required, but they do not carry much weight. Grades are viewed as the best predictors for success. General admissions require a class rank within the top 40 percent or B average and an 850 SAT. If applicants have below a 2.5 GPA and an 850 SAT, they may be referred to Edward Williams College, a two-year college located on the Teaneck campus that requires an 18 ACT or 600 SAT. Admission decisions are made after careful review.

ADDITIONAL INFORMATION

Edward Williams College, a two-year liberal arts college on the campus, offers services and accommodations to students with learning disabilities who are not admissible to Fairleigh Dickinson. FDU students already enrolled in the university may request LD assessments on campus for no charge. Skills class for no college credit are offered in math and writing. Tutorial sessions incorporate a variety of teaching techniques. There is a 13:1 ratio between student and LD specialists. Support sessions are small, individualized, and flexible. In their sophomore year, students can request tutoring for three courses. Students with disabilities are entitled to priority registration. Most students are seen by 3–4 different LD specialists who regularly exchange views on academic and counseling issues. Services include recorded textbooks, extended testing times and other class support, technological support, and supervised study to meet with specialists in study rooms.

LEARNING DISABILITY PROGRAM/SERVICES

Learning Disability Program/Services: Regional Center for College Students with LD
Director: Dr. Brenda Jackson
  E-mail: jackson@fdu.edu
  Telephone: 973-443-8935
  Fax: 973-443-8932

LEARNING DISABILITY SERVICES

Requests for the following services/accommodations will be evaluated individually based on appropriate and current documentation.

Allowed in exams
  Calculator: Yes
  Dictionary: No
  Computer: Yes
  Spellchecker: Yes
  Extended test time: Yes
  Scribes: No
  Proctors: Yes
  Oral exams: Yes
  Note-takers: No

Distraction-reduced environment: Yes
Tape recording in class: Yes
Books on tape from RFBD: Yes
Taping of books not from RFBD: No
**Accommodations for students with
  ADHD:** No
Reading machine: Yes
Other assistive technology: Yes
Priority registration: Yes

Added costs for services: No
LD specialists: Yes
Professional tutors: 8
Peer tutors: No
Max. hours/wk. for services: NR
**How professors are notified of
  LD/ADHD:** By both student and
  director

GENERAL ADMISSIONS INFORMATION

Director of Admissions: Bernetta Millonde
Telephone: 800-338-8803

ENTRANCE REQUIREMENTS

Academic units required: 4 English, 3 math, 2 science (2 science labs), 2 foreign language, 2 social studies, 2 history, 3 academic electives. **Academic units recommended:** 3 math, 3 science (3 science labs), 2 foreign language, 2 social studies, 2 history, 3 academic electives. High school diploma is required, and GED is accepted. ACT with or without Writing component accepted. TOEFL required of all international applicants: minimum paper TOEFL 550, minimum computer TOEFL 213.

Application deadline: Rolling
Notification: Rolling
Average GPA: NR
ACT Composite middle 50% range:
  NR

SAT Math middle 50% range:
  460–570
SAT Critical Reading middle 50%
  range: 460–560
SAT Writing middle 50% range:
  460–560

Graduated top 10% of class: 11%
Graduated top 25% of class: 31%
Graduated top 50% of class: 66%

COLLEGE GRADUATION REQUIREMENTS

Course waivers allowed: No
Course substitutions allowed: Yes
In what course: Mathematics and foreign language substitutions are available if appropriate to students with LD enrolled in the Regional Center for College Students with Learning Disabilities.

ADDITIONAL INFORMATION

Environment: FDU's College at Florham is in Morris County, New Jersey, bridging the towns of Florham Park and Madison.

Student Body
  Undergrad enrollment: 2,564
  Women: 53%
  Men: 47%
  Percent out-of-state: 14%

Cost Information
  Tuition: $25,946
  Room & board: $8,250
Housing Information
  University housing: Yes
  Percent living on campus: 60%

Greek System
  Fraternity: Yes
  Sorority: Yes
Athletics: Division III

Fairleigh Dickinson University—Florham Campus

FAIRLEIGH DICKINSON UNIVERSITY— METROPOLITAN CAMPUS

1000 River Road, Teaneck, NJ 07666-1966
Phone: 201-692-2553 • Fax: 201-692-7319
E-mail: globaleducation@fdu.edu • Web: www.fdu.edu
Support: SP • Institution type: 4-year private

LEARNING DISABILITY PROGRAM AND SERVICES

The Regional Center for College Students with LD offers a structured plan of intensive advisement, academic support, and counseling services that is tailored to the unique needs of students with LD. The goal is to provide a framework within which college students with LD will develop the confidence to succeed in their studies and the independence to do their best. Planning, learning strategies, professional tutors, counseling, and accommodations are the cornerstones of the Regional Center. Staffed by professionals with services at both the Teaneck and the Madison campus, the LD program and special services are free of charge. Assistance to students is intensive, and the program is fully integrated into the course work. Students are in touch with faculty on a regular basis. The program encourages involvement in the community—particularly service-type activities relevant to the students with LD. Performance data are routinely reviewed to identify students in need of more intensive help. Once admitted, students are invited to attend a summer orientation session. During this time, students meet with center staff to develop an IEP to develop a class schedule with the right balance.

LD/ADHD ADMISSIONS INFORMATION

College entrance tests required: Yes
Interview required: No
Essay recommended: No
Documentation required for LD: WAIS–III, WJPEB
Documentation required for ADHD: Diagnosis and
 psychoeducational evaluation
Submitted to: Regional Center for College Students with LD
Special Ed. HS course work accepted: Yes

Specific course requirements of all applicants: Yes
Separate application required: Yes
# of LD applications submitted each year: 250
# of LD applications accepted yearly: 50
Total # of students receiving LD services: 150
Acceptance into program means acceptance into
 college: Students are accepted jointly by the Regional
 Center for College Students with Learning Disabilities and the
 Office of Admissions.

ADMISSIONS

Admissions decisions are made jointly by the Admissions Office and the LD program director. Criteria include documentation of LD made by licensed professionals dated within 24 months of the application; an IQ in average to above-average range; evidence of adequate performance in mainstream college-prep high school courses; and evidence of motivation as reflected in recommendations. Students enrolled in all special education high school classes are usually not admissible. Lower level mainstream classes are acceptable from high schools offering different levels in the same subjects. ACT/SAT results are required, but they do not carry much weight. Grades are viewed as the best predictors for success. General admissions require a class rank within the top 40 or B average and an 850 SAT. If applicants are below a 2.5 GPA and an 850 SAT, they may be referred to Edward Williams College, a two-year college located on the Teaneck campus that requires an 18 ACT or 600 SAT. Admission decisions are made after careful review.

ADDITIONAL INFORMATION

Edward Williams College, a two-year liberal arts college on the campus, offers services and accommodations to students with learning disabilities who are not admissible to Fairleigh Dickinson. FDU students already enrolled in the university may request LD assessments on campus for no charge. Skills class for no college credit are offered in math and writing. Tutorial sessions incorporate a variety of teaching techniques. There is a 13:1 ratio between students and LD specialists. Support sessions are small, individualized, and flexible. In their sophomore year, students can request tutoring for three courses. Students have priority registration. Most students are seen by 3–4 different LD specialists who regularly exchange views on academic and counseling issues. Services include recorded textbooks, extended testing times and other class support, technological support, and supervised study to meet with specialists in study rooms.

LEARNING DISABILITY PROGRAM/SERVICES

Learning Disability Program/Services: Regional Center for College Students with LD

Director: Dr. Mary Farrell
  E-mail: farrell@fdu.edu
  Telephone: 201-692-2087
  Fax: 201-692-2813

Contact Person: Dr. Robert Greenfield
  E-mail: greenfie@fdu.edu
  Telephone: 201-692-2460
  Fax: 201-692-2813

LEARNING DISABILITY SERVICES

Requests for the following services/accommodations will be evaluated individually based on appropriate and current documentation.

Allowed in exams
  Calculator: Yes
  Dictionary: No
  Computer: Yes
  Spellchecker: Yes
Extended test time: Yes
Scribes: No
Proctors: Yes
Oral exams: Yes
Note-takers: No

Distraction-reduced environment: Yes
Tape recording in class: Yes
Books on tape from RFBD: Yes
Taping of books not from RFBD: No
Accommodations for students with ADHD: Yes
Reading machine: No
Other assistive technology: No
Priority registration: Yes

Added costs for services: No
LD specialists: Yes
Professional tutors: 10
Peer tutors: No
Max. hours/wk. for services: NR
How professors are notified of LD/ADHD: By student and director

GENERAL ADMISSIONS INFORMATION

Director of Admissions: Bernetta Millonde
Telephone: 201-692-2553

ENTRANCE REQUIREMENTS

Academic units required: 4 English, 3 math, 2 science (2 science labs), 2 foreign language, 2 social studies, 2 history, 3 academic electives. **Academic units recommended:** 3 math, 3 science (3 science labs), 2 foreign language, 2 social studies, 2 history, 3 academic electives. High school diploma is required, and GED is accepted. ACT with or without Writing component accepted. TOEFL required of all international applicants: minimum paper TOEFL 550, minimum computer TOEFL 213.

Application deadline: Rolling
Notification: Rolling
Average GPA: NR

SAT Math middle 50% range:
  450–560
SAT Critical Reading middle 50% range: 430–540
SAT Writing middle 50% range:
  430–530

Graduated top 10% of class: 14%
Graduated top 25% of class: 40%
Graduated top 50% of class: 72%

COLLEGE GRADUATION REQUIREMENTS

Course waivers allowed: No
Course substitutions allowed: Yes
In what course: Math and foreign language

ADDITIONAL INFORMATION

Environment: The Teaneck campus is located on the banks of the Hackensack River. It is within walking distance of Edward Williams Junior College.

Student Body
  Undergrad enrollment: 3,403
  Women: 57%
  Men: 43%
  Percent out-of-state: 14%

Cost Information
  Tuition: $24,072
  Room & board: $8,250
Housing Information
  University housing: Yes
  Percent living on campus: 23%

Greek System
  Fraternity: Yes
  Sorority: Yes
Athletics: Division I

GEORGIAN COURT UNIVERSITY

900 Lakewood Avenue, Lakewood, NJ 08701-2697
Phone: 732-987-2200 • Fax: 732-987-2000
E-mail: admissions@georgian.edu • Web: www.georgian.edu
Support: SP • Institution type: 4-year private

LEARNING DISABILITY PROGRAM AND SERVICES

The Learning Center (TLC) is an assistance program designed to provide an environment for students with mild to moderate learning disabilities who desire a college education. The program is not one of remediation, but it is an individualized support program to assist candidates in becoming successful college students. Emphasis is placed on developing self-help strategies and study techniques. To be eligible for the TLC program, all applicants must submit the following: documentation of a learning disability by a certified professional within a school system or state-certified agency; the documentation must be current, having been completed within the past 3 years and must include the identification and description of the learning disability, including the student's level of academic performance and the effect the disabilty has on the student's learning; a recent IEP; other evaluations or recommendations from professionals who have recently provided services to the student; and additional documentation on request. All applicants must have a personal interview.

LD/ADHD ADMISSIONS INFORMATION

College entrance tests required: Yes
Interview required: Yes
Essay recommended: No
Documentation required for LD: Psychoeducational
  evaluation by a child study team, IEP documentation or
  private consultant documentation, physicians' and other
  professionals' notes as they apply to each individual ADA
  accommodation
Documentation required for ADHD: In addition to what is
  listed above, all appropriate documentation regarding ADHD
  by a certified professional in the field should be submitted.
Submitted to: Both Admissions and the Learning Center
Special Ed. HS course work accepted: No
Specific course requirements of all applicants: Yes

Separate application required: No
# of LD applications submitted each year: 50
# of LD applications accepted yearly: 40
Total # of students receiving LD services: 45
**Acceptance into program means acceptance into
  college:** Students are simultaneously admitted into The
  Learning Center and Georgian Court College.

ADMISSIONS

Applicants must meet the following criteria: 16 academic units that include 4 years of English, 2 years of a foreign language, 2 years of math, 1 year of science lab, 1 year history, and electives. The class rank and transcript should give evidence of the ability to succeed in college. Students must submit SAT scores. Conditional admission may be offered to some applicants. The Associate Director of Admissions is the liaison between the admissions staff and the TLC.

ADDITIONAL INFORMATION

College graduation requirements are not waived for TLC students. Reduced course load is recommended for students with learning disabilities, and program completion may take longer than 4 years. A social worker and counselor are on the staff of the TLC to help students as well. The TLC offers the following: an individualized support program; scheduled tutorial sessions with a learning disabilities specialist; faculty liaisons; academic counseling; priority registration; organizational skills training in time management, test-taking, note-taking, and outlining; study techniques; memory and concentration techniques; techniques for planning and writing research papers; and content tutoring if needed.

LEARNING DISABILITY PROGRAM/SERVICES

Learning Disability Program/Services: The Learning Center (TLC)
Director: Patricia A. Cohen
  E-mail: parisi@georgian.edu
  Telephone: 732-987-2650 or 732-987-2659
  Fax: 732-987-2026

LEARNING DISABILITY SERVICES

Requests for the following services/accommodations will be evaluated individually based on appropriate and current documentation.

Allowed in exams
  Calculator: Yes
  Dictionary: Yes
  Computer: Yes
  Spellchecker: Yes
Extended test time: Yes
Scribes: Yes
Proctors: Yes
Oral exams: Yes
Note-takers: Yes

Distraction-reduced environment: Yes
Tape recording in class: Yes
Books on tape from RFBD: Yes
Taping of books not from RFBD: No
Accommodations for students with ADHD: Yes
Reading machine: No
Other assistive technology: No
Priority registration: Yes

Added costs for services: Yes
LD specialists: Yes
Professional tutors: 6
Peer tutors: No
Max. hours/wk. for services: Varies
How professors are notified of LD/ADHD: By both student and director

GENERAL ADMISSIONS INFORMATION

Director of Admissions: Ann Diehl
Telephone: 732-364-2200

ENTRANCE REQUIREMENTS

Academic units required: 4 English, 2 math, 1 science (1 science lab), 2 foreign language, 1 history, 6 academic electives. High school diploma is required, and GED is accepted. ACT with or without Writing component accepted. TOEFL required of all international applicants: minimum paper TOEFL 550, minimum computer TOEFL 213.

Application deadline: 8/1
Notification: Rolling
Average GPA: 3.16
ACT Composite middle 50% range: NR

SAT Math middle 50% range: 390–490
SAT Critical Reading middle 50% range: 400–500
SAT Writing middle 50% range: NR

Graduated top 10% of class: 8%
Graduated top 25% of class: 27%
Graduated top 50% of class: 69%

COLLEGE GRADUATION REQUIREMENTS

Course waivers allowed: No
Course substitutions allowed: Yes
In what course: Foreign language, if applicable

ADDITIONAL INFORMATION

Environment: Georgian Court College is a small private institution centrally located in New Jersey.

Student Body
  Undergrad enrollment: 1,701
  Women: 93%
  Men: 7%
  Percent out-of-state: 1%

Cost Information
  Tuition: $18,380
  Room & board: $7,600
Housing Information
  University housing: Yes
  Percent living on campus: 15%

Greek System
  Fraternity: Yes
  Sorority: Yes
Athletics: Division II

KEAN UNIVERSITY

PO Box 411, 1000 Morris Avenue, Union, NJ 07083-0411
Phone: 908-737-7100 • Fax: 908-737-7105
E-mail: admitme@kean.edu • Web: www.kean.edu
Support: CS • Institution type: 4-year public

LEARNING DISABILITY PROGRAM AND SERVICES

Kean University believes qualified students with difficulties processing oral and written material have the potential to earn a college degree if they are provided with certain individualized support services. These services are designed to help students develop skills to be independent, involved, responsible learners and use their own assets to become successful learners. Students with LD attend the same classes and meet the same academic requirements as their peers. Once admitted to Kean University, students who choose to register with Project Excel may do so by providing complete documentation of a diagnosed disability. Students are asked to complete a Project Excel application after admission to Kean and answer questions such as: in what academic areas are you most and least successful; describe how the LD affects your academic work; what support services are needed for success; describe any past special services received; identify high school mainstream courses; and when was your LD diagnosed.

LD/ADHD ADMISSIONS INFORMATION

College entrance tests required: Yes
Interview required: No
Essay recommended: No
Documentation required for LD: Psychoeducational battery completed within the past 3 years, test scores, diagnosis of LD, and professional summary. All guidelines are available at: www.kean.edu/~pexcel.
Documentation required for ADHD: Full written evaluation and diagnosis of ADHD performed by a qualified practioner. All guidelines are available at: www.kean.edu/~pexcel.
Submitted to: Project Excel
Special Ed. HS course work accepted: No

Specific course requirements of all applicants: Yes
Separate application required: No
# of LD applications submitted each year: 15–20
# of LD applications accepted yearly: 15–19
Total # of students receiving LD services: 110–120
Acceptance into program means acceptance into college: Students must be admitted and enrolled in the university first and then may request services through Project Excel.

ADMISSIONS

There is no special admissions process for students with LD. It is recommended that students self-disclose in the admissions process. All applicants must meet the same admission criteria, which include 4 years of English, 3 years of math, 2 years of social studies, 2 years of science, and 5 elective credits. Courses taken in special education may be considered. SAT/ACT results are required, and the average SAT range is 950–1020. The minimum GPA is 2.8. The student must be highly motivated, able to do college work, be of at least average intelligence, have a documented learning disability, have areas of academic strength, and make a commitment to work responsibly and attend classes, tutoring, workshops, and counseling sessions. Students are encouraged to apply by early March.

ADDITIONAL INFORMATION

Project Excel does not provide remedial or developmental instruction. A number of services are available through Project Excel: diagnostic assessments; academic, career, and personal advisement and counseling; development of a college education plan (CEP) for the individual student; student advocacy with faculty; and referral to other college services as appropriate such as tutoring in basic skills and course materials. All information about the student's LD is held in strict confidence. Information shared on- or off-campus is only done with the student's signed consent. LD assessments are available for a fee of $250 for a professional assessment and $150 for an assessment from a student intern. All students in Project Excel select from the same schedule of classes and attend with all other students in the college.

LEARNING DISABILITY PROGRAM/SERVICES

Learning Disability Program/Services: Project Excel
Director: Marie Segal, EdD
  E-mail: pexcel@kean.edu
  Telephone: 908-737-5400
  Fax: 908-737-5405
Contact Person: Ellen Gottdenker, LDT-C, Mentor
  E-mail: pexcel@kean.edu
  Telephone: 908-737-5400
  Fax: 908-737-5405

LEARNING DISABILITY SERVICES

Requests for the following services/accommodations will be evaluated individually based on appropriate and current documentation.

Allowed in exams
  Calculator: Yes
  Dictionary: Yes
  Computer: Yes
  Spellchecker: Yes
Extended test time: Yes
Scribes: No
Proctors: Yes
Oral exams: Yes
Note-takers: No

Distraction-reduced environment: Yes
Tape recording in class: Yes
Books on tape from RFBD: Yes
Taping of books not from RFBD: No
Accommodations for students with ADHD: Yes
Reading machine: Yes
Other assistive technology: Yes
Priority registration: Yes

Added costs for services: No
LD specialists: Yes
Professional tutors: Yes
Peer tutors: Yes
Max. hours/wk. for services: NR
How professors are notified of LD/ADHD: By student

GENERAL ADMISSIONS INFORMATION

Director of Admissions: Audley W. Bridges
Telephone: 908-737-7109

ENTRANCE REQUIREMENTS
Academic units required: 4 English, 3 math, 2 science (2 science labs), 2 history, 5 academic electives.
Academic units recommended: 2 foreign language, 2 social studies. High school diploma is required, and GED is accepted. ACT with or without Writing component accepted.

Application deadline: 5/31
Notification: Rolling
Average GPA: 2.90
ACT Composite middle 50% range: NR

SAT Math middle 50% range: 430–530
SAT Critical Reading middle 50% range: 410–510
SAT Writing middle 50% range: NR

Graduated top 10% of class: 7%
Graduated top 25% of class: 22%
Graduated top 50% of class: 59%

COLLEGE GRADUATION REQUIREMENTS

Course waivers allowed: No
Course substitutions allowed: No

ADDITIONAL INFORMATION

Environment: The college is located on 151 acres in a suburban area 20 miles west of New York City.

Student Body
  Undergrad enrollment: 9,650
  Women: 63%
  Men: 37%
  Percent out-of-state: 2%

Cost Information
  In-state tuition: $7,500
  Out-of-state tuition: $10,139
  Room & board: $8,880
Housing Information
  University housing: Yes
  Percent living on campus: 15%

Greek System
  Fraternity: Yes
  Sorority: Yes
Athletics: Division III

MONMOUTH UNIVERSITY (NJ)

Admissions, 400 Cedar Avenue, West Long Branch, NJ 07764-1898
Phone: 732-571-3456 • Fax: 732-263-5166
E-mail: admission@monmouth.edu • Web: www.monmouth.edu
Support: CS • Institution type: 4-year private

LEARNING DISABILITY PROGRAM AND SERVICES

Monmouth University recognizes the special needs of students with disabilities who are capable, with appropriate assistance, of excelling in a demanding college environment. Comprehensive support services and a nurturing environment contribute to their success. Monmouth's commitment is to provide a learning process and atmosphere that allows students to pursue their educational goals, realize their full potential, contribute actively to their community and society, and determine the direction of their lives. Students are enrolled in regular courses and are not isolated from the rest of the student body in any manner. Students with documented disabilities may request reasonable modifications, accommodations, or auxiliary aids. It is important that students disclose their disability and provide the required learning accommodations to DSS. Much of their success has to do with individual recognition of their specific learning needs combined with supportive faculty. Monmouth is very proud of the many important contributions of students with learning disabilities to life at the university.

LD/ADHD ADMISSIONS INFORMATION

College entrance tests required: Yes
Interview required: No
Essay recommended: No
Documentation required for LD: Psychoeducational evaluation
Documentation required for ADHD: Yes
Submitted to: Disability Services for Students
Special Ed. HS course work accepted: No

Specific course requirements of all applicants: Yes
Separate application required: No
# of LD applications submitted each year: NR
# of LD applications accepted yearly: NR
Total # of students receiving LD services: 208
Acceptance into program means acceptance into college: Students are accepted jointly into the college and the learning disabilities program.

ADMISSIONS

There is no special admissions process for students with diagnosed learning disabilities. General admission requirements include 4 years of English, 3 years of math, 2 years of social science, 2 years of science, and 5 electives from English, math, science, social studies, and/or a foreign language. Courses taken in the special education department may be accepted. The minimum GPA is 2.25. Students are encouraged to self-disclose if they believe that their high school performance needs an explanation.

ADDITIONAL INFORMATION

Students with documented disabilities may request reasonable modifications, accommodations, or auxiliary aids that will enable them to participate in and benefit from postsecondary educational programs and activities. These may include extended time on tests, reader assistance, and note-takers. Monmouth University also offers a summer transition session during the university's freshman orientation and assistance with advocacy such as serving as liaison between the student and the professors.

LEARNING DISABILITY PROGRAM/SERVICES

Learning Disability Program/Services: Department of Disability Services for Students
Director: Skip Carey
  Telephone: 732-571-3460
  Fax: 732-263-5126
Contact Person: Carolyne Chirichello
  Telephone: 732-571-3456
  Fax: 732-263-5166

LEARNING DISABILITY SERVICES

Requests for the following services/accommodations will be evaluated individually based on appropriate and current documentation.

Allowed in exams
  Calculator: Yes
  Dictionary: Yes
  Computer: Yes
  Spellchecker: Yes
Extended test time: Yes
Scribes: Yes
Proctors: Yes
Oral exams: Yes
Note-takers: Yes

Distraction-reduced environment: Yes
Tape recording in class: Yes
Books on tape from RFBD: Yes
Taping of books not from RFBD: No
**Accommodations for students with
  ADHD:** Yes
Reading machine: Yes
Other assistive technology: Yes
Priority registration: Yes

Added costs for services: Yes
LD specialists: Yes
Professional tutors: No
Peer tutors: No
Max. hours/wk. for services:
  Unlimited
**How professors are notified of
  LD/ADHD:** By both student and
  director

GENERAL ADMISSIONS INFORMATION

Director of Admissions: Lauren Vento Cifelli
Telephone: 732-571-3456

ENTRANCE REQUIREMENTS

Academic units required: 4 English, 3 math, 2 science (1 science lab), 2 history, 5 academic electives. **Academic units recommended:** 2 foreign language, 2 social studies. High school diploma is required, and GED is accepted. ACT with Writing component required. TOEFL required of all international applicants: minimum paper TOEFL 550, minimum computer TOEFL 213.

Application deadline: 3/1
Notification: 4/01
Average GPA: 3.17
ACT Composite middle 50% range:
  20–25

SAT Math middle 50% range:
  500–580
**SAT Critical Reading middle 50%
  range:** 490–570
SAT Writing middle 50% range:
  480–570

Graduated top 10% of class: 9%
Graduated top 25% of class: 32%
Graduated top 50% of class: 72%

COLLEGE GRADUATION REQUIREMENTS

Course waivers allowed: Yes
In what course: Case-by-case determination (Most majors do not require foreign languages.)
Course substitutions allowed: Yes
In what course: Case-by-case determination (Most majors do not require foreign languages.)

ADDITIONAL INFORMATION

Environment: The college is located on 125 acres in a suburb 60 miles south of New York City.

Student Body
  Undergrad enrollment: 4,577
  Women: 58%
  Men: 42%
  Percent out-of-state: 9%

Cost Information
  Tuition: $21,248
  Room & board: $8,472
Housing Information
  University housing: Yes
  Percent living on campus: 44%

Greek System
  Fraternity: Yes
  Sorority: Yes
  Athletics: Division I

NEW JERSEY CITY UNIVERSITY

2039 Kennedy Boulevard, Jersey City, NJ 07305
Phone: 888-441-6528 • Fax: 201-200-2044
E-mail: admissions@njcu.edu • Web: www.njcu.edu
Support: SP • Institution type: 4-year public

LEARNING DISABILITY PROGRAM AND SERVICES

Project Mentor is a support program that opens the door to higher education for students with learning disabilities by providing them with a faculty mentor—a teacher, advisor, and facilitator—for their entire college career. A low-cost, 4-week precollege summer orientation program prepares freshmen students for success in the academic setting. (Residential students pay for food and housing). In addition to the traditional university admissions process, there is an alternate admissions pathway through Project Mentor. Faculty mentors, advisement, priority registration, special tutorials, compensatory strategy development, counseling, and advocacy are among the many services that are available to student participants throughout the academic year.

LD/ADHD ADMISSIONS INFORMATION

College entrance tests required: Yes
Interview required: No
Essay recommended: Yes
Documentation required for LD: Educational and psychological evaluations and IEPs (current, preferably completed within the past 3 years)
Documentation required for ADHD: Yes
Submitted to: Project Mentor
Special Ed. HS course work accepted: NR

Specific course requirements of all applicants: Yes
Separate application required: Yes
# of LD applications submitted each year: 15–20
# of LD applications accepted yearly: 15–20
Total # of students receiving LD services: 110–120
Acceptance into program means acceptance into college: Admission is given to the college and Project Mentor at the same time.

ADMISSIONS

Students with LD may gain admission through one of two procedures: (1) the traditional university admissions process or (2) Project Mentor's alternate admissions process. These two procedures operate concurrently, and their outcomes are independent of each other. A student who is admitted traditionally may receive all of the support and advocacy services available by providing LD documentation. To be considered for alternate admissions, students must submit recent documentation of the LD and evidence of motivation and successful academic performance. The Project Mentor Admissions Committee analyzes the documentation to gain a better understanding of the student's academic strengths and how the disability may impact academic performance. Members of the Project Mentor Admissions Committee will make their recommendations for admission to NJCU based on special criteria for candidates with LD who possess academic promise. Admitted students into Project Mentor must attend a summer program. All applicants to Project Mentor are requested to schedule an interview, submit recommendations or telephone calls from a high school counselor and/or teacher, and have a recent child study team evaluation. The admissions process involves a review of the psychoeducational report. Project Mentor is looking for students with the intellectual potential to achieve in a four-year college setting who were mostly in mainstream college-prep classes in high school. Although SAT scores are required, they are not used for admission purposes. All applications from students with learning disabilities are referred to Project Mentor. Project faculty review applications and make recommendations to the Admissions Office for acceptance, rejection, or trial status for a precollege summer orientation program. The staff considers each candidate individually.

ADDITIONAL INFORMATION

Students meet once a week with mentors. Sessions might include instruction, counseling, and/or referral to services available to all students at the college. Exclusive tutorials for Project Mentor students are staffed by highly trained professionals. Mentors help the students negotiate accommodations with their professors. Extending the limits on examinations, providing tutorial assistance, and permitting tape recording of lectures are among the types of accommodations provided. Professors try to provide for the special needs of students with learning differences/disabilities while maintaining appropriate academic standards.

LEARNING DISABILITY PROGRAM/SERVICES

Learning Disability Program/Services: Project Mentor
Director: Jennifer Aitken
  E-mail: jaitken@njcu.edu
  Telephone: 201-200-2091
  Fax: 201-200-3083

LEARNING DISABILITY SERVICES

Requests for the following services/accommodations will be evaluated individually based on appropriate and current documentation.

Allowed in exams
  Calculator: Yes
  Dictionary: Yes
  Computer: Yes
  Spellchecker: Yes
Extended test time: Yes
Scribes: Yes
Proctors: Yes
Oral exams: Yes
Note-takers: Yes

Distraction-reduced environment: Yes
Tape recording in class: Yes
Books on tape from RFBD: Yes
Taping of books not from RFBD: Yes
Accommodations for students with ADHD: Yes
Reading machine: No
Other assistive technology: Yes
Priority registration: Yes

Added costs for services: No
LD specialists: Yes
Professional tutors: 7
Peer tutors: Yes
Max. hours/wk. for services: Unlimited
How professors are notified of LD/ADHD: By both student and director

GENERAL ADMISSIONS INFORMATION

Director of Admissions: Carmen Panlilio
Telephone: 201-200-3378

ENTRANCE REQUIREMENTS

Academic units required: 4 English, 4 math, 4 science (2 science labs), 4 social studies. **Academic units recommended:** 4 English, 4 math, 4 science (3 science labs), 2 foreign language, 4 social studies. High school diploma is required, and GED is accepted. TOEFL required of all international applicants: minimum paper TOEFL 500, minimum computer TOEFL 150.

Application deadline: 4/1
Notification: Rolling
Average GPA: 2.7
ACT Composite middle 50% range: NR

SAT Math middle 50% range: 410–510
SAT Critical Reading middle 50% range: 410–490
SAT Writing middle 50% range: NR

Graduated top 10% of class: 8%
Graduated top 25% of class: 24%
Graduated top 50% of class: 62%

COLLEGE GRADUATION REQUIREMENTS

Course waivers allowed: No
Course substitutions allowed: Yes
In what course: Each case is reviewed on an individual basis.

ADDITIONAL INFORMATION

Environment: The college is located on 150 acres in a suburban area 20 miles west of New York City.

Student Body
  Undergrad enrollment: 6,115
  Women: 63%
  Men: 37%
  Percent out-of-state: 1%

Cost Information
  In-state tuition: $6,300
  Out-of-state tuition: $11,400
  Room & board: $7,810
Housing Information
  University housing: Yes
  Percent living on campus: 4%

Greek System
  Fraternity: Yes
  Sorority: Yes
Athletics: Division III

RIDER UNIVERSITY

2083 Lawrenceville Road, Lawrenceville, NJ 08648-3099
Phone: 609-896-5042 • Fax: 609-895-6645
E-mail: admissions@rider.edu • Web: www.rider.edu
Support: CS • Institution type: 4-year private

LEARNING DISABILITY PROGRAM AND SERVICES

The Education Enhancement Program offers a range of services to help students with documented LD obtain appropriate accommodations. These services include screening and referral, supplementary assessment, and instructional services. The goal of the program is to assist students in becoming more independent and efficient learners. A learning disability specialist meets individually with students who have learning disabilities and/or attention deficit hyperactivity disorder. Students must initiate the request for this meeting and must supply documentation of the disability. These learning disability specialists conduct an intake interview and, based on the information resulting from this interview, refer students to appropriate support services. They also determine the appropriate academic adjustments.

LD/ADHD ADMISSIONS INFORMATION

College entrance tests required: Yes
Interview required: No
Essay recommended: Yes
Documentation required for LD: Educational and
  psychological tests completed within the past 3 years.
  Please see website for complete documentation guidelines.
Documentation required for ADHD: Please see website for
  complete documentation guidelines.
Submitted to: Education Enhancement Program
Special Ed. HS course work accepted: No

Specific course requirements of all applicants: Yes
Separate application required: No
# of LD applications submitted each year: NR
# of LD applications accepted yearly: NR
Total # of students receiving LD services: NR
**Acceptance into program means acceptance into
  college:** Students must be admitted to and enrolled in the
  university first and then request services.

ADMISSIONS

There is no special admissions process for students with learning disabilities. All students must submit the general university application. Admissions criteria are based on the following: high school academic record and GPA of 2.0 or better, SAT or ACT test results, and a college writing sample (essay). Courses required include 16 acceptable units from a college-prep curriculum: 4 years of English and 2 years of math, science, foreign language, social science, and humanities. For students with a learning disability, proper documentation recognizing the differing abilities of the student is requested. The Rider Achievement Program is for academically admissible students who are just below the admissions criteria for the regularly admitted student. The Educational Opportunity Fund Program is the state-funded program for academically disadvantaged or economically disadvantaged students.

ADDITIONAL INFORMATION

The Rider Learning Center provides individual and small group tutoring in writing, reading comprehension, and study strategies. The staff offers study strategy workshops, and students have access to computers. The Mathematics Skill Lab provides a math course for students who do not meet the placement criteria for college-level math. The course is taught via individual tutoring, structured workshops, and computer-assisted instruction. The MSL staff offers weekly tutorial sessions for finite math, helps students prepare for the Algebra and Trigonometry Qualifying Exam, and provides tutoring for other courses. Tutoring Services provides a peer tutoring program for students needing extra help. The Education Enhancement Program offers a course in college reading and an introduction to academic reading.

LEARNING DISABILITY SERVICES

Learning Disability Program/Services: Education Enhancement Program/Services for Students with Disabilities
Director: Jacqueline Simon, EdD
  E-mail: serv4dstu@rider.edu
  Telephone: 609-895-5492
  Fax: 609-895-5507

LEARNING DISABILITY SERVICES

Requests for the following services/accommodations will be evaluated individually based on appropriate and current documentation.

Allowed in exams
  Calculator: Yes
  Dictionary: Yes
  Computer: Yes
  Spellchecker: Yes
Extended test time: Yes
Scribes: Yes
Proctors: Yes
Oral exams: Yes
Note-takers: Yes

Distraction-reduced environment: Yes
Tape recording in class: Yes
Books on tape from RFBD: Yes
Taping of books not from RFBD: Yes
Accommodations for students with ADHD: Yes
Reading machine: No
Other assistive technology: Yes
Priority registration: Yes

Added costs for services: No
LD specialists: Yes
Professional tutors: 3–5
Peer tutors: 50–75
Max. hours/wk. for services: 3
How professors are notified of LD/ADHD: By both student and director

GENERAL ADMISSIONS INFORMATION

Director of Admissions: Susan C. Christian, Dean of Enrollment
Telephone: 609-895-5768

ENTRANCE REQUIREMENTS

Academic units required: 4 English, 2 math, 2 science, 2 foreign language, 2 social studies. **Academic units recommended:** 4 math, 4 science (2 science labs), 2 foreign language, 2 social studies, 2 history. High school diploma is required, and GED is accepted. ACT with or without Writing component accepted. TOEFL required of all international applicants: minimum paper TOEFL 563, minimum computer TOEFL 202.

Application deadline: Rolling
Notification: Within 3–4 weeks of receipt of application
Average GPA: 3.24
ACT Composite middle 50% range: 18–21

SAT Math middle 50% range: 480–570
SAT Critical Reading middle 50% range: 470–570
SAT Writing middle 50% range: NR

Graduated top 10% of class: 13%
Graduated top 25% of class: 40%
Graduated top 50% of class: 75%

COLLEGE GRADUATION REQUIREMENTS

Course waivers allowed: No
Course substitutions allowed: Yes
In what course: Substitutions are considered on a case-by-case basis only and may be considered for foreign language and math. The common practice is for students to accomplish the courses with academic support and accommodations.

ADDITIONAL INFORMATION

Environment: The college is located on a 353-acre campus between Princeton and Trenton, New Jersey.

Student Body
  Undergrad enrollment: 4,369
  Women: 60%
  Men: 40%
  Percent out-of-state: 25%

Cost Information
  Tuition: $24,220
  Room & board: $9,280
Housing Information
  University housing: Yes
  Percent living on campus: 57%

Greek System
  Fraternity: Yes
  Sorority: Yes
Athletics: Division I

SETON HALL UNIVERSITY

Enrollment Services, 400 South Orange Avenue, South Orange, NJ 07079
Phone: 973-761-9332 • Fax: 973-275-2040
E-mail: thehall@shu.edu • Web: www.shu.edu
Support: CS • Institution type: 4-year private

LEARNING DISABILITY PROGRAM AND SERVICES

Student Support Services is an academic program that addresses the needs of all eligible undergraduates. The program provides individual and group tutoring in many disciplines. Academic, career, and other counseling services are also available. The program provides individual and group tutoring in many disciplines. Special emphasis is placed on mathematics, science labs, and business. Student Support Services is especially attentive to the needs of students who can provide professional documentation of specific disabilities. Every effort is made to accommodate the special academic needs of these students by recommending extended test time and a distraction-free testing environments. To self-identify for services, students should complete and submit the self-identification form with the appropriate documentation.

LD/ADHD ADMISSIONS INFORMATION

College entrance tests required: Yes
Interview required: No
Essay recommended: No
Documentation required for LD: Psychoeducational evaluation. Applicants should be reminded that the requirement for higher education eligibility for services is substantial limitation. Visit the DSS website for information at http://studentaffairs.shu.edu/dss.
Documentation required for ADHD: A full evaluation is required. A Connors rating scale and/or a prescription form from a physician will not be accepted. Visit the DSS website for information at http://studentaffairs.shu.edu/dss.
Submitted to: Student Support Services
Special Ed. HS course work accepted: No

Specific course requirements of all applicants: Yes
Separate application required: No
# of LD applications submitted each year: NR
# of LD applications accepted yearly: NR
Total # of students receiving LD services: NR
Acceptance into program means acceptance into college: Students must be admitted to and enrolled in the university first and then request services.

ADMISSIONS

There is no special admission process for students with learning disabilities, and all applicants must meet the same admission criteria. Courses required include 4 years of English, 3 years of math, 1 year of science lab, 2 years of a foreign language, 2 years of social studies, and 4 electives. If students have been waived from a world language via their IEP, the requirement will be waived if it is not a core requirement of a particular program. The minimum SAT is 900. Students need to rank in the top 40 percent of their class, and a minimum 2.5 GPA is preferred.

ADDITIONAL INFORMATION

In coordinating its activities with other departments of the university (such as Residence Life and Academic Services), Student Support Services works to assure that the university remains in compliance with all federal laws and regulations. The DSS office provides the following services to individuals with LD (with appropriate documentation): reduced course load, extended time to complete assignments, tape recorders, note-taking, taped texts, readers, extended time for in class assignments, assistive technology (calculator, word processor, etc.), extended time for testing, and a distraction-free environment.

LEARNING DISABILITY PROGRAM/SERVICES

Learning Disability Program/Services: Student Support Services
Director: Linda Raye Walter
E-mail: walterli@shu.edu
Telephone: 973-313-6003
Fax: 973-761-9185

LEARNING DISABILITY SERVICES

Requests for the following services/accommodations will be evaluated individually based on appropriate and current documentation.

Allowed in exams
Calculator: Yes
Dictionary: Yes
Computer: Yes
Spellchecker: Yes
Extended test time: Yes
Scribes: Yes
Proctors: Yes
Oral exams: Yes
Note-takers: Yes

Distraction-reduced environment: Yes
Tape recording in class: Yes
Books on tape from RFBD: No
Taping of books not from RFBD: Yes
Accommodations for students with ADHD: Yes
Reading machine: Yes
Other assistive technology: Yes
Priority registration: Yes

Added costs for services: No
LD specialists: Yes
Professional tutors: Yes
Peer tutors: Yes
Max. hours/wk. for services: Unlimited
How professors are notified of LD/ADHD: By both student and director

GENERAL ADMISSIONS INFORMATION

Director of Admissions: Robert Herr
Telephone: 973-275-2498

ENTRANCE REQUIREMENTS
Academic units required: 4 English, 3 math, 1 science, 2 foreign language, 2 social studies, 4 academic electives. High school diploma is required, and GED is accepted. ACT with Writing component required. TOEFL required of all international applicants: minimum paper TOEFL 550, minimum computer TOEFL 213.

Application deadline: 3/1
Notification: Rolling
Average GPA: 3.15
ACT Composite middle 50% range: NR

SAT Math middle 50% range: 500–600
SAT Critical Reading middle 50% range: 480–590
SAT Writing middle 50% range: NR

Graduated top 10% of class: 28%
Graduated top 25% of class: 60%
Graduated top 50% of class: 88%

COLLEGE GRADUATION REQUIREMENTS

Course waivers allowed: Yes
In what course: Course waivers for mathematics and world languages are available as long as they are not core courses required for the student's major.
Course substitutions allowed: Yes
In what course: Students may request course substitutions through the DSS office for mathematics and world languages that are then approved by the dean of each school or college by recommendation of the DSS office.

ADDITIONAL INFORMATION

Environment: The university is located on 58 acres in a suburban area 14 miles west of New York City.

Student Body
Undergrad enrollment: 4,951
Women: 55%
Men: 45%
Percent out-of-state: 26%

Cost Information
Tuition: $23,400
Room & board: $10,466
Housing Information
University housing: Yes
Percent living on campus: 44%

Greek System
Fraternity: Yes
Sorority: Yes
Athletics: Division I

COLLEGE OF SANTA FE

1600 St. Michaels Drive, Santa Fe, NM 87505-7634
Phone: 505-473-6133 • Fax: 505-473-6129
E-mail: admissions@csf.edu • Web: www.csf.edu
Support: S • Institution type: 4-year private

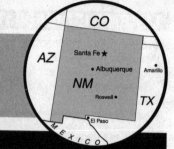

LEARNING DISABILITY PROGRAM AND SERVICES

The Center for Academic Excellence is a federally funded Title IV support services program designed to assist eligible students to graduate from CSF. There is no formal disabilities program at the college, but the students do have access to many services and accommodations. Students may receive services in basic skills instruction for reading, study strategies, writing, math, humanities, and science. Students work with the professional staff to set up a support program that meets their specific needs. The initial meeting is during registration. To be eligible for services, students with learning disabilities must provide a current psychoeducational evaluation that identifies their learning disability. Once this documentation is on file with the Center for Academic Excellence, students may meet with staff to identify the necessary accommodations and services needed to be successful in college.

LD/ADHD ADMISSIONS INFORMATION

College entrance tests required: Yes
Interview required: Yes
Essay recommended: Yes
Documentation required for LD: Prepared by an appropriate professional; current, within the past 3 years; include a specific diagnosis and an interpretive summary.
Documentation required for ADHD: Psychoeducational measurement battery of tests are preferred.
Submitted to: Center for Academic Excellence
Special Ed. HS course work accepted: Yes

Specific course requirements of all applicants: Yes
Separate application required: No
# of LD applications submitted each year: NR
# of LD applications accepted yearly: NR
Total # of students receiving LD services: 75–100
Acceptance into program means acceptance into college: Students are admitted to the college and to the Center for Academic Excellence after applying for services.

ADMISSIONS

There is no separate admission process for students with LD/ADHD. Students with LD/ADHD are required to meet the general admission criteria. This includes course requirements of 3 years of English, 2 years of math, 2 years of science, 2 years of social science, and a recommendation of 2 years of a foreign language. Each applicant is evaluated individually. All traditional first-time candidates for admission are required to go through an on-campus interview process. If students are unable to come to campus because of distance or time, the college will arrange a telephone interview. If admitted, students with a GPA inconsistent with their level of ability arrange for academic support from the Center for Academic Excellence. Copies of diagnostic examinations not more than 3 years old must document the student's learning disability or ADHD. The results of these tests are sent to the Center for Academic Excellence after the student is admitted.

ADDITIONAL INFORMATION

Throughout the academic year, the Disabilities Service Office works to support the needs of students with disabilities by providing an initial interview, assessment of accommodation needs, and ongoing support. Services provided by the college could include, but are not limited to, the following: alternative testing, specialized tutoring, academic advisement and career planning, note-takers, interpreters for the hearing impaired, screen-reader software, other assistive technology, peer tutoring, resource information, and referrals. CAE offers students free tutoring in most subjects taught at the College of Santa Fe. Tutoring helps students more fully understand course material and develop academic strategies helpful in all courses. Individual tutoring is available from professional staff as well as peer tutors. Peer tutors are CSF students who have excellent academic records, have taken the courses they tutor, and have been trained to work with students with a wide range of needs and learning styles. Tutors also facilitate study groups for many courses offered at the college. These groups provide opportunities to discuss course content, compare notes with other students, and develop success strategies. Accommodations are provided on an individual basis.

LEARNING DISABILITY PROGRAM/SERVICES

Learning Disability Program/Services: Center for Academic Excellence
Director: Erika Ellis
  E-mail: eellis@csf.edu
  Telephone: 505-473-6552
  Fax: 505-473-6124

LEARNING DISABILITY SERVICES

Requests for the following services/accommodations will be evaluated individually based on appropriate and current documentation.

Allowed in exams
  Calculator: Yes
  Dictionary: Yes
  Computer: Yes
  Spellchecker: Yes
Extended test time: Yes
Scribes: Yes
Proctors: Yes
Oral exams: Yes
Note-takers: Yes

Distraction-reduced environment: Yes
Tape recording in class: Yes
Books on tape from RFBD: Yes
Taping of books not from RFBD: Yes
Accommodations for students with ADHD: Yes
Reading machine: Yes
Other assistive technology: Yes
Priority registration: No

Added costs for services: No
LD specialists: No
Professional tutors: 3
Peer tutors: 25–40
Max. hours/wk. for services: 3
How professors are notified of LD/ADHD: By both student and director

GENERAL ADMISSIONS INFORMATION

Director of Admissions: Jeff Miller
Telephone: 505-473-6133

ENTRANCE REQUIREMENTS
Academic units required: 3 English, 2 math, 2 science (2 science labs), 2 social studies, 6 academic electives.
Academic units recommended: 4 English, 3 math, 3 science (2 science labs), 2 foreign language, 2 social studies, 2 history, 4 academic electives. High school diploma is required, and GED is accepted. ACT with Writing component required. TOEFL required of all international applicants: minimum paper TOEFL 550, minimum computer TOEFL 213.

Application deadline: Rolling
Notification: Rolling
Average GPA: 3.09
ACT Composite middle 50% range: 20–25

SAT Math middle 50% range: 460–590
SAT Critical Reading middle 50% range: 520–640
SAT Writing middle 50% range: NR

Graduated top 10% of class: 7%
Graduated top 25% of class: 30%
Graduated top 50% of class: 63%

COLLEGE GRADUATION REQUIREMENTS

Course waivers allowed: Yes
In what course: This is done on an individual basis, depending on the experience of the individual student.
Course substitutions allowed: Yes
In what course: Again, it is done on a case-by-case basis, but substitution is common for all students here.

ADDITIONAL INFORMATION

Environment: The college is located on 118 acres in a suburban area of Santa Fe.

Student Body
  Undergrad enrollment: 1,225
  Women: 58%
  Men: 42%
  Percent out-of-state: 73%

Cost Information
  Tuition: $22,200
  Room & board: $6,702
Housing Information
  University housing: Yes
  Percent living on campus: 60%

Greek System
  Fraternity: No
  Sorority: No
  Athletics: NAIA

College of Santa Fe

NEW MEXICO INSTITUTE OF MINING AND TECHNOLOGY

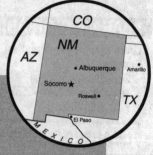

Campus Station, 801 Leroy Place, Socorro, NM 87801
Phone: 505-835-5424 • Fax: 505-835-5989
E-mail: admission@admin.nmt.edu • Web: www.nmt.edu
Support: S • Institution type: 4-year public

LEARNING DISABILITY PROGRAM AND SERVICES

New Mexico Tech does not have a specific program for students with LD. Services for students with disabilities are available in the Counseling and Student Health Center. Students must present recent documentation completed within the previous 3 years. The documentation should be sent to Services for Students with Disabilities. New Mexico Tech sends a letter to all admitted students asking those with disabilities to contact Services for Students with Disabilities. There is a special application required after admission and enrollment to receive services or accommodations. The counseling staff works with students with disabilities on an individual basis to accommodate their special needs. Students may also use the counseling service to reduce their stress, think through problems or difficulties, clarify options, and express and explore feelings.

LD/ADHD ADMISSIONS INFORMATION

College entrance tests required: Yes
Interview required: No
Essay recommended: No
Documentation required for LD: Psychoeducational evaluation
Documentation required for ADHD: Yes
Submitted to: Services for Students with Disabilities
Special Ed. HS course work accepted: NR

Specific course requirements of all applicants: Yes
Separate application required: Yes
# of LD applications submitted each year: NR
# of LD applications accepted yearly: NR
Total # of students receiving LD services: 24
Acceptance into program means acceptance into college: Students must be admitted to and enrolled in the university first and then request services.

ADMISSIONS

There is no special admission process for students with LD. The minimum GPA is a 2.5. The college requires an ACT composite score of 21 or higher or an SAT score of 970 or higher. The college will accept the SAT, but prefers the ACT. The GED is accepted with a score of 50 or higher. High school course requirements include 4 years of English, 2 years of science (including biology, physics, chemistry, and earth science), 3 years of math, and 3 years of social science, of which one must be history. Students are encouraged to self-disclose their disability during the admission process.

ADDITIONAL INFORMATION

Students will work with staff to determine appropriate accommodations or services. These services may include coordinating academic accommodations, extended time for tests, calculators in exams, skills classes in study strategies and time management, and tutorial services available for all students on campus.

LEARNING DISABILITY PROGRAM/SERVICES

Learning Disability Program/Services: Services for Students with Disabilities
Director: Laurie Tacheny Borden
  E-mail: ltborden@admin.nmt.edu
  Telephone: 505-835-5443
  Fax: 505-835-5959

LEARNING DISABILITY SERVICES

Requests for the following services/accommodations will be evaluated individually based on appropriate and current documentation.

Allowed in exams
  Calculator: Yes
  Dictionary: No
  Computer: Yes
  Spellchecker: Yes
Extended test time: Yes
Scribes: Yes
Proctors: Yes
Oral exams: Yes
Note-takers: Yes

Distraction-reduced environment: Yes
Tape recording in class: Yes
Books on tape from RFBD: Yes
Taping of books not from RFBD: Yes
Accommodations for students with
  ADHD: Yes
Reading machine: No
Other assistive technology: Yes
Priority registration: Yes

Added costs for services: No
LD specialists: No
Professional tutors: No
Peer tutors: 50
Max. hours/wk. for services:
  Unlimited
How professors are notified of
  LD/ADHD: By both student and
  director

GENERAL ADMISSIONS INFORMATION

Director of Admissions: Mike Kloeppel
Telephone: 505-835-5424

ENTRANCE REQUIREMENTS

Academic units required: 4 English, 3 math, 2 science (2 science labs), 2 social studies, 1 history, 3 academic electives. **Academic units recommended:** 4 English, 4 math, 4 science (3 science labs), 2 foreign language, 3 social studies, 1 history. High school diploma is required, and GED is accepted. ACT with or without Writing component accepted. TOEFL required of all international applicants: minimum paper TOEFL 540, minimum computer TOEFL 207.

Application deadline: 8/1
Notification: Rolling
Average GPA: 3.60
ACT Composite middle 50% range:
  23–29

SAT Math middle 50% range:
  570–670
SAT Critical Reading middle 50%
  range: 550–670
SAT Writing middle 50% range: NR

Graduated top 10% of class: 32%
Graduated top 25% of class: 67%
Graduated top 50% of class: 91%

COLLEGE GRADUATION REQUIREMENTS

Course waivers allowed: No
Course substitutions allowed: No

ADDITIONAL INFORMATION

Environment: The campus is located 75 miles from Albuquerque.

Student Body
  Undergrad enrollment: 1,170
  Women: 28%
  Men: 72%
  Percent out-of-state: 13%

Cost Information
  In-state tuition: $3,600
  Out-of-state tuition: $10,873
  Room & board: $5,090
Housing Information
  University housing: Yes
  Percent living on campus: 59%

Greek System
  Fraternity: No
  Sorority: No
Athletics: Intramural

NEW MEXICO STATE UNIVERSITY

PO Box 30001, MSC 3A, Las Cruces, NM 88003-8001
Phone: 505-646-3121 • Fax: 505-646-6330
E-mail: admissions@nmsu.edu • Web: www.nmsu.edu
Support: S • Institution type: 4-year public

LEARNING DISABILITY PROGRAM AND SERVICES

Services for Students with Disabilities is a component of the Office of Student Development. The staff are committed to providing information and services that assist students with disabilities in personal and academic adjustment to the university community. Services for Students with Disabilities provides assistance with procuring auxiliary aids, coordinating services and resources, and discussing special needs and accommodations, and the staff serve as consultants regarding questions about various accommodations. They work with students to ensure that they have access to all of the programs and services that will affect their full participation in the campus community. Students are encouraged to contact Services for Students with Disabilities to discuss their needs and to register for the program. Students should complete the petition for Services for Students with Disabilities and return it with the appropriate documentation for evaluation and review. A review committee will determine their eligibility and the specific services and accommodations to be provided, and students will be notified by a coordinator. This process takes time, and students are encouraged to start the process as soon as possible.

LD/ADHD ADMISSIONS INFORMATION

College entrance tests required: Yes
Interview required: No
Essay recommended: No
Documentation required for LD: Psychoeducational evaluation
Documentation required for ADHD: Yes
Submitted to: Services for Students with Disabilities
Special Ed. HS course work accepted: Yes

Specific course requirements of all applicants: Yes
Separate application required: No
# of LD applications submitted each year: NR
# of LD applications accepted yearly: NR
Total # of students receiving LD services: 90
Acceptance into program means acceptance into college: Students must be admitted to and enrolled in the university first and then request services.

ADMISSIONS

Admission criteria are the same for all students. Admission can be granted on a regular status or provisional status. Regular admission requires high school GPA of 2.5 and 21 ACT or 970 SAT. Course requirements include 4 years of English, 2 years of science, 3 years of math, and 3 years of social studies (1 must be history). Provisional status is possible for students who have a high school GPA of 2.1 and 18 ACT. Students admitted provisionally must take at least 6, but not more than 12, credits in a regular semester and at least 3, but not more than 6, credits in a summer session.

ADDITIONAL INFORMATION

The Center for Learning Assistance offers students the skills they need to excel in college. Students work with learning facilitators to develop or maximize the skills needed for college success. Assistance is offered in time management, concentration, memory, test preparation, test-taking, listening/note-taking, textbook-reading techniques, math and science study skills, reasoning skills, writing, spelling, and grammar. Student Support Services is a program of academic and personal support with the goal of improving the retention and graduation of undergraduate students with disabilities. A mentor is provided for all participants to help motivate them, and tutors help with study skills in specific subjects. Students may have tutors in two subjects and can meet weekly. Other services available are early registration, note-taking services, readers, and test accommodations including extended time, a quiet location, scribes, readers, or other assistance with exams. All services are free.

LEARNING DISABILITY PROGRAM/SERVICES

Learning Disability Program/Services: Services for Students with Disabilities (SSD)
Director: Michael Armendariz
  E-mail: ssd@nmsu.edu
  Telephone: 505-646-6840
  Fax: 505-646-5222

LEARNING DISABILITY SERVICES

Requests for the following services/accommodations will be evaluated individually based on appropriate and current documentation.

Allowed in exams
  Calculator: Yes
  Dictionary: No
  Computer: Yes
  Spellchecker: Yes
Extended test time: Yes
Scribes: Yes
Proctors: Yes
Oral exams: Yes
Note-takers: Yes

Distraction-reduced environment: Yes
Tape recording in class: Yes
Books on tape from RFBD: Yes
Taping of books not from RFBD: Yes
Accommodations for students with ADHD: Yes
Reading machine: Yes
Other assistive technology: Yes
Priority registration: Yes

Added costs for services: No
LD specialists: No
Professional tutors: No
Peer tutors: 50
Max. hours/wk. for services: Unlimited
How professors are notified of LD/ADHD: By both student and director

GENERAL ADMISSIONS INFORMATION

Director of Admissions: Angela Mora-Riley
Telephone: 505-646-3121

ENTRANCE REQUIREMENTS

Academic units required: 4 English, 3 math, 2 science (2 science labs), 1 foreign language. High school diploma is required, and GED is accepted. TOEFL required of all international applicants: minimum paper TOEFL 500.

Application deadline: Rolling
Notification: Rolling
Average GPA: 3.40
ACT Composite middle 50% range: 17–23

SAT Math middle 50% range: NR
SAT Critical Reading middle 50% range: NR
SAT Writing middle 50% range: NR

Graduated top 10% of class: 17%
Graduated top 25% of class: 44%
Graduated top 50% of class: 76%

COLLEGE GRADUATION REQUIREMENTS

Course waivers allowed: Yes
In what course: Students need to negotiate with the college in which they are majoring.
Course substitutions allowed: Yes
In what course: Students need to negotiate with the college in which they are majoring.

ADDITIONAL INFORMATION

Environment: The university is located on 5,800 acres in a suburban area 40 miles north of El Paso, Texas.

Student Body
  Undergrad enrollment: 12,157
  Women: 55%
  Men: 45%
  Percent out-of-state: 16%

Cost Information
  In-state tuition: $4,230
  Out-of-state tuition: $13,804
  Room & board: $5,576
Housing Information
  University housing: Yes
  Percent living on campus: 16%

Greek System
  Fraternity: Yes
  Sorority: Yes
Athletics: Division I

ADELPHI UNIVERSITY

Levermore Hall 114, One South Avenue, Garden City, NY 11530
Phone: 516-877-3050 • Fax: 516-877-3039
E-mail: admissions@adelphi.edu • Web: www.adelphi.edu
Support: SP • Institution type: 4-year private

LEARNING DISABILITY PROGRAM AND SERVICES

The approach of the Learning Disabilities Program at Adelphi is to provide an atmosphere where students with LD/ADHD can realize their potential. The program is specially designed for students unable to process oral and written materials in conventional ways, but who excel in other ways. Each student is provided with the support of an interdisciplinary team of experienced professionals in tutoring and counseling. All instruction, counseling, and assessment are provided by more than 15 professionals with advanced degrees in special education and social work. Students meet individually with an educator and a counselor who work as a team. There is a mandatory 5-week summer program prior to freshman year. Students must attend tutoring sessions two times a week, participate in all the program's services, and sign an agreement acknowledging their academic commitment. Students attend classes in their chosen major and meet standard academic requirements. The goal is independence in the academic and the real world.

LD/ADHD ADMISSIONS INFORMATION

College entrance tests required: No
Interview required: Yes
Essay recommended: Yes
Documentation required for LD: WAIS–III, WJ–III, and specific LD diagnosis with psychoeducational evaluation
Documentation required for ADHD: Comprehensive evaluation with written interpretive report
Submitted to: Learning Disabilities Program
Special Ed. HS course work accepted: No

Specific course requirements of all applicants: NR
Separate application required: Yes
# of LD applications submitted each year: 300–400
# of LD applications accepted yearly: 75–100
Total # of students receiving LD services: 105
Acceptance into program means acceptance into college: Yes.

ADMISSIONS

The Admissions Committee reviews all submitted materials for a total picture of strengths and disabilities. Applicants with LD who show an ability to succeed academically are invited to interview. They must submit a high school transcript, documentation of LD, ACT/SAT scores, and a recent testing. The director of the program is actively involved in the admissions decision and conducts a highly individualized assessment of each applicant and their documentation. Motivation, college-prep courses, average or higher IQ (WAIS–III), interview, documentation, and a recommendation from an LD specialist are factors that are used in making an admission decision. Prior to applying, applicants should attend an information session conducted by the program. The program seeks highly motivated and socially mature individuals with average to superior intelligence that are capable of handling full academic schedules. Judgment of the professional staff will determine the applicant's eligibility for the program.

ADDITIONAL INFORMATION

Students receive intensive academic tutoring and individual counseling that begins in the summer program. Course content and requirements are never compromised for students with learning disabilities, but program procedures do help to ease the way in the classroom. For example, in individual tutorials, professional special educators teach how to get the most of studies; instructors are privately notified in writing and by phone if program students are in their classes; students may tape-record class lectures if note-taking is difficult; and individual counseling enables students to understand their behavior, reduce anxiety, and grow emotionally. Approximately 25 percent of these students make the dean's list.

LEARNING DISABILITY PROGRAM/SERVICES

Learning Disability Program/Services: Learning Disabilities Program
Director: Susan Spencer
  E-mail: LDProgram@adelphi.edu
  Telephone: 516-877-4710
  Fax: 516-877-4711

LEARNING DISABILITY SERVICES

Requests for the following services/accommodations will be evaluated individually based on appropriate and current documentation.

Allowed in exams
  Calculator: Yes
  Dictionary: Yes
  Computer: Yes
  Spellchecker: Yes
Extended test time: Yes
Scribes: Yes
Proctors: Yes
Oral exams: Yes
Note-takers: Yes

Distraction-reduced environment: Yes
Tape recording in class: Yes
Books on tape from RFBD: Yes
Taping of books not from RFBD: No
Accommodations for students with ADHD: Yes
Reading machine: Yes
Other assistive technology: Yes
Priority registration: Yes

Added costs for services: Yes
LD specialists: Yes
Professional tutors: No
Peer tutors: No
Max. hours/wk. for services: 3
How professors are notified of LD/ADHD: By both student and director

GENERAL ADMISSIONS INFORMATION

Director of Admissions: Christine Murphy
Telephone: 516-877-3050

ENTRANCE REQUIREMENTS

Academic units recommended: 4 English, 3 math, 3 science, 2 foreign language, 4 electives from social studies, history, English, math, science, or foreign language. High school diploma is required, and GED is accepted. ACT with Writing component required. TOEFL required of all international applicants: minimum paper TOEFL 550, minimum computer TOEFL 213.

Application deadline: NR
Notification: Rolling
Average GPA: 3.30
ACT Composite middle 50% range: 20–25

SAT Math middle 50% range: 490–590
SAT Critical Reading middle 50% range: 480–580
SAT Writing middle 50% range: 480–590

Graduated top 10% of class: 17%
Graduated top 25% of class: 48%
Graduated top 50% of class: 85%

COLLEGE GRADUATION REQUIREMENTS

Course waivers allowed: No
Course substitutions allowed: No

ADDITIONAL INFORMATION

Environment: The university is located on a 75-acre campus 20 miles from New York City.

Student Body
  Undergrad enrollment: 4,916
  Women: 73%
  Men: 27%
  Percent out-of-state: 8%

Cost Information
  Tuition: $19,800
  Room & board: $9,500
Housing Information
  University housing: Yes
  Percent living on campus: 23%

Greek System
  Fraternity: Yes
  Sorority: Yes
Athletics: Division II

COLGATE UNIVERSITY

13 Oak Drive, Hamilton, NY 13346
Phone: 315-228-7401 • Fax: 315-228-7544
E-mail: admission@mail.colgate.edu • Web: www.colgate.edu
Support: CS • Institution type: 4-year private

LEARNING DISABILITY PROGRAM AND SERVICES

Colgate provides for a small student body a liberal arts education that will expand individual potential and ability to participate effectively in society's affairs. There are many resources available for all students. Colgate's goal is to offer resources and services within the campus-wide support system that are responsive to the various talents, needs, and preferences of students with disabilities. For the university to understand and prepare for the accommodations that may be requested, students are asked to complete a confidential self-assessment questionnaire and provide appropriate documentation about their disability. The Director of Academic Support works with students and faculty to assure that the needs of students with disabilities are met, serves as clearinghouse for information about disabilities, provides training and individual consultation for all members of the Colgate community, and provides academic counseling and individualized instruction. Seeking help early and learning to be a self-advocate are essential to college success.

LD/ADHD ADMISSIONS INFORMATION

College entrance tests required: Yes
Interview required: No
Essay recommended: No
Documentation required for LD: Current; complete guidelines provided on request.
Documentation required for ADHD: Current; complete guidelines provided on request.
Submitted to: Academic Support
Special Ed. HS course work accepted: No

Specific course requirements of all applicants: Yes
Separate application required: No
# of LD applications submitted each year: NR
# of LD applications accepted yearly: NR
Total # of students receiving LD services: NR
Acceptance into program means acceptance into college: Students must be admitted to and enrolled in the university first and then request services.

ADMISSIONS

There is no special admission process for students with learning disabilities. The Office of Admissions reviews the applications of all candidates for admission. The admissions staff looks for evidence of substantial achievement in a rigorous secondary school curriculum, one counselor recommendation, standardized testing, a personalized essay, and extracurricular involvement. Also valued are qualities such as curiosity, originality, thoughtfulness, and persistence. Admission is very competitive. Criteria include 16 courses in a college-preparatory program (20 recommended): 4 years of English, 3–4 years of math, 3–4 years of science, 3–4 years of social studies, and 3 years of a foreign language. The ACT average is 29 or the SAT Reasoning Test average is 1348. Three SAT Subject Tests of the applicant's choice are required if the applicant submits the SAT Reasoning Test. However, SAT Subject Tests are not required if the applicant submits the ACT.

ADDITIONAL INFORMATION

Students are encouraged to seek help early; meet with professors at the beginning of each semester to discuss approaches and accommodations that will meet their needs; and seek assistance from the Director of Academic Support and Disability Services, administrative advisor, and faculty advisor. Modifications in the curriculum are made on an individual basis. Colgate provides services in support of academic work on an as-needed basis, such as assistance with note-takers, tape-recorded lectures, tutors, readers, and assistive technology. There is a Writing Center, Math Clinic and departmental tutoring, and skills help is available in writing, reading, and study strategies. Services and accommodations are available for undergraduate and graduate students.

LEARNING DISABILITY PROGRAM/SERVICES

Learning Disability Program/Services: Academic Program Support and Disability Services
Director: Lynn Waldman
  E-mail: lwaldman@mailcolgate.edu
  Telephone: 315-228-7375
  Fax: 315-228-7975

LEARNING DISABILITY SERVICES

Requests for the following services/accommodations will be evaluated individually based on appropriate and current documentation.

Allowed in exams
  Calculator: Yes
  Dictionary: Yes
  Computer: Yes
  Spellchecker: Yes
Extended test time: Yes
Scribes: Yes
Proctors: Yes
Oral exams: Yes
Note-takers: Yes

Distraction-reduced environment: Yes
Tape recording in class: Yes
Books on tape from RFBD: Yes
Taping of books not from RFBD: Yes
Accommodations for students with ADHD: Yes
Reading machine: Yes
Other assistive technology: Yes
Priority registration: Yes

Added costs for services: No
LD specialists: Yes
Professional tutors: No
Peer tutors: Yes
Max. hours/wk. for services: Unlimited
How professors are notified of LD/ADHD: By student

GENERAL ADMISSIONS INFORMATION

Director of Admissions: Gary L. Ross
Telephone: 315-228-7401

ENTRANCE REQUIREMENTS

Academic units required: 4 English, 3 math, 3 science (2 science labs), 3 foreign language, 3 social studies, 1 history. **Academic units recommended:** 4 English, 4 math, 4 science (3 science labs), 4 foreign language, 4 social studies, 3 history. High school diploma is required, and GED is accepted. ACT with or without Writing component accepted. TOEFL required of all international applicants: minimum paper TOEFL 600, minimum computer TOEFL 250.

Application deadline: 1/15
Notification: 4/1
Average GPA: 3.60
ACT Composite middle 50% range: 28–32

SAT Math middle 50% range: 640–710
SAT Critical Reading middle 50% range: 620–720
SAT Writing middle 50% range: NR

Graduated top 10% of class: 70%
Graduated top 25% of class: 92%
Graduated top 50% of class: 100%

COLLEGE GRADUATION REQUIREMENTS

Course waivers allowed: No
Course substitutions allowed: Yes
In what course: Foreign language—all requests are considered case-by-case.

ADDITIONAL INFORMATION

Environment: The university is located in a small town about 45 miles from Syracuse.

Student Body
  Undergrad enrollment: 2,756
  Women: 52%
  Men: 48%
  Percent out-of-state: 70%

Cost Information
  Tuition: $34,795
  Room & board: $8,530
Housing Information
  University housing: Yes
  Percent living on campus: 91%

Greek System
  Fraternity: Yes
  Sorority: Yes
Athletics: Division I

Colgate University

CONCORDIA COLLEGE (NY)

171 White Plains Road, Bronxville, NY 10708
Phone: 914-337-9300 • Fax: 914-395-4636
E-mail: admission@concordia-ny.edu • Web: www.concordia-ny.edu
Support: CS • Institution type: 4-year private

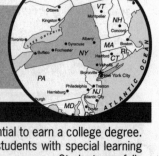

LEARNING DISABILITY PROGRAM AND SERVICES

Concordia Connection is a program for students with LD who have demonstrated the potential to earn a college degree. Their commitment is to provide an intimate, supportive, and caring environment where students with special learning needs can experience college as a successful and rewarding endeavor. This is a mainstream program. Students are fully integrated into the college. During the fall and spring semesters, students are registered for four or five classes. Additionally, students are registered for a one-credit independent study, which incorporates a weekly, 1-hour group session with the director and staff that focuses on the development of individualized learning strategies. Progress is monitored, and an assessment of learning potential and academic levels is provided. The program's assistant director serves as the freshman advisor and coordinates support services. Enrollment is limited to 15 students. A 3-day summer orientation and academic seminar is required for all new Concordia Connection students.

LD/ADHD ADMISSIONS INFORMATION

College entrance tests required: Yes
Interview required: No
Essay recommended: Yes
Documentation required for LD: WAIS–R or WJ-III, IEP, recommendations from teacher or counselor
Documentation required for ADHD: WAIS–R or WJ-III, psychoeducational report documenting ADHD
Submitted to: Admissions
Special Ed. HS course work accepted: No

Specific course requirements of all applicants: Yes
Separate application required: No
# of LD applications submitted each year: 30–45
# of LD applications accepted yearly: 10–16
Total # of students receiving LD services: 32–50
Acceptance into program means acceptance into college: Students must be admitted to and enrolled in the university first and then request services. Some are reviewed by the LD program, which provides a recommendation to the Admissions Office.

ADMISSIONS

Students wishing to apply should submit the following documents to the Admissions Office: a Concordia application and the student's current transcript; SAT/ACT scores; documentation of LD, which must minimally include a WAIS–R profile with subtest scores that was completed within the past year and the student's most recent IEP; recommendations from an LD specialist and a guidance counselor; and an essay describing the nature of the LD, the effect on learning patterns, and the student's reason for pursuing college. Visits are encouraged. Applicants must be high school graduates, have a diagnosed LD, have college-prep courses, and be emotionally stable and committed to being successful. General admissions criteria include a B average, ACT/SAT scores (used to assess strengths and weaknesses rather than for acceptance or denial), and college-preparatory courses in high school (foreign language is recommended but not required). Students with LD who self-disclose and provide documentation will be reviewed by the Admissions Office and the Director of Concordia Connection.

ADDITIONAL INFORMATION

The Concordia Connection provides services to all students. These include test-taking modifications, taped text books, computer access, and tutoring. Although there are no charges for students requesting peer tutoring, there is a $2,500 per semester charge for program services. Skills courses for credit are offered in time management, organizational skills, and study skills. The 3-day summer orientation helps students get acquainted with support services, get exposure to academic expectations, review components and requirements of the freshman year, develop group cohesion, and explore individualized needs and strategies for seeking assistance.

LEARNING DISABILITY PROGRAM/SERVICES

Learning Disability Program/Services: The Concordia Connection Program
Director: George Groth, PsyD
  E-mail: ghg@concordia-ny.edu
  Telephone: 914-337-9300, ext. 2361
  Fax: 914-395-4500

LEARNING DISABILITY SERVICES

Requests for the following services/accommodations will be evaluated individually based on appropriate and current documentation.

Allowed in exams
  Calculator: Yes
  Dictionary: Yes
  Computer: Yes
  Spellchecker: Yes
Extended test time: Yes
Scribes: Yes
Proctors: Yes
Oral exams: Yes
Note-takers: Yes

Distraction-reduced environment: Yes
Tape recording in class: Yes
Books on tape from RFBD: Yes
Taping of books not from RFBD: No
Accommodations for students with
  ADHD: Yes
Reading machine: No
Other assistive technology: No
Priority registration: Yes

Added costs for services: Yes
LD specialists: Yes
Professional tutors: 3–6
Peer tutors: 10–20
Max. hours/wk. for services: 10
How professors are notified of
  LD/ADHD: By both student and
  director

GENERAL ADMISSIONS INFORMATION

Director of Admissions: Amy Becher
Telephone: 914-337-9300

ENTRANCE REQUIREMENTS

Academic units required: 4 English, 3 math, 2 science (2 science labs), 2 foreign language, 2 social studies, 2 history. High school diploma is required, and GED is accepted. ACT without Writing component accepted. TOEFL required of all international applicants: minimum paper TOEFL 550, minimum computer TOEFL 213.

Application deadline: 3/15
Notification: Rolling
Average GPA: 2.70
ACT Composite middle 50% range:
  17–22

SAT Math middle 50% range:
  410–530
SAT Critical Reading middle 50%
  range: 420–520
SAT Writing middle 50% range: NR

Graduated top 10% of class: 5%
Graduated top 25% of class: 14%
Graduated top 50% of class: 44%

COLLEGE GRADUATION REQUIREMENTS

Course waivers allowed: No
Course substitutions allowed: Yes
In what course: Substitution of American Sign Language for foreign language

ADDITIONAL INFORMATION

Environment: The college is in a suburban area approximately 15 miles north of New York City.

Student Body
  Undergrad enrollment: 587
  Women: 58%
  Men: 42%
  Percent out-of-state: 27%

Cost Information
  Tuition: $20,700
  Room & board: $8,230
Housing Information
  University housing: Yes
  Percent living on campus: 68%

Greek System
  Fraternity: No
  Sorority: No
Athletics: Division II

CORNELL UNIVERSITY

Undergraduate Admissions, 410 Thurston Avenue, Ithaca, NY 14850
Phone: 607-255-5241 • Fax: 607-255-0659
E-mail: admissions@cornell.edu • Web: www.cornell.edu
Support: S • Institution type: 4-year private

LEARNING DISABILITY PROGRAM AND SERVICES

Cornell University is committed to ensuring that students with disabilities have equal access to all university programs and activities. Policy and procedures have been developed to provide students with as much independence as possible, preserve confidentiality, and provide students with disabilities the same exceptional opportunities available to all Cornell students. Student Disability Services (SDS), in concert with the Center for Learning and Teaching, provides a unique, integrated model to serve the needs of students with disabilities. A major goal of SDS is to develop self-advocacy skills for students with disabilities. This consists of having a clear understanding of the disability, an understanding of how the disability affects functioning within the university community, and the ability to communicate this information.

LD/ADHD ADMISSIONS INFORMATION

College entrance tests required: Yes
Interview required: No
Essay recommended: No
Documentation required for LD: Current comprehensive psychoeducational evaluation based on adult norms
Documentation required for ADHD: Current comprehensive psychoeducational evaluation
Submitted to: Student Disability Services
Special Ed. HS course work accepted: Yes

Specific course requirements of all applicants: Yes
Separate application required: No
# of LD applications submitted each year: NR
# of LD applications accepted yearly: NR
Total # of students receiving LD services: 135–160
Acceptance into program means acceptance into college: Students must be admitted to and enrolled in the university first and then request services.

ADMISSIONS

Cornell does not have a special admissions process for students with learning disabilities. All students applying to Cornell are expected to meet admissions criteria. General admission requirements include 16 units of English, math, science, social studies, and foreign language. Each of the seven undergraduate colleges has its own specific requirements. Admission is very competitive and most of the admitted students rank in the top 20 percent of the class, at least, and have taken AP and honors courses in high school. Disability documentation should not be sent along with the admissions application, but should be sent directly to Student Disability Services after acceptance to Cornell.

ADDITIONAL INFORMATION

Students are encouraged to complete a disability self-identification form that is included in acceptance materials. Once Student Disability Services has received current and complete documentation of a disability, it will work with students to determine appropriate accommodations. Diagnostic testing, remedial courses, and tutors specifically selected to work with students with LD are not available at Cornell. The Learning Strategies Center provides general supportive services including classes and workshops in reading comprehension, organizational skills, note-taking, and exam preparation. The Learning Strategies Center is open to all students.

LEARNING DISABILITY PROGRAM/SERVICES

Learning Disability Program/Services: Student Disability Services
Director: Katherine Fahey
  E-mail: clt_sds@cornell.edu
  Telephone: 607-254-4545
  Fax: 607-255-1562
Contact Person: Katherine Fahey/Michele Fish
  E-mail: clt_sds@cornell.edu
  Telephone: 607-254-4545
  Fax: 607-255-1562

LEARNING DISABILITY SERVICES

Requests for the following services/accommodations will be evaluated individually based on appropriate and current documentation.

Allowed in exams	**Distraction-reduced environment:** Yes	**Added costs for services:** No
Calculator: Yes	**Tape recording in class:** Yes	**LD specialists:** No
Dictionary: Yes	**Books on tape from RFBD:** Yes	**Professional tutors:** No
Computer: Yes	**Taping of books not from RFBD:** Yes	**Peer tutors:** Yes
Spellchecker: Yes	**Accommodations for students with**	**Max. hours/wk. for services:**
Extended test time: Yes	**ADHD:** Yes	Unlimited
Scribes: Yes	**Reading machine:** No	**How professors are notified of**
Proctors: Yes	**Other assistive technology:** Yes	**LD/ADHD:** By student
Oral exams: No	**Priority registration:** No	
Note-takers: Yes		

GENERAL ADMISSIONS INFORMATION

Director of Admissions: Jason Locke
Telephone: 607-255-5241

ENTRANCE REQUIREMENTS

Academic units required: 4 English, 3 math. **Academic units recommended:** 3 science (3 science labs), 3 foreign language, 3 social studies, 3 history. High school diploma or equivalent is not required. ACT with Writing component required. TOEFL required of all international applicants: minimum paper TOEFL 550, minimum computer TOEFL 250.

Application deadline: 1/1	**SAT Math middle 50% range:**	**Graduated top 10% of class:** 84%
Notification: 4/1	660–760	**Graduated top 25% of class:** 97%
Average GPA: NR	**SAT Critical Reading middle 50%**	**Graduated top 50% of class:** 100%
ACT Composite middle 50% range:	**range:** 620–730	
28–32	**SAT Writing middle 50% range:** NR	

COLLEGE GRADUATION REQUIREMENTS

Course waivers allowed: No
Course substitutions allowed: Yes
In what course: Foreign language

ADDITIONAL INFORMATION

Environment: Cornell is located 45 minutes from Syracuse on the southern end of Lake Cayuga in the Finger Lakes region.

Student Body	**Cost Information**	**Greek System**
Undergrad enrollment: 13,523	**Tuition:** $32,800	**Fraternity:** Yes
Women: 49%	**Room & board:** $10,776	**Sorority:** Yes
Men: 51%	**Housing Information**	**Athletics:** Division I
Percent out-of-state: 62%	**University housing:** Yes	
	Percent living on campus: 46%	

Cornell University

DOWLING COLLEGE

Idle Hour Boulevard, Oakdale, NY 11769-1999
Phone: 800-369-5464 • Fax: 631-563-3827
E-mail: admissions@dowling.edu • Web: www.dowling.edu
Support: SP • Institution type: 4-year private

LEARNING DISABILITY PROGRAM AND SERVICES

Dowling College's Program for College Students with Learning Disabilities is a small, individualized program that provides for cognitive development. The college is looking for students who are committed to life-long learning who have taken academically demanding courses in high school. They seek students who are eager and willing to persevere to achieve their goals. Additionally, students need to be interested and involved in community and extracurricular activities. There is a fee of $1,500 per semester for services from the LD program. Students must submit a recent psychoevaluation and an IEP to be eligible to receive services or accommodations. Students are encouraged to make sure that their IEP includes all of the necessary accommodations. Students sign a contract promising to attend tutoring sessions and all of their classes. Services are available all 4 years.

LD/ADHD ADMISSIONS INFORMATION

College entrance tests required: Yes
Interview required: No
Essay recommended: No
Documentation required for LD: Psychological evaluation and an IEP
Documentation required for ADHD: Yes
Submitted to: Admissions
Special Ed. HS course work accepted: NR

Specific course requirements of all applicants: NR
Separate application required: Yes
# of LD applications submitted each year: 20
# of LD applications accepted yearly: 6–11
Total # of students receiving LD services: 25
Acceptance into program means acceptance into college: Students must be admitted to and enrolled in the university first and then request services.

ADMISSIONS

Students must be admitted to Dowling College first and then may request an application to the Program for College Students with LD. Applicants to Dowling College are encouraged to submit either the ACT or SAT. Students should have 16 academic courses in high school, including 4 years of English. Students are encouraged to have an interview. Once a student with LD has been admitted to the college, they may submit an application to the LD program. Both student and parent are required to complete an application. Students must submit their most recent IEP and psychoeducational evaluation. An interview is required, and the LD program director looks for students with tenacity and motivation. Approximately 25 students are admitted to the program each year.

ADDITIONAL INFORMATION

The Program for Students with Learning Disabilities offers support services in word processing and language development, a liaison between professors and students, weekly writing workshops, and a freshman college orientation for course requirements geared to the specific needs of students with LD. There is no Learning Resource Center, but students have access to tutors who are available in the library. Tutors are trained to provide academic support. There is a lab school at which students with learning disabilities may receive special tutoring two times a week in learning strategies. Students are eligible to receive all accommodations or services that are listed in their most recent IEP. The Hausman Center will arrange reasonable accommodations that will not compromise academic standards and will provide services such as extended time for tests, NCR paper available, proctored exams, and scribes; work with the Suffolk Cooperative Library System for access to books and tapes; and liaison with outside agencies, professors, and other college offices.

LEARNING DISABILITY PROGRAM/SERVICES

Learning Disability Program/Services: Program for College Students with Learning Disabilities
Director: Dr. Dorothy Stracher
  E-mail: Strached@dowling.edu
  Telephone: 631-244-3306
  Fax: 631-244-5036

LEARNING DISABILITY SERVICES

Requests for the following services/accommodations will be evaluated individually based on appropriate and current documentation.

Allowed in exams
  Calculator: Yes
  Dictionary: Yes
  Computer: Yes
  Spellchecker: Yes
Extended test time: Yes
Scribes: Yes
Proctors: Yes
Oral exams: Yes
Note-takers: Yes

Distraction-reduced environment: Yes
Tape recording in class: Yes
Books on tape from RFBD: Yes
Taping of books not from RFBD: Yes
Accommodations for students with ADHD: Yes
Reading machine: Yes
Other assistive technology: Yes
Priority registration: Yes

Added costs for services: Yes
LD specialists: Yes
Professional tutors: 25
Peer tutors: No
Max. hours/wk. for services: Unlimited
How professors are notified of LD/ADHD: By director

GENERAL ADMISSIONS INFORMATION

Director of Admissions: Bridget Mastruzo
Telephone: 631-244-3436

ENTRANCE REQUIREMENTS
Academic units recommended: 4 English, 3 math, 2 science, 3 social studies, 4 electives. High school diploma is required, and GED is accepted.

Application deadline: Rolling
Notification: Rolling
Average GPA: 2.80
ACT Composite middle 50% range: NR

SAT Math middle 50% range: 410–520
SAT Critical Reading middle 50% range: 410–520
SAT Writing middle 50% range: NR

Graduated top 10% of class: 6%
Graduated top 25% of class: 19%
Graduated top 50% of class: 50%

COLLEGE GRADUATION REQUIREMENTS

Course waivers allowed: Yes
In what course: Foreign language
Course substitutions allowed: Yes
In what course: Foreign language

ADDITIONAL INFORMATION

Environment: The university is located 50 miles from New York City.

Student Body
  Undergrad enrollment: 3,627
  Women: 61%
  Men: 39%
  Percent out-of-state: 10%

Cost Information
  Tuition: $14,529
  Room & board: $8,998
Housing Information
  University housing: Yes
  Percent living on campus: 17%

Greek System
  Fraternity: No
  Sorority: No
Athletics: Division II

HOFSTRA UNIVERSITY

Admissions Center, Bernon Hall, Hempstead, NY 11549
Phone: 516-463-6700 • Fax: 516-463-5100
E-mail: admitme@hofstra.edu • Web: www.hofstra.edu
Support: SP • Institution type: 4-year private

LEARNING DISABILITY PROGRAM AND SERVICES

The Program for Academic Learning Skills (PALS) seeks candidates who have been diagnosed with LD and show above-average intellectual ability and emotional stability. The program concentrates on identifying qualified applicants for entrance to the university and on enhancing the skills that will help students achieve academic success. This program is part of the Division of Special Studies. Normally, candidates will be accepted into PALS for a period of 1 academic year. In the first semester, students enroll in courses offered through DSS, and in the second semester, they enroll in regular Hofstra classes. In addition, among applicants not acceptable through regular admissions, PALS seeks candidates with substantially higher than average intellectual ability and emotional stability who are willing to work hard and are socially mature, but who have experienced a variety of learning disabilities. These may be demonstrated by problems in oral and written language expression that reflect linguistic and semantic confusions and problems with organizational skills that are demonstrated by disorientations in space and time. These problems contribute to deficiencies in listening, reading, writing, and problem solving as they relate to academic achievement. PALS believes that these difficulties do not always stand in the way of academic success, nor should they stand in the way of entrance to a university community. The School for University Studies, therefore, concentrates on selecting the best applicants and on enhancing the skills that will help them achieve academic success at Hofstra University.

LD/ADHD ADMISSIONS INFORMATION

College entrance tests required: No
Interview required: Yes
Essay recommended: No
Documentation required for LD: WAIS–III, completed within the past year; achievement testing; full psychoeducational report with a diagnostic statement
Documentation required for ADHD: Yes
Submitted to: Admissions
Special Ed. HS course work accepted: NR

Specific course requirements of all applicants: NR
Separate application required: No
# of LD applications submitted each year: 293
# of LD applications accepted yearly: 96
Total # of students receiving LD services: 71
Acceptance into program means acceptance into college: Students who are admitted to PALS are automatically admitted to the university.

ADMISSIONS

Students with LD who are not admissible as regular students are invited to interview and may be offered admission to PALS. The Division of Special Studies, which administers PALS, has always conducted a highly individualized admissions process. Students with LD who may be in the bottom 30 percent of their high school class and have an 800–850 SAT may be eligible for the PALS program. The interview is very important, and students may be asked to write an essay at this time. Only 18 of the 100 students accepted into the Division of Special Studies are learning disabled. PALS is looking for students who have self-knowledge and understanding of their strengths and weaknesses, as well as a willingness to work hard. There are no specific high school course requirements for PALS. In cooperation with the Admissions Office, candidates are encouraged to apply for admission for the fall semester. Admission decisions are made jointly by PALS and the Office of Admissions. Only in exceptional cases will applicants be admitted midyear.

ADDITIONAL INFORMATION

Students with LD who are not admissible as regular students are invited to interview, and there are course waivers available. The university prefers, however, to substitute courses where possible. Once admitted, the student meets with a specialist two times a week, and information regarding progress is shared with the student's family. Basic skills courses are offered in spelling, learning strategies, study strategies, time management, written language, and social skills. Accommodations available to LD students (non-PALS) include time extensions on exams, access to quiet locations for exams, assistance with contracting classmates for note-taking, access to a computer lab for creating papers and taking exams, computer technology (voice-activation, PCs, electronic readers), and notification to professors of accommodations (on request). Currently content tutoring is not available through PALS, but is available for all students through the university's tutoring center.

LEARNING DISABILITY PROGRAM/SERVICES

Learning Disability Program/Services: Program for Academic Learning Skills (PALS)
E-mail: Diane.Herbert@hofstra.edu
Telephone: 516-463-5761
Fax: 516-463-4049

LEARNING DISABILITY SERVICES

Requests for the following services/accommodations will be evaluated individually based on appropriate and current documentation.

Allowed in exams
  Calculator: Yes
  Dictionary: Yes
  Computer: Yes
  Spellchecker: Yes
Extended test time: Yes
Scribes: Yes
Proctors: Yes
Oral exams: Yes
Note-takers: No

Distraction-reduced environment: Yes
Tape recording in class: No
Books on tape from RFBD: No
Taping of books not from RFBD: No
Accommodations for students with
  ADHD: Yes
Reading machine: Yes
Other assistive technology: Yes
Priority registration: No

Added costs for services: Yes
LD specialists: Yes
Professional tutors: No
Peer tutors: No
Max. hours/wk. for services:
  Unlimited
How professors are notified of
  LD/ADHD: By both student and
  director

GENERAL ADMISSIONS INFORMATION

Director of Admissions: Jessica Eads
Telephone: 516-463-6710

ENTRANCE REQUIREMENTS

Academic units required: 4 English, 3 math, 3 science (1 science lab), 2 foreign language, 3 social studies.
Academic units recommended: 4 math, 4 science (2 science labs), 3 foreign language, 4 social studies. High school diploma is required, and GED is accepted. ACT with Writing component required. TOEFL required of all international applicants: minimum paper TOEFL 550, minimum computer TOEFL 213.

Application deadline: NR
Notification: Rolling
Average GPA: 3.26
ACT Composite middle 50% range:
  22–26

SAT Math middle 50% range:
  550–630
**SAT Critical Reading middle 50%
  range:** 530–620
SAT Writing middle 50% range: NR

Graduated top 10% of class: 23%
Graduated top 25% of class: 46%
Graduated top 50% of class: 80%

COLLEGE GRADUATION REQUIREMENTS

Course waivers allowed: No
Course substitutions allowed: Yes
In what course: Students requesting accommodations for foreign language requirements must meet with the PALS director soon after beginning their first semester.

ADDITIONAL INFORMATION

Environment: Hempstead is a residential community in Long Island just outside New York City.

Student Body
  Undergrad enrollment: 8,383
  Women: 53%
  Men: 47%
  Percent out-of-state: 32%

Cost Information
  Tuition: $23,800
  Room & board: $9,800
Housing Information
  University housing: Yes
  Percent living on campus: 47%

Greek System
  Fraternity: Yes
  Sorority: Yes
  Athletics: Division I

IONA COLLEGE

715 North Avenue, New Rochelle, NY 10801
Phone: 914-633-2502 • Fax: 914-633-2642
E-mail: icad@iona.edu • Web: www.iona.edu
Support: SP • Institution type: 4-year private

LEARNING DISABILITY PROGRAM AND SERVICES

The College Assistance Program (CAP) offers comprehensive support and services for students with LD/ADHD. CAP is designed to encourage success by providing instruction tailored to individual strengths and needs. Students take standard full-time course requirements to ensure the level of quality education expected of all degree candidates. Professional tutors teach individually appropriate strategies that cross disciplines. CAP staff encourages students to become involved members of the college community. All CAP freshmen must participate in a 3-week summer orientation. During the orientation, the staff instructs and guides students in intensive writing instruction and study and organizational and time management skills; students are oriented to the college and services; individual learning styles are explored; opportunities are provided for the students to practice self-advocacy; several workshops are offered in areas that meet the student's specific needs; and individual fall classes are developed. Semester services include supplementary advisement, counseling, regularly scheduled weekly skill-based tutoring with an LD professional, study groups, skills workshops, and provision of appropriate documented accommodations.

LD/ADHD ADMISSIONS INFORMATION

College entrance tests required: Yes
Interview required: Yes
Essay recommended: No
Documentation required for LD: A complete psychoeducational report including aptitude and achievement testing performed within the past 2 years
Documentation required for ADHD: Students should have a complete psychoeducational report that includes aptitude and achievement testing to rule out or address learning disabilities. In addition, reports should include diagnostic testing results and interpretation demonstrating attention deficit hyperactivity disorder.

Submitted to: College Assistance Program
Special Ed. HS course work accepted: No
Specific course requirements of all applicants: Yes
Separate application required: No
# of LD applications submitted each year: 150–250
# of LD applications accepted yearly: 15–20
Total # of students receiving LD services: 60–70
Acceptance into program means acceptance into college: Students must be admitted and enrolled at the college first and then may request admission to CAP.

ADMISSIONS

All applicants must meet the same admission criteria, which include 4 years of English, 1 year of American history, 1 year of social studies, 2 years of a foreign language (waivers granted), 1 year of natural science, and 3 years of math. Students should send the following to the CAP office: a complete psychological evaluation conducted within the past 2 years that includes the WAIS–III or WAIS–R subtest scores, a comprehensive report, a copy of the most recent IEP, and two letters of recommendation (one from an LD instructor). A personal interview is required. CAP is designed for students with LD and ADHD who have been mainstreamed in their academic courses in high school. Students should be average or above average in intellectual ability, socially mature, emotionally stable, and motivated to work hard.

ADDITIONAL INFORMATION

CAP services include a freshman summer college transition program, supplementary academic advising and program planning based on each student's learning style, priority registration, 2 hours per week of scheduled skill-based individual tutoring with a professional learning specialist (additional tutoring sessions are possible), small group tutoring and workshops, testing accommodations, alternative testing procedures, special equipment, self-advocacy training, referrals to additional services on campus, and counseling services. The CAP director works with faculty to help them understand the problems faced by students with LD and explore creative ways to support the learning process. The Samuel Rudin Academic Resource Center (ARC) offers free services to all students who wish to improve their learning skills or who want academic support. ARC provides free reasonable services to all students with documented LD/ADHD.

LEARNING DISABILITY PROGRAM/SERVICES

Learning Disability Program/Services: College Assistance Program (CAP)
Director: Linda Refsland
 E-mail: LRefsland@iona.edu
 Telephone: 914-633-2159
 Fax: 914-633-2011
Contact Person: Linda Robertello
 E-mail: LRefsland@iona.edu
 Telephone: 914-633-2582
 Fax: 914-633-2011

LEARNING DISABILITY SERVICES

Requests for the following services/accommodations will be evaluated individually based on appropriate and current documentation.

Allowed in exams
 Calculator: Yes
 Dictionary: Yes
 Computer: Yes
 Spellchecker: Yes
Extended test time: Yes
Scribes: Yes
Proctors: Yes
Oral exams: No
Note-takers: Yes

Distraction-reduced environment: Yes
Tape recording in class: Yes
Books on tape from RFBD: Yes
Taping of books not from RFBD: Yes
Accommodations for students with
 ADHD: Yes
Reading machine: Yes
Other assistive technology: Yes
Priority registration: Yes

Added costs for services: Yes
LD specialists: Yes
Professional tutors: 10
Peer tutors: No
Max. hours/wk. for services:
 Unlimited
How professors are notified of
 LD/ADHD: By both student and
 director

GENERAL ADMISSIONS INFORMATION

Director of Admissions: Thomas Weede
Telephone: 914-633-2120

ENTRANCE REQUIREMENTS

Academic units required: 4 English, 3 math, 2 science (2 science labs), 2 foreign language, 1 social studies, 1 history, 1 academic elective. **Academic units recommended:** 4 English, 4 math, 3 science (2 science labs), 2 foreign language, 2 social studies, 2 history, 3 academic electives. High school diploma is required, and GED is accepted. ACT with or without Writing component accepted. TOEFL required of all international applicants: minimum paper TOEFL 550, minimum computer TOEFL 213.

Application deadline: 2/15
Notification: 3/20
Average GPA: 3.40
ACT middle 50% range: NR

SAT Math middle 50% range:
 530–620
SAT Critical Reading middle 50%
 range: 520–620
SAT Writing middle 50% range: NR

Graduated top 10% of class: 31%
Graduated top 25% of class: 54%
Graduated top 50% of class: 93%

COLLEGE GRADUATION REQUIREMENTS

Course waivers allowed: No
Course substitutions allowed: Yes
In what course: Foreign language

ADDITIONAL INFORMATION

Environment: The college is located on 56 acres 20 miles northeast of New York City.

Student Body
 Undergrad enrollment: 3,407
 Women: 55%
 Men: 45%
 Percent out-of-state: 20%

Cost Information
 Tuition: $21,518
 Room & board: $9,998
Housing Information
 University housing: Yes
 Percent living on campus: 30%

Greek System
 Fraternity: Yes
 Sorority: Yes
Athletics: Division I

Iona College

KEUKA COLLEGE

Office of Admissions, Keuka Park, NY 14478 -0098
Phone: 315-279-5254 • Fax: 315-536-5386
E-mail: admissions@mail.keuka.edu • Web: www.keuka.edu
Support: CS • Institution type: 4-year private

LEARNING DISABILITY PROGRAM AND SERVICES

The Academic Support Program will assist students in becoming competent, independent learners able to achieve their maximum potential in academic endeavors. Students with documented disabilities who are admitted and enrolled are encouraged to request services either in advance of the new semester or immediately at the beginning of the semester. Every effort is made to provide services and accommodations as quickly and appropriately as possible. It is the student's responsibility to contact the Academic Support Program Office. The coordinator will meet with the student and review the documentation to create a plan of services and accommodations. The provision of services will be based on the specific diagnoses and recommendations of the professional performing the assessments. Students are encouraged to ensure that the diagnoses and all recommendations for accommodations are clearly stated within the report. Students who are eligible for testing accommodations will be required to make these arrangements with the professor prior to every test of the semester, as well as signing up for each test with the Academic Support Program Office.

LD/ADHD ADMISSIONS INFORMATION

College entrance tests required: No
Interview required: No
Essay recommended: No
Documentation required for LD: Psychoeducational evaluation
Documentation required for ADHD: Evaluation from a medical doctor
Submitted to: Academic Support Program
Special Ed. HS course work accepted: Yes
Specific course requirements of all applicants: NR

Separate application required: No
# of LD applications submitted each year: NR
# of LD applications accepted yearly: NR
Total # of students receiving LD services: 86
Acceptance into program means acceptance into college: Students must be admitted to and enrolled in the university first and then request services.

ADMISSIONS

There is no special admissions process available, and all students are expected to meet the general admission criteria. Students are expected to rank in the top 50 percent of their high school class and have a minimum 2.8 GPA. Course requirements include 4 years of English, 3 years of history, 1 year of social studies, 2–3 years of math and science, and 2 years of a foreign language. An essay is required, and a campus visit and an interview is recommended.

ADDITIONAL INFORMATION

The provision of support is based on the specific diagnosis and recommendations of the professional performing the assessments. Examples of some support services offered by the Academic Support Program are testing accommodations, tutors (group and individual), individual appointments with professional staff members, career counseling, and books on tape. Workshops for all students are offered in note-taking strategies, testing strategies, and time management and study skills. A coaching program for students with ADHD is also offered. Students are encouraged to request services either in advance of the new semester or immediately at the beginning of the semester.

LEARNING DISABILITY PROGRAM/SERVICES

Learning Disability Program/Services: Academic Support Program
Director: Carole K. Lillis
  E-mail: clillis@mail.keuka.edu
  Telephone: 315-279-5636
  Fax: 315-279-5626
Contact Person: Jennifer Robinson
  E-mail: clillis@mail.keuka.edu
  Telephone: 315-279-5636
  Fax: 315-279-5626

LEARNING DISABILITY SERVICES

Requests for the following services/accommodations will be evaluated individually based on appropriate and current documentation.

Allowed in exams
  Calculator: Yes
  Dictionary: Yes
  Computer: Yes
  Spellchecker: Yes
Extended test time: Yes
Scribes: Yes
Proctors: Yes
Oral exams: Yes
Note-takers: Yes

Distraction-reduced environment: Yes
Tape recording in class: Yes
Books on tape from RFBD: Yes
Taping of books not from RFBD: Yes
Accommodations for students with
  ADHD: Yes
Reading machine: Yes
Other assistive technology: Yes
Priority registration: Yes

Added costs for services: No
LD specialists: Yes
Professional tutors: 3
Peer tutors: 40
Max. hours/wk. for services: No
How professors are notified of
  LD/ADHD: By student

GENERAL ADMISSIONS INFORMATION

Director of Admissions: Carolanne Marquis, Vice President of Keuka College
Telephone: 315-279-5262

ENTRANCE REQUIREMENTS
Academic units recommended: 4 English, 3 math, 3 science (2 science labs), 3 foreign language, 1 social studies, 2 history. High school diploma is required, and GED is accepted. ACT with or without Writing component accepted. TOEFL required of all international applicants: minimum paper TOEFL 500, minimum computer TOEFL 300.

Application deadline: NR
Notification: Rolling
Average GPA: 3.00
ACT Composite middle 50% range:
  NR

SAT Math middle 50% range:
  425–540
SAT Critical Reading middle 50%
  range: 410–520
SAT Writing middle 50% range: NR

Graduated top 10% of class: 5%
Graduated top 25% of class: 22%
Graduated top 50% of class: 58%

COLLEGE GRADUATION REQUIREMENTS

Course waivers allowed: No
Course substitutions allowed: Yes
In what course: When appropiate and agreed on by the student, instructor, division chair, and registrar.

ADDITIONAL INFORMATION

Environment: The college is located 50 miles from Rochester.

Student Body
  Undergrad enrollment: 1,369
  Women: 70%
  Men: 30%
  Percent out-of-state: 6%

Cost Information
  Tuition: $18,850
  Room & board: $8,210
Housing Information
  University housing: Yes
  Percent living on campus: 81%

Greek System
  Fraternity: No
  Sorority: No
Athletics: Division III

LONG ISLAND U.—C.W. POST

720 Northern Boulevard, Brookville, NY 11548
Phone: 516-299-2900 • Fax: 516-299-2137
E-mail: enroll@cwpost.liu.edu • Web: www.liu.edu
Support: SP • Institution type: 4-year private

LEARNING DISABILITY PROGRAM AND SERVICES

The Academic Resource Center (ARC) is a comprehensive support program designed for students with learning disabilities to help them achieve their academic potential in a university setting. The objective is to encourage students to become independent learners and self-advocates. Students participate in mainstream college courses and assume full responsibility for attendance in class and at the ARC. Students work with learning assistants on a one-on-one basis. Graduate assistants are students enrolled in the School of Education who are pursuing master's degrees. The graduate assistants help students make the transition from high school to college. They assist students in time management, organizational skills, note-taking techniques, study skills, and other learning strategies. Students are responsible for attendance and participation in meetings with the learning assistants. ARC staff communicates with professors, and students are tutored by learning assistants. Students learn time management, reading, study and test-taking strategies, organizational skills, and note-taking techniques. The ARC provides an environment that helps students demonstrate positive attitudes toward themselves and learning.

LD/ADHD ADMISSIONS INFORMATION

College entrance tests required: Yes
Interview required: Yes
Essay recommended: Yes
Documentation required for LD: WAIS–III completed within the past 3 years, an IEP, and any other relevant testing (e.g., WJ–III)
Documentation required for ADHD: In addition to the above documents, the student must submit a report from a neuropsychologist/neuropsychiatrist that clearly diagnoses ADHD. Testing must no older than 3 years.
Submitted to: Academic Resource Center
Special Ed. HS course work accepted: Yes

Specific course requirements of all applicants: NR
Separate application required: Yes
# of LD applications submitted each year: 200
# of LD applications accepted yearly: 50–60
Total # of students receiving LD services: 85–125
Acceptance into program means acceptance into college: Students must be admitted to and enrolled in the university first and then request services.

ADMISSIONS

Acceptance into the university is separate and distinct from acceptance into the ARC. Students admitted to the university and who identify themselves as learning disabled are sent information and an application to apply to the ARC. Applications must include a diagnostic evaluation describing the specific LD, WAIS-R, and a handwritten essay indicating why the student is requesting admittance into the ARC. Once all of the information is on file, the student will be invited to interview. This interview is an integral part of the admission process. Some students may be admitted through the General Studies Program if their GPA or test scores are low. During an interview, students must convince the admissions counselor that they have changed and are now willing to focus on studies. Motivation is very important. Students with an SAT below 800 or a Verbal score below 450 are required to have either a B-minus average or 400 Math SAT. If students have a deficiency, the people responsible for testing must write letters stating what specifically in the test data indicates the students should be granted a waiver.

ADDITIONAL INFORMATION

Ancillary services include note-takers in individual course lectures, subject tutors, proctors, assistance securing books on tape, amanuensis for test-taking, audio and video tapes to supplement learning, assistance with planning and scheduling classes, study and social skills workshops, and a mentor program. Other services include individualized learning strategies on a one-on-one basis two times a week, extended time and readers for exams, academic advisement and faculty liaisons, and assistance in formulating an overall plan and structure when approaching an assignment. The program is a 4-year program, but the majority of students opt to handle their own class work at the end of their sophomore year. Freshmen are limited to taking only 12 credits for their first semester, and all must enroll in a freshman seminar. There are no special or remedial classes.

LEARNING DISABILITY PROGRAM/SERVICES

Learning Disability Program/Services: Academic Resource Center
Director: Susan Rock
   E-mail: srock@liu.edu
   Telephone: 516-299-3057
   Fax: 516-299-2126

LEARNING DISABILITY SERVICES

Requests for the following services/accommodations will be evaluated individually based on appropriate and current documentation.

Allowed in exams
   Calculator: Yes
   Dictionary: Yes
   Computer: Yes
   Spellchecker: Yes
Extended test time: Yes
Scribes: Yes
Proctors: Yes
Oral exams: NR
Note-takers: Yes

Distraction-reduced environment: Yes
Tape recording in class: Yes
Books on tape from RFBD: Yes
Taping of books not from RFBD: Yes
Accommodations for students with ADHD: Yes
Reading machine: Yes
Other assistive technology: Yes
Priority registration: No

Added costs for services: Yes
LD specialists: Yes
Professional tutors: 15–20
Peer tutors: 10
Max. hours/wk. for services: Unlimited
How professors are notified of LD/ADHD: By both student and director

GENERAL ADMISSIONS INFORMATION

Director of Admissions: Beth Carson
Telephone: 516-299-2900

ENTRANCE REQUIREMENTS

Academic units required: 4 English, 2 math, 2 science (2 science labs), 2 foreign language, 3 social studies, 1 academic elective. **Academic units recommended:** 4 English, 4 math, 4 science (4 science labs), 4 foreign language, 4 social studies. High school diploma is required, and GED is accepted. TOEFL required of all international applicants: minimum paper TOEFL 500.

Application deadline: Rolling
Notification: Rolling
Average GPA: 3.00
ACT Composite middle 50% range: NR

SAT Math middle 50% range: 500–600
SAT Critical Reading middle 50% range: 500–550
SAT Writing middle 50% range: NR

Graduated top 10% of class: 10%
Graduated top 25% of class: 26%
Graduated top 50% of class: 61%

COLLEGE GRADUATION REQUIREMENTS

Course waivers allowed: Yes
In what course: A specific computer course can be taken to staisfy the core math requirement. English 7 and 8 (anthology courses) can be taken instead of a foreign language. These are for core requirements only.
Course substitutions allowed: Yes
In what course: A specific computer course can be taken to staisfy the core math requirement. English 7 and 8 (anthology courses) can be taken instead of a foreign language. These are for core requirements only.

ADDITIONAL INFORMATION

Environment: The college is located in Long Island, about 30 minutes from New York City.

Student Body
   Undergrad enrollment: 5,748
   Women: 57%
   Men: 43%
   Percent out-of-state: 6%

Cost Information
   Tuition: $23,370
   Room & board: $9,100
Housing Information
   University housing: Yes
   Percent living on campus: 37%

Greek System
   Fraternity: Yes
   Sorority: Yes
Athletics: Division II

MANHATTANVILLE COLLEGE

2900 Purchase Street, Admissions Office, Purchase, NY 10577
Phone: 914-323-5124 • Fax: 914-694-1732
E-mail: admissions@mville.edu • Web: www.mville.edu
Support: SP • Institution type: 4-year private

LEARNING DISABILITY PROGRAM AND SERVICES

The Higher Education Learning Program (HELP) is designed to help motivated and committed students with learning disabilities successfully meet the academic challenge of the college experience. HELP offers a range of support services for students with learning disabilities throughout their years of college. HELP remains focused on instruction and applications of compensatory strategies to college content courses. HELP offers a credit-bearing writing course; it is specifically designed for students with learning disabilities and fulfills the college's writing requirement. Students in HELP, as well as all students at the college, are entitled to reasonable accommodations and modifications. Students in HELP are assisted by tutors in developing those advocacy skills needed to secure accommodations and modifications.

LD/ADHD ADMISSIONS INFORMATION

College entrance tests required: Yes
Interview required: No
Essay recommended: No
Documentation required for LD: A psychoeducational diagnosis or neuropsychological report completed within the past 5 years
Documentation required for ADHD: A psychoeducational diagnosis or neuropsychological report completed within the past 5 years
Submitted to: HELP
Special Ed. HS course work accepted: NR

Specific course requirements of all applicants: Yes
Separate application required: No
# of LD applications submitted each year: NR
# of LD applications accepted yearly: NR
Total # of students receiving LD services: 85
Acceptance into program means acceptance into college: Admission is a joint decision between the Office of Admissions and HELP, but students are admitted to the college first then the program.

ADMISSIONS
Applicants must meet the requirements for general admission. These criteria include 3.0 GPA and 4 years of English, 2 years of math, 2 years of science, 2 years of a foreign language, and 2 years of history. The average ACT is 24, and the average for the SAT is 1015. Applicants must also submit diagnostic testing identifying the learning disability.

ADDITIONAL INFORMATION
The core of the program is one-on-one tutoring in learning strategies directly applicable to course work. Services are individualized to accommodate the specific needs of each student and are coordinated and implemented by trained learning disabilities professionals.

LEARNING DISABILITY PROGRAM/SERVICES

Learning Disability Program/Services: Higher Education Learning Program
Director: Jean Baldassare
  E-mail: Baldassarej@mville.edu
  Telephone: 914-323-3186
  Fax: 914-798-2764

LEARNING DISABILITY SERVICES

Requests for the following services/accommodations will be evaluated individually based on appropriate and current documentation.

Allowed in exams
  Calculator: Yes
  Dictionary: NR
  Computer: Yes
  Spellchecker: NR
Extended test time: Yes
Scribes: Yes
Proctors: Yes
Oral exams: Yes
Note-takers: No

Distraction-reduced environment: Yes
Tape recording in class: Yes
Books on tape from RFBD: Yes
Taping of books not from RFBD: Yes
Accommodations for students with ADHD: Yes
Reading machine: Yes
Other assistive technology: NR
Priority registration: No

Added costs for services: Yes
LD specialists: Yes
Professional tutors: 7–10
Peer tutors: Yes
Max. hours/wk. for services: 3
How professors are notified of LD/ADHD: By both student and director

GENERAL ADMISSIONS INFORMATION

Director of Admissions: Erica Padilla
Telephone: 914-323-5124

ENTRANCE REQUIREMENTS
Academic units required: 4 English, 2 math, 2 science, 2 social studies, 2 foreign language, 5 academic electives. High school diploma is required, and GED is accepted. TOEFL required of all international applicants: minimum paper TOEFL 550, minimum computer TOEFL 217.

Application deadline: 3/1
Notification: Rolling
Average GPA: 3.0
ACT Composite middle 50% range: 20–25

SAT Math middle 50% range: 500–610
SAT Critical Reading middle 50% range: 500–620
SAT Writing middle 50% range: NR

Graduated top 10% of class: 21%
Graduated top 25% of class: 47%
Graduated top 50% of class: 80%

COLLEGE GRADUATION REQUIREMENTS

Course waivers allowed: No
Course substitutions allowed: No

ADDITIONAL INFORMATION

Environment: The college is located on a 100-acre campus in a suburban area 25 miles north of New York City.

Student Body
  Undergrad enrollment: 1,762
  Women: 67%
  Men: 33%
  Percent out-of-state: 36%

Cost Information
  Tuition: $28,540
  Room & board: $12,240
Housing Information
  University housing: Yes
  Percent living on campus: 80%

Greek System
  Fraternity: No
  Sorority: No
  Athletics: Division III

MARIST COLLEGE

3399 North Road, Poughkeepsie, NY 12601-1387
Phone: 845-575-3226 • Fax: 845-575-3215
E-mail: admissions@marist.edu • Web: www.marist.edu
Support: SP • Institution type: 4-year private

LEARNING DISABILITY PROGRAM AND SERVICES

Marist College believes that bright, motivated students with specific learning disabilities are more similar than they are different from other college students and can achieve a higher education. Marist offers a program of support for students with learning disabilities through the Learning Disabilities Program. Students receive a complement of academic services designed to meet individual needs. The program focuses on the development and use of strategies to promote independence and personal success. The philosophy of the program does not emphasize remediation but rather the development of compensatory strategies. Each student is enrolled in credit-bearing courses and completes the same degree requirements as all students. Program staff work closely with faculty and administration, and students are encouraged to discuss their learning disabilities with faculty. The goal is for each student to achieve the maximum level of independence possible and become an effective self-advocate. Participation in the program is available on a continual basis for as long as the LD specialist and the student agree is necessary.

LD/ADHD ADMISSIONS INFORMATION

College entrance tests required: Yes
Interview required: Yes
Essay recommended: Yes
Documentation required for LD: Psychoeducation evaluation
Documentation required for ADHD: Yes
Submitted to: Learning Disabilities Program
Special Ed. HS course work accepted: No

Specific course requirements of all applicants: NR
Separate application required: Yes
# of LD applications submitted each year: 200
# of LD applications accepted yearly: 50
Total # of students receiving LD services: 70
Acceptance into program means acceptance into college: Students are admitted jointly into the college and the LD program.

ADMISSIONS

Students with LD must submit an application for admission and all required materials to the Office of Admissions. A supplementary application for the LD support program must also be completed and sent directly to the OSS. Additionally, students must submit to the OSS the results of the WAIS–R, including subtest scores; their calculated IQ and an accompanying narrative; achievement testing with current levels of functioning in reading, mathematics, and written language; an unedited essay describing the impact of the LD on academic achievement; and a $20 fee. ACT/SAT scores are required of students with LD. After applications have been reviewed, those most qualified and suited to the program will be invited to interview. Students accepted into the program should have an acceptance and understanding of their LD; know their academic strengths and weaknesses; have taken college-prep courses; provide recommendations that communicate strengths, motivation to succeed, and willingness to accept and access supports; and have sound study skills and work habits. Admission to the program is competitive, and students are encouraged to apply early. There is no early decision option.

ADDITIONAL INFORMATION

Upon enrollment students, complete a comprehensive survey of their abilities and attitudes toward academics. This survey is combined with diagnostic evaluations and the comprehensive record of students' performance to develop an individual support service plan. Students meet an LD specialist two times a week and typically concentrate on writing skills, note-taking, organizational skills, study skills, and testing strategies. Accommodations may include adaptive testing procedures, note-takers/tape recorders, scribes, taped textbooks/personal readers, and use of adaptive equipment. A program fee is charged only for the services of the learning specialist. Students in the program also have access to content tutors and a counselor who can address academic, career, and personal issues. Services and accommodations are available for undergraduate and graduate students.

LEARNING DISABILITY PROGRAM/SERVICES

Learning Disability Program/Services: Office of Special Services(OSS)/ Learning Disabilities Program
Director: Linda Cooper
  E-mail: SpecServ@marist.edu
  Telephone: 845-575-3274
  Fax: 845-575-3011
Contact Person: Gale Canale
  E-mail: SpecServ@marist.edu

LEARNING DISABILITY SERVICES

Requests for the following services/accommodations will be evaluated individually based on appropriate and current documentation.

Allowed in exams
  Calculator: Yes
  Dictionary: Yes
  Computer: Yes
  Spellchecker: Yes
Extended test time: Yes
Scribes: Yes
Proctors: Yes
Oral exams: Yes
Note-takers: Yes

Distraction-reduced environment: Yes
Tape recording in class: Yes
Books on tape from RFBD: Yes
Taping of books not from RFBD: Yes
Accommodations for students with ADHD: Yes
Reading machine: Yes
Other assistive technology: Yes
Priority registration: Yes

Added costs for services: Yes
LD specialists: Yes
Professional tutors: 4
Peer tutors: 60
Max. hours/wk. for services: 1.5
How professors are notified of LD/ADHD: By student

GENERAL ADMISSIONS INFORMATION

Director of Admissions: Kenton Rhinehart
Telephone: 845-575-3226

ENTRANCE REQUIREMENTS

Academic units required: 4 English, 3 math, 3 science (2 science labs), 2 foreign language, 2 social studies, 1 history, 2 academic electives. **Academic units recommended:** 4 math, 4 science (3 science labs), 3 foreign language. High school diploma is required, and GED is accepted. ACT with Writing component required. TOEFL required of all international applicants: minimum paper TOEFL 550, minimum computer TOEFL 213.

Application deadline: 2/15
Notification: 3/15
Average GPA: 3.30
ACT Composite middle 50% range: 20–26

SAT Math middle 50% range: 540–630
SAT Critical Reading middle 50% range: 530–610
SAT Writing middle 50% range: 530–620

Graduated top 10% of class: 26%
Graduated top 25% of class: 78%
Graduated top 50% of class: 95%

COLLEGE GRADUATION REQUIREMENTS

Course waivers allowed: Yes
In what course: Substitutions are made in math.
Course substitutions allowed: Yes
In what course: Substitutions are made in math.

ADDITIONAL INFORMATION

Environment: The college is located on 120 acres in upstate New York, 75 miles from New York City.

Student Body
  Undergrad enrollment: 4,873
  Women: 57%
  Men: 43%
  Percent out-of-state: 40%

Cost Information
  Tuition: $22,066
  Room & board: $8,590
Housing Information
  University housing: Yes
  Percent living on campus: 72%

Greek System
  Fraternity: Yes
  Sorority: Yes
Athletics: Division I

MARYMOUNT MANHATTAN COLLEGE

221 East Seventy-first Street, New York, NY 10021
Phone: 212-517-0430 • Fax: 212-517-0448
E-mail: admissions@mmm.edu • Web: www.mmm.edu
Support: SP • Institution type: 4-year private

LEARNING DISABILITY PROGRAM AND SERVICES

Marymount Manhattan College's Program for Academic Access includes a full range of support services that center on academic and personal growth for students with learning disabilities. Students who have been admitted to the full-time program are required to demonstrate commitment to overcoming learning difficulties through regular attendance and tutoring. Academic advisement and counseling is provided to assist in developing a program plan suited to individual needs. The college is looking for highly motivated students with a commitment to compensate for their learning disabilities and fully participate in the tutoring program. Once admitted into the program, students receive a program plan suited to their needs, based on a careful examination of the psychoeducational evaluations. Full-time students sign a contract to regularly attend tutoring provided by professionals experienced within the field of LD. In addition to assisting students in the development of skills and strategies for their course work, LD specialists coach participants in the attitudes and behavior necessary for college success. Professors assist learning specialists in carefully monitoring students' progress throughout the academic year and arranging for accommodations. Students must submit a current and complete psychoeducational evaluation that provides clear and specific evidence of the disability and its limitations on academic functioning in the diagnosis summary statement. Students with ADHD must have a licensed physician, psychiatrist, or psychologist provide a complete and current documentation of the disorder.

LD/ADHD ADMISSIONS INFORMATION

College entrance tests required: Yes
Interview required: Yes
Essay recommended: Yes
Documentation required for LD: Psychoeducational evaluation completed within the past 3 years
Documentation required for ADHD: Signed letter from a psychiatrist or psychologist with diagnostic code
Submitted to: Program for Academic Success
Special Ed. HS course work accepted: Yes

Specific course requirements of all applicants: Yes
Separate application required: No
# of LD applications submitted each year: 40
# of LD applications accepted yearly: 30
Total # of students receiving LD services: 30
Acceptance into program means acceptance into college: Students may be admitted to the college through the Program for Academic Access.

ADMISSIONS

Admission to Marymount Manhattan College's Program for Academic Access is based on a diagnosis of dyslexia, ADHD, or other primary learning disability; intellectual potential within the average to superior range; and a serious commitment in attitude and work habits to meeting the program and college academic requirements. Prospective students are required to submit a high school transcript or GED. Students are expected to have taken college-prep courses in high school, but foreign language is not required for admission. ACT or SAT results are preferred but not required. Results of a recent complete psychoeducational evaluation; letters of recommendation from teachers, tutors, or counselors; and a personal interview are also required. Students may be admitted to the college through the Program for Academic Access. Students interested in being considered for admission through the program must self-disclose their LD/ADHD in a personal statement with the regular application. There is no fixed deadline for the application; however, there are a limited number of slots available.

ADDITIONAL INFORMATION

There are three LD professionals associated with the program. Students have access to 2 hours of tutoring per week plus drop-in tutoring. Skills classes are offered in study skills, reading, and vocabulary development, and workshops in overcoming procrastination are also available. The following services are offered to students with appropriate documentation: the use of calculators, computers, and spellcheckers during exams; extended time on tests; proctors; oral exams; distraction-free testing environments; tape recorders in class; books on tape; separate and alternative forms of testing; and priority registration. The program fee is $3,000 per academic year above tuition.

LEARNING DISABILITY PROGRAM/SERVICES

Learning Disability Program/Services: Program for Academic Success
Director: Ann Jablon, PhD
  E-mail: ajablon@mmm.edu
  Telephone: 212-774-0721
  Fax: 212-517-0419

LEARNING DISABILITY SERVICES

Requests for the following services/accommodations will be evaluated individually based on appropriate and current documentation.

Allowed in exams
  Calculator: Yes
  Dictionary: No
  Computer: Yes
  Spellchecker: Yes
Extended test time: Yes
Scribes: No
Proctors: Yes
Oral exams: Yes
Note-takers: Yes

Distraction-reduced environment: Yes
Tape recording in class: Yes
Books on tape from RFBD: Yes
Taping of books not from RFBD: Yes
Accommodations for students with ADHD: Yes
Reading machine: No
Other assistive technology: Yes
Priority registration: Yes

Added costs for services: Yes
LD specialists: Yes
Professional tutors: No
Peer tutors: No
Max. hours/wk. for services: 2
How professors are notified of LD/ADHD: By student

GENERAL ADMISSIONS INFORMATION

Director of Admissions: Jim Rogers
Telephone: 212-517-0430

ENTRANCE REQUIREMENTS
Academic units required: 4 English, 3 math, 2 science, 3 social studies, 4 academic electives. **Academic units recommended:** 3 science, 2 foreign language. High school diploma is required, and GED is accepted. ACT without Writing component accepted. TOEFL required of all international applicants: minimum paper TOEFL 550, minimum computer TOEFL 213.

Application deadline: 3/5
Notification: Rolling
Average GPA: 3.10
ACT Composite middle 50% range: 20–25

SAT Math middle 50% range: 460–570
SAT Critical Reading middle 50% range: 500–600
SAT Writing middle 50% range: NR

Graduated top 10% of class: NR
Graduated top 25% of class: NR
Graduated top 50% of class: NR

COLLEGE GRADUATION REQUIREMENTS

Course waivers allowed: No
Course substitutions allowed: No

ADDITIONAL INFORMATION

Environment: The campus is located on the upper east side of Manhattan.

Student Body
  Undergrad enrollment: 1,871
  Women: 77%
  Men: 23%
  Percent out-of-state: 51%

Cost Information
  Tuition: $18,748
  Room & board: $12,090
Housing Information
  University housing: Yes
  Percent living on campus: 65%

Greek System
  Fraternity: No
  Sorority: No
Athletics: NR

NEW YORK UNIVERSITY

22 Washington Square North, New York, NY 10011
Phone: 212-998-4500 • Fax: 212-995-4902
E-mail: admissions@nyu.edu • Web: www.nyu.edu
Support: CS • Institution type: 4-year private

LEARNING DISABILITY PROGRAM AND SERVICES

Success in college depends on such things as motivation, intelligence, talent, problem-solving abilities, and hard work. For students with LD these traits must be complemented by an understanding of their learning style and their ways of compensating for their disability. Access to Learning strives to help students capitalize on their strengths and minimize the impact of their LD, and provides support services and accommodations to all NYU students with learning disabilities. There is no fee. The program can assist students in coping with their LD while working toward independence, competence, and a college degree. Students with LD requesting accommodations or services must provide appropriate documentation, which must be clear and show a specific diagnosis of LD, and evidence of a substantial limitation to academic functioning, and must be recent and performed by a qualified professional. Students with ADHD must provide documentation showing a clear and specific diagnosis of ADHD; documentation must be comprehensive, specify the criteria for the diagnosis and an interpretive summary, and must have been performed by a qualified professional.

LD/ADHD ADMISSIONS INFORMATION

College entrance tests required: Yes
Interview required: No
Essay recommended: No
Documentation required for LD: Current psychoeducational or neuropsychological evaluation
Documentation required for ADHD: Yes
Submitted to: Access to Learning
Special Ed. HS course work accepted: Yes
Specific course requirements of all applicants: NR

Separate application required: No
# of LD applications submitted each year: NR
# of LD applications accepted yearly: NR
Total # of students receiving LD services: NR
Acceptance into program means acceptance into college: Students must be admitted to and enrolled in the university first and then request services.

ADMISSIONS

NYU is a competitive university that provides a challenging academic environment. Any student who applies, including students with LD, must demonstrate the potential to do well. As part of the admissions decision, a learning disability specialist may be consulted for recommendations for students who self-disclose their LD. General admission criteria include: 4 English, 3 math, 3 science, 2 foreign language, and 3 social studies; SAT/ACT and two SAT Subject Tests are required (except for Tisch School of the Arts or for the studio art or any of the music programs in the Steinhardt School of Education). Students applying for programs in the Steinhardt School that do not require an audition or portfolio are required to submit scores from two SAT Subject Tests. NYU has separate Admissions Committees for each college. The Director of the Admissions Committee and others may also review files. The admissions representative responsible for a specific geographic area of the country or world may also contribute to the review of an application. The evaluation involves a comprehensive review of the applicant's academic background, including the relative strength of the high school program and the student's performance in courses and SAT/ACT. NYU will also consider the personal statements and application essay, letters of recommendations and activities both in school and in the community. Finally, NYU considers special talents, alumni affiliation, socioeconomic background, geographic location, and race or ethnicity.

ADDITIONAL INFORMATION

Students can meet with a learning specialist to help develop compensatory skills, work on testing strategies, time management, reading efficiency, organization, effective writing, proofreading, note-taking, and study skills. There are weekly support meetings with peers; test accommodations, which could include extended time, private test rooms, use of a computer or calculator, reader, scribe, and alternative formats for tests; assistance in arranging for taping of lectures and ordering books on tape; priority seating; and technology such as Franklin Spellers, computers, and readers. Not all students need all of these services. An accommodation plan is made with each student based on individual needs, keeping in mind the goal of encouraging independence. It is possible for a student with LD to petition for a waiver of certain course requirements. The decision to allow for a waiver is made on a case-by-case basis by an academic standards committee.

LEARNING DISABILITY PROGRAM/SERVICES

Learning Disability Program/Services: Henry and Lucy Moses Center for Students with Disabilities
Director: Yolanda Cacciolo
  E-mail: yolanda.cacciolo@nyu.edu
  Telephone: 212-998-4980
  Fax: 212-995-4114

LEARNING DISABILITY SERVICES

Requests for the following services/accommodations will be evaluated individually based on appropriate and current documentation.

Allowed in exams
  Calculator: Yes
  Dictionary: Yes
  Computer: Yes
  Spellchecker: Yes
Extended test time: Yes
Scribes: Yes
Proctors: Yes
Oral exams: Yes
Note-takers: Yes

Distraction-reduced environment: Yes
Tape recording in class: Yes
Books on tape from RFBD: Yes
Taping of books not from RFBD: Yes
Accommodations for students with ADHD: Yes
Reading machine: Yes
Other assistive technology: Yes
Priority registration: Yes

Added costs for services: No
LD specialists: Yes
Professional tutors: No
Peer tutors: Yes
Max. hours/wk. for services: 2
How professors are notified of LD/ADHD: By student

GENERAL ADMISSIONS INFORMATION

Director of Admissions: Barbara Hall
Telephone: 212-998-4500

ENTRANCE REQUIREMENTS
Academic units required: 4 English, 3 math, 3 science (2 science labs), 2 foreign language, 4 history. **Academic units recommended:** 4 math, 3 foreign language. High school diploma is required, and GED is accepted. ACT with Writing component required. TOEFL required of all international applicants: minimum paper TOEFL 600, minimum computer TOEFL 250.

Application deadline: 1/15
Notification: 4/1
Average GPA: 3.60
ACT Composite middle 50% range: 27–31

SAT Math middle 50% range: 610–710
SAT Critical Reading middle 50% range: 600–700
SAT Writing middle 50% range: 600–700

Graduated top 10% of class: 67%
Graduated top 25% of class: 95%
Graduated top 50% of class: 100%

COLLEGE GRADUATION REQUIREMENTS

Course waivers allowed: Yes
Course substitutions allowed: Yes
In what course: Determined by an academic standards committee on a case-by-case basis

ADDITIONAL INFORMATION

Environment: The university has an urban campus in New York City.

Student Body
  Undergrad enrollment: 20,604
  Women: 62%
  Men: 38%
  Percent out-of-state: 66%

Cost Information
  Tuition: $33,420
  Room & board: $11,780
Housing Information
  University housing: Yes
  Percent living on campus: 51%

Greek System
  Fraternity: Yes
  Sorority: Yes
  Athletics: Division III

ROCHESTER INST. OF TECHNOLOGY

60 Lomb Memorial Drive, Rochester, NY 14623-5604
Phone: 585-475-6631 • Fax: 585-475-7424
E-mail: admissions@rit.edu • Web: www.rit.edu
Support: SP • Institution type: 4-year private

LEARNING DISABILITY PROGRAM AND SERVICES

The Learning Development Center offers a variety of services for students. Disability Services reviews requests for accommodations and approves accommodations and coordinates services. Learning Support Services provides regularly scheduled check-ins with a specialist who provides coaching in organizational skills, study strategies, and advocacy. This service is intended for any student who anticipates difficulty navigating the college environment. Lunch n' Learning Workshops are a series of 1-hour workshops dealing with specific study topics or strategies such as procrastination, test preparation, time management, and study skills. The Office of Special Services offers peer tutoring 2 hours per week to all RIT students.

LD/ADHD ADMISSIONS INFORMATION

College entrance tests required: Yes
Interview required: No
Essay recommended: No
Documentation required for LD: Comprehensive psychological evaluation completed within the past 3 years
Documentation required for ADHD: Diagnosis by qualified professional
Submitted to: Learning Development Center
Special Ed. HS course work accepted: NR

Specific course requirements of all applicants: Yes
Separate application required: No
# of LD applications submitted each year: NR
# of LD applications accepted yearly: NR
Total # of students receiving LD services: NR
Acceptance into program means acceptance into college: Students must be admitted to the institute and DSO/LSS separately.

ADMISSIONS

There is no special admissions process for students with learning disabilities. However, students with learning disabilities may include a supporting essay. Although an interview is not required, it is recommended. The required scores on the SAT or ACT will depend on the college the student is applying to within RIT. For the College of Liberal Arts, the mid 50 percent SAT score is 1090–1270, or for the ACT, it is 24–28. It is also helpful to identify compensatory strategies used in high school and what will be needed for success in college. The admission decision is made jointly by the program chairperson and Director of Admissions. Applicants are encouraged to indicate a second and third program choice. If RIT is unable to offer an admission to the first choice program, an applicant may be qualified for admission to one of the alternative choices. Factors considered in a general admission decision include, but are not limited to: overall GPA and rank in class, rigor of course work, grades in content courses, appropriateness of courses for academic major, competitiveness of high school, standardized test(s), recommendation from school counselor, recommendations from those familiar with the student's academic performance, and an essay.

ADDITIONAL INFORMATION

RIT is currently serving over 600 students with disabilities of which 388 are currently students with learning disabilities or attention deficit hyperactivity disorder. There are eight specialists on staff. Requests for accommodations and services are evaluated individually based on appropriate and current documentation. Services and accommodations that may be provided include the use of calculators, dictionaries, computers, or spellcheckers on exams, extended test times, scribes, proctors, note-takers, and distraction-free environments, books on tape, assistive technology, and priority registration. Disability information is confidential. Students distribute copies of letters to professors that list approved accommodations only. Course substitutions are allowed depending on documentation. There are fees for Learning Support Services.

LEARNING DISABILITY PROGRAM/SERVICES

Learning Disability Program/Services: Learning Development Center (LDC)
Director: Susan Ackerman, Coordinator
 E-mail: smacst@rit.edu
 Telephone: 585-475-7804
 Fax: 585-475-2215

LEARNING DISABILITY SERVICES

Requests for the following services/accommodations will be evaluated individually based on appropriate and current documentation.

Allowed in exams
 Calculator: Yes
 Dictionary: No
 Computer: Yes
 Spellchecker: Yes
Extended test time: Yes
Scribes: Yes
Proctors: Yes
Oral exams: Yes
Note-takers: Yes

Distraction-reduced environment: Yes
Tape recording in class: Yes
Books on tape from RFBD: Yes
Taping of books not from RFBD: Yes
Accommodations for students with
 ADHD: Yes
Reading machine: No
Other assistive technology: Yes
Priority registration: Yes

Added costs for services: Yes
LD specialists: Yes
Professional tutors: No
Peer tutors: Yes
Max. hours/wk. for services: 12
How professors are notified of
 LD/ADHD: By student

GENERAL ADMISSIONS INFORMATION

Director of Admissions: Dr. Daniel Shelley
Telephone: 585-475-6631

ENTRANCE REQUIREMENTS
Academic units required: 4 English, 2 math, 2 science (1 science lab), 4 social studies, 10 academic electives.
Academic units recommended: 4 English, 3 math, 3 science (2 science labs), 3 foreign language, 4 social studies, 5 academic electives. High school diploma is required, and GED is accepted. ACT with or without Writing component accepted. TOEFL required of all international applicants: minimum paper TOEFL 550, minimum computer TOEFL 215.

Application deadline: 2/1
Notification: Rolling
Average GPA: 3.7
ACT Composite middle 50% range:
 23–28

SAT Math middle 50% range:
 570–670
SAT Critical Reading middle 50%
 range: 530–630
SAT Writing middle 50% range: NR

Graduated top 10% of class: 30%
Graduated top 25% of class: 62%
Graduated top 50% of class: 89%

COLLEGE GRADUATION REQUIREMENTS

Course waivers allowed: No
Course substitutions allowed: Yes
In what course: Courses may be substituted depending on documentation and for nonrequired courses only.

ADDITIONAL INFORMATION

Environment: RIT is located on a 1,300-acre campus five miles south of the city of Rochester, the third largest city in New York State.

Student Body
 Undergrad enrollment: 12,532
 Women: 31%
 Men: 69%
 Percent out-of-state: 45%

Cost Information
 Tuition: $23,949
 Room & board: $8,748
Housing Information
 University housing: Yes
 Percent living on campus: 65%

Greek System
 Fraternity: Yes
 Sorority: Yes
 Athletics: Division III

ST. BONAVENTURE UNIVERSITY

PO Box D, St. Bonaventure, NY 14778
Phone: 716-375-2400 • Fax: 716-375-4005
E-mail: admissions@sbu.edu • Web: www.sbu.edu
Support: S • Institution type: 4-year private

LEARNING DISABILITY PROGRAM AND SERVICES

St. Bonaventure does not operate a specialized LD program but does provide services to students with identified disabilities. In the spirit of the federal mandates, reasonable accommodations are made for otherwise qualified students with disabilities. St. Bonaventure's Teaching and Learning Center is an intrinsic element of the university's goal of academic excellence. The credo is to assist, not do. Once authentic, current documentation has been received, a careful review of the records will be conducted and an evaluation of appropriate accommodations will be made. Students who wait to identify themselves until after registration may find that some accommodations are not immediately available. Students with learning disabilities/attention deficit hyperactivity disorder who wish to request accommodations must meet with the coordinator of Services for Students with Disabilities. It is the student's responsibility to deliver accommodation letters to professors after accommodations have been arranged. Accommodations are arranged each semester. Students are encouraged to discuss the disability with professors and arrange for specific accommodations for test-taking and other course requirements. Students must contact the coordinator of Services for Students with Disabilities to request a course substitution. The students need to accept responsibility for their own academic excellence, and assistance will be provided.

LD/ADHD ADMISSIONS INFORMATION

College entrance tests required: Yes
Interview required: No
Essay recommended: No
Documentation required for LD: WAIS–R or WAIS–III and an IEP (some memory and/or perceptual test) completed within the past 3 years
Documentation required for ADHD: Same as above
Submitted to: Services for Students with Disabilities
Special Ed. HS course work accepted: Yes

Specific course requirements of all applicants: Yes
Separate application required: No
# of LD applications submitted each year: NR
# of LD applications accepted yearly: NR
Total # of students receiving LD services: 50–100
Acceptance into program means acceptance into college: Students must be admitted to and enrolled in the university first and then request services.

ADMISSIONS
Students with learning disabilities must meet regular admission standards and complete the same admissions process as all applicants. The mid 50 percent ACT score range is 23–24, and for SAT it is 1070–1110. The minimum GPA is a 3.0. Course requirements include 4 years of English, 4 years of social studies, 3 years of math, 3 years of science, and 2 years of a foreign language. Special education courses may be considered. It is recommended that students self-disclose their disability in a personal statement. Once students are accepted and have enrolled, they are encouraged to self-disclose their learning disability, if this has not already been done, and provide appropriate documentation to the Office of Services for Students with Disabilities. Documentation is reviewed and appropriate accommodations are arranged.

ADDITIONAL INFORMATION
Students with LD may obtain assistance with assessing learning strengths and weaknesses and consult one-on-one or in groups to acquire a greater command of a subject, get help with a specific assignment, or discuss academic challenges. Services might include, but are not limited to: alternative testing arrangements, taped texts and classes, access to word processors/spellchecker, note-takers, tutors, peer mentors, time management and study skills training, and weekly individual appointments. To order books on tape from RFBD, students should allow 3 months to secure these books in time. Assistance can be offered in requesting books on tape. Tutoring services are available to all students and are not intended to be a substitute for independent study or preparation.

LEARNING DISABILITY PROGRAM/SERVICES

Learning Disability Program/Services: Services for Students with Disabilities
Director: Nancy A. Matthews
  E-mail: nmatthew@sbu.edu
  Telephone: 716-375-2065
  Fax: 716-375-2072

LEARNING DISABILITY SERVICES

Requests for the following services/accommodations will be evaluated individually based on appropriate and current documentation.

Allowed in exams
  Calculator: Yes
  Dictionary: Yes
  Computer: Yes
  Spellchecker: Yes
Extended test time: Yes
Scribes: Yes
Proctors: Yes
Oral exams: Yes
Note-takers: Yes

Distraction-reduced environment: Yes
Tape recording in class: Yes
Books on tape from RFBD: Yes
Taping of books not from RFBD: Yes
**Accommodations for students with
  ADHD:** Yes
Reading machine: No
Other assistive technology: Yes
Priority registration: No

Added costs for services: No
LD specialists: Yes
Professional tutors: 1
Peer tutors: 60–100
Max. hours/wk. for services:
  Unlimited
**How professors are notified of
  LD/ADHD:** By both student and
  director

GENERAL ADMISSIONS INFORMATION

Director of Admissions: James M. DiRisio
Telephone: 716-375-2400

ENTRANCE REQUIREMENTS

Academic units required: 4 English, 3 math, 3 science, 2 foreign language, 4 social studies. **Academic units recommended:** 4 English, 3 math, 3 science (3 science labs), 2 foreign language, 4 social studies. High school diploma is required, and GED is accepted. ACT with or without Writing component accepted. TOEFL required of all international applicants: minimum paper TOEFL 550, minimum computer TOEFL 213.

Application deadline: 4/15
Notification: Rolling
Average GPA: 3.13
ACT Composite middle 50% range:
  19–23

SAT Math middle 50% range:
  470–570
**SAT Critical Reading middle 50%
  range:** 480–570
SAT Writing middle 50% range: NR

Graduated top 10% of class: 11%
Graduated top 25% of class: 31%
Graduated top 50% of class: 68%

COLLEGE GRADUATION REQUIREMENTS

Course waivers allowed: No
Course substitutions allowed: Yes
In what course: Math and foreign languages with appropriate documentation

ADDITIONAL INFORMATION

Environment: The university is located on 600 acres in a rural area 70 miles southeast of Buffalo.

Student Body
  Undergrad enrollment: 2,072
  Women: 49%
  Men: 51%
  Percent out-of-state: 24%

Cost Information
  Tuition: $21,650
  Room & board: $7,760
Housing Information
  University housing: Yes
  Percent living on campus: 77%

Greek System
  Fraternity: No
  Sorority: No
Athletics: Division I

ST. LAWRENCE UNIVERSITY

Payson Hall, Canton, NY 13617
Phone: 315-229-5261 • Fax: 315-229-5818
E-mail: admissions@stlawu.edu • Web: www.stlawu.edu
Support: S • Institution type: 4-year private

LEARNING DISABILITY PROGRAM AND SERVICES

The Office of Special Needs provides services to members of the university who either have identified themselves or believe they may have some type of learning disability. The office has several purposes: to serve students who are learning-challenged by documented disabilities; help students get the academic help that they need; put students in touch with other people on campus who can help; advise and counsel students; and educate everyone on campus about special needs. The office works with students in developing IEPs for the purpose of receiving reasonable accommodations in their educational and residential life concerns. The service will also make referrals and advocate at several on-campus services, and if necessary, connect with state or regional support agencies. There is a Writing Center for help with writing assignments, peer tutors for general assistance with academic work, and a Counseling Center and Health Center. As appropriate to the disability, documentation should include a diagnostic statement identifying the disability, date of the current diagnostic evaluation, and the date of the original diagnosis; a description of the diagnostic criteria and/or diagnostic test used; a description of the current functional impact of the disability; treatments, medications, and assistive devices/services currently prescribed or in use; a description of the expected progression or stability of the impact of the disability over time; and the credentials of the diagnosing professionals. Recommendations from professionals with a history of working with the individual provide valuable information for the review process. They will be included in the evaluation of requests for accommodation and/or auxiliary aids.

LD/ADHD ADMISSIONS INFORMATION

College entrance tests required: Yes
Interview required: No
Essay recommended: No
Documentation required for LD: Psychoeducational evaluation
Documentation required for ADHD: Yes
Submitted to: Office of Special Needs
Special Ed. HS course work accepted: Yes

Specific course requirements of all applicants: NR
Separate application required: No
# of LD applications submitted each year: NR
# of LD applications accepted yearly: NR
Total # of students receiving LD services: 130–141
Acceptance into program means acceptance into college: Students must be admitted to and enrolled in the university first and then request services.

ADMISSIONS

There is no special admissions process for students with learning disabilities. All applicants must meet the same admission criteria, which include recommended courses of 4 years of English, 3 years of math, 3 years of science, 3 years of a foreign language, and 3 years of social studies, and SAT/ACT scores (the average SAT is 1130). An interview is recommended and can be done off campus with an alumni representative.

ADDITIONAL INFORMATION

Students need to be self-starters (to seek out the service early and follow through). As soon as possible, students should provide the official documents that describe the learning disability—so that the office can help develop the IEP—and notify the professors and people in various offices about the learning disability. The Director of Services sends a memo to each professor that describes the student's IEP, discloses that the student is a documented and endorsed learning-challenged student on file with the Office of Special Needs, and lists the accommodations necessary for the student to be successful in the course. Services and accommodations are available for undergraduate and graduate students.

LEARNING DISABILITY PROGRAM/SERVICES

Learning Disability Program/Services: Office of Academic Services for Students with Special Needs
Director: John Meagher, Director
  E-mail: jmeagher@stlawu.edu
  Telephone: 315-229-5104
  Fax: 315-229-7453

LEARNING DISABILITY SERVICES

Requests for the following services/accommodations will be evaluated individually based on appropriate and current documentation.

Allowed in exams
  Calculator: Yes
  Dictionary: Yes
  Computer: Yes
  Spellchecker: Yes
Extended test time: Yes
Scribes: Yes
Proctors: Yes
Oral exams: No
Note-takers: Yes

Distraction-reduced environment: Yes
Tape recording in class: Yes
Books on tape from RFBD: Yes
Taping of books not from RFBD: No
Accommodations for students with ADHD: Yes
Reading machine: Yes
Other assistive technology: Yes
Priority registration: Yes

Added costs for services: No
LD specialists: No
Professional tutors: No
Peer tutors: 75
Max. hours/wk. for services: Unlimited
How professors are notified of LD/ADHD: By both student and director

GENERAL ADMISSIONS INFORMATION

Director of Admissions: Teresa Cowdrey
Telephone: 315-229-5261

ENTRANCE REQUIREMENTS
Academic units recommended: 4 English, 3 math, 3 science, 3 foreign language, 3 social studies, 2 history. High school diploma is required, and GED is accepted. ACT with or without Writing component accepted. TOEFL required of all international applicants: minimum paper TOEFL 600, minimum computer TOEFL 250.

Application deadline: 2/15
Notification: 3/30
Average GPA: 3.49
ACT Composite middle 50% range: 25–28

SAT Math middle 50% range: 550–640
SAT Critical Reading middle 50% range: 550–640
SAT Writing middle 50% range: 540–630

Graduated top 10% of class: 33%
Graduated top 25% of class: 67%
Graduated top 50% of class: 91%

COLLEGE GRADUATION REQUIREMENTS

Course waivers allowed: No
Course substitutions allowed: No

ADDITIONAL INFORMATION

Environment: The university is located on 1,000 acres in a rural area 80 miles south of Ottawa, Canada.

Student Body
  Undergrad enrollment: 2,145
  Women: 52%
  Men: 48%
  Percent out-of-state: 53%

Cost Information
  Tuition: $33,690
  Room & board: $8,630
Housing Information
  University housing: Yes
  Percent living on campus: 99%

Greek System
  Fraternity: Yes
  Sorority: Yes
Athletics: Division III

ST. THOMAS AQUINAS COLLEGE

125 Route 340, Sparkill, NY 10976
Phone: 914-398-4100 • Fax: 914-398-4114
E-mail: admissions@stac.edu • Web: www.stac.edu
Support: SP • Institution type: 4-year private

LEARNING DISABILITY PROGRAM AND SERVICES

St. Thomas Aquinas College (STAC) Exchange services are comprehensive and specialized, based on research and actual experiences with bright college students with LD. The STAC Exchange has adapted to the increasing diversity of college students with LD/ADHD, with a present emphasis on individualized services. STAC focuses on the development of effective learning strategies by critically evaluating and educating students about their specific needs and abilities. The aim is to break the pattern of dependency often created in students with learning deficits, foster a spirit of independent and active learning, teach students to maximize their strengths and compensate for their weaknesses, and inspire confidence in the students' own abilities. At the heart of the program are mentoring sessions. Students meet twice weekly with a professional mentor in one-on-one sessions tailored to meet specific needs. Mentors are not tutors but guides who help students develop learning strategies, improve organizational and editing skills, understand course concepts, and negotiate academic life. Study groups and workshops are also available, and incoming freshmen must attend a 4-day residential summer program to help prepare them for college life.

LD/ADHD ADMISSIONS INFORMATION

College entrance tests required: Yes
Interview required: Yes
Essay recommended: Yes
Documentation required for LD: Psychological report, including adult intelligence tests (WAIS–III), and educational evaluation (decoding, reading comprehension, spelling, writing, and mathematics); testing must not be more than 3 years old.
Documentation required for ADHD: Same as above, plus documentation of ADHD; testing must not be more than 3 years old.

Submitted to: STAC
Special Ed. HS course work accepted: Yes
Specific course requirements of all applicants: Yes
Separate application required: Yes
# of LD applications submitted each year: 90–120
# of LD applications accepted yearly: 20–25
Total # of students receiving LD services: 50–75
Acceptance into program means acceptance into college: Students are admitted to the college and then to STAC.

ADMISSIONS

The STAC Exchange has a separate application and admissions process from the college itself. Admission to the program is limited to those students the program feels it can effectively serve and is, therefore, extremely competitive. Students must be accepted by the college before their STAC Exchange application is evaluated. SAT or ACT scores are required for regular college admission. The following must be submitted to The STAC Exchange: a completed STAC application, high school transcripts (college transcripts for transfers), a letter of recommendation from a teacher, the applicant's most recent IEP if available, and a comprehensive diagnostic assessment indicating an LD/ADHD that was completed within the past 3 years. This diagnostic assessment must include an adult intelligence test (WAIS–III), measures of achievement, evaluation of social/emotional functioning, and the specific effects of the LD/ADHD on the student's current academic performance. Reports are required; scores on an IEP are insufficient documentation. Students must also have a personal interview with STAC Exchange staff to be admitted into the program. Transfer applications are accepted.

ADDITIONAL INFORMATION

STAC has a director, an assistant director, and a trained staff of mentors. Mentors are professionals with post-college education and experience in some aspect of teaching. The director and assistant director are hands-on administrators who also provide mentoring. Mentoring differs from traditional tutoring in that students come to sessions having already attended classes and prepared initial course work. STAC Exchange students are required to attend regularly scheduled sessions with their own mentor and are encouraged to drop in for additional help as needed. Workshops/seminars on organization and time management, note-taking, test-taking, interview skills, resume writing, and self-advocacy are provided based on needs and interests. Study groups in specific areas are offered dependent on student need and staff expertise. STAC Exchange students are also provided with academic counseling, course advisement, and priority registration. The required summer program for incoming STAC freshmen is designed to identify the specific needs of each student to begin preparing them for academic rigors of higher education and build a sense of trust and community within the group. This summer program also integrates the first half of a three-credit academic course whose topic may vary from year to year.

LEARNING DISABILITY PROGRAM/SERVICES

Learning Disability Program/Services: The STAC Exchange
Director: Richard F. Heath, PhD
  E-mail: pathways@stac.edu
  Telephone: 845-398-4230
  Fax: 845-398-4229

LEARNING DISABILITY SERVICES

Requests for the following services/accommodations will be evaluated individually based on appropriate and current documentation.

Allowed in exams
  Calculator: Yes
  Dictionary: Yes
  Computer: Yes
  Spellchecker: Yes
Extended test time: Yes
Scribes: Yes
Proctors: Yes
Oral exams: Yes
Note-takers: Yes

Distraction-reduced environment: Yes
Tape recording in class: Yes
Books on tape from RFBD: Yes
Taping of books not from RFBD: No
Accommodations for students with ADHD: Yes
Reading machine: Yes
Other assistive technology: Yes
Priority registration: Yes

Added costs for services: Yes
LD specialists: Yes
Professional tutors: 9
Peer tutors: N/A
Max. hours/wk. for services: Unlimited
How professors are notified of LD/ADHD: By student

GENERAL ADMISSIONS INFORMATION

Director of Admissions: Tracey Howard-Ubelhoer
Telephone: 914-398-8136

ENTRANCE REQUIREMENTS

Academic units required: 4 English, 3 math, 3 science (2 science labs), 3 foreign language, 4 social studies, 1 history. **Academic units recommended:** 3 academic electives. High school diploma is required, and GED is accepted. ACT with or without Writing component accepted. TOEFL required of all international applicants: minimum paper TOEFL 530, minimum computer TOEFL 173.

Application deadline: NR
Notification: Rolling
Average GPA: 2.60
ACT Composite middle 50% range: 17–22

SAT Math middle 50% range: 410–510
SAT Critical Reading middle 50% range: 410–510
SAT Writing middle 50% range: NR

Graduated top 10% of class: 5%
Graduated top 25% of class: 35%
Graduated top 50% of class: 50%

COLLEGE GRADUATION REQUIREMENTS

Course waivers allowed: No
Course substitutions allowed: Yes
In what course: Foreign language, only with appropriate documentation; two culture course substitutions from an approved list are then required. Speech, only with appropriate documentation; one communications course substitution from an approved list is then required.

ADDITIONAL INFORMATION

Environment: The school is located on 43 acres in a suburban area 15 miles from New York City.

Student Body
  Undergrad enrollment: 1,416
  Women: 55%
  Men: 45%
  Percent out-of-state: 29%

Cost Information
  Tuition: $18,400
  Room & board: $9,400
Housing Information
  University housing: Yes
  Percent living on campus: 41%

Greek System
  Fraternity: Yes
  Sorority: Yes
Athletics: NAIA

STATE UNIVERSITY OF NEW YORK— ALFRED STATE COLLEGE

Huntington Administration•Building, Alfred, NY 14802
Phone: 607-587-4215 • Fax: 607-587-4299
E-mail: admissions@alfredstate.edu • Web: www.alfredstate.edu
Support: S • Institution type: 4-year public

LEARNING DISABILITY PROGRAM AND SERVICES

The goal of the Office of Services for Students with Disabilities (SSD) is to ensure that students with disabilities and appropriate documentation have equal access to programs, activities, and services offered to other students. Once students present appropriate documentation, services are provided depending on individual needs. The Student Development Center has a team of dedicated professionals committed to fostering the personal and academic growth of all students. The centralized nature of the center allows for an important link among college supportive services dedicated to maximizing student growth and student success. The Alfred State Opportunity Program (ASOP) is a special admissions program designed to improve the student's opportunity to be academically successful. Reduced course loads and college-preparatory developmental courses assist students in meeting curricular prerequisites. Students should contact learning assistance and must provide adequate documentation before accommodations/services will be provided. The Services for Students with Disabilities counselor determines the extent of services provided.

LD/ADHD ADMISSIONS INFORMATION

College entrance tests required: Yes
Interview required: No
Essay recommended: No
Documentation required for LD: Psychoeducational evaluation
Documentation required for ADHD: Yes
Submitted to: Services for Students with Disabilities
Special Ed. HS course work accepted: Yes

Specific course requirements of all applicants: NR
Separate application required: No
# of LD applications submitted each year: NR
# of LD applications accepted yearly: NR
Total # of students receiving LD services: 222
Acceptance into program means acceptance into college: Students must be admitted to and enrolled in the university first and then request services.

ADMISSIONS
There is no special admission process for students with learning disabilities. All applicants must meet the same admission criteria. The minimum core courses that are preferred include 4 years of English, 3 years of math, 3 years of science, 3 years of social science, 2 years of a foreign language, and 1 year of art. The minimum GPA is 74 percent. ASOP allows students to take 3 years to complete a 2-year program.

ADDITIONAL INFORMATION
Services available through SSD include individual academic skills development, note-takers and scribes, readers, peer tutors, taped texts, testing accommodations, extended curricular programs, referral to other offices and agencies, specialized equipment loans, advocacy, and registration assistance. ASOP provides counseling, extensive advising, and tutoring. Peer and professional tutors are available by appointment and provide course-specific assistance such as answers to questions, clarification of information, and drill and/or review for exams. Academic Skills Assistance for reading improvement, student success, and study skills can be provided through individual appointments, small group seminars, classroom instruction, or computer tutorials.

LEARNING DISABILITY PROGRAM/SERVICES

Learning Disability Program/Services: Services for Students with Disabilities (SSD)
Director: Heather Meacham
  E-mail: meacham@alfredstate.edu
  Telephone: 607-587-4122
  Fax: 607-587-3210

LEARNING DISABILITY SERVICES

Requests for the following services/accommodations will be evaluated individually based on appropriate and current documentation.

Allowed in exams
  Calculator: Yes
  Dictionary: Yes
  Computer: Yes
  Spellchecker: Yes
Extended test time: Yes
Scribes: Yes
Proctors: Yes
Oral exams: No
Note-takers: Yes

Distraction-reduced environment: Yes
Tape recording in class: Yes
Books on tape from RFBD: Yes
Taping of books not from RFBD: Yes
Accommodations for students with ADHD: Yes
Reading machine: Yes
Other assistive technology: Yes
Priority registration: Yes

Added costs for services: No
LD specialists: No
Professional tutors: 2
Peer tutors: 75
Max. hours/wk. for services: As needed
How professors are notified of LD/ADHD: By director

GENERAL ADMISSIONS INFORMATION

Director of Admissions: Deborah Goodrich
Telephone: 800-4-Alfred

ENTRANCE REQUIREMENTS

Academic units recommended: 4 English, 4 math, 4 science, 4 social studies, 2 foreign language, 1 art. High school diploma is required, and GED is accepted. ACT with or without Writing component accepted. TOEFL required of all international applicants: minimum paper TOEFL 500, minimum computer TOEFL 173.

Application deadline: Rolling
Notification: Rolling
Average GPA: 2.80
ACT Composite middle 50% range: 18–24

SAT Math middle 50% range: 440–560
SAT Critical Reading middle 50% range: 410–510
SAT Writing middle 50% range: NR

Graduated top 10% of class: NR
Graduated top 25% of class: NR
Graduated top 50% of class: NR

COLLEGE GRADUATION REQUIREMENTS

Course waivers allowed: No
Course substitutions allowed: No

ADDITIONAL INFORMATION

Environment: The university has a rural campus 70 miles from Rochester.

Student Body
  Undergrad enrollment: 3,231
  Women: 36%
  Men: 64%
  Percent out-of-state: 11%

Cost Information
  In-state tuition: $4,350
  Out-of-state tuition: $7,210
  Room & board: $8,040
Housing Information
  University housing: Yes
  Percent living on campus: 66%

Greek System
  Fraternity: Yes
  Sorority: Yes
Athletics: Division III

STATE UNIVERSITY OF NEW YORK AT BINGHAMTON

PO Box 6001, Binghamton, NY 13902-6001
Phone: 607-777-2171 • Fax: 607-777-4445
E-mail: admit@binghamton.edu • Web: www.binghamton.edu
Support: S • Institution type: 4-year public

LEARNING DISABILITY PROGRAM AND SERVICES

The Services for Students with Disabilities office provides assistance to students with physical or learning disabilities. They operate on the philosophy that the individuals they serve are students first and their disabilities are secondary. Support services assist students in taking advantage of the opportunities at Binghamton and in making their own contributions to the university community.

LD/ADHD ADMISSIONS INFORMATION

College entrance tests required: Yes
Interview required: No
Essay recommended: Yes
Documentation required for LD: Psychoeducational evaluation
Documentation required for ADHD: Psychoeducational evaluation
Submitted to: SSD
Special Ed. HS course work accepted: NR

Specific course requirements of all applicants: NR
Separate application required: No
# of LD applications submitted each year: NR
# of LD applications accepted yearly: NR
Total # of students receiving LD services: 79
Acceptance into program means acceptance into college: Students must be admitted to and enrolled in the university first and then request services.

ADMISSIONS

Binghamton University welcomes applications from all qualified individuals. While there are no special admissions procedures or academic programs expressly for students with disabilities, the Services for Students with Disabilities Office provides a wide range of support services to enrolled students. Diagnostic tests are not required for admissions, but students are encouraged to meet with the director of Services for Students with Disabilities and provide documentation to determine appropriate accommodations. Through nonmatriculated enrollment, students can take courses but are not enrolled in a degree program. If they do well, they may then apply for matriculation, using credits earned toward their degree. General admission criteria includes 4 years of English, 2.5 years of math, 2 years of social science, 2 years of science, and 2 years of 2 foreign languages or 3 years of 1 foreign language. The mid 50 percent score range on the SAT is 1100–1330.

ADDITIONAL INFORMATION

Students with LD/ADHD may use all campus-wide services, plus receive accommodations and services through SSD. Accommodations that are available for students with appropriate documentation include extended testing times; low-distraction environments for tests; scribes; proctors; use of calculators, dictionaries, computers, and spellchecker during exams; and assistive technology including voice recognition software, screen readers software, print enlargement, assistive listening devices, and variable speed tape recorders on loan. Tutorial services are provided for 4 hours per week to undergraduate students at no charge. However, SSD can arrange for more than 4 hours per week at the student's expense. The university's Center for Academic Excellence provides peer tutoring to any student at no cost. The university has offered courses in college study, coping skills, and applying study skills to career research. Availability of these courses each year is dependent on staffing. Students are provided memos of reasonable accommodation written by the SSD director or learning disabilities specialist to be given to their professors. Services and accommodations are available for undergraduate and graduate students.

LEARNING DISABILITY PROGRAM/SERVICES

Learning Disability Program/Services: Services for Students with Disabilities (SSD)
Director: B. Jean Fairbairn
  E-mail: bjfairba@binghamton.edu
  Telephone: 607-777-2686
  Fax: 607-777-6893

LEARNING DISABILITY SERVICES

Requests for the following services/accommodations will be evaluated individually based on appropriate and current documentation.

Allowed in exams
  Calculator: Yes
  Dictionary: Yes
  Computer: Yes
  Spellchecker: Yes
Extended test time: Yes
Scribes: Yes
Proctors: Yes
Oral exams: Yes
Note-takers: Yes

Distraction-reduced environment: Yes
Tape recording in class: Yes
Books on tape from RFBD: Yes
Taping of books not from RFBD: Yes
Accommodations for students with ADHD: Yes
Reading machine: Yes
Other assistive technology: Yes
Priority registration: Yes

Added costs for services: No
LD specialists: Yes
Professional tutors: No
Peer tutors: Yes
Max. hours/wk. for services: 5
How professors are notified of LD/ADHD: By student

GENERAL ADMISSIONS INFORMATION

Director of Admissions: Cheryl Brown
Telephone: 607-777-2171

ENTRANCE REQUIREMENTS

Academic units required: 4 English, 3 math, 2 science, 3 foreign language, 2 social studies. **Academic units recommended:** 4 math, 4 science, 3 foreign language, 3 history. High school diploma is required, and GED is accepted. ACT with Writing component required. TOEFL required of all international applicants: minimum paper TOEFL 550, minimum computer TOEFL 213.

Application deadline: 2/15
Notification: 4/1
Average GPA: 3.70
ACT Composite middle 50% range: 25–29

SAT Math middle 50% range: 610–690
SAT Critical Reading middle 50% range: 570–650
SAT Writing middle 50% range: NR

Graduated top 10% of class: 49%
Graduated top 25% of class: 84%
Graduated top 50% of class: 98%

COLLEGE GRADUATION REQUIREMENTS

Course waivers allowed: No
Course substitutions allowed: Yes
In what course: Varies, depending on the nature and severity of the student's disability, the student's current and comprehensive diagnostic documentation, and the student's major of study.

ADDITIONAL INFORMATION

Environment: The university has a suburban campus near Binghamton.

Student Body
  Undergrad enrollment: 11,470
  Women: 48%
  Men: 52%
  Percent out-of-state: 7%

Cost Information
  In-state tuition: $4,350
  Out-of-state tuition: $10,610
  Room & board: $8,588
Housing Information
  University housing: Yes
  Percent living on campus: 56%

Greek System
  Fraternity: Yes
  Sorority: Yes
Athletics: Division I

STATE UNIVERSITY OF NEW YORK— CANTON

French Hall, SUNY—Canton, Canton, NY 13617
Phone: 315-386-7123 • Fax: 315-386-7929
E-mail: admissions@canton.edu • Web: www.canton.edu
Support: S • Institution type: 2-year public

LEARNING DISABILITY PROGRAM AND SERVICES

At the State University of New York—Canton, College of Technology, the Accommodative Services Program is equipped to help students with learning disabilities make a smooth transition to college and receive the necessary accommodations to ensure their academic success. The mission of the Office of Accommodative Services is to create a comprehensively accessible environment where individuals are viewed on the basis of ability, not disability. This supports the mission of SUNY—Canton, a technical college, offering 2- and 4-year degrees to a diverse student body. Prospective students are welcome to contact the Accommodative Services office with any questions. Although students with learning disabilities may register at the office at any time during their stay at SUNY—Canton, they are encouraged to do so as early as possible. Students must register at the office to obtain the special resources and services. It is the students' responsibility to self-disclose, provide appropriate documentation, and request accommodations.

LD/ADHD ADMISSIONS INFORMATION

College entrance tests required: Yes
Interview required: No
Essay recommended: No
Documentation required for LD: A psychological educational evaluation with adult norms
Documentation required for ADHD: A psychological educational evaluation with adult norms and/or current (no more than 3 years old) documentation from an MD or a licensed health-care professional.
Submitted to: Accommodative Services
Special Ed. HS course work accepted: No

Specific course requirements of all applicants: NR
Separate application required: No
# of LD applications submitted each year: NR
# of LD applications accepted yearly: NR
Total # of students receiving LD services: 165
Acceptance into program means acceptance into college: Students must be admitted to and enrolled in the university first and then request services.

ADMISSIONS
All students follow the same admissions procedure and are evaluated similarly for specific course placement. The Office of Accommodative Services is not directly involved in the admission process, but will usually meet with students (and families) during admission interviews. There are no specific course requirements as the requirements vary per curriculum, and foreign language is not required for admission. All students must have a high school diploma or the GED equivalent. No ACT/SAT tests are required for admission to the 2-year programs. However, ACT or SAT is required for the 4-year bachelor programs. Compass tests are used for placement. A student may be required to take our compass exam for placement in English. Students are exempt if they achieve a minimum NYS English Regents score of 75, achieve a minimum SAT verbal score of 420, or achieve a minimum ACT score of 17 on the English and Reading sections.

ADDITIONAL INFORMATION
A number of support services are offered on campus: an Academic Advisement Center, an Academic Computing Center, the Canton special services program, Counseling Center, Educational Opportunity Program, Learning Center, Math Lab, Writing Center, tutoring, and Science Learning Center. Services or accommodations could include testing accommodations; scribes, proctors; note-takers; books on tape; assistive technology; use of calculators, dictionaries, computers, or spellchecker in exams; distraction-free environments for tests; and priority registration. Acceptance into the university ensures that students will receive the services they request when they provide appropriate documentation.

LEARNING DISABILITY PROGRAM/SERVICES

Learning Disability Program/Services: Accommodative Services (AS)
Director: Veigh Mehan Lee, Coordinator
E-mail: leev@canton.edu
Telephone: 315-386-7392
Fax: 315-379-3877

LEARNING DISABILITY SERVICES

Requests for the following services/accommodations will be evaluated individually based on appropriate and current documentation.

Allowed in exams
  Calculator: Yes
  Dictionary: Yes
  Computer: Yes
  Spellchecker: Yes
Extended test time: Yes
Scribes: Yes
Proctors: Yes
Oral exams: Yes
Note-takers: Yes

Distraction-reduced environment: Yes
Tape recording in class: Yes
Books on tape from RFBD: Yes
Taping of books not from RFBD: Yes
Accommodations for students with ADHD: Yes
Reading machine: Yes
Other assistive technology: Yes
Priority registration: Yes

Added costs for services: No
LD specialists: No
Professional tutors: 12–25
Peer tutors: 12
Max. hours/wk. for services: As needed
How professors are notified of LD/ADHD: By director

GENERAL ADMISSIONS INFORMATION

Director of Admissions: Dave Gerlach
Telephone: 315-386-7123

ENTRANCE REQUIREMENTS

Academic units recommended: 4 English, 2 math, 2 science, 4 social studies. High school diploma is required, and GED is accepted. TOEFL required of all international applicants: minimum paper TOEFL 550, minimum computer TOEFL 213.

Application deadline: Rolling
Notification: Rolling
Average GPA: NR
ACT Composite middle 50% range: NR

SAT Math middle 50% range: NR
SAT Critical Reading middle 50% range: NR
SAT Writing middle 50% range: NR

Graduated top 10% of class: NR
Graduated top 25% of class: NR
Graduated top 50% of class: NR

COLLEGE GRADUATION REQUIREMENTS

Course waivers allowed: Yes
In what course: Depends on disability
Course substitutions allowed: Yes
In what course: Depends on disability

ADDITIONAL INFORMATION

Environment: The 550-acre campus is 135 miles northeast of Syracuse.

Student Body
  Undergrad enrollment: 2,119
  Women: 48%
  Men: 52%
  Percent out-of-state: 43%

Cost Information
  In-state tuition: $3,200
  Out-of-state tuition: $5,000
  Room & board: $6,490
Housing Information
  University housing: Yes
  Percent living on campus: 43%

Greek System
  Fraternity: Yes
  Sorority: Yes
Athletics: Division III

STATE UNIVERSITY OF NEW YORK— DELHI

Bush Hall, Two Main Street, Delhi, NY 13753
Phone: 607-746-4550 • Fax: 607-746-4104
E-mail: enroll@Delhi.edu • Web: www.delhi.edu
Support: CS • Institution type: 2-year public

LEARNING DISABILITY PROGRAM AND SERVICES

SUNY—Delhi provides students with learning disabilities with academic support services and equipment, including tutors, exams in distraction-free environments, remedial courses in math and English, and enlarged-video-display computer terminals. The Coordinator of Services often confers with students regarding their unique learning, study, and time management needs.

LD/ADHD ADMISSIONS INFORMATION

College entrance tests required: No
Interview required: No
Essay recommended: No
Documentation required for LD: Should be no more than 3 years old prior to admission and use adult standards (norms); IQ and achievment testing required
Documentation required for ADHD: Same as above, and if student is on medication, a doctor's statement
Submitted to: Center for Academic Services
Special Ed. HS course work accepted: NR

Specific course requirements of all applicants: Yes
Separate application required: No
# of LD applications submitted each year: NR
# of LD applications accepted yearly: NR
Total # of students receiving LD services: NR
Acceptance into program means acceptance into college: Students must be admitted to and enrolled in the university first and then request services.

ADMISSIONS

The admission requirements are the same for all students. It is always helpful if students with learning disabilities present themselves as confident, independent, goal-oriented, and self-directed learners. The minimum GPA is 2.0, and course requirements depend on the major. Courses taken in special education may be considered. Students are encouraged to self-disclose the disability in a personal statement. Admissions counselors will refer students to the coordinator if the student provides information about a disability. To be eligible for services, students must disclose information about their learning disability/attention deficit hyperactivity disorder and meet with the coordinator of Services for Students with Disabilities. ASSET scores are used for placement within courses.

ADDITIONAL INFORMATION

The Coordinator of Services for Students with Learning Disabilities is available to answer any questions regarding academic and non-academic matters. The coordinator also serves as a campus referral service. There are writing, tutoring, and computer labs available for all students. Skills classes are offered in test-taking strategies, time management, and study skills. Services and accommodations available with appropriate documentation include extended testing times for exams; distraction-free environments; use of calculators, dictionaries, computers, and spellchecker during exams; scribes; proctors; note-takers; books on tape; assistive technology; and course substitutions for math or foreign language. Additionally, there are computer stations with built-in software to read tests independently, electronic books for qualified students, and a Writing and Math Center. The Educational Opportunity Program is designed for students who have the ability and talent to succeed in college, but have had limited academic and financial options to prove their dedication. It provides supplemental support in the areas of tutoring, counseling, and financial aid to eligible students. Students enrolled in the program must meet specific criteria. If accepted into the program, students must also sign a contract that outlines expectations and the steps students must take to succeed.

LEARNING DISABILITY PROGRAM/SERVICES

Learning Disability Program/Services: The Center for Academic Services (AS)
Director: Linda Weinberg, Coordinator
  E-mail: weinbell@delhi.edu
  Telephone: 607-746-4593
  Fax: 607-746-4368

LEARNING DISABILITY SERVICES

Requests for the following services/accommodations will be evaluated individually based on appropriate and current documentation.

Allowed in exams
  Calculator: Yes
  Dictionary: Yes
  Computer: Yes
  Spellchecker: Yes
Extended test time: Yes
Scribes: Yes
Proctors: Yes
Oral exams: Yes
Note-takers: Yes

Distraction-reduced environment: Yes
Tape recording in class: Yes
Books on tape from RFBD: No
Taping of books not from RFBD: No
Accommodations for students with ADHD: Yes
Reading machine: Yes
Other assistive technology: Yes
Priority registration: No

Added costs for services: No
LD specialists: Yes
Professional tutors: 4
Peer tutors: 10
Max. hours/wk. for services: 2
How professors are notified of LD/ADHD: By student

GENERAL ADMISSIONS INFORMATION

Director of Admissions: Robert W. Mazzei
Telephone: 607-746-4550

ENTRANCE REQUIREMENTS

Academic units required: 4 English, 1 math, 1 science, 3 social studies, 1 history. **Academic units recommended:** 2 math, 2 science (1 science lab). High school diploma is required, and GED is accepted.

Application deadline: Rolling
Notification: Rolling
Average GPA: NR
ACT Composite middle 50% range: NR

SAT Math middle 50% range: NR
SAT Critical Reading middle 50% range: NR
SAT Writing middle 50% range: NR

Graduated top 10% of class: NR
Graduated top 25% of class: NR
Graduated top 50% of class: NR

COLLEGE GRADUATION REQUIREMENTS

Course waivers allowed: No
Course substitutions allowed: Yes
In what course: Math and foreign language

ADDITIONAL INFORMATION

Environment: The university is on 1,100 acres in a small town setting in upstate New York.

Student Body
  Undergrad enrollment: 1,791
  Women: 44%
  Men: 56%
  Percent out-of-state: 4%

Cost Information
  In-state tuition: $4,350
  Out-of-state tuition: $10,610
  Room & board: $6,830
Housing Information
  University housing: Yes
  Percent living on campus: 70%

Greek System
  Fraternity: Yes
  Sorority: Yes
Athletics: Division III

STATE UNIVERSITY OF NEW YORK— FARMINGDALE

Admissions Office, 2350 Broadhollow Road, Farmingdale, NY 11735
Phone: 631-420-2200 • Fax: 631-420-2633
E-mail: admissions@farmingdale.edu • Web: www.farmingdale.edu
Support: S • Institution type: 4-year public

LEARNING DISABILITY PROGRAM AND SERVICES

There is no learning disabilities program at the college, but the Office for Students with Disabilities is dedicated to the principle that equal opportunity to realize one's full potential should be available to all students. In keeping with this philosophy, the staff offers individualized services to students with disabilities in accordance with their needs. Students may meet individually with a learning disability specialist or in group meetings. Services include academic remediation with emphasis on compensatory strategies, study skills strategies training, test accommodations, time management instruction, tutoring, and self-understanding of disability. The services offered strive to instill independence, self-confidence, and self-advocacy skills.

LD/ADHD ADMISSIONS INFORMATION

College entrance tests required: Yes
Interview required: Yes
Essay recommended: No
Documentation required for LD: WAIS–III, WJ–III
Documentation required for ADHD: Diagnosis and report by a qualified professional
Submitted to: Office of Support Services
Special Ed. HS course work accepted: Yes

Specific course requirements of all applicants: Yes
Separate application required: No
# of LD applications submitted each year: NR
# of LD applications accepted yearly: NR
Total # of students receiving LD services: 145–155
Acceptance into program means acceptance into college: Students must be admitted and enrolled in the university first (they can appeal a denial) and then request services.

ADMISSIONS

There is no special admissions procedure for applicants with learning disabilities. The Precollege Pathways Program has more flexible entrance requirements. Elementary Algebra is the minimum requirement in math. Students should self-identify on the application. Admission decisions are made by the Office of Admissions. Students should submit psychoeducational reports and letters of recommendation and request a personal interview. Students are required to take the SAT/ACT. The university has rolling admissions. Almost all of the programs accept students throughout the year.

ADDITIONAL INFORMATION

The university would like the student's high school IEP and WAIS–R results to help identify the services necessary to help the student be successful. Services and accommodations available with appropriate documentation include extended testing times; distraction-free environments; use of calculators, dictionaries, computers, and spellchecker during exams; note-takers; scribes; proctors; assistive technology; professional tutors; and tape recording in class. Students are responsible for arranging for accommodations with professors.

LEARNING DISABILITY PROGRAM/SERVICES

Learning Disability Program/Services: Support Services for Students with Disabilities
Director: Malka Edelman
  E-mail: malka.edelman@farmingdale.edu
  Telephone: 631-420-2411
  Fax: 631-420-2163

LEARNING DISABILITY SERVICES

Requests for the following services/accommodations will be evaluated individually based on appropriate and current documentation.

Allowed in exams
  Calculator: Yes
  Dictionary: Yes
  Computer: Yes
  Spellchecker: Yes
Extended test time: Yes
Scribes: Yes
Proctors: Yes
Oral exams: Yes
Note-takers: Yes

Distraction-reduced environment: Yes
Tape recording in class: Yes
Books on tape from RFBD: Yes
Taping of books not from RFBD: Yes
**Accommodations for students with
  ADHD:** Yes
Reading machine: Yes
Other assistive technology: Yes
Priority registration: No

Added costs for services: No
LD specialists: Yes
Professional tutors: No
Peer tutors: Yes
Max. hours/wk. for services:
  Unlimited
**How professors are notified of
  LD/ADHD:** By student

GENERAL ADMISSIONS INFORMATION

Director of Admissions: James Hall
Telephone: 631-420-2200

ENTRANCE REQUIREMENTS

Academic units required: 4 English, 2 math, 1 science (1 science lab), 4 social studies. **Academic units recommended:** 4 English, 4 math, 3 science (3 science labs), 4 social studies. High school diploma is required, and GED is accepted. TOEFL required of all international applicants: minimum paper TOEFL 500, minimum computer TOEFL 173.

Application deadline: NR
Notification: Rolling
Average GPA: NR
ACT Composite middle 50% range:
  NR

SAT Math middle 50% range: NR
**SAT Critical Reading middle 50%
  range:** NR
SAT Writing middle 50% range: NR

Graduated top 10% of class: NR
Graduated top 25% of class: NR
Graduated top 50% of class: NR

COLLEGE GRADUATION REQUIREMENTS

Course substitutions allowed: Yes
In what course: Foreign language and math

ADDITIONAL INFORMATION

Environment: Farmingdale is a small town within easy access to New York City.

Student Body
  Undergrad enrollment: 3,909
  Women: 47%
  Men: 53%
  Percent out-of-state: 2%

Cost Information
  In-state tuition: $4,350
  Out-of-state tuition: $10,300
  Room & board: $6,810
Housing Information
  University housing: Yes
  Percent living on campus: 10%

Greek System
  Fraternity: No
  Sorority: No
Athletics: Division III

STATE UNIVERSITY OF NEW YORK— POTSDAM

44 Pierrepont Avenue, Potsdam, NY 13676
Phone: 315-267-2180 • Fax: 315-267-2163
E-mail: admissions@potsdam.edu • Web: www.potsdam.edu
Support: S • Institution type: 4-year public

LEARNING DISABILITY PROGRAM AND SERVICES

The State University of New York College—Potsdam is committed to the full inclusion of all individuals who can benefit from educational opportunities. Accommodative Services provides academic accommodations for all qualified students who have documented learning, emotional, and/or physical disabilities and a need for accommodations. The ultimate goal is to promote individuals' independence within the academic atmosphere of the university. Students are assisted in this process by the support services and programs available to all Potsdam students. Students must submit (written) documentation of the disability and the need for accommodations. After forwarding documentation, students are encouraged to make an appointment to meet with the coordinator to discuss accommodations. All accommodations are determined on an individual basis. Accommodative Services makes every effort to ensure access to academic accommodations.

LD/ADHD ADMISSIONS INFORMATION

College entrance tests required: Yes
Interview required: No
Essay recommended: No
Documentation required for LD: Comprehensive assessment
  by a licensed profesional
Documentation required for ADHD: Yes
Submitted to: Support Services
Special Ed. HS course work accepted: No

Specific course requirements of all applicants: Yes
Separate application required: No
# of LD applications submitted each year: NR
# of LD applications accepted yearly: NR
Total # of students receiving LD services: 45–50
Acceptance into program means acceptance into
  college: Students must be admitted to and enrolled in the
  university first and then request services.

ADMISSIONS

Students with learning disabilities must meet the same admission criteria as all applicants to the university. General admissions requirements include an ACT of 20-plus or SAT of 960, 3.0 GPA, and 17 core courses including 3 years of math, 2 years of science, 4 years of social studies, 4 years of English, 3 years of a foreign language, and 1 year of fine or performing arts. There is no conditional or probational admission plan. Students are encouraged to self-disclose their disability and provide appropriate documentation to Accommodative Services.

ADDITIONAL INFORMATION

Accommodations available through Accommodative Services include note-takers; test readers/books on tape; alternative testing such as extended time and/or distraction-reduced environment, exam readers/scribes, and use of word processor with spellchecker; and lending of some equipment. Additional services can include special registration and academic advising. Accommodative Services will assist students requesting non-academic auxiliary aids or services in locating the appropriate campus resources to address the request. The College Counseling Center provides psychological services. The early warning system asks each instructor to indicate at midpoint in each semester if a student is making unsatisfactory academic progress. Results of this inquiry are sent to the student and advisor. Student Support Services provides academic support, peer mentoring, and counseling. Tutoring is available for all students one-on-one or in small groups.

LEARNING DISABILITY PROGRAM/SERVICES

Learning Disability Program/Services: Student Support Services
Director: Diana Fisher
  Telephone: 315-267-3267
  Fax: 315-267-3268

LEARNING DISABILITY SERVICES

Requests for the following services/accommodations will be evaluated individually based on appropriate and current documentation.

Allowed in exams	**Distraction-reduced environment:** Yes	**Added costs for services:** No
Calculator: Yes	**Tape recording in class:** Yes	**LD specialists:** No
Dictionary: Yes	**Books on tape from RFBD:** Yes	**Professional tutors:** No
Computer: Yes	**Taping of books not from RFBD:** Yes	**Peer tutors:** 180
Spellchecker: Yes	**Accommodations for students with**	**Max. hours/wk. for services:** 3
Extended test time: Yes	**ADHD:** Yes	**How professors are notified of**
Scribes: Yes	**Reading machine:** Yes	**LD/ADHD:** By student
Proctors: Yes	**Other assistive technology:** Yes	
Oral exams: Yes	**Priority registration:** Yes	
Note-takers: Yes		

GENERAL ADMISSIONS INFORMATION

Director of Admissions: Thomas Nesbitt
Telephone: 315-267-2180

ENTRANCE REQUIREMENTS

Academic units required: 4 English, 3 math, 2 science (1 science lab), 4 social studies, 1 fine arts. **Academic units recommended:** 4 English, 4 math, 4 science (2 science labs), 4 foreign language, 4 social studies, 1 fine arts. High school diploma is required, and GED is accepted. ACT with or without Writing component accepted. TOEFL required of all international applicants: minimum paper TOEFL 550, minimum computer TOEFL 213.

Application deadline: Open	**SAT Math middle 50% range:**	**Graduated top 10% of class:** 13%
Notification: Rolling	480–590	**Graduated top 25% of class:** 35%
Average GPA: 3.20	**SAT Critical Reading middle 50%**	**Graduated top 50% of class:** 70%
ACT Composite middle 50% range:	**range:** 470–580	
20–24	**SAT Writing middle 50% range:** NR	

COLLEGE GRADUATION REQUIREMENTS

Course waivers allowed: Yes
In what course: Waivers only done on an individual basis
Course substitutions allowed: Yes
In what course: Substitutions only done on an individual basis

ADDITIONAL INFORMATION

Environment: The university is located on 240 acres in a rural area.

Student Body	**Cost Information**	**Greek System**
Undergrad enrollment: 3,610	**In-state tuition:** $4,350	**Fraternity:** Yes
Women: 56%	**Out-of-state tuition:** $10,610	**Sorority:** Yes
Men: 44%	**Room & board:** $8,170	**Athletics:** Division III
Percent out-of-state: 2%	**Housing Information**	
	University housing: Yes	
	Percent living on campus: 54%	

STATE UNIVERSITY OF NEW YORK— STONY BROOK UNIVERSITY

Office of Admissions, Stony Brook, NY 11794-1901
Phone: 631-632-6868 • Fax: 631-632-9898
E-mail: enroll@stonybrook.edu • Web: www.stonybrook.edu
Support: CS • Institution type: 4-year public

LEARNING DISABILITY PROGRAM AND SERVICES

Disability Support Services (DSS) coordinates advocacy and support services for students with disabilities. These services assist integrating students' needs with the resources available at the university to eliminate physical or programmatic barriers and ensure an accessible academic environment. All information and documentation of student disabilities is confidential. Students are responsible for identifying and documenting their disabilities through the DSS office. Students receive assistance with special housing and transportation, recruitment of readers, interpreters, note-takers, test accommodations, and counseling. A learning disabilities specialist is available to refer students for diagnostic testing and educational programming, meet accommodation needs, and provide in-service training to the university community. A Supported Education Program offering individual counseling and group sessions is available for students with psychological disabilities. Students who anticipate requiring assistance should contact Disability Support Services as early as possible to allow time for implementing recommended services.

LD/ADHD ADMISSIONS INFORMATION

College entrance tests required: Yes
Interview required: No
Essay recommended: No
Documentation required for LD: Psychoeducational
  evaluation that has been completed within the past 3 years
Documentation required for ADHD: Yes
Submitted to: DSS
Special Ed. HS course work accepted: No

Specific course requirements of all applicants: Yes
Separate application required: No
# of LD applications submitted each year: NR
# of LD applications accepted yearly: NR
Total # of students receiving LD services: 145
**Acceptance into program means acceptance into
  college:** Students must be admitted to and enrolled in the
  university first and then request services.

ADMISSIONS

Admission decisions are based on grades, GPA and/or class rank, and ACT/SAT. There is no separate or special admission because there are no developmental or remedial classes. However, each applicant who is identified as having a disability is given the special consideration of being reviewed by an admissions counselor and a DSS staff member jointly. All special circumstances are taken into consideration. Students are encouraged to self-disclose their disability in the application process. The Director of Disabilities Services will review documentation from students with learning disabilities and provide a recommendation to the Office of Admissions. Courses required for admission include 4 units of English, 4 units of social studies, 3 units of mathematics (4 units required for engineering), 3 units of science (4 units required for engineering), and 2 or 3 units of a foreign language. The average high school GPA is 91.

ADDITIONAL INFORMATION

Types of services and accommodations available are pre-registration advisement, liaisoning with faculty and staff, taped texts, learning strategies and time management training, assistance in locating tutors, assistance in arranging for note-takers and readers, tutorial computer programs, proctoring and/or modified administration of exams, support groups, referrals to appropriate campus resources, peer advising, and aid in vocational decision making. Services and accommodations are available to undergraduate and graduate students. No skills classes are offered.

LEARNING DISABILITY PROGRAM/SERVICES

Learning Disability Program/Services: Disabilities Support Services (DSS)
Director: Joanna Harris
  E-mail: j.jharris@notes.cc.sunysb.edu
  Telephone: 631-632-6748
  Fax: 631-632-6747
Contact Person: Donna Molloy, Learning Disabilities Specialist
  E-mail: j.jharris@notes.cc.sunysb.edu

LEARNING DISABILITY SERVICES

Requests for the following services/accommodations will be evaluated individually based on appropriate and current documentation.

Allowed in exams
  Calculator: NR
  Dictionary: No
  Computer: Yes
  Spellchecker: Yes
Extended test time: Yes
Scribes: Yes
Proctors: Yes
Oral exams: No
Note-takers: Yes

Distraction-reduced environment: Yes
Tape recording in class: Yes
Books on tape from RFBD: Yes
Taping of books not from RFBD: No
Accommodations for students with ADHD: Yes
Reading machine: Yes
Other assistive technology: Yes
Priority registration: Yes

Added costs for services: No
LD specialists: Yes
Professional tutors: No
Peer tutors: No
Max. hours/wk. for services: 2
How professors are notified of LD/ADHD: By student

GENERAL ADMISSIONS INFORMATION

Director of Admissions: Matthew Whalen
Telephone: 631-632-6868

ENTRANCE REQUIREMENTS

Academic units required: 4 English, 3 math, 3 science, 2 foreign language, 4 social studies. **Academic units recommended:** 4 math, 4 science, 3 foreign language. High school diploma is required, and GED is accepted. ACT with Writing component required. TOEFL required of all international applicants: minimum paper TOEFL 550, minimum computer TOEFL 213.

Application deadline: 3/1
Notification: 2/1
Average GPA: 3.60
ACT Composite middle 50% range: NR

SAT Math middle 50% range: 570–670
SAT Critical Reading middle 50% range: 510–610
SAT Writing middle 50% range: NR

Graduated top 10% of class: NR
Graduated top 25% of class: NR
Graduated top 50% of class: NR

COLLEGE GRADUATION REQUIREMENTS

Course waivers allowed: No
Course substitutions allowed: Yes
In what course: Subsitutions possible for foreign language

ADDITIONAL INFORMATION

Environment: The university is located on 1,100 acres in a suburban area on Long Island, 60 miles from New York City.

Student Body
  Undergrad enrollment: 14,639
  Women: 50%
  Men: 50%
  Percent out-of-state: 4%

Cost Information
  In-state tuition: $4,350
  Out-of-state tuition: $10,610
  Room & board: $8,394
Housing Information
  University housing: Yes
  Percent living on campus: 52%

Greek System
  Fraternity: Yes
  Sorority: Yes
Athletics: Division I

State University of New York—Stony Brook University

STATE UNIVERSITY OF NEW YORK— UNIVERSITY AT ALBANY

Office of Undergraduate Admissions, UAB 101, 1400 Washington Avenue, Albany, NY 12222 • Phone: 518-442-5435 • Fax: 518-442-5383
E-mail: ugadmissions@albany.edu • Web: www.albany.edu
Support: S • Institution type: 4-year public

LEARNING DISABILITY PROGRAM AND SERVICES

The mission at SUNY at Albany is to provide a quality educational program to students with dyslexia/learning disabilities. The Learning Disabilities Resource Program is a division of Student Affairs that seeks to empower students with LD to become successful decision makers and problem solvers. It also promotes increased sensitivity to and appreciation for the uniqueness of students with LD. The goal is to provide general support for students as they attempt to gain access to services and accommodations necessary to their success. The program provides a Writing Center staffed by faculty, advocacy, assistance with recommended courses, and tutoring assistance, and is willing to explore innovative ways of providing the most efficient assistance possible. The Mentor Program provides extra academic assistance and support for students with LD/ADHD. The mentor is a graduate student with a distinguished academic record who is paired with the mentee. They meet twice a week and develop problem-solving techniques. The mentor does not function as a content tutor, but does provide oversight and supervision for academic course work. The cost for the Mentor Program is $675 per semester.

LD/ADHD ADMISSIONS INFORMATION

College entrance tests required: Yes
Interview required: No
Essay recommended: No
Documentation required for LD: Current psychological/educational evaluation (completed within the past 3 years)
Documentation required for ADHD: Medical documenation is sufficient for individual appointments. Psychoeducational evaluation (completed within the past 3 years) will need to be submitted to support any academic accommodations.
Submitted to: LDRP
Special Ed. HS course work accepted: NR

Specific course requirements of all applicants: Yes
Separate application required: NR
# of LD applications submitted each year: NR
# of LD applications accepted yearly: NR
Total # of students receiving LD services: 65–90
Acceptance into program means acceptance into college: Students must be admitted to and enrolled in the university first and then request services.

ADMISSIONS

There is no special application for applicants with learning disabilities. Applicants who self-disclose may have their application files reviewed by the director of the LDRP and the Office of Admissions. Letters of recommendation, auxiliary testing, and a personal interview are helpful. Students must present 18 units from high school acceptable to the university, a 950 SAT score, and a high school average of at least 85 percent, and must rank in the top one-third of their class.

ADDITIONAL INFORMATION

Services include pre-admission review of the applicant's file in conjunction with admissions and individual counseling and advisement to applicants and their families; counseling and support; auxiliary aids and services such as testing accommodations, assistance in locating note-takers and tutors, reading services, and loan of tape recorders; information and referral to campus resources; and consultation and advocacy. Students diagnosed with ADHD who have documented LD may receive support from the LDRP or, in some cases, from the Office of Disabled Student Services. The Learning Disabilities Resource Program empowers students to become successful decision makers and problem solvers within a safe, accessible, diverse environment. LDRP offers counseling, testing accommodation, and consultation and advocacy services, while promoting increased sensitivity to and appreciation for the uniqueness of students with learning disabilities.

LEARNING DISABILITY PROGRAM/SERVICES

Learning Disability Program/Services: Learning Disabilities Resource Program
Director: Nancy Belowich-Negron
  E-mail: nbelowich@uamail.albany.edu
  Telephone: 518-442-5490
  Fax: 518-442-5589

LEARNING DISABILITY SERVICES

Requests for the following services/accommodations will be evaluated individually based on appropriate and current documentation.

Allowed in exams
  Calculator: Yes
  Dictionary: No
  Computer: Yes
  Spellchecker: Yes
Extended test time: Yes
Scribes: Yes
Proctors: Yes
Oral exams: Yes
Note-takers: Yes

Distraction-reduced environment: Yes
Tape recording in class: Yes
Books on tape from RFBD: Yes
Taping of books not from RFBD: No
Accommodations for students with ADHD: Yes
Reading machine: Yes
Other assistive technology: Yes
Priority registration: Yes

Added costs for services: No
LD specialists: Yes
Professional tutors: Yes
Peer tutors: Yes
Max. hours/wk. for services: Unlimited
How professors are notified of LD/ADHD: By student

GENERAL ADMISSIONS INFORMATION

Director of Admissions: Robert Andrea
Telephone: 800-293-7869

ENTRANCE REQUIREMENTS

Academic units required: 4 English, 2 math, 2 science (2 science labs), 1 foreign language, 3 social studies, 2 history, 4 academic electives. **Academic units recommended:** 4 math, 3 science (3 science labs), 3 foreign language. High school diploma is required, and GED is accepted. ACT with Writing component required. TOEFL required of all international applicants: minimum paper TOEFL 550, minimum computer TOEFL 213.

Application deadline: 3/1
Notification: Rolling
Average GPA: 3.26
ACT Composite middle 50% range: NR

SAT Math middle 50% range: 520–610
SAT Critical Reading middle 50% range: 500–590
SAT Writing middle 50% range: NR

Graduated top 10% of class: 14%
Graduated top 25% of class: 31%
Graduated top 50% of class: 87%

COLLEGE GRADUATION REQUIREMENTS

Course waivers allowed: No
Course substitutions allowed: Yes
In what course: Determined on a case-by-case basis with supporting documentation

ADDITIONAL INFORMATION

Environment: The university has an urban campus on 515 acres located on the fringe of the state capital.

Student Body
  Undergrad enrollment: 11,680
  Women: 50%
  Men: 50%
  Percent out-of-state: 6%

Cost Information
  In-state tuition: $4,350
  Out-of-state tuition: $10,610
  Room & board: $8,604
Housing Information
  University housing: Yes
  Percent living on campus: 61%

Greek System
  Fraternity: Yes
  Sorority: Yes
  Athletics: Division I

SYRACUSE UNIVERSITY

200 Crouse-Hinds Hall, Office of Admissions, Syracuse, NY 13244-2130
Phone: 315-443-3611 • Fax: 315-443-4226
E-mail: orange@syr.edu • Web: www.syracuse.edu
Support: CS • Institution type: 4-year private

LEARNING DISABILITY PROGRAM AND SERVICES

The Center for Academic Achievement provides an integrated network of academic support, counseling, and advising services to meet the individual needs of students with diagnosed learning disabilities. Every student with learning disabilities who is accepted to the university is eligible for services and must provide diagnostic information from which appropriate academic accommodations are determined. The staff is very supportive and sensitive to the needs of the students. Services are provided by a professional staff that sincerely cares about the needs of every student. The program enables students to develop a sense of independence as they learn to advocate for themselves and become involved in their college education.

LD/ADHD ADMISSIONS INFORMATION

College entrance tests required: Yes
Interview required: Yes
Essay recommended: Yes
Documentation required for LD: Psychoeducational evaluation
Documentation required for ADHD: Yes
Submitted to: CAA
Special Ed. HS course work accepted: No

Specific course requirements of all applicants: Yes
Separate application required: Yes
# of LD applications submitted each year: NR
# of LD applications accepted yearly: NR
Total # of students receiving LD services: 450
Acceptance into program means acceptance into college: Students must be admitted to and enrolled in the university first and then request services.

ADMISSIONS

All students must meet regular admission standards and submit the general application form. General admission criteria include 4 years of English, 3–4 years of math, 3–4 years of science, 3–4 years of social studies, and 2 years of a foreign language; an ACT of 25 or SAT of 1100-plus; and a B average (80 percent or a 3.0 GPA). However, consideration will be given to standardized testing scores in light of the disability. Students with learning disabilities may request substitutions for high school math or foreign language if documentation can substantiate a disability in any one of these areas. Students should include current testing and documentation. Students can write an accompanying letter describing their learning disability, their goals, and the services needed. Students' grades should show an upward trend. In the event that an applicant is denied admission to a specific course of study, an alternative offer may be suggested.

ADDITIONAL INFORMATION

Students with identified learning disabilities are provided with an integrated network of academic and counseling services to meet their individual needs. Services include note-takers, proofreaders, readers for exams and textbooks, tutors, counseling, and advising. Accommodations include time extensions for exams, papers, or projects; alternative testing methods; and spelling waivers. The Center for Academic Achievement provides each student with an accommodation letter to be used when the students meet with instructors to verify their LD status. To take advantage of these support services, diagnosed students must submit recent documentation of their learning disability. The Summer Institute Program is a 6-week program designed to enrich students' academic experience and ensure a smooth transition from high school to college with academic advising, orientation, tutoring, and career planning and counseling. Services are offered to undergraduate and graduate students.

LEARNING DISABILITY PROGRAM/SERVICES

Learning Disability Program/Services: Center for Academic Achievement (CAA)
Director: Stephen H. Simon
  E-mail: shsimon@syr.edu
  Telephone: 315-443-4498
  Fax: 315-443-1312

LEARNING DISABILITY SERVICES

Requests for the following services/accommodations will be evaluated individually based on appropriate and current documentation.

Allowed in exams
  Calculator: Yes
  Dictionary: NR
  Computer: Yes
  Spellchecker: Yes
Extended test time: Yes
Scribes: Yes
Proctors: Yes
Oral exams: Yes
Note-takers: Yes

Distraction-reduced environment: Yes
Tape recording in class: Yes
Books on tape from RFBD: Yes
Taping of books not from RFBD: Yes
Accommodations for students with ADHD: Yes
Reading machine: Yes
Other assistive technology: Yes
Priority registration: No

Added costs for services: No
LD specialists: Yes
Professional tutors: No
Peer tutors: Yes
Max. hours/wk. for services: 18
How professors are notified of LD/ADHD: By student

GENERAL ADMISSIONS INFORMATION

Director of Admissions: Susan E. Donovan
Telephone: 315-443-3611

ENTRANCE REQUIREMENTS
Academic units required: 4 English, 3 math, 3 science (3 science labs), 2 foreign language, 3 social studies, 5 academic electives. **Academic units recommended:** 4 English, 3 math, 3 science (3 science labs), 3 foreign language, 3 social studies, 5 academic electives. High school diploma is required, and GED is accepted. ACT with Writing component required. TOEFL required of all international applicants: minimum paper TOEFL 560, minimum computer TOEFL 217.

Application deadline: 1/1
Notification: Rolling
Average GPA: 3.60
ACT Composite middle 50% range: 24–29

SAT Math middle 50% range: 570–680
SAT Critical Reading middle 50% range: 550–650
SAT Writing middle 50% range: NR

Graduated top 10% of class: 45%
Graduated top 25% of class: 78%
Graduated top 50% of class: 97%

COLLEGE GRADUATION REQUIREMENTS

Course waivers allowed: No
Course substitutions allowed: Yes
In what course: Students can petition for substitutions for math or foreign language. Substitutions must be approved by each college.

ADDITIONAL INFORMATION

Environment: The school is located on 200 acres set on a hill overlooking the city of Syracuse.

Student Body
  Undergrad enrollment: 11,546
  Women: 55%
  Men: 45%
  Percent out-of-state: 57%

Cost Information
  Tuition: $28,820
  Room & board: $10,420
Housing Information
  University housing: Yes
  Percent living on campus: 75%

Greek System
  Fraternity: Yes
  Sorority: Yes
Athletics: Division I

UTICA COLLEGE

1600 Burrstone Road, Utica, NY 13502-4892
Phone: 315-792-3006 • Fax: 315-792-3003
E-mail: admiss@utica.edu • Web: www.utica.edu
Support: CS • Institution type: 4-year private

LEARNING DISABILITY PROGRAM AND SERVICES

Utica College is dedicated to ensuring reasonable access to programs and continuously seeks to augment and improve their services. The Academic Support Services Center provides counseling and academic support to an increasing number of students who identify themselves as LD. Accommodations are determined as a result of a diagnostic evaluation. Students are responsible for initiating a request for accommodations, for providing verification of a disability, and for contacting the support office as early as possible after admission to the college. The Coordinator of Student Services determines eligibility for services based on documentation, consults with students about appropriate accommodations, assists students in self-monitoring the effectiveness of the accommodations, coordinates auxiliary services, reviews disability documentation and development of a needs assessment, provides information regarding legal rights and responsibilities of students, provides personal and educational counseling, and serves as an advocate.

LD/ADHD ADMISSIONS INFORMATION

College entrance tests required: No
Interview required: No
Essay recommended: Yes
Documentation required for LD: A written evaluation, including a discrepancy analysis, completed by an appropriate professional. Please contact Learning Services for guidelines.
Documentation required for ADHD: A written evaluation completed by an appropriate professional. Please contact Learning Services for guidelines.
Submitted to: Admissions and Academic Support Services
Special Ed. HS course work accepted: No

Specific course requirements of all applicants: Yes
Separate application required: No
# of LD applications submitted each year: NR
# of LD applications accepted yearly: NR
Total # of students receiving LD services: NR
Acceptance into program means acceptance into college: Students must be admitted to and enrolled in the university first and then request services.

ADMISSIONS

Utica College does not require standardized tests. Students are evaluated on an individual basis. Students should have 4 years of English, 3 years of social studies, 3 years of math, 3 years of science, and 2 years of a foreign language. Special education courses are not accepted. Students with LD are encouraged to request an interview. Documentation of an LD should be sent to admissions and support services. Students are encouraged to self-disclose the LD during the admission process.

ADDITIONAL INFORMATION

Student Services provides accommodations to students with LD based on appropriate and current documentation. Current documentation includes a written evaluation with a discrepancy analysis that is completed by a licensed psychologist or certified learning disability specialist, indicating the specific learning disability and the academic accommodations needed. Services could include priority registration, specific skill remediation, learning and study strategy development, referrals for diagnostic evaluation, time management training, and individual peer tutoring. Other accommodations could include such items as use of a tape recorder, time extensions for tests and/or alternative testing methods, note-takers, scribes, readers, tutors, and use of a proofreader to correct spelling on assignments outside of class. A disabilities form is provided stating what accommodations are appropriate in each individual case. It is the student's responsibility to notify instructors of the disability.

LEARNING DISABILITY PROGRAM/SERVICES

Learning Disability Program/Services: Learning Services/Academic Support Services Center
Director: Kateri Teresa Henkel, Coordinator
  E-mail: khenkel@utica.edu
  Telephone: 315-792-3032
  Fax: 315-223-2504

LEARNING DISABILITY SERVICES

Requests for the following services/accommodations will be evaluated individually based on appropriate and current documentation.

Allowed in exams
  Calculator: Yes
  Dictionary: Yes
  Computer: Yes
  Spellchecker: Yes
  Extended test time: Yes
  Scribes: No
  Proctors: No
  Oral exams: Yes
  Note-takers: Yes

Distraction-reduced environment: Yes
Tape recording in class: Yes
Books on tape from RFBD: No
Taping of books not from RFBD: Yes
Accommodations for students with ADHD: Yes
Reading machine: No
Other assistive technology: Yes
Priority registration: Yes

Added costs for services: No
LD specialists: Yes
Professional tutors: 2
Peer tutors: No
Max. hours/wk. for services: Yes
How professors are notified of LD/ADHD: By student

GENERAL ADMISSIONS INFORMATION

Director of Admissions: Patrick Quinn
Telephone: 315-792-3006

ENTRANCE REQUIREMENTS

Academic units required: 4 English, 3 math, 3 science, 2 foreign language, 3 social studies, 1 academic elective. High school diploma is required, and GED is accepted. ACT with or without Writing component accepted. TOEFL required of all international applicants: minimum paper TOEFL 525, minimum computer TOEFL 195.

Application deadline: Open
Notification: Rolling
Average GPA: 2.98
ACT Composite middle 50% range: 19–23

SAT Math middle 50% range: 430–540
SAT Critical Reading middle 50% range: 420–530
SAT Writing middle 50% range: 410–520

Graduated top 10% of class: 10%
Graduated top 25% of class: 30%
Graduated top 50% of class: 65%

COLLEGE GRADUATION REQUIREMENTS

Course waivers allowed: No
Course substitutions allowed: Yes
In what course: Foreign language substitutions are determined individually based on documentation and are allowed if the course is not an essential component of the major.

ADDITIONAL INFORMATION

Environment: The school has a suburban campus located 50 miles east of Syracuse

Student Body
  Undergrad enrollment: 2,339
  Women: 60%
  Men: 40%
  Percent out-of-state: 16%

Cost Information
  Tuition: $22,030
  Room & board: $9,056
Housing Information
  University housing: Yes
  Percent living on campus: 41%

Greek System
  Fraternity: Yes
  Sorority: Yes
  Athletics: Division III

APPALACHIAN STATE UNIVERSITY

Office of Admissions, ASU Box 32004, Boone, NC 28608-2004
Phone: 828-262-2120 • Fax: 828-262-3296
E-mail: admissions@appstate.edu • Web: www.appstate.edu
Support: CS • Institution type: 4-year public

LEARNING DISABILITY PROGRAM AND SERVICES

The University Learning Disability Program is part of a larger academic support service called the Learning Assistance Program. The LD program is designed to provide academic services for students who self-identify on a voluntary basis and attend regular classes. Students with learning disabilities are totally integrated throughout the university community. Students are expected to communicate with their instructors regarding their specific needs. The Coordinator of Services works with students and faculty to implement needed services and accommodations. The needs of each student are considered and treated individually in consultation with the student and are based on current documentation of the learning disability.

LD/ADHD ADMISSIONS INFORMATION

College entrance tests required: Yes
Interview required: No
Essay recommended: No
Documentation required for LD: A comprehensive psychoeducational evaluation that is current within the past 3 years
Documentation required for ADHD: A comprehensive psychoeducational evaluation that is current within the past 3 years
Submitted to: Disabiltity Services
Special Ed. HS course work accepted: No

Specific course requirements of all applicants: Yes
Separate application required: Yes
# of LD applications submitted each year: 100
# of LD applications accepted yearly: 100
Total # of students receiving LD services: 234
Acceptance into program means acceptance into college: Students must be accepted and enrolled at the university first and then must identify and provide documentation to be eligible for assistance.

ADMISSIONS
Students with learning disabilities are admitted to the university through the regular admission procedure. The minimum admissions requirements include 4 years of English, 3 years of math, 3 years of science (1 in biology and 1 in a physical science), 2 years of social science. Two years of a foreign language and 1 course in math and foreign language in the student's senior year are recommended. Applicants may self-disclose on their applications. This information would support their application for admission. A personal statement, letters of recommendations, and school activities provide additional useful information. Once students have been accepted by the university, a form is provided with which the students can identify their disabilities. This identification process is necessary for the students to have access to the services of the LD program. Students not regularly admissible may request a review of their application with additional or updated information.

ADDITIONAL INFORMATION
Tutoring is provided on a one-on-one basis for assistance with course content, as well as guidance in developing or improving learning skills. Tutors are trained in working with each student. Basic skills courses are available in memory skills, oral presentation, and note-taking strategies, reading textbooks, written language, math, time management techniques, and study strategies. Skills courses for no credit are offered in English and math. LD/ADHD coaching is available through the Office of Disability Services (ODS). Coaching is provided by ODS graduate assistants and consists of one-on-one meetings to minimize the frustrations of ADHD/LD and maximize your ability using feedback, guidance, and an ongoing partnership. Skills addressed include establishing and achieving semester goals, study and test strategies, time management and organizational planning, note-taking tips, and planning projects. Services and accommodations are available for undergraduates and graduates.

LEARNING DISABILITY PROGRAM/SERVICES

Learning Disability Program/Services: Office of Disability Services
Director: Suzanne T. Wehner
  E-mail: wehnerst@appstate.edu
  Telephone: 828-262-2291
  Fax: 828-262-6834

LEARNING DISABILITY SERVICES

Requests for the following services/accommodations will be evaluated individually based on appropriate and current documentation.

Allowed in exams	**Distraction-reduced environment:** Yes	**Added costs for services:** No
Calculator: Yes	**Tape recording in class:** Yes	**LD specialists:** Yes
Dictionary: Yes	**Books on tape from RFBD:** Yes	**Professional tutors:** 2
Computer: Yes	**Taping of books not from RFBD:** No	**Peer tutors:** 150
Spellchecker: Yes	**Accommodations for students with**	**Max. hours/wk. for services:**
Extended test time: Yes	**ADHD:** Yes	Unlimited
Scribes: Yes	**Reading machine:** Yes	**How professors are notified of**
Proctors: Yes	**Other assistive technology:** Yes	**LD/ADHD:** By student
Oral exams: Yes	**Priority registration:** Yes	
Note-takers: Yes		

GENERAL ADMISSIONS INFORMATION

Director of Admissions: Dr. Harry Williams, Acting Vice Chancellor for Enrollment
Telephone: 828-262-2120

ENTRANCE REQUIREMENTS

Academic units required: 4 English, 4 math, 3 science (1 science lab), 2 foreign language, 2 social studies, 1 history. High school diploma is required, and GED is not accepted. ACT with Writing component required. TOEFL required of all international applicants: minimum paper TOEFL 500.

Application deadline: NR	**SAT Math middle 50% range:**	**Graduated top 10% of class:** 16%
Notification: 10/15	530–620	**Graduated top 25% of class:** 50%
Average GPA: 3.74	**SAT Critical Reading middle 50%**	**Graduated top 50% of class:** 87%
ACT Composite middle 50% range:	**range:** 510–600	
20–25	**SAT Writing middle 50% range:**	
	480–580	

COLLEGE GRADUATION REQUIREMENTS

Course waivers allowed: No
Course substitutions allowed: No

ADDITIONAL INFORMATION

Environment: The university has a 255-acre campus in a small town 90 miles northwest of Winston-Salem.

Student Body	**Cost Information**	**Greek System**
Undergrad enrollment: 13,114	**In-state tuition:** $3,000	**Fraternity:** Yes
Women: 50%	**Out-of-state tuition:** $13,000	**Sorority:** Yes
Men: 50%	**Room & board:** $5,760	**Athletics:** Division I
Percent out-of-state: 9%	**Housing Information**	
	University housing: Yes	
	Percent living on campus: 38%	

BREVARD COLLEGE

One Brevard College Drive, Brevard, NC 28712
Phone: 828-884-8300 • Fax: 828-884-3790
E-mail: admissions@brevard.edu • Web: www.brevard.edu
Support: CS • Institution type: 4-year private

LEARNING DISABILITY PROGRAM AND SERVICES

Brevard College does not offer a special program or curriculum for students with LD. However, students with a documented LD or other disability can receive assistance from the Office for Students with Special Needs and Disabilities. The college has excellent LD support services, as well as the Learning Enhancement Center, where any student can receive services such as counseling on academic matters; tutoring in a specific subject; advice on organizing work and/or managing time; assistance with reading skills, study skills, and test-taking skills; and private note-taking. Through private meetings with the director, students can review their documentation and identify academic accommodations, which are adjustments to course policies. The Director of the Office for Students with Special Needs and Disabilities works with students to determine what accommodations would be good to use and how to obtain these accommodations. The director can talk to professors about the LD and accommodations.

LD/ADHD ADMISSIONS INFORMATION

College entrance tests required: Yes
Interview required: No
Essay recommended: No
Documentation required for LD: A recent psychoeducational assessment
Documentation required for ADHD: A recent psychoeducational assessment or a diagnostic statement from a medical professional currently treating the condition
Submitted to: Admissions

Special Ed. HS course work accepted: Yes
Specific course requirements of all applicants: NR
Separate application required: No
# of LD applications submitted each year: NR
# of LD applications accepted yearly: NR
Total # of students receiving LD services: 63
Acceptance into program means acceptance into college: Students must be admitted to and enrolled in the university first and then request services.

ADMISSIONS

There is no special admission process for students with LD. However, every applicant is unique, and this is why Brevard College asks for quite a bit of information from applicants and from those who know the applicants and their learning style. If applicants are aware of a learning disability, they are encouraged to provide information: for example, testing and reports, recommendations, and assessments. Applicants must provide official transcripts from all secondary schools and colleges attended and letters of recommendation from their counselor, a teacher of English, and one other teacher or adult who has worked with the student and knows the student well. ACT/SAT is required but there is no cutoff point relative to admission. Brevard looks for strong verbal ability as represented in an applicant's writing samples submitted with the application. Special admissions procedures require an on-campus interview. This gives the college a chance to know what the student struggles with, what the student feels confident about, and what the student wants to achieve. The admission process changes only when the student does not meet the general admissions requirements and wants special consideration due to a disability. Students should enclose with their application a statement that says he or she has a disability, which admission requirements the student feels the disability impacts and how it does so, what alternative or additional info the student wants considered, and documentation of the disability. Disability services will review the individual circumstances and consider providing advocacy. Special admission is available for students who are nondegree candidates, auditors, and dual-enrolled high school students. One who enters via special admission is not eligible for a degree program but is eligible to receive college credit (unless auditing a course).

ADDITIONAL INFORMATION

Students have access to the Career Counseling Center, the Math Lab, and the Writing Center. The Learning Enhancement Center provides individualized and personalized assistance via such academic services as academic counseling; course schedule advisement; tutor referrals; guidance with time management, project organization, study skills, textbook reading skills, concentration development, test anxiety reduction, and test-taking skills; note-taking; limited textbook taping services; and distraction-reduced test sites. Brevard College also provides developmental courses in math, computers, and reading for students in need of a better academic foundation. Students placed in a developmental course will need to complete it successfully before certain college-level courses can be taken.

LEARNING DISABILITY PROGRAM/SERVICES

Learning Disability Program/Services: Office for Students with Special Needs and Disabilities
Director: Susan Kuehn
  E-mail: skuehn@brevard.edu
  Telephone: 828-884-8131
  Fax: 828-884-8293

LEARNING DISABILITY SERVICES

Requests for the following services/accommodations will be evaluated individually based on appropriate and current documentation.

Allowed in exams
  Calculator: Yes
  Dictionary: Yes
  Computer: Yes
  Spellchecker: Yes
Extended test time: Yes
Scribes: Yes
Proctors: Yes
Oral exams: Yes
Note-takers: Yes

Distraction-reduced environment: Yes
Tape recording in class: Yes
Books on tape from RFBD: Yes
Taping of books not from RFBD: Yes
Accommodations for students with ADHD: Yes
Reading machine: Yes
Other assistive technology: Yes
Priority registration: Yes

Added costs for services: No
LD specialists: Yes
Professional tutors: 5–15
Peer tutors: 5–10
Max. hours/wk. for services: Unlimited
How professors are notified of LD/ADHD: By student

GENERAL ADMISSIONS INFORMATION

Director of Admissions: Joretta Nelson
Telephone: 828-884-8313

ENTRANCE REQUIREMENTS

Academic units recommended: 4 English, 3 math, 3 science (1 science lab), 2 foreign language, 4 social studies, 1 history, 4 academic electives. High school diploma is required, and GED is accepted. SAT/ACT with or without Writing component accepted. TOEFL required of all international applicants: minimum paper TOEFL 537, minimum computer TOEFL 203.

Application deadline: Rolling
Notification: Rolling
Average GPA: 3.13
ACT Composite middle 50% range: 17–23

SAT Math middle 50% range: 408–608
SAT Critical Reading middle 50% range: 389–595
SAT Writing middle 50% range: NR

Graduated top 10% of class: 5%
Graduated top 25% of class: 22%
Graduated top 50% of class: 53%

COLLEGE GRADUATION REQUIREMENTS

Course waivers allowed: No
Course substitutions allowed: Yes
In what course: Substitutions are done on a case-by-case basis.

ADDITIONAL INFORMATION

Environment: Brevard College is a residential campus located in a small town 33 miles from Asheville, North Carolina.

Student Body
  Undergrad enrollment: 664
  Women: 44%
  Men: 56%
  Percent out-of-state: 47%

Cost Information
  Tuition: $16,820
  Room & board: $6,150
Housing Information
  University housing: Yes
  Percent living on campus: 74%

Greek System
  Fraternity: No
  Sorority: No
  Athletics: Division II

DAVIDSON COLLEGE

PO Box 7156, Davidson, NC 28035-5000
Phone: 704-894-2230 • Fax: 704-894-2016
E-mail: admission@davidson.edu • Web: www.davidson.edu
Support: CS • Institution type: 4-year private

LEARNING DISABILITY PROGRAM AND SERVICES

Students enroll in Davidson with a proven record of academic achievement and the ability to utilize resources, persevere, and excel. The college provides services and accommodations to allow students an opportunity to continue to be successful. Special procedures have been developed for students handicapped by learning disabilities. Students who seek adapted instruction on the basis of a learning disability undergo an evaluation by college-designated learning specialists, usually at the student's expense. The results of the evaluation, made available to the college with the student's permission, may include recommendations for compensatory learning strategies to be used by the student and recommendations for services and accommodations to be provided by the college. Using these recommendations as a guide, the Student Learning Support Committee works with the student to develop a learning plan that enhances learning strengths and compensates for learning difficulties. If the learning plan recommends adjustment to academic requirements, the recommendation is considered by the Curriculum Requirements Committee and may result in the approval of the recommendation or the substitution of the academic requirement. All students seeking accommodations on the basis of an LD must provide recent documentation. The Dean of Students, with the student's permission, will notify professors of an individual student's need for adaptations. Accommodations are not universal in nature but are designed to meet the specific need of the individual to offset a specific disability.

LD/ADHD ADMISSIONS INFORMATION

College entrance tests required: Yes
Interview required: No
Essay recommended: No
Documentation required for LD: Documentation is not required until matriculation.
Documentation required for ADHD: Documentation is required once the student is matriculated.
Submitted to: Dean of Student Services
Special Ed. HS course work accepted: No

Specific course requirements of all applicants: Yes
Separate application required: No
# of LD applications submitted each year: NR
# of LD applications accepted yearly: NR
Total # of students receiving LD services: 54
Acceptance into program means acceptance into college: Students must be admitted to and enrolled in the university first and then request services.

ADMISSIONS

There is no special admission process for students with LD, though the Admissions Office may seek comments from support staff knowledgeable about LD. Students are encouraged to self-disclose their ADHD. The admission process is very competitive, and the disclosure can help the Admissions Office more fairly evaluate the transcript. This disclosure could address any specific academic issues related to the LD, such as no foreign language in high school because of the specific LD or lower grades in math as a result of a math disability. The GPA is recalculated to reflect rigor with 97 percent of the accepted students having a recalculated GPA of 3.0. Students have completed at least 4 years of English, 3 years of math, 2 years of the same foreign language, 2 years of science, and 2 years of history/social studies. Courses taken in special education are not accepted. The mid 50 percent of students have an ACT between 28 and 31 or SAT between 1240 and 1420. Interviews are not required but are recommended.

ADDITIONAL INFORMATION

Support services and accommodations available include, but are not limited to: referrals for appropriate diagnostic evaluation; individual coaching and instruction in compensatory strategies and study skills; consultation with faculty and staff; student support groups as requested; classroom accommodations such as extra test-taking time, taped texts, note-takers, use of tape recorders, use of computers with spellcheckers, and individual space for study or test-taking; reduced course loads; and course substitutions or waivers (rarely). There are a Math Center, Writing Lab, peer tutoring, and skill class in time management available for all students. There is one full-time and one part-time LD specialist on staff and peer tutoring for all students as needed.

LEARNING DISABILITY PROGRAM/SERVICES

Learning Disability Program/Services: Dean of Students Office
Director: Kathy Bray Merrell, Associate Dean of Students
  E-mail: kamerrel@davidson.edu
  Telephone: 704-894-2225
  Fax: 704-894-2849

LEARNING DISABILITY SERVICES

Requests for the following services/accommodations will be evaluated individually based on appropriate and current documentation.

Allowed in exams
  Calculator: Yes
  Dictionary: Yes
  Computer: Yes
  Spellchecker: Yes
Extended test time: Yes
Scribes: Yes
Proctors: Yes
Oral exams: No
Note-takers: Yes

Distraction-reduced environment: Yes
Tape recording in class: Yes
Books on tape from RFBD: Yes
Taping of books not from RFBD: No
Accommodations for students with ADHD: Yes
Reading machine: No
Other assistive technology: No
Priority registration: No

Added costs for services: No
LD specialists: Yes
Professional tutors: No
Peer tutors: 100
Max. hours/wk. for services: Unlimited
How professors are notified of LD/ADHD: By both student and director

GENERAL ADMISSIONS INFORMATION

Director of Admissions: Dr. Nancy Cable
Telephone: 704-894-2230

ENTRANCE REQUIREMENTS

Academic units required: 4 English, 3 math, 2 science, 2 foreign language, 2 social studies and history.
Academic units recommended: 4 math, 4 science, 4 foreign language, 4 social studies and history. High school diploma is required, and GED is not accepted. ACT with or without Writing component accepted. TOEFL required of all international applicants: minimum paper TOEFL 600, minimum computer TOEFL 250.

Application deadline: 1/2
Notification: 4/1
Average GPA: 3.9
ACT Composite middle 50% range: 27–31

SAT Math middle 50% range: 630–720
SAT Critical Reading middle 50% range: 620–720
SAT Writing middle 50% range: NR

Graduated top 10% of class: 79%
Graduated top 25% of class: 97%
Graduated top 50% of class: 99%

COLLEGE GRADUATION REQUIREMENTS

Course waivers allowed: No
Course substitutions allowed: Yes
In what course: Substitutions in any appropriate course

ADDITIONAL INFORMATION

Environment: The campus is located 20 miles from Charlotte, North Carolina.

Student Body
  Undergrad enrollment: 1,660
  Women: 50%
  Men: 50%
  Percent out-of-state: 81%

Cost Information
  Tuition: $29,119
  Room & board: $8,590
Housing Information
  University housing: Yes
  Percent living on campus: 91%

Greek System
  Fraternity: Yes
  Sorority: No
Athletics: Division I

DUKE UNIVERSITY

2138 Campus Drive, Box 90586, Durham, NC 27708-0586
Phone: 919-684-3214 • Fax: 919-681-8941
E-mail: undergrad-admissions@duke.edu• Web: www.admissions.duke.edu
Support: CS • Institution type: 4-year private

LEARNING DISABILITY PROGRAM AND SERVICES

Duke University does not provide a formal, highly structured program for students with LD. The university does provide, however, significant academic support services for students through the Academic Resource Center (ARC). Students who submit appropriate documentation of their learning disability to the ARC clinical director are eligible for assistance in obtaining reasonable academic adjustments and auxiliary aids. In addition, the ARC clinical director and instructors can provide individualized instruction in academic skills and learning strategies, academic support counseling, and referrals for other services. Students with learning disabilities voluntarily access and use the services of the ARC, just as they might access and use other campus resources. Student interactions with the ARC staff are confidential. The goals of the support services for students with learning disabilities are in keeping with the goals of all services provided through the ARC: to help students achieve their academic potential within the context of a competitive university setting, promote a disciplined approach to study, and foster active, independent learners.

LD/ADHD ADMISSIONS INFORMATION

College entrance tests required: Yes
Interview required: No
Essay recommended: No
Documentation required for LD: Current psychoeducational testing completed within the past 3 years
Documentation required for ADHD: Current psychoeducational testing completed within the past 3 years
Submitted to: ARC
Special Ed. HS course work accepted: No

Specific course requirements of all applicants: NR
Separate application required: No
# of LD applications submitted each year: 15
# of LD applications accepted yearly: 15
Total # of students receiving LD services: 30–50
Acceptance into program means acceptance into college: Students must be admitted to and enrolled in the university first and then request services.

ADMISSIONS

There is no special admission process for students with learning disabilities. All applicants must meet the general Duke admissions criteria. Admission to Duke is highly competitive, and most applicants are in the top 10 percent of their class. Most applicants have completed a demanding curriculum in high school, including many Advanced Placement and honors courses. Services and accommodations may be requested after enrollment in Duke.

ADDITIONAL INFORMATION

Assistance is available as needed from the student's academic dean and the clinical director of ARC. Students are encouraged to consult with their faculty advisor and the ARC well in advance of registration to determine the appropriate measures for particular courses. There is one staff member with special learning disability training and three staff members who are writing/learning strategy instructors. Documentation and diagnostic tests are required for accommodations, not admissions. Students may also receive peer tutoring in introductory-level courses in several disciplines through the ARC peer tutoring program. Up to 12 hours of tutoring in each course is offered at no additional charge. Students need to understand their LD, be able to self-advocate, and know what accommodations are necessary to assist them in being successful in college. Students are expected to work out reasonable accommodations with each of their professors. Outside testing referrals are made at the student's expense.

LEARNING DISABILITY PROGRAM/SERVICES

Learning Disability Program/Services: Student Disability Access Office/Academic Resource Center (ARC)
Director: Emma Swain
  E-mail: eswain@duke.edu
  Telephone: 919-668-1267
  Fax: 919-668-3977
Contact Person: Jim Baker, Disability Specialist
  E-mail: jbaker@duke.edu
  Telephone: 919-668-1267
  Fax: 919-668-3977

LEARNING DISABILITY SERVICES

Requests for the following services/accommodations will be evaluated individually based on appropriate and current documentation.

Allowed in exams
  Calculator: No
  Dictionary: Yes
  Computer: Yes
  Spellchecker: No
Extended test time: Yes
Scribes: Yes
Proctors: Yes
Oral exams: Yes
Note-takers: Yes

Distraction-reduced environment: Yes
Tape recording in class: Yes
Books on tape from RFBD: Yes
Taping of books not from RFBD: Yes
Accommodations for students with ADHD: Yes
Reading machine: No
Other assistive technology: Yes
Priority registration: No

Added costs for services: No
LD specialists: Yes
Professional tutors: No
Peer tutors: 80
Max. hours/wk. for services: Unlimited
How professors are notified of LD/ADHD: By both student and director

GENERAL ADMISSIONS INFORMATION

Director of Admissions: Christoph Guttentag
Telephone: 919-684-3214

ENTRANCE REQUIREMENTS
Academic units recommended: 4 English, 4 math, 4 science, 4 foreign language, 4 social studies. High school diploma is required, and GED is not accepted.

Application deadline: 1/2
Notification: 4/1
Average GPA: NR
ACT Composite middle 50% range: 29–34

SAT Math middle 50% range: 690–800
SAT Critical Reading middle 50% range: 690–770
SAT Writing middle 50% range: NR

Graduated top 10% of class: 90%
Graduated top 25% of class: 98%
Graduated top 50% of class: 100%

COLLEGE GRADUATION REQUIREMENTS

Course waivers allowed: No
Course substitutions allowed: No

ADDITIONAL INFORMATION

Environment: The university is on 8,500 acres in a suburban area 285 miles southwest of Washington, DC.

Student Body
  Undergrad enrollment: 6,259
  Women: 48%
  Men: 52%
  Percent out-of-state: 85%

Cost Information
  Tuition: $31,420
  Room & board: $8,950
Housing Information
  University housing: Yes
  Percent living on campus: 82%

Greek System
  Fraternity: Yes
  Sorority: Yes
  Athletics: Division I

EAST CAROLINA UNIVERSITY

Office of Undergraduate Admissions, 106 Whichard Building,
Greenville, NC 27858-4353 • Phone: 252-328-6640 • Fax: 252-328-6945
E-mail: admis@ecu.edu • Web: www.ecu.edu
Support: CS • Institution type: 4-year public

LEARNING DISABILITY PROGRAM AND SERVICES

Through the Department for Disability Support Services, the university seeks to meet individual needs by coordinating and implementing internal policy regarding programs, services, and activities for individuals with disabilities. The department functions as a source of information and advice and as a communication link among individuals with disabilities, faculty and staff members, state rehab agencies, and the community at large. The overall purpose of the university's program for students with learning disabilities is to provide auxiliary support services, so they may derive equal benefits from all that East Carolina University has to offer. Individuals with learning disabilities and attention deficit hyperactivity disorder are required to provide the department with proper documentation of their disability. An acceptable psychoeducational evaluation administered within the past 3 years must be submitted to qualify for services. Students should schedule a meeting with the department well in advance of the beginning of their first semester to prevent delays in the planning of services. Students with LD or ADHD will receive a letter describing the services required to give to their instructors. With the exception of tutorial services for personal use, academic support services are provided at no cost.

LD/ADHD ADMISSIONS INFORMATION

College entrance tests required: Yes
Interview required: No
Essay recommended: No
Documentation required for LD: Current psychoeducational battery
Documentation required for ADHD: Diagnostic summary from qualified clinician
Submitted to: Disability Support Services
Special Ed. HS course work accepted: Yes

Specific course requirements of all applicants: Yes
Separate application required: No
# of LD applications submitted each year: NR
# of LD applications accepted yearly: NR
Total # of students receiving LD services: 100–150
Acceptance into program means acceptance into college: Students must be admitted to and enrolled in the university first and then request services.

ADMISSIONS

A student with a disability applies for admission and is considered for admission in the same manner as any other applicant. Neither the nature nor the severity of one's disability is used as a criterion for admission. Students with learning disabilities are admitted solely on academic qualifications. Out-of-state students must present slightly higher GPAs and test scores, but the minimum is 2.0 depending on the SAT score. Test scores vary, but the minimum out-of-state ACT is 19 and in-state is 17, and the average ACT is 21. The minimum SAT out-of-state is 1000 and in-state is 900, and the average SAT is 1030. Students must have taken 4 years of English, 2 years of social science, and 3 years of science (1 year biology and 1 year physical science); 3 years of math and 2 years of a foreign language are recommended.

ADDITIONAL INFORMATION

Once admitted to the university, students must self-identify and register with the Department for Disability Support Services. Students must show official verification of their disability. Students will be assigned to academic advisors from the department. Once students enter their major fields of study, the department will still be available to provide advising assistance but never to the exclusion of the individual's assigned academic advisor. Alternative testing accommodations may include extended time, a noise-free environment, reader-assisted test-taking, and other arrangements that satisfy the needs of the student. A maximum of double time can be allowed for students to complete a test or an exam. The university offers a modified language sequence for students enrolled in Spanish. There are several laboratories available, including a Writing Center, a Reading Center, a Mathematics Center, an Academic Support Center, and a computer lab. Students pay for private tutoring. Skills classes for any student are available in time management, test-taking and anxiety study strategies, and academic motivation.

LEARNING DISABILITY PROGRAM/SERVICES

Learning Disability Program/Services: Department for Disability Support Services
Director: Liz Johnston
  E-mail: johnstone@mail.ecu.edu
  Telephone: 252-328-6799
  Fax: 252-328-4883
Contact Person: Diane Majewski
  E-mail: majewskid@mail.ecu.edu
  Telephone: 252-328-6799
  Fax: 252-328-4883

LEARNING DISABILITY SERVICES

Requests for the following services/accommodations will be evaluated individually based on appropriate and current documentation.

Allowed in exams
  Calculator: Yes
  Dictionary: Yes
  Computer: Yes
  Spellchecker: Yes
Extended test time: Yes
Scribes: Yes
Proctors: Yes
Oral exams: Yes
Note-takers: Yes

Distraction-reduced environment: Yes
Tape recording in class: Yes
Books on tape from RFBD: Yes
Taping of books not from RFBD: Yes
Accommodations for students with ADHD: Yes
Reading machine: Yes
Other assistive technology: Yes
Priority registration: Yes

Added costs for services: No
LD specialists: Yes
Professional tutors: No
Peer tutors: 2
Max. hours/wk. for services: Unlimited
How professors are notified of LD/ADHD: By student

GENERAL ADMISSIONS INFORMATION

Director of Admissions: Thomas E. Powell
Telephone: 252-328-6640

ENTRANCE REQUIREMENTS

Academic units required: 4 English, 4 math, 3 science (1 science lab), 2 foreign language, 2 social studies, 4 academic electives. **Academic units recommended:** 1 fine arts; 1 social studies (must be U.S. History). High school diploma is required, and GED is accepted. TOEFL required of all international applicants: minimum paper TOEFL 550, minimum computer TOEFL 213.

Application deadline: 3/15
Notification: Rolling
Average GPA: 3.42
ACT Composite middle 50% range: 17–22

SAT Math middle 50% range: 470–560
SAT Critical Reading middle 50% range: 450–540
SAT Writing middle 50% range: 440–530

Graduated top 10% of class: 11%
Graduated top 25% of class: 37%
Graduated top 50% of class: 75%

COLLEGE GRADUATION REQUIREMENTS

Course waivers allowed: No
Course substitutions allowed: No

ADDITIONAL INFORMATION

Environment: The school is located on over 370 acres within the city of Greenville, 85 miles from Raleigh.

Student Body
  Undergrad enrollment: 18,445
  Women: 60%
  Men: 40%
  Percent out-of-state: 13%

Cost Information
  In-state tuition: $4,000
  Out-of-state tuition: $14,000
  Room & board: $6,940
Housing Information
  University housing: Yes
  Percent living on campus: 24%

Greek System
  Fraternity: Yes
  Sorority: Yes
  Athletics: Division I

ELON UNIVERSITY

100 Campus Drive, 2700 Campus Box, Elon, NC 27244-2010
Phone: 336-278-3566 • Fax: 336-278-7699
E-mail: admissions@elon.edu • Web: www.elon.edu
Support: S • Institution type: 4-year private

LEARNING DISABILITY PROGRAM AND SERVICES

Elon University is committed to the principle of equal opportunity. We assist students with disabilities in finding approaches and accommodations that provide them an opportunity to benefit from the many programs offered on campus. Faculty, staff, administrators, and students work together to find approaches and accommodations that enable students to benefit from the wide variety of programs and activities on campus.

LD/ADHD ADMISSIONS INFORMATION

College entrance tests required: Yes
Interview required: No
Essay recommended: No
Documentation required for LD: Formal psychoeducational evaluation
Documentation required for ADHD: Five of the following seven: psychological evaluation, physical exam, developmental history, family history and parent interview, in-depth clinical interview, TOVA, and diagnostic criteria for ADHD as described in DSM–IV
Submitted to: Disability Services
Special Ed. HS course work accepted: No

Specific course requirements of all applicants: Yes
Separate application required: No
# of LD applications submitted each year: NR
# of LD applications accepted yearly: NR
Total # of students receiving LD services: NR
Acceptance into program means acceptance into college: Students must be admitted and enrolled prior to requesting services.

ADMISSIONS

Students with disabilities must meet the same admissions criteria as other students. There is no special disabilities admissions application. Minimum GPA is 2.4. Course requirements include 3 years of algebra, 4 years of English, 2 years of a foreign language, 1 year of history, and 1 year of science. Students may be admitted with one deficiency.

ADDITIONAL INFORMATION

Though Elon does not have a formal disabilities program, we aim to make the campus, our academic programs, and our activities accessible. Students must provide current documentation to request accommodations. Students with disabilities are encouraged to be proactive and develop an ongoing conversation with their professors and service providers. Every Elon student is assigned an advisor, a university professor or an administrator who will work with students to plan, problem-solve, and explore interests and majors. Advisors are also a contact for getting information regarding programs, tutors, special needs, or just general information.

LEARNING DISABILITY PROGRAM/SERVICES

Learning Disability Program/Services: Disabilities Services
Director: Priscilla Lipe
  E-mail: plipe@elon.edu
  Telephone: 336-278-6500
  Fax: 336-278-6514

LEARNING DISABILITY SERVICES

Requests for the following services/accommodations will be evaluated individually based on appropriate and current documentation.

Allowed in exams
  Calculator: Yes
  Dictionary: Yes
  Computer: Yes
  Spellchecker: Yes
Extended test time: Yes
Scribes: Yes
Proctors: NR
Oral exams: No
Note-takers: Yes

Distraction-reduced environment: Yes
Tape recording in class: Yes
Books on tape from RFBD: Yes
Taping of books not from RFBD: No
Accommodations for students with
  ADHD: Yes
Reading machine: Yes
Other assistive technology: No
Priority registration: Yes

Added costs for services: No
LD specialists: No
Professional tutors: No
Peer tutors: 35
Max. hours/wk. for services:
  Unlimited
How professors are notified of
  LD/ADHD: By both student and
  director

GENERAL ADMISSIONS INFORMATION

Director of Admissions: Susan Klopman
Telephone: 336-278-3566

ENTRANCE REQUIREMENTS

Academic units required: 4 English, 3 math, 3 science (1 science lab), 2 foreign language, 1 social studies, 1 history. **Academic units recommended:** 4 math, 3 foreign language, 3 social studies. High school diploma is required, and GED is accepted. ACT with Writing component required. TOEFL required of all international applicants: minimum paper TOEFL 550, minimum computer TOEFL 213.

Application deadline: 1/10
Notification: 12/20
Average GPA: 3.90
ACT Composite middle 50% range:
  23–28

SAT Math middle 50% range:
  570–650
SAT Critical Reading middle 50%
  range: 560–650
SAT Writing middle 50% range: NR

Graduated top 10% of class: 30%
Graduated top 25% of class: 64%
Graduated top 50% of class: 92%

COLLEGE GRADUATION REQUIREMENTS

Course waivers allowed: No
Course substitutions allowed: Yes
In what course: Not generally, but on a case-by-case basis—rarely in foreign language and even more rarely in math, especially if the course is required in the student's major.

ADDITIONAL INFORMATION

Environment: The campus is on a 575-acre campus located in the Piedmont Triad area of North Carolina.

Student Body
  Undergrad enrollment: 4,849
  Women: 60%
  Men: 40%
  Percent out-of-state: 71%

Cost Information
  Tuition: $20,171
  Room & board: $6,850
Housing Information
  University housing: Yes
  Percent living on campus: 57%

Greek System
  Fraternity: Yes
  Sorority: Yes
Athletics: Division I

GUILFORD COLLEGE

5800 West Friendly Avenue, Greensboro, NC 27410
Phone: 336-316-2100 • Fax: 336-316-2954
E-mail: admission@guilford.edu • Web: www.guilford.edu
Support: S • Institution type: 4-year private

LEARNING DISABILITY PROGRAM AND SERVICES

The Academic Skills Center serves the learning needs of a diverse campus by providing professional and peer tutoring, workshops, advocacy, and realistic encouragement. The focus is on self-advocacy and the articulation of both strengths and weaknesses. Faculty tutors work one-on-one with students on time management, study skills, test-taking, reading, math, science, and Spanish. A large student tutoring service offers course-specific tutoring. The tutoring service also provides editors for students who need help checking final drafts. The center sponsors workshops and seminars on subjects pertaining to academic success. Faculty allow the usual accommodations requested by students: extra time, permission to use a computer for in-class work, testing in a less distracting environment, tape-recording classes, and so on.

LD/ADHD ADMISSIONS INFORMATION

College entrance tests required: No
Interview required: No
Essay recommended: No
Documentation required for LD: Psychoeducational evaluation within the past 3 years
Documentation required for ADHD: Diagnosis with DSM–IV code
Submitted to: ASC
Special Ed. HS course work accepted: Yes

Specific course requirements of all applicants: NR
Separate application required: N/A
# of LD applications submitted each year: NR
# of LD applications accepted yearly: NR
Total # of students receiving LD services: NR
Acceptance into program means acceptance into college: Students must be admitted to and enrolled in the university first and then request services.

ADMISSIONS

Students with LD must meet the same criteria as other students. The general admission criteria include the mid 50 percent range for the ACT of 20–28 (or the SAT, 1030–1270) and a 2.8–3.4 GPA. Typically, admitted students have 4 years of English, 3 years of math, 3–4 years natural science, 3 years of social studies, and 2 years of a foreign language. With appropriate documentation, students with LD can substitute some high school courses in areas that impact their ability to learn. The ASC director reviews files to make certain that the college can provide appropriate support services.

ADDITIONAL INFORMATION

Guilford is a writing-intensive place. The writing program is revision-driven and utilizes peer-editing and response groups. The Academic Skills Center (ASC) offers individualized professional tutoring in writing as well as opportunities to work with trained student writing tutors. The ASC offers other services, including faculty tutors to work one-on-one with students on time management, study skills, test-taking, reading, math, science, and Spanish. A large student tutoring service offers course-specific tutoring. The center also sponsors workshops and seminars on subjects pertaining to academic success. Students are encouraged to speak with professors early concerning particular needs. Guilford waives the foreign language requirement if students submit appropriate documentation and petition through ASC.

LEARNING DISABILITY PROGRAM/SERVICES

Learning Disability Program/Services: Academic Skills Center
Director: Melissa Daniel
 E-mail: mdaniel@guilford.edu
 Telephone: 336-316-2200
 Fax: 336-316-2946
Contact Person: Rita Sullivant
 E-mail: mdaniel@guilford.edu
 Telephone: 336-316-2837
 Fax: 336-316-2946

LEARNING DISABILITY SERVICES

Requests for the following services/accommodations will be evaluated individually based on appropriate and current documentation.

Allowed in exams
 Calculator: Yes
 Dictionary: Yes
 Computer: Yes
 Spellchecker: Yes
Extended test time: Yes
Scribes: Yes
Proctors: No
Oral exams: Yes
Note-takers: Yes

Distraction-reduced environment: Yes
Tape recording in class: Yes
Books on tape from RFBD: No
Taping of books not from RFBD: Yes
**Accommodations for students with
 ADHD:** Yes
Reading machine: Yes
Other assistive technology: Yes
Priority registration: No

Added costs for services: No
LD specialists: No
Professional tutors: 4–13
Peer tutors: 20–40
Max. hours/wk. for services: NR
**How professors are notified of
 LD/ADHD:** By student

GENERAL ADMISSIONS INFORMATION

Director of Admissions: B. Randy Doss
Telephone: 336-316-2100

ENTRANCE REQUIREMENTS

Academic units recommended: 4 English, 3 math, 3 science, 3 social studies, 2 foreign language. High school diploma is required, and GED is accepted. ACT with or without Writing component accepted. TOEFL required of all international applicants: minimum paper TOEFL 550, minimum computer TOEFL 213.

Application deadline: 2/15
Notification: Rolling
Average GPA: 3.14
ACT Composite middle 50% range:
 20–26

SAT Math middle 50% range:
 500–610
**SAT Critical Reading middle 50%
 range:** 520–630
SAT Writing middle 50% range: NR

Graduated top 10% of class: 20%
Graduated top 25% of class: 51%
Graduated top 50% of class: 83%

COLLEGE GRADUATION REQUIREMENTS

Course waivers allowed: No
Course substitutions allowed: Yes
In what course: Foreign language

ADDITIONAL INFORMATION

Environment: The college is located on a suburban campus in a culturally diverse city in Greensboro, North Carolina.

Student Body
 Undergrad enrollment: 2,582
 Women: 62%
 Men: 38%
 Percent out-of-state: 62%

Cost Information
 Tuition: $22,690
 Room & Board: $6,530
Housing Information
 University housing: Yes
 Percent living on campus: 75%

Greek System
 Fraternity: No
 Sorority: No
 Athletics: Division III

LENOIR-RHYNE COLLEGE

Admissions Office, LRC Box 7227, Hickory, NC 28603
Phone: 828-328-7300 • Fax: 828-328-7378
E-mail: admission@lrc.edu • Web: www.lrc.edu
Support: CS • Institution type: 4-year private

LEARNING DISABILITY PROGRAM AND SERVICES

The Lenoir-Rhyne College Disability Services Office strives to provide the highest quality service to each student with a disability through appropriate modification of college policies, practices, and procedures. It is the mission of the office to ensure that every student with a disability has an equal chance to benefit from college programs. Furthermore, the office emphasizes personal independence and responsibility on the part of the student in the provision of services. The office will also serve as a campus and community resource for information about people with disabilities and the issues that affect them.

LD/ADHD ADMISSIONS INFORMATION

College entrance tests required: Yes
Interview required: No
Essay recommended: No
Documentation required for LD: Full psychoeducational evaluation with IQ scores listed
Documentation required for ADHD: Full psychoeducational evaluation with IQ scores listed
Submitted to: Disability Services
Special Ed. HS course work accepted: N/A

Specific course requirements of all applicants: Yes
Separate application required: No
# of LD applications submitted each year: 25
# of LD applications accepted yearly: 20
Total # of students receiving LD services: 40–50
Acceptance into program means acceptance into college: Students not admitted are reviewed by the LD program, which provides a recommendation to admissions. Once admitted, students may request services.

ADMISSIONS

There is no special admissions process for students with learning disabilities. All students are reviewed on an individual case-by-case basis. Basic admissions criteria include a 2.0 GPA, a class rank within the top 50 percent, an 850 on the SAT or 17 on the ACT, and 4 years of English, 3 years of math, 1 year of history, and 2 years of a foreign language (substitutions are allowed).

ADDITIONAL INFORMATION

The Advising and Academic Services Center offers a variety of services to help students achieve academic success through group peer tutoring, advising and assessment, and academic skills counseling. With appropriate documentation, students with LD/ADHD may be provided with some of the following services and accommodations: the use of calculators, dictionaries, computers, or spellcheckers during exams; extended time on tests; distraction-free environments; scribes; proctors; oral exams; note-takers; tape recorders in class; books on tape; and substitution of the foreign language requirement. Students placed on academic probation by the college are monitored by the center. Also, the center provides access to supplementary computerized learning materials, such as Learning Plus for prospective educators and computerized test preps for standardized tests such as the GMAT.

LEARNING DISABILITY PROGRAM/SERVICES

Learning Disability Program/Services: Disability Services
Director: Dr. Janette L. Sims
  E-mail: SimsJ@lrc.edu
  Telephone: 828-328-7296
  Fax: 828-267-3441

LEARNING DISABILITY SERVICES

Requests for the following services/accommodations will be evaluated individually based on appropriate and current documentation.

Allowed in exams
  Calculator: Yes
  Dictionary: Yes
  Computer: Yes
  Spellchecker: Yes
Extended test time: Yes
Scribes: Yes
Proctors: Yes
Oral exams: Yes
Note-takers: Yes

Distraction-reduced environment: Yes
Tape recording in class: Yes
Books on tape from RFBD: Yes
Taping of books not from RFBD: No
Accommodations for students with ADHD: Yes
Reading machine: Yes
Other assistive technology: No
Priority registration: No

Added costs for services: No
LD specialists: Yes
Professional tutors: No
Peer tutors: 20–25
Max. hours/wk. for services: Unlimited
How professors are notified of LD/ADHD: By both student and director

GENERAL ADMISSIONS INFORMATION

Director of Admissions: Rachel Nichols
Telephone: 828-328-7300

ENTRANCE REQUIREMENTS

Academic units required: 4 English, 3 math, 1 science (1 science lab), 2 foreign language, 1 social studies, 1 history. High school diploma is required, and GED is accepted. TOEFL required of all international applicants: minimum paper TOEFL 500.

Application deadline: NR
Notification: Rolling
Average GPA: 3.47
ACT Composite middle 50% range: 17–24

SAT Math middle 50% range: 470–580
SAT Critical Reading middle 50% range: 460–570
SAT Writing middle 50% range: NR

Graduated top 10% of class: 18%
Graduated top 25% of class: 50%
Graduated top 50% of class: 82%

COLLEGE GRADUATION REQUIREMENTS

Course waivers allowed: No
Course substitutions allowed: Yes
In what course: Substitution of foreign language is available.

ADDITIONAL INFORMATION

Environment: The college is located in a small town north of Charlotte.

Student Body
  Undergrad enrollment: 1,358
  Women: 64%
  Men: 36%
  Percent out-of-state: 29%

Cost Information
  Tuition: $18,900
  Room & board: $6,600
Housing Information
  University housing: Yes
  Percent living on campus: 60%

Greek System
  Fraternity: Yes
  Sorority: Yes
Athletics: Division II

NORTH CAROLINA STATE UNIVERSITY

PO Box 7103, Raleigh, NC 27695
Phone: 919-515-2434 • Fax: 919-515-5039
E-mail: undergrad_admissions@ncsu.edu • Web: www.ncsu.edu
Support: CS • Institution type: 4-year public

LEARNING DISABILITY PROGRAM AND SERVICES

Services for students with learning disabilities are handled by the LD coordinator through Disability Services for Students. The functions of the coordinator include identifying students with learning disabilities, helping to accommodate and interpret the needs of these students to the faculty, and providing services to students according to their individual needs. Support groups meet periodically to provide workshops, mutual support, and awareness of disability issues to the university community. The purpose of the services is to ensure that students with documented learning disabilities receive appropriate accommodations to equalize their opportunities while studying at NCSU.

LD/ADHD ADMISSIONS INFORMATION

College entrance tests required: Yes
Interview required: No
Essay recommended: No
Documentation required for LD: Psychoeducational
  evaluation
Documentation required for ADHD: Yes
Submitted to: Disability Services
Special Ed. HS course work accepted: NR

Specific course requirements of all applicants: Yes
Separate application required: No
# of LD applications submitted each year: NR
# of LD applications accepted yearly: NR
Total # of students receiving LD services: 260–300
**Acceptance into program means acceptance into
  college:** Students not admitted are reviewed by the LD
  program, which provides a recommendation to admissions.
  Once admitted, students may request services.

ADMISSIONS

Admission to the university for students with learning disabilities is determined on the basis of academic qualifications, and they are considered in the same manner as any other applicant. There is no pre-admission question regarding a learning disability. A cover letter from applicants stating that a learning disability exists alerts the admission staff to consider that there may be unusual circumstances. Self-disclosure of the learning disability could explain the high school record, such as late diagnosis and onset of LD accommodations or difficulty in particular subjects. General admission criteria include an ACT of 23–29 or SAT of 1100–1300; more than 75 percent of the students have a 3.5 GPA. Course requirements include 4 years of English, 3 years of math, 3 years of social studies, 3 years of science, and 2 years of a foreign language.

ADDITIONAL INFORMATION

All enrolled students may receive services and accommodations through the coordinator of learning disabilities of the DSS if they present appropriate documentation. The documentation should include a written report with a statement specifying areas of learning disabilities. Services and accommodations available with appropriate documentation include extended testing times for exams; distraction-free testing environments; use calculators, dictionaries, computers, or spellcheckers during exams; proctors; scribes; note-takers; books on tape; assistive technology; and priority registration. If new needs are identified, services are modified or developed to accommodate them.

LEARNING DISABILITY PROGRAM/SERVICES

Learning Disability Program/Services: Disability Services for Students (DSS)
Director: Cheryl Branker, EdD
  E-mail: cheryl_branker@ncsu.edu
  Telephone: 919-515-7653
  Fax: 919-513-2840

LEARNING DISABILITY SERVICES

Requests for the following services/accommodations will be evaluated individually based on appropriate and current documentation.

Allowed in exams	**Distraction-reduced environment:** Yes	**Added costs for services:** No
Calculator: Yes	**Tape recording in class:** Yes	**LD specialists:** Yes
Dictionary: Yes	**Books on tape from RFBD:** Yes	**Professional tutors:** No
Computer: Yes	**Taping of books not from RFBD:** Yes	**Peer tutors:** 20–25
Spellchecker: Yes	**Accommodations for students with**	**Max. hours/wk. for services:**
Extended test time: Yes	**ADHD:** Yes	Unlimited
Scribes: Yes	**Reading machine:** Yes	**How professors are notified of**
Proctors: Yes	**Other assistive technology:** Yes	**LD/ADHD:** By both student and
Oral exams: Yes	**Priority registration:** Yes	director
Note-takers: Yes		

GENERAL ADMISSIONS INFORMATION

Director of Admissions: Thomas H. Griffin
Telephone: 919-515-2434

ENTRANCE REQUIREMENTS

Academic units required: 4 English, 3 math, 3 science (1 science lab), 2 foreign language, 3 social studies, 1 history, 1 academic elective. **Academic units recommended:** 4 English, 4 math, 4 science (2 science labs), 2 foreign language, 1 social studies, 1 history, 4 academic electives. High school diploma is required, and GED is not accepted. ACT with Writing component required. TOEFL required of all international applicants: minimum paper TOEFL 550, minimum computer TOEFL 213.

Application deadline: 2/1	**SAT Math middle 50% range:**	**Graduated top 10% of class:** 37%
Notification: Rolling	560–660	**Graduated top 25% of class:** 79%
Average GPA: 4.11	**SAT Critical Reading middle 50%**	**Graduated top 50% of class:** 98%
ACT Composite middle 50% range:	**range:** 520–620	
21–26	**SAT Writing middle 50% range:**	
	510–600	

COLLEGE GRADUATION REQUIREMENTS

Course waivers allowed: No
Course substitutions allowed: Yes
In what course: Students may apply to substitute courses to satisfy the foreign lanuage proficiency requirement.

ADDITIONAL INFORMATION

Environment: The university sits on 623 acres in the central part of the state and has an adjacent 900-acre research campus.

Student Body	**Cost Information**	**Greek System**
Undergrad enrollment: 21,438	**In-state tuition:** $4,700	**Fraternity:** Yes
Women: 42%	**Out-of-state tuition:** $16,900	**Sorority:** Yes
Men: 58%	**Room & board:** $7,373	**Athletics:** Division I
Percent out-of-state: 7%	**Housing Information**	
	University housing: Yes	
	Percent living on campus: 34%	

ST. ANDREWS PRESBYTERIAN COLLEGE

1700 Dogwood Mile, Laurinburg, NC 28352
Phone: 910-277-5555 • Fax: 910-277-5087
E-mail: admissions@sapc.edu • Web: www.sapc.edu
Support: CS • Institution type: 4-year private

LEARNING DISABILITY PROGRAM AND SERVICES

St. Andrews Presbyterian College acknowledges its responsibility, both legally and educationally, to serve students with learning disabilities by providing reasonable accommodations. These services do not guarantee success, but endeavor to assist students in pursuing a quality postsecondary education. Disability and Academic Support Services provide a full range of learning disability support services. The services are meant to help students devise strategies for meeting college demands and to foster independence, responsibility, and self-advocacy. Disability and Academic Support Services is committed to ensuring that all information regarding a student is kept confidential.

LD/ADHD ADMISSIONS INFORMATION

College entrance tests required: Yes
Interview required: No
Essay recommended: No
Documentation required for LD: Educational and psychological testing, including subtest scores from the WAIS–R/WAID III. Complete documentation guidelines available on request.
Documentation required for ADHD: Educational and psychological testing and a DSM–IV diagnosis from qualified professional. Complete documentation guidelines available on request.
Submitted to: Admissions Office
Special Ed. HS course work accepted: Yes

Specific course requirements of all applicants: NR
Separate application required: Yes
# of LD applications submitted each year: NR
# of LD applications accepted yearly: NR
Total # of students receiving LD services: 40–60
Acceptance into program means acceptance into college: Students must be admitted to and enrolled in the university first and then request services.

ADMISSIONS

Each application is reviewed on an individual basis. Factors considered are an SAT minimum of 700 or ACT minimum of 17 and students' high school profiles and courses attempted, as well as a minimum GPA of 2.0; an essay and counselor and/or teacher recommendations are optional but strongly recommended. Courses recommended include 4 years of English, 3 years of math, 3 years of science, 1 year of social studies, 1 year of history, and 2 years of a foreign language. Prospective students are strongly encouraged to visit the campus. Students with learning disabilities complete the regular admissions application. Students with a diagnosis of attention deficit hyperactivity disorder are required to show achievement and ability testing (adult version) that validates the DSM–IV diagnosis. All students must meet the same admissions criteria. For the Admissions Committee to make the most informed decision, students are encouraged to self-disclose the existence of a learning disability in their personal statement. Any other personal information indicating the student's ability to succeed in college should also be included with the application. All documentation of a specific learning disability should be sent separately.

ADDITIONAL INFORMATION

All accommodations are based on the submitted current documentation. Each case is reviewed individually. Disability Services reserves the right to determine eligibility for services based on the quality of the submitted documentation. The services and accommodations include note-taking, extended time on tests, alternative test formats, separate locations for tests, books on tape through Recordings for the Blind and Dyslexic or from readers, and content tutoring through individual departments. Franklin Language Masters and audiotape equipment are available for loan. All computers in computer labs are equipped with spellchecker. A Learning Resource Center is planned to open in the near future.

LEARNING DISABILITY PROGRAM/SERVICES

Learning Disability Program/Services: Disability Academic Support Services
Director: Dorothy Wells
  E-mail: ods@sapc.edu
  Telephone: 910-277-5331
  Fax: 910-277-5746

LEARNING DISABILITY SERVICES

Requests for the following services/accommodations will be evaluated individually based on appropriate and current documentation.

Allowed in exams	**Distraction-reduced environment:** Yes	**Added costs for services:** No
Calculator: Yes	**Tape recording in class:** Yes	**LD specialists:** Yes
Dictionary: Yes	**Books on tape from RFBD:** Yes	**Professional tutors:** NR
Computer: Yes	**Taping of books not from RFBD:** Yes	**Peer tutors:** 5–15
Spellchecker: Yes	**Accommodations for students with**	**Max. hours/wk. for services:**
Extended test time: Yes	**ADHD:** Yes	Unlimited
Scribes: Yes	**Reading machine:** Yes	**How professors are notified of**
Proctors: Yes	**Other assistive technology:** Yes	**LD/ADHD:** By both student and
Oral exams: Yes	**Priority registration:** No	director
Note-takers: Yes		

GENERAL ADMISSIONS INFORMATION

Director of Admissions: Cynthia Robinson
Telephone: 910-277-5555

ENTRANCE REQUIREMENTS

Academic units recommended: 4 English, 3 math, 3 science, 2 foreign language, 1 social studies, 2 academic electives. High school diploma is required, and GED is accepted. ACT with or without Writing component accepted. TOEFL required of all international applicants: minimum paper TOEFL 550, minimum computer TOEFL 280.

Application deadline: No	**SAT Math middle 50% range:** NR	**Graduated top 10% of class:** NR
Notification: Rolling	**SAT Critical Reading middle 50%**	**Graduated top 25% of class:** NR
Average GPA: 3.03	**range:** NR	**Graduated top 50% of class:** NR
ACT Composite middle 50% range:	**SAT Writing middle 50% range:** NR	
NR		

COLLEGE GRADUATION REQUIREMENTS

Course waivers allowed: No
Course substitutions allowed: Yes
In what course: Foreign language

ADDITIONAL INFORMATION

Environment: The college is located on 600 acres in a small town 40 miles southwest of Fayetteville.

Student Body	**Cost Information**	**Greek System**
Undergrad enrollment: 768	**Tuition:** $17,300	**Fraternity:** No
Women: 60%	**Room & board:** $6,000	**Sorority:** No
Men: 40%	**Housing Information**	**Athletics:** Division II
Percent out-of-state: 48%	**University housing:** Yes	
	Percent living on campus: 92%	

THE UNIVERSITY OF NORTH CAROLINA at CHAPEL HILL

Jackson Hall 153A—Campus Box #2200, Chapel Hill, NC 27599-2200
Phone: 919-966-3621 • Fax: 919-962-3045
E-mail: unchelp@admissions.unc.edu • Web: www.unc.edu
Support: CS • Institution type: 4-year public

LEARNING DISABILITY PROGRAM AND SERVICES

Learning Disabilities Services (LDS) is one of seven units of Academic Support Services in the College of Arts and Sciences. The mission of LDS is to assist students in achieving their academic potential within the regular, academically competitive university curriculum. This is a comprehensive program with a team of LD specialists that meets both the letter and the spirit of the law. LDS works with students who are eligible for services and is the service provider to students with documented LD/ADHD. LDS has developed innovative services for students with ADHD and LD in college students. A student's documented disability becomes the foundation for accommodations; the student's desire to discover new ways to learn becomes the foundation for direct services. Accommodations are changes made by the university in how the students take in or express information. This is why the accommodations are determined on a case-by-case basis and based on each student's specific documented disability. Direct services focus on changes that students can make in how they learn. Services are offered in addition to the accommodations required by law. Students can meet as often as weekly in one-on-one sessions to learn more about their disability, develop self-advocacy skills, obtain referrals, and practice learning strategies.

LD/ADHD ADMISSIONS INFORMATION

College entrance tests required: Yes
Interview required: No
Essay recommended: Yes
Documentation required for LD: Psychoeducational
  evaluation
Documentation required for ADHD: Yes
Submitted to: LDS
Special Ed. HS course work accepted: Yes

Specific course requirements of all applicants: Yes
Separate application required: No
# of LD applications submitted each year: NR
# of LD applications accepted yearly: NR
Total # of students receiving LD services: 250
**Acceptance into program means acceptance into
  college:** Students must be admitted to and enrolled in the
  university first and then request services.

ADMISSIONS

In terms of admission criteria for students with LD, nonenrolled students can choose to voluntarily share documentation of their disability. If the student discloses a disability during admissions, his or her application is reviewed by Subcommittee D of the Admissions Committee. This subcommittee is made up of a number of campus professionals with expertise in disabilities, including the Director of the Learning Disabilities Services. If a student who is reviewed by this subcommittee is admitted, the student is then automatically eligible to use LDS. Students with disabilities who apply for admissions have the right to refrain from disclosing. If, after being admitted, a student wishes to use LDS, that student would then submit documentation to be reviewed by the LD team.

ADDITIONAL INFORMATION

Accommodations provided include note-takers, taped textbooks, tutors in math or foreign languages, extended time on tests, distraction-free test environments, readers during exams, scribes to write dictated test answers, and computers for writing test answers. Using the student's current course work, LDS can teach a range of strategies, including how to plan, draft, and edit papers; how to take lecture notes and reading notes; how to read critically and efficiently; how to manage time; and how to prepare for and take exams. Group experiences are available to students each semester based on their expressed interests. These can include support groups that promote understanding, acceptance, and pride; academic workshops that allow students to help one another learn specific skills; seminars that provide topical information from campus experts as well as other students; and panel discussions between students and university personnel. Currently, there are 100 students with LD and 150 with ADHD.

LEARNING DISABILITY PROGRAM/SERVICES

Learning Disability Program/Services: Learning Disabilities Services (LDS)
Director: Jane Benson
  E-mail: jbenson@E-mail.unc.edu
  Telephone: 919-962-7227
  Fax: 919-962-3674
Contact Person: Kim Allison
  E-mail: jbenson@E-mail.unc.edu

LEARNING DISABILITY SERVICES

Requests for the following services/accommodations will be evaluated individually based on appropriate and current documentation.

Allowed in exams
  Calculator: Yes
  Dictionary: Yes
  Computer: Yes
  Spellchecker: Yes
Extended test time: Yes
Scribes: Yes
Proctors: Yes
Oral exams: Yes
Note-takers: Yes

Distraction-reduced environment: Yes
Tape recording in class: Yes
Books on tape from RFBD: NR
Taping of books not from RFBD: Yes
**Accommodations for students with
  ADHD:** Yes
Reading machine: Yes
Other assistive technology: Yes
Priority registration: Yes

Added costs for services: No
LD specialists: Yes
Professional tutors: No
Peer tutors: Referral
Max. hours/wk. for services: 2
**How professors are notified of
  LD/ADHD:** By director

GENERAL ADMISSIONS INFORMATION

Director of Admissions: Stephen Farmer
Telephone: 919-966-3621

ENTRANCE REQUIREMENTS

Academic units required: 4 English, 3 math, 3 science (1 science lab), 2 foreign language, 2 social studies, 2 academic electives, 1 U.S. history. **Academic units recommended:** 4 English, 4 math, 4 science (1 science lab), 4 foreign language, 3 social studies. High school diploma is required, and GED is not accepted. ACT with Writing component required. TOEFL required of all international applicants: minimum paper TOEFL 600, minimum computer TOEFL 250.

Application deadline: 1/15
Notification: 1/31, 3/31
Average GPA: 4.37
ACT Composite middle 50% range:
  25–30

SAT Math middle 50% range:
  610–700
**SAT Critical Reading middle 50%
  range:** 590–690
SAT Writing middle 50% range:
  580–680

Graduated top 10% of class: 76%
Graduated top 25% of class: 96%
Graduated top 50% of class: 99%

COLLEGE GRADUATION REQUIREMENTS

Course waivers allowed: No
Course substitutions allowed: No

ADDITIONAL INFORMATION

Environment: The university is located in a suburban town near Raleigh.

Student Body
  Undergrad enrollment: 16,706
  Women: 59%
  Men: 41%
  Percent out-of-state: 17%

Cost Information
  In-state tuition: $4,600
  Out-of-state tuition: $18,400
  Room & board: $6,846
Housing Information
  University housing: Yes
  Percent living on campus: 44%

Greek System
  Fraternity: Yes
  Sorority: Yes
Athletics: Division I

The University of North Carolina at Chapel Hill

THE UNIVERSITY OF NORTH CAROLINA AT CHARLOTTE

9201 University City Boulevard, Charlotte, NC 28223-0001
Phone: 704-687-2213 • Fax: 704-687-6483
E-mail: unccadm@E-mail.uncc.edu • Web: www.uncc.edu
Support: CS • Institution type: 4-year public

LEARNING DISABILITY PROGRAM AND SERVICES

The mission of Disability Services reflects the university's commitment to diversity by providing educational opportunities for persons with disabilities. This primary purpose is facilitated through ongoing research and development activities; development and presentation of educational seminars, workshops, and training designed to increase knowledge of disability-related issues; and a case management system approach to service delivery. The professional staff in Disability Services assists students with learning disabilities to meet their individual needs. In all possible cases, UNC—Charlotte will use existing resources for educational auxiliary aids. Services could include registration assistance, orientation to available services, IEPs, special testing arrangements, counseling, and peer support services.

LD/ADHD ADMISSIONS INFORMATION

College entrance tests required: Yes
Interview required: No
Essay recommended: No
Documentation required for LD: Current psychoeducational evaluation
Documentation required for ADHD: History and testing showing type of ADHD
Submitted to: Admissions and Disability Services
Special Ed. HS course work accepted: Yes

Specific course requirements of all applicants: NR
Separate application required: No
# of LD applications submitted each year: NR
# of LD applications accepted yearly: NR
Total # of students receiving LD services: NR
Acceptance into program means acceptance into college: Students must be admitted to and enrolled in the university first and then request services.

ADMISSIONS

All applicants must meet the general admissions requirements and any special requirements for acceptance into a particular program of study. Students go through the regular application process. Courses required include 4 years of English, 3 years of math, 3 years of science, 1 year of science lab, 2 years of a foreign language, 2 years of social studies (1 year of history recommended), and 2 years of electives. Applicants with learning disabilities are encouraged to provide information about their learning disability at the time of application for admission. The university reserves the right to withhold the admission of any applicant who fails to meet any of the requirements for admission. Students who are not otherwise qualified and who provide documentation of a learning disability may be reviewed by the Disability Services, which will give a recommendation to the Office of Admissions. Once students have been admitted and enrolled they may request the necessary services.

ADDITIONAL INFORMATION

Services offered include academic advisement and priority registration, assistive technology, taped textbooks, special test administration, note-takers, broad-based case management activities to include orientation and assessment for services, individual consultation and counseling 30 minutes each week, workshops, and referrals for tutorial services and learning. There is a Tutoring Center and a Writing Center. Currently, there are 127 students with LD and 91 students with ADHD receiving services on campus. Students with ADHD must provide documentation that includes a diagnosis and a verification of the diagnosis.

LEARNING DISABILITY PROGRAM/SERVICES

Learning Disability Program/Services: Disability Services
Director: Jo Ann A. Fernald
E-mail: jfernal1@E-mail.uncc.edu
Telephone: 704-687-4355
Fax: 704-687-3226

LEARNING DISABILITY SERVICES

Requests for the following services/accommodations will be evaluated individually based on appropriate and current documentation.

Allowed in exams
 Calculator: Yes
 Dictionary: No
 Computer: Yes
 Spellchecker: Yes
Extended test time: Yes
Scribes: No
Proctors: No
Oral exams: Yes
Note-takers: Yes

Distraction-reduced environment: Yes
Tape recording in class: Yes
Books on tape from RFBD: Yes
Taping of books not from RFBD: No
Accommodations for students with ADHD: Yes
Reading machine: Yes
Other assistive technology: Yes
Priority registration: Yes

Added costs for services: No
LD specialists: Yes
Professional tutors: No
Peer tutors: Yes
Max. hours/wk. for services: N/A
How professors are notified of LD/ADHD: By both student and director

GENERAL ADMISSIONS INFORMATION

Director of Admissions: Tina McEntire
Telephone: 704-687-2213

ENTRANCE REQUIREMENTS

Academic units required: 4 English, 3 math, 3 science (1 science lab), 2 foreign language, 2 social studies.
Academic units recommended: 1 foreign language. High school diploma is required, and GED is accepted. ACT with Writing component required. TOEFL required of all international applicants: minimum paper TOEFL 507, minimum computer TOEFL 180.

Application deadline: 7/1
Notification: Rolling
Average GPA: 3.54
ACT Composite middle 50% range: 19–24

SAT Math middle 50% range: 490–590
SAT Critical Reading middle 50% range: 470–560
SAT Writing middle 50% range: 460–550

Graduated top 10% of class: 13%
Graduated top 25% of class: 54%
Graduated top 50% of class: 90%

COLLEGE GRADUATION REQUIREMENTS

Course waivers allowed: No
Course substitutions allowed: Yes
In what course: Foreign language substitution if supported by documentation and only done on a case-by-case basis

ADDITIONAL INFORMATION

Environment: The university is located on 1,000 acres 8 miles northeast of Charlotte.

Student Body
 Undergrad enrollment: 16,885
 Women: 52%
 Men: 48%
 Percent out-of-state: 9%

Cost Information
 In-state tuition: $3,500
 Out-of-state tuition: $13,900
 Room & board: $5,790
Housing Information
 University housing: Yes
 Percent living on campus: 26%

Greek System
 Fraternity: Yes
 Sorority: Yes
Athletics: Division I

The University of North Carolina at Charlotte

THE UNIVERSITY OF NORTH CAROLINA
AT GREENSBORO

1400 Spring Garden Street, Greensboro, NC 27402-6170
Phone: 336-334-5243 • Fax: 336-334-4180
E-mail: admissions@uncg.edu • Web: www.uncg.edu
Support: CS • Institution type: 4-year public

LEARNING DISABILITY PROGRAM AND SERVICES

The University of North Carolina—Greensboro is committed to equality of educational opportunities for qualified students with disabilities. The goal of Disabled Student Services is to provide a full range of academic accommodations. Students who need tests offered in a nontraditional format may request this service. Modifications may include extended test times, private rooms, readers, scribes, or the use of word processors for essay examinations. Documentation must verify the use of special accommodations. The Disability Services Office provides a handbook for students to use as a helpful guide in making their experience at UNCG a positive one.

LD/ADHD ADMISSIONS INFORMATION

College entrance tests required: Yes
Interview required: No
Essay recommended: No
Documentation required for LD: See our website.
Documentation required for ADHD: See our website.
Submitted to: Disabled Student Services
Special Ed. HS course work accepted: NR

Specific course requirements of all applicants: Yes
Separate application required: No
# of LD applications submitted each year: NR
# of LD applications accepted yearly: NR
Total # of students receiving LD services: 200
Acceptance into program means acceptance into college: Students must be admitted to and enrolled in the university first and then request services.

ADMISSIONS
There is no special admissions process for students with learning disabilities. Admission is competitive and based on academic qualifications. Students with learning disabilities must submit the regular application and are considered for admission in the same manner as any other applicant. No pre-admission inquiry regarding the learning disability is made. It is highly recommended that the SAT or ACT be taken with accommodations (if eligible) if this gives a better estimate of the student's ability.

ADDITIONAL INFORMATION
Trained staff members are available for counseling to assist students with academic and/or personal problems. Voluntary note-takers are solicited through DSS, and photocopying is available. Students will meet with their faculty advisor to discuss courses that need to be taken, and DSS will stamp the students' registration cards to verify that they are registered with DSS and warrant priority registration. Assistance in securing taped textbooks through Recording for the Blind is provided, and a file of available readers is available for instances when materials are not available through RFB. Students are provided with information regarding campus tutorials and labs. Individual tutors are provided when it seems necessary. Students can receive help with study skills and time management techniques.

LEARNING DISABILITY PROGRAM/SERVICES

Learning Disability Program/Services: Disabled Student Services
Director: Mary Culkin
  E-mail: meculkin@uncg.edu
  Telephone: 336-334-5440
  Fax: 336-334-4412

LEARNING DISABILITY SERVICES

Requests for the following services/accommodations will be evaluated individually based on appropriate and current documentation.

Allowed in exams
  Calculator: Yes
  Dictionary: Yes
  Computer: Yes
  Spellchecker: Yes
Extended test time: Yes
Scribes: Yes
Proctors: Yes
Oral exams: Yes
Note-takers: Yes

Distraction-reduced environment: Yes
Tape recording in class: Yes
Books on tape from RFBD: Yes
Taping of books not from RFBD: Yes
Accommodations for students with ADHD: Yes
Reading machine: Yes
Other assistive technology: Yes
Priority registration: Yes

Added costs for services: No
LD specialists: Yes
Professional tutors: No
Peer tutors: Yes
Max. hours/wk. for services: Depends on needs
How professors are notified of LD/ADHD: By both student and director

GENERAL ADMISSIONS INFORMATION

Director of Admissions: Lise Keller
Telephone: 336-334-5243

ENTRANCE REQUIREMENTS

Academic units required: 4 English, 4 math, 3 science (1 science lab), 2 foreign language, 1 social studies, 1 history. High school diploma is required, and GED is not accepted. ACT with Writing component required. TOEFL required of all international applicants: minimum paper TOEFL 550, minimum computer TOEFL 213.

Application deadline: 3/1
Notification: Rolling
Average GPA: 3.51
ACT Composite middle 50% range: NR

SAT Math middle 50% range: 480–570
SAT Critical Reading middle 50% range: 460–570
SAT Writing middle 50% range: 450–560

Graduated top 10% of class: 14%
Graduated top 25% of class: 43%
Graduated top 50% of class: 86%

COLLEGE GRADUATION REQUIREMENTS

Course waivers allowed: No
Course substitutions allowed: Yes
In what course: Decided on a case-by-case basis in foreign language (an extreme exception rather than the rule). All substitutions must be approved by a faculty committee. Currently, the univeristy offers a modified foreign language program.

ADDITIONAL INFORMATION

Environment: The university is located on 178 acres in an urban area in Greensboro.

Student Body
  Undergrad enrollment: 12,757
  Women: 68%
  Men: 32%
  Percent out-of-state: 7%

Cost Information
  In-state tuition: $3,400
  Out-of-state tuition: $14,700
  Room & board: $5,513
Housing Information
  University housing: Yes
  Percent living on campus: 33%

Greek System
  Fraternity: Yes
  Sorority: Yes
Athletics: Division I

The University of North Carolina at Greensboro

THE UNIVERSITY OF NORTH CAROLINA AT WILMINGTON

601 South College Road, Wilmington, NC 28403-5904
Phone: 910-962-3243 • Fax: 910-962-3038
E-mail: admissions@uncw.edu • Web: www.uncw.edu
Support: CS • Institution type: 4-year public

LEARNING DISABILITY PROGRAM AND SERVICES

The university's goal is to provide access to all of its academic programs, support services, and extracurricular activities and enrich students' academic and vocational experiences while in college. The coordinator of Disability Services (DS) meets with the student to appraise special needs, make referrals, and arrange for special accommodations. The university has devoted much time and energy to meeting the requirements of Section 504 and the ADA. This effort is exemplified by the accommodating services offered through DS for students with learning disabilities and by special cooperation of the faculty. As the number of students with learning disabilities attending UNCW increases, so does the university's commitment to making facilities and programs more accessible.

LD/ADHD ADMISSIONS INFORMATION

College entrance tests required: Yes
Interview required: No
Essay recommended: No
Documentation required for LD: Psychoeducational evaluation completed within the past 3 years.
Documentation required for ADHD: Documentation must be current—completed within the past 3 years. Reports must include a specific diagnosis of ADHD.
Submitted to: Disability Services
Special Ed. HS course work accepted: No

Specific course requirements of all applicants: Yes
Separate application required: N/A
# of LD applications submitted each year: NR
# of LD applications accepted yearly: NR
Total # of students receiving LD services: 250
Acceptance into program means acceptance into college: Students must be admitted to and enrolled in the university first and then request services.

ADMISSIONS
Students with learning disabilities must meet the same entrance requirements as all other applicants. Course requirements include 4 years of English, 3 years of math, 3 years of science, 3 years of social studies, and 2 years of a foreign language. UNCW requires one recommendation from a guidance counselor or a core academic teacher. Most students admitted to UNCW have SAT test scores between 1160 and 1230 or, ACT scores between 26 and 28, and the average GPA is 3.68. The university prefers that students respond to the essay question posed by UNCW rather than sending an essay they have prepared for another institution.

ADDITIONAL INFORMATION
Services are provided based on individual needs as assessed through recent diagnostic information and a personal interview. As new needs are identified, services may be modified or developed to accommodate them. Newly accepted students interested in services should complete and sign the disclosure form that is included with the letter of acceptance. This information should then be forwarded to the Student Development Center. Current documentation must be sent to the coordinator of DS after acceptance to the university. Diagnostic testing must be conducted by a licensed professional, and an adequate report must include specific educational recommendations. Priority registration is available to all returning students registered with DSS. There are no special classes or programs designed just for students with learning disabilities. Services and accommodations are offered to undergraduate and graduate students.

LEARNING DISABILITY PROGRAM/SERVICES

Learning Disability Program/Services: Disability Services (DS)
Director: Peggy Turner, PhD
  E-mail: turnerm@uncw.edu
  Telephone: 910-962-7555
  Fax: 910-962-7556
Contact Person: Chris Stone
  E-mail: turnerm@uncw.edu
  Telephone: 910-962-7555
  Fax: 910-962-7556

LEARNING DISABILITY SERVICES

Requests for the following services/accommodations will be evaluated individually based on appropriate and current documentation.

Allowed in exams
  Calculator: Yes
  Dictionary: Yes
  Computer: Yes
  Spellchecker: Yes
Extended test time: Yes
Scribes: Yes
Proctors: Yes
Oral exams: Yes
Note-takers: Yes

Distraction-reduced environment: Yes
Tape recording in class: Yes
Books on tape from RFBD: No
Taping of books not from RFBD: Yes
Accommodations for students with
  ADHD: Yes
Reading machine: Yes
Other assistive technology: Yes
Priority registration: Yes

Added costs for services: No
LD specialists: Yes
Professional tutors: No
Peer tutors: Yes
Max. hours/wk. for services: Depends
  on needs
How professors are notified of
  LD/ADHD: By student

GENERAL ADMISSIONS INFORMATION

Director of Admissions: Terrence M. Curran, Associate Provost
Telephone: 910-962-3243

ENTRANCE REQUIREMENTS

Academic units required: 4 English, 3 math, 3 science (1 science lab), 2 foreign language, 3 social studies, 1 history, 5 academic electives. High school diploma is required, and GED is accepted. ACT with Writing component required. TOEFL required of all international applicants: minimum paper TOEFL 550, minimum computer TOEFL 213.

Application deadline: 2/1
Notification: ending date: 4/01
Average GPA: 3.68
ACT Composite middle 50% range:
  21–24

SAT Math middle 50% range:
  540–630
SAT Critical Reading middle 50%
  range: 520–610
SAT Writing middle 50% range:
  500–590

Graduated top 10% of class: 22%
Graduated top 25% of class: 62%
Graduated top 50% of class: 92%

COLLEGE GRADUATION REQUIREMENTS

Course waivers allowed: No
Course substitutions allowed: Yes
In what course: Determined strictly on a case-by-case basis

ADDITIONAL INFORMATION

Environment: The university is located on a 650-acre urban campus.

Student Body
  Undergrad enrollment: 10,479
  Women: 58%
  Men: 42%
  Percent out-of-state: 14%

Cost Information
  In-state tuition: $3,600
  Out-of-state tuition: $13,600
  Room & board: $6,722
Housing Information
  University housing: Yes
  Percent living on campus: 27%

Greek System
  Fraternity: Yes
  Sorority: Yes
Athletics: Division I

WAKE FOREST UNIVERSITY

PO Box 7305, Reynolda Station, Winston-Salem, NC 27109
Phone: 336-758-5201 • Fax: 336-758-4324
E-mail: admissions@wfu.edu • Web: www.wfu.edu
Support: CS • Institution type: 4-year private

LEARNING DISABILITY PROGRAM AND SERVICES

The Learning Assistance Center (LAC) offers support for academic success. For students with documented disabilities, the program director will work with the student and members of the faculty to help implement any approved course accommodations. The students with learning disabilities have a series of conferences with staff members who specialize in academic skills and who help design an overall study plan to improve scholastic performance in those areas needing assistance. If special course accommodations are needed, the program director will serve as an advocate for the students with members of the faculty.

LD/ADHD ADMISSIONS INFORMATION

College entrance tests required: Yes
Interview required: No
Essay recommended: Yes
Documentation required for LD: Psychoeducational
evaluation completed within the past year
Documentation required for ADHD: Yes
Submitted to: LAC
Special Ed. HS course work accepted: No

Specific course requirements of all applicants: Yes
Separate application required: No
# of LD applications submitted each year: NR
# of LD applications accepted yearly: NR
Total # of students receiving LD services: 116
**Acceptance into program means acceptance into
college:** Students must be admitted to and enrolled in the
university first and then request services.

ADMISSIONS

There are no special admissions procedures for students with learning disabilities. Students with LD submit the general Wake Forest University application and are expected to meet the same admission criteria as all applicants. Wake Forest does not accept the ACT. The mid 50 percent range for the SAT is 1240–1360. Course requirements include 4 years of English, 3 years of math, 1 year of science, 2 years of social studies, and 2 years of a foreign language. Students should self-disclose to the Learning Assistance Center after admission. Services are available to all enrolled students with documentation on file. Students are encouraged to provide a recent psychoeducational evaluation.

ADDITIONAL INFORMATION

The Learning Assistance Program staff will assist students with learning disabilities to learn new approaches to studying and methods for improving reading and comprehension, note-taking, time management, study organization, memory, motivation, and self-modification. The LAC offers peer tutoring services. In addition to one-on-one tutoring in most academic subjects, the LAC provides collaborative learning groups comprised of two to five students. The LAC also assists students who present special academic needs. Accommodations are determined based on appropriate documentation. Applications are accepted for course substitutions. All students with or without learning disabilities are eligible for group or individual tutoring in basic academic subjects. The tutors are advanced undergraduates or graduate students who have demonstrated mastery of specific subject areas and are supervised by the LAC staff for their tutoring activities. The LAC also offers all students individual academic counseling to help develop study, organization, and time management strategies that are important for successful college-level learning.

LEARNING DISABILITY PROGRAM/SERVICES

Learning Disability Program/Services: Learning Assistance Center (LAC)
Director: Van D. Westervelt, PhD
E-mail: lacenter@wfu.edu
Telephone: 336-758-5929
Fax: 336-758-1991

LEARNING DISABILITY SERVICES

Requests for the following services/accommodations will be evaluated individually based on appropriate and current documentation.

Allowed in exams
  Calculator: Yes
  Dictionary: Yes
  Computer: Yes
  Spellchecker: Yes
Extended test time: Yes
Scribes: No
Proctors: No
Oral exams: No
Note-takers: No

Distraction-reduced environment: Yes
Tape recording in class: Yes
Books on tape from RFBD: No
Taping of books not from RFBD: No
Accommodations for students with
  ADHD: Yes
Reading machine: No
Other assistive technology: No
Priority registration: No

Added costs for services: No
LD specialists: Yes
Professional tutors: No
Peer tutors: 90
Max. hours/wk. for services: NR
How professors are notified of
  LD/ADHD: By both student and
director

GENERAL ADMISSIONS INFORMATION

Director of Admissions: Martha B. Allman
Telephone: 336-758-5201

ENTRANCE REQUIREMENTS

Academic units required: 4 English, 3 math, 1 science, 2 foreign language, 2 social studies. **Academic units recommended:** 4 English, 4 math, 4 science, 4 foreign language, 4 social studies. High school diploma is required, and GED is accepted. ACT with Writing component required. TOEFL required of all international applicants: minimum paper TOEFL 600, minimum computer TOEFL 250.

Application deadline: 1/15
Notification: 4/1
Average GPA: NR
ACT Composite middle 50% range:
  NR

SAT Math middle 50% range:
  710–710
SAT Critical Reading middle 50%
  range: 690–610
SAT Writing middle 50% range: NR

Graduated top 10% of class: 62%
Graduated top 25% of class: 88%
Graduated top 50% of class: 98%

COLLEGE GRADUATION REQUIREMENTS

Course waivers allowed: No
Course substitutions allowed: Yes
In what course: Foreign language only. If there is a documented language-based LD and a good faith effort has been made by the student to learn a foreign language without success, then two courses from an approved list of classics and humanities courses may be substituted.

ADDITIONAL INFORMATION

Environment: The 550-acre campus is located in the Piedmont region of North Carolina.

Student Body
  Undergrad enrollment: 4,313
  Women: 51%
  Men: 49%
  Percent out-of-state: 74%

Cost Information
  Tuition: $32,040
  Room & board: $8,800
Housing Information
  University housing: Yes
  Percent living on campus: 70%

Greek System
  Fraternity: Yes
  Sorority: Yes
Athletics: Division I

WESTERN CAROLINA UNIVERSITY

242 HFR Administration, Cullowhee, NC 28723
Phone: 828-227-7317 • Fax: 828-227-7319
E-mail: admiss@E-mail.wcu.edu • Web: www.wcu.edu
Support: CS • Institution type: 4-year public

LEARNING DISABILITY PROGRAM AND SERVICES

The Disabled Student Services Program attempts to respond to the needs of students with learning disabilities by making services and equipment available as needed and by making judicious use of reading and tutoring services. Each student in the program is assigned a counselor/advisor. The students must meet with this counselor at least twice a month to discuss topics such as academic progress, study skills, adjustment to college life, career decision-making, and personal concerns. In addition, students may take specially designed classes in English, reading, and study skills.

LD/ADHD ADMISSIONS INFORMATION

College entrance tests required: Yes
Interview required: No
Essay recommended: No
Documentation required for LD: Psychoeducational evaluation completed within the past 3 years
Documentation required for ADHD: Yes
Submitted to: DSS
Special Ed. HS course work accepted: No

Specific course requirements of all applicants: Yes
Separate application required: No
# of LD applications submitted each year: NR
# of LD applications accepted yearly: NR
Total # of students receiving LD services: 100–120
Acceptance into program means acceptance into college: Students must be admitted to and enrolled in the university first and then request services.

ADMISSIONS

Students with learning disabilities are admitted under the same standards as students who do not have learning disabilities. The minimum GPA is 2.0, and the course requirements include 4 years of English, 3 years of math, 3 years of science, 3 years of social studies, and 2 years of a foreign language (recommended). The nonstandardized ACT/SAT is acceptable. Students who are admitted are encouraged to take the Summer Term Enrichment Program (STEP) to jumpstart their introduction to college. Students not admissible through the regular admission process may be offered a probationary admission and must begin in the summer prior to freshman year. The admission decision is made by the Admissions Office.

ADDITIONAL INFORMATION

To qualify for services, students must be enrolled at the university, must have been evaluated within the past 3 years, must be willing to participate in additional evaluation to confirm the disability, and must be willing to participate in planning support services. The following services or accommodations are available for students with appropriate documementation: the use of calculators, dictionaries, computers, or spellcheckers during exams; extended time on tests; distraction-free environments; scribes; proctors; oral exams; note-takers; tape recorders in class; taped texts; and priority registration. All students have access to tutoring, writing and math centers, a Technology Assistance Center, and counseling and psychological services. Admitted students should maintain good class attendance, strive for good grades, cooperate with counselors and advisors, set realistic career goals, and meet with the LD team. Services and accommodations are available for undergraduate and graduate students.

LEARNING DISABILITY PROGRAM/SERVICES

Learning Disability Program/Services: Disabled Student Services
Director: Kimberly Marcus
  E-mail: kmarcus@E-mail.wcu.edu
  Telephone: 828-227-7234
  Fax: 828-227-7036

LEARNING DISABILITY SERVICES

Requests for the following services/accommodations will be evaluated individually based on appropriate and current documentation.

Allowed in exams
  Calculator: Yes
  Dictionary: Yes
  Computer: Yes
  Spellchecker: Yes
Extended test time: Yes
Scribes: Yes
Proctors: Yes
Oral exams: Yes
Note-takers: Yes

Distraction-reduced environment: Yes
Tape recording in class: Yes
Books on tape from RFBD: Yes
Taping of books not from RFBD: Yes
Accommodations for students with ADHD: Yes
Reading machine: Yes
Other assistive technology: Yes
Priority registration: Yes

Added costs for services: No
LD specialists: Yes
Professional tutors: Varies
Peer tutors: 20–50
Max. hours/wk. for services: NR
How professors are notified of LD/ADHD: By student

GENERAL ADMISSIONS INFORMATION

Director of Admissions: Alan Kines
Telephone: 877-WCU-4-YOU

ENTRANCE REQUIREMENTS

Academic units required: 4 English, 3 math, 3 science (3 science labs), 2 foreign language, 2 social studies, 1 history, 5 academic electives. **Academic units recommended:** 4 English, 3 math, 3 science (3 science labs), 2 foreign language, 2 social studies, 1 history, 7 academic electives. High school diploma is required, and GED is accepted. ACT with Writing component required. TOEFL required of all international applicants: minimum paper TOEFL 550, minimum computer TOEFL 213.

Application deadline: 8/1
Notification: Rolling
Average GPA: 3.26
ACT Composite middle 50% range: 17–21

SAT Math middle 50% range: 470–560
SAT Critical Reading middle 50% range: 460–550
SAT Writing middle 50% range: 430–530

Graduated top 10% of class: 8%
Graduated top 25% of class: 28%
Graduated top 50% of class: 62%

COLLEGE GRADUATION REQUIREMENTS

Course waivers allowed: Yes
In what course: Individually considered
Course substitutions allowed: Yes
In what course: Individually considered

ADDITIONAL INFORMATION

Environment: The university is located on 400 acres in a rural area 50 miles southwest of Asheville.

Student Body
  Undergrad enrollment: 7,051
  Women: 52%
  Men: 48%
  Percent out-of-state: 4%

Cost Information
  In-state tuition: $4,874
  Out-of-state tuition: $14,457
  Room & board: $4,902
Housing Information
  University housing: Yes
  Percent living on campus: 42%

Greek System
  Fraternity: Yes
  Sorority: Yes
Athletics: Division I

WINGATE UNIVERSITY

Campus Box 3059, Wingate, NC 28174
Phone: 704-233-8200 • Fax: 704-233-8110
E-mail: admit@wingate.edu • Web: www.wingate.edu
Support: CS • Institution type: 4-year private

LEARNING DISABILITY PROGRAM AND SERVICES

Wingate University provides a program designed to assist students with diagnosed specific learning disabilities and dyslexia. Wingate University is aware that students with learning disabilities may be successful in the college environment, provided their special needs are recognized and proper services are made available to them. The coordinator works closely with each student in an effort to maximize the opportunity for a successful college experience. While each student will have specific needs, there are some modes of assistance available to assist each student with the maximum support necessary. This assistance will include identifying strengths and weaknesses, balancing course selections, preregistration, and access to word processing, oral testing, extra testing times, taped texts, and tutoring. Success will be determined by the amount of motivation and initiative of the individual student in seeking available assistance.

LD/ADHD ADMISSIONS INFORMATION

College entrance tests required: Yes
Interview required: Yes
Essay recommended: Yes
Documentation required for LD: Psychoeducational evaluation
Documentation required for ADHD: Yes
Submitted to: Disability Services
Special Ed. HS course work accepted: Yes

Specific course requirements of all applicants: NR
Separate application required: No
# of LD applications submitted each year: NR
# of LD applications accepted yearly: NR
Total # of students receiving LD services: 70–80
Acceptance into program means acceptance into college: Students must be admitted to and enrolled in the university first and then request services.

ADMISSIONS

All applicants must submit the general application and meet the same admission requirements as mainstream students. There is no special process for students with learning disabilities. Applicants must submit either the SAT or ACT, two letters of recommendation, and a short statement or an essay and have a 2.7 GPA. Course requirements include 4 years of English, 3 years of math, 2 years of history, 2 years of science, 1 year of social studies, and 2 years of a foreign language. Once students are admitted and enrolled, they should provide current documentation to Specific Learning Disabilities Office to receive appropriate accommodations and services.

ADDITIONAL INFORMATION

Services for enrolled students include developing a plan for study, including choice of major, proper class load, dealing with and informing faculty, regular evaluation sessions, and additional guidance through the college's counseling program. With appropriate documentation students may receive accommodations such as extended testing times; distraction-free environments for tests; use of calculators, dictionaries, computers, and spellcheckers during exams; scribes; proctors; note-takers; tape recording in class; books on tape; peer tutoring; and priority registration. There are no waivers or substitutions for college graduation requirements.

LEARNING DISABILITY PROGRAM/SERVICES

Learning Disability Program/Services: Disability Services
Director: Linda Stedje-Larsen
  E-mail: stedje@wingate.edu
  Telephone: 704-233-8269
  Fax: 704-233-8265

LEARNING DISABILITY SERVICES

Requests for the following services/accommodations will be evaluated individually based on appropriate and current documentation.

Allowed in exams
  Calculator: Yes
  Dictionary: Yes
  Computer: Yes
  Spellchecker: Yes
Extended test time: NR
Scribes: NR
Proctors: NR
Oral exams: NR
Note-takers: NR

Distraction-reduced environment: Yes
Tape recording in class: Yes
Books on tape from RFBD: Yes
Taping of books not from RFBD: No
Accommodations for students with ADHD: Yes
Reading machine: Yes
Other assistive technology: No
Priority registration: Yes

Added costs for services: No
LD specialists: Yes
Professional tutors: No
Peer tutors: Yes
Max. hours/wk. for services: Unlimited
How professors are notified of LD/ADHD: By student

GENERAL ADMISSIONS INFORMATION

Director of Admissions: Rhett Brown
Telephone: 704-233-8200

ENTRANCE REQUIREMENTS
Academic units recommended: 4 English, 3 math, 2 science (1 science lab), 2 foreign language, 2 social studies. High school diploma is required, and GED is accepted. ACT with or without Writing component accepted. TOEFL required of all international applicants: minimum paper TOEFL 550, minimum computer TOEFL 213.

Application deadline: Rolling
Notification: Rolling
Average GPA: 3.10
ACT Composite middle 50% range: 19–24

SAT Math middle 50% range: 460–565
SAT Critical Reading middle 50% range: NR
SAT Writing middle 50% range: NR

Graduated top 10% of class: 19%
Graduated top 25% of class: 41%
Graduated top 50% of class: 72%

COLLEGE GRADUATION REQUIREMENTS

Course waivers allowed: No
Course substitutions allowed: No

ADDITIONAL INFORMATION

Environment: The university is located on 330 acres in a small town 25 miles east of Charlotte.

Student Body
  Undergrad enrollment: 1,378
  Women: 53%
  Men: 47%
  Percent out-of-state: 37%

Cost Information
  Tuition: $16,000
  Room & board: $6,750
Housing Information
  University housing: Yes
  Percent living on campus: 84%

Greek System
  Fraternity: Yes
  Sorority: Yes
Athletics: Division II

MINOT STATE U.—BOTTINEAU

105 Simrall Boulevard, Bottineau, ND 58318
Phone: 800-542-6866 • Fax: 701-288-5499
E-mail: groszk@misu.nodak.edu • Web: www.misu-b.nodak.edu
Support: CS • Institution type: 4-year public

LEARNING DISABILITY PROGRAM AND SERVICES

The Learning Center provides a variety of academic support services to eligible students with LD. The Learning Center also provides individualized or small group instruction in English, algebra, biology, basic computer use, and other areas. Individuals are also provided with services that best meet their needs. In addition, study skills and reading improvement classes are offered for credit. An LD specialist/math instructor and an English/social studies instructor provide assistance in this program. Students planning to enroll at MSU—Bottineau should send documentation of their disability that is no more than 3 years old to the Learning Center. The documentation should include an intelligence assessment (preferably the WAIS–R), achievement testing (such as the Woodcock-Johnson psychoeducational battery), and education recommendations such as accommodations provided in high school and a recent IEP. Students should visit the Learning Center as soon as they arrive on campus. Students will be asked to complete an application, and the Learning Center instructor will review the students' class schedules and arrange for tutoring if deemed necessary.

LD/ADHD ADMISSIONS INFORMATION

College entrance tests required: Yes
Interview required: No
Essay recommended: No
Documentation required for LD: Documentation is needed only if the student requests accommodations. It should include a psychological evaluation and a recent IEP.
Documentation required for ADHD: Yes
Submitted to: Learning Center
Special Ed. HS course work accepted: Yes

Specific course requirements of all applicants: NR
Separate application required: No
# of LD applications submitted each year: NR
# of LD applications accepted yearly: NR
Total # of students receiving LD services: 10–20
Acceptance into program means acceptance into college: Students must be admitted to and enrolled in the university first and then request services.

ADMISSIONS

Minot State University has an open admission policy. Applicants must present a high school diploma or equivalent such as a GED. Standardized tests are not required. Students are encouraged to self-disclose their disability during the application process so that the university may provide information about accessing support once enrolled. All students who enroll are asked to complete a questionnaire that asks them to identify academic support services that they feel they may need once on campus.

ADDITIONAL INFORMATION

The Learning Center offers free tutoring and is open to all students. Sessions are adapted to fit a student's schedule. Individual tutoring is available. Students may receive accommodations that include class scheduling, though priority registration is not offered. Skills courses are offered in note-taking strategies, test-taking tips, and memory aids. There is a one-credit reading improvement course that helps improve reading comprehension. Additional accommodations based on appropriate documentation could include extended testing times, note-takers, distraction-free testing environments, tape recorders in class, and auxiliary taping of books not available through RFBD. Partners Affiliated for Student Success is a consortium of educational institutions and businesses dedicated to assisting learners as they move from high school education to postsecondary education to work.

LEARNING DISABILITY PROGRAM/SERVICES

Learning Disability Program/Services: Learning Center
Director: Ms. Jan Nahinurk
  E-mail: jan.nahinurk@misu.nodak.edu
  Telephone: 701-228-5479
  Fax: 701-228-5614

LEARNING DISABILITY SERVICES

Requests for the following services/accommodations will be evaluated individually based on appropriate and current documentation.

Allowed in exams
  Calculator: Yes
  Dictionary: Yes
  Computer: Yes
  Spellchecker: Yes
Extended test time: Yes
Scribes: NR
Proctors: NR
Oral exams: Yes
Note-takers: Yes

Distraction-reduced environment: Yes
Tape recording in class: Yes
Books on tape from RFBD: Yes
Taping of books not from RFBD: Yes
Accommodations for students with ADHD: Yes
Reading machine: No
Other assistive technology: Yes
Priority registration: No

Added costs for services: No
LD specialists: Yes
Professional tutors: 2
Peer tutors: 2–5
Max. hours/wk. for services: Varies
How professors are notified of LD/ADHD: By both student and director

GENERAL ADMISSIONS INFORMATION

Director of Admissions: Paula Berg
Telephone: 800-542-6866

ENTRANCE REQUIREMENTS

High school diploma is required, and GED is accepted.

Application deadline: Rolling
Notification: Rolling
Average GPA: 3.1
ACT Composite middle 50% range: NR

SAT Math middle 50% range: NR
SAT Critical Reading middle 50% range: NR
SAT Writing middle 50% range: NR

Graduated top 10% of class: NR
Graduated top 25% of class: NR
Graduated top 50% of class: NR

COLLEGE GRADUATION REQUIREMENTS

Course waivers allowed: No
Course substitutions allowed: No

ADDITIONAL INFORMATION

Environment: The campus is located in a small town 80 miles from Minot, North Dakota.

Student Body
  Undergrad enrollment: 450
  Women: 52%
  Men: 48%
  Percent out-of-state: 14%

Cost Information
  In-state tuition: $3,300
  Out-of-state tuition: $7,800
  Room & board: $3,400
Housing Information
  University housing: Yes
  Percent living on campus: 51%

Greek System
  Fraternity: No
  Sorority: No
Athletics: NAIA

Minot State University—Bottineau

NORTH DAKOTA STATE UNIVERSITY

PO Box 5454, Fargo, ND 58105
Phone: 701-231-8643 • Fax: 701-231-8802
E-mail: ndsu.admission@ndsu.edu • Web: www.ndsu.edu
Support: S • Institution type: 4-year public

LEARNING DISABILITY PROGRAM AND SERVICES

The mission of Disabilities Services is to assist students with disabilities in obtaining optimal access to educational programs, facilities, and employment at NDSU. Toward this end, the staff collaborates with other Counseling Center staff in providing consultation to students regarding accommodations that are therapeutic to their development as human beings and students. Disabilities Services works to provide equal access to academic programs, promote self-awareness and advocacy, educate the student body and faculty on disability-related issues, and provide reasonable and appropriate accommodations. The staff educates faculty regarding the accommodation needs of students and works to ensure compliance with the Americans with Disabilities Act.

LD/ADHD ADMISSIONS INFORMATION

College entrance tests required: Yes
Interview required: N/A
Essay recommended: N/A
Documentation required for LD: Psychoeducational evaluation
Documentation required for ADHD: yes
Submitted to: Disability Services
Special Ed. HS course work accepted: N/A

Specific course requirements of all applicants: Yes
Separate application required: No
# of LD applications submitted each year: NR
# of LD applications accepted yearly: NR
Total # of students receiving LD services: NR
Acceptance into program means acceptance into college: Students must be admitted to and enrolled in the university first and then request services.

ADMISSIONS

Students with learning disabilities submit the general application form and are expected to meet the same admission standards as all other applicants. The ACT range is 20–22, and the minimum GPA is 2.5. Applicants are expected to have taken high school courses in math, including algebra; English; science labs; and social studies. Students with learning disabilities may include a self-disclosure or information explaining or documenting their disability. When necessary, an admission decision is made jointly by the coordinator of the program and the Admissions Office. Disabilities Services would review the documentation and provide a recommendation to admissions. Students can be admitted conditionally on probation and are required to take a study skills course.

ADDITIONAL INFORMATION

Skills courses are offered in study strategies, reading, computers, math, and science. A technology lab/resource room is available for student use. Assessment, counseling, and remedial support are coordinated through the Center for Student Counseling and Personal Growth. In addition, individual counseling, group support, career counseling, and personal/academic enrichment classes are offered. The NDSU Student Support Services Program provides tutoring and small group instruction. Students with appropriate documentation may request alternative testing accommodations. Skills classes are offered for credit for students with learning disabilities and ADHD. Additionally, Disabilities Services offers support groups for students with ADHD. Services and accommodations are available for undergraduate and graduate students.

LEARNING DISABILITY PROGRAM/SERVICES

Learning Disability Program/Services: Disability Services
Director: Bunnie Johnson-Messelt
  E-mail: Bunnie.Johnson-Messelt@ndsu.nodak.edu
  Telephone: 701-231-7671
  Fax: 701-231-6318
Contact Person: Bunnie Johnson-Messelt or Jennifer Erickson
  E-mail: Bunnie.Johnson-Messelt@ndsu.nodak.edu
  Telephone: 701-231-7671
  Fax: 701-231-6318

LEARNING DISABILITY SERVICES

Requests for the following services/accommodations will be evaluated individually based on appropriate and current documentation.

Allowed in exams	**Distraction-reduced environment:** Yes	**Added costs for services:** No
Calculator: Yes	**Tape recording in class:** Yes	**LD specialists:** No
Dictionary: NR	**Books on tape from RFBD:** Yes	**Professional tutors:** No
Computer: NR	**Taping of books not from RFBD:** Yes	**Peer tutors:** 20–50
Spellchecker: NR	**Accommodations for students with**	**Max. hours/wk. for services:**
Extended test time: Yes	**ADHD:** Yes	Unlimited
Scribes: Yes	**Reading machine:** Yes	**How professors are notified of**
Proctors: Yes	**Other assistive technology:** Yes	**LD/ADHD:** By student
Oral exams: Yes	**Priority registration:** Yes	
Note-takers: Yes		

GENERAL ADMISSIONS INFORMATION

Director of Admissions: Jobey Lichtblau
Telephone: 701-231-8643

ENTRANCE REQUIREMENTS

Academic units required: 4 English, 3 math, 3 science (3 science labs), 3 social studies. **Academic units recommended:** 2 foreign language. High school diploma is required, and GED is accepted. ACT with or without Writing component accepted. TOEFL required of all international applicants: minimum paper TOEFL 525, minimum computer TOEFL 193.

Application deadline: 8/15	**SAT Math middle 50% range:**	**Graduated top 10% of class:** 16%
Notification: Rolling	500–650	**Graduated top 25% of class:** 40%
Average GPA: 3.33	**SAT Critical Reading middle 50%**	**Graduated top 50% of class:** 74%
ACT Composite middle 50% range:	**range:** 470–630	
20–25	**SAT Writing middle 50% range:** NR	

COLLEGE GRADUATION REQUIREMENTS

Course waivers allowed: No
Course substitutions allowed: No

ADDITIONAL INFORMATION

Environment: The university is located in a small city 250 miles from Minneapolis, Sioux Falls, and Winnipeg, Canada.

Student Body	**Cost Information**	**Greek System**
Undergrad enrollment: 10,596	**In-state tuition:** $11,244	**Fraternity:** Yes
Women: 45%	**Out-of-state tuition:** $19,217	**Sorority:** Yes
Men: 55%	**Room & board:** $5,477	**Athletics:** Division I
Percent out-of-state: 46%	**Housing Information**	
	University housing: Yes	
	Percent living on campus: 30%	

North Dakota State University

BOWLING GREEN STATE UNIVERSITY

110 McFall Center, Bowling Green, OH 43403
Phone: 419-372-2478 • Fax: 419-372-6955
E-mail: admissions@bgsu.edu • Web: www.bgsu.edu
Support: S • Institution type: 4-year public

LEARNING DISABILITY PROGRAM AND SERVICES

The philosophy of the university is to level the playing field for students with LD and/or ADHD through the provision of appropriate accommodations and advocacy. The Office of Disability Services (ODS) is evidence of BGSU's commitment to provide people a support system that assists in conquering obstacles that persons with disabilities may encounter as they pursue their educational goals and activities. ODS provides services on an as-needed basis. The Study Skills Lab is open to all BGSU students, and the extent of participation is determined by the student. No grades are given in the lab, participation is voluntary, and the program is individualized. The lab is not a tutorial service, but students will be shown efficient techniques for studying, reading textbooks, taking notes, and time management and strategies for effective test-taking and test preparation.

LD/ADHD ADMISSIONS INFORMATION

College entrance tests required: Yes
Interview required: No
Essay recommended: No
Documentation required for LD: Psychoeducational evaluation
Documentation required for ADHD: Neuropsychological evaluation, developmental history
Submitted to: Office of Disability Services
Special Ed. HS course work accepted: Yes

Specific course requirements of all applicants: Yes
Separate application required: No
# of LD applications submitted each year: NR
# of LD applications accepted yearly: NR
Total # of students receiving LD services: 325–350
Acceptance into program means acceptance into college: Students must be admitted to and enrolled in the university first and then request services.

ADMISSIONS

There is no special application or special admissions process. Core courses preferred include 4 years of English, 3 years of math, 3 years of science, 3 years of social studies, 2 years of a foreign language, and 1 year of art. Students with LD may substitute foreign language with another core course. The minimum GPA is approximately 2.0. Students with LD submit the regular application and are encouraged to self-disclose their LD and arrange an interview with ODS to allow staff to discuss any documentation they may require and any concerns of the student. Additional information such as school or medical history that describes specific strengths and weaknesses is helpful in determining the services necessary once the student is admitted. Information documenting the LD should be sent to ODS. Students should submit the results of a psychoeducational evaluation or other testing and documentation that establishes the presence of a specific LD. Students should indicate accommodations that have worked successfully in high school. There is a summer freshman program for freshmen applicants who do not meet the academic standards for fall admission.

ADDITIONAL INFORMATION

General services include priority registration; advising by sharing information on instructor's teaching and testing styles; a writing lab for effective strategies; a study skills center for effective study skills, test-taking strategies, time management techniques, and textbook-reading skills; a math lab, a walk-in lab for understanding basic and advanced concepts; computerized technology; note-takers, readers, and scribes; letters to professors explaining the disability and modifications needed; advocacy; and books on tape. To be eligible for test accommodations, students are required to provide documentation that provides a clear indication/recommendation for the need requested. Staff works with the student to reach a consensus on the type of accommodation to be provided. Test accommodations may include extended time, oral exams, take-home exams, open-book exams, readers, scribes, computers and spellcheckers or grammar checkers, calculators, scratch paper, speller's dictionaries, question clarification, modification of test response format, and quiet rooms.

LEARNING DISABILITY PROGRAM/SERVICES

Learning Disability Program/Services: Office of Disability Services
Director: Rob Cunningham
 E-mail: rcunnin@bgsu.edu
 Telephone: 419-372-8495
 Fax: 419-372-8496

LEARNING DISABILITY SERVICES

Requests for the following services/accommodations will be evaluated individually based on appropriate and current documentation.

Allowed in exams
 Calculator: Yes
 Dictionary: Yes
 Computer: Yes
 Spellchecker: Yes
Extended test time: Yes
Scribes: Yes
Proctors: Yes
Oral exams: Yes
Note-takers: Yes

Distraction-reduced environment: Yes
Tape recording in class: Yes
Books on tape from RFBD: Yes
Taping of books not from RFBD: Yes
**Accommodations for students with
 ADHD:** Yes
Reading machine: Yes
Other assistive technology: Yes
Priority registration: Yes

Added costs for services: No
LD specialists: No
Professional tutors: No
Peer tutors: Yes
Max. hours/wk. for services:
 Unlimited
**How professors are notified of
 LD/ADHD:** By student

GENERAL ADMISSIONS INFORMATION

Director of Admissions: Gary Swegan
Telephone: 419-372-BGSU

ENTRANCE REQUIREMENTS

Academic units required: 4 English, 3 math, 3 science (2 science labs), 2 foreign language, 3 social studies, 1 visual/performing arts. **Academic units recommended:** 4 English, 3 math, 3 science (2 science labs), 2 foreign language, 3 social studies, 1 visual/performing arts. High school diploma is required, and GED is accepted. ACT with or without Writing component accepted. TOEFL required of all international applicants: minimum paper TOEFL 500, minimum computer TOEFL 173.

Application deadline: 7/15
Notification: Rolling
Average GPA: 3.23
ACT Composite middle 50% range:
 19–24

SAT Math middle 50% range:
 450–570
**SAT Critical Reading middle 50%
 range:** 450–560
SAT Writing middle 50% range: NR

Graduated top 10% of class: 14%
Graduated top 25% of class: 36%
Graduated top 50% of class: 70%

COLLEGE GRADUATION REQUIREMENTS

Course waivers allowed: Yes
In what course: Primarily foreign language; other requests will be considered.
Course substitutions allowed: Yes
In what course: Primarily foreign language; other requests will be considered.

ADDITIONAL INFORMATION

Environment: The 1,250-acre campus is in a small town 25 miles south of Toledo.

Student Body
 Undergrad enrollment: 15,875
 Women: 54%
 Men: 46%
 Percent out-of-state: 9%

Cost Information
 In-sate tuition: $9,060
 Out-of-state: $16,368
 Room & board: $6,588
Housing Information
 University housing: Yes
 Percent living on campus: 43%

Greek System
 Fraternity: Yes
 Sorority: Yes
 Athletics: NCAA Division I

CASE WESTERN RESERVE UNIVERSITY

103 Tomlinson Hall, 10900 Euclid Avenue, Cleveland, OH 44106-7055
Phone: 216-368-4450 • Fax: 216-368-5111
E-mail: admission@case.edu • Web: www.case.edu
Support: S • Institution type: 4-year private

LEARNING DISABILITY PROGRAM AND SERVICES

The goals of Educational Support Services (ESS) are to provide reasonable accommodations and serve as an advocate for individuals with diagnosed learning disabilities. ESS ensures that students with disabilities have access to services and accommodations needed to make the college experience a positive and successful one. ESS provides academic support, special accommodations, and personal encouragement. The associate director of Disability Resources will work closely with students and design an individual plan for accommodations. Included in that plan are strategies for disclosure to professors as well as identifying specific accommodations that will be needed for each course.

LD/ADHD ADMISSIONS INFORMATION

College entrance tests required: Yes
Interview required: No
Essay recommended: Yes
Documentation required for LD: Neuropsychological evaluation is preferred.
Documentation required for ADHD: Yes
Submitted to: Educational Support Services
Special Ed. HS course work accepted: No

Specific course requirements of all applicants: Yes
Separate application required: No
# of LD applications submitted each year: NR
# of LD applications accepted yearly: NR
Total # of students receiving LD services: 40
Acceptance into program means acceptance into college: Students must be admitted to and enrolled in the university first and then request services.

ADMISSIONS

Students with learning disabilities are encouraged to apply to CWRU. Admission is highly competitive, but all applicants are evaluated on an individual basis. Students who feel additional information would be helpful to the Admissions Committee are encouraged to provide diagnostic information about their individual situation. General admission criteria include 4 years of English, 3 years of math, 3 years of social science, 1 year of science, and 2–4 years of a foreign language. Students must also submit a writing sample and are encouraged to have an interview. Most admitted students rank in the top 20 percent of their class and have an SAT Reasoning score of 1180–1380 or an ACT score of 27–31.

ADDITIONAL INFORMATION

Skills courses are offered in study and learning strategies, time management, and reading. It is helpful for students to provide information regarding the nature of their disability so that services may be accommodated to their needs. High-performing students do well with the peer tutors available through ESS. These tutors are students who have successfully completed the appropriate course work and have been approved by faculty. Special arrangements are made by ESS for students to have alternative testing such as additional time and proctored examinations in alternative settings. Students with LD are eligible for books on tape through RFBD. The ESS center has reading improvement software, word processing, and all network applications. A reading strategies tutorial program for 1 credit and taught by a graduate student is also available for students with LD.

LEARNING DISABILITY PROGRAM/SERVICES

Learning Disability Program/Services: Disability Services in Educational Support Services (ESS)
Director: Susan Sampson, Coordinator
  E-mail: sms17@po.cwru.edu
  Telephone: 216-368-5230
  Fax: 216-368-8826

LEARNING DISABILITY SERVICES

Requests for the following services/accommodations will be evaluated individually based on appropriate and current documentation.

Allowed in exams
  Calculator: Yes
  Dictionary: Yes
  Computer: Yes
  Spellchecker: Yes
Extended test time: Yes
Scribes: Yes
Proctors: Yes
Oral exams: Yes
Note-takers: Yes

Distraction-reduced environment: Yes
Tape recording in class: Yes
Books on tape from RFBD: Yes
Taping of books not from RFBD: Yes
**Accommodations for students with
  ADHD:** Yes
Reading machine: Yes
Other assistive technology: Yes
Priority registration: Yes

Added costs for services: No
LD specialists: No
Professional tutors: No
Peer tutors: 30–60
Max. hours/wk. for services:
  Unlimited
**How professors are notified of
  LD/ADHD:** By student

GENERAL ADMISSIONS INFORMATION

Director of Admissions: Elizabeth Woyczynski
Telephone: 216-368-4450

ENTRANCE REQUIREMENTS

Academic units required: 4 English, 3 math, 3 science (1 science lab), 2 foreign language, 3 social studies.
Academic units recommended: 4 math, (2 science labs), 3 foreign language, 4 social studies. High school diploma is required, and GED is accepted. ACT with Writing component required. TOEFL required of all international applicants: minimum paper TOEFL 550, minimum computer TOEFL 213.

Application deadline: 1/15
Notification: 4/1
Average GPA: NR
ACT Composite middle 50% range:
  26–31

SAT Math middle 50% range:
  630–730
**SAT Critical Reading middle 50%
  range:** 600–700
SAT Writing middle 50% range:
  590–680

Graduated top 10% of class: 68%
Graduated top 25% of class: 93%
Graduated top 50% of class: 99%

COLLEGE GRADUATION REQUIREMENTS

Course waivers allowed: No
Course substitutions allowed: No

ADDITIONAL INFORMATION

Environment: The university is located on 128 acres four miles east of downtown Cleveland.

Student Body
  Undergrad enrollment: 3,998
  Women: 41%
  Men: 59%
  Percent out-of-state: 45%

Cost Information
  Tuition: $30,240
  Room & board: $9,280
Housing Information
  University housing: Yes
  Percent living on campus: 79%

Greek System
  Fraternity: Yes
  Sorority: Yes
Athletics: Division III

CENTRAL OHIO TECHNICAL COLLEGE

1179 University Drive, Newark, OH 43055-1767
Phone: 740-366-9222 • Fax: 740-364-9531
E-mail: jmerrin@cotc.edu • Web: www.cotc.edu
Support: CS • Institution type: 2-year public

LEARNING DISABILITY PROGRAM AND SERVICES

The goals of Disability Services (DS) are to foster self-advocacy and independence. Disability Services provides counseling and accommodations for students with learning disabilities. Placement tests are given after admissions. The tutoring program and Disability Services are the academic support units. They provide programs and services to students desiring to strengthen their academic skills. Students need to self-identify before scheduling classes. Early notice is needed for some services, such as alternate testing and recorded textbooks. The college advocates meeting the unique needs of students with disabilities. Accommodations provided allow for equal access to higher education. Students with learning disabilities make up the largest category of all students with disabilities attending the college. This permanent disorder does not impair the normally average to above-average IQ of these students, but it does mean that different teaching/learning strategies may be needed. A student with a diagnosed learning disability who has been to DS will present an authorized accommodation form signed by a DS staff member to a faculty member. The faculty member and student then arrange to meet the accommodations.

LD/ADHD ADMISSIONS INFORMATION

College entrance tests required: No
Interview required: No
Essay recommended: No
Documentation required for LD: Psychoeducational evaluation
Documentation required for ADHD: Yes
Submitted to: Disability Services
Special Ed. HS course work accepted: No

Specific course requirements of all applicants: No
Separate application required: No
# of LD applications submitted each year: NR
# of LD applications accepted yearly: NR
Total # of students receiving LD services: NR
Acceptance into program means acceptance into college: Students must be admitted and enrolled at the college, and then their requests for supportive services will be reviewed.

ADMISSIONS

Admission is open to all applicants with a high school diploma or the GED, except in health programs. There are no specific course requirements. ACT/SAT tests are not required. The application process is the same for all students. There is no requirement to provide disability-related information to the Admissions Office. Documentation of your disability should be sent directly to DS. Eligibility for services/accommodations from DS is a separate process from admissions. To receive accommodations, the student's diagnostic test results and diagnosis must not be older than 3 years. All prospective students are encouraged to contact DS in the early stages of their college planning. Preadmission services include information about academic support services, transition issues, admission requirements, and appropriate documentation and meetings with staff disability professionals.

ADDITIONAL INFORMATION

The Tutoring Lab and the Assistive Teaching Lab are for students with learning disabilities and ADHD. All students are automatically eligible for services. The tutoring program includes peer tutoring in almost any course, scheduled at the student's convenience for 2 hours each week per course. The Assistive Technology Lab has resources to improve reading, math, and language skills; word processing; and study aids for some courses and national tests. The Study Skills Workshop Series provides assistance in improving study skills and 50-minute workshops on time management, learning styles/memory, test preparation and taking, reading textbooks effectively, and note-taking. Students also have access to proctors, individualized instruction designed to meet special needs, advocacy assistance, diagnosis counseling, coaching, and assistance with accommodations.

LEARNING DISABILITY PROGRAM/SERVICES

Learning Disability Program/Services: Office for Disability Services (DS)
Director: Connie S. Zang
  E-mail: czang@cotc.edu
  Telephone: 740-366-9246
  Fax: 740-364-9646

LEARNING DISABILITY SERVICES

Requests for the following services/accommodations will be evaluated individually based on appropriate and current documentation.

Allowed in exams	**Distraction-reduced environment:** Yes	**Added costs for services:** No
Calculator: Yes	**Tape recording in class:** Yes	**LD specialists:** Yes
Dictionary: No	**Books on tape from RFBD:** Yes	**Professional tutors:** 1
Computer: Yes	**Taping of books not from RFBD:** Yes	**Peer tutors:** 25–40
Spellchecker: No	**Accommodations for students with**	**Max. hours/wk. for services:**
Extended test time: Yes	**ADHD:** Yes	Unlimited
Scribes: Yes	**Reading machine:** Yes	**How professors are notified of**
Proctors: Yes	**Other assistive technology:** Yes	**LD/ADHD:** By student
Oral exams: No	**Priority registration:** No	
Note-takers: Yes		

GENERAL ADMISSIONS INFORMATION

Director of Admissions: John Merrin
Telephone: 740-366-9393

ENTRANCE REQUIREMENTS

Open admissions. High school diploma or GED accepted. ACT score of 14 on the English section and 15 on the Math section. Some programs have additional requirements.

Application deadline: Rolling	**SAT Math middle 50% range:** NR	**Graduated top 10% of class:** NR
Notification: Rolling	**SAT Critical Reading middle 50%**	**Graduated top 25% of class:** NR
Average GPA: NR	**range:** NR	**Graduated top 50% of class:** NR
ACT Composite middle 50% range: NR	**SAT Writing middle 50% range:** NR	

COLLEGE GRADUATION REQUIREMENTS

Course waivers allowed: No
Course substitutions allowed: Yes
In what course: Varies, on case-by-case basis

ADDITIONAL INFORMATION

Environment: The campus is located in a small town with easy access to Columbus.

Student Body	**Cost Information**	**Greek System**
Undergrad enrollment: 2,903	**In-state tuition:** $4,400	**Fraternity:** No
Women: 74%	**Out-of-state tuition:** $11,000	**Sorority:** No
Men: 26%	**Room & board:** $5,400	**Athletics:** NJCAA
Percent out-of-state: 1%	**Housing Information**	
	University housing: Yes	
	Percent living on campus: 1%	

COLLEGE OF MOUNT ST. JOSEPH

5701 Delhi Road, Cincinnati, OH 45233
Phone: 513-244-4531 • Fax: 513-244-4629
E-mail: admission@mail.msj.edu • Web: www.msj.edu
Support: SP • Institution type: 4-year private

LEARNING DISABILITY PROGRAM AND SERVICES

Project EXCEL is a comprehensive academic support program for students with learning disabilities enrolled in the college. The program's goals are to assist students in the transition from a secondary program to a college curriculum and promote the development of learning strategies and compensatory skills that will enable students to achieve success in a regular academic program. The structure of the program and supportive environment at the Mount give Project EXCEL its singular quality. Project EXCEL offers students individualized attention and a variety of support services to meet specific needs, including supervised tutoring by professional tutors; monitoring of student progress; instruction in learning strategies, time management, and coping skills; and academic advising with attention to students' specific learning needs. Students admitted to the program must maintain a 2.25 overall GPA, and their progress is evaluated on an ongoing basis.

LD/ADHD ADMISSIONS INFORMATION

College entrance tests required: Yes
Interview required: Yes
Essay recommended: Yes
Documentation required for LD: Psychoeducational evaluation that less than 3 years old
Documentation required for ADHD: Yes
Submitted to: Project EXCEL
Special Ed. HS course work accepted: No

Specific course requirements of all applicants: Yes
Separate application required: Yes
# of LD applications submitted each year: 60
# of LD applications accepted yearly: 32
Total # of students receiving LD services: 75
Acceptance into program means acceptance into college: Students are either admitted directly into EXCEL and the college or EXCEL reviews applicants and makes recommendations to admissions. Applicants may also be admitted directly into the college.

ADMISSIONS

Admission to Project EXCEL is multistep and includes the following: an interview with the program director, completed general admission application, completed Project EXCEL forms (general information, applicant goal and self-assessment, and educational data completed by high school), psychoeducational evaluation, transcript, an ACT minimum of 15 or an SAT minimum of 700–740, and a recommendation. The application is reviewed by the Project EXCEL director and Project EXCEL Admissions Committee. The diagnostic evaluation must indicate the presence of specific LD and provide reasonable evidence that the student can successfully meet college academic requirements. Academic performance problems that exist concomitantly with a diagnosed ADHD will be considered in the review of the student's diagnostic profile. Students can be admitted to the college through Project EXCEL. Students not meeting all EXCEL admission requirements may be admitted part-time or on a probationary basis. Apply early. Other students not meeting admission requirements can take up to 6 hours per semester to a maximum of 13 hours. At that point, if they have a 2.0-plus GPA, they are admitted to the college.

ADDITIONAL INFORMATION

Project EXCEL students are assisted with course and major selection. Students are offered individualized attention and a variety of support services to meet specific needs, including supervised tutoring, monitoring of student progress, access to a writing lab, note-takers, accommodated testing, instruction in learning strategies, time management, coping skills, liaisons with faculty, and academic advising with attention to specific learning needs. Students enroll in regular classes and must fulfill the same course requirements as all Mount students. The curriculum is closely supervised, and specialized instruction is offered in writing, reading, and study skills to fit the individual needs of the students. The program director serves as a student advisor.

LEARNING DISABILITY PROGRAM/SERVICES

Learning Disability Program/Services: Project EXCEL
Director: Jane Pohlman
E-mail: jane_pohlman@mail.msj.edu
Telephone: 513-244-4623
Fax: 513-244-4222

LEARNING DISABILITY SERVICES

Requests for the following services/accommodations will be evaluated individually based on appropriate and current documentation.

Allowed in exams
  Calculator: Yes
  Dictionary: Yes
  Computer: Yes
  Spellchecker: Yes
Extended test time: Yes
Scribes: Yes
Proctors: Yes
Oral exams: Yes
Note-takers: Yes

Distraction-reduced environment: Yes
Tape recording in class: Yes
Books on tape from RFBD: Yes
Taping of books not from RFBD: Yes
Accommodations for students with ADHD: Yes
Reading machine: Yes
Other assistive technology: No
Priority registration: No

Added costs for services: Yes
LD specialists: Yes
Professional tutors: 15
Peer tutors: No
Max. hours/wk. for services: Unlimited
How professors are notified of LD/ADHD: By both student and director

GENERAL ADMISSIONS INFORMATION

Director of Admissions: Peggy Minnich
Telephone: 513-244-4531

ENTRANCE REQUIREMENTS

Academic units required: 4 English, 2 math, 2 science (1 science lab), 2 foreign language, 1 social studies, 1 history, 1 academic elective, 1 fine arts. **Academic units recommended:** 4 English, 4 math, 4 science (2 science labs), 2 foreign language, 2 social studies, 2 history, 1 academic elective, 2 fine arts. High school diploma is required, and GED is accepted. ACT with or without Writing component accepted. TOEFL required of all international applicants: minimum paper TOEFL 510, minimum computer TOEFL 180.

Application deadline: 8/15
Notification: Rolling
Average GPA: 3.22
ACT Composite middle 50% range: 19–23

SAT Math middle 50% range: 430–540
SAT Critical Reading middle 50% range: 430–540
SAT Writing middle 50% range: NR

Graduated top 10% of class: 9%
Graduated top 25% of class: 33%
Graduated top 50% of class: 71%

COLLEGE GRADUATION REQUIREMENTS

Course waivers allowed: No
Course substitutions allowed: No

ADDITIONAL INFORMATION

Environment: The Mount is a Catholic, coeducational, liberal arts college located approximately 15 miles from downtown Cincinnati.

Student Body
  Undergrad enrollment: 1,883
  Women: 68%
  Men: 32%
  Percent out-of-state: 15%

Cost Information
  Tuition: $19,650
  Room & board: $6,300
Housing Information
  University housing: Yes
  Percent living on campus: 21%

Greek System
  Fraternity: No
  Sorority: No
Athletics: Division III

HOCKING COLLEGE

3301 Hocking Parkway, Nelsonville, OH 45764
Phone: 740-753-3591 • Fax: 740-753-1452
E-mail: admissions@hocking.edu • Web: www.hocking.edu
Support: CS • Institution type: 2-year public

LEARNING DISABILITY PROGRAM AND SERVICES

The Access Center Office of Disability Support Services (ACODS) is dedicated to serving the various needs of individuals with disabilities and promoting their full participation in college life. The educational coordinator for students with disabilities helps all students with learning disabilities successfully adjust to college life by finding the right fit between the instructional offerings of Hocking College and their own individualized learning and personal needs. This is accomplished in part by working with assessment and counseling professionals to assist students in identifying individualized programs of study and means for success by more closely aligning interests and abilities with instructors and program effectiveness. The accommodation process is one of collaboration between students and instructors with support from ACODS. Eligibility is determined on the basis of the presence of a disability and a need for services and accommodations to support an equal educational opportunity. Information from the disability documentation, the student's stated experience with services and accommodations that have been effective in the past, and ACODS professional judgment will be drawn on in making the eligibility determination. The Access Center assists students with physical disabilities, health problems, and/or learning disabilities. The Access Center can make students' adjustment to college life easy by finding the right fit at Hocking College for their learning styles.

LD/ADHD ADMISSIONS INFORMATION

College entrance tests required: Yes
Interview required: No
Essay recommended: No
Documentation required for LD: Psychoeducational
  evaluation is preferred.
Documentation required for ADHD: Psychoeducational
  evaluation is preferred.
Submitted to: ACODS
Special Ed. HS course work accepted: N/A

Specific course requirements of all applicants: No
Separate application required: Yes
# of LD applications submitted each year: NR
# of LD applications accepted yearly: NR
Total # of students receiving LD services: 171
**Acceptance into program means acceptance into
  college:** Students must be admitted to and enrolled in the
  university first and then request services.

ADMISSIONS

The college has open enrollment for any student with a high school diploma or equivalent. Students are not required to take any specific courses or have any specific test score on the ACT/SAT. Students requesting accommodations or services for learning disabilities must be admitted and enrolled, and then they may request services. Current documentation should be submitted.

ADDITIONAL INFORMATION

ACODS staff and the student work together to identify individual needs and then determine which of the support services and accommodations would enable the student to achieve academic potential. Strategies used to assist students with disabilities include assistance with instructional and supportive needs; aligning interests and abilities with instructors and program effectiveness; assuring individual program implementation consistent with the identified needs of the student; evaluating problematic situations regarding modes of presentation that affect student performance and potential for success; assisting on course assignments, troubleshooting learning problems, and assisting in solutions to situations that inhibit success; helping to obtain tutoring services; priority scheduling; liaising with community agencies; and serving as an advocate. For those who qualify, the Access Center staff can assist with advising, tutoring, and test-taking and also arrange for campus transportation and classroom access. In addition, the Access Center can link students with other college services and external service agencies. Eligibility is determined on the basis of the presence of a disability and a need for services and accommodations to support an equal educational opportunity. Documentation of the disability is required as well as the student's stated experience with services and accommodations that have been effective in the past. Quest for Success is a program designed especially for new students to help them prepare to start technical classes in the fall. Additional services include professional tutors in some mathematics and communications courses, Compu-Lenz to enlarge type on a computer screen and reduce glare, academic advising, and an educational coordinator to act as a liaison with college instructors and community agencies.

LEARNING DISABILITY PROGRAM/SERVICES

Learning Disability Program/Services: Office of Disability Services (ACODS)
Director: Kim Forbes Powell
  E-mail: forbes_k@hocking.edu.
  Telephone: 740-753-3591
  Fax: 740-753-4495

LEARNING DISABILITY SERVICES

Requests for the following services/accommodations will be evaluated individually based on appropriate and current documentation.

Allowed in exams
  Calculator: Yes
  Dictionary: No
  Computer: Yes
  Spellchecker: Yes
Extended test time: Yes
Scribes: Yes
Proctors: Yes
Oral exams: Yes
Note-takers: Yes

Distraction-reduced environment: Yes
Tape recording in class: Yes
Books on tape from RFBD: Yes
Taping of books not from RFBD: Yes
Accommodations for students with ADHD: Yes
Reading machine: Yes
Other assistive technology: Yes
Priority registration: No

Added costs for services: No
LD specialists: Yes
Professional tutors: 3
Peer tutors: 25–40
Max. hours/wk. for services: Unlimited
How professors are notified of LD/ADHD: By student

GENERAL ADMISSIONS INFORMATION

Director of Admissions: Lynn Hull
Telephone: 740-753-7049

ENTRANCE REQUIREMENTS

Academic Units Recommended: 4 English, 3 math, 3 science, 4 social studies, 2 foreign language. Open admissions. High school diploma or GED accepted. Specific ACT or SAT scores are not required.

Application deadline: Rolling
Notification: Rolling
Average GPA: NR
ACT Composite middle 50% range: NR

SAT Math middle 50% range: NR
SAT Critical Reading middle 50% range: NR
SAT Writing middle 50% range: NR

Graduated top 10% of class: NR
Graduated top 25% of class: NR
Graduated top 50% of class: NR

COLLEGE GRADUATION REQUIREMENTS

Course waivers allowed: NR
Course substitutions allowed: Yes
In what course: Any with an appropriate substitution

ADDITIONAL INFORMATION

Environment: The college is located on 150 acres in a rural area with easy access to Columbus.

Student Body
  Undergrad enrollment: 5,070
  Women: 46%
  Men: 54%
  Percent out-of-state: 14%

Cost Information
  In-state tuition: $3,018
  Out-of-state tuition: $6,048
  Room & board: $3,300
Housing Information
  University housing: Yes
  Percent living on campus: 10%

Greek System
  Fraternity: Yes
  Sorority: Yes
Athletics: Intramural

KENT STATE UNIVERSITY

161 Michael Schwartz Center, Kent, OH 44242-0001
Phone: 330-672-2444 • Fax: 330-672-2499
E-mail: admissions@kent.edu • Web: www.kent.edu
Support: CS • Institution type: 4-year public

LEARNING DISABILITY PROGRAM AND SERVICES

The goals and philosophy of the Student Disability Services (SDS) program are to promote student independence and self-advocacy at the college level. The university believes that the ability to do college work is highly correlated with grades in high school. Students with learning disabilities who receive accommodations in high school and who are academically successful are most likely to be successful at KSU. If an LD support system has been available and the student has been diligent but still has a low GPA in high school, lack of skills or disabilities may be too severe for that student to be successful at KSU. Students should meet with an SDS staff member 6 months before enrollment to discuss needs and accommodations.

LD/ADHD ADMISSIONS INFORMATION

College entrance tests required: Yes
Interview required: Yes
Essay recommended: No
Documentation required for LD: Psychoeducational
evaluation; see www.kent.edu/sds
Documentation required for ADHD: Yes
Submitted to: Student Disability Services
Special Ed. HS course work accepted: No

Specific course requirements of all applicants: NR
Separate application required: No
# of LD applications submitted each year: NR
# of LD applications accepted yearly: NR
Total # of students receiving LD services: NR
**Acceptance into program means acceptance into
college:** Students must be admitted to and enrolled in the
university first and then request services.

ADMISSIONS

Students with LD must meet the same admission criteria as all other applicants. There is no special admissions procedure for students with LD. However, the high school may adjust GPA if the student was not diagnosed until late in high school. Documentation of the student's disability is required. In addition to having completed standard college-preparatory courses, applicants should be able to type or use a computer and a calculator and have skills in performing addition, subtraction, multiplication, and division using natural numbers, integers, fractions, and decimals. Students should also have highly developed study skills based on their specific strengths. The minimum GPA for admission is 2.2, and the minimum college entrance test scores are 21 ACT or 870 SAT. Students who have been in the upper 60 percent of their high school class and have an ACT score of 19-plus or SAT of 900-plus do very well at KSU.

ADDITIONAL INFORMATION

It is recommended that all documentation be submitted prior to enrolling, as services include academic assistance in selecting courses. All students with documentation of a learning disability may utilize the academic and counseling services, such as academic advising; developmental education courses for freshmen students with deficits in reading, writing, and math; individual and small group tutoring; support groups; and individual and group study skills help through the Academic Success Center. The peer mentoring program matches a student with a personal study coach—someone who can help them acquire the skills and motivation necessary for academic success. Supplemental Instruction (SI) is a national program that offers peer-facilitated group study sessions for students enrolled in large, high-risk liberal arts and science courses. (High-risk courses are courses that have a D, F, or withdrawal rate of at least 30 percent.) The basic difference between SI and other tutoring services offered at the Academic Success Center is that SI leaders actually attend classes along with the students they are tutoring. Each SI leader has already taken the course and earned an A or a B. The writing tutoring program is designed to help all students strengthen their writing skills and develop gradually as independent writers. Writing sessions at the Academic Success Center are process oriented. Services and accommodations are available for undergraduate and graduate students.

LEARNING DISABILITY PROGRAM/SERVICES

Learning Disability Program/Services: Student Disability Services
Director: Mary DeMichele Reeves
E-mail: mreeves1@kent.edu
Telephone: 330-672-3391
Fax: 330-672-3763
Contact Person: Laura McGlothlin
E-mail: mreeves1@kent.edu
Telephone: 330-672-3391
Fax: 330-672-3763

LEARNING DISABILITY SERVICES

Requests for the following services/accommodations will be evaluated individually based on appropriate and current documentation.

Allowed in exams
  Calculator: Yes
  Dictionary: Yes
  Computer: Yes
  Spellchecker: Yes
Extended test time: Yes
Scribes: Yes
Proctors: Yes
Oral exams: No
Note-takers: Yes

Distraction-reduced environment: Yes
Tape recording in class: Yes
Books on tape from RFBD: Yes
Taping of books not from RFBD: Yes
**Accommodations for students with
  ADHD:** Yes
Reading machine: No
Other assistive technology: Yes
Priority registration: Yes

Added costs for services: No
LD specialists: Yes
Professional tutors: 3
Peer tutors: 50
Max. hours/wk. for services: 4
**How professors are notified of
  LD/ADHD:** By student

GENERAL ADMISSIONS INFORMATION

Director of Admissions: Nancy Dellavecchia
Telephone: 330-672-2444

ENTRANCE REQUIREMENTS

Academic units recommended: 4 English, 3 math, 3 science (2 science labs), 3 foreign language, 3 social studies, 1 art. High school diploma is required, and GED is accepted. ACT without Writing component accepted. TOEFL required of all international applicants: minimum paper TOEFL 525, minimum computer TOEFL 197.

Application deadline: 8/1
Notification: Rolling
Average GPA: 3.15
ACT Composite middle 50% range:
  18–24

SAT Math middle 50% range:
  460–590
**SAT Critical Reading middle 50%
  range:** 460–580
SAT Writing middle 50% range: NR

Graduated top 10% of class: 12%
Graduated top 25% of class: 32%
Graduated top 50% of class: 68%

COLLEGE GRADUATION REQUIREMENTS

Course waivers allowed: No
Course substitutions allowed: Yes
In what course: Decisions are made by individual colleges, and they depend on the student's major.

ADDITIONAL INFORMATION

Environment: The university is a residential campus located on 1,200 acres 45 miles southeast of Cleveland.

Student Body
  Undergrad enrollment: 17,793
  Women: 59%
  Men: 41%
  Percent out-of-state: 10%

Cost Information
  In-state tuition: $8,430
  Out-of-state tuition: $15,862
  Room & board: $7,810
Housing Information
  University housing: Yes
  Percent living on campus: 35%

Greek System
  Fraternity: Yes
  Sorority: Yes
Athletics: Division I

Kent State University

MIAMI UNIVERSITY

301 South Campus Avenue, Oxford, OH 45056
Phone: 513-529-2531 • Fax: 513-529-1550
E-mail: admissions@muohio.edu • Web: www.muohio.edu
Support: CS • Institution type: 4-year public

LEARNING DISABILITY PROGRAM AND SERVICES

The Learning Disabilities Program staff coordinates university and community resources to meet the academic and personal needs of students with LD; assist faculty in understanding the characteristics and needs of these students; and provide services on an individual basis to students with appropriate documentation. All students with LD or ADHD are ultimately responsible for their own academic adjustment. Appropriate services and accommodations are determined through a flexible, interactive process that involves the student and the coordinator and are arranged through dialogue with faculty and staff responsible for implementing many of these services or accommodations. Decisions about services and accommodations for students with LD are made on the basis of the disability documentation and the functional limitations caused by the disability, as well as the current needs of the student. Students with ADHD must meet with the LD coordinator to initiate services after discussing disability-related needs and providing verification of the disability.

LD/ADHD ADMISSIONS INFORMATION

College entrance tests required: Yes
Interview required: No
Essay recommended: No
Documentation required for LD: Documentation guidelines are available online.
Documentation required for ADHD: Documentation guidelines are available online.
Submitted to: Admissions Office
Special Ed. HS course work accepted: NR

Specific course requirements of all applicants: NR
Separate application required: No
# of LD applications submitted each year: Yes
# of LD applications accepted yearly: NR
Total # of students receiving LD services: NR
Acceptance into program means acceptance into college: Students must be admitted to and enrolled in the university first and then request services.

ADMISSIONS

Students with LD are admitted to Miami through the regular admission process; therefore, it is important to ensure that the information in the application accurately reflects a student's academic ability and potential. Students with academic deficiencies may still be qualified for admission. Students may choose to self-disclose LD or ADHD on their application, either through a personal essay or the extenuating circumstances statement. Also, students may voluntarily choose to submit other information that may help the Admissions Office to understand their unique learning strengths and needs. Applicants with LD are encouraged to meet with the LD coordinator during the college search process to discuss the LD support program, the nature and extent of their disability, the types of accommodations that may be needed, and the program and course requirements in their field of study.

ADDITIONAL INFORMATION

Support services for students with LD include transition information; admission counseling; priority registration; classroom accommodations such as test modifications, extended exam times, and so on; academic assistance such as tutoring and study skills assistance; mentoring in learning strategies, time management, and coping strategies; liaison with faculty; campus advocacy; counseling; and career awareness. The Orton Student Association is a student organization that provides a support system—academically, socially, emotionally, and personally—to students with LD. The group encourages and promotes student and faculty awareness of these conditions through outreach efforts. The Terry A. Gould LD Fund is an endowed account providing funds for instructional materials, program expenses, and conference opportunities for students with LD. The Office of Learning Assistance works with students encountering academic difficulties. The tutorial assistance program provides peer tutors. The Bernard B. Rinella Jr. Learning Center has special services designed to help students experiencing academic problems. In meeting with a learning specialist, students' existing learning strategies will be assessed, and new effective strategies will be introduced. Topics of time management, note-taking, test-taking, writing, and organization will be covered. New study strategies will be reinforced through individual conferences with a learning specialist, peer mentoring, and/or tutoring.

LEARNING DISABILITY PROGRAM/SERVICES

Learning Disability Program/Services: Office of Disability Resources
Director: J. Andrew Zeisler
  E-mail: zeisleja@muohio.edu
  Telephone: 513-529-1541
  Fax: 513-529-8799

LEARNING DISABILITY SERVICES

Requests for the following services/accommodations will be evaluated individually based on appropriate and current documentation.

Allowed in exams
  Calculator: Yes
  Dictionary: Yes
  Computer: Yes
  Spellchecker: Yes
Extended test time: Yes
Scribes: Yes
Proctors: Yes
Oral exams: Yes
Note-takers: Yes

Distraction-reduced environment: Yes
Tape recording in class: Yes
Books on tape from RFBD: Yes
Taping of books not from RFBD: Yes
Accommodations for students with ADHD: Yes
Reading machine: Yes
Other assistive technology: Yes
Priority registration: Yes

Added costs for services: No
LD specialists: Yes
Professional tutors: No
Peer tutors: 100–220
Max. hours/wk. for services: Unlimited
How professors are notified of LD/ADHD: By student

GENERAL ADMISSIONS INFORMATION

Director of Admissions: Ann Larson (interim)
Telephone: 513-529-2531

ENTRANCE REQUIREMENTS

Academic units recommended: 4 English, 3 math, 3 science, 2 foreign language, 3 social studies, 1 fine arts. High school diploma is required, and GED is accepted. ACT with Writing component required. TOEFL required of all international applicants: minimum paper TOEFL 533, minimum computer TOEFL 200.

Application deadline: 1/31
Notification: 3/15
Average GPA: 3.66
ACT Composite middle 50% range: 24–29

SAT Math middle 50% range: 570–660
SAT Critical Reading middle 50% range: 540–640
SAT Writing middle 50% range: NR

Graduated top 10% of class: 38%
Graduated top 25% of class: 74%
Graduated top 50% of class: 98%

COLLEGE GRADUATION REQUIREMENTS

Course waivers allowed: No
Course substitutions allowed: Yes
In what course: Foreign language and math only if it is determined not to be an essential component of the curriculum and/or major.

ADDITIONAL INFORMATION

Environment: The university is in a small town northwest of Cincinnati.

Student Body
  Undergrad enrollment: 14,471
  Women: 54%
  Men: 46%
  Percent out-of-state: 29%

Cost Information
  In-state tuition: $8,496
  Out-of-state tuition: $21,011
  Room & board: $8,140
Housing Information
  University housing: Yes
  Percent living on campus: 48%

Greek System
  Fraternity: Yes
  Sorority: Yes
Athletics: Division I

Miami University

MUSKINGUM COLLEGE

163 Stormont Drive, New Concord, OH 43762
Phone: 614-826-8137 • Fax: 614-826-8100
E-mail: adminfo@muskingum.edu • Web: www.muskigum.edu
Support: SP • Institution type: 4-year private

LEARNING DISABILITY PROGRAM AND SERVICES

The PLUS Program provides students who have disabilities with the opportunity to reach their academic potential. A learning strategies instructional model administered by a professional staff is the basis for PLUS support. Students may revise full program participation to maintenance (reduced fee) or independence (no fee) based on academic achievement. A full range of accommodations in addition to a structured tutorial are provided through the Center for Advancement of Learning, the framework for academic support at Muskingum College. Program participants must partake in a minimum of 1 hour of individual tutoring time per week for each class. The program offers no remedial or developmental instruction, encourages individual responsibility for learning, and acknowledges successful individual efforts. The program offers qualified students individual or small group content-based learning strategies, instruction, and content tutorial support. Parent contact is made each semester for students participating in the PLUS Program.

LD/ADHD ADMISSIONS INFORMATION

College entrance tests required: Yes
Interview required: Yes
Essay recommended: Yes
Documentation required for LD: Psychoeducational evaluation
Documentation required for ADHD: Psychoeducational evaluation with documentation of ADHD
Submitted to: PLUS Program
Special Ed. HS course work accepted: NR

Specific course requirements of all applicants: NR
Separate application required: No
# of LD applications submitted each year: NR
# of LD applications accepted yearly: 60–70
Total # of students receiving LD services: 130–160
Acceptance into program means acceptance into college: Admissions to the PLUS Program is an automatic admission to the college.

ADMISSIONS

Admission for students with LD is based on a careful evaluation of all the materials submitted. Students must submit a completed application for admission (check the box for PLUS Program), ACT/SAT scores, a current psychoeducational evaluation documenting the disability and administered by a licensed psychologist or a medical diagnosis of ADHD, a copy of a current IEP and transition plan, and a detailed request for and description of auxiliary accommodations being requested. The student is evaluated for potential for academic success as a participant in the PLUS Program. Admission policies are flexible for students with LD, but a good distribution among college-prep courses is helpful. Students should submit recommendations from teachers or guidance counselors. Applicants are reviewed, and selected candidates are invited to interview. Space in the program is limited, and early application submission is encouraged. The admission decision is made jointly by the program director and admissions director. A summer transitions program is available to students who are admitted to the college and the PLUS Program. Some students admitted to the PLUS Program may be required to attend the transitions program.

ADDITIONAL INFORMATION

PLUS assigns students to academic and program advisors. Professionals provide tutorial services and coordinate appropriate testing and instructional accommodations. Students are provided with a combination of individual and small group tutorial support. Students participating in the full program must maintain a minimum of one contact hour of tutoring per week for each course. PLUS maintenance is recommended for upperclassmen as they progress successfully in college. High school juniors and seniors with LD can participate in a comprehensive, two-week summer experience, First Step, to help them make the transition to college. The primary emphasis of this program is on the application of learning strategies within the context of a college-level expository course. The program focuses on social and emotional changes associated with the transition to college.

LEARNING DISABILITY PROGRAM/SERVICES

Learning Disability Program/Services: PLUS Program, Center for Advancement of Learning
Director: Dr. Eileen Henry, EdD, MBA
   E-mail: ehenry@muskingum.edu
   Telephone: 740-826-8284
   Fax: 740-826-8285
Contact Person: Michelle Butler
   E-mail: ehenry@muskingum.edu
   Telephone: 740-826-8280
   Fax: 740-826-8285

LEARNING DISABILITY SERVICES

Requests for the following services/accommodations will be evaluated individually based on appropriate and current documentation.

Allowed in exams	**Distraction-reduced environment:** Yes	**Added costs for services:** Yes for
Calculator: Yes	**Tape recording in class:** Yes	PLUS
Dictionary: Yes	**Books on tape from RFBD:** Yes	**LD specialists:** Yes
Computer: Yes	**Taping of books not from RFBD:** Yes	**Professional tutors:** 22
Spellchecker: Yes	**Accommodations for students with**	**Peer tutors:** No
Extended test time: Yes	**ADHD:** Yes	**Max. hours/wk. for services:** 6.5
Scribes: Yes	**Reading machine:** Yes	**How professors are notified of**
Proctors: Yes	**Other assistive technology:** Yes	**LD/ADHD:** By both student and
Oral exams: Yes	**Priority registration:** Yes	director
Note-takers: Yes		

GENERAL ADMISSIONS INFORMATION

Director of Admissions: Beth DaLonzo
Telephone: 740-826-8137

ENTRANCE REQUIREMENTS

Academic units required: 4 English, 2 math, 2 science (1 science lab), 2 foreign language, 1 social studies, 2 history. **Academic units recommended:** 4 English, 3 math, 3 science (2 science labs), 2 foreign language, 1 social studies, 2 history. High school diploma is required, and GED is accepted. ACT with or without Writing component accepted. TOEFL required of all international applicants: minimum paper TOEFL 550.

Application deadline: 8/1	**SAT Math middle 50% range:**	**Graduated top 10% of class:** 23%
Notification: Rolling	450–610	**Graduated top 25% of class:** 45%
Average GPA: 3.28	**SAT Critical Reading middle 50%**	**Graduated top 50% of class:** 72%
ACT Composite middle 50% range:	range: 450–610	
19–24	**SAT Writing middle 50% range:**	
	460–590	

COLLEGE GRADUATION REQUIREMENTS

Course waivers allowed: No
Course substitutions allowed: No

ADDITIONAL INFORMATION

Environment: The college is located on 215 acres in a rural area 70 miles east of Columbus.

Student Body	**Cost Information**	**Greek System**
Undergrad enrollment: 1,633	**Tuition:** $16,600	**Fraternity:** Yes
Women: 51%	**Room & board:** $6,740	**Sorority:** Yes
Men: 49%	**Housing Information**	**Athletics:** Division III
Percent out-of-state: 10%	**University housing:** Yes	
	Percent living on campus: 85%	

NOTRE DAME COLLEGE

4545 College Road, South Euclid, OH 44121
Phone: 216-381-1680 • Fax: 216-373-5278
E-mail: admissions@ndc.edu • Web: www.notredamecollege.edu
Support: SP • Institution type: 4-year private

LEARNING DISABILITY PROGRAM AND SERVICES

The Mission of the Academic Support Center (ASC) is to provide quality educational opportunities and support services above and beyond those required by law to individuals with documented learning disabilities who are traditionally underserved in postsecondary education. The mission of the Academic Support Center parallels the mission of Notre Dame College, which is to educate a diverse population in liberal arts for personal, professional, and global responsibility. The services provided by the ASC are structured and comprehensive, thus enabling a student with a documented learning disability to succeed in college. Prior to being admitted to the center, the student must meet the admission requirements of Notre Dame College. To participate in the ASC, the student must submit documentation of a learning disability. This documentation must include a psychoeducational evaluation that has been conducted within the past 3 years. Refer to Web link on documentation.

LD/ADHD ADMISSIONS INFORMATION

College entrance tests required: Yes
Interview required: No
Essay recommended: Yes
Documentation required for LD: Psychoeducational evaluation conducted within the past 3 years and a current IEP
Documentation required for ADHD: Psychoeducational evaluation conducted within the past 3 years and a current IEP
Submitted to: ASC
Special Ed. HS course work accepted: N/A

Specific course requirements of all applicants: NR
Separate application required: No
# of LD applications submitted each year: 30–40
# of LD applications accepted yearly: 15–20
Total # of students receiving LD services: 23
Acceptance into program means acceptance into college: Students must be admitted and enrolled prior to requesting services.

ADMISSIONS

In fulfilling its mission, Notre Dame College seeks to attract students of diverse religious, racial, educational, and socioeconomic backgrounds and those of various ages and personal experiences. Notre Dame College admits students who demonstrate potential for success in rigorous academic work. The credentials of each applicant are individually evaluated with consideration to a combination of academic record, entrance examination performance, and evidence of potential for success in college studies. The following distribution of courses is considered to be standard academic preparation: 4 units of English, 3 units of math (including Algebra I, Geometry, and Algebra II), 3 units of science with laboratory experience, 3 units of social studies, 2 units of a foreign language, and 1 unit of fine arts.

ADDITIONAL INFORMATION

Services offered through the Academic Support Center include a fall orientation program, support group meetings, individual tutoring geared to subject matter, individual tutoring sessions with a writing specialist, academic advising, training and use of adaptive equipment, workshops on study skills, workshops on organizational skills, accommodations based on documentation, summer programs, and books on tape. The Dwyer Learning Center provides free educational support to all Notre Dame students to help them achieve academic success.

LEARNING DISABILITY PROGRAM/SERVICES

Learning Disability Program/Services: Disability Services
Director: Dr. T. J. Arant
  E-mail: tjarant@ndc.edu
  Telephone: 216-373-5310
  Fax: 216-373-5287
Contact Person: Anne Buffa
  E-mail: tjarant@ndc.edu
  Telephone: 216-373-5224
  Fax: 216-373-5187

LEARNING DISABILITY SERVICES

Requests for the following services/accommodations will be evaluated individually based on appropriate and current documentation.

Allowed in exams		
Calculator: Yes	**Distraction-reduced environment:** Yes	**Added costs for services:** Yes
Dictionary: Yes	**Tape recording in class:** Yes	**LD specialists:** Yes
Computer: Yes	**Books on tape from RFBD:** Yes	**Professional tutors:** 5–10
Spellchecker: Yes	**Taping of books not from RFBD:** Yes	**Peer tutors:** N/A
Extended test time: Yes	**Accommodations for students with**	**Max. hours/wk. for services:** N/A
Scribes: Yes	**ADHD:** Yes	**How professors are notified of**
Proctors: Yes	**Reading machine:** Yes	**LD/ADHD:** By student
Oral exams: Yes	**Other assistive technology:** Yes	
Note-takers: Yes	**Priority registration:** Yes	

GENERAL ADMISSIONS INFORMATION

Director of Admissions: David A. Armstrong, Esq.
Telephone: 216-373-5214

ENTRANCE REQUIREMENTS

Academic units recommended: 4 English, 3 math, 3 science (3 science labs), 2 foreign language, 3 social studies, 1 fine arts. High school diploma is required, and GED is accepted. ACT with or without Writing component accepted. TOEFL required of all international applicants: minimum paper TOEFL 550, minimum computer TOEFL 213.

Application deadline: NR	**SAT Math middle 50% range:**	**Graduated top 10% of class:** 4%
Notification: Rolling	393–520	**Graduated top 25% of class:** 22%
Average GPA: 2.95	**SAT Critical Reading middle 50%**	**Graduated top 50% of class:** 62%
ACT Composite middle 50% range:	**range:** 440–528	
17–21	**SAT Writing middle 50% range:** NR	

COLLEGE GRADUATION REQUIREMENTS

Course waivers allowed: Yes
In what course: To be determined on an individual basis
Course substitutions allowed: Yes
In what course: Logic may be substituted for math with proper documentation. NDC does not require a foreign language.

ADDITIONAL INFORMATION

Environment: Notre Dame College is located in South Euclid, Ohio, a suburb under 30 minutes east of downtown Cleveland, Ohio. The college sits on a wooded 53-acre campus.

Student Body	Cost Information	Greek System
Undergrad enrollment: 835	**Tuition:** $18,670	**Fraternity:** No
Women: 63%	**Room & board:** $6,648	**Sorority:** No
Men: 37%	**Housing Information**	**Athletics:** NAIA
Percent out-cf-state: 3%	**University housing:** Yes	
	Percent living on campus: 29%	

OBERLIN COLLEGE

101 North Professor Street, Oberlin College, Oberlin, OH 44074
Phone: 440-775-8411 • Fax: 440-775-6905
E-mail: college.admissions@oberlin.edu • Web: www.oberlin.edu
Support: CS • Institution type: 4-year private

LEARNING DISABILITY PROGRAM AND SERVICES

Personnel from the Office of Services for Students with Disabilities (OSSD) provide services, as well as coordinate accommodations, to meet the needs of students who have disabilities. Their goal is to maximize the student's entire educational potential while helping him or her develop and maintain independence. The program philosophy is one that encourages self-advocacy. Students who are diagnosed by OSSD personnel as having LD, as well as those who can provide documentation of a current diagnosis of LD, are eligible for services. To verify a previously diagnosed LD, a student must provide a psychological assessment, educational test results, and a recent copy of an IEP that specifies placement in a learning disabilities program. These documents will be reviewed by personnel from OSSD to determine eligibility. Students requesting services are interviewed by a learning disability counselor before a service plan is developed or initiated.

LD/ADHD ADMISSIONS INFORMATION

College entrance tests required: Yes
Interview required: No
Essay recommended: No
Documentation required for LD: A recent psychological evaluation.
Documentation required for ADHD: Yes
Submitted to: SSD
Special Ed. HS course work accepted: Yes

Specific course requirements of all applicants: Yes
Separate application required: No
# of LD applications submitted each year: NR
# of LD applications accepted yearly: NR
Total # of students receiving LD services: 200
Acceptance into program means acceptance into college: Students must be admitted to and enrolled in the university first and then request services.

ADMISSIONS

There is no special admissions procedure for students with LD. All applicants must meet the same admission requirements. Courses required include 4 years of English and math and at least 3 years of social science and science. The average GPA is typically a B average or better. ACT scores range between 25 and 30; SAT Reasoning test scores range between 1100 and 1320, and SAT Subject Test scores range between 560 and 680 on each Subject Test. Students who self-disclose and provide documentation may have their files read by OSSD personnel, who will provide a recommendation to the Office of Admissions. Students who can provide valid and recent documentation of a psychoeducational diagnosis of LD may receive services.

ADDITIONAL INFORMATION

A Learning Resource Center and an Adaptive Technology Center are available for all students. Skills classes are offered for college credit in reading, study skills, and writing. OSSD can arrange one or all of the following services for students with learning disabilities: quiet space for exams; extended examination times, up to twice the time typically allotted, based on diagnosis; oral exams; scribes; individual academic, personal, and vocational counseling; peer support groups for the development of academic strategies and psychosocial adjustments; computer resources for additional academic skill development and assistance; taped textbooks based on careful planning and lead time; priority academic scheduling; peer tutoring; diagnostic testing; new student orientation assistance; and faculty/staff consultation. In addition, OSSD can provide information about other support services sponsored by the college.

LEARNING DISABILITY PROGRAM/SERVICES

Learning Disability Program/Services: Office of Services for Students with Disabilities
Director: Jane Boomer
  E-mail: jane.boomer@oberlin.edu
  Telephone: 440-775-8464
  Fax: 440-775-5589

LEARNING DISABILITY SERVICES

Requests for the following services/accommodations will be evaluated individually based on appropriate and current documentation.

Allowed in exams
  Calculator: Yes
  Dictionary: Yes
  Computer: Yes
  Spellchecker: Yes
Extended test time: Yes
Scribes: Yes
Proctors: Yes
Oral exams: Yes
Note-takers: Yes

Distraction-reduced environment: Yes
Tape recording in class: Yes
Books on tape from RFBD: Yes
Taping of books not from RFBD: Yes
**Accommodations for students with
  ADHD:** Yes
Reading machine: Yes
Other assistive technology: Yes
Priority registration: Yes

Added costs for services: No
LD specialists: Yes
Professional tutors: No
Peer tutors: 38
Max. hours/wk. for services:
  Unlimited
**How professors are notified of
  LD/ADHD:** By both student and
  director

GENERAL ADMISSIONS INFORMATION

Director of Admissions: Debra Chermonte
Telephone: 440-775-8411

ENTRANCE REQUIREMENTS

Academic units required: 4 English, 4 math, 3 science, 3 foreign language, 3 social studies. High school diploma is required, and GED is accepted. ACT with Writing component required. TOEFL required of all international applicants: minimum paper TOEFL 600, minimum computer TOEFL 200.

Application deadline: 1/15
Notification: 4/1
Average GPA: 3.58
ACT Composite middle 50% range:
  27–31

SAT Math middle 50% range:
  620–710
**SAT Critical Reading middle 50%
  range:** 650–750
SAT Writing middle 50% range: NR

Graduated top 10% of class: 68%
Graduated top 25% of class: 90%
Graduated top 50% of class: 97%

COLLEGE GRADUATION REQUIREMENTS

Course waivers allowed: No
Course substitutions allowed: Yes
In what course: Case-by-case

ADDITIONAL INFORMATION

Environment: The college is located on 440 acres in a small town 35 miles southwest of Cleveland.

Student Body
  Undergrad enrollment: 2,829
  Women: 55%
  Men: 45%
  Percent out-of-state: 90%

Cost Information
  Tuition: $34,216
  Room & board: $8,720
Housing Information
  University housing: Yes
  Percent living on campus: 86%

Greek System
  Fraternity: No
  Sorority: No
  Athletics: Division III

THE OHIO STATE UNIVERSITY—COLUMBUS

Undergraduate Admissions, 110 Enarson Hall, 154 West Twelfth Avenue,
Columbus, OH 43210 • Phone: 614-292-3980 • Fax: 614-292-4818
E-mail: askabuckeye@osu.edu • Web: www.osu.edu
Support: CS • Institution type: 4-year public

LEARNING DISABILITY PROGRAM AND SERVICES

The mission of the Office for Disability Services (ODS) is threefold: to ensure that students can freely and actively participate in all facets of university life, to provide and coordinate support services and programs to maximize educational potential, and to increase the level of awareness among all members of the university community. ODS helps students in their efforts to attain an excellent college education by promoting self-advocacy skills, self-understanding, and independence. Staff members are specialists in learning disabilities. Students are assigned to a counselor who understands their disability. Counselors assist and advise students about how to make the most of college life and, more important, advise students on how to succeed academically. Disability Services matches services with students' needs. The staff recommends specific services, but students select the services that are suitable for them based on recommendations.

LD/ADHD ADMISSIONS INFORMATION

College entrance tests required: Yes
Interview required: No
Essay recommended: No
Documentation required for LD: WAIS and W-J
Documentation required for ADHD: A diagnostic report that includes the diagnosis and date; criteria used for diagnosis (e.g., DSM–IV)
Submitted to: ODS
Special Ed. HS course work accepted: No

Specific course requirements of all applicants: Yes
Separate application required: No
# of LD applications submitted each year: NR
# of LD applications accepted yearly: NR
Total # of students receiving LD services: 300
Acceptance into program means acceptance into college: Students must be admitted to and enrolled in the university first and then request services.

ADMISSIONS

Students with LD are admitted under the same criteria as regular applicants. However, consideration can be given to students with LD with support from ODS in instances where the student's rank, GPA, or lack of courses, such as foreign language, have affected performance in high school. Applicants interested in services should submit a general application for admission; complete the section under optional personal statement that gives students the opportunity to provide information if they feel that their high school performance was adversely affected by special circumstances; and submit documentation of the disability to ODS, including the latest IEP and the results of the last psychoeducational testing. ODS will review the application, look at course work and deficiencies, review services received in high school and determine if the student's needs can be met at OSU if the student is not normally admissible, look at when a diagnosis was made and at the IEP, and make a recommendation to the Admissions Office. Students exceeding the minimum curriculum in math, natural resources, or foreign language will be given additional consideration. Other factors considered include the competitiveness of the high school, accelerated courses taken, if the applicant is a first-generation college student, or the student's cultural, economic, racial, or geographic diversity; outstanding talents; extracurricular activities; significant work experiences; or leadership positions.

LEARNING DISABILITY PROGRAM/SERVICES

Learning Disability Program/Services: Office for Disability Services (ODS)
Director: Lois Burke (Interim)
  E-mail: burke.4@osu.edu
  Telephone: 614-292-3307
  Fax: 614-292-4190

LEARNING DISABILITY SERVICES

Requests for the following services/accommodations will be evaluated individually based on appropriate and current documentation.

Allowed in exams
  Calculator: Yes
  Dictionary: Yes
  Computer: Yes
  Spellchecker: Yes
Extended test time: Yes
Scribes: Yes
Proctors: Yes
Oral exams: Yes
Note-takers: Yes

Distraction-reduced environment: Yes
Tape recording in class: Yes
Books on tape from RFBD: Yes
Taping of books not from RFBD: Yes
Accommodations for students with
  ADHD: Yes
Reading machine: Yes
Other assistive technology: Yes
Priority registration: Yes

Added costs for services: No
LD specialists: Yes
Professional tutors: No
Peer tutors: Yes
Max. hours/wk. for services: N/A
How professors are notified of
  LD/ADHD: By student

GENERAL ADMISSIONS INFORMATION

Director of Admissions: Dr. Mabel Freeman
Telephone: 614-247-6281

ENTRANCE REQUIREMENTS

Academic units required: 4 English, 3 math, 2 science (2 science labs), 2 foreign language, 2 social studies, 1 academic elective, 1 visual/performing arts. **Academic units recommended:** 4 English, 4 math, 4 science (3 science labs), 3 foreign language, 3 social studies, 1 academic elective, 1 visual/performing arts. High school diploma is required, and GED is accepted. ACT with Writing component required. TOEFL required of all international applicants: minimum paper TOEFL 527, minimum computer TOEFL 197.

Application deadline: 2/1
Notification: Rolling
Average GPA: NR
ACT Composite middle 50% range:
  24–29

SAT Math middle 50% range:
  560–670
SAT Critical Reading middle 50%
  range: 530–640
SAT Writing middle 50% range:
  520–630

Graduated top 10% of class: 43%
Graduated top 25% of class: 80%
Graduated top 50% of class: 98%

COLLEGE GRADUATION REQUIREMENTS

Course waivers allowed: No
Course substitutions allowed: Yes
In what course: On a case-by-case basis and with appropriate supporting disability documentation, some students can petition for a substitution of the foreign language requirement if it is not essential for the major. Math substitutions are rare.

ADDITIONAL INFORMATION

Environment: The campus is in an urban area four miles from downtown Columbus.

Student Body
  Undergrad enrollment: 37,239
  Women: 47%
  Men: 53%
  Percent out-of-state: 10%

Cost Information
  In-state tuition: $8,298
  Out-of-state tuition: $20,193
  Room & board: $6,720
Housing Information
  University housing: Yes
  Percent living on campus: 24%

Greek System
  Fraternity: Yes
  Sorority: Yes
Athletics: Division I

OHIO UNIVERSITY

120 Chubb Hall, Athens, OH 45701
Phone: 740-593-4100 • Fax: 740-593-0560
E-mail: admissions@ohio.edu • Web: www.ohio.edu
Support: S • Institution type: 4-year public

LEARNING DISABILITY PROGRAM AND SERVICES

The Office for Institutional Equity helps students with disabilities coordinate the services needed to enjoy full participation in academic programs and campus life. Students are heard, advised, and assisted in achieving goals. Students are urged to have confidence in their abilities and feel comfortable talking with their professors about their disability. Accommodations are a result of collaborative efforts among the student, faculty, and staff of the Office for Institutional Equity. The goal is to identify and strategize a plan to assist the student in achieving success in his or her educational pursuits. Students should provide the Office for Institutional Equity with a course schedule the first week of the quarter so that professors can be notified of the student's status in the class. Students also need to communicate with professors in advance of requesting accommodations. Extra time to complete assignments and take tests can be arranged. Students should also take advantage of the tutoring sessions that can be arranged. It is very important that students understand the accommodations requested may not be the ones considered reasonable by the university.

LD/ADHD ADMISSIONS INFORMATION

College entrance tests required: Yes
Interview required: No
Essay recommended: No
Documentation required for LD: Psychoeducational evaluation
Documentation required for ADHD: Yes
Submitted to: Disability Student Services
Special Ed. HS course work accepted: Yes

Specific course requirements of all applicants: Yes
Separate application required: No
# of LD applications submitted each year: NR
# of LD applications accepted yearly: NR
Total # of students receiving LD services: 400
Acceptance into program means acceptance into college: Students must be admitted to and enrolled in the university first and then request services.

ADMISSIONS

Applicants with learning disabilities are expected to meet the same admission criteria as all other applicants. General admission requires applicants to be in the top 30 percent of their class with 21 ACT or 990 SAT, or top 50 percent with 23 ACT or 1060 SAT. The mid 50 percent range for the ACT is 22–26, and for the SAT it is 1030–1200. Students taking the ACT must submit the optional Writing section. Course requirements include 4 years of English, 3 years of science and social studies, 3 years of math, and 2 years of a foreign language. Students can be admitted with deficiencies. Applicants with learning disabilities who meet the criteria should send documentation to special services after admission. Those students not meeting the admission criteria are encouraged to self-disclose by writing a narrative explaining the impact of the disability condition on their academic career as well as sending relevant documentation. This disclosure and accompanying documentation will be reviewed by admissions. Students, in general, must demonstrate the ability to perform in a mainstream academic setting where support is available when needed. Counselor recommendations are very helpful for students who do not meet the traditional criteria.

ADDITIONAL INFORMATION

General services provided include advising referrals, academic adjustments and classroom accommodations, priority scheduling, free tutoring through the Academic Advancement Center (4 hours per course per week), and tutoring in writing and reading skills. Skills classes are offered in learning strategies, college reading skills, reading, speed, and vocabulary. Services are available to undergraduate and graduate students.

LEARNING DISABILITY PROGRAM/SERVICES

Learning Disability Program/Services: Office for Institutional Equity/Disability Student Services
Director: Katherine Fahey
  E-mail: fahey@oak.cats.ohiou.edu
  Telephone: 740-593-2620
  Fax: 740-593-0790

LEARNING DISABILITY SERVICES

Requests for the following services/accommodations will be evaluated individually based on appropriate and current documentation.

Allowed in exams
  Calculator: Yes
  Dictionary: Yes
  Computer: Yes
  Spellchecker: Yes
Extended test time: Yes
Scribes: Yes
Proctors: No
Oral exams: Yes
Note-takers: No

Distraction-reduced environment: Yes
Tape recording in class: Yes
Books on tape from RFBD: Yes
Taping of books not from RFBD: No
Accommodations for students with ADHD: Yes
Reading machine: Yes
Other assistive technology: Yes
Priority registration: Yes

Added costs for services: No
LD specialists: No
Professional tutors: No
Peer tutors: 300
Max. hours/wk. for services: 4
How professors are notified of LD/ADHD: By student

GENERAL ADMISSIONS INFORMATION

Director of Admissions: David Garcia
Telephone: 740-593-4100

ENTRANCE REQUIREMENTS

Academic units required: 4 English, 3 math, 3 science, 2 foreign language, 3 social studies, 1 visual/performing arts. High school diploma is required, and GED is accepted. ACT with Writing component required.

Application deadline: 2/1
Notification: Rolling
Average GPA: 3.35
ACT Composite middle 50% range: 21–26

SAT Math middle 50% range: 490–600
SAT Critical Reading middle 50% range: 490–600
SAT Writing middle 50% range: 480–590

Graduated top 10% of class: 15%
Graduated top 25% of class: 42%
Graduated top 50% of class: 81%

COLLEGE GRADUATION REQUIREMENTS

Course waivers allowed: No
Course substitutions allowed: Yes
In what course: Any substitution would be specific to each individual and his or her learning disability. This is not done as a general rule.

ADDITIONAL INFORMATION

Environment: The university is in a small town south of Ohio State University.

Student Body
  Undergrad enrollment: 16,872
  Women: 52%
  Men: 48%
  Percent out-of-state: 13%

Cost Information
  In-state tuition: $8,316
  Out-of-state tuition: $17,170
  Room & board: $7,839
Housing Information
  University housing: Yes
  Percent living on campus: 45%

Greek System
  Fraternity: Yes
  Sorority: Yes
Athletics: Division I

UNIVERSITY OF CINCINNATI

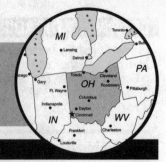

PO Box 210091, Cincinnati, OH 45221-0091
Phone: 513-556-1100 • Fax: 513-556-1105
E-mail: admissions@uc.edu • Web: www.uc.edu
Support: CS • Institution type: 4-year public

LEARNING DISABILITY PROGRAM AND SERVICES

The University of Cincinnati does not have a specific structured learning disability program. However, students with learning disabilities who use academic accommodations and support services available through Disability Services and other resources of the university find they can be successful in achieving their academic objectives. The goal of Disability Services is to provide the necessary accommodations to students for them to become successful and independent learners. Remedial developmental courses are available along with campus-wide tutoring. To receive support services, students need to submit documentation from a licensed professional to the Disability Services Office. Service staff will work with students and faculty to arrange for special needs or accommodations.

LD/ADHD ADMISSIONS INFORMATION

College entrance tests required: Yes
Interview required: No
Essay recommended: No
Documentation required for LD: Appropriate test protocals, including scores, will be accepted from licensed diagnostic professionals.
Documentation required for ADHD: Appropriate test protocals, including scores, will be accepted from licensed diagnostic professionals.
Submitted to: Disability Student Services
Special Ed. HS course work accepted: Yes

Specific course requirements of all applicants: Yes
Separate application required: N/A
# of LD applications submitted each year: NR
# of LD applications accepted yearly: NR
Total # of students receiving LD services: NR
Acceptance into program means acceptance into college: Students must be admitted to and enrolled in the university first and then request services.

ADMISSIONS

There is no special admissions procedure for students with learning disabilities. The Admissions Office looks at each individual situation; there is no set rule for admissions and waivers. All students submit the general university application form. Course requirements and waivers depend on the college within the university. General course requirements include 4 years of English, 3 years of math (4 for engineering), 2 years of science, 2 years of social studies, and 2 years of a foreign language (not required in business; students can substitute American Sign Language). University College is a two-year associate degree program that has an open-door policy, no minimum GPA, no required tests, and no course requirements for entrance. Students may transfer to other majors after 1 year if they are doing well or may transfer into one of the four-year majors after receiving an associate's degree. Students with learning disabilities are encouraged to request an interview with the Disability Services Office, which their parents may attend.

ADDITIONAL INFORMATION

Disabilities Services provides services and accommodations that are mandated under federal law. Support services include note-taking, tutors, readers, taped textbooks, testing accommodations, scribes, loan of equipment, and library disability services. Peer tutoring is available as an accommodation at no cost. Students with appropriate documentation may request course substitutions in math or foreign language. Skills classes are offered for all students in time management, organizational skills, and study skills. University College offers developmental courses in effective reading, English, and mathematics as well as a college study course.

LEARNING DISABILITY PROGRAM/SERVICES

Learning Disability Program/Services: Disability Student Services
Director: Debra Merchant, JD
  E-mail: debra.merchant@uc.edu
  Telephone: 513-556-6823
  Fax: 513-556-1383

LEARNING DISABILITY SERVICES

Requests for the following services/accommodations will be evaluated individually based on appropriate and current documentation.

Allowed in exams
  Calculator: Yes
  Dictionary: Yes
  Computer: Yes
  Spellchecker: Yes
Extended test time: Yes
Scribes: Yes
Proctors: Yes
Oral exams: Yes
Note-takers: Yes

Distraction-reduced environment: Yes
Tape recording in class: Yes
Books on tape from RFBD: Yes
Taping of books not from RFBD: Yes
Accommodations for students with ADHD: Yes
Reading machine: Yes
Other assistive technology: Yes
Priority registration: Yes

Added costs for services: No
LD specialists: Yes
Professional tutors: No
Peer tutors: 15–20
Max. hours/wk. for services: Unlimited
How professors are notified of LD/ADHD: By student

GENERAL ADMISSIONS INFORMATION

Director of Admissions: Thomas Canepa
Telephone: 513-556-1100

ENTRANCE REQUIREMENTS

Academic units required: 4 English, 3 math, 2 science, 2 foreign language, 2 social studies, 2 academic electives. **Academic units recommended:** 4 math, 3 science, 1 history. High school diploma is required, and GED is accepted. ACT with Writing component required. Minimum paper TOEFL 515.

Application deadline: 9/1
Notification: Rolling
Average GPA: 3.35
ACT Composite middle 50% range: 21–27

SAT Math middle 50% range: 510–630
SAT Critical Reading middle 50% range: 490–600
SAT Writing middle 50% range: 470–590

Graduated top 10% of class: 21%
Graduated top 25% of class: 45%
Graduated top 50% of class: 77%

COLLEGE GRADUATION REQUIREMENTS

Course waivers allowed: No
Course substitutions allowed: Yes
In what course: Math and foreign language

ADDITIONAL INFORMATION

Environment: The university is located on 392 acres in downtown Cincinnati.

Student Body
  Undergrad enrollment: 19,217
  Women: 51%
  Men: 49%
  Percent out-of-state: 11%

Cost Information
  In-state tuition: $8,800
  Out-of-state tuition: $22,600
  Room & board: $8,800
Housing Information
  University housing: Yes
  Percent living on campus: 20%

Greek System
  Fraternity: Yes
  Sorority: Yes
  Athletics: Division I

UNIVERSITY OF DAYTON

300 College Park, Dayton, OH 45469-1300
Phone: 937-229-4411 • Fax: 937-229-4729
E-mail: admission@udayton.edu • Web: www.udayton.edu
Support: CS • Institution type: 4-year private

LEARNING DISABILITY PROGRAM AND SERVICES

Every individual student with a disability is guaranteed equal access to all educational programs and activities at the University of Dayton. Qualified persons with disabilities who have been accepted at the University of Dayton are those who have met the university's standards. Students with disabilities must submit a copy of the results of a psychoeducational assessment or a physical and/or a psychological assessment by a qualified evaluator for the delivery of academic support and/or special services. Students who have provided appropriate documentation and have been interviewed by the coordinator of the Office for Students with Disabilities are considered registered under the university policies. There is no obligation for any student to identify a disability; however, students who wish to receive special and/or reasonable accommodations must submit proper documentation, participate in an assessment interview with the coordinator for Students with Disabilities, and request in writing the need for specific services.

LD/ADHD ADMISSIONS INFORMATION

College entrance tests required: Yes
Interview required: No
Essay recommended: No
Documentation required for LD: Psychoeducational
  evaluation
Documentation required for ADHD: Yes
Submitted to: Office for Students with Disabilities
Special Ed. HS course work accepted: N/A

Specific course requirements of all applicants: Yes
Separate application required: No
# of LD applications submitted each year: NR
# of LD applications accepted yearly: NR
Total # of students receiving LD services: NR
**Acceptance into program means acceptance into
  college:** Students must be admitted and enrolled prior to
  requesting services.

ADMISSIONS

Applications for admission are reviewed for specific academic majors or, when applicable, for undeclared status in an academic division. Five factors are considered when applications are assessed: your selection of courses in preparation for college, your grade record and pattern throughout high school, your class standing or ranking, results of either the SAT or ACT, and your character and record of leadership and service. Balanced consideration is given to all aspects of your college preparation. While no minimum GPA, class rank, or standardized test score is specified, these measures must provide evidence of your readiness for college studies in your chosen academic program.

ADDITIONAL INFORMATION

Because the university recognizes that students have individually unique academic and personal strengths and weaknesses, the Office of Learning Enhancement and Academic Development (LEAD) provides support services to students, such as drop-in tutoring (peer-facilitated), with additional support models (supplemental instruction) linked to specific classes as well as tutor-supported English and math sections, and writing support across the curriculum. The Write Place tutors work with all students in their efforts to become better writers. LEAD offers a developmental math course designed to help students improve basic skills.

LEARNING DISABILITY PROGRAM/SERVICES

Learning Disability Program/Services: Office of Students with Disabilities
Director: Timothy King, PhD
  E-mail: Timothy.King@notes.udayton.edu
  Telephone: 937-229-2066
  Fax: 937-229-3270
Contact Person: Brenda D. Cooper, Program Coordinator
  E-mail: Timothy.King@notes.udayton.edu
  Telephone: 937-229-2066
  Fax: 937-229-3270

LEARNING DISABILITY SERVICES

Requests for the following services/accommodations will be evaluated individually based on appropriate and current documentation.

Allowed in exams
  Calculator: Yes
  Dictionary: Yes
  Computer: Yes
  Spellchecker: Yes
Extended test time: Yes
Scribes: Yes
Proctors: Yes
Oral exams: Yes
Note-takers: Yes

Distraction-reduced environment: Yes
Tape recording in class: Yes
Books on tape from RFBD: Yes
Taping of books not from RFBD: No
Accommodations for students with ADHD: Yes
Reading machine: No
Other assistive technology: Yes
Priority registration: Yes

Added costs for services: No
LD specialists: Yes
Professional tutors: No
Peer tutors: Yes
Max. hours/wk. for services: Varies
How professors are notified of LD/ADHD: By student

GENERAL ADMISSIONS INFORMATION

Director of Admissions: Robert F. Durkle
Telephone: 937-229-4411

ENTRANCE REQUIREMENTS

Academic units required: 2 units of foreign language are required for admission to the College of Arts and Sciences. **Academic units recommended:** 4 English, 3 math, 2 science, 3 social studies, 4 academic electives. High school diploma is required, and GED is accepted. ACT with or without Writing component accepted. TOEFL required of all international applicants: minimum paper TOEFL 523, minimum computer TOEFL 193.

Application deadline: Rolling
Notification: Rolling
Average GPA: 3.48
ACT Composite middle 50% range: 23–28

SAT Math middle 50% range: 530–650
SAT Critical Reading middle 50% range: 510–620
SAT Writing middle 50% range: NR

Graduated top 10% of class: 22%
Graduated top 25% of class: 49%
Graduated top 50% of class: 80%

COLLEGE GRADUATION REQUIREMENTS

Course waivers allowed: No
Course substitutions allowed: Yes
In what course: Each student's request would be reviewed on a case-by-case basis to discuss a course substitution.

ADDITIONAL INFORMATION

Environment: The University of Dayton is an urban campus in Dayton, Ohio.

Student Body
  Undergrad enrollment: 7,230
  Women: 50%
  Men: 50%
  Percent out-of-state: 34%

Cost Information
  Tuition: $24,880
  Room & board: $7,600
Housing Information
  University housing: Yes
  Percent living on campus: 75%

Greek System
  Fraternity: Yes
  Sorority: Yes
  Athletics: Division I

UNIVERSITY OF TOLEDO

2801 West Bancroft, Toledo, OH 43606
Phone: 419-530-8700 • Fax: 419-530-5713
E-mail: enroll@utnet.utoledo.edu • Web: www.utoledo.edu
Support: S • Institution type: 4-year public

LEARNING DISABILITY PROGRAM AND SERVICES

The University of Toledo sees its students as people first. The university strives always to provide a nurturing environment that can help strengthen the student as a whole human being—mind, body, and spirit. The goal of the Office of Accessibility is to provide comprehensive academic support services to allow for equal opportunity in pursuing a postsecondary education. Students with learning disabilities should identify the nature of their disability and/or attention deficit hyperactivity disorder and provide this information to the Office of Accessibility along with current psychoeducational evaluation or medical diagnosis of ADHD. Students should provide information about the support services received in high school. The Office of Accessibility respects the right to privacy for each student and maintains confidentiality. The support service personnel, faculty directly involved with the student's classes, academic advisors, and administrative staff members exchange information with the Office of Accessibility pertaining to the nature of the student's disability, accommodations requested, and academic status. Students must sign a form indicating their understanding of the release of information for the Office of Accessibility and giving permission to release the information.

LD/ADHD ADMISSIONS INFORMATION

College entrance tests required: Yes
Interview required: No
Essay recommended: No
Documentation required for LD: Psychoeducational
  evaluation
Documentation required for ADHD: Psychoeducational
  evaluation
Submitted to: Office of Accessibility
Special Ed. HS course work accepted: Yes

Specific course requirements of all applicants: Yes
Separate application required: No
# of LD applications submitted each year: NR
# of LD applications accepted yearly: 50–75
Total # of students receiving LD services: 200–225
**Acceptance into program means acceptance into
  college:** Students must be admitted to and enrolled in the
  university first and then request services.

ADMISSIONS

There is no separate admissions process for students with learning disabilities. All students must meet the same admission criteria. Admissions standards include a GPA of at least 2.0 or the equivalent of a C GPA; 18 ACT or higher for Ohio residents and 21 ACT or 1000 SAT score for non-Ohio residents; 4 years of English, 3 years of math, 3 years of science, 3 years of social studies, and 2 years of a foreign language; and high school graduation requirements fulfilled or successful passing score on the GED. Ohio residents not meeting these requirements are reviewed on an individual basis for admission consideration. Some programs, including engineering, nursing, physical therapy, pharmacy, pre-medical, pre-dentistry, and pre-veterinary, have higher requirements.

ADDITIONAL INFORMATION

The Office of Accessibility requests a program information form giving background information and disability-related information. There are no limitations on the number of students who can receive services and accommodations. Students are automatically accepted into the program once they are admitted to the university and provide appropriate documentation. The following support services are provided if supported by documentation: note-taking services; reader services, texts on tape, and a one-on-one reader; extension of time for quizzes and tests and proctors to help with reading or/and writing; tutoring services; counseling for academic advising, social/interpersonal counseling, and disability advising; instructor contact, personal memos, and liaison between students and professors; registration assistance, advanced registration, and priority registration; scholarship funds; Challenged Individuals Association for students; and adaptive technology.

LEARNING DISABILITY PROGRAM/SERVICES

Learning Disability Program/Services: Office of Accessibility
Director: Angela M. Paprocki, MEd
  E-mail: angela.paprocki@utoledo.edu
  Telephone: 419-530-4981
  Fax: 419-530-6137

LEARNING DISABILITY SERVICES

Requests for the following services/accommodations will be evaluated individually based on appropriate and current documentation.

Allowed in exams
  Calculator: Yes
  Dictionary: Yes
  Computer: Yes
  Spellchecker: Yes
Extended test time: Yes
Scribes: Yes
Proctors: Yes
Oral exams: Yes
Note-takers: Yes

Distraction-reduced environment: Yes
Tape recording in class: Yes
Books on tape from RFBD: No
Taping of books not from RFBD: No
Accommodations for students with ADHD: Yes
Reading machine: No
Other assistive technology: Yes
Priority registration: Yes

Added costs for services: No
LD specialists: No
Professional tutors: No
Peer tutors: 75–80
Max. hours/wk. for services: Unlimited
How professors are notified of LD/ADHD: By student

GENERAL ADMISSIONS INFORMATION

Director of Admissions: Jennifer Kwiatkowski (Interim)
Telephone: 419-530-5720

ENTRANCE REQUIREMENTS
Academic units required: 4 English, 3 math, 3 science, 3 social studies, 2 foreign language. **Academic units recommended:** 4 English, 3 math, 3 science (1 science lab), 2 foreign language, 3 social studies, 1 history. High school diploma is required, and GED is accepted. ACT with Writing component required. TOEFL required of all international applicants: minimum paper TOEFL 500, minimum computer TOEFL 173.

Application deadline: NR
Notification: Rolling
Average GPA: 3.08
ACT Composite middle 50% range: 19–25

SAT Math middle 50% range: 460–600
SAT Critical Reading middle 50% range: 450–570
SAT Writing middle 50% range: NR

Graduated top 10% of class: 16%
Graduated top 25% of class: 37%
Graduated top 50% of class: 64%

COLLEGE GRADUATION REQUIREMENTS

Course waivers allowed: No
Course substitutions allowed: Yes
In what course: Foreign language if considered appropriate. Each case is decided on an individualized basis.

ADDITIONAL INFORMATION

Environment: The University of Toledo is located on a 305-acre campus in Toledo, Ohio.

Student Body
  Undergrad enrollment: 15,288
  Women: 49%
  Men: 51%
  Percent out-of-state: 8%

Cost Information
  In-state tuition: $7,490
  Out-of-state tuition: $16,300
  Room & board: $8,800
Housing Information
  University housing: Yes
  Percent living on campus: 18%

Greek System
  Fraternity: Yes
  Sorority: Yes
Athletics: Division I

University of Toledo

URSULINE COLLEGE

2550 Lander Road, Pepper Pike, OH 44124-4398
Phone: 440-449-4203 • Fax: 440-684-6138
E-mail: admission@ursuline.edu • Web: www.ursuline.edu
Support: SP • Institution type: 4-year private

LEARNING DISABILITY PROGRAM AND SERVICES

Ursuline College is a small Catholic college committed to helping students with learning disabilities succeed in their courses and become independent learners. The Program for Students with Learning Disabilities (PSLD) is a voluntary, comprehensive fee-paid program. PSLD's goals include providing a smooth transition to college life, helping students learn to apply the most appropriate learning strategies in college courses, and teaching self-advocacy skills. To be eligible for PSLD, a student must present documentation of an LD, which consists of a WAIS–R, the Woodcock-Johnson, and any other standardized measures of achievement. The psychoeducational evaluation must clearly indicate that the student has a specific learning disability and should have been conducted within the past 3 years. Students must have average to above-average intellectual ability and an appropriate academic foundation to succeed in a four-year liberal arts college.

LD/ADHD ADMISSIONS INFORMATION

College entrance tests required: Yes
Interview required: Yes
Essay recommended: No
Documentation required for LD: WAIS-R, Woodcock-Johnson
Documentation required for ADHD: Testing—psychological/medical
Submitted to: PSLD
Special Ed. HS course work accepted: Yes

Specific course requirements of all applicants: Yes
Separate application required: No
# of LD applications submitted each year: 12
# of LD applications accepted yearly: 12
Total # of students receiving LD services: 12
Acceptance into program means acceptance into college: Students must be admitted to and enrolled in the university first and then request services.

ADMISSIONS

To participate in PSLD, students must first meet with the LD specialist to discuss whether the program is suitable for them. Students must then meet the requirements for clear or conditional admission to the college by applying to the Admissions Office and completing all regular admission procedures. Students with learning disabilities must meet the same requirements for admission to the college as all other students: a 2.5 GPA and an ACT score of 17 or an SAT score of 850 for a clear admission. Courses recommended include 4 years of English, 3 years of social studies, 3 years of math, 3 years of science, and 2 years of a foreign language. A student may receive a conditional admission if the GPA and ACT are lower. Course deficiencies must be removed prior to graduation from college. Students with conditional admission are limited to 12 credit hours per semester for the first year. The final admission decision is made by the Office of Admissions.

ADDITIONAL INFORMATION

PSLD features an orientation that provides a smooth transition to the college, acquaints students with mentors and other students in PSLD, and introduces students to high-tech equipment and computers in the LRC; individual biweekly 1-hour sessions with an LD specialist to work on developing time management and organizational skills, design learning strategies for success in college, and learn note-taking and test-taking skills; individual weekly 1-hour sessions with a writing specialist who provides assistance with writing assignments in specific courses and who helps with developing skills in writing effective sentences, paragraphs, and essays; weekly academic-skills support groups with an LD specialist to learn coping skills, develop self-advocacy skills, and receive support for dealing with classroom issues; and academic advising for guidance on choosing appropriate courses and scheduling an appropriate number of credits each semester.

LEARNING DISABILITY PROGRAM/SERVICES

Learning Disability Program/Services: Program for Students with Learning Disabilities (PSLD)
Director: Eileen D. Kohut
  E-mail: EKohut@ursuline.edu
  Telephone: 440-646-8123
  Fax: 440-644-6114
Contact Person: Jill Carroll
  E-mail: EKohut@ursuline.edu
  Telephone: 440-449-2049
  Fax: 440-684-6114

LEARNING DISABILITY SERVICES

Requests for the following services/accommodations will be evaluated individually based on appropriate and current documentation.

Allowed in exams
  Calculator: Yes
  Dictionary: Yes
  Computer: Yes
  Spellchecker: Yes
Extended test time: Yes
Scribes: Yes
Proctors: Yes
Oral exams: Yes
Note-takers: Yes

Distraction-reduced environment: Yes
Tape recording in class: Yes
Books on tape from RFBD: Yes
Taping of books not from RFBD: Yes
Accommodations for students with
  ADHD: Yes
Reading machine: Yes
Other assistive technology: Yes
Priority registration: Yes

Added costs for services: No
LD specialists: Yes
Professional tutors: 6
Peer tutors: 1
Max. hours/wk. for services: 3
How professors are notified of
  LD/ADHD: By student

GENERAL ADMISSIONS INFORMATION

Director of Admissions: NR
Telephone: 440-449-4203

ENTRANCE REQUIREMENTS

Academic units recommended: 4 English, 3 math, 3 science (2 science labs), 2 foreign language, 3 social studies, 1 fine/performing arts, 1 physical education/health. High school diploma is required, and GED is accepted. ACT with or without Writing component accepted. TOEFL required of all international applicants: minimum paper TOEFL 500, minimum computer TOEFL 173.

Application deadline: Rolling
Notification: Within 3 weeks of
  completed application
Average GPA: 3.17
ACT Composite middle 50% range:
  18–22

SAT Math middle 50% range:
  420–530
SAT Critical Reading middle 50%
  range: 450–530
SAT Writing middle 50% range: NR

Graduated top 10% of class: 27%
Graduated top 25% of class: 44%
Graduated top 50% of class: 82%

COLLEGE GRADUATION REQUIREMENTS

Course waivers allowed: Yes
In what course: Waiving of courses is done on an individual basis.
Course substitutions allowed: No

ADDITIONAL INFORMATION

Environment: The college is located in a suburban area about 20 miles from Cleveland.

Student Body
  Undergrad enrollment: 1,159
  Women: 93%
  Men: 7%
  Percent out-of-state: 5%

Cost Information
  Tuition: $19,860
  Room & board: $6,684
Housing Information
  University housing: Yes
  Percent living on campus: 16%

Greek System
  Fraternity: No
  Sorority: No
  Athletics: NAIA

WRIGHT STATE UNIVERSITY

3640 Colonel Glenn Highway, Dayton, OH 45435
Phone: 937-775-5700 • Fax: 937-775-5795
E-mail: admissions@wright.edu • Web: www.wright.edu
Support: CS • Institution type: 4-year public

LEARNING DISABILITY PROGRAM AND SERVICES

Students with disabilities are encouraged to participate in all facets of university life according to their abilities and interests and to develop independence and responsibility to the fullest extent possible. The philosophy of the university is intended to stimulate students to pursue the career of study regardless of their learning disability. Through the Office of Disability Services, the university provides a comprehensive array of services on a campus with a long history of commitment to students with physical, visual, and/or learning disabilities. A pre-service interview is required of all prospective students to discuss service needs. Eligibility for services is determined after documentation is received and the student has an individual interview.

LD/ADHD ADMISSIONS INFORMATION

College entrance tests required: Yes
Interview required: Yes
Essay recommended: No
Documentation required for LD: Psychoeducational report that includes a diagnosis, summary of assessment findings, description of current substantial limitations, aptitude and cognitive ability testing.
Documentation required for ADHD: Psychoeducational report that includes a diagnosis, summary of assessment findings, description of current substantial limitations, rating scales to supplement the DSM–IV diagnosis.

Submitted to: Office of Disability Services
Special Ed. HS course work accepted: No
Specific course requirements of all applicants: Yes
Separate application required: Yes
# of LD applications submitted each year: 55–75
# of LD applications accepted yearly: NR
Total # of students receiving LD services: 125–155
Acceptance into program means acceptance into college: Students must be admitted to and enrolled in the university first and then request services.

ADMISSIONS

The university has an open admission policy for in-state students. ACT/SAT is used for placement, not admission. The mid 50 percent range for the ACT is 18–24, and for the SAT, it is 990–1140. Students with LD must meet the same criteria as all applicants and must be accepted to the university prior to requesting services. However, out-of-state students are encouraged to self-disclose their learning disability and submit documentation to the Office of Disability Services prior to applying to the university if they would like to discuss eligibility for admission and services available on campus and determine if Wright State is a good fit for them. It is recommended that students self-disclose the LD if GPA or test scores are low and the student feels that LD disclosure is important in explaining academic or testing information. The Director of Disability Services encourages students and their families to visit and interview. Admissions will ask ODS to review documentation, transcripts, and so on, and meet with the student to determine readiness for college. Students with a college-prep curriculum in high school have been more successful at Wright State than those who took a general curriculum. The final decision rests with the Admissions Office.

ADDITIONAL INFORMATION

Please contact the Office of Disability Services for additional eligibility requirements once a student is accepted to the program.

LEARNING DISABILITY PROGRAM/SERVICES

Learning Disability Program/Services: Office of Disability Services (ODS)
Director: Jeff Vernooy
  E-mail: jeffrey.vernooy@wright.edu
  Telephone: 937-775-5680
  Fax: 937-775-5699
Contact Person: Cassandra Mitchell
  E-mail: jeffrey.vernooy@wright.edu
  Telephone: 937-775-5680
  Fax: 937-775-5699

LEARNING DISABILITY SERVICES

Requests for the following services/accommodations will be evaluated individually based on appropriate and current documentation.

Allowed in exams
  Calculator: Yes
  Dictionary: Yes
  Computer: Yes
  Spellchecker: Yes
Extended test time: Yes
Scribes: Yes
Proctors: Yes
Oral exams: Yes
Note-takers: Yes

Distraction-reduced environment: Yes
Tape recording in class: Yes
Books on tape from RFBD: Yes
Taping of books not from RFBD: Yes
Accommodations for students with
  ADHD: Yes
Reading machine: Yes
Other assistive technology: Yes
Priority registration: No

Added costs for services: No
LD specialists: Yes
Professional tutors: No
Peer tutors: 40–50
Max. hours/wk. for services: 10
How professors are notified of
  LD/ADHD: By student

GENERAL ADMISSIONS INFORMATION

Director of Admissions: Cathy Davis
Telephone: 937-775-5700

ENTRANCE REQUIREMENTS

Academic units required: 4 English, 3 math, 3 science (3 science labs), 2 foreign language, 3 social studies. High school diploma is required, and GED is accepted. ACT with or without Writing component accepted. TOEFL required of all international applicants: minimum paper TOEFL 500, minimum computer TOEFL 173.

Application deadline: Rolling
Notification: Rolling
Average GPA: 3.09
ACT Composite middle 50% range:
  18–21

SAT Math middle 50% range:
  430–560
SAT Critical Reading middle 50%
  range: 430–570
SAT Writing middle 50% range: NR

Graduated top 10% of class: 15%
Graduated top 25% of class: 36%
Graduated top 50% of class: 67%

COLLEGE GRADUATION REQUIREMENTS

Course waivers allowed: Yes
In what course: Math
Course substitutions allowed: Yes
In what course: Foreign language

ADDITIONAL INFORMATION

Environment: The university is located on 645 acres 8 miles northeast of Dayton.

Student Body
  Undergrad enrollment: 11,770
  Women: 56%
  Men: 44%
  Percent out-of-state: 4%

Cost Information
  In-state tuition: $7,278
  Out-of-state tuition: $14,004
  Room & board: $7,180
Housing Information
  University housing: Yes
  Percent living on campus: 22%

Greek System
  Fraternity: Yes
  Sorority: Yes
Athletics: Division I

Wright State University

XAVIER UNIVERSITY (OH)

3800 Victory Parkway, Cincinnati, OH 45207-5311
Phone: 513-745-3301 • Fax: 513-745-4319
E-mail: xuadmit@xavier.edu • Web: www.xavier.edu
Support: CS • Institution type: 4-year private

LEARNING DISABILITY PROGRAM AND SERVICES

The Learning Assistance Center's (LAC) mission is three-fold: to ensure that all students with disabilities can freely and actively participate in every aspect of college life, to provide academic support services so that students with disabilities have equal educational access, and to seek to educate the community at large. Our office provides reasonable academic adjustments and support services that are individualized and flexible. With a goal of equal educational access in mind, the LAC creates opportunities and promotes the same educational experiences, services, and enrichment to persons with disabilities that are offered to those who are not disabled.

LD/ADHD ADMISSIONS INFORMATION

College entrance tests required: Yes
Interview required: No
Essay recommended: Yes
Documentation required for LD: Psychoeducational evaluation
Documentation required for ADHD: Yes
Submitted to: LAC
Special Ed. HS course work accepted: Yes

Specific course requirements of all applicants: Yes
Separate application required: No
# of LD applications submitted each year: NR
# of LD applications accepted yearly: NR
Total # of students receiving LD services: 310
Acceptance into program means acceptance into college: Students must be admitted to and enrolled in the university first and then request services.

ADMISSIONS

There is no special admissions process for students with learning disabilities. However, there is a freshman success program for some admitted students who would benefit from a reduced course load and more guidance and mentoring. The middle 50 percent GPA is 3.28–3.97; the middle 50 percent class rank is 65–93 percent; the middle 50 percent ACT score is 23–29; and the middle 50 percent SAT score is 1080–1270.

ADDITIONAL INFORMATION

All students have access to the Math Lab, Writing Center, and Tutoring Center. Additionally, there are study skills classes offered in time management and test-taking strategies. Students with learning disabilities and/or ADHD also have access to support groups, special testing, and mentoring. Accommodations and services are available for undergraduates and graduates. Documentation required for a student with LD is a copy of the last IEP and results of the last psychoeducational test battery (no more than 3 years old). Students with ADHD should submit a copy of a recent diagnostic report that states the DSM–IV diagnosis, symptoms, instruments and procedures used to make the diagnosis, and the dosage, type and frequency of your current medication. In addition to this documentation, students must fill out paperwork and sign a release form at the beginning of each semester. This enables the staff at the Learning Assistance Center to contact professors and arrange for accommodations.

LEARNING DISABILITY PROGRAM/SERVICES

Learning Disability Program/Services: Learning Assistance Center (LAC)
Director: Ann Dinan, PhD
E-mail: dinan@xavier.edu
Telephone: 513-745-3280
Fax: 513-745-3387

LEARNING DISABILITY SERVICES

Requests for the following services/accommodations will be evaluated individually based on appropriate and current documentation.

Allowed in exams
Calculator: Yes
Dictionary: Yes
Computer: Yes
Spellchecker: Yes
Extended test time: Yes
Scribes: Yes
Proctors: Yes
Oral exams: Yes
Note-takers: Yes

Distraction-reduced environment: Yes
Tape recording in class: Yes
Books on tape from RFBD: Yes
Taping of books not from RFBD: Yes
Accommodations for students with ADHD: Yes
Reading machine: Yes
Other assistive technology: Yes
Priority registration: Yes

Added costs for services: No
LD specialists: Yes
Professional tutors: No
Peer tutors: 35
Max. hours/wk. for services: Unlimited
How professors are notified of LD/ADHD: By director

GENERAL ADMISSIONS INFORMATION

Director of Admissions: Marc Camille
Telephone: 513-745-2941

ENTRANCE REQUIREMENTS

Academic units recommended: 4 English, 3 math, 3 science, 2 foreign language, 3 social studies, 5 academic electives, 1 health/physical education. High school diploma is required, and GED is accepted. ACT with or without Writing component accepted. TOEFL required of all international applicants: minimum paper TOEFL 530, minimum computer TOEFL 197.

Application deadline: 2/1
Notification: 1/15 and 3/15
Average GPA: 3.63
ACT Composite middle 50% range: 23–29

SAT Math middle 50% range: 540–640
SAT Critical Reading middle 50% range: 530–640
SAT Writing middle 50% range: 510–620

Graduated top 10% of class: 33%
Graduated top 25% of class: 63%
Graduated top 50% of class: 90%

COLLEGE GRADUATION REQUIREMENTS

Course waivers allowed: No
Course substitutions allowed: Yes
In what course: Only substitutions are offered. These are usually in math and foreign language. Students are encouraged to petition the Deans Committee on course substitutions early in the Xavier careers. Documentation must support substitutions.

ADDITIONAL INFORMATION

Environment: The university is located 5 miles from downtown Cincinatti.

Student Body
Undergrad enrollment: 3,770
Women: 57%
Men: 43%
Percent out-of-state: 40%

Cost Information
Tuition: $24,660
Room & board: $7,400
Housing Information
University housing: Yes
Percent living on campus: 46%

Greek System
Fraternity: No
Sorority: No
Athletics: Division I

OKLAHOMA STATE UNIVERSITY

219 Student Union, Stillwater, OK 74078
Phone: 800-233-5019 • Fax: 405-744-7092
E-mail: admissions@okstate.edu • Web: www.osu.okstate.edu
Support: S • Institution type: 4-year public

LEARNING DISABILITY PROGRAM AND SERVICES

Oklahoma State University does not have a formal learning disabilities program, but uses a service-based model to assist students in obtaining the necessary accommodations for specific learning disabilities through Student Disability Services (SDS). Students with learning disabilities may request priority enrollment and a campus orientation to assist in scheduling classes. Other services developed in coordination with SDS work to minimize the students' difficulties in relation to course work. These services could include test accommodations, course substitutions, and independent study. The underlying philosophy of this program is to provide assistance to students to facilitate their academic progress. SDS also acts as a resource for faculty and staff.

LD/ADHD ADMISSIONS INFORMATION

College entrance tests required: Yes
Interview required: No
Essay recommended: No
Documentation required for LD: Adult-normed evaluations of ability and achievement; e.g., WAIS-R (ability), Woodcock Johnson-R (achievement), and clear diagnostic statement
Documentation required for ADHD: TOVA, Connor's checklist, clinical interiew, and clear diagnostic statement
Submitted to: Student Disability Services
Special Ed. HS course work accepted: No

Specific course requirements of all applicants: Yes
Separate application required: No
# of LD applications submitted each year: NR
# of LD applications accepted yearly: NR
Total # of students receiving LD services: 180—190
Acceptance into program means acceptance into college: Student must be admitted and enrolled in the university first and then request services.

ADMISSIONS

There is not a special admissions policy for students with learning disabilities. Applicants with learning disabilities must meet the same specific requirements of the program in which they wish to enroll. General admission requirements include ACT 22 or higher or SAT 1020 or higher, 3.0 GPA, and courses in English, math, science, and history. Students with appropriate documentation may be allowed to substitute courses for math or foreign language. The Alternative Admission program allows students to present evidence of potential success. It is available to students whose high school achievement is slightly below the standards specified in the performance requirements and/or are deficient in no more than one curricular unit. Space is limited and only those applicants showing the best potential for academic success will be admitted. Eight percent of all students may be admitted on probation. Once admitted, a strong effort is made to monitor students' progress and to familiarize them with skills and attitudes that will contribute to their academic success. After remediating any deficiencies they might have and completing at least one semester of satisfactory work, students generally may transfer to the major of their choice. Admitted students are encouraged to contact SDS to discuss special services or accommodations.

ADDITIONAL INFORMATION

There is a Math Lab and a Writing Center for all students. All students with LD/ADHD requesting accommodations or services must provide appropriate and current documentation. All diagnostic testing and documentation should be sent to Student Disability Services. There are currently 180 students with learning disabilities and 60 with ADHD receiving services on campus. The university also operates the Oklahoma City Technical Institute, which offers 2-year, career-oriented programs.

LEARNING DISABILITY PROGRAM/SERVICES

Learning Disability Program/Services: Student Disability Services (SDS)
Director: Michael Shuttic
   E-mail: m.shuttic@okstate.edu
   Telephone: 405-744-7116
   Fax: 405-744-8380

LEARNING DISABILITY SERVICES

Requests for the following/services accommodations will be evaluated individually based on appropriate and current documentation.

Allowed in exams	**Distraction-reduced environment:** Yes	**LD specialists:** No
Calculator: Yes	**Tape recording in class:** Yes	**Professional tutors:** NR
Dictionary: Yes	**Books on tape from RFBD:** Yes	**Peer tutors:** No
Computer: Yes	**Taping of books not from RFBD:** Yes	**Max. hours/wk. for services:**
Spellchecker: Yes	**Accommodations for students with**	Unlimited
Extended test time: Yes	**ADHD:** Yes	**How professors are notified of**
Scribes: Yes	**Reading machine:** Yes	**LD/ADHD:** By student and director
Proctors: Yes	**Other assistive technology:** Yes	
Oral exams: Yes	**Priority registration:** Yes	
Notetakers: Yes	**Added costs for services:** No	

GENERAL ADMISSIONS INFORMATION

Director of Admissions: Karen Lucas
Telephone: 405-744-3087

ENTRANCE REQUIREMENTS

Academic units required: 4 English, 3 math, 2 science (2 science labs), 2 social studies, 1 history, 3 academic electives. **Academic units recomended:** 2 foreign language, 1 computer science. High school diploma is required, and GED is accepted. ACT with or without Writing component accepted. TOEFL required of all international applicants, minimum paper TOEFL 500, minimum computer TOEFL 173.

Application deadline: NR	**SAT Math middle 50% range:**	**Graduated top 10% of class:** 27%
Notification: Rolling	510–640	**Graduated top 25% of class:** 55%
Average GPA: 3.54	**SAT Critical Reading middle 50%**	**Graduated top 50% of class:** 86%
ACT Composite middle 50% range:	**range:** 490–610	
22–27	**SAT Writing middle 50% range:**	
	NR	

COLLEGE GRADUATION REQUIREMENTS

Course waivers allowed: Yes
In what course: No waiver. Substitution possible based on degree requirements and major
Course substitutions allowed: Yes
In what course: Math, foreign language

ADDITIONAL INFORMATION

Environment: The 415-acre campus is located in a small city 65 miles north of Oklahoma City.

Student Body	**Cost Information**	**Greek System**
Undergrad enrollment: 18,600	In-state tuition: $4,300	Fraternity: Yes
Women: 49%	Out-of-state tuition: $12,300	Sorority: Yes
Men: 51%	Room & board: $6,015	Athletics: Division I
Percent out-of-state: 16%	**Housing Information**	
	University housing: Yes	
	Percent living on campus: 38%	

UNIVERSITY OF OKLAHOMA

1000 Asp Avenue, Norman, OK 73019-4076
Phone: 405-325-2252 • Fax: 405-325-7124
E-mail: admrec@ou.edu • Web: www.ou.edu
Support: S • Institution type: 4-year public

LEARNING DISABILITY PROGRAM AND SERVICES

The Office of Disability Services provides support services and is committed to the goal of achieving equal educational opportunity and full participation for students with disabilities. In many cases, these services are developed in response to expressed student needs. There are no special LD or remedial classes. Students are encouraged to be self advocates in making requests for reasonable academic accommodations. Assistance is to be used to support the accomplishment of educational goals. The coordinator of services sponsors the OU Association for Disabled Students, a student organization that provides a recognized forum for support, regular meetings, and social and recreational activities. Students must provide psychoeducational evaluations documenting learning disabilities in order to receive services. The evaluation should include full-scale, performance, and verbal IQ scores; scores from aptitude achievement comparisons; and a summary and recommendations.

LD/ADHD ADMISSIONS INFORMATION

College entrance tests required: Yes
Interview required: No
Essay recommended: No
Documentation required for LD: Current comprehensive report of a psychoeducational assessment
Documentation required for ADHD: Current comprehensive report of a psychoeducational assessment
Submitted to: Office of Disability Services
Special Ed. HS course work accepted: No

Specific course requirements of all applicants: Yes
Separate application required: No
# of LD applications submitted each year: NR
# of LD applications accepted yearly: NR
Total # of students receiving LD services: 225
Acceptance into program means acceptance into college: Student must be admitted and enrolled in the university first and then request services.

ADMISSIONS

Admission requirements for students with learning disabilities are the same as for all other students. Course requirements include 4 years of English, 2 years of science, 3 years of math, 2 years of social studies, 1 unit in economics, geography, government or non-Western culture, and 3 additional subjects. The university strongly recommends additional course work in music, art, drama, or speech. ACT score required is 22 or higher and/or SAT 1010 or higher. The expected GPA is 3.0., and top 33 percent of the graduating class. Applicants who do not meet the general admission criteria but who believe they are prepared to be successful in college are encouraged to apply. Careful attention will be given to an applicant's written comments concerning background and educational goals, personal interviews, as well as letters of recommendation from counselors, teachers, principals, and employers attesting to the student's motivation and potential for academic success.

ADDITIONAL INFORMATION

After receiving academic advisement from the college, the student should make an appointment with Disabled Student Services. The office will also provide a personal campus orientation upon request. Services offered, based on individual needs, include alternative testing, readers, scribes, note-takers (who are volunteers), tutors, tape-recorded texts, and library assistance. Tutoring is provided on a one-on-one basis by peer tutors. Services are available for undergraduate and graduate students.

LEARNING DISABILITY PROGRAM/SERVICES

Learning Disability Program/Services: Office of Disability Services
Director: Suzette Dyer
  E-mail: sdyer@ou.edu
  Telephone: 405-325-3852
  Fax: 405-325-4491

LEARNING DISABILITY SERVICES

Requests for the following/services accommodations will be evaluated individually based on appropriate and current documentation.

Allowed in exams
  Calculator: Yes
  Dictionary: Yes
  Computer: Yes
  Spellchecker: Yes
Extended test time: Yes
Scribes: Yes
Proctors: Yes
Oral exams: Yes
Notetakers: Yes

Distraction-reduced environment: Yes
Tape recording in class: Yes
Books on tape from RFBD: Yes
Taping of books not from RFBD: NR
Accommodations for students with
  ADHD: Yes
Reading machine: Yes
Other assistive technology: Yes
Priority registration: Yes

Added costs for services: No
LD specialists: No
Professional tutors: No
Peer tutors: 25-50
Max. hours/wk. for services: As needed
How professors are notified of LD/ADHD: By director

GENERAL ADMISSIONS INFORMATION

Director of Admissions: Patricia Lynch, Director
Telephone: 405-325-2252

ENTRANCE REQUIREMENTS

Academic units required: 4 English, 3 math, 2 science (2 science labs), 2 social studies, 1 history, 3 academic electives. **Academic units recommended:** 3 foreign language, 1 computer science. High school diploma is required, and GED is accepted. ACT with or without Writing component accepted. TOEFL required of all international applicants, minimum paper TOEFL 550, minimum computer TOEFL 213.

Application deadline: 4/1
Notification: Rolling
Average GPA: 3.6
ACT Composite middle 50% range: 23–28

SAT Math middle 50% range: NR
SAT Critical Reading middle 50% range: NR
SAT Writing middle 50% range: NR

Graduated top 10% of class: 35%
Graduated top 25% of class: 68%
Graduated top 50% of class: 92%

COLLEGE GRADUATION REQUIREMENTS

Course substitutions allowed: Yes
In what course: Students may petition for a substitution in foreign language.

ADDITIONAL INFORMATION

Environment: The 3,107-acre campus is located in a suburb 17 miles south of Oklahoma City.

Student Body
  Undergrad enrollment: 20,287
  Women: 51%
  Men: 49%
  Percent out-of-state: 24%

Cost Information
  In-state tuition: $4,400
  Out-of-state tuition: $12,300
  Room & board: $6,863
Housing Information
  University housing: Yes
  Percent living on campus: 28%

Greek System
  Fraternity: Yes
  Sorority: Yes
Athletics: Division I

THE UNIVERSITY OF TULSA

600 South College Avenue, Tulsa, OK 74104
Phone: 918-631-2307 • Fax: 918-631-5003
E-mail: admission@utulsa.edu • Web: www.utulsa.edu
Support: CS • Institution type: 4-year private

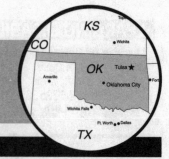

LEARNING DISABILITY PROGRAM AND SERVICES

The Center for Student Academic Support offers a comprehensive range of academic support services and accommodations to students with disabilities. The goal is to provide services which will, in combination with the resources and talents of the student, maximize the students' independence for full participation in the curriculum and provide an opportunity to achieve career goals. The policy of the University of Tulsa, in keeping with the Americans with Disabilities Act, is to provide reasonable accommodations for students with disabilities, including students with learning disabilities. Students who have specific disabilities that might impact their full access and participation in university programs are urged to provide the relevant documentation and make an appointment with the Coordinator of the Center for Student Academic Support.

LD/ADHD ADMISSIONS INFORMATION

College entrance tests required: Yes
Interview required: No
Essay recommended: Yes
Documentation required for LD: Psychoeducational evaluation; consult the university website for Learning Disabilities (LD) Documentation Guidelines for the Diagnosing Professional.
Documentation required for ADHD: Consult the university website for Learning Disabilities (LD) Documentation Guidelines for the Diagnosing Professional.
Submitted to: Center for Student Academic Support
Special Ed. HS course work accepted: Yes

Specific course requirements of all applicants: Yes
Separate application required: Yes
# of LD applications submitted each year: 60
# of LD applications accepted yearly: 60
Total # of students receiving LD services: 50–75
Acceptance into program means acceptance into college: Student must be admitted and enrolled in the university first and then request services.

ADMISSIONS

All students must meet the general admissions requirements. Students with disabilities are not required to disclose information about the disability, but may voluntarily disclose or request information from CSAS. The university does not consider disabilities in the decision-making process, even if there is knowledge of the disability, without a request and disclosure by the applicant. Students may provide verification of the disability that should be submitted directly to CSAS. General admission requirements include: 4 years of English, 3 years of math, 4 years of science, and 2 years of foreign language. No course substitutions are allowed. The average ACT is above 21 and for the SAT is 1080–1140. Students applying to the nursing or athletic training programs must submit a special application. Conditional admission is available for freshmen and probational admission is an option for transfer students. The student with learning disabilities also needs to complete the application form and intake sheet. Also required is documentation presented from a doctor stating diagnostic material and diagnosis of the disorder.

ADDITIONAL INFORMATION

Accommodations students might qualify for depending upon their documentation and needs include: extended time on tests, priority registration, testing in self-contained environment, use of spelling aids on written exams, texts on tape, note-takers, preferential seating, tests given orally, and enlarged print tests. Concerns regarding requests for a referral for evaluation of a learning disability should be directed to the Coordinator of the Center for Student Academic Support. Students with LD must provide documentation that includes tests of intellect and of achievement administered by a professional. Students with documented ADHD must provide behavior checklist (one completed by a doctor), a test of intellect, a test of attention, and a clinical interview that includes a history of the ADHD.

LEARNING DISABILITY PROGRAM/SERVICES

Learning Disability Program/Services: Center for Student Academic Support
Director: Dr. Jane Corso
  E-mail: jane-corso@utulsa.edu
  Telephone: 918-631-2315
  Fax: 918-631-3459

LEARNING DISABILITY SERVICES

Requests for the following/services accommodations will be evaluated individually based on appropriate and current documentation.

Allowed in exams	**Distraction-reduced environment:** Yes	**Added costs for services:** No
Calculator: Yes	**Tape recording in class:** Yes	**LD specialists:** Yes
Dictionary: Yes	**Books on tape from RFBD:** Yes	**Professional tutors:** 9
Computer: Yes	**Taping of books not from RFBD:** Yes	**Peer tutors:** 140
Spellchecker: Yes	**Accommodations for students with**	**Max. hours/wk. for services:**
Extended test time: Yes	**ADHD:** Yes	Unlimited
Scribes: Yes	**Reading machine:** Yes	**How professors are notified of**
Proctors: Yes	**Other assistive technology:** Yes	**LD/ADHD:** By both student and
Oral exams: NR	**Priority registration:** Yes	director
Notetakers: Yes		

GENERAL ADMISSIONS INFORMATION

Director of Admissions: Mr. John C. Corso
Telephone: 918-631-2307

ENTRANCE REQUIREMENTS

Academic units required: 4 English, 3 math, 4 science (2 science labs), 2 foreign language, 1 social studies, 2 history, 1 academic elective. High school diploma is required, and GED is accepted. ACT with or without Writing component accepted. TOEFL required of all international applicants, minimum paper TOEFL 500, minimum computer TOEFL 173.

Application deadline: NR	**SAT Math middle 50% range:**	**Graduated top 10% of class:** 59%
Notification: Rolling	540–690	**Graduated top 25% of class:** 79%
Average GPA: 3.70	**SAT Critical Reading middle 50%**	**Graduated top 50% of class:** 94%
ACT Composite middle 50% range:	**range:** 530–690	
23–30	**SAT Writing middle 50% range:**	
	NR	

COLLEGE GRADUATION REQUIREMENTS

Course waivers allowed: Yes
In what course: Depends on the nature of the disability
Course substitutions allowed: Yes
In what course: Depends on the nature of the disability

ADDITIONAL INFORMATION

Environment: The campus is in an urban area.

Student Body	**Cost Information**	**Greek System**
Undergrad enrollment: 2,830	**Tuition:** $21,690	**Fraternity:** Yes
Women: 50%	**Room & board:** $7,504	**Sorority:** Yes
Men: 50%	**Housing Information**	**Athletics:** NCAA Division I
Percent out-of-state: 36%	**University housing:** Yes	
	Percent living on campus: 60%	

The University of Tulsa

OREGON STATE UNIVERSITY

104 Kerr Administration Building, Corvallis, OR 97331-2106
Phone: 541-737-4411 • Fax: 541-737-2482
E-mail: osuadmit@oregonstate.edu • Web: www.oregonstate.edu
Support: S • Institution type: 4-year public

LEARNING DISABILITY PROGRAM AND SERVICES

Oregon State University is committed to providing equal opportunity for higher education to academically qualified students without regard to disability. Services for Students with Disabilities (SSD) strives to be sensitive to the individual needs of students by offering a variety of services. Services rendered are dependent on the type of learning disability. Services are provided to ensure an equal opportunity to succeed but do not guarantee success. Self-advocacy and independence are promoted. SSD is available for all students who need extra services. The Educational Opportunities Program (EOP) offers students who are learning disabled, economically disadvantaged, or first-generation college-bound a variety of remedial courses for credit. The EOP tries to provide tutoring for any undergraduate class if tutors are available. To be recognized as a person with a learning disability, students are required to submit documentation from a qualified educational evaluator. Preferred diagnostic testing would include at least one test in each of the following categories: cognitive, achievement, and processing. Other documentation specifying a learning disability without testing in the three categories mentioned must include an in-depth valid assessment of the disability by a qualified professional.

LD/ADHD ADMISSIONS INFORMATION

College entrance tests required: Yes
Interview required: No
Essay recommended: No
Documentation required for LD: Psychoeducational evaluation
Documentation required for ADHD: Appropriate documentation from a psychologist/psychiatrist must include educational testing.
Submitted to: Services for Students with Disabilities
Special Ed. HS course work accepted: No

Specific course requirements of all applicants: Yes
Separate application required: No
# of LD applications submitted each year: NR
# of LD applications accepted yearly: NR
Total # of students receiving LD services: NR
Acceptance into program means acceptance into college: Student must be admitted and enrolled in the university first and then request services.

ADMISSIONS

All students must submit the general application for admission. If a student does not meet admissions requirements, admission will be denied. Enclosed with the notification, the student will receive information regarding petitioning for special admission. Students who want to petition their admission on the basis of a learning disability must submit all information required in the petition. Petitioning students must utilize the services of the EOP. The director of SSD helps to make admission decisions and may recommend the EOP for the student with LD. Regular admission requires a 3.0 GPA and special admit for students with 2.5. Course requirements include: 4 years of English, 3 years of math, 3 years of social studies, 3 years of sciences, and 2 years of foreign language. Students requesting services should self-identify; submit documentation of their LD, including educational history and diagnostic testing administered by professionals; and include information describing cognitive strengths and weaknesses, recommendations for accommodations or services, and any other additional information in the form of a family history. Students must also submit a handwritten 1–2 page statement outlining educational goals and explaining motivation to succeed at OSU. Students admitted through the EOP must start in the summer and attend a required SSD orientation in the beginning of fall. The EOP admission decision is made jointly between admissions and the EOP.

ADDITIONAL INFORMATION

Students with LD, whether admitted regularly or as special admits, are encouraged to apply for additional assistance from the EOP, which can provide special counseling, tutoring, and intensive practice in study skills. Accommodations in instruction and related academic work may include alternative test methods such as extended testing time and use of resources such as calculators and dictionaries. Accommodations are negotiated with instructors, academic departments, and the college as appropriate. Personal counseling is available through the Counseling Center. The director acts as a liaison between students and faculty.

LEARNING DISABILITY PROGRAM/SERVICES

Learning Disability Program/Services: Services for Students with Disabilities (SSD)
Director: Tracy Bentley-Townlin, PhD
  E-mail: Tracey.Bentley@oregonstate.edu
  Telephone: 541-737-4098
  Fax: 541-737-7354

LEARNING DISABILITY SERVICES

Requests for the following/services accommodations will be evaluated individually based on appropriate and current documentation.

Allowed in exams
  Calculator: Yes
  Dictionary: No
  Computer: Yes
  Spellchecker: Yes
Extended test time: Yes
Scribes: Yes
Proctors: Yes
Oral exams: Yes
Notetakers: Yes

Distraction-reduced environment: Yes
Tape recording in class: Yes
Books on tape from RFBD: Yes
Taping of books not from RFBD: Yes
Accommodations for students with ADHD: Yes
Reading machine: Yes
Other assistive technology: Yes
Priority registration: Yes

Added costs for services: No
LD specialists: No
Professional tutors: NR
Peer tutors: Yes
Max. hours/wk. for services: N/A
How professors are notified of LD/ADHD: By both student and director

GENERAL ADMISSIONS INFORMATION

Director of Admissions: Michele Sandlin
Telephone: 800-291-4192

ENTRANCE REQUIREMENTS

Academic units required: 4 English, 3 math, 2 science (1 science lab), 2 foreign language, 3 social studies.
Academic units recommended: 2 science lab. High school diploma is required, and GED is accepted. ACT with Writing component required. TOEFL required of all international applicants, minimum paper TOEFL 550, minimum computer TOEFL 213.

Application deadline: 9/1
Notification: Rolling
Average GPA: 3.49
ACT Composite middle 50% range: 20–26

SAT Math middle 50% range: 480–610
SAT Critical Reading middle 50% range: 460–580
SAT Writing middle 50% range: NR

Graduated top 10% of class: 19%
Graduated top 25% of class: 47%
Graduated top 50% of class: 83%

COLLEGE GRADUATION REQUIREMENTS

Course waivers allowed: No
Course substitutions allowed: Yes
In what course: On a case-by-case basis, depending on the major selected and documentation.

ADDITIONAL INFORMATION

Environment: The university is located on 530 acres in a small town 85 miles south of Portland.

Student Body
  Undergrad enrollment: 15,196
  Women: 46%
  Men: 54%
  Percent out-of-state: 14%

Cost Information
  In-state Tuition: $4,700
  Out-of-state Tuition: $17,500
  Room & board: $6,450
Housing Information
  University housing: Yes
  Percent living on campus: 22

Greek System
  Fraternity: Yes
  Sorority: Yes
Athletics: Division I

UNIVERSITY OF OREGON

1217 University of Oregon, Eugene, OR 97403-1217
Phone: 541-346-3201 • Fax: 541-346-5815
E-mail: uoadmit@uoregon.edu • Web: www.uoregon.edu
Support: CS • Institution type: 4-year public

LEARNING DISABILITY PROGRAM AND SERVICES

At the University of Oregon, Disability Services coordinates services and provides advocacy and support to students with documented learning disabilities. Eligibility for services must be supported by professional documentation of disability and need for services. Accommodations are determined on a case-by-case basis. Students who feel they are eligible for services should meet with the Counselor for Students with Disabilities. At this meeting students will be able to discuss the documentation process, services available, and their educational goals. Disability Services will work with students and faculty members to best accommodate needs. A general letter explaining the particular disability and suggested accommodations will be written, by request, to share with faculty at the students' discretion. This letter is reissued each academic term to designated instructors. Students with learning disabilities should be motivated, hard-working, and willing to take responsibility for meeting their educational goals.

LD/ADHD ADMISSIONS INFORMATION

College entrance tests required: Yes
Interview required: No
Essay recommended: Yes
Documentation required for LD: Psychoeducational evaluation
Documentation required for ADHD: Yes
Submitted to: Both Admissions and Disability Services
Special Ed. HS course work accepted: Yes

Specific course requirements of all applicants: Yes
Separate application required: No
# of LD applications submitted each year: NR
# of LD applications accepted yearly: NR
Total # of students receiving LD services: 350
Acceptance into program means acceptance into college: Student must be admitted and enrolled in the university first and then request services.

ADMISSIONS

Students with learning disabilities must meet the same admission criteria as all other applicants. Courses recommended for admission include: 4 years of English, 3 years of math, 2 years of science, 2 years of foreign language, 3 years of social studies, and 2 electives. The average SAT is 1140 and the average GPA is 3.3. Students not meeting the regular admission requirements who have extenuating circumstances due to a learning disability may request additional consideration of their application by a special committee. A completed application form, a writing sample, two letters of recommendation, and documentation of the disability with information about how it has influenced the student's ability to meet minimum admission requirements are required for special admission consideration based on disability.

ADDITIONAL INFORMATION

Students are encouraged to take an active role in utilizing the services. Once admitted, students should meet with the counselor to discuss educational goals. Documentation will be put on file. Services available include note-takers; books on tape; modification of testing procedures, including additional testing time, audiotape answers, having someone write dictated answers, large print, or taking the exam in a quiet location; Adaptive Technology Lab; and faculty liaison to assist in communicating needs to instructors and to help negotiate reasonable accommodations in courses and programs. The Office of Academic Advising provides counseling and assessment of progress toward graduation. There is a support group for "unique learners." The university requires two writing classes for graduation. In addition, the BS degree requires 1 year of college math. Two years of foreign language is required for a BA degree. Writing and math labs are available.

LEARNING DISABILITY PROGRAM/SERVICES

Learning Disability Program/Services: Disability Services
Director: Steve Pickett, MS, CRC
  E-mail: spickett@uoregon.edu
  Telephone: 541-346-1155
  Fax: 541-346-6013

LEARNING DISABILITY SERVICES

Requests for the following/services accommodations will be evaluated individually based on appropriate and current documentation.

Allowed in exams	**Distraction-reduced environment:** Yes	**Added costs for services:** Yes
Calculator: Yes	**Tape recording in class:** Yes	**LD specialists:** Yes
Dictionary: Yes	**Books on tape from RFBD:** Yes	**Professional tutors:** Yes
Computer: Yes	**Taping of books not from RFBD:** Yes	**Peer tutors:** Yes
Spellchecker: Yes	**Accommodations for students with**	**Max. hours/wk. for services:** NR
Extended test time: Yes	**ADHD:** Yes	**How professors are notified of**
Scribes: Yes	**Reading machine:** Yes	**LD/ADHD:** By both student and
Proctors: Yes	**Other assistive technology:** Yes	director
Oral exams: Yes	**Priority registration:** Yes	
Notetakers: Yes		

GENERAL ADMISSIONS INFORMATION

Director of Admissions: Martha Pitts, Assistant Vice President for Enrollment Management and Director of Admissions
Telephone: 541-346-3201

ENTRANCE REQUIREMENTS

Academic units required: 4 English, 3 math, 2 science, 2 foreign language, 3 social studies. **Academic units recommended:** 1 science lab, 2 additional units in required college preparatory areas recommended. High school diploma is required, and GED is accepted. ACT with Writing component required. TOEFL required of all international applicants, minimum paper TOEFL 500, minimum computer TOEFL 173.

Application deadline: NR	**SAT Math middle 50% range:**	**Graduated top 10% of class:** 23%
Notification: Rolling	500–611	**Graduated top 25% of class:** 56%
Average GPA: 3.50	**SAT Critical Reading middle 50%**	**Graduated top 50% of class:** 89%
ACT Composite middle 50% range:	range: 488–606	
NR	**SAT Writing middle 50% range:**	
	NR	

COLLEGE GRADUATION REQUIREMENTS

Course waivers allowed: No
Course substitutions allowed: Yes
In what course: In extreme cases with appropriate documentation.

ADDITIONAL INFORMATION

Environment: The university is located on 250 acres in an urban area of Eugene.

Student Body	**Cost Information**	**Greek System**
Undergrad enrollment: 16,282	**In-state tuition:** $5,600	**Fraternity:** Yes
Women: 53%	**Out-of-state tuition:** $17,400	**Sorority:** Yes
Men: 47%	**Room & board:** $7,827	**Athletics:** Division I
Percent out-of-state: 22%	**Housing Information**	
	University housing: Yes	
	Percent living on campus: 22%	

University of Oregon

WESTERN OREGON UNIVERSITY

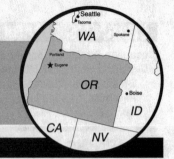

345 North Monmouth Avenue, Monmouth, OR 97361
Phone: 503-838-8211 • Fax: 503-838-8067
E-mail: wolfgram@wou.edu • Web: www.wou.edu
Support: S • Institution type: 4-year public

LEARNING DISABILITY PROGRAM AND SERVICES

The mission of the Office of Disability Services (ODS) is to remove barriers to learning for students with disabilities and to help ensure that these students access the tools and processes they need to create a successful experience at Western and beyond. These goals are realized by providing support services and information to help students develop skills such as self-advocacy, independence, identification and use of resources, appropriate use of problem-solving techniques, and accepting responsibility for one's actions. ODS strives to meet the individual needs of students with disabilities. The Student Enrichment Program (SEP) is designed to help students find success in college. The program's goals are to help SEP students develop writing, math, learning, and critical-thinking skills; maintain the necessary GPA to achieve individual goals; develop interpersonal communication skills; and achieve autonomy and maintain a sense of self-worth. Students who could benefit from SEP are those who enter the university without being completely prepared. SEP staff focuses on working with individual needs. Eligibility is based on federal guidelines determined by first-generation college-bound, financial need, or physical or learning disability; additionally, the student must have demonstrated academic need for the program.

LD/ADHD ADMISSIONS INFORMATION

College entrance tests required: No
Interview required: No
Essay recommended: No
Documentation required for LD: Psychoeducational evaluation completed within the past 3 years
Documentation required for ADHD: Yes
Submitted to: Office of Disability Services
Special Ed. HS course work accepted: No

Specific course requirements of all applicants: Yes
Separate application required: Yes
# of LD applications submitted each year: NR
# of LD applications accepted yearly: NR
Total # of students receiving LD services: 60–70
Acceptance into program means acceptance into college: Student must be admitted and enrolled in the university first and then request services.

ADMISSIONS

General admission requires a 2.75 GPA and ACT/SAT scores, which are used only as alternatives to the required GPA. Course requirements include 4 years of English, 3 years of math, 2 years of science, 3 years of social science, and 2 years of the same foreign language. Alternatives to course requirements require either a score of 470 or above on three SAT Subject Tests. The combined score must be 1410 or above. A limited number of students who do not meet the regular admission requirements, alternatives, or exceptions may be admitted through special action of an Admissions Committee. These students must submit by January 1 for the first session and April 1 for the second session a personal letter of petition stating why they don't meet the admission requirements and what they are doing to make up deficiencies, and three letters of recommendation from school and community members.

ADDITIONAL INFORMATION

Skills classes are offered in academic survival strategies (no credit) and critical thinking (college credit). Other services include advocacy, computer stations, note-takers, readers and taping services, alternative testing, advisement, and assistance with registration. CEP offers counseling; basic math courses; advising; individualized instruction in reading, study skills, writing, and critical thinking; monitor programs; and workshops on study skills, research writing, math anxiety, rapid reading, note-taking, and time management. Services and accommodations are available for undergraduate and graduate students.

LEARNING DISABILITY PROGRAM/SERVICES

Learning Disability Program/Services: Office of Disability Services
Director: Phillip A. Pownall, MS
  E-mail: pownallp@wou.edu
  Telephone: 503-838-8250
  Fax: 503-838-8721

LEARNING DISABILITY SERVICES

Requests for the following/services accommodations will be evaluated individually based on appropriate and current documentation.

Allowed in exams
  Calculator: Yes
  Dictionary: Yes
  Computer: Yes
  Spellchecker: Yes
Extended test time: Yes
Scribes: Yes
Proctors: Yes
Oral exams: Yes
Notetakers: Yes

Distraction-reduced environment: Yes
Tape recording in class: Yes
Books on tape from RFBD: No
Taping of books not from RFBD: No
Accommodations for students with ADHD: Yes
Reading machine: No
Other assistive technology: Yes
Priority registration: Yes

Added costs for services: No
LD specialists: No
Professional tutors: No
Peer tutors: Yes
Max. hours/wk. for services: N/A
How professors are notified of LD/ADHD: By both student and director

GENERAL ADMISSIONS INFORMATION

Director of Admissions: David McDonald
Telephone: 877-877-1593

ENTRANCE REQUIREMENTS

Academic units required: 4 English, 3 math, 2 science, 2 foreign language, 3 social studies, 1 history. **Academic units recommended:** 1 science lab. High school diploma is required, and GED is accepted. ACT with Writing component required. TOEFL required of all international applicants, minimum paper TOEFL 500, minimum computer TOEFL 180.

Application deadline: NR
Notification: NR
Average GPA: 3.20
ACT Composite middle 50% range: 17–23

SAT Math middle 50% range: 430–530
SAT Critical Reading middle 50% range: 420–530
SAT Writing middle 50% range: 400–510

Graduated top 10% of class: 13%
Graduated top 25% of class: 36%
Graduated top 50% of class: 73%

COLLEGE GRADUATION REQUIREMENTS

Course waivers allowed: No
Course substitutions allowed: Yes
In what course: Decisions are made on a case-by-case basis.

ADDITIONAL INFORMATION

Environment: The university is located on 134 acres in a rural area 15 miles west of Salem.

Student Body
  Undergrad enrollment: 4,103
  Women: 59%
  Men: 41%
  Percent out-of-state: 9%

Cost Information
  In-state tuition: $4,300
  Out-of-state tuition: $13,650
  Room & board: $7,030
Housing Information
  University housing: Yes
  Percent living on campus: 26%

Greek System
  Fraternity: No
  Sorority: No
Athletics: Division II

CLARION U. OF PENNSYLVANIA

Admissions Office, 840 Wood Street, Clarion, PA 16214
Phone: 814-393-2306 • Fax: 814-393-2030
E-mail: admissions@clarion.edu • Web: www.clarion.edu
Support: CS • Institution: 4-year public

LEARNING DISABILITY PROGRAM AND SERVICES

Clarion does not have a special admissions policy for students with learning disabilities nor does it offer a structured LD program. The Office of Disability Support Services works to ensure educational parity for students with learning disabilities within a mainstream setting. Academic accommodations and support focuses on minimizing the effects of the disability. The Center for Academic Enrichment is the university's primary vehicle for providing a Tutoring Center and is available to all students but especially beneficial for students with learning disabilities. These services are free of charge and include extensive peer tutoring, study skills workshops, and individual "learning to learn" activities.

LD/ADHD ADMISSIONS INFORMATION

College entrance tests required: Yes
Interview required: Yes
Essay recommended: No
Documentation required for LD: Psychoeducational evaluation
Documentation required for ADHD: Yes
Submitted to: Disability Support Services
Special Ed. HS course work accepted: Yes

Specific course requirements of all applicants: Yes
Separate application required: No
# of LD applications submitted each year: NR
# of LD applications accepted yearly: NR
Total # of students receiving LD services: 75
Acceptance into program means acceptance into college: Student must be admitted and enrolled in the university first and then request services.

ADMISSIONS

Students with learning disabilities who wish to be admitted to the university must meet regular admission requirements. Course requirements include 4 years of English, 2 years of math (4 recommended), 3 years of science (4 recommended), 2 years of a foreign language (recommended), and 4 years of social studies. As part of the application process, students are encouraged to provide documentation of their learning disability to establish a clear need for individualized support services. Students should also include a copy of their Individualized Educational Program from high school. Students not meeting the general admission criteria may be admitted by either the Academic Support Acceptance (these students are referred to Student Support Services) or Summer Start (probationary admittance).

ADDITIONAL INFORMATION

The Disability Support Services staff serve as liaisons between students and faculty to provide special considerations when appropriate. Accommodations are based on documentation,for example, psychoeducational evaluations for students with learning disabilities. The nature of the student's disability, as well as the student's functional limitation, is considered when accommodations are determined. Accommodations could include extended time for exams, reader for exams, scribes for exams, word processor for exams, alternate test location, objective exams (when possible), essay exams (when possible), oral exams (when possible), word processor for written assignments, extended time for in-class assignments, taped lectures, tapes of textbooks, note-taking assistance, assistive technology, priority registration, and liaising with agencies. The program also provides academic advising, special topic seminars, reading/study skills workshops, and referral to other campus resources such as the Tutoring and Writing Centers. Services and accommodations are available to undergraduate and graduate students.

LEARNING DISABILITY PROGRAM/SERVICES

Learning Disability Program/Services: Disability Support Services
Director: Jennifer May
  E-Mail: jmay@clarion.edu
  Telephone: 814-393-2095
  Fax: 814-393-2368

LEARNING DISABILITY SERVICES

Requests for the following/services accommodations will be evaluated individually based on appropriate and current documentation.

Allowed in exams
  Calculator: NR
  Dictionary: NR
  Computer: NR
  Spellchecker: NR
Extended test time: Yes
Scribes: Yes
Proctors: Yes
Oral exams: Yes
Notetakers: Yes

Distraction-reduced environment: Yes
Tape recording in class: Yes
Books on tape from RFBD: Yes
Taping of books not from RFBD: Yes
Accommodations for students with ADHD: Yes
Reading machine: Yes
Other assistive technology: Yes
Priority registration: Yes

Added costs for services: No
LD specialists: Yes
Professional tutors: 0
Peer tutors: 20
Max. hours/wk. for services: 1
How professors are notified of LD/ADHD: By student

GENERAL ADMISSIONS INFORMATION

Director of Admissions: Mr. William Bailey
Telephone: 800-672-7171

ENTRANCE REQUIREMENTS

Academic units required: 4 English, 2 math, 3 science, 4 social studies. **Academic units recommended:** 4 English, 4 math, 4 science (1 science lab), 2 foreign language, 4 social studies. High school diploma is required, and GED is accepted. ACT with or without Writing component accepted. TOEFL required of all international applicants, minimum paper TOEFL 500, minimum computer TOEFL 173.

Application deadline: NR
Notification: Rolling
Average GPA: 3.00
ACT Composite middle 50% range: NR

SAT Math middle 50% range: 420–530
SAT Critical Reading middle 50% range: 420–520
SAT Writing middle 50% range: NR

Graduated top 10% of class: 9%
Graduated top 25% of class: 27%
Graduated top 50% of class: 62%

COLLEGE GRADUATION REQUIREMENTS

Course waivers allowed: Yes
In what course: Determined case-by-case
Course substitutions allowed: Yes
In what course: Determined case-by-case

ADDITIONAL INFORMATION

Environment: The university is located on 100 acres in a small town 85 miles northeast of Pittsburgh.

Student Body
  Undergrad enrollment: 5,724
  Women: 61%
  Men: 39%
  Percent out-of-state: 6%

Cost Information
  In-state tuition: $6,500
  Out-of-state tuition: $11,500
  Room & board: $5,546
Housing Information
  University housing: Yes
  Percent living on campus: 35%

Greek System
  Fraternity: Yes
  Sorority: Yes
Athletics: Division II

COLLEGE MISERICORDIA

301 Lake Street, Dallas, PA 18612
Phone: 570-674-6264 • Fax: 570-675-2441
E-mail: admiss@misericordia.edu • Web: www.misericordia.edu
Support: SP • Institution: 4-year private

LEARNING DISABILITY PROGRAM AND SERVICES

All students who participate in the Alternate Learners Project (ALP) are enrolled in regular college classes. In most cases, they take a carefully selected, reduced credit load each semester. Students who participate in ALP are supported by an assortment of services delivered by a specially trained full-time staff. Services include "Learning Strategies," which are designed to make students more efficient, and accommodations designed to work around student's disabilities whenever possible. Upon entry each student develops an Individual Education Program and signs a contract agreeing to weekly meetings with mentors. The ultimate goal of ALP is to help students with learning disabilities succeed in college.

LD/ADHD ADMISSIONS INFORMATION

College entrance tests required: Yes
Interview required: Yes
Essay recommended: Yes
Documentation required for LD: Recent and complete psychoeducational report
Documentation required for ADHD: Recent and complete psychoeducational report or medical report
Submitted to: Admissions Office and ALP
Special Ed. HS course work accepted: No

Specific course requirements of all applicants: Yes
Separate application required: No
# of LD applications submitted each year: 125
# of LD applications accepted yearly: 25
Total # of students receiving LD services: 50
Acceptance into program means acceptance into college: There is a joint acceptance between ALP and the Office of Admissions.

ADMISSIONS

College Misericordia's experience with students with learning disabilities is that students who are highly motivated and socially mature have an excellent chance to be successful. Each applicant has to secure a standard admissions form, enclose a written cover letter summarizing the learning disability, and indicate a desire to participate in the ALP. Additionally, a copy of the psychoeducational report should be submitted along with the high school transcript and three letters of recommendation (one must be written by a special education professional). Class rank is usually above the top 60 percent. ACT/SAT are required but not used in any way for LD admissions. Students and their parents will be invited to interviews. This interview is very important. The program director reviews all information and recommends an action to the Admissions Department, which, after careful review, acts on the recommendation. The admission decision is made jointly by the program director and the Director of Admissions.

ADDITIONAL INFORMATION

All students served by ALP are asked to attend a summer program ($1,600) to learn strategies, understand needed accommodations, and learn about the college. Accommodations, such as Kurzweil Personal Readers, Franklin Spellcheckers, word processors, voice-activated computers, scanners, books on tape, tape recording procedures, editing services, note-taking services, and alternative test-taking procedures allow students to work around their disabilities. The ALP arranges the accommodations students need. The college, not ALP, offers several skills courses (non-credited) in basic areas such as reading, writing, and math. Services and accommodations are available for undergraduate and graduate students. College Misericordia offers a summer program for high school students with learning disabilities.

LEARNING DISABILITY PROGRAM/SERVICES

Learning Disability Program/Services: Alternative Learners Project (ALP)
Director: Dr. Joseph Rogan
    E-Mail: Jrogan@misericordia.edu
    Telephone: 570-674-6347
    Fax: 570-675-2441

LEARNING DISABILITY SERVICES

Requests for the following/services accommodations will be evaluated individually based on appropriate and current documentation.

Allowed in exams
  Calculator: Yes
  Dictionary: Yes
  Computer: Yes
  Spellchecker: Yes
Extended test time: Yes
Scribes: Yes
Proctors: Yes
Oral exams: Yes
Notetakers: Yes

Distraction-reduced environment: Yes
Tape recording in class: Yes
Books on tape from RFBD: Yes
Taping of books not from RFBD: No
Accommodations for students with
  ADHD: No
Reading machine: Yes
Other assistive technology: Yes
Priority registration: Yes

Added costs for services: No
LD specialists: Yes
Professional tutors: 7
Peer tutors: 100
Max. hours/wk. for services:
  Unlimited
How professors are notified of
  LD/ADHD: By director

GENERAL ADMISSIONS INFORMATION

Director of Admissions: Glenn Bozinski
Telephone: 570-674-6434

ENTRANCE REQUIREMENTS

Academic units required: 4 English, 4 math, 4 science, 4 social studies. High school diploma is required, and GED is accepted. ACT with or without Writing component accepted. TOEFL required of all international applicants, minimum paper TOEFL 500, minimum computer TOEFL 75.

Application deadline: NR
Notification: Rolling
Average GPA: 3.14
ACT Composite middle 50% range:
  20–25

SAT Math middle 50% range:
  440–570
SAT Critical Reading middle 50%
  range: 440–550
SAT Writing middle 50% range:
  NR

Graduated top 10% of class: 17%
Graduated top 25% of class: 41%
Graduated top 50% of class: 72%

COLLEGE GRADUATION REQUIREMENTS

Course waivers allowed: Yes
In what course: Varies with curriculum/program
Course substitutions allowed: Yes
In what course: Varies

ADDITIONAL INFORMATION

Environment: The college is located on a 100-acre campus in a suburban small town 9 miles south of Wilkes-Barre.

Student Body
  Undergrad enrollment: 2,001
  Women: 72%
  Men: 28%
  Percent out-of-state: 16%

Cost Information
  Tuition: $19,800
  Room & board: $8,640
Housing Information
  University housing: Yes
  Percent living on campus: 38%

Greek System
  Fraternity: No
  Sorority: No
Athletics: Division III

DICKINSON COLLEGE

PO Box 1773, Carlisle, PA 17013-2896
Phone: 717-245-1231 • Fax: 717-245-1442
E-mail: admit@dickinson.edu • Web: www.dickinson.edu
Support: S • Institution: 4-year private

LEARNING DISABILITY PROGRAM AND SERVICES

Dickinson College is committed to providing reasonable accommodations to qualified individuals with disabilities. Students with disabilities will be integrated as completely as possible into the college community. Dickinson does not offer a specialized curriculum. In order to receive support services, students must submit documentation in accordance with college policy for documenting a disability.

LD/ADHD ADMISSIONS INFORMATION

College entrance tests required: No
Interview required: No
Essay recommended: Yes
Documentation required for LD: A recent evaluation within 3 years
Documentation required for ADHD: A recent evaluation within 3 years
Submitted to: Support Program/Services
Special Ed. HS course work accepted: No

Specific course requirements of all applicants: NR
Separate application required: No
# of LD applications submitted each year: NR
# of LD applications accepted yearly: NR
Total # of students receiving LD services: NR
Acceptance into program means acceptance into college: Student must be admitted and enrolled in the university first and then request services.

ADMISSIONS

There is no special admissions process for students with learning disabilities. Students should include a separate statement concerning their interest in disability services. ACT/SAT tests are optional for admission, but required for academic scholarship consideration. Students should have a minimum of 4 years of English, 3 years of math, 3 years of science, 2 years of social studies, and 2 years of sequential foreign language in high school. Candidates are evaluated on the quality of the courses they have taken, their grades, the quality of the school from which they are applying, and their demonstrated willingness to involve themselves in their school and community.

ADDITIONAL INFORMATION

Skills classes are available in time management, note-taking, test-taking strategies, reading and writing. Substitutions may be requested in foreign language, but only after attempting a language and demonstrating effort to pass the course. Support services could include: extended testing time; distraction-free environment; scribes; proctors; note-takers; books on tape; peer tutors; and the use of calculator, dictionary, computer or spellchecker in exams. Workshops for all students on campus (including those with disabilities) are available in time management, test-taking strategies, and study skills.

LEARNING DISABILITY PROGRAM/SERVICES

Learning Disability Program/Services: Academic Resource Services
Director: Jorja Waybrant
E-Mail: waybranj@dickinson.edu
Telephone: 717-245-1080
Fax: 717-245-1618

LEARNING DISABILITY SERVICES

Requests for the following/services accommodations will be evaluated individually based on appropriate and current documentation.

Allowed in exams
Calculator: Yes
Dictionary: Yes
Computer: Yes
Spellchecker: Yes
Extended test time: Yes
Scribes: Yes
Proctors: Yes
Oral exams: Yes
Notetakers: Yes

Distraction-reduced environment: Yes
Tape recording in class: Yes
Books on tape from RFBD: Yes
Taping of books not from RFBD: No
Accommodations for students with ADHD: Yes
Reading machine: Yes
Other assistive technology: No
Priority registration: No

Added costs for services: No
LD specialists: No
Professional tutors: 0
Peer tutors: 40–50
Max. hours/wk. for services: Unlimited
How professors are notified of LD/ADHD: By student

GENERAL ADMISSIONS INFORMATION

Director of Admissions: Christopher Seth Allen, Dean of Admissions
Telephone: 800-644-1773

ENTRANCE REQUIREMENTS

Academic units required: 4 English, 3 math, 3 science (2 science labs), 2 foreign language, 2 social studies, 2 academic electives. **Academic units recommended:** 3 foreign language. High school diploma is required, and GED is accepted. ACT with or without Writing component accepted. TOEFL required of all international applicants, minimum paper TOEFL 600, minimum computer TOEFL 250.

Application deadline: 2/1
Notification: 3/31
Average GPA: NR
ACT Composite middle 50% range: 26–30

SAT Math middle 50% range: 600–680
SAT Critical Reading middle 50% range: 600–690
SAT Writing middle 50% range: NR

Graduated top 10% of class: 53%
Graduated top 25% of class: 84%
Graduated top 50% of class: 97%

ADDITIONAL INFORMATION

Environment: The college is located on a 103 acre suburban campus.

Student Body
Undergrad enrollment: 2,369
Women: 56%
Men: 44%
Percent out-of-state: 73%

Cost Information
Tuition: $33,470
Room & board: $8,480
Housing Information
University housing: Yes
Percent living on campus: 92%

Greek System
Fraternity: Yes
Sorority: Yes
Athletics: Division III

DREXEL UNIVERSITY

3141 Chestnut Street, 81-210, Philadelphia, PA 19104-2875
Phone: 215-895-1401 • Fax: 215-895-1402
E-mail: disability@drexel.edu • Web: www.drexel.edu/ODS
Support: CS • Institution type: 4-year private

LEARNING DISABILITY PROGRAM AND SERVICES

Drexel University does not have a specific learning disability program, but services are provided through the Office of Disability Services (ODS). The professional staff works closely with the students who have special needs to ensure that they have the opportunity to participate fully in Drexel University's programs and activities. Drexel's ODS offers an individualized transition program for students with disabilities upon request. Students need to contact the ODS.

LD/ADHD ADMISSIONS INFORMATION

College entrance tests required: Yes
Nonstandardized tests accepted: Yes
Interview required: No
Essay required: No
Documentation required for LD: Psycoeducational evaluations
Documentation required for ADHD: Yes
Documentation submitted to: Office of Disability Services (ODS)
Special Ed. HS course work accepted: No

Specific course requirements of all applicants: Yes
Separate application required for services: No
# of LD applications submitted early: N/A
# of LD applications accepted yearly: N/A
Total # receiving LD/ADHD services: 200
Acceptance into program means acceptance into college: Students must be admitted and enrolled at the university first, then they may request services.

ADMISSIONS

The regular admission requirements are the same for all students, and there is no special process for students with learning disabilities or any other type of disability. Students are encouraged to self disclose and provide current documentation of their disabilities to the ODS. General admission criteria include recommended courses of 4 years of English, 3 years of math, 1 year of science, 1 year of social studies, 7 electives (chosen from English, math, science, social studies, foreign language, history, or mechanical drawing). The average SAT score is 1180, and the average GPA is 3.4; an interview is recommended. For additional information, contact the Admissions Office at Drexel University directly.

ADDITIONAL INFORMATION

Accommodations may be provided, if appropriate and reasonable, and may include extra time for exams, adaptive technologies, note-takers, priority scheduling, instruction modifications, reduced course loads, and course substitutions. All accommodation eligibility is determined on a case-by-case basis. Tutors are not an accommodation in college, but are available for all students at Drexel through the Learning Centers. Currently there are nearly 200 students with LD eligible for services and accommodations.

LEARNING DISABILITY PROGRAM/SERVICES

Learning Disability Program/Services: Office of Disability Services
Director: Michelle M. Peters, M.Ed.
  E-mail: michelle.m.peters@drexel.edu
  Phone: 215-895-1401
  Fax: 215-895-1402
 Disability Specialist: Jeanette Dugger, M.A.
  E-mail: jeanette.k.dugger@drexel.edu
  Phone: 215-895-1401
  Fax: 215-895-1402

LEARNING DISABILITY SERVICES

Requests for the following services/accommodations will be evaluated individually based on appropriate and current documentation.

Allowed in Exams
  Calculator: Yes
  Dictionary: Yes
  Computer: Yes
  Spellchecker: Yes
Extended test time: Yes
Scribes: Yes
Proctors: Yes
Oral exams: Yes
Note-takers: Yes

Distraction-reduced environment: Yes
Tape recording in class: Yes
Books on tape from RFBD: Yes
Taping of books not from RFBD: Yes
**Accommodations for students with
  ADHD:** Yes
Reading machine: Yes
Other assistive technology: Yes
Priority registration: Yes

Added costs: No
LD Specialists: 1
Professional tutors: Yes
Peer tutors: Yes
Max hrs for serv: Varies
**How professors are notified of
  LD/ADHD:** By the student

GENERAL ADMISSIONS INFORMATION

Director of Admissions: Dana R. Davies
Telephone: 215-895-2400

ENTRANCE REQUIREMENTS

Academic units required: 3 math, 1 science (1 science lab). **Academic units recommended:** 4 English, 3 math, 1 science (1 science lab), 1 foreign language, 1 social studies, 7 electives. High school diploma or GED is required. Minimum TOEFL is 550 written or 213 computer-based. TOEFL required of all international applicants.

Application deadline: 3/1
Notification: Rolling
Average GPA: 3.5
ACT Composite middle 50% range:
  N/A

SAT Math middle 50% range: NR
**SAT Critical Reading middle 50%
  range:** NR
SAT Writing middle 50% range: NR

Graduated top 10%: 30%
Graduated top 15%: 42%
Graduated top 25%: 66%

ADDITIONAL INFORMATION

Environment: The campus is located on 38 acres near the center of Philadelphia.

Student Body
Undergrad enrollment: 12,906
Women: 44%
Men: 56%
Out-of-state: 39%

Cost Information
Tuition: $27,200 (5-year)
Room & board: $11,570
Housing Information
University housing: Yes
Percent living campus: 25%

Greek System
  Fraternity: NR
  Sorority: NR
Athletics: NR

EAST STROUDSBURG U. OF PA

200 Prospect Street, East Stroudsburg, PA 18301-2999
Phone: 570-422-3542 • Fax: 570-422-3933
E-mail: undergrads@po-box.esu.edu • Web: www.esu.edu
Support: CS • Institution: 4-year public

LEARNING DISABILITY PROGRAM AND SERVICES

There is no special program for students with learning disabilities at East Stroudsburg University. However, the university is committed to supporting otherwise qualified students with learning disabilities in their pursuit of an education. Disability Services offers students with LD academic and social support and acts as their advocate on campus. Students are encouraged to meet with the coordinator, once accepted, to schedule classes and to develop compensatory skills. Tutors are trained to be sensitive to individual learning styles. Students who request accommodations or academic adjustments are responsible for providing required documentation to the Office of Disability Services and for requesting those accommodations or academic adjustments. East Stroudsburg University will need documentation of the disability that consists of an evaluation by an appropriate professional and describes the current impact of the disability as it relates to the accommodation request. To receive services, students with disabilities must identify that they have a disability, submit appropriate documentation, and request services.

LD/ADHD ADMISSIONS INFORMATION

College entrance tests required: Yes
Interview required: No
Essay recommended: Yes
Documentation required for LD: Psychoeducational evaluation; must have been completed no earlier than 10th grade
Documentation required for ADHD: Medical evaluation that includes medical histsory, diagnostic assessment instruments, diagnosis, and functional limitations
Submitted to: Disability Services
Special Ed. HS course work accepted: Yes

Specific course requirements of all applicants: Yes
Separate application required: No
# of LD applications submitted each year: 0
# of LD applications accepted yearly: 0
Total # of students receiving LD services: 130
Acceptance into program means acceptance into college: Student must be admitted and enrolled in the university first and then request services.

ADMISSIONS

Students with LD file the general application and are encouraged to complete the section titled "Disabilities Information" and forward documentation of their disability to Disability Services. Notification of a learning disability is used as a part of the admissions process only if the student is denied admission. At this time the Admissions Office waits for a recommendation from the learning disability specialist. The Office of Academic Support may request that the Admissions Office re-evaluate the student's application in light of information on the disability. For general admission, academic achievement is the primary factor considered in the selection process. ESU looks for a good match between what each applicant can contribute to the university and how the university can meet each applicant's expectations through a whole-person assessment. ESU is interested in student contributions to their school and community, activities and achievements, aspirations, and anything else that would help evaluate potential success at ESU. SAT or ACT—are used as a common yardstick to help in the selection process. SAT Subject Tests are not required.

ADDITIONAL INFORMATION

There is a pre-admission summer program for Pennsylvania residents only called the "Summer Intensive Study Program." Drop-in labs are offered in math and writing, as are study skills workshops. Students with learning disabilities may work individually with the Disability Services Coordinator. All students enrolled in the university have the opportunity to take skills classes in reading, composition, and math. Other services include workshops in time management and test-taking strategies as well as support groups. The Learning Center provides individual and group tutoring by professional and peer tutors free of charge to ESU students. Tutors are assigned on a first-come, first-served basis, and students must complete and submit a request form in order to receive tutoring. Although tutoring is not an accommodation for a disability, new peer and professional tutors participate in a tutor training program that includes strategies for tutoring students with disabilities. Services and accommodations are available for undergraduate and graduate students.

LEARNING DISABILITY PROGRAM/SERVICES

Learning Disability Program/Services: Office of Disability Services
Director: Edith F. Miller, EdD
  E-Mail: emiller@po-box.esu.edu
  Telephone: 570-422-3954
  Fax: 717-422-3898

LEARNING DISABILITY SERVICES

Requests for the following/services accommodations will be evaluated individually based on appropriate and current documentation.

Allowed in exams
  Calculator: Yes
  Dictionary: No
  Computer: Yes
  Spellchecker: Yes
Extended test time: Yes
Scribes: Yes
Proctors: No
Oral exams: Yes
Note-takers: Yes

Distraction-reduced environment: Yes
Tape recording in class: Yes
Books on tape from RFBD: Yes
Taping of books not from RFBD: Yes
Accommodations for students with ADHD: Yes
Reading machine: Yes
Other assistive technology: Yes
Priority registration: Yes

Added costs for services: No
LD specialists: Yes
Professional tutors: 70
Peer tutors: 50
Max. hours/wk. for services: 2
How professors are notified of LD/ADHD: By student

GENERAL ADMISSIONS INFORMATION

Director of Admissions: Alan Chesterton
Telephone: 570-422-3542

ENTRANCE REQUIREMENTS

Academic units recomended: 4 English, 4 math, 3 science (2 science labs), 2 foreign language, 3 social studies, 3 history. High school diploma is required, and GED is accepted. ACT with or without Writing component accepted. TOEFL required of all international applicants, minimum paper TOEFL 500, minimum computer TOEFL 173.

Application deadline: 4/1
Notification: Rolling
Average GPA: 3.14
ACT Composite middle 50% range:
  NR

SAT Math middle 50% range:
  440–540
SAT Critical Reading middle 50% range: 440–520
SAT Writing middle 50% range:
  430–510

Graduated top 10% of class: 5%
Graduated top 25% of class: 24%
Graduated top 50% of class: 64%

COLLEGE GRADUATION REQUIREMENTS

Course waivers allowed: No
Course substitutions allowed: No

ADDITIONAL INFORMATION

Environment: The 813-acre campus is set in the foothills of the Pocono Mountains.

Student Body
  Undergrad enrollment: 5,750
  Women: 58%
  Men: 42%
  Percent out-of-state: 23%

Cost Information
  In-state tuition: $5,900
  Out-of-state tuition: $12,900
  Room & board: $5,302
Housing Information
  University housing: Yes
  Percent living on campus: 47%

Greek System
  Fraternity: Yes
  Sorority: Yes
  Athletics: Division II

EDINBORO U. OF PENNSYLVANIA

Biggers House, Edinboro, PA 16444
Phone: 814-732-2761 • Fax: 814-732-2420
E-mail: eup_admissions@edinboro.edu • Web: www.edinboro.edu
Support: CS • Institution type: 4-year public

LEARNING DISABILITY PROGRAM AND SERVICES

Edinboro is actively involved in providing services for students with learning disabilities. The Office for Students with Disabilities (OSD) provides services that are individually directed by the program staff according to expressed needs. There are different levels of services offered depending on the student's needs. Level I offers supervised study sessions with trained mentors up to 10 hours per week; a writing specialist by appointment 1–2 hours weekly; a required appointment every 2 weeks with professional staff to review progress; and all services in Basic Service. Level 2 requires a 2.5 GPA and one semester at Level I, and includes peer mentoring up to 3 hours weekly and all services in Basic Service. Basic Service provides assistance in arranging academic accommodations, including alternate test arrangements; priority scheduling; consultation with staff; and tape-recorded textbooks. Level I and 2 are fee-for-service levels.

LD/ADHD ADMISSIONS INFORMATION

College entrance tests required: Yes
Interview required: No
Essay recommended: No
Documentation required for LD: Psychoeducational evaluation
Documentation required for ADHD: Yes
Submitted to: Support Program/Services
Special Ed. HS course work accepted: Yes

Specific course requirements of all applicants: NR
Separate application required: No
# of LD applications submitted each year: 40–100
# of LD applications accepted yearly: 40–60
Total # of students receiving LD services: 285
Acceptance into program means acceptance into college: Student must be admitted and enrolled in the university first and then request services.

ADMISSIONS

Students with LD submit the general application form. Upon receipt of the application from the Admissions Office, it is suggested that students identify any special services that may be required and contact the OSD so that a personal interview may be scheduled. Occasionally, OSD staff is asked for remarks on certain files, but it is not part of the admission decision. Students must provide a multifactor educational assessment; standard scores in reading, vocabulary and comprehension, math, and spelling; an individual intelligence test administered by a psychologist, including a list of the tests given; and a list of recommended accommodations. Evaluations submitted must have seen completed recently. Students are reviewed for academic promise, motivation, and positive attitude.

ADDITIONAL INFORMATION

Students with LD are paired with peer advisors who help them with study skills, organizational skills, and time management skills. Students are recommended for different levels of services based on their needs. Students are not required to select a particular level, but OSD strongly recommends that students enroll for Level I if they have less than a 2.5 GPA. Specific academic scheduling needs may be complex, but students working through the OSD are given priority in academic scheduling. The Life Skills Center is a training area designed to enable students with disabilities to maximize their personal independence while completing their academic programs. Extensive tutoring is available for all students.

LEARNING DISABILITY PROGRAM/SERVICES

Learning Disability Program/Services: Office for Students with Disabilities (OSD)
Director: Robert McConnell, PhD
  E-mail: mcconnell@Edinboro.edu
  Telephone: 814-732-2462
  Fax: 814-732-2866
Contact Person: Kathleen Strosser
  E-mail: strosser@Edinboro.edu
  Telephone: 814-732-2462
  Fax: 814-732-2866

LEARNING DISABILITY SERVICES

Requests for the following/services accommodations will be evaluated individually based on appropriate and current documentation.

Allowed in exams
  Calculator: Yes
  Dictionary: Yes
  Computer: Yes
  Spellchecker: Yes
Extended test time: Yes
Scribes: Yes
Proctors: Yes
Oral exams: No
Note-takers: No

Distraction-reduced environment: Yes
Tape recording in class: Yes
Books on tape from RFBD: Yes
Taping of books not from RFBD: Yes
Accommodations for students with ADHD: Yes
Reading machine: Yes
Other assistive technology: Yes
Priority registration: Yes

Added costs for services: Yes
LD specialists: Yes
Professional tutors: 1
Peer tutors: 80–100
Max. hours/wk. for services: 12
How professors are notified of LD/ADHD: By student

GENERAL ADMISSIONS INFORMATION

Director of Admissions: Terrence J. Carlin
Telephone: 888-8GO-BORO

ENTRANCE REQUIREMENTS

Academic units recommended: 4 English, 3 math, 3 science, 2 foreign language, 4 social studies, 3 academic electives, 1 keyboarding/computer. High school diploma is required, and GED is accepted. ACT with Writing component required. TOEFL required of all international applicants, minimum paper TOEFL 500, minimum computer TOEFL 173.

Application deadline: NR
Notification: Rolling
Average GPA: 3.24
ACT Composite middle 50% range:
  16–21

SAT Math middle 50% range:
  410–520
SAT Critical Reading middle 50% range: 410–530
SAT Writing middle 50% range:
  NR

Graduated top 10% of class: 6%
Graduated top 25% of class: 21%
Graduated top 50% of class: 51%

COLLEGE GRADUATION REQUIREMENTS

Course waivers allowed: No
Course substitutions allowed: Yes
In what course: Case-by-case basis; request reviewed by committee.

ADDITIONAL INFORMATION

Environment: Edinboro University is located on 600 acres in a small town 20 miles south of Erie.

Student Body
  Undergrad enrollment: 6,162
  Women: 57%
  Men: 43%
  Percent out-of-state: 10%

Cost Information
  In-state tuition: $6,200
  Out-of-state tuition: $11,100
  Room & board: $5,718
Housing Information
  University housing: Yes

  Percent living on campus: 27%
Greek System
  Fraternity: Yes
  Sorority: Yes
Athletics: Division II

Edinboro University of Pennsylvania

GANNON UNIVERSITY

University Square, Erie, PA 16541
Phone: 814-871-7240 • Fax: 814-871-5803
E-mail: NR • Web: www.gannon.edu
Support: SP • Institution type: 4-year private

LEARNING DISABILITY PROGRAM AND SERVICES

Gannon's Program for Students with Learning Disabilities (PSLD) provides special support services for students who have been diagnosed with either LD or ADHD who are highly motivated for academic achievement. PSLD faculty are committed to excellence and strive to offer each student individually designed instruction. Students in the program may select any academic major offered by the university. Freshman-year support includes weekly individual sessions with instructor-tutors and a writing specialist, and small group meetings with a reading specialist. They also provide an advocacy seminar course that includes participation in small group counseling. There is limited space in PSLD, and students should check the appropriate box on the admissions application if this service applies.

LD/ADHD ADMISSIONS INFORMATION

College entrance tests required: Yes
Interview required: Yes
Essay recommended: Yes
Documentation required for LD: WAIS or WISC
Documentation required for ADHD: Official letter of documentation from a licensed professional (usually a medical doctor)
Submitted to: Admissions Office and PSLD
Special Ed. HS course work accepted: Yes

Specific course requirements of all applicants: Yes
Separate application required: No
# of LD applications submitted each year: 45
# of LD applications accepted yearly: 15
Total # of students receiving LD services: 40–60
Acceptance into program means acceptance into college: The Director of PSLD accepts students into the program and the university.

ADMISSIONS

Besides the regular application and interview there is a special admissions process for students with LD. Students must check the box on the application indicating interest in the Learning Disabilities Program. Applicants must submit a psychoeducational evaluation, a high school transcript, two letters of recommendation, and a paragraph about why there is a need for support services. The program director and assistant director make an initial decision and advise the Admissions Office on their decision. Students who are admitted conditionally must enter as undeclared majors until they can achieve a 2.0 GPA. Special education high school courses are accepted in certain situations.

ADDITIONAL INFORMATION

Specific features of the program include biweekly tutoring sessions with the program instructors to review course material, learn study skills relevant to material from courses, and focus on specific needs; weekly sessions with the writing specialist for reviewing, editing, and brainstorming. A one-credit Advocacy Seminar course is part of the course load of first and second semester. This course covers self-advocacy, motivational techniques, college survival skills, the law and LD, and learning styles and strategies. Additional services available are computer access taped textbooks, taping of classes, extended time on exams, scribes, and oral exams. There is a $600 fee for support services.

LEARNING DISABILITY PROGRAM/SERVICES

Learning Disability Program/Services: Program for Students with Learning Disabilities
Director: Sister Joyce Lowrey, SSJ, MEd
  E-mail: lowrey@gannon.edu
  Telephone: 814-871-5326
  Fax: 814-871-7499
 Contact Person: Jane Kanter
  E-mail: lowrey@gannon.edu
  Telephone: 814-871-5360
  Fax: 814-871-7499

LEARNING DISABILITY SERVICES

Requests for the following/services accommodations will be evaluated individually based on appropriate and current documentation.

Allowed in exams
  Calculator: Yes
  Dictionary: No
  Computer: Yes
  Spellchecker: Yes
Extended test time: Yes
Scribes: Yes
Proctors: Yes
Oral exams: Yes
Notetakers: No

Distraction-reduced environment: Yes
Tape recording in class: Yes
Books on tape from RFBD: Yes
Taping of books not from RFBD: Yes
Accommodations for students with ADHD: Yes
Reading machine: Yes
Other assistive technology: No
Priority registration: N/A
Added costs for services: Yes

LD specialists: Yes
Professional tutors: 5
Peer tutors: 2
Max. hours/wk. for services: 3
How professors are notified of LD/ADHD: By both student and director

GENERAL ADMISSIONS INFORMATION

Director of Admissions: Terrance Kizina, Director
Telephone: 814-871-5759

ENTRANCE REQUIREMENTS

Academic units required: 4 English, 12 combination of remaining academic units based on planned major. High school diploma is required, and GED is accepted. ACT with or without Writing component accepted. TOEFL required of all international applicants, minimum paper TOEFL 500, minimum computer TOEFL 173.

Application deadline: NR
Notification: Rolling
Average GPA: 3.26
ACT Composite middle 50% range: 19–24

SAT Math middle 50% range: 460–580
SAT Critical Reading middle 50% range: 460–540
SAT Writing middle 50% range: NR

Graduated top 10% of class: 19%
Graduated top 25% of class: 44%
Graduated top 50% of class: 75%

COLLEGE GRADUATION REQUIREMENTS

Course waivers allowed: No
Course substitutions allowed: Yes
In what course: Substitutions for foreign language and mathematics in certain circumstances.

ADDITIONAL INFORMATION

Environment: The university is located on 13 acres in Erie, an urban area 135 miles north of Pittsburgh.

Student Body
  Undergrad enrollment: 2,457
  Women: 60%
  Men: 40%
  Percent out-of-state: 21%

Cost Information
Housing Information
  Tuition: $18,690
  Room & Board: $7,410
  University housing: Yes
  Percent living on campus: 47%

Greek System
  Fraternity: Yes
  Sorority: Yes
Athletics: Division II

KUTZTOWN U. OF PENNSYLVANIA

Admissions Office, PO Box 730, Kutztown, PA 19530-0730
Phone: 610-683-4060 • Fax: 610-683-1375
E-mail: admission@kutztown.edu • Web: www.kutztown.edu
Support: CS • Institution type: 4-year public

LEARNING DISABILITY PROGRAM AND SERVICES

The philosophy of the university is to provide equal opportunity to all individuals. Services for Students with Disabilities provide all necessary and reasonable services while fostering independence in the students. The services provided are in accordance with the needs of the students and the academic integrity of the institution. The office acts as an information and referral resource, provides direct services, coordinates services provided by other departments/agencies, and serves as a liaison between students with disabilities and u niversity personnel working with students. Since information regarding a student's disability is not obtained through the admission process, it is the student's responsibility upon acceptance to the university to identify him- or herself to the program. Students are encouraged to do this as early as possible upon admission or even when contemplating applying to the university. This will provide an opportunity to assess the university's capability of responding to special needs and the services available at the university. The ADA/504 coordinator works together with all university offices to help provide specific services as warranted by a diagnosis or clear need, as well as provide creative solutions to problems with which students with disabilities are confronted.

LD/ADHD ADMISSIONS INFORMATION

College entrance tests required: Yes
Interview required: No
Essay recommended: No
Documentation required for LD: Psychoeducational evaluation
Documentation required for ADHD: Yes
Submitted to: Services for Students with Disabilities
Special Ed. HS course work accepted: Yes

Specific course requirements of all applicants: Yes
Separate application required: No
# of LD applications submitted each year: NR
# of LD applications accepted yearly: NR
Total # of students receiving LD services: 278
Acceptance into program means acceptance into college: Students must be admitted to and enrolled in the university first and then request services.

ADMISSIONS

There is no special admissions process for students with learning disabilities. All applicants are expected to meet the same admission criteria, which include college-prep courses and an SAT Reasoning score of 900 or an ACT score of 19, with exceptions. Admission requirements are not so high that they impede access. An Admissions Exceptions Committee considers applications that may warrant exceptions to the general admission standards. Students may enter through Extended Learning, and upon earning 21 credits, a student may be considered for regular matriculation. In-state residents who do not predict a 2.0 GPA may be considered for a 5-week summer developmental studies session.

ADDITIONAL INFORMATION

The Coordinator of Human Diversity Programming is the initial resource person and record keeper who validates the existence of a disability and the need for any specific accommodations, and contacts faculty and other individuals who have reason to receive information. Academic assistance is provided through the Tutoring Center. Students with LD are eligible to receive services and accommodations prescribed in the psychoeducational evaluation, extended time on exams, use of tape recorder, use of calculator, testing in a separate location, readers, spellchecker and grammar check on written assignments, scribes, 4-track cassette, tutorial assistance, early advisement and pre-registration, computer assistive technology, and referrals. Individualized study skills assessments are made, and tutorial assistance is provided. Skills classes are offered in study skills, stress management, and remedial math, English and reading, and ESL. Tutors are available to all students, and arrangements are made at no cost to the student.

LEARNING DISABILITY PROGRAM/SERVICES

Learning Disability Program/Services: Services for Students with Disabilities
Director: Patricia Richter
  E-mail: richter@kutztown.edu
  Telephone: 610-683-4108
  Fax: 610-683-1520

LEARNING DISABILITY SERVICES

Requests for the following services/accommodations will be evaluated individually based on appropriate and current documentation.

Allowed in exams
  Calculator: Yes
  Dictionary: Yes
  Computer: Yes
  Spellchecker: Yes
Extended test time: Yes
Scribes: Yes
Proctors: Yes
Oral exams: Yes
Note-takers: Yes

Distraction-reduced environment: Yes
Tape recording in class: Yes
Books on tape from RFBD: Yes
Taping of books not from RFBD: Yes
Accommodations for students with ADHD: Yes
Reading machine: Yes
Other assistive technology: Yes
Priority registration: Yes

Added costs for services: No
LD specialists: Yes
Professional tutors: No
Peer tutors: Yes
Max. hours/wk. for services: Unlimited
How professors are notified of LD/ADHD: By both student and director

GENERAL ADMISSIONS INFORMATION

Director of Admissions: Dr. William Stahler
Telephone: 610-683-4060

ENTRANCE REQUIREMENTS

Academic units recommended: 4 English, 3 math, 3 science, 2 foreign language, 4 social studies. High school diploma is required, and GED is accepted. ACT with or without Writing component accepted. TOEFL required of all international applicants: minimum paper TOEFL 500, minimum computer TOEFL 173.

Application deadline: NR
Notification: Rolling
Average GPA: 3.10
ACT Composite middle 50% range: 18–21

SAT Math middle 50% range: 440–540
SAT Critical Reading middle 50% range: 450–540
SAT Writing middle 50% range: 430–530

Graduated top 10% of class: 6%
Graduated top 25% of class: 25%
Graduated top 50% of class: 64%

COLLEGE GRADUATION REQUIREMENTS

Course waivers allowed: No
Course substitutions allowed: Yes
In what course: Only with strong diagnostic recommendation through the Undergraduate Exceptions Committee, foreign language and math

ADDITIONAL INFORMATION

Environment: The university is located on 325 acres in a rural area 90 miles north of Philadelphia.

Student Body
  Undergrad enrollment: 8,616
  Women: 58%
  Men: 42%
  Percent out-of-state: 9%

Cost Information
  In-state tuition: $6,000
  Out-of-state tuition: $12,900
  Room & board: $6,628
Housing Information
  University housing: Yes
  Percent living on campus: 49%

Greek System
  Fraternity: Yes
  Sorority: Yes
Athletics: Division II

LEHIGH UNIVERSITY

27 Memorial Drive West, Bethlehem, PA 18015
Phone: 610-758-3100 • Fax: 610-758-4361
E-mail: admissions@lehigh.edu • Web: www.lehigh.edu
Support: CS • Institution type: 4-year private

LEARNING DISABILITY PROGRAM AND SERVICES

Lehigh University is committed to ensuring reasonable accommodations to students who are substantially limited by a diagnosed disability. Lehigh students with learning disabilities have met the same competitive requirements for admission as all other Lehigh students. Once admitted, students may request support services with appropriate documentation. Students requesting academic accommodations are required to submit for review current documentation of their disability. If a student is not certain whether he or she has a learning disability, the Director of Academic Support Services can conduct a comprehensive intake interview and screening process. If a complete diagnostic evaluation seems appropriate, the student will be provided with referrals to community-based professionals who can perform a comprehensive evaluation at the student's expense. The ultimate goal is to ensure that students with disabilities have an opportunity to grow independently to their fullest potential at a competitive university. It is the responsibility of students with disabilities to identify themselves to the appropriate university contact person and provide the required documentation to receive accommodations. Given the specific nature of each person's disability, reasonable accommodations will be determined on an individual basis by the appropriate university contact person. Students who are eligible for accommodations must sign a professor notification and accommodation form at the beginning of each semester that students are requesting accommodations.

LD/ADHD ADMISSIONS INFORMATION

College entrance tests required: Yes
Interview required: No
Essay recommended: No
Documentation required for LD: A current, comprehensive psychoeducational evaluation is required. Please check the guidelines for documentation on Lehigh's website.
Documentation required for ADHD: A current, comprehensive psychoeducational or neuropsychological evaluation.
Submitted to: Office of Academic Support Services

Special Ed. HS course work accepted: No
Specific course requirements of all applicants: Yes
Separate application required: No
# of LD applications submitted each year: 25
# of LD applications accepted yearly: 25
Total # of students receiving LD services: 94
Acceptance into program means acceptance into college: Students must be admitted and enrolled prior to requesting services.

ADMISSIONS

There is no special admission process for students with learning disabilities. All applicants must meet the same admission criteria. Applicants must submit either the SAT Reasoning Test or the ACT with the optional Writing section. An on-campus interview is recommended. Applicants' evaluations are based on many factors, including a challenging college-prep curriculum that included AP and honors courses.

ADDITIONAL INFORMATION

The Peer Mentor Program assists first-year students with the transition from high school to a competitive university. The peer mentors are composed of upperclass students who have a diagnosed learning disability or attention deficit hyperactivity disorder. Each mentor has demonstrated leadership capability and has been academically successful at Lehigh University. First-year students are matched with a peer mentor by college and/or major. The rationale for matching students in this manner is because upperclass students of the same major and/or college have most likely taken the same courses and professors and have experienced the same challenges as the freshman with whom they have been matched. The first-year students who have participated in the Peer Mentor Program and who have worked with the Office of Academic Support Services have traditionally performed significantly better than students who have not participated in support services. Program participation is voluntary, and students may choose to withdraw from the program at any time. The Center for Writing and Math provides assistance with any writing assignments, including brainstorming, rough-draft preparations, and critiques of final draft and assistance in calculus and other math courses. The Center for Academic Success has peer tutors available in most freshman- and sophomore-level courses. Ten free hours of tutoring per course per semester are provided. The tutors provide assistance with study skills, note-taking skills, and time management techniques.

LEARNING DISABILITY PROGRAM/SERVICES

Learning Disability Program/Services: Office of Academic Support Services
Director: Cheryl A. Ashcroft
  E-mail: caa4@lehigh.edu
  Telephone: 610-758-4152
  Fax: 610-758-5293

LEARNING DISABILITY SERVICES

Requests for the following services/accommodations will be evaluated individually based on appropriate and current documentation.

Allowed in exams
  Calculator: No
  Dictionary: No
  Computer: Yes
  Spellchecker: No
Extended test time: Yes
Scribes: Yes
Proctors: Yes
Oral exams: No
Note-takers: Yes

Distraction-reduced environment: No
Tape recording in class: Yes
Books on tape from RFBD: Yes
Taping of books not from RFBD: No
Accommodations for students with ADHD: Yes
Reading machine: Yes
Other assistive technology: No
Priority registration: No

Added costs for services: No
LD specialists: Yes
Professional tutors: 3
Peer tutors: 30
Max. hours/wk. for services: NR
How professors are notified of LD/ADHD: By both student and director

GENERAL ADMISSIONS INFORMATION

Director of Admissions: J. Bruce Gardiner
Telephone: 610-758-3100

ENTRANCE REQUIREMENTS
Academic units required: 4 English, 3 math, 2 science (2 science labs), 2 foreign language, 2 social studies, 3 academic electives. High school diploma or equivalent is not required. ACT with Writing component required. TOEFL required of all international applicants: minimum paper TOEFL 570, minimum computer TOEFL 230.

Application deadline: 1/1
Notification: NR
Average GPA: NR
ACT Composite middle 50% range: NR

SAT Math middle 50% range: 640–720
SAT Critical Reading middle 50% range: 580–670
SAT Writing middle 50% range: NR

Graduated top 10% of class: 90%
Graduated top 25% of class: 99%
Graduated top 50% of class: 100%

COLLEGE GRADUATION REQUIREMENTS

Course waivers allowed: No
Course substitutions allowed: No

ADDITIONAL INFORMATION

Environment: Lehigh is located 60 miles north of Philadelphia and 80 miles southwest of New York City.

Student Body
  Undergrad enrollment: 4,719
  Women: 42%
  Men: 58%
  Percent out-of-state: 73%

Cost Information
  Tuition: $35,310
  Room & board: $9,340
Housing Information
  University housing: Yes
  Percent living on campus: 70%

Greek System
  Fraternity: Yes
  Sorority: Yes
Athletics: Division I

MARYWOOD UNIVERSITY

2300 Adams Avenue, Scranton PA 18509
Phone: 570-348-6211 • Fax: 570-961-4763
E-mail: yourfuture@marywood.edu • Web: www.marywood.edu
Support: S • Institution Type: 4-year private

LEARNING DISABILITY PROGRAM AND SERVICES

Marywood University is committed to providing an environment that is accessible to all students, regardless of disability type. Through the Office of Disability Services, we have helped facilitate the education of students who have disabilities by coordinating a variety of services that support the unique academic needs of permanently and temporarily disabled students. The Office of Disability Services also works to ensure policies, procedures, and practices within the university environment do not discriminate against students because they have a disability. The Office of Disability Services provides individualized support to all students with disabilities. This support includes academic advising, advocacy, awareness, and accommodations. The Office of Disability Services assists students in developing strategies for time management, organization, study skills, test preparation, and transition to and beyond life at the university. We also assist with solving problems and provide information about other community resources.

LD/ADHD ADMISSIONS INFORMATION

College entrance tests required: Yes
Interview required: No
Essay required: No
Documentation required for LD: Complete psychoeducational report; IEP/504 service plan suggested, no more than 4 years old.
Documentation required for ADD: Complete psychoeducational report; IEP/504 service plan suggested, no more than 4 years old.
Specific course requirements of all applicants: Yes
Submitted to: Admissions and Disability Services

Special Ed HS course work accepted: Yes
Separate application required for program services: No
# of LD applications submitted each year: NR
# of LD applications accepted each year: NR
Total # of students receiving LD services: N/A
Acceptance into program means acceptance into college: Students must be admitted based upon standard acceptance criteria with allowance for accommodations.

ADMISSIONS

All applicants must meet the same admission criteria. There is an extensive application process, including official high school transcripts (and college if applicable), letters of recommendation, SAT/ACT and a review by the Admissions Office/Committee. Admissions requirements include approximately top 50 percent of high school class or high school 6-semester overall GPA of 2.25 or equivalent, 900 or higher SAT (CR+M only), or 19 ACT composite score. High school units required include 4 units of English, 3 units of social science, 2 units of math, 1 unit of lab science, and 6 additional units to fulfill graduation requirements. Some students who meet established eligibility requirements including adjusted family income levels may be admitted through the ACT 101 program. This program requires attendance of a summer program at Marywood University. For further information concerning the ACT 101 program, please contact that office directly. Marywood University makes all efforts to avoid any possible prejudice in the admissions process. Students with disabilities are encouraged to self-disclose and request an interview with the Disability Services Director. The director can then make an informed recommendation to the Admissions Office/Committee regarding a student's ability to succeed at Marywood.

ADDITIONAL INFORMATION:

Students with disabilities may also find the services provided through the Academic Excellence Center to be helpful. These services are available for all Marywood students. The Academic Excellence Center (AEC) supports students in their efforts to become excellent learners and provides dynamic learning assistance services to increase student achievement and foster active involvement in the learning process. Services include tutoring, college-level study skill information, and a Writing Center staffed by both peer tutors and a professional writing tutor.

LEARNING DISABILITY PROGRAM/SERVICES

Learning Disability Program/Services: Office of Disability Services
Coordinator: Diane Taylor (interim)
  E-mail: dtaylor@marywood.edu
  Telephone: 570-340-6045
  Fax: 570-340-6028

LEARNING DISABILITY SERVICES

Requests for the following/services accommodations will be evaluated individually based on appropriate and current documentation.

Allowed in exams
  Calculator: Yes
  Dictionary: Yes
  Computer: Yes
  Spellchecker: Yes
Extended test time: Yes
Scribes: Yes
Proctors: Yes
Oral Exams: Yes
Note-takers: Yes

Distraction reduced environment: Yes
Tape recording in class: Yes
Books on tape from RFBD: Yes
Taping of books not from RFBD: No
Accommodations for students with ADD: Yes
Reading machine: Yes
Other assistive technology: Yes
Priority registration: No
Added costs for services: No

LD specialists: No
Professional tutors: 1
Peer tutors: 120
Max. hours/wk. for services: Unlimited
How professors are notified of LD/ADD: By both student and coordinator

GENERAL ADMISSIONS INFORMATION

Director of Admissions: Robert Reese
Telephone: 570-348-6234

ENTRANCE REQUIREMENTS
Academic units required: 4 English, 3 social science, 2 math, 1 science lab, 6 additional units.
High school Diploma is required, and GED is accepted. SAT is preferred, and ACT is accepted. TOEFL is required of all international applicants.

Application Deadline: Rolling
Notification: Rolling
Average GPA: 3.30

Average SAT Math: 514
Average SAT Verbal: 513
Average ACT: VI

Graduated top 10% of class: 19%
Graduated top 25% of class: 45%
Graduated top 50% of class: 81%

COLLEGE GRADUATION REQUIREMENTS

Course waivers allowed: No
Course substitutions allowed: Yes
In what courses: Foreign Language, math and others on case-by-case basis

ADDITIONAL INFORMATION

Environment: Situated on a hill top, Marywood's scenic 115-acre campus is part of an attractive residential area of the city of Scranton in northeastern Pennsylvania.

Student Body
  Undergraduate enrollment: 1,896
  Women: 72%
  Men: 28%
  Percent out-of-state: 24%

Cost Information:
  Tuition: $21,840
  Room & board: $9,690
Housing Information:
  University housing: Yes
  Percent living on campus: 70%

Greek System:
  Fraternity: No
  Sorority: No
Athletics: NCAA Division III

MERCYHURST COLLEGE

Admissions, 501 East Thirty-eighth Street, Erie, PA 16546
Phone: 814-824-2202 • Fax: 814-824-2071
E-mail: admissions@mercyhurst.edu • Web: www.mercyhurst.edu
Support: SP • Institution type: 4-year private

LEARNING DISABILITY PROGRAM AND SERVICES

The specialized program at Mercyhurst College is designed to assist students who have been identified as having LD. The emphasis is on students' individual strengths, abilities, and interests, as well as learning deficits. This program consists of a structured, individualized set of experiences designed to assist students with LD to get maximum value from their educational potential and earn a college degree. Students selecting the structured program for students with learning differences pay an additional fee for this service and must submit a recent psychological evaluation that includes the WAIS or WISC–R scores (completed within the past 2 years); three letters of recommendation, one each from a math, English, and LD teacher or guidance counselor; SAT/ACT scores; and a written statement from a professional documenting the student's learning disability. Students choosing the structured program option must attend a summer session prior to entrance; classes may include learning strategies, basic writing, communications, career planning, and computer competency. The program lasts 5 weeks and costs approximately $1,600 (includes room, board, and tuition). Students with learning differences who feel that they do not require a structured program may opt to receive support services through the Academic Support Center at no additional charge.

LD/ADHD ADMISSIONS INFORMATION

College entrance tests required: Yes
Interview required: Yes
Essay recommended: No
Documentation required for LD: Aptitude tests (e.g., WAIS–R or WAIS–III with subtest scores), achievement tests (e.g., WAIT), information processing tests (e.g., short- and long-term memory), conducted within the past 3 years
Documentation required for ADHD: Students must provide DSM–IV diagnosis and pharmacological history. Forms need to be completed by a licensed medical provider.
Submitted to: Admissions Office
Special Ed. HS course work accepted: No

Specific course requirements of all applicants: Yes
Separate application required: No
# of LD applications submitted each year: 80
# of LD applications accepted yearly: 35
Total # of students receiving LD services: 75
Acceptance into program means acceptance into college: Students must be admitted to and enrolled in the university first and then request services.

ADMISSIONS

To be eligible for any of the services at Mercyhurst, students with learning disabilities must adhere to the regular admission requirements and meet the regular admission criteria. General admission criteria include a 2.5 GPA; ACT 19-plus or SAT 900-plus; and 4 years of English, 2 years of social science, 3 years of math, 2 years of science, and 2 years of a foreign language (waivers and substitutions are determined on an individual basis). Students who do not meet the regular admissions standards are referred to Mercyhurst—McAuley and/or Mercyhurst—Northeast for consideration into the 2-year division. Some students may be admitted on probation pending the completion of developmental course work. The college reserves the right to reject any student not meeting admission standards. The admission decisions are made jointly by the director of Programs for Students with Learning Differences and the Office of Admissions. Upon acceptance to the college, if the student wishes special services, he or she must identify him- or herself to the Admissions Office and, at that time, choose to receive services in one of two options available to students with documented learning differences. These programs are a structured program and a basic service program.

ADDITIONAL INFORMATION

The Structured Program for Students with Learning Differences provides special services, including an advisory board, advocacy, alternative testing, books on tape though RFBD, community skills, drop-in services, access to a Kurzweil Personal Reader, midterm progress reports, note-takers, peer tutoring, professional advising/priority registration, a special 5-week summer orientation program prior to freshman year, special section of basic writing, special section of math problem solving, study hall (required of all freshman), and a support group.

LEARNING DISABILITY PROGRAM/SERVICES

Learning Disability Program/Services: Program for Students with Learning Differences
Director: Dianne Rogers
  E-mail: drogers@mercyhurst.edu
  Telephone: 814-824-2450
  Fax: 814-824-2436

LEARNING DISABILITY SERVICES

Requests for the following services/accommodations will be evaluated individually based on appropriate and current documentation.

Allowed in exams
  Calculator: Yes
  Dictionary: Yes
  Computer: Yes
  Spellchecker: Yes
Extended test time: Yes
Scribes: Yes
Proctors: Yes
Oral exams: Yes
Note-takers: Yes

Distraction-reduced environment: Yes
Tape recording in class: Yes
Books on tape from RFBD: Yes
Taping of books not from RFBD: Yes
Accommodations for students with ADHD: Yes
Reading machine: Yes
Other assistive technology: Yes
Priority registration: Yes

Added costs for services: Yes
LD specialists: Yes
Professional tutors: No
Peer tutors: 30
Max. hours/wk. for services: Unlimited
How professors are notified of LD/ADHD: By both student and director

GENERAL ADMISSIONS INFORMATION

Director of Admissions: J.P. Cooney
Telephone: 814-824-2202

ENTRANCE REQUIREMENTS

Academic units recommended: 4 English, 3 math, 3 science (1 science lab), 2 foreign language, 2 social studies, 2 history. High school diploma is required, and GED is accepted. ACT without Writing component accepted. TOEFL required of all international applicants: minimum paper TOEFL 550, minimum computer TOEFL 300.

Application deadline: Rolling
Notification: Rolling
Average GPA: 3.40
ACT Composite middle 50% range: 19–25

SAT Math middle 50% range: 490–590
SAT Critical Reading middle 50% range: 480–590
SAT Writing middle 50% range: NR

Graduated top 10% of class: 18%
Graduated top 25% of class: 43%
Graduated top 50% of class: 79%

COLLEGE GRADUATION REQUIREMENTS

Course waivers allowed: Yes
In what course: Foreign language
Course substitutions allowed: Yes
In what course: Foreign language, others as determined by faculty chair

ADDITIONAL INFORMATION

Environment: The 80-acre campus of Mercyhurst overlooks Lake Erie.

Student Body
  Undergrad enrollment: 3,537
  Women: 62%
  Men: 34%
  Percent out-of-state: 34%

Cost Information
  Tuition: $21,175
  Room & board: $7,450
Housing Information
  University housing: Yes
  Percent living on campus: 58%

Greek System
  Fraternity: No
  Sorority: No
Athletics: Division II

MESSIAH COLLEGE

PO Box 3005, One College Avenue, Grantham, PA 17027
Phone: 717-691-6000 • Fax: 717-796-5374
E-mail: admiss@messiah.edu • Web: www.messiah.edu
Support: S • Institution type: 4-year private

LEARNING DISABILITY PROGRAM AND SERVICES

Messiah College is committed to making reasonable accommodations for qualified students who present evidence of a disability. Documentation is reviewed, and, if adequate for determining eligibility, a plan of assistance is worked out with the student. The Disabilities Services (DS) staff assists the student in identifying accommodations needed in various classes and in communicating these needs to faculty. Students must make an appointment with DS to receive assistance in reviewing documentation and determining appropriate accommodations. DS may also require additional documentation or evaluations for determination of eligibility. Any costs incurred for evaluation are the responsibility of the student. Students who do not have documentation, but who think they may have a disability, may seek assistance from DS in locating screening services on campus. Students who are encouraged to pursue determination of eligibility or support services, but choose not to at the time, will be asked to sign a form indicating their preference in waiving their rights temporarily. Students may change their minds at a later date, as long as they are actively enrolled at Messiah College.

LD/ADHD ADMISSIONS INFORMATION

College entrance tests required: Yes
Interview required: No
Essay recommended: No
Documentation required for LD: Complete psychoeducational report from a qualified examiner. An IEP/504 service plan is recommended to verify needs for accommodation.
Documentation required for ADHD: Complete psychoeducational report from a qualified examiner. An IEP/504 service plan is recommended to verify needs for accommodation.
Submitted to: Disability Services
Special Ed. HS course work accepted: Yes

Specific course requirements of all applicants: Yes
Separate application required: No
# of LD applications submitted each year: NR
# of LD applications accepted yearly: NR
Total # of students receiving LD services: 20–25
Acceptance into program means acceptance into college: Students must be admitted to and enrolled in the university first and then request services.

ADMISSIONS

All applicants must meet the same admission criteria. There is an extensive application process that includes submitting letters of recommendation, ACT/SAT scores, a high school transcript, and essays and a review by the Admissions Officer/Committee. Admission requirements include a minimum 3.0 GPA, 20 ACT or 1000 SAT, and 4 units of English, 2 units of math, 2 units of natural sciences, 2 units of social studies, and 6 electives (2 of these should be in foreign language). Foreign language is recommended, but alternatives are considered with appropriate documentation. Some applicants who are borderline candidates may be reviewed and admitted through a program called START. These students are required to attend a 2-week orientation prior to the beginning of freshman year. Messiah College makes all efforts to avoid any possible prejudice in the admission process. Students with disabilities are encouraged to self-disclose and request an interview with the DS director. The director can review the student's file and make a recommendation to the Office of Admissions regarding a student's ability to succeed in college. Additionally, self-disclosure of a disability alerts the DS office to the fact that the student has a potential disability that may make them eligible for accommodations.

ADDITIONAL INFORMATION

Commonly provided accommodations by Disability Services include extended time for test-taking, proctored exams in alternate locations, assistance with getting notes, hard copies of transparencies, advocacy with instructors, taped textbooks for nonreaders, peer tutoring, and referral source for other required services. Additionally, the Learning Center provides a range of tutorial services through trained peer tutors, and the Writing Center provides peer tutors for written projects. Developmental Services offers assistance with time management, motivation, goal setting, reading skills, note-taking, learning theory, and taking exams.

LEARNING DISABILITY PROGRAM/SERVICES

Learning Disability Program/Services: Disability Services
Director: Keith W. Drahn, PhD
  E-mail: kdrahn@messiah.edu
  Telephone: 717-796-5358
  Fax: 717-796-5217
Contact Person: Carol Wickey
  E-mail: kdrahn@messiah.edu
  Telephone: 717-796-5358

LEARNING DISABILITY SERVICES

Requests for the following services/accommodations will be evaluated individually based on appropriate and current documentation.

Allowed in exams
  Calculator: Yes
  Dictionary: Yes
  Computer: Yes
  Spellchecker: Yes
Extended test time: Yes
Scribes: Yes
Proctors: Yes
Oral exams: Yes
Note-takers: Yes

Distraction-reduced environment: Yes
Tape recording in class: Yes
Books on tape from RFBD: Yes
Taping of books not from RFBD: Yes
Accommodations for students with ADHD: Yes
Reading machine: Yes
Other assistive technology: Yes
Priority registration: Yes

Added costs for services: No
LD specialists: No
Professional tutors: No
Peer tutors: 16
Max. hours/wk. for services: Unlimited
How professors are notified of LD/ADHD: By student

GENERAL ADMISSIONS INFORMATION

Director of Admissions: Scott Morrell
  Telephone: 717-796-5374

ENTRANCE REQUIREMENTS
Academic units required: 4 English, 2 math, 2 science (2 science labs), 2 foreign language, 2 social studies, 4 academic electives. **Academic units recommended:** 4 English, 3 math, 3 science (3 science labs), 2 foreign language, 2 social studies, 2 history, 4 academic electives. High school diploma is required, and GED is accepted. ACT without Writing component accepted. TOEFL required of all international applicants: minimum paper TOEFL 550, minimum computer TOEFL 213.

Application deadline: Rolling
Notification: Rolling
Average GPA: 3.76
ACT Composite middle 50% range: 23–28

SAT Math middle 50% range: 540–650
SAT Critical Reading middle 50% range: 550–660
SAT Writing middle 50% range: NR

Graduated top 10% of class: 39%
Graduated top 25% of class: 71%
Graduated top 50% of class: 94%

COLLEGE GRADUATION REQUIREMENTS

Course waivers allowed: No
Course substitutions allowed: Yes
In what course: Foreign language substitutions from an approved list of courses

ADDITIONAL INFORMATION

Environment: The college is located on a hilly 400-acre campus within a 15-minute drive of Harrisburg.

Student Body
  Undergrad enrollment: 2,916
  Women: 63%
  Men: 37%
  Percent out-of-state: 48%

Cost Information
  Tuition: $22,600
  Room & board: $7,060
Housing Information
  University housing: Yes
  Percent living on campus: 84%

Greek System
  Fraternity: No
  Sorority: No
  Athletics: Division III

PENN. STATE U.—UNIVERSITY PARK

201 Shields Building, Box 3000, University Park, PA 16802-3000
Phone: 814-865-5471 • Fax: 814-863-7590
E-mail: admissions@psu.edu • Web: www.psu.edu
Support: S • Institution type: 4-year public

LEARNING DISABILITY PROGRAM AND SERVICES

The goal of Penn State's academic support services for students with learning disabilities is to ensure that students receive appropriate accommodations so that they can function independently and meet the academic demands of a competitive university. Students with learning disabilities should be able to complete college-level courses with the help of support services and classroom accommodations. To receive any of the support services, students must submit documentation of their learning disability to the learning disability specialist in the Office for Disability Services (ODS). Documentation should be a psychoeducational report from a certified or licensed psychologist completed within the past 3 years. The report should include measures of intellectual functioning (WAIS–III preferred) and measures of achievement that describe current levels of functioning in reading, mathematics, and written language. Students with ADHD should have the professional who diagnosed them complete the ADHD Verification Form and submit it to the Office for Disability Services.

LD/ADHD ADMISSIONS INFORMATION

College entrance tests required: Yes
Interview required: No
Essay recommended: No
Documentation required for LD: Psychoeducational evaluation
Documentation required for ADHD: Psychoeducational evaluation and diagnosis of ADHD
Submitted to: Support Program/Services
Special Ed. HS course work accepted: Yes
Specific course requirements of all applicants: NR
Separate application required: No
# of LD applications submitted each year: NR

# of LD applications accepted yearly: NR
Total # of students receiving LD services: 279
Acceptance into program means acceptance into college: Students must be admitted to and enrolled in the university first and then request services.

ADMISSIONS

There is no special application process for students with learning disabilities or attention deficit hyperactivity disorder, and these students are considered for admission on the same basis as other applicants. The minimum 50 percent of admitted students have a GPA between 3.47 and 3.85 and an ACT score between 26 and 30 or an SAT score between 1160 and 1340. Course requirements include 4 years of English, 3 years of math, 3 years of science, 2 years of a foreign language, and 3 years of social studies. If the applicant's high school grades and test scores are low, students may submit a letter explaining why their ability to succeed in college is higher than indicated by their academic records. The Admissions Office will consider this information as it is voluntarily provided. The acceptable ACT or SAT score will depend on the high school grades and class rank of the student. Two-thirds of the evaluation is based on high school grades and one-third on test scores. Once admitted, students must submit documentation of their learning disability to receive support services. Students may seek admission as a provisional or nondegree student if they do not meet criteria required for admission as a degree candidate. Any student may enroll as a nondegree student.

ADDITIONAL INFORMATION

Students with LD are encouraged to participate in the Buddy Program; incoming students are matched with a senior buddy who is a current student with a disability and is available to share experiences with a junior buddy. Other services include providing audiotaped textbooks, arranging course substitutions with academic departments (when essential requirements are not involved), providing test accommodations, and providing individual counseling. Assistance with note-taking is offered through the ODS. Services are offered in a mainstream setting. The Learning Assistance Center operates a Math Center, Tutoring Center, Writing Center, and Computer Learning Center. Students may receive academic help either individually or in small groups for a number of different courses. One-on-one academic assistance is available through the Office of Disability Services. Graduate clinicians provide individual assistance with study skills, time management, and compensatory learning strategies. Currently, 234 students with LD and 109 with ADHD are receiving services or accommodations.

LEARNING DISABILITY PROGRAM/SERVICES

Learning Disability Program/Services: Office for Disability Services (ODS)
Director: Bill Welsh
E-mail: wjw9@psu.edu
Telephone: 814-863-1807
Fax: 814-863-3217

LEARNING DISABILITY SERVICES

Requests for the following services/accommodations will be evaluated individually based on appropriate and current documentation.

Allowed in exams
Calculator: Yes
Dictionary: No
Computer: Yes
Spellchecker: No
Extended test time: Yes
Scribes: Yes
Proctors: Yes
Oral exams: Yes
Note-takers: Yes

Distraction-reduced environment: Yes
Tape recording in class: Yes
Books on tape from RFBD: Yes
Taping of books not from RFBD: Yes
Accommodations for students with ADHD: Yes
Reading machine: Yes
Other assistive technology: Yes
Priority registration: Yes

Added costs for services: No
LD specialists: No
Professional tutors: No
Peer tutors: Yes
Max. hours/wk. for services: Unlimited
How professors are notified of LD/ADHD: By student

GENERAL ADMISSIONS INFORMATION

Director of Admissions: Dr. Randall C. Deike
Telephone: 814-865-5471

ENTRANCE REQUIREMENTS

Academic units required: 4 English, 3 math, 3 science, 2 foreign language, 3 social studies. High school diploma is required, and GED is accepted. ACT with or without Writing component accepted. TOEFL required of all international applicants: minimum paper TOEFL 550, minimum computer TOEFL 213.

Application deadline: Rolling
Notification: Rolling
Average GPA: 3.53
ACT Composite middle 50% range: NR

SAT Math middle 50% range: 560–660
SAT Critical Reading middle 50% range: 520–620
SAT Writing middle 50% range: NR

Graduated top 10% of class: 37%
Graduated top 25% of class: 77%
Graduated top 50% of class: 98%

COLLEGE GRADUATION REQUIREMENTS

Course waivers allowed: No
Course substitutions allowed: Yes
In what course: Possibly foreign language if not essential to the major

ADDITIONAL INFORMATION

Environment: The school is located on more than 5,000 acres in a small city 90 miles west of Harrisburg.

Student Body
Undergrad enrollment: 35,711
Women: 45%
Men: 55%
Percent out-of-state: 23%

Cost Information
In-state tuition: $11,646
Out-of-state tuition: $22,194
Room & board: $6,850
Housing Information
University housing: Yes
Percent living on campus: 38%

Greek System
Fraternity: Yes
Sorority: Yes
Athletics: Division I

SETON HILL UNIVERSITY

One Seton Hill Drive, Greensburg, PA 15601
Phone: 724-838-4255 • Fax: 724-830-1294
E-mail: admit@setonhill.edu • Web: www.setonhill.edu
Support: S • Institution type: private

LEARNING DISABILITY PROGRAM AND SERVICES

Students who are eligible for, and are requesting, accommodations under the Americans with Disabilities ACT are required to register with the Coordinator of Disabled Student Services. Students work individually with the disability services coordinator to determine what learning or environmental supports are needed based on the documentation and recommendations for accommodations in the report. An individualized plan of accommodation will be developed with the student. It is the student's responsibility to implement the plan. The student should advise the coordinator of Disability Services if they experience any difficulties with their accommodation plan.

LD/ADHD ADMISSIONS INFORMATION

College entrance tests required: Yes
Interview required: No
Essay recommended: No
Documentation required for LD: Psychoeducational evaluation
Documentation required for ADHD: Statement of documented disability of ADHD from a qualified medical professional who is not related to the applicant
Submitted to: Disability Services
Special Ed. HS course work accepted: NR

Specific course requirements of all applicants: Yes
Separate application required: No
# of LD applications submitted each year: NR
# of LD applications accepted yearly: NR
Total # of students receiving LD services: NR
Acceptance into program means acceptance into college: Students must be admitted to and enrolled in the university first and then request services.

ADMISSIONS

The admissions process is the same for all students. Those with documentation supporting a disability are given the option of meeting with the disability services coordinator. There is a summer program that targets math, English, and study skills. These are required programs for students with weak transcripts or SAT/ACT scores who otherwise meet admissions standards. Students with documented learning disabilities may request course substitutions for deficiencies in entrance courses based on the LD. Preadmission interviews are not required but are recommended.

ADDITIONAL INFORMATION

Accommodations may include, but are not limited to, priority registration, preferential seating, note-taking services, tape-recorded lectures, extended time for projects, extended time for quizzes and tests, testing in distraction-free environments, alternative testing formats, tutoring, counseling, course substitutions, use of assisted technologies (e.g., spellcheckers), computer-based programs, and scribe services. Students are responsible for notifying professors about their disability and requesting accommodations. Course substitution requests are reviewed and considered on an individual basis. Skills classes for college credit are offered in time management techniques, note-taking strategies, test-taking strategies, and text reading.

LEARNING DISABILITY PROGRAM/SERVICES

Learning Disability Program/Services: Disability Services
Director: Teresa A. Bassi
  E-mail: bassi@setonhill.edu
  Telephone: 724-838-4295
  Fax: 724-830-4233

LEARNING DISABILITY SERVICES

Requests for the following services/accommodations will be evaluated individually based on appropriate and current documentation.

Allowed in exams	**Distraction-reduced environment:** Yes	**Added costs for services:** No
Calculator: Yes	**Tape recording in class:** Yes	**LD specialists:** No
Dictionary: Yes	**Books on tape from RFBD:** Yes	**Professional tutors:** No
Computer: Yes	**Taping of books not from RFBD:** Yes	**Peer tutors:** 60
Spellchecker: Yes	**Accommodations for students with**	**Max. hours/wk. for services:**
Extended test time: Yes	**ADHD:** Yes	Unlimited
Scribes: Yes	**Reading machine:** Yes	**How professors are notified of**
Proctors: Yes	**Other assistive technology:** Yes	**LD/ADHD:** By student
Oral exams: Yes	**Priority registration:** Yes	
Note-takers: Yes		

GENERAL ADMISSIONS INFORMATION

Director of Admissions: Kim McCarty
Telephone: 724-838-4255

ENTRANCE REQUIREMENTS

Academic units required: 4 English, 2 math, 1 science (1 science lab), 2 social studies, 4 academic electives.
Academic units recommended: 4 English, 2 math, 1 science (1 science lab), 2 foreign language, 2 social studies, 4 academic electives. High school diploma is required, and GED is accepted. ACT without Writing component accepted. TOEFL required of all international applicants: minimum paper TOEFL 550, minimum computer TOEFL 213.

Application deadline: 8/15	**SAT Math middle 50% range:**	**Graduated top 10% of class:** 18%
Notification: Rolling	440–560	**Graduated top 25% of class:** 40%
Average GPA: 3.16	**SAT Critical Reading middle 50%**	**Graduated top 50% of class:** 73%
ACT Composite middle 50% range:	**range:** 450–550	
NR	**SAT Writing middle 50% range:** NR	

COLLEGE GRADUATION REQUIREMENTS

Course waivers allowed: Yes
In what course: All appropriate waivers are reviewed and considered. Essential elements of a students program of student cannot be waived.
Course substitutions allowed: Yes
In what course: All appropriate substitutions are reviewed and considered. Essential elements of a students program of student cannot be substituted.

ADDITIONAL INFORMATION

Environment: The campus is located 35 miles east of Pittsburgh.

Student Body	**Cost Information**	**Greek System**
Undergrad enrollment: 1,374	**Tuition:** $23,180	**Fraternity:** No
Women: 62%	**Room & board:** $7,230	**Sorority:** No
Men: 38%	**Housing Information**	**Athletics:** NCAA
Percent out-of-state: 20%	**University housing:** Yes	
	Percent living on campus: 61%	

TEMPLE UNIVERSITY

1801 North Broad Street, Philadelphia, PA 19122-6096
Phone: 215-204-7200 • Fax: 215-204-5694
E-mail: tuadm@temple.edu • Web: www.temple.edu
Support: CS • Institution type: 4-year public

LEARNING DISABILITY PROGRAM AND SERVICES

Disability Resources and Services (DRS) is the primary department for disability-related information and services. DRS arranges academic adjustments and accommodations for students. Students must meet with their DRS advisor and review recommended academic adjustments. Documentation submitted for consideration should contain the specific diagnosis and indicate the source used to make this determination. Students may take a copy of an accommodation letter prepared by DRS staff to their professors at the start of each semester. Faculty members cannot retroactively provide academic adjustments for course requirements for students who have not previously presented a letter supporting such requests. Faculty may not alter the essential function of a course. Discussions of disability-related needs and ways to adjust course requirements can be developed. As changes occur, updated information describing new requests must be provided.

LD/ADHD ADMISSIONS INFORMATION

College entrance tests required: Yes
Interview required: No
Essay recommended: No
Documentation required for LD: Psychoeducational test results and recommendations
Documentation required for ADHD: Psychoeducational, neurological, or other relevant medical assessment with educationally based recommendations
Submitted to: DRS
Special Ed. HS course work accepted: Yes

Specific course requirements of all applicants: Yes
Separate application required: No
# of LD applications submitted each year: NR
# of LD applications accepted yearly: NR
Total # of students receiving LD services: 450
Acceptance into program means acceptance into college: Students must be admitted to and enrolled in the university first and then request services.

ADMISSIONS

DRS staff encourage students with LD/ADHD to use available accommodations/adjustments when taking standardized admissions examinations. In situations where standardized exams do not reflect academic potential because of a disability, applicants are encouraged to discuss anticipated strategies for success and explanations of past performance in a personal statement. General admission requirements include 4 years of English, 3–4 years of math, 2–3 years of a foreign language, 3 years of social studies, 1 year of science, 1 year of art, and 5 years other liberal arts/college-prep courses. Students may begin with a reduced load of courses. A 6-week summer program is available for selected students (not specifically designed for students with LD).

ADDITIONAL INFORMATION

Making the grade is a summer postsecondary transition program developed for high school graduates who have disabilities. Program goals include developing interpersonal skills, developing time management strategies, experiencing residential life, developing strategies for reading and writing, developing note-taking and organizational techniques, developing test-taking proficiencies, articulating an understanding of personal strengths and goals, and practicing self-advocacy approaches. There is a Math Lab, a Writing Lab, tutoring, and a study skills program. Assistive technology available includes Dragon Naturally Speaking, Jaws, LDDeluxe, and Alphasmart. Skills classes are offered in time management, test strategies, and reading strategies. Career recruitment, peer coaching, and support counseling are also available. Students experiencing difficulty in areas such as foreign language or math that are not essential to a specific major should meet with DRS staff to discuss alternatives and procedures.

LEARNING DISABILITY PROGRAM/SERVICES

Learning Disability Program/Services: Disability Resources and Services (DRS)
Director: John Bennett
   E-mail: john.bennett@temple.edu
   Telephone: 215-204-1280
   Fax: 215-204-6794

LEARNING DISABILITY SERVICES

Requests for the following services/accommodations will be evaluated individually based on appropriate and current documentation.

Allowed in exams
   Calculator: Yes
   Dictionary: Yes
   Computer: Yes
   Spellchecker: Yes
Extended test time: Yes
Scribes: Yes
Proctors: Yes
Oral exams: Yes
Note-takers: Yes

Distraction-reduced environment: Yes
Tape recording in class: Yes
Books on tape from RFBD: Yes
Taping of books not from RFBD: Yes
Accommodations for students with
   ADHD: Yes
Reading machine: Yes
Other assistive technology: Yes
Priority registration: N/A

Added costs for services: No
LD specialists: Yes
Professional tutors: No
Peer tutors: No
Max. hours/wk. for services: N/A
How professors are notified of
   LD/ADHD: By student

GENERAL ADMISSIONS INFORMATION

Director of Admissions: Dr. Timm Rinehart
Telephone: 215-204-8556

ENTRANCE REQUIREMENTS

Academic units required: 4 English, 3 math, 2 science (1 science lab), 2 foreign language, 3 social studies, 1 history, 1 academic elective. **Academic units recommended:** 4 English, 4 math, 3 science (2 science labs), 2 foreign language, 2 social studies, 2 history, 3 academic electives. High school diploma is required, and GED is accepted. ACT with Writing component required. TOEFL required of all international applicants: minimum paper TOEFL 527, minimum computer TOEFL 197.

Application deadline: 4/1
Notification: Rolling
Average GPA: 3.26
ACT Composite middle 50% range:
   20–25

SAT Math middle 50% range:
   500–600
SAT Critical Reading middle 50%
   range: 490–590
SAT Writing middle 50% range:
   480–580

Graduated top 10% of class: 18%
Graduated top 25% of class: 50%
Graduated top 50% of class: 88%

COLLEGE GRADUATION REQUIREMENTS

Course waivers allowed: Yes
In what course: Foreign language, math
Course substitutions allowed: Yes
In what course: Students can petition for substitutions for math or foreign language. Substitutions must be approved by each college's academic committee. Documentation that specifically recommends this as an accommodation must be on file in the LDSS.

ADDITIONAL INFORMATION

Environment: The university is located on a 76-acre urban campus.

Student Body
   Undergrad enrollment: 24,070
   Women: 55%
   Men: 45%
   Percent out-of-state: 22%

Cost Information
   In-state tuition: $9,680
   Out-of-state tuition: $17,724
   Room & board: $8,230
Housing Information
   University housing: Yes
   Percent living on campus: 20%

Greek System
   Fraternity: Yes
   Sorority: Yes
Athletics: Division I

Temple University

UNIVERSITY OF PITTSBURGH

4227 Fifth Avenue, First Floor, Alumni Hall, Pittsburgh, PA 15260
Phone: 412-624-7488 • Fax: 412-648-8815
E-mail: oafa@pitt.edu • Web: www.pitt.edu
Support: CS • Institution type: 4-year public

LEARNING DISABILITY PROGRAM AND SERVICES

To access services, students must refer themselves to Disability Resource Services (DRS) and submit documentation of their learning disability. Once eligibility is established, students meet regularly with a DRS learning specialist who will assist the student in accessing resources and developing an individualized, comprehensive educational program. The objective of DRS is to work closely with students to empower them to plan and implement a successful academic experience. The Transition Program is a program designed to assist students with LD in their transition into the university through the exploration and development of self-awareness and self-advocacy skills and to educate students in the use of learning strategies designed to compensate for limitations imposed by their disability. The objective of this program is to positively impact the retention, matriculation, and academic performance of students with LD through the provision of transferable skills necessary for academic work and to foster self-reliance and independence. Participants attend one group session weekly to discuss self-advocacy, rights and responsibilities, and general skills and strategies. Students also meet weekly with a DRS learning specialist to focus on individualized strategies and skills. There is no fee for these services.

LD/ADHD ADMISSIONS INFORMATION

College entrance tests required: Yes
Interview required: N/A
Essay recommended: N/A
Documentation required for LD: Full neuropsychological evaluation completed withinn the past 5 years
Documentation required for ADHD: Neuropsychological evaluation or comprehensive report from a qualified professional
Submitted to: DRS
Special Ed. HS course work accepted: No

Specific course requirements of all applicants: Yes
Separate application required: No
# of LD applications submitted each year: NR
# of LD applications accepted yearly: NR
Total # of students receiving LD services: 222
Acceptance into program means acceptance into college: Students must be admitted to and enrolled in the university first and then request services.

ADMISSIONS

Students with Learning Disabilities must meet the admission criteria established for all applicants. These criteria include an ACT score of 22 or an SAT score of 1000, a class rank in top 40 percent, and college-prep courses. Students may be admitted on probation for one term, and having met the continuation policy at a minimum GPA of 2.0, will be permitted to continue. This applies only in the College of General Studies.

ADDITIONAL INFORMATION

DRS individually designs and recommends services to enhance the skills and personal development of the student. Services available may include exam accommodations; use of calculators, dictionaries, computers, or spellcheckers during exams; scribes; proctors; distraction-free environments; taped textbooks; instructional strategy assistance; and adaptive computers. There are two LD specialists on staff. Students with documented disabilities may schedule weekly one-on-one meetings to identify potential barriers to success and to learn new strategies to reach academic goals. General topics include executive functioning skills; test analysis; note-taking; active reading; utilizing accommodations; disability counseling; and self-advocacy. Students are encouraged to meet regularly with the disability specialist to review the effectiveness of services received, to update information, or to discuss changes in service.

LEARNING DISABILITY PROGRAM/SERVICES

Learning Disability Program/Services: Disability Resources and Services (DRS)
Director: Lynnett Van Slyke
 E-mail: vanslyke@pitt.edu
 Telephone: 412-648-7890
 Fax: 412-624-3346
Contact Person: Leigh Culley
 E-mail: vanslyke@pitt.edu
 Telephone: 412-648-7890
 Fax: 412-624-3346

LEARNING DISABILITY SERVICES

Requests for the following services/accommodations will be evaluated individually based on appropriate and current documentation.

Allowed in exams
 Calculator: Yes
 Dictionary: No
 Computer: Yes
 Spellchecker: Yes
Extended test time: Yes
Scribes: Yes
Proctors: Yes
Oral exams: No
Note-takers: No

Distraction-reduced environment: Yes
Tape recording in class: Yes
Books on tape from RFBD: Yes
Taping of books not from RFBD: No
Accommodations for students with ADHD: Yes
Reading machine: No
Other assistive technology: Yes
Priority registration: No

Added costs for services: No
LD specialists: Yes
Professional tutors: No
Peer tutors: No
Max. hours/wk. for services: N/A
How professors are notified of LD/ADHD: By student

GENERAL ADMISSIONS INFORMATION

Director of Admissions: Betsy A. Porter
Telephone: 412-624-7488

ENTRANCE REQUIREMENTS

Academic units required: 4 English, 3 math, 3 science (3 science labs), 1 foreign language, 1 social studies, 4 academic electives. **Academic units recommended:** 4 math, 4 science, 3 foreign language, 3 social studies, 2 history. High school diploma is required, and GED is not accepted. ACT with Writing component required. TOEFL required of all international applicants: minimum paper TOEFL 550, minimum computer TOEFL 213.

Application deadline: Rolling
Notification: Rolling
Average GPA: NR
ACT Composite middle 50% range: 24–29

SAT Math middle 50% range: 570–670
SAT Critical Reading middle 50% range: 560–660
SAT Writing middle 50% range: NR

Graduated top 10% of class: 43%
Graduated top 25% of class: 80%
Graduated top 50% of class: 98%

COLLEGE GRADUATION REQUIREMENTS

Course waivers allowed: No
Course substitutions allowed: Yes

ADDITIONAL INFORMATION

Environment: The university is located on a 132-acre urban campus.

Student Body
 Undergrad enrollment: 16,796
 Women: 51%
 Men: 49%
 Percent out-of-state: 15%

Cost Information
 In-state tuition: $11,430
 Out-of-state tuition: $20,785
 Room & board: $7,800
Housing Information
 University housing: Yes
 Percent living on campus: 44%

Greek System
 Fraternity: Yes
 Sorority: Yes
Athletics: Division I

University of Pittsburgh

WIDENER UNIVERSITY

One University Place, Chester, PA 19013
Phone: 610-499-4126 • Fax: 610-499-4676
E-mail: admissions.office@widener.edu • Web: www.widener.edu
Support: CS • Institution type: 4-year private

LEARNING DISABILITY PROGRAM AND SERVICES

Enable is a structured mainstream support service designed to assist students enrolled in one of Widener's standard academic programs. Students wishing to use Enable services must submit a copy of their psychological testing results, including intelligence and achievement testing that describes the nature of the learning disability. Each student in Enable is provided each week with two private counseling sessions with a learning specialist. Typically, these sessions focus on time management, study skills, social and emotional adjustment, and academic planning. Enable serves as a campus advocate for the needs of students with LD by making sure that accommodations are provided when appropriate. Participation in Enable is included in the basic tuition charge. Thus, there is no extra fee for the services offered through Enable.

LD/ADHD ADMISSIONS INFORMATION

College entrance tests required: Yes
Interview required: No
Essay recommended: Yes
Documentation required for LD: A comprehensive psychological and educational assessment, including tests of cognitive ability, academic achievement, and information processing
Documentation required for ADHD: Same as above
Submitted to: Enable
Special Ed. HS course work accepted: Yes

Specific course requirements of all applicants: NR
Separate application required: No
# of LD applications submitted each year: NR
# of LD applications accepted yearly: NR
Total # of students receiving LD services: 200
Acceptance into program means acceptance into college: Students must be admitted to and enrolled in the university first and then request services.

ADMISSIONS
Students with learning disabilities submit the general application form. Admission decisions are made jointly by the Office of Admissions and the Director of Enable. Students should submit documentation, an essay, and recommendations. ACT scores range between 17 and 27 and SAT scores range between 750 and 1300. There are no specific course requirements for admissions. High school GPA range is 2.0–4.0.

ADDITIONAL INFORMATION
Enable is a personalized academic advising and counseling service designed to help students with learning disabilities who meet university entrance requirements cope with the rigors of academic life. Students are assigned counselors who help them understand and accept their disabilities; provide academic advice; individualize learning strategies; teach self-advocacy; and link the students with the Reading and Academic Skills Center, Math Lab, Writing Center, and tutoring services. This office assures that professors understand which accommodations are needed. The Writing Center provides assistance with writing assignments and is staffed by professors. The Math Center offers individualized and group tutoring and is staffed by professors and experienced tutors. The Reading Skills Center assists in improving reading comprehension and study skills. Skills classes are available in college reading, math, and English; only 3 credits are accepted for college credit. The Academic Skills Program assists students who receive less than a 2.0 GPA in the fall semester.

LEARNING DISABILITY PROGRAM/SERVICES

Learning Disability Program/Services: Enable
Director: Rebecca Corsey McKeogh, PsyD
  E-mail: rebecc.mckeogh@widener.edu
  Telephone: 610-499-4179
  Fax: 610-499-1192

LEARNING DISABILITY SERVICES

Requests for the following services/accommodations will be evaluated individually based on appropriate and current documentation.

Allowed in exams
  Calculator: Yes
  Dictionary: Yes
  Computer: Yes
  Spellchecker: Yes
Extended test time: Yes
Scribes: Yes
Proctors: Yes
Oral exams: Yes
Note-takers: Yes

Distraction-reduced environment: Yes
Tape recording in class: Yes
Books on tape from RFBD: Yes
Taping of books not from RFBD: Yes
Accommodations for students with ADHD: Yes
Reading machine: Yes
Other assistive technology: Yes
Priority registration: Yes

Added costs for services: No
LD specialists: Yes
Professional tutors: 1
Peer tutors: Yes
Max. hours/wk. for services: Unlimited
How professors are notified of LD/ADHD: By student

GENERAL ADMISSIONS INFORMATION

Director of Admissions: Irina B. Capaldi
Telephone: 610-499-4126

ENTRANCE REQUIREMENTS

Academic units required: 4 English, 3 math, 3 science, 2 foreign language, 3 social studies, 3 academic electives.
Academic units recommended: 4 English, 4 math, 4 science (2 science labs), 2 foreign language, 4 social studies, 3 academic electives. High school diploma is required, and GED is accepted. TOEFL required of all international applicants: minimum paper TOEFL 500, minimum computer TOEFL 173.

Application deadline: Rolling
Notification: Rolling
Average GPA: 3.16
ACT Composite middle 50% range: NR

SAT Math middle 50% range: 450–560
SAT Critical Reading middle 50% range: 440–530
SAT Writing middle 50% range: NR

Graduated top 10% of class: 12%
Graduated top 25% of class: 32%
Graduated top 50% of class: 67%

COLLEGE GRADUATION REQUIREMENTS

Course waivers allowed: No
Course substitutions allowed: No

ADDITIONAL INFORMATION

Environment: The university's 105-acre campus is located 15 miles south of Philadelphia.

Student Body
  Undergrad enrollment: 3,050
  Women: 57%
  Men: 43%
  Percent out-of-state: 36%

Cost Information
  Tuition: $26,350
  Room & board: $9,640
Housing Information
  University housing: Yes
  Percent living on campus: 57%

Greek System
  Fraternity: Yes
  Sorority: Yes
Athletics: Division III

BROWN UNIVERSITY

PO Box 1876, 45 Prospect Street, Providence, RI 02912
Phone: 401-863-2378 • Fax: 401-863-9300
E-mail: admission_undergraduate@brown.edu • Web: www.brown.edu
Support: CS • Institution type: 4-year private

LEARNING DISABILITY PROGRAM AND SERVICES

The Students with Alternative Learning Styles is a mainstreaming program providing accommodations and services to enable students with LD to succeed at Brown. Counseling is available, as well as the Writing Center, Computer Center, and Student-to-Student (a peer counseling group). Testing accommodations are available. Students may petition to take a reduced course load. Accommodations are made that are suitable and reasonable for each individual situation. A particular accommodation is not necessarily useful to all students. Students are invited to offer suggestions of accommodations that have worked for them in the past. Disability Support Services will work closely with each student to provide reasonable accommodations.

LD/ADHD ADMISSIONS INFORMATION

College entrance tests required: Yes
Interview required: N/A
Essay recommended: N/A
Documentation required for LD: A current, complete psychoeducational evaluation, WAIS-III, achievement testing such as the Woodcock-Johnson IV, and information processing testing as appropriate are required.
Documentation required for ADHD: Prefer same documentation we request to document a learning disability
Submitted to: Disability Support Services

Special Ed. HS course work accepted: No
Specific course requirements of all applicants: NR
Separate application required: No
# of LD applications submitted each year: NR
# of LD applications accepted yearly: NR
Total # of students receiving LD services: 126
Acceptance into program means acceptance into college: Students must be admitted to and enrolled in the university first and then request services.

ADMISSIONS

Admission is very competitive, and all students are required to submit the same application form and meet the same standards. Brown is a highly competitive university, and students have been enrolled in AP and honors courses in high school. If a student does disclose an area of disability, Brown admissions will carefully review any information submitted.

ADDITIONAL INFORMATION

Students requesting accommodations and/or support services must provide documentation of the existence of an LD. With appropriate documentation, students may have access to the following services: note-takers; distraction-free testing environments; tape recorders; auxiliary taping of books; self-advocacy workshop; academic advising and study skills counseling; examination modifications as necessary, such as additional time, a quiet room, or use of a word processor, or in rare cases, in alternate format; extended deadlines for some paper assignments; the option of taking a reduced course load with a prorated tuition; referral to off-campus professional tutors; referral to off-campus neuropsychologists for diagnosis; and other assistive technology. There is a Writing Center, an Academic Center, and professional tutors (for a fee) available for all students. There are no specific graduation requirements, and students determine what group of courses to take. Services and accommodations are available for undergraduate and graduate students.

LEARNING DISABILITY PROGRAM/SERVICES

Learning Disability Program/Services: Disability Support Services
Director: Catherine Axe
  E-mail: dss@brown.edu
  Telephone: 401-863-9588
  Fax: 401-863-1999
Contact Person: Admissions Office
  E-mail: dss@brown.edu
  Telephone: 401-863-2378

LEARNING DISABILITY SERVICES

Requests for the following services/accommodations will be evaluated individually based on appropriate and current documentation.

Allowed in exams	**Distraction-reduced environment:** Yes	**Added costs for services:** No
Calculator: Yes	**Tape recording in class:** Yes	**LD specialists:** Yes
Dictionary: Yes	**Books on tape from RFBD:** Yes	**Professional tutors:** Yes
Computer: Yes	**Taping of books not from RFBD:** Yes	**Peer tutors:** 400
Spellchecker: Yes	**Accommodations for students with**	**Max. hours/wk. for services:**
Extended test time: Yes	**ADHD:** Yes	Unlimited
Scribes: Yes	**Reading machine:** Yes	**How professors are notified of**
Proctors: Yes	**Other assistive technology:** Yes	**LD/ADHD:** By student
Oral exams: Yes	**Priority registration:** No	
Note-takers: Yes		

GENERAL ADMISSIONS INFORMATION

Director of Admissions: Michael Goldberger
Telephone: 401-863-2378

ENTRANCE REQUIREMENTS

Academic units required: 4 English, 3 math, 3 science (2 science labs), 3 foreign language, 2 history, 1 academic elective. **Academic units recommended:** 4 English, 4 math, 4 science (3 science labs), 4 foreign language, 2 history, 1 academic elective. High school diploma is required, and GED is not accepted. ACT with Writing component required. TOEFL required of all international applicants: minimum paper TOEFL 600, minimum computer TOEFL 250.

Application deadline: 1/1	**SAT Math middle 50% range:**	**Graduated top 10% of class:** 90%
Notification: 4/1	670–770	**Graduated top 25% of class:** 99%
Average GPA: NR	**SAT Critical Reading middle 50%**	**Graduated top 50% of class:** 100%
ACT Composite middle 50% range:	range: 660–760	
27–33	**SAT Writing middle 50% range:** NR	

COLLEGE GRADUATION REQUIREMENTS

Course waivers allowed: No
Course substitutions allowed: Yes
In what course: Varies

ADDITIONAL INFORMATION

Environment: The university is located on 146 acres in the urban area of Providence, Rhode Island.

Student Body	**Cost Information**	**Greek System**
Undergrad enrollment: 5,927	**Tuition:** $33,200	**Fraternity:** Yes
Women: 53%	**Room & board:** $8,796	**Sorority:** Yes
Men: 47%	**Housing Information**	**Athletics:** Division I
Percent out-of-state: 96%	**University housing:** Yes	
	Percent living on campus: 85%	

BRYANT UNIVERSITY

1150 Douglas Pike, Suite 3, Smithfield, RI 02917-1285
Phone: 401-232-6100 • Fax: 401-232-6741
E-mail: admission@bryant.edu • Web: www.bryant.edu
Support: CS • Institution type: 4-year private

LEARNING DISABILITY PROGRAM AND SERVICES

The Academic Center for Excellence (ACE) is dedicated to helping Bryant students achieve their goal of academic success. Basically, the center provides study skills training to help students become self-reliant, independent, and confident learners. This is achieved through this internationally accredited peer tutoring program and study skills instruction by professional staff. Group sessions as a mode of instruction are encouraged, and the staff engages in a partnership with to students to help them achieve their goals. The learning specialist provides support for students with LD. Consideration is given for reasonable modifications, accommodations, or auxiliary aids that will enable qualified students to have access to, participate in, and benefit from the full range of their educational programs and activities offered to all students. As a liaison among students, faculty, and administration, ACE encourages students with LD requiring special accommodations to schedule an appointment with a learning specialist as soon as they register for courses each semester.

LD/ADHD ADMISSIONS INFORMATION

College entrance tests required: Yes
Interview required: No
Essay recommended: No
Documentation required for LD: Psychoeducational evaluation
Documentation required for ADHD: Psychoeducational evaluation
Submitted to: ACE
Special Ed. HS course work accepted: No

Specific course requirements of all applicants: Yes
Separate application required: No
# of LD applications submitted each year: NR
# of LD applications accepted yearly: NR
Total # of students receiving LD services: 120
Acceptance into program means acceptance into college: Students must be admitted to and enrolled in the university first and then request services.

ADMISSIONS

If students self-disclose during the admission process, the Office of Admissions will forward documentation to the Academic Center for Excellence. If students do not self-disclose, they must schedule an appointment at ACE to do so. Students may elect to self-disclose and provide current documentation that should be sent to admissions and to ACE. General admission criteria include an average GPA of 3.0 and 4 years of English, 2 years of social studies, at least 1 year of science lab, and 3 years of college-prep mathematics. Interviews are recommended. A probationary/conditional admission is available.

ADDITIONAL INFORMATION

Students with documented disabilities may receive accommodations and services based solely on the disability and appropriate services. Some of the accommodations could include extended testing times; readers; distraction-free environments; scribes; proctors; oral exams; note-takers; use of calculators, computers, and spellcheckers; and books on tape through the RFBD. ACE provides learning specialists to assist students in college-level study skills development. Learning specialists also help students find out what learning and study strategies work best for them. The College Reading and Learning Association provides the peer tutoring program, and one-on-one tutoring is available in a variety of subjects. Students can drop in to work with a specialist or peer tutor in the learning labs. Study skills workshops are offered covering topics such as time management, note-taking skills, test preparation, and combating procrastination. The ACE course is a 7-week, voluntary enrollment study strategies course designed to help students maintain superior GPAs. The Writing Center provides one-on-one conferencing in writing for all subjects. There are writing consultants, writing specialists, ESL writing specialists, and writing workshops available at the center.

LEARNING DISABILITY PROGRAM/SERVICES

Learning Disability Program/Services: Academic Center for Excellence (ACE)
Director: Laurie L. Hazard, EdD
  E-mail: lhazard@bryant.edu
  Telephone: 401-232-6746
  Fax: 401-232-6038
Contact Person: Sally Riconscente
  E-mail: lhazard@bryant.edu
  Telephone: 401-232-6746
  Fax: 401-232-6038

LEARNING DISABILITY SERVICES

Requests for the following services/accommodations will be evaluated individually based on appropriate and current documentation.

Allowed in exams
  Calculator: Yes
  Dictionary: Yes
  Computer: Yes
  Spellchecker: Yes
Extended test time: Yes
Scribes: Yes
Proctors: Yes
Oral exams: Yes
Note-takers: Yes

Distraction-reduced environment: Yes
Tape recording in class: Yes
Books on tape from RFBD: Yes
Taping of books not from RFBD: Yes
Accommodations for students with
  ADHD: Yes
Reading machine: No
Other assistive technology: Yes
Priority registration: No

Added costs for services: No
LD specialists: Yes
Professional tutors: 6
Peer tutors: 50
Max. hours/wk. for services:
  Unlimited
How professors are notified of
  LD/ADHD: By both student and
  director

GENERAL ADMISSIONS INFORMATION

Director of Admissions: Michelle Beauregard
Telephone: 401-232-6100

ENTRANCE REQUIREMENTS

Academic units required: 4 English, 4 math, 3 science (2 science labs), 2 foreign language, 2 history/social sciences. **Academic units recommended:** 4 history/social sciences. High school diploma is required, and GED is accepted. ACT with Writing component required. TOEFL required of all international applicants: minimum paper TOEFL 550, minimum computer TOEFL 213.

Application deadline: 2/1
Notification: 3/15
Average GPA: 3.42
ACT Composite middle 50% range:
  21–25

SAT Math middle 50% range:
  540–620
SAT Critical Reading middle 50%
  range: 500–580
SAT Writing middle 50% range:
  510–590

Graduated top 10% of class: 24%
Graduated top 25% of class: 63%
Graduated top 50% of class: 93%

COLLEGE GRADUATION REQUIREMENTS

Course waivers allowed: No
Course substitutions allowed: No

ADDITIONAL INFORMATION

Environment: The campus is located in a suburban area 12 miles from Providence.

Student Body
  Undergrad enrollment: 3,231
  Women: 42%
  Men: 58%
  Percent out-of-state: 84%

Cost Information
  Tuition: $26,110
  Room & board: $10,909
Housing Information
  University housing: Yes
  Percent living on campus: 81%

Greek System
  Fraternity: Yes
  Sorority: Yes
Athletics: Division II

JOHNSON & WALES UNIVERSITY

Eight Abbott Park Place, Providence, RI 02903-3703
Phone: 401-598-2310 • Fax: 401-598-2948
E-mail: admissions.pvd@jwu.edu • Web: www.jwu.edu
Support: CS • Institution type: 2- and 4-year private

LEARNING DISABILITY PROGRAM AND SERVICES

Johnson & Wales University is dedicated to providing reasonable accommodations to allow students with learning disabilities to succeed in their academic pursuits. While maintaining the highest academic integrity, the university strives to balance scholarship with support services that will assist special needs students to function in the postsecondary learning process. It is important that these students identify themselves and present the appropriate neurological, medical, and/or psychoeducational documentation as soon as possible. Recommendations for specific accommodations will be based on the student's individual needs and learning style. The goal of the Student Success Department is to support students in their efforts to develop their talents, empower them to direct their own learning, and lead them on the pathways of success.

LD/ADHD ADMISSIONS INFORMATION

College entrance tests required: No
Interview required: No
Essay recommended: No
Documentation required for LD: Psychoeducational report
Documentation required for ADHD: Medical documentation
Submitted to: Center for Academic Support
Special Ed. HS course work accepted: Yes

Specific course requirements of all applicants: Yes
Separate application required: No
# of LD applications submitted each year: NR
# of LD applications accepted yearly: NR
Total # of students receiving LD services: 550
Acceptance into program means acceptance into college: Students must be admitted to and enrolled in the university first and then request services.

ADMISSIONS

There is no special application process. Standardized tests are not required for admission, and foreign language is not required for admission. After the regular admissions process has been completed and the student is accepted, the student should self-identify and verify the learning disability with the appropriate neurological, medical, and/or psychoeducational documentation. This would include tests administered by the student's high school or a private testing service within the past 3 years. Once admitted, a special needs advisor will meet with the student, and recommendations for specific accommodations will be based on the student's individual needs and learning styles. Any student admitted conditionally will be closely monitored by an academic counselor and must maintain a GPA of 2.0 (2 terms below a 2.0 may result in dismissal).

ADDITIONAL INFORMATION

Academic counselors establish initial contact with probational, conditional, and special needs students. Counselors monitor and review grades and enforce academic policies. Accommodations could include a decelerated course load, preferential scheduling, oral exams or extended time on exams, note-takers, use of tape recorder in class, an LD support group, individualized tutoring, and a special needs advisor. Career counselors and personal counselors are also available. Program of Assisted Studies (PAS) provides a structured delivery of fundamental math, language, and major skills courses with a strong emphasis on learning strategy instruction and professional advising and tutoring. The Learning Center offers group and/or one-on-one tutoring, writing skills, culinary skills, grammar fundamentals, study groups, and supplemental instruction groups. Freshman requirements include a course in study and social adjustment skills and a course to teach effective job-search techniques, including career planning, personal development, resume writing, and interview techniques. Services and accommodations are available for undergraduate and graduate students.

LEARNING DISABILITY PROGRAM/SERVICES

Learning Disability Program/Services: Center for Academic Support
Director: Meryl Berstein
  E-mail: mberstein@jwu.edu
  Telephone: 401-598-4689
  Fax: 401-598-4657

LEARNING DISABILITY SERVICES

Requests for the following services/accommodations will be evaluated individually based on appropriate and current documentation.

Allowed in exams
  Calculator: Yes
  Dictionary: Yes
  Computer: Yes
  Spellchecker: Yes
Extended test time: Yes
Scribes: Yes
Proctors: Yes
Oral exams: Yes
Note-takers: Yes

Distraction-reduced environment: Yes
Tape recording in class: Yes
Books on tape from RFBD: Yes
Taping of books not from RFBD: Yes
Accommodations for students with
  ADHD: Yes
Reading machine: Yes
Other assistive technology: Yes
Priority registration: Yes

Added costs for services: No
LD specialists: Yes
Professional tutors: 18
Peer tutors: 18
Max. hours/wk. for services:
  Unlimited
How professors are notified of
  LD/ADHD: By both student and
  director

GENERAL ADMISSIONS INFORMATION

Director of Admissions: Maureen Dumas
Telephone: 401-598-2310

ENTRANCE REQUIREMENTS

Academic units recommended: 4 English, 3 math, 3 science, 2 social studies. High school diploma is required, and GED is accepted. ACT with or without Writing component accepted.

Application deadline: Rolling
Notification: Rolling
Average GPA: 2.84
ACT Composite middle 50% range: NR

SAT Math middle 50% range: NR
SAT Critical Reading middle 50% range: NR
SAT Writing middle 50% range: NR

Graduated top 10% of class: NR
Graduated top 25% of class: NR
Graduated top 50% of class: NR

COLLEGE GRADUATION REQUIREMENTS

Course waivers allowed: Yes
In what course: Foreign language
Course substitutions allowed: Yes
In what course: Foreign language

ADDITIONAL INFORMATION

Environment: The university is located on 100 acres, with easy access to Boston.

Student Body
  Undergrad enrollment: 9,066
  Women: 52%
  Men: 48%
  Percent out-of-state: 69%

Cost Information
  Tuition: $20,800
  Room & board: $8,550
Housing Information
  University housing: Yes
  Percent living on campus: 41%

Greek System
  Fraternity: Yes
  Sorority: Yes
Athletics: Division III

PROVIDENCE COLLEGE

Harkins 222, 549 River Avenue, Providence, RI 02918
Phone: 401-865-2535 • Fax: 401-865-2826
E-mail: pcadmiss@providence.edu • Web: www.providence.edu
Support: CS • Institution type: 4-year private

LEARNING DISABILITY PROGRAM AND SERVICES

There is no formal program for students with LD. However, the Director of the Office of Academic Services and the faculty of the college are very supportive and are diligent about providing comprehensive services. The goal of the college is to be available to assist students whenever help is requested. After admission, the Disability Support Services coordinator meets with the LD students during the summer, prior to entry, to help them select the appropriate courses for freshman year. Students are monitored for 4 years. The college makes every effort to provide reasonable accommodations.

LD/ADHD ADMISSIONS INFORMATION

College entrance tests required: No
Interview required: N/A
Essay recommended: N/A
Documentation required for LD: No documentation is required for admission.
Documentation required for ADHD: No
Submitted to: Office of Academic Support
Special Ed. HS course work accepted: N/A

Specific course requirements of all applicants: Yes
Separate application required: No
# of LD applications submitted each year: NR
# of LD applications accepted yearly: NR
Total # of students receiving LD services: NR
Acceptance into program means acceptance into college: Students must be admitted to and enrolled in the university first and then request services.

ADMISSIONS

There is no special admissions process for students with learning disabilities. However, an interview is highly recommended, during which individualized course work is examined. General course requirements include 4 years of English, 3 years of math, 3 years of a foreign language, 2 years of science lab, 2 years of social studies, and 2 years of electives. Students with learning disabilities who have lower test scores but a fairly good academic record may be accepted. The Admission Committee has the flexibility to overlook poor test scores for students with learning disabilities. Those who have higher test scores and reasonable grades in college-prep courses (C-plus/B) may also gain admission. Students should self-identify as learning disabled on their application. Also, with appropriate documentation, a student may substitute a required entrance course such as a foreign language with a college-prep class.

ADDITIONAL INFORMATION

The following services and accommodations are available for students presenting appropriate documentation: the use of calculators, dictionaries, computers, and spellcheckers during exams; extended time on tests; distraction-free testing environments; scribes; proctors; oral exams; note-takers; tape recorders in class; assistive technology; and priority registration. Skills seminars, for no credit, are offered in study techniques and test-taking strategies. All students have access to the Tutorial Center and Writing Center. Services and accommodations are available for undergraduate and graduate students.

LEARNING DISABILITY PROGRAM/SERVICES

Learning Disability Program/Services: Office of Academic Services—Disabilty Support Services
Director: Andrew Christensen, Assistant Director for Disability Services
  E-mail: oas@providence.edu
  Telephone: 401-865-1121
  Fax: 401-865-1219

LEARNING DISABILITY SERVICES

Requests for the following services/accommodations will be evaluated individually based on appropriate and current documentation.

Allowed in exams
  Calculator: Yes
  Dictionary: Yes
  Computer: Yes
  Spellchecker: Yes
Extended test time: Yes
Scribes: Yes
Proctors: Yes
Oral exams: Yes
Note-takers: Yes

Distraction-reduced environment: Yes
Tape recording in class: Yes
Books on tape from RFBD: No
Taping of books not from RFBD: Yes
Accommodations for students with ADHD: Yes
Reading machine: Yes
Other assistive technology: Yes
Priority registration: Yes

Added costs for services: No
LD specialists: Yes
Professional tutors: No
Peer tutors: 30–35
Max. hours/wk. for services: Unlimited
How professors are notified of LD/ADHD: By student

GENERAL ADMISSIONS INFORMATION

Director of Admissions: Christopher Lydon
Telephone: 401-865-2535

ENTRANCE REQUIREMENTS

Academic units required: 4 English, 4 math, 3 science (2 science labs), 3 foreign language, 2 social studies, 2 history. **Academic units recommended:** 4 English, 4 math, 4 science (2 science labs), 3 foreign language, 2 social studies, 2 history. High school diploma is required, and GED is not accepted. ACT with Writing component required. TOEFL required of all international applicants: minimum paper TOEFL 550, minimum computer TOEFL 213.

Application deadline: 1/15
Notification: 4/1
Average GPA: 3.46
ACT Composite middle 50% range: 23–28

SAT Math middle 50% range: 560–650
SAT Critical Reading middle 50% range: 540–640
SAT Writing middle 50% range: 560–650

Graduated top 10% of class: 45%
Graduated top 25% of class: 83%
Graduated top 50% of class: 97%

COLLEGE GRADUATION REQUIREMENTS

Course waivers allowed: Yes
In what course: Depends on student's disability
Course substitutions allowed: Yes
In what course: Depends on student's disabilty

ADDITIONAL INFORMATION

Environment: Providence College has a 105-acre campus located in a small city 50 miles south of Boston.

Student Body
  Undergrad enrollment: 3,990
  Women: 56%
  Men: 44%
  Percent out-of-state: 88%

Cost Information
  Tuition: $26,780
  Room & board: $9,765
Housing Information
  University housing: Yes
  Percent living on campus: 80%

Greek System
  Fraternity: No
  Sorority: No
Athletics: Division I

RHODE ISLAND COLLEGE

Undergrad. Admissions, 600 Mt. Pleasant Avenue, Providence, RI 02908
Phone: 401-456-8234 • Fax: 401-456-8817
E-mail: admissions@ric.edu • Web: www.ric.edu
Support: CS • Institution type: public

LEARNING DISABILITY PROGRAM AND SERVICES

Rhode Island College strives to create and promote an environment that is conducive to learning for all students. Necessary accommodations require that administration, faculty, and staff be consistent and use flexibility in making adaptations, and that the students be flexible in adapting to and using alternative modes of learning and instruction. Students with disabilities may self-identify at any point, but are encouraged to do so at admission. A registration card is sent to all new students. Filling out this card and returning it to the Office of Student Life starts the process. Faculty is responsible for stating at the beginning of each semester verbally or in writing that the instructor is available to meet individually with students who require accommodations. The college wants students to feel comfortable requesting assistance, and faculty and fellow students are encouraged to be friendly and supportive. The college feels that the presence of students with individual ways of learning and coping serves as a learning experience for the professor, student, and class.

LD/ADHD ADMISSIONS INFORMATION

College entrance tests required: Yes
Interview required: No
Essay recommended: No
Documentation required for LD: Psychoeducational evaluation
Documentation required for ADHD: Yes
Submitted to: Both Admissions Office and Office of Student Life
Special Ed. HS course work accepted: No

Specific course requirements of all applicants: NR
Separate application required: Yes
# of LD applications submitted each year: Yes
# of LD applications accepted yearly: NR
Total # of students receiving LD services: 177
Acceptance into program means acceptance into college: Students must be admitted to and enrolled in the university first and then request services.

ADMISSIONS

Admission requirements are the same for all applicants. Freshman requirements include 4 years of English, 2 years of a foreign language, 3 years of mathematics (Algebra I, Algebra II, and geometry), 2 years of social studies, 2 years of science (biology and chemistry or physics), 0.5 unit in the arts, and 4.5 additional college-preparatory units. Most accepted students rank in the upper 50 percent of their class. SAT or ACT scores required. Students with LD/ADHD should submit the general application for admission. If a student does not meet admission requirements and is considered as a conditional admit, this would be done regardless of having an LD or ADHD.

ADDITIONAL INFORMATION

The Student Life Office provides the following services for students with appropriate documentation: one-on-one consultation, note-taking arrangements, use of a tape recorders in class, readers/recorders, registration assistance, disability discussion groups, and assistive technology. The Office of Academic Support and Information Services provides the following for all students: academic advisement, an Academic Development Center, a Math Learning Center, tutorial services, and a Writing Center. Students may request substitutions in courses not required by their major.

LEARNING DISABILITY PROGRAM/SERVICES

Learning Disability Program/Services: Disability Services, Student Life Office
Director: Scott Kane, Associate Dean of Student Life
  E-mail: skane@ric.edu
  Telephone: 401-456-8061
  Fax: 401-456-8702
Contact Person: Ann M. Roccio, Coordinator of Students with Disabilities
  E-mail: skane@ric.edu
  Telephone: 401-456-8061
  Fax: 401-456-8702

LEARNING DISABILITY SERVICES

Requests for the following services/accommodations will be evaluated individually based on appropriate and current documentation.

Allowed in exams
  Calculator: Yes
  Dictionary: Yes
  Computer: Yes
  Spellchecker: Yes
Extended test time: Yes
Scribes: Yes
Proctors: No
Oral exams: Yes
Note-takers: Yes

Distraction-reduced environment: Yes
Tape recording in class: Yes
Books on tape from RFBD: Yes
Taping of books not from RFBD: Yes
Accommodations for students with ADHD: Yes
Reading machine: Yes
Other assistive technology: Yes
Priority registration: Yes

Added costs for services: No
LD specialists: Yes
Professional tutors: No
Peer tutors: Yes
Max. hours/wk. for services: Unlimited
How professors are notified of LD/ADHD: By both student and director

GENERAL ADMISSIONS INFORMATION

Director of Admissions: Holly L. Shadoian
Telephone: 401-456-8234

ENTRANCE REQUIREMENTS

Academic units required: 4 English, 3 math, 2 science (2 science labs), 2 foreign language, 2 social studies, 4 academic electives, 1 art and computer literacy (0.5 each). High school diploma is required, and GED is accepted. TOEFL required of all international applicants: minimum paper TOEFL 550.

Application deadline: 5/1
Notification: Rolling
Average GPA: NR
ACT Composite middle 50% range: NR

SAT Math middle 50% range: 430–540
SAT Critical Reading middle 50% range: 440–550
SAT Writing middle 50% range: NR

Graduated top 10% of class: NR
Graduated top 25% of class: NR
Graduated top 50% of class: NR

COLLEGE GRADUATION REQUIREMENTS

Course waivers allowed: Yes
In what course: English and others if not required by student's major
Course substitutions allowed: Yes
In what course: English and others if not required by student's major

ADDITIONAL INFORMATION

Environment: The campus is located a few miles from downtown Providence.

Student Body
  Undergrad enrollment: 6,531
  Women: 68%
  Men: 32%
  Percent out-of-state: NR

Cost Information
  In-state tuition: $3,700
  Out-of-state tuition: $19,500
  Room & board: $6,136
Housing Information
  University housing: Yes
  Percent living on campus: NR

Greek System
  Fraternity: Yes
  Sorority: Yes
Athletics: Division III

UNIVERSITY OF RHODE ISLAND

Undergrad. Admissions Office, 14 Upper College Road, Kingston, RI 02881
Phone: 401-874-7000 • Fax: 401-874-5523
E-mail: uriadmit@etal.uri.edu • Web: www.uri.edu
Support: CS • Institution type: 4-year public

LEARNING DISABILITY PROGRAM AND SERVICES

Disability Services for Students assists students in arranging accommodations, facilitate communication between students and professors, and help them to develop effective coping skills like time management, study skills, stress management, and so on. Accommodations are provided to meet the specific needs of individual students. Students are encouraged to have an ongoing relationship with DSS, and the professional staff is able to meet with students as often as desired. Students with LD/ADHD who want to access services or accommodations must provide DSS with current documentation and communicate what needs are requested. Students are also expected to keep up with their requested accommodations (pick up, deliver, and return letters in timely manner) and be involved in the decision-making process when it comes to their needs. Students are encouraged to make accommodation requests as early as possible prior to the beginning of each semester.

LD/ADHD ADMISSIONS INFORMATION

College entrance tests required: Yes
Interview required: No
Essay recommended: No
Documentation required for LD: Full psychoeducational evaluation, including aptitude, achievement, and information processing testing
Documentation required for ADHD: Same as above or full diagnostic letter from a psychiatrist or neurologist
Submitted to: Admissions Office
Special Ed. HS course work accepted: N/A

Specific course requirements of all applicants: Yes
Separate application required: No
# of LD applications submitted each year: NR
# of LD applications accepted yearly: NR
Total # of students receiving LD services: 500
Acceptance into program means acceptance into college: Students must be admitted to and enrolled in the university first and then request services.

ADMISSIONS

All applicants are expected to meet the general admission criteria. There is not a special process for students with LD/ADHD. General admission requirements expect students to rank in the upper 50 percent of their high school class and complete college-preparatory courses in English, math, social studies, science, and foreign language. If there is current documentation of a language-based LD, there is a waiver for the foreign language admissions requirement, but students must self-disclose during the admission process.

ADDITIONAL INFORMATION

Students need to provide the Disability Services for Students Office with current documentation of their disability that includes psychoeducational testing completed by a professional evaluator. DSS assists students in arranging for accommodations, help to facilitate communication between students and professors, work with students to develop effective coping strategies, assist students with identifying appropriate resources and provide referrals, and offer support groups for students with ADHD and a group working toward enhanced awareness of disability issues. Accommodations are based solely on documented disabilities, and eligible students have access to services such as priority registration, extended time on exams, permission to tape record lectures, and access to a note-taker.

LEARNING DISABILITY PROGRAM/SERVICES

Learning Disability Program/Services: Disability Services for Students
Director: Pamela A. Rohland
  E-mail: rohland@uri.edu
  Telephone: 401-874-2098
  Fax: 401-874-5574

LEARNING DISABILITY SERVICES

Requests for the following services/accommodations will be evaluated individually based on appropriate and current documentation.

Allowed in exams
  Calculator: Yes
  Dictionary: Yes
  Computer: Yes
  Spellchecker: Yes
Extended test time: Yes
Scribes: Yes
Proctors: Y/N
Oral exams: Y/N
Note-takers: Yes

Distraction-reduced environment: Yes
Tape recording in class: Yes
Books on tape from RFBD: Yes
Taping of books not from RFBD: Yes
Accommodations for students with
  ADHD: Yes
Reading machine: Yes
Other assistive technology: Yes
Priority registration: Yes

Added costs for services: No
LD specialists: Yes
Professional tutors: No
Peer tutors: No
Max. hours/wk. for services: N/A
How professors are notified of
  LD/ADHD: By both student and
  director

GENERAL ADMISSIONS INFORMATION

Director of Admissions: Cynthia Bonn
Telephone: 401-874-7100

ENTRANCE REQUIREMENTS

Academic units required: 4 English, 3 math, 2 science (1 science lab), 2 foreign language, 2 social studies, 5 academic electives. High school diploma is required, and GED is accepted. ACT with Writing component required. TOEFL required of all international applicants: minimum paper TOEFL 550, minimum computer TOEFL 213.

Application deadline: 2/1
Notification: Rolling
Average GPA: 3.12
ACT Composite middle 50% range:
  NR

SAT Math middle 50% range:
  510–610
SAT Critical Reading middle 50%
  range: 490–585
SAT Writing middle 50% range: NR

Graduated top 10% of class: 21%
Graduated top 25% of class: NR
Graduated top 50% of class: NR

COLLEGE GRADUATION REQUIREMENTS

Course waivers allowed: No
Course substitutions allowed: Yes
In what course: On a case-by-case basis for eligible students

ADDITIONAL INFORMATION

Environment: The campus is located 30 miles from Providence.

Student Body
  Undergrad enrollment: 11,542
  Women: 56%
  Men: 44%
  Percent out-of-state: 39%

Cost Information
  In-state tuition: $7,200
  Out-of-state tuition: $19,900
  Room & board: $8,466
Housing Information
  University housing: Yes
  Percent living on campus: 40%

Greek System
  Fraternity: Yes
  Sorority: Yes
Athletics: Division I

CLEMSON UNIVERSITY

105 Sikes Hall, Box 345124, Clemson, SC 29634-5124
Phone: 864-656-2287 • Fax: 864-656-2464
E-mail: cuadmissions@clemson.edu • Web: www.clemson.edu
Support: S • Institution type: 4-year public

LEARNING DISABILITY PROGRAM AND SERVICES

Student Disability Services coordinates the provision of reasonable accommodations for students with disabilities. All reasonable accommodations are individualized, flexible, and confidential based on the nature of the disability and the academic environment. Students requesting accommodations must provide current documentation of the disability from a physician or licensed professional. High school IEP, 504 plan, and/or letter from a physician or other professional will not be sufficient to document a learning disability. While such documentation can be helpful in establishing the student's learning history, a recent (fewer than 3 years old) psychological evaluation is still necessary to confirm current needs. Reasonable accommodations will be made in the instructional process to ensure full educational opportunities. The objective is to provide appropriate services to accommodate the student's learning differences, not to lower scholastic requirements.

LD/ADHD ADMISSIONS INFORMATION

College entrance tests required: Yes
Interview required: No
Essay recommended: No
Documentation required for LD: Psychoeducational evaluation completed within the past 3 years
Documentation required for ADHD: Yes
Submitted to: Student Disability Services
Special Ed. HS course work accepted: Yes

Specific course requirements of all applicants: Yes
Separate application required: No
# of LD applications submitted each year: NR
# of LD applications accepted yearly: NR
Total # of students receiving LD services: 590
Acceptance into program means acceptance into college: Students must be admitted to and enrolled in the university first and then request services.

ADMISSIONS

All students must satisfy the same admission criteria for the university. There is no separate application process for students with learning disabilities. General admission requirements include an ACT score of 22–27 or an SAT Reasoning score of 1080–1260, and course requirements include 4 years of English, 3 years of math, 3 years of science lab, 3 years of a foreign language, and 3 years of social studies. Students may request a waiver of the foreign language requirement by submitting a request to the exceptions committee. It is recommended that students self-disclose their learning disability if they need to explain the lack of a foreign language in their background or other information that will help admissions to understand their challenges.

ADDITIONAL INFORMATION

Appropriate accommodations are discussed with each student individually and confidentially. Some of the accommodations offered are assistive technology; note-takers, readers, and transcribers; course substitutions; exam modifications, including computers, extended time, private and quiet rooms, readers, and scribes; priority registration; and taped lectures. All students have access to peer tutoring, a writing lab, and departmental tutoring. Assistive technology available includes screen readers, scanners, Dragon Dictate, and grammar-check. Skills courses are offered in time management techniques, test strategies, and study skills. Peer Academic Coaching is a collaborative process between students and a trained peer coach to improve academic and self-management skills through structure, support, and compensatory strategies. Any student is eligible to participate in peer academic coaching. There are currently 230 students with learning disabilities and 310 students with ADHD receiving services.

LEARNING DISABILITY PROGRAM/SERVICES

Learning Disability Program/Services: Student Disability Services
Director: Bonnie Martin
  E-mail: bmartin@clemson.edu
  Telephone: 864-656-6848
  Fax: 864-656-6849

LEARNING DISABILITY SERVICES

Requests for the following services/accommodations will be evaluated individually based on appropriate and current documentation.

Allowed in exams
  Calculator: Yes
  Dictionary: Yes
  Computer: Yes
  Spellchecker: Yes
Extended test time: Yes
Scribes: Yes
Proctors: Yes
Oral exams: Yes
Note-takers: Yes

Distraction-reduced environment: Yes
Tape recording in class: Yes
Books on tape from RFBD: Yes
Taping of books not from RFBD: Yes
Accommodations for students with ADHD: Yes
Reading machine: Yes
Other assistive technology: Yes
Priority registration: Yes

Added costs for services: No
LD specialists: No
Professional tutors: No
Peer tutors: Yes
Max. hours/wk. for services: Unlimited
How professors are notified of LD/ADHD: By both student and director

GENERAL ADMISSIONS INFORMATION

Director of Admissions: Robert S. Barkley
Telephone: 864-656-2287

ENTRANCE REQUIREMENTS
Academic units required: 4 English, 3 math, 3 science (3 science labs), 3 foreign language, 3 social studies, 1 history, 2 academic electives, 1 physical education or ROTC. **Academic units recommended:** 4 math, (4 science labs). High school diploma is required, and GED is accepted. ACT with Writing component required. TOEFL required of all international applicants: minimum paper TOEFL 550, minimum computer TOEFL 213.

Application deadline: 5/1
Notification: Rolling
Average GPA: 4.08
ACT Composite middle 50% range: 25–29

SAT Math middle 50% range: 590–680
SAT Critical Reading middle 50% range: 540–640
SAT Writing middle 50% range: NR

Graduated top 10% of class: 45%
Graduated top 25% of class: 74%
Graduated top 50% of class: 93%

COLLEGE GRADUATION REQUIREMENTS

Course waivers allowed: No
Course substitutions allowed: Yes
In what course: Math and foreign language, depending on program of study

ADDITIONAL INFORMATION

Environment: The university is located on 1,400 acres in a small town.

Student Body
  Undergrad enrollment: 13,959
  Women: 46%
  Men: 54%
  Percent out-of-state: 32%

Cost Information
  In-state tuition: $9,868
  Out-of-state tuition: $20,292
  Room & board: $5,874
Housing Information
  University housing: Yes
  Percent living on campus: 44%

Greek System
  Fraternity: Yes
  Sorority: Yes
Athletics: Division I

LIMESTONE COLLEGE

1115 College Drive, Gaffey, SC 29340-3799
Phone: 864-488-4549 • Fax: 864-487-8706
E-mail: admiss@limestone.edu • Web: www.limestone.edu
Support: CS • Institution type: 4-year private

LEARNING DISABILITY PROGRAM AND SERVICES

The Program for Alternative Learning Styles (PALS) was developed to service students with learning disabilities. Therefore, only students with documented learning disabilities are eligible to receive program services. For program purposes, LD refers to students with average to above average intelligence (above 90) who have a discrepancy between measured intelligence and achievement. PALS's biggest advantage is the follow-up system that is in place for the PALS students. Each student is very carefully monitored as to his or her progress in each course he or she takes. The students who are not successful are typically those students who do not take advantage of the system. With the follow-up system, the students in PALS are in no danger of falling between the cracks. The tracking system is specifically designed to keep the professors, the director, and the students informed about their progress toward a degree from Limestone College.

LD/ADHD ADMISSIONS INFORMATION

College entrance tests required: No
Interview required: Yes
Essay recommended: No
Documentation required for LD: Wechsler Adult Intelligence Scale (WAIS) and Woodcock-Johnson (WJ–III) or Wechsler Individual Achievement Test (WIAT) and Woodcock-Johnson
Documentation required for ADHD: Letters from doctors, psychiatrists, or psychologists. The above testing is also required for program records.
Submitted to: PALS
Special Ed. HS course work accepted: Yes

Specific course requirements of all applicants: Yes
Separate application required: No
# of LD applications submitted each year: 27
# of LD applications accepted yearly: 20
Total # of students receiving LD services: 21
Acceptance into program means acceptance into college: Students are admitted simultaneously into the college and PALS program.

ADMISSIONS

Students who self-disclose their LD and want the services of PALS must first be admitted to Limestone College either fully or conditionally. Students must submit a high school transcript with a diploma or GED certificate, SAT or ACT scores, and the general college application. The minimum GPA is a 2.0. To receive services through PALS, students must submit their most recent psychological report (completed within the past 3 years) documenting the existence of the LD. Only evaluations by certified school psychologists will be accepted. In addition, only intelligence test scores from the Stanford Binet and/or Wechsler Scales will be acceptable. All available information is carefully reviewed prior to acceptance. Students may be admitted provisionally provided they are enrolled in PALS. Students interested in PALS must arrange for an interview with the director of PALS to learn what will be expected of the student and what the program will and will not do for the student. After the interview is completed, students will be notified of their eligibility for the PALS and be given the opportunity to sign a statement indicating their wish to participate or not to participate.

ADDITIONAL INFORMATION

During the regular academic year, students will receive special instruction in the area of study skills. The director of PALS is in constant communication with students concerning grades, tutors, professors, accommodations, time management, and study habits. Tutorial services are provided on an individual basis so that all students can reach their maximum potential. Skills classes are offered in math and reading. Other services include counseling, time management skills, and screening for the best ways to make accommodations. All freshmen or new students are required to pay the full fee for the first year of services ($3,000). After the first two semesters, that fee will be reduced by 50 percent for all students who meet the following GPA requirements: a 2.0 GPA after two semesters; 2.3 GPA after four semesters; and 2.5 GPA after six semesters.

LEARNING DISABILITY PROGRAM/SERVICES

Learning Disability Program/Services: Program for Alternative Learning Styles (PALS)
Director: Karen Kearse, MEd
  E-mail: kkearse@limestone.edu
  Telephone: 864-488-8377
  Fax: 864-487-8706

LEARNING DISABILITY SERVICES

Requests for the following services/accommodations will be evaluated individually based on appropriate and current documentation.

Allowed in exams
  Calculator: Yes
  Dictionary: Yes
  Computer: Yes
  Spellchecker: Yes
Extended test time: Yes
Scribes: Yes
Proctors: Yes
Oral exams: Yes
Note-takers: Yes

Distraction-reduced environment: Yes
Tape recording in class: Yes
Books on tape from RFBD: Yes
Taping of books not from RFBD: Yes
Accommodations for students with
  ADHD: Yes
Reading machine: Yes
Other assistive technology: Yes
Priority registration: No

Added costs for services: Yes
LD specialists: Yes
Professional tutors: 4–8
Peer tutors: 16–24
Max. hours/wk. for services:
  Unlimited
How professors are notified of
  LD/ADHD: By director

GENERAL ADMISSIONS INFORMATION

Director of Admissions: Chris Phenicie (Vice President for Admissions)
Telephone: 864-488-4549

ENTRANCE REQUIREMENTS

Academic units required: 4 English, 3 math, 2 science (2 science labs), 3 social studies. High school diploma is required, and GED is accepted. ACT with or without Writing component accepted. TOEFL required of all international applicants: minimum paper TOEFL 500, minimum computer TOEFL 173.

Application deadline: 8/26
Notification: Rolling
Average GPA: 3.01
ACT Composite middle 50% range:
  17–22

SAT Math middle 50% range:
  450–550
SAT Critical Reading middle 50%
  range: 440–530
SAT Writing middle 50% range: NR

Graduated top 10% of class: 4%
Graduated top 25% of class: 21%
Graduated top 50% of class: 56%

COLLEGE GRADUATION REQUIREMENTS

Course waivers allowed: No
Course substitutions allowed: No

ADDITIONAL INFORMATION

Environment: The campus is located in an urban area 45 miles south of Charlotte.

Student Body
  Undergrad enrollment: 728
  Women: 43%
  Men: 57%
  Percent out-of-state: 42%

Cost Information
  Tuition: $15,000
  Room & board: $6,200
Housing Information
  University housing: Yes
  Percent living on campus: 51%

Greek System
  Fraternity: No
  Sorority: No
Athletics: Division II

SOUTHERN WESLEYAN UNIVERSITY

Wesleyan Drive, PO Box 1020, Central, SC 29630-1020
Phone: 864-644-5550 • Fax: 864-644-5972
E-mail: admissions@swu.edu • Web: www.swu.edu
Support: S • Institution type: 4-year private

LEARNING DISABILITY PROGRAM AND SERVICES

Southern Wesleyan University provides the environment for success. In accepting students with learning disabilities, the university is committed to providing special services and assistance to these students. Services are provided after an assessment of the students' particular needs. The objectives of the SWU program are to help students with learning disabilities make a smooth transition from high school to college and provide faculty with methods to accommodate and help students succeed and become increasingly independent.

LD/ADHD ADMISSIONS INFORMATION

College entrance tests required: Yes
Interview required: No
Essay recommended: No
Documentation required for LD: Written diagnosis or reassessment (preferably including all test results) by an appropriately certified professional within the past 3 years before student's enrollment at Southern Wesleyan
Documentation required for ADHD: Written diagnosis or reassessment by an appropriately certified professional within the past 3 years before student's enrollment at Southern Wesleyan

Submitted to: Services to Students with Disabilities
Special Ed. HS course work accepted: NR
Specific course requirements of all applicants: Yes
Separate application required: No
# of LD applications submitted each year: NR
# of LD applications accepted yearly: NR
Total # of students receiving LD services: NR
Acceptance into program means acceptance into college: Students are admitted directly into the university and to Special Services for Students with Disabilities with appropriate documentation.

ADMISSIONS

Applicants with learning disabilities are reviewed on the basis of high school transcript, SAT or ACT, personal interview, recommendations, and psychoeducational evaluation. Students may be conditionally admitted with less than a C average, an SAT score lower than 740 or an ACT score lower than 19, or a class rank in the bottom 50 percent. High school courses should include 4 years of English, 2 years of math, 2 years of science, and 2 years of social studies. Applicants not meeting these requirements may be admitted conditionally (on academic warning), on probation, or provisionally.

ADDITIONAL INFORMATION

There is a liaison person between faculty and students. Professors are available to students after class. Modifications can be made in test-taking, which could include extended time and a quiet place to take exams. Additionally, students may receive assistance with note-taking. All services are offered in response to students' requests.

LEARNING DISABILITY PROGRAM/SERVICES

Learning Disability Program/Services: Services to Students with Disabilities
Director: Carol Sinnamon
   E-mail: csinnamon@swu.edu
   Telephone: 864-644-5133
   Fax: 864-644-5973

LEARNING DISABILITY SERVICES

Requests for the following services/accommodations will be evaluated individually based on appropriate and current documentation.

Allowed in exams
   Calculator: Yes
   Dictionary: Yes
   Computer: Yes
   Spellchecker: Yes
Extended test time: Yes
Scribes: Yes
Proctors: Yes
Oral exams: Yes
Note-takers: Yes

Distraction-reduced environment: Yes
Tape recording in class: Yes
Books on tape from RFBD: Yes
Taping of books not from RFBD: Y/N
Accommodations for students with ADHD: Yes
Reading machine: No
Other assistive technology: Yes
Priority registration: No

Added costs for services: No
LD specialists: No
Professional tutors: 1
Peer tutors: 5–8
Max. hours/wk. for services: NR
How professors are notified of LD/ADHD: By both student and director

GENERAL ADMISSIONS INFORMATION

Director of Admissions: Chad Peters
Telephone: 864-644-5558

ENTRANCE REQUIREMENTS

Academic units required: 4 English, 2 math, 2 science, 2 social studies. High school diploma is required, and GED is accepted. ACT without Writing component accepted. TOEFL required of all international applicants: minimum paper TOEFL 500, minimum computer TOEFL 173.

Application deadline: 8/1
Notification: No set date
Average GPA: 3.5
ACT Composite middle 50% range: 17–23

SAT Math middle 50% range: 450–570
SAT Critical Reading middle 50% range: 430–560
SAT Writing middle 50% range: 430–550

Graduated top 10% of class: 14%
Graduated top 25% of class: 33%
Graduated top 50% of class: 69%

COLLEGE GRADUATION REQUIREMENTS

Course waivers allowed: No
Course substitutions allowed: No

ADDITIONAL INFORMATION

Environment: The college is centrally located among Charlotte, North Carolina, and Atlanta, Georgia and within sight of the Blue Ridge Mountains.

Student Body
   Undergrad enrollment: 1,783
   Women: 64%
   Men: 36%
   Percent out-of-state: 33%

Cost Information
   Tuition: $15,700
   Room & board: $6,400
Housing Information
   University housing: Yes
   Percent living on campus: 62%

Greek System
   Fraternity: No
   Sorority: No
Athletics: NAIA

THE UNIVERSITY OF SOUTH CAROLINA— COLUMBIA

Office of Undergraduate Admissions, Columbia, SC 29208
Phone: 803-777-7700 • Fax: 803-777-0101
E-mail: admissions@sc.edu • Web: www.sc.edu
Support: CS • Institution type: 4-year public

LEARNING DISABILITY PROGRAM AND SERVICES

The university's Office of Disability Services (ODS) provides educational support and assistance to students with LD who have the potential for success in a competitive university setting. The Office of Disability Services is specifically designed to empower them with the confidence to become self-advocates and to take an active role in their education. The university works with each student on an individualized basis to match needs with appropriate services. The services are tailored to provide educational support and assistance to students based on their specific needs. The Office of Disability Services recommends and coordinates support services with faculty, administrators, advisors, and deans. The nature and severity of LD may vary considerably. All requests are based on documented diagnostic information regarding each student's specific learning disability. The first step in accessing services from the Office of Disability Services is to self-disclose the disability and arrange an interview. During the interview, staff members will discuss the student's educational background and determine which services best fit his or her needs.

LD/ADHD ADMISSIONS INFORMATION

College entrance tests required: Yes
Interview required: Yes
Essay recommended: No
Documentation required for LD: Psychoeducational evaluation completed within the past 3 years
Documentation required for ADHD: Medical doctor's letter and psychoeducational evaluation completed within the past 3 years
Submitted to: ODS
Special Ed. HS course work accepted: No

Specific course requirements of all applicants: Yes
Separate application required: No
# of LD applications submitted each year: NR
# of LD applications accepted yearly: NR
Total # of students receiving LD services: 300
Acceptance into program means acceptance into college: Students must be admitted and enrolled in the university first (they can appeal a denial) and then request services.

ADMISSIONS

There is no special application or admission process for students with LD. Required scores on the SAT and ACT vary with class rank. Applicants must have a cumulative C-plus average on defined college-preparatory courses, including 4 years of English, 3 years of math, 3 years of science, 2 years of the same foreign language, 4 years of electives, and 1 year of physical education, as well as a 1200 SAT or 27 ACT. If they are denied admission or feel they do not meet the required standards, students may petition the Admissions Committee for an exception to the regular admissions requirements. Once admitted, students should contact the Educational Support Services Center to arrange an interview to determine which services are necessary to accommodate their needs.

ADDITIONAL INFORMATION

Services are individually tailored to provide educational support and assistance. All requests are based on documented diagnostic information. The program is designed to provide educational support and assistance, including analysis of learning needs to determine appropriate interventions, consulting with the faculty about special academic needs, monitoring of progress by a staff member, study skills training, and tutorial referrals. Special program accommodations may include a reduced course load of 9–12 hours, waivers/substitutions for some courses, and expanded pass/fail options. Special classroom accommodations may include tape recorders, note-takers, and extended time on tests.

LEARNING DISABILITY PROGRAM/SERVICES

Learning Disability Program/Services: Office of Student Disability Services
Director: Karen Pettus
 E-mail: karen@gwm.sc.edu or pettus@sc.edu
 Telephone: 803-777-4331
 Fax: 803-777-6741

LEARNING DISABILITY SERVICES

Requests for the following services/accommodations will be evaluated individually based on appropriate and current documentation.

Allowed in exams
 Calculator: Yes
 Dictionary: Yes
 Computer: Yes
 Spellchecker: Yes
 Extended test time: Yes
 Scribes: Yes
 Proctors: Yes
 Oral exams: No
 Note-takers: Yes

Distraction-reduced environment: Yes
 Tape recording in class: Yes
 Books on tape from RFBD: Yes
 Taping of books not from RFBD: Yes
 Accommodations for students with ADHD: Yes
 Reading machine: Yes
 Other assistive technology: Yes
 Priority registration: Yes

Added costs for services: No
 LD specialists: Yes
 Professional tutors: No
 Peer tutors: No
 Max. hours/wk. for services: 42.5
 How professors are notified of LD/ADHD: By student

GENERAL ADMISSIONS INFORMATION

Director of Admissions: R. Scott Verzyl
Telephone: 803-777-7700

ENTRANCE REQUIREMENTS

Academic units required: 4 English, 3 math, 3 science (3 science labs), 2 foreign language, 2 social studies, 1 history, 4 academic electives, 1 physical education or ROTC. High school diploma is required, and GED is accepted. ACT with Writing component required. TOEFL required of all international applicants: minimum paper TOEFL 550, minimum computer TOEFL 210.

Application deadline: 12/1
Notification: Rolling
Average GPA: 3.90
ACT Composite middle 50% range: 23–28

SAT Math middle 50% range: 540–640
SAT Critical Reading middle 50% range: 520–620
SAT Writing middle 50% range: NR

Graduated top 10% of class: 29%
Graduated top 25% of class: 63%
Graduated top 50% of class: 93%

COLLEGE GRADUATION REQUIREMENTS

Course waivers allowed: Yes
In what course: Students with learning disabilities may petition their college for substitution of the required foreign language if the requirement is not an integral part of the degree program.
Course substitutions allowed: Yes
In what course: Students with learning disabilities may petition their college for substitution of the required foreign language if the requirement is not an intregal part of the degree program.

ADDITIONAL INFORMATION

Environment: The university is located on 242 acres in downtown Columbia.

Student Body
 Undergrad enrollment: 18,133
 Women: 54%
 Men: 46%
 Percent out-of-state: 11%

Cost Information
 In-state tuition: $7,408
 Out-of-state tuition: $19,836
 Room & board: $6,520
 Housing Information
 University housing: Yes
 Percent living on campus: 40%

Greek System
 Fraternity: Yes
 Sorority: Yes
 Athletics: Division I

BLACK HILLS STATE UNIVERSITY

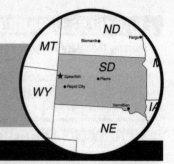

1200 University Street Unit 9502, Spearfish, SD 57799-9502
Phone: 605-642-6343 • Fax: 605-642-6254
E-mail: admissions@bhsu.edu • Web: www.bhsu.edu
Support: CS • Institution type: 2- and 4-year, public

LEARNING DISABILITY PROGRAM AND SERVICES

Student Support Services ensures equal access and opportunities to educational programs for students with learning disabilities. Within the program, the disabilities services coordinator arranges accommodations, counseling services, and campus awareness activities for students with disabilities. The algebra advisor, language/learning skills instructor, and academic and career advisor provide tutoring and advising services to encourage students with disabilities to achieve academic success.

LD/ADHD ADMISSIONS INFORMATION

College entrance tests required: Yes
Interview required: No
Essay recommended: No
Documentation required for LD: Psychoeducational evaluation
Documentation required for ADHD: Medical or psychological evaluation/documentation of ADHD
Submitted to: Student Assistance Center
Special Ed. HS course work accepted: No

Specific course requirements of all applicants: Yes
Separate application required: Yes
# of LD applications submitted each year: NR
# of LD applications accepted yearly: NR
Total # of students receiving LD services: 70
Acceptance into program means acceptance into college: Students must be admitted to and enrolled in the university first and then request services.

ADMISSIONS

General admission requirements include a C average, an ACT of 20, or a rank in the upper 65 percent of graduation class for residents or upper half for nonresidents. In addition, students must complete the following high school course work: 4 years of English, 2 years of science lab, 3 years of math (or 2 years of math and 2 years of science lab), 3 years of social studies, 0.5 year of fine arts, and 0.5 year of computer science. Students who do not meet the admission requirements for general admissions will be admitted to the junior college at Black Hills State. Course deficiencies must be satisfied within 2 years of admittance. There is complete open enrollment for summer courses also. Transfer students who do not meet admission requirements will be admitted on probationary status.

ADDITIONAL INFORMATION

The Student Assistance Center offers peer tutoring to all students in most subject areas. Basic skills instruction is available in English and math, and a university learning skills course provides an introduction to college-level studies. The Center for Academic Success at Black Hills State University is a student-centered, service-oriented office focused on ensuring student persistence and success. The center provides assistance and information to all students, faculty, and staff in an effort to facilitate academic success, student persistence, and student level of satisfaction with the university experience. Staff provides information and advisement on a number of topics related to study skills success and personal development. They use various valid and reliable inventories to assist students in identifying their academic strengths, personal interests, learning styles, and academic and career goals. They also draw up personal success plans with students early in the semester to clearly define goals, and they follow up on student progress throughout the semester to ensure that plans are put into action and monitored regularly. Testing and tutoring services are also available in the Center for Academic Success.

LEARNING DISABILITY PROGRAM/SERVICES

Learning Disability Program/Services: Student Assistance Center
Director: Larry Vrooman, MS, CRC
 E-mail: larryvrooman@bhsu.edu
 Telephone: 605-642-6099
 Fax: 605-642-6690

LEARNING DISABILITY SERVICES

Requests for the following services/accommodations will be evaluated individually based on appropriate and current documentation.

Allowed in exams
 Calculator: Yes
 Dictionary: Yes
 Computer: Yes
 Spellchecker: Yes
Extended test time: Yes
Scribes: Yes
Proctors: Yes
Oral exams: Yes
Note-takers: Yes

Distraction-reduced environment: Yes
Tape recording in class: Yes
Books on tape from RFBD: Yes
Taping of books not from RFBD: Yes
Accommodations for students with ADHD: Yes
Reading machine: Yes
Other assistive technology: Yes
Priority registration: No

Added costs for services: No
LD specialists: Yes
Professional tutors: 4
Peer tutors: 3–10
Max. hours/wk. for services: 40
How professors are notified of LD/ADHD: By both student and director

GENERAL ADMISSIONS INFORMATION

Director of Admissions: Steve Ochsner
Telephone: 605-642-6343

ENTRANCE REQUIREMENTS

Academic units required: 4 English, 3 math, 3 science (3 science labs), 3 social studies, 0.5 fine arts. High school diploma is required, and GED is accepted. ACT with or without Writing component accepted. TOEFL required of all international applicants: minimum paper TOEFL 520.

Application deadline: NR
Notification: NR
Average GPA: 3.0
ACT Composite middle 50% range: 18–23

SAT Math middle 50% range: NR
SAT Critical Reading middle 50% range: NR
SAT Writing middle 50% range: NR

Graduated top 10% of class: 6%
Graduated top 25% of class: 23%
Graduated top 50% of class: 56%

COLLEGE GRADUATION REQUIREMENTS

Course waivers allowed: No
Course substitutions allowed: No

ADDITIONAL INFORMATION

Environment: The university is located on 123 acres in a small town 45 miles northwest of Rapid City.

Student Body
 Undergrad enrollment: 3,166
 Women: 63%
 Men: 37%
 Percent out-of-state: 18%

Cost Information
 In-state tuition: $4,600
 Out-of-state tuition: $9,600
 Room & board: $3,200
Housing Information
 University housing: Yes
 Percent living on campus: 25%

Greek System
 Fraternity: Yes
 Sorority: Yes
 Athletics: NAIA

SOUTH DAKOTA STATE UNIVERSITY

SAD 200, BOX 2201, Brookings, SD 57007-0649
Phone: 605-688-4121 • Fax: 605-688-6891
E-mail: sdsu.admissions@sdstate.edu • Web: www3.sdstate.edu
Support: S • Institution type: 4-year public

LEARNING DISABILITY PROGRAM AND SERVICES

South Dakota State University is committed to providing equal opportunities for higher education to academically qualified students with LD who have a reasonable expectation of college success. The university does not offer a specialized curriculum, but it does share responsibility with students for modifying programs to meet individual needs. Students needing specialized tutoring service in reading and writing may have to seek assistance from Vocational Rehabilitation or personally pay for such help.

LD/ADHD ADMISSIONS INFORMATION

College entrance tests required: Yes
Interview required: No
Essay recommended: No
Documentation required for LD: WAIS–III, WISC–R, WRAT
Documentation required for ADHD: Our website has a link to a documentation form that we ask students to have their medical professional complete.
Submitted to: DS
Special Ed. HS course work accepted: NR

Specific course requirements of all applicants: Yes
Separate application required: Yes
# of LD applications submitted each year: NR
# of LD applications accepted yearly: NR
Total # of students receiving LD services: 55
Acceptance into program means acceptance into college: Students must be admitted to and enrolled in the university first and then request services.

ADMISSIONS

Students with LD are required to submit the general application form. If they do not meet all of the course requirements, they may be admitted conditionally based on ACT scores or class rank. Courses required include 4 years of English, 2–3 years of math, 0.5 year of computer science, 3 years of social studies, 2–3 years of science, and 0.5 year of art or music. Students deficient in course requirements need an ACT of 22 (in-state or Minnesota) or 23 (out of state).

ADDITIONAL INFORMATION

A skills course is available entitled Mastering Lifelong Skills. Test proctoring for additional time, as well as reading or writing assistance with classroom exams, can be arranged. DSS will also assist students who are LD with finding readers or note-takers.

LEARNING DISABILITY PROGRAM/SERVICES

Learning Disability Program/Services: Disability Services (DS)
Director: Nancy Hartenhoff-Crooks, MS, Coordinator
  E-mail: nancy.crooks@sdstate.edu
  Telephone: 605-688-4504
  Fax: 605-688-4987

LEARNING DISABILITY SERVICES

Requests for the following services/accommodations will be evaluated individually based on appropriate and current documentation.

Allowed in exams
  Calculator: Yes
  Dictionary: No
  Computer: Yes
  Spellchecker: Yes
Extended test time: Yes
Scribes: Yes
Proctors: Yes
Oral exams: Yes
Note-takers: No

Distraction-reduced environment: Yes
Tape recording in class: Yes
Books on tape from RFBD: No
Taping of books not from RFBD: No
Accommodations for students with ADHD: Yes
Reading machine: Yes
Other assistive technology: Yes
Priority registration: No

Added costs for services: No
LD specialists: No
Professional tutors: No
Peer tutors: 25–32
Max. hours/wk. for services: Unlimited
How professors are notified of LD/ADHD: By both student and director

GENERAL ADMISSIONS INFORMATION

Director of Admissions: Tracy Welsh
Telephone: 605-688-4121

ENTRANCE REQUIREMENTS

Academic units required: 4 English, 3 math, 3 science (3 science labs), 3 social studies, 0.5 fine arts. High school diploma is required, and GED is accepted. ACT with or without Writing component accepted. TOEFL required of all international applicants: minimum paper TOEFL 500, minimum computer TOEFL 1.

Application deadline: NR
Notification: Rolling
Average GPA: NR
ACT Composite middle 50% range: 20–25

SAT Math middle 50% range: NR
SAT Critical Reading middle 50% range: NR
SAT Writing middle 50% range: NR

Graduated top 10% of class: NR
Graduated top 25% of class: NR
Graduated top 50% of class: NR

COLLEGE GRADUATION REQUIREMENTS

Course waivers allowed: No
Course substitutions allowed: No

ADDITIONAL INFORMATION

Environment: The school is located on 220 acres in a rural area 50 miles north of Sioux Falls.

Student Body
  Undergrad enrollment: 9,003
  Women: 50%
  Men: 50%
  Percent out-of-state: 28%

Cost Information
  In-state tuition: $5,000
  Out-of-state tuition: $9,900
  Room & board: $5,029
Housing Information
  University housing: Yes
  Percent living on campus: 33%

Greek System
  Fraternity: Yes
  Sorority: Yes
Athletics: Division I

THE UNIVERSITY OF SOUTH DAKOTA

414 East Clark, Vermillion, SD 57069
Phone: 605-677-5434 • Fax: 605-677-6323
E-mail: admissions@usd.edu • Web: www.usd.edu
Support: CS• Institution type: 2- and 4-year public

LEARNING DISABILITY PROGRAM AND SERVICES

The University of South Dakota Disability Services (USDDS) operates on the premise that students at the university are full participants in the process of obtaining appropriate accommodations for their disabilities. Students are encouraged to make their own decisions and become self-advocates for appropriate accommodations or services. The three main goals are to help students become self-advocates, provide better transition services into and out of college, and to provide better instructional and support services. The university strives to ensure that all individuals with legally defined disabilities have access to the full range of the university's programs, services, and activities.

LD/ADHD ADMISSIONS INFORMATION

College entrance tests required: Yes
Interview required: N/A
Essay recommended: N/A
Documentation required for LD: NR
Documentation required for ADHD: NR
Submitted to: USDDS
Special Ed. HS course work accepted: Yes

Specific course requirements of all applicants: Yes
Separate application required: Yes
# of LD applications submitted each year: NR
# of LD applications accepted yearly: NR
Total # of students receiving LD services: NR
Acceptance into program means acceptance into
  college: Student must be admitted and enrolled in the university first and then request services.

ADMISSIONS

The general admission requirements include standing in the top 60 percent of the class, an ACT score of 18 or above, or a GPA of 2.6 with a C or higher in the required high school courses. Course requirements include 4 years of English or ACT English subtest of 17 or above or AP English score of 2 or above; 3 years of math or ACT math sub score of 17 or above or AP Calculus score of 2 or above; 3 years of lab science or ACT Science-Reasoning sub score of 17 or above or AP Science of 2 or above; 3 years of social studies or ACT Reading sub score of 17 or above or AP Social Studies score of 2 or above; and 0.5 year of fine arts or AP fine arts score of 2 or above. Students are expected to be proficient in computer skills or they may be required to take specific computer skills courses at the university. Applicants to the Associate Degree Program must meet the same criteria as general admissions or complete the General Equivalency Diploma with a combined score of at least 225 and a minimum score of 40 on each test. Applications submitted from students with deficiencies are reviewed on an individual basis. Nontraditional students (21 years or older) may be admitted at the university's discretion. There is an alternative option for the Director of Admissions to seek a recommendation from the Director of Disability Services regarding admission questions for individuals with disabilities.

ADDITIONAL INFORMATION

Services are individualized for each student's learning needs. USDDS staff provides the following activities: planning, developing, delivering, and evaluating direct service programs; meeting individually with students for academic and related counseling and skill building; ensuring that students receive reasonable and appropriate accommodations that match their needs; consulting with faculty; and providing academic, career, and personal counseling referrals. Classroom accommodations include test modification, note-taking assistance, readers, books on tape, specialized computer facilities, and tutors.

LEARNING DISABILITY PROGRAM/SERVICES

Learning Disability Program/Services: Disability Services, Center for Disabilities (USDDS)
Director: Ernetta L. Fox
  E-mail: dservice@usd.edu
  Telephone: 605-677-6389
  Fax: 605-677-3172

LEARNING DISABILITY SERVICES

Requests for the following/services accommodations will be evaluated individually based on appropriate and current documentation.

Allowed in exams
  Calculator: Yes
  Dictionary: Yes
  Computer: Yes
  Spellchecker: Yes
Extended test time: Yes
Scribes: Yes
Proctors: Yes
Oral exams: Yes
Note-takers: Yes

Distraction-reduced environment: Yes
Tape recording in class: Yes
Books on tape from RFBD: Yes
Taping of books not from RFBD: Yes
Accommodations for students with ADHD: Yes
Reading machine: Yes
Other assistive technology: Yes
Priority registration: No
Added costs for services: No

LD specialists: Yes
Professional tutors: NR
Peer tutors: Yes
Max. hours/wk. for services: Unlimited
How professors are notified of LD/ADHD: By student

GENERAL ADMISSIONS INFORMATION

Director of Admissions: Cecil Foster
Telephone: 605-677-5434

ENTRANCE REQUIREMENTS

Academic units required: 4 English, 3 math, 3 science (3 science labs), 3 social studies, 1 fine arts **Academic units recommended:** 4 English, 4 math, 4 science, (3 science labs), 2 foreign language, 3 social studies, 1 fine arts. High school diploma is required, and GED is accepted. ACT with or without Writing component accepted. TOEFL required of all international applicants: minimum paper TOEFL 550, minimum computer TOEFL 213.

Application deadline: NR
Notification: Rolling
Average GPA: 3.27
ACT Composite middle 50% range: 20–25

SAT Math middle 50% range: 470–620
SAT Critical Reading middle 50% range: 460–580
SAT Writing middle 50% range: NR

Graduated top 10% of class: 11%
Graduated top 25% of class: 32%
Graduated top 50% of class: 69%

COLLEGE GRADUATION REQUIREMENTS

Course waivers allowed: No
Course substitutions allowed: No

ADDITIONAL INFORMATION

Environment: Located 35 miles from Sioux City

Student Body
  Undergrad enrollment: 5,751
  Women: 61%
  Men: 39%
  Percent out-of-state: 26%

Cost Information
  In-state tuition: $4,800
  Out-of-state tuition: $9,800
  Room & board: $4,964
Housing Information
  University housing: Yes
  Percent living on campus: 31%

Greek System
  Fraternity: Yes
  Sorority: Yes
Athletics: Division II

LEE UNIVERSITY

PO Box 3450, Cleveland, TN 37320-3450
Phone: 423-614-8500 • Fax: 423-614-8533
E-mail: admissions@leeuniversity.edu • Web: www.leeuniversity.edu
Support: CS • Institution type: 4-year private

LEARNING DISABILITY PROGRAM AND SERVICES

Lee University provides an Academic Support Program for students. This service is free to students. It is the goal of the Lee University Academic Support Program to empower students to actualize all the academic potential that they can. The college offers a peer tutorial program that hires the best students on campus to share their time, experience, and insight in the course or courses that are most difficult for the students who need tutoring. In addition, the college provides direct assistance for any student to verify a learning disability. For these students, Lee University provides support teams, testing adjustments, classroom adjustments, tutoring, and personal monitoring. Students must initiate the request for special accommodations by applying at the Academic Support Program Office. Lee University is committed to the provision of reasonable accommodations for students with disabilities.

LD/ADHD ADMISSIONS INFORMATION

College entrance tests required: Yes
Interview required: No
Essay recommended: No
Documentation required for LD: Psychoeducational evaluation
Documentation required for ADHD: Yes
Submitted to: Both Admissions Office and Academic Support Program
Special Ed. HS course work accepted: Yes

Specific course requirements of all applicants: NR
Separate application required: No
# of LD applications submitted each year: NR
# of LD applications accepted yearly: NR
Total # of students receiving LD services: NR
Acceptance into program means acceptance into college: Students must be admitted to and enrolled in the university first and then request services.

ADMISSIONS
Each applicant is reviewed on a case-by-case basis. Each student must be able to perform successfully with limited support. The ACT minimum is 17; for the SAT it is 860. The minimum required GPA is 2.0. There are no specific course requirements. Students who do not meet the college policy for entrance are referred to a special committee for possible probational acceptance.

ADDITIONAL INFORMATION
The Academic Support Program is staffed by professional counselors, math and reading instructors, and a tutoring coordinator. The center has listening and study lab instructional materials, group study/discussion rooms, and tutoring services. The program provides readers and books on tape. Benefits included in the program are tutoring sessions with friendly and comfortable surroundings; 2 hours of tutoring per week per subject; and tutoring in any subject, including biology, psychology, English, mathematics, religion, science, sociology, history, and foreign language. Freshmen are channeled into a gateway class, which provides study skills and time management skills.

LEARNING DISABILITY PROGRAM/SERVICES

Learning Disability Program/Services: Academic Support Program
Director: Gayle Gallaher
  E-mail: AcademicSupport@LeeUniversity.edu
  Telephone: 423-614-8181
  Fax: 423-614-8179

LEARNING DISABILITY SERVICES

Requests for the following services/accommodations will be evaluated individually based on appropriate and current documentation.

Allowed in exams
  Calculator: NR
  Dictionary: No
  Computer: No
  Spellchecker: No
Extended test time: Yes
Scribes: Yes
Proctors: Yes
Oral exams: Yes
Note-takers: Yes

Distraction-reduced environment: Yes
Tape recording in class: Yes
Books on tape from RFBD: Yes
Taping of books not from RFBD: No
Accommodations for students with
  ADHD: Yes
Reading machine: Yes
Other assistive technology: Yes
Priority registration: No

Added costs for services: No
LD specialists: Yes
Professional tutors: NR
Peer tutors: 50
Max. hours/wk. for services: NR
How professors are notified of
  LD/ADHD: By student

GENERAL ADMISSIONS INFORMATION

Director of Admissions: Phil Cook
Telephone: 423-614-8500

ENTRANCE REQUIREMENTS

Academic units required: 4 English, 3 math, 2 science, 1 foreign language, 2 social studies, 1 history. **Academic units recommended:** 4 English, 3 math, 2 science, 1 foreign language, 2 social studies, 1 history, 1 computer skills. High school diploma is required, and GED is accepted. ACT with or without Writing component accepted. TOEFL required of all international applicants: minimum paper TOEFL 450, minimum computer TOEFL 133.

Application deadline: 9/1
Notification: Rolling
Average GPA: 3.36
ACT Composite middle 50% range:
  20–27

SAT Math middle 50% range:
  450–600
SAT Critical Reading middle 50% range: 470–600
SAT Writing middle 50% range: NR

Graduated top 10% of class: 19%
Graduated top 25% of class: 46%
Graduated top 50% of class: 74%

COLLEGE GRADUATION REQUIREMENTS

Course waivers allowed: No
Course substitutions allowed: No

ADDITIONAL INFORMATION

Environment: The college is located on 40 acres in a small town 25 miles from Chattanooga.

Student Body
  Undergrad enrollment: 3,580
  Women: 56%
  Men: 44%
  Percent out-of-state: 61%

Cost Information
  Tuition: $10,392
  Room & board: $5,276
Housing Information
  University housing: Yes
  Percent living on campus: 45%

Greek System
  Fraternity: Yes
  Sorority: Yes
Athletics: NAIA

MIDDLE TENNESSEE STATE U.

Office of Admissions, Murfreesboro, TN 37132
Phone: 800-433-6878 • Fax: 615-898-5478
E-mail: admissions@mtsu.edu • Web: www.mtsu.edu
Support: CS • Institution type: 4-year public

LEARNING DISABILITY PROGRAM AND SERVICES

The Learning Disabilities Program is a part of the Disabled Student Services office. The LD program offers comprehensive support services for students diagnosed with LD and ADHD. Eligibility for the program requires admission to MTSU and documentation of the disability. The LD program is designed to ensure students have an equal opportunity to pursue an education. Students with LD are held to the same academic standards as all students; however, accommodations are available to assist meeting these requirements. Accommodations are determined on an individual basis considering the student's strengths, course requirements, and documentation. To register with the LD program, students schedule an appointment with the coordinator, complete the registration form, and provide the most current documentation of the disability.

LD/ADHD ADMISSIONS INFORMATION

College entrance tests required: Yes
Interview required: No
Essay recommended: No
Documentation required for LD: Psychoeducational evaluation
Documentation required for ADHD: Physician statement
Submitted to: Disabled Student Services
Special Ed. HS course work accepted: No

Specific course requirements of all applicants: Yes
Separate application required: No
# of LD applications submitted each year: NR
# of LD applications accepted yearly: NR
Total # of students receiving LD services: 250–350
Acceptance into program means acceptance into college: Students must be admitted to and enrolled in the university first and then request services.

ADMISSIONS

There is no special admission process for students with LD. All students must meet the same general admission requirements. The minimum GPA is a 2.3. Students should have 4 years of English, 2 years of math, 2 years of science, 2 years of social studies, 2 years of a foreign language, and 1 year of visual and performing arts. Course substitutions are not allowed. The average ACT score is 21; the average SAT score is 970. Students are encouraged to self-disclose a disability in a personal statement during the admission process, though this is not required.

ADDITIONAL INFORMATION

Students are encouraged to initiate contact with the LD program coordinator early in the semester to determine the necessary accommodations. Once enrolled in courses, students schedule regular meetings with the coordinator to monitor progress and/or determine the need for adjustments to the accommodations. Services/resources provided include orientation to the LD program; orientation to an Adaptive Technology Center; assistance with the admission process; advising and strategic scheduling of classes; early registration of classes; tutorial services; test accommodations; note-takers, readers, scribes, and books on tape; exploration of time management/note-taking strategies; career planning and employment strategies; and resume preparation. The Adaptive Technology Center provides training support for students, faculty, and staff with disabilities in the use of adaptive/assistive technology application and devices. All disability documentation is conditional and is not released without the consent of the student.

LEARNING DISABILITY PROGRAM/SERVICES

Learning Disability Program/Services: Disabled Student Services
Director: John Harris
 E-mail: jharris@mtsu.edu
 Telephone: 615-898-2783
 Fax: 615-898-4893

LEARNING DISABILITY SERVICES

Requests for the following services/accommodations will be evaluated individually based on appropriate and current documentation.

Allowed in exams
 Calculator: Yes
 Dictionary: Yes
 Computer: Yes
 Spellchecker: Yes
Extended test time: Yes
Scribes: Yes
Proctors: Yes
Oral exams: Yes
Note-takers: Yes

Distraction-reduced environment: Yes
Tape recording in class: Yes
Books on tape from RFBD: Yes
Taping of books not from RFBD: Yes
Accommodations for students with ADHD: Yes
Reading machine: Yes
Other assistive technology: Yes
Priority registration: Yes

Added costs for services: No
LD specialists: Yes
Professional tutors: No
Peer tutors: Yes
Max. hours/wk. for services: Unlimited
How professors are notified of LD/ADHD: By both student and director

GENERAL ADMISSIONS INFORMATION

Director of Admissions: Lynn Palmer
Telephone: 800-433-6878

ENTRANCE REQUIREMENTS

Academic Units Required: 4 English, 3 math, 2 science, 2 social studies, 1 fine arts, 1 elective. SAT/ACT required. ACT of 22 required if GPA is less than 3.0.

Application deadline: 7/1
Notification: Rolling
Average GPA: 2.96
ACT Composite middle 50% range: NR

SAT Math middle 50% range: NR
SAT Critical Reading middle 50% range: NR
SAT Writing middle 50% range: NR

Graduated top 10% of class: 17%
Graduated top 25% of class: 51%
Graduated top 50% of class: 64%

COLLEGE GRADUATION REQUIREMENTS

Course waivers allowed: Yes
In what course: On an individual basis
Course substitutions allowed: Yes
In what course: On an individual basis

ADDITIONAL INFORMATION

Environment: The university is located 32 miles from Nashville.

Student Body
 Undergrad enrollment:
 Women: NR
 Men: NR
 Percent out-of-state: 5%

Cost Information
 In-state tuition: $3,900
 Out-of-state tuition: $11,800
 Room & board: $4,025
Housing Information
 University housing: Yes
 Percent living on campus: 25%

Greek System
 Fraternity: Yes
 Sorority: Yes
Athletics: Division I

THE UNIVERSITY OF MEMPHIS

229 Administration Building, Memphis, TN 38152
Phone: 901-678-2111 • Fax: 901-678-3053
E-mail: recruitment@memphis.edu • Web: www.memphis.edu
Support: CS • Institution type: 4-year public

LEARNING DISABILITY PROGRAM AND SERVICES

The university's LD/ADHD program is designed to enhance academic strengths, provide support for areas of weakness, and build skills to help students with LD and ADHD compete in the college environment. The program encourages development of life-long learning skills as well as personal responsibility for academic success. Training in college survival skills and regular meetings with the staff are emphasized during the first year to aid in the transition to college. Specific services are tailored to individual needs, considering one's strengths, weaknesses, course requirements, and learning styles. Students are integrated into regular classes and are held to the same academic standards as other students; however, academic accommodations are available to assist them in meeting requirements. The LD/ADHD program places responsibility on students to initiate services and follow through with services once they are arranged. Most students who use the appropriate services are successful in their academic pursuits.

LD/ADHD ADMISSIONS INFORMATION

College entrance tests required: Yes
Interview required: No
Essay recommended: No
Documentation required for LD: WAIS–III, WJ–III
Documentation required for ADHD: Yes
Submitted to: Admissions Office and LD/ADHD Program
Special Ed. HS course work accepted: Yes

Specific course requirements of all applicants: Yes
Separate application required: No
# of LD applications submitted each year: 150–200
# of LD applications accepted yearly: 150–200
Total # of students receiving LD services: 250–325
Acceptance into program means acceptance into college: Students must be admitted to and enrolled in the university first and then request services.

ADMISSIONS

If applicants with learning disabilities or ADHD choose to disclose their disability and provide professional medical documentation, exceptions to the regular admissions criteria may be made on an individual basis. Course requirements include 4 years of English, 2 years of science, 2 years of a foreign language, 2 years of social studies, and 1 year of visual and performing arts. It is recommended that students self-disclose their LD during the admission process if they do not meet regular admission requirements. Exceptions are made only for applicants who have at least a 17 ACT composite, a 2.0 GPA, and no more than three high school curriculum deficiencies, only one of which can be math. Applicants who request admissions exceptions will be asked to provide two academic recommendations and a personal letter in addition to the documentation. Students requesting admissions exceptions based on learning disabilities or attention deficit hyperactivity disorder will have their documentation reviewed by the LD coordinator to determine if the documentation is sufficient to meet qualifying criteria.

ADDITIONAL INFORMATION

Transitional studies courses are available in basic math, algebra, and composition for credit; however, they do not apply toward a degree. One-on-one instruction is available in note-taking, time management techniques, and organization skills. The university also offers orientation (highly advised for incoming students) for students with learning disabilities, early registration, use of computers and adaptive software, preferential classroom seating, and two special sections of Introduction to the university geared to the needs of students with LD and ADHD. Services and accommodations are available for undergraduate and graduate students.

LEARNING DISABILITY PROGRAM/SERVICES

Learning Disability Program/Services: LD/ADHD Program
Director: Susan Te Paske
  E-mail: stepaske@memphis.edu
  Telephone: 901-678-2880
  Fax: 901-678-3070
Contact Person: Jennifer Murchison
  E-mail: stepaske@memphis.edu
  Telephone: 901-678-2880
  Fax: 901-678-3070

LEARNING DISABILITY SERVICES

Requests for the following services/accommodations will be evaluated individually based on appropriate and current documentation.

Allowed in exams
  Calculator: Yes
  Dictionary: Yes
  Computer: Yes
  Spellchecker: Yes
Extended test time: Yes
Scribes: Yes
Proctors: Yes
Oral exams: Yes
Note-takers: Yes

Distraction-reduced environment: Yes
Tape recording in class: Yes
Books on tape from RFBD: Yes
Taping of books not from RFBD: Yes
Accommodations for students with ADHD: Yes
Reading machine: Yes
Other assistive technology: Yes
Priority registration: Yes

Added costs for services: No
LD specialists: Yes
Professional tutors: 2
Peer tutors: 1–3
Max. hours/wk. for services: 6
How professors are notified of LD/ADHD: By student

GENERAL ADMISSIONS INFORMATION

Director of Admissions: David Wallace
Telephone: 901-678-2111

ENTRANCE REQUIREMENTS

Academic units required: 4 English, 3 math, 2 science, 2 foreign language, 2 social studies, 1 visual/performing arts. **Academic units recommended:** 4 math, 3 science, 2 social studies. High school diploma is required, and GED is accepted. TOEFL required of all international applicants: minimum paper TOEFL 500.

Application deadline: 8/1
Notification: Rolling
Average GPA: NR
ACT Composite middle 50% range: NR

SAT Math middle 50% range: NR
SAT Critical Reading middle 50% range: NR
SAT Writing middle 50% range: NR

Graduated top 10% of class: NR
Graduated top 25% of class: NR
Graduated top 50% of class: NR

COLLEGE GRADUATION REQUIREMENTS

Course waivers allowed: Yes
In what course: Foreign language
Course substitutions allowed: Yes
In what course: Foreign language

ADDITIONAL INFORMATION

Environment: The university is located on 1,159 acres in an urban area.

Student Body
  Undergrad enrollment: 15,600
  Women: 57%
  Men: 43%
  Percent out-of-state: 7%

Cost Information
  In-state tuition: $5,000
  Out-of-state tuition: $14,800
  Room & board: $6,000
Housing Information
  University housing: Yes
  Percent living on campus: 14%

Greek System
  Fraternity: Yes
  Sorority: Yes
Athletics: Division I

The University of Memphis

THE U. OF TENNESSEE AT CHATTANOOGA

615 McCallie Avenue, 131 Hooper Hall, Chattanooga, TN 37403
Phone: 423-425-4662 • Fax: 423-425-4157
E-mail: Yancy-Freeman@utc.edu • Web: www.utc.edu
Support: CS • Institution type: 4-year public

LEARNING DISABILITY PROGRAM AND SERVICES

The College Access Program (CAP) at the university provides academic, social, and emotional support for students with learning disabilities. CAP provides academic advisement, tutoring in all course work, career planning, counseling, social skills development, survival skills, career advisement, word processing skills, extended time on tests, freshmen orientation, and psychological testing. Start Smart is a summer seminar for CAP students to prepare them for university course work and general adjustment to the university.

LD/ADHD ADMISSIONS INFORMATION

College entrance tests required: Yes
Interview required: No
Essay recommended: No
Documentation required for LD: WJ–III, WAIS–III,
   achievement battery completed within the past 3 years
Documentation required for ADHD: Yes
Submitted to: Admissions Office and CAP
Special Ed. HS course work accepted: N/A

Specific course requirements of all applicants: Yes
Separate application required: Yes
# of LD applications submitted each year: 20
# of LD applications accepted yearly: 20
Total # of students receiving LD services: 75
**Acceptance into program means acceptance into
   college:** Students must be admitted an enrolled at the
   university first to participate in CAP.

ADMISSIONS

Students with learning disabilities submit a general application to the Admissions Office and a special application to CAP. Applicants to CAP should also submit an LD evaluation, a transcript, and two letters of recommendation. Minimum admissions requirements are a 2.0 GPA; an ACT score 16 or an SAT score of 760; and 4 years of English, 3 years of math, 2 years of science lab, 1 year of American history, 1 year of European history, world history, or world geography, 2 years of a foreign language, and 1 year of fine arts. Students may be admitted conditionally if they fall below these guidelines and have only 1 unit deficiency. If the course deficiency is in the area of the LD, an Appeals Committee will sometimes allow a probationary admittance if CAP also accepts the student. Students admitted on condition must earn at least a 1.0 GPA their first semester or suspension will result. The Dean of Admissions or Admission Committee may recommend conditions for acceptance. Application to the Office for Students with Disabilities is a separate process and is not relevant to the admissions process.

ADDITIONAL INFORMATION

CAP does not, as a matter of policy, seek on a student's behalf a waiver of any course work. Students admitted conditionally may be required to carry a reduced course load, take specific courses, have a specific advisor, and take specific programs of developmental study. Upperclass and graduate student tutors trained to work with students with learning disabilities hold regularly scheduled and individualized tutoring sessions. The coordinator matches tutors with CAP students according to learning styles. Social skills development activities may involve video and role-playing situations in group form as well as during informal gatherings. There is a monthly publication, *The CAPsule*, for CAP students and parents. UTC offers developmental math and English courses for institutional credit. Services and accommodations are available for undergraduate and graduate students.

LEARNING DISABILITY PROGRAM/SERVICES

Learning Disability Program/Services: College Access Program (CAP)
Director: Debra Anderson
  E-mail: OSD-CAP@utc.edu
  Telephone: 423-425-4006
  Fax: 423-425-2288

LEARNING DISABILITY SERVICES

Requests for the following services/accommodations will be evaluated individually based on appropriate and current documentation.

Allowed in exams	**Distraction-reduced environment:** Yes	**Added costs for services:** Yes
Calculator: Yes	**Tape recording in class:** Yes	**LD specialists:** Yes
Dictionary: No	**Books on tape from RFBD:** Yes	**Professional tutors:** 3–5
Computer: Yes	**Taping of books not from RFBD:** No	**Peer tutors:** 3–5
Spellchecker: Yes	**Accommodations for students with**	**Max. hours/wk. for services:**
Extended test time: Yes	**ADHD:** Yes	Unlimited
Scribes: No	**Reading machine:** Yes	**How professors are notified of**
Proctors: No	**Other assistive technology:** Yes	**LD/ADHD:** By student
Oral exams: Yes	**Priority registration:** No	
Note-takers: Yes		

GENERAL ADMISSIONS INFORMATION

Director of Admissions: Yancy Freeman
Telephone: 423-425-4662

ENTRANCE REQUIREMENTS

Academic units required: 4 English, 3 math, 2 science (2 science labs), 2 foreign language, 2 social studies, 2 history, 2 fine arts. High school diploma is required, and GED is accepted. ACT with or without Writing component accepted. TOEFL required of all international applicants: minimum paper TOEFL 500, minimum computer TOEFL 200.

Application deadline: NR	**SAT Math middle 50% range:** NR	**Graduated top 10% of class:** NR
Notification: After processing	**SAT Critical Reading middle 50%**	**Graduated top 25% of class:** 41%
application	**range:** NR	**Graduated top 50% of class:** 81%
Average GPA: 3.17	**SAT Writing middle 50% range:** NR	
ACT Composite middle 50% range:		
19–24		

COLLEGE GRADUATION REQUIREMENTS

Course waivers allowed: No
Course substitutions allowed: No

ADDITIONAL INFORMATION

Environment: The university is located on 60 acres in an urban area in Chattanooga.

Student Body	**Cost Information**	**Greek System**
Undergrad enrollment: 7,381	**In-state tuition:** $4,688	**Fraternity:** Yes
Women: 57%	**Out-of-state tuition:** $14,084	**Sorority:** Yes
Men: 43%	**Room & board:** $7,384	**Athletics:** Division I
Percent out-of-state: 6%	**Housing Information**	
	University housing: Yes	
	Percent living on campus: 30%	

The University of Tennessee at Chattanooga

THE U. OF TENNESSEE AT KNOXVILLE

320 Student Service Building, Circle Park Dr., Knoxville, TN 37996-0230
Phone: 865-974-2184 • Fax: 865-974-6341
E-mail: admissions@tennessee.edu • Web: www.tennesee.edu
Support: CS • Institution type: 4-year public

LEARNING DISABILITY PROGRAM AND SERVICES

The mission of the Office of Disability Services is to provide each student with a disability an equal opportunity to participate in the university's programs and activities. Students who are requesting support services are required to submit documentation to verify eligibility under the ADA of 1990. The documentation must include medical or psychological information from a certified professional. It is each student's responsibility to meet the essential qualifications and institutional standards; disclose the disability in a timely manner to ODS; provide appropriate documentation; inform ODS of accommodation needs; talk with professors about accommodations in the classroom, as needed; inform ODS of barriers to a successful education; maintain and return borrowed equipment; keep all appointments with ODS staff members or call to cancel or reschedule; be involved in their academic planning and course selection; and monitor their own progress toward graduation.

LD/ADHD ADMISSIONS INFORMATION

College entrance tests required: Yes
Interview required: No
Essay recommended: No
Documentation required for LD: Psychoeducational evaluation
Documentation required for ADHD: Yes
Submitted to: ODS
Special Ed. HS course work accepted: N/A

Specific course requirements of all applicants: Yes
Separate application required: Yes
# of LD applications submitted each year: NR
# of LD applications accepted yearly: NR
Total # of students receiving LD services: NR
Acceptance into program means acceptance into college: Students must be admitted and enrolled prior to requesting services.

ADMISSIONS

There is no special admission process for students with learning disabilities. The Office of Admissions makes every attempt to judge each application on its academic merits. The university does not ask if a prospective student has a disability prior to admission. If an applicant believes that their academic record does not accurately reflect their situation, then the student should self-identify. It is not recommended that the student include documentation with their admission materials. Documentation of a disability is not needed until the time of enrollment. Prospective students who include documentation with their application and are admitted are not guaranteed services. They need to contact ODS directly. If you feel more information is needed for you to compete at an equal level with others seeking admission, you may consider voluntarily self-identifying your disability and the circumstances to the Admissions Office. Qualified candidates with a disability will not be denied admissions solely on the basis of their disability. Applicants are required to have 4 years of English; 2 years of algebra; 1 year of geometry, trigonometry, advanced math, or calculus; 2 years of natural science, including at least 1 year of biology, chemistry, or physics; 1 year of American history; 1 year of European history, world history, or world geography; 2 years of a single foreign language; and 1 year of visual and performing arts. A minimum high school GPA of 2.0 is required.

ADDITIONAL INFORMATION

The goals of ODS are to provide access to appropriate accommodations and support services; provide referrals and information for a variety of campus resources, including transportation and housing; encourage and assist students with disabilities to develop greater independence; increase faculty and staff understanding of the various needs of students with disabilities; and assist the university in interpreting legal mandates that address students with disabilities. Disability Services works with each student on a case-by-case basis to determine and implement appropriate accommodations based on documentation. Services could include note-takers, alternative testing arrangements such as extra time, books on tape, computers with speech input, separate testing rooms, tape recorders, and foreign language substitutions. Content tutors are available on campus through different departments.

LEARNING DISABILITY PROGRAM/SERVICES

Learning Disability Program/Services: Office of Disability Services (ODS)
Director: Emily Singer
  E-mail: ods@utk.edu
  Telephone: 865-974-6087
  Fax: 865-974-9552

LEARNING DISABILITY SERVICES

Requests for the following services/accommodations will be evaluated individually based on appropriate and current documentation.

Allowed in exams
  Calculator: Yes
  Dictionary: Yes
  Computer: Yes
  Spellchecker: Yes
Extended test time: Yes
Scribes: Yes
Proctors: Yes
Oral exams: Yes
Note-takers: Yes

Distraction-reduced environment: Yes
Tape recording in class: Yes
Books on tape from RFBD: Yes
Taping of books not from RFBD: Yes
**Accommodations for students with
  ADHD:** Yes
Reading machine: Yes
Other assistive technology: Yes
Priority registration: Yes

Added costs for services: No
LD specialists: Yes
Professional tutors: No
Peer tutors: Yes
Max. hours/wk. for services: N/A
**How professors are notified of
  LD/ADHD:** By student

GENERAL ADMISSIONS INFORMATION

Director of Admissions: Nancy McGlasson
Telephone: 865-974-2184

ENTRANCE REQUIREMENTS

Academic units required: 4 English, 3 math, 2 science (1 science lab), 2 foreign language, 1 social studies, 2 history,
1 visual/performing arts. High school diploma is required, and GED is accepted. ACT with or without Writing component
accepted. TOEFL required of all international applicants: minimum paper TOEFL 523, minimum computer TOEFL 193.

Application deadline: 2/1
Notification: 1/31 and 3/31
Average GPA: 3.60
ACT Composite middle 50% range:
  23–28

SAT Math middle 50% range:
  530–640
**SAT Critical Reading middle 50%
  range:** 520–630
SAT Writing middle 50% range: NR

Graduated top 10% of class: 42%
Graduated top 25% of class: 27%
Graduated top 50% of class: 68%

COLLEGE GRADUATION REQUIREMENTS

Course waivers allowed: No
Course substitutions allowed: Yes
In what course: Foreign languages, if appropriate

ADDITIONAL INFORMATION

Environment: The campus is located on a suburban campus in Knoxville.

Student Body
  Undergrad enrollment: 20,298
  Women: 51%
  Men: 49%
  Percent out-of-state: 14%

Cost Information
  In-state tuition: $5,290
  Out-of-state tuition: $16,338
  Room & board: $6,400
Housing Information
  University housing: Yes
  Percent living on campus: 34%

Greek System
  Fraternity: Yes
  Sorority: Yes
Athletics: Division I

THE U. OF TENNESSEE AT MARTIN

200 Hall-Moody, Administrative Building, Martin, TN 38238
Phone: 731-881-7020 • Fax: 731-881-7029
E-mail: admitme@utm.edu • Web: www.utm.edu
Support: CS • Institution type: 4-year public

LEARNING DISABILITY PROGRAM AND SERVICES

The university believes students with learning disabilities can achieve success in college without academic compromise and can become productive, self-sufficient members of society. A preliminary interview will include a review of previous assessments of the disability and the collection of background information. If the results of the PACE evaluation show that the academic and social needs of the student can be met by PACE services, the student will work with a learning disabilities specialist to develop an individually designed program. University staff who work with PACE students receive training in understanding learning disabilities and teaching strategies that meet the individual student's needs. Graduate supervisors coordinate support services. PACE is designed to complement and supplement existing university support services available for all students.

LD/ADHD ADMISSIONS INFORMATION

College entrance tests required: Yes
Interview required: No
Essay recommended: No
Documentation required for LD: Psychoeducational
  evaluation
Documentation required for ADHD: Yes
Submitted to: Admissions Office and PACE
Special Ed. HS course work accepted: No

Specific course requirements of all applicants: Yes
Separate application required: No
# of LD applications submitted each year: NR
# of LD applications accepted yearly: NR
Total # of students receiving LD services: NR
Acceptance into program means acceptance into college: Students must be admitted and enrolled prior to requesting services.

ADMISSIONS

Basically, applicants must meet regular admission criteria, including an ACT score of 16 and a 2.6 GPA, or an ACT score of 19 and a 2.2 GPA. Some applicants are considered through qualified admission with an ACT score of 14 and a 2.25 GPA. Course requirements include 4 years of English, 3 years of math, 2 years of science, 2 years of social studies, and 2 years of a foreign language. Each student is considered based on background, test scores, strengths/weaknesses, and motivation. Qualified students with learning disabilities should apply directly to both the PACE Center and the Office of Admissions. Students must complete all steps in both admission processes before an admission decision can be made. An interview is required for students applying to the PACE Program. Documentation should be sent to PACE. To be certain consideration is given to the learning disability, university decisions on acceptance are determined by both the PACE Center and the Admissions Office. Applicants are selected on the basis of intellectual potential (average to superior), motivation, academic preparation, and willingness to work hard.

ADDITIONAL INFORMATION

All freshmen students with LD selected to participate in PACE and admitted for fall semester must attend the second summer session program. Students take one selected university class in the mornings. In the afternoons, PACE staff teach learning strategies that can be applied to all future courses so that the students will have hands-on experience using the skills. The summer program will also address improvements in reading, spelling, written language, or math skills. Equally important are small group sessions to help students improve social skills. Students with ADHD must have comprehensive documentation to receive accommodations and services. There is a Math Lab and an English Writing Center. Students with appropriate documentation may be eligible to receive the following services: extended testing times; distraction-free testing environments; use of calculators, dictionaries, computers, and spellcheckers during exams; proctors; oral exams; note-takers; taper recorders in class; books of tape; and tutoring. Services and accommodations are provided to undergraduate and graduate students.

LEARNING DISABILITY PROGRAM/SERVICES

Learning Disability Program/Services: Program Access for College Enhancement (PACE)
Director: Michelle Arant
  E-mail: marant@utm.edu
  Telephone: 901-587-7195
  Fax: 901-587-7956
Contact Person: Beth Vise
  E-mail: marant@utm.edu
  Telephone: 901-587-7195
  Fax: 901-587-7956

LEARNING DISABILITY SERVICES

Requests for the following services/accommodations will be evaluated individually based on appropriate and current documentation.

Allowed in exams
  Calculator: NR
  Dictionary: NR
  Computer: NR
  Spellchecker: NR
Extended test time: Yes
Scribes: Yes
Proctors: Yes
Oral exams: Yes
Note-takers: Yes

Distraction-reduced environment: Yes
Tape recording in class: Yes
Books on tape from RFBD: Yes
Taping of books not from RFBD: Yes
**Accommodations for students with
  ADHD:** Yes
Reading machine: Yes
Other assistive technology: Yes
Priority registration: NR

Added costs for services: NR
LD specialists: Yes
Professional tutors: 2
Peer tutors: 20
Max. hours/wk. for services:
  Unlimited
**How professors are notified of
  LD/ADHD:** By student

GENERAL ADMISSIONS INFORMATION

Director of Admissions: Judy Rayburn
Telephone: 731-881-7020

ENTRANCE REQUIREMENTS

Academic units required: 4 English, 3 math, 2 science (1 science lab), 2 foreign language, 2 history, 1 fine/performing arts. High school diploma is required, and GED is accepted. ACT with or without Writing component accepted. TOEFL required of all international applicants: minimum paper TOEFL 500, minimum computer TOEFL 173.

Application deadline: 8/1
Notification: Rolling
Average GPA: 3.34
ACT Composite middle 50% range:
  19–24

SAT Math middle 50% range: NR
**SAT Critical Reading middle 50%
  range:** NR
SAT Writing middle 50% range: NR

Graduated top 10% of class: 20%
Graduated top 25% of class: 50%
Graduated top 50% of class: 85%

COLLEGE GRADUATION REQUIREMENTS

Course waivers allowed: No
Course substitutions allowed: No

ADDITIONAL INFORMATION

Environment: The university is located on a 200-acre campus in a small town 100 miles north of Memphis.

Student Body
  Undergrad enrollment: 5,612
  Women: 56%
  Men: 44%
  Percent out-of-state: 5%

Cost Information
  In-state: $4,660
  Out-of-state: $13,500
  Room & board: $4,310
Housing Information
  University housing: Yes
  Percent living on campus: 29%

Greek System
  Fraternity: Yes
  Sorority: Yes
Athletics: Division I

ABILENE CHRISTIAN UNIVERSITY

ACU Box 29000, Abilene, TX 79699
Phone: 325-674-2650 • Fax: 325-674-2130
E-mail: info@admissions.acu.edu • Web: www.acu.edu
Support: CS • Institution type: 4-year private

LEARNING DISABILITY PROGRAM AND SERVICES

Alpha Academic Services is a Student Support Service Program funded under Title IV legislation governing TRIO programs. The program strives to assist students in programs that move them toward independence in learning and living. The staff is specially trained instructors, peer tutors, counselors, and administrators who focus on the problems encountered by college students. Staff members help qualifying students find and apply solutions to their problems. Students qualify for services if they are a first-generation college student, economically disadvantaged, or a student with disabilities. Alpha means one-on-one help, and the instruction and tutoring are tailored to the student's unique needs. Students with learning disabilities may receive special accommodation services to assist them in achieving success in their university studies. Documentation of the disability is required to receive disability accommodations. Students must make an appointment to determine if they qualify to receive services.

LD/ADHD ADMISSIONS INFORMATION

College entrance tests required: Yes
Interview required: Yes
Essay recommended: Yes
Documentation required for LD: Psychological assessment for LD by a qualified professional. Recommended tests include WAIS–R and WJPB.
Documentation required for ADHD: Psychological assessment for ADHD such as Brown ADHD Screening
Submitted to: Both Admissions and Alpha Academic Services
Special Ed. HS course work accepted: Yes

Specific course requirements of all applicants: Yes
Separate application required: Yes
# of LD applications submitted each year: 30–40
# of LD applications accepted yearly: 25–30
Total # of students receiving LD services: 100–130
Acceptance into program means acceptance into college: Students must be admitted to and enrolled in the university first and then request services.

ADMISSIONS

All students must be admitted to the university and meet the same criteria for admission. There is no special admission process for students with learning disabilities. Regular admissions criteria include 20 ACT or 930-plus SAT; college-preparatory courses including 4 years of English, 3 years of math, 3 years of science, and 2 years of a foreign language; and no specific GPA. Some students not meeting the admission criteria may be admitted conditionally. Students admitted conditionally must take specified courses in a summer term and demonstrate motivation and ability. Freshman applicants need to take the SAT Reasoning Test or ACT with Writing component.

ADDITIONAL INFORMATION

Alpha Academic Services provides opportunities for individual instruction in basic skills areas such as writing, math, or study skills; assessment of learning preferences, strengths, and weaknesses; instruction and tutoring designed to fit the student's particular learning preferences and strengths and academic needs; classroom help if needed such as readers, note-takers, alternative testing arrangements; personal, career, and academic counseling; and workshops on topics such as time management skills, resume writing, career placement, and study skills.

LEARNING DISABILITY PROGRAM/SERVICES

Learning Disability Program/Services: Alpha Academic Services
Director: Gloria Bradshaw
  E-mail: bradshawg@acu.edu
  Telephone: 325-674-2275
  Fax: 325-674-6847
Contact Person: Gloria Bradshaw, Ada Dodd, or Jamie Jimenez
  E-mail: bradshawg@acu.edu
  Telephone: 325-674-2667
  Fax: 325-674-6847

LEARNING DISABILITY SERVICES

Requests for the following services/accommodations will be evaluated individually based on appropriate and current documentation.

Allowed in exams
  Calculator: Yes
  Dictionary: Yes
  Computer: Yes
  Spellchecker: Yes
Extended test time: Yes
Scribes: Yes
Proctors: Yes
Oral exams: Yes
Note-takers: Yes

Distraction-reduced environment: Yes
Tape recording in class: Yes
Books on tape from RFBD: Yes
Taping of books not from RFBD: Yes
Accommodations for students with ADHD: Yes
Reading machine: Yes
Other assistive technology: Yes
Priority registration: No

Added costs for services: No
LD specialists: Yes
Professional tutors: 3
Peer tutors: 12–20
Max. hours/wk. for services: Unlimited
How professors are notified of LD/ADHD: By student

GENERAL ADMISSIONS INFORMATION

Director of Admissions: Robert Heil
Telephone: 325-674-2650

ENTRANCE REQUIREMENTS

Academic units recommended: 4 English, 3 math, 3 science (2 science labs), 2 foreign language. High school diploma is required, and GED is accepted. ACT without Writing component accepted. TOEFL required of all international applicants: minimum paper TOEFL 525, minimum computer TOEFL 197.

Application deadline: 8/1
Notification: Rolling
Average GPA: 3.51
ACT Composite middle 50% range: 20–27

SAT Math middle 50% range: 490–630
SAT Critical Reading middle 50% range: 480–620
SAT Writing middle 50% range: NR

Graduated top 10% of class: 18%
Graduated top 25% of class: 47%
Graduated top 50% of class: 80%

COLLEGE GRADUATION REQUIREMENTS

Course waivers allowed: No
Course substitutions allowed: Yes
In what course: As appropriate with petition for reasonable substitute

ADDITIONAL INFORMATION

Environment: The campus is in a suburban area 150 miles from Fort Worth.

Student Body
  Undergrad enrollment: 4,099
  Women: 55%
  Men: 45%
  Percent out-of-state: 19%

Cost Information
  Tuition: $15,190
  Room & board: $5,600
Housing Information
  University housing: Yes
  Percent living on campus: 42%

Greek System
  Fraternity: Yes
  Sorority: Yes
Athletics: Division II

Abilene Christian University

LAMAR UNIVERSITY

PO Box 10009, Beaumont, TX 77710
Phone: 409-880-8888 • Fax: 409-880-8463
E-mail: admissions@hal.lamar.edu • Web: www.lamar.edu
Support: S • Institution type: 4-year public

LEARNING DISABILITY PROGRAM AND SERVICES

Services are designed to help students become successful on the Lamar campus. Students with learning disabilities could qualify for registration assistance, tutoring, and other personalized services. Students are encouraged to notify the coordinator of services that specific disabilities exist and the modifications needed, and preferably a conference prior to registration will allow the appropriate accommodations to be made. Prior to registration, students are requested to notify the Coordinator of Services for Students with Disabilities regarding assistance and/or accommodation they anticipate will be needed during the course of instruction for which they plan to register.

LD/ADHD ADMISSIONS INFORMATION

College entrance tests required: Yes
Interview required: Yes
Essay recommended: No
Documentation required for LD: Psychoeducational evaluation administered after sixteenth birthday; should contain relevant developmental, psychological, social, and educational history; IQ test or subtest scores
Documentation required for ADHD: Psychoeducational evaluation administered after sixteenth birthday; should contain relevant developmental, psychological, social, and educational history; DSM–IV diagnosis

Submitted to: SSWD
Special Ed. HS course work accepted: No
Specific course requirements of all applicants: NR
Separate application required: Yes
# of LD applications submitted each year: NR
# of LD applications accepted yearly: NR
Total # of students receiving LD services: NR
Acceptance into program means acceptance into college: Students must be admitted to and enrolled in the university first and then request services.

ADMISSIONS

Applicants with learning disabilities must meet the general admission requirements. Services will be offered to enrolled students who notify the Coordinator of Services for Students with Disabilities. Students must be in the top half of their class and complete 14 credits to be admitted unconditionally, including 4 years of English, 3 years of math (Algebra I–II and geometry or higher), 2 years of science (physical science, biology, chemistry, physics, or geology), 2.5 years of social science, and 2.5 years of electives (foreign language is recommended). Those not in the top half must achieve a minimum composite score of 1000 SAT/21 ACT. Some students may be considered on an individual approval basis if they fail to meet unconditional admission. These students are subject to mandatory advisement; they must maintain a 6-credit limit in the summer and 14 in the fall term and successfully complete 9 hours with a 2.0 GPA. Students must meet these provisions or leave after one year.

ADDITIONAL INFORMATION

SSWD offers a variety of services designed to assist students in becoming full participating members of the university. Services or accommodations could include priority registration; alternative testing accommodations; copying of class notes; classroom accommodations; counseling for academic, personal, and vocational needs; note-takers; readers; textbooks on tape; and tutoring. Professional staff assists students with questions, problem solving, adjustment, decision making, goal planning, testing, and development of learning skills. Skills classes in study skills are offered, including developmental writing, reading, and math for credit. Students are referred to other offices and personnel in accordance with the needs and intents of the individual. Services and accommodations are available for undergraduate and graduate students.

LEARNING DISABILITY PROGRAM/SERVICES

Learning Disability Program/Services: Services for Students with Disabilities (SSWD)
Director: Callie Trahan
  E-mail: callie.trahan@lamar.edu
  Telephone: 409-880-8347
  Fax: 409-880-2225

LEARNING DISABILITY SERVICES

Requests for the following services/accommodations will be evaluated individually based on appropriate and current documentation.

Allowed in exams
  Calculator: Yes
  Dictionary: Yes
  Computer: Yes
  Spellchecker: Yes
Extended test time: Yes
Scribes: Yes
Proctors: Yes
Oral exams: Yes
Note-takers: Yes

Distraction-reduced environment: Yes
Tape recording in class: Yes
Books on tape from RFBD: Yes
Taping of books not from RFBD: Yes
**Accommodations for students with
  ADHD:** Yes
Reading machine: Yes
Other assistive technology: Yes
Priority registration: Yes

Added costs for services: No
LD specialists: No
Professional tutors: No
Peer tutors: Yes
Max. hours/wk. for services: 15
**How professors are notified of
  LD/ADHD:** By student

GENERAL ADMISSIONS INFORMATION

Director of Admissions: Jim Rush
Telephone: 409-880-8888

ENTRANCE REQUIREMENTS
Academic units recommended: 4 English, 3 math, 2 science, 2 social studies, 2 academic electives. High school diploma is required, and GED is accepted. TOEFL required of all international applicants: minimum paper TOEFL 500.

Application deadline: 8/1
Notification: Rolling
Average GPA: NR
ACT Composite middle 50% range:
  NR

SAT Math middle 50% range: NR
**SAT Critical Reading middle 50%
  range:** NR
SAT Writing middle 50% range: NR

Graduated top 10% of class: 10%
Graduated top 25% of class: 27%
Graduated top 50% of class: 90%

COLLEGE GRADUATION REQUIREMENTS

Course waivers allowed: No
Course substitutions allowed: Yes
In what course: Appropriateness of a core course substitution is determined by the Coordinating Board of the State of Texas.

ADDITIONAL INFORMATION

Environment: The university is located on 200 acres in an urban area 90 miles east of Houston.

Student Body
  Undergrad enrollment: 9,057
  Women: 55%
  Men: 45%
  Percent out-of-state: 1%

Cost Information
  In-state tuition: $2,600
  Out-of-state tuition: $9,010
  Room & board: $4,200
Housing Information
  University housing: Yes
  Percent living on campus: 11%

Greek System
  Fraternity: Yes
  Sorority: Yes
Athletics: Division I

MIDWESTERN STATE UNIVERSITY

3410 Taft Boulevard, Wichita Falls, TX 76308-2099
Phone: 940-397-4334 • Fax: 940-397-4672
E-mail: admissions@mwsu.edu • Web: www.mwsu.edu
Support: S • Institution type: 4-year public

LEARNING DISABILITY PROGRAM AND SERVICES

In accordance with Section 504 of the Federal Rehabilitation Act of 1973 and the Americans with Disabilities Act of 1990, Midwestern State University endeavors to make reasonable adjustments in its policies, practices, services, and facilities to ensure equal opportunity for qualified persons with disabilities to participate in all educational programs and activities. Students requiring special accommodation or auxiliary aids must apply for such assistance through the Office of Disability Accommodations. The Office of Disability Accommodations focuses on helping students to negotiate all aspects of adapting to college life. These include academic, personal, career, and social concerns. To obtain services, students must be accepted for admissions at MSU, complete an application form from the Office of Disability Accommodations, and supply verification of the disability.

LD/ADHD ADMISSIONS INFORMATION

College entrance tests required: Yes
Interview required: No
Essay recommended: No
Documentation required for LD: WAIS–III, WJ–III
Documentation required for ADHD: Psychiatrist's or psychologist's report
Submitted to: ODA
Special Ed. HS course work accepted: Yes

Specific course requirements of all applicants: Yes
Separate application required: Yes
# of LD applications submitted each year: NR
# of LD applications accepted yearly: NR
Total # of students receiving LD services: 30
Acceptance into program means acceptance into college: Students must be admitted to and enrolled in the university first and then request services.

ADMISSIONS
Unconditional acceptance by the university is available to the student who graduates from an accredited high school with course work as follows: 4 years of English, 3 years of math, 2 years of science; a class rank within the top 60 percent; and an ACT of 20-plus or SAT score of 840-plus. Admission by review is an alternative admission with the same high school units as mentioned previously, but a high school rank 40–60 percent, an ACT score of 14–19, or an SAT score of 560–839. Students whose high school transcript does not reflect ranking must submit scores of 1110 on the SAT Reasoning Test or 24 composite on the ACT to be considered for unconditional admission.

ADDITIONAL INFORMATION
The Office of Disability Accommodations arranges accommodations for the student with special needs. Help includes priority registration; testing arrangements; classroom accessibility; special equipment; and counseling for personal, academic, or vocational concerns. Skills courses for credit are offered in study skills and time management techniques. The conditions for students admitted under advised admission are as follows: students will enroll in no more than 14 semester hours of credit in a long semester and no more than 3 hours in each summer session; in the first semester of enrollment, the student is required to enroll in designated courses of MWSU 1233, College Connections, as part of their class schedule; students will remain in the advised admission program until they have completed 24 semester hours at Midwestern State University and are in good academic standing according to the Table of Academic Standards listed in the university catalog. The Academic Support Center (ASC) will monitor students. Once advised by their faculty advisor, students must take their approved schedule of classes to the ASC for removal of a registration hold. Services and accommodations are available for undergraduate and graduate students.

LEARNING DISABILITY PROGRAM/SERVICES

Learning Disability Program/Services: Office of Disability Accommodations (ODA)
Director: Debra J. Higginbotham
E-mail: debra.higginbotham@mwsu.edu
Telephone: 940-397-4140
Fax: 940-397-4180

LEARNING DISABILITY SERVICES

Requests for the following services/accommodations will be evaluated individually based on appropriate and current documentation.

Allowed in exams
Calculator: Yes
Dictionary: Yes
Computer: Yes
Spellchecker: Yes
Extended test time: Yes
Scribes: Yes
Proctors: Yes
Oral exams: Yes
Note-takers: Yes

Distraction-reduced environment: Yes
Tape recording in class: Yes
Books on tape from RFBD: Yes
Taping of books not from RFBD: No
Accommodations for students with ADHD: Yes
Reading machine: Yes
Other assistive technology: Yes
Priority registration: Yes

Added costs for services: No
LD specialists: No
Professional tutors: No
Peer tutors: Yes
Max. hours/wk. for services: Yes
How professors are notified of LD/ADHD: By student

GENERAL ADMISSIONS INFORMATION

Director of Admissions: Barbara Merkle
Telephone: 940-397-4334

ENTRANCE REQUIREMENTS

Academic units required: 4 English, 3 math, 2 science, 6 academic electives. High school diploma is required, and GED is accepted. ACT with Writing component required. TOEFL required of all international applicants: minimum paper TOEFL 550, minimum computer TOEFL 213.

Application deadline: 8/7
Notification: Rolling
Average GPA: 3.41
ACT Composite middle 50% range: 18–23

SAT Math middle 50% range: 450–560
SAT Critical Reading middle 50% range: 440–550
SAT Writing middle 50% range: 440–540

Graduated top 10% of class: 12%
Graduated top 25% of class: 37%
Graduated top 50% of class: 73%

COLLEGE GRADUATION REQUIREMENTS

Course waivers allowed: No
Course substitutions allowed: Yes
In what course: Substitutions require an individual review by Disability Support Services, the chair of the department, and the Vice President of Academics.

ADDITIONAL INFORMATION

Environment: The campus is located 135 miles northwest of Dallas.

Student Body
Undergrad enrollment: 5,358
Women: 58%
Men: 42%
Percent out-of-state: 5%

Cost Information
In-state: $4,716
Out-of-state: $12,700
Room & board: $5,230
Housing Information
University housing: Yes
Percent living on campus: 20%

Greek System
Fraternity: Yes
Sorority: Yes
Athletics: Division II

SCHREINER UNIVERSITY

2100 Memorial Boulevard, Kerrville, TX 78028-5697
Phone: 830-792-7217 • Fax: 830-792-7226
E-mail: admissions@schreiner.edu • Web: www.schreiner.edu
Support: SP • Institution type: 2- and 4-year private

LEARNING DISABILITY PROGRAM AND SERVICES

Students admitted to the Learning Support Services program must be highly motivated, have the intellectual potential for success in a rigorous academic program, and have the ability to meet the demands of college life. Extensive learning support is given to each student, and the ultimate goal is for students to be able to succeed without special help. The Learning Support Services (LSS) program is staffed by LD specialists and many tutors. Students with learning disabilities are enrolled in regular college courses and receive individual tutorial assistance in each subject. Students in the program are held to the same high standards and complete the same curriculum requirements as all other degree candidates. In addition to the LSS staff, the Schreiner University faculty is dedicated to helping students realize their full potential.

LD/ADHD ADMISSIONS INFORMATION

College entrance tests required: Yes
Interview required: Yes
Essay recommended: Yes
Documentation required for LD: WAIS-III and individually administered achievement test such as WIAT or Woodcock-Johnson
Documentation required for ADHD: Letter from a medical doctor or psychologist
Submitted to: Admissions and Learning Support Services
Special Ed. HS course work accepted: No

Specific course requirements of all applicants: Yes
Separate application required: No
# of LD applications submitted each year: 110
# of LD applications accepted yearly: 30
Total # of students receiving LD services: 35
Acceptance into program means acceptance into college: Students admitted into the Learning Support Services program are automatically admitted into the college.

ADMISSIONS

Proof of high school diploma and all significant materials relevant to the specific learning disability must be submitted. Applicants should be enrolled in regular, mainstream English courses in high school. We recommend that students take a college-preparatory curriculum. However, admission would not be denied to a qualified candidate if some course work was not included. The Woodcock-Johnson Achievement Battery is preferred, but other tests are accepted. An interview is required and is an important part of the admissions decision. Applicants are considered individually and selected on the basis of their intellectual ability, motivation, academic preparation, and potential for success. For a candidate to be considered for admission, the following are required: all secondary school transcripts (transfer students must also supply transcripts of all attempted college work); medical or psychological statement of learning disability or attention deficit hyperactivity disorder; written report of the results of the WAIS-III, including all subtest scores and verbal, performance, and full-scale IQ scores taken within 12 months of application for admission; current individual achievement test results showing level of proficiency in reading comprehension, word identification, word attack, spelling, writing (written language), math calculation, and applied mathematics; and a completed application with application fee must be submitted to the Office of Admissions. LSS students are admitted contingent on their participation in the program. Students admitted into LSS are automatically admitted into the college.

ADDITIONAL INFORMATION

The Learning Support Services Program is tailored to meet the needs of each participating student. Every LSS staff member is committed to helping students develop the independent study skills and strategies that are necessary for academic success. Individualized services may include study skills development; regularly scheduled tutoring for all classes; alternative testing options, including readers, scribes, and extended time; use of recorded textbooks; arrangements made for note-takers in lecture classes; and a freshman seminar class that addresses issues of specific concern to college students with learning disabilities. Individual skill development is available in study strategies, test-taking, note-taking, reading, math, and written language. There is a professional counselor on staff.

LEARNING DISABILITY PROGRAM/SERVICES

Learning Disability Program/Services: Learning Support Services (LSS)
Director: Jude Gallik, PhD
  E-mail: jgallik@schreiner.edu
  Telephone: 830-792-7256
  Fax: 803-792-7448
Contact Person: Any admission counselor
  E-mail: jgallik@schreiner.edu
  Telephone: 800-343-4919
  Fax: 830-792-7226

LEARNING DISABILITY SERVICES

Requests for the following services/accommodations will be evaluated individually based on appropriate and current documentation.

Allowed in exams
  Calculator: No
  Dictionary: No
  Computer: Yes
  Spellchecker: Yes
Extended test time: Yes
Scribes: Yes
Proctors: Yes
Oral exams: Yes
Note-takers: Yes

Distraction-reduced environment: Yes
Tape recording in class: Yes
Books on tape from RFBD: No
Taping of books not from RFBD: Yes
Accommodations for students with ADHD: Yes
Reading machine: Yes
Other assistive technology: No
Priority registration: No

Added costs for services: Yes
LD specialists: Yes
Professional tutors: 15
Peer tutors: No
Max. hours/wk. for services: None
How professors are notified of LD/ADHD: By both student and director

GENERAL ADMISSIONS INFORMATION

Director of Admissions: Todd Brown
Telephone: 830-792-7217

ENTRANCE REQUIREMENTS

Academic units recommended: 4 English, 3 math, 2 science (2 science labs), 2 social studies. High school diploma is required, and GED is accepted. ACT with Writing component required. TOEFL required of all international applicants: minimum paper TOEFL 550, minimum computer TOEFL 213.

Application deadline: 8/1
Notification: NR
Average GPA: 3.53
ACT Composite middle 50% range: 18–23

SAT Math middle 50% range: 430–550
SAT Critical Reading middle 50% range: 440–545
SAT Writing middle 50% range: 430–540

Graduated top 10% of class: 11%
Graduated top 25% of class: 40%
Graduated top 50% of class: 72%

COLLEGE GRADUATION REQUIREMENTS

Course waivers allowed: No
Course substitutions allowed: No

ADDITIONAL INFORMATION

Environment: The college is located on 175 acres in a rural wooded area 60 miles northwest of San Antonio.

Student Body
  Undergrad enrollment: 876
  Women: 58%
  Men: 42%
  Percent out-of-state: 2%

Cost Information
  Tuition: $15,479
  Room & board: $7,566
Housing Information
  University housing: Yes
  Percent living on campus: 54%

Greek System
  Fraternity: Yes
  Sorority: Yes
Athletics: Division III

SOUTHERN METHODIST UNIVERSITY

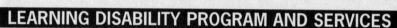

PO Box 750181, Dallas, TX 75275-0181
Phone: 214-768-3417 • Fax: 214-768-0202
E-mail: enrol_serv@smu.edu • Web: www.smu.edu
Support: CS • Institution type: 4-year private

LEARNING DISABILITY PROGRAM AND SERVICES

The goal of Services for Students with Disabilities is to provide students with disabilities services or reasonable accommodations to reduce the effects that a disability may have on their performance in a traditional academic setting. The Coordinator of Services for Students with Disabilities provides individual attention and support for students needing assistance with any aspect of their campus experience such as notifying professors, arranging accommodations, referrals, and accessibility. Students requesting LD assistance need to bring in their class schedules as soon as possible after receiving them to arrange accommodations in the desired classes. All students with LD who are requesting accommodations should have made their request with the Coordinator of Services for Students with Disabilities within 30 days after the first day of classes. A student with ADHD must provide a report from either a physician or licensed psychologist that elaborates on how the student meets the diagnostic criteria for ADHD, limitations the student is likely to experience in an academic environment that are directly related to the disability (substantial limitation), and suggested accommodations with explanation of why the accommodations are needed to mitigate impact of ADHD on the student.

LD/ADHD ADMISSIONS INFORMATION

College entrance tests required: Yes
Interview required: No
Essay recommended: No
Documentation required for LD: A full psychoeducational assessment conducted in the past 3 years.
Documentation required for ADHD: Report from either a licensed psychologist or physician trained in diagnosing ADHD. Evaluation needs to be conducted within 3 years of the time student seeks accommodations.
Submitted to: Services for Students with Disabilities

Special Ed. HS course work accepted: N/A
Specific course requirements of all applicants: Yes
Separate application required: No
# of LD applications submitted each year: NR
# of LD applications accepted yearly: NR
Total # of students receiving LD services: 216
Acceptance into program means acceptance into college: Students must be admitted to and enrolled in the university first and then request services.

ADMISSIONS

There is no special admissions process for students with LD. If their standardized tests were administered under nonstandard conditions, this will not weigh unfavorably into the admission decision. Regular admission criteria include 4 years of English, 3 years of math, 3 years of science, 3 years of social studies, and 2 years of a foreign language. Only foreign language may be waived with other appropriate and approved academic classes taken as substitutions. Candidates who exceed the minimum requirements are advantaged in the selection process.

ADDITIONAL INFORMATION

All students have access to tutoring, Writing Centers, study skills workshops, and classes to improve reading rate, comprehension, and vocabulary. Skills classes are offered in time management techniques, test-taking strategies, note-taking strategies, organizational skills, concentration, memory, and test anxiety. There are currently 170 students with learning disabilities and 146 students with ADHD receiving services.

LEARNING DISABILITY PROGRAM/SERVICES

Learning Disability Program/Services: Services for Students with Disabilities
Director: Rebecca Marin, Coordinator
  E-mail: rmarin@smu.edu
  Telephone: 214-768-4557
  Fax: 214-768-1255

LEARNING DISABILITY SERVICES

Requests for the following services/accommodations will be evaluated individually based on appropriate and current documentation.

Allowed in exams
  Calculator: Yes
  Dictionary: Yes
  Computer: Yes
  Spellchecker: Yes
Extended test time: Yes
Scribes: Yes
Proctors: Yes
Oral exams: Yes
Note-takers: Yes

Distraction-reduced environment: Yes
Tape recording in class: Yes
Books on tape from RFBD: Yes
Taping of books not from RFBD: Yes
**Accommodations for students with
  ADHD:** Yes
Reading machine: Yes
Other assistive technology: Yes
Priority registration: Yes

Added costs for services: No
LD specialists: Yes
Professional tutors: No
Peer tutors: 50–60
Max. hours/wk. for services: NR
**How professors are notified of
  LD/ADHD:** By both student and
  director

GENERAL ADMISSIONS INFORMATION

Director of Admissions: Ron Moss
Telephone: 214-768-2058

ENTRANCE REQUIREMENTS
Academic units required: 4 English, 3 math, 3 science (2 science labs), 2 foreign language, 3 social studies, 2 history. **Academic units recommended:** 4 English, 4 math, 4 science (3 science labs), 3 foreign language, 2 social studies, 3 history. High school diploma is required, and GED is not accepted. ACT with or without Writing component accepted. TOEFL required of all international applicants: minimum paper TOEFL 550, minimum computer TOEFL 213.

Application deadline: 3/15
Notification: Rolling
Average GPA: 3.50
ACT Composite middle 50% range:
  24–29

SAT Math middle 50% range:
  580–670
**SAT Critical Reading middle 50%
  range:** 560–650
SAT Writing middle 50% range:
  550–650

Graduated top 10% of class: 35%
Graduated top 25% of class: 70%
Graduated top 50% of class: 91%

COLLEGE GRADUATION REQUIREMENTS

Course waivers allowed: No
Course substitutions allowed: Yes
In what course: Foreign language and math

ADDITIONAL INFORMATION

Environment: The university is located on a 163-acre suburban campus.

Student Body
  Undergrad enrollment: 6,199
  Women: 54%
  Men: 46%
  Percent out-of-state: 35%

Cost Information
  Tuition: $27,400
  Room & board: $10,825
Housing Information
  University housing: Yes
  Percent living on campus: 45%

Greek System
  Fraternity: Yes
  Sorority: Yes
Athletics: Division I

TEXAS A&M U.—COLLEGE STATION

Admissions Counseling, College Station, TX 77843-1265
Phone: 979-845-3741 • Fax: 979-847-8737
E-mail: admissions@tamu.edu • Web: www.tamu.edu
Support: S • Institution type: 4-year public

LEARNING DISABILITY PROGRAM AND SERVICES

The Department of Disability Services exits to promote an academic experience for all students that is fully inclusive and accessible. The philosophy of Disability Services is to empower students with the skills needed to act as their own advocate and succeed in the mainstream of the university environment. Services include testing, accommodations, note-takers, adaptive technology, interpreters, and registration assistance.

LD/ADHD ADMISSIONS INFORMATION

College entrance tests required: Yes
Interview required: No
Essay recommended: No
Documentation required for LD: Comprehensive psychoeducational testing, intelligence and achievement scores, written report, WISC–III or WAIS–R with Woodcock-Johnson
Documentation required for ADHD: Psychoeducational testing along with documentation from qualified evaluator diagnosing the ADHD. Documentation should match the DSM–IV–TR criteria.

Submitted to: Disability Services
Special Ed. HS course work accepted: No
Specific course requirements of all applicants: Yes
Separate application required: Yes
# of LD applications submitted each year: NR
# of LD applications accepted yearly: NR
Total # of students receiving LD services: 375
Acceptance into program means acceptance into college: Students must be admitted to and enrolled in the university first and then request services.

ADMISSIONS

General application requirements require that students submit an essay, ACT (with optional essay) or new SAT scores, and have at least 4 years of English, 3.5 years of math (Algebra I and II, geometry, and 0.5 credit of advanced math), 3 years of science (2 must be in biology, chemistry, or physics), and recommend 2 years of the same foreign language. Students ranked in the top 10 percent of their class are automatically admissible if they have taken the required courses. Students not in the top 10 percent but ranked in the top 25 percent must have a 1300 on the SAT with a score of 600-plus in math and verbal or a 30 on the ACT and have the course requirements. Applicants with learning disabilities submit the general application form and are considered under the same guidelines as all applicants. Students may have their application reviewed by requesting special consideration based on their disability and by providing letters of recommendation from their high school counselor stating what accommodations are needed in college to be successful. Admissions will be affected by the student's record indicating success with provided accommodations along with any activities and leadership skills. Students not meeting academic criteria for automatic admission may be offered admission to a summer provisional program. These students must take 9–12 credits and receive a grade of C in each of the courses.

ADDITIONAL INFORMATION

Accommodations are provided on an individual basis as needs arise. Disability Services is a resource for information, including, but not limited to, tutoring services, study and time management skills training, community resources, disability awareness, and various university services. Skills classes in math, reading, and writing are offered to the entire student body though the Student Learning Center. Some of these classes may be taken for college credit. Services and accommodations are available for undergraduate and graduate students. Services include an adaptive technology laboratory equipped with state-of-the-art technology for students with disabilities, including text-to-speech scanning for personal computer use.

LEARNING DISABILITY PROGRAM/SERVICES

Learning Disability Program/Services: Disability Services
Director: Dr. Anne Reber
  E-mail: anne@disability.tamu.edu
  Telephone: 979-845-1637
  Fax: 979-458-1214

LEARNING DISABILITY SERVICES

Requests for the following services/accommodations will be evaluated individually based on appropriate and current documentation.

Allowed in exams
  Calculator: Yes
  Dictionary: Yes
  Computer: Yes
  Spellchecker: Yes
Extended test time: Yes
Scribes: Yes
Proctors: Yes
Oral exams: Yes
Note-takers: Yes

Distraction-reduced environment: Yes
Tape recording in class: Yes
Books on tape from RFBD: Yes
Taping of books not from RFBD: Yes
Accommodations for students with ADHD: Yes
Reading machine: Yes
Other assistive technology: Yes
Priority registration: Yes

Added costs for services: No
LD specialists: No
Professional tutors: No
Peer tutors: No
Max. hours/wk. for services: NR
How professors are notified of LD/ADHD: By student

GENERAL ADMISSIONS INFORMATION

Director of Admissions: Dr. Scott McDonald
Telephone: 979-458-0509

ENTRANCE REQUIREMENTS

Academic units required: 4 English, 3.5 math, 3 science (2 science labs), 2 foreign language, 2 social studies, 1 history. **Academic units recommended:** 4 English, 3 math, 3 science (2 science labs), 2 foreign language, 2 social studies, 1 history, 1 computer course. High school diploma is required, and GED is accepted. ACT with Writing component required. TOEFL required of all international applicants: minimum paper TOEFL 550.

Application deadline: 2/1
Notification: Rolling
Average GPA: NR
ACT Composite middle 50% range: 23–28

SAT Math middle 50% range: 560–660
SAT Critical Reading middle 50% range: 520–630
SAT Writing middle 50% range: 500–610

Graduated top 10% of class: 46%
Graduated top 25% of class: 77%
Graduated top 50% of class: 90%

COLLEGE GRADUATION REQUIREMENTS

Course waivers allowed: Yes
In what course: Math and foreign language have been the only ones requested.
Course substitutions allowed: Yes
In what course: Math and foreign language courses are the only ones that have been requested. Courses are substituted, not waived.

ADDITIONAL INFORMATION

Environment: The school is located on more than 5,000 acres in a college town of 100,000 residents that is about 90 miles from Houston.

Student Body
  Undergrad enrollment: 36,473
  Women: 48%
  Men: 52%
  Percent out-of-state: 3%

Cost Information
  In-state tuition: $6,300
  Out-of-state tuition: $14,600
  Room & board: $7,660
Housing Information
  University housing: Yes

Percent living on campus: 25%
Greek System
  Fraternity: Yes
  Sorority: Yes
Athletics: Division I

TEXAS A&M U.—KINGSVILLE

MSC 105, Kingsville, TX 78363
Phone: 361-593-2315 • Fax: 361-593-2195
E-mail: ksossrx@tamuk.edu • Web: www.tamuk.edu
Support: S • Institution type: 4-year public

LEARNING DISABILITY PROGRAM AND SERVICES

The university is committed to providing an environment in which every student is encouraged to reach the highest level of personal and educational achievement. Students with disabilities may have special concerns and even special needs. Services vary according to the nature of the disability and are provided by the Center for Life Services and Wellness. Counseling services offer educational, vocational, and personal consultations, as well as tutoring, testing, and academic advising. Students with LD have access to note-takers, readers, writers, and other assistance that the university can provide. All students entering college as freshmen (or transfers with less than 30 hours) have the university's commitment to improve student achievement, retention, depth, and quality of instruction and services.

LD/ADHD ADMISSIONS INFORMATION

College entrance tests required: Yes
Interview required: Yes
Essay recommended: No
Documentation required for LD: Psychoeducational evaluation
Documentation required for ADHD: Yes
Submitted to: SSD
Special Ed. HS course work accepted: Yes

Specific course requirements of all applicants: Yes
Separate application required: No
# of LD applications submitted each year: NR
# of LD applications accepted yearly: NR
Total # of students receiving LD services: 190
Acceptance into program means acceptance into college: Students must be admitted to and enrolled in the university first and then request services.

ADMISSIONS

All applicants must meet the same general admission criteria. Admission is very similar to open door admissions, and thus, most applicants are admitted either conditionally or unconditionally or on probation. Average ACT scores are 16-plus; for the SAT, they are 610-plus. There are no specific courses required for entrance; however, it is recommended that students take 4 years of English, 3 years of math, 3 years of science, 4 years of social studies, 3 years of a foreign language, 0.5 year of health, 1.5 years of physical education, 1 year of computer science, 1 year of art/speech, and 3 years of electives. Students with LD are encouraged to self-disclose during the application process. There are two types of admission plans: conditional and unconditional. Unconditional admission is met by achieving 970-plus on the SAT. Conditional admission is achieved by scoring 810–960 on the SAT.

ADDITIONAL INFORMATION

Each freshman receives academic endorsement; developmental educational classes in writing, math, or reading (if necessary); access to tutoring or study groups; and academic rescue programs for students in academic jeopardy. Skills classes are offered for no credit in stress management and test anxiety. Letters are sent to faculty each semester, hand delivered by the student. DSS provides tutoring on a limited basis. Testing accommodations are available, but students are responsible for scheduling the tests. Accommodations include extended testing times, private rooms, scribes, and readers. DSS will also proctor the exam and return the test to the instructor. DSS relies on a volunteer program for note-takers. Services and accommodations are available to undergraduate and graduate students.

LEARNING DISABILITY PROGRAM/SERVICES

Learning Disability Program/Services: Services for Students with Disabilities (SSD)
Director: Jeanie Alexander, MS
  E-mail: kacja01@tamuk.edu
  Telephone: 361-593-3268
  Fax: 361-593-2006

LEARNING DISABILITY SERVICES

Requests for the following services/accommodations will be evaluated individually based on appropriate and current documentation.

Allowed in exams
  Calculator: Yes
  Dictionary: Yes
  Computer: Yes
  Spellchecker: Yes
Extended test time: Yes
Scribes: Yes
Proctors: Yes
Oral exams: Yes
Note-takers: Yes

Distraction-reduced environment: Yes
Tape recording in class: Yes
Books on tape from RFBD: Yes
Taping of books not from RFBD: Yes
Accommodations for students with ADHD: Yes
Reading machine: No
Other assistive technology: Yes
Priority registration: No

Added costs for services: No
LD specialists: No
Professional tutors: No
Peer tutors: Yes
Max. hours/wk. for services: NR
How professors are notified of LD/ADHD: By student

GENERAL ADMISSIONS INFORMATION

Director of Admissions: NR
Telephone: 361-593-2315

ENTRANCE REQUIREMENTS

Academic units recommended: 4 English, 3 math, 3 science, 3 foreign language, 4 social studies, 3 history, 0.5 health, 1.5 physical education, 1 computer science, 1 art/speech, 3 academic electives. High school diploma is required, and GED is accepted.

Application deadline: Rolling
Notification: Rolling
Average GPA: NR
ACT Composite middle 50% range: NR

SAT Math middle 50% range: NR
SAT Critical Reading middle 50% range: NR
SAT Writing middle 50% range: NR

Graduated top 10% of class: NR
Graduated top 25% of class: NR
Graduated top 50% of class: NR

COLLEGE GRADUATION REQUIREMENTS

Course waivers allowed: Yes
In what course: Case-by-case decision made by provost
Course substitutions allowed: Yes
In what course: Case-by-case decision made by provost

ADDITIONAL INFORMATION

Environment: The 246-acre university campus is located 40 miles southwest of Corpus Christi.

Student Body
  Undergrad enrollment: 4,373
  Women: 47%
  Men: 53%
  Percent out-of-state: 2%

Cost Information
  In-state tuition: $3,200
  Out-of-state tuition: $8,900
  Room & board: $3,966
Housing Information
  University housing: Yes
  Percent living on campus: 30%

Greek System
  Fraternity: Yes
  Sorority: Yes
Athletics: Division I

TEXAS STATE U.—SAN MARCOS

429 North Guadalupe Street, San Marcos, TX 78666
Phone: 512-245-2364 • Fax: 512-245-9020
E-mail: admissions@txstate.edu • Web: www.txstate.edu
Support: CS • Institution type: 4-year public

LEARNING DISABILITY PROGRAM AND SERVICES

The mission of the Office of Disability Services (ODS) is to assist students with disabilities to independently achieve their educational goals and enhance their leadership development by ensuring equal access to all programs, activities, and services. This is accomplished through a decentralizing approach in providing education and awareness so that programs, activities, and services are conducted in the most integrated setting appropriate. Students with learning disabilities are encouraged to self-identify and submit documentation once admitted. By identifying and assessing student needs, ODS provides direct services and refers students to appropriate resources on and off campus. ODS also promotes awareness of the special needs and abilities of students with disabilities through educational events and outreach activities.

LD/ADHD ADMISSIONS INFORMATION

College entrance tests required: Yes
Interview required: No
Essay recommended: No
Documentation required for LD: Refer to
  www.ods.txstate.edu/learningdisabilityguideline.htm.
Documentation required for ADHD: Refer to
www.ods.txstate.edu/addguide.htm.
Submitted to: Admissions and Disability Services
Special Ed. HS course work accepted: NR

Specific course requirements of all applicants: Yes
Separate application required: Yes
# of LD applications submitted each year: NR
# of LD applications accepted yearly: NR
Total # of students receiving LD services: 357
Acceptance into program means acceptance into
  college: Students must be admitted to and enrolled in the
  university first and then request services.

ADMISSIONS

Students with LD must meet the same admission requirements as other applicants. A student whose educational and/or personal goals for success have been negatively impacted due to disability-related reasons may provide a supplemental essay with their application for admission. This information may be considered by the Admission Office during the review process. General admission requirements include 4 years of English, 3 years of math, 2 years of science, 3 years of social studies, 0.5 year economics, and 2 years of a foreign language; and a 2.0 GPA or class rank. A 22 ACT and 850 SAT are the average scores. Students who are not accepted are free to write letters of appeal to the Admissions Office. All decisions are made by the Admissions Office. Probationary admission plans are available. Students not meeting the required rank in class may be admitted by review through Predicted Academic Success Option (PASO): Students in the top three-fourths may submit their seventh semester transcript and a request that a PASO formula be attempted. (Students who rank in the fourth quarter are not eligible for PASO). The formula used is an individual's high school rank in combination with ACT or SAT scores. If admitted, these students are placed on a one-semester contract set by the Director of Admissions.

ADDITIONAL INFORMATION

Specialized support services are based on the individual student needs. Services available could include advance registration; books on tape; special testing accommodations; readers; note-takers; liaison and advocacy between students, faculty, and staff; assistance with tutoring; and an academic excellence seminar. Student Support Services provides one-on-one tutoring in limited subject areas. Remedial courses and an effective learning course are offered. An academic support group course covering various topics is offered for credit. Services and accommodations are available for undergraduate and graduate students. The following campus agencies provide students with special academic support services: ODS, Learning Resource Center, and Student Learning Assistance Center.

LEARNING DISABILITY PROGRAM/SERVICES

Learning Disability Program/Services: Office of Disability Services (ODS)
Director: Tina Schultz
  E-mail: ts12@txstate.edu
  Telephone: 512-245-3451
  Fax: 512-245-3452

Contact Person: Jenni Ward
  E-mail: ts12@txstate.edu
  Telephone: 512-245-3451
  Fax: 512-245-3452

LEARNING DISABILITY SERVICES

Requests for the following services/accommodations will be evaluated individually based on appropriate and current documentation.

Allowed in exams
  Calculator: Yes
  Dictionary: Yes
  Computer: Yes
  Spellchecker: Yes
Extended test time: Yes
Scribes: Yes
Proctors: Yes
Oral exams: Yes
Note-takers: Yes

Distraction-reduced environment: Yes
Tape recording in class: Yes
Books on tape from RFBD: Yes
Taping of books not from RFBD: Yes
Accommodations for students with
  ADHD: Yes
Reading machine: No
Other assistive technology: Yes
Priority registration: Yes

Added costs for services: No
LD specialists: Yes
Professional tutors: NR
Peer tutors: NR
Max. hours/wk. for services:
  Unlimited
How professors are notified of
  LD/ADHD: By student

GENERAL ADMISSIONS INFORMATION

Director of Admissions: Christy Kangas
Telephone: 512-245-2364

ENTRANCE REQUIREMENTS

Academic units required: 4 English, 3 math, 3 science (2 science labs), 2 foreign language, 3 social studies, 3 academic electives, 5 computer literacy, 1 physical education, 1.5 fine arts, 1 economics, 0.5 health, 0.5 speech.
Academic units recommended: 4 English, 3 math, 3 science (2 science labs), 2 foreign language, 3 social studies, 3 academic electives, 5 comupter literacy, 1 physical education, 1.5 fine arts, 1 economics, 0.5 health, 0.5 speech. High school diploma is required, and GED is accepted. ACT with Writing component required. TOEFL required of all international applicants: minimum paper TOEFL 550, minimum computer TOEFL 213.

Application deadline: 5/1
Notification: Rolling
Average GPA: NR
ACT Composite middle 50% range:
  21–25

SAT Math middle 50% range:
  500–590
SAT Critical Reading middle 50%
  range: 480–570
SAT Writing middle 50% range: NR

Graduated top 10% of class: 14%
Graduated top 25% of class: 52%
Graduated top 50% of class: 95%

COLLEGE GRADUATION REQUIREMENTS

Course waivers allowed: No
Course substitutions allowed: Yes
In what course: Foreign language

ADDITIONAL INFORMATION

Environment: The 1,091-acre campus is located 30 miles south of Austin and within easy access of San Antonio.

Student Body
  Undergrad enrollment: 23,568
  Women: 55%
  Men: 45%
  Percent out-of-state: 1%

Cost Information
  In-state tuition: $5,200
  Out-of-state tuition: $15,500
  Room & board: $5,610
Housing Information
  University housing: Yes
  Percent living on campus: 23%

Greek System
  Fraternity: Yes
  Sorority: Yes
Athletics: Division I

Texas State University—San Marcos

TEXAS TECH UNIVERSITY

PO Box 45005, Lubbock, TX 79409-5005
Phone: 806-742-1480 • Fax: 806-742-0062
E-mail: admissions@ttu.edu • Web: www.ttu.edu
Support: S • Institution type: 4-year public

LEARNING DISABILITY PROGRAM AND SERVICES

It is the philosophy of Texas Tech University to serve each student on a case-by-case basis. All services rendered are supported by adequate documentation. We firmly believe that all students should be and will become effective self-advocates. Students with disabilities attending Texas Tech will find numerous programs designed to provide services and promote access to all phases of university activity. Such programming is coordinated through the Dean of Students's Office with the assistance of an advisory committee of both disabled and non-disabled students, faculty, and staff. Services to disabled students are offered through a decentralized network of university and nonuniversity resources. This means that many excellent services are available, but it is up to the student to initiate them. Each student is encouraged to act as his or her own advocate and take the major responsibility for securing services and accommodations. The Disabled Student Services team, Dean of Students's Office, faculty, and staff are supportive in this effort.

LD/ADHD ADMISSIONS INFORMATION

College entrance tests required: Yes
Interview required: No
Essay recommended: No
Documentation required for LD: Psychoeducational evaluation
Documentation required for ADHD: Yes
Submitted to: PASS
Special Ed. HS course work accepted: Yes

Specific course requirements of all applicants: Yes
Separate application required: Yes
# of LD applications submitted each year: NR
# of LD applications accepted yearly: NR
Total # of students receiving LD services: 600
Acceptance into program means acceptance into college: Students must be admitted to and enrolled in the university first and then request services.

ADMISSIONS

There is no special admissions process for students with LD, and all applicants must meet the same criteria. All students must have 4 years of English, 3 years of math, 2.5 years of social studies, 2 years of science, and 3.5 years of electives. Any applicant who scores a 1200 on the SAT or a 29 on the ACT is automatically admitted regardless of class rank. Some students are admissible who do not meet the stated requirements, but they must have a 2.0 GPA for a provisional admission. After a student is admitted, Disabled Student Services requires documentation that provides a diagnosis and an indication of the severity of the disability and offers recommendations for accommodations for students to receive services.

ADDITIONAL INFORMATION

Support services through Disabled Student Services include academic support services, which can help students develop habits enabling them to get a good education. Students may receive academic support services in the PASS (Programs for Academic Support Services) Center, which is open to all students on campus. Services offered free of charge include tutor referral services (paid by student); study skills group; hour-long workshops that target a variety of subjects from overcoming math anxiety to preparing for finals; a self-help learning lab with videotapes; computer-assisted instruction; individual consultations assisting students with specific study problems; and setting study skills improvement goals. All students with LD are offered priority registration. Services and accommodations are available for undergraduate and graduate students.

LEARNING DISABILITY PROGRAM/SERVICES

Learning Disability Program/Services: Programs for Academic Support Services
Director: Larry K. Phillippe
  E-mail: larry.phillippe@ttu.edu
  Telephone: 806-742-2405
  Fax: 806-742-4837

LEARNING DISABILITY SERVICES

Requests for the following services/accommodations will be evaluated individually based on appropriate and current documentation.

Allowed in exams
  Calculator: Yes
  Dictionary: NR
  Computer: Yes
  Spellchecker: Yes
Extended test time: Yes
Scribes: Yes
Proctors: Yes
Oral exams: Yes
Note-takers: Yes

Distraction-reduced environment: Yes
Tape recording in class: Yes
Books on tape from RFBD: Yes
Taping of books not from RFBD: No
Accommodations for students with
  ADHD: Yes
Reading machine: Yes
Other assistive technology: Yes
Priority registration: Yes

Added costs for services: No
LD specialists: No
Professional tutors: No
Peer tutors: 25–35
Max. hours/wk. for services:
  Unlimited
How professors are notified of
  LD/ADHD: By student

GENERAL ADMISSIONS INFORMATION

Director of Admissions: Djuana Young
Telephone: 806-742-1480

ENTRANCE REQUIREMENTS

Academic units required: 4 English, 3 math, 2 science (2 science labs), 2 foreign language. High school diploma is required, and GED is accepted. ACT with Writing component required. TOEFL required of all international applicants: minimum paper TOEFL 550, minimum computer TOEFL 213.

Application deadline: 5/1
Notification: Rolling
Average GPA: NR
ACT Composite middle 50% range:
  21–26

SAT Math middle 50% range:
  520–620
SAT Critical Reading middle 50%
  range: 500–590
SAT Writing middle 50% range:
  470–570

Graduated top 10% of class: 22%
Graduated top 25% of class: 54%
Graduated top 50% of class: 88%

COLLEGE GRADUATION REQUIREMENTS

Course waivers allowed: Yes
In what course: Possible in math or foreign language
Course substitutions allowed: Yes
In what course: Possible in math or foreign language

ADDITIONAL INFORMATION

Environment: The university is located on 1,839 acres in an urban area in Lubbock.

Student Body
  Undergrad enrollment: 22,838
  Women: 45%
  Men: 55%
  Percent out-of-state: 4%

Cost Information
  In-state tuition: $6,100
  Out-of-state tuition: $14,400
  Room & board: $7,288
Housing Information
  University housing: Yes
  Percent living on campus: 24%

Greek System
  Fraternity: Yes
  Sorority: Yes
Athletics: Division I

UNIVERSITY OF HOUSTON

Office of Admissions, 122 East Cullen Building, Houston, TX 77204-2023
Phone: 713-743-1010 • Fax: 713-743-9633
E-mail: admissions@uh.edu • Web: www.uh.edu
Support: CS • Institution type: 4-year public

LEARNING DISABILITY PROGRAM AND SERVICES

The Center for Students with Disabilities provides a wide variety of academic support services to students with all types of disabilities. Its goal is to help ensure that these otherwise qualified students are able to successfully compete with non-disabled students by receiving equal educational opportunities in college as mandated by law. Through advocacy efforts and a deliberate, ongoing, public education program, the staff strives to heighten the awareness of needs, legal rights, and abilities of persons with handicapping conditions.

LD/ADHD ADMISSIONS INFORMATION

College entrance tests required: Yes
Interview required: No
Essay recommended: No
Documentation required for LD: WAIS–R, WJ–III, or a neuropsychological evaluation completed within the past 3 years
Documentation required for ADHD: Yes
Submitted to: Center for Students with Disabilities
Special Ed. HS course work accepted: Yes

Specific course requirements of all applicants: Yes
Separate application required: No
# of LD applications submitted each year: NR
# of LD applications accepted yearly: NR
Total # of students receiving LD services: 280
Acceptance into program means acceptance into college: Students must be admitted to and enrolled in the university first and then request services.

ADMISSIONS

General admission requirements are as follows: class rank within the top 10 percent, and there is no minimum score for the SAT or ACT. Students falling into the following quarters should have the corresponding SAT or ACT scores: first quarter, 920 SAT or 19 ACT; second quarter 1010 SAT or 21 ACT; third quarter, 1100 SAT or 24 ACT; or fourth quarter, 1180 SAT or 26 ACT. Courses required are 2 years of English, 3 years of math, 2 years of science, and 3 years of social studies. Applicants who do not qualify for admission may request a further review through the individual admission process. The review will be based on an overall assessment of each applicant's circumstances in respect to potential for academic success. If an applicant to a program with different requirements does not meet the stated standards but does meet the general admission requirements, then that applicant may be admitted to the university with an undeclared status.

ADDITIONAL INFORMATION

Students who come from an educationally and/or economically disadvantaged background may be eligible to participate in the UH Challenger Program, which is designed to provide intense support to students who face obstacles in their efforts to successfully complete college. Services to all students include tutoring, counseling, financial aid advisement, and social enrichment. Remedial reading, writing, and study skills courses for 3 hours of noncollege credit are offered. There are also remedial courses for credit in English and college algebra. Other services include assistance with petitions for course substitutions, peer support groups, free carbonized paper for note-taking, textbooks and class handouts put on tape by office staff or volunteer readers, and advocacy for student's legal rights to reasonable and necessary accommodations in their course work. Extended tutoring is available at the Learning Support Services and Math Lab.

LEARNING DISABILITY PROGRAM/SERVICES

Learning Disability Program/Services: Center for Students with Disabilities
Director: Cheryl Amoruso
  E-mail: camoruso@mail.uh.edu
  Telephone: 713-743-5400
  Fax: 713-743-5396
Contact Person: Scott Crain, Counselor
  E-mail: camoruso@mail.uh.edu
  Telephone: 713-743-5400
  Fax: 713-743-5396

LEARNING DISABILITY SERVICES

Requests for the following services/accommodations will be evaluated individually based on appropriate and current documentation.

Allowed in exams	**Distraction-reduced environment:** Yes	**Added costs for services:** No
Calculator: Yes	**Tape recording in class:** Yes	**LD specialists:** Yes
Dictionary: Yes	**Books on tape from RFBD:** Yes	**Professional tutors:** No
Computer: Yes	**Taping of books not from RFBD:** Yes	**Peer tutors:** Yes
Spellchecker: Yes	**Accommodations for students with**	**Max. hours/wk. for services:** 2–4
Extended test time: Yes	**ADHD:** Yes	**How professors are notified of**
Scribes: Yes	**Reading machine:** Yes	**LD/ADHD:** By student
Proctors: Yes	**Other assistive technology:** Yes	
Oral exams: Yes	**Priority registration:** Yes	
Note-takers: Yes		

GENERAL ADMISSIONS INFORMATION

Director of Admissions: Dr. Susanna Finnell
Telephone: 713-743-9570

ENTRANCE REQUIREMENTS

Academic units required: 4 English, 3 math, 2 science (2 science labs), 2 social studies, 2 history. **Academic units recommended:** 2 foreign language. High school diploma is required, and GED is accepted. ACT with or without Writing component accepted. TOEFL required of all international applicants: minimum paper TOEFL 550, minimum computer TOEFL 213.

Application deadline: 4/1	**SAT Math middle 50% range:** 490–610	**Graduated top 10% of class:** 22%
Notification: Rolling	**SAT Critical Reading middle 50%**	**Graduated top 25% of class:** 53%
Average GPA: 3.35	range: 460–580	**Graduated top 50% of class:** 83%
ACT Composite middle 50% range: 19–24	**SAT Writing middle 50% range:** NR	

COLLEGE GRADUATION REQUIREMENTS

Course waivers allowed: Yes
In what course: Foreign language course waivers have been granted most recently.
Course substitutions allowed: Yes
In what course: Foreign language course substitutions have been granted most recently.

ADDITIONAL INFORMATION

Environment: The university is located on 540 acres in an urban area three miles from Houston.

Student Body	**Cost Information**	**Greek System**
Undergrad enrollment: 26,243	**In-state tuition:** $4,260	**Fraternity:** Yes
Women: 51%	**Out-of-state tuition:** $12,510	**Sorority:** Yes
Men: 49%	**Room & board:** $6,418	**Athletics:** Division I
Percent out-of-state: 2%	**Housing Information**	
	University housing: Yes	
	Percent living on campus: 7%	

UNIVERSITY OF NORTH TEXAS

PO Box 311277, Denton, TX 76203-1277
Phone: 940-565-2681 • Fax: 940-565-2408
E-mail: undergrad@unt.edu • Web: www.unt.edu
Support: S • Institution type: 4-year public

LEARNING DISABILITY PROGRAM AND SERVICES

The goal of the Office of Disability Accommodations is to ensure that qualified students with disabilities have access to reasonable and appropriate services and learning resources needed to facilitate matriculation and successful completion of academic programs at the university. The office serves as a liaison to ensure that assistance and/or accommodation and adjustments are available for students with disabilities to enable them full access to the educational facilities and services at the university. The office provides consultation and assistance to academic and general service offices in making adaptations and adjustments for students with disabilities. It also provides alternative testing sites and proctors when the academic department is unable to provide assistance.

LD/ADHD ADMISSIONS INFORMATION

College entrance tests required: Yes
Interview required: No
Essay recommended: No
Documentation required for LD: Completed within the last 5 years and should include a psychoeducational evaluation, including the WAIS III, WRAT-R, Nelson-Denny reading test and other appropriate assessments.
Documentation required for ADHD: Yes
Submitted to: Office of Disability Accommodations
Special Ed. HS course work accepted: No

Specific course requirements of all applicants: Yes
Separate application required: No
# of LD applications submitted each year:
# of LD applications accepted yearly: NR
Total # of students receiving LD services: 225
Acceptance into program means acceptance into college: Students must be admitted and enrolled at the university first and then may request services. Students denied admission may appeal the decision.

ADMISSIONS

Students must apply directly to the Admissions Office and meet the current requirements. Course requirements include 4 years of English, 4 years of math, 3 years of science, 3 years of a foreign language, 4 years of social studies, and 3 years of electives. When a student makes a written request for waivers for admission requirements, the request is sent to an individual approval review committee for consideration. Students in the top 10 percent of their high school class must submit ACT/SAT scores, but no specific score is required; students in the remainder of top quarter need a minimum 920 SAT I or 19 ACT; the second quarter need a minimum 1010 SAT I or 21 ACT; the third quarter need a minimum 1100 SAT I or 24 ACT; and the fourth quarter need a minimum 1180 SAT I or 27 ACT. If a student is not accepted, there is an appeal process on the basis of the learning disability. These students may need letters of support, a statement of commitment from the student, and an evaluation of the documentation by the Disability Office. Admission decisions are made by the Office of Admissions and the Office of Disability Accommodations.

ADDITIONAL INFORMATION

The Center for Development Studies provides tutoring to build academic knowledge and skills in various subject areas, academic counseling to plan class schedules and evaluate areas of strengths and weaknesses, personal counseling to develop greater self-understanding and learn ways to cope with adjustments to college and the pressures of life, and study skills assessment for evaluating and improving academic performance. Skills courses for credit are offered in time management, career choice, and study skills. Students requesting a distraction-free environments for tests must provide the appropriate documentation. Calculators, dictionaries, computers, and spellcheckers are allowed with instructor's approval. Services and accommodations are available for undergraduate and graduate students.

LEARNING DISABILITY PROGRAM/SERVICES

Learning Disability Program/Services: Office of Disability Accommodations (ODA)
Director: Steve Pickett, MS, CRC
    E-mail: steve@dsa.admin.unt.edu
    Telephone: 940-565-4323
    Fax: 940-565-4376

Contact Person: Dee Wilson
    E-mail: steve@dsa.admin.unt.edu

LEARNING DISABILITY SERVICES

Requests for the following services/accommodations will be evaluated individually based on appropriate and current documentation.

Allowed in exams
  Calculator: NR
  Dictionary: NR
  Computer: NR
  Spellchecker: NR
Extended test time: Yes
Scribes: Yes
Proctors: Yes
Oral exams: Yes
Note-takers: Yes

Distraction-reduced environment: Yes
Tape recording in class: Yes
Books on tape from RFBD: Yes
Taping of books not from RFBD: Yes
**Accommodations for students with
  ADHD:** Yes
Reading machine: Yes
Other assistive technology: Yes
Priority registration: Yes

Added costs for services: No
LD specialists: Yes
Professional tutors: No
Peer tutors: Yes
Max. hours/wk. for services:
  Unlimited
**How professors are notified of
  LD/ADHD:** By both student and
  director

GENERAL ADMISSIONS INFORMATION

Director of Admissions: Marcilla Collinsworth
Telephone: 940-565-2681

ENTRANCE REQUIREMENTS

Academic units required: 4 English, 4 math, 3 science, 3 foreign language, 4 social studies, 2 history, 3 academic electives. **Academic units recommended:** 4 English, 4 math, 3 science, 3 foreign language, 2 social studies, 2 history, 2 academic electives, 4.5 health, 1.5 physical education, 1 computer science, 1 fine arts. High school diploma is required, and GED is accepted. ACT with or without Writing component accepted. TOEFL required of all international applicants: minimum paper TOEFL 550, minimum computer TOEFL 213.

Application deadline: 8/19
Notification: Rolling
Average GPA: NR
ACT Composite middle 50% range:
  21–26

SAT Math middle 50% range:
  510–620
**SAT Critical Reading middle 50%
  range:** 500–610
SAT Writing middle 50% range: NR

Graduated top 10% of class: 20%
Graduated top 25% of class: 50%
Graduated top 50% of class: 89%

COLLEGE GRADUATION REQUIREMENTS

Course waivers allowed: Yes
In what course: This is looked at on an approval basis by each department. Approval is not automatic; it is dependent on the student's situation.
Course substitutions allowed: Yes
In what course: This is looked at on an approval basis by each department. Approval is not automatic; it is dependent on the student's situation.

ADDITIONAL INFORMATION

Environment: The university is located on 425 acres in an urban area 35 miles north of the Dallas/Fort Worth area.

Student Body
  Undergrad enrollment: 26,598
  Women: 55%
  Men: 45%
  Percent out-of-state: 3%

Cost Information
  In-state tuition: $4,215
  Out-of-state tuition: $12,465
  Room & board: $5,625
Housing Information
  University housing: Yes
  Percent living on campus: 21%

Greek System
  Fraternity: Yes
  Sorority: Yes
Athletics: Division I

UNIVERSITY OF TEXAS—EL PASO

500 West University Avenue, El Paso, TX 79968-0510
Phone: 915-747-5890 • Fax: 915-747-8893
E-mail: futureminer@utep.edu • Web: www.utep.edu
Support: S • Institution type: 4-year public

LEARNING DISABILITY PROGRAM AND SERVICES

The Disabled Student Services Office DSSO provides a program of support and advocacy for students with LD. Services offered include peer support group, assistance with learning strategies, note-takers for lectures, scribe/readers, extended time for in-class work, and altered test formats, such as oral exams. There is also a Tutoring and Learning Center whose free services include study skill assistance, subject-area tutoring, life management skills, exam reviews, peer mentoring, and distance tutoring.

LD/ADHD ADMISSIONS INFORMATION

College entrance tests required: Yes
Interview required: No
Essay recommended: No
Documentation required for LD: Current diagnostic report, comprehensive and include aptitude and achievement testing, and specific evidence of a learning disability
Documentation required for ADHD: Information regarding onset, longevity, and severity of the symptoms; complete psychoeducational evaluation that includes a cognitive assessment with a report of the interpretation of data; impact of ADHD on educational setting; medication history and current recommendations regarding medication, the exact DSM–IV diagnosis, and information concerning co-morbidity should also be included in the evaluation.

Submitted to: Disabled Student Services
Special Ed. HS course work accepted: Yes
Specific course requirements of all applicants: Yes
Separate application required: N/A
# of LD applications submitted each year: NR
# of LD applications accepted yearly: NR
Total # of students receiving LD services: 79
Acceptance into program means acceptance into college: Students must be admitted to and enrolled in the university first and then request services.

ADMISSIONS

There is no special admissions process for students with learning disabilities. General admission criteria requires students to have a high school diploma and ACT/SAT results, and they are not interested in class rank or GPA. Course requirements include 4 years of English, 3 years of math, 3 years of science, 4 years of social studies, 3 years of a foreign language, 0.5 year of health, 1 year of fine arts, 1.5 years of physical education, and 1 year of computer science. For students not otherwise eligible to enter due to grades or scores, a study skills class is required plus other courses from a course list.

ADDITIONAL INFORMATION

To receive services, students must meet with the director of DSSO. Students need to provide current documentation from an appropriate licensed professional. Services offered to students, when appropriate, are diagnostic testing, peer support group, assistance with learning strategies, and priority registration. Classroom accommodations include note-takers, assistive technology, scribes, readers, extended testing times, and exam modifications. In the Tutoring and Learning Center, students can access study skills assistance, subject area tutoring, life management skills assistance, and a special needs room with state of the art technology. Currently there are 60 students with LD and 17 with ADHD receiving services.

LEARNING DISABILITY PROGRAM/SERVICES

Learning Disability Program/Services: Disabled Student Services Office
Director: James B. Saunders Jr.
 E-mail: jsaunders@utep.edu
 Telephone: 915-747-5148
 Fax: 915-747-8712
Contact Person: Hector E. Flores
 E-mail: jsaunders@utep.edu
 Telephone: 915-747-5148
 Fax: 915-747-8712

LEARNING DISABILITY SERVICES

Requests for the following services/accommodations will be evaluated individually based on appropriate and current documentation.

Allowed in exams
 Calculator: Yes
 Dictionary: Yes
 Computer: Yes
 Spellchecker: Yes
Extended test time: Yes
Scribes: Yes
Proctors: Yes
Oral exams: Yes
Note-takers: Yes

Distraction-reduced environment: Yes
Tape recording in class: Yes
Books on tape from RFBD: Yes
Taping of books not from RFBD: Yes
Accommodations for students with ADHD: Yes
Reading machine: Yes
Other assistive technology: Yes
Priority registration: Yes

Added costs for services: No
LD specialists: No
Professional tutors: No
Peer tutors: No
Max. hours/wk. for services: 40
How professors are notified of LD/ADHD: By both student and director

GENERAL ADMISSIONS INFORMATION

Director of Admissions: Tammie Aragon-Campos
Telephone: 915-747-5890

ENTRANCE REQUIREMENTS

Academic units recommended: 4 English, 4 math, 3 science, 3 foreign language, 4 social studies, 2 history. High school diploma is required, and GED is accepted.

Application deadline: 7/31
Notification: When admission file is complete
Average GPA: 3.10
ACT Composite middle 50% range: 16–21

SAT Math middle 50% range: 400–520
SAT Critical Reading middle 50% range: NR
SAT Writing middle 50% range: NR

Graduated top 10% of class: 18%
Graduated top 25% of class: 40%
Graduated top 50% of class: 71%

COLLEGE GRADUATION REQUIREMENTS

Course waivers allowed: No
Course substitutions allowed: Yes
In what course: Math and foreign language

ADDITIONAL INFORMATION

Environment: The university is located on a 360-acre urban campus.

Student Body
 Undergrad enrollment: 16,486
 Women: 55%
 Men: 45%
 Percent out-of-state: 3%

Cost Information
 In-state tuition: $4,800
 Out-of-state tuition: $12,500
 Room & Board: $8,900
Housing Information
 University housing: Yes
 Percent living on campus: 3%

Greek System
 Fraternity: Yes
 Sorority: Yes
Athletics: Division I

University of Texas—El Paso

UNIVERSITY OF TEXAS— PAN AMERICAN

Admissions & New Student Services, 1201 West University Drive,
VC 1.133, Edinburg, TX 78541 • Phone: 956-381-2201
Fax: 956-381-2212 • E-mail: recruitment@utpa.edu
Web: www.utpa.edu • Support: CS • Institution type: 4-year public

LEARNING DISABILITY PROGRAM AND SERVICES

The Office of Services for Persons with Disabilities (OSPD) is a component of the Division of Enrollment and Student Services at the University of Texas—Pan American. It is designed and committed to providing support services to meet the educational, career, and personal needs of persons with disabilities attending or planning to attend the university. Students requesting accommodations must put their requests in writing and must provide documentation from a professional who is qualified to diagnose and verify the particular disability; and the testing and documentation must be current (completed within the past 3 years). OSPD will use the documentation to properly prepare an assistance plan for the student to use while enrolled at the university. It typically takes at least 30 days to process requests for services or accommodations.

LD/ADHD ADMISSIONS INFORMATION

College entrance tests required: Yes
Interview required: Yes
Essay recommended: No
Documentation required for LD: Psychoeducational evaluation
Documentation required for ADHD: Yes
Submitted to: Office of Services for Persons with Disabilities
Special Ed. HS course work accepted: No

Specific course requirements of all applicants: NR
Separate application required: Yes
# of LD applications submitted each year: NR
# of LD applications accepted yearly: NR
Total # of students receiving LD services: 50
Acceptance into program means acceptance into college: Students must be admitted to and enrolled in the university first and then request services.

ADMISSIONS

Students with learning disabilities must meet the same admission requirements as all other applicants. The criteria for entering freshmen are a high school diploma denoting graduation with honors or Advanced Placement; a class rank in the top 50 percent or 20-plus ACT or 1200-plus SAT; and 4 years of English, 4 years of math, 3 years of science, 4 years of social studies, 3 years of a foreign language, 1 year of fine arts, 1.5 years of physical education, 0.5 year of health, 0–1 year of computers, and 2.5 years of electives. Students not meeting these criteria may enroll through the Provisional Enrollment Program (PEP). PEP students must attend orientation, be advised by Counseling Center, select classes prescribed, and participate in noncredit programs to develop study and academic skills. PEP students with a total of 9 or more hours may fulfill criteria for regular admission by meeting specific requirements in GPA and completion of attempted hours. PEP students who do not have a 2.0 GPA after 9 hours can take an additional semester if they have at least a 1.5 GPA and meet successful completion of attempted hours. Some students not eligible to continue may petition the Admissions Committee.

ADDITIONAL INFORMATION

OSPD provides the following services: assessment for special needs; note-takers; readers and writers; advisement, counseling, and guidance; assistance with admissions, orientation, and registration; referral services to other university units; liaison between students, faculty, staff, and others; resolution of problems/concerns; computer hardware and software; and reading machines. Skills classes for credit are offered in time management, test-taking strategies, note-taking skills, reading text, and stress management. OSPD assists students in preparing appeals and works with faculty/administrators to secure waivers. Services and accommodations are available for undergraduate and graduate students.

LEARNING DISABILITY PROGRAM/SERVICES

Learning Disability Program/Services: Office of Services for Persons with Disabilities (OSPD)
Director: Rick Gray (RN, MBA)
  E-mail: grayr@panam.edu
  Telephone: 956-316-7005
  Fax: 956-316-7034
Contact Person: Maureen F. McClain, Associate Director
  E-mail: grayr@panam.edu
  Telephone: 956-316-7005
  Fax: 956-316-7034

LEARNING DISABILITY SERVICES

Requests for the following services/accommodations will be evaluated individually based on appropriate and current documentation.

Allowed in exams
  Calculator: Yes
  Dictionary: Yes
  Computer: Yes
  Spellchecker: Yes
Extended test time: Yes
Scribes: Yes
Proctors: Yes
Oral exams: Yes
Note-takers: Yes

Distraction-reduced environment: Yes
Tape recording in class: Yes
Books on tape from RFBD: Yes
Taping of books not from RFBD: Yes
**Accommodations for students with
  ADHD:** Yes
Reading machine: Yes
Other assistive technology: Yes
Priority registration: Yes

Added costs for services: No
LD specialists: No
Professional tutors: No
Peer tutors: 50
Max. hours/wk. for services: 40
**How professors are notified of
  LD/ADHD:** By both student and
  director

GENERAL ADMISSIONS INFORMATION

Director of Admissions: Dr. Magdalena Williams
Telephone: 956-381-2201

ENTRANCE REQUIREMENTS

Academic units required: 4 English, 4 math, 3 science, 2 foreign language, 4 social studies, 4 academic electives.
Academic units recommended: 3 academic electives. High school diploma is required, and GED is accepted. ACT with or without Writing component accepted. TOEFL required of all international applicants: minimum paper TOEFL 500, minimum computer TOEFL 173.

Application deadline: 8/10
Notification: As received
Average GPA: NR
ACT Composite middle 50% range:
  16–21

SAT Math middle 50% range:
  420–530
**SAT Critical Reading middle 50%
  range:** 400–510
SAT Writing middle 50% range:
  400–510

Graduated top 10% of class: 17%
Graduated top 25% of class: 44%
Graduated top 50% of class: 75%

COLLEGE GRADUATION REQUIREMENTS

Course waivers allowed: No
Course substitutions allowed: Yes
In what course: On a case-by-case basis

ADDITIONAL INFORMATION

Environment: The campus is in a small town near the Mexican border.

Student Body
  Undergrad enrollment: 13,991
  Women: 58%
  Men: 42%
  Percent out-of-state: 1%

Cost Information
  In-state tuition: $2,900
  Out-of-state tuition: $9,500
  Room & board: $5,095
Housing Information
  University housing: Yes
  Percent living on campus: 10%

Greek System
  Fraternity: Yes
  Sorority: Yes
Athletics: Division I

University of Texas—Pan American

BRIGHAM YOUNG UNIVERSITY

A-153 ASB, Provo, UT 84602-1110
Phone: 801-422-2507 • Fax: 801-422-0005
E-mail: admissions@byu.edu • Web: www.byu.edu
Support: CS • Institution type: 4-year private

LEARNING DISABILITY PROGRAM AND SERVICES

The Services to Students with Learning Disabilities program works to provide individualized programs to meet the specific needs of each student, assisting in developing strengths to meet the challenges, and making arrangements for accommodations and special services as required. Students with learning disabilities or ADHD should consult with an University Accessibility Program advisor and submit current medical and/or psychological documentation for evaluation. All accommodations are given on an individual basis and are available after approval from an UAC advisor.

LD/ADHD ADMISSIONS INFORMATION

College entrance tests required: Yes
Interview required: No
Essay recommended: No
Documentation required for LD: Psychoeducational evaluation
Documentation required for ADHD: Current diagnosis from a qualified professional
Submitted to: Services to Students with LD
Special Ed. HS course work accepted: Yes

Specific course requirements of all applicants: Yes
Separate application required: Yes
# of LD applications submitted each year: 90
# of LD applications accepted yearly: 60
Total # of students receiving LD services: 101
Acceptance into program means acceptance into college: Students must be admitted to and enrolled in the university first and then request services.

ADMISSIONS

There is no special admission process for students with learning disabilities. Suggested courses include 4 years of English, 3–4 years of math, 2–3 years of science, 2 years of history or government, 2 years of a foreign language, and 2 years of literature or writing. Evaluations are made on an individualized basis with a system weighted for college-prep courses and core classes.

ADDITIONAL INFORMATION

Workshops are offered for noncredit. The following are some examples of topics: math anxiety, memory, overcoming procrastination, self-appreciation, stress management, test-taking, textbook comprehension, time management, and communication. Additional services include counseling support and advising. When a specific disability may preclude a student from participating at an equal level with non-disabled peers, one course may be substituted for another at the discretion of the academic department. Testing may be available in oral, computerized, non-Scantron, or another format according to student needs and professor discretion. Some students with learning disabilities or ADHD may register for fewer than 8.5 credit hours while maintaining full-time status. However, financial aid course load requirements must be taken into consideration. Professors can authorize alternative exam times or breaks. Volunteer note-takers and test scribes/proctors may be provided. Services and accommodations are available for undergraduate and graduate students.

LEARNING DISABILITY PROGRAM/SERVICES

Learning Disability Program/Services: University Accessibility Center
Director: Michael Brooks
E-mail: michael_brooks@byu.edu
Telephone: 801-422-2767
Fax: 801-422-0174

LEARNING DISABILITY SERVICES

Requests for the following services/accommodations will be evaluated individually based on appropriate and current documentation.

Allowed in exams	**Distraction-reduced environment:** Yes	**Added costs for services:** No
Calculator: Yes	**Tape recording in class:** Yes	**LD specialists:** Yes
Dictionary: Yes	**Books on tape from RFBD:** Yes	**Professional tutors:** No
Computer: Yes	**Taping of books not from RFBD:** Yes	**Peer tutors:** 100
Spellchecker: Yes	**Accommodations for students with**	**Max. hours/wk. for services:** N/A
Extended test time: Yes	**ADHD:** Yes	**How professors are notified of**
Scribes: Yes	**Reading machine:** Yes	**LD/ADHD:** By both student and
Proctors: Yes	**Other assistive technology:** Yes	director
Oral exams: Yes	**Priority registration:** Yes	
Note-takers: Yes		

GENERAL ADMISSIONS INFORMATION

Director of Admissions: Tom Gourley
Telephone: 801-422-2507

ENTRANCE REQUIREMENTS

Academic units required: 4 English, 3 math, 2 science (2 science labs), 2 foreign language, 2 history, 2 literature or writing. **Academic units recommended:** 4 English, 4 math, 3 science (3 science labs), 4 foreign language. High school diploma is required, and GED is accepted. ACT with or without Writing component accepted. TOEFL required of all international applicants: minimum paper TOEFL 500, minimum computer TOEFL 173.

Application deadline: 2/1	**SAT Math middle 50% range:**	**Graduated top 10% of class:** 49%
Notification: Rolling	570–670	**Graduated top 25% of class:** 35%
Average GPA: 3.73	**SAT Critical Reading middle 50%**	**Graduated top 50% of class:** 99%
ACT Composite middle 50% range:	**range:** 550–660	
25–29	**SAT Writing middle 50% range:** NR	

COLLEGE GRADUATION REQUIREMENTS

Course waivers allowed: No
Course substitutions allowed: Yes
In what course: General education, foreign language, and/or math

ADDITIONAL INFORMATION

Environment: The university is located in a suburban area 45 miles south of Salt Lake City.

Student Body	**Cost Information**	**Greek System**
Undergrad enrollment: 30,798	**In-state tuition:** $3,620	**Fraternity:** No
Women: 49%	**Out-of-state tuition:** $5,100	**Sorority:** No
Men: 51%	**Room & board:** $5,640	**Athletics:** Division I
Percent out-of-state: 72%	**Housing Information**	
	University housing: Yes	
	Percent living on campus: 20%	

SOUTHERN UTAH UNIVERSITY

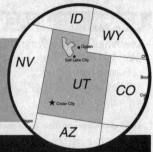

Admissions Office, 351 West University Boulevard, Cedar City, UT 84720
Phone: 435-586-7740 • Fax: 435-865-8223
E-mail: adminfo@suu.edu • Web: www.suu.edu
Support: S • Institution type: 4-year public

LEARNING DISABILITY PROGRAM AND SERVICES

The philosophy of Student Support Services (SSS) is to promote self-sufficiency and achievement. SSS assists college students with developmental classes, skills courses, academic and tutorial support, and advisement. In particular, disabled students are encouraged and supported in advocating for themselves. The university provides a full variety of services and accommodations for all disabled students. The academic support coordinator assists students with enrollment in SSS and helps them identify academic areas where they feel a need to strengthen skills to assure college success.

LD/ADHD ADMISSIONS INFORMATION

College entrance tests required: Yes
Interview required: No
Essay recommended: No
Documentation required for LD: WRAT, WAIS, Woodcock-Johnson
Documentation required for ADHD: WAIS—III, WJ–III, MMPI–2, WURS
Submitted to: Student Support Services
Special Ed. HS course work accepted: No

Specific course requirements of all applicants: Yes
Separate application required: No
# of LD applications submitted each year: 30
# of LD applications accepted yearly: 30
Total # of students receiving LD services: 63
Acceptance into program means acceptance into college: Students must be admitted to and enrolled in the university first and then request services.

ADMISSIONS

Students with learning disabilities submit the general application form. Students must have at least a 2.0 GPA and show competency in English, math, science, and social studies. The university uses an admissions index derived from the combination of the high school GPA and results of either the ACT or SAT. If students are not admissible through the regular process, special consideration by a committee review can be gained through reference letters and a personal letter. The university is allowed to admit 5 percent in flex admission. These applications are reviewed by a committee consisting of the Director of Support Services and representatives from the Admissions Office. Students are encouraged to self-disclose their learning disability and submit documentation.

ADDITIONAL INFORMATION

Student Support Services, a project funded by the U.S. Department of Education, assists college students with developmental classes, skills courses, academic and tutorial support, and advisement. Tutoring is available in small groups or one-on-one, free of charge. Basic skills classes, for credit, are offered in English, reading, math, math anxiety, language, and study skills. The English writing support that SSS offers is a section of English 1000, which students take in conjunction with English 1010. This class is recommended for any student entering SUU with a score of 16 or lower on the ACT Writing subset or those needing additional support in writing. SSS staff will also work individually with students to improve writing skills.

LEARNING DISABILITY PROGRAM/SERVICES

Learning Disability Program/Services: Student Support Services (SSS)
Director: Carmen R. Alldredge
  E-mail: alldredge@suu.edu
  Telephone: 435-865-8022
  Fax: 435-865-8235

LEARNING DISABILITY SERVICES

Requests for the following services/accommodations will be evaluated individually based on appropriate and current documentation.

Allowed in exams
  Calculator: No
  Dictionary: Yes
  Computer: Yes
  Spellchecker: Yes
Extended test time: Yes
Scribes: Yes
Proctors: Yes
Oral exams: Yes
Note-takers: Yes

Distraction-reduced environment: Yes
Tape recording in class: Yes
Books on tape from RFBD: Yes
Taping of books not from RFBD: Yes
Accommodations for students with ADHD: Yes
Reading machine: Yes
Other assistive technology: Yes
Priority registration: Yes

Added costs for services: No
LD specialists: No
Professional tutors: 6
Peer tutors: 6–30
Max. hours/wk. for services: Unlimited
How professors are notified of LD/ADHD: By both student and director

GENERAL ADMISSIONS INFORMATION

Director of Admissions: Dale Orton
Telephone: 435-586-7740

ENTRANCE REQUIREMENTS

Academic units recommended: 4 English, 3 math, 3 science (1 science lab), 2 foreign language, 3 social studies. High school diploma is required, and GED is accepted. ACT with or without Writing component accepted. TOEFL required of all international applicants: minimum paper TOEFL 50.

Application deadline: 8/1
Notification: Decision sent immediately
Average GPA: 3.42
ACT Composite middle 50% range: 18–24

SAT Math middle 50% range: 450–570
SAT Critical Reading middle 50% range: 440–590
SAT Writing middle 50% range: NR

Graduated top 10% of class: 28%
Graduated top 25% of class: 55%
Graduated top 50% of class: 82%

COLLEGE GRADUATION REQUIREMENTS

Course waivers allowed: No
Course substitutions allowed: No

ADDITIONAL INFORMATION

Environment: The university is in a small town 150 miles north of Las Vegas.

Student Body
  Undergrad enrollment: 5,268
  Women: 57%
  Men: 43%
  Percent out-of-state: 14%

Cost Information
  In-state tuition: $3,600
  Out-of-state tuition: $11,200
  Room & board: $5,400
Housing Information
  University housing: Yes
  Percent living on campus: 13%

Greek System
  Fraternity: Yes
  Sorority: Yes
Athletics: Division I

UNIVERSITY OF UTAH

201 South 1460 East, Room 250 S, Salt Lake City, UT 84112
Phone: 801-581-7281 • Fax: 801-585-7864
E-mail: admissions@sa.utah.edu • Web: www.utah.edu
Support: CS • Institution type: 4-year public

LEARNING DISABILITY PROGRAM AND SERVICES

The Center for Disability Services at the University of Utah provides accommodations and support for students with disabilities who have current physical or psychological documentation that qualifies them for services. The goal is to provide assistance to encourage and enhance student's independence, maintain ongoing cooperative efforts to develop and maintain an accessible physical environment, and provide educational efforts to create a supportive psychological environment for students to achieve their educational objectives. A cooperative relationship is maintained with relevant campus departments to ensure the University of Utah complies with federal and state regulations regarding students with disabilities.

LD/ADHD ADMISSIONS INFORMATION

College entrance tests required: Yes
Interview required: No
Essay recommended: No
Documentation required for LD: Psychoeducational evaluation
Documentation required for ADHD: Yes
Submitted to: Center for Disability Services
Special Ed. HS course work accepted: No

Specific course requirements of all applicants: Yes
Separate application required: No
# of LD applications submitted each year: NR
# of LD applications accepted yearly: NR
Total # of students receiving LD services: 239
Acceptance into program means acceptance into college: Students must be admitted to and enrolled in the university first and then request services.

ADMISSIONS

There is no special application process for students with learning disabilities. All applicants to the university must meet the general admission requirements. Students who do not meet the admission requirements as a direct result of their disability may be admitted on the condition that course deficiencies are filled prior to earning 30 semester hours at the university. Conditional admission is determined by the Center for Disability Services and the Admissions Office. Students must provide appropriate information regarding their disability and any services they received in high school due to their disability. Self-disclosure is recommended only if the student needs to inform the Admissions Office they are working with the Center for Disability Services to consider conditional admission. Otherwise disclosure is not recommended, but it is left to the student to make the decision.

ADDITIONAL INFORMATION

The University of Utah is committed to providing reasonable accommodations to students whose disabilities may limit their ability to function in the academic setting. To meet the needs of students and to make university activities, programs, and facilities accessible, the Center for Disability Services can provide the following services to students who provide documentation of a disability: assistance with admissions, registration, and graduation; orientation to the campus; referrals to campus and community services; guidelines for obtaining CDS services; general and academic advising related to disability; investigation of academic strengths and weaknesses; develop effective learning strategies; coordinate with academic and departmental advisors regarding program goals; coordinate reasonable accommodations of disability-related limitations with faculty and staff; liaison between student and faculty or staff; provide readers, scribes, note-takers, textbooks, and printed material recorded onto cassettes; and arrange for exam accommodations. The Center for Disability Services has the right to set procedures to determine whether the student qualifies for services and how the services will be implemented. Additionally, the center has the responsibility to adjust or substitute academic requirements that unfairly discriminate against the student with a disability and that are not essential to the integrity of a student's academic program. Students must provide appropriate documentation.

LEARNING DISABILITY PROGRAM/SERVICES

Learning Disability Program/Services: Center for Disability Services
Director: Joe Pete Wilson
 E-mail: Joepete@sa.utah.edu
 Telephone: 801-581-5020
 Fax: 801-581-5487

LEARNING DISABILITY SERVICES

Requests for the following services/accommodations will be evaluated individually based on appropriate and current documentation.

Allowed in exams
 Calculator: Yes
 Dictionary: Yes
 Computer: Yes
 Spellchecker: Yes
Extended test time: Yes
Scribes: Yes
Proctors: Yes
Oral exams: Yes
Note-takers: Yes

Distraction-reduced environment: Yes
Tape recording in class: Yes
Books on tape from RFBD: Yes
Taping of books not from RFBD: Yes
Accommodations for students with ADHD: Yes
Reading machine: Yes
Other assistive technology: Yes
Priority registration: Yes

Added costs for services: No
LD specialists: Yes
Professional tutors: 10
Peer tutors: 110
Max. hours/wk. for services: Unlimited
How professors are notified of LD/ADHD: By both student and director

GENERAL ADMISSIONS INFORMATION

Director of Admissions: Timothy Ebner
Telephone: 801-581-6240

ENTRANCE REQUIREMENTS

Academic units required: 4 English, 2 math, 3 science (2 science labs), 2 foreign language, 1 history, 4 academic electives. High school diploma is required, and GED is accepted. ACT with or without Writing component accepted. TOEFL required of all international applicants: minimum paper TOEFL 500, minimum computer TOEFL 173.

Application deadline: 4/1
Notification: Rolling, within 2 weeks of file completion
Average GPA: 3.52
ACT Composite middle 50% range: 21–27

SAT Math middle 50% range: 500–640
SAT Critical Reading middle 50% range: 500–630
SAT Writing middle 50% range: NR

Graduated top 10% of class: 23%
Graduated top 25% of class: 50%
Graduated top 50% of class: 82%

COLLEGE GRADUATION REQUIREMENTS

Course waivers allowed: Yes
In what course: Math requirement for general education for BS, and foreign language requirement for BA
Course substitutions allowed: Yes
In what course: Math and foreign language

ADDITIONAL INFORMATION

Environment: The university is located in Salt Lake City.

Student Body
 Undergrad enrollment: 21,249
 Women: 44%
 Men: 56%
 Percent out-of-state: 16%

Cost Information
 In-state tuition: $4,300
 Out-of-state tuition: $13,902
 Room & board: $5,800
Housing Information
 University housing: Yes
 Percent living on campus: 12%

Greek System
 Fraternity: Yes
 Sorority: Yes
Athletics: Division I

UTAH STATE UNIVERSITY

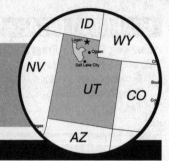

0160 Old Main Hill, Logan, UT 84322-0160
Phone: 435-797-1079 • Fax: 435-797-3708
E-mail: admit@cc.usu.edu • Web: www.usu.edu
Support: CS • Institution type: 4-year public

LEARNING DISABILITY PROGRAM AND SERVICES

The mission of the Disability Resource Center (DRC) is to provide support services to students with learning disabilities (and physical disabilities) to assist them in meeting their academic and personal goals. Staff members coordinate university support services and help the students identify their needs and overcome educational or attitudinal barriers that may prevent them from reaching their full educational potential. The DRC works to tailor services to students' individual needs. Many students use a combination of services to assist them academically, including campus orientation, registration referral, and academic advising to help students feel comfortable and promote academic services.

LD/ADHD ADMISSIONS INFORMATION

College entrance tests required: Yes
Interview required: No
Essay recommended: No
Documentation required for LD: Psychoeducational evaluation
Documentation required for ADHD: Full evaluation from an individual with experience in doing evaluations
Submitted to: Disability Resource Center
Special Ed. HS course work accepted: Yes

Specific course requirements of all applicants: Yes
Separate application required: Yes
# of LD applications submitted each year: NR
# of LD applications accepted yearly: NR
Total # of students receiving LD services: 150
Acceptance into program means acceptance into college: Students must be admitted to and enrolled in the university first and then request services.

ADMISSIONS

All students submit the regular application. Course requirements include 4 years of English, 3 years of math, 3 years of science, 1 year of science lab, 2 years of a foreign language (recommended), 1 year of history, and 4 years of electives. If the Admissions Committee does not admit the student with a learning disability, the Disability Resource Center will consult with admissions on special admits. Students who know they have a learning disability should contact the DRC to find out the details. Each student is assessed individually for admission. Consideration is given to waiving certain entrance requirements, such as flexibility on the GPA, course requirements, and SAT or ACT scores (lower than 17 on the ACT).

ADDITIONAL INFORMATION

Basic skills courses are offered in time management, learning strategies, and reading, math, and study strategies. The DRC has developed an assistive technology lab with computers and adaptive equipment to promote independence in conducting research and completing class assignments. Scholarships are available. Testing accommodations include extended time, readers, scribes, and distraction-reduced testing rooms. Note-takers in the class provide notes for eligible students. Notes are sent to the student by e-mail or WebCT. Priority registration is available for students who have individual scheduling needs or to aid in providing high-demand DRC services.

LEARNING DISABILITY PROGRAM/SERVICES

Learning Disability Program/Services: Disability Resource Center (DRC)
Director: Diane Craig Baum
  E-mail: Diane.Baum@usu.edu
  Telephone: 435-797-2444
  Fax: 435-797-0130

LEARNING DISABILITY SERVICES

Requests for the following services/accommodations will be evaluated individually based on appropriate and current documentation.

Allowed in exams
  Calculator: Yes
  Dictionary: Yes
  Computer: Yes
  Spellchecker: Yes
Extended test time: Yes
Scribes: Yes
Proctors: Yes
Oral exams: Yes
Note-takers: Yes

Distraction-reduced environment: Yes
Tape recording in class: Yes
Books on tape from RFBD: Yes
Taping of books not from RFBD: Yes
**Accommodations for students with
  ADHD:** Yes
Reading machine: Yes
Other assistive technology: Yes
Priority registration: Yes

Added costs for services: No
LD specialists: Yes
Professional tutors: No
Peer tutors: Yes
Max. hours/wk. for services: NR
**How professors are notified of
  LD/ADHD:** By student

GENERAL ADMISSIONS INFORMATION

Director of Admissions: Jenn Putnam
Telephone: 435-797-1079

ENTRANCE REQUIREMENTS

Academic units required: 4 English, 3 math, 3 science (1 science lab), 1 history, 4 academic electives. **Academic units recommended:** 2 foreign language. High school diploma is required, and GED is accepted. ACT with or without Writing component accepted. TOEFL required of all international applicants: minimum paper TOEFL 500, minimum computer TOEFL 173.

Application deadline: Rolling
Notification: When accepted
Average GPA: 3.54
ACT Composite middle 50% range:
  21–27

SAT Math middle 50% range:
  490–620
**SAT Critical Reading middle 50%
  range:** 470–620
SAT Writing middle 50% range: NR

Graduated top 10% of class: 25%
Graduated top 25% of class: 51%
Graduated top 50% of class: 81%

COLLEGE GRADUATION REQUIREMENTS

Course waivers allowed: No
Course substitutions allowed: No

ADDITIONAL INFORMATION

Environment: The university is located on 332 acres 96 miles north of Salt Lake City.

Student Body
  Undergrad enrollment: 12,572
  Women: 48%
  Men: 52%
  Percent out-of-state: 27%

Cost Information
  In-state tuition: $3,949
  Out-of-state tuition: $11,449
  Room & board: $4,500
Housing Information
  University housing: Yes
  Percent living on campus: 14%

Greek System
  Fraternity: Yes
  Sorority: Yes
Athletics: Division I

CHAMPLAIN COLLEGE

163 South Willard Street, PO Box 670, Burlington, VT 05402-0670
Phone: 802-860-2727 • Fax: 802-860-2767
E-mail: admission@champlain.edu • Web: www.champlain.edu
Support: S • Institution type: 4-year private

LEARNING DISABILITY PROGRAM AND SERVICES

Champlain College does not offer a special program for students with LD. Support services and academic accommodations are available when needed. Students with LD meet individually with a counselor at the start of the semester and are assisted in developing a plan of academic support. The counselor acts as liaison between the student and faculty. The Student Resource Center offers peer tutoring, writing assistance, accounting lab, math lab, and a study skill workshop series in note-taking; mastering a college text; writing, revising, and editing papers; and personal counseling. Students must provide documentation of the disability to Support Services for Students with Disabilities, which should include the most recent educational evaluation performed by a qualified individual, and a letter from any educational support service provider who has recently worked with the student would be most helpful. The letter should include information about the nature of the disability and the support services and/or program modifications provided.

LD/ADHD ADMISSIONS INFORMATION

College entrance tests required: Yes
Interview required: No
Essay recommended: Yes
Documentation required for LD: The most recent psychoeducational evaluation, including WISC or WAIS–III and achievement testing.
Documentation required for ADHD: Yes
Submitted to: Support Services
Special Ed. HS course work accepted: Yes

Specific course requirements of all applicants: Yes
Separate application required: No
# of LD applications submitted each year: NR
# of LD applications accepted yearly: NR
Total # of students receiving LD services: 100–130
Acceptance into program means acceptance into college: Students must be admitted to and enrolled in the university first and then request services.

ADMISSIONS

There is no special admissions procedure for students with LD. Admissions are fairly flexible, though some requirements for certain majors are more difficult. Upward grade trend is very helpful, and a good senior year is looked on favorably. Recommendations are crucial. Students may elect to self-disclose the LD during the admission process, and the college will take this information into consideration when making admission decisions. Students may take a reduced load of 12 credits and still be considered full-time. The average ACT for applicants is a 20, and for the SAT, it is 1100. The minimum GPA is a 2.0.

ADDITIONAL INFORMATION

Students with learning disabilities who self-disclose receive a special needs form after they have enrolled in college courses from the Coordinator of Support Services for Students with Disabilities. The coordinator meets with each student during the first week of school. The first appointment includes a discussion about the student's disability and the academic accommodations that will be needed. Accommodations could include, but are not limited to, tutoring, extended time for tests (in the Resource Center), readers for tests, use of computers during exams, peer note-takers, tape recording lectures, and books on tape. With the student's permission, faculty members receive a letter describing the student's disability and discussing appropriate accommodations. The coordinator will continue to act as a liaison between students and faculty, consult with tutors, monitor students' academic progress, and consult with faculty as needed. Freshman focus, a course designed to assist students in making a smooth transition to college, is available for students in certain majors.

LEARNING DISABILITY PROGRAM/SERVICES

Learning Disability Program/Services: Support Services for Students with Disabilities
Director: Allyson Krings, Coordinator and Counselor
  E-mail: krings@champlain.edu
  Telephone: 802.651.5961
  Fax: 802.860.2764

LEARNING DISABILITY SERVICES

Requests for the following services/accommodations will be evaluated individually based on appropriate and current documentation.

Allowed in exams
  Calculator: Yes
  Dictionary: Yes
  Computer: Yes
  Spellchecker: Yes
Extended test time: Yes
Scribes: Yes
Proctors: Yes
Oral exams: Yes
Note-takers: Yes

Distraction-reduced environment: Yes
Tape recording in class: Yes
Books on tape from RFBD: Yes
Taping of books not from RFBD: Yes
Accommodations for students with ADHD: Yes
Reading machine: Yes
Other assistive technology: Yes
Priority registration: No

Added costs for services: No
LD specialists: No
Professional tutors: No
Peer tutors: 30
Max. hours/wk. for services: N/A
How professors are notified of LD/ADHD: By student

GENERAL ADMISSIONS INFORMATION

Director of Admissions: Dr. Laryn Runco
Telephone: 802-860-2727

ENTRANCE REQUIREMENTS
Academic units required: 4 English, 3 math, 3 science (2 science labs), 4 history, 4 academic electives.
Academic units recommended: 4 math, 4 science (3 science labs), 2 foreign language, 2 social studies. High school diploma is required, and GED is accepted. ACT with or without Writing component accepted. TOEFL required of all international applicants: minimum paper TOEFL 500, minimum computer TOEFL 173.

Application deadline: 1/31
Notification: 3/25
Average GPA: 3.00
ACT Composite middle 50% range: 20–25

SAT Math middle 50% range: 500–610
SAT Critical Reading middle 50% range: 500–590
SAT Writing middle 50% range: NR

Graduated top 10% of class: 10%
Graduated top 25% of class: 15%
Graduated top 50% of class: 85%

COLLEGE GRADUATION REQUIREMENTS

Course waivers allowed: No
Course substitutions allowed: No

ADDITIONAL INFORMATION

Environment: The college is located on 16 acres in a small city surrounded by rural area mountains and Lake Champlain.

Student Body
  Undergrad enrollment: 1,928
  Women: 50%
  Men: 50%
  Percent out-of-state: 59%

Cost Information
  Tuition: $22,550
  Room & board: $10,910
Housing Information
  University housing: Yes
  Percent living on campus: 40%

Greek System
  Fraternity: No
  Sorority: No
Athletics: Intramural

GREEN MOUNTAIN COLLEGE

One College Circle, Poultney, VT 05764-1199
Phone: 802-287-8000 • Fax: 802-287-8099
E-mail: admiss@greenmtn.edu • Web: www.greenmtn.edu
Support: S • Institution type: 4-year private

LEARNING DISABILITY PROGRAM AND SERVICES

Green Mountain College provides accommodations for students with documented learning differences. The college believes that every student has the potential for academic success and strives to support students while teaching them independence and self-advocacy. The Learning Center (LC) functions as the primary source of information regarding academic issues relating to disabilities. Students seeking academic accommodations must self-identify and submit valid documentation of their learning needs. The LC staff determines which students are eligible for academic accommodations and works with the student and staff to develop and implement an accommodation plan that will allow the student an opportunity to succeed at college. Progress is monitored to ensure access to the necessary supports and to assist in fostering self-advocacy. The LC has six main functions: to provide academic support, primarily through one-on-one, small group, general content area tutoring; to serve as the campus Writing Center; to support courses specifically designed for underprepared students; to provide support for foreign students; to be the campus center for academic issues relating to disabilities; and to provide workshops and seminars and events with the goal of improving learning skills.

LD/ADHD ADMISSIONS INFORMATION

College entrance tests required: Yes
Interview required: No
Essay recommended: No
Documentation required for LD: Documentation necessary to substantiate the LD that is comprehensive. Diagnostic interview, assessment, specific diagnosis, actual test scores from standardized instruments, and rationale for accommodation.
Documentation required for ADHD: Yes
Submitted to: Support Program/Services
Special Ed. HS course work accepted: Yes

Specific course requirements of all applicants: NR
Separate application required: No
# of LD applications submitted each year: NR
# of LD applications accepted yearly: NR
Total # of students receiving LD services: 50
Acceptance into program means acceptance into college: Students must be admitted and enrolled at the college and then reviewed for LC services.

ADMISSIONS

There is no special admissions process for students with learning disabilities. Students face the same admission criteria, which include: ACT score of 19 or SAT score of 900; 2.0 GPA; 4 years of English, 2–3 years of history/social studies, 2 years of science (with lab), 3 years of math, and 2 years of a foreign language. All applications are carefully considered with the best interest of both the student and the college in mind. Green Mountain College has a probationary admission that limits the course load of the new student while requiring the student to make use of support services.

ADDITIONAL INFORMATION

The Learning Center provides support services to all students which include: counseling and monitoring of academic progress for students on an individual basis and, when appropriate, making referrals to related college departments; offering and facilitating group sessions for students experiencing similar academic concerns; coordinating the delivery of services for students with disabilities that impact academic performance including responding to requests for reasonable and appropriate accommodations; conducting educational workshops designed to facilitate the mastery of study strategies and learning skills and to improve overall academic performance; coordinating the college tutorial program in consultation with individual academic departments; and collaborating with existing college components. The tutoring program uses a three-tiered approach: a drop-in clinic for immediate but temporary academic assistance; individually scheduled tutoring; or a more extensive schedule of one, two, or three tutoring sessions per week for tutorial help throughout a course. The Writing Center is open during drop-in hours. All new students take placement tests to assess their achievement in reading and mathematics. Students whose work is unsatisfactory are requested to rewrite assignments with the help of the Learning Center staff. Students underprepared in math are advised to take Basic Math or Beginning Algebra, and tutoring is available.

LEARNING DISABILITY PROGRAM/SERVICES

Learning Disability Program/Services: The Learning Center (LC)
Director: Raina Robins
  E-mail: robinsr@greenmtn.edu
  Telephone: 802-287-8287
  Fax: 802-287-8288

LEARNING DISABILITY SERVICES

Requests for the following/services accommodations will be evaluated individually based on appropriate and current documentation.

Allowed in exams	**Distraction-reduced environment:** Yes	**Added costs for services:** No
Calculator: Yes	**Tape recording in class:** Yes	**LD specialists:** No
Dictionary: Yes	**Books on tape from RFBD:** Yes	**Professional tutors:** 4
Computer: Yes	**Taping of books not from RFBD:** No	**Peer tutors:** 15–19
Spellchecker: Yes	**Accommodations for students with**	**Max. hours/wk. for services:**
Extended test time: Yes	**ADHD:** Yes	Unlimited
Scribes: Yes	**Reading machine:** Yes	**How professors are notified of**
Proctors: Yes	**Other assistive technology:** No	**LD/ADHD:** By both student and
Oral exams: No	**Priority registration:** No	director
Notetakers: Yes		

GENERAL ADMISSIONS INFORMATION

Director of Admissions: Jessica Day
Telephone: 802-287-8207

ENTRANCE REQUIREMENTS

Academic units required: 4 English, 3 math, 3 science (2 science labs), 2 foreign language, 3 social studies, 1 history, 5 academic electives. Academic units recomended: 4 math, 4 science, 3 foreign language, 3 social studies, 2 history. High school diploma is required, and GED is accepted. ACT with or without Writing component accepted. TOEFL required of all international applicants: minimum paper TOEFL 500, minimum computer TOEFL 173.

Application deadline: NR	**SAT Math middle 50% range:** NR	**Graduated top 10% of class:** NR
Notification: Rolling	**SAT Critical Reading middle 50%**	**Graduated top 25% of class:** NR
Average GPA: NR	**range:** NR	**Graduated top 50% of class:** NR
ACT Composite middle 50% range:	**SAT Writing middle 50% range:**	
NR	NR	

COLLEGE GRADUATION REQUIREMENTS

Course waivers allowed: No
Course substitutions allowed: No

ADDITIONAL INFORMATION

Environment: The campus is in a small town near Rutland.		
Student Body	**Cost Information**	**Greek System**
Undergrad enrollment: 721	**Tuition:** $22,662	**Fraternity:** No
Women: 50%	**Room & board:** $8,426	**Sorority:** No
Men: 50%	**Housing Information**	**Athletics:** Division III
Percent out-of-state: 85%	**University housing:** Yes	
	Percent living on campus: 81%	

JOHNSON STATE COLLEGE

337 College Hill, Johnson, VT 05656-9408
Phone: 802-635-1219 • Fax: 802-635-1230
E-mail: jscadmissions@jsc.vsc.edu • Web: www.jsc.vsc.edu
Support: CS • Institution type: 4-year public

LEARNING DISABILITY PROGRAM AND SERVICES

Johnson State College provides services to students with learning disabilities through the special services counselor. The fundamental purpose is to provide students with the appropriate services necessary to allow full participation in all Johnson State College academic programs. Students with learning disabilities are integrated fully into the college community. There is also a TRIO Program for 235 students meeting eligibility criteria, which include at least one of the following areas: be enrolled in one or more basic skills courses; earned SAT scores below 300 on either Verbal or Math sections; earned a GED; has below-average high school grades; has not completed Algebra II or its equivalent in high school; or was conditionally accepted to the college. Students must also meet one of three criteria: have a documented disability, be a first-generation college student, and be economically disadvantaged. Eligible students receive intensive support services through the Academic Support Services program. The Learning Resource Center provides a friendly and supportive environment for any student who is academically struggling or under prepared to meet his or her educational goals. Services include group and peer tutoring, access to a math lab, a writer's workshop, and supplemental/instruction.

LD/ADHD ADMISSIONS INFORMATION

College entrance tests required: Yes
Interview required: No
Essay recommended: No
Documentation required for LD: Cognitive measurement WAIS–R and achievement tests within the past 3 years.
Documentation required for ADHD: Completed by school personnel and diagnosing physician.
Submitted to: Academic Support Services
Special Ed. HS course work accepted: N/A

Specific course requirements of all applicants: Yes
Separate application required: No
# of LD applications submitted each year: NR
# of LD applications accepted yearly: NR
Total # of students receiving LD services: 57
Acceptance into program means acceptance into college: Students must be admitted to and enrolled in the university first and then request services.

ADMISSIONS

As a state college, no formula is used to determine who is admitted to Johnson State College. In deciding which students have the greatest potential for success here, our admissions counselors consider a range of information about each individual candidate. Admissions counselors carefully evaluate each student's academic preparation as reflected by transcripts, course selection, letters of recommendation, SAT or ACT scores, and class rank. We also look closely at personal qualities such as motivation, ambition, and individualism as demonstrated through involvement in extracurricular activities and community service. Upon consultation with the Academic Support Services Office, all students with learning disabilities who self-disclose and demonstrate the academic ability to be successful are accepted. Modifications to entrance requirements are accommodated if a student is otherwise admissible. Course requirements include 4 years of English, 2 years of science, 2 years of social science, and 3 years of math. The high school GPA minimum is 2.0. The SAT score range is 700–940; for the ACT it is 15–20 for the middle 50 percent of students admitted.

ADDITIONAL INFORMATION

Academic Support Services provides tutoring, academic advising, personal counseling, career exploration, college survival skills training workshops, and assistance with establishing appropriate and reasonable accommodations. Students should be self-advocates and are responsible for notifying instructors to arrange for accommodations. The Transition Year Experience (TYE) is available to all students who are conditionally accepted to JSC. It begins 1 week prior to freshman year and continues through 15 weeks of the fall semester. This innovative learning experience will help make the transition from high school to college a more positive and rewarding experience for students needing strong academic and individual support. Students earn a total of four college credits through the TYE designed to teach critical inquiry, study skills, general college survival skills, and self-advocacy.

LEARNING DISABILITY PROGRAM/SERVICES

Learning Disability Program/Services: Academic Support Services
Director: Karen Madden, PhD
  E-mail: karen.madden@jsc.vsc.edu
  Telephone: 802-635-1259
  Fax: 802-635-1454
Contact Person: Dian Duranleau
  E-mail: karen.madden@jsc.vsc.edu
  Telephone: 802-635-1259
  Fax: 802-635-1454

LEARNING DISABILITY SERVICES

Requests for the following services/accommodations will be evaluated individually based on appropriate and current documentation.

Allowed in exams
  Calculator: Yes
  Dictionary: Yes
  Computer: Yes
  Spellchecker: Yes
Extended test time: Yes
Scribes: Yes
Proctors: Yes
Oral exams: No
Note-takers: Yes

Distraction-reduced environment: Yes
Tape recording in class: Yes
Books on tape from RFBD: Yes
Taping of books not from RFBD: Yes
Accommodations for students with
  ADHD: Yes
Reading machine: Yes
Other assistive technology: Yes
Priority registration: No

Added costs for services: No
LD specialists: Yes
Professional tutors: 4
Peer tutors: 15–25
Max. hours/wk. for services:
  Unlimited
How professors are notified of
  LD/ADHD: By student

GENERAL ADMISSIONS INFORMATION

Director of Admissions: Penny Paradee Howrigan
Telephone: 800-635-253

ENTRANCE REQUIREMENTS

Academic units required: 4 English, 3 math, 2 science (1 science lab), 2 social studies, 2 history. **Academic units recommended:** 4 English, 4 math, 3 science (2 science labs), 1 foreign language, 3 social studies, 3 history. High school diploma is required, and GED is accepted. ACT with Writing component required. TOEFL required of all international applicants: minimum paper TOEFL 500, minimum computer TOEFL 173.

Application deadline: Rolling
Notification: Rolling
Average GPA: NR
ACT Composite middle 50% range:
  20–28

SAT Math middle 50% range:
  430–550
SAT Critical Reading middle 50%
  range: 430–600
SAT Writing middle 50% range: NR

Graduated top 10% of class: 6%
Graduated top 25% of class: 24%
Graduated top 50% of class: 52%

COLLEGE GRADUATION REQUIREMENTS

Course waivers allowed: No
Course substitutions allowed: Yes
In what course: Lower math may be substituted for one of the two math requirements if there is a math LD only.

ADDITIONAL INFORMATION

Environment: The college is located in a rural area 45 miles northeast of Burlington.

Student Body
  Undergrad enrollment: 1,554
  Women: 60%
  Men: 40%
  Percent out-of-state: 22%

Cost Information
  In-state tuition: $5,980
  Out-of-state tuition: $12,920
  Room & board: $6,454
Housing Information
  University housing: Yes
  Percent living on campus: 38%

Greek System
  Fraternity: No
  Sorority: No
  Athletics: Division III

Johnson State College

LANDMARK COLLEGE

PO Box 820, Putney, VT 05346-0820
Phone: 802-387-6718 • Fax: 802-387-6868
E-mail: admissions@landmark.edu • Web: www.landmark.edu
Support: SP • Institution type: 2-year private

LEARNING DISABILITY PROGRAM AND SERVICES

Landmark College is designed exclusively for high-potential students with dyslexia, specific learning disabilities, and/or ADHD. It is the only accredited college in the nation for students with LD/ADHD. More than 100 members of the faculty and professional staff devote their entire attention to providing the finest possible program for these students. The goal is to prepare students to enter or return to college. At Landmark, students do not bypass difficulties by using note-takers, taped books, or taking exams orally. Students must do their own work, and Landmark teaches them how. Landmark's approach is unique and includes an individually designed tutorial program, very small classes, structured assignments, and an emphasis on constantly improving language and study skills. Coaching Services provides a specific and unique type of support. They are designed for students who struggle with the various aspects of academic work production known as "executive functioning." These include planning and prioritizing, organizing, remembering to do intended tasks, getting started, sustaining motivation, self-monitoring, managing multiple tasks, and following through to completion.

LD/ADHD ADMISSIONS INFORMATION

College entrance tests required: No
Interview required: Yes
Essay recommended: Yes
Documentation required for LD: Psychoeducational evaluation
Documentation required for ADHD: Psychoeducational evaluation
Submitted to: Admissions
Special Ed. HS course work accepted: Yes

Specific course requirements of all applicants: NR
Separate application required: No
# of LD applications submitted each year: 800
# of LD applications accepted yearly: 400
Total # of students receiving LD services: 100–125
Acceptance into program means acceptance into college: The program and the college are one and the same.

ADMISSIONS

Landmark College serves students whose academic skills have not been developed to a level equal to their intellectual capacity. Students must have average to superior intellectual potential; diagnosis of dyslexia, specific LD, or ADHD; and high motivation. Applicants must have a willingness to undertake a rigorous academic program that does not provide bypass methods such as note-takers, books on tape, or oral exams. Focus instead is on individualized, intensive development and honing of academic skills. Qualified students must have a testing session and interview. An admission decision is made at this time. ACT/SAT are not required. There are no specific course requirements for admission, but students must take courses that lead to a high school diploma or the GED. Students may apply for admission for summer, fall, or spring semesters.

ADDITIONAL INFORMATION

Skills Development Summer Sessions ($7,300) help students develop the language and study skills needed for success in college. This program is open to students from other colleges or recent high school graduates, as well as those planning to attend Landmark. Students can get help with writing, reading, study skills, and understanding their own learning styles. Skills classes are offered to students on campus in study skills, math, written language, oral language, and content courses. In addition to the types of services found at typical institutions of higher learning, we have services that support any additional needs, due to learning disabilities or ADHD. Students can access support for skills development, coaching, class support, academic planning, advising, understanding their learning profile, and planning for future academic or professional goals. Typically, students work with your academic advisors to develop a plan. This determines which services students will access at any given time throughout the pursuit of their degree. All of these services are staffed by professional faculty and staff members.

LEARNING DISABILITY PROGRAM/SERVICES

Learning Disability Program/Services: Landmark College
Director: John Kipp, Academic Dean
  E-mail: jkipp@landmark.edu
  Telephone: 802-387-4767
  Fax: 802-387-6868
Contact Person: Dale M. Herold
  E-mail: jkipp@landmark.edu
  Telephone: 802-387-6718
  Fax: 802-387-6868

LEARNING DISABILITY SERVICES

Requests for the following services/accommodations will be evaluated individually based on appropriate and current documentation.

Allowed in exams	**Distraction-reduced environment:** Yes	**Added costs for services:** No
Calculator: Yes	**Tape recording in class:** Yes	**LD specialists:** Yes
Dictionary: Yes	**Books on tape from RFBD:** NR	**Professional tutors:** 90
Computer: Yes	**Taping of books not from RFBD:** No	**Peer tutors:** No
Spellchecker: Yes	**Accommodations for students with**	**Max. hours/wk. for services:**
Extended test time: Yes	**ADHD:** Yes	Unlimited
Scribes: No	**Reading machine:** Yes	**How professors are notified of**
Proctors: No	**Other assistive technology:** Yes	**LD/ADHD:** N/A
Oral exams: Yes	**Priority registration:** No	
Note-takers: No		

GENERAL ADMISSIONS INFORMATION

Director of Admissions: Dale Herold
Telephone: 802-387-6718

ENTRANCE REQUIREMENTS

High school diploma is required, and GED is accepted. TOEFL required of all international applicants: minimum paper TOEFL 200, minimum computer TOEFL 40.

Application deadline: Rolling	**SAT Math middle 50% range:** NR	**Graduated top 10% of class:** NR
Notification: Rolling	**SAT Critical Reading middle 50%**	**Graduated top 25% of class:** NR
Average GPA: NR	**range:** NR	**Graduated top 50% of class:** NR
ACT Composite middle 50% range: NR	**SAT Writing middle 50% range:** NR	

COLLEGE GRADUATION REQUIREMENTS

Course waivers allowed: No
Course substitutions allowed: No

ADDITIONAL INFORMATION

Environment: The college is located on 125 acres overlooking the Connecticut River Valley hills of Vermont and New Hampshire.

Student Body	**Cost Information**	**Greek System**
Undergrad enrollment: 429	**Tuition:** $40,500	**Fraternity:** No
Women: 27%	**Room & board:** $7,500	**Sorority:** No
Men: 73%	**Housing Information**	**Athletics:** NCAA Div. III
Percent out-of-state: 96%	**University housing:** Yes	
	Percent living on campus: 97%	

NEW ENGLAND CULINARY INSTITUTE

56 College Street, Montpelier, VT 05602
Phone: 877-223-6324 • Fax: 802-225-3280
E-mail: admissions@neci.edu • Web: www.neci.edu
Support: CS • Institution type: 2- and 4-year private

LEARNING DISABILITY PROGRAM AND SERVICES

The New England Culinary Institute is in business to provide educational programs in the culinary arts, food and beverage management, basic cooking, and related areas that prepare students for employment and advancement in the hospitality industry. Students with LD/ADHD have found success at the institute, though sometimes it might take these students longer to finish a specific course or complete all of the graduation requirements. Some students with LD/ADHD may find the production kitchen learning environment, with its intensity, pressure, and long hours, a very demanding place. Almost all of the courses have a strong academic component, which requires comprehension and retention of a great deal of new information. Students with LD/ADHD often find the most success in the Associate's Degree of Occupational Studies program. Additionally, students are more successful if they have a strong work ethic and have had some experience in the food industry. The Learning Services Office provides services to all students, and the coordinator is available 5 days a week to work with students one-on-one. The goal of the Learning Services Office is to provide support to maximize culinary learning.

LD/ADHD ADMISSIONS INFORMATION

College entrance tests required: No
Interview required: No
Essay recommended: No
Documentation required for LD: Psychoeducational evaluation or high school IEP
Documentation required for ADHD: Psychoeducational evaluation or high school IEP
Submitted to: Learning Services
Special Ed. HS course work accepted: Yes

Specific course requirements of all applicants: NR
Separate application required: No
# of LD applications submitted each year: NR
# of LD applications accepted yearly: NR
Total # of students receiving LD services: 10
Acceptance into program means acceptance into college: Students must be admitted to and enrolled in the university first and then request services.

ADMISSIONS

There is no special admission process for students with LD/ADHD. Students who are applying for the AOS program must have a high school diploma or equivalency certificate and must submit an essay and a minimum of one to three letters of recommendation. Interviews are recommended. Applicants may also be required to spend some time in the kitchen with one of the chefs. Students interested in the BA program must complete an associate's degree first. Applicants with LD/ADHD with appropriate documentation will be eligible to access accommodations once they are admitted and enrolled. Some students may wish to complete a certificate in basic cooking first to determine their commitment and skills in the culinary arts.

ADDITIONAL INFORMATION

Students with LD/ADHD must provide appropriate documentation and meet with the Learning Center director to receive services. The director will verify the documentation, review the requests, and meet with the student to explain the learning services. Instructors are notified with student permission. Self-advocacy information is provided, and a learning contract (if necessary) is written and signed by the student. Accommodations such as oral and untimed tests, alternate test sites, use of a dictionary during nonvocabulary tests, note-taking, individualized tutoring, use of calculators and computers, tape-recording of lectures, and paper writing assistance can be accessed through Learning Services. These services also include one-on-one tutorials, small group workshops to refresh math skills, review sessions, opportunity to retake tests, computers, software to help with writing papers, reference books, and a quiet study/work space. This is a self-serve resource, and they will try to work out all requests.

LEARNING DISABILITY PROGRAM/SERVICES

Learning Disability Program/Services: Learning Services
Director: Jackie Burke
  E-mail: jackieb@neci.edu
  Telephone: 802-764-2135
  Fax: 802-764-2180

LEARNING DISABILITY SERVICES

Requests for the following services/accommodations will be evaluated individually based on appropriate and current documentation.

Allowed in exams
  Calculator: Yes
  Dictionary: Yes
  Computer: Yes
  Spellchecker: Yes
Extended test time: Yes
Scribes: Yes
Proctors: Yes
Oral exams: Yes
Note-takers: Yes

Distraction-reduced environment: Yes
Tape recording in class: Yes
Books on tape from RFBD: Yes
Taping of books not from RFBD: Yes
Accommodations for students with ADHD: Yes
Reading machine: No
Other assistive technology: Yes
Priority registration: No

Added costs for services: No
LD specialists: Yes
Professional tutors: No
Peer tutors: 10–25
Max. hours/wk. for services: Unlimited
How professors are notified of LD/ADHD: By both student and director

GENERAL ADMISSIONS INFORMATION

Director of Admissions: Sherri Gilmore
Telephone: 802-225-3219

ENTRANCE REQUIREMENTS

Academic units recommended: 4 English, 3 math, 2 science (1 science lab). High school diploma is required, and GED is accepted. TOEFL required of all international applicants: minimum paper TOEFL 550, minimum computer TOEFL 213.

Application deadline: Rolling
Notification: Within 2 weeks
Average GPA: NR
ACT Composite middle 50% range: NR

SAT Math middle 50% range: NR
SAT Critical Reading middle 50% range: NR
SAT Writing middle 50% range: NR

Graduated top 10% of class: NR
Graduated top 25% of class: NR
Graduated top 50% of class: NR

COLLEGE GRADUATION REQUIREMENTS

Course waivers allowed: No
Course substitutions allowed: Yes
In what course: Foreign language, but only after course is attempted

ADDITIONAL INFORMATION

Environment: The institute is located in the city of Montpelier, 45 miles from Burlington.

Student Body
  Undergrad enrollment: 533
  Women: 35%
  Men: 65%
  Percent out-of-state: 85%

Cost Information
  Tuition: $23,835
  Room & board: $6,565
Housing Information
  University housing: Yes
  Percent living on campus: 85%

Greek System
  Fraternity: No
  Sorority: No
Athletics: Intramural

NORWICH UNIVERSITY

Admissions Office, 27 ID White Avenue, Northfield, VT 05663
Phone: 802-485-2001 • Fax: 802-485-2032
E-mail: nuadm@norwich.edu • Web: www.norwich.edu
Support: CS • Institution type: 4-year private

LEARNING DISABILITY PROGRAM AND SERVICES

The Learning Support Center (LSC) offers comprehensive support services in all areas of academic life. While Norwich does not have a formal program for students with learning disabilities, the university does offer support services on a voluntary basis. Students are instructed by the center staff in a wide range of study and college survival skills. The center's staff work closely with advisors and faculty members and are strong advocates for students with learning disabilities. The university stresses autonomy by providing a level of support that assists students with becoming responsible, thinking adults who are well acquainted with their own needs and able to articulate them. Services are provided by a staff of professionals that includes LD specialists, study skills/writing specialists, and a basic math specialist. The professional staff is supplemented by a trained, well-supervised student tutorial staff.

LD/ADHD ADMISSIONS INFORMATION

College entrance tests required: Yes
Interview required: No
Essay recommended: No
Documentation required for LD: Comprehensive
   cognitive/achievement. An IEP alone will not be accepted.
Documentation required for ADHD: Minimum of psychiatric/
   psychological protocol targeting ADHD; prefer comprehensive
   evaluation as for LD. As recent as possible; an IEP alone will
   not be accepted.
Submitted to: Learning Support Center

Special Ed. HS course work accepted: No
Specific course requirements of all applicants: Yes
Separate application required: No
# of LD applications submitted each year: NR
# of LD applications accepted yearly: NR
Total # of students receiving LD services: NR
Acceptance into program means acceptance into
   college: Students must be admitted to and enrolled in the
   university first and then request services.

ADMISSIONS

Students with learning disabilities submit a general application. Admission criteria include high school GPA of a C or better; an SAT score of 850 or equivalent ACT; participation in activities; and strong college recommendations from teachers, counselors, or coaches. There are no course waivers for admission. The university is flexible on ACT/SAT test scores. If grades and other indicators are problematic is recommended that students provide detailed information to give a better understanding the disability. A complete psychodiagnostic evaluation is required. A small number of students who do not meet the general admission requirements may be admitted if they show promise. An interview is highly recommended. In some cases, the Director of Learning Support may review the admissions file and make a recommendation. There are limited conditional admission slots. Students are required to go to a college and take courses if their high school grades and/or SAT scores are below requirement.

ADDITIONAL INFORMATION

A telephone conversation or personal meeting with the LSC support personnel is encouraged prior to the start of college, so that work can begin immediately on preparing an individualized program. Students are responsible for meeting with each professor to discuss accommodations. Services begin with Freshman Placement Testing designed to assess each individual's level of readiness for college-level reading, writing, and math. Other services include course advising with an assigned academic advisor and advocacy for academic petitions. Services and accommodations are available for undergraduate and graduate students.

LEARNING DISABILITY PROGRAM/SERVICES

Learning Disability Program/Services: Learning Support Center (LSC)
Director: Paula A. Gills
  E-mail: gills@norwich.edu
  Telephone: 802-485-2130
  Fax: 802-485-2684

LEARNING DISABILITY SERVICES

Requests for the following services/accommodations will be evaluated individually based on appropriate and current documentation.

Allowed in exams
  Calculator: Yes
  Dictionary: Yes
  Computer: Yes
  Spellchecker: Yes
Extended test time: Yes
Scribes: Yes
Proctors: Yes
Oral exams: Yes
Note-takers: No

Distraction-reduced environment: Yes
Tape recording in class: Yes
Books on tape from RFBD: Yes
Taping of books not from RFBD: No
Accommodations for students with ADHD: Yes
Reading machine: No
Other assistive technology: No
Priority registration: Yes

Added costs for services: No
LD specialists: Yes
Professional tutors: 9
Peer tutors: 25–30
Max. hours/wk. for services: N/A
How professors are notified of LD/ADHD: By both student and director

GENERAL ADMISSIONS INFORMATION

Director of Admissions: Karen McGrath
Telephone: 802-485-2001

ENTRANCE REQUIREMENTS

Academic units required: 4 English, 3 math, 2 science (2 science labs). **Academic units recommended:**
4 English, 4 math, 3 science (2 science labs), 2 foreign language. High school diploma is required, and GED is accepted. TOEFL required of all international applicants: minimum paper TOEFL 500, minimum computer TOEFL 1.

Application deadline: Rolling
Notification: Rolling
Average GPA: NR
ACT Composite middle 50% range: NR

SAT Math middle 50% range: 440–570
SAT Critical Reading middle 50% range: 440–560
SAT Writing middle 50% range: NR

Graduated top 10% of class: 8%
Graduated top 25% of class: 21%
Graduated top 50% of class: 43%

COLLEGE GRADUATION REQUIREMENTS

Course waivers allowed: No
Course substitutions allowed: Yes
In what course: Foreign language, only with proof of inability to successfully function and after having gone through a lengthy petition process.

ADDITIONAL INFORMATION

Environment: Two campuses in Northfield (traditional) and Montpelier (low residency), 50 miles southeast of Burlington.

Student Body
  Undergrad enrollment: 2,099
  Women: 20%
  Men: 80%
  Percent out-of-state: 77%

Cost Information
  Tuition: $20,800
  Room & board: $7,300
Housing Information
  University housing: Yes
  Percent living on campus: 81%

Greek System
  Fraternity: No
  Sorority: No
Athletics: Division III

UNIVERSITY OF VERMONT

Admissions Office, 194 South Prospect Street, Burlington, VT 05401-3596
Phone: 802-656-3370 • Fax: 802-656-8611
E-mail: admissions@uvm.edu • Web: www.uvm.edu
Support: CS • Institution type: 4-year public

LEARNING DISABILITY PROGRAM AND SERVICES

The university provides a multidisciplinary program for students with LD. ACCESS works closely with students having learning problems to ensure that campus-wide resources are used effectively. Initially, a comprehensive assessment is revised to identify students' strengths and weaknesses in learning. This information is used to carefully design classroom and study accommodations to compensate for learning problems. Through this process, students and program staff have identified a number of techniques and strategies to enable success at class and study tasks. The academic advising process for students with LD involves two offices: The academic advisor assigned by the college and the professional staff of ACCESS who review tentative semester schedules to balance course format, teaching style, and workload with a student's learning strengths. The Learning Cooperative offers individual tutoring and assistance with reading, writing, study skills, and time management. The Writing Center assists with proofing and feedback on writing assignments. There is a developmental course called "Conquering College." This is an individualized support service program designed to equalize educational opportunities for students with learning disabilities.

LD/ADHD ADMISSIONS INFORMATION

College entrance tests required: Yes
Interview required: No
Essay recommended: No
Documentation required for LD: Psychoeducational
  evaluation
Documentation required for ADHD: Psychoeducational and
  medical examination
Submitted to: ACCESS
Special Ed. HS course work accepted: Yes
Specific course requirements of all applicants: Yes

Separate application required: No
# of LD applications submitted each year: NR
# of LD applications accepted yearly: NR
Total # of students receiving LD services: NR
Acceptance into program means acceptance into
  college: Students must be admitted to and enrolled in the
  university first and then request services. Some students are
  reviewed by the LD program, which provides consultation to
  admissions.

ADMISSIONS

Students submit a regular UVM application to admissions and all documentation of their disability to ACCESS. Students are encouraged to voluntarily provide documentation of their disability. ACCESS reviews documentation and consults with admissions as to how the student's disability has effected their academic record. A clear understanding of the students' strengths and weaknesses in learning and the influence of the disability on the current and past educational process will enable a broader assessment of ability to meet the academic qualifications, requirements, and rigors of UVM. Students with LD should submit a current educational evaluation that includes a measure of cognitive functioning and documentation of the learning problems. Students with ADHD are encouraged to provide documentation and information on how the ADHD had an impact on the educational setting. Course requirements include 4 years of English, 3 years of social science, 3 years of math, 2 years physical sciences, and 2 years of a foreign language. (Math and foreign language can be waived with appropriate documentation.) Special education courses are acceptable if the student's high school gives high school credit for the courses. Self-disclosing in the application is a matter of personal choice. However, at UVM, disclosing a disability will absolutely not have a negative impact on a student's admissibility.

ADDITIONAL INFORMATION

UVM provides a multidisciplinary program for students with LD emphasizing development of academic accommodations; academic adjustments, including note-taking, course substitution, course load reduction, extended test time, alternate test formats and computer/spellchecker; auxiliary services, including taped tests, readers, tutoring, writing skill development, proofing services, reading skill development; academic advising and course selection; priority registration; learning strategies and study skills training; LD support group and counseling; faculty consultation and in-service training; and diagnostic screening and evaluation referral. Students with ADHD with appropriate documentation may receive help with class schedules, study activities to fit individual learning styles, support services, or accommodations in test conditions, course loads, and/or program requirements because of the severity of the disability.

LEARNING DISABILITY PROGRAM/SERVICES

Learning Disability Program/Services: ACCESS
Director: Marsha Camp
  E-mail: Access@uvm.edu
  Telephone: 802-656-7753
  Fax: 802-656-0739
Contact Person: Aaron Ferguson
  E-mail: Access@uvm.edu
  Telephone: 802-656-7753
  Fax: 802-656-0739

LEARNING DISABILITY SERVICES

Requests for the following services/accommodations will be evaluated individually based on appropriate and current documentation.

Allowed in exams
  Calculator: Yes
  Dictionary: Yes
  Computer: Yes
  Spellchecker: Yes
Extended test time: Yes
Scribes: Yes
Proctors: Yes
Oral exams: Yes
Note-takers: Yes

Distraction-reduced environment: Yes
Tape recording in class: Yes
Books on tape from RFBD: Yes
Taping of books not from RFBD: Yes
Accommodations for students with ADHD: Yes
Reading machine: Yes
Other assistive technology: Yes
Priority registration: Yes

Added costs for services: Yes
LD specialists: Yes
Professional tutors: 1
Peer tutors: 1–30
Max. hours/wk. for services: 1–2
How professors are notified of LD/ADHD: By both student and director

GENERAL ADMISSIONS INFORMATION

Director of Admissions: Susan A. Wertheimer (Interim)
Telephone: 802-656-4667

ENTRANCE REQUIREMENTS

Academic units required: 4 English, 3 math, 2 science (1 science lab), 2 foreign language, 3 social studies. High school diploma is required, and GED is accepted. ACT with Writing component required. TOEFL required of all international applicants: minimum paper TOEFL 550, minimum computer TOEFL 213.

Application deadline: 1/15
Notification: 3/31
Average GPA: NR
ACT Composite middle 50% range: 22–27

SAT Math middle 50% range: 540–640
SAT Critical Reading middle 50% range: 530–630
SAT Writing middle 50% range: NR

Graduated top 10% of class: 23%
Graduated top 25% of class: 62%
Graduated top 50% of class: 95%

COLLEGE GRADUATION REQUIREMENTS

Course waivers allowed: No
Course substitutions allowed: No

ADDITIONAL INFORMATION

Environment: The university is located on 425 acres by Lake Champlain 90 miles south of Montreal.

Student Body
  Undergrad enrollment: 9,040
  Women: 55%
  Men: 45%
  Percent out-of-state: 64%

Cost Information
  In-state tuition: $10,700
  Out-of-state tuition: $24,816
  Room & board: $7,642
Housing Information
  University housing: Yes
  Percent living on campus: 53%

Greek System
  Fraternity: Yes
  Sorority: Yes
Athletics: Division I

VERMONT TECHNICAL COLLEGE

PO Box 500, Randolph Center, VT 05061
Phone: 802-728-1242 • Fax: 802-728-1321
E-mail: Admissions@vtc.edu • Web: www.vtc.edu
Support: CS • Institution type: 2-year public

LEARNING DISABILITY PROGRAM AND SERVICES

The goal of Services for Students with Disabilities is to ensure equal access to all VTC programs for all qualified students with disabilities, to help students develop the necessary skills to be effective at VTC and beyond, and to further students' understanding of how their disabilities affect them in school, work, and social settings. The learning specialist at Vermont Technical College is responsible for coordinating services to ensure accessibility and usability of all programs, services, and activities of the college by people with disabilities and is a resource for information and advocacy toward their full participation in all aspects of campus life. The learning specialist collaborates with the entire campus community to provide services in the most appropriate setting to meet the access needs of the individual.

LD/ADHD ADMISSIONS INFORMATION

College entrance tests required: Yes
Interview required: Yes
Essay recommended: No
Documentation required for LD: WAIS–III, WJ–III
Documentation required for ADHD: Yes
Submitted to: Services for Students with Disabilities
Special Ed. HS course work accepted: Yes

Specific course requirements of all applicants: Varies
Separate application required: No
# of LD applications submitted each year: NR
# of LD applications accepted yearly: NR
Total # of students receiving LD services: 70
Acceptance into program means acceptance into college: Students must be admitted to and enrolled in the university first and then request services.

ADMISSIONS

There is no special admissions process for students with learning disabilities. In general, students have a GPA of 80 percent or higher. There is no cutoff score for the SAT. The program director can make recommendations to waive certain admission criteria if they discriminate against a student with a learning disability and other evidence of a student's qualifications exist. General course requirements include Algebra I and II, geometry, and physics or chemistry for engineering programs. Many students meet with the disabilities coordinator during the application process to discuss their needs. The Summer Bridge Program, an alternative admission plan, is a 4-week math/physics and language arts program used as preparation for marginal freshmen who do not require the 3-year program option. The 3-year alternative admission option is for engineering students who need longer than 2 years to complete the program.

ADDITIONAL INFORMATION

The disabilities coordinator provides a variety of services, which include assessment of students' academic needs, coordination of tutoring to provide assistance with course material, and a disabilities forum for students to share experiences and academic strategies that they have learned with other students. Individual tutoring is provided in writing and study skills, such as time management, effective textbook reading, learning strategies, and stress management. Other accommodations could include individualized accommodations for test-taking, note-taking assistance, consultation and advocacy throughout the campus community, liaison with community-based disability service agencies, information and referral, academic adjustments, academic coaching, study skills instruction, assistive technology training, academic and career counseling, and coordination of accommodations. There is a Learning Center open to all students on campus.

LEARNING DISABILITY PROGRAM/SERVICES

Learning Disability Program/Services: Services for Students with Disabilities
Director: Robin Goodall
  E-mail: rgoodall@vtc.edu
  Telephone: 802-728-1278
  Fax: 802-728-1714

LEARNING DISABILITY SERVICES

Requests for the following services/accommodations will be evaluated individually based on appropriate and current documentation.

Allowed in exams
  Calculator: Yes
  Dictionary: Yes
  Computer: Yes
  Spellchecker: Yes
Extended test time: Yes
Scribes: Yes
Proctors: Yes
Oral exams: Yes
Note-takers: Yes

Distraction-reduced environment: Yes
Tape recording in class: Yes
Books on tape from RFBD: Yes
Taping of books not from RFBD: Yes
Accommodations for students with ADHD: Yes
Reading machine: Yes
Other assistive technology: Yes
Priority registration: Yes

Added costs for services: No
LD specialists: Yes
Professional tutors: No
Peer tutors: Yes
Max. hours/wk. for services: Unlimited
How professors are notified of LD/ADHD: By student

GENERAL ADMISSIONS INFORMATION

Director of Admissions: Dwight Cross
Telephone: 802-728-1242

ENTRANCE REQUIREMENTS

Admissions are based on a total picture of applicants, including transcript, ACT or SAT, recommendations, and activities. Courses required vary depending on major.

Application deadline: Rolling
Notification: Rolling
Average GPA: NR
ACT Composite middle 50% range: NR

SAT Math middle 50% range: NR
SAT Critical Reading middle 50% range: NR
SAT Writing middle 50% range: NR

Graduated top 10% of class: NR
Graduated top 25% of class: NR
Graduated top 50% of class: NR

COLLEGE GRADUATION REQUIREMENTS

Course waivers allowed: No
Course substitutions allowed: No

ADDITIONAL INFORMATION

Environment: The college is located on 54 acres in a rural area.

Student Body
  Undergrad enrollment: 1,333
  Women: 41%
  Men: 59%
  Percent out-of-state: 20%

Cost Information
  In-state tuition: $5,608
  Out-of-state tuition: $11,328
  Room & board: $4,834
Housing Information
  University housing: Yes
  Percent living on campus: 60%

Greek System
  Fraternity: No
  Sorority: No
Athletics: Intramural and intercollegiate

THE COLLEGE OF WILLIAM & MARY

PO Box 8795, Williamsburg, VA 23187-8795
Phone: 757-221-4223 • Fax: 757-221-1242
E-mail: admiss@wm.edu • Web: www.wm.edu
Support: CS • Institution type: 4-year public

LEARNING DISABILITY PROGRAM AND SERVICES

Disability services at the College of William & Mary are available to all students with disabilities. Reasonable requested accommodations are evaluated on an individual and flexible basis. Program goals include fostering independence, encouraging self-determination, emphasizing accommodations over limitations, and creating an accessible environment to ensure that individuals are viewed on the basis of ability and not disability. Individual accommodations needs are considered on a case-by-case basis in consultation with the student. The staff works with students and faculty to implement reasonable supports. Students anticipating the need for academic support must provide pertinent documentation in a timely manner to facilitate the provision of the service. Additional documentation may be requested and accommodation requests can be denied if they do not seem to be substantially supported. Documentation for LD/ADHD must include a comprehensive report of psychoeducational or neuropsychological assessment. The documentation must demonstrate the impact of the disability on major life activities and support all of the recommended accommodations.

LD/ADHD ADMISSIONS INFORMATION

College entrance tests required: Yes
Interview required: No
Essay recommended: No
Documentation required for LD: Psychoeducational evaluation
Documentation required for ADHD: Yes
Submitted to: Disability Services
Special Ed. HS course work accepted: No

Specific course requirements of all applicants: Yes
Separate application required: No
# of LD applications submitted each year: NR
# of LD applications accepted yearly: NR
Total # of students receiving LD services: NR
Acceptance into program means acceptance into college: Students must be admitted to and enrolled in the university first and then request services.

ADMISSIONS
Students go through a regular admissions process. Students must take either the SAT Reasoning test or ACT, and three SAT Subject Tests are recommended. Results of nonstandardized test administrations and documentation of disability may be submitted in support of any application, but are not essential for full consideration. Once admitted, students are fully mainstreamed and are expected to maintain the same academic standards as all other students.

ADDITIONAL INFORMATION
The staff of Disability Services works with the student and the faculty to implement reasonable accommodations such as peer note-takers, alternative test forms, textbook recording services, study skills training, and peer support groups. Disability-Related Program Access includes assistance with priority registration, liaison to the university, assistance with academic adjustments and curriculum alternatives, advocacy, in-service training for faculty and staff, and acquisition of adaptive equipment and/or software. The staff works closely with all college departments to identify appropriate options for accommodating students with disabilities.

LEARNING DISABILITY PROGRAM/SERVICES

Learning Disability Program/Services: Disability Services
Director: Lisa Bickley
　E-mail: ljbick@wm.edu
　Telephone: 757-221-2510
　Fax: 757-221-2538

LEARNING DISABILITY SERVICES

Requests for the following services/accommodations will be evaluated individually based on appropriate and current documentation.

Allowed in exams
　Calculator: NR
　Dictionary: NR
　Computer: Yes
　Spellchecker: NR
Extended test time: Yes
Scribes: Yes
Proctors: NR
Oral exams: NR
Note-takers: Yes

Distraction-reduced environment: Yes
Tape recording in class: NR
Books on tape from RFBD: Yes
Taping of books not from RFBD: NR
Accommodations for students with
　ADHD: Yes
Reading machine: Yes
Other assistive technology: Yes
Priority registration: Yes

Added costs for services: No
LD specialists: Yes
Professional tutors: No
Peer tutors: Yes
Max. hours/wk. for services: NR
How professors are notified of
　LD/ADHD: By student

GENERAL ADMISSIONS INFORMATION

Director of Admissions: Henry Broaddus
Telephone: 757-221-4223

ENTRANCE REQUIREMENTS

Academic units recommended: 4 English, 4 math, 4 science (3 science labs), 4 foreign language, 4 social studies. High school diploma is required, and GED is not accepted. ACT with or without Writing component accepted. TOEFL required of all international applicants: minimum paper TOEFL 600, minimum computer TOEFL 250.

Application deadline: 1/1
Notification: 4/1
Average GPA: NR
ACT Composite middle 50% range:
　28–32

SAT Math middle 50% range:
　630–710
SAT Critical Reading middle 50%
　range: 630–730
SAT Writing middle 50% range: NR

Graduated top 10% of class: 85%
Graduated top 25% of class: 97%
Graduated top 50% of class: 100%

COLLEGE GRADUATION REQUIREMENTS

Course waivers allowed: No
In what course: N/A
Course substitutions allowed: Yes
In what course: Foreign language

ADDITIONAL INFORMATION

Environment: Located 50 miles from Richmond

Student Body
　Undergrad enrollment: 5,651
　Women: 54%
　Men: 46%
　Percent out-of-state: 32%

Cost Information
　In-state tuition: $8,490
　Out-of-state tuition: $25,048
　Room & board: $6,932
Housing Information
　University housing: Yes
　Percent living on campus: 76%

Greek System
　Fraternity: Yes
　Sorority: Yes
Athletics: Division I

FERRUM COLLEGE

PO Box 1000, Ferrum, VA 24088
Phone: 540-365-4290 • Fax: 540-365-4366
E-mail: admissions@ferrum.edu • Web: www.ferrum.edu
Support: CS • Institution type: 4-year private

LEARNING DISABILITY PROGRAM AND SERVICES

Ferrum College does not have a program for students with learning disabilities, but does provide services to students with disabilities documentation. Ferrum also does not offer a comprehensive program or monitoring services. Students motivated to accept the assistance and academic accommodations offered frequently find Ferrum's services to be excellent. The Academic Support Division combines library and media services with the Academic Resource Center and the first-year experience so that all academic support programs can function in unison and be housed under one roof. The division offers classes in academic skill development, Ferrum 101, mentoring, service-learning, and career development. Services offered include academic counseling, tutoring, assistance for the learning disabled, as well as traditional library, media, and information services.

LD/ADHD ADMISSIONS INFORMATION

College entrance tests required: Yes
Interview required: No
Essay recommended: No
Documentation required for LD: Current psychoeducational evaluation and statement of eligibility or other comparable documentation provided by a qualified professional
Documentation required for ADHD: Current documentation with a statement of identification from a qualified professional
Submitted to: Admissions Office and Academic Resource Center

Special Ed. HS course work accepted: N/A
Specific course requirements of all applicants: Yes
Separate application required: No
# of LD applications submitted each year: NR
# of LD applications accepted yearly: NR
Total # of students receiving LD services: NR
Acceptance into program means acceptance into college: Students must be admitted and enrolled at the university first and then may request services. Students denied admission may appeal the decision.

ADMISSIONS

Ferrum is proactive in terms of the admissions process for students with documentation of a disability. All students first go through the admissions process. If students are not admitted through the general admissions process, the committee can be requested to reconsider with the presentation of the documentation and a recommendation from the disability service provider. Those applicants who do not meet general admission criteria are encouraged to have an interview with the Office of Admissions. General admission criteria include 4 years of English, 1 year of math (3 recommended), 1 year of science (3 recommended), 2 years of a foreign language, and 3 years of social studies (recommended). The SAT/ACT is required (the average ACT is 18, and the average SAT is 1040); the average GPA is 2.6.

ADDITIONAL INFORMATION

The Academic Resources Center is a learning center available for students with learning disabilities as well as all other students on campus. Some of the tutoring is provided by volunteer professors. Skills classes are offered for credit in study skills. Other accommodations could include extended time for testing, oral testing, test clarification, reader services, quiet testing environment, and adaptive equipment for testing, including computers, word processors, zoom text, and tape recorders. Ferrum College offers a summer program for precollege freshmen with learning disabilities.

LEARNING DISABILITY PROGRAM/SERVICES

Learning Disability Program/Services: Academic Resources Center
Director: Nancy S. Beach
  E-mail: nbeach@ferrum.edu
  Telephone: 540-365-4529
  Fax: 540-365-4271

LEARNING DISABILITY SERVICES

Requests for the following services/accommodations will be evaluated individually based on appropriate and current documentation.

Allowed in exams
  Calculator: Yes
  Dictionary: Yes
  Computer: Yes
  Spellchecker: Yes
Extended test time: Yes
Scribes: Yes
Proctors: Yes
Oral exams: Yes
Note-takers: Yes

Distraction-reduced environment: Yes
Tape recording in class: Yes
Books on tape from RFBD: Yes
Taping of books not from RFBD: Yes
Accommodations for students with ADHD: Yes
Reading machine: Yes
Other assistive technology: Yes
Priority registration: No

Added costs for services: No
LD specialists: Yes
Professional tutors: No
Peer tutors: 15–25
Max. hours/wk. for services: Unlimited
How professors are notified of LD/ADHD: By both student and director

GENERAL ADMISSIONS INFORMATION

Director of Admissions: Gilda Woods
Telephone: 540-365-4290

ENTRANCE REQUIREMENTS

Academic units recommended: 4 English, 3 math, 2 science (1 science lab), 2 foreign language, 3 social studies, 2 academic electives. High school diploma is required, and GED is accepted. TOEFL required of all international applicants: minimum paper TOEFL 550.

Application deadline: Rolling
Notification: 30 days after receipt of completed application
Average GPA: 2.64
ACT Composite middle 50% range: NR

SAT Math middle 50% range: 400–545
SAT Critical Reading middle 50% range: 390–540
SAT Writing middle 50% range: NR

Graduated top 10% of class: 6%
Graduated top 25% of class: 19%
Graduated top 50% of class: 46%

COLLEGE GRADUATION REQUIREMENTS

Course waivers allowed: No
Course substitutions allowed: Yes
In what course: Course substitution is discussed on a case-by-case basis and determined by the Academic Standards Committee.

ADDITIONAL INFORMATION

Environment: The college is located in a rural area south of Roanoke.

Student Body
  Undergrad enrollment: 951
  Women: 40%
  Men: 60%
  Percent out-of-state: 18%

Cost Information
  Tuition: $17,900
  Room & board: $8,300
Housing Information
  University housing: Yes
  Percent living on campus: 80%

Greek System
  Fraternity: No
  Sorority: No
Athletics: Division III

GEORGE MASON UNIVERSITY

Undergraduate Admissions Office, 4400 University Drive MSN 3A4,
Fairfax, VA 22030-4444 • Phone: 703-993-2400 • Fax: 703-993-2392
E-mail: admissions@gmu.edu • Web: www.gmu.edu
Support: S • Institution type: 4-year public

LEARNING DISABILITY PROGRAM AND SERVICES

The university does not maintain a specific program for students with LD. George Mason is, however, committed to providing appropriate services and accommodations to allow identified students with disabilities to access programs. The Disability Resource Center is responsible for assuring that students receive the services to which they are entitled. Students must provide documentation and complete a faculty contact sheet to receive documentation. DRC must confirm the students' requests for services.

LD/ADHD ADMISSIONS INFORMATION

College entrance tests required: Yes
Interview required: No
Essay recommended: No
Documentation required for LD: Psychoeducational evaluation
Documentation required for ADHD: Yes
Submitted to: Disability Resource Center
Special Ed. HS course work accepted: Yes

Specific course requirements of all applicants: Yes
Separate application required: No
# of LD applications submitted each year: NR
# of LD applications accepted yearly: NR
Total # of students receiving LD services: 400
Acceptance into program means acceptance into college: Students must be admitted to and enrolled in the university first and then request services.

ADMISSIONS

Students with LD must submit the general George Mason University undergraduate application and meet the same requirements as all other applicants. Students are encouraged to self-disclose and provide documentation of their disability. Letters of recommendation are helpful for explaining weaknesses or problematic areas. Students who have deficiencies in required courses may request a waiver of the requirement. These requests are considered on an individual basis. General admission criteria include 4 years of English, 3 years of math (4 recommended), 1 year of science (3 recommended), 3 years of a foreign language, 3 years of social studies (4 recommended), and 3–4 year of electives; an ACT/SAT score; and an interview.

ADDITIONAL INFORMATION

Students with LD may request extended testing times or alternative formats for exams, extended time for in-class writing assignments or short-term projects, note-takers, or use of a word processor for essay exams if documentation supports these modifications. Learning Services is a resource center for all students on campus. The center offers self-help skills classes in time management, organizational skills, and test-taking strategies. A freshman orientation class is offered for credit, and some sections of this class are geared toward academic skills. The staff at the Office of Disability Services collaborate with students individually to help choose the most effective reasonable accommodations; coordinate implementations of accommodations; act as a liaison between students and faculty/administration on concerns relating to accommodations, and services are available for prospective students, community groups, and secondary education personnel interested in learning more about accommodations and services at George Mason.

LEARNING DISABILITY PROGRAM/SERVICES

Learning Disability Program/Services: Disability Resource Center
Director: Christopher Moy
  E-mail: cmoy@gmu.edu
  Telephone: 703-993-2474
  Fax: 703-993-4306

LEARNING DISABILITY SERVICES

Requests for the following services/accommodations will be evaluated individually based on appropriate and current documentation.

Allowed in exams
  Calculator: Yes
  Dictionary: Yes
  Computer: Yes
  Spellchecker: Yes
Extended test time: Yes
Scribes: Yes
Proctors: Yes
Oral exams: Yes
Note-takers: Yes

Distraction-reduced environment: Yes
Tape recording in class: Yes
Books on tape from RFBD: Yes
Taping of books not from RFBD: Yes
Accommodations for students with ADHD: Yes
Reading machine: Yes
Other assistive technology: Yes
Priority registration: Yes

Added costs for services: Yes
LD specialists: No
Professional tutors: No
Peer tutors: Yes
Max. hours/wk. for services: Unlimited
How professors are notified of LD/ADHD: By student

GENERAL ADMISSIONS INFORMATION

Director of Admissions: Andrew Flagel
Telephone: 703-993-2400

ENTRANCE REQUIREMENTS

Academic units required: 4 English, 3 math, 1 science (1 science lab), 3 foreign language, 3 social studies, 3 academic electives. **Academic units recommended:** 4 English, 4 math, 3 science (3 science labs), 3 foreign language, 4 social studies, 4 academic electives. High school diploma is required, and GED is accepted. ACT with or without Writing component accepted. TOEFL required of all international applicants: minimum paper TOEFL 570, minimum computer TOEFL 230.

Application deadline: 1/15
Notification: 4/1
Average GPA: 3.36
ACT Composite middle 50% range: 20–25

SAT Math middle 50% range: 510–610
SAT Critical Reading middle 50% range: 500–600
SAT Writing middle 50% range: 490–590

Graduated top 10% of class: 15%
Graduated top 25% of class: 48%
Graduated top 50% of class: 94%

COLLEGE GRADUATION REQUIREMENTS

Course waivers allowed: No
Course substitutions allowed: Yes
In what course: Foreign language and, in some instances, analytical reasoning with specific documentation provided

ADDITIONAL INFORMATION

Environment: The university is located on 682 acres in a suburban area 18 miles southwest of Washington, DC.

Student Body
  Undergrad enrollment: 17,812
  Women: 54%
  Men: 46%
  Percent out-of-state: 12%

Cost Information
  In-state tuition: $5,800
  Out-of-state tuition: $17,100
  Room & board: $6,750
Housing Information
  University housing: Yes
  Percent living on campus: 23%

Greek System
  Fraternity: Yes
  Sorority: Yes
Athletics: Division I

George Mason University

HAMPTON UNIVERSITY

Office of Admissions, Hampton University, Hampton, VA 23668
Phone: 757-727-5328 • Fax: 757-727-5095
E-mail: admit@hamptonu.edu • Web: www.hamptonu.edu
Support: S • Institution type: 4-year private

LEARNING DISABILITY PROGRAM AND SERVICES

Hampton University is committed to assisting students with disabilities. They seek to help students achieve their academic potential within the academically competitive curriculum by providing a variety of accommodations. In the classroom, students may use a tape recorder and calculator, have a note-taker, obtain selective seating, and ask for extended time for assignments. In an examination, they may have extended time, an alternate test form, a reader/scribe, an oral proctor, and a distraction-free environment. For services not available through Disability Services, referrals to other sources are made.

LD/ADHD ADMISSIONS INFORMATION

College entrance tests required: Yes
Interview required: No
Essay recommended: No
Documentation required for LD: Medical documentation of the disability by a licensed practitioner not older than 3 years
Documentation required for ADHD: Medical documentation of the disability by a licensed practitioner not older than 3 years
Submitted to: Student Support Services

Special Ed. HS course work accepted: Yes
Specific course requirements of all applicants: Yes
Separate application required: No
# of LD applications submitted each year: NR
# of LD applications accepted yearly: NR
Total # of students receiving LD services: 30–40
Acceptance into program means acceptance into college: Students must be admitted to and enrolled in the university first and then request services.

ADMISSIONS

There is no special admission process for students with learning disabilities. All students are expected to meet the same admission criteria, which include 4 years of English, 3 years of math, 2 years of science, 2 years of history, and 6 electives; a minimum SAT of 800; a class rank in the top 50 percent; and a minimum GPA of 2.0. Each applicant should present satisfactory credentials as to his or her ability, character, and health. Some students may be admitted through the Summer Bridge Program if SAT scores are below 800 or the students are deficient in course requirements. These students take placement exams to determine the need for English, writing, reading, or science courses. Twenty percent of the class is admitted through the Summer Bridge Program.

ADDITIONAL INFORMATION

Accommodations in the classroom could include tape recorders or calculators, extended time for assignments, and note-takers. Accommodations in an examination could include distraction-free environments, extended time, alternate test formats, readers/scribes, printed copies of oral instructions, and oral proctors. A student who would like to receive disability services must contact the Section 504 compliance officer and provide documentation of the disability that is not older than 3 years. This compliance officer is responsible for qualifying students with disabilities for reasonable academic accommodations within the university. The Precollege Program is open to all students. Freshmen on probation may take two nonrepeating courses in summer school. If they earn a C or better, they may return for sophomore year.

LEARNING DISABILITY PROGRAM/SERVICES

Learning Disability Program/Services: Student Suppport Services
Director: Jean S. Williamson
E-mail: jean.williamson@hamptonu.edu
Telephone: 757-727-5493
Fax: 757-727-5998

LEARNING DISABILITY SERVICES

Requests for the following services/accommodations will be evaluated individually based on appropriate and current documentation.

Allowed in exams
  Calculator: Yes
  Dictionary: Yes
  Computer: Yes
  Spellchecker: Yes
Extended test time: Yes
Scribes: Yes
Proctors: Yes
Oral exams: Yes
Note-takers: Yes

Distraction-reduced environment: Yes
Tape recording in class: Yes
Books on tape from RFBD: Yes
Taping of books not from RFBD: No
Accommodations for students with ADHD: Yes
Reading machine: No
Other assistive technology: No
Priority registration: Yes

Added costs for services: No
LD specialists: No
Professional tutors: No
Peer tutors: Yes
Max. hours/wk. for services: Unlimited
How professors are notified of LD/ADHD: By student

GENERAL ADMISSIONS INFORMATION

Director of Admissions: Angela Boyd
Telephone: 757-727-5328

ENTRANCE REQUIREMENTS

Academic units required: 4 English, 3 math, 2 science (2 science labs), 2 social studies, 6 academic electives.
Academic units recommended: 2 foreign language. High school diploma is required, and GED is accepted. TOEFL required of all international applicants: minimum paper TOEFL 550, minimum computer TOEFL 214.

Application deadline: Rolling
Notification: Rolling, 3 weeks after receipt of completed application
Average GPA: 3.20
ACT Composite middle 50% range: 17–26

SAT Math middle 50% range: 464–606
SAT Critical Reading middle 50% range: 481–552
SAT Writing middle 50% range: NR

Graduated top 10% of class: 20%
Graduated top 25% of class: 45%
Graduated top 50% of class: 90%

COLLEGE GRADUATION REQUIREMENTS

Course waivers allowed: No
Course substitutions allowed: Yes
In what course: Foreign language, case-by-case basis

ADDITIONAL INFORMATION

Environment: The university is located on 204 acres 15 miles west of Norfolk.

Student Body
  Undergrad enrollment: 5,056
  Women: 64%
  Men: 36%
  Percent out-of-state: 69%

Cost Information
  Tuition: $13,358
  Room & board: $6,746
Housing Information
  University housing: Yes
  Percent living on campus: 59%

Greek System
  Fraternity: Yes
  Sorority: Yes
Athletics: Division I

JAMES MADISON UNIVERSITY

Sonner Hall, MSC 0101, Harrisonburg, VA 22807
Phone: 540-568-5681 • Fax: 540-568-3332
E-mail: admissions@jmu.edu • Web: www.jmu.edu
Support: CS • Institution type: 4-year public

LEARNING DISABILITY PROGRAM AND SERVICES

The Office of Disability Service (ODS) does not have a formal LD program, but students with learning disabilities are assisted individually and are eligible for appropriate accommodations. The mission of the ODS is to ensure that all students with disabilities can freely and actively participate in all facets of university life: to provide and coordinate support services and programs that enable students with disabilities maximize their educational potential and assist students in the developmental process of transition to higher education, independence, and effective self-advocacy. The director functions as a liaison between students and the university community and provides support in obtaining accommodations for equalizing academic success in the classroom. If the applicant is eligible for reevaluation through the school system, it is strongly advised to take advantage of the service before leaving high school. Current documentation with recommendations for postsecondary accommodations are crucial for providing appropriate services in college. Course substitution requests are dealt with on an individual basis. They may be appropriate for students for whom a particular subject has been a continuously documented obstacle to academic progress. Students should notify ODS upon enrollment if they want to seek a substitution for a course requirement. Substitutions are not guaranteed.

LD/ADHD ADMISSIONS INFORMATION

College entrance tests required: Yes
Interview required: No
Essay recommended: No
Documentation required for LD: Current comprehensive
  psychoeducational evaluation. Visit
  www.jmu.edu/disabilityserv/ldguide.shtm for guidelines.
Documentation required for ADHD: Yes
Submitted to: Office of Disability Services
Special Ed. HS course work accepted: Yes

Specific course requirements of all applicants: Yes
Separate application required: No
# of LD applications submitted each year: NR
# of LD applications accepted yearly: NR
Total # of students receiving LD services: NR
**Acceptance into program means acceptance into
  college:** Students must be admitted to and enrolled in the
  university first and then request services.

ADMISSIONS

The admissions team at JMU is highly sensitive and knowledgeable concerning students with learning disabilities and the admissions process. Admission decisions are made without regard to disabilities. All prospective students are expected to present academic credentials at or above the minimum standards for admission as established by the Admissions Committee. After admission to JMU, documentation will be forwarded to ODS. Current recommendations for postsecondary accommodations are crucial for providing appropriate services in college. There are no specific courses required for admission into James Madison; however, students are expected to complete a solid college-prep curriculum. The mid 50 percent range for the ACT is 24–28, and for the SAT, it is 1110–1250. The mid 50 percent range for GPAs is 3.31–3.75. SAT Subject Tests are required in Writing and foreign language where applicable. The university uses class rank as one of the criteria reviewed, but does not use GPA.

ADDITIONAL INFORMATION

Some of the commonly used services are priority registration; the Support Lab, which houses equipment; academic advisors and services; and course-scheduling information. Classroom accommodations include extended time for tests and written assignments, testing in distraction-free environments, modification of exam formats, volunteer note-takers, use of tape recorders in class, oral testing, scribes, use of computers for tests, and individual assistance as needed. Other university services include a reading and writing lab, a counseling and student development center, and academic advising. Basic workshops for no credit are offered in study skills and self-advocacy. Services and accommodations are available for undergraduate and graduate students.

LEARNING DISABILITY PROGRAM/SERVICES

Learning Disability Program/Services: Office of Disability Services (ODS)
Director: Valerie Schoolcraft
E-mail: disability-svcs@jmu.edu
Telephone: 540-568-6705
Fax: 540-568-7099

LEARNING DISABILITY SERVICES

Requests for the following services/accommodations will be evaluated individually based on appropriate and current documentation.

Allowed in exams
Calculator: Yes
Dictionary: Yes
Computer: Yes
Spellchecker: Yes
Extended test time: Yes
Scribes: Yes
Proctors: Yes
Oral exams: Yes
Note-takers: Yes

Distraction-reduced environment: Yes
Tape recording in class: Yes
Books on tape from RFBD: Yes
Taping of books not from RFBD: Yes
Accommodations for students with ADHD: Yes
Reading machine: Yes
Other assistive technology: Yes
Priority registration: Yes

Added costs for services: No
LD specialists: Yes
Professional tutors: No
Peer tutors: No
Max. hours/wk. for services: N/A
How professors are notified of LD/ADHD: By student

GENERAL ADMISSIONS INFORMATION

Director of Admissions: Michael D. Walsh
Telephone: 540 568 5681

ENTRANCE REQUIREMENTS

Academic units required: 4 English, 4 math, 4 science (3 science labs), 3 foreign language, 3 social studies.
Academic units recommended: 4 English, 5 math, 4 science (4 science labs), 4 foreign language, 4 social studies. High school diploma is required, and GED is accepted. ACT with or without Writing component accepted. TOEFL required of all international applicants: minimum paper TOEFL 570, minimum computer TOEFL 230.

Application deadline: 1/15
Notification: 4/1
Average GPA: 3.69
ACT Composite middle 50% range: 24–26

SAT Math middle 50% range: 530–620
SAT Critical Reading middle 50% range: 520–610
SAT Writing middle 50% range: 520–610

Graduated top 10% of class: 31%
Graduated top 25% of class: 78%
Graduated top 50% of class: 98%

COLLEGE GRADUATION REQUIREMENTS

Course waivers allowed: NR
Course substitutions allowed: NR

ADDITIONAL INFORMATION

Environment: The university is located in the Shenandoah Valley surrounded by the Blue Ridge Mountains and the Allegheny Mountain Range, 120 miles from Washington, DC.

Student Body
Undergrad enrollment: 15,653
Women: 61%
Men: 39%
Percent out-of-state: 30%

Cost Information
In-state tuition: $5,800
Out-of-state tuition: $15,300
Room & board: $6,496
Housing Information
University housing: Yes
Percent living on campus: 37%

Greek System
Fraternity: Yes
Sorority: Yes
Athletics: Division I

James Madison University

LIBERTY UNIVERSITY

1971 University Boulevard, Lynchburg, VA 24502
Phone: 434-582-5905 • Fax: 800-542-2311
E-mail: admissions@liberty.edu • Web: www.liberty.edu
Support: CS • Institution type: 4-year private

LEARNING DISABILITY PROGRAM AND SERVICES

The primary purpose of the Bruckner Learning Center is to offer reading and study skills assistance to all students. The center provides individualized peer tutoring regularly or on a drop-in basis for English or math. There are three one-semester hour courses provided for students wishing to develop reading and study skills: College Study Strategies, College Reading Improvement, and Individualized Laboratory in Reading and Study Strategies. Students with a disability who self-identify may be eligible for accommodations such as priority class registration, academic advising from trained faculty, deaf interpreters, and confidential requests for classroom accommodations (additional time on tests, note-taking help, and so on).

LD/ADHD ADMISSIONS INFORMATION

College entrance tests required: Yes
Interview required: No
Essay recommended: No
Documentation required for LD: The student's latest IEP and/or psychological testing profile or other written information that describes the learning disability
Documentation required for ADHD: Diagnosis from a qualified professional
Submitted to: Both Admissions Office and Office of Disability Services
Special Ed. HS course work accepted: No

Specific course requirements of all applicants: Yes
Separate application required: No
# of LD applications submitted each year: NR
# of LD applications accepted yearly: NR
Total # of students receiving LD services: 100
Acceptance into program means acceptance into college: Students must be admitted to and enrolled in the university first and then request services.

ADMISSIONS

All applicants must submit an official transcript from an accredited high school and/or college, an official copy of a state high school equivalency diploma, or an official copy of the GED test results. The minimum acceptable unweighted GPA is 2.0. All applicants must submit ACT or SAT results prior to admission. The minimum acceptable scores are an SAT score of 800 or an ACT score of 17. Courses required for admission include 4 years of English, 2 or 3 years of college-prep mathematics, 2 years of science lab, 2 years of social science, and at least 4 units of elective credits in subjects such as art, music, or drama. Applicants who fail to meet the minimum required GPA will be evaluated using other indicators of collegiate ability and may be admitted on academic warning.

ADDITIONAL INFORMATION

If a student's entrance test scores indicate a deficiency in English or math, then the student will enroll in a basic composition class or fundamentals of math class. With the student's permission, instructors are provided with a written communication providing information about the student's specific disability and suggestions of appropriate accommodations. Students with a specific learning disability can be assigned to a faculty advisor who has had training in LD. This person advises students concerning academic loads and acts as a liaison between instructors and students regarding classroom accommodations. The Bruckner Learning Center provides individualized peer tutoring in most subjects on a weekly or drop-in basis. The Office of Disability Academic Support coordinates services for students with documented disabilities. Students who self-identify may be eligible for accommodations such as priority class registration, academic advising from trained faculty, deaf interpreters, and confidential requests for classroom accommodations (e.g., additional time on tests, note-taking help). The ODAS office provides the following support services: early registration, disability documentation notification, academic accommodations, progress reports, one-on-one mentoring/advising, and an Assistive Technology Lab.

LEARNING DISABILITY PROGRAM/SERVICES

Learning Disability Program/Services: Office of Disability Academic Support
Director: Mr. Denny McHaney
  E-mail: wdmchane@liberty.edu
  Telephone: 434-582-2159
  Fax: 434-582-7567

LEARNING DISABILITY SERVICES

Requests for the following services/accommodations will be evaluated individually based on appropriate and current documentation.

Allowed in exams
  Calculator: No
  Dictionary: No
  Computer: No
  Spellchecker: Yes
Extended test time: Yes
Scribes: Yes
Proctors: Yes
Oral exams: Yes
Note-takers: Yes

Distraction-reduced environment: Yes
Tape recording in class: Yes
Books on tape from RFBD: Yes
Taping of books not from RFBD: No
Accommodations for students with
  ADHD: Yes
Reading machine: No
Other assistive technology: Yes
Priority registration: Yes

Added costs for services: No
LD specialists: Yes
Professional tutors: No
Peer tutors: 30
Max. hours/wk. for services:
  Unlimited
How professors are notified of
  LD/ADHD: By director

GENERAL ADMISSIONS INFORMATION

Director of Admissions: Richard Plyter
Telephone: 434-592-3072

ENTRANCE REQUIREMENTS

Academic units recommended: 4 English, 3 math, 2 science (2 science labs), 2 foreign language, 2 social studies, 4 academic electives. High school diploma is required, and GED is accepted. ACT with or without Writing component accepted. TOEFL required of all international applicants: minimum paper TOEFL 500, minimum computer TOEFL 173.

Application deadline: Rolling
Notification: Rolling
Average GPA: 3.17
ACT Composite middle 50% range:
  18–24

SAT Math middle 50% range:
  420–540
SAT Critical Reading middle 50%
  range: 440–550
SAT Writing middle 50% range: NR

Graduated top 10% of class: 4%
Graduated top 25% of class: 13%
Graduated top 50% of class: 41%

COLLEGE GRADUATION REQUIREMENTS

Course waivers allowed: No
Course substitutions allowed: No

ADDITIONAL INFORMATION

Environment: The 5,200-acre university is located in a suburban area 45 miles east of Roanoke.

Student Body
  Undergrad enrollment: 13,296
  Women: 52%
  Men: 48%
  Percent out-of-state: 67%

Cost Information
  Tuition: $14,850
  Room & board: $5,400
Housing Information
  University housing: Yes
  Percent living on campus: 40%

Greek System
  Fraternity: No
  Sorority: No
Athletics: Division I

OLD DOMINION UNIVERSITY

108 Rollins Hall, 5115 Hampton Boulevard, Norfolk, VA 23529-0050
Phone: 757-683-3685 • Fax: 757-683-3255
E-mail: admit@odu.edu • Web: www.odu.edu
Support: CS • Institution type: 4-year public

LEARNING DISABILITY PROGRAM AND SERVICES

Student Support Services is a TRIO Program funded by the U.S. Department of Education providing academic support. The program is oriented to meet the needs of students according to their development level. Typically, students are newly diagnosed or recently transitioning to campus. The program assists students in achieving and maintaining the academic performance level required for satisfactory academic standing at the university, thereby, increasing their chances of graduating. Services include on-site orientation programs, taped materials, and tutorial services by peers, oral testing, untimed testing, and individual counseling. The students are respected as the primary source of knowledge of their needs.

LD/ADHD ADMISSIONS INFORMATION

College entrance tests required: Yes
Interview required: No
Essay recommended: No
Documentation required for LD: WAIS–III, WISC–R, and
  WJ–III completed within the past 3 years
Documentation required for ADHD: Yes
Submitted to: Disability Services
Special Ed. HS course work accepted: Yes

Specific course requirements of all applicants: Yes
Separate application required: No
# of LD applications submitted each year: 40–60
# of LD applications accepted yearly: 50
Total # of students receiving LD services: 275
Acceptance into program means acceptance into
  college: Students must be admitted to and enrolled in the
  university first and then request services.

ADMISSIONS

There is no special admissions process for students with learning disabilities. Students are encouraged to include a cover letter identifying their learning disabilities and explaining weaknesses that may have affected their academic records. If students self-identify during the admissions process, the information may be used to support their application, but may not be used to their detriment. Clear and specific evidence and identification of a learning disability must be stated, and the report must be conducted and written by a qualified professional. Students not meeting regular admission standards may be admitted through the Academic Opportunity Program. This is for 300 students with low test scores but high GPAs. Others may be admitted through a summer transition program or individual admission for nontraditional students. General admission criteria include 4 years of English, 3 years of math, 3 years of science, 2 years of a foreign language, 3 years of social studies, and 3 years of history; ACT/SAT scores (with a minimum SAT of 850 and at least a 400 in the Verbal and Math sections); a rank in the top half of the class; and a minimum GPA of 2.0.

ADDITIONAL INFORMATION

Counseling and advising; study skills instruction; reading, writing, and math instruction; and tutorial assistance are available. Program staff design support services that focus on students' learning styles and special needs. There is a special section of Spanish for students with learning disabilities to meet the foreign language requirements, as well as developmental math, reading, spelling, and writing classes.

LEARNING DISABILITY PROGRAM/SERVICES

Learning Disability Program/Services: Disability Services
Director: Sheryn Milton, MEd
  E-mail: disabilityservices@odu.edu
  Telephone: 757-683-4655
  Fax: 757-683-5356
Contact Person: Kate Broderick
  E-mail: disabilityservices@odu.edu

LEARNING DISABILITY SERVICES

Requests for the following services/accommodations will be evaluated individually based on appropriate and current documentation.

Allowed in exams
  Calculator: Yes
  Dictionary: Yes
  Computer: Yes
  Spellchecker: Yes
Extended test time: Yes
Scribes: Yes
Proctors: Yes
Oral exams: Yes
Note-takers: Yes

Distraction-reduced environment: Yes
Tape recording in class: Yes
Books on tape from RFBD: Yes
Taping of books not from RFBD: Yes
Accommodations for students with
  ADHD: Yes
Reading machine: Yes
Other assistive technology: Yes
Priority registration: Yes

Added costs for services: No
LD specialists: Yes
Professional tutors: No
Peer tutors: N/A
Max. hours/wk. for services: NR
How professors are notified of
  LD/ADHD: By both student and director

GENERAL ADMISSIONS INFORMATION

Director of Admissions: Alice McAdory
Telephone: 757-683-3648

ENTRANCE REQUIREMENTS

Academic units recommended: 4 English, 3 math, 3 science, 3 foreign language, 3 social studies, 3 history. High school diploma is required, and GED is accepted. ACT with Writing component required. TOEFL required of all international applicants: minimum paper TOEFL 550, minimum computer TOEFL 213.

Application deadline: 5/1
Notification: Rolling
Average GPA: 3.30
ACT Composite middle 50% range:
  19–22

SAT Math middle 50% range:
  490–580
SAT Critical Reading middle 50%
  range: 480–570
SAT Writing middle 50% range:
  460–560

Graduated top 10% of class: 14%
Graduated top 25% of class: 46%
Graduated top 50% of class: 87%

COLLEGE GRADUATION REQUIREMENTS

Course waivers allowed: No
Course substitutions allowed: Yes
In what course: All students must complete 3 credits in math. A special 1-year Spanish course is available for students registered with DS.

ADDITIONAL INFORMATION

Environment: The university is located on 46 acres in a suburban area of Norfolk.

Student Body
  Undergrad enrollment: 14,845
  Women: 59%
  Men: 41%
  Percent out-of-state: 9%

Cost Information
  In-state tuition: $5,910
  Out-of-state tuition: $16,470
  Room & board: $6,640
Housing Information
  University housing: Yes
  Percent living on campus: 29%

Greek System
  Fraternity: Yes
  Sorority: Yes
Athletics: Division I

UNIVERSITY OF VIRGINIA

Office of Admissions, PO Box 400160, Charlottesville, VA 22906
Phone: 434-982-3200 • Fax: 434-924-3587
E-mail: undergradadmission@virginia.edu • Web: www.virginia.edu
Support: CS • Institution type: 4-year public

LEARNING DISABILITY PROGRAM AND SERVICES

The University of Virginia is committed to providing equal access to educational and social opportunities for all disabled students. The Learning Needs and Evaluation Center (LNEC) is housed within the university's Center for Counseling and Psychological Services and serves as the coordinating agency for services to all students with disabilities. The LNECs assists students with disabilities to become independent self-advocates who are able to demonstrate their abilities both in the classroom and as members of the university community. The center provides a number of services, including review of documentation supporting the disability, determination of appropriate academic accommodations, academic support services for students requiring assistance, and serving as a liaison with faculty and administrators. Information can be shared, with the student's permission, with university personnel who have an educational need to know. Once a learning disability is documented, the center assigns appropriate and reasonable accommodations and serves as a liaison with faculty and administrators. The center's primary purpose is to support the academic well-being of students with disabilities.

LD/ADHD ADMISSIONS INFORMATION

College entrance tests required: Yes
Interview required: No
Essay recommended: No
Documentation required for LD: Psychoeducational
  evaluation
Documentation required for ADHD: Yes
Submitted to: LNEC
Special Ed. HS course work accepted: NR

Specific course requirements of all applicants: Yes
Separate application required: No
# of LD applications submitted each year: NR
# of LD applications accepted yearly: NR
Total # of students receiving LD services: NR
**Acceptance into program means acceptance into
  college:** Students must be admitted to and enrolled in the
  university first and then request services.

ADMISSIONS

The students with learning disabilities go through the same admissions procedure as all incoming applicants. After admission to the university, students must contact the LNEC to receive services. Students with learning disabilities admitted to the university have qualified for admission because of their abilities. No criteria for admission are waived because of a disability. All applicants to UVA have outstanding grades, a high rank in their high school class, excellent performance in advanced placement and honor courses, superior performance on ACT/SAT Reasoning and SAT Subject Tests, extracurricular success, special talents, and interests and goals. Letters of recommendation are required.

ADDITIONAL INFORMATION

Following acceptance of an offer of admission to the university, students with an LD or ADHD are advised to contact the LNEC to identify their need for services. All students seeking accommodations while at the university must provide acceptable documentation of their disability, including, but not limited to, a neuropsychological or psychoeducational evaluation report, completed by a licensed clinical psychologist or clinical neuropsychologist, that has been completed within 3 years of matriculation. The Learning Needs and Evaluation Center addresses such things as personal social skills; alternative speaking, reading, and writing methods; and referrals for tutors. Staff also consult with students about academic difficulties. Classes are offered in study skills and time management. Services and accommodations are available for undergraduate and graduate students.

LEARNING DISABILITY PROGRAM/SERVICES

Learning Disability Program/Services: Learning Needs and Evaluation Center (LNEC)
Director: Allison Anderson, PhD
  E-mail: LNEC@virginia.edu
  Telephone: 434-243-5181
  Fax: 434-243-5188
Contact Person: Debbie Shoemaker, MA
  E-mail: LNEC@virginia.edu

LEARNING DISABILITY SERVICES

Requests for the following services/accommodations will be evaluated individually based on appropriate and current documentation.

Allowed in exams
  Calculator: Yes
  Dictionary: Yes
  Computer: Yes
  Spellchecker: Yes
Extended test time: Yes
Scribes: Yes
Proctors: Yes
Oral exams: Yes
Note-takers: Yes

Distraction-reduced environment: Yes
Tape recording in class: Yes
Books on tape from RFBD: Yes
Taping of books not from RFBD: Yes
Accommodations for students with
  ADHD: Yes
Reading machine: Yes
Other assistive technology: Yes
Priority registration: NR

Added costs for services: No
LD specialists: Yes
Professional tutors: No
Peer tutors: No
Max. hours/wk. for services: NR
How professors are notified of
  LD/ADHD: By both student and
  director

GENERAL ADMISSIONS INFORMATION

Director of Admissions: John A. Blackburn
Telephone: 434-982-3200

ENTRANCE REQUIREMENTS

Academic units required: 4 English, 4 math, 2 science, 2 foreign language, 1 social studies. **Academic units recommended:** 5 math, 4 science, 5 foreign language, 4 social studies. High school diploma is required, and GED is accepted. ACT with Writing component required. TOEFL required of all international applicants: minimum paper TOEFL 600, minimum computer TOEFL 250.

Application deadline: 1/2
Notification: 4/1
Average GPA: 4.07
ACT Composite middle 50% range:
  26–31

SAT Math middle 50% range:
  620–720
SAT Critical Reading middle 50%
  range: 600–710
SAT Writing middle 50% range:
  610–710

Graduated top 10% of class: 88%
Graduated top 25% of class: 97%
Graduated top 50% of class: 100%

COLLEGE GRADUATION REQUIREMENTS

Course waivers allowed: No
Course substitutions allowed: Yes
In what course: Considerations of alternate courses for the foreign language requirement following an attempt by the student to complete standard language courses

ADDITIONAL INFORMATION

Environment: The 2,440-acre campus is located in a small city 70 miles northwest of Richmond.

Student Body
  Undergrad enrollment: 13,440
  Women: 55%
  Men: 45%
  Percent out-of-state: 28%

Cost Information
  In-state tuition: $7,798
  Out-of-state tuition: $25,398
  Room & board: $7,000
Housing Information
  University housing: Yes
  Percent living on campus: 44%

Greek System
  Fraternity: Yes
  Sorority: Yes
Athletics: Division I

VIRGINIA INTERMONT COLLEGE

1013 Moore Street, Bristol, VA 24201-4298
Phone: 276-466-7856 • Fax: 276-466-7855
E-mail: viadmit@vic.edu • Web: www.vic.edu
Support: CS • Institution type: 4-year private

LEARNING DISABILITY PROGRAM AND SERVICES

Student Support Services provides free supportive services to students who participate in the program. There are extensive services offered to those with LD. The objective of the services is to help students stay in school and graduate. The department consists of a director/counselor, school psychologist/LD specialist, tutor coordinator, and an administrative assistant. Students work voluntarily with the staff as individuals or as a team to develop individual plans of support. Staff members act as advocates for students with faculty and administration and provide general faculty awareness and understanding of overall student needs without disclosure of confidentiality. Virginia Intermont staff and faculty have a commitment to the significance of the individual and to the value of personalizing education. The college provides quality education with extensive support services and accommodations, rather than altering admissions criteria or course requirements. Once admitted, students are encouraged to submit documentation of any special needs. This is usually in the form of psychoeducational test data and an IEP from high school. All accommodations are provided at the request of students with documentation.

LD/ADHD ADMISSIONS INFORMATION

College entrance tests required: Yes
Interview required: No
Essay recommended: No
Documentation required for LD: Psychoeducational assessment completed within past 3 years
Documentation required for ADHD: Clinical assessment and diagnosis from a medical doctor, psychologist, or psychiatrist
Submitted to: Student Support Services
Special Ed. HS course work accepted: No

Specific course requirements of all applicants: Yes
Separate application required: No
# of LD applications submitted each year: NR
# of LD applications accepted yearly: NR
Total # of students receiving LD services: 30–40
Acceptance into program means acceptance into college: Students must be admitted to and enrolled in the university first and then request services.

ADMISSIONS

There is no special admissions procedure for the student with a learning disability. Documentation related to a learning disability may be submitted to the Office of Admissions with the general application or may be submitted separately to the Office of Student Support Services. Testing done by a high school psychologist is acceptable. The average ACT is 21; the average SAT is 885. The minimum GPA reuired is 2.0. Course requirements include a minimum of 15 units: 4 years of English, 2 years of math, 1 year of science lab, 2 years of social science, and 6 years of electives. Virginia Intermont is more concerned with the student's quality of preparation than with the precise numerical distribution of requirements. A conditional admit may be offered if the high school GPA or SAT scores are below requirements. Students not having the proper high school preparation or not meeting the normal admissions criteria may be required, if admitted, to take developmental courses as needed in math, English, reading, and/or study strategies. These courses would not count toward graduation, and the student would be limited to 14 hours in the first semester.

ADDITIONAL INFORMATION

Students with LD will be offered appropriate accommodations recommended by the learning specialist based on the documentation. Accommodations and/or services available to eligible students include individual personal and academic counseling, freshman placement test accommodations, scribes, computer tests, extended time on tests, taped tests, peer and staff tutoring emphasizing unique techniques as needed, support groups, academic advising, diagnostic testing, liaison with faculty, tape recording of classes, assistance with course selection and registration, and optional reduced course load. A few accommodations require appointments, though generally there is an open door policy. Education 100 (1 credit), taught by Student Support Services staff, is designed for students interested in improving academic skills. Topics covered in this course are individual learning styles, time-study management, note-taking, textbook reading, memory strategies, test-taking strategies, and test anxiety reduction.

LEARNING DISABILITY PROGRAM/SERVICES

Learning Disability Program/Services: Student Support Services
Director: Talmage Dobbins
  E-mail: tdobbins@vic.edu
  Telephone: 276-466-7905
  Fax: 276-645-6493
Contact Person: Barbara Holbrook
  E-mail: tdobbins@vic.edu

LEARNING DISABILITY SERVICES

Requests for the following services/accommodations will be evaluated individually based on appropriate and current documentation.

Allowed in exams	**Distraction-reduced environment:** Yes	**Added costs for services:** No
Calculator: Yes	**Tape recording in class:** Yes	**LD specialists:** Yes
Dictionary: Yes	**Books on tape from RFBD:** Yes	**Professional tutors:** No
Computer: Yes	**Taping of books not from RFBD:** Yes	**Peer tutors:** 12–30
Spellchecker: Yes	**Accommodations for students with**	**Max. hours/wk. for services:**
Extended test time: Yes	**ADHD:** Yes	Unlimited
Scribes: Yes	**Reading machine:** No	**How professors are notified of**
Proctors: Yes	**Other assistive technology:** No	**LD/ADHD:** By both student and
Oral exams: Yes	**Priority registration:** No	director
Note-takers: Yes		

GENERAL ADMISSIONS INFORMATION

Director of Admissions: Anne Shumaker
Telephone: 276-466-7856

ENTRANCE REQUIREMENTS

Academic units required: 4 English, 2 math, 1 science (1 science lab), 2 social studies, 6 academic electives. High school diploma is required, and GED is accepted. ACT with Writing component required. TOEFL required of all international applicants: minimum paper TOEFL 500, minimum computer TOEFL 173.

Application deadline: Rolling	**SAT Math middle 50% range:**	**Graduated top 10% of class:** 8%
Notification: Rolling	410–540	**Graduated top 25% of class:** 20%
Average GPA: 3.20	**SAT Critical Reading middle 50%**	**Graduated top 50% of class:** 58%
ACT Composite middle 50% range:	**range:** 410–530	
17–25	**SAT Writing middle 50% range:** NR	

COLLEGE GRADUATION REQUIREMENTS

Course waivers allowed: No
Course substitutions allowed: Yes
In what course: Substitutions are rarely granted but must be considered by a committee.

ADDITIONAL INFORMATION

Environment: The college is located on a 16-acre campus in the Blue Ridge Mountains.

Student Body	**Cost Information**	**Greek System**
Undergrad enrollment: 885	**Tuition:** $16,895	**Fraternity:** No
Women: 69%	**Room & board:** $6,095	**Sorority:** No
Men: 31%	**Housing Information**	**Athletics:** NAIA
Percent out-of-state: 68%	**University housing:** Yes	
	Percent living on campus: 60%	

EASTERN WASHINGTON UNIVERSITY

526 Fifth Street, Cheney, WA 99004
Phone: 509-359-2397 • Fax: 509-359-6692
E-mail: admissions@mail.ewu.edu • Web: www.ewu.edu
Support: S • Institution type: 4-year public

LEARNING DISABILITY PROGRAM AND SERVICES

Although the university does not offer a specialized curriculum, personnel work with students to modify programs to meet individual needs. Disability Support Services (DSS) is dedicated to the coordination of appropriate and reasonable accommodations for students with disabilities. These accommodations are based on individual needs so that each student may receive an equal opportunity to learn to participate in campus life, to grow emotionally and socially, and to successfully complete a program of study that will enable him or her to be self-supporting and remain as independent as possible. This is facilitated through support services, information sharing, advisement, and referral when requested. Students who require services and support need to contact DSS so that the disability can be verified, specific needs determined, and timely accommodations made. In most cases, documentation by a professional service provider will be necessary. Information is kept strictly confidential. However, it is important to share information that will enable DSS staff to provide appropriate, reasonable, and timely services tailored to individual needs.

LD/ADHD ADMISSIONS INFORMATION

College entrance tests required: Yes
Interview required: No
Essay recommended: No
Documentation required for LD: Statement of diagnosis and list of tests administered and their interpretation (aptitude, achievement, information processing, and/or functional)
Documentation required for ADHD: Current and comprehensive (include evidence of early impairment, current impairment, relevant testing info, alternative diagnosis ruled out, and prepared by a professional with comprehensive training in the diagnosis and treatment of ADHD.
Submitted to: Admissions Office and DSS

Special Ed. HS course work accepted: Yes
Specific course requirements of all applicants: Yes
Separate application required: No
# of LD applications submitted each year: NR
# of LD applications accepted yearly: NR
Total # of students receiving LD services: 80–90
Acceptance into program means acceptance into college: Students must be admitted to and enrolled in the university first and then request services.

ADMISSIONS

Individuals with disabilities are admitted via the standard admissions criteria that apply to all students. General admissibility is based on an index using GPA and test scores. The minimum GPA accepted is a 2.0. Required courses include 4 years of English, 3 years of math, 3 years of social science, 2 years of science (1 year of lab), 2 years of a foreign language (American Sign Language accepted), and 1 year of arts or academic electives. Special education courses are acceptable if they are courses that are regularly taught in the high school. However, all applicants must complete the required core courses. Students who do not meet the grade and test score admission scale may provide additional information to the Admission Office and request consideration through the special talent admissions process.

ADDITIONAL INFORMATION

Examples of services for students with specific learning disabilities include taped texts; equipment loans; alternative testing arrangements such as oral exams, extended time on tests, relocation of testing site; note-takers; tutorial assistance (available to all students); referral to a Learning Skills Center, Writers' Center, and/or Mathematics Lab; accessible computer stations; and a Kurzweil reading machine. Examples of services for students with ADHD are consultation regarding reasonable and effective accommodations with classroom professors; alternative testing; books on tape; note-takers; taped lectures; equipment loans; referrals to a Learning Skills Center, a Math Lab, a Writers' Center, and counseling and psychological services; information on ADHD; and informal counseling. Skills classes for credit are offered in math, reading, time management, study skills, and writing skills. FOCUS is a structured first-year experience for selected, provisionally admitted students. The experience includes advising; academic instruction in math, English, and study strategies; and professional mentoring. Services and accommodations are offered to undergraduate and graduate students.

LEARNING DISABILITY PROGRAM/SERVICES

Learning Disability Program/Services: Disability Support Services (DSS)
Director: Robert A. Campbell
  E-mail: rcampbell@mail.ewu.edu
  Telephone: 509-359-6871
  Fax: 509-359-7458
Contact Person: Pam McDermott
  E-mail: rcampbell@mail.ewu.edu

LEARNING DISABILITY SERVICES

Requests for the following services/accommodations will be evaluated individually based on appropriate and current documentation.

Allowed in exams
  Calculator: Yes
  Dictionary: Yes
  Computer: Yes
  Spellchecker: Yes
Extended test time: Yes
Scribes: Yes
Proctors: Yes
Oral exams: Yes
Note-takers: Yes

Distraction-reduced environment: Yes
Tape recording in class: Yes
Books on tape from RFBD: Yes
Taping of books not from RFBD: Yes
Accommodations for students with
  ADHD: Yes
Reading machine: Yes
Other assistive technology: Yes
Priority registration: Yes

Added costs for services: No
LD specialists: No
Professional tutors: 7
Peer tutors: 33
Max. hours/wk. for services: NR
How professors are notified of
  LD/ADHD: By both student and
  director

GENERAL ADMISSIONS INFORMATION

Director of Admissions: Shannon Carr
Telephone: 509-359-2397

ENTRANCE REQUIREMENTS

Academic units required: 4 English, 3 math, 2 science (1 science lab), 2 foreign language, 3 social studies, 1 fine arts or another unit chosen from previously listed subjects. **Academic units recommended:** 4 English, 4 math, 3 science, 2 foreign language, 4 social studies, 1 fine arts or another unit chosen from previously listed subjects. High school diploma is required, and GED is accepted. ACT with Writing component required. TOEFL required of all international applicants: minimum paper TOEFL 525, minimum computer TOEFL 195.

Application deadline: 8/15
Notification: Rolling
Average GPA: 3.30
ACT Composite middle 50% range: NR

SAT Math middle 50% range: NR
SAT Critical Reading middle 50% range: NR
SAT Writing middle 50% range: NR

Graduated top 10% of class: NR
Graduated top 25% of class: NR
Graduated top 50% of class: NR

COLLEGE GRADUATION REQUIREMENTS

Course waivers allowed: Yes
In what course: Possible waiver for foreign language. This must be supported by documentation.
Course substitutions allowed: Yes
In what course: Possible substitutions in math and foreign language. These must be supported by documentation.

ADDITIONAL INFORMATION

Environment: The university is located on 35 acres in a small town 18 miles southwest of Spokane.

Student Body
  Undergrad enrollment: 9,553
  Women: 58%
  Men: 42%
  Percent out-of-state: 9%

Cost Information
  In-state tuition: $4,695
  Out-of-state tuition: $14,200
  Room & board: $6,549
Housing Information
  University housing: Yes
  Percent living on campus: 19%

Greek System
  Fraternity: Yes
  Sorority: Yes
Athletics: Division I

THE EVERGREEN STATE COLLEGE

2700 Evergreen Pkwy. NW, Office of Admissions, Olympia, WA 98505
Phone: 360-867-6170 • Fax: 360-867-6576
E-mail: admissions@evergreen.edu • Web: www.evergreen.edu
Support: S • Institution type: public

LEARNING DISABILITY PROGRAM AND SERVICES

The Evergreen State College has consistently provided an integrated learning community for students. Students take one program that unifies classes around a central theme, taught by two or three faculty from different academic disciplines. Students receive a narrative evaluation from the faculty. The student's accomplishments and achievements will be detailed to provide graduate schools and employers with a comprehensive overview of his or her undergraduate education. Students are eligible to receive accommodations through Access Services. Depending on the disability, professional documentation may be presented from a medical doctor, psychologist, psychiatrist, neuro-psychologist, school psychologist, other professional diagnostician or medical professional who is a specialist in the field of the specific disability.

LD/ADHD ADMISSIONS INFORMATION

College entrance tests required: Yes
Interview required: No
Essay recommended: No
Documentation required for LD: Psychoeducational
evaluation
Documentation required for ADHD: Yes
Submitted to: Access Services
Special Ed. HS course work accepted: No

Specific course requirements of all applicants: Yes
Separate application required: No
# of LD applications submitted each year: NR
# of LD applications accepted yearly: NR
Total # of students receiving LD services: NR
Acceptance into program means acceptance into
college: Students must be admitted and enrolled prior to requesting services.

ADMISSIONS

Students entering directly from high school will be considered for admission upon the following: A GPA minimum of 2.0 cumulative for full consideration, and 2.8 or above recommended and ACT or SAT. The most important factor is academic achievement demonstrated by the nature and distribution of your high school course work. After the high school course work has been reviewed, an admissions formula is used to determine an "admission index." The index combines the cumulative GPA and the composite test score from the SAT or ACT test. The best composite score will be used in this calculation if the student takes the ACT or SAT test more than once. Typically, applicants who have at least an admissions index score of 25 or higher are admitted. An optional personal statement is not required but is recommended. This statement might describe academic interests, goals and why the student believes Evergreen is the right college for the student. Students might also consider submitting letters of recommendation and essays. Submissions should be limited to one page and clearly address the student's academic history and preparation for rigorous study. Applicants with index scores below 25 are encouraged to submit a personal statement. The index can be found at www.evergreen.edu/admissions/publications/pdf/grid.pdf.

ADDITIONAL INFORMATION

KEY Student Services is designed for students who are the first in their family to go to college or meet federal guidelines for low-income status, or have a recently documented physical or learning disability and have academic need. Students who participate in KEY Student Support Services have access to numerous tools and resources intended to help them stay in school and earn a college degree. Experienced staff works individually with each student, identifying and providing resources that will be of greatest value. Services may include: needs assessment to determine strengths and weaknesses and support needed to accomplish goals; academic and career planning: free academic tutoring; and referral and advocacy from KEY staff trained to identify student needs and provide linkages to vital support services on campus and in the community; social and cultural events which include a quarterly gathering to "eat, meet, and greet," and to enjoy guest speakers, holiday celebrations and lively conversation.

LEARNING DISABILITY PROGRAM/SERVICES

Learning Disability Program/Services: Access Services
Director: Linda Pickering
  E-mail: pickeril@evergreen.edu
  Telephone: 360-867-6364
  Fax: 360-867-5349
Contact Person: Meredith Inocencio
  E-mail: pickeril@evergreen.edu
  Telephone: 360-867-6348
  Fax: 360-867-5349

LEARNING DISABILITY SERVICES

Requests for the following services/accommodations will be evaluated individually based on appropriate and current documentation.

Allowed in exams
  Calculator: Yes
  Dictionary: Yes
  Computer: Yes
  Spellchecker: Yes
Extended test time: Yes
Scribes: Yes
Proctors: Yes
Oral exams: Yes
Note-takers: Yes

Distraction-reduced environment: Yes
Tape recording in class: Yes
Books on tape from RFBD: Yes
Taping of books not from RFBD: Yes
Accommodations for students with
  ADHD: Yes
Reading machine: Yes
Other assistive technology: Yes
Priority registration: No

Added costs for services: No
LD specialists: No
Professional tutors: 10
Peer tutors: 3–5
Max. hours/wk. for services: NR
How professors are notified of
  LD/ADHD: By both student and
  director

GENERAL ADMISSIONS INFORMATION

Director of Admissions: Richard (Steve) Hunter
Telephone: 360-867-6170

ENTRANCE REQUIREMENTS

Academic units required: 4 English, 3 math, 2 science (1 science lab), 2 foreign language, 3 social studies, 1 academic elective, 1 fine or visual/performing arts elective or other college-prep elective from the areas listed previously. High school diploma is required, and GED is accepted. ACT with or without Writing component accepted. TOEFL required of all international applicants: minimum paper TOEFL 550, minimum computer TOEFL 213.

Application deadline: Rolling
Notification: Rolling
Average GPA: 3.07
ACT Composite middle 50% range:
  21–27

SAT Math middle 50% range:
  470–590
SAT Critical Reading middle 50%
  range: 520–650
SAT Writing middle 50% range: NR

Graduated top 10% of class: 10%
Graduated top 25% of class: 31%
Graduated top 50% of class: 63%

COLLEGE GRADUATION REQUIREMENTS

Course waivers allowed: No
Course substitutions allowed: No

ADDITIONAL INFORMATION

Environment: The campus is in Olympia, Washington—1 hour south of Seattle and 2 hours north of Portland, Oregon.

Student Body
  Undergrad enrollment: 3,931
  Women: 55%
  Men: 45%
  Percent out-of-state: 23%

Cost Information
  In-state tuition: $4,371
  Out-of-state tuition: $14,562
  Room & board: $7,140
Housing Information
  University housing: Yes
  Percent living on campus: 21%

Greek System
  Fraternity: No
  Sorority: No
  Athletics: NAIA

The Evergreen State College

WASHINGTON STATE UNIVERSITY

PO Box 641067, Pullman, WA 99164-1067
Phone: 509-335-5586 • Fax: 509-335-4902
E-mail: admiss2@wsu.edu • Web: www.wsu.edu
Support: S • Institution type: 4-year public

LEARNING DISABILITY PROGRAM AND SERVICES

The Disability Resource Center (DRC) assists students who have a disability by providing academic services. The program may also refer students to other service programs that may assist them in achieving their academic goals. DRC will help students overcome potential obstacles so that they may be successful in their area of study. All academic adjustments are authorized on an individual basis. DRC coordinates services for students with LD. The program offers academic support in many areas. To be eligible for assistance, students must be currently enrolled at Washington State University. They also must submit documentation of their disability. For a learning disability, the student must submit a written report that includes test scores and evaluation. It is the student's responsibility to request accommodations if desired. It is important to remember that even though two individuals may have the same disability, they may not necessarily need the same academic adjustments. DRC works with students and instructors to determine and implement appropriate academic adjustments. Many adjustments are simple, creative alternatives for traditional ways of learning.

LD/ADHD ADMISSIONS INFORMATION

College entrance tests required: Yes
Interview required: No
Essay recommended: No
Documentation required for LD: WAIS–R or WISC–R (completed within the past 3 years)
Documentation required for ADHD: WAIS–R or WISC–R
Submitted to: Disability Resource Center
Special Ed. HS course work accepted: Yes

Specific course requirements of all applicants: Yes
Separate application required: NR
# of LD applications submitted each year: NR
# of LD applications accepted yearly: NR
Total # of students receiving LD services: 283
Acceptance into program means acceptance into college: Students must be admitted and enrolled in the university first (they can appeal a denial) and then request services.

ADMISSIONS

All students must meet the general admission requirements. The university looks at the combination of scores on the ACT/SAT and the applicant's high school GPA. The standard admission criteria are based on an index score determined by 75 percent GPA and 25 percent SAT/ACT. Courses required include 3 years of English, 3 years of math, 2 years of science, 2 years of a foreign language, 3 years of social studies, 1 year of an elective. Only 15 percent of new admissions may be admitted under special admission. Documentation of the learning disability and diagnostic tests given less than 3 years before applying to the university are required if requesting accommodations or services.

ADDITIONAL INFORMATION

General assistance to students with learning disabilities includes pre-admission counseling; information about disabilities; referral to appropriate community resources; academic, personal, and career counseling; information about accommodations; information about the laws pertaining to individuals with disabilities; and self-advocacy. Typical academic adjustments for students with learning disabilities may include note-takers and/or audiotape class sessions; alternative testing arrangements; textbook taping or one-on-one readers; extended time for exams; essay exams taken on computer; and use computers with voice output and spellcheckers. Services and accommodations are available for undergraduate and graduate students.

LEARNING DISABILITY PROGRAM/SERVICES

Learning Disability Program/Services: Disability Resource Center (DRC)
Director: Susan Schaeffer, PhD   **Contact Person:** Disability Specialist
  E-mail: schaeff@wsu.edu   **E-mail:** schaeff@wsu.edu
  Telephone: 509-335-1566
  Fax: 509-335-8511

LEARNING DISABILITY SERVICES

Requests for the following services/accommodations will be evaluated individually based on appropriate and current documentation.

Allowed in exams
  Calculator: No
  Dictionary: No
  Computer: Yes
  Spellchecker: Yes
Extended test time: Yes
Scribes: Yes
Proctors: Yes
Oral exams: Yes
Note-takers: Yes

Distraction-reduced environment: Yes
Tape recording in class: Yes
Books on tape from RFBD: Yes
Taping of books not from RFBD: Yes
Accommodations for students with ADHD: Yes
Reading machine: No
Other assistive technology: No
Priority registration: Yes

Added costs for services: No
LD specialists: No
Professional tutors: No
Peer tutors: 50
Max. hours/wk. for services: Unlimited
How professors are notified of LD/ADHD: By student

GENERAL ADMISSIONS INFORMATION

Director of Admissions: Wendy Peterson
Telephone: 509-335-5586

ENTRANCE REQUIREMENTS

Academic units required: 3 English, 3 math, 2 science (1 science lab), 2 foreign language, 3 social studies, 1 history, 1 academic elective. **Academic units recommended:** 4 English, 4 math, 2 science (1 science lab), 2 foreign language, 2 social studies, 1 history, 1 academic elective. High school diploma is required, and GED is accepted. ACT with Writing component required. TOEFL required of all international applicants: minimum paper TOEFL 520, minimum computer TOEFL 190.

Application deadline: Rolling
Notification: Rolling
Average GPA: 3.45
ACT Composite middle 50% range: NR

SAT Math middle 50% range: 500–610
SAT Critical Reading middle 50% range: 480–590
SAT Writing middle 50% range: NR

Graduated top 10% of class: 38%
Graduated top 25% of class: 62%
Graduated top 50% of class: 91%

COLLEGE GRADUATION REQUIREMENTS

Course waivers allowed: Yes
In what course: Foreign language
Course substitutions allowed: Yes
In what course: Foreign language

ADDITIONAL INFORMATION

Environment: The university is located on 600 acres in a small town 80 miles south of Spokane.

Student Body
  Undergrad enrollment: 18,995
  Women: 52%
  Men: 48%
  Percent out-of-state: 8%

Cost Information
  In-state tuition: $5,900
  Out-of-state tuition: $15,072
  Room & board: $6,890
Housing Information
  University housing: Yes
  Percent living on campus: 33%

Greek System
  Fraternity: Yes
  Sorority: Yes
Athletics: Division I

DAVIS AND ELKINS COLLEGE

100 Campus Drive, Elkins, WV 26241
Phone: 304-637-1230 • Fax: 304-637-1800
E-mail: admiss@davisandelkins.edu • Web: www.davisandelkins.edu
Support: SP • Institution type: 4-year private

LEARNING DISABILITY PROGRAM AND SERVICES

Davis and Elkins offers a comprehensive support program for college students with learning disabilities. The goals blend with the college's commitment to diversity and providing a personalized education. The program goes well beyond accommodations or services by providing individualized instruction to meet each student's needs. The goal of the LD program is to enable students diagnosed with LD/ADHD to function to the best of their ability. To meet this goal, each student meets at least weekly for a regularly scheduled session with one of the three experienced learning disabilities specialists. The main focus of these meetings is to develop learning strategies and academic skills. Students may request extra assistance and use the lab as a study area. There is a $2,600 fee for first-year students. Applicants must submit complete and current documentation of their disability.

LD/ADHD ADMISSIONS INFORMATION

College entrance tests required: Yes
Interview required: No
Essay recommended: Yes
Documentation required for LD: Complete psychological and academic battery completed within the past 3 years
Documentation required for ADHD: Complete psychological and academic battery completed within the past 3 years.
Submitted to: Admissions Office and Supported Learning Program

Special Ed. HS course work accepted: No
Specific course requirements of all applicants: Yes
Separate application required: Yes
# of LD applications submitted each year: 30–50
# of LD applications accepted yearly: 25–30
Total # of students receiving LD services: 35
Acceptance into program means acceptance into college: Applications to the university and the LD program are separate.

ADMISSIONS

All applications are screened by the learning disabilities program director and the Director of Admissions. Students must be admitted to Davis and Elkins College prior to being considered for the program. The admissions counselors have been trained to recognize potentially successful students with learning disabilities. Students requesting admission to the program must meet admissions requirements; complete a separate application to the program; send current documentation completed within the past 3 years; provide recommendations for participation in the program by a counselor or a learning specialist; provide a copy of a recent IEP, if available; complete a handwritten essay requesting services and indicating why services are being requested; and have a personal meeting with a member of the Supported Learning Program to discuss needs and expectations.

ADDITIONAL INFORMATION

Services include individual sessions with certified LD specialists, individualized programs focusing on improved writing skills, test-taking techniques, note-taking and textbook usage, and time management strategies. Specialists help students develop a personalized program focusing on improving written work, identifying class expectations and preparing work to that level of expectation, test-taking skills, using textbooks and taking notes, and managing time effectively. Students also receive advising and registration assistance based on assessment information. Personnel in the LD program also assist the students with course selection and registration; orientation to college life; monitoring of classes throughout the year and interpreting feedback from professors; coordinating of tutoring, additional counseling, and career planning; and modifying instructional programs as needed.

LEARNING DISABILITY PROGRAM/SERVICES

Learning Disability Program/Services: Supported Learning Program
Director: Mary Ellen Schubert
  E-mail: schubert@davisandelkins.edu
  Telephone: 304-637-1384
  Fax: 304-637-1482

LEARNING DISABILITY SERVICES

Requests for the following services/accommodations will be evaluated individually based on appropriate and current documentation.

Allowed in exams
  Calculator: Yes
  Dictionary: Yes
  Computer: Yes
  Spellchecker: Yes
Extended test time: Yes
Scribes: Yes
Proctors: Yes
Oral exams: Yes
Note-takers: Yes

Distraction-reduced environment: Yes
Tape recording in class: Yes
Books on tape from RFBD: Yes
Taping of books not from RFBD: Yes
Accommodations for students with ADHD: Yes
Reading machine: No
Other assistive technology: Yes
Priority registration: N/A

Added costs for services: Yes
LD specialists: Yes
Professional tutors: No
Peer tutors: 2–10
Max. hours/wk. for services: Unlimited
How professors are notified of LD/ADHD: By both student and director

GENERAL ADMISSIONS INFORMATION

Director of Admissions: Renee Heckel
Telephone: 304-637-1974

ENTRANCE REQUIREMENTS

Academic units required: 4 English, 3 science (1 science lab), 1 foreign language, 3 social studies, 2 math (must include Algebra I or II and geometry). High school diploma is required, and GED is accepted. ACT with Writing component required. TOEFL required of all international applicants: minimum paper TOEFL 450, minimum computer TOEFL 133.

Application deadline: Rolling
Notification: Rolling
Average GPA: 3.06
ACT Composite middle 50% range: 18–22

SAT Math middle 50% range: 420–510
SAT Critical Reading middle 50% range: 420–530
SAT Writing middle 50% range: NR

Graduated top 10% of class: 12%
Graduated top 25% of class: 33%
Graduated top 50% of class: 71%

COLLEGE GRADUATION REQUIREMENTS

Course waivers allowed: Yes
In what course: Individual requests are reviewed by the dean.
Course substitutions allowed: Yes
In what course: Individual requests are reviewed by the dean.

ADDITIONAL INFORMATION

Environment: The college is located in a community of 10,000 residents in the foothills of the Allegheny Mountain Range.

Student Body
  Undergrad enrollment: 624
  Women: 63%
  Men: 37%
  Percent out-of-state: 23%

Cost Information
  Tuition: $17,210
  Room & board: $6,300
Housing Information
  University housing: Yes
  Percent living on campus: 49%

Greek System
  Fraternity: Yes
  Sorority: Yes
Athletics: Division II

MARSHALL UNIVERSITY

One John Marshall Drive, Huntington, WV 25755
Phone: 304-696-3160 • Fax: 304-696-3135
E-mail: admissions@marshall.edu • Web: www.marshall.edu
Support: SP • Institution type: 4-year public

LEARNING DISABILITY PROGRAM AND SERVICES

Higher Education for Learning Problems (HELP) encourages a feeling of camaraderie among the students enrolled in the program. HELP provides an individual tutoring program in course work, exceptions in testing, and a remedial program. Students work with LD specialists one-on-one to improve reading, writing, and language skills. Counseling is provided on site, and the large professional staff offers a variety of additional services. This program boasts a 95 percent success rate with students.

LD/ADHD ADMISSIONS INFORMATION

College entrance tests required: Yes
Interview required: Yes
Essay recommended: Yes
Documentation required for LD: A copy of the psychological and educational diagnosis. The psychological evaluation must be less than 3 years. The educational evaluation should have been completed within the last year.
Documentation required for ADHD: A copy of the psychological and educational diagnosis. The psychological evaluation must be less than 3 years. The educational evaluation should have been completed within the last year.
Submitted to: Admissions and HELP

Special Ed. HS course work accepted: Yes
Specific course requirements of all applicants: Yes
Separate application required: Yes
# of LD applications submitted each year: 100
# of LD applications accepted yearly: 25–35
Total # of students receiving LD services: 150
Acceptance into program means acceptance into college: Students should apply to HELP first and then request admission to Marshall.

ADMISSIONS

Students with learning disabilities must follow a special admissions procedure. These students must submit an application; an updated psychological and educational evaluation; a one-page, handwritten statement by the student (no assistance) regarding why college is desirable; and two recommendations stating why the recommenders feel the student should attend college. Interviews are required. Marshall also requires a minimum GPA of 2.0, a minimum ACT score of 17 or a minimum SAT score of 810 (tests are unimportant for LD admit), plus 4 years of English, 3 years of social studies, and 2 years of math. Students should schedule an interview before January and submit an application to HELP no less than 1 year in advance of the proposed entry date to college. All applications must be received by December 31. Marshall University has a probationary admission if the reason for a low GPA or low test scores is convincing. There is a required 5-week summer HELP Program for these incoming freshmen.

ADDITIONAL INFORMATION

The summer learning disabilities program is offered through HELP to incoming freshmen with learning disabilities. The program includes teachers with master's degrees in learning disabilities, a graduate assistant for each teacher who assists with tutoring course work (tutors are matched to students who have a learning style compatible to the teaching style of the tutor), small study groups with no more than five members to each group, and training in note-taking, study skills, test-taking, and time management. The program strives to improve students' basic skills in reading, spelling, written language, and mathematics and the students' self-esteem and confidence. The cost is $1,000 for West Virginia residents, $1,300 for Metro area residents, and $2,000 for non–West Virginia residents. This does not include registration for classes students may take through the university. Students sign a release allowing HELP to talk to professors and parents. There is also a summer program for elementary and secondary students with learning disabilities.

LEARNING DISABILITY PROGRAM/SERVICES

Learning Disability Program/Services: Higher Education for Learning Problems (HELP)
Director: Lynne M. Weston, EdS
  E-mail: weston@marshall.edu
  Telephone: 304-696-6317
  Fax: 304-696-3231
Contact Person: Diane Williams
  E-mail: weston@marshall.edu
  Telephone: 304-696-6314
  Fax: 304-696-3231

LEARNING DISABILITY SERVICES

Requests for the following services/accommodations will be evaluated individually based on appropriate and current documentation.

Allowed in exams
  Calculator: Yes
  Dictionary: Yes
  Computer: Yes
  Spellchecker: Yes
Extended test time: Yes
Scribes: Yes
Proctors: Yes
Oral exams: Yes
Note-takers: Yes

Distraction-reduced environment: Yes
Tape recording in class: Yes
Books on tape from RFBD: Yes
Taping of books not from RFBD: Yes
**Accommodations for students with
  ADHD:** Yes
Reading machine: Yes
Other assistive technology: Yes
Priority registration: Yes

Added costs for services: Yes
LD specialists: Yes
Professional tutors: 10
Peer tutors: No
Max. hours/wk. for services:
  Unlimited
**How professors are notified of
  LD/ADHD:** By both student and
  director

GENERAL ADMISSIONS INFORMATION

Director of Admissions: Dr. Tammy Johnson
Telephone: 304-696-3160

ENTRANCE REQUIREMENTS

Academic units required: 4 English, 3 math, 3 science (2 science labs), 3 social studies. High school diploma is required, and GED is accepted. ACT with or without Writing component accepted. TOEFL required of all international applicants: minimum paper TOEFL 500, minimum computer TOEFL 173.

Application deadline: Rolling
Notification: Rolling
Average GPA: 3.30
ACT Composite middle 50% range:
  20–25

SAT Math middle 50% range:
  450–570
**SAT Critical Reading middle 50%
  range:** 460–570
SAT Writing middle 50% range:
  450–560

Graduated top 10% of class: NR
Graduated top 25% of class: NR
Graduated top 50% of class: NR

COLLEGE GRADUATION REQUIREMENTS

Course waivers allowed: Yes
In what course: Foreign language, math
Course substitutions allowed: Yes
In what course: Foreign language, math

ADDITIONAL INFORMATION

Environment: Marshall University has a 55-acre urban campus located 140 miles east of Lexington, Kentucky.

Student Body
  Undergrad enrollment: 8,931
  Women: 56%
  Men: 44%
  Percent out-of-state: 19%

Cost Information
  In-state tuition: $4,150
  Out-of-state tuition: $11,054
  Room & board: $6,492
Housing Information
  University housing: Yes
  Percent living on campus: 20%

Greek System
  Fraternity: Yes
  Sorority: Yes
Athletics: Division I

WEST VIRGINIA UNIVERSITY

Admissions Office, PO Box 6009, Morgantown, WV 26506-6009
Phone: 304-293-2121 • Fax: 304-293-3080
E-mail: go2wvu@mail.wvu.edu • Web: www.wvu.edu
Support: S • Institution type: 4-year public

LEARNING DISABILITY PROGRAM AND SERVICES

The Office of Disability Services is available to all students on the campus of West Virginia University. Services are provided to better enable qualified students with disabilities to maximize their academic potential. It is the student's responsibility to provide documentation for the diagnosis prior to receiving accommodations based on that disability. Each student's academic accommodations will be determined by the university on an individual basis. To meet the adult criteria of disability under federal laws, individuals must provide documentation of how the significant impairment substantially limits their academic functioning. A "significant impairment" means below-average functioning. An IEP is not documentation of a disability for the purposes of providing accommodations at the college level.

LD/ADHD ADMISSIONS INFORMATION

College entrance tests required: Yes
Interview required: No
Essay recommended: No
Documentation required for LD: Recent psychoeducational evaluation
Documentation required for ADHD: Yes
Submitted to: Office of Disability Services
Special Ed. HS course work accepted: No

Specific course requirements of all applicants: Yes
Separate application required: Yes
# of LD applications submitted each year: NR
# of LD applications accepted yearly: NR
Total # of students receiving LD services: NR
Acceptance into program means acceptance into college: Students must be admitted and enrolled in the university first (they can appeal a denial) and then request services.

ADMISSIONS

There is no special admissions process for students with LD and ADHD. In-state students must have a 2.0 GPA, and out-of-state students must have a 2.25 GPA. Additionally, all applicants must have 4 years of English, 3 years of social studies, 3 years of math, and 2 years of science lab, and course work in a foreign language is recommended. Students are not encouraged to self-disclose a disability in a personal statement during the application process. Appropriate services/accommodations will be determined after the student is admitted.

ADDITIONAL INFORMATION

Requirements for the documentation of an LD include the following: a signed, dated comprehensive psychoeducational evaluation report indicating how the LD impacts academic performance and contributes to a significant impairment in academic functioning. The report should address aptitude, achievement, and processing and should include the WAIS and full Woodcock-Johnson battery. A description of the functional limitations that impact against the educational effort must be included in the diagnostic report. Additionally, a documented history of previous accommodations received should be included. Documentation of ADHD must be in the form of a signed and dated report by a psychiatrist, neuropsychologist, or licensed psychologist trained in the differential diagnosis. Additional information is required. There are no LD specialists on staff; however, counselors are available to provide services to all students. Some accommodations that are available with appropriate documentation include priority registration, course substitutions, extended testing times, note-takers, distraction-free environments, books on tape, and assistive technology.

LEARNING DISABILITY PROGRAM/SERVICES

Learning Disability Program/Services: Office of Disability Services
Director: Jennifer McIntosh
  E-mail: jennifer.mcintosh@mail.wvu.edu
  Telephone: 304-293-5496
  Fax: 304-293-3861

Contact Person: Rebecca Berger
  E-mail: jennifer.mcintosh@mail.wvu.edu
  Telephone: 304-299-6700
  Fax: 304-293-3861

LEARNING DISABILITY SERVICES

Requests for the following services/accommodations will be evaluated individually based on appropriate and current documentation.

Allowed in exams
  Calculator: No
  Dictionary: Yes
  Computer: Yes
  Spellchecker: Yes
Extended test time: Yes
Scribes: Yes
Proctors: No
Oral exams: Yes
Note-takers: Yes

Distraction-reduced environment: Yes
Tape recording in class: Yes
Books on tape from RFBD: No
Taping of books not from RFBD: Yes
Accommodations for students with
  ADHD: Yes
Reading machine: No
Other assistive technology: Yes
Priority registration: Yes

Added costs for services: No
LD specialists: No
Professional tutors: No
Peer tutors: 65
Max. hours/wk. for services:
  Unlimited
How professors are notified of
  LD/ADHD: By student

GENERAL ADMISSIONS INFORMATION

Director of Admissions: Cheng Khoo
Telephone: 304-293-4515

ENTRANCE REQUIREMENTS

Academic units required: 4 English, 3 math, 3 science (2 science labs), 3 social studies. **Academic units recommended:** 2 foreign language. High school diploma is required, and GED is accepted. ACT with Writing component required. TOEFL required of all international applicants: minimum paper TOEFL 550, minimum computer TOEFL 173.

Application deadline: Rolling
Notification: Rolling
Average GPA: 3.00
ACT Composite middle 50% range:
  20–26

SAT Math middle 50% range:
  480–580
SAT Critical Reading middle 50%
  range: 460–560
SAT Writing middle 50% range: NR

Graduated top 10% of class: 17%
Graduated top 25% of class: 40%
Graduated top 50% of class: 73%

COLLEGE GRADUATION REQUIREMENTS

Course waivers allowed: Yes
In what course: Foreign language
Course substitutions allowed: Yes
In what course: Foreign language

ADDITIONAL INFORMATION

Environment: The campus is located 70 miles from Pittsburgh, Pennsylvania.

Student Body
  Undergrad enrollment: 20,590
  Women: 46%
  Men: 54%
  Percent out-of-state: 43%

Cost Information
  In-state tuition: $4,476
  Out-of-state tuition: $13,840
  Room & board: $6,630
Housing Information
  University housing: Yes
  Percent living on campus: 26%

Greek System
  Fraternity: Yes
  Sorority: Yes
Athletics: Division I

WEST VIRGINIA WESLEYAN COLLEGE

59 College Avenue, Buckhannon, WV 26201
Phone: 304-473-8510 • Fax: 304-473-8108
E-mail: admission@wvwc.edu • Web: www.wvwc.edu
Support: SP• Institution type: 4-year private

LEARNING DISABILITY PROGRAM AND SERVICES

The college holds a strong commitment to providing excellent support to students with documented disabilities. An individually structured program has been designed to accommodate students with varying needs. Master-level professionals in the fields of learning disabilities, reading, education, and counseling work to help each student design strategies for academic success. Accommodation plans are determined through a review of the documentation provided by the student and the recommendations of the student's comprehensive advisor who works closely with each individual. Students who want to receive LD services must submit an educational assessment, completed within the last 2 to 3 years, to the director of the Student Academic Support Services. Documentation must include the WAIS and the Woodcock-Johnson Standard Achievement Battery. Alternate achievement assessment will be considered with the approval of the director. Both numeric scores and a narrative report that interpret a perceived or diagnosed LD are required. A copy of the IEP would be helpful. Documentation must be submitted in a timely manner to plan specialized advising, preferential registration, and the implementation of the appropriate accommodations.

LD/ADHD ADMISSIONS INFORMATION

College entrance tests required: Yes
Interview required: No
Essay recommended: Yes
Documentation required for LD: Psychoeducational evaluation. Both narrative and numeric reporting is necessary.
Documentation required for ADHD: Psychological or medical documentation.
Submitted to: Admissions Office and SASS
Special Ed. HS course work accepted: Yes

Specific course requirements of all applicants: Yes
Separate application required: No
# of LD applications submitted each year: 80–100
# of LD applications accepted yearly: 70–90
Total # of students receiving LD services: 75–90
Acceptance into program means acceptance into college: Students are admitted jointly into the college and SASS.

ADMISSIONS

The director of Student Academic Support Services reviews the application of students who self-disclose a LD or ADHD. Applicants are encouraged to submit a psychological evaluation if they believe it will help develop an accurate picture of student potential. Interviews are encouraged but not required unless it is determined that an interview could help the admissions team gain a better understanding of the applicant. The Academic Dean has the authority to offer special admission to some students not admitted through the regular application process. Application decisions are made jointly by the Director of Admissions and the Director of Student Academic Support Services. No foreign language is required for admission. The mid 50 percent for ACT is 18–27, and for the SAT, 800–1400. It is to the student's advantage to self-disclose a disability. If a student chooses to self-disclose, the educational assessment is interpreted by the Director of Special Services, who may recommend admission based on the evaluation of the student's potential for success in college.

ADDITIONAL INFORMATION

SASS provides the following services when appropriate: individualized support from a comprehensive advisor who plans and coordinates accommodations for student needs and acts as a liaison with other departments, annual individualized accommodation plan with yearly updates of appropriate accommodations, preferential registration and specialized academic advising for the first three semesters, extended time and separate testing location for qualified students, limited noncredit practical as needed to support composition courses, note-takers when necessary and appropriate, alternative textbook formats, and individual peer tutoring. Some class offerings include college study strategies, developmental math, Lindamood-Bell Learning Program, memory techniques, note-taking, techniques of reading, test-taking, time management, and visual thinking.

LEARNING DISABILITY PROGRAM/SERVICES

Learning Disability Program/Services: Learning Center
Director: Dr. Shawn Mahoney Kuba
  E-mail: kuba_s@wvwc.edu
  Telephone: 304-473-8563
  Fax: 304-473-8497
Contact Person: Shawn Mahoney Kuba
  E-mail: kuba_s@wvwc.edu

LEARNING DISABILITY SERVICES

Requests for the following services/accommodations will be evaluated individually based on appropriate and current documentation.

Allowed in exams		
Calculator: Yes	**Distraction-reduced environment:** Yes	**Added costs for services:** No
Dictionary: Yes	**Tape recording in class:** Yes	**LD specialists:** Yes
Computer: Yes	**Books on tape from RFBD:** Yes	**Professional tutors:** 5
Spellchecker: Yes	**Taping of books not from RFBD:** Yes	**Peer tutors:** 14–18
Extended test time: Yes	**Accommodations for students with**	**Max. hours/wk. for services:** 57
Scribes: Yes	**ADHD:** Yes	**How professors are notified of**
Proctors: Yes	**Reading machine:** Yes	**LD/ADHD:** By student
Oral exams: Yes	**Other assistive technology:** Yes	
Note-takers: Yes	**Priority registration:** Yes	

GENERAL ADMISSIONS INFORMATION

Director of Admissions: Christopher Coons
Telephone: 304-473-8510

ENTRANCE REQUIREMENTS

Academic units recommended: 4 English, 3 math, 3 science (3 science labs), 2 foreign language, 3 social studies. High school diploma is required, and GED is accepted. ACT with or without Writing component accepted. TOEFL required of all international applicants: minimum paper TOEFL 500, minimum computer TOEFL 200.

Application deadline: Rolling	**SAT Math middle 50% range:**	**Graduated top 10% of class:** 24%
Notification: Rolling	435–560	**Graduated top 25% of class:** 51%
Average GPA: 3.29	**SAT Critical Reading middle 50%**	**Graduated top 50% of class:** 77%
ACT Composite middle 50% range:	range: 440–560	
20–26	**SAT Writing middle 50% range:**	
	430–550	

COLLEGE GRADUATION REQUIREMENTS

Course waivers allowed: No
Course substitutions allowed: No

ADDITIONAL INFORMATION

Environment: The college is located on 80 acres 135 miles from Pittsburgh in the Appalachian foothills.

Student Body	Cost Information	Greek System
Undergrad enrollment: 1,153	**Tuition:** $21,300	**Fraternity:** Yes
Women: 54%	**Room & board:** $5,550	**Sorority:** Yes
Men: 46%	**Housing Information**	**Athletics:** Division II
Percent out-of-state: 47%	**University housing:** Yes	
	Percent living on campus: 81%	

ALVERNO COLLEGE

3400 South 43rd Street, PO Box 343922, Milwaukee, WI 53234-3922
Phone: 414-382-6100 • Fax: 414-382-6354
E-mail: admissions@alverno.edu • Web: www.alverno.edu
Support: S • Institution type: 4-year private

LEARNING DISABILITY PROGRAM AND SERVICES

Alverno College is a small liberal arts college for women with approximately 2,000 students. The Instructional Services Center (ISC) provides academic support to Alverno students and assists Alverno applicants in meeting admissions requirements. ISC offers courses in reading, writing, critical thinking, math, and algebra to develop academic skills as required on the basis of new student assessment results. ISC also offers tutorial support, course-based study groups, and workshops to provide an opportunity for small groups of students to study together under the direction of a peer tutor or an ISC teacher. There is also a Coordinator of Support Services for Students with Disabilities who assists the student to meet her academic potential by understanding of her learning needs, developing strategies and accommodations to maximize her strengths, and developing of self-advocacy with faculty.

LD/ADHD ADMISSIONS INFORMATION

College entrance tests required: Yes
Interview required: No
Essay recommended: No
Documentation required for LD: WAIS–III, WJ-III, WRAT-R—all completed within the past 4 to 6 years
Documentation required for ADHD: Relevant historical information, description of current functional limitations pertaining to academic settings, and recommendations for strategies and accommodations by qualified professional.
Submitted to: Student Accessibility
Special Ed. HS course work accepted: NR

Specific course requirements of all applicants: Yes
Separate application required: No
# of LD applications submitted each year: NR
# of LD applications accepted yearly: NR
Total # of students receiving LD services: 45
Acceptance into program means acceptance into college: Students must be admitted and enrolled in the university first (they can appeal a denial) and then request services.

ADMISSIONS

Admission criteria are the same for all students coming directly from high school. General admission requirements include 19-plus ACT; 17 academic credits in college-prep courses with recommendations, including 4 years of English, 2 years of a foreign language, 3 years of math, 3 years of science, and 3 years of social studies; a minimum GPA of 2.5; and a class rank within the top half of the applicant's graduating class. There is a college transition program for students who do not meet the admissions criteria but have academic potential.

ADDITIONAL INFORMATION

Classes are offered at a beginning level in reading, writing, math, and algebra. Students may not substitute courses for math courses required to graduate, but intensive assistance is provided. Tutoring is provided through ISC, and an academic support group for students with LD meets every 2 to 3 weeks to discuss topics such as self-advocacy, problem solving, writing letters, and communicating with professors. The college has a Math Resource Center and a Writing Resource Center available for all students. Alverno's unique emphasis on learning the abilities needed to put knowledge to use—commonly called "ability-based education"—has gained national praise. Alverno College's faculty has developed and implemented ability-based undergraduate education, redefining education in terms of abilities needed for effectiveness in the worlds of work, family, and civic community. The distinctive feature of an ability-based approach is the expectation that students should be able to do something with what they know. The specific abilities identified by the faculty as central to the approach to liberal arts and professional education are communication, analysis, problem solving, valuing in decision making, social interaction, development of a global perspective, effective citizenship, and aesthetic engagement.

LEARNING DISABILITY PROGRAM/SERVICES

Learning Disability Program/Services: Student Accessibility
Director: Colleen Barnett
 E-mail: colleen.barnett@alverno.edu
 Telephone: 414-382-6026
 Fax: 414-382-6354

LEARNING DISABILITY SERVICES

Requests for the following services/accommodations will be evaluated individually based on appropriate and current documentation.

Allowed in exams
 Calculator: Yes
 Dictionary: Yes
 Computer: Yes
 Spellchecker: Yes
Extended test time: Yes
Scribes: Yes
Proctors: Yes
Oral exams: Yes
Note-takers: Yes

Distraction-reduced environment: Yes
Tape recording in class: Yes
Books on tape from RFBD: Yes
Taping of books not from RFBD: Yes
Accommodations for students with
 ADHD: Yes
Reading machine: Yes
Other assistive technology: Yes
Priority registration: No

Added costs for services: No
LD specialists: No
Professional tutors: 10
Peer tutors: 75
Max. hours/wk. for services: NR
How professors are notified of
 LD/ADHD: By both student and
 director

GENERAL ADMISSIONS INFORMATION

Director of Admissions: Mary Kay Farrell
Telephone: 414-382-6100

ENTRANCE REQUIREMENTS

Academic units required: 4 English, 3 math, 3 science, 3 social studies, 2 foreign language. High school diploma is required, and GED is accepted. ACT with or without Writing component accepted. TOEFL required of all international applicants: minimum paper TOEFL 520, minimum computer TOEFL 190.

Application deadline: Rolling
Notification: Rolling
Average GPA: 3.04
ACT Composite middle 50% range:
 17–22

SAT Math middle 50% range: NR
SAT Critical Reading middle 50%
 range: NR
SAT Writing middle 50% range: NR

Graduated top 10% of class: NR
Graduated top 25% of class: NR
Graduated top 50% of class: NR

COLLEGE GRADUATION REQUIREMENTS

Course waivers allowed: No
Course substitutions allowed: No

ADDITIONAL INFORMATION

Environment: The campus is located in a suburban area on the southwest side of Milwaukee.

Student Body
 Undergrad enrollment: 2,123
 Women: 100%
 Percent out-of-state: 2%

Cost Information
 Tuition: $15,994
 Room & board: $5,954
Housing Information
 University housing: Yes
 Percent living on campus: 9%

Greek System
 Fraternity: No
 Sorority: Yes
 Athletics: NCAA Div. III

Alverno College

BELOIT COLLEGE

700 College Street, Beloit, WI 53511
Phone: 608-363-2500 • Fax: 608-363-2075
E-mail: admiss@beloit.edu • Web: www.beloit.edu
Support: S • Institution type: 4-year private

LEARNING DISABILITY PROGRAM AND SERVICES

The goal of the Educational Development Program (EDP) at Beloit College is to provide support services and accommodations individually tailored to the needs of each student to enable the successful completion of the baccalaureate degree. EDP is a campus resource that provides opportunities for students to succeed. Beloit College students can qualify for EDP services based on any one of the following: parents' educational attainment, family income, and documented need for accommodations. EDP is funded through Beloit College in cooperation with the U.S. Department of Education. Participation is on a first-come, first-served basis for those who qualify and by the discretion of project staff.

LD/ADHD ADMISSIONS INFORMATION

College entrance tests required: Yes
Interview required: No
Essay recommended: N/A
Documentation required for LD: Psychoeducational
  evaluation completed within the past 3 years
Documentation required for ADHD: Yes
Submitted to: Educational Development Program
Special Ed. HS course work accepted: Yes

Specific course requirements of all applicants: Yes
Separate application required: No
# of LD applications submitted each year: NR
# of LD applications accepted yearly: NR
Total # of students receiving LD services: 17–23
**Acceptance into program means acceptance into
  college:** Students must be admitted to and enrolled in the
  university first and then request services.

ADMISSIONS

There is no special admissions procedure for students with learning disabilities. Each student is reviewed individually, and the final decision is made by the Office of Admissions. The college is competitive in admissions, but there are no cutoffs for GPA or test scores. Sixteen academic courses are required for admission. Courses recommended include 4 years of English, 3 years of math, 3 years of science, 3 years of science lab, 2 years of a foreign language, and 3 years of social studies.

ADDITIONAL INFORMATION

The Beloit Learning Resource Center offers additional services to the students in the areas of tutoring, study skills and time management, math and science tutoring and study groups, improvement of writing skills, advising, mentoring, reading speed and comprehension, and computer usage. Counseling services are offered in personal counseling, career guidance, and crisis intervention. Individual and self-help programs and small group workshops are available. Assessment tools are offered to help students determine individual strengths and weakness in reading rate, comprehension, and vocabulary, and there are a variety of handouts covering a wide range of academic skill areas such as studying, math, footnoting, and test-taking.

LEARNING DISABILITY PROGRAM/SERVICES

Learning Disability Program/Services: Learning Support Services Center/EDP
Director: Diane Arnzen
  E-mail: arnzend@beloit.edu
  Telephone: 608-363-2572
  Fax: 608-363-7059

LEARNING DISABILITY SERVICES

Requests for the following services/accommodations will be evaluated individually based on appropriate and current documentation.

Allowed in exams
  Calculator: Yes
  Dictionary: Yes
  Computer: Yes
  Spellchecker: Yes
Extended test time: Yes
Scribes: Yes
Proctors: Yes
Oral exams: Yes
Note-takers: Yes

Distraction-reduced environment: Yes
Tape recording in class: Yes
Books on tape from RFBD: Yes
Taping of books not from RFBD: Yes
**Accommodations for students with
  ADHD:** Yes
Reading machine: No
Other assistive technology: Yes
Priority registration: No

Added costs for services: No
LD specialists: No
Professional tutors: No
Peer tutors: 70–95
Max. hours/wk. for services: N/A
**How professors are notified of
  LD/ADHD:** By both student and
director

GENERAL ADMISSIONS INFORMATION

Director of Admissions: Nancy Monnich Benedict, Vice President of Enrollment
Telephone: 608-363-2380

ENTRANCE REQUIREMENTS

Academic units recommended: 4 English, 3 math, 3 science (3 science labs), 2 foreign language, 3 social studies, 4 history. High school diploma is required, and GED is accepted. ACT with or without Writing component accepted. TOEFL required of all international applicants: minimum paper TOEFL 525, minimum computer TOEFL 197.

Application deadline: Rolling
Notification: Rolling
Average GPA: 3.46
ACT Composite middle 50% range:
  25–29

SAT Math middle 50% range:
  560–650
**SAT Critical Reading middle 50%
  range:** 600–730
SAT Writing middle 50% range: NR

Graduated top 10% of class: 35%
Graduated top 25% of class: 70%
Graduated top 50% of class: 97%

COLLEGE GRADUATION REQUIREMENTS

Course waivers allowed: No
Course substitutions allowed: No

ADDITIONAL INFORMATION

Environment: The college is located 50 miles south of Madison and 90 miles northwest of Chicago.

Student Body
  Undergrad enrollment: 1,329
  Women: 58%
  Men: 42%
  Percent out-of-state: 81%

Cost Information
  Tuition: $29,980
  Room & board: $6,408
Housing Information
  University housing: Yes
  Percent living on campus: 87%

Greek System
  Fraternity: Yes
  Sorority: Yes
Athletics: Division III

MARIAN COLLEGE OF FOND DU LAC

45 South National Avenue, Fond du Lac, WI 54935
Phone: 920-923-7650 • Fax: 920-923-8755
E-mail: admissions@mariancollege.edu • Web: www.mariancollege.edu
Support: S • Institution type: 4-year private

LEARNING DISABILITY PROGRAM AND SERVICES

The Student Development Center offers services for students with learning disabilities. The ultimate goal of the center is to provide the academic, social, and emotional support to students so they may maintain at least a 2.0 GPA and persevere to earn a college degree. The Student Development Center strives to provide a neutral area within which students can be accepted for who they are and can begin moving toward meeting their own personal and academic goals.

LD/ADHD ADMISSIONS INFORMATION

College entrance tests required: Yes
Interview required: No
Essay recommended: No
Documentation required for LD: Psychoeducational
  evaluation completed within 5 years
Documentation required for ADHD: Psychoeducational
  evaluation completed within 3 years
Submitted to: Disability Services
Special Ed. HS course work accepted: No

Specific course requirements of all applicants: Yes
Separate application required: No
# of LD applications submitted each year: 15–20
# of LD applications accepted yearly: 15–20
Total # of students receiving LD services: NR
**Acceptance into program means acceptance into
  college:** Students must be admitted to and enrolled in the
  university first and then request services.

ADMISSIONS

There is no special application or admissions procedure for students with learning disabilities. Admission criteria include a 2.0 GPA, a class rank within top 50 percent, and an ACT score of 18. All students, not just those with LD, are asked to meet two-thirds of these criteria. Students who do not meet two-thirds may be admitted on probation through a program called EXCEL. Students will be asked to submit 3 letters of recommendation supporting their ability to succeed in college-level course work. Students also may be asked to schedule a visit to Marian for a pre-admission interview during which their skills, attitudes, motivation, and self-understanding will be informally assessed. Students admitted provisionally may be admitted with limited credit status and may be required to take a freshman seminar course. Special education course work is accepted, but students are encouraged to be fully mainstreamed by senior year with minimal monitoring. Students who self-disclose their disability are given information on services available through the Student Development Center.

ADDITIONAL INFORMATION

Disability Services offers the following services and accommodations to students with appropriate documentation: note-takers, audio books, audio players, scan and read software, distraction-free test environments, extended exam times, and test readers/scribes. The following support is also provided: organizational and study skills training, liaison with instructors/advisors, consultation, advocacy, referrals, and resource materials. The peer tutoring program helps students gain the confidence and skills necessary to successfully complete course work. To receive assistance, students must disclose their disability. Skill classes are offered in English, math, and study skills, as well as computer-assisted instruction in math and basic skill areas. Other services include information on community, state, and national resources, assistance in writing and proofreading papers and assignments, tutors (individual and group), liaison service, assistance in working with instructors, and course scheduling. Calculators are allowed in exams for students with a documented disability in math, and dictionaries are allowed in exams for students with a documented disability in written language. Assistance is determined for each individual based on assessment. All students have access to the tutoring program, the Writing Lab, and the Computer Lab. Services are available for undergraduate and graduate students.

LEARNING DISABILITY PROGRAM/SERVICES

Learning Disability Program/Services: Disability Services
Director: Lisa Rogers
  E-mail: lmrogers65@mariancollege.edu
  Telephone: 920-923-7162
  Fax: 920-926-2113

LEARNING DISABILITY SERVICES

Requests for the following services/accommodations will be evaluated individually based on appropriate and current documentation.

Allowed in exams
  Calculator: Yes
  Dictionary: Yes
  Computer: Yes
  Spellchecker: Yes
Extended test time: Yes
Scribes: Yes
Proctors: Yes
Oral exams: Yes
Note-takers: Yes

Distraction-reduced environment: Yes
Tape recording in class: Yes
Books on tape from RFBD: Yes
Taping of books not from RFBD: No
Accommodations for students with ADHD: Yes
Reading machine: Yes
Other assistive technology: Yes
Priority registration: Yes

Added costs for services: No
LD specialists: No
Professional tutors: No
Peer tutors: Yes
Max. hours/wk. for services: Unlimited
How professors are notified of LD/ADHD: By director

GENERAL ADMISSIONS INFORMATION

Director of Admissions: Eric Peterson
Telephone: 920-923-7643

ENTRANCE REQUIREMENTS

Academic units required: 4 English, 2 math, 1 science (1 science lab), 1 history. **Academic units recommended:** 3 math, 2 science, 2 foreign language. High school diploma is required, and GED is accepted. ACT with or without Writing component accepted. TOEFL required of all international applicants: minimum paper TOEFL 525, minimum computer TOEFL 193.

Application deadline: Rolling
Notification: Rolling
Average GPA: 3.05
ACT Composite middle 50% range: 18–22

SAT Math middle 50% range: NR
SAT Critical Reading middle 50% range: NR
SAT Writing middle 50% range: NR

Graduated top 10% of class: 9%
Graduated top 25% of class: 29%
Graduated top 50% of class: 66%

COLLEGE GRADUATION REQUIREMENTS

Course waivers allowed: No
Course substitutions allowed: Yes
In what course: Directed study-type classes to fulfill math requirement or students can work one-on-one with a tutor and weekly with an instructor. Other students have been given one year to complete a semester course. Students must attempt the required course.

ADDITIONAL INFORMATION

Environment: Marian College is located on 50 acres in a suburb of Fond du Lac, 60 miles north of Milwaukee.

Student Body
  Undergrad enrollment: 1,969
  Women: 73%
  Men: 27%
  Percent out-of-state: 4%

Cost Information
  Tuition: $17,300
  Room & board: $5,200
Housing Information
  University housing: Yes
  Percent living on campus: 29%

Greek System
  Fraternity: Yes
  Sorority: Yes
Athletics: Division III

MARQUETTE UNIVERSITY

PO Box 1881, Milwaukee, WI 53201-1881
Phone: 414-288-7302 • Fax: 414-288-3764
E-mail: admissions@marquette.edu • Web: www.marquette.edu
Support: S • Institution type: 4-year private

LEARNING DISABILITY PROGRAM AND SERVICES

The Office of Disability Services (ODS) is the designated office at Marquette University to coordinate accommodations for all students with identified and documented disabilities. Accommodations are determined on a case-by-case basis. To obtain educational opportunities, the student must seek assistance in a timely manner, preferably prior to the start of classes. Relevant documentation from an appropriate licensed professional that gives a diagnosis of the disability and how it impacts the student's participation in courses, programs, jobs, and activities at Marquette is important. The student and a staff member from ODS will discuss the student's disability and how it will impact the requirements of the student's courses. Based on this evaluation, the ODS coordinator provides a range of individualized accommodations. For students who suspect they have a disability, a free informal screening for possible LD or ADHD can be provided by ODS. This screening process can determine if the student should have a formal testing battery done.

LD/ADHD ADMISSIONS INFORMATION

College entrance tests required: Yes
Interview required: No
Essay recommended: No
Documentation required for LD: Psychoeducational
  evaluation
Documentation required for ADHD: Yes
Submitted to: Office of Disability Services
Special Ed. HS course work accepted: No

Specific course requirements of all applicants: Yes
Separate application required: No
# of LD applications submitted each year: NR
# of LD applications accepted yearly: NR
Total # of students receiving LD services: NR
**Acceptance into program means acceptance into
  college:** Students must be admitted to and enrolled in the
  university first and then request services.

ADMISSIONS

There is no special admissions process for students with LD and ADHD. All applicants for admission must meet the same admission criteria. Marquette requires applicants to rank in the top 50 percent of their high school class (most rank in the top 25 percent) and have 4 years of English, 2–4 years of math and science, 2–3 years of social studies, 2 years of a foreign language, and additional subjects. Freshman Frontier Program offers admission to a small number of incoming freshman who show potential, though they may have low ACT/SAT scores but a reasonable GPA.

ADDITIONAL INFORMATION

ODS provides a number of accommodations for students with LD and ADHD, including taped texts and alternative testing arrangements. If a student's disability requires a backup note-taker, ODS assists students in locating or hiring note-takers and will provide non-carbon-required paper. Other methods of acquiring class material may include the use of a tape recorder in class for later transcription and photocopying class notes or copies of lecture notes. Advance notice of assignments, alternative ways of completing an assignment, computer technology, assistive listening devices, taped textbooks, and course or program modifications are also available. To assist students with reading-related disabilities, the Kurzweil Omni 3000 Education System is available. Students also have access to the Campus Writing Center, tutors, and general study skills assistance from the Office of Student Educational Services.

LEARNING DISABILITY PROGRAM/SERVICES

Learning Disability Program/Services: Office of Disability Services
Director: Karen Desotelle
 E-mail: Karen.Desotelle@marquette.edu
 Telephone: 414-288-1645
 Fax: 414-288-5799

LEARNING DISABILITY SERVICES

Requests for the following services/accommodations will be evaluated individually based on appropriate and current documentation.

Allowed in exams
 Calculator: Yes
 Dictionary: Yes
 Computer: Yes
 Spellchecker: Yes
Extended test time: Yes
Scribes: Yes
Proctors: Yes
Oral exams: Yes
Note-takers: Yes

Distraction-reduced environment: Yes
Tape recording in class: Yes
Books on tape from RFBD: Yes
Taping of books not from RFBD: Yes
Accommodations for students with ADHD: Yes
Reading machine: Yes
Other assistive technology: No
Priority registration: Yes

Added costs for services: No
LD specialists: No
Professional tutors: No
Peer tutors: 35–55
Max. hours/wk. for services: NR
How professors are notified of LD/ADHD: By student

GENERAL ADMISSIONS INFORMATION

Director of Admissions: Robert Blust
Telephone: 414-288-7004

ENTRANCE REQUIREMENTS

Academic units required: 4 English, 2 math, 2 science (2 science labs), 2 foreign language, 2 social studies, 2 academic electives. **Academic units recommended:** 4 English, 4 math, 3 science (3 science labs), 2 foreign language, 3 social studies, 5 academic electives. High school diploma is required, and GED is accepted. ACT without Writing component accepted. TOEFL required of all international applicants: minimum paper TOEFL 520, minimum computer TOEFL 190.

Application deadline: 12/1
Notification: 1/31
Average GPA: NR
ACT Composite middle 50% range: 24–29

SAT Math middle 50% range: 550–660
SAT Critical Reading middle 50% range: 540–640
SAT Writing middle 50% range: 530–630

Graduated top 10% of class: 35%
Graduated top 25% of class: 67%
Graduated top 50% of class: 92%

COLLEGE GRADUATION REQUIREMENTS

Course waivers allowed: Yes
In what course: Foreign language, math, and others as appropriate
Course substitutions allowed: Yes
In what course: Foreign language, math, and others as appropriate

ADDITIONAL INFORMATION

Environment: Marquette University located in Milwaukee, 1 hour south of Madison and 1 hour north of Chicago.

Student Body
 Undergrad enrollment: 7,812
 Women: 54%
 Men: 46%
 Percent out-of-state: 53%

Cost Information
 Tuition: $24,670
 Room & board: $8,120
Housing Information
 University housing: Yes
 Percent living on campus: 52%

Greek System
 Fraternity: Yes
 Sorority: Yes
Athletics: Division I

Marquette University

RIPON COLLEGE

PO Box 248, Ripon, WI 54971
Phone: 920-748-8114 • Fax: 920-748-8335
E-mail: adminfo@ripon.edu • Web: www.ripon.edu
Support: S • Institution type: 4-year private

LEARNING DISABILITY PROGRAM AND SERVICES

The Educational Development Program (EDP) provides a wide variety of services on the campus, including academic and personal counseling, study skills information, and tutoring. Although the focus of the program is on first-generation students, students of higher need, and students who are learning disabled, other students who feel they might qualify are encouraged to contact the EDP office. EDP is a voluntary program that has been in existence at Ripon College since 1974. For the many students who have used its services, EDP has provided a network of support for academic, financial, and personal concerns. A group of peer contacts serves EDP by meeting regularly with students to facilitate communication between EDP participants and the office staff. For students who qualify, EDP offers free tutoring in specific subject areas. (All-campus tutoring is also available.) The tutors are upperclass students who have been recommended by their professors and trained by the EDP staff. These tutors serve as a supplement to faculty assistance. The aim of the tutoring program is to help students develop independent learning skills and improve their course grades. Although federal guidelines require a restriction on who qualifies, the door to EDP remains open to all eligible students.

LD/ADHD ADMISSIONS INFORMATION

College entrance tests required: Yes
Interview required: Yes
Essay recommended: No
Documentation required for LD: Psychoeducational evaluation
Documentation required for ADHD: Complete test file
Submitted to: Educational Development Program
Special Ed. HS course work accepted: No

Specific course requirements of all applicants: Yes
Separate application required: No
# of LD applications submitted each year: NR
# of LD applications accepted yearly: NR
Total # of students receiving LD services: 10
Acceptance into program means acceptance into college: Students must be admitted to and enrolled in the university first and then request services.

ADMISSIONS

Students with learning disabilities are screened by admissions and must meet the same admission criteria as all other applicants. There is no set GPA required (the average GPA is 3.4); courses required include 4 years of English, algebra, and geometry; 2 years of natural science, 2 years of social studies, and 7 additional units. A pre-admission interview is required. Students with learning disabilities who self-disclose are referred to Student Support Services when making prospective visits to the campus to ascertain specific needs and abilities of the student.

ADDITIONAL INFORMATION

EDP provides tutoring in subject areas; skills classes for no credit in time management, note-taking, test-taking strategies, reading college texts, writing papers, studying for and taking exams, and setting goals; and counseling/guidance. Student Support Services provides intensive study groups, LD support groups, and internships. EDP provides students with peer contacts who provide students with one-on-one support and are useful in helping students adjust to college life, provide a contact for the student to go to with problems or issues, organize group tutoring, and help students open their minds and see hope in their future.

LEARNING DISABILITY PROGRAM/SERVICES

Learning Disability Program/Services: Student Support Services/EDP
Director: Dan Krhin
  E-mail: krhind@ripon.edu
  Telephone: 920-748-8107
  Fax: 920-748-8382

LEARNING DISABILITY SERVICES

Requests for the following services/accommodations will be evaluated individually based on appropriate and current documentation.

Allowed in exams
  Calculator: Yes
  Dictionary: No
  Computer: Yes
  Spellchecker: Yes
Extended test time: Yes
Scribes: Yes
Proctors: Yes
Oral exams: Yes
Note-takers: Yes

Distraction-reduced environment: Yes
Tape recording in class: Yes
Books on tape from RFBD: Yes
Taping of books not from RFBD: Yes
Accommodations for students with
  ADHD: Yes
Reading machine: Yes
Other assistive technology: Yes
Priority registration: No

Added costs for services: No
LD specialists: No
Professional tutors: No
Peer tutors: 50
Max. hours/wk. for services:
  Unlimited
How professors are notified of
  LD/ADHD: By both student and
  director

GENERAL ADMISSIONS INFORMATION

Director of Admissions: Steven Schuetz
Telephone: 920-748-8185

ENTRANCE REQUIREMENTS
Academic units required: 4 English, 2 math, 2 science, 2 social studies. **Academic units recommended:** 4 math, 4 science, 2 foreign language, 4 social studies. High school diploma is required, and GED is accepted. ACT with or without Writing component accepted. TOEFL required of all international applicants: minimum paper TOEFL 550, minimum computer TOEFL 220.

Application deadline: Rolling
Notification: Rolling
Average GPA: 3.47
ACT Composite middle 50% range:
  21–27

SAT Math middle 50% range:
  480–610
SAT Critical Reading middle 50%
  range: 490–620
SAT Writing middle 50% range: NR

Graduated top 10% of class: 26%
Graduated top 25% of class: 56%
Graduated top 50% of class: 86%

COLLEGE GRADUATION REQUIREMENTS

Course waivers allowed: No
Course substitutions allowed: No

ADDITIONAL INFORMATION

Environment: The college is located in a small town north of Milwaukee.

Student Body
  Undergrad enrollment: 963
  Women: 54%
  Men: 46%
  Percent out-of-state: 26%

Cost Information
  Tuition: $22,162
  Room & board: $6,060
Housing Information
  University housing: Yes
  Percent living on campus: 87%

Greek System
  Fraternity: Yes
  Sorority: Yes
Athletics: Division III

U. OF WISCONSIN—EAU CLAIRE

105 Garfield Avenue, Eau Claire, WI 54701
Phone: 715-836-5415 • Fax: 715-836-2409
E-mail: admissions@uwec.edu • Web: www.uwec.edu
Support: S • Institution type: 4-year public

LEARNING DISABILITY PROGRAM AND SERVICES

The university does not have a separate program for students with learning disabilities. However, appropriate services are provided. Documentation of a learning disability is required to receive services. Students should meet with staff in the Students with Disabilities Office 2 months before enrolling to ensure that needed documentation is in place. Academic adjustments or accommodations will be provided to meet the students' needs based on the documentation provided.

LD/ADHD ADMISSIONS INFORMATION

College entrance tests required: Yes
Interview required: No
Essay recommended: No
Documentation required for LD: Psychoeducational evaluation
Documentation required for ADHD: Psychoeducational and medical evaluation
Submitted to: Student Disabilities Office
Special Ed. HS course work accepted: No

Specific course requirements of all applicants: Yes
Separate application required: No
# of LD applications submitted each year: NR
# of LD applications accepted yearly: NR
Total # of students receiving LD services: NR
Acceptance into program means acceptance into college: Students must be admitted to and enrolled in the university first and then request services.

ADMISSIONS

Individuals with learning disabilities complete the standard university application form and must meet the regular university admission criteria. After a student is admitted, a copy of the diagnosis and assessment of the disability, including educational recommendations, should be submitted to Services for Students with Disabilities. Applicants for admission should rank in the top 50 percent of their class with an ACT of 23 or an SAT of 1000. Courses required include 4 years of English, 3 years of math, 3 years of natural science, 3 years of social science, 2 years of a foreign language, and 2 courses in any academic course or art, music, speech, and computer science. Students not admitted in the fall may find a January admission somewhat less competitive. Students must submit an ACT score and take placement tests in English, math, and other appropriate areas. Conditional student status is given during the summer and second semester of the academic year.

ADDITIONAL INFORMATION

Students must provide documentation prior to receiving appropriate accommodations. Some of the accommodations provided with appropriate documentation could include tutoring individually or in groups, readers, scribes, note-takers, taped textbooks, proofreaders, and exam accommodations, including extended time, readers, and separate testing rooms. The Academic Skills Center offers individualized tutoring in math preparation and background, composition, reading, and study skills. Many departments on campus provide tutors to help students with course content. Students take a form identifying appropriate accommodation requests completed by SSD staff to instructors. Students who are denied accommodations can appeal any denial by filing a complaint with the Affirmative Action Review Board. Services and accommodations are available to undergraduate and graduate students.

LEARNING DISABILITY PROGRAM/SERVICES

Learning Disability Program/Services: Services for Students with Disabilities (SSD)
Director: Kathleen Hurley
  E-mail: hurleyks@uwec.edu
  Telephone: 715-836-4542
  Fax: 715-836-3712
Contact Person: Tricia Tollefson
  E-mail: hurleyks@uwec.edu

LEARNING DISABILITY SERVICES

Requests for the following services/accommodations will be evaluated individually based on appropriate and current documentation.

Allowed in exams
  Calculator: Yes
  Dictionary: Yes
  Computer: Yes
  Spellchecker: Yes
Extended test time: Yes
Scribes: Yes
Proctors: Yes
Oral exams: Yes
Note-takers: Yes

Distraction-reduced environment: Yes
Tape recording in class: Yes
Books on tape from RFBD: Yes
Taping of books not from RFBD: Yes
**Accommodations for students with
  ADHD:** Yes
Reading machine: Yes
Other assistive technology: Yes
Priority registration: Yes

Added costs for services: No
LD specialists: No
Professional tutors: No
Peer tutors: 40–50
Max. hours/wk. for services: NR
**How professors are notified of
  LD/ADHD:** By student

GENERAL ADMISSIONS INFORMATION

Director of Admissions: Kristina Anderson
Telephone: 715-836-5415

ENTRANCE REQUIREMENTS

Academic units required: 4 English, 3 math, 3 science, 2 foreign language, 3 social studies, 2 academic electives. High school diploma is required, and GED is accepted. ACT with or without Writing component accepted. TOEFL required of all international applicants: minimum paper TOEFL 525, minimum computer TOEFL 197.

Application deadline: Rolling
Notification: Rolling
Average GPA: NR
ACT Composite middle 50% range:
  22–26

SAT Math middle 50% range:
  530–650
**SAT Critical Reading middle 50%
  range:** 500–650
SAT Writing middle 50% range:
  510–630

Graduated top 10% of class: 17%
Graduated top 25% of class: 54%
Graduated top 50% of class: 97%

COLLEGE GRADUATION REQUIREMENTS

Course waivers allowed: Yes
In what course: If appropriate documentation is provided, waivers may be permitted in the area of foreign language.
Course substitutions allowed: Yes
In what course: If appropriate documentation is provided, substitutions may be permitted in the area of foreign language.

ADDITIONAL INFORMATION

Environment: The 333-acre campus is in an urban setting 95 miles east of Minneapolis.

Student Body
  Undergrad enrollment: 9,901
  Women: 59%
  Men: 41%
  Percent out-of-state: 21%

Cost Information
  In-state tuition: $5,502
  Out-of-state tuition: $15,200
  Room & board: $4,936
Housing Information
  University housing: Yes
  Percent living on campus: 36%

Greek System
  Fraternity: Yes
  Sorority: Yes
Athletics: Division III

University of Wisconsin—Eau Claire

U. OF WISCONSIN—LA CROSSE

1725 State Street, LaCrosse, WI 54601-3742
Phone: 608-785-8939 • Fax: 608-785-8940
E-mail: admissions@uwlax.edu • Web: www.uwlax.edu
Support: CS • Institution type: 4-year public

LEARNING DISABILITY PROGRAM AND SERVICES

The goal of the Disability Resource Services Office provides academic accommodations for students with learning disabilities in order for them to participate fully at the university. A number of academic and personal support services are available. Students must provide documentation (completed within the past 3 years) to verify their disability. The mission is to identify, reduce, or eliminate barriers in education for students with disabilities within the most integrated setting possible.

LD/ADHD ADMISSIONS INFORMATION

College entrance tests required: Yes
Interview required: No
Essay recommended: No
Documentation required for LD: Psychoeducational evaluation completed within the past 3 years, WAIS, and the Woodcock-Johnson Achievement Test
Documentation required for ADHD: Documentation of testing results from a qualified psychologist
Submitted to: Disability Resource Services
Special Ed. HS course work accepted: No

Specific course requirements of all applicants: Yes
Separate application required: Yes
# of LD applications submitted each year: 30
# of LD applications accepted yearly: NR
Total # of students receiving LD services: 140
Acceptance into program means acceptance into college: Students must be admitted to and enrolled in the university first and then request services.

ADMISSIONS

Admission criteria include an ACT of 23 and a class rank in the top 35 percent. There is limited admission for students with learning disabilities if they are close to the regular admission requirements. Students with learning disabilities are encouraged to self-disclose their disability. These applications are automatically referred to the program director who will then request a recent psychological report, 3 letters of recommendation, and a personal interview. The Admissions Office is sensitive to the director's opinions and will admit students recommended who can succeed, even if these students do not meet standard admissions requirements.

ADDITIONAL INFORMATION

The program director writes a letter to all of the student's professors explaining the student's learning disability and describing necessary modifications. The program director meets with freshmen every 2 weeks. A support group meets twice a month. Services include taped texts, testing accommodations, and note-takers. Students are encouraged to get tutoring through the academic departments. Tutorial assistance is offered through each department within the university. Skills classes are offered in reading, remedial English, and mathematics. Services and accommodations are available for undergraduate and graduate students.

LEARNING DISABILITY PROGRAM/SERVICES

Learning Disability Program/Services: Disability Resource Services
Director: June Reinert, Coordinator
  E-mail: reinert.june@uwlax.edu
  Telephone: 608-785-6900
  Fax: 608-785-6910

LEARNING DISABILITY SERVICES

Requests for the following services/accommodations will be evaluated individually based on appropriate and current documentation.

Allowed in exams
  Calculator: Yes
  Dictionary: Yes
  Computer: Yes
  Spellchecker: Yes
Extended test time: Yes
Scribes: Yes
Proctors: Yes
Oral exams: Yes
Note-takers: Yes

Distraction-reduced environment: Yes
Tape recording in class: Yes
Books on tape from RFBD: Yes
Taping of books not from RFBD: Yes
Accommodations for students with ADHD: Yes
Reading machine: Yes
Other assistive technology: Yes
Priority registration: Yes

Added costs for services: No
LD specialists: Yes
Professional tutors: No
Peer tutors: Yes
Max. hours/wk. for services: Unlimited
How professors are notified of LD/ADHD: By student

GENERAL ADMISSIONS INFORMATION

Director of Admissions: Kathryn Kiefer
Telephone: 608-785-8939

ENTRANCE REQUIREMENTS
Academic units required: 4 English, 3 math, 3 science (2 science labs), 3 social studies, 4 academic electives.
Academic units recommended: 4 English, 4 math, 4 science (2 science labs), 3 foreign language, 4 social studies, 2 academic electives. High school diploma is required, and GED is accepted. ACT with or without Writing component accepted. TOEFL required of all international applicants: minimum paper TOEFL 550, minimum computer TOEFL 213.

Application deadline: Rolling
Notification: Rolling
Average GPA: NR
ACT Composite middle 50% range: 23–26

SAT Math middle 50% range: 520–630
SAT Critical Reading middle 50% range: 490–622
SAT Writing middle 50% range: NR

Graduated top 10% of class: 26%
Graduated top 25% of class: 71%
Graduated top 50% of class: 76%

COLLEGE GRADUATION REQUIREMENTS

Course waivers allowed: Yes
In what course: Decision is made on an individual basis.
Course substitutions allowed: Yes
In what course: Decision is made on an individual basis.

ADDITIONAL INFORMATION

Environment: The university is located on 119 acres in a small city 140 miles west of Madison.

Student Body
  Undergrad enrollment: 8,097
  Women: 59%
  Men: 41%
  Percent out-of-state: 15%

Cost Information
  In-state tuition: $5,555
  Out-of-state tuition: $15,200
  Room & board: $4,970
Housing Information
  University housing: Yes
  Percent living on campus: 36%

Greek System
  Fraternity: Yes
  Sorority: Yes
Athletics: Division III

U. OF WISCONSIN—MADISON

Armory and Gymnasium, 716 Langdon Street, Madison, WI 53706-1481
Phone: 608-262-3961 • Fax: 608-262-7706
E-mail: onwisconsin@admissions.wisc.edu • Web: www.wisc.edu
Support: CS • Institution type: 4-year public

LEARNING DISABILITY PROGRAM AND SERVICES

The McBurney Disability Resource Center LD Support Services seeks to provide students with equal access to the programs and activities of the university. LD staff work with students, other staff, and faculty to promote students' independence and ensure assessment of their abilities, not disabilities. LD staff work with students to determine disability-related accommodations and academic services that will maximize a student's opportunity for success. The LD staff consists of two part-time professionals. More than 450 undergraduate and graduate students with LD/ADHD are currently registered with the McBurney Center. Students with LD who tend to do well have graduated from competitive high school or college programs and are reasonably independent, proactive in seeking assistance, and use accommodations similar to those offered here.

LD/ADHD ADMISSIONS INFORMATION

College entrance tests required: Yes
Interview required: No
Essay recommended: Yes
Documentation required for LD: Current and completed by qualified professional; must include a clinical interview and the neuropsychological or psychoeducational evaluation.
Documentation required for ADHD: Evidence of early impairment, current impairment, diagnostic interview, alternative diagnoses or explanations ruled out, neuropsychological or psychoeducational assessment, specific psychological diagnosis, and clinical summary
Submitted to: McBurney Center

Special Ed. HS course work accepted: No
Specific course requirements of all applicants: Yes
Separate application required: No
# of LD applications submitted each year: NR
# of LD applications accepted yearly: NR
Total # of students receiving LD services: 150–450
Acceptance into program means acceptance into college: Students must be admitted to and enrolled in the university first and then request services.

ADMISSIONS

The admission process is the same for all applicants. Applicants not meeting regular admission criteria who self-disclose a disability can have their documentation reviewed by an Admissions Office liaison and then sent to the McBurney Center. The disability could become a factor in admission when documentation is provided that clearly establishes the presence of a disability, shows it's impact on the student's education, and a record of academic achievement that meets guidelines suggesting potential success. Factors in the alternative admissions review process include disability information, grades, rank, test scores, course requirements completed, and potential for success. Examples of LD information include the date of diagnosis or onset of the disability and the ramifications of the disability on curricular requirements. If course requirements are directly impacted by the disability, resulting in low grades or the absence of courses, the GPA will be reviewed with and without those courses.

ADDITIONAL INFORMATION

The documentation must be completed by a professional qualified to diagnose an LD. The report must include results of a clinical interview and descriptions of the testing procedures; instruments used; test and subtest results reported in standard scores, as well as percentile rank and grade scores where useful; and interpretation and recommendations based on data gathered. It must be comprehensive and include test results where applicable in intelligence, reading, math, spelling, written language, language processing, and cognitive processing skills. Testing should carefully examine areas of concern/weakness, as well as areas of strengths; documentation should include a clear diagnostic statement based on the test results and personal history. Students may be eligible for advocacy/liaison with faculty and staff, alternative testing accommodations, curriculum modifications, disability management advising, learning skills training, liaison with vocational rehab, access to the McBurney Learning Resource Room, note-takers, peer support groups, priority registration, taped texts, and course materials.

LEARNING DISABILITY PROGRAM/SERVICES

Learning Disability Program/Services: McBurney Disability Resource Center
Director: Cathleen Trueba
  E-mail: mcburney@odos.wisc.edu
  Telephone: 608-263-2741
  Fax: 608-265-2998

LEARNING DISABILITY SERVICES

Requests for the following services/accommodations will be evaluated individually based on appropriate and current documentation.

Allowed in exams
  Calculator: Yes
  Dictionary: NR
  Computer: Yes
  Spellchecker: NR
Extended test time: Yes
Scribes: Yes
Proctors: Yes
Oral exams: Yes
Note-takers: Yes

Distraction-reduced environment: Yes
Tape recording in class: Yes
Books on tape from RFBD: Yes
Taping of books not from RFBD: Yes
Accommodations for students with
  ADHD: Yes
Reading machine: Yes
Other assistive technology: Yes
Priority registration: Yes

Added costs for services: No
LD specialists: Yes
Professional tutors: No
Peer tutors: Yes
Max. hours/wk. for services: .5
How professors are notified of
  LD/ADHD: By student

GENERAL ADMISSIONS INFORMATION

Director of Admissions: Robert Seltzer
Telephone: 608-262-3961

ENTRANCE REQUIREMENTS
Academic units required: 4 English, 3 math, 3 science, 2 foreign language, 3 social studies, 2 academic electives.
Academic units recommended: 4 English, 4 math, 4 science, 4 foreign language, 4 social studies, 2 academic electives. High school diploma is required, and GED is accepted. ACT with Writing component required. TOEFL required of all international applicants: minimum paper TOEFL 550, minimum computer TOEFL 213.

Application deadline: 2/1
Notification: Rolling
Average GPA: 3.67
ACT Composite middle 50% range:
  26–30

SAT Math middle 50% range:
  610–710
SAT Critical Reading middle 50%
  range: 560–670
SAT Writing middle 50% range:
  570–670

Graduated top 10% of class: 58%
Graduated top 25% of class: 93%
Graduated top 50% of class: 100%

COLLEGE GRADUATION REQUIREMENTS

Course waivers allowed: No
Course substitutions allowed: Yes
In what course: Foreign language

ADDITIONAL INFORMATION

Environment: The university is located in an urban area in the state capital.

Student Body
  Undergrad enrollment: 28,462
  Women: 53%
  Men: 47%
  Percent out-of-state: 31%

Cost Information
  In-state tuition: $6,730
  Out-of-state tuition: $20,730
  Room & board: $6,920
Housing Information
  University housing: Yes
  Percent living on campus: 26%

Greek System
  Fraternity: Yes
  Sorority: Yes
Athletics: Division I

University of Wisconsin—Madison

U. OF WISCONSIN—MILWAUKEE

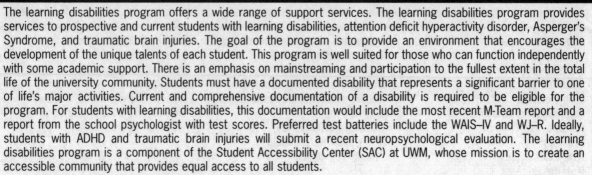

PO Box 749, Milwaukee, WI 53201
Phone: 414-229-2222 • Fax: 414-229-6940
E-mail: uwmlook@uwm.edu • Web: www.uwm.edu
Support: CS • Institution type: 4-year public

LEARNING DISABILITY PROGRAM AND SERVICES

The learning disabilities program offers a wide range of support services. The learning disabilities program provides services to prospective and current students with learning disabilities, attention deficit hyperactivity disorder, Asperger's Syndrome, and traumatic brain injuries. The goal of the program is to provide an environment that encourages the development of the unique talents of each student. This program is well suited for those who can function independently with some academic support. There is an emphasis on mainstreaming and participation to the fullest extent in the total life of the university community. Students must have a documented disability that represents a significant barrier to one of life's major activities. Current and comprehensive documentation of a disability is required to be eligible for the program. For students with learning disabilities, this documentation would include the most recent M-Team report and a report from the school psychologist with test scores. Preferred test batteries include the WAIS–IV and WJ–R. Ideally, students with ADHD and traumatic brain injuries will submit a recent neuropsychological evaluation. The learning disabilities program is a component of the Student Accessibility Center (SAC) at UWM, whose mission is to create an accessible community that provides equal access to all students.

LD/ADHD ADMISSIONS INFORMATION

College entrance tests required: Yes
Interview required: No
Essay recommended: No
Documentation required for LD: Comprehensive and current psychoeducational or neuropsychological assessment
Documentation required for ADHD: A comprehensive and current psychoeducational or neuropsychological assessment
Submitted to: Learning Disabilities Program
Special Ed. HS course work accepted: Yes

Specific course requirements of all applicants: Yes
Separate application required: Yes
# of LD applications submitted each year: 50
# of LD applications accepted yearly: 25–50
Total # of students receiving LD services: 100–125
Acceptance into program means acceptance into college: Students must be admitted to and enrolled in the university first and then request services. Some students may apply directly through AOC.

ADMISSIONS
Students apply directly to the Admissions Office. The LD program does not make admission decisions. Students should send documentation to the LD program, and once admitted, students will be contacted by the LD program. The director of the LD program can assist students with the admission process and can make informal recommendations to the admission office on an individual basis. Students not regularly admissible, who are serious about continuing their education and show potential for university study may apply through the Academic Opportunity Center (AOC). Students should submit a UWM application, transcripts, take AOC placement tests, submit ACT/SAT scores, and schedule an interview. Approximately 60–75 students submit applications yearly through AOC. There is no limit to the number of students who can be admitted through the AOC each year.

ADDITIONAL INFORMATION
Students are encouraged to provide the LD Program with the required documentation and application as early as possible. Students who meet eligibility criteria receive individual counseling and guidance. In addition, students may be eligible for academic accommodations based on specific disability-related needs. These accommodations may include, but are not limited to, priority registration, note-taking assistance, exam accommodations, taped textbooks, use of computers, tutoring, and progress reports.

LEARNING DISABILITY PROGRAM/SERVICES

Learning Disability Program/Services: Learning Disabilities Program
Director: Laurie Petersen
  E-mail: lauriep@uwm.edu
  Telephone: 414-229-6239
  Fax: 414-229-2237

LEARNING DISABILITY SERVICES

Requests for the following services/accommodations will be evaluated individually based on appropriate and current documentation.

Allowed in exams
  Calculator: Yes
  Dictionary: Yes
  Computer: Yes
  Spellchecker: Yes
Extended test time: Yes
Scribes: Yes
Proctors: Yes
Oral exams: Yes
Note-takers: Yes

Distraction-reduced environment: Yes
Tape recording in class: Yes
Books on tape from RFBD: Yes
Taping of books not from RFBD: Yes
Accommodations for students with ADHD: Yes
Reading machine: Yes
Other assistive technology: Yes
Priority registration: Yes

Added costs for services: No
LD specialists: Yes
Professional tutors: No
Peer tutors: Yes
Max. hours/wk. for services: 3
How professors are notified of LD/ADHD: By student

GENERAL ADMISSIONS INFORMATION

Director of Admissions: Beth Weckmueller
Telephone: 414-229-2222

ENTRANCE REQUIREMENTS

Academic units required: 4 English, 3 math, 3 science (1 science lab), 3 social studies, 2 academic electives, 2 from the previously listed areas, computer science, fine arts, or other appropriate courses. High school diploma is required, and GED is accepted. ACT with or without Writing component accepted. TOEFL required of all international applicants: minimum paper TOEFL 500.

Application deadline: 8/1
Notification: Rolling
Average GPA: 3.10
ACT Composite middle 50% range: 20–24

SAT Math middle 50% range: 490–610
SAT Critical Reading middle 50% range: 470–600
SAT Writing middle 50% range: 470–580

Graduated top 10% of class: 7%
Graduated top 25% of class: 26%
Graduated top 50% of class: 67%

COLLEGE GRADUATION REQUIREMENTS

Course waivers allowed: No
Course substitutions allowed: Yes
In what course: On an individual basis determinations will be made for course substitutions, generally in math and foreign language courses.

ADDITIONAL INFORMATION

Environment: The university is located on 90 acres in a residential area 90 miles north of Chicago.

Student Body
  Undergrad enrollment: 22,066
  Women: 52%
  Men: 48%
  Percent out-of-state: 2%

Cost Information
  In-state tuition: $5,868
  Out-of-state tuition: $18,000
  Room & board: $5,314
Housing Information
  University housing: Yes
  Percent living on campus: NR

Greek System
  Fraternity: Yes
  Sorority: Yes
Athletics: Division I

UNIVERSITY OF WISCONSIN—OSHKOSH

Dempsey Hall 135, 800 Algoma Boulevard, Oshkosh, WI 54901
Phone: 920-424-0202 • Fax: 920-424-1098
E-mail: oshadmuw@uwosh.edu • Web: www.uwosh.edu
Support: CS • Institution type: 4-year public

LEARNING DISABILITY PROGRAM AND SERVICES

Project Success is a language remediation project that is based on mastering the entire sound structure of the English language. These students are academically able and determined to succeed, in spite of a pronounced problem in a number of areas. Help is offered in the following ways: direct remediation of deficiencies through the Orton-Gillingham Technique, one-on-one tutoring assistance, math and writing labs, guidance and counseling with scheduling course work and interpersonal relations, untimed exams, and by providing an atmosphere that is supportive. The goal is for students to become language independent in and across all of these major educational areas: math, spelling, reading, writing, comprehension, and study skills. As full-time university students, they will acquire language independence by mastering the entire phonetic structure of the American English language.

LD/ADHD ADMISSIONS INFORMATION

College entrance tests required: Yes
Interview required: No
Essay recommended: Yes
Documentation required for LD: Full psychoeducational testing completed within the past 3 years
Documentation required for ADHD: Yes
Submitted to: Admissions Office and Project Success
Special Ed. HS course work accepted: Yes

Specific course requirements of all applicants: Yes
Separate application required: No
# of LD applications submitted each year: 50–70
# of LD applications accepted yearly: 40
Total # of students receiving LD services: 200
Acceptance into program means acceptance into college: Students are accepted jointly to Project Success and the university; however, they must submit separate applications for the program and the university.

ADMISSIONS

Students should apply to Project Success in their junior year of high school. Applicants apply by writing a letter, in their own handwriting, indicating interest in the program and why they are interested. Applications are processed on a first-come, first-served basis. Those interested should apply at least 1 to 2 years prior to the student's desired entrance sememster. Students and parents will be invited to interview. The interview is used to assess family dynamics in terms of support for the student and reasons for wanting to attend college. The director is looking for motivation, stability, and the ability of the students to describe the disability. Acceptance into Project Success does not grant acceptance into the university. Admission to the university and acceptance into Project Success is a joint decision, but a separate process is required for each. General admissions procedures must be followed before acceptance into Project Success can be offered. ACT/SAT or GPA are not critical. Students who are admitted to UW—Oshkosh and Project Success not in full standing (all high school units completed, top 40 percent of graduating class, and ACT of 22-plus) must attend the Project Success summer program prior to freshman year.

ADDITIONAL INFORMATION

Incoming freshmen to Project Success must participate in an 8-week summer school program consisting of simultaneous multisensory instructional procedures (SMSIP). This program is used to teach study skills, reading, spelling, writing, and mathematical operations. The Project Success program offers the following remedial and support services for all students enrolled in its program: organizational tutors, mathematics courses/tutoring, remedial reading and spelling courses, English/written expression courses/tutoring, and content area tutoring. Additionally, students are eligible for untimed testing opportunities. Although Project Success does not offer taped texts, students are not prohibited from using them. Student requesting taped texts are referred to the UW—Oshkosh Disability Services office. Services and accommodations are available for undergraduate and graduate students.

LEARNING DISABILITY PROGRAM/SERVICES

Learning Disability Program/Services: Project Success
Director: John Palmer
  E-mail: palmer@uwosh.edu
  Telephone: 920-424-3100

LEARNING DISABILITY SERVICES

Requests for the following services/accommodations will be evaluated individually based on appropriate and current documentation.

Allowed in exams
  Calculator: Yes
  Dictionary: Yes
  Computer: Yes
  Spellchecker: No
Extended test time: Yes
Scribes: No
Proctors: Yes
Oral exams: No
Note-takers: No

Distraction-reduced environment: Yes
Tape recording in class: Yes
Books on tape from RFBD: NR
Taping of books not from RFBD: Yes
Accommodations for students with ADHD: Yes
Reading machine: No
Other assistive technology: Yes
Priority registration: Yes

Added costs for services: No
LD specialists: Yes
Professional tutors: No
Peer tutors: 80
Max. hours/wk. for services: NR
How professors are notified of LD/ADHD: By both student and director

GENERAL ADMISSIONS INFORMATION

Director of Admissions: Jill Endries
Telephone: 920-424-0202

ENTRANCE REQUIREMENTS

Academic units required: 4 English, 3 math, 3 science (2 science labs), 3 social studies, 1 history, 4 academic electives. **Academic units recommended:** 4 math, 4 science (4 science labs). High school diploma is required, and GED is accepted. ACT with or without Writing component accepted. TOEFL required of all international applicants: minimum paper TOEFL 525, minimum computer TOEFL 197.

Application deadline: 8/1
Notification: Rolling
Average GPA: 3.27
ACT Composite middle 50% range: 20–24

SAT Math middle 50% range: NR
SAT Critical Reading middle 50% range: NR
SAT Writing middle 50% range: NR

Graduated top 10% of class: 11%
Graduated top 25% of class: 39%
Graduated top 50% of class: 89%

COLLEGE GRADUATION REQUIREMENTS

Course waivers allowed: Yes
In what course: UW—Oshkosh has special accommodations in place relating to the foreign language requirement.
Course substitutions allowed: Yes
In what course: Foreign language and several others in select areas

ADDITIONAL INFORMATION

Environment: The campus is located 3 hours north of Chicago and 2 hours northeast of Madison.

Student Body
  Undergrad enrollment: 9,598
  Women: 59%
  Men: 41%
  Percent out-of-state: 2%

Cost Information
  In-state tuition: $5,364
  Out-of-state tuition: $15,200
  Room & board: $5,164
  Housing Information
    University housing: Yes
    Percent living on campus: 25%

Greek System
  Fraternity: Yes
  Sorority: Yes
  Athletics: Division III

University of Wisconsin—Oshkosh

U. OF WISCONSIN—STEVENS POINT

Student Services Center, Stevens Point, WI 54481
Phone: 715-346-2441 • Fax: 715-346-3957
E-mail: admiss@uwsp.edu • Web: www.uwsp.edu
Support: S • Institution type: 4-year public

LEARNING DISABILITY PROGRAM AND SERVICES

The university does not have a formal program or a specialized curriculum for students with LD; rather it provides all of the services appropriate to ensure equal access to all programs. The university's philosophy is to provide what is mandated to enhance the student's academic success and also to convey its concern for the student's total well-being. The Director of Disability Services is a strong advocate for students. Students are encouraged to meet with the director prior to admissions for information about the services. A full range of accommodations are provided. The services provide a multisensory approach to developing compensatory skills, not remediation, and utilize a developmental model for advising as well as psychosocial adjustment. Students should make an appointment at the beginning of each semester and should not miss appointments. Students should also register with RFBD for taped texts, make their needs known, and be a self-advocate. The Office of Disability Services (ODS) provides students with accommodations that are appropriate for the disability. Together, ODS and the student can work toward effective accommodations and utilization of support services and establish a working relationship based on trust and communication.

LD/ADHD ADMISSIONS INFORMATION

College entrance tests required: Yes
Interview required: No
Essay recommended: No
Documentation required for LD: WAIS or WISC–R, WJ–III, and ETS, as appropriate
Documentation required for ADHD: Yes
Submitted to: Office of Disability Services
Special Ed. HS course work accepted: No

Specific course requirements of all applicants: Yes
Separate application required: No
# of LD applications accepted yearly: NR
Total # of students receiving LD services: NR
Acceptance into program means acceptance into college: Students must be admitted to and enrolled in the university first and then request services.

ADMISSIONS

There is no separate admission procedure for students with learning disabilities. However, students are encouraged to make a pre-admission inquiry and talk to the director of ODS. Students with learning disabilities who do not meet the combined class rank and ACT test score criteria should send a letter of recommendation from the high school LD specialist or counselor. Students should also meet with the director of Disabled Student Services at Stevens Point if support is needed in the application process. The Director of Admissions has the flexibility to admit students with learning disabilities on a case-by-case basis. Applicants should rank in the top 25 percent of their high school graduating class or have an ACT score of 21 or higher (or an SAT Reasoning score of 990) and have a GPA of 3.25 or higher (on a 4-point scale) or have a 21 or higher on the ACT (or a 990 of the SAT) and rank in the top 50 percent of their high school graduating class. Applicants who meet one of the following requirements will be considered on an individual basis: rank in the top 50 percent of their high school graduating class, have a high school GPA of 3.0 or better, or earn an ACT composite score of 21 or higher (or an SAT Reasoning score of 990).

ADDITIONAL INFORMATION

ODS provides accommodations that are appropriate to the disability, orientation assistance, taped textbooks, note-takers, proctors and scribes, adaptive testing, priority registration, assistance with life skills and advising, referral to tutoring and writing assistance, time management and study strategies training, notification to faculty/staff regarding necessary accommodations, assessment and referral services for those not yet diagnosed, and a commitment to keeping scheduled appointments and a corresponding commitment to being timely. The Tutoring-Learning Center schedules 30-minute tutoring sessions and small-group tutoring; tutoring is free for students wanting help with reading or writing assignments. Tutoring in subject areas is done in groups, and there is a $10 enrollment fee; however, for most students, the fee is covered by various support programs.

LEARNING DISABILITY PROGRAM/SERVICES

Learning Disability Program/Services: Office of Disability Services (ODS)
Director: Jim Joque
  E-mail: jjoque@uwsp.edu
  Telephone: 715-346-3365
  Fax: 715-346-2558

LEARNING DISABILITY SERVICES

Requests for the following services/accommodations will be evaluated individually based on appropriate and current documentation.

Allowed in exams
  Calculator: Yes
  Dictionary: Yes
  Computer: Yes
  Spellchecker: Yes
Extended test time: Yes
Scribes: Yes
Proctors: Yes
Oral exams: Yes
Note-takers: Yes

Distraction-reduced environment: Yes
Tape recording in class: Yes
Books on tape from RFBD: Yes
Taping of books not from RFBD: Yes
**Accommodations for students with
  ADHD:** Yes
Reading machine: Yes
Other assistive technology: Yes
Priority registration: Yes

Added costs for services: No
LD specialists: No
Professional tutors: 3
Peer tutors: No
Max. hours/wk. for services: 2
**How professors are notified of
  LD/ADHD:** By student

GENERAL ADMISSIONS INFORMATION

Director of Admissions: Catherine Glennon
Telephone: 715-346-2441

ENTRANCE REQUIREMENTS

Academic units required: 4 English, 3 math, 3 science, 3 social studies, 4 academic electives. **Academic units recommended:** 2 foreign language. High school diploma is required, and GED is accepted. ACT with or without Writing component accepted. TOEFL required of all international applicants: minimum paper TOEFL 523, minimum computer TOEFL 193.

Application deadline: Rolling
Notification: Rolling
Average GPA: 3.40
ACT Composite middle 50% range:
  20–25

SAT Math middle 50% range: NR
**SAT Critical Reading middle 50%
  range:** NR
SAT Writing middle 50% range: NR

Graduated top 10% of class: 15%
Graduated top 25% of class: 46%
Graduated top 50% of class: 92%

COLLEGE GRADUATION REQUIREMENTS

Course waivers allowed: No
Course substitutions allowed: Yes
In what course: Foreign language and math

ADDITIONAL INFORMATION

Environment: The University of Wisconsin—Stevens Point is located on 335 acres 110 miles north of Madison.

Student Body
  Undergrad enrollment: 8,589
  Women: 53%
  Men: 47%
  Percent out-of-state: 6%

Cost Information
  In-state tuition: $5,000
  Out-of-state tuition: $15,100
  Room & board: $4,322
Housing Information
  University housing: Yes
  Percent living on campus: 37%

Greek System
  Fraternity: Yes
  Sorority: Yes
  Athletics: Division III

U. OF WISCONSIN—WHITEWATER

800 West Main Street, Baker Hall, Whitewater, WI 53190-1791
Phone: 262-472-1440 • Fax: 262-472-1515
E-mail: uwwadmit@uww.edu • Web: www.uww.edu
Support: CS • Institution type: 4-year public

LEARNING DISABILITY PROGRAM AND SERVICES

The University of Wisconsin—Whitewater offers support services for students with learning disabilities, including tutoring, teaching strategies for long-term success, test-taking accommodations, and note-takers. The program is based on the philosophy that students with learning disabilities can learn specific strategies that will enable them to become independent learners who can be successful in a college setting. Project ASSIST offers a 4-week high school to college program for incoming freshmen during the summer prior to first-year entry into the university. The intent of this program is to help students make a smooth transition from high school to university life. Any student with a learning disability who is accepted to UW—Whitewater is eligible to attend the summer program. There is a charge for room and board for the 4 weeks (residence and meal plan), the 3-credit course based on the university's fee schedule for in- and out-of-state tuition, and a separate fee for Project ASSIST.

LD/ADHD ADMISSIONS INFORMATION

College entrance tests required: Yes
Interview required: No
Essay recommended: Yes
Documentation required for LD: Diagnostic interview, WAIS–III, Woodcock-Johnson, information processing
Documentation required for ADHD: History of early impairment, evidence of current impairment, diagnostic interview, any relevant testing, clearly stated specific diagnosis, and rationale for specific accommodations
Submitted to: Project ASSIST and Admissions Office
Special Ed. HS course work accepted: No

Specific course requirements of all applicants: Yes
Separate application required: No
# of LD applications submitted each year: 75–90
# of LD applications accepted yearly: 60–70
Total # of students receiving LD services: 200–225
Acceptance into program means acceptance into college: Students must be admitted to and enrolled in the university first and then request services. Project ASSIST reviews some applications and makes recommendations to admissions.

ADMISSIONS

All applicants must meet the same criteria for admission. General criteria include an ACT score of 18 (or a lower ACT score if the student is in the top 50 percent of his or her class). Students apply to the university admissions first; after a decision is made to admit or deny, the Director of Project ASSIST reviews the file to decide whether to make an exception for admission or whether the student may use services. If the director needs to make an exception for admissions, then the student is required to participate in the summer transition program, and the student receives two years of support. The summer transition program is only offered to students with learning disabilities.

ADDITIONAL INFORMATION

Students may have LD assessments on campus for $250. Skills courses are offered for no credit in reading comprehension and writing. The summer transition program offers a three-credit study skills class that emphasizes such things as note-taking skills, test-taking strategies, time management skills, word processing skills, and verbal and written language skills. The students also write a research paper during which time they become proficient on the word processor, as well as, becoming proficient at how to use the library. This course is a developmental course, which means that though the students get a grade for the course and the grade is averaged into their cumulative GPA, the course does not count toward the total hours needed for graduation. Students in the summer transition program also take a Project ASSIST class where they learn about their learning disabilities, strengths and weaknesses, as well as their learning styles and how these affect their success in the classroom. Students begin to practice advocating for themselves with their professors and receive help with registration for the fall semester. The focus of the class is also on time management, organization, and various learning strategies.

LEARNING DISABILITY PROGRAM/SERVICES

Learning Disability Program/Services: Center for Students with Disabilities
Director: Dr. Elizabeth Watson
  E-mail: watson@uww.edu
  Telephone: 262-472-4711
  Fax: 262-472-4865

LEARNING DISABILITY SERVICES

Requests for the following services/accommodations will be evaluated individually based on appropriate and current documentation.

Allowed in exams
  Calculator: Yes
  Dictionary: Yes
  Computer: Yes
  Spellchecker: Yes
Extended test time: Yes
Scribes: Yes
Proctors: Yes
Oral exams: Yes
Note-takers: Yes

Distraction-reduced environment: Yes
Tape recording in class: Yes
Books on tape from RFBD: Yes
Taping of books not from RFBD: Yes
Accommodations for students with ADHD: Yes
Reading machine: No
Other assistive technology: Yes
Priority registration: Yes

Added costs for services: Yes
LD specialists: Yes
Professional tutors: No
Peer tutors: 35–40
Max. hours/wk. for services: Unlimited
How professors are notified of LD/ADHD: By student

GENERAL ADMISSIONS INFORMATION

Director of Admissions: Stephen J. McKellips
Telephone: 262-472-1440

ENTRANCE REQUIREMENTS
Academic units required: 4 English, 3 math, 3 science (1 science lab), 3 social studies, 4 academic electives.
Academic units recommended: 4 math, 4 science, 2 foreign language, 4 social studies. High school diploma is required, and GED is accepted. ACT with or without Writing component accepted. TOEFL required of all international applicants: minimum paper TOEFL 500, minimum computer TOEFL 214.

Application deadline: Rolling
Notification: Rolling
Average GPA: NR
ACT Composite middle 50% range: 20–24

SAT Math middle 50% range: 480–600
SAT Critical Reading middle 50% range: NR
SAT Writing middle 50% range: 470–610

Graduated top 10% of class: 9%
Graduated top 25% of class: 32%
Graduated top 50% of class: 77%

COLLEGE GRADUATION REQUIREMENTS

Course waivers allowed: No
Course substitutions allowed: Yes
In what course: Some math and foreign language requirements

ADDITIONAL INFORMATION

Environment: The university is located in a small town southwest of Milwaukee.

Student Body
  Undergrad enrollment: 4,822
  Women: 8%
  Men: 92%
  Percent out-of-state: 4%

Cost Information
  In-state tuition: $5,568
  Out-of-state tuition: $15,500
  Room & board: $4,322
Housing Information
  University housing: Yes
  Percent living on campus: 40%

Greek System
  Fraternity: Yes
  Sorority: Yes
Athletics: Division III

University of Wisconsin—Whitewater

LARAMIE COUNTY COMMUNITY COLLEGE

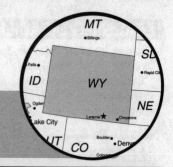

1400 East College Drive, Laramie, WY 82007 • Phone: 800-522-2993
E-mail: LearnMore@lccc.wy.edu • Web: www.lccc.cc.wy.us
Support: CS • Institution type: 2-year public

LEARNING DISABILITY PROGRAM AND SERVICES

The Disability Resource Center (DRC) at Laramie County Community College provides comprehensive, confidential services for LCCC students with documented disabilities. Services and adaptive equipment to reduce mobility, sensory, and perceptual problems are available through the DRC, and all services are provided free of charge to LCCC students. High school students are encouraged to contact the DRC during their junior year to gather information.

LD/ADHD ADMISSIONS INFORMATION

College entrance tests required: No
Interview required: No
Essay recommended: No
Documentation required for LD: LCCC adheres to the documentation guidelines published on the Disability Resource Center website: www.lccc.wy.edu/DRC.
Documentation required for ADHD: LCCC adheres to the documentation guidelines published on the Disability Resource Center website: www.lccc.wy.edu/DRC.
Submitted to: Support Program/Services
Special Ed. HS course work accepted: Yes

Specific course requirements of all applicants: NR
Separate application required: No
# of LD applications submitted each year: NR
# of LD applications accepted yearly: NR
Total # of students receiving LD services: NR
Acceptance into program means acceptance into college: Students must be admitted and enrolled prior to requesting services.

ADMISSIONS

Admission is open to all high school graduates or GED recipients. To register students for classes, LCCC needs to assess the student's skill level in three key areas (reading, English, and math). Admission to LCCC is not based on these scores. There are no specific course requirements.

ADDITIONAL INFORMATION

Students requesting services will be required to provide a copy of current documentation. Laramie County Community College has adopted and strictly adheres to documentation guidelines as developed by the Consortium of Support Programs for Students with Disabilities, representing the postsecondary institutions of Colorado and Wyoming. Examples of services available include testing accommodations, readers/taped tests, scribes, extended time on exams, quiet rooms, use of calculators, special seating, textbooks on tape, tape recording of lectures, note-takers, assistive listening devices, assistive technology equipment, hardware and software programs, and priority registration. Appropriate accommodations are determined on a case-by-case basis between the DRC staff and the student.

LEARNING DISABILITY PROGRAM/SERVICES

Learning Disability Program/Services: Disability Resource Center
Director: Lisa Dignan
  E-mail: DRC@lccc.wy.edu
  Telephone: 307-778-1359
  Fax: 307-778-1262

LEARNING DISABILITY SERVICES

Requests for the following services/accommodations will be evaluated individually based on appropriate and current documentation.

Allowed in exams
  Calculator: Yes
  Dictionary: Yes
  Computer: Yes
  Spellchecker: Yes
Extended test time: Yes
Scribes: Yes
Proctors: Yes
Oral exams: Yes
Note-takers: Yes

Distraction-reduced environment: Yes
Tape recording in class: Yes
Books on tape from RFBD: Yes
Taping of books not from RFBD: Yes
Accommodations for students with
  ADHD: Yes
Reading machine: Yes
Other assistive technology: Yes
Priority registration: Yes

Added costs for services: No
LD specialists: Yes
Professional tutors: 5–15
Peer tutors: 10–20
Max. hours/wk. for services:
  Unlimited
How professors are notified of
  LD/ADHD: By director

GENERAL ADMISSIONS INFORMATION

Director of Admissions: Holly Allison, Coordinator of Admissions
Telephone: 307-778-1117

ENTRANCE REQUIREMENTS

Open admissions but selective for some majors. Interview is required for equine science. ACT/SAT not required. High school diploma or GED accepted.

Application deadline: Rolling
Notification: Rolling
Average GPA: NR
ACT Composite middle 50% range:
  NR

SAT Math middle 50% range: NR
SAT Critical Reading middle 50%
  range: NR
SAT Writing middle 50% range: NR

Graduated top 10% of class: NR
Graduated top 25% of class: NR
Graduated top 50% of class: NR

COLLEGE GRADUATION REQUIREMENTS

Course waivers allowed: No
Course substitutions allowed: Yes
In what course: Decided on a case-by-case basis depending on the documented disability and the student's course of study

ADDITIONAL INFORMATION

Environment: LCCC is 100 miles north of Denver, Colorado.

Student Body
  Undergrad enrollment: 4,584
  Women: 60%
  Men: 40%
  Percent out-of-state: 12%

Cost Information
  In-state tuition: $2,004
  Out-of-state tuition: $4,860
  Room & board: $6,000
Housing Information
  University housing: Yes
  Percent living on campus: 2%

Greek System
  Fraternity: No
  Sorority: No
Athletics: NJCAA

UNIVERSITY OF WYOMING

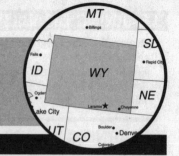

Department 3435, 1000 East University Avenue, Laramie, WY 82071
Phone: 307-766-5160 • Fax: 307-766-4042
E-mail: Why-Wyo@uwyo.edu • Web: www.uwyo.edu
Support: CS • Institution type: 4-year public

LEARNING DISABILITY PROGRAM AND SERVICES

University Disability Support Services (UDSS) offers academic support services to students with learning disabilities and physically handicapped students. Its goals are to promote the independence and self-sufficiency of students and encourage the provision of equal opportunities in education for students with disabilities. Any student enrolled at UW who has a documented disability is eligible for assistance. UDSS provides disability-related accommodations and services, technical assistance, consultations, and resource information. Recommended documentation includes a clear statement of the LD (documentation should be current, preferably having been completed within the past 3 years); a summary of assessment procedures and evaluation instruments used to make the diagnosis and a summary of the results, including standardized or percentile scores that support the diagnosis (LD testing must be comprehensive, including a measure of both aptitude and achievement in the areas of reading, mathematics, and written language); a statement of strengths and needs that will impact the student's ability to meet the demands of college; and suggestions of reasonable accommodations that may be appropriate. Accommodations are collaboratively determined by the student and the assigned disability support service coordinator.

LD/ADHD ADMISSIONS INFORMATION

College entrance tests required: Yes
Interview required: No
Essay recommended: No
Documentation required for LD: A comprehensive diagnostic report; specifically state diagnosis
Documentation required for ADHD: A current, diagnostic report from a qualified professional that provides a specific diagnosis
Submitted to: University Disability Support Services
Special Ed. HS course work accepted: Yes

Specific course requirements of all applicants: Yes
Separate application required: Yes
# of LD applications submitted each year: 50–75
# of LD applications accepted yearly: NR
Total # of students receiving LD services: 50–75
Acceptance into program means acceptance into college: Students must be admitted to and enrolled in the university first and then request services.

ADMISSIONS

Students with learning disabilities must meet general admission requirements. If the students are borderline and have a documented learning disability, they are encouraged to self-identify to the director. Students who were diagnosed late in high school or began utilizing services late may be able to explain how this had an impact on academics. Students with learning disabilities who meet the general admission criteria request LD services after being admitted. Conditional admission is granted with a GPA of 2.5 or a GPA of 2.25 and an ACT score of 20 or an SAT score of 960. Students with learning disabilities not meeting admission criteria and not qualifying for assured or conditional admission may have their applications reviewed by the LD program director. The LD director will make a recommendation to the Office of Admissions.

ADDITIONAL INFORMATION

Services include priority registration, readers, assistance with study skills, note-taking, test preparation, word processing orientation, equipment loan assistance, tutor referral, and advocacy for students via the University Committee on Campus Access for the Disabled. Auditory systems are also used to provide access to print mediums for persons with LD. Synthesized speech reinforces visual cues. Grammar-checking software is available to proof documents and improve writing skills; writing skills may also be improved through the use of word prediction software. Dragon Dictate, a voice recognition program, may benefit those students who have learning disabilities that affect written expression. All students must take one course in math or quantitative reasoning to graduate.

LEARNING DISABILITY PROGRAM/SERVICES

Learning Disability Program/Services: University Disability Support Services (UDSS)
Director: Chris Primus
  E-mail: cfprimus@uwyo.edu
  Telephone: 307-766-6189
  Fax: 307-766-4010

LEARNING DISABILITY SERVICES

Requests for the following services/accommodations will be evaluated individually based on appropriate and current documentation.

Allowed in exams
  Calculator: Yes
  Dictionary: Yes
  Computer: Yes
  Spellchecker: Yes
Extended test time: Yes
Scribes: Yes
Proctors: Yes
Oral exams: Yes
Note-takers: Yes

Distraction-reduced environment: Yes
Tape recording in class: Yes
Books on tape from RFBD: Yes
Taping of books not from RFBD: Yes
Accommodations for students with ADHD: Yes
Reading machine: Yes
Other assistive technology: Yes
Priority registration: Yes

Added costs for services: No
LD specialists: Yes
Professional tutors: No
Peer tutors: Yes
Max. hours/wk. for services: NR
How professors are notified of LD/ADHD: By both student and director

GENERAL ADMISSIONS INFORMATION

Director of Admissions: Sara Axelson, Associate Vice President for Enrollment Management
  Telephone: 307-766-5160

ENTRANCE REQUIREMENTS

Academic units required: 4 English, 3 math, 3 science (3 science labs), 3 cultural context electives (recommended), 3 behavioral or social sciences, 3 visual/performing arts, 3 humanities or earth/space sciences. **Academic units recommended:** 4 English, 4 math, 4 science (3 science labs), 2 foreign language, 3 cultural context electives, 3 behavioral or social sciences, 3 visual/performing arts, 3 humanities or earth/space sciences. High school diploma is required, and GED is accepted. ACT with or without Writing component accepted. TOEFL required of all international applicants: minimum paper TOEFL 525, minimum computer TOEFL 197.

Application deadline: 8/10
Notification: Rolling
Average GPA: NR
ACT Composite middle 50% range: NR

SAT Math middle 50% range: NR
SAT Critical Reading middle 50% range: NR
SAT Writing middle 50% range: NR

Graduated top 10% of class: NR
Graduated top 25% of class: NR
Graduated top 50% of class: NR

COLLEGE GRADUATION REQUIREMENTS

Course waivers allowed: No
Course substitutions allowed: Yes
In what course: Substitutions are possible for foreign language and some math course requirements.

ADDITIONAL INFORMATION

Environment: The university is located on 785 acres in a small town 128 miles north of Denver.

Student Body
  Undergrad enrollment: 9,757
  Women: 56%
  Men: 44%
  Percent out-of-state: 27%

Cost Information
  In-state tuition: $3,400
  Out-of-state tuition: $9,800
  Room & board: $7,274
Housing Information
  University housing: Yes
  Percent living on campus: 20%

Greek System
  Fraternity: Yes
  Sorority: Yes
Athletics: Division I

SHERIDAN COLLEGE

1430 Trafalgar Road, Oakville, ON L6H 2L1 Canada
Phone: 905-815-4007 • Fax: 905-815-4004
E-mail: international@sheridanc.on.ca • Web: www.sheridanc.on.ca
Support: S • Institution type: public

LEARNING DISABILITY PROGRAM AND SERVICES

Sheridan College has limited services available for students with learning disabilities. Students who have been enrolled in special education classes in high school may find that the college does not have the extensive services necessary for them to be successful. Students need to be self-sufficient because the two advisor/counselors are able to allot only a small percentage of their time to work with students with disabilities. Students requesting accommodations must provide psychoeducational evaluations and have these sent to the Counseling/Testing Offices. The college reserves the right to evaluate if it can serve the needs of students.

LD/ADHD ADMISSIONS INFORMATION

College entrance tests required: No
Interview required: No
Essay recommended: No
Documentation required for LD: Copies of the most recent diagnostic testing and reports clarifying the results are needed.
Documentation required for ADHD: Copies of the most recent diagnostic testing and reports clarifying the results are needed.
Submitted to: Admissions Office
Special Ed. HS course work accepted: N/A

Specific course requirements of all applicants: No
Separate application required: Yes
# of LD applications submitted each year: 10
# of LD applications accepted yearly: 8
Total # of students receiving LD services: 10
Acceptance into program means acceptance into college: Students must be admitted to and enrolled in the university first and then request services.

ADMISSIONS

There are no special admission procedures or criteria for students with learning disabilities. The college has open admissions, and any student with a high school diploma or GED is eligible to attend. All students are treated the same and must submit the general college application for admission. Any information on learning disabilities provided is voluntarily given by the student. Students with learning disabilities must submit psychoeducational evaluations. The admission decision is made by the director of the program.

ADDITIONAL INFORMATION

The college offers tutoring, quiet places to take tests, readers, extended testing times, recorders, note-takers, and the availability of a few Franklin Spellers. Remediation courses are offered in arithmetic skills, spelling, vocabulary, reading, writing, and algebra. Other aids for students with learning disabilities include test-taking strategies training, books on tape, tutoring one-on-one or in small groups in the Learning Center, and GED preparation and testing. Support services include career testing and evaluation, peer counseling, and personal and career development.

LEARNING DISABILITY PROGRAM/SERVICES

Learning Disability Program/Services: Enrollment Services
Director: Zane Garstad
  E-mail: zgarstad@sheridan.edu
  Telephone: 307-674-6446
  Fax: 307-674-7205
Contact Person: Lisa Wallace
  E-mail: zgarstad@sheridan.edu
  Telephone: 307-674-6446
  Fax: 307-674-7205

LEARNING DISABILITY SERVICES

Requests for the following services/accommodations will be evaluated individually based on appropriate and current documentation.

Allowed in exams	**Distraction-reduced environment:** Yes	**Added costs for services:** No
Calculator: Yes	**Tape recording in class:** Yes	**LD specialists:** No
Dictionary: Yes	**Books on tape from RFBD:** Yes	**Professional tutors:** No
Computer: Yes	**Taping of books not from RFBD:** Yes	**Peer tutors:** Yes
Spellchecker: Yes	**Accommodations for students with**	**Max. hours/wk. for services:**
Extended test time: Yes	**ADHD:** Yes	Unlimited
Scribes: Yes	**Reading machine:** No	**How professors are notified of**
Proctors: Yes	**Other assistive technology:** Yes	**LD/ADHD:** By student
Oral exams: Yes	**Priority registration:** No	
Note-takers: Yes		

GENERAL ADMISSIONS INFORMATION

Director of Admissions: NR
Telephone: 905-815-4007

ENTRANCE REQUIREMENTS

High school diploma is required, and GED is not accepted.

Application deadline: 6/1	**SAT Math middle 50% range:** NR	**Graduated top 10% of class:** NR
Notification: NR	**SAT Critical Reading middle 50%**	**Graduated top 25% of class:** NR
Average GPA: NR	**range:** NR	**Graduated top 50% of class:** NR
ACT Composite middle 50% range:	**SAT Writing middle 50% range:** NR	
NR		

COLLEGE GRADUATION REQUIREMENTS

Course waivers allowed: Yes
In what course: Would have to be very particular circumstances
Course substitutions allowed: Yes
In what course: Would have to be very particular circumstances

ADDITIONAL INFORMATION

Environment: The college is located on 64 acres in Sheridan.

Student Body	**Cost Information**	**Greek System**
Undergrad enrollment: $3,500	**In-state tuition:** $3,600	**Fraternity:** No
Women: 66%	**Out-of-state tuition:** $9,200	**Sorority:** No
Men: 34%	**Room & board:** $4,000	**Athletics:** NJCAA
Percent out-of-state: 9%	**Housing Information**	
	University housing: Yes	
	Percent living on campus: 7%	

QUICK CONTACT REFERENCE LIST

ALABAMA

School	Location	Contact	Program	Phone
Alabama St. U.	Montgomery, AL 36101	Jessyca Darrington	Learning Disabilities Program	334-229-4382
Auburn U.	Auburn U., AL 36849	Dr. Kelly Haynes	Students w/ Disabilities	334-844-2096
Auburn U.	Montgomery, AL 36124-4023	Tamara Massey	Special Services	334-244-3754
Birmingham-Southern C.	Birmingham, AL 35254	Jane S. Seigel	Learning Disabilities Program	205-226-4696
Faulkner U.	Montgomery, AL 36109	Pat Morrow	Project Key	334-386-7185
Gadsden St. C.C.	Gadsden, AL 35999	Danny Wilborn	Student Services	256-549-8346
Huntingdon C.	Montgomery, AL 36106-2148	Sandy Montgomery	Student Activities & Career Resources	334-833-4432
Jacksonville St. U.	Jacksonville, AL 36265	Daniel Miller	Academic Center for Excellence	256-782-8380
Judson C.	Marion, AL 36756	Dr. Mark Tew	LD Services	334-683-5104
Miles C.	Birmingham, AL 35208	Sarah Johnson	Student Support Services	205-929-1820
Samford U.	Birmingham, AL 35229	Anne Sherman	Counseling Services	205-726-4078
Spring Hill C.	Mobile, AL 36608	Ashley Dunklin	Student Academic Support	251-380-3470
Stillman C.	Tuscaloosa, AL 35403	Jaqueline Currie	Student Development Center	250-366-8894
Troy St. U.	Troy, AL 36082	Deborah G. Sellors	Adaptive Needs Program	334-670-3220
Troy St. U.—Dothan	Dothan, AL 36304	Keith Seagle	Learning Disability Services	334-983-6556 ext. 221
Tuskegee U.	Tuskegee, AL 36088	Minnie R. Austin	Learning Disability Services	334-727-8837
U. of Alabama—Birmingham	Birmingham, AL 35294-1150	Angela Stowe	Disability Support	205-934-4205
U. of Alabama—Huntsville	Huntsville, AL 35899	Dr. Jared Dinehart, PhD	Disability Support Services	256-824-6203
U. of Alabama—Tuscaloosa	Tuscaloosa, AL 35487	Judy Thorpe	Office of Disabilities Services	205-348-4285
U. of Montevallo	Montevallo, AL 35115	Deborah S. McCune	Services for Students w/ Disabilities	205-665-6250
U. of North Alabama	Florence, AL 35632	Jennifer Adams	Student-Life Development Services	256-765-4214
U. of South Alabama	Mobile, AL 36688-0002	Andrea Agnew	Special Student Services	251-460-7212
U. of West Alabama	Livingston, AZ 35470	Danny Buckalew	Learning Disabilities Services	205-652-3581

ALASKA

School	Location	Contact	Program	Phone
Sheldon Jackson C.	Sitka, AK 99835	David Dobler	Learning Assistance Program	907-747-5220
U. of Alaska—Anchorage	Anchorage, AK 99508-8046	Kaela Parks	Disability Support Services	907-786-4530
U. of Alaska—Fairbanks	Fairbanks, AK 99775-7480	Mary Mathews	Disability Services	907-474-7043
U. of Alaska—Southeast	Juneau, AK 99801-8681	Susan Wylie	Disability Coordinator	907-796-6000

ARIZONA

School	Location	Contact	Program	Phone
Arizona St. U.	Tempe, AZ 85287-3202	Carol Takao	Disability Resource Services	602-965-1234
Arizona St. U. West	Phoenix, AZ 85069-7100	Adele Darr	Disability Outreach & Education	480-965-1232

Institution	Contact	Service	Address	Phone
Coconino C.C.	Nancy Elliot	Disability Resources	Flagstaff, AZ 86004	928-226-4243
Embry-Riddle Aero. U. (AZ)	Nancy Jensen	Student Success Program	Prescott, AZ 86301-3720	928-777-3700
Gateway C.C.	Emily Bluestine	Special Services	Phoenix, AZ 85034	602-286-8170
Mesa C.C.	Mora Shahan	Disability Resources and Services	Mesa, AZ 85202	480-461-7447
Northern Arizona U.	Jane Mulrooney	Disability Support Services	Flagstaff, AZ 86011-4084	928-523-8773
Phoenix C.	Gene Heppard	Special Services	Phoenix, AZ 85013	602-285-7477
Pima C.C.	Jane Irey	Disabled Student Resources	Tucson, AZ 85702	520-206-7699
Prescott C.	Patricia Quinn-Kane	Learning Disability Program	Prescott, AZ 86301	928-350-1009
U. of Arizona	Dr. Jeff Orgera	SALT	Tucson, AZ 85921	520-621-1242
U. of Phoenix	Beth Barilla	Office of Admissions	Phoenix, AZ 85040-1958	480-317-6200

ARKANSAS

Institution	Contact	Service	Address	Phone
Arkansas St. U.	Dr. Jenifer Rice Mason	Disability Services	Jonesboro, AR 72467	870-972-3964
Arkansas Tech U.	Carolyn Crawford	Disability Services	Russellville, AR 72801-2222	479-968-0302
Harding U.	Dr. Jim Johnston	Student Support Services (SSS)	Searcy, AR 72149	501-279-4416
Henderson St. U.	Vickie Faust	Disability Services	Arkadelphia, AR 71999-0001	870-230-5453
Hendrix C.	Dionne Jackson	Counseling Center	Conway, AR 72032	501-450-1482
John Brown U.	Becky Lambert	Disability Services	Siloam Springs, AR 72761	479-524-7217
Lyon C.	Dr. John M. Peek	Disability Services	Batesville, AR72503-2317	870-698-4202
NW Arkansas C.C.	Mike Kurk	Learner Development Center	Bentonville, AR 72712	479-619-4384
Ouachita Baptist U.	Neil Hunter	Disability Services	Arkadelphia, AR 71998	870-245-5591
S. Arkansas U.	Paula Washington-Woods	Student Disability Special Services	Magnolia, AR 71753-5000	870-235-4145
U. of Arkansas—Fayetteville	Anne L. Jannarone	Student Support Services	Fayetteville, AR 72701	479-575-3104
U. of Arkansas—Little Rock	Susan Queller	Disability Support Services	Little Rock, AR 72204	501-569-3143
U. of Arkansas—Pine Bluff	Michael Washington	Office of Veterans & Disability Services	Pine Bluff, AR 71601-2799	870-575-8560
U. of Central Arkansas	Crystal Hill	Disability Services	Conway, AR 72035	501-450-3135
U. of the Ozarks	Julia Frost	Jones Learning Center	Clarksville, AR 72830	479-979-1401
Williams Baptist C.	Gary Gregory	Learning Disabilities	Walnut Ridge, AR 72476	870-759-4178

CALIFORNIA

Institution	Contact	Service	Address	Phone
Alliant Intl. U.	Baby Medina	Disability Services	San Diego, CA 92131	858-635-4471
Art Center C. of Design	Kit Baron	Disability Services	Pasadena, CA 91103	626-396-2373
Azusa Pacific U.	Nina Ashur	Learning Enrichment Center	Azusa, CA 91702	626-815-6000 ext. 332
Bakersfield C.	Mary Dunwoody	Support Services Program	Bakersfield, CA 93305	661-395-4334

College	Location	Contact	Service	Phone
Biola U.	La Mirada, CA 90639	Kevin Grant	Disability Services	562-906-4542
Butte C.C.	Oroville, CA 95965	Richard Dunn	Services for Students with Disabilities	530-895-2455
Cabrillo C.	Santa Cruz, CA 95060	Shelly Skye	Disabled Student Services	831-479-6390
Cabrillo C.	Aptos, CA 95003	Cathy Brogoitti	Learning Skills Program	831-479-6220
California Baptist U.	Riverside, CA 92504	Jim Paulus	Disability Services	951-343-4690
California C. of Arts	Oakland, CA 94618-1426	Virginia Jardim	Learning Resource Center	510-594-3756
California Institute of Arts	Valencia CA 91355	Yvonne Guy	Disability Services	661-253-7891
California Institute of Tech.	Pasadena, CA 91125	Dr. Erica O'Neal	Disability Services	626-395-6322
California Lutheran U.	Thousand Oaks, CA 91360	Damien Pena	Center for Academic & Accessibility	805-493-3878
California Polytechnic St. U.	San Luis Obispo, CA 93407	J. Trey Duffy	Disability Resource Center	805-756-1395
California St. Polytechnic U.	Pomona, CA 91768	Dr. Catherine Schmitt Whitaker	Disabled Student Services	909-869-5257
California St. U.	Turlock, CA 95832	Lee Bettencourt	Disabled Student Services	209-667-3159
California St. U.—Bakersfield	Bakersfield, CA 93311	Janice Clalussen	Services for Students with Disabilities	661-664-3360
California St. U.—Chico	Chico, CA 95929-0720	Billie Jackson	Disabilities Support Services	530-898-5959
California St. U.—East Bay	Hayward, CA 94542	Paul Hippolitus	Studen Disability Resource Center	510-885-3868
California St. U.—Fullerton	Fullerton, CA 92634	Paul K. Miller	Disabled Student Services	714-278-3112
California St. U.—Hayward	Hayward, CA 94542	Janet Brockmann	Learning Disabled Resources	510-885-3868
California St. U.—Long Beach	Long Beach, CA 90840	David Sanfilippo	Disabled Student Services	562-985-5401
California St. U.—Monterey Bay	Seaside, CA 93955-8001	Margaret Keith	Student Disability Resources	831-582-3672
California St. U.—Northridge	Northridge, CA 91328-1286	Dr. Mary Ann Cummins Prager	Students with Disabilities Resource	818-677-2684
California St. U.—Sacramento	Sacramento, CA 95819	Judy Dean	Services for Students With LD	916-278-6955
Calif. St. U.—San Bernardino	San Bernardino, CA 92407	Beth Jaworski	Services to Students with Disabilities	909-537-3589
California St. U.—San Marcos	San Marcos, CA 92096-0001	John Segoria	Disabled Student Services	760-750-4905
California St. U.—Stanislaus	Turlock, CA 95382	Ona Baker	Disability Resource Center	209-667-3159
Cerritos C.C.	Norwalk, CA 90650	Dr. Lucinda Aborn	Disabled Students Programs & Svcs	562-860-2451 ext. 2335
Chapman U.	Orange, CA 92866	Dr. Lynn Mayer	Center for Academic Success	714-997-6828
Charles R. Drew U. of Med	Los Angeles, CA 90059	Maranda Montgomery	Student Education Center	323-563-3638
Citrus C.C.	Glendora, CA 91741	Jennifer Mcleod	Disabled Student Program	626-914-8675
City C. San Francisco	Orinda, CA 94563	Kathleen Kerr Schocket	Disabled Student Services	415-452-5481
Claremont McKenna C.	Claremont, CA 91711	Jefferson Huang	Dean of Students	909-621-8117
C. of Redwoods	Crescent City, CA 95531	Sandra Nightingale	Disabled Student Spec.	707-465-2324
College of the Siskiyous	Weed, CA 96094	Dr. Kathleen Gabriel	Disabled Student Services	530-938-5297

Institution	Location	Contact	Office/Program	Phone
Columbia C.C.	Sonora, CA 95370	Mario Cordova	Disabled Student Programs & Services	209-588-5130
Concordia U.	Irvine, CA 92612-3299	Becky Peters	Disability Services	949-854-8002 ext. 1836
Cuesta C.	San Luis Obispo, CA 93403	Ilene French	Academic Support	805-546-3148
De Anza C.	Sunnyvale, CA 94087	Benita Rashall, MS	Educational Diagnostic Center	408-864-8959
Dominican U. of California	San Rafeal, CA 94901-2298	Kathryn Mulholland	Tutoring and Disability Services	415-257-0187
East Los Angeles C.	Monterey Pk, CA 90025	Grace Marillo Hernandez	DSPS	323-265-8787
El Camino C.	Torrance, CA 90506	Susan Brouillette	Special Resource Center	310-660-3296
Evergreen Valley C.	San Jose, CA 95135	Robin Salak	Disabled Students Program	408-223-6756
Foothill C.	Los Altos, CA 94022	Margo Dobbins	STEP	650-949-7038
Fresno Pacific U.	Fresno, CA 93702	Don Sparks	Student Development Program	559-453-3696
Grossmont C.	Ramona, CA 92065	Carl Fielden	Disabled Students Programs & Services	619-644-7112
Harvey Mudd C.	Claremont, CA 91711	Jenne Noda	Dean of Students	909-621-8125
Holy Names U.	Oakland, CA 94619	Laura Lydon	Disability Support Services	510-436-1658
Humboldt St. U.	Arcata, CA 95521-8299	Kevin O'Brien	Disabled Student Services	707-826-4678
Humphreys C.	Stockton, CA 95207	Jess Bonds	Disability Services	209-235-2920
John F. Kennedy U.	Orinda, CA 94563	Lisa Noshe-Pitro	Student Disability Services	925-969-3447
Lake Tahoe C.C.	So. Lake Tahoe, CA 96150	Bob Albrecht	Disability Resource Center	530-541-4660 ext. 249
Laney College	El Sobrante, CA 94803	Carol Dalissio	Disabled Student Program Services	510-464-3432
Life Pacific C.	San Dimas, CA 91773-3298	Pat Crowder	Life Challenges & PCS	909-599-5433 ext. 363
Long Beach City C.	Long Beach, CA 90808	Mark Matsui	Disabled Student Program Services	562-938-4111
Los Angeles City C.	Los Angeles, CA 90039	Susan Matranga	LD Services	323-953-4000 ext. 2270
Loyola Marymount U.	Los Angeles, CA 90045	Priscilla F. Levine, LCSW	Disability Support Services	310-338-4535
Master's C.	Newhall, CA 91322	Marion McElwee	Disability Services	661-259-3540 ext. 3851
Menlo C.	Atherton, CA 94027	Janet Miller, MA, CET	Academic Success Center	650-543-3854
Mills C.	Oakland, CA 94613	Jeff Miller	Disability Services	510-430-2264
Mount St. Mary's C.	Los Angeles, CA 90049	Michele Lewis	Disability Services	310-954-4141
Norte Dame de Namur U.	Belmont, CA 94002-1908	Joanne Rossi	PASS	650-508-3613
Occidental C.	Los Angeles, CA 90041	Raul Villa	Center for Academic Excellence	323-259-2545
Orange Coast C.	Costa Mesa, CA 92628	Kevin Smith	Learning Center	714-432-5535
Oxnard C.	Oxnard, CA 93033	Orlean Bowers	Disabled Students Program & Services	805-986-5830
Pasadena City C.	Pasadena, CA 91106	Lisa Paiz	Disabled Student Services	626-585-7127
Pacific Oaks C.	Pasadena, CA 31103	Patricia Meda	CARE Center	626-397-1338
Pacific Union C.	Angwin, CA 94508	Nancy Jacobo	Disability Support Services	707-965-7685

College	Location	Contact	Office	Phone
Patten U.	Oakland, CA 94601	Inez Bailey	Enrollment Services	510-261-8500 ext. 7765
Pepperdine U.	Malibu, CA 90263	Tammy Selby	Disability Services	310-506-6500
Pitzer C.	Claremont, CA 91711	Rochelle D. Brown	Academic Support Services	909-607-3553
Reedley College	Reedley, CA 93654-2099	Dr. Janice Emerzian	Disabled Students Programs & Services	559-638-0332
Pitzer C.	Claremont, CA 91711	Rochelle D. Brown	Academic Support Services	909-607-3553
Point Loma Nazarene U.	San Diego, CA 92106	Patricia Curley	Academic Advising	619-849-2486
Pomona C.	Claremont, CA 91711	Toni Clark	Disability Services	909-621-8017
Saddleback C.	Carlsbad, CA 92008	Randy Anderson	Special Services	949-582-4885
St. Mary's C. of CA	Moraga, CA 94556	Jeannine Chavez-Parfitt	Academic Support Center	925-631-4358
San Diego City C.	San Diego, CA 92101	Barbara Mason	Disabled Student Program & Service	619-230-2513
San Diego St. U.	San Diego, CA 92182	Mary Shojai	Disabled Student Program & Service	619-594-6473
San Francisco Art Institute	San Francisco, CA 94133	Susan Green	Center for Individual Learning	415-771-7020 ext. 4471
San Francisco St. U.	San Francisco, CA 94132	Gene Chelberg	Disability Programs & Resource Center	415-338-6356
San Jose St. U.	San Jose, CA 95192	Martin Schulter	Disability Resource Center	408-924-6000
Santa Barbara City C.	Santa Barbara, CA 93109	Janet Shapiro	Disabled Student Services	805-965-0581
Santa Clara U.	Santa Clara, CA 95053	Ann Ravenscroft	Disability Resources	408-554-4111
Santa Monica C.	Santa Monica, CA 90405	Mary Jane Well	Center for Students with Disabilities	310-434-4265
Santa Rosa Junior C.	Santa Rosa, CA 95401	Patie Wegman	Disability Resource Department	707-527-4278
Scripps C.	Claremont, CA 91711	Carol Entler	Disability Services	909621-8089
Sierra C.	Rocklin, CA 95677	Kaylene Hallberg	Learning Opportunities Center	916-789-2939
Simpson U.	Redding, CA 96003-8606	Mike Schill	Growth and Development	530-226-4179
Sonoma St. U.	Rohnert Park, CA 94928	Rose T. Lawrence	Disabled Student Services	707-664-2677
Stanford U.	Stanford, CA 94305-3005	Joan Bisagno	Office of Accessible Education	650-723-1066
Taft C.	Taft, CA 93268	Jeff Ross	Disabled Student Services	661-763-7776
U. of California—Berkeley	Berkeley, CA 94720-4250	Ed Rogers	Disabled Students' Program	510-642-0518
U. of California—Davis	Davis, CA 95616	Signe Morton	Learning Disability Center	530-752-3184
U. of California—Irvine	Irvine, CA 92717	Dr. Jane Serrantino	Office of Disability Services	949-824-7494
U. of California—Los Angeles	Los Angeles, CA 90095	Kathy Molini	Office for Students with Disabilities	310-825-1501
U. of California—Riverside	Riverside, CA 92521	Marcia Theise Schiffer	Services for Students w/ Disabilities	951-827-4538
U. of California—San Diego	La Jolla, CA 92093-0337	Roberta Gimblett	Office for Students with Disabilities	858-534-4382
U. of California—Santa Barbara	Santa Barbara, CA 93106	Gary White	Disabled Student Program	805-893-2182
U. of California—Santa Cruz	Santa Cruz, CA 95064	Peggy Church	Disability Resource Center	831-459-2089
U. of Judaism	Bel Air, CA 90077	Matt Davidson	Disability Services	310-440-1250

Institution	City, State ZIP	Contact	Service	Phone
U. of La Verne	La Verne, CA 91750	Cynthia Denne	Disability Services	909-593-3511 ext. 4441
U. of Redlands	Redlands, CA 92373-0999	Jen Ostermiller	Academic Support Services	909-748-8108
U. of San Diego	San Diego, CA 92110-2492	Dr. Don Kirson	Disabled Student Services	619-260-4655
U. of San Francisco	San Francisco, CA 94117	Tom Merrell	Student Disability Services	415-422-6876
U. of Southern California	Los Angeles, CA 90089	Dr. Edward Roth	Disability Services & Programs	213-740-0776
U. of the Pacific	Stockton, CA 95211	Lisa Cooper	Office of Services for Students with Disabilities	209-946-2458
Vanguard U. of Southern CA	Costa Mesa, CA 92626	Barbi Rouse	Learning Skills	714-556-3610
Westmont C.	Santa Barbara, CA 93108	Michelle Hardley	Academic Resource Center	805-565-6159
Whittier C.	Whittier, CA 90608	Rosalba B. Rios, MS	Disability Services	562-907-4840
Woodbury C.	Burbank, CA 91510	Emmanuel Lopez	Academic Advising	818-252-5129

COLORADO

Institution	City, State ZIP	Contact	Service	Phone
Colorado Christian C.	Lakewood, CO 80226	Kristen Parker	Academic Services	303-963-3267
Colorado C.	Colorado Springs, CO 80903	Kristen Wiegers	Services for Students with Disabilities	303-273-3377
Colorado Mt. C.	Glenwood Springs, CO 81601	Cheri White	Developmental Education	970-945-8256
Colorado School of Mines	Golden, CO 80401-1869	Ron Brummett	Student Development & Career Center	303-273-3297
Colorado St. U.	Fort Collins, CO 80523	Rosemary Kreston	Resources for Disabled Students	970-491-6385
Mesa St. C.	Grand Junction, CO 81502-2647	Nancy Conklin	Education Access Service	970-248-1826
Metropolitan St. C. of Denver	Denver, CO 80217-3362	Gregory Sullivan	Access Center	303-556-8387
Northeastern Junior C.	Sterling, CO 80751	Lori Gill	Study Skills Services	970-521-6670
Regis U.	Denver, CO 80221-1099	Marijo (Joie) Williams	Disability Services	303-458-4941
U. of Colorado—Boulder	Boulder, CO 80309-0107	Cindy Donohue	Disability Services	303-492-8671
U. of Colorado—Col. Springs	Colorado Springs, CO 80933	Kaye Simonton	Disability Services	719-262-3354
U. of Colorado—Denver	Denver, CO 80217	Lisa McGill	Disability Support Department	303-556-8388
U. of Denver	Denver, CO 80208	Ted F. May	LEP	303-871-2372
U. of Northern Colorado	Greeley, CO 80639	Nancy Kauffman	Disability Access Center	970-351-2289
Colorado State U.—Pueblo	Pueblo, CO 81001	John Meisper	Disabilities Resources Office	719-549-2663
Western St. C. of Colorado	Gunnison, CO 81231	Julie Luekenga	Disability Services	970-943-7056

CONNECTICUT

Institution	City, State ZIP	Contact	Service	Phone
Albertus Magnus C.	New Haven, CT 06511	Deborah Frattini	Academic Development Center	203-773-8564
Briarwood C.	Southington, CT 06489	Cynthia Clark	Services for Students with LD	860-628-4751
Central Connecticut St. U.	New Britain, CT 06050	Natalie Byers	Special Student Services	860-832-1957
Eastern Connecticut St. U.	Willimantic, CT 06226	Pamela Starr	Counseling for Students w/ Disabilities	860-465-5573

College	Contact	Address	Service	Phone
Fairfield U.	David Ryan-Soderlund	Fairfield, CT 06430-5195	Academic & Disability Support Services	203-254-4000 ext. 2615
Housatonic C.	Lynn Langella	Bridgeport, CT 06608	Disability Support Services	203-332-5018
Mitchell C.	Peter F. Love, PhD	New London, CT 06320	Learning Resource Center	860-701-5144
Post U.	Lauren Ferrara	Waterbury, CT 06723	Disability Services	203-596-4677
Quinnipiac C.	John Jarvis	Hamden, CT 06518	Learning Services	203-582-5390
Sacred Heart U.	Jill Angotta	Fairfield, CT 06825	Special Services	203-365-4730
St. Joseph C.	Jacqueline Sironen	West Hartford, CT 06117	Disability Services	860-231-5428
Southern Connecticut St. U.	Suzanne Tucker	New Haven, CT 06515	Disability Resource Office	203-392-6828
Trinity C.	Fred Alford	Hartford, CT 06106	Disability Services	860-297-2157
U. of Bridgeport	Carole Weiner	Bridgeport, CT 06604	Disability Services	203-576-4454
U. of Connecticut	Nadine Brennan	W. Hartford, CT 06117	Disability Support Services	860-570-9232
U. of Connecticut	David Parker, PhD	Storrs, CT 06269	Univ. Program for College Students with LD	860-486-0178
U. of Hartford	Lynne Golden	West Hartford, CT 06117	Learning Plus	860-768-5129
U. of New Haven	Linda Copney-Okeke	West Haven, CT 06516	Disability Services & Resources	203-932-7331
Wesleyan U.	Vancenia Rutherford	Middletown, CT 06459-0265	Learning Disabilities Services	860-685-2600
Western Connecticut St. U.	Jack Sikora	Danbury, CT 06810	Disability Services	203-837-8946
Yale U.	Carolyn Barrett	New Haven, CT 06520	Resource Office for Disabilities	203-432-2324

DELAWARE

College	Contact	Address	Service	Phone
Delaware St. U.	Laura Kurtz	Dover, DE 19901	Disabilities Services	302-857-6388
Delaware Tech C.C.	Bonnie Hall	Georgetown, DE 19947	Student Support Services	302-856-5400 ext. 3360
U. of Delaware	Lysbet J. Murray	Newark, DE 19716-6210	Academic Success Services	302-831-1639
Wesley C.	Christine McDermott	Dover, DE 19901-3875	Academic Support Services	302-736-2491

DISTRICT OF COLUMBIA

College	Contact	Address	Service	Phone
American U.	Kathy Schwartz	Washington, DC 20016	Academic Support Center	202-885-3360
Catholic U. of America, The	Emily Singer	Washington, DC 20064-0001	Disability Support Services	202-319-5211
Corcoran C. of Art	Elizabeth C. Smith	Washington DC 20006-4804	Disability Services	202-639-1814
Gallaudet U.	Patricia Tesar	Washington, DC 20002	Prog for Students w/ Other Disabilities	202-651-5256
George Washington U.	Christy Willis	Washington, DC 20052	Disability Support Services	202-994-8250
Georgetown U.	Jane Holahan	Washington, DC 20057	Learning Services	202-687-8354
Howard U.	Dr. Barbara Williams	Washington, DC	Special Student Services	202-238-2420
Trinity C. (DC)	Melissa Earnest	Washington, DC 20017-1094	Career Services	202-884-9681

Institution	City, State ZIP	Contact	Service	Phone
U. of District of Columbia	Washington, DC 20008	Sandra Carter	Services for Students w/Disabilities	202-274-5531

FLORIDA

Institution	City, State ZIP	Contact	Service	Phone
Baptist C. of Florida	Graceville, GL 32440	Stephanie W. Orr	Disability Services	800-328-2660 ext. 465
Barry U.	Miami Shores, FL 33161-6695	Leslie Rouder	Clinical Center for Advanced Learning	305-899-3461
Beacon C.	Leesburg, FL 34748	Deborah Brodbeck	Office of President	352-787-7660
Broward C.C.	Ft. Lauderdale, FL 33301	Beverly Cranmer	Disability Services	954-201-7655
Clearwater Christian C.	Clearwater, FL 33759-4595	Linda Wiggins	Disability Services	727-726-1153
Eckerd C.	St. Petersburg, FL 33711	Laura E. Schlack	Disability Support Services	727-864-8331
Edison C.C.	Fort Meyers, FL 33906	Joseph Kay	Disability Services	239-489-9112
Edward Waters C.	Jacksonville, FL 32009	Dr. Emmanuel Okakor	Disability Services	904-470-8052
Embry-Riddle Aeronaut. U. (FL)	Daytona Beach, FL 32114	Vanessa Lloyd	Disability Services	386-226-7916
Flafle C.	St. Augustine, FL 32084	Deborah Larew	Services for Students w/ Disabilities	905-819-6460
Florida A&M U.	Tallahassee, FL 32307	Dr. Nathaniel Holmes	Learning Development & Evaluation Ctr.	850-599-3180
Florida Atlantic U.	Boca Raton, FL 33431	Nicole Rokos	Office for Students with Disabilities	561-297-3880
Florida Gulf Coast U.	Fort Myers, FL 33965-6565	Cori Bright	Disability Services	239-590-7956
Florida Institute of Tech.	Melborne, FL 32901-6975	Rodney Bowers	Academic Support Services	321-674-7110
Florida International U.	Miami, FL 33199	Beverly Trott	Disability Services	305-348-3532
Florida Memorial C.	Miami, FL 33054	Dr. Harold Clarke, Jr.	Disability Services	305-626-3711
Florida St. U.	Tallahassee, FL 32306	Bea Awoniyi	Student Disability Resource Center	850-644-9566
Gulf Coast C.C.	Panama City, FL 32401	Linda Van Dalen	Disability Support Services	850-872-3834
Hillsborough C.C.	Tampa, FL 33631-3127	Janice Jeffers-Long	Disabled Services	813-253-7914
Indian River C.C.	Fort Pierce, FL 34981	Rhoda Brant	Disability Services	772-462-4700
Jacksonville U.	Jacksonville, FL 32211	Dr. John Balog	Disabled Students Services	904-256-7070
Lynn U.	Boca Raton, FL 33431	Dr. Marsha A. Glines	Institute for Achievement & Learning	561-237-7881
Miami Int'l. U. of Art	Miami, FL 33132	Shari Saperstein	Student Affairs	305-428-5900
New C. of Florida	Sarasota, FL 34243-2197	Christopher J. Pantzis	Student Disability Services	941-359-4254
Northwood U.—Florida Campus	West Palm Beach, FL 33409	Holly Genser	Learning Center	561-478-5585
Nova Southeastern U.	Ft. Lauderdale, FL 33314	Arlene Giczkowski	Academic Services	954-262-7189
Pensacola Jr. C.	Pensacola, FL 32504	Dr. James Nickles	Disability Support Services	850-484-1637
Ringling School of Art	Sarasota, FL 34234-5895	Virginia Demers	Academic Resource Center	800-255-7695
Rollins C.	Winter Park, FL 32789-4499	Karen Hater	Student Resources Center	407-646-2354
Saint Thomas U.	Miami, FL 33054	Maritza Rivera	Academic Enhancement	305-628-6564

College	City, State Zip	Contact	Office	Phone
Santa Fe C.C.	Gainesville, FL 32606	Claudia Munnis	Disability Resource Center	352-395-5948
Seminole C.C.	Sanford, FL 32773	Dorothy Paishon	Disabled Support Services	407-328-2109
St. Leo U.	Saint Leo, FL 33574-6665	Dr. Joanne MacEachran	Learning Resource Center	352-588-8462
St. Petersburg Jr. C.	St. Petersburg, FL 33733	Dr. Linda Giar	Disability Services	727-341-3721
Southeastern U.	Lakeland, FL 33801	Misty Mancini	Academic Success Center	863-667-5157
Stetson U.	Deland, FL 32723	Karen Cole, PhD	Academic Resource Center	386-822-7127
Tallahassee CC	Tallahassee, FL 32340	Judy Barnes	Disability Support Services	850-201-8430
Trinity Baptist C.	Jacksonville, FL 32221	Larry Appleby	Disability Services	800-786-2206
U. of Central Florida	Orlando, FL 32816	Dr. Philip Kalfin	Student Disability Services	407-823-2371
U. of Florida	Gainesville, FL 32611	Jim Faubel	Disability Resources Center	352-392-8565 ext. 200
U. of Miami	Coral Gables, FL 33146	Mayra Diaz	Academic Resource Center	305-284-2374
U. of North Florida	Jacksonville, FL 32224-2645	Dr. Robert E. Lee	Disability Resource Center	904-620-2769
U. of South Florida	Tampa, FL 33620	Dr. Mary Sarver	Student Disability Services	813-974-4309
U. of Tampa	Tampa, FL 33606-1490	Robert Ruday	Student Disability Services	813-253-6204
U. of West Florida	Pensacola, FL 32514-5750	Lusharon Wiley	Dean of Students	850-474-2387
Warner Southern C.	Lake Wales, FL 33859	Jason Roe	Disability Services	863-638-7212

GEORGIA

College	City, State Zip	Contact	Office	Phone
Agnes Scott C.	Decatur, GA 30030	Jennifer Cannady	Academic Advising	404-471-6200
Andrew C.	Cuthbert, GA 31740	Sherri Taylor	FOCUS	229-732-5908
Armstrong St. C.	Savannah, GA 31419	Amelia Castillian	Disability Services	912-927-5271
Art Institute of Atlanta	Atlanta, GA 30328	April Shavkin	Disability Services	770-689-4908
Augusta State U.	August, GA 30904-2200	Angie Kitchens	Testing & Disability Services	706-737-1469
Berry C.	Mount Berry, GA 30149	Martha Van Cise	Academic Support	706-233-4080
Brenau U.	Gainesville, GA 30501	Vincent Yamilkoski, EdD	Learning Center	770-534-6134
Brewton-Parker C.	Mt. Vernon, GA 30445	Juanita Kissell	Disability Services	912-583-3222
Clark Atlanta U.	Atlanta, GA 30314	Ricky Robinson	Student Assistance	404-880-8771
Clayton College & St. U.	Morrow, GA 30260	Nicole Palazzo	Disability Resource Center	770-961-3719
Columbus C.	Columbus, GA 31907	Joy Norman	Disability Services	706-568-2330
Covenant C.	Lookout Mountain, GA 30750	Rodney Miller	Disability Services	706-419-1135
Darton C.	Albany, GA 31707	Tanya Anderson	Disabled Student Services	229-430-6867
Georgia Perimeter College	Clarkston, GA 30021	Mavis Clark	Ctr. for Disability Services	678-891-3385
Emmanuel College	Franklin Springs, GA 30639	Lee Phillips	Counseling Services	706-245-7226
Emory U.	Atlanta, GA 30322	Gloria Weaver	Disability Services	404-727-6016

Institution	Location	Contact	Service	Phone
Ft. Valley St. U.	Fort Valley, GA 31030-4313	Alfred Conteh	Differently Abled Services	476-825-6744
Gainesville C.	Gainesville, GA 30503	Carolyn Swindle	Disability Services	770-718-3855
Georgia C. and St. U.	Milledgeville, GA 31061	Dr. Craig Smith	Dept. of Special Ed. & Educational Leadership	478-445-4577
Georgia Institute of Tech.	Atlanta, GA 30332-0320	Denise Johnson	Disabled Student Services	404-894-9191
Georgia Southern U.	Statesboro, GA 30460	Wayne Akins	Disabled Student Services	912-871-1566
Georgia St. U.	Atlanta, GA 30302-4009	Rodney E. Pennamon	Disability Services	404-463-9044
Kennesaw St. U.	Kennesaw, GA 30144-5591	Carol Pope	Disabled Student Services	770-423-6443
Life U.	Marietta, GA 30060	Dr. Lisa Rubin	Academic Assistance Center	770-426-2725
LaGrange C.	La Grange, GA 30240	Pamela Tremblay	Disability Services	706-880-8313
Mercer U.	Macon, GA 31207-0003	Michele Currie	Disability Services	478-301-2686
Morehouse C.	Atlanta, GA 30314	Carolyn S. Walker	Disability Services	404-215-2636
North Georgia C. & St. U.	Dahlonega, GA 30597	Elizabeth McIntosh	Student Disability Resources	706-867-2782
Oglethorpe U.	Atlanta, GA 30319	RoseMary Watkins	Learning Resources Services	404-364-8869
Paine C.	Augusta, GA 30901-3182	Dr. Elias Etinge	Disability Services	706-821-8302
Piedmont C.	Demorest, GA 30535	Debra Taylor	Academic Support Services	706-778-3000
Reinhardt C.	Waleska, GA 30183	Sylvia Robertson	Academic Support Office	770-720-5567
Shorter C.	Rome, GA 30165-4898	Michele Turner	Academic Support Center	706-233-7323
South U.—Georgia	Savannah, GA 33411	Lisa Brightberg	Disability Services	912-201-8170
Southern Polytechnic St. U.	Marietta, GA 30060	Phyllis Weatherly	Counseling & Disability Services	678-915-7226
Spelman C.	Atlanta, GA 30314	Merrine McDonald	Student Disability Services	404-270-5293
The Savannah C. of Art	Savannah, GA 31402-3146	Lita Clary	Disability Services	912-525-4665
Truett-McConnell C.	Cleveland, GA 30528	Neil Hoyle	Special Support Services	706-865-2134
U. of Georgia	Athens, GA 30602	Dr. Karen Kalivoda	Learning Disabilities Center	706-542-8719
U. of West Georgia	Carrolton, GA 30118	Ann Phillips, PhD	Disability Services	678-839-6428
Valdosta St. U.	Valdosta, GA 31698	Kimberly Godden	Access Office for Students with Disabilities	229-245-2498
Wesleyan C.	Macon, GA 31210-4462	Jerri Crowell	Academic Center	478-757-5219

HAWAII

Institution	Location	Contact	Service	Phone
Brigham Young U.	Laie Oahu, HI 96762-1294	Leilani Auna	Services for Students with Special Needs	808-293-3999
Chaminade U. of Honolulu	Honolulu, HI 96816	Don Kopf	Student Affairs	808-735-4845
Hawaii C.C.	Hilo, HI 96720	Karen Kane	Ha'awi Kokua Program	808-933-0702
Hawaii Pacific U.	Honolulu, HI 96813	Sara Seto	Office of Admissions	808-544-0238
U. of Hawaii—Hilo	Hilo, HI 96720-4091	Susan Shirachi	Disability Services	808-933-0816
U. of Hawaii—Manoa	Honolulu, HI 96822	Ann C. Ito	KOKUA Program	808-956-7511

IDAHO

Institution	Location	Contact	Service	Phone
Albertson C. of Idaho	Caldwell, ID 83605	Linette Alan	Disability Services	208-459-5683
Boise St. U.	Boise, ID 83725	Elyse Taylor	Special Services	208-426-1583
Idaho St. U.	Pocatello, ID 83209-8270	Dennis Toney	ADA Disabilities Center	208-282-3599
Lewis-Clark St. C.	Lewiston, ID 83501	Debbie Mundell	Disability Services	208-792-2211
Northwest Nazarene U.	Nampa, ID 83686	Barbara Howard	Academic Support Center	208-467-8669
U. of Idaho	Moscow, ID 83844-4140	Gloria R. Jensen	Disability Support Services	208-885-7200

ILLINOIS

Institution	Location	Contact	Service	Phone
Augustana C.	Rock Island, IL 61201-2296	Evelyn Campbell	Dean of Students Office	309-794-7533
Aurora U.	Aurora, IL 60506	Susan Lausier	Disability Services	630-844-5267
Benedictine U.	Lisle, IL 60532-0900	Tina Sonderby	Academic Resource Center	630-829-6512
Blackburn C.	Carlinville, IL 62626	Rob Weis	Counseling Office/Learning Center	800-233-3550
Bradley U.	Peoria, IL 61625	Carolyn Griffith	Learning Assistance	309-794-7533
Chicago St. U.	Chicago, IL 60628	Dr. Cherly Green	Abilities Office	773-995-4401
C. of Du Page	Glen Ellyn, IL 60137	Jacqueline Reuland	Special Student Services	630-942-2567
C. of Lake County	Grayslake, IL 60030	Beth Remedi	Disability Student Services	847-543-2473
Columbia C. (IL)	Chicago, IL 60605-1996	Sandra Saunders	Services for Students with Disabilities	312-344-8134
Concordia U.	River Forest, IL 60305-1499	Carol Gilbert	Learning Assistance	708-809-3042
DePaul University	Chicago, IL 60604	Karen Meyer	Productive Learning Strategies	773-325-7290
Eastern Illinois U.	Charleston, IL 61920-3099	Kathy Waggoner	Disability Services	217-581-6583
Elgin C.C.	Elgin, IL 60123	Annabelle Rhoades	Disability Services	847-697-1000
Elmhurst C.	Elmhurst, IL 60126	Maureen Connolly	Disability Services	630-617-3753
Eureka C.	Eureka, IL 61530-1500	JoAnne Woiwode	Learning Center	309-467-6520
Governors St. U.	University Park, IL 60466	Robin Sweeney	Disability Services	708-534-4508
Greenville C.	Greenville, IL 62246-0159	Dr. Will Boyd	Disability Services	618-664-6613
Harper C.	Palatine, IL 60067	Tom Thompson	Center for Students with Disabilities	847-925-6266
Illinois C.	Jacksonville, IL 62650-2299	Judy Norris	Templeton Counseling Center	217-245-3073
Illinois Institute of Technology	Chicago, IL 60616	Elizabeth Lyongs	Academic Resource Center	312-567-7959
Illinois St. U.	Normal, IL 61790	Ann M. Cadwell	Disability Concerns	309-438-5853
Illinois Wesleyan U.	Bloomington, IL 61702-2900	Roger Schnaitter	Disability Services	309-556-3255
Ivy Tech St. C.	Evansville, IL 47710	Cindy Kates	Special Needs	812-429-1386
John Wood C.C.	Quincy, IL 62301	Rose-Marie Akers	Support Services Center	217-224-6500

Institution	Location	Contact	Office/Program	Phone
Joliet Junior C.	Joliet, IL 60436	Jewell Dennis	Project Achieve	815-729-9020 ext. 2455
Kankakee C. C.	Kankakee, IL 60901	Joylenne Keiser	Special Population & Instruc. Support	815-802-8482
Knox C.	Galesburg, IL 61401	John Haslem	Center for Teaching and Learning	309-341-7151
Lake Forest C.	Lake Forest, IL 60045	Marta Tonegutti	Dean's Office	847-735-5200
Lakeland C.	Mattoon, IL 61938	Heather Nohren	Special Needs Office	217-234-5259
Lewis U.	Romeoville, IL 60446-2200	Denise Rich	Disability Resources	815-836-5284
Lincoln C.	Lincoln, IL 62656	Stephanie Gaddy, EdD	Disability Services	800-569-0556
Loyola U. of Chicago	Chicago, IL 60611	Maggie Rogers	Services for Students with Disabilities	773-508-2741
MacMurray C.	Lebanon, IL 62254-1299	Randy Myers	Disability Services	217-479-7222
McHenry C.C.	Crystal Lake, IL 60012	Bev Albright	Special Needs	815-455-8676
McKendree C.	Lebanon, IL 62254-1299	Clarissa Melvin	Academic Support	618-537-6850
Millikin U.	Decatur, IL 62522-2084	Linda M. Slagell	Disability Services	217-420-6622
Monmouth C.	Monmouth, IL 61462	Jacquelyn Condon	Student Affairs	309-457-2133
Morraine Valley C.C.	Palos Hills, IL 60465	Debbie Sievers	Center for Disability Services	708-974-5330
Morton C.	Cicero, IL 60650	Chris Martin	Special Needs	708-656-8000
National-Louis U.	Evanston, IL 60201	Erin Haulotte	Center for Academic Development	847-947-5491
North Central C.	Naperville, IL 60566	Jennifer Peppin	Learning Disability Services	630-637-5264
North Park U.	Chicago, IL 60625-4895	Talia Campbell	Academic Services	773-244-5726
Northeastern Illinois U.	Chicago, IL 60625	Victoria Amey-Flippin	HELP Program	773-442-5495
Northern Illinois U.	DeKalb, IL 60115	Nancy Kasinski	Ctr. for Access-Ability Resources	815-753-9734
Northwestern U.	Evanston, IL 60204	Margie Roe	Services for Students with Disabilities	847-491-2690
Oakton Community C.	Des Plaines, IL 60116	Teresa O'Sullivan	ASSIST	847-635-1759
Olivet Nazarene U.	Bourbonnais, IL 60914	Sue Rattin	Disability Services	815-928-5150
Parkland C.	Champaign, IL 61821	Marilyn Ryan	Disability Services	217-351-2364
Quincy U.	Quincy, IL 62301	Linda Godley	Disability Services	217-228-5288
Robert Morris C.	Chicago, IL 60605	Monique Jones	Student Services	312-935-2003
Rockford C.	Rockford, IL 61108-2393	Lorraine Hoover	Disability Support Services	815-226-4022
Roosevelt U.	Chicago, IL 60605	Nancy Litke	Learning Support Services Program	312-341-3810
St Francis Med. Center C. of Nurs.	Peoria, IL 61603	Sally McLaughlin	Disability Services	309-655-7100
Saint Xavier U.	Chicago, IL 60655	Julie Ashley	Student Success/Learning Assist. Ctr.	773-298-3308
Schl. of Art Inst. of Chicago	Chicago, IL 60603	Heather Walsh	Learning Center	312-499-4278
Shimer C.	Waukegan, IL 60079-0500	Elaine Vincent	Disability Services	312-235-3500

Institution	Location	Contact	Office	Phone
SIU-Carbondale	Carbondale, IL 62901-4710	Kathleen Piesko	Achieve Program	618-453-7754
SIU-Edwardsville	Edwardsville, IL 62026	Jane Floyd-Hendey	Office of Disabled Student Services	618-650-3782
St. Anthony C. of Nursing	Rockford, IL 61108-2468	Nancy Sanders	Student Affairs Office	815-395-5100
Trinity Christian C.	Palos Heights, IL 60463	Nancy Kwasteniet	Services for Student Success	708-239-4765
Trinity International C.	Deerfield, IL	Felix Theonugraha	Dean of Students Office	847-317-4063
U. of Chicago	Chicago, IL 60637	Aneesah Ali	Assistance for Disabled Students	773-702-5671
U. of Illinois—Chicago	Chicago, IL 60680	Roxanna Stupp	Disability Services	312-413-2183
U. of Illinois—Springfield	Springfield, IL 62703-5407	Karla Carwile	Disability Services	217-206-6666
U. of Ill.—Urbana-Champaign	Urbana, IL 61801	Brad Hendrick	Disability Resources & Educational Services	217-333-4600
U. of St. Francis	Joliet, IL 60435	Pat Vivio	Office of Disability Services	815-740-3204
Waubonsee C.C.	Sugar Grove, IL 60554	Iris Hansen	Access Ctr. for Students w/ Disabilities	630-466-2564
Western Illinois U.	Macomb, IL 61455-1390	Tara Miller	Disability Support Services	309-298-2512
Wheaton C.	Weaton, IL 60187	Paul E. Johnson	Registrars Office	630-752-5044

INDIANA

Institution	Location	Contact	Office	Phone
Anderson U.	Anderson, IN 46012	Rinda Vogelgesang	Kissinger Learning Center	765-641-4226
Ball St. U.	Muncie, IN 47306	Larry Markle	Office of Disabled Students	765-285-5293
Bethel C.	Mishawaka, IN 46545	Carolyn Arthur	Academic Support Center	574-257-3356
Butler U.	Indianapolis, IN 46208	Michele Atterson	Student Disabilities Center	317-940-9308
Calumet C. of St. Joseph	Whiting, IN 46394	Valerie Rister	Student Support Services	219-473-4388
DePauw U.	Greencastle, IN 46135	Diane D. Hightower	Academic Services	765-658-4027
Earlham C.	Richmond, IN 47374	Donna Keesling	Center for Academic Enrichment	765-983-1200 ext. 1341
Franklin C.	Franklin, IN 46131-2623	Bethany Tidball	Academic Resource Center	317-738-8288
Goshen C.	Goshen, IN 46526-4794	Lois Martin	Academic Support Center	574-535-7576
Grace C. and Seminary	Winona Lake, IN 46590	Peggy Underwood	Academic Achievement Center	574-372-5100 ext. 6422
Hanover C.	Hanover, IN 47243	Dr. Kenneth Prince	Disability Services	812-866-7051
Huntington C.	Huntington, IN 46750	Kris Chafin	Learning Center	260-359-4290
Indiana St. U.	Terre Haute, IN 47809	Rita Worrall	Student Support Services	812-237-2301
Indiana U. SE	New Albany, IN 47150	Hannah Wallace	Disabilities Services	812-941-2243
Indiana U. East	Richmond, IN 47374-1289	Sheryl Stafford	Student Support Services	765-973-8319
Indiana U.—Bloomington	Bloomington, IN 47405-7700	Martha P. Jacques	Disabled Student Services	812-855-7578
Indiana U.—Kokomo	Kokomo, IN 46904-9003	Gerry Stroman	Disability Services	765-455-9309
Indiana U.—Northwest	Gary, IN 46408	Jason Griffith	Student Services	219-980-6943
Indiana U.—Purdue Univ.	Indianapolis, IN 46202-5143	Pamela King	Adaptive Educational Services	317-274-3241

Institution	City/State	Contact	Service	Phone
Indiana U.—South Bend	South Bend, IN 46634-7111	Valerie St. Germain	Division of Disabled Student Services	574-520-4256
Indiana Wesleyan U.	Marion, IN 46953-4999	Nathan L. Herring, M.A.	Student Support Services	765-677-2257
IPFW-Ft. Wayne	Ft. Wayne, IN 46805	Eric Wheenfeld	Services for Students with Disabilities(SSD)	260-481-6657
IVY Tech	Fort Wayne, IN 46805	Debra Clarke	Disability Services	260-480-4207
Manchester C.	N. Manchester, IN 46962	Denise L.S. Howe, Ed.S.	Learning Support Services	260-982-5076
Marion C.	Indianapolis, IN 46222	Marge Batic	Learning and Counseling Center	317-955-6150
Purdue U.—Calumet	Hammond, IN 46323-2094	Michaeline Florek	Student Support Services	219-989-2455
Purdue U.—North Central	Westville, IL 46391	Jodi James	Disability Services	219-785-5374
Purdue U.—West Lafayette	West Lafayette, IN 47907	Heather Stout	Adaptive Program	765-494-1247
Rose-Human Institute of Tech.	Terre Haute, IN 47803	Karen DeGrange	Special Programs	812-877-8285
St. Joseph's C.	Rensselaer, IN 47978	Lesile Frere	Counseling Services	219-866-6116
St. Mary-of-the-Wood C.	St. Mary-of-the-Wood, IN 47876	John Lotz	Learning Resource Center	812-535-5271
Taylor U.	Upland, IN 46989	Edwin Welch	Academic Support Services	765-998-5523
Tri-St. U.	Angola, IN 46703	Marline Sweet	Special Students	260-665-4172
U. of Evansville	Evansville, IN 47722	Sylvia Buck	Counselling & Testing Center	812-479-2663
U. of Indianapolis	Indianapolis, IN 46227	Candace Joles	BUILD	317-788-3536
U. of Notre Dame	Notre Dame, IN 46556	Scott Howland	Office for Students w/ Disabilities	574-631-7157
U. of Saint Francis	Fort Wayne, IN 46808	Michelle Kruyer	Student Learning Center	260-434-7677
U. of Southern Indiana	Evansville, IN 47712	James Browning	Counseling Center	812-464-1867
Valparaiso U.	Valparaiso, IN 46383	Christina Grabarek	Disability Support Services	219-464-5790
Vincennes U.	Vincennes, IN 47591	Jane Kavanaugh	STEP	812-888-4485
Wabash C.	Crawfordsville, IN 47933	Julia Rosenberg	Writing Center—Academic Support	765-361-6024

IOWA

Institution	City/State	Contact	Service	Phone
Briar Cliff U.	Sioux City, IA 51104	Sister Jean Beringer	Student Support Services	712-279-5232
Buena Vista U.	Storm Lake, IA 50588	Mary Gill	Disability Services	712-749-2205
Central C.	Pella, IA 50219	Nancy Kroese	Student Support Services	641-628-5247
Clarke C.	Dubuque, IA 52001	Myra Benzer	Learning Center	563-588-8107
Coe C.	Cedar Rapids, IA 52402	Lois Kabela-Coates	Academic Achievement Program	319-399-8547
Cornell C.	Mount Vernon, IA 52341	John Harp	Dean's Office	319-895-4234
Des Moines Area C.C.	Ankney, IA 50021	Pamela Parker	Special Needs	515-964-6850
Dordt C.	Sioux Center, IA	Marlilis Van Der Zwaag	Services for Students with Disabilities	
Drake U.	Des Moines, IA 50311	Michelle Laughlin	Disability Resource Center	515-271-1835
Faith Baptist & Theological Seminary	Ankeny, IA 50021	Cole Alan	Office of Admissions	515-965-2025 ext. 233

College	Address	Contact	Office	Phone
Graceland U.	Lamoni, IA 50140	Susan Knotts	Student Support Services	641-784-5421
Grand View C.	Des Moines, IA 50316-1599	Carolyn Wassenaar	Academic Success	515-263-2971
Grinnell C.	Grinnell, IA 50112	Joyce Stern	Academic Advising Office	641-269-3702
Hawkeye C.C.	Waterloo, IA 50704	Barbara Hill	Student Development	319-296-4014
Indian Hills C.C.	Ottumwa, IA 52501	Mary Stewart	Academic Services	641-683-5218
Iowa Central C.C.	Ft. Dodge, IA 50501	Heather Lundberg	Special Needs	515-576-7201
Iowa St. U.	Ames, IA 50011-2011	Steve Moats	Student Disability Resources	515-294-7220
Iowa Wesleyan C.	Mount Pleasant, IA 52641	Preston VanLoon	Academic Resource Center	319-385-6376
Iowa Western C.C.	Council Bluffs, IA 51502	Dedrick Bell	Special Needs	712-325-3479
Loras C.	Dubuque, IA 52001	Dianne Gibson	Learning Disabilities Program	563-588-7134
Luther C.	Decorah, IA 52101-1045	G.R. Rosales	Student Academic Support Services	563-387-1270
Morningside College	Sioux City, IA 51106-1751	Robbie Rohlena	Academic Support Center	800-831-0806 ext. 5104
Mount Mercy C.	Cedar Rapids, IA 52402	Mary Jean Stanton	Disability Services	319-363-8213 ext. 1204
Mount Saint Clare C.	Clinton, IA 52733-2967	Dean Gary Cooper	Student Affairs	563-242-4023
Northwestern C.	Orange City, IA 51041	Patti Thayer	Academic Support Services	712-707-7045
Saint Ambrose U.	Davenport, IA 52803-2898	Ryan C. Saddler	Services for Students with Disabilities	563-333-6275
Scott CC E. Iowa CC	Bettonderf, IA 52722	Jan Weis	Student Support Services	563-441-4072
Simpson C.	Indianola, IA 50125	Todd Little	Academic Resource Center	515-961-1524
Southeastern C.C.	W. Burlington, IA 52655	Shari Smith	Office for Students with Disabilities	319-752-2731 ext.8140
U. of Dubuque	Dubuque, IA 52001-5050	Susanna Robey	Academic Support Center	563-589-3218
U. of Iowa	Iowa City, IA 52242	Dau-shen Ju, PhD	Student Disability Services	319-335-1462
U. of Northern Iowa	Cedar Falls, IA 5061	David Towle, PhD	Disability Services	319-273-2676
Waldorf C.	Forest City, IA 50436	Michelle Sprout Murray	Learning Disability Program	641-584-8207
Wartburg C.	Waverly, IA 50677	Alexander Smith	Student Life	319-352-8260
William Penn U.	Oskaloosa, IA 52577	Dr. Fred Allen	Academic Resource Center	641-673-1102

KANSAS

College	Address	Contact	Office	Phone
Baker University	Baldwin City, KS 66006	Cindy Novelo	Learning Resource Center	785-594-8349
Benedictine College	Atchison, KS 66002	Kelly Vowels	Admission and Financial Aid Office	800-467-5340 ext.7418
Bethany C.	Lindsborg, KS 67456-1897	Tom Claassen	Academic Support Services	785-227-3311
Bethel C.	N. Newton, KS 67117	Daniel Quinlin, PhD	Center for Academic Development	316-284-5333
Butler City C.C.	Eldorado, KS 67042	Teresa Eastman	Special Needs & Services	316-322-3166
Central Christian C. of Kansas	McPherson, KS 67460-5799	Karen Mayse	Guidence Center	620-241-0723 ext. 312
Colby CC.	Colby, KS 67701	Monica Kane	Student Support Services	785-462-3984

Institution	Location	Contact	Service	Phone
Emporia St. U.	Emporia, KS 66801-5087	Trudi Benjamin	Project Challenge	620-341-5097
Friends U.	Wichita, KS 67213	Carole Obermeyer	Student Affairs	316-295-5779
Hutchinson C.C.	Hutchinson, KS 67502	Jill Crank	Disability Services	620-665-3554
Johnson County C.C.	Overland Park, KS 66210	Holly Dressler	Student Access Center	913-469-8500 ext. 3974
Kansas City C.C.	Kansas City, KS 66112	Valerie Webb	Academic Resource Center	913-288-7670
Kansas St. U.	Manhattan, KS 66506	Andrea Blair, M.Ed	Disability Support Services	785-532-6441
Manhattan Christian C.	Manhattan, KS 66502	Lauren Sanders	Student Development	785-539-3571
McPherson C.	McPherson, KS 67460	Kevin Hadduck	Disability Services	620-242-0507
MidAmerica Nazarene U.	Olathe, KS 66062	Cynthia Lindsey	Learning Resources Center	913-791-3387
Newman University	Wichita, KS 67213	Alicia Smith	Student Support Services	316-942-4291 ext. 2146
Pittsburg State U.	Pittsburg, KS 66762-5880	Dr. Jamie Wood	Learning Center	620-235-4193
Pratt C.C.	Pratt, KS 67124	Spencer Baker	Student Success	620-672-5641 ext. 215
U. of Kansas	Lawrence, KS 66045	Mary Ann Rasnak	Services for Students with Disabilities	785-864-2620
U. of St. Mary	Levenworth, KS 66048	Keith Hansen	Student Life	913-682-5151
Wichita St. U.	Wichita, KS 67260	Grady Landrum	Resource Center for Independence	316-978-6970

KENTUCKY

Institution	Location	Contact	Service	Phone
Bellarmine C.	Louisville, KY 40205	Dr. Myrna Boland	Office of Student Affairs	502-452-8480
Berea C.	Berea, KY 40404	Bev Penkalski	Special Needs	859-985-3150
Bluegrass Comm. & Tech. College	Lexington, KY 40506-0235	Veronica Miller	Disability Support Services	859-246-6530
Brescia C.	Owensboro, KY 42301	Dr. Dolores Kiesler	Student Support Services	270-686-4259
Centre C.	Danville, KY 40422	Mary Gulley	Disability Services	859-238-5223
Cumberland C.	Williamsburg, KY 40769	Jim Ross	Academic Services	606-539-4214
Eastern Kentucky U.	Richmond, KY 40475	Teresa Belluscio	Project SUCCESS	859-622-2933
Georgetown C.	Georgetown, KY 40324	Edward Marshall	Disability Services	502-863-7074
Kentucky Christian U.	Grayson, KY 41143	Chad Leach	Special Student Services	606-474-3257
Kentucky Wesleyan C.	Owensboro, KY 42302	Marisue Coy	PLUS Center	207-852-3300
Lexington C.C.	Lexington, KY 40506-0235	Veronica Miller	Disability Support Services	859-246-6200
Lindsey Wilson C.	Columbia, KY 42728	David Ludden	Learning Disabilities	270-384-8080
Mid-Continent C.	Mayfield, KY 42066	Debra McCuiston	A.C.E. Program	270-247-8521 ext. 354
Morehead St. U.	Morehead, KY 40351	Eveanglina Day	Disability Services	606-783-5188
Murray St. U.	Murray, KY 42071	Annazette McCain	Office of Equal Opportunity	270-809-3155
Northern Kentucky U.	Highland Heights, KY 41099	Sue Roth	Disability Services	859-572-5180
Southeast C.C.	Cumberland, KY 40823	Ruth Lewis	Student Support Services	606-589-2145 ext. 13054

College	Location	Contact	Office	Phone
Thomas More C.	Crestview Hill, KY 41017	Barbara S. Davis	Student Support Services	859-344-3521
U. of Kentucky	Lexington, KY 40506	Jake Karnes	Disability Resource Center	859-257-2754
U. of Louisville	Louisville, KY 40292	Cathy Patus	Disability Resource Center	502-852-6938
Western Kentucky U.	Bowling Green, KY 42101	Matt Davis	Student Disability Services	270-745-5004

LOUISIANA

College	Location	Contact	Office	Phone
Louisiana C.	Pineville, LA 71359-0560	Betty P. Matthews	Program to Assist Student Success	318-487-7629
LSU—Baton Rouge	Baton Rouge, LA 70803	Benjamin Cornwell	Office of Disability Services	225-578-4401
Loyola U. New Orleans	New Orleans, LA 70118	Sarah Smith	Acad. Enrichment and Disibility Svcs.	504-865-2990
McNeese St. U.	Lake Charles, LA 70609	Timothy Delany	Services for Students with Disabilities	337-475-5916
Nicholls St. U.	Thibodaux, LA 70310	Stacey Guidry	Office of Disability Services	985-448-4429
Northwestern St. U. of Louisiana	Natchitoches, LA 71497	Steve Hicks	Disability Services	318-357-6950
Our Lady of Holy Cross C.	New Orleans, LA 70131	Kristine Hatfield	Enrollment Services	504-398-2185
Southeastern Louisiana U.	Hammond, LA 70402	Sharon Eaton	Disability Services	504-549-2247
Southern U. & A&M C.	Baton Rouge, LA 70813	Patricia Herbert	Special Education	225-771-3950
Southern U. of New Orleans	New Orleans, LA 70126	Dr. Zelma Frank	Student Support Services	504-286-5106
Tulane U.	New Orleans, LA 70118-5680	Dr. Jillandra Rovaris	Disability Services	504-862-8433
U. of New Orleans	New Orleans, LA 70148	Janice G. Lyn, PhD	Disabled Student Services	504-280-6222
U. of Louisiana—Lafayette	Lafayette, LA 70504	Dr. Carol Landry	Services for Students w/ Disabilities	337-482-5252
U. of Louisiana,—Monroe	Monroe, LA 71209	Lisa Miller	Office of Admissions	318-342-5430

MAINE

College	Location	Contact	Office	Phone
Bates C.	Lewiston, ME 04240-9917	Mary Gravel	Dean's Office	207-786-6219
Bowdoin C.	Brunswick, ME 04011-8441	Joanne Canning	Dean's Office	207-725-3866
Colby C.	Waterville, ME 04901-8840	Mark Serdjenian	Dean's Office	207-872-3106
C. of Atlantic	Bar Harbor, ME 04609	Ken Hill	Disability Services	207-288-5015
Eastern Maine Tech C.	Bangor, ME 04401	Dr. Elizabeth Warden	Academic Support Center	207-974-4658
Husson C.	Bangor, ME 04401	John Rubino	Disability Services	207-941-7109
Kennebec Valley Tech	Fairfield, ME 04937	Karen Normandin	Students With Disabilities	207-453-5019
Maine C. of Art	Portland, ME 04101	Stacy Wilson	Student Affairs	207-879-5742
N. Maine Tech C.	Presque Isle, ME 04769	Tammy Nelson	Student Affairs—TRIO	207-768-2793
St. Joseph's C.	Standish, ME 04054	Joyce Coburn	Dean of College	207-893-6642
Southern Maine C. C.	South Portland, ME 04106	Mark Krogman	Disability Services	207-741-5629
Thomas C.	Waterville, ME 04901	Ellen McQuiston	Center for Academic Support	207-859-1214

Institution	Location	Contact	Office	Phone
Unity C.	Unity, ME 04988-0532	James Horan	Learning Resource Center	207-948-3131 ext. 241
U. of Maine—Augusta	Bangor, ME 04401-4367	Phil Watkins	Cornerstone Program	207-621-3157
U. of Maine—Farmington	Farmington, ME 04938	Claire Nelson	Acad. Svcs. for Students w/ Disab.	207-778-7295
U. of Maine—Fort Kent	Fort Kent, ME 04743	Anglea Theriault	Disability Services	807-834-7530
U. of Maine—Machias	Machias, ME 04654	Jean Schild	Student Resources	207-255-1228
U. of Maine—Orono	Orono, ME 04469-5757	Ann Smith	Onward Program/Disabilities	207-581-2319
U. of Maine—Presque Isle	Presque Isle, ME 04769	Mary Kate Barbosa	Student Support Services	207-768-9613
U. of New England	Biddeford, ME 04005	Susan Church	Disability Services	207-283-0170
U. of Southern Maine	Portland, ME 04104	Joyce Branaman	Support for Students with Disabilities	207-780-4706

MARYLAND

Institution	Location	Contact	Office	Phone
Allegheny C.	Cumberland, MD 21502	Carol Davis	Student Support Center	301-784-5551
Anne Arundel C.C.	Arnold, MD 21012	Mimi Stoops	Disabled Student Services	410-777-2306
Baltimore City C.C.	Baltimore, MD 21215	Nicole Wilson	Disability Support Services Center	410-462-8585
Capitol C.	Laurel, MD 20708	Melinda Bunnell-Phyne	Dean of Student's Office	301-369-2800 ext. 3046
Carroll C.C.	Westminster, MD 21157	Joyce Sebian	Student Support Services	410-386-8329
Catonsville C.C.	Catonsville, MD 21228	Jill Hodge	Special Student Population	410-455-4718
Cecil C.C.	North East, MD 20901	Tomeka Swan	Academic Advising	410-287-6060 ext. 556
C. of Norte Dame of Maryland	Baltimore, MD 21210	Winifred Daisley	Disability Support Services	410-532-5379
C. of Southern MD—La Plata	La Plata, MD 20646	Glennis Daniels-Bacchus	Academic Support Services	301-934-2251 ext. 7614
Columbia Union C.	Takoma Park, MD 20912	Selma Chaij	Center for Learning Resources	301-891-4184
Coppin St. U.	Baltimore, MD 21216-3698	Elaine Howell	Counseling Center	410-951-3939
Essex C.C.	Baltimore, MD 21237	Beth Hunsinger	Office of Special Services	410-780-6741
Frostburg St. U.	Frostburg, MD 21532	Leroy Pullen	Disability Support Services	301-687-4483
Goucher C.	Baltimore, MD 21204-2794	Frona Brown	Disability Specialist	410-337-6178
Harford C.C.	Bel Air, MD 21015	Lorraine Peniston	Learninng Support Services	410-836-4414
Hood C.	Fredrick, MD 21701	Tom Kranz	Disability Services	301-696-3421
Howard C.C.	Columbia, MD 21044	Joan King	Learning Assistance Center	410-772-4822
John Hopkins U.	Baltimore, MD 21218	Peggy Hayeslip	Equal Oppurtunity Center	410-516-8075
Loyola C. (MD)	Baltimore, MD 21210	Leslie Brown	Center for Academic Services and Support	410-617-2663
McDaniel College	Westminster, MD 21157	Kevin Selby	Academic Skills Center	410-857-2504
Montgomery C.	Rockville, MD 20850	Chanel Riley	Disability Support Services	301-279-5058
Morgan St. U.	Baltimore, MD 21251	Dr. Renee Harding	Counseling Center	443-885-3130
Mount St. Mary's U.	Emmitsburg, MD 21727	Denise Marjarum	Learning Services	301-447-5006

College	Location	Contact	Service	Phone
Salisbury U.	Salisbury, MD 21801	Lea Wimbrow	Student Services	410-543-6080
Towson U.	Towson, MD 21252-0001	Susan Willemin	Disability Support Services	410-704-2638
U. of Baltimore	Baltimore, MD 21201	Jacquelyn Truelove-DeSimone	Disability Support Services	410-837-4775
U. of Maryland—C. Park	College Park, MD 20742-5235	Jo Ann Hutchinson, PhD	Disability Support Services	301-314-7682
U. of Maryland—Eastern Shore	Princess Anne, MD 21853	Dorling K. Joseph	Disabled Student Services	410-651-6461
U. of Maryland—U. College	Adelphi, MD 20783	Noelle Atwell	Disability Services	301-985-7260

MASSACHUSETTS

College	Location	Contact	Service	Phone
American International C.	Springfield, MA 01109-3184	Prof. Mary M. Saltus	Supportive Learning Services	413-205-3426
Amherst C.	Amherst, MA 01002	Charri Boykin-East	Services for Students with LD	413-542-2529
Anna Maria C.	Paxton, MA 01612	Dennis Vanasse	Learning Center	508-849-3356
Art Institute of Boston—Lesley U.	Boston, MA 02215-2598	Maureen Riley	Center for Academic Achievement	617-349-8459
Assumption C.	Worcester, MA 01615	Dr. Eloise Knowlton	Disabled Students Services	508-767-7487
Babson C.	Babson Park, MA 02157-0310	Erin Evans	Disability Services/Office of Class Dean	781-239-4508
Bay Path C.	Longmeadow, MA 01106	Brenda Hardin	Office of Disability Services	413-565-1353
Becker C.	Worchester, MA 01609	Madeleine Entel	Center for Academic Success	508-373-9704
Bentley C.	Waltham, MA 2452	Christopher Kennedy	Counseling & Student Development	781-891-2274
Berklee C. of Music	Boston, MA 02215	Robert Mulvey	Learning Center	617-747-2310
Berkshire C.C.	Pittsfield, MA 01201	Lorel Maynard	Services for Disabled Students	413-499-4660 ext. 220
Boston Architectural Center	Boston, MA 02115	Jenifer Marshall	Disability Services	617-858-0259
Boston C.	Chestnut Hill, MA 02167	Kathleen Duggan	Academic Development Center	617-552-8055
Boston U.	Boston, MA 02215	Allan Macurdy	Learning Disability Support Services	617-353-3658
Brandeis U.	Waltham, MA 02254	Beth Rogers-Kay	Dean's Office-Academic Affairs	781-736-3470
Bridgewater St. C.	Bridgewater, MA 02325	Pat Connolly	Office for Students with Disabilities	508-531-1214
Clark U.	Worcester, MA 01610-1477	Jane Daigneault	Academic Advising Center	508-793-7468
C. of the Holy Cross	Worcester, MA 01610-2395	Dr. Matthew Toth	Disability Services	508-793-3363
Curry C.	Milton, MA 02186	Dr. Lisa Ijiri	Program for Advancement of Learning	617-333-2250
Dean C.	Franklin, MA 02038	Erin Lowery-Corkran, PhD	Disability Support Services	508-541-1764
Elms C.	Chicopee, MA 01013	Anne Marie Smith	Office of Students with Disabilities	413-265-2333
Emerson C.	Boston, MA 02116-1511	Dr. Anthony Bashir	Disability Services Office	617-824-8415
Emmanuel C.	Boston, MA 02115	Susan Mayo	Disability Services	617-735-9923
Endicott C.	Beverly, MA 01915	Laura Rossi-Le	Student Support Program	978-232-2292
Fitchburg St. C.	Fitchburg, MA 01420-2697	Dawn Stevenson, Med, ORT/L	Disability Services	978-665-3427
Framingham St. C.	Framingham, MA 01701	LaDonna Bridges	Academic Support	508-626-4906

College	Contact	Address	Office	Phone
Gordon C.	Ann Seavey	Wenham, MA 01984-1899	Academic Support	978-867-4743
Hampshire C.	Joel Dansky	Amherst, MA 01002	Center for Academic Support and Advising	413-559-5423
Harvard and Radcliffe C.s	Louise Russell	Cambridge, MA 02318	Student Disability Resource Center	617-496-8707
Holyoke C.C.	Maureen Conroy	Holyoke, MA 01040	College Disability Services	413-552-2582
Lasell C.	Rosalie Frolick	Newton, MA 02466	Academic Achivement Center	617-243-2306
Lesley C.	Laura Patey	Cambridge, MA 02138	Disability Services	617-349-8194
Mass. C. of Liberal Arts	Claire Smith	North Adams, MA 01247	Learning Services Center	413-662-5318
Mass. C. of Pharmacy & Health	Kristine Souza	Boston, MA 02115-5896	Academic Support Services	617-732-2800
Mass. Institute of Technology	Kathleen Cahill	Cambridge, MA 02139	Disability Serivices	617-253-1674
Mass. Maritime Academy	Betty Anne Bevis	Bussards Bay, MA 02532-1803	Disability Resource	508-830-5000
Mass Bay C.C.	Rita Heywood	Wellesley Hills, MA 02181	Disability Services	781-239-2626
Massasoit C.C.	Andrea Henry	Brockton, MA 02402	Disability Services	508-588-9100
Merrimack C.	Timothy Montgomery	North Andover, MA 01845	Disability Services	978-837-5140
Montserrart C. of Art	Brian Pellinen	Beverly, MA 01915	Academic Affairs	978-921-4242 ext. 1603
Mt. Holyoke C.	John Body III	South Hadley, MA 01075	Office of Learning Skills	413-538-2504
Mt. Ida C.	Jill Mehler	Newton, MA 01259	Learning Opportunities Program	617-928-4648
Mt. Wachusett C.C.	Nancy Kennedy	Gardner, MA 01440	Students with Disabilities	978-630-9178
Nichols C.	Edward J. Kolek	Dudley, MA 01571	Advising Services	508-213-2293
Northeaster U.	Dean G. Ruth Kukiela Bork	Boston, MA 02115	Disability Resource Program	617-373-2730
N. Adams St. C.	Theresa Miller	N. Adams, MA 01247	Learning Center	413-662-5309
North Shore C.C.	Susan Graham	Danvers, MA 01923	SSC—Disabilities Services	978-762-4000 ext. 4036
Northeastern U.	Ruth K. Bork	Boston, MA 02115	Disability Resource Center	617-373-2675
Pine Manor C.	Mary Walsh	Chestnut Hill, MA 02167	Learning Resource Center	617-731-7181
Quinsigamond C.C.	Lori Corcoran	Worcester, MA 01606	Disabilities Services	508-854-4471
Regis C.	Lis Smith-Freeman	Weston, MA 02493-1571	Disability Services	781-768-7384
Simmons C.	Krista Stokes	Boston, MA 02115	Academic Support	617-521-2465
Smith C.	Laura Rauscher	Northampton, MA 01063	Office of Disability Services	413-585-2071
Springfield C.	Deborah Dickens	Springfield, MA 01109	Student Support Service	413-748-3768
Springfield Tech C.C.	Mary Moriarty	Springfield, MA 01105	Office of Disability Services	413-755-4785
St. C. at N. Adams	Terry Miller	N. Adams, MA 01247	Ctr. for Acad. Advancement Learning	413-662-5309
Stonehill C.	Richard Grant	Easton, MA 02357-5610	Academic Services	508-565-1306
Suffolk U.	Christopher Giordano	Boston, MA 02114-4280	Dean of Students Office	617-573-8239
Tufts U.	Sandra Baer	Medford, MA 02155	Academic Resource Center	617-627-5571

College	Location	Contact	Service	Phone
U. Mass.—Amherst	Amherst, MA 01003	Madeline L. Peters	Learning Disabilities Support Services	413-545-0892
U. Mass.—Boston	Boston, MA 02125-3393	Stacey Foskett	Roth Center for Disability Services	617-287-7430
U. Mass.—Dartmouth	North Dartmouth, MA 02747	Carole J. Johnson	Disabled Student Services	508-999-8711
U. Mass.—Lowell	Lowell, MA 01854	Chandrika Sharma	Disability Services	978-934-4574
Wellesley C.	Wellesley, MA 02481	Jim Wice	Learning & Teaching Center	781-283-2434
Wentworth Institute of Technology	Boston, MA 02115-5998	Judith Moss	Disability Services	617-989-4393
Western New England C.	Springfield, MA 01119	Bonnie Alpert	Student Disability Services	413-782-1257
Wheaton C. (MA)	Norton, MA 02766	Martha Bledsoe	Academic Support Services	508-286-8215
Wheelock C.	Boston, MA 02215	Paul Hastings	Disability Support Services	617-879-2304
Williams C.	Williamstown, MA 01267	Peter Grudin	Assoc. Dean for Student Services	413-597-4264
Worcester Poly. Institute	Worcester, MA 01609	Joann VanDyke	Office of Academic Advising	508-831-5381
Worcester St. C.	Worcester, MA 01602-2597	Dennis Lindblom	Disability Services Office	508-793-8000

MICHIGAN

College	Location	Contact	Service	Phone
Adrian C.	Adrian, MI 49221-2575	Jane McCloskey	ACCESS	517-265-5161 ext. 4093
Albion College	Albion, MI 49224	David Hawsey	Disability Services	517-629-0756
Alma C.	Alma, MI 48801-1599	Patricia Chase	Center for Student Development	989-463-7225
Andrews U.	Berrien Springs, MI 49104	Karen Tilstra	Student Services	269-471-6205
Aquinas C.	Grand Rapids, MI 49506-1799	Sarah Cox	Academic Achievement Center	616-632-2166
Calvin C.	Grand Rapids, MI 49546	James Mackenzie, PhD	Student Academic Services	616-957-6113
Central Michigan U.	Mount Pleasant, MI 48859	Michelle Howard	Academic Assistance	989-774-3465
C. of Creative Studies	Detroit, MI 48202	Sylvia Austermiller	Student Success Services	313-664-7680
Concordia U.	Ann Arbor, MI 48105	Kathryn Klintworth	Disability Services	734-995-7479
Cornerstone U.	Grand Rapids, MI 49525	Anna Maddox	Learning Center	616-949-5300
Davenport U.	Grand Rapids, MI 49503	Celeste Belcher-Girard	Disability Services	866-922-3884
Delta C.	Universal City, MI 48710	Michael Cooper	Learning Disabilities Services	989-686-9322
Eastern Michigan U.	Ypsilanti, MI 48197	Donald J. Anderson	Disability Services	734-487-2470
Ferris St. U.	Big Rapids, MI 49307	Eunice Merwin	Disabilities Services	231-591-3772
Finlandia U.	Hancock, MI 49930	Kirsti Arko	Disability Support Services	906-487-7276
Grand Rapids C.C.	Grand Rapids, MI 49503	Anne Sherman	Disability Support Services	616-234-4140
Grand Valley St. U.	Allendale, MI 49401	Kathleen Vanderveen	Academic Support (OAS)	616-331-2490
Hillsdale C.	Hillsdale, MI 49242	Abigail Clevenger	Academic Support	517-437-7341 ext. 8597
Hope C.	Holland, MI 49422-9000	Jacqueline Heisler	Academic Support Center	616-395-7830
Itaska C.C.	Grand Rapids, MI 55744	Anne Vidovic	Support Services	218-327-4167

Institution	Location	Contact	Service	Phone
Kalamazoo C.	Kalamazoo, MI 49006	Karen Joshua-Wathel	Dean of Students	269-337-7209
Kellogg C.C.	Battle Creek, MI 49017	L. Marshall Washington	Support Services	269-965-3931 ext. 2627
Kettering U.	Flint, MI 48504	Deborah Williams-Roberts	Wellness Center	810-762-9650
Kuyper C.	Grand Rapids, MI 49525	Melvin Flikkema	Academic Support	616-988-3649
Lansing C.C.	Lansing, MI 48901	Jennifer Lack	Counseling Services	517-483-5263
Lawrence Tech. U.	Southfield, Mi 48075	Diana Richard	Disability Services	248-204-4110
Madonna U.	Livonia, MI 48150-1173	Michael Meldrum	Educational Support Services	734-432-5641
Marygrove C.	Detroit, MI 48221	Veronica Killebrew	Support Services	313-927-1200 ext. 1427
Michigan St. U.	East Lansing, MI 48824	Michael Hudson	Resource Center for Persons with Disabilities	517-353-9642
Michigan Tech U.	Houghton, MI 49931	Dr. Gloria Melton	Student Afairs	906-487-2212
North Central Michigan C.	Petoskey, MI 49770	Katherine Flewelling	Educational Opportunity Program	231-348-6687
Northern Michigan U.	Marquette, MI 49855	Lynn Walden	Disability Services	906-227-1737
Northwood U.—Midland	Midland, MI 48640	Rachelle Puffpaff	Special Needs Services	989-837-4216
Oakland C.C.	Auburn Hills, MI 48309	Mary Jo Lord	PASS Office	248-232-4080
Oakland U.	Rochester, MI 48309	Linda Sisson	Disability Support Services	248-370-2100
Olivet C.	Olivet, MI 49076	Diana Batwright	Disability Services	269-749-6637
Rochester C.	Rochester Hills, MI 48307	Paula Bonbrisco	Student Support Center	248-218-2014
Saginaw Valley St. U.	University Ctr, MI 48152	Cynthia Woiderski	Disability Services—Student Affairs	989-964-4168
Schoolcraft C.C.	Livonia, MI 48152	Dr. Debra Daiek	Academic Assessment Services	734-462-4436
SW Michigan C.	Dowagiac, MI 49047	Susan Sullivan	Special	269-687-4801
Spring Arbor U.	Spring Arbor, MI	Carolee Hamilton	Disability Center	517-750-6479
U. of Michigan—Ann Arbor	Ann Arbor, MI 48109	Stuart Segal, PhD	Services for Students with Disabilities	734-763-3000
U. of Michigan—Dearborn	Dearborn, MI48128-1491	Dennis Underwood	Counseling & Support Services	313-593-5430
U. of Michigan—Flint	Flint, MI 48502	Zach Pomlinson	Student Development Center	810-762-3456
Walsh C.	Troy, MI 48007-7006	Kathy Bentley	Academic Advising	248-823-1386
Wayne St. U.	Detroit, MI 48202	Jane DePriester-Morandini	Education Access Service	313-577-1851
Western Michigan U.	Kalamazoo, MI 49008	Beth DenHartigh	Disabled Student Resources and Services	269 387-2116

MINNESOTA

Institution	Location	Contact	Service	Phone
Augsburg C.	Minneapolis, MN 55454	Karena Jones	CLASS Program	612-330-1053
Bethel C.	St. Paul, MN 55112	Gretchen Wrobel	Disability Services	651-638-6403
Bimidji St. U.	Bimidji, MN 55601	Kathy Heagen	Disability Services	218-755-3883
Carleton C.	Northfield, MN 55057	Hudlin Wagner	Support Services	507-646-4075
C. of Saint Benedict	Saint Joseph, MN 56374	Michelle Sauer	Academic Advising	320-363-5011

College	Location	Contact	Office/Service	Phone
C. of St. Catherine, The	Saint Paul, MN 55105	Barbara Mandel	O'Neill Learning Center	651-590-6563
C. of St. Scholastica, The	Duluth, MN 55811-4199	Jay Newcomb	Academic Support Services	218-723-6552
Concordia C.—Moorhead	Moorhead, MN 56562	Monica Kersting	Disability Counseling	218-299-3514
Concordia C.—Saint Paul	Saint Paul, MN 55104-5494	David Schreiber	Students with Disabilities	651-641-8272
Crown C.	St. Bonifacius, MN 55375	Don Bouchard	Disability Counseling	952-446-4216
Fond du Lac C.C.	Cloquet, MN 55720	Bill Kallis	Office of Students with Disabilities	218-879-0815
Gustavus Adolphus C.	St. Peter, MN 56082	Henry Toutain	Academic Advising: Dean of Students	507-933-7526
Hamline U.	Saint Paul, MN 55104	Deb Holtz	Disability Services	651-523-2521
Hibbing C.C.	Hibbing, MN 55746	Shelly Flaten	Disability Services	218-262-6745
Inver Hills C.C.	Inver Grove Hgts, MN 55076	Tim Boyer	Disabled Student Services	651-450-8628
Lake Superior C.	Duluth, MN 55811	Georgia Robillard	Disability Services	218-733-7650
Century College	White Bear Lk, MN 55110	Ed Sapinski	Access Center	651-779-3354
Macalester C.	St. Paul, MN 55105	Micheal Dickel	Learning Center	651-696-6118
Mesabi C.C.	Virginia, MN 55792	Lindsay Grott	Disability Services	218-749-0319
Minneapolis C.C.	Minneapolis, MN 55403	Jane Larson	Office for Students with Disabilities	612-659-6730
Minnesota State U.—Mankato	Mankato, MN 56002	Julie Snow	Center for Academic Success	507-389-1199
Minnesota State U.—Moorhead	Moorhead, MN 56563	Greg Toutges	Disability Services	218-477-5859
N. Hennepin C.C.	Brooklyn Pk, MN 55445	Connie Sherman	Disability Access Services	763-493-0556
Normandale C.C.	Bloomington, MN 55431	Debbie Tillman	Office for Students with Disabilities	952-487-7035
North Central U.	Minneapolis, MN 55404	Rachel Gray	Disability Services	612-343-4190
Northwestern C.	St. Paul, MN 55113-1598	David Golias	Disability Services	651-631-7446
Riverland C.C.	Austin, MN 55912	Sharon Stiehm	Student Success Center	507-433-0646
Rochester C.C.	Rochester, MN 55904	Travis Kromminga	Disability Services	507-280-2968
Saint Cloud St. U.	Saint Cloud, MN 56301-4498	Owen Zimpel	Student Disability Services	320-308-3117
Saint John's U.	Collegeville, MN 56321-7155	Susan Douma	Academic Advising	320-363-3246
Saint Mary's U.	Winona, MN 55987-1399	Joe Dulak	Academic Skills Center	507-457-1414
St. Olaf C.	Northfield, MN 55057-1098	Ruth Bolstad	Student Disability Service	507-786-3288
Southwest St. U.	Marshall, MN 56258	Pam Ekstrom	Learning Resources	507-537-7672
U. of Minnesota	Crookston, MN 56716	Laurie Wilson	Office for Students w/ Disabilities	218-281-8587
U. of Minnesota—Duluth	Duluth, MN 55812-2496	Penny Cragun	Learning Disability Program	218-726-8727
U. of Minnesota—Minneapolis	Minneapolis, MN 55455	Sheila Fox-Wassink	Disability Services	612-624-2893
U. of Minnesota—Morris	Morris, MN 56267	Ferolyn Angell	Academic Assistance Office	320-589-6163
U. of Minnesota—Twin Cities	Minneapolis, MN 55455-0213	Derek Snow	Disability Services	612-624-4120

Institution	Location	Contact	Service	Phone
U. of St. Thomas	St. Paul, MN 55105-1096	Kimberly Schumann	Enhancement Program	651-962-6315
Winona St. U.	Winona, MN 55987	Nancy Dumke	Disability Resource Center	507-457-2391

MISSISSIPPI

Institution	Location	Contact	Service	Phone
Bellhaven C.	Jackson, MS 39202	Erin Price	Academic Support	601-968-8990
Blue Mountain C.	Blue Mountain, MS 38610-0160	Sharon Enzor		662-685-4771
Jackson St. U	Jackson, MS 39217	Vinson Ballard	Disability Services	601-979-3704
Millsaps C.	Jackson, MS 39210-0001	Patrick Cooper	Disability Services	601-974-1228
Mississippi C.	Clinton, MS 39058	Dr. Buddy Wagner	Counseling & Testing Center	601-325-3354
Mississippi St. U.	Mississippi, MS 39762	Julie Berry	Student Support Services	662-325-3335
Mississippi U. for Women	Columbus, MS 39701	Carol Frazier	Academic Support Services	662-241-7471
Rust C.	Holy Springs, MS 38635	Chiquita Walls	Disability Services	662-252-8000 ext. 4909
U. of Mississippi	University, MS 38677	Ardessa Minor	Services for Students with Disabilities	662-915-7128
U. of Southern Mississippi	Hattiesburg, MS 39406	Suzy B. Hebert	Office of Disability Accmmodations	601-266-5024
William Carey C.	Hattiesburg, MS 39401-5499	Clara Reedy	Student Support Services	601-318-6209

MISSOURI

Institution	Location	Contact	Service	Phone
Avila U.	Kansas City, MO 64145	Suzanne Franklin	Learning Center	816-501-3666
Barnes-Jewish C. of Nurs. & AH	St. Louis, MO 33132	Malou Jaime	Student Support Services	314-454-8686
Blue River C.C.	Blue Springs, MO 64015-7242	Leah Shelton	ACCESS Office	816-220-6651
Central Missouri St. U.	Warrensburg, MO 64093	Barbara Mayfield	Office of Accessibility	660-543-4421
C. of the Ozarks	Point Lookout, MO 65726	Cheryl Marley	Academic Dean's Office	417-334-6411 ext. 2278
Columbia C.	Columbia, MO 65216	Shirley Wilbur	Student Support Center	573-875-7626
Culver-Stockton C.	Canton, MO 63435	Dr. Jayme Long	Academic Support Services	573-288-6451
Drury C.	Springfield, MO 65802-9977	Lawrence Anderson	Assistive Student Services	417-873-7419
Evangel U.	Springfield, MO 65802	Dr. Laynah Rogers	Academic Development Center	417-865-2811
Fontbonne C.	St. Louis, MO 63105	Jane Snyder	Academic Resource Center	314-719-3627
Hannibal-LaGrange C.	Hannibal, MO 63401	Dr. Garry Breland	Academic Affairs	573-221-3675 ext. 253
Harris-Stowe St. C.	St. Louis, MO 63103	Robert Bandon	Disability Services	314-340-3649
Kansas City Art Institute	Kansas City, MO 64111-1762	Andrea Kahn	Academic Resource Center	816-802-3466
Lincoln U.	Jefferson City, MO 65102-0029	Cynthia Washington	Disability Services	573-681-5167
Lindenwood U.	St. Charles, MO 63301-1695	Tonie Isenhour	Disability Services	636-949-4784
Longview Comm. C.	Lee Summit, MO 64081-2105	Connie Flick-Hruska	ACCESS Office	816-672-2252
Maple Woods C.C.	Kansas City, MO 64156	Kim Fernandes	ACCESS Office	816-437-3192

School	City, State ZIP	Contact	Office	Phone
Maryville U. of St. Louis	St. Louis, MO 63141-7299	Julie Kindred	Academic Success Center	314-529-9374
Mineral Area C.	Park Hills, MO 63601	Lisa Leftridge	Special Services	573-518-2152
Missouri Southern St. C.	Joplin, MO 64801-1595	Melissa Locher	Learning Center	417-625-9516
Missouri State U.	Springfield, MO 65897	Steve Capps, PhD	Learning Diagnostic Clinic	417-836-4787
Missouri Valley C.	Marshall, MO 65340	Virginia Zank	Learning Center	660-831-4226
Missouri Western St. U.	Saint Joseph, MO 64507	Ellen Kisker	Non-Traditional Student Services	816-271-4280
Northwest Missouri St. U.	Maryville, MO 64468	Phil Kenkel	Director Student Support Services	660-562-1861
Park U.	Parkville, Mo 64152	Debra Mcarthur	Academic Support Services	816-584-6332
Penn Valley C.C.	Kansas City, MO 64110	Connie Spies	Access Office	816-759-4152
Saint Louis U.	Saint Louis, MO 63103	Vicki Wroblewski	Student Disabilities Center	314-977-3838
Southwest Baptist U.	Bolivar, MO 65613	Dr. Stephanie Miller	Disability Services	417-328-1797
Southwest Missouri St. U.	Springfield, MO 65804	Dr. Steve Capps	Learning Diagnostic Clinic	417-836-4787
St. Charles City C.C.	St. Peters, MO 63376	Pam Bova	Disabled Student Services	636-922-8247
St. Louis C C.—Florissant Valley	St. Louis, MO 63135	Suelaine Matthews	ACCESS Office	314-513-4551
St. Louis C.C.—Forest Park	St. Louis, MO 63110	Deborah Carter	ACCESS Office	314-644-9260
St. Louis C.C.—Meramec	St. Louis, MO 63122	Linda Nissenbaum	ACCESS Office	314-984-7654
Stephens C.	Columbia, MO 65215	Deb Duren	Student Services	573-876-7212
Three River C.C.	Poplar Bluff, MO 63901	Dr. Joseph Mick	Student Support Services	573-840-9650
Truman St. U.	Kirksville, MO 63501	Vicki Wehner	Disability Services	660-785-4478
U. of Missouri—Columbia	Columbia, MO 65203	Sarah Colby Weaver, PhD	Office of Disability Services	573-882-4696
U. of Missouri—Kansas City	Kansas City, MO 64110-2499	Scott Laurent	Services for Students with Disabilities	816-235-5696
U. of Missouri—Rolla	Rolla, MO 65409	Connie Arthur	Disability Support Services	573-341-4211
U. of Missouri—Saint Louis	Saint Louis, MO 63121	Marilyn Ditto-Pernell	Disability Access Services	314-516-6554
Washington U.	Saint Louis, MO 63130-4899	Christine Duden Street	Disability Resource Center	314-935-4153
Webster U.	St. Louis, MO 63119	Barbara Stewart	Academic Support Center	314-968-7495
Westminster C.	Fulton, MO 65251-1299	Hank Ottinger	Learning Disabilities Program	573-592-5304
William Jewell C.	Liberty, MO 64068	Beth Gentry-Epley	Counseling and Testing	816-415-5946
William Woods U.	Fulton, MO 65251	Margie White	Disability Services	573-592-1194

MONTANA

School	City, State ZIP	Contact	Office	Phone
Carroll C.	Helena, MT 59625-0002	Joan Stottlemyer	Academic Resource Center	406-447-4504
Montana St. U.	Billings, MT 59101-0298	Trudy Carey	Disability Support Services	406-657-2283
Montana St. U.	Bozeman, MT 59717	Brenda York	Disability Services	406-994-2824
Montana Tech. College	Butte, MT 59701	Eletha Suttey	Disability Services	406-496-3730

Institution	Location	Contact	Service	Phone
Montana State U.—Northern	Harve, MT 59501	William Linier	Assistant Dean of Students	406-265-4117
Rocky Mountain C.	Billings, MT 59102	Dr. Jane Van Dyk	Services for Academic Success	406-657-1128
U. of Great Falls	Great Falls, MT 59405	Twila Croft	Center for Academic Excellence	406-791-5213
U. of Montana	Missoula, MT 59812	James Marks	Disability Services for Students	406-243-2243
The U. of Montana—Western	Dillon, MT 59725	Nicole Hazelbaker	Disability Services	406-683-7565

NEBRASKA

Institution	Location	Contact	Service	Phone
Bellevue U.	Bellevue, NE 68005	Terra Beethe	Special Needs Services	402-682-4012
Concordia C.	Seward, NE 68434	Tanya Jarthow	Academic Support	402-643-7377
Creighton U.	Omaha, NE 68178	Wade Pearson	Educational Opportunity Program	402-280-2195
Dana C.	Blair, NE 68008	Lori Nielsen	Academic Support Services	402-426-7334
Doane C.	Crete, NE 68333	Sheri Hanigan	Academic Support	402-826-8554
Grace U.	Omaha, NE 68108-3629	Beth Sanchez	Dean of Women	402-449-2849
Hastings C.	Hastings, NE 68901-7621	Kathleen Haverly	Disability Services	402-461-7386
Nebraska Methodist C.	Omaha, NE 68114	Gina Toman	Student Development Services	402-354-4977
Metropolitan C.C.	Omaha, NE 68103	Melinda Classen	Special Needs Program	402-457-2580
Midland Lutheran C.	Fremont, NE 68025	Lori Moseman	Academic Support Center	402-941-6257
Southeast C.C.	Lincoln, NE 68510	Teresa Webster	Disability Services	402-437-2620
Union C.	Lincoln, NE 68506-4300	Debbie Forshee-Sweeney	Teaching Learning Center	402-486-2506
U. of Nebraska—Kearney	Kearney, NE 68849	Gail Zeller	Academic Success	308-865-8988
U. of Nebraska—Lincoln	Lincoln, NE 68588-0417	Veva Cheney	Services for Students w/ Disabilities	402-472-3787
U. of Nebraska—Medical Center	Omaha, NE 68198-4265	Ronda Stevens	Student Disability Services	402-559-5553
U. of Nebraska—Omaha	Omaha, NE 68182	Kate Clark	Disability Services	402-554-2896
Wayne St. C.	Wayne, NE 68787	Jamie Mackling	STRIDE	402-375-7321
West Nebraska C.C.	Scottsbluff, NE 69361-1899	Norm Stephenson	Counseling Center	308-635-6090

NEVADA

Institution	Location	Contact	Service	Phone
Truckee Meadows C.C.	Reno, NV 89512	Lee Geldmacher	Disabled Student Services	775-673-7286
U. of Nevada—Las Vegas	Las Vegas, NV 89154	Clark Hochstetler	Disability Resource Center	702-895-0866
U. of Nevada—Reno	Reno, NV 89557	Mary Zabel	Disability Resource Center	775-784-6000
Western Nevada C.C.	Carson City, NV 89703	Susan Trist	ADA Support Services	775-445-3275

NEW HAMPSHIRE

Institution	Location	Contact	Service	Phone
Colby-Sawyer C.	New London, NH 03257	Anne Chalker	Academic Services for Student	603-526-3711
Dartmouth C.	Hanover, NH 03755	Ward Newmeyer	Student Disabilities Center	603-646-2014

College	Contact	Service	Location	Phone
Franklin Pierce C.	Trish Moore	Academic Services	Rindge, NH 03461-0060	603-899-4044
Keene St. C.	Jane Warner	Office of Disability Services	Keene, NH 03435	603-358-2353
New England C.	Anna Carlson	Academic Advising & Support Ctr.	Henniker, NH 03242	603-428-2218
New Hampshire Tech	Beverly Boggess	Support Services	Concord, NH 03301	603-271-7723
Plymouth St. U.	Susan Keefe	Disability Services	Plymouth, NH 03264-1595	603-535-2270
Rivier College	Dina DiGregorio Karlon	Special Needs Services	Nashua, NH 03060	603-897-8497
St. Anselm C.	Anne Harrington	Academic Advisment	Manchester, NH 03102	603-641-7465
Southern New Hampshire U.	Hyla Jaffe	Disability Services	Manchester, NH 03108	603-668-2211
U. of New Hampshire	Maxine Little	Support for Students with Disabilities	Durham, NH 03824	603-862-2607

NEW JERSEY

College	Contact	Service	Location	Phone
Bergen C.C.	Lynn Gold	Office of Special Services	Paramus, NJ 07652	201-612-5273
Bloomfield C.	Janette Lawrence	Learning Needs	Bloomfield, NJ 07003	973-748-9000
Brookdale C.C.	Elaine Foley	Director of Disability Services	Lincroft, NJ 07738	732-224-2730
Caldwell College	Abbe Benowitz	Office of Disability Services	Caldwell, NJ 07006-9165	973-618-3645
Camden County C.	Anne-Marie Hoyle	PACS Program	Blackwood, NJ 08012	856-227-7200 ext. 4372
Centenary C.	Chris Selena	Disability Services	Hackettstown, NJ 07840	908-852-1400 ext. 2251
C. of New Jersey, The	Terri Yamiolkowski	Office for Students w/ Differing Abilities	Ewing, NJ 06628-0718	609-771-2571
C. of St. Elizabeth	Virginia Reiner	Academic Skills Center	Morristown, NJ 07960-6989	973-290-4325
County C. of Morris	Dr. David Nast	Horizons Program	Randolph, NJ 07869	973-328-5284
Drew U.	Edye Lawler	Academic Dean's Office	Madison, NJ 07940	973-408-3514
Fairleigh Dickinson U.-Florham Campus	Dr. Brenda Jackson	Reg. Ctr. for Coll. Students with LD	Madison, NJ 07940	973-443-8935
Fairleigh Dickinson U.	Dr. Mary L. Farrell	Reg. Ctr. for College Students with LD	Teaneck, NJ 07666	201-692-2087
Georgian Court C.	Patricia Cohen	The Learning Center	Lakewood, NJ 08701	732-987-2650
Kean U.	Dr. Marie Segal	Project Excel	Union, NJ 07083-0411	908-737-5400
Middlesex C.C.	Elaine Weir-Daidone	Project Connections	Edison, NJ 08818	732-906-2546
Monmouth U.	Skip Carey	Department of Disability Services for Students	W. Long Branch, NJ 07764	732-571-3460
Mountclair St. U.	Linda Smith	Disability Services	Montclair, NJ 07043	973-655-5431
New Jersey City U.	Jennifer Aitken	Project Mentor	Jersey City, NJ 07305	201-200-2091
New Jersey Institute of Tech.	Phyllis Bolling	Disability Services	Newark, NJ 070102-1982	973-596-3420
Ocean County C.	Maureen Reustle	Disability Resource Center	Toms River, NJ 08754	732-255-0456
Princeton U.	Maria Flores-Mills	Disability Services	Princeton, NJ 08544-0430	609-258-3054
Raritan Valley C.C.	Cathy Doyle	Disability Services	Somerville, NJ 08876	908-526-1200 ext. 8330
Richard Stockton C. of NJ	Frances H. Bottone	Learning Access Program	Pomona, NJ 08240-0195	609-652-4988

Institution	Contact	Service	Location	Phone
Rider U.	Jacqueline Simon, EdD	Education Enrichment Program	Lawrenceville, NJ 08648	609-895-5492
Rowan U.	Melissa Arnott	Academic Success Center	Glassboro, NJ 08028	856-256-4260
Rutgers U.	Altyman Brown	Learning Center	Piscataway, NJ 08854-8097	973-353-5608
Rutgers U.	Clayton Walton	Dean's Office	Newark, NJ 07102-1896	973-353-5300
Salem C.C.	Naydeen Gonzalez-DeJesus	Special Population	Carneys Point, NJ 08069	856-351-2759
Seton Hall U.	Linda Raye Walter	Disability Support Services	South Orange, NJ 07079	973-313-6003
St. Peter's C.	Lucille L. Foster	Special Needs Students	Jersey City, NJ 07306-5997	201-761-6032
Stevens Institute of Tech.	Ken Nilsen	Dean of Students	Hoboken, NJ 07030	201-216-5699
Sussex C.C.	Kathleen Okay	LD Program	Newton, NJ 07860	973-300-2153
Thomas Edison St. C.	Barbara Aikins	Learners Services	Trenton, NJ 08608-1176	609-984-1141 ext. 3415
Westminster Choir C. of Rider U.	Barbara Blandford	Services for Students w/ Disabilities	Princeton, NJ 08540	609-896-5000 ext. 7365
William Paterson U. of NJ	Jakie Safont	Disability Services	Wayne, NJ 07470	973-720-2351

NEW MEXICO

Institution	Contact	Service	Location	Phone
C. of Santa Fe	Erika Ellis	Center for Academic Excellence	Santa Fe, NM 84505	505-473-6552
C. of Southwest	Mary Harris	Office of Special Services	Hobbs, NM 88240	505-392-6561 ext. 1056
Eastern New Mexico U.	Bernita Davis	Services for Students with Disabilities	Portales, NM 88130	505-562-2280
New Mexico Highlands U.	David Esquibel	Disability & Testing Services	Las Vegas, NM 87701	505-454-3252
New Mexico Junior C.	Cynthia Zambrelli	Special Needs Services	Hobbs, NM 88240	505-392-5041
N.M. Inst. of Mining & Tech.	Laurie Tacheny Borden	Services for Students with Disabilities	Socorro, NM 87801	505-835-5443
New Mexico St. U.	Michael Armendariz	Services for Students with Disabilities	Las Cruces, NM 88003	505-646-6840
Santa Fe C.C.	Jill Douglas	Special Services	Santa Fe, NM 87502	505-428-1331
U. of New Mexico	Joan Green	Special Services Program	Albuquerque, NM 87131	505-277-3506
Western New Mexico U.	Karen Correa	Special Needs Services	Silver City, NM 88062	505-538-6498

NEW YORK

Institution	Contact	Service	Location	Phone
Adelphi U.	Susan Spencer	Learning Disabilities Program	Garden City, NY 11530	516-877-4710
Bard C.	Lucille Larney, PhD	Academic Resource Center	Annandale, NY 12504	845-758-6822 ext. 6637
Barnard C.	Susan Quinby	Disability Services	New York, NY 10027	212-854-4634
Canisius C.	Ann-Marie Dobies	Disabled Student Services	Buffalo, NY 14208	716-888-3748
CUNY—Baruch C.	Barbara Sirios	Disability Services	New York, NY 10010	646-312-4590
CUNY—Bronx C.C.	Caren Horowitz	Disability Services	Bronx, NY 10453	718-289-5874
CUNY—Brooklyn C.	Roberta Adleman	Services for Students with Disabilities	Brooklyn, NY 11210	718-951-5538
CUNY—C. of Staten Island	Margaret Venditti	Disability Services	Staten Island, NY 10314	718-982-2510

College	Location	Contact	Office	Phone
CUNY—Hunter C.	New York, NY 10021	Don Cohen	Office of Students with Disabilities	212-772-4857
CUNY—John Jay C. of Criminal Justice	New York, NY 10019	Matthew McGee	Services for Individuals with Disabilities	212-237-8031
CUNY—Kingsborough C.C.	Brooklyn, NY 11235	Anthony Colarossi	Special Services	718-368-5175
CUNY—LaGuardia C.C.	Long Island City, NY 11101	Matthew Joffre	Office for Students with Disabilities	718-482-5278
CUNY—Lehman C.	Bronx, NY 10468	Mary Parra	Disability Issues	718-960-8441
CUNY—Medgar Evers C.	Brooklyn, NY 11225	Anthony Phifer	Differently Abled Student Services	718-270-5027
CUNY—New York City C. of Tech.	Brooklyn, NY 11201	Faith Fogelman	Student Support Services	718-260-5143
Clarkson U.	Potsdam, NY 13699	Helen McLean-Pletcher	Accommodative Services	315-268-7643
Colgate U.	Hamilton, NY 13346	Lynn Waldman	Academic Program Support	315-228-7375
C. of New Rochelle	New Rochelle, NY 10805-2339	Joan Bristol	Student Services	914-654-5364
C. of Saint Rose, The	Albany, NY 12203	Jenny Rossin	Office of Students with Disabilities	518-454-5299
Columbia U.	New York, NY 10027	Sarah Damsky	Disability Services	212-854-2388
Concordia C. (NY)	Bronxville, NY 10708	George Groth	The Concordia Connection	914-337-9300 ext. 2361
Cooper Union	New York, NY 10003	Linda Lemiesz	Dean of Students	212-353-4115
Cornell U.	Ithaca, NY 14850	Katherine Fahey	Student Disability Services	607-254-4545
Corning C.C.	Corning, NY 14830	Judy Northrop	Counseling for Students with Disabilities	607-962-9262
Culinary Institute of America	Hyde Park, NY 12538	Jack Rittel	The Learning Strategies Center	845-451-1219
Daemen C.	Amherst, NY 14226	Dr. Kathleen Boone	Disability Support Services	716-839-8301
Dominican C.	Orangeburg, NY 10692-1210	Jerome Cashman	Disability Services	845-359-7800 ext. 4035
Dowling C.	Oakdale, NY 11769-1999	Dr. Dorothy Stracher	College Students with Learning Disabilities	631-244-3306
D'Youville C.	Buffalo, NY 14201	Isabel Vecchio	Disability Services	716-881-7728
Eastman School of Music	Rochester, NY 14627	Donna Brink-Fox	Dean of Academic Affairs	585-274-1020
Elmira C.	Elmira, NY 14901	Carolyn Draht	Education Services	607-735-1922
Eugene Lang C. of New School U.	New York, NY 10011	Jason Luchs	Student Disability Services	212-229-5626 ext. 3135
Fashion Institue of Technology	New York, NY 10001-5992	Liz Holly Mortenen	Disability Support Services	212-217-8900
Five Towns C.	Dix Hills, NY 11746-5871	Susan Barr	Academic Support Services	631-656-2129
Fordham U.	New York, NY 10458	Christina Bertsch	Disabled Student Services	718-817-4362
Hamilton C.	Clinton, NY 13323	Allen Harrison	Disabled Student Services	315-859-4021
Hartwick C.	Oneonta, NY 13820-4020	Joan Lambiaso	Academic Center for Excellence	607-431-4435
Hilbert C.	Hamburg, NY 14075-1597	Katherine Monroe	Academic Services	716-649-7900 ext. 395
Hobart & William Smith C.	Geneva, NY 14456	Samuel Vann	Center for Teaching and Learning	315-781-3351
Hofstra U.	Hempstead, NY 11549	Diane Herbert	PALS Program	516-463-5761
Houghton C.	Houghton, NY 14744	Dr. Susan M. Hice	Student Academic Services	716-567-9262

Institution	City, State	Contact	Program/Service	Phone
Iona C.	New Rochelle, NY 10801	Linda Refsland	College Assistance Program	914-633-2159
Ithaca C.	Ithaca, NY 14850-7020	Sandy Simkin	Academic Support Services	607-274-1005
Keuka College	Keuka Park, NY 14478-0098	Carole Lillis	Academic Support Program	315-279-5636
Le Moyne C.	Syracuse, NY 13214	Roger Purdy	Academic Support Center	315-445-4118
Long Island U.—Brooklyn	Brooklyn, NY 11021	Jeff Lambert	Special Educational Services	718-488-1044
Long Island U.—C.W. Post	Brookville, NY 11548-1300	Susan Rock	Academic Resource Center	516-299-3057
Manhattan C.	Riverdale, NY 10471	Dr. Ross Pollack	Learning Disabilites Program	718-862-7101
Manhattan School of Music	New York, NY 10027	Elsa Jean Davidson	Dean of Students	212-749-2802 ext. 4036
Manhattanville C.	Purchase, NY 10577	Jean Baldassare	Higher Education Learning Program	914-323-3186
Marist C.	Poughkeepsie, NY 12601-1387	Linda Cooper	Office of Special Services/LD Program	845-575-3274
Marymount C.	Tarrytown, NY 10591	Polly Waldman	Learning Services	914-332-8310
Marymount Manhattan C.	New York, NY 10021	Ann Jablon, PhD	Program for Academic Access	212-774-0721
Mercy C.	Dobbs Ferry, NY 10522	Terry Rich	Support Services	914-948-3666 ext. 3304
Molloy C.	Rockville Centre, NY 11570	Barbara Merola	STEEP Program	516-678-5000 ext. 6381
NY Institute of Technology	Old Westbury, NY 11568-8000	Alice Burke	Student Services	516-686-7683
New York U.	New York, NY 10011	Yolanda Cacciolo	Henry & Lucy Moses Ctr for Stnts with Disab.	212-998-4980
Niagara U.	Niagara University, NY 14109	Dianne Stoelting	Office of Academic Support	716-286-8076
NYU Teaching & Learning Ctn.	New York, NY 10003	Dr. Jane Herzog	Para Educator for Young Adults	212-998-5800
Onondaga C.C.	Syracuse, NY 13215	Nancy Hazzard	Svcs. for Students w/ Special Needs	315-498-2119
Paul Smith C.	Paul Smith's, NY 12970	Carol A. Lamb	Special Services	518-327-6415
Rensselaer Polytechnic Inst.	Troy, NY 12180	Debra Hamilton	Disability Services	518-276-2746
Roberts Wesleyan C.	Rochester, NY 14624	Bonnie Whitney	Learning Center	585-594-6270
Rochester Inst. of Technology	Rochester, NY 14623	Susan Ackerman	Learning Development Center	585-475-7804
Rockland C.C.	Suffern, NY 10901	Marge Zemek	Office of Disability Services	845-574-4316
Saint Bonaventure U.	St. Bonaventure, NY 14778	Nancy A. Mathews	Services for Students with Disabilities	716-375-2065
Saint Francis C.	Brooklyn Heights, NY 11201	Deborah Seaton	Student Health Services	718-489-5366
Saint John's U. (NY)	Jamaica, NY 11439	Jackie Lochrie	Director of Student Services	718-990-6568
Saint Lawrence U.	Canton, NY 13617	John Meagher	Academic Svcs for Students with Special Needs	315-229-5104
Saint Thomas Aquinas C.	Sparkill, NY 10976	Richard Heath, PhD	The STAC Exchange	845-398-4230
Schenectady C.C.	Schenectady, NY 12305	Tom Dotson	Disabled Student Services	518-381-1344
SUNY—Alfred State College	Alfred, NY 14802	Heather Meacham	Services for Students with Disabilities	607-587-4122
SUNY at Binghamton	Binghamton, NY 13902	Jean Fairbairn	Services for Student with Disabilities	607-777-2686
SUNY—Brockport	Brockport, NY 14420-2915	Maryellen Post	Office for Students with Disabilities	585-395-5409

College	Location	Contact	Service	Phone
SUNY—Broome C.C.	Binghamton, NY 134902	Lisa Hughes	Learning Disabilities	607-778-5316
SUNY—Canton	Canton, NY 13617	Veigh Mehan Lee	Accommodative Services	315-386-7392
SUNY—Cayuga C.C.	Auburn, NY 13021	Robert Meeks	Office of Disability Services	315-255-1743 ext. 2422
SUNY—C. of Technology	Cobelskill, NY 12043	Lynn K. Abarno	Disability Support Services	518-255-5282
SUNY—Columbia Greene C.C.	Hudson, NY 12534	Catherine Tretheway	Dean of Students	518-828-4181 x3437
SUNY—Cortland	Cortland, NY 13045	Ute Gomez	Disabilities Services	607-753-2066
SUNY—Delhi	Delhi, NY 13753	Linda Weinberg	Center for Academic Services	607-746-4593
SUNY—Farmingdale	Farmingdale, NY 11735	Malka Edelman	Support Svcs. for Stdnts. w/ Disabilities	631-420-2411
SUNY—Finger Lakes C.C.	Canandaigua, NY 14424	Amy Nichols	Services for Students w/Disabilities	585-394-3500 ext. 70390
SUNY—Fredonia	Fredonia, NY 14063	Adam Hino	Disabled Student Support	716-673-3270
SUNY—Geneseo	Geneseo, NY 14454-1471	Tabitha Buggie-Hunt	Office of the Dean	585-245-5112
SUNY—Hudson Valley C.C.	Troy, NY 12180	Jennifer Miller	Disability Resource Center	518-629-7552
SUNY—Jamestown C.C.	Jamestown, NY 14702	Nancy Callahan	Main Street Center	716-665-5220
SUNY—Jefferson C.C.	Watertown, NY 13601	Sheree Trainham	Learning Skills Center	315-786-2288
SUNY—Mohawk Valley C.C.	Utica, NY 13501	Lynn Igoe	Services for Students with Disabilities	315-792-5413
SUNY—Nassau C.C.	Garden City, NY 11530	Janis Schimsky	Center for Students with Disabilities	516-572-7138
SUNY—New Paltz	New Paltz, NY 12561	Portia Altman	Disability Resource Center	845-257-3020
SUNY—Old Westbury	Old Westbury, NY 11568	Lisa Whitten, PhD	Disability Services	516-876-3009
SUNY—Oneonta	Oneonta, NY 13820	Craig Levins	Learning Support Services	607-436-2137
SUNY—Oswego	Oswego, NY 13126	Starr Knapp	Office of Disabled Student Services	315-312-3358
SUNY—Plattsburgh	Plattsburgh, NY 12901-2681	Michele Carpentier	Student Support Services	518-564-2810
SUNY—Potsdam	Potsdam, NY 13676	Diana Fisher	Student Support Services	315-267-3267
SUNY—Purchase	Purchase, NY 10577	Ronnie Mait	Special Services	914-251-6035
SUNY—Stony Brook U.	Stony Brook, NY 11794	Joanna Harris	Disabilities Support Services	631-632-6748
SUNY—University at Albany	Albany, NY 12222	Nancy Belowich-Negron	Learning Disabilities Resource Program	518-442-5490
SUNY—University at Buffalo	Buffalo, NY 14222-1095	Marianne Savino	Disability Services	716-878-4500
Syracuse U.	Syracuse, NY 13244	Stephen H. Simon	Center for Academic Acievement	315-443-4498
Tompkins Cortland C.C.	Dryden, NY 13035	Catherine Wunderlich	Baker Center for Learning	607-844-8211 ext. 4375
U. of Buffalo	Buffalo, NY 14260	Randall Borst	Office of Disability Services	716-645-2608
U. of Rochester	Rochester, NY 14627-0251	Vicki Roth	Learning Assistance Services	585-275-9049
Union C.	Schenectady, NY 12308	Shelly Shinebarger	Director—Student Support Services	518-388-6061
Utica C. of Syracuse U.	Utica, NY 13502-4892	Kateri Teresa Henkel	Academic Support Services	315-792-3032
Vassar C.	Poughkeepsie, NY 12604	Belinda Guthrie	Office of Disability Services	845-437-7584

Institution	Location	Contact	Service	Phone
Vaughn C. of Aeronautics & Tech.	Flushing, NY 11369	Reynold Ali	Academic Support Services	718-429-6600 ext. 133
Wagner C.	Staten Island, NY 10301	Dina Assante	Academic Advisement Center	718-390-3278
Wells C.	Aurora, NY 13026	Diane Koester	Academic Advising	315-364-3241
Westchester C.C.	Valhalla, NY 10595	Marcia Kalkut	Disabled Students	914-606-6552
Yeshiva U.	New York, NY 10033	Dr. Chaim Nissel	Student Affairs	212-960-5480
CUNY—York C.	Jamaica, NY 11451	Jeffrey Silva	Disability Services	718-262-2073

NORTH CAROLINA

Institution	Location	Contact	Service	Phone
Appalachian St. U.	Boone, NC 28608	Suzanne T. Wehner	Office of Disability Services	828-262-2291
Asheville-Buncombe Tech.	Asheville, NC 28801	Annie Clingenpeel	Special Needs	828-254-1921 ext. 141
Barton C.	Wilson, NC 27893	Courtney Manning	Disability Services	252-399-6587
Belmont Abbey C.	Belmont, NC 28012	Stacy Davis	Academic Assistance	704-825-6776
Bennett C.	Greensboro, NC 27401	Darnita Howard	Center for Teaching, Learning, and Technology	336-517-1567
Brevard College	Brevard, NC 28712	Susan Kuehn	Office for Stmts w/Special Needs & Disabilities	828-884-8131
Campbell U.	Buies Creek, NC 27506	Laura Rich	Student Support Services	800-334-4111
Catawba C.	Salisbury, NC 28144	Nan Zimmerman	Academic Resource Center	704-637-4259
Central Piedmont C.C.	Charlotte, NC 28235	Patricia Adams	Services for Students with Disabilities	704-330-6556
Chowan College	Murfreesboro, NC 27855	Marion Foster	Learning Center	252-398-3604
Davidson C.	Davidson, NC 28036	Kathy Brey Merrell	Dean of Students Office	704-894-2225
Duke U.	Durham, NC 27708	Emma Swain	Student Disability Access Office	919-668-1267
East Carolina U.	Greenville, NC 27858	Liz Johnston	Disability Support Services	252-328-6799
Elizabeth City State U.	Elizabeth City, NC 27909	Annie Hedgebeth	Center for Special Needs Students	252-335-3527
Elon University	Elon, NC 27244	Priscilla Lipe	Disability Services	336-278-6500
Gardner-Webb U.	Boiling Springs, NC 28071	Cheryl Potter	Disability Services	704-406-4270
Greensboro C.	Greensboro, NC 27401-1875	Julie Yindra	Disability Services	336-272-7102 ext. 591
Guilford C.	Greensboro, NC 27410	Melissa Daniel	Academic Skills Center	336-316-2200
Guilford Tech C.C.	Jamestown, NC 27282	Angela Leak	Academic Support Services	336-334-4822 ext. 2325
High Point U.	High Point, NC 27262-3598	Irene Ingersoll	Disability Services	336-841-9037
Johnson C. Smith U.	Charlotte, NC 28216	James Cuthbertson	Student Support Services	708-378-1282
Lees-McRae C.	Banner Elk, NC 28604	Tamara Tressler-Blewitt	Center for Student Success	828-898-5241 ext. 2561
Lenoir-Rhyne C.	Hickory, NC 28603	Dr. Janette L. Sims	Disability Services	828-328-7296
Livingstone C.	Salisbury, NC 28144	Judith Cowan	Disability Services	704-216-6065
Mars Hill C.	Mars Hill, NC 28754	Chris Kain	Special Education	828-689-1495
Meredith C.	Raleigh, NC 27607-5298	Betty-Shannon Prevatt	Disability Services	919-760-8427

College	Location	Contact	Service	Phone
Methodist C.	Fayetteville, NC 28311-1498	Linda Szulc	Disability Services	910-630-7251
Mt. Olive C.	Mount Olive, NC 28365	Carlette Whitesides	Teaching and Learning Center	919-658-2502 ext. 1185
Nash Community C.	Rocky Mount, NC 27804	Cynthia Hinnant	Compensatory Education Dept.	252-443-4011 ext. 8315
North Carolina School of the Arts	Winston-Salem, NC 27127-2189	Tom Murray	Counseling Center	336-770-3277
North Carolina St. U.	Raleigh, NC 27695	Cheryl Branker, EdD	Disability Services for Students	919-515-7653
Richmond C.C.	Hamlet, NC 28345	Traci Etheridge	Student Development	910-410-1728
Rockingham C.C.	Wentworth, NC 27375	LaVonne James	Student Development	336- 342-4261 ext. 2243
St. Andrews Presbyterian C.	Laurinburg, NC 28352	Dorthy Wells	Disability Academic Support Services	910-277-5331
Southwestern C.C.	Sylva, NC 28779	Cheryl Contino-Conner	Student Support Services	828-586-4091 ext. 245
UNC at Chapel Hill, The	Chapel Hill, NC 27599	Jane Benson	Learning Disabilities Services	919-962-7227
UNC at Charlotte, The	Charlotte, NC 28223-0001	Joanne Ferneld	Disability Services	704-687-4355
UNC at Greensboro, The	Greensboro, NC 27402-6170	Mary Culkin	Disabled Student Services	336-334-5440
UNC at Pembroke, The	Pembroke, NC 28372	Mary Helen Walker	Disability Support Services	910-521-6695
UNC at Wilmington, The	Wilmington, NC 28403	Peggy Turner, PhD	Disability Services	910-962-7555
Wake Forest U.	Winston-Salem, NC 27109	Van D. Westervelt, PhD.	Learning Assistance Center	336-758-5929
Wake Tech C.C.	Raleigh, NC 27603	Janet Kilhen	Disability Support Services	919-662-3615
West Piedmont C.C.	Morgantown, NC 28655	David Collins	Disabled Student Services	828-438-6044
Western Carolina U.	Cullowhee, NC 28723	Kimberly Marcus	Disabled Student Services	828-227-7234
Wingate U.	Wingate, NC 28174	Linda Stedje-Larsen	Disability Services	704-233-8269
Winston-Salem St. U.	Winston-Salem, NC 27110	Myra Waddell	Academic Resource Center	336-750-2394

NORTH DAKOTA

College	Location	Contact	Service	Phone
Bismarck St. C.	Bismarck, ND 58506	Marlene Swenson-Seaworth	Disability Support Services	701-224-5554
Dickinson St. U.	Dickinson, ND 58601-4896	Dr. Mary Jo Gonzales	Student Support Services	701-483-2999
Jamestown C.	Jamestown, ND 58405	Dan Kunzman	Office of Admissions	701-252-3467
Maryville St. U.	Maryville, ND 58257	Greta Kyllo	Academic Support Services	701-788-4747
Minot St. U.	Minot, ND 58707	Jan Nahinurk	Learning Center	701-228-5479
North Dakota St. C.	Wahpeton, ND 58076-0002	Joy Eichhorn	Study Svcs. for Students w/ Disabilities	701-671-2623
North Dakota St. U.	Fargo, ND 58105-5226	Bunnie Johnson-Messelt	Disability Services	701-231-7671
United Tribes Tech C.	Bismarck, ND 58504	Carol Johnson	Student Support Services	701-255-3285 ext. 1465
U. of Mary	Bismarck, ND 58504	Mary Jo Woken	Learning Skill Services	701-355-8264
Williston St. C.	Williston, ND 58801	Penny Soiseth	Enrollment Services	701-774-4220
U. of North Dakota—Grand Forks	Grand Forks, ND 58202	Deb Glennen	Disabled Student Support Services	701-777-3425
Valley City St. U.	Valley City, ND 58072	Jan Drake	Student Academic Services	701-845-7298

Institution	Location	Contact	Service	Phone
Antioch C.	Yellow Spring, OH 45387	John A. Smith	Academic Support Services	937-769-1166
Art Academy of Cincinnati	Cincinnati, OH 45202	Dabby Blatt	Learning Assistance	513-562-6261
Ashland U.	Ashland, OH 44805	Suzanne Salvo	Disability Services	419-289-4142 ext. 5953
Baldwin-Wallace C.	Berea, OH 44017	Carol Templeman	Svcs for Students w/ Disabilities	440-826-2188 x 2116
Bowling Green St. U.	Bowling Green, OH 43403	Robert D. Cunningham	Office of Disability Services	419-372-8495
Capital U.	Columbus, OH 43209	Lydia Block	Disability Concerns	614-236-6284
Case Western Reserve U.	Cleveland, OH 44106	Susan Sampson	Disability Support Services	216-368-5230
Central Ohio Tech C.	Newark, OH 43055	Connie Zang	Office for Disability Services	740-366-9246
Clark St. C.C.	Springfield, OH 45505	Marie Ann Kaiser	Office of Student Services	937-328-6019
Cleveland Institute of Art	Cleveland, OH 44106	Todd Emery	Office of Academic Services	216-421-7465
Cleveland Institute of Music	Cleveland, OH 44106	William Fay	Office of Admissions	216-795-3107
Cleveland St. U.	Cleveland, OH 44115	Kate Yurick	Disability Services	216-687-2015
C. of Mount Saint Joseph	Cincinnati, OH 45233-1630	Jane Pohlman	Project Excel	513-244-4623
C. of Wooster	Wooster, OH 44691	Pamela Rose	Learning Center	330-263-2595
Columbus C. of Art and Design	Columbis, OH 43215	Roderick Jungbauer	Disability Services	614-222-3292
Columbus St. C.C.	Columbus, OH 43216	Wayne Cocchi	Disability Services	614-227-2629
Cuyahoga C.C. Western	Parma, OH 44130	Paul Shane	Access Office for Accommodation	216-987-2052
Denison U.	Granville, OH 43023	Jennifer Grube Vestal	Office of Academic Support	740-587-5719
Franciscan U. of Seubenville	Stubenville, OH 43952-1763	Rose Kline	Disability Services	740-284-5358
Franklin U.	Columbus, OH 43215-5399	Carla Waugh	Student Services	614-341-6256
Heidelburg C.	Tiffin, OH 44883	William Miller	Learning Center	419-448-2301
Hiram C.	Hiram, OH 44234	Dr. Lynn B. Taylor	Counseling	330-569-5952
Hocking C.	Nelsonville, OH 45764	Kim Forbes Powell	Office of Disability Services	740-753-3591
John Carroll U.	University Heights, OH 44118	Allison West	Services for Students with Disabilities	216-397-4967
Kent St. U.	Kent, OH 44242-0001	Mary De Michele Reeves	Student Accessibility Services	330-672-3391
Kenyon C.	Gambier, OH 43022	Erin Salva	Academic Advising	740-427-5145
Lake Erie C.	Painesville, OH 44077	John Meehl	Academic Services	440-375-7111
Lakeland C.C.	Kirtland, OH 44095	Alan Kirsh	Services for Students with Disabilities	440-953-7245
Lorain City C.C.	Elyria, OH 44035	Theodora Scott	Office for Special Needs Services	440-366-4058
Lourdes C.	Sylvania, OH 43560	Kim Grieve	Disability Services	419-824-3834
Malone C.	Canton, OH 44709	Patty Little	Student Retention	330-471-8359
Marietta C.	Marietta, OH 45750	Dr. Michael Harding	Counseling Center	740-376-4477

College	Location	Contact	Office	Phone
Miami U.—Hamilton	Hamilton, OH 45011	Mary Vogel	Special Services	513-785-3211
Miami U.	Oxford, OH 45056	J. Andrew Zeisler	Office of Disability Resources	513-529-1541
Mt. Union C.	Alliance, OH 44601	Karen Saracusa	Disability Support Services	330-823-7372
Mt. Vernon Nazarene U.	Mount Vernon, OH 43050	Dr. Carol Matthews	Academic Support Services	740-392-6868 ext. 4536
Muskingum C.	New Concord, OH 43762	Dr. Eileen Henry, EdD, MBA	PLUS Program	740-826-8284
North Central State C.	Mansfield, OH 44901	Sandra Luckie	Disability Services	419-755-4727
Notre Dame C. of Ohio	Cleveland, OH 44121	Dr. T.J. Arant	Disability Services	216-373-5310
Oberlin C.	Oberlin, OH 44074	Jane Boomer	Off. of Serv. for Students w/ Disab.	440-775-8464
Ohio Dominican C.	Coumbus, OH 42319	Amy Spencer	Academic Development	614-251-4511
Ohio Northern U.	Ada, OH 45810	Anne Lippert	Student Affairs	419-772-2034
Ohio St. U.	Marion, OH 43302	Margaret Hazelett	Learning Disabilities Services	740-389-6786 ext. 6247
Ohio St. U.—Columbus	Columbus, OH 43210-1200	Lois Burke	Office for Disability Services	614-292-3307
Ohio St. U.—Newark	Newark, OH 43055	Dr. Phyllis Tompson	Learning Assistance Services	740-366-9246
Ohio U.—Athens	Athens, OH 45701	Katherine Fahey	Office for Institutional Equity	740-593-2620
Ohio Wesleyan U.	Delaware, OH 43015	Dr. Lydia Block	Academic Advising	740-368-3275
Otterbein C.	Westerville, OH 43081	Ellen Kasulis	Academic Support Center	614-823-1362
Owens C.C.	Toledo, OH 43699	Beth Scheffert	Disability Resource Services	419-661-7007
Raymond Walters C.	Cincinnati, OH 45236	John Kraimer	Disability Services	513-729-8625
Shawnee St. U.	Portsmouth, OH 45662	Scott Douthat	Office of Special Needs Services	740-351-3276
Sinclair C.C.	Dayton, OH 45402	Robin Moore-Cooper	Disability Services	937-512-5113
Terra St. C.C.	Fremont, OH 43420	Gina Staccone-Smeal	Disability Services	419-559-2208
Union Institute U.	Cincinnati, OH 45206	Neil Meier	Disability Services	513-861-3116
U. of Akron	Akron, OH 44325-2001	Mara Byers	Services for Students with Disabilities	330-972-7928
U. of Cincinnati	Cincinnati, OH 45221-0091	Debra Merchant, JD	Disability Student Services	513-556-6823
U. of Dayton	Dayton, OH 45469-1611	Timothy King, PhD	Office of Students with Disabilities	937-229-2066
U. of Findlay	Findlay, OH 45840	Lori Colchagoff	Supporting Skills System	419-424-5532
U. of Rio Grande	Rio Grande, OH 45674	Marshall Kimmel	Disability Services	740-245-7339
U. of Toledo	Toledo, OH 43606-3390	Angela M. Paprocki, MEd	Office of Accessibility	419-530-4981
Urbana U.	Urbana, OH 43078	Shawan Benson	Disability Services	937-484-1286
Ursuline C.	Pepper Pike, OH 44124-4398	Eileen D. Kohut	Program for Students with LD	440-646-8123
Walsh U.	Canton, OH 44720	Ellen Kutz	Disability Services	330-490-7302
Washington St. C.C.	Marietta, OH 45750	Patti Zakowski	Student Development	740-374-8716 ext. 2503
Wilmington C.	Wilmington, OH 45177	Steve Spencer	Disability Services	937-382-6661

Whittenberg U.	Springfield, OH 45501	Lynne Banion	Academic Services	937-327-7924
Wright St. U.	Dayton, OH 45435	Jeff Vernooy	Office of Disability Services	937-775-5680
Xavier U.	Cincinnati, OH 45207-2612	Ann Dinan, PhD	Learning Assistance Center	513-745-3280
Youngstown St. U.	Youngstown, OH 44555	Jain Savage	Disability Services	330-941-1372

OKLAHOMA

Cameron U.	Lawton, OK 73505	Jennifer Pruchniki	Disability Services	580-581-2209
East Central U.	Ada, OK 74820	Dwain West	Student Support Services	580-310-5300
Northeastern St. U.	Tahlequah, OK 74464	Donna Agee	Student Affairs	918-456-5511 ext. 2120
Oklahoma Baptist U.	Shawnee, OK 74804	Canaan Crane	Student Services	405-878-2416
Oklahoma Christian U.	Oklahoma City, OK 73136-1100	Amy Jenzen	Student Life	405-425-5907
Oklahoma City C.C.	Oklahoma City, OK 73159	Pat Stowe	Services to Students with Disabilities	405-682-1611
Oklahoma St. U.	Stillwater, OK 74078	Michael Shuttic	Student Disability Services	405-744-7116
Oklahoma Wesleyan U.	Bartlesville, OK 74006	Ruth Ann Colaw	Disability Support Services	918-335-6209
Oral Roberts U.	Tulsa, OK 74171	Danny Ziriax	Student Support Services	918-495-7018
Southern Nazarene U.	Bethany, OK 73008	Loral Henck	Student Support Services	405-491-6694
Southeastern Oklahoma St. U.	Durant, OK 74701-0609	May Susan Dodson	Student Support Services	580-745-2254
St. Gregory's U.	Shawnee, OK 74804	Melody Harrington	Disability Support Services	405-878-5310
Tulsa Junior C.	Tulsa, OK 74119	Yolanda Williams	Disabled Student Resource Center	918-595-7115
U. of Central Oklahoma	Edmound, OK 73034	Kimberly Fields	Disability Support Services	405-974-2549
U. of Oklahoma	Norman, OK 73019	Suzette Dyer	Office of Disability Services	405-325-3852
U. of Tulsa	Tulsa, OK 74104	Dr. Jane Corso	Center for Student Academic Support	918-631-2315

OREGON

Blue Mountain C.C.	Pendelton, OR 97801	Amy Spiegel	Services for Students with Disabilities	541-278-5807
Chemeketa C.C.	Salem, OR 97309	Rebecca Woods	Office for Students with Disabilities	503-399-5192
Concordia U.	Portland, OR 97211	Terry McGlassen	Couseling and Learning Services	503-493-6545
Corban C.	Salem, OR 97301	Daren Milionis	Career and Academic Services	503-375-7012
Eastern Oregon U.	La Grande, OR 97850	Pat Arnson	Learning Center	541-962-3081
George Fox U.	Newberg, OR 97132	Rick Muthiah	Disability Services	503-554-2314
Lane C.C.	Eugene, OR 97405	Nancy Hart	Disabled Student Services	541-463-3000
Lewis & Clark C.	Portland, OR 97219-7899	Dale Holloway	Student Support Services	503-768-7175
Linfield C.	McMinnville, OR 97128-6894	Judith Haynes	Learning Support Services	503-883-2444
Linn-Benton C.C.	Albany, OR 97321	Lynne A. Cox	Disability Services	541-917-4808

Institution	Location	Contact	Service	Phone
Marylhurst U.	Marylhurst, OR 97036-0261	Gerri Stanfield	Disability Services	503-636-8141 ext. 3344
Mt. Hood C.C.	Gresham, OR 97030	Liz Johnson	Disability Services	503-491-7650
Northwest Christian C.	Eugene, OR 97401	Angela Doty	Career Development & Service Learning	541-684-7345
Oregon Institute of Technology	Klamath Falls, OR 97601	Ron McCutcheon	Campus Access and Equality	541-885-1031
Oregon St. U.	Corvallis, OR 97331-2133	Tracy Bentley-Townlin, PhD	Services for Students with Disabilities	541-737-4098
Pacific U.	Forest Grove, OR 97116	Edna Gehring	Learning Support Services	503-352-2107
Portland St. U.	Portland, OR 97207	Margaret McIlmoyl	Disability Resource Center	503-725-4150
Rogue C.C.	Grants Pass, OR 97527	Bonnie Reeg	Support Services	541-956-7337
Southern Oregon St. U.	Ashland, OR 97520-5032	Theresa Lowrie	Disabled Student Services	541-552-6213
Umpqua C.C.	Roseburg, OR 97470	Barbara Stoner	Disability Services	541-440-7655
U. of Oregon	Eugene, OR 97403-1217	Steve Pickett, MS, CRC	Disability Services	541-346-1155
U. of Portland	Portland, OR 97203	Melanie Gangle	Disability Services	503-943-7134
Warner Pacific C.	Portland, OR 97215	Rod Johanson	Career Services	503-517-1000 ext. 1010
Western Oregon U.	Monmouth, OR 97361	Phil Pownall	Office of Disability Services	503-838-8250
Willamette U.	Salem, OR 97301	Deb Loers	Disability Services	503-370-6471

PENNSYLVANIA

Institution	Location	Contact	Service	Phone
Albright C.	Reading, PA 19612	Tiffenia Archie	Learning Center - Academic Support	610-921-7662
Allegheny C.	Meadville, PA 16335	Nancy Sheridan	Learning Commons	814-332-2898
Alvernia C.	Reading, PA 19607-1799	Catherine Emery	Office of Admissions	888-258-3764 ext. 8221
Arcadia U.	Glenside, PA 19038-3295	Linda Pizzi	Education Enhancement Center	215-572-4086
Bloomsburg U. of Pennsylvania	Bloomsburg, PA 17815	Peter B. Walters	Accommodative Services	570-389-4491
Bryn Athyn C. of the New Church	Bryn Athyn, PA 19009	Carol Odhner	Disability Services	276-502-2547
Bryn Mawr C.	Bryn Mawr, PA 19010-2899	Stephanie Bell	Access Services	610-526-7351
Bucknell U.	Lewisburg, PA 17837-9988	Elaine Garrett	Admissions Svcs. for Disabled Students	570-577-1301
Bucks County C.C.	Newton, PA 18940	Marie Stevens Cooper	Program for Students with Disabilities	215-968-8463
Cabrini C.	Randor, PA 19087	Anne Abbuhl	Disabilities Support Services	610-902-8572
California U. of Pennsylvania	California, PA 15419	Cheryl Bilitski	Office for Students with Disabilities	724-938-5781
Carlow C.	Pittsburgh, PA 15213	Andrea Beranek	College Learning Center	412-578-6136
Carnegie Mellon U.	Pittsburgh, PA 15213	Larry Powell	Equal Opportunity Services	412-268-2012
Cedar Crest C.	Allentown, PA 18104-6796	Karen Schoenborn	Academic Services	610-606-4628
Chatham C.	Pittsburgh, PA 15232	Janet James	College Learning Center	412-365-1611
Chestnut Hill C.	Philadelphia, PA 19118-2693	Catharine Fee	Academic Advising	215-248-7199
Cheyney U. of PA	Cheyney, PA 19319	Etta Baldwin	Academic Success Center	610-339-2275 ext. 2319

Institution	Location	Contact	Service	Phone
Clarion U. of Pennsylvania	Clarion, PA 16214	Jennifer May	Disability Support Services	814-393-2095
C. Misericordia	Dallas, PA 18612	Dr. Joseph Rogan	Alternative Learning Project	570-674-6347
C.C. of Allegheny County	Pittsburgh, PA 15212	Mary Beth Doyle	Support Svcs. for Stdnts. w/ Disabilities	412-237-4614
C.C. of Philadelphia	Philadelphia, PA 19130	Joan Monroe	Educational Support Services	215-751-8478
CCAC C. North	Pittsburgh, PA 15237	Kathleen White	Support Services	412-369-3686
Delaware Valley C.	Doylestown, PA 18901	Sharon Malka	Learning Support Services	215-489-2490
DeSales U.	Center Valley, PA 18034	Dr. Rosalind Edman	Learning Center	610-282-1100 ext. 1293
Dickinson C.	Carlisle, PA 17013-2896	Jorja Waybrant	Learning Support	717-245-1080
Drexel U.	Philadelphia, PA 19104	Michelle M. Peters	Office of Disability Services	215-895-1401
Duquesne U.	Pittsburgh, PA 15282	David Lachowski	Learning Skills Center	412-396-6035
Eastern U.	St. Davids, PA 19087-3696	Lisa Hemlick, PhD	Cushing Center for Counseling	610-341-5837
East Stroudsburg U. of PA	East Stroudsburg, PA 18301-2999	Dr. Edith F. Miller	Office of Disability Services	570-422-3954
Edinboro U. of Pennsylvania	Edinboro, PA 16444	Robert McConnell, PhD	Office for Students with Disabilities	814-732-2462
Elizabethtown C.	Elizabethtown, PA 17022-2298	Shirley Deichert	Disability Services	717-361-1227
Franklin & Marshall C.	Lancaster, PA 17604-3003	Kenneth John, PhD	Counseling Services	717-291-4083
Gannon U.	Erie, PA 16541	Sr. Joyce Lowrey, SSJ	Program for Students w/ LD	814-871-5326
Geneva C.	Beaver Falls, PA 15010	Nancy Smith	ACCESS Center	
Gettysburg C.	Gettysburg, PA 17325	Dr. GailAnn Rickert	Academic Advising	717-337-6579
Grove City College	Grove City, PA 16127	Diana King	Disability Services	724-458-2700
Gwynedd-Mercy C.	Gwyned Valley, PA 19437-0901	Rachelle Guido	Disability Services	215-646-7300 ext. 427
Harcum Jr C.	Bryn Mawr, PA 19010	Gail Sklar	AccESS Development	610-526-6036
Haverford C.	Haverford, PA 19041-1392	Rick Webb	Counseling & Psychological Services	610-896-1290
Holy Family U.	Philadelphia, PA 19114-2094	Diana R. Piperata, PhD	Disability Services	215-637-7700 ext. 3232
Immaculata U.	Immaculata, PA 19345-0702	Valerie Vogal	Academic Deans Office	610-647-4400 ext. 3728
Indiana U. of Penn	Indiana, PA 15705	Dr. Catherine Dugan	Advising and Testing Center	724-357-4067
Juniata C.	Huntingdon, PA 16652	Sarah M. Clarkson	Academic Support	814-641-3161
King's C.	Wilkes-Baree, PA 18711	Jacintha Burke	Academic Skills Center	570-208-5800
Kutztown U. of Pennsylvania	Kutztown, PA 19530	Patricia Ritcher	Services for Students with Disabilities	610-683-4108
LaRoche C.	Pittsburgh, PA 15327	Diana Forsyth	Academic Enrichment	412-536-1231
LaSalle U.	Philadelphia, PA 19141-1199	Rose Lee Pauline	Teaching and Learning Center	215-951-1014
Lebanon Valley College	Annville, PA 17003-0501	Yvonne Foster	Office of Disability Services	717-867-6071
Lehigh U.	Bethlehem, PA 18015	Cheryl A. Ashcroft	Office of Academic Support Services	610-758-4152
Lincoln U.	Lincoln University, PA 19352	Nancy Kenner	Disability Services	610-932-8300 ext. 7624

College	Location	Office/Service	Contact	Phone
Lock Haven U. of Pennsylvania	Lock Haven, PA 17745	Student Support Services	Dr. Reynol Junco	570-893-2926
Luzerne Cty. C.C.	Naanticoke, PA 18634	Learning Support Services	Anna Mary McHugh	570-740-0771
Lycoming C.	Williamsport, PA 17701	Academic Resource Center	Daniel Hertsock	570-321-4294
Mansfield U. of PA	Mansfield, PA 16933	Disability Services	Hemlock Manor,	570-662-4798
Marywood U.	Scranton, PA 18509-1598	Office of Disability Services	Diane Taylor	570-340-6045
Mercyhurst C.	Erie, PA 16546	Program for Students with LD	Dianne Rogers	814-824-2450
Messiah C.	Grantham, PA 17027-0800	Disability Services	Keith Drahn, PhD	717-796-5358
Millersville U. of PA	Millersville, PA 17551-0302	Learning Services	Sherylnn Bessick	717-872-3178
Montgomery College C.C.	Blue Bell, PA 19422	Services for Students with Disabilities	Saul Finkle	215-641-6574
Moore C. of Art & Design	Philadelphia, PA 19103	Educational Support Services	Claudine Thomas	215-965-4061
Moravian C.	Bethlehem, PA 18018	Learning Services	Laurie M. Roth	610-861-1510
Mount Aloysius C.	Cresson, PA 16630	Disability Services	Sister Linda Karas	814-886-6336
Muhlenberg C.	Allentown, PA 18104-5596	Academic Support Services	Wendy Cole	484-664-3433
Neumann C.	Aston, PA 19014-1298	Disability Services	James Kain	610-361-5349
Northampton C.C.	Bethlehem, PA 18017	Services for Disabled Students	Laraine Demshock	610-861-5342
Peirce C.	Philadelphia, PA 19102	Dean of Students	Rita Toliver-Roberts	888-467-3472 ext. 8654
Pennsylvania C. of Technology	Williamsport, PA 17701	Disability Support Services	Sharon Waters	570-327-4765
Penn St. U.—Delaware	Media, PA 19063-5596	Support Services	Sharon Manco	610-892-1461
Penn St. U.—Erie, The Behrend C.	Erie, PA 16563	Services for Students with Disabilities	Andres Herrera	814-898-6111
Penn St. U.—Fogelsville	Fogelsville, PA 18051-9999	Disability Services	Bill Welsh	814-863-1807
Penn St. U.—Mont Alto	Mont Alto, PA 17237-9703	Learning Center	Nanette Hatzes	717-749-6045
Penn St. U.—Schuylkill	Schuylkill Haven, PA 17972-2208	Disability Services	Bill Welsh	814-863-1807
Pennsylvania St. U.—U. Park	Univ. Park, PA 16802-3000	Office for Disability Services	Bill Welsh	814-863-1807
Philadelphia Biblical U.	Langhorne, PA 19047-2990	Disability Services	Jean Minto	215-702-4270
Philadelphia U.	Philadelphia, PA 19144	Disability Service Office	Amy Schwab	215-951-6830
Point Park U.	Pittsburg, PA 15222	Academic Success	Patricia Boykin	412-392-4738
Robert Morris C.	Moon Township, PA 15108	Center For Student Success	Cassandra L. Oden	412-262-8349
Rosemont C.	Rosemont, PA 19010-1699	Dean of Students	Marilyn Moller	610-527-0200 ext. 2400
Saint Francis U. (PA)	Loretto, PA 15940	Academic Center for Enrichment	Denise Kovach	814-472-3176
Saint Joseph's U. (PA)	Philadelphia, PA 19131	Services for Students with Disabilities	Jim Scott	610-660-1774
Saint Vincent C. (PA)	Latrobe, PA 15650-2690	Disability Support Services	Sandy Quinlivan	724-805-2371
Seton Hill University	Greensburg, PA 15601	Disability Services	Teresa A. Bassi	724-838-4295
Shippensburg U. of Penn.	Shippensburg, PA 17257-2299	Office of Disability Services	Paula Madey	717-477-1329

Institution	Location	Office	Contact	Phone
Slippery Rock U. of PA	Slippery Rock, PA 16057	Office for Students with Disabilities	Linda Quidone	724-738-4877
Susquehanna U.	Selinsgrove, PA 17870	Counseling Center	Anna Beth Payne, PhD	570-372-4751
Swarthmore C.	Swarthmore, PA 19081	Disability Services	James L. Bock	610-328-8000
Temple U.	Philadelphia, PA 19122-6096	Disability Resources & Services	John Bennett	215-204-1280
Thiel C.	Greenville, PA 16125	Office of Special Needs	Susan Cowan	724-589-2063
Thomas Jefferson U., Col. of Health	Philadelphia, PA 19107	Student Affairs	William Thygeson	215-503-8189
U. of Arts, The	Philadelphia, PA 19102	Disability Services	Neila Douglas	215-717-6616
U. of Pennsylvania	Philadelphia, PA 19104	Student Disability Services	Matthew Tominey	215-573-9235
U. of Pittsburg-Bradford	Bradford, PA 16701	Academic Success Center	Anna Johnson	814-362-7609
U. of Pittsburg-Greensburg	Greensburg, PA 15601	Disability Services	Lou Ann Sears	724-836-7098
U. of Pittsburg-Johnstown	Johnstown, PA 15904	Learning Resources Center	Theresa Horner	814-269-7001
U. of Pittsburg-Pittsburgh	Pittsburgh, PA 15260	Disability Resources & Services	Lynnett Van Slyke	412-648-7890
U. of Scranton	Scranton, PA 18510-4699	Learning Enrich. Spclst-Learning Resources Cntr	Mary Ellen Pichiarello	570-941-4039
Ursinus C.	Collegeville, PA 19426	Dean of Admissions	Robert McCullough	610-409-3200
Villanova U.	Villanova, PA 19085	Learning Support Services	Nancy Mott	610-519-5636
Washington & Jefferson C.	Washington, PA 15301	Student Resource Center	Catherine Sherman	724-223-6008
Westminster C.	New Wilmington, PA 16172	Disability Support Services	Yvonne Van Bruggen	724-946-7192
West Chester U. of PA	West Chester, PA 19383	Disability Services	Martin Patwell	610-436-3217
Widener U.	Chester, PA 19013-5792	ENABLE	Rebecca Corsey-Mckeogh, PhD	610-499-4179
Wilkes U.	Wilkes-Barre, PA 18766	Learning Center	Thomas Thomas	570-408-4154
Wilson College	Chambersburg, PA 17201	Learning Resource Center	Pam Cleary	717-264-4141 x3351
York C. of PA	York, PA 17405-7199	Academic Advising	Dr. Carol Bair	717-815-1531

RHODE ISLAND

Institution	Location	Office	Contact	Phone
Brown U.	Providence, RI 02912	Disability Support Services	Catherine Axe	401-863-9588
Bryant C.	Smithfield, RI 02917	Academic Center for Excellence	Laurie L. Hazard, EdD	401-232-6746
C.C. of Rhode Island	Warwick, RI 02856	Student Access and Mentoring	Tracy Karasinski	401-825-2402
Johnson & Wales	Providence, RI 02903	Center for Academic Support	Meryl Berstein	401-598-4689
Providence C.	Providence, RI 02918	Office of Academic Services	Andrew Christensen	401-865-1121
Rhode Island College	Providence, RI 02908	Disability Services	Scott Kane	401-456-8061
Roger Williams U.	Bristol, RI 02809	Center for Academic Development	Lisa Bauer	401-254-3736
Salve Regina U.	Newport, RI 02840-4192	Disability Services	Susan Pratt	401-341-3150
U. of Rhode Island	Kingston, RI 02881	Disability Services for Students	Pamela Rohland	401-874-2098

SOUTH CAROLINA

Institution	Location	Contact	Office	Phone
Anderson C.	Anderson, SC 29621	Linda Carlson	Academic Services	864-231-2026
Citadel, The	Charleston, SC 29409	Dr. Barbara Zaremba	Academic Support Special Services	843-953-6877
Clemson U.	Clemson, SC 29634	Bonnie Martin	Student Disability Services	864-656-6848
Coastal Carolina U.	Conway, SC 29528-6054	Seleah L. Crosland	Counseling Services	843-349-2307
Coker C.	Hartsville, SC 29550	Dr. Steve Terry	Disability Services	843-383-8035
C. of Charleston	Charleston, SC 29424	Bobbie D. Lindstrom	Center for Disability Services	843-953-1431
Columbia International U.	Columbia, SC 29203	Cynthia Morgan	Academic Services	800-777-2227 ext. 5611
Converse C.	Spartanburg, SC 29302	Kathleen Miller	Academic Support	864-577-2028
Erskine C.	Due West, SC 29639	Robyn Agnew	Student Services	864-379-8701
Francis Marion U.	Florence, SC 295001	Rebecca Lawson	Counseling & Testing	843-673-1828
Furman U.	Greenville, SC 29613	Gina Parris	Disability Services	864-294-2322
Lander U.	Greenwood, SC 29649-2099	Leslie Glover	Student Support Services	864-388-8972
Limestone C.	Gaffney, SC 29340	Karen Kearse, MEd	Program for Alternative Learning Styles (PALS)	864-488-8377
Newberry C.	Newberry, SC 29108	Don Johnson-Taylor	Institutional Research and Disabilities	803-321-5112
North Greeville C.	Tigerville, SC 29688	Nancy Isgett	Learning Disability Services	864-977-7129
Presbyterian C.	Clinton, SC 29325	Robert Holyer	Office of Provost	864-833-8233
Southern Wesleyan U.	Central, SC 29630-1020	Carol Sinnamon	Services to Students with Disabilities	864-644-5133
USC—Lancaster	Lancaster, SC 29721	Trach Taylor	Academic Success Center	803-313-7066
USC—Aiken	Aiken, SC 29801	Barbara Riverdahl	Disability Services	803-641-3609
USC—Columbia	Columbia, SC 29208	Karen Pettus	Office of Student Disability Services	803-777-4331
USC—Spartanburg	Spartanburg, SC 29303	Jim Gorske	Disability Services	864-503-5195
Winthrop U.	Rock Hill, SC 29733	Gena Smith	Students with Disabilities Services	803-323-2233
Wofford C.	Spartanburg, SC 29303-3663	Elizabeth Wallace	Health Services and Couseling	864-597-4371
York Tech C.	Clover, SC 29730	Sally Herlong	Disability Services—Special Resources Office	803-325-2896

SOUTH DAKOTA

Institution	Location	Contact	Office	Phone
Augustana C. (SD)	Sioux Falls, SD 57197	Susan Bies	Svcs. for Students with Special Needs	605-274-5503
Black Hills St. U.	Spearfish, SD 57799	Larry Vrooman, MS, CRC	Student Assistant Center	605-642-6099
Dakota St. U.	Madison, SD 57042	Robert Jackson	ADA Academic Services	605-256-5823
Dakota Wesleyan U.	Mitchell, SD 57301-4398	Amy Novak	Student Support Services	605-995-2661
Mount Marty C.	Yankton, SD 57078	James Foster	Academic Affairs	605-668-1584
National American U.	Rapid City, SD 57709	Dr. Sam Kerr	HR Services	605-721-5214
Northern St. U.	Aberdeen, SD 57401	Karen Gerety	Office of Disability Services	605-626-2371

Institution	Location	Contact	Office	Phone
South Dakota Scl of Mines & Tech.	Rapid City, SD 57701	Jolie McCoy	Disability Services	605-394-1924
South Dakota St. U.	Brookings, SD 57007-1198	Nancy Hartenhoff-Crooks, MS	Disability Services	605-688-4504
U. of Sioux Falls	Sioux Falls, SD 57105	Mark Patterson	Career Services	605-331-6740
U. of South Dakota—Vermillion	Vermillion, SD 57069	Ernetta Fox	Disability Services	605-677-6389

TENNESSEE

Institution	Location	Contact	Office	Phone
Austin Peay St. U.	Clarksville, TN 37044	Beulah Oldham	Office of Disability Services	931-221-6230
Chattanooga St. Tech C.C.	Chattanooga, TN 37406	Kathy Lutes	Disability Services	423-697-4452
Christian Brothers U.	Memphis, TN 38104	Karen Conway	Student Disability Services	901-321-3536
Cleveland St. CC.	Cleveland, TN 37320	Amy Derrick	Disabilities Support Services	423-472-7141 ext. 288
Crichton C.	Memphis, TN 38111-1375	Robert Wharton	Academic Affairs	901-320-9700
Cumberland U.	Lebanon, TN 37087-3408	Eddie Pawlawski	Student Affairs	615-547-1225
East Tennessee St. U.	Johnson City, TN 37614-0731	Martha Edde-Adams	Disability Services	423-439-8494
Lambuth U.	Jackson, TN 38301	Donna Overstreet	Student Academic Support	731-425-3297
Lipscomb U.	Nashville, TN 37204-3951	Ashley Dumas	Disability Services	615-279-5737
Lee U.	Cleveland, TN 37311	Gayle Gallaher	Academic Support Program	423-614-8181
Martin Methodist C.	Pulaski, TN 38472	Dennis Haskins	Student Resources Center	931-363-9895
Maryville C.	Maryville, TN 37804-5907	Lori Hunter	Learning Center	865-981-8124
Middle Tennessee State U.	Murfreesboro, TN 37132	John Harris	Disabled Student Services	615-898-2783
Milligan C.	Milligan College, TN 37682	Mark Matson	Dean's Office	423-461-8720
Pellissippi St. Tech C.	Knoxville, TN 37933	Sarah McMurray	Services for Students with Disabilities	865-539-7091
Rhodes C.	Memphis, TN 38112	Melissa Butler	Disability Services	901-843-3994
Southern Adventist U.	Collegeedale, TN 37315	Sheila Smith	Learning Success Services	423-236-2574
Tennessee St. U.	Nashville, TN 37209-1561	Patricia Scudder	Disability Services	615-963-7400
Tennessee Tech U.	Cookeville, TN 38505	Sammie Young	Disabled Services	931-372-6318
Tennessee Wesleyan C.	Athens, TN 37371-0040	Dr. Catherine Emanuel	Academic Success Center	423-746-5305
Trevecca Nazarene U.	Nashville, TN 37210	Amy Murphy	Academic Support	615-248-1346
Tusculum C.	Greeneville, Tn 37743	Lisa Johnson	Academic Resource Center	423-636-5693
Union U.	Jackson, TN 38305	Paul Deschenes	Counseling Services	731-661-5322
U. of Memphis	Memphis, TN 38152-6687	Susan Te Paske	LD/ADHD Program	901-678-2880
U. of Tenn. at Martin, The	Martin, TN 38238	Michelle Arant	PACE	901-587-7195
U. of Tenn. at Chattanooga, The	Chattanooga, TN 37403	Debra Anderson	College Access Program	423-425-4006
U. of Tenn. at Knoxville, The	Knoxville, TN 37996	Emily Singer	Office of Disability Services	865-974-6087
Vanderbilt U.	Nashville, TN 37203-1700	Melissa Smith	Opportunity Development Center	615-322-4705

College	Location	Contact	Service	Phone
Abilene Christian U.	Abilene, TX 79699	Gloria Bradshaw	Alpha Academic Services	325-674-2275
Amarillo C.	Amarillo, TX 79178	Brenda Rossnagel	disAbility Services	806-371-5436
Angelo St. U.	San Angelo, TX 76909	Mr. Nolen Mears	Student Services	325-942-2191
Austin C.C.	Cedar Park, TX 78613	Amber Kelly	Students Services	512-223-2012
Baylor U.	Waco, TX 76798	Dea Vasek	Access & Learning Accomodations	254-710-3605
Central Texas C.	Killeen, TX 76540	Marie Cedillo	Project PASS	254-526-1293
Dallas Baptist U.	Dallas, TX 75211-9299	Mark Hale	Student Affairs	214-333-5101
East Texas Baptist U.	Marshall, TX 75670	Bob Flannery	Advising and Career Development	903-923-2079
El Paso C.C.	El Paso, TX 79998	Jan Lockhart	Center for Students with Disabilities	915-831-2426
Hardin-Simmons U.	Abilene, TX 79698-1000	Kaci Murphy	Disability Support Services	325-670-5842
Houston Baptist U.	Houston, TX 77074-3298	Dr. Renee Borns	Academic Advising	281-649-2521
Howard Payne U.	Brownwood, TX 76801	Amy Dodson	Disabled Student Services	325-649-8618
Jarvis Christian U.	Hawkins, TX 75765-1470	Lorene Holmes	Career Management Services	903-769-5700
Lamar U.	Beaumont, TX 77710	Callie Trahan	Services for Students with Disabilities	409-880-8347
Lamar U.—Orange	Orange, TX 77630	Judy Shoate	Disability Services	409-882-3379
Laredo C.C.	Laredo, TX 78040	Marta Salas	Special Population	956-721-5137
LaTourneau U.	Longview, TX 75607-7001	William Franklin, PhD	Student Services	903-233-4460
Lee C.	Baytown, TX 77522	Joann Szabo	Disabilities Services	281-425-6384
Lubbock Christian U.	Lubbock, TX 79407	Dana Turner	Disability Services	806-720-7486
McMurry U.	Abilene, TX 79697	James Greer	Counseling and Testing	325-793-4880
Midwestern St. U.	Wichita Falls, TX 76308-2099	Debra Higginbotham	Office of Disability Accommodations	940-397-4140
Northwood U. Texas Campus	Cedar Hill, TX 75104	Rene Rojas	Academic Office	972-293-5465
Our Lady of the Lake U.	San Antonio, TX 78207-4689	Theresa Gately	Center for Academic Achivement	210-434-6711 ext. 2731
Prairie View A&M U.	Praire View, TX 77446	Belinda Lewis	Disability Support Services	936-857-3311
Rice U.	Houston, TX 77251-1892	Jean Ashmore	Disability Services	713-348-5841
Saint Edward's U.	Austin, TX 78704	Lorrain Perea	Student Disability Office	512-448-8660
Sam Houston St. U.	Huntsville, Tx 77341	Kelley Osborn	Counseling Center	936-294-1720
Schreiner U.	Kerrville, TX 78028-5697	Jude Gallick, PhD	Learning Support Services	830-792-7256
Southern Methodist U.	Dallas, TX 75275-0355	Rebecca Marin	Services for Students with Disabilities	214-768-4557
Southwestern U.	Georgetown, TX 78627-0770	Kimele Carter	Academic Services	512-863-1536
St. Mary's U. of San Antonio	San Antonio, TX 78228	Patrice Buckner	Student Life	210-436-3714
Stephen F. Austin St. U.	Nonacogdoches, TX 75962	Chuck Lopez	Disability Services	936-468-3004

Institution	Address	Contact	Service	Phone
Texas A&M U.—Corpus Christi	Corpus Christi, TX 78412-5503	Rachel A. Fox	Services for Students with Disabilities	361-825-5816
Texas A&M U.—Galveston	Galveston, TX 77553-1675	Dr. Bob Sidylek	Counseling Center	409-740-4587
Texas A&M U.—Kingsville	Kingsville, TX 78363	Jeanie Alexander, MS	Services for Students with Disabilities	361-593-3268
Texas A&M U.—C. Station	College Station, TX 77843	Dr. Anne Reber	Disability Services	979-845-1637
Texas Christian U.	Fort Worth, TX 76129	Stacy Moore-Helms	Student Disability Services	817-257-7486
Texas Lutheran U.	Seguin, TX 78156-5999	Terry A. Weers	Disability Support Services	830-372-8009
Texas St. U.—San Marcos	San Marcos, TX 78666	Tina Schultz	Office of Disability Services	512-245-3451
Texas Tech U.	Lubbock, TX 79409-5005	Larry Phillippe	Program for Academic Support Services	806-742-2405
Texas Wesleyan U.	Fort Worth, TX 76105-1536	Mike Ellison	Counseling Center	817-531-4444
Texas Woman's U.	Denton, TX 76204-5679	Joanne Nunnelly	Disability Support Services	940-898-3835
Tyler Jr. C.	Tyler, TX 75711	Vickie Geisel	Suport Services	903-510-2615
U. of Houston	Houston, TX 77204-3022	Cheryl Amoruso	Center for Students with Disabilities	713-743-5400
U. of Houston—Downtown	Houston, TX 77002-1001	Duraese Hall	Disabled Student Services	713-221-8430
U of the Incarnate World	San Antonio, TX 78209-6397	Ada Soto	Student Disability Services	210-805-5813
U. of Mary Hardin-Baylor	Belton, TX 76513	Nate Williams	Counseling and Testing	254-295-4696
U. of North Texas	Denton, TX 76203-5358	Steve Pickett, MS, CRC	Office of Disability Accommodations	940-565-4323
U. of St. Thomas	Houston, TX 77006-4696	Dr. Rose Signorello	Counceling Services	713-525-3162
U. of Texas—Arlington	Arlington, TX 76019-0111	Dianne Hengst	Office for Students with Disabilities	817-272-3364
U. of Texas—Austin	Austin, TX 78712	Jennifer Maedgen	Services for Students with Disabilities	512-471-6259
U. of Texas—Dallas	Richardson, TX 75083-0688	Kerry Tate	Disability Services	972-883-2098
Univesity of Texas—El Paso	El Paso, TX 79968	James B. Saunders Jr.	Disabled Student Services	915-747-5148
U. of Texas—Pan American	Edinburg, TX 78539	Rick Gray	Off. of Serv. for Persons with Disabilities	956-316-7005
U. of Texas—Permian Basin	Odessa, TX 79762-0001	Efren Castro	PASS Office	432-552-2630
U. of Texas—San Antonio	San Antonio, TX 78249-0617	Lorraine Harrison	Disability Services	210-458-4157
U. of Texas—Tyler	Tyler, TX 75799	Ida McDonald	Testing Center	903-566-7079
West Texas A&M U.	Canyon, TX 79016	Jon Davis	Student Disability Services	806-651-2335
Wiley C.	Marshall, TX 75670	Dr. Robert Watkins	Academic Affairs	903-923-2429

UTAH

Institution	Address	Contact	Service	Phone
Brigham Young U. (UT)	Provo, UT 84602-1110	Michael Brooks	University Accessibility Center	801-422-2767
C. of Eastern Utah	Price, UT 84501	Mandy Krajnc	Disability Support Services	435-613-5670
Snow C.	Ephraim, UT 84627	Katie Larsen	Student Support Services	435-283-7321
Southern Utah U.	Cedar City, UT 84720	Carmen Alldredge	Student Support Services	435-865-8022
U. of Utah	Salt Lake City, UT 84112	Joe Pete Wilson	Center for Disability Services	801-581-5020

College	Location	Contact	Office	Phone
Utah St. U.	Logan, UT 84322	Diane Craig Baum	Disability Resource Center	435-797-2444
Utah Valley State College	Orem, UT 84058	Sherine Miller	Accessibility Services	801-863-8747
Weber St. U.	Ogden, UT 84408-1103	Jeff Morris	Disabilities Center	801-626-6413
Westminster C.	Salt Lake City, UT 84105-3697	Ginny DeWitt	START Center	801-832-2281

VERMONT

College	Location	Contact	Office	Phone
Bennington C.	Bennington, VT 05701	Wendy Hirsch	Dean of Studies	801-832-4400
Burlington C.	Burlington, VT 05401	Michael Ohler	Student Support Services	802-862-9616 ext. 124
Castleton St. C.	Castleton, VT 05735	Kelley Gilmour	Academic Support Center	802-468-1321
Champlain C.	Burlington, VT 05402-0670	Allyson Krings	Support Services for Students w/Disabilities	802-651-5961
C. of St. Joseph	Rutland, VT 05701	Charlotte Gillam	Project Success	802-773-5900 ext. 3239
Green Mountain C.	Poultney, VT 05764-1199	Raina Robins	Learning Center	802-287-8287
Johnson St. C.	Johnson, VT 05656	Karen Madden, PhD	Academic Support Services	802-635-1259
Landmark C.	Putney, VT 05346	John Kipp	Academic Support	802-387-4767
Lyndon St. C.	Lyndonville, VT 05851	Mary Etter	Academic Support Services	802-626-6210
Marlboro C.	Marlboro, VT 05344	Catherine O'Callaghan	Advising	802-258-9235
Middlebury C.	Middlebury, VT 05753-6002	Jodi Litchfield	ADA Office	802-443-5936
New England Culinary School		Jakie Burke	Learning Services	802-764-2135
Norwich U.	Northfield, VT 05663	Paula Gills	Learning Support Center	802-485-2130
Saint Michael's C.	Colchester, VT 05439	Antonia Messuri	Dean's Office	802-654-2466
Southern Vermont C.	Bennington, VT 05201	David Lindenberg	Disabilities Support Program	802-447-6360
U. of Vermont	Burlington, VT 05401	Marsha Camp	ACCESS	802-656-7753
Vermont Technical C.	Randolph Center, VT 05061	Robin Goodall	Services for Students with Disabilities	802-728-1278

VIRGINIA

College	Location	Contact	Office	Phone
Averett U.	Danville, VA 24541	Kathie Tune	Dean of Admissions	434-791-7301
Blue Ridge C.C.	Weyers Cave, VA 24486	Beth Styers	Disability Services	540-234-9261 ext. 2252
Bridgewater C.	Bridgewater, VA 22812-1599	Dr. Arthur Hessler	Dean of Students	540-828-5608
Bluefield C.	Bluefield, VA 24605	Brad Bowl	Students with Disabilities	276-326-4277
Christopher Newport U.	Newport News, VA 23606	Debbie Witt	Services to Students with Disabilities	757-594-8763
C. of William & Mary, The	Williamsburg, VA 23187-8795	Lisa Bickley	Disability Services	757-221-2510
Eastern Mennonite U.	Harrisonburg, VA 22801	Joyce Coryell Hedrick	Disability Support Services	540-432-4233
Emory & Henry C.	Emory, VA 24327	Lisa Honeycutt	Academic Support Services	276-944-6145
Ferrum C.	Ferrum, VA 24088	Nancy Beach	Academic Resource Center	540-365-4262

College	Location	Contact	Department	Phone
George Mason U.	Fairfax, VA 22030-4444	Christopher Moy	Disability Resource Center	703-993-2474
Hampden-Sydney C.	Hampden-Sydney, VA 23943	Elizabeth Ford	Academic Success Center	434-223-6286
Hampton U.	Hampton, VA 23668	Jean S. Williamson	Student Support Services	757-727-5493
Hollins C.	Roanoke, VA 24020	Rita Foster	Student Support Services	540-362-6298
James Madison U.	Harrisonburg, VA 22807	Valerie Schoolcraft	Office of Disability Services	540-568-6705
Liberty U.	Lynchburg, VA 24502	Dr. Dennis McHaney	Office of Disability Academic Support	434-582-2159
Longwood C.	Farmville, VA 23909	Dr. Sally Scott	Office of Disability Support Services	434-395-2391
Lynchburg C.	Lynchburg, VA 24501	Jessica Baldwin	Academic Advising	434-544-8152
Mary Baldwin C.	Staunton, VA 24401	Beverly Askegaard	Learning Skills Center	540-887-7250
Mary Washington C.	Fredericksburg, VA 22401	Stephanie Smith	Academic Services	540-654-1266
Marymount U.	Arlington, VA 22207	Kelly Desenti	Disabled Student Services	703-284-1615
New River C.C.	Dublin, VA 24060	Jeananne Dixon	LEAP Center	540-674-3600 ext. 4358
Old Dominion U.	Norfolk, VA 23529-0050	Sheryn Milton, MEd	Disability Services	757-683-4655
Patrick Henry C.C.	Martinsville, VA 24115	Scott Guebert	Student Support Services	276-656-0257
Radford U.	Radford, VA 24142	Joann Stephens-Forrest	Disability Resouce Office	540-831-6350
Randolph-Macon C.	Ashland, VA 23005	Jack Trammell	Disability Support Services	804-752-7343
Roanoke C.	Salem, VA 24153-3794	Hillary Holland	Academic Services	540-375-2248
Saint Paul's C.	Lawrenceville, VA 23868	Walter Dean	Student Support Services	434-848-6453
Shenandoah U.	Winchester, VA 22601	Adrienne Rogerson	Academic Success Center	540-665-4928
Sweet Briar C.	Sweet Briar, VA 24595	Laura Symons	Academic Resource Center	434-381-6278
Thomas Nelson C.C.	Hampton, VA 23670	Nancy Bailey	Disabled Student Services	757-825-2833
Tidewater C.C.	Portsmouth, VA 23703	Linda W. Harris	LD Services	757-822-1213
U. of Richmond	Richmond, VA 23173	Hope Walton	Academic Skills Center	804-289-8626
U. of Virginia	Charlottesville, VA 22906	Allison Anderson, PhD	Learning Needs & Evaluation Center	434-243-5181
U. of Virginia—College at Wise	Wise, VA 24293	Narda Porter	Student Support Services	276-328-0177
Virginia Commonwealth U.	Richmond, VA 23284	Joyce Knight	Disability Support Services	804-828-2253
Virginia Intermont College	Bristol, VA 24201-4298	Talmage Dobbins	Student Support Services	276-466-7905
Virginia Military Institute	Lexington, VA 24450-0304	Mollie Messinmer	Miller Academic Center	540-464-7765
Virginia St. U.	Petersburg, VA 23806	Rosezelia W. Roy	Students with Disabilities Program	804-524-5061
Virginia Tech	Blacksburg, VA 24061	Susan Angle	Services for Students with Disabilities	540-231-3788
Virginia Union U.	Richmond, VA 23220	Linda Jackson	Academic Enpowerment Center	804-342-3885
Virginia Wesleyan C.	Norfolk, VA 23502-5599	Fayne C. Pearson	Learning Center	757-455-3246

College	Location	Contact	Service	Phone
Virginia Western Comm C.	Roanoke, VA 24038	Martha Richardson	Reach Student Support Services	540-857-7286
Washington and Lee U.	Lexington, VA 24450-0303	Janet Ikeda	Student Academic Support	540-458-8746

WASHINGTON

College	Location	Contact	Service	Phone
Bates Tech C.	Tacoma, WA 98405	Daniel Eberle	Special Needs	253-596-1698
Central Washington U.	Ellensburg, WA 98926-7463	Pamela Wilson	Disability Support Services	509-963-2171
City U.	Bellevue, WA 98005	Esther Hunt	Disability Resource Center	800-426-5596
Cornish C. of the Arts	Seattle, WA 98121	Cheryl Coatney	Student Affairs Program	206-726-5098
Eastern Washington U.	Cheney, WA 99004	Robert Campbell	Disability Support Services	509-359-6871
Everett C.C.	Everette, WA 98201	Kathy Cook	Center for Disability Services	425-388-9273
Evergreen St. C., The	Olympia, WA 98505	Linda Pickering	Access Services	360-867-6364
Gonzaga U.	Spokane, WA 99258	Kathy Shearer	Disabilities Support Services	509-323-4134
Heritage U.	Toppenish, WA 98948	Jackie Meyer-Graza	Eagles Program	509-865-8514
North Seattle C.C.	Seattle, WA 98103	Suzanne Sewell	Educational Access Center	206-527-7307
Northwest U.	Kirkland, WA 98083	Amy Jones	Academic Success Center	425-889-7823
Pacific Lutheran U.	Tacoma, WA 98447-0003	Ruth Tweeten	Academic Assistance	253-535-7206
Pierce C.	Tacoma, WA 98446	Brenda McKinney	Disability Support Services	253-964-6526
Saint Martin's U.	Lacey, WA 98503	Laura Puryear-Finnell	Disability Support Services	360-438-4580
Seattle Pacific U.	Seattle, WA 98119	Bethany Anderson	Center for Learning	206-281-2272
Seattle U.	Seattle, WA 98122	Carol Schneider	Student Learning Center	206-296-5740
Spokane Falls C.C.	Spokane, WA 99204	Ben Webinger	Support Services	509-533-3437
Tacoma C.C.	Tacoma, WA 98465	Kathryn Held	Services for Students with Disabilities	253-566-5328
U. of Puget Sound	Tacoma, WA 98416	Ivey West	Disability Services	253-879-2692
U. of Washington	Seattle, WA 98195-5840	Dyane Haynes	Disabled Student Services	206-543-8924
Walla Walla C.	College Place, WA 99324-1198	Sue Huett	Disability Support Services	509-527-2366
Washington St. U.	Pullman, WA 99164-4122	Susan Schaeffer, PhD	Disability Resource Center	509-335-1566
Western Washington U.	Bellingham, WA 98225	David Brunnemer	Disabled Student Services	360-650-3083
Whatcom C.C.	Bellingham, WA 98226	Bill Culwell	Disabled Student Services	360-676-2170 ext. 3320
Whitman C.	Walla Walla, WA 99362-2083	Clare Carson	Academic Resource Center	509-527-5213
Whitworth C.	Spokane, WA 99251	Andrew Pyrc	Disability Support Services	509-777-4534
Yakima Valley C.C.	Yakima, WA 98907	Bob Chavez	Disability Services	509-574-4968

WEST VIRGINIA

Bethany C.	Bethany, WV 26032	Rebecca Pauls	Disability Support Services	304-829-7899
Bluefield St. C.	Bluefield, WB 24701	Carolyn Kirby	Student Support Services	304-327-4098
Concord C.	Athens, WV 24712	Nancy Ellison	Office of Disability Services	304-384-6086
Davis & Elkins C.	Elkins, WV 26241	Mary Ellen Schubert	Supported Learning Program	304-637-1384
Fairmount St. U.	Fairmont, WV 26554	Andrea Pammer	Disability Services	304-367-4686
Glenville St. C.	Glenville, WV 26351	Daniel Reed	Academic Support Center	304-462-4118
Marshall U.	Huntington, WV 25755	Lynne M. Weston, EdS	HELP	304-696-6317
Mountain St. U.	Beckley, WV 25802	Reginald Garcon	Student Affairs	304-929-1434
Ohio Valley U.	Vienna, WV 26105-8000	Kathy Muller	Academic Support	304-865-6082
Shepherd U.	Shepherdstown, WV 25443-3210	Christina Johnson	Disability Support Services	304-876-5453
U. of Charleston	Charleston, WV 25304	Catherine Moors	Learning Support Services	304-357-4931
West Liberty St. C.	West Liberty, WV 26074-0295	Traci Jordan	Center for Student Success	304-336-8216
West Virginia St. C.	Institute, WV 25112-1000	Kelly Toledo	Collegiate Support Services	304-766-3000
West Virginia Tech	Montgomery, WV 25136	Kitty Polaski	Student Support Services	304-442-3498
West Virginia U.	Morgantown, WV 26506-6009	Jennifer McIntosh	Disability Services	304-293-5496
West Virginia Wesleyan C.	Buckhannon, WV 26201	Dr. Shawn Mahoney Kuba	Learning Center	304-473-8563
Wheeling Jesuit U.	Wheeling, WV 26003	Kathy Tagg	Academic Resource Center	304-243-2427

WISCONSIN

Alverno C.	Milwaukee, WI 53234-3922	Colleen Barnett	Student Accessibility	414-382-6026
Bellin C. of Nursing	Green Bay, WI 54305	Jo Woelfel	Disability Support Services	920-433-3465
Beloit C.	Beloit, WI 53511	Diane Arnzen	Learning Support Services Center	608-363-2572
Cardinal Stritch C.	Milwaukee, WI 53217-3985	Marcia Laskey	Academic Support	414-410-4168
Carroll C. (WI)	Waukesha, WI 53186	Jennifer Maney	Walter Young Center	262-524-7335
Carthage C.	Kenosha, WI 53140	Diane Schowalter	Office of Academic Advising	262-551-5802
Concordia U. (WI)	Mequon, WI 53097	Jean Timpel	Learning Resource Center	262-243-4216
Edgewood C.	Madison, WI 53711	Deborah Tobin	Disability Services	608-663-8347
Gateway Technical C.	Kenosha, WI 53144	Jack Sullivan	Special Needs	262-564-2320
Lawrence U.	Appleton, WI 54912-0599	Martha Hemwall	Disability Services	920-832-6530
Marian C. of Fond Du Lac	Fond du Lac, WI 54935	Lisa Rogers	Disability Services	920-923-7162
Marquette U.	Milwaukee, WI 53201-1881	Karen Desotelle	Disability Services	414-288-1645
Milwaukee Inst. of Art & Des.	Milwaukee, WI 53202	Jennifer Crandall	Academic Support	414-847-3344
Milwaukee School of Eng.	Milwaukee, WI 53202-3109	Amy Cisnell	Student Support Services	414-277-7281

College	Location	Contact	Service	Phone
Mount Mary C.	Milwaukee, WI 53222	Marci Ocker	Disability Services	414-258-4210 ext. 324
Northland C.	Ashland, WI 54806	Judi Holevatz	Office of Special Needs	715-682-1340
Ripon C.	Ripon, WI 54971	Daniel J. Krhin	Student Support Services	920-748-8107
Saint Norbert C.	De Pere, WI 54115	Karen Goode-Bartholomew	Academic Support Services	920-403-1326
Silver Lake C.	Manitowoc, WI 54220	George Grinde	Disability Services	920-686-6125
U of Wisc.—Baraboo/Sauk County	Baraboo, WI 53913	Ruth Joyce	Student Services	608-355-5230
U. of Wisconsin—Eau Claire	Eau Claire, WI 54701	Kathleen Hurley	Services for Students with Disabilities	715-836-4542
U. of Wisconsin—Green Bay	Green Bay, WI 53411-7001	Lynn Niemi	Disability Services	920-465-2841
U. of Wisconsin—LaCrosse	LaCrosse, WI 54601-3742	June Reinert	Disability Resource Services	608-785-6900
U. of Wisconsin—Madison	Madison, WI 53706	Cathleen Trueba	McBurney Disability Resource Center	608-263-2741
U. of Wisconsin—Milwaukee	Milwaukee, WI 53201	Laurie Peterson	Learning Disabilities Program	414-229-6239
U. of Wisconsin—Oshkosh	Oshkosh, WI 54901-8662	John Palmer	Disability Services	920-424-3100
U. of Wisconsin—Parkside	Kenosha, WI 53141	Renee Sartin-Kirby	Learning Disabilities Support Services	262-595-2610
U. of Wisconsin—Platteville	Platteville, WI 53818	Becky Peters	Student Support Services	608-342-1818
U. of Wisconsin—River Falls	River Falls, WI 54022	Carmen Croonquist	Challenge Program	715-425-3884
U. of Wisconsin—Stevens Pt.	Stevens Point, WI 54481	Jim Joque	Disability Services	715-346-3365
U. of Wisconsin—Stout	Menomonie, WI 54751	Debroah Shefchik	Disabilities Services	715-232-2995
U. of Wisconsin—Superior	Superior, WI 54880	Mary Lee Vance	Special Services	715-394-8185
U. of Wisconsin—Whitewater	Whitewater, WI 53190	Dr. Elizabeth Watson	Center for Students with Disabilities	262-472-4711
Viterbo U.	La Crosse, WI 54601	Jane Eady	Learning Center	608-796-3190
West Wisconsin Tech. C.	La Crosse, WI 54602	Kristina Puent	Disability Services	608-785-9875
Wisconsin Indianhead Tech.	Shell Lake, WI 54871	Anne Freagon	Disability Services	715-468-2815 ext. 5350
Wisconsin Lutheran C.	Milwaukee, WI 53226	Karen Sitz	Student Support	414-443-8797

WYOMING

College	Location	Contact	Service	Phone
Central Wyoming C	Riverton, WY	Marilú Duncan	Student Support Services	307-855-2227
Laramie County C.C.	Cheyenne, WY 82007	Lisa Digman	Diability Resource Center	307-778-1359
Sheridan C.	Sheridan, WY 82801	Elizabeth Stearns-Sims	Learning Center	307-674-6446
U. of Wyoming	Laramie, WY 82071	Chris Primus	University Disability Support Services	307-766-6189

CANADA/ALBERTA

College	Location	Contact	Service	Phone
Grace MacEwan C.C.	Edmonton, AB T51 2P2	Abigail Parrish-Craig	Counseling & Special Services	780-497-5811
Lethbridge C.C.	Lethbridge, AB T1K 1L6	Julie Deimert	Support Services	403-329-7268
N. Alberta Inst. Tech.	Edmonton AB T5G 2R1	Diana Culo	Services to Disabled Students	780-378-6133

Institution	Location	Contact	Service	Phone
S. Alberta Inst. Tech.	Calgary AB T2M OL4	Ursula Gardynik	Disability Support Services	403-284-7023
U. of Alberta	Edmonton AB T6G 2E8	Marion Vosahlo	Disabled Student Services	780-492-3381
U. of Calgary	Calgary AB T2N 1N4	Patricia Pardo	Disability Resource Centre	403-220-8237

CANADA/BRITISH COLUMBIA

Institution	Location	Contact	Service	Phone
Camosun C.	Victoria BC V8P 4X8	Susan McArthur	Adult Special Education	250-370-3325
Capilano C.	N. Vancouver BC V71 3H5	Dr. Jan Shiell	Disability Support Services	604-983-7526
C. of New Caledonia	Pr. George BC V2N 1P8	Fran Miller	Disability Support Services	250-561-5848 ext. 248
Kwantlen College	Surrey V3T BC 5H8	Susanne Dadson	Services for Stud. With Disabilities	604-599-2003
Langara C.	Vancover BC V5Y 2Z6	Tera-Jean Wenc	Disability Services	604-323-5635
Okanagan C.	Kelowna BC V1Y 4X8	Judy Colpitts	Disability Services	250-762-5445 ext. 4119
Simon Fraser U.	Burnaaby BC V5A 1S6	Mitchell Stoddard	Centre for Students with Disabilities	604-291-3112
U. of N. British Colum.	Prince Grge BC V2L 5P2	Maureen Hewlett	Disability Services	250-960-6355
U. of British Columbia	Vancouver BC V6T 1Z1	Ruth Warick	Disabilities Resource Center	604-822-5844
U. of Victoria	Victoria BC V8W 3P2	Laurie Keenan	Student & Ancillary Services	250-721-8223

CANADA/MANITOBA

Institution	Location	Contact	Service	Phone
U. of Manitoba	Winnipeg MB R3T 2N2	Caroyln Christie	Disabilities Services	204-474-6213
U. of Winnipeg	Winnipeg MB R3B 2E9	Andrea Johnston	Disability Resource Center	204-786-9771

CANADA/NEW BRUNSWICK

Institution	Location	Contact	Service	Phone
Mt. Allison U.	Sackville NB E0A 3C0	Jane Drover	Center for Learning Assistance	506-364-2527
U. of New Brunswick	Fredericton NB E3B 6E3	Patricia Kirby	Disability Services	506-453-3515

CANADA/NEWFOUNDLAND

Institution	Location	Contact	Service	Phone
Mem. U. Newfoundland	St. John's NF A1G 5S7	Dr. Donna Hardy-Cox	Student Development	709-737-3057

CANADA/NOVA SCOTIA

Institution	Location	Contact	Service	Phone
Dalhousie U.	Halifax NS B3H 4J2	Paul Szymanowski	Student Accessibility Services	902-494-2836
NSCAD U.	Halifax NS B3J 3J6	Bill Travis	Disability Resources	902-494-8313
St. Mary's U.	Halifax NS B3H 3C3	David Leitch	Support for Disabled Students	902-420-5449

CANADA/ONTARIO

Institution	Location	Contact	Service	Phone
Algoma U. C.	S. Ste. Marie ON P6A 2G4	Barbara Muio	Learning Center	705-949-2301 ext. 4221
Cambrian C.	Sudbury ON P3A 3V8	Susan Alcorn MacKay	Disability Services	705-566-8101 ext. 7420
Canadore C.	N. Bay ON P1B 8K9	Dawson Pratt	Special Needs Services	705-474-7600 ext. 5213
Carleton U.	Ottawa ON K1S 5B6	Dr. Nancy McIntyre	Paul Menton Centre for Students w/ Disabilities	613-520-6608
Centennial C.	Scarborough ON M1K 5E9	Irene Volinets	Special Needs	416-289-5000 ext. 2254

College	Location	Contact	Service	Phone
Durham C.	Oshawa ON L1H 7L7	Willona Blanche	Special Needs—(REACH)	905-721-3123
Fanshawe C.	London ON N5V 1W2	Lois Wey	Counseling & Student Life	519-452-4304
George Brown C.	Toronto ON M5T 2T9	Stephanie Burke	Special Needs	416-415-5000 ext. 6370
Humber College	Toronto ON M9W 5L7	Maureen Carnegie	Services for Students with Disabilities	416-675-5090
Lakehead U.	Thunder Bay ON P7B 5E1	Donna Grau	Learning Assistance	807-343-8087
Loyalist College	Belleville ON K8N 5B9	Katherine O'Rourke	Stnt Office for Alternative Resources	613-969-1913 ext. 2256
Mohawk College	Hamilton ON L8N 3T2	Rachel Mathews	Disability Services	905-575-2389
Nippissing U.	N. Bay ON P1B 8L7	Dan Pletzer	Disability Services	705-474-3450 ext. 4331
Ontarion C. of Art	Toronto ON M5T 1W1	David Greig	Services for Students with Disabilities	416-977-6000 ext. 288
Queen's U.	Kingston ON K7L 3N6	Allyson Harrison	Disability Services	613-533-6311
Seneca College	N. York ON M2J 2X5	Arthur Burke	Special Needs	416-491-5050 ext. 3150
St. Clair C.	Windsor ON N9A 6S4	Mark Colangelo	Disability Services	519-972-2727 ext. 4266
St. Lawrence C.	Brockville ON K6V 5X3	Doug Hone	Special Needs	613-345-0660 ext. 3235
Sheridan C.	Oakville ON L6H 2L1	Zane Garstad	Enrollment Services	307-674-6446
Trent U.	Peterborough ON K9J 7B8	Eunice Lund-Lucas	Special Needs	705-748-1011 ext. 1637
U. of W. Ontario	London ON N6A 3K7	Denise Dunleavey	Services for Students with Disabilities (SDC)	519-661-2147
U. of Waterloo	Waterloo ON N2L 3G1	Rose Padacz	Services for Disabled Persons	519-888-4567 ext. 35231
U. of Windsor	Windsor ON N9B 3P4	Brooke White	Special Needs Office	519-253-3000 ext. 3287
York U.	N. York ON M3J 1P3	Marc Wilchesky	LD Programs—Counseling & Dev. Cntr.	416-736-5297

CANADA/PRINCE EDWARD ISLAND

College	Location	Contact	Service	Phone
Holland College	Charlottetown PE C1A 4Z1	June Harper	Counseling	902-984-6833

CANADA/QUEBEC

College	Location	Contact	Service	Phone
Concordia U.	Montreal PQ H4B 1R6	Leo Bissonnette	Office for Students with Disabilities	514-848-2424 ext. 3518
Dawson C.	Montreal PQ H3Z 1A4	Alice Havel	Centre for Students with Disabilities	514-931-8731 ext. 1211
John Abbott C.	St. An. Belvue. PQ H9X 3L9	Brenda Rowe	Special Needs Learning Center	514-457-6610
McGill U.	Montreal PQ H3A 1X1	Joan Wolforth	Special Services	514-398-6009

CANADA/SASKATCHEWAN

College	Location	Contact	Service	Phone
SIAST-Kelsey	Saskatoon SK S7K 6B1	Tony Kessler	Dept. of Disabilities Services	306-933-6445
U. of Saskatchewan	Saskatoon SK S7N 0W0	Maxine Kinakin	Disabled Student Services	306-966-5673

CANADA/YUKON

Yukon C.	Yukon YT Y1A 5K4	Catalina Colaci	Learning Assistance Center-Service for Students with Disabilities	867-668-8785

PUERTO RICO

Pontifical Catholic U. of Puerto Rico	Ponce, PR 00717-0777	Wanda Soto	Disability Support Services	800-981-5040 ext. 1451
U. of Puerto Rico—Humacao	Humacao, PR 00791-4300	Carmen Sepulveda	SERPI	787-850-9383
U. of Puerto Rico—Mayaguez	Mayaguez, PR 00631-9000	Teresita Cruz	Students with Disabilities	787-265-3862

UNITED KINGDOM

American International U.—Rich. The	Rich.-upon Thames TW10 6JP, Eng.	Dr. John O'Connell	Disability Support Services	617-450-5617

ALPHABETICAL LIST OF COLLEGES BY LEVEL OF SUPPORT SERVICES

SP: STRUCTURED PROGRAMS

College/University	State	Support
Adelphi University	New York	SP
American International College	Massachusetts	SP
American University	District of Columbia	SP
Augsburg College	Minnesota	SP
Barry University	Florida	SP
Beacon College	Florida	SP
Brenau University	Georgia	SP
College Misericordia	Pennsylvania	SP
College of Mount St. Joseph	Ohio	SP
Curry College	Massachusetts	SP
Davis and Elkins College	West Virginia	SP
Dean College	Massachusetts	SP
Dowling College	New York	SP
Fairleigh Dickinson University—Florham Campus	New Jersey	SP
Fairleigh Dickinson University—Metropolitan Campus	New Jersey	SP
Finlandia University	Michigan	SP
Florida A&M University	Florida	SP
Gannon University	Pennsylvania	SP
Georgian Court College	New Jersey	SP
Hofstra University	New York	SP
Iona College	New York	SP
Landmark College	Vermont	SP
Long Island University—C.W. Post	New York	SP
Loras College	Iowa	SP
Louisiana College	Louisiana	SP
Lynn University	Florida	SP
Manhattanville College	New York	SP
Marist College	New York	SP
Marshall University	West Virginia	SP
Marymount Manhattan College	New York	SP
Mercyhurst College	Pennsylvania	SP
Missouri State University	Missouri	SP
Mitchell College	Connecticut	SP
Mount Ida College	Massachusetts	SP
Muskingum College	Ohio	SP
National-Louis University	Illinois	SP
New Jersey City University	New Jersey	SP
Norte Dame College	Ohio	SP
Northeastern University	Massachusetts	SP
Reinhardt College	Georgia	SP
Rochester Institute of Technology	New York	SP
St. Thomas Aquinas College	New York	SP

College/University	State	Support
Schreiner College	Texas	SP
Southern Illinois University—Carbondale	Illinois	SP
University of Arizona	Arizona	SP
University of Denver	Colorado	SP
University of Indianapolis	Indiana	SP
University of the Ozarks	Arkansas	SP
Ursuline College	Ohio	SP
Vincennes University	Indiana	SP
Waldorf College	Iowa	SP
West Virginia Wesleyan College	West Virginia	SP
Westminster College	Missouri	SP

CS: COORDINATED SERVICES

College/University	State	Support
Abilene Christian University	Texas	CS
Adrian College	Michigan	CS
Anderson University	Indiana	CS
Appalachian State University	North Carolina	CS
Arizona State University	Arizona	CS
Black Hills State University	South Dakota	CS
Boston College	Massachusetts	CS
Boston University	Massachusetts	CS
Brevard College	North Carolina	CS
Brigham Young University	Utah	CS
Brown University	Rhode Island	CS
Bryant College	Rhode Island	CS
Caldwell College	New Jersey	CS
California Polytechnic State University—San Luis Obispo	California	CS
California State Polytechnic University—Pomona	California	CS
California State University—Chico	California	CS
California State University—Fullerton	California	CS
California State University—Long Beach	California	CS
California State University—Northridge	California	CS
California State University—San Bernardino	California	CS
Calvin College	Michigan	CS
Catholic University of America	District of Columbia	CS
Central Ohio Technical College	Ohio	CS
Clarion University of Pennsylvania	Pennsylvania	CS
Clark University	Massachusetts	CS
Colby-Sawyer College	New Hampshire	CS
Colgate University	New York	CS
College of St. Catherine, The	Minnesota	CS
College of the Siskiyous	California	CS
College of William and Mary, The	Virginia	CS
Concordia College	New York	CS

Davidson College	North Carolina	CS
DePaul University	Illinois	CS
Drexel University	Pennsylvania	CS
Duke University	North Carolina	CS
East Carolina University	North Carolina	CS
East Stroudsburg University of Pennsylvania	Pennsylvania	CS
Eastern Kentucky University	Kentucky	CS
Edinboro University of Pennsylvania	Pennsylvania	CS
Emerson College	Massachusetts	CS
Emory University	Georgia	CS
Evangel College	Missouri	CS
Fairfield University	Connecticut	CS
Ferris State University	Michigan	CS
Ferrum College	Virginia	CS
Florida Atlantic University	Florida	CS
Florida State University	Florida	CS
George Washington University	District of Columbia	CS
Georgia Southern University	Georgia	CS
Georgia State University	Georgia	CS
Grand View College	Iowa	CS
Harding University	Arkansas	CS
Hocking College	Ohio	CS
Illinois State University	Illinois	CS
Indiana University	Indiana	CS
Iowa State University	Iowa	CS
Jacksonville State University	Alabama	CS
James Madison University	Virginia	CS
Johnson & Wales University	Rhode Island	CS
Johnson State College	Vermont	CS
Kansas City Art Institute	Missouri	CS
Kansas State University	Kansas	CS
Kean University	New Jersey	CS
Kent State University	Ohio	CS
Keuka College	New York	CS
Kutztown University of Pennsylvania	Pennsylvania	CS
Laramie County Community College	Wyoming	CS
Lee University	Tennessee	CS
Lehigh University	Pennsylvania	CS
Lenoir-Rhyne College	North Carolina	CS
Liberty University	Virginia	CS
Limestone College	South Carolina	CS
Lincoln College	Illinois	CS
Louisiana State University	Louisiana	CS
Loyola University—Chicago	Illinois	CS
Manchester College	Indiana	CS

McDaniel College	Maryland	CS
Menlo College	California	CS
Miami University	Ohio	CS
Michigan State University	Michigan	CS
Middle Tennessee State University	Tennessee	CS
Minot State University—Bottineau	North Dakota	CS
Monmouth University	New Jersey	CS
Montana Tech of the University of Montana	Montana	CS
Morningside College	Iowa	CS
New England College	New Hampshire	CS
New England Culinary Institute	Vermont	CS
New York University	New York	CS
North Carolina State University	North Carolina	CS
Northern Illinois University	Illinois	CS
Northwestern University	Illinois	CS
Norwich University	Vermont	CS
Oberlin College	Ohio	CS
Ohio State University—Columbus	Ohio	CS
Old Dominion University	Virginia	CS
Pine Manor College	Massachusetts	CS
Pittsburg State University	Kansas	CS
Providence College	Rhode Island	CS
Reedley College	California	CS
Regis University	Colorado	CS
Rhode Island College	Rhode Island	CS
Rider University	New Jersey	CS
Rocky Mountain College	Montana	CS
Roosevelt University	Illinois	CS
Saint Ambrose University	Iowa	CS
St. Andrew's Presbyterian College	North Carolina	CS
San Diego State University	California	CS
San Francisco State University	California	CS
San Jose State University	California	CS
Santa Clara University	California	CS
Santa Monica College	California	CS
Santa Rosa Junior College	California	CS
Seton Hall University	New Jersey	CS
Sierra College	California	CS
Southern Connecticut State University	Connecticut	CS
Southern Illinois University—Edwardsville	Illinois	CS
Southern Methodist University	Texas	CS
Southwest Texas State University	Texas	CS
Springfield College	Massachusetts	CS
Stanford University	California	CS
SUNY—Delhi	New York	CS

SUNY—Stony Brook University	New York	CS
Syracuse University	New York	CS
Temple University	Pennsylvania	CS
Texa State University—San Marcos	Texas	CS
Towson University	Maryland	CS
Union College	Nebraska	CS
Unity College	Maine	CS
University of California—Berkeley	California	CS
University of California—Los Angeles	California	CS
University of California—San Diego	California	CS
University of California—Santa Barbara	California	CS
University of Central Florida	Florida	CS
University of Cincinnati	Ohio	CS
University of Colorado—Boulder	Colorado	CS
University of Colorado—Colorado Springs	Colorado	CS
University of Connecticut	Connecticut	CS
University of Dayton	Ohio	CS
University of Delaware	Delaware	CS
University of Dubuque	Iowa	CS
University of Florida	Florida	CS
University of Georgia	Georgia	CS
University of Hartford	Connecticut	CS
University of Houston	Texas	CS
University of Illinois at Urbana-Champaign	Illinois	CS
University of Iowa	Iowa	CS
University of Kansas	Kansas	CS
University of Kentucky	Kentucky	CS
University of Maryland—College Park	Maryland	CS
University of Maryland—Eastern Shore	Maryland	CS
University of Massachusetts—Amherst	Massachusetts	CS
University of Memphis, The	Tennessee	CS
University of Michigan	Michigan	CS
University of Missouri—Columbia	Missouri	CS
University of Nevada—Reno	Nevada	CS
University of New Hampshire	New Hampshire	CS
University of North Carolina at Chapel Hill, The	North Carolina	CS
University of North Carolina at Charlotte, The	North Carolina	CS
University of North Carolina at Greensboro, The	North Carolina	CS
University of North Carolina at Wilmington, The	North Carolina	CS
University of Oregon	Oregon	CS
University of Pittsburgh	Pennsylvania	CS
University of Rhode Island	Rhode Island	CS
University of Saint Francis	Indiana	CS
University of San Francisco	California	CS
University of South Carolina—Columbia	South Carolina	CS

College/University	State	
University of South Dakota, The	South Dakota	CS
University of Southern California	California	CS
University of Tennessee at Chattanooga, The	Tennessee	CS
University of Tennessee at Knoxville, The	Tennessee	CS
University of Tennessee at Martin, The	Tennessee	CS
University of Tulsa, The	Oklahoma	CS
University of Utah	Utah	CS
University of Vermont	Vermont	CS
University of Virginia	Virginia	CS
University of Wisconsin—La Crosse	Wisconsin	CS
University of Wisconsin—Madison	Wisconsin	CS
University of Wisconsin—Milwaukee	Wisconsin	CS
University of Wisconsin—Oshkosh	Wisconsin	CS
University of Wisconsin—Whitewater	Wisconsin	CS
University of Wyoming	Wyoming	CS
Utah State University	Utah	CS
Utica College	New York	CS
Vermont Technical College	Vermont	CS
Virginia Intermont College	Virginia	CS
Wake Forest University	North Carolina	CS
Washington University in St. Louis	Missouri	CS
Western Carolina University	North Carolina	CS
Western Connecticut State University	Connecticut	CS
Western Illinois University	Illinois	CS
Western Kentucky University	Kentucky	CS
Wheelock College	Massachusetts	CS
Widener University	Pennsylvania	CS
Wingate University	North Carolina	CS
Wright State University	Ohio	CS
Xavier University	Ohio	CS

S: SERVICES

College/University	State	Support
Alfred State College	New York	S
Alverno College	Wisconsin	S
Beloit College	Wisconsin	S
Bluegrass Community and Technical College	Kentucky	S
Bowling Green State University	Ohio	S
Case Western Reserve University	Ohio	S
Champlain College	Vermont	S
Clemson University	South Carolina	S
College of Santa Fe	New Mexico	S
Colorado State University—Pueblo	Colorado	S
Cornell University	New York	S
Dickinson College	Pennsylvania	S

Drake University	Iowa	S
Eastern Illinois University	Illinois	S
Eastern Washington University	Washington	S
Elon University	North Carolina	S
Emory University	Georgia	S
Evergreen State College, The	Washington	S
Fitchburg State College	Massachusetts	S
Frostburg State University	Maryland	S
George Mason University	Virginia	S
Grand Valley State University	Michigan	S
Green Mountain College	Vermont	S
Grinnell College	Iowa	S
Guilford College	North Carolina	S
Hampton University	Virginia	S
Indian Hills Community College	Iowa	S
Indiana Wesleyan University	Indiana	S
Lamar University	Texas	S
Loyola Marymount University	California	S
Marian College of Fond du Lac	Wisconsin	S
Marquette University	Wisconsin	S
Marywood University	Pennsylvania	S
Messiah College	Pennsylvania	S
Midwestern State University	Texas	S
Minnesota State University—Moorhead	Minnesota	S
Montana State University—Billings	Montana	S
New Mexico Institute of Mining and Technology	New Mexico	S
New Mexico State University	New Mexico	S
Nicholls State University	Louisiana	S
North Dakota State University	North Dakota	S
Northern Arizona University	Arizona	S
Northern Michigan University	Michigan	S
Occidental College	California	S
Ohio University	Ohio	S
Oklahoma State University	Oklahoma	S
Oregon State University	Oregon	S
Penn State University—University Park	Pennsylvania	S
Ripon College	Wisconsin	S
Rivier College	New Hampshire	S
St. Bonaventure University	New York	S
St. Lawrence University	New York	S
St. Olaf College	Minnesota	S
Seton Hill University	Pennsylvania	S
Sheridan College	Wyoming	S
Shimer College	Illinois	S
Smith College	Massachusetts	S

Sonoma State University	California	S
South Dakota State University	South Dakota	S
Southern Maine Comm. College	Maine	S
Southern Wesleyan University	South Carolina	S
Southern Utah University	Utah	S
SUNY—Alfred State College	New York	S
SUNY at Binghamton	New York	S
SUNY—Canton	New York	S
SUNY—Farmingdale	New York	S
SUNY—Potsdam	New York	S
SUNY—University at Albany	New York	S
Texas A&M University—College Station	Texas	S
Texas A&M University—Kingsville	Texas	S
Texas Tech University	Texas	S
Thomas More College	Kentucky	S
University of Alabama in Huntsville, The	Alabama	S
University of Alabama at Tuscaloosa, The	Alabama	S
University of Alaska—Anchorage	Alaska	S
University of Alaska—Fairbanks	Alaska	S
University of Arkansas–Fayetteville	Arkansas	S
University of Idaho	Idaho	S
University of Kansas	Kansas	S
University of Maine at Machias	Maine	S
University of Montana	Montana	S
University of Montana—Western	Montana	S
University of Nebraska—Lincoln	Nebraska	S
University of Nevada—Las Vegas	Nevada	S
University of New England	Maine	S
University of New Haven	Connecticut	S
University of New Orleans	Louisiana	S
University of North Texas	Texas	S
University of Northern Colorado	Colorado	S
University of Northern Iowa	Iowa	S
University of Notre Dame	Indiana	S
University of Oklahoma	Oklahoma	S
University of Redlands	California	S
University of Saint Thomas (MN)	Minnesota	S
University of Southern Indiana	Indiana	S
University of Southern Mississippi	Mississippi	S
University of Texas—El Paso	Texas	S
University of Texas—Pan American	Texas	S
University of Toledo	Ohio	S
University of the Pacific	California	S
University of Wisconsin—Eau Claire	Wisconsin	S
University of Wisconsin—Stevens Point	Wisconsin	S

Washington State University	Washington	S
Wayne State College	Nebraska	S
West Virginia University	West Virginia	S
Western Oregon University	Oregon	S
Western State College of Colorado	Colorado	S
Wheaton College (MA)	Massachusetts	S
Whittier College	California	S
Winona State University	Minnesota	S

ADDENDUM: INDEPENDENT LIVING OPTIONS

The following programs are options for students who may have LD/ADHD or other disabilities, but who want to continue to pursue independent living skills and education beyond high school.

Allen Institute Center for Innovative Learning
PO Box 100, 85 Jones Street
plove@alleninstitute.info
Hebron, CT 06248-0100
www.alleninstitute.info
866-666-6919
860-228-9670 (fax)

Anchor to Windward
PO Box 813
66 Clifton Avenue
Marblehead , MA 01945
www.anchortowindward.org
info@AnchortoWindward.org
978-740-0013
978-740-0014 (fax)

Bancroft Neurohealth
425 Kings Highway East
HADHDonfield, NJ 08033-0018
www.bancroftneurohealth.org/Corporate/
contactus.html
856-429-0010

Berkshire Center
18 Park Street
Lee, MA 01238
www.berkshirecenter.org
admissions@berkshirecenter.org
1-877-Know-CIP
413-243-3351 (fax)

Berkshire Hills Music Academy
48 Woodbridge Street
South Hadley, MA 01075
www.berkshirehills.org
info@berkshirehills.org
413-540-9720 (fax)
413-534-3875

Brehm Preparatory School
Options Program at Brehm
1245 East Grand, Carbondale, IL 62901
www.brehm.org
admissionsinfo@brehm.org
618-457-0371
618-529-1248 fax

Casa de Amma
27231 Calle Arroyo
San Juan Capistrano, CA 92675
www.casadeamma.org
949-496-9901

Center For Adaptive Living
3350-A Clayton Road
Concord, CA 94519
www.centerforadaptivelearning.org
info@centerforadaptivelearning.org
925-827-3863
925-827-4080 (fax)

Chapel Haven
1040 Whalley Avenue
Westville, CT 06515
www.chapelhaven.org
jlefkowitz@chapelhaven.org
203-397-1714 ext. 113
203-392-3698 (fax)

Chapel Haven West
University of Arizona
Tucson, Arizona
jlefkowitz@chapelhaven.org
www.chapelhaven.org
203-397-1714

Cloister Creek
1280 Highway 138 Southwest
Conyers, GA 30094
http://yp.bellsouth.com/sites/cloistercreek
770-483-0748
770-918-8217 (fax)

College Excel
86 Southwest Century Drive
Box 199
Bend, OR 97702
www.collegexcel.com
info@collegeexcel.com
541-388-3043

College Living Experience
6555 Nova Drive, Suite #300
Davie, Fl 33317
www.cleinc.net
800-486-5058
954-370-1895 (fax)

College Living Experience
Skokie, Illinois
847-509-8281
www.cleinc.net
www.esa-education.com

Elmhurst Life Skills Academy ELSA
190 Prospect Avenue
Elmhurst, Illinois 60126
http://public.elmhurst.edu/elsa
elsa@elmhurst.edu
630-617-3752
630-617-6417 (fax)

Brevard Center
3716 North Wickham Road Suite 1
Melbourne, FL 32935
www.brevardcenter.org
866-603-1900
321-259-1907 (fax)

Evaluation and Developmental Center
500-C South Lewis Lane
Southern Illinois University
Carbondale, IL 62901
www.siu.edu/~rehabedc/support/edc_index.html
rehab@siu.edu
618-453-2331

Foundation for Independent Living
5311 Northeast Thirty-third Avenue
Fort Lauderdale, FL 33308
www.filinc.org/fjaug2001.html
csutherland@filinc.org
954-968-6472
954-968-5045 (fax)

Gersh College Experience at Daemen College
150 Broadhollow Road
Suite 120
Melville, New York 11747
www.gershacademy.org/college/daemen.html
info@gershacademy.org
631-385-3342
631-427-6332

The Horizons School
2018 Fifteenth Avenue South
Birmingham, AL 35205
www.horizonsschool.org
jkcarter@horizonsschool.org
800-822-6242
205-322-6605 (fax)

Independence Center
3640 South Sepulveda Boulevard, Suite 102
Los Angeles, CA 90034
www.independencecenter.com
judym@independencecenter.com
310-202-7102
310-202-7180 (fax)

Life Development Institute
18001 North Seventy-ninth Avenue
Suite E71
Glendale, AZ 85308
www.life-development-inst.org/
kadams@life-development-inst.org
623-773-2774
623-773-2788 (fax)

Life Skills Inc.
44 Morris Street
Webster, MA 01570
http://swcrcinc.org
swcrc@swcrcinc.org
508-943-0700
508-949-6129 (fax)

Living Independently Forever, Inc.
8620 West Emerald Street 130
Boise, ID 83704
https://secure1.fiberpipe.net/lifeincidaho/default.asp
mwilson@Lifeincidaho.com
208-888-0076
208-888-335 (fax)

Maplebrook School
5142 Route 22
Amenia, NY 12501
15-3Y 1-5327
www.maplebrookschool.org
admin@maplebrookschool.org
845-373-9511
845-373-7029 fax

Minnesota Life College
7501 Logan Avenue South
Suite 2A
Richfield, MN 55423
www.minnesotalifecollege.com
612-869-4008
612-869-0443 (fax)

Moving Forward Toward Independence
1020 Clinton Street
Suite 210
Napa, CA 94559
www.moving-forward.org
707-259-1125 or 707-251-8603

New York Institute of Technology
Vocational Independence Program
Central Islip Campus
Central Islip, NY 11722
www.vip-at-nyit.org
info@vip-at-nyit.org
631-348-3354
631-529-1248 (fax)

Optimum Performance Institute
3080 Eucalyptus Hill Road
Santa Barbara, CA 93108
www.optimumperformanceinstitute.com
anne@opiliving.com
888 558-0617
805-969-1642 (fax)

OPTIONS at Brehm
1245 East Grand Avenue
Carbondale, IL 62901
www.brehm.org/options
admissionsinfo@brehm.org
618-457-0371
618-529-1248 (fax)

Pace Program
National-Louis University
2840 Sheridan Road
Evanston, IL 60201
www2.nl.edu/PACE
cburns@nl.edu
847-256-5150

Pathway at UCLA Extension
10995 Le Conte Avenue
Suite 413
Los Angeles, CA 90024
www.uclaextension.edu/index.cfm?href=/
departmentalpages/index.cfm&department=/
pathway/index.cfm
pathway@uclaextension.edu
310-794-1235

Program at the Brevard Center
3716 North Wickham Road, Suite 1
Melbourne, FL 32935
www.brevardcenter.org
321-259-1900

Riverview School
551 Route 6A
East Sandwich, MA 02537

Project Grow
549 Route 6A, East Sandwich
Cape Cod, MA 02537

Riverview School
www.riverviewschool.org
admissions@riverviewschool.org
508-833-7000
508-833-7001 (fax)
www.riverviewschool.org/admissions_grow.asp
grow@riverviewschool.org
508-888-3699
508-833-7628 fax

Threshold Program at Lesley University
29 Everett Street
Cambridge, MA 02138
www.lesley.edu/threshold/threshold_home.htm
threshld@mail.lesley.edu
617-349-8181 or 800-999-1959, ext. 8181

Strive U
28 Foden Road
South Portland, ME 04106
www.pslstrive.org/index.html
info@pslstrive.org
207-774-6278
207-774-7695 (fax)

Vista Vocational & Life Skills Center
1356 Old Clinton Road
Westbrook, CT 06498
www.vistavocational.org/welcome.htm
admissions@vistavocational.org.
860-399-8080
860-399-3103

Wellspring Foundation
PO Box 370
Bethlehem, CT 06751
www.wellspring.org
christa.pelletier@wellspring.org
203- 266-8000
203-266-8030 (fax)

RECOMMENDED WEBSITES

Independent Educational Consultants Association
www.IECAonline.com

LDA of America
www.ldanatl.org

Council for Exceptional Children
www.cec.sped.org

Council for Learning Disabilities
www.cldinternational.org

INDEX

ABOUT THE AUTHORS

Marybeth Kravets, MA, has been a counselor and college consultant at Deerfield High School, a public high school, in Deerfield, Illinois since 1979. She has acted as an educational consultant to high schools, colleges, and families. She received her BA in education from the University of Michigan in Ann Arbor, and her MA in Counseling from Wayne State University in Detroit, Michigan. She is a past president of the National Association for College Admission Counseling (NACAC) and previously served as the president of the Illinois Association for College Admission Counseling. In addition to coauthoring the *K&W Guide*, she also coauthored, with Dr. Michael Koehler, *Counseling Secondary Students with Learning Disabilities: Ready To Use Guidelines, Techniques and Materials to Help Students Prepare for College and Work* (The Center for Applied research in Education, A Simon & Schuster Company), and has written articles for many professional journals. She has been a guest on the NBC'S *Today Show* several times and has appeared on many other radio and television programs. She has presented at major conferences in the United States and Europe. She is married to Alan Kravets and has four children and seven grandchildren. For additional information or to contact Marybeth Kravets for consultation, write or call:

K&W
PO Box 197
Deerfield, IL 60015-0187
847-236-1985
mbkrav@aol.com

Imy F. Wax, MS, is a licensed psychotherapist and educational consultant currently in private family practice. She has worked with adolescents and their families in high schools and social service settings. She received her BS from Mills College of Education in New York, New York, and her MS from Hunter College in New York, New York. Imy is a member of several professional and parental organizations. She has presented at both professional and parental conferences on such topics as "The Emotional Expectations of Parenting a Child with Learning Disabilities," and has written numerous articles in professional and parental journals. Imy conducts workshops for parents on raising children with learning disabilities and/or attention deficit hyperactivity disorder, as well as for school districts on the college process. She has appeared as a guest on the NBC's *Today Show*, as well as other television and radio shows. She is married to Howard Wax and has four children, two with learning disabilities and one who also has attention deficit hyperactivity disorder. Her daughter was the inspiration for this book. For additional information or to contact Imy Wax for consultation or for presentations, write or call:

K&W
PO Box 187
Deerfield, IL 60015-0187
847-945-0913
imywax@aol.com

Notes

NOTES

NOTES

NOTES

FINDING THE FUNDS:

What you should know about paying for your college education

A year attending a public college on average costs $12,796. Going to a private one will cost you $30,367 per year. Laying down what could be as much as $120,000 if not more over four years is a lot. That's the equivalent of almost 500 iPods, 12,000 movie tickets, or 444,444 packs of instant noodles.

Your parents have a tough job ahead of them. Just about everyone needs some kind of financial assistance. Fortunately, you have many different options, including grants, scholarships, work-study, federal loans, and private loans. Read on to learn about these options and share this with your parents.

OTHER PEOPLE'S MONEY

Scholarships and Grants
These are the best forms of financial aid because they don't have to be paid back. Scholarships are offered to students with unique abilities that the school is seeking to infuse into the student body, such as exceptional talent in music, art, or athletics. However, most scholarships require that you pass and maintain a minimum GPA requirement and some grants may not extend through all four years of your undergraduate education.

Federal grants for undergraduate study include Pell Grants, Federal Supplemental Educational Opportunity Grants (FSEOG), Academic Competitiveness Grants (ACG), and national SMART grants. Pell Grants are the most common type of federal grant awarded to undergraduate students, and form the base upon which supplemental aid from other financing sources may be added. Moreover, Pell Grant recipients receive priority for FSEOG awards, which are provided to students with exceptional financial need, and for National SMART Grants for math and science students.

Academic Competitiveness Grants (ACG) are a brand new kind of grant that began in the 2006–07 academic year. They are for students who have attended secondary school programs that have been qualified by the government as achieving a high standard of academic rigor. As with Federal Supplemental Educational Opportunity Grants, ACG awards are generally provided as a supplement to students already receiving Federal Pell Grants.

Additionally, your state residency or the state where the school you wish to attend is located also opens you up to state-funded grants and scholarships. Remember to check out the state grant application deadlines found on the FAFSA website mentioned below.

Note that as you advance through your undergraduate education, that progress itself makes you eligible for additional federal, state, and private grant and scholarship opportunities.

Maximize your eligibility for free money by completing the Free Application for Federal Student Aid ("FAFSA") online annually at http://www.fafsa.ed.gov. Visit the Department of Education's student aid portal at http://studentaid.ed.gov for the latest information on federal aid available to students like you. According to the National Center for Education Statistics, approximately 63% of all undergraduates receive some form of financial aid. There is approximately $80 billion in federal grants, loans and work-study funds available out there. Even if you don't think you'll qualify, it is worth it to fill out this form.

Work-study
Federal work-study is another way to lessen the burden of college tuition. Work-study is an actual part-time job, with pay of at least the current federal minimum wage—sometimes higher depending on the type of work you do.

Another advantage of federal work-study is that the program can sometimes place you in jobs related to your field of study. So, while you might be able to get equivalent wages working at a local restaurant or retail store, with work-study, you can sometimes gain resume-building experience related to your degree – in a school laboratory or research center, for example.

How much work-study you receive depends on your level of financial need and the funding level provided by your school. Be aware that work-study alone isn't going to be enough to pay for your education. But, it can be a good way to lessen the sting.

LOANS

When scholarships, grants, and work-study don't cover the full cost of attendance, many students take out loans to help out with the rest.

Avoid loans if you can. A loan can best be described as renting money. There's a cost and it may not be an easy cost to bear.

Here's an interesting anecdote. Many students graduate college without knowing what types of loans they received, who the lender was, and how much they owe. The first time many students become aware of the scope of their obligation is when they receive their first bill—six months after graduation.

This is often because students are passive participants in the financial aid process and do not educate themselves or ask questions. Most students receive a list of "preferred lenders" from their financial aid office and simply go with the lender recommended to them. Over the course of the previous year, relationships between financial aid offices and lenders have been called into question by State Attorneys General, the Department of Education and regulators. Financial aid offices in certain cases received revenue from lenders in exchange for being placed on the "preferred lender list." Some schools have even rented out their name and logo for use on loan applications. These practices occur without disclosure to parents and students.

It is important to know that the "preferred lenders" may not offer the best deals on your loan options. While your financial aid office may be very helpful with scholarships and grants, and is legally required to perform certain duties with regard to federal loans, many do not have staff researching the lowest cost options at the time you are borrowing.

Remember that your tuition payment equals revenue for the school. When borrowing to pay tuition, you can choose to borrow from any lender. That means you can shop for the lowest rate. Keep reading. This will tell you how.

TYPES OF LOANS

The federal government and private commercial lenders offer educational loans to students. Federal loans are usually the "first resort" for borrowers because many are subsidized by the federal government and offer lower interest rates. Private loans have the advantage of fewer restrictions on borrowing limits, but may have higher interest rates and more stringent qualification criteria.

Federal Loans
There are three federal loan programs. The Federal Perkins Loan Program where your school lends you money made available by government funds, the Federal Direct Loan Program (FDLP) where the government lends its money directly to students; and the Federal Family Education Loan Program (FFELP) where financial institutions such as MyRichUncle lend their own money but the government guarantees them. While most schools participate in the Federal Perkins Program, institutions tend to favor either the FFELP or FDLP. You will borrow from FFELP or FDLP depending on which program your school has elected to participate in.

The Federal Perkins Loan is a low-interest (5%) loan for students with exceptional need. Many students who do not qualify or who may need more funds can borrow FFELP or FDLP student loans. Under both programs, the Stafford loan is the typical place to start. The Stafford loan program features a fixed interest rate and yearly caps on the maximum amount a student can borrow. Stafford loans can either be subsidized (the government pays the interest while the student is in school) or unsubsidized (the student is responsible for the interest that accrues while in school). Starting July 1, 2007, the maximum amount an independent freshman student can borrow is $7,500.

It is often assumed that the government sets the rate on student loans. The government does not set the rate of interest. It merely indicates the maximum rate lenders can charge. These lenders are free to charge less than the specified rate of 6.8% for Stafford loans. There is also an origination fee of up to 2% dropping to 1.5% on July 1, 2007. In some cases you may also be charged up to a 1% guarantee fee. Any fees will be taken out of your disbursement.

The government only lends money directly to you under the Federal Direct Loan Program. Lenders provide loans guaranteed by the federal government in the Federal Family Education Loan program.

Historically lenders have hovered at the maximum rate because most loans were distributed via the financial aid office whereby a few lenders received most of the loans. The end result was limited competition. At 1,239 institutions, one lender received more than 90% of the number of Stafford loans in 2006.

Certain lenders offer rate reductions, also known as borrower benefits, conditioned on the borrower making a certain number of on-time payments. Unfortunately, it is estimated that 90% of borrowers never qualify for these reductions.

Last year, MyRichUncle challenged this process by launching a price war. The company cut interest rates on Stafford loans and introduced widespread price competition. These interest rate cuts are effective when students enter repayment and do not have any further qualification requirements. In addition, students only lose the rate reduction if they default.

Parents can also borrow a PLUS loan. The Parent PLUS Loan program allows the parents of dependent students to take out loans to supplement the aid packages of their children. The program allows parents to borrow money to cover any cost not already met by the student's financial aid package up to the full cost of attendance. Unlike the Stafford Loan, eligibility for the Parent PLUS loan is not determined by the FAFSA. A parent fills out a loan application and signs a master promissory note. Eligibility is contingent upon whether the parent has an adverse credit history. Adverse credit history is defined as being no more than 90 days delinquent on any debt, having not declared bankruptcy in the last five years, and having not been the subject of a default determination on a foreclosure, a repossession, a tax lien, a wage garnishment, or a write-off of Title IV debt in the last five years.

The maximum rate a lender can charge for Parent PLUS loans is 8.5%. PLUS loans also have an origination fee of up to 3%, and a guarantee fee of up to 1%. Any fees will be taken out of your disbursement.

Your financial aid office is legally required to certify for lenders that you are enrolled and based on your financial aid package, the amount in Federal loans you are eligible to borrow. You are free to choose any lender even if the lender is not on your financial aid office's preferred lender list.

To shop for low cost Federal loans, call a number of lenders before applying to determine their rates and fees. This is an effective approach because your application will not impact the price. Once you are comfortable that you have the lowest cost option, apply and submit the Master Promissory Note to your lender of choice.

Private Loans

Private student loans can make it possible to cover the costs of higher education when other sources of funding have been exhausted. Additionally, when you apply for federal loans, you can borrow up to what your institution has pre-defined as the annual cost of attendance. If your anticipated expenses are above and beyond this pre-defined cost because of your unique needs, it will take a series of appeals before your institution will allow you to borrow more federal loans. Private loans help you meet your true expectation of what you will need financially. Private loans can pay expenses that federal loans can't, such as application and testing fees and the cost of transportation.

When you apply for a private loan, the lending institution will check your credit history including your credit score and determine your capacity to pay back the money you borrow. For individuals whose credit history is less than positive, lenders may require a co-borrower: a credit-worthy individual who also agrees to be accountable to the terms of the loan. While private loans do not have annual borrowing limits, they often have higher interest rates, and interest rate caps are higher than those set by Federal loans. Generally, the loans are variable rate loans, so the interest rate may go up or down, changing the cost.

To shop for a private loan, after you've researched several options, apply to as many of them as you feel comfortable. Once you are approved, compare rates. Pick the lowest cost option.

EXTRA LESSONS

Borrow the minimum
Just because someone is offering to lend you thousands upon thousands of dollars doesn't mean you should necessarily take them up on that offer. At some point, you'll have to repay the debt and you'll have to do it responsibly. Wouldn't it be better to use your money for something more worthwhile to you?

Know your rights
Currently, student lending is an industry that is under heavy scrutiny. It is important, now more than ever, for parents and students to have an active voice and to make educational and financial choices that are right for them. Some schools work with "preferred lenders" when offering federal and private loans. You are not required to choose a loan from one of these lenders if you can find a better offer. With respect to Federal loans the financial aid office has a legislated role which is to certify for the lending institution that you the borrower are indeed enrolled and the amount you are eligible for. They are not legally empowered to dictate your choice of lender and must certify your loan from the lender of your choice. You have the right to shop for and to secure the best rates possible for your loans. Don't get bullied into choosing a different lender, simply because it is preferred by an institution. Instead, do your homework and make sure you understand all of your options.

Know what you want
When it's all said and done, you will have to take a variety of factors into account in order to choose the best school for you and for your future. You shouldn't have to mortgage your future to follow a dream, but you also shouldn't downgrade this opportunity just to save a few bucks.

An out-of-the-box approach
Community colleges are a viable option for those ultimately seeking a four-year degree. Articulation agreements between community colleges and major four-year institutions allow students to complete their general education requirements at community colleges and have them transferred to a four-year institution. If you are really keen on graduating from that fancy four year college of your choice, transferring in from a community college is a cheaper path to getting that same degree. At an average cost of $2,272 per year, it is a thought worth exploring.

MYRICHUNCLE

Who we are:
MyRichUncle is a national student loan company offering federal (Stafford, PLUS and GradPLUS) and private loans to undergraduate, graduate, and professional students. **MyRichUncle** knows that getting a student loan can be a complicated and intimidating process, so we changed it. We believe students are credit-worthy borrowers, and that student loan debt should be taken seriously by borrowers and lenders alike. We propose changes in the student loan industry that will better serve parents, schools, and most importantly, students.

Why it matters:
Your student loan will be your responsibility. When you enter into a loan agreement, you're entering into a long-term relationship with your lender—15 years, on average. The right student loan with the right lender can help you avoid years of unnecessary fees and payments.

What we do:
MyRichUncle pays close attention to the obstacles students face. Removing these obstacles drives everything we do. **MyRichUncle** discounts federal loan rates at repayment rather than requiring years of continuous payments to earn the discount, which saves you money right from the start. We help you plan ahead, so you can choose the best loans and save.

Our credentials:
MyRichUncle is a NASDAQ listed company. Our symbol is UNCL. In 2006, **MyRichUncle** was featured in FastCompany Magazine's Fast 50 and in Businessweek's Top Tech Entrepreneurs. **MyRichUncle** and its parent company, MRU Holdings, are financed by a number of leading investment banks and venture capitalists, including subsidiaries of Merrill Lynch, Lehman Brothers, Battery Ventures and Nomura Holdings.

MYRICHUNCLE
STUDENT LOANS

Call us:
1-800-926-5320

or learn more online:
MYRICHUNCLE.COM